- Chapter 5—new examination of the beneficial economic function of the modern state to correct market failure, the occurrence of market externalities, the financial collapse that led to the Great Recession, the market failure of monopolies, and the global policy coordination of the G-20 in response to the Great Recession.
- Chapter 6—new discussion of the trade-off between popular participation in the government and the representation of many viewpoints and effective governance; new section comparing executive-legislative institutions; new Methods in Context box asks, "When do politicians constrain bureaucrats, and when do they not?"
- Chapter 7—more information on the SNTV and AV electoral systems; recent scholarship on the decline of partisan loyalty and increased electoral volatility; new discussion of patron-client relationships; new Methods in Context box examines what might explain the trend of major parties' declining share of the vote.
- Chapter 8—explores the dictator's dilemma in greater depth: How do authoritarian regimes rely on military forces to maintain power, and how do they seek to influence the citizenry through co-optation and repression? New case studies consider China's evolution from a communist to modernizing authoritarian regime, whether Iran is a theocracy or a military dictatorship, and Nigeria's weakening institutions under military rule; new mini case on the unraveling of semi-authoritarian regimes in Egypt and Tunisia.
- Chapter 9—new Methods in Context box examines comparativists' research on whether modernization causes democracy; new case study on Mexico and its transition from a semi-authoritarian regime.
- Chapter 10—considers the wide-ranging results of globalization; examines how various countries were impacted by the Great Recession; new Methods in Context box explores whether democracies or dictatorships produce better development; mini case considers Turkey as a potential Middle Eastern "tiger."
- Chapter 11—discusses using tax expenditures to achieve social policy goals and how welfare states are changing in response to globalization; new Methods in Context box explores comparativists' research asking "Can democracy make you healthier?"
- Chapter 12—considers communitarianism's role behind inclusion policies and the use of quotas for women's representation in politics; new case study on Mexico examines anticlericalism in a Catholic country.

introducingCP.cqpress.com

A rich student companion Web site features chapter summaries, interactive quizzes, and key concept flashcards.

Instructor's Resources

Helpful materials include a test bank, discussion questions, PowerPoint lecture slides, a syllabus transition guide for first-time users, instructor's manual, and a guide for teaching assistants on leading discussion sections. Go to http://college.cqpress.com/sites/introducingCPIR/ to register and download materials.

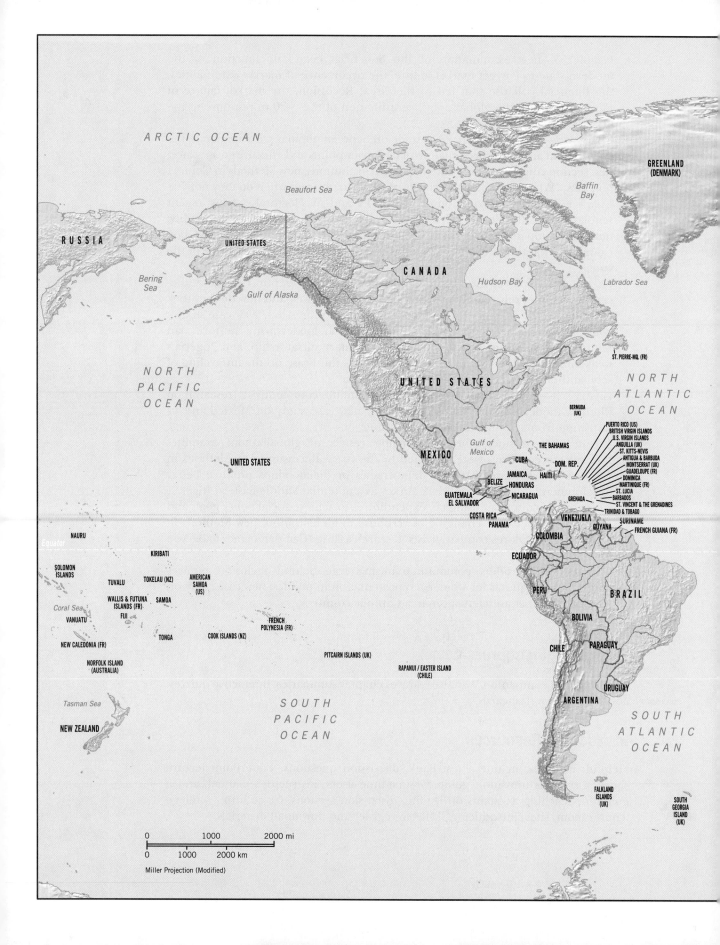

ARCTIC OCEAN

Beaufort Sea

Baffin Bay

GREENLAND (DENMARK)

RUSSIA

UNITED STATES

CANADA

Bering Sea

Gulf of Alaska

Hudson Bay

Labrador Sea

NORTH PACIFIC OCEAN

UNITED STATES

ST. PIERRE-MQ. (FR)

NORTH ATLANTIC OCEAN

BERMUDA (UK)

PUERTO RICO (US)
BRITISH VIRGIN ISLANDS
U.S. VIRGIN ISLANDS
ANGUILLA (UK)
ST. KITTS-NEVIS
ANTIGUA & BARBUDA
MONTSERRAT (UK)
GUADELOUPE (FR)
DOMINICA
MARTINIQUE (FR)
ST. LUCIA
BARBADOS
ST. VINCENT & THE GRENADINES
TRINIDAD & TOBAGO

THE BAHAMAS

MEXICO

Gulf of Mexico

CUBA

DOM. REP.

JAMAICA

HAITI

BELIZE

HONDURAS

GUATEMALA
EL SALVADOR

NICARAGUA

GRENADA

UNITED STATES

COSTA RICA

PANAMA

VENEZUELA

GUYANA

SURINAME

FRENCH GUIANA (FR)

COLOMBIA

Equator

NAURU

ECUADOR

SOLOMON ISLANDS

KIRIBATI

PERU

BRAZIL

TUVALU

TOKELAU (NZ)

AMERICAN SAMOA (US)

BOLIVIA

Coral Sea

WALLIS & FUTUNA ISLANDS (FR)

SAMOA

VANUATU

FIJI

FRENCH POLYNESIA (FR)

CHILE

PARAGUAY

NEW CALEDONIA (FR)

TONGA

COOK ISLANDS (NZ)

PITCAIRN ISLANDS (UK)

URUGUAY

NORFOLK ISLAND (AUSTRALIA)

RAPANUI / EASTER ISLAND (CHILE)

ARGENTINA

Tasman Sea

SOUTH PACIFIC OCEAN

SOUTH ATLANTIC OCEAN

NEW ZEALAND

FALKLAND ISLANDS (UK)

SOUTH GEORGIA ISLAND (UK)

0   1000   2000 mi

0   1000   2000 km

Miller Projection (Modified)

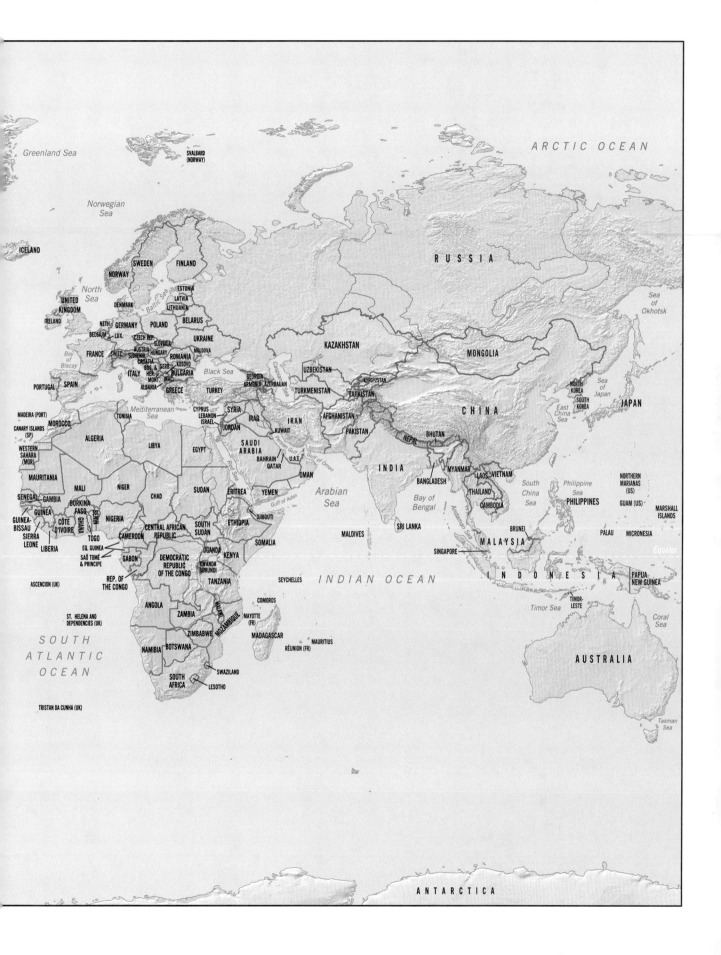

Introducing Comparative Politics

Concepts and Cases in Context

2nd Edition

CAROL ANN DROGUS

STEPHEN ORVIS

Hamilton College

Los Angeles | London | New Delhi
Singapore | Washington DC

CQ Press
2300 N Street, NW, Suite 800
Washington, DC 20037

Phone: 202-729-1900; toll-free, 1-866-4CQ-PRESS (1-866-427-7737)

Web: www.cqpress.com

Cover design: Matthew Simmons, Myself Included Design
Typesetting: C&M Digitals (P) Ltd.
Map composition: International Mapping Associates

⊗ The paper used in this publication exceeds the requirements of the American National Standard for Information Sciences—Permanence of Paper for Printed Library Materials, ANSI Z39.48-1992.

Printed and bound in Canada

15   14   13   12   11   1   2   3   4   5

Library of Congress Cataloging-in-Publication Data

Drogus, Carol Ann.
  Introducing comparative politics: concepts and cases in context/Carol Ann Drogus, Stephen Orvis. — 2nd ed.
p. cm.
  Includes bibliographical references and index.
  ISBN 978-1-60871-668-5 (pbk.: alk. paper) 1. Comparative government.
2. Comparative government—Case studies. I. Orvis, Stephen Walter II. Title.

 JF51.D76 2011
  320.3—dc23

                                                                2011023853

To Nick and Will, in the hope that their generation
will better understand the world,
in order to improve it.

About the Authors

 **Carol Ann Drogus** is Associate Dean of Students for Off-Campus Study at Hamilton College. She is a specialist on Brazil, religion, and women's political participation. She taught introduction to comparative politics for more than fifteen years, as well as courses on Latin American politics, gender and politics, and women in Latin America. She has written two books and numerous articles on the political participation of women in religious movements in Brazil.

 **Stephen Orvis** is professor of government at Hamilton College. He is a specialist on sub-Saharan Africa (Kenya in particular), identity politics, democratic transitions, and the political economy of development. He has been teaching introduction to comparative politics for more than twenty years, as well as courses on African politics, nationalism and the politics of identity, political economy of development, and weak states. He has written a book and articles on agricultural development in Kenya, as well as several articles on civil society in Africa and Kenya, and is currently doing research on political institutions in Africa.

Brief Contents

Contents	**xi**
Regional and Country Coverage	**xx**
Timelines, Figures, Tables, Maps, and Boxes	**xxiv**
Preface	**xxvii**

PART I: A Framework for Understanding Comparative Politics — **2**

Chapter 1: Introduction	**4**
Chapter 2: The Modern State	**38**
Chapter 3: States and Citizens	**94**
Chapter 4: States and Identity	**142**
Chapter 5: States and Markets	**188**

PART II: Political Systems and How They Work — **242**

Chapter 6: Governing Institutions in Democracies	**244**
Chapter 7: Institutions of Participation and Representation in Democracies	**308**
Chapter 8: Authoritarian Institutions	**368**
Chapter 9: Regime Change	**422**

PART III: Issues and Policies — **482**

Chapter 10: Globalization, Economic Sovereignty, and Development	**484**
Chapter 11: Public Policies When Markets Fail: Welfare, Health, and the Environment	**538**
Chapter 12: Policies and Politics of Inclusion and Clashing Values	**604**

Glossary	**663**
Index	**677**

Contents

Regional and Country Coverage   xx

Timelines, Figures, Tables, Maps, and Boxes   xxiv

Preface   xxvii

PART I: A Framework for Understanding Comparative Politics   2

Chapter 1: Introduction   4

The Big Issues   6

Comparative Politics: What Is It? Why Study It? How to Study It?   10

- Methods in Context: Critically Examining How Comparativists Do Research   16

Three Key Questions in Comparative Politics   16

Conclusion   26

Plan of the Book   33

- Where and Why   34

Key Concepts   35

Works Cited   35

Resources for Further Study   36

Web Resources   37

Chapter 2: The Modern State   38

Characteristics of the Modern State   40

- In Context: New States and the United Nations   41

Mini Case: Somaliland: Internal versus External Sovereignty   45

Historical Origins of Modern States   46

Strong, Weak, and Failed States   51

- Where and Why: Failed and Sustainable States   52

Mini Case: Afghanistan's Failed State   56

Mini Case: Sierra Leone and Liberia: Collapsed States   58

Case Studies of State Formation   **60**

• Country and Concept: The Modern State   61

Case Study: United Kingdom: A Strong, Modern State   62

Case Study: The United States: A Consciously Crafted State   64

Case Study: Japan: Determined Sovereignty   67

Case Study: Germany: The First Modern Welfare State   69

Case Study: Brazil: A Moderately Strong, and Now Legitimate,
    Modern State   72

Case Study: Russia: Strong External Sovereignty with Weak Rule of Law   74

Case Study: Mexico: Challenges to Internal Sovereignty   77

Case Study: Iran: Claiming Legitimacy via Theocracy   80

Case Study: India: Enduring Democracy in a Moderately Weak State   82

Case Study: China: Economic Legitimacy over Political Reform   84

Case Study: Nigeria: An Extremely Weak State   87

Conclusion   **90**

Key Concepts   **92**

Works Cited   **93**

Resources for Further Study   **93**

Web Resources   **93**

Chapter 3: States and Citizens   **94**

• Country and Concept: Modern Regimes   96

Regimes, Ideologies, and Citizens   **100**

• Where and Why: Authoritarian versus Democratic Rule   102

Case Study: United Kingdom: "Cradle of Democracy"   108

Case Study: Russia: The First Self-Proclaimed Communist Regime   112

Case Study: Germany: Rise of the Nazi Party and a Totalitarian State   116

Mini Case: Tanzania's One-Party Regime   121

Case Study: Brazil: The Bureaucratic Authoritarian State, 1964–1985   123

Case Study: Nigeria: Neopatrimonial Military Rule, 1966–1979 and
    1983–1999   125

Case Study: Mexico: Semi-Authoritarianism under the PRI   128

Case Study: The Islamic Republic of Iran: Theocratic State, 1979–   134

Conclusion   **137**

Key Concepts   **139**

Works Cited   **139**

Resources for Further Study   **140**

Web Resources   **141**

Chapter 4: States and Identity   142

- Country and Concept: Ethnicity, Race, and Religion   144

The Debate over Identity   147

Nations and Nationalism   150

Case Study: Nationalism in Germany   153

Ethnicity and Religion   155

Mini Case: Consociationalism in Northern Ireland   158

- Methods in Context: Explaining Ethnic Violence   160

Case Study: Nigeria's Strange History of Ethnicity and Religion   165

Mini Case: Rwanda: Trying to Understand Genocide   168

Race   170

Case Study: Racial Politics in the United States   171

Case Study: Race in Brazil   178

- In Context: Race and Ethnicity in Latin America   180

Conclusion   182

Key Concepts   185

Works Cited   185

Resources for Further Study   186

Web Resources   187

Chapter 5: States and Markets   188

- Country and Concept: States and Markets   190

The Market, Capitalism, and the State   190

Key Economic Debates   197

- Where and Why: The Successes and Failures of SAPs   202

Globalization: A New World Order or Déjà Vu All Over Again?   204

States and Markets around the World   209

Case Study: The United States: The Free-Market Model   210

- In Context: Central Banks   211

Case Study: Germany: The Social Market Economy   216

Mini Case: The European Union, Economic Sovereignty, and Globalization   220

Case Study: Japan: The Developmental State and Its Crisis   222

Mini Case: Chile: Early Neoliberal Reformer   227

Case Study: Mexico: From Protectionism to Neoliberalism   229

Case Study: Nigeria: A Weak State, Oil, and Corruption   232

- In Context: Nigeria as an Oil Exporter   235

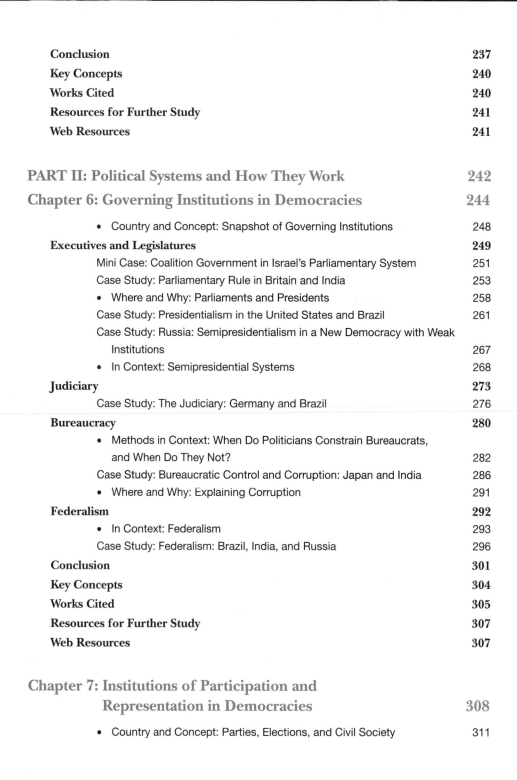

Conclusion   237
Key Concepts   240
Works Cited   240
Resources for Further Study   241
Web Resources   241

PART II: Political Systems and How They Work   242

Chapter 6: Governing Institutions in Democracies   244

- Country and Concept: Snapshot of Governing Institutions   248

Executives and Legislatures   249
Mini Case: Coalition Government in Israel's Parliamentary System   251
Case Study: Parliamentary Rule in Britain and India   253
- Where and Why: Parliaments and Presidents   258
Case Study: Presidentialism in the United States and Brazil 261
Case Study: Russia: Semipresidentialism in a New Democracy with Weak
  Institutions   267
- In Context: Semipresidential Systems   268

Judiciary   273
Case Study: The Judiciary: Germany and Brazil   276

Bureaucracy   280
- Methods in Context: When Do Politicians Constrain Bureaucrats,
  and When Do They Not?   282
Case Study: Bureaucratic Control and Corruption: Japan and India   286
- Where and Why: Explaining Corruption   291

Federalism   292
- In Context: Federalism   293
Case Study: Federalism: Brazil, India, and Russia   296

Conclusion   301
Key Concepts   304
Works Cited   305
Resources for Further Study   307
Web Resources   307

Chapter 7: Institutions of Participation and
   Representation in Democracies   308

- Country and Concept: Parties, Elections, and Civil Society 311

Formal Institutions: The Electoral System   **312**
- Where and Why: Women in Power   317

Formal Institutions: Political Parties and Party Systems   **319**
- Methods in Context: What's the Trouble with Political Parties?   324

Mini Case: France and the Shift toward a Two-Party System   327

Civil Society   **329**

Patron-Client Relationships   **337**

Case Studies in Participation and Representation   **338**

Case Study: The United Kingdom and the United States: FPTP and
Pluralist Systems in Different Contexts   339
- In Context: FPTP   343

Case Study: Germany: Two-and-a-Half-Party System and
Neocorporatism under Threat   347

Case Study: Japan: From Dominant-Party to Two-Party System?   352
- In Context: SNTV   353

Case Study: India: From Dominant-Party to Multiparty Democracy   357

Conclusion   **362**

Key Concepts   **365**

Works Cited   **365**

Resources for Further Study   **367**

Web Resources   **367**

Chapter 8: Authoritarian Institutions   368

- Country and Concept: Authoritarian Rule   371

Governing Institutions in Authoritarian Regimes   **372**
- Where and Why: Institutional Limits on Dictators' Rule   374

Mini Case: The "Politics of Survival" in Mobutu's Zaire   377

Case Study: China: From Communist to Modernizing Authoritarian Rule   379
- In Context: The Decline of Communism   382

Case Study: Iran: Theocracy or Military Dictatorship?   385

Case Study: Nigeria: Weakening Institutions under Military Rule   390
- In Context: Authoritarian Rule in Sub-Saharan Africa (SSA),
1970–2010   392

Elections, Parties, and Civil Society in Authoritarian Regimes   **394**

Mini Case: Egypt and Tunisia: The Unraveling of Semi-Authoritarian
Regimes   399

Case Study: China: Growing Participation but Not Democracy
or Semi-Authoritarian Rule   402

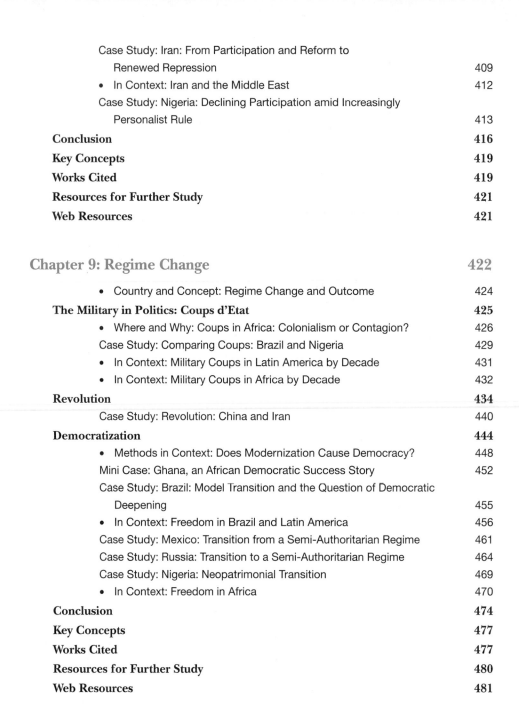

Case Study: Iran: From Participation and Reform to
    Renewed Repression   409
- In Context: Iran and the Middle East   412
Case Study: Nigeria: Declining Participation amid Increasingly
    Personalist Rule   413

Conclusion   **416**

Key Concepts   **419**

Works Cited   **419**

Resources for Further Study   **421**

Web Resources   **421**

Chapter 9: Regime Change   **422**

- Country and Concept: Regime Change and Outcome   424

The Military in Politics: Coups d'Etat   **425**
- Where and Why: Coups in Africa: Colonialism or Contagion?   426
Case Study: Comparing Coups: Brazil and Nigeria   429
- In Context: Military Coups in Latin America by Decade   431
- In Context: Military Coups in Africa by Decade   432

Revolution   **434**
Case Study: Revolution: China and Iran   440

Democratization   **444**
- Methods in Context: Does Modernization Cause Democracy?   448
Mini Case: Ghana, an African Democratic Success Story   452
Case Study: Brazil: Model Transition and the Question of Democratic
    Deepening   455
- In Context: Freedom in Brazil and Latin America   456
Case Study: Mexico: Transition from a Semi-Authoritarian Regime   461
Case Study: Russia: Transition to a Semi-Authoritarian Regime   464
Case Study: Nigeria: Neopatrimonial Transition   469
- In Context: Freedom in Africa   470

Conclusion   **474**

Key Concepts   **477**

Works Cited   **477**

Resources for Further Study   **480**

Web Resources   **481**

PART III: Issues and Policies   482

Chapter 10: Globalization, Economic Sovereignty, and Development   484

- Country and Concept: Globalization, Economic Sovereignty, and Development   487

Wealthy Countries: Globalization and Economic Sovereignty   488

Case Study: United Kingdom: Radical Reform in a Liberal Market Economy   492

Case Study: Germany: Struggling to Reform a Coordinated Market Economy   496

- In Context: Government and Growth in the EU   500

Development and Globalization   501

- Methods in Context: Do Democracies or Dictatorships Produce Better Development?   508

Mini Case: Turkey: A Middle Eastern "Tiger"?   512

- Where and Why: Asian Miracle versus African Malaise   514

Case Study: China: An Emerging Powerhouse   518

Case Study: India: Development and Democracy   522

Case Study: Brazil: Does Globalization Allow a Different Path?   526

- In Context: Brazilian Economic Growth   528

Case Study: Iran: Struggling with the Blessings of Oil   530

Conclusion   532

Key Concepts   535

Works Cited   535

Resources for Further Study   537

Web Resources   537

Chapter 11: Public Policies When Markets Fail: Welfare, Health, and the Environment   538

- Country and Concept: Welfare, Health, and the Environment   540

"Welfare": Social Policy in Comparative Perspective   542

Mini Case: Sweden's Welfare State   546

- Where and Why: The Development of Welfare States   548

Case Study: Germany: Reforming the Christian Democratic Welfare State   554

- In Context: The German Welfare State   556
Case Study: The United States: Reforming the Liberal Welfare State   557
Case Study: Brazil: Starting a Welfare State in a Developing Economy   561

Health Care and Health Policy   **564**
- In Context: Health Care in Wealthy Countries, 2009   567
- Methods in Context: Can Democracy Make You Healthier?   568
Case Study: Germany: Pioneer of Modern Health Policy   571
Case Study: United Kingdom: Reforming the NHS   574
Case Study: U.S. Health Policy: Trials and Tribulations of the Market Model   577

Environmental Problems and Policy   **581**
Case Study: The United States: Pioneer That Lost Its Way?   586
Case Study: China: Searching for Sustainable Development   589
Case Study: Nigeria and Oil: A Question of Environmental Justice and
Sustainable Development   593

Conclusion   **597**

Key Concepts   **600**

Works Cited   **600**

Resources for Further Study   **603**

Web Resources   **603**

**Chapter 12: Policies and Politics of Inclusion and
Clashing Values**   **604**
- Country and Concept: Policies and Politics of Inclusion and
Clashing Values   606

The Debate over Inclusion and Group Rights   **608**

Religion: Recognition, Autonomy, and the Secular State   **612**
Mini Case: Islamic Head Scarves in France and Turkey   613
- Where and Why: Explaining Policy Differences toward
Muslims in Europe   617
Case Study: United Kingdom: Religious Challenge to Multiculturalism   618
Case Study: India: Secularism in a Religious and Religiously
Plural Society   622
Case Study: Mexico: Anticlericalism in a Catholic Country   626

**Gender: The Continuing Struggle for Equal Social Status, Representation,
and Participation**   **629**
Mini Case: Women in Saudi Arabia and Kuwait   633
Case Study: Russia: Women through Social and Political Transformation   636

Case Study: Iran: Social Gains, Political and Cultural Restrictions,
and Islamic Feminism   640
• In Context: Women in Iran and the Middle East   643

Sexual Orientation: Assimilation or Liberation?   **645**
Case Study: The United States: Birthplace of a Movement but Limited
Policy Change   649
Case Study: Brazil: LGBT Rights in a New Democracy   652

Conclusion   **655**
Key Concepts   **658**
Works Cited   **658**
Resources for Further Study   **660**
Web Resources   **661**

Glossary   **663**
Index   **677**

REGIONAL AND COUNTRY COVERAGE

Country	Feature	Page
AFRICA		
Somaliland: Internal versus External Sovereignty	Mini Case	45
Sierra Leone and Liberia: Collapsed States	Mini Case	58
Nigeria: An Extremely Weak State	Case Study	87
Tanzania's One-Party Regime	Mini Case	121
Nigeria: Neopatrimonial Military Rule, 1966–1979 and 1983–1999	Case Study	125
Nigeria's Strange History of Ethnicity and Religion	Case Study	165
Rwanda: Trying to Understand Genocide	Mini Case	168
Nigeria: A Weak State, Oil, and Corruption	Case Study	232
Nigeria as an Oil Exporter	In Context	235
The "Politics of Survival" in Mobutu's Zaire	Mini Case	377
Nigeria: Weakening Institutions under Military Rule	Case Study	390
History of Military Intervention in Nigeria	Timeline	391
Authoritarian Rule in Sub-Saharan Africa (SSA), 1970–2010	In Context	392
Egypt and Tunisia: The Unraveling of Semi-Authoritarian Regimes	Mini Case	399
Nigeria: Declining Participation amid Increasingly Personalist Rule	Case Study	413
Coups in Africa: Colonialism or Contagion?	Where and Why	426
Comparing Coups: Brazil and Nigeria	Case Study	429
Military Coups in Africa by Decade	In Context	432
Ghana, an African Democratic Success Story	Mini Case	452
Nigeria: Neopatrimonial Transition	Case Study	469
Freedom in Africa	In Context	470
Asian Miracle versus African Malaise	Where and Why	514
Nigeria and Oil: A Question of Environmental Justice and Sustainable Development	Case Study	593
AMERICAS		
The United States: A Consciously Crafted State	Case Study	64
Brazil: A Moderately Strong, and Now Legitimate, Modern State	Case Study	72
Mexico: Challenges to Internal Sovereignty	Case Study	77
Brazil: The Bureaucratic Authoritarian State, 1964–1985	Case Study	123
Mexico: Semi-Authoritarianism under the PRI	Case Study	128
Racial Politics in the United States	Case Study	171
Race in Brazil	Case Study	178
Race and Ethnicity in Latin America	In Context	180
The United States: The Free-Market Model	Case Study	210
Chile: Early Neoliberal Reformer	Mini Case	227
Mexico: From Protectionism to Neoliberalism	Case Study	229
Presidentialism in the United States and Brazil	Case Study	261
The Judiciary: Germany and Brazil	Case Study	276

Country	Feature	Page
Federalism: Brazil, India, and Russia	Case Study	296
The United Kingdom and the United States: FPTP and Pluralist Systems in Different Contexts	Case Study	339
Comparing Coups: Brazil and Nigeria	Case Study	429
Military Coups in Latin America by Decade	In Context	431
Brazil: Model Transition and the Question of Democratic Deepening	Case Study	455
Freedom in Brazil and Latin America	In Context	456
Mexico: Transition from a Semi-Authoritarian Regime	Case Study	461
Brazil: Does Globalization Allow a Different Path?	Case Study	526
Brazilian Economic Growth	In Context	528
The United States: Reforming the Liberal Welfare State	Case Study	557
Brazil: Starting a Welfare State in a Developing Economy	Case Study	561
U.S. Health Policy: Trials and Tribulations of the Market Model	Case Study	577
The United States: Pioneer That Lost Its Way?	Case Study	586
Mexico: Anticlericalism in a Catholic Country	Case Study	626
The United States: Birthplace of a Movement but Limited Policy Change	Case Study	649
Brazil: LGBT Rights in a New Democracy	Case Study	652
Afghanistan's Failed State	Mini Case	56
Japan: Determined Sovereignty	Case Study	67
India: Enduring Democracy in a Moderately Weak State	Case Study	82
China: Economic Legitimacy over Political Reform	Case Study	84
Japan: The Developmental State and Its Crisis	Case Study	222
Parliamentary Rule in Britain and India	Case Study	253
Bureaucratic Control and Corruption: Japan and India	Case Study	286
Federalism: Brazil, India, and Russia	Case Study	296
Japan: From Dominant-Party to Two-Party System?	Case Study	352
India: From Dominant-Party to Multiparty Democracy	Case Study	357
China: From Communist to Modernizing Authoritarian Rule	Case Study	379
China: Growing Participation but Not Democracy or Semi-Authoritarian Rule	Case Study	402
Revolution: China and Iran	Case Study	440
Asian Miracle versus African Malaise	Where and Why	514
China: An Emerging Powerhouse	Case Study	518
India: Development and Democracy	Case Study	522
China: Searching for Sustainable Development	Case Study	589
India: Secularism in a Religious and Religiously Plural Society	Case Study	622

ASIA

REGIONAL AND COUNTRY COVERAGE *(cont.)*

Country	Feature	Page
EUROPE		
United Kingdom: A Strong, Modern State	Case Study	62
Germany: The First Modern Welfare State	Case Study	69
Russia: Strong External Sovereignty with Weak Rule of Law	Case Study	74
United Kingdom: "Cradle of Democracy"	Case Study	108
Russia: The First Self-Proclaimed Communist Regime	Case Study	112
Germany: Rise of the Nazi Party and a Totalitarian State	Case Study	116
Nationalism in Germany	Case Study	153
Consociationalism in Northern Ireland	Mini Case	158
Germany: The Social Market Economy	Case Study	216
The European Union, Economic Sovereignty, and Globalization	Mini Case	220
Parliamentary Rule in Britain and India	Case Study	253
Russia: Semipresidentialism in a New Democracy with Weak Institutions	Case Study	267
The Judiciary: Germany and Brazil	Case Study	276
Federalism: Brazil, India, and Russia	Case Study	296
France and the Shift toward a Two-Party System	Mini Case	327
The United Kingdom and the United States: FPTP and Pluralist Systems in Different Contexts	Case Study	339
Germany: Two-and-a-Half-Party System and Neocorporatism under Threat	Case Study	347
Russia: Transition to a Semi-Authoritarian Regime	Case Study	464
United Kingdom: Radical Reform in a Liberal Market Economy	Case Study	492
Germany: Struggling to Reform a Coordinated Market Economy	Case Study	496
Government and Growth in the EU	In Context	500
Sweden's Welfare State	Mini Case	546
Germany: Reforming the Christian Democratic Welfare State	Case Study	554
The German Welfare State	In Context	556
Germany: Pioneer of Modern Health Policy	Case Study	571
United Kingdom: Reforming the NHS	Case Study	574
Islamic Head Scarves in France and Turkey	Mini Case	613
Explaining Policy Differences toward Muslims in Europe	Where and Why	617
United Kingdom: Religious Challenge to Multiculturalism	Case Study	618
Russia: Women through Social and Political Transformation	Case Study	636
MIDDLE EAST		
Iran: Claiming Legitimacy via Theocracy	Case Study	80
The Islamic Republic of Iran: Theocratic State, 1979–	Case Study	134
Coalition Government in Israel's Parliamentary System	Mini Case	251
Iran: Theocracy or Military Dictatorship?	Case Study	385
Egypt and Tunisia: The Unraveling of Semi-Authoritarian Regimes	Mini Case	399
Iran: From Participation and Reform to Renewed Repression	Case Study	409
Iran and the Middle East	In Context	412
Revolution: China and Iran	Case Study	440

Country	Feature	Page
Turkey: A Middle Eastern "Tiger"?	Mini Case	512
Iran: Struggling with the Blessings of Oil	Case Study	530
Islamic Head Scarves in France and Turkey	Mini Case	613
Women in Saudi Arabia and Kuwait	Mini Case	633
Iran: Social Gains, Political and Cultural Restrictions, and Islamic Feminism	Case Study	640
Women in Iran and the Middle East	In Context	643

Timelines, Figures, Tables, Maps, and Boxes

Timelines

The Modern State	91
Political Institutions	330
History of Military Intervention in Nigeria	391

Figures

6.1	Typical Parliamentary System	250
6.2	Typical Presidential System	260
6.3	Typical Semipresidential System	266
7.1	What Affects Turnout?	316
7.2	Contrasting Models of State-Interest Group Interaction	333
8.1	China's Governing Institutions	381
8.2	Iran's Governing Institutions	387
10.1	Globalization's Effects on Economic Policies: Two Views	490
10.2	Employment Growth and Unemployment Rates in Germany, 1997–2010	499
11.1	Poverty and Inequality in Welfare States	552

Tables

1.1	What Explains Political Behavior?	28
1.2	Who Rules?	33
2.1	The Shifting Borders of Modern States: Not Recognized, Limited Recognition, and Majority Recognition States	42
2.2	Failed States, 2010	54
2.3	Sustainable States, 2010	54
4.1	Racial Disparity in the United States	176
4.2	Racial Representation in Congress	176
5.1	Economic Overview	208
5.2	Profile of Japan's Economy, 1970–2009	226
7.1	Results of the 2005 United Kingdom Parliamentary Election	314
7.2	Results of Sweden's 2010 Parliamentary Election	315
7.3	British National Election Results, 2010	340
7.4	German General Election Results, 1998–2009	351

7.5	Japan's House of Representatives Election Results, 1996–2009	355
10.1	Economic Globalization Index	503
11.1	Comparison of Welfare State Outcomes	550
11.2	Social Expenditure, in Percentage of GDP, 2007	550

Maps

2.1	Spread of Modern States	50
3.1	Spread of Democracy by Era	106
4.1	Civil Wars and Ethnic Fragmentation	164
6.1	Three Major Types of Electoral Democracy	259
6.2	Code- versus Common-Law Countries	274
6.3	Annual Corruption Scores, 2010	285
7.1	World Electoral Systems	318
9.1	Coups in Africa	427
9.2	Democratic Institutionalization	451
11.1	Global Variations in CO_2 Emissions	585
12.1	Gender Inequality	631
12.2	Women in Legislative Seats Worldwide	636
12.3	Gay Rights	648

Boxes

Scientific Method in Comparative Politics	13
Major Political Ideologies and Regimes	100
What Is Democracy?	107
What about Gender?	149
What's in a Name? Tribe, Ethnicity, and Nation	156
The Role of the State in the Market	204
Von Beyme's Categorization of Political Parties	322
Was the American Revolution Really a Revolution?	436
What about Terrorism?	438

PREFACE

The teaching of introductory comparative politics has long been divided, and to some extent confounded, by the question of "country" or "concept": Should the course be taught, as it traditionally has been, as a series of country studies highlighting the key similarities and differences among political institutions around the world, or should it be focused on the important concepts in the discipline? Throughout twenty years of teaching Introduction to Comparative Politics, we have been frustrated by this "either/or" proposition, as well as by the textbooks that have been built upon it. The country approach is far too descriptive, and it is not easy to tease major concepts out of country case studies in any sustained way. This makes it difficult for students to get to the intellectual "meat" of our discipline. A purely conceptual approach, on the other hand, leaves students with little concrete knowledge, even when they're given examples here and there. We want our students to know the difference between a president and a prime minister. We've found that it is impossible for them to assess theories in an empirical vacuum. Students need the context that studying actual country cases provides.

We traded syllabi back and forth over the years, trying to combine the two approaches. Our goal was to introduce a set of related concepts and then immediately examine in some detail how they matter in the real world in a comparative context. To do this, we started using two textbooks, one conceptual and the other country based, in an iterative fashion. But the parts never fit together well, even if written by the same team. In particular, we found that the conceptual books didn't lend themselves well to connecting key theoretical concepts to case study material. We also found that the case studies in most country-based books were either too detailed, leaving the student overwhelmed by unnecessary information, or too simplistic, leaving the student without adequate knowledge with which to understand the utility of the theoretical concepts.

This textbook tries to resolve this country-or-concept dilemma, using what we've come to think of as a "hybrid" approach. The book is organized conceptually, but each chapter introduces concepts and then immediately uses them to examine a series of topical, interesting, and relevant case studies. For instance, chapter 5 on states and markets lays out the key concepts in political economy and major economic theories and inserts case studies, where they best fit, of the U.S. laissez-faire model, the German social market economy, the Japanese developmental state, Mexico's history of import substitution industrialization and recent move toward global integration, and Nigeria's underdevelopment and oil dependence.

We use eleven countries throughout the book as "touchstones" (approximately five cases in each chapter), returning to these countries to illustrate the debates we address. The eleven countries—Brazil, China, Germany, India, Iran, Japan, Mexico,

Nigeria, Russia, the United Kingdom, and the United States—span the globe, illustrate a wide array of current and past regimes, and avoid a Eurocentrism still too common in the field of comparative politics. Since we know, however, that not all aspects of comparative politics can best be represented by these eleven countries alone, we also include what we call "mini cases" throughout the book. These briefer cases are interspersed throughout the chapters where they make the most sense and cover some of the most important topics of current research. In this way we are able to introduce students to such topics as democratization in Ghana, genocide in Rwanda, the 2011 regime changes in Egypt and Tunisia, and Turkey's economic development model.

By the end of the book, students not only will have been introduced to a wide array of important concepts and theoretical debates but also will have learned a lot about the most interesting aspects of each of the eleven countries. We do not and cannot systematically examine all elements of all eleven as a standard country-by-country book would. Instead, after a brief overview of each country in chapter 2 to give students a basic context, we identify the most conceptually interesting elements of each country. For instance, for Japan, we cover the developmental state, the role of that state's bureaucracy and level of corruption, its electoral system, and the country's recent efforts to deal with globalization and resuscitate economic growth. For Germany, we cover the rise and structure of the Nazi regime, Germany's cultural nationalism and citizenship debates, the social market economy, the role of the country's powerful judiciary, its electoral system, and its effort to reform the social market economy and welfare state in the face of globalization and EU integration. The case studies are organized and written in a way that allows students to understand the context of the interesting debates and concepts without having to read an entire "country chapter" on each. And the cases are not overly long, which leaves faculty members the option of lecturing to fill in any additional detail that they may feel important or to provide comparisons with cases not covered in a chapter.

Rather than using any one theoretical or methodological approach, in chapter 1 we introduce students to the broad debates in the field to show throughout the book how comparativists have used various theories and methodologies to understand political phenomena. We do not generally offer definitive conclusions about which approach is best for understanding a particular issue, preferring instead to show students the strengths and weaknesses of each. Occasionally, we make clear that one approach has become the "conventional wisdom" in the field or that we believe it is the most accurate way to analyze a particular phenomenon, but we do this in the context of a broader debate. Our primary focus on eleven countries gives the book an implicit bias toward comparative case studies over large-N quantitative methodology, but we introduce students to the core ideas and benefits of the latter and refer to large-N studies throughout the book as well. We believe our approach will allow faculty to generate debates among students over key approaches and methodologies. By focusing on the key conceptual debates and illustrating them in the real world, the book enables instructors to move their introductory students beyond the memorization of basic information and toward an ability to assess and debate the real issues in our discipline.

The book also moves firmly away from the traditional Cold War division of the world into first-, second-, and third-world countries. While many textbooks claim to do this, we have found that they typically suffer from a "Cold War hangover," with the old division lurking just beneath the surface. We consciously set out to show that many theoretical concepts in the discipline are useful in a wide array of settings, that political phenomena are not fundamentally different in one part of the world than they are in another. For instance, we illustrate the parliamentary system not only with Britain but also with India, we use both Germany and Brazil to analyze the role of the judiciary and judicial review in a democracy, and we examine women's struggle for equality in Russia and Iran. Throughout, we try to show how long-standing concepts and debates in the discipline illuminate current "hot topics."

ORGANIZATION OF THE BOOK

This book is divided into three main parts. It examines the theories and concepts that inform and drive research as a way to frame our investigation, then moves to a survey of political institutions and institutional change, and, finally, to an examination of several current policy debates. Part I introduces the major theoretical approaches to the discipline and focuses on the modern state and its relationship to citizens and civil society, regimes, identity groups, and the market economy. It provides an introduction to the discipline and its key concepts in the modern world, applying them to case studies throughout. Chapter 1 provides a broad overview of key conceptual debates and divides the field into three broad questions to help students organize these debates: What explains political behavior? Who rules? and Where and why? These orient students by grouping the many debates in the field into broad categories tied to clear and compelling questions. "What explains political behavior?" gets at the heart of the discipline's major disputes, which we divide among rational-actor theories, theories of political culture and ideology, and structural theories. "Who rules?" addresses the dispersion of political power, focusing mainly on the debate between pluralist and elite theorists. While that debate is typically subsumed under the study of American politics, we think it helps illuminate important areas of comparative politics as well. "Where and why?" introduces students to the importance of and approaches to comparison.

The rest of Part I focuses on the modern state and its relationship to other key areas of modern politics. Chapter 2 defines and provides an overview of the modern state and uses a brief history of the modern state in our eleven case studies to give students an overview of each. Chapter 3 examines modern states in relation to citizens, civil society, and political regimes, arguing that the latter are based first and foremost on political ideologies that define the relationship between state and citizen. Chapter 4 looks at the debate over political identity and the state's relationship to nations, ethnic and religious groups, and racial groups. Chapter 5 examines the abstract and historical relationship between the state and the market economy, including key concepts in political economy, economic theories, and globalization. Each of these chapters uses case studies to illustrate and assess the concepts and debates it introduces.

Part II examines political institutions in both democratic and authoritarian regimes as well as regime transitions. It is the "nuts-and-bolts" section of the book, providing what traditionally has been a core feature of the course. While this part of the book is essential, we have endeavored to keep it as succinct as possible to allow room to develop the thematic and theoretical elements of Part I as well as the contemporary policy debates of Part III. Chapters 6 and 7 examine political institutions in democratic regimes. Chapter 6 focuses on governing institutions: executive/legislative systems, the judiciary, the bureaucracy, and federalism. The theme throughout is the question of accountability in democracies. Chapter 7 looks at institutions of participation and representation: electoral systems, parties and party systems, and interest groups and social movements. It focuses primarily on how to achieve different kinds of representation and the potential trade-off between active participation and effective governance. Chapter 8 looks at institutions in authoritarian regimes, drawing on the previous two chapters to show how similar institutions function quite differently in nondemocratic regimes. Chapter 9, on regime transition, not only focuses on democratic transitions but also sets them in the longer-term debate over regime change, looking first at military coups and social revolutions.

Part III examines some key current policy issues that have been foreshadowed earlier in the book. The conceptual and empirical knowledge that the students have gained in Parts I and II are used to address important current issues. Chapter 10 looks at different states' efforts to respond effectively to globalization, revisiting in a more current context the debates developed in chapter 5. It looks at the debate over convergence versus the varieties of capitalism approach in understanding the response to globalization in wealthy countries, as well as developing countries' efforts to respond to globalization in order to further develop; the chapter includes a discussion of the global financial crisis and its implications. The theme of chapter 11 is market failure, examining social policy, health policy, and environmental policy in turn. It draws on chapters 5 and 10, as well as material from Part II, to look at different approaches to current hot topics such as universal health care and climate change. Chapter 12 returns to themes first developed in a theoretical and historical framework in chapter 4 on identity politics. Its theme is how states respond to demands for inclusion in full citizenship by groups typically not included in the past and the clashes of fundamental values those demands raise in the areas of religion, gender, and sexual orientation.

KEY FEATURES

A number of pedagogical features reappear throughout the chapters. Each of them is designed to help students marry the conceptual and country-specific material in the most effective way possible. We think students can manage the concepts without losing sight of the important facts they've learned about the countries if they're given the right tools. The three questions set out in chapter 1 are introduced at the start of each chapter in the form of specific chapter-opener questions relevant to the content of the chapter. They are intended to provide students with key material to consider as they read the chapter, study the cases, and then debate in class. The chapters sometimes provide conclusive answers to some of the opener questions, but more often they show students different ways the questions can be answered or approached. The questions are addressed systematically in each chapter in the introduction and conclusion, creating a well-integrated presentation of concept and context. Each chapter also opens with a map showing the countries used as case studies and mini cases. This feature helps readers locate chapters in which specific countries are discussed, facilitating the development of country-specific knowledge.

"Country and Concept" tables in the introductions of chapters 2 through 12 showcase empirical material. These provide key data of relevance for our eleven case study countries. The text refers to the tables at various points, but students and faculty can use these for much more, comparing the countries across the variables and asking questions about what might explain the observable variation.

As described earlier, each chapter after chapter 1 includes mini cases as well as case studies of some of our eleven countries. Mini cases are one-shot interesting examples of particular themes. They illustrate alternatives to the models our case studies provide, or in some cases they introduce students to "classic" case studies not included in our eleven. For instance, we include mini cases on Sierra Leone and Liberia when discussing failed states, Ghana when discussing the third wave of democratic transitions, and Northern Ireland when presenting consociationalism.

Most chapters have a "Where and Why" feature that provides a brief overview of a major theoretical debate in comparative politics relevant to the chapter but not directly addressed in the main text. Chapter 5 on political economy, for instance, outlines the debate over why structural adjustment programs have been more successful in some countries than in others, and chapter 11 includes one on why different kinds of welfare states have developed in different countries.

Most chapters also include one or more "In Context" features that present basic data. These allow students to set a case study or idea into a comparative (and sometimes provocative) context. Students can use these to assess how representative some of our case studies are or to see the distribution of an institution, type of event, or set of factors around the world. For example, the "In Context" in chapter 4 focuses on identity politics in Latin America and shows racial and ethnic demography across the entire region. This is set next to the case study of race relations in Brazil.

In several chapters, we include a "Methods in Context" box, a new feature in which we examine a major question of relevance to that particular chapter, looking at different research hypotheses and methods and usually focusing on one or two recent works that use the latest techniques to try to resolve the question. Chapter 9, for instance, includes a "Methods in Context" box on the question of modernization and democratization, looking at the debate over the last decade between Adam Przeworski and Ronald Inglehart.

In addition to these themed features, readers will find many original tables, figures, and maps throughout the book that illustrate key relationships or variables around the world. Students will find end-of-chapter lists of key concepts with page references to help their study and review, as well as a list of works cited and a list of important references for further research. We hope the design of the book strikes a balance as well: colorful and well illustrated to help engage student attention, but without adding significantly to cost.

ANCILLARIES

Because we know from experience that making the leap into a new textbook is no small chore, we also offer a full suite of high-quality instructor and student ancillary materials (prepared by Nathan Gonzalez, University of California, Los Angeles). Specifically tailored to *Introducing Comparative Politics: Concepts and Cases in Context*, all of these materials are available online.

Adopters can access the instructor resources at http://college.cqpress.com/sites/introducingCPIR/to register and download the following:

- A comprehensive test bank with more than 600 multiple-choice, fill-in-the-blank, and short- and long-essay questions. The test bank is available in Word as well as fully loaded in Respondus, a flexible and easy-to-use test-generation software that allows instructors to build, customize, and even integrate exams into course management systems.
- A set of 180 PowerPoint lecture slides tailored around the core concepts of the book.
- A set of graphics from the text, including all of the maps, tables, and figures, in PowerPoint and *.pdf* formats for classroom presentations.

Students also have access to a companion Web site at http://introducingCP.cqpress.com. Organized by chapter, the Web site offers opportunities to self-test and study, including clear and concise chapter summaries for each chapter, multiple-choice quizzes, and interactive flashcards based on the key concepts of the book.

ACKNOWLEDGMENTS

We have developed numerous debts in the process of writing this book. Perhaps the longest standing is to our students over twenty years of teaching Introduction to Comparative Politics at Hamilton College. Figuring out how to teach the course in a way that is interesting, relevant, and clear to them led us to develop the approach taken in this book. We kept them in mind as we wrote the book: Will it be clear to them? Will it interest them? Will it help them see the important concepts and how they matter in the real world?

We owe a substantial thank you to the office of the Dean of Faculty at Hamilton College as well. It has provided support for research assistants for this project over four years and two editions, primarily from the Steven Sands Fund for Faculty Innovation. The office also provided sabbatical support for Steve Orvis on Hamilton's program at Pembroke College, Oxford University, where the first elements of this project were written. Additional thanks go to the fellows and staff at Pembroke College for providing a hospitable venue for a sabbatical leave for research and writing on the first edition. Deep thanks go as well to seven especially talented Hamilton College undergraduates who worked for us as research assistants on the two editions, pulling together vital data and information for many of the book's case studies. They are Henry Anreder, Luke Forster, Laura Gault, Derek King, Katie McGuire, Joshua Meah, and Natalie Tarallo. They were invaluable help for two faculty taking on a project of this magnitude. Thanks go also to Andrew Rogan and Dawn Woodward for assistance in preparing the bibliographies in the book. We are very grateful to Amy Forster Rothbart and Nathan Gonzalez for ably crafting all of the ancillary materials for this book. Thanks also to Nathan Gonzalez for drafting the initial case studies on Mexico added to the second edition.

The staff at CQ Press has been pleasant, professional, and efficient throughout this process. Our association began with a chance meeting between one of us and a sales representative from CQ Press, in which "complaints were made" about the quality of textbooks in the field and the sales rep asked the inevitable: "So how would you write one?" A quick response was met with the sales rep's enthusiastic statement: "We're looking for a book just like that! Can my acquisitions editor call you to talk about it?" We said sure, but, to be honest, didn't expect to hear from anyone. A week later the phone rang—Charisse Kiino, now editorial director for CQ Press's College Publishing Group, was on the line to talk through the ideas further. This led to a long process through which Charisse expertly led us, starting with developing a proposal and draft chapter and responding to the first round of reviews. Charisse patiently walked us through the process with constant good cheer and support. Our development editor for the first edition (now acquisitions editor), Elise Frasier, was invaluable, putting forth tremendous ideas for pedagogical elements of the book that we would have never thought of on our own, doing much of the research to develop these elements (with the help of her interns Serena Golden and Joe Farrell, whom we thank as well), and being herself an insightful reader and critic of the text.

For the second edition, Nancy Matuszak served as development editor and expertly guided us through the substantial revision process, helping us improve the work in innumerable ways, and we greatly appreciate all of her hard work. Finally, our production editor Gwenda Larsen and copyeditor Paula Fleming have been fabulous in the final stages of the project, improving the prose in innumerable places, pointing out inconsistencies, and working with us in an open, honest, and professional way that has made a tedious process as easy as it could be. We deeply appreciate the work of all at CQ Press who have made the process of writing this book as painless as we could imagine it being.

We wish also to thank the numerous reviewers who read chapters of the book at various stages. Their comments led us to revise a number of elements, drop others, and further develop still others. They have collectively made it a much better book that we hope will serve students well. They are:

William Avilés, *University of Nebraska–Kearney*

Jody Baumgartner, *East Carolina University*

Dilchoda Berdieva, *Miami University*

Michael Bernhard, *University of Florida*

Gitika Commuri, *California State University–Bakersfield*

Jeffrey Conroy-Krutz, *Michigan State University*

William Crowther, *University of North Carolina–Greensboro*

Andrea Duwel, *Santa Clara University*

Clement M. Henry, *University of Texas–Austin*

Eric H. Hines, *University of Montana*

Christian B. Jensen, *University of Iowa*

Eric Langenbacher, *Georgetown University*

Ricardo Laremont, *SUNY Binghamton*

Carol S. Leff, *University of Illinois–Urbana Champaign*

Paul Lenze, *Washington State University*

Mona Lyne, *University of Missouri–Kansas City*

Mary McCarthy, *Drake University*

Scott Morgenstern, *University of Pittsburgh*

Nils Ringe, *University of Wisconsin–Madison*

David Sacko, *U.S. Air Force Academy*

Brian Shoup, *Mississippi State University*

Anthony Spanakos, *Manhattanville College*

Boyka Stefanova, *University of Texas–San Antonio*

Sarah Tenney, *The Citadel*

Erica Townsend-Bell, *University of Iowa*

Kellee Tsai, *Johns Hopkins University*

Thomas Turner, *Virginia Commonwealth University*

Dwayne Woods, *Purdue University*

Eleanor E. Zeff, *Drake University*

Darren Zook, *University of California–Berkeley*

Last, but far from least, we have to extend thanks to our children, Nick and Will. They didn't contribute ideas or critique the book, but they showed real enthusiasm for understanding things like who the prime minister of Britain is and why there is a Monster Raving Loony Party, and they endured and even participated in occasional dinner table debates on things like the relative merits of parliamentary systems and different concepts of citizenship. Most of all, they gave of themselves in the form of great patience. This project became more of an obsession, at least at key points, than our work usually is. It took us away from them more than we like and made our family life rather hectic, especially in the final year of writing both the first and second editions. They bore it well, going on with their lives in their typically independent way. We deeply appreciate that, and hope we can make it up to them now that the writing is done.

Introducing Comparative Politics

PART I

A woman demonstrates against the fraudulent elections in Myanmar in November 2010. The long-ruling military regime seems to be trying to improve its democratic image via elections, but the opposition boycotted, calling them a sham.

Credit: CKN/Getty Images

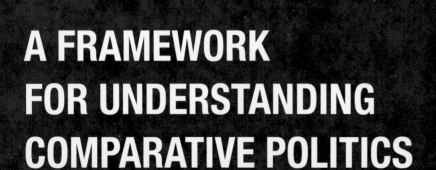

A FRAMEWORK FOR UNDERSTANDING COMPARATIVE POLITICS

Chapter	Brazil	China	Germany	India	Iran	Japan	Mexico	Nigeria	Russia	UK	US
1. Introduction											
2. The Modern State	•	•	•	•	•	•	•	•	•	•	•
3. States and Citizens	•		•		•		•	•	•		•
4. States and Identity	•		•						•		•
5. States and Markets			•			•	•	•			•

Country	Population	Age structure	Monetary unit	Major natural resources
Brazil	201,103,330	0–14 years: 26.7%; 15–64 years: 66.8%; 65 years and over: 6.4%	Real	Bauxite, gold, hydropower, iron ore, manganese, nickel, petroleum, phosphates, platinum, timber, tin, uranium
China	1,330,141,295 including Hong Kong, Macao, Taiwan	0–14 years: 19.8%; 15–64 years: 72.1%; 65 years and over: 8.1%	Yuan	Aluminum, antimony, coal, iron ore, lead, magnetite, manganese, mercury, molybdenum, natural gas, petroleum, tin, tungsten, uranium, vanadium, zinc, hydropower potential
Germany	82,282,988	0–14 years: 13.7; 15–64 years: 66.1%; 65 years and over: 20.3%	Euro	Arable land, coal, construction materials, copper, iron ore, lignite, natural gas, nickel, potash, salt, timber, uranium
India	1,173,108,018	0–14 years: 30.5%; 15–64 years: 64.3%; 65 years and over: 5.2%	Rupee	Arable land, bauxite, coal (world's fourth-largest reserves), chromite, diamonds, iron ore, limestone, manganese, mica, natural gas, petroleum, titanium ore
Iran	76,923,300	0–14 years: 21.7%; 15–64 years: 72.9%; 65 years and over: 5.4%	Rial	Coal, chromium, copper, iron ore, lead, manganese, natural gas, petroleum, sulfur, zinc
Japan	126,804,433	0–14 years: 13.5%; 15–64 years: 64.3%; 65 years and over: 22.2%	Yen	Negligible mineral resources, fish
Mexico	112,468,855	0–14 years: 29.1%; 15–64 years: 64.6%; 65 years and over: 6.2%	Peso	Petroleum, silver, copper, gold, lead, zinc, natural gas, timber
Nigeria	152,217,341	0–14 years: 41.5%; 15–64 years: 55.5%; 65 years and over: 3.1%	Naira	Arable land, coal, iron ore, lead, limestone, natural gas, niobium, petroleum, tin, zinc
Russia	139,390,205	0–14 years: 14.8%; 15–64 years: 71.5%; 65 years and over: 13.7%	Ruble	Broad natural resource base, including major deposits of coal, natural gas, oil, timber, and many strategic minerals
United Kingdom	62,348,447	0–14 years: 16.7%; 15–64 years: 67.1%; 65 years and over: 16.2%	Pound sterling	Arable land, chalk, clay, coal, gold, gypsum, iron ore, lead, limestone, natural gas, petroleum, potash, salt, sand, silica, slate, tin, zinc
United States	310,232,863	0–14 years: 20.2%; 15–64 years: 67%; 65 years and over: 12.8%	Dollar	Bauxite, coal, copper, gold, iron, lead, mercury, molybdenum, natural gas, nickel, petroleum, phosphates, potash, silver, timber, tungsten, uranium, zinc

Source: CIA, The World Factbook, https://www.cia.gov/library/publications/the-world-factbook/index.html.

Who Rules?

- How much power do different people or groups have in different political systems?
- Is power widely shared or concentrated among a few individuals?

What Explains Political Behavior?

- Do self-interest, beliefs, or underlying structural forces best explain how people act in the political realm?
- What kinds of evidence can help us determine why political actors do what they do?

Where and Why?

- What can be learned from comparing political behavior and outcomes across countries?

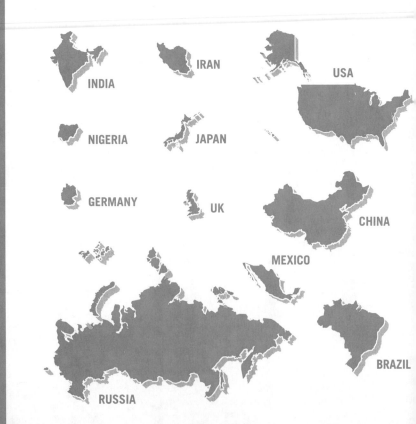

INDIA

IRAN

USA

NIGERIA

JAPAN

GERMANY

UK

CHINA

MEXICO

RUSSIA

BRAZIL

1

INTRODUCTION

To Americans today, understanding political developments and disputes around the world has never seemed more important. This increased awareness of world politics stems largely from the attacks of September 11, 2001, on the World Trade Center and Pentagon. The 9/11 plot was conceived in Afghanistan and carried out primarily by individuals originally from Saudi Arabia. In the wake of the attacks, the United States invaded Afghanistan in search of terrorists and stayed to engage in a difficult process of democratization. The United States then invaded Iraq, ostensibly to rid it of weapons of mass destruction, but again ended up trying to build a democracy. U.S. policy tried to help a new Iraqi leadership navigate extremely difficult and, to Americans, unfamiliar political differences among Shiite Arabs, Sunni Arabs, and Kurds.

Many Americans now see the world as more complicated and less comprehensible than it was during the post–Cold War era (1989–2001), when the international realm seemed peaceful and stable and foreign politics was of little importance. Indeed, Francis Fukuyama, an official in the George H. W. Bush administration, called the end of the Cold War "the end of history" (1992). The end of Communist rule in the Soviet Union and Eastern Europe seemed to foreshadow a period in which liberal democracies and market economies would spread, erasing the differences that made countries and their politics so incomprehensible to one another. Understanding political differences among countries appeared at once easier and less important.

In reality, the post–Cold War era was not nearly as peaceful, and change not nearly as homogenizing, as Fukuyama and others believed. Instead, it was a period of dramatic political change: Communist rule collapsed, several countries split into two or more new countries, the number of ethnic and religious civil wars increased significantly, and two full-scale genocides took place. Yet the number of countries that could claim to have democratic governments also increased substantially, and East Asia, led by China, achieved unprecedented economic growth that lifted more people out of poverty more quickly than ever before in history. So while 9/11 and its aftermath may have refocused Americans' attention on the differences among nations and the perplexities of understanding them, those differences are not new.

Diversity of political, economic, and social life among nations persists in every period of history. The field of comparative politics focuses primarily on the

Secular Iraquiya coalition leader Iyad Allawi, Iraqi prime minister Nuri al-Maliki, Iraqi president Jalal Talabani, and Kurdish president Masoud Barzani (right to left) attend a parliament session in Baghdad in November 2010. Elections in March 2010 resulted in no majority support in parliament for any of the major leaders, requiring the formation of a coalition government. After more than six months, al-Maliki (the Shiite leader) ultimately forged a coalition with other Shiite, some Sunni, and Kurdish leaders to form a working government. Limited Sunni participation, however, left observers concerned about long-term Sunni support for the new government.

Credit: Reuters/Landov

fundamental and long-standing questions raised by this diversity: Why do governments form? Why does a group of people come to see itself as a nation? Why do nations sometimes fall apart? How can a government convince people that it has the right to rule? Do some forms of government last longer than others? Do some forms of government serve their people's interests better than others? How do democracies form, and how do they fall apart? Can democracy work anywhere or only in particular countries and at particular times? Are certain political institutions more democratic than others? Can government policy reduce poverty and improve economic well-being? This book introduces you to the many and often conflicting answers to these questions that political scientists have proposed by examining these and other questions comparatively. It will also help you start to assess which of these answers are the most convincing and why.

THE BIG ISSUES

Despite an unprecedented focus among Americans on international politics, current "hot-button" political issues around the world are just the latest manifestations of a set of enduring issues that students of comparative politics have been studying for the last half century. We could list many such issues, but for the moment, let's focus on just five to illustrate the major areas of interest in comparative politics: political development, regime type and change, participation and representation, policy-making processes, and political economy. The logical starting point is the question of **political development.**

Political Development You may be accustomed to seeing development applied to the field of economics, where it relates to the growth of modern industrial economies, but the word has important political dimensions as well. Historically, the biggest political development question is how and why modern nations and states arose. Why did the entity now known as France, and a group of people that thinks of itself as French, come into existence? Is this process similar for all countries? If not, how and why does it vary?

Political scientists initially thought about these issues in a European historical context, but since World War II most questions about political development have emerged out of the experience of former European colonies in Latin America, Africa, and Asia. As these colonies gained independence, the relationship between the two types of development—economic and political—came into focus. Most observers assumed that former colonies would go through a process of economic development dubbed **modernization**—the transformation of poor agrarian societies into wealthy industrial societies. Political scientists initially assumed that as this transformation occurred, political systems that were more or less democratic also would emerge.

In truth, neither economic nor political development has occurred as planned in the former colonies. Some countries, such as South Korea, have achieved rapid economic transformation and have established electoral democracies. Many others, however, have not. Democracy has emerged in some very poor countries, while nondemocratic governments have presided over great economic change in others. In many countries, a sense of being a nation has never fully emerged, and some have even collapsed completely into civil war. Even though the assumptions of modernization have not systematically answered the question of how economic and political development are related, scholars continue to examine it because finding an answer remains crucial, as the cases of Afghanistan and Iraq demonstrate so vividly today.

Regime Type and Change Closely related to the issue of political development is the question of regime type and regime change. Americans often use regime to refer to some sort of "bad" government: we (democracies) have governments, whereas they (nondemocracies) have regimes. Political scientists, however, think of regimes in more neutral terms, as sets of fundamental rules and institutions that govern political activity. Germany has existed as a state and a nation since at least the 1860s, but it has had several different regimes. Otto von Bismarck and Kaiser Wilhelm ruled over the first regime of a united Germany—a modernizing authoritarian regime—until its destruction in World War I. Out of that emerged a second regime, the democratic Weimar Republic. Its instability led to the rise of the fascist Nazi regime under Adolf Hitler. The Cold War split the country into two states, each with its own regime—a democratic one in West Germany and a Communist one in East Germany. The reunification of Germany in 1990 brought both countries under the democratic regime as the Communist regime crumbled entirely. Germany has continuously existed for well over a century as one state (and, for a time, two), but it has had five different regimes.

political development: The processes through which modern nations and states arise and how political institutions and regimes evolve

modernization: The transformation of poor agrarian societies into wealthy industrial societies, usually seen as the process by which postcolonial societies become more like societies in the West

democracy: A regime in which citizens have basic rights of open association and expression and the ability to change the government through some sort of electoral process

authoritarian regime: A regime lacking democratic characteristics, ruled by a single leader or small group of leaders

For greater ease of comparison, political scientists try to classify regimes by designating them as belonging to certain categories, or regime types. Two broad categories are democratic and authoritarian regimes. Many definitions of a democracy exist, but for purposes of systematic comparison, most political scientists adhere to what is often called the "minimal definition" of a **democracy** as a regime in which citizens have basic rights of open association and expression and the ability to change the government through some sort of electoral process. This is not to say that democratic regimes are all the same. Besides being "more" or "less" democratic, they are also organized in different ways, for example, as presidential or parliamentary systems (see chapter 6).

Conversely, an **authoritarian regime** is simply a regime lacking democratic characteristics. As with democratic regimes, numerous kinds of authoritarian regimes exist. The most important of these in the twentieth century were fascist regimes such as Nazi Germany, communist regimes such as the Soviet Union, modernizing authoritarian regimes like that of the shah of Iran or the military government of Brazil from 1964 to 1985, and theocratic regimes such as the Islamic Republic of Iran since 1979.

In recent years, a third broad regime category has come into being. The semi-authoritarian regime includes some elements of democracy such as elections, but the ruling party has sufficient control over democratic processes to ensure that it remains in power. Most of these regimes have emerged out of attempts to create new democracies during the last two decades.

Britain's Prince Philip passes the Instruments of Independence to Kenyan nationalist leader Jomo Kenyatta at Kenya's independence ceremony on December 12, 1963. Kenyatta presided over a relatively successful economy but also created a one-party dictatorship that lasted until 1992. Even after opposition parties were allowed and democratic elections began, Kenyatta's party continued to rule for another ten years, finally relinquishing power after losing an election in 2002.

Credit: AP Photo/Dennis Lee Royle

Once the various regime categories are identified, we can ask questions about how they differ and how they are similar. On the surface, the answer seems obvious: democracies have elections, and authoritarian regimes have dictators. In fact, the differences and similarities are much more complex. Some formally democratic regimes have significant informal limits on citizen input and participation, whereas some authoritarian regimes allow dissent and even power sharing within certain bounds. We define and explore the main regime categories in detail, as well as various subtypes of each category, in chapter 3.

As our earlier German example suggests, we also need to ask questions about regime change, the process through which one regime is transformed into another. Recent dramatic political changes often influence what events and processes political scientists explore when looking at regime change. For much of the last century, most political science research focused on revolution, spurred by the overthrow of Russia's autocratic regime in 1917 and the triumph of Chinese Communists in 1949. In the 1950s and 1960s, researchers looking primarily at Latin America also developed theories about the causes of democratic breakdowns brought about by military coups d'etat.

However, the spread of democracy since the late 1970s has shifted scholarly attention to the form of regime change most common today: democratic transition. Scholars studying democratic transitions ask questions about when and why authoritarian regimes give way to democracies, what kind of democracies are likely to emerge in particular circumstances, how truly democratic new democracies are, and how likely they are to last.

Participation and Representation Closely related to the issues of regime type and democratization are popular participation and representation. Since Aristotle, if not before, political scientists and political philosophers have sought to understand why and how people participate in the political process, as well as how that participation differs across cultures and regimes. In some countries citizens participate as part of self-conscious identity groups, such as ethnic, religious, or racial groups (see chapter 4). In other countries identity groups have little relevance to politics. When and why do these differences emerge? What are the effects of strong "identity politics" on the stability of democracy? In relatively poor, agrarian societies, participation is often individual in nature, with citizens seeking out individuals above them in the political system who can help them secure what they need. In more industrial societies, citizens may band together in what is called civil society to pursue common interests via the political process. **Civil society** is defined as the sphere of organized, nongovernmental, nonviolent activity by groups larger than individual families or firms. The most familiar elements of civil society in the United States are interest groups such as the Sierra Club or a chamber of commerce.

Political participation also occurs through the medium of political parties, of course. Different regimes have quite distinct kinds of parties and electoral systems that encourage different kinds of citizen participation, but whatever the type, parties are meant to represent citizens' concerns in the formal political process. It is no surprise then that political scientists want to know which electoral system most accurately represents the interests of citizens in the political process. How can citizens ensure that their representatives actually represent them? Can representation exist in authoritarian regimes? How do different societies conceptualize political representation in different cultural contexts? Each of these questions is an enduring element of comparative politics, and is discussed in chapters 7 and 8.

civil society: The sphere of organized, nongovernmental, nonviolent activity by groups larger than individual families or firms

Policymaking Another major issue in comparative politics is policymaking. All governments, whatever the regime, ultimately make policies that govern society. How do different regimes decide which policies to pursue? What role do different political institutions have in the policy-making process? Who is most influential in the process and why? Do the policies that finally gain approval reflect the will of the people? Which decisions should be made at the level of the national government, and which should be delegated to more local governments such as states or provinces? Different regimes provide different answers to these questions.

political economy: The study of the interaction between political and economic phenomena

Political Economy **Political economy** is the study of the interaction between political and economic phenomena. In the modern world, virtually all governments are concerned with and (at least in theory) held responsible for the economic well-being of their societies. Political economists try to determine what kinds of economic policies are most likely to prove beneficial in particular cultural, social, and political contexts. Do some types of regimes produce better economic outcomes than others? Many observers have argued, for instance, that modernizing authoritarian regimes can achieve more rapid economic growth in poor countries than democratic regimes can, but in recent years political scientists have found substantial evidence that the relationship is far less black and white. Some authoritarian regimes, such as China's, have been quite capable of achieving growth, whereas others, including Nigeria, have not. Similarly, some kinds of democratic regimes seem capable of achieving beneficial economic outcomes even as others do not. A detailed comparative study of regimes and economic success can help unravel the answer to this all-important question.

comparativists: Political scientists who study comparative politics

These big issues do not encompass all of comparative politics, but they do raise the most prominent questions that **comparativists**, political scientists who study comparative politics, have been grappling with for the past half century. Today these questions are alive and well in the countries making headlines, from Pakistan and Afghanistan to Libya and Egypt. Comparativists try to look beyond the momentary hot topics to systematically examine these enduring questions, seeking ever clearer understanding of how politics works in the world and how it might be made better. Doing this requires some thought about how to study a very complex subject.

politics: The process by which human communities make collective decisions

comparative politics: One of the major subfields of political science, in which the primary focus is on comparing power and decision making across countries

COMPARATIVE POLITICS: WHAT IS IT? WHY STUDY IT? HOW TO STUDY IT?

political science: The systematic study of politics and power

Politics can be defined as the process by which human communities make collective decisions. These communities can be of any size, from small villages or neighborhoods to nations and international organizations. **Comparative politics** is one of the major subfields of **political science,** the systematic study of politics. Politics always involves elements of power, the first concept we need to examine closely.

first dimension of power: The ability of one person or group to get another person or group to do something it otherwise would not do

A definition of power may seem pretty straightforward, but political scientists have long debated its exact meaning. Political theorist Steven Lukes (1974) usefully categorized power into three dimensions. The **first dimension of power** is the ability of one person or group to get another person or group to do something it otherwise would not do. The focus here is on behavior: making someone do something. A **second dimension of power**, first articulated by Peter Bachrach and Morton Baratz (1962), sees power as the ability not only to make people do something but to keep them from doing something. Bachrach and Baratz argued that a key element of

second dimension of power: The ability not only to make people do something but to keep them from doing something

political power is the ability to keep certain groups and issues out of the political arena by creating political processes and setting the political agenda to allow certain groups to participate and voice their concerns while preventing others from doing so. A **third dimension of power,** which Lukes contributed, is the ability to shape or determine individual or group political demands by causing people to think about political issues in ways that are contrary to their own interests. The ability to influence how people think produces the power to prevent certain political demands from ever being articulated. We will examine the role of all three of these dimensions of power in this chapter and in the rest of the book.

What Is Comparative Politics?
In comparative politics, the primary focus is on power and decision making within national boundaries. This includes the politics of entire countries as well as more local-level politics. Politics among national governments and beyond national boundaries is generally the purview of the field of **international relations,** and while comparativists certainly take into account the domestic effects of international events, we do not try to explain the international events themselves. Perhaps it is self-evident, but comparativists also compare; we systematically examine political phenomena in more than one place and during more than one period, and we try to develop a generalized understanding of and an explanation for political activity that seem to apply to many different situations.

Why Study Comparative Politics?
For one thing, comparativists are interested in understanding political events and developments in various countries. Why did the Taliban come to power in Afghanistan? Why did the Conservative Party rule Britain continuously from 1979 to 1997, and why was the Labour Party able to defeat it and rule until 2010? Also, as the Taliban example shows, understanding political events in other countries can be very important to foreign policy. If the U.S. government had understood better and paid more attention to events in Afghanistan in the 1990s, perhaps the attacks of September 11, 2001, could have been prevented, or at least government officials might have been better prepared to respond to them.

Systematic comparison of different political systems and events around the world also can generate important lessons from one place that can be applied in another. Americans often see their system of government, with a directly elected president, as a very successful and stable model of democracy. Certainly it has been used successfully elsewhere as well, but not everywhere. Much evidence suggests that in a situation of intense political conflict, such as an ethnically divided country after a civil war, a system with a single and powerful elected president might not be the best option. Only one candidate from one side can win this coveted post, and the sides that lose the election might choose to restart the war rather than live with the results. A democratic system that gives all major groups some share of political power at the national level might work better in such a situation. That conclusion is not obvious when examining the United States alone. A systematic comparison of a number of different countries, however, reveals this possibility.

A third reason for examining politics comparatively is to develop broad theories about how politics works. A **theory** is an abstract argument that provides a systematic explanation of some phenomenon. The theory of evolution, for instance, makes an argument about how species change over time in response to their environments. The social sciences, including political science, use two different kinds of theories. An **empirical theory** is an argument that explains what actually occurs. Empirical theorists first *describe* a pattern and then attempt to *explain* what causes it. The theory of evolution is an empirical theory in that evolutionary biologists do not argue

third dimension of power: The ability to shape or determine individual or group political demands by causing people to think about political issues in ways that are contrary to their own interests

international relations: The study of politics among national governments and beyond national boundaries

theory: An abstract argument that provides a systematic explanation of some phenomena

empirical theory: An argument explaining what actually occurs; empirical theorists first notice and describe a pattern and then attempt to explain what causes it

whether evolution is inherently good or bad; they simply describe evolutionary patterns and explain their causes. A good empirical theory should also allow theorists to *predict* what will happen. For example, a comparison of democratic systems in post–civil war situations would lead us to predict that presidential systems are more likely to lead to renewed conflict.

On the other hand, a **normative theory** is an argument that explains what *ought* to occur. For instance, socialists support a normative theory that the government and economy *ought* to be structured in a way that produces a relatively equal distribution of wealth. While comparativists certainly hold various normative theories, most of the discipline of comparative politics focuses on empirical theory. We attempt to explain the political world around us, and we do this by looking across multiple cases to come up with generalizations about politics.

Comparison is important because an empirical theory cannot be proved or disproved on the basis of a single case, although that single case may suggest a theory. For instance, the U.S. case suggests a theory about presidentialism as an inherently stable form of government. Once an empirical theory has been developed, however, it must be tested multiple times in different situations to see if it explains behavior across many cases. If it does not, the theory must be modified or abandoned in light of the evidence.

How Do Comparativists Study Politics?

Clearly, political scientists do not have perfect scientific conditions in which to do research. We do not have a controlled laboratory, because we certainly cannot control the real world of politics. Physicists can use a laboratory to control all elements of an experiment, and they can repeat that same experiment to achieve identical results because molecules do not notice what the scientists are doing, think about the situation, and change their behavior. In political science, however, political actors think about the changes going on around them and modify their behavior accordingly. Research completed by political scientists and disseminated via publication and teaching can influence the real world of politics. By making public the results of our research, we sometimes cause those we are studying to change their behavior, thus making our original ideas no longer applicable.

Despite these limitations, comparativists use the scientific method (as explained in the "Scientific Method in Comparative Politics" box) to try to gain as systematic evidence as possible. We use several research methods to try to overcome at least some of the difficulties our complex field of study presents. **Research methods** are systematic processes used to ensure that the study of a specific item or situation is as objective and unbiased as possible.

One common research method we use is the **single case study,** which examines a particular political phenomenon in just one country or community. A case study can generate ideas for new theories, or it can test existing theories developed from different cases. A single case, of course, can never be definitive proof of anything beyond that case itself, but it can be suggestive of further research and can be of interest to people researching that particular country. Deviant case studies examining a country that does not fit a widely held pattern can be particularly helpful in highlighting the limits of even widely supported theories. Case studies also build on past scholarship on that particular country, examining new questions that prior scholars had overlooked and deepening our knowledge about the country. Typically, they are based on physical research in the country; the researcher may consult historical and government archives and interview political actors or the general public to gain direct insight into the country. Scholars engaging in case study research search for common patterns within the case or use a method known as process tracing, which involves careful examination of the historical linkages

normative theory: An argument explaining what ought to occur rather than what does occur; contrast with empirical theory

research methods: Systematic processes used to ensure that the study of a specific item or situation is as objective and unbiased as possible

single case study: Research method that examines a particular political phenomenon in just one country or community and can generate ideas for theories or test theories developed from different cases

Scientific Method in Comparative Politics

While political science can never be a pure science because of imperfect laboratory conditions (i.e., the real world, over which we have very little control), political scientists nonetheless think in scientific terms. Most use key scientific concepts, including the following:

- Theory: Abstract argument explaining a phenomenon
- Hypothesis: A claim that certain things cause other things to happen or change
- Variable: A measurable phenomenon that changes across time or space
- Dependent variable: The phenomenon a scientist is trying to explain
- Independent variable: The thing that explains the dependent variable
- Control: Holding variables constant so that the effects of one independent variable at a time can be examined

The questions in political science are complex enough that one must usually account for several independent variables simultaneously to come close to a complete explanation of a dependent variable. In quantitative studies, each variable is explicitly measured, and complex statistical techniques can allow simultaneous examination of how all the independent variables correlate with the dependent variable. This in turn suggests the extent to which each independent variable explains variation in the dependent variable. For instance, one recent study of civil wars by Paul Collier and Anke Hoeffler (2001) included, among other variables, measurements of poverty, ethnic fragmentation, and dependence on natural resources to explain where civil wars start and how long they last. Through the study of these variables, the researchers concluded that the presence of natural resources is more closely correlated with civil war than is ethnic fragmentation.

Using the scientific method in political science is quite complex because we do not control our laboratory and the political world is opaque. Often, the first challenge we face in our research is to define the variables clearly and measure them accurately. We conceive of the variables by developing hypotheses. For example, Collier and Hoeffler would have asked themselves, What constitutes a "civil war"? How much violence must occur and for how long before a particular country is considered to be having a civil war? In 2007, critics of the U.S. presence in Iraq argued that Iraq was experiencing a civil war, while defenders of the United States denied this, so should the internal conflict in Iraq in 2007 be counted as a civil war or not?

A second challenge we face is figuring out how to include all the potentially relevant variables in our research. In a laboratory, scientists control many of the variables they work with, holding them constant so that they can examine the effects of one independent variable at a time on the dependent variable. Political scientists can rarely do this directly, as we cannot hold variables constant. Therefore, we measure the simultaneous effects of all the independent variables through quantitative studies. Single-case studies and the comparative method attempt to control variables via careful selection of cases. For instance, a comparative case study examining the same questions Collier and Hoeffler studied might select as cases only poor countries, hypothesizing that the presence of natural resources only causes civil wars in poor countries. The question becomes, In the context of poverty, is ethnic fragmentation or the presence of natural resources more important in causing civil war? If, on the other hand, we think poverty itself affects the likelihood of civil war, we might select several cases from poor countries and several others from rich countries to see if the presence of natural resources has a different effect in the different contexts. None of this provides the perfect control that a laboratory can achieve but rather attempts to mimic those conditions as closely as possible to arrive at scientifically defensible conclusions.

between potential causes and effects. They do this in order to demonstrate as definitively as possible what caused what in the case being studied. Case studies serve as important sources of information and ideas for comparativists using more comparative methods.

Scholars use the **comparative method** to examine the same phenomenon in several cases, and they try to mimic laboratory conditions by selecting cases carefully. Two approaches are common. The **most similar systems design** selects cases that are alike in a number of ways but differ on the key question under examination. This method is often used by comparativists who focus exclusively on one region of the world, and it at least implicitly assumes that the countries in the region have certain similarities. For instance, Michael Bratton and Nicholas van de Walle (1997) looked at transitions to democracy in Africa, arguing that all African countries share certain similarities in patterns of political behavior that are distinct from patterns in Latin America, where the main theories of democratization were developed. African transitions, they argued, are distinct from transitions elsewhere in the world in particular ways. On the other hand, the **most different systems design** looks at countries that differ in many ways but are similar in terms of the particular political process or outcome in which the research is interested. For instance, scholars of revolution look at the major cases of revolution around the world—a list of seemingly very different countries like France, Russia, China, Vietnam, Cuba, Nicaragua, and Iran— and ask what common elements can be found that explain why these countries had revolutions. Both comparative methods have their strengths and weaknesses, but their common goal is to use careful case selection and systematic examination of key variables in every case to mimic laboratory methods as closely as possible.

With about 200 countries in the world, however, no one can systematically examine every single case in depth on any subject. For large-scale studies, political scientists rely on a third method: **quantitative statistical techniques.** When evidence can be reduced to sets of numbers, statistical methods can be used to systematically compare a huge number of cases. Recent research on the causes of civil war, for instance, looked at all identifiable civil wars over several decades, literally hundreds of cases. The results indicated that ethnic divisions, which often seem to be the cause of civil war, are not as important as had been assumed. Although they may play a role, civil war is much more likely when groups are fighting over control of a valuable resource such as oil. Where no such resource exists, ethnic divisions are far less likely to result in war (Collier and Hoeffler 2001).

Each of these methods has its advantages and disadvantages. A single case study allows a political scientist to look at a phenomenon in great depth and come to a more thorough understanding of a particular case (usually a country). The comparative method retains some, but not all, of this depth and gains the advantage of systematic comparison from which more generalizable conclusions can be drawn. Quantitative techniques can show broad patterns, but only for questions involving evidence that can be presented numerically, and they provide little depth on any particular case. Case studies are best at generating new ideas and insights that can lead to new theories. Quantitative techniques are best at showing the tendency of two or more phenomena to vary together, such as civil war and the presence of valuable resources. Understanding how phenomena are connected, and what causes what, often requires case studies that can provide greater depth to see the direct connections involved.

No matter how much political scientists attempt to mimic laboratory sciences, the subject matter will not allow the kind of scientific conclusions that exist in chemistry or biology. The real world of politics is too complex and self-consciously changing to yield any universal theories that are supported in the long run by completely convincing evidence. As the world changes, ideas and theories have to adapt to

comparative method: The means by which scholars try to mimic laboratory conditions by careful selection of cases

most similar systems design: A common approach of the comparative method that selects cases that are alike in a number of ways but differ on a key question under examination

most different systems design: A common approach of the comparative method that looks at countries that differ in many ways but that are similar in terms of the particular political process or outcome in which the research is interested

quantitative statistical techniques: Research method used for large-scale studies that reduces evidence to sets of numbers so that statistical analysis can systematically compare a huge number of cases

explain what goes on in it. That does not mean that old theories are not useful; they very often are. It does mean that no theory will ever become a universal and unchanging law, like the law of gravity. The political world simply isn't that certain.

Comparative politics will also never become a true science because political scientists have their own human passions and positions regarding the various debates they study. A biologist might become determined to gain fame or fortune by proving a particular theory, even if laboratory tests don't support it (e.g., Woo Suk Hwang of South Korea, who fabricated stem cell research results). Biologists, however, do not usually become ethically or morally committed to finding particular research results, nor do they tend to engage in particular kinds of research because of their moral beliefs.

On the other hand, political scientists do act on their moral concerns, and that is entirely justifiable. Normative theories affect political science because our field is in part the study of people. Our ethical and moral positions often influence the very questions we ask. Those who ask questions about the level of "cheating" in the welfare system, for instance, are typically critics of the system who tend to think the government is wasting money on welfare payments to people who could get by without them. Those who ask questions about the effects of budget cuts on the poor, on the other hand, probably believe the government should be involved in alleviating poverty. These ethical positions do not mean that the evidence can or should be ignored. For example, research suggested that the 1996 welfare reform in the United States neither reduced the income of the poor as much as critics initially feared nor helped the poor get jobs and rise out of poverty as much as its proponents predicted (Jacobson 2001). Good political scientists can approach a subject like this with a set of moral concerns but recognize the results of careful empirical research nonetheless. Their normative position may not change, but they might modify their support for particular solutions to problems in light of new evidence.

Normative questions can be important and legitimate purposes for research projects. This book includes extensive discussions of different kinds of democratic political institutions. We systematically compare them, in part to understand their effects in particular contexts. One of the potential trade-offs, we argue, is between greater levels of representation and participation on the one hand and efficient policymaking on the other. We demonstrate this by looking at abstract logic and the actual functioning of different institutions in particular countries. But this analysis is only interesting if we care about this trade-off. We have to hold a normative position on which of the two—representation and participation or efficient policymaking—is more important and why. Only then can we use the lessons learned from our empirical examination to make recommendations about which institutions a country ought to adopt.

Where does this leave the field of comparative politics? Is there a way to study politics comparatively and systematically that can actually provide convincing answers? The answer to the latter is "only partially." The answer to the former is that it leaves us aware of our own biases but still leaves us room to use various methods to generate the most systematic evidence possible to come to logical conclusions. We approach the subject with our normative concerns, our own ideas about what a "good society" should be and what role a government should have in it. We try to do research on interesting questions as scientifically and systematically as possible to develop the best evidence we can to provide a solid basis for government policy. And because we care passionately about the issues, we ought to study them as rigorously as possible. Comparative politics is all about trying to find the most convincing answers possible to crucial political questions.

METHODS IN CONTEXT

Critically Examining How Comparativists Do Research

In an introductory course, students first have to learn some basic information about the concepts used in the field as well as major elements of the modern political world. These provide the basic language and empirical information we need as we develop our understanding of the field of comparative politics. With that information under our belts, we can then start asking bigger and more complicated questions that often have no settled answers. On these questions, comparativists have done extensive research using various methods to try to find convincing empirical evidence.

In several chapters of this book, we explore a few of these complex questions in "Methods in Context," where we focus on such big questions in comparative politics as whether democracies or dictatorships are better at fostering economic development. We begin by introducing the debates, many of which have histories going back decades (at least). We then outline the arguments on each side of the debate, providing an intellectual history of the questions and their various answers. After examining the arguments, we turn to the most recent scholarship on these enduring questions to see what we can learn from it, focusing on one or more recent and particularly innovative attempts to find answers. The research methods used in comparative politics have advanced greatly over the last generation. Most earlier research relied on single- or comparative-case studies to make its claims, with scholars often using different case studies at different times to come to different conclusions. More recently, the availability of larger sets of data and closer attention to careful comparative case study methods have often yielded exciting new insights.

HYPOTHESES

First, we need to set out clearly the hypotheses, which serve as the competing, theory-based answers to the question. We must also understand the theories from which the hypotheses are derived. Having outlined carefully specified and conceptually plausible answers to the question, we can seek to verify them empirically via some type of methodologically justified research.

RESEARCH AND ANALYSIS

Clearly identified hypotheses provide a set of explicit variables that the researcher must then find a way to measure in order to test the relationships among them. In other words, the researcher asks, "What causes what?" We identify

THREE KEY QUESTIONS IN COMPARATIVE POLITICS

Comparative politics is a huge field that encompasses all political activity except international relations. The questions that can be asked and the debates that can be held are virtually limitless. Spanning this huge range, however, are three major questions. The first two are fundamental to the field of political science, of which comparative politics is a part. The third is comparativists' particular contribution to the broader field of political science.

Probably the most common question political scientists ask is, What explains political behavior? The heart of the discipline of political science is trying to understand why people do what they do in the world of politics. We can ask, Why do voters vote the way they do? Why do interest groups champion particular causes so

the variables and learn how they are measured in the most recent scholarship in the field. This includes not only the variables the hypotheses identify as the main causes of what we are examining but also other variables that ideally we need to control for, as if in a laboratory, to understand precisely the relationships among our key variables. In comparative politics, this is often not an easy process. How do we measure, for instance, whether a country is a "democracy" or a "dictatorship"? As we'll see in chapters 8 and 9, the distinctions are not always as clear as they might seem. When do we measure the variables? Should we assume that a democracy will make immediate progress toward greater economic development, meaning that we can look at both variables in the same year? Or should we assume that we need to allow a ten- (or twenty- or thirty-) year lag between the start of democracy and its effect on economic development? Measuring the variables is often one of the most difficult and controversial parts of political science research.

These variables can be tested using either comparative case studies or quantitative statistical techniques or both. Much of the best recent research uses large, quantitative statistical techniques to identify broad patterns of relationships among the key variables and comparative case studies to examine closely the mechanisms by which the most important independent variables cause change in the dependent variable (i.e., the relationship between the presence of democracy or dictatorship and the successful pursuit of economic development). We will review the best recent research on the question we address, looking at the methods used and the conclusions the researchers arrived at.

QUESTIONS IN CONTEXT

Even with the best methods, these large questions typically remain only partly answered. Often, the extent to which we accept research results depends on whether or not we accept the researchers' choice of variables, the way they measure them, and the statistical techniques they use. While you as introductory students are not yet in a position to assess critically all of these issues, you nonetheless can think for yourselves about whether the methods and measurements used seem to reflect accurately the underlying reality the research is trying to examine. We will leave you with questions to think about and discuss along these lines, to spur your own critical thinking on the big issues at hand.

passionately? Why does the U.S. Supreme Court make the decisions it does? Why did the United States invade Iraq? By asking these questions, we seek to discover why individuals, groups, institutions, or countries take particular political actions. Comparativists ask all but the last of these questions—we usually leave the question of why one country invades another to the field of international relations. Political scientists have developed many theories to explain various kinds of political actions. Below, we discuss them in terms of three broad approaches that focus on individual motivation, culture and ideology, and underlying structures.

The second large question animating political science is, Who rules? Who has power in a particular country, political institution, or political situation and why? Formal power is often clear in modern states; particular officials have prescribed functions and rules that give them certain powers. For example, the U.S. Congress passes legislation, which the president has the power to sign or veto and which the Supreme Court can rule as constitutional or not. But does the legislation Congress passes reflect the will of the citizens? Are citizens really ruling through their elected representatives (as the U.S. Constitution implies), or are powerful lobbyists calling the shots, or can members of Congress do whatever they want once in office? The Constitution and laws can't fully answer this broader question of who really has a voice, is able to participate, and therefore has power.

Virtually all questions in political science derive from these two fundamental questions, and virtually all empirical theories are involved in the debate these two questions raise. Comparativists add a third particular focus by asking, Where and why do particular types of political behavior occur? If we can explain why Americans on the left side of the political spectrum vote for Democrats, can we use the same explanation for the voting patterns of Germans and Brazilians with left-leaning views? If special interests have the real power over economic policy in the U.S. presidential system, is this the case in Britain's parliamentary democracy as well? Why have military coups d'etat happened rather frequently in Latin America and Africa but very rarely in Europe and North America? Comparativists start with the same basic theories used by other political scientists to try to explain political behavior and understand who really has power; we then add a comparative dimension to develop explanations that work in different times and places. In addition to helping develop more scientific theories, comparing different cases and contexts can help us determine which lessons from one situation are applicable to another.

These three main questions—What explains political behavior? Who rules? Where and why?—guide this book. Each chapter touches on each of them in one way or another. As is true for most political scientists, explaining political behavior occupies much of our attention. But we also raise the question of who really has power in particular situations and why. Each chapter also includes a separate box asking a where and why question, one that has been the subject of significant attention in the field. In addition, each chapter opens with key questions specific to the subject matter in that chapter but that also derive from the three overarching questions. As we examine specific material, we introduce new questions and concepts, but all originate in the three main questions and the broad theoretical approaches to answering them that we outline below.

What Explains Political Behavior?

The core activity in all political science is explaining political behavior: Why do people, groups, and governments act as they do in the political arena? It's easy enough to observe and describe behavior, but what explains it? In daily discussions we tend to attribute the best of motives to those with whom we agree—they are "acting in the best interests" of the community or nation. We tend to see those with whom we disagree, on the other hand, as acting selfishly or even with evil intent. You can see this tendency in the way Americans use the phrase "special interest." We perceive groups whose causes or ideological leanings we agree with as benevolent and general; those we disagree with are "special interests." Logically, however, any **political actor,** meaning any person or group engaged in political behavior, can be motivated by a variety of factors. Political scientists have developed three broad answers to the question of what explains political behavior: individual motivation, culture and ideology, and underlying structures. Each answer includes within it several theoretical approaches.

political actor: Any person or group engaged in political behavior

Individual Motivation It is a common assumption that most people involved in politics are in it for their own good. Even when political actors claim to be working for the greater good or for some specific principle, many people suspect they are just hiding their own self-interested motives behind such claims. The assumption of self-interest (broadly defined) is also a major element in political science theories about political behavior.

Rational choice theory assumes that individuals are rational and that they bring a set of self-defined preferences into the political arena. This does not mean that all people are greedy or selfish but rather that they rationally pursue their preferences, whatever those may be. The theory borrows heavily from the field of modern economics, which makes the same assumptions in analyzing behavior in the market. Scholars use this model to explain political behavior and its results by making assumptions about political actors' preferences, by modeling the political context in which they pursue those preferences, and by demonstrating how political outcomes can be explained as the result of the interactions of those actors in that context. For instance, the allocation of money for building new roads is the result of an agreement among members of a congressional committee. All of the members of the committee have certain interests or preferences, based mainly on the stated desires of the voters in the districts they represent as well as the members' own desire for re-election. The committee members pursue those interests rationally, and the final bill is a negotiated settlement reflecting the relative power of the various committee members, as well as their interests within the context of the committee and Congress more broadly.

Rational choice theorists start their analyses at the level of the individual, but they often seek to explain group behavior. They model group behavior from their assumptions about the preferences of individual members of groups. Group behavior is essentially considered a result of the collective actions of rational individual actors in the group in a particular context. Racial or ethnic minority groups, women's groups, or environmental and religious groups can all be analyzed in this way. Rational choice theorists would argue, for instance, that environmentalists are just as rational and self interested as oil companies but simply have different preferences. Environmentalists gain benefits from breathing clean air and walking through unpolluted forests; they pursue those preferences in the same way that the oil industry pursues its opposition to environmental regulations. While self-defined preferences may be easier to see when analyzing battles over material goods and money, they exist throughout the political arena. Rational choice theorists thus are not interested in the third dimension of power we mentioned earlier, the ability to influence how people think about politics and thus perhaps change people's preferences. They instead accept people's preferences as given and rational and then ask how those preferences influence political behavior and outcomes.

This raises one of the major criticisms of rational choice theories. Critics contend that rational choice theorists have some difficulty explaining outcomes because it is often difficult to know in advance exactly which individuals or groups might be involved in a particular political dispute and exactly how they will define their preferences. When a new political issue arises, individuals or groups have to figure out if they are interested in it and, if so, what preferences they will hold and pursue. In economics, this usually isn't a problem. It's a pretty safe assumption that people engage in economic activity to make money: businesses seek to maximize profits, and workers look for the highest wage. Knowing preferences in advance is much more difficult in political science. For instance, how can a rational choice theorist explain the electoral choice of a voter who is both a devout Catholic and

rational choice theory: An explanation of political behavior that assumes that individuals are rational beings who bring to the political arena a set of self-defined preferences and adequate knowledge and ability to pursue those preferences

a union member if the two available candidates are (a) a Democrat who favors raising the minimum wage and other workers' benefits but also favors legalized abortion and (b) a Republican with the opposite views? Will that person vote as a Catholic or as a union member? How can we use rational choice theory to figure out his preferences in this situation?

Many comparativists also ask whether rational choice theories can explain the different political behavior seen around the world. For most of the twentieth century, for example, the most important French labor unions were closely affiliated with the Communist Party and pursued many objectives tied to Party beliefs, beyond the basic "shop floor" issues of wages and working conditions. In the United States, by contrast, no major unions were tied to communist or socialist parties, and unions focused much more on improving wages and working conditions with less concern for broader social changes. In Britain, labor unions were not Communists, but they created their own party, the Labour Party, to represent their interests in government. Rational choice theorists might be able to explain political outcomes involving these unions after correctly understanding the preferences of each, but they have a hard time explaining why unions in different countries seem to develop strikingly different sets of preferences. Did something about the working conditions of these three countries produce different definitions of "self-interest," or do different workers define their interests differently based on factors other than rational calculation?

psychological theories: Explanations of political behavior based on psychological analysis of political actors' motives

Psychological theories also focus on individual motivation. They explain political behavior on the basis of individuals' psychological experiences or dispositions. This approach stands in opposition to rational choice theory's assumption of rational behavior. Instead, psychological theories look for nonrational explanations for political behavior. Comparativists who study individual leaders often use this approach, trying to explain leaders' choices and actions by understanding personal backgrounds and psychological states. Psychological theories are also sometimes used to explain group identity and behavior (e.g., strong attachments to racial or ethnic groups) and the willingness to join a group engaging in political actions outside the norms and values of a particular society at a particular time (e.g., revolutions, political violence, and genocide). Therefore, psychological theories are often interested in the third dimension of power: influences on the formation of individual political demands. In these cases, rational choice explanations seem unhelpful. Critics of the psychological approach question whether the inherent focus on the individual that is fundamental to psychological theories makes them irrelevant to explaining group behavior. If so, their utility in political science is limited. Explanations beyond the level of individual motivation, however, might help explain these situations.

Culture and Ideology Culture and ideology are probably second only to self-interest in popular ideas about political behavior. If people think someone is acting out of something other than self-interest, they usually assume that something to be a value or belief. Environmentalists care about the environment; regardless of their own personal interests, they think everyone ought to have clean air to breathe and forests to walk through. People who are against abortion believe that life begins at conception and therefore abortion is murder; self-interest has nothing to do with it. Political scientists have developed various formal theories that relate to this commonsense notion that values and beliefs matter. These approaches focus on either political culture or political ideology.

political culture: A set of widely held attitudes, values, beliefs, and symbols about politics

A **political culture** is a set of widely held attitudes, values, beliefs, and symbols about politics. It provides people with ways to understand the political arena, justifications for a particular set of political institutions and practices, and definitions of appropriate political behaviors. Political cultures emerge from various historical processes and can change over time, although they usually change rather slowly as they are often deeply embedded in a society. They tend to endure, in part, because of **political socialization,** the process through which people, especially young people, learn about politics and are taught a society's common political values and beliefs. Theories of political culture argue that the attitudes, values, beliefs, and symbols that constitute a given country's political culture are crucial explanations of political behavior in that country. Widely accepted cultural values, they argue, can influence all three dimensions of power: getting people to do something, preventing them from doing something, and influencing their political demands.

Two broad schools of thought within political culture theory exist: modernist and postmodernist. **Modernists** believe that clear attitudes, values, and beliefs can be identified within any particular political culture. The best-known example of this approach was presented by Gabriel Almond and Sidney Verba in their 1963 book, *The Civic Culture.* Based on a broad survey of citizens of five countries in North America and Europe, the authors developed a **typology,** or list of different types, of political cultures. They saw each country as dominated primarily by one particular type of political culture and argued that more stable and democratic countries, such as the United States and Great Britain, had a **civic culture.** This meant that their citizens held democratic values and beliefs that supported their democracies; these attitudes led citizens to participate actively in politics but also to defer enough to the leadership to let it govern effectively. On the other hand, the authors described Mexico as an authoritarian culture in which citizens viewed themselves primarily as subjects with no right to control their government, suggesting that these attitudes helped to produce the semi-authoritarian regime that ruled the country until 2000.

political socialization: The process through which people, especially young people, learn about politics and are taught a society's common political values and beliefs

modernists: Theorists of political culture who believe that clear sets of attitudes, values, and beliefs can be identified in each country that change very rarely and explain much about politics there

typology: A classification of some set of phenomena into distinct types for purposes of analysis

civic culture: A political culture in which citizens hold values and beliefs that support democracy, including active participation in politics but also enough deference to the leadership to let it govern effectively

A woman votes in Guinea on November 7, 2010. The West African state's first free election since independence from France in 1958 raises a major set of questions in comparative politics about new democracies: What explains their likely success? How much do ideology, political culture, and institutional history matter to a democracy's survival? Can democracies thrive in any society, or must certain prerequisites exist first?

Credit: Emmanuel Braun/Reuters/Landov

subcultures: Groups that hold partially different beliefs and values from the main political culture of a country

Critics of the modernist approach question the assumption that any country has a clearly defined political culture that is relatively fixed and unchanging, and they contest the argument that cultural values cause political outcomes rather than the other way around. They note that **subcultures** (distinct political cultures of particular groups) exist in all societies. Racial or religious minorities, for instance, may not fully share the political attitudes and values of the majority. The assumption that we can identify a single, unified political culture that is key to understanding a particular country can mask some of the most important political conflicts within the country. Furthermore, political attitudes themselves may be symptoms rather than causes of political activity or a governmental system. For example, Mexican citizens in the 1960s may not have viewed themselves as active participants in government for a very rational reason: they had lived for forty years under one party that had effectively suppressed all meaningful opposition and participation. They really did not have any effective voice in government or any chance for effective participation. According to this view, the political institutions in Mexico created the political attitudes of Mexicans, rather than vice versa.

Some political scientists also accuse modernists of ethnocentrism, in that many modernist approaches argue that Anglo-American values are superior to others for establishing stable democracies. Still other critics suggest that political culture is more malleable than *The Civic Culture* assumed. The attitudes that surveys identified in the 1960s were just that, attitudes of the 1960s. Over time, as societies change and new political ideas arise, attitudes and values change accordingly, sometimes with breathtaking speed (Almond and Verba 1989). Many cultural theorists, for instance, have argued that both Arab and Islamic cultures tend to have nondemocratic values that support the authoritarian regimes widespread in the Middle East. The revolts in 2011 that toppled regimes in Tunisia and Egypt suggest that those theorists either misunderstood the cultures or those cultures were subject to rapid change.

postmaterialist: A set of values in a society in which most citizens are economically secure enough to move beyond immediate economic (materialist) concerns to "quality of life" issues like human rights, civil rights, women's rights, environmentalism, and moral values

A somewhat more recent modernist approach examines change in political culture. Ronald Inglehart (1971) coined the term **postmaterialist** in the 1970s to describe what he saw as a new predominant element in political culture in wealthy democracies. He argued that as a result of the post–World War II economic expansion, by the 1960s and 1970s most citizens in wealthy societies were less concerned about economic (materialist) issues and more concerned with "quality of life" issues. They had become "postmaterialist." Economic growth had allowed most citizens to attain a level of material comfort that led to a change in attitudes and values. Individuals had become more concerned with ideas like human rights, civil rights, women's rights, environmentalism, and moral values.

This postmaterialist shift in political culture led to a sea change in the issues that politicians came to care about and the outcomes of elections. It explained, for instance, why many self-identified Catholic voters in the United States shifted from voting Democratic in the middle of the twentieth century to voting Republican by the end of that century. In the 1950s they voted their mostly working-class economic interests, supporting the party that created what many saw as "pro-worker" policies. Later, as they moved into greater security as part of an expanding middle class, they came to care more about postmaterial moral values, such as their religious opposition to abortion, and they shifted their party allegiance accordingly. As the bulk of American voters went through this shift in political culture, political battles focused less on economic issues and more on debates over the moral and cultural values that many analysts see dividing the country more recently. This brings up some interesting questions: In situations of economic decline and instability, such as the crisis that began in 2008, do voters revert to caring primarily about material concerns? Will any voter reversion to a materialist outlook be a long-term change? Or will such a change be temporary, lasting only until economic security returns and postmaterial values once again become predominant?

Inglehart's (1971) approach, and others like it, shows how political culture can change over time and how current political culture could be seen as the result of other changes in society. Nonetheless, Inglehart and others continued to argue that it was useful to think about societies as having identifiable political cultures that explain much political behavior. A different approach to political culture is the **postmodernist** approach, which criticizes the assumption that one clear set of values can be identified that has a clear meaning to all members of a society and defines the politics of that society at a particular time. Postmodernists, influenced primarily by postmodern French philosophers such as Michel Foucault, see cultures not as sets of fixed and clearly defined values but rather as sets of symbols subject to interpretation. When examining political culture, postmodernists focus primarily on **political discourse,** meaning the ways in which a society speaks and writes about politics. They argue that a culture has a set of symbols that, through a particular historical process, has come to be highly valued but is always subject to varying interpretations. These symbols do not have fixed values upon which all members of a society agree; instead, political actors can use them by interpreting them through political discourse. Influencing discourse can be a means to gain power in its third dimension: influencing how people think about politics.

One example of a symbol that political actors use in political discourse is "family values." Politicians in the United States seldom say they are opposed to family values. In the 1980s Republicans under President Ronald Reagan used this concept in their campaign discourse very effectively to paint themselves as supporters of the core concerns of middle-class families. As a result, Democrats and their policies came to be seen at times as threatening to the ideal of the nuclear family. In the 1990s under President Bill Clinton, Democrats were able to gain back some political advantage by reinterpreting family values to mean what they argued was support for "real" American families: single mothers trying to raise kids on their own or two-income families in which the parents were worried about the quality of after-school programs and the cost of a college education. Democrats created a new discourse about family values that allowed them to connect that powerful symbol to the kinds of government programs they supported. Family values, the postmodernists would argue, are not a fixed set of values that all agree on but rather a symbol through which political leaders build support by developing a particular discourse at a particular time. Such symbols are always subject to reinterpretation in this way.

Critics of the postmodern approach argue that it really cannot explain anything. If everything is subject to interpretation, then how can one explain anything or form any prediction other than "things will change as new interpretations arise"? Postmodernists respond that the discourses themselves matter by setting symbolic boundaries within which political actors must engage to mobilize political support. The ability of political leaders to interpret these symbols to develop support for themselves and their policies is a central element to understanding political activity in any country.

A recent example of this approach is discussed in a book by political scientist Michael Schatzberg (2001) in which he examined African politics. He argued that each society has a "moral matrix of legitimate governance" that places boundaries on what is "politically thinkable." In Africa that moral matrix involves symbols of the family and of the political leader as "father-chief." This symbol, however, is not fixed. The father is seen as the head and leader of the family, and as such he is due respect, but he also is responsible for the well-being of his children. In addition, he is expected eventually to turn over his position to someone in the next generation.

postmodernist: An approach that sees cultures not as sets of fixed and clearly defined values but rather as sets of symbols subject to interpretation

political discourse: The ways in which people speak and write about politics; postmodern theorists argue that political discourse influences political attitudes, identity, and actions

Political discourse in Africa, then, is often about what a leader owes his "children"—the citizens—and how well he is providing for them, but it is also about when the leader will relinquish power to the next generation. While the image of the father may appear undemocratic to Westerners, it can also be interpreted in ways that are much more democratic, ways that involve concern for the well-being of citizens and the transfer of power from one generation to the next. The moral matrix sets boundaries on what is acceptable, but it leaves room for many political battles within these boundaries. Political culture, in this view, affects political behavior by constraining it within certain boundaries and providing the discourse through which political actors debate one another and mobilize political support.

Advocates of political culture, whether modernist or postmodernist, argue that explaining political behavior requires understanding the effects of political culture at the broadest level. A related but distinct way to examine the effect of values and beliefs is the study of **political ideology,** a systematic set of beliefs about how a political system ought to be structured. Political ideologies typically are quite powerful, overarching worldviews that incorporate both normative and empirical theories and explicitly state an understanding of how the political world does operate and how it ought to operate. Political ideology is distinct from political culture in that it is much more consciously elaborated. In chapter 3 we examine the predominant political ideologies of the last century: liberalism, communism, fascism, modernizing authoritarianism, and theocratic ideology.

Advocates of a particular political ideology attempt to mobilize support for their position by proclaiming a vision of a just and good society as a goal toward which political actors should strive. The most articulate proponents of a particular political ideology can expound on its points, define its key terms, and argue for why it is right. Communists, for instance, envision a communist society in which all people are equal and virtually all serious conflicts disappear, meaning government itself can disappear. They appeal to people's sense of injustice by pointing out the inequality that is inherent in the existing order in a capitalist society, and they encourage people to work with them through various means to achieve a better society in the future.

A political ideology may be related to a particular political culture, but political ideologies are conscious and well-developed sets of beliefs rather than the vague sets of values or attitudes that typically constitute a political culture. Some scholars take political ideology at face value, at least implicitly accepting the idea that political leaders, and perhaps their followers as well, should be taken at their word. These scholars believe that political actors have thought about politics and adopted a particular set of beliefs that they use as a basis for their own political actions and for judging the actions of others. Comparativists Evelyne Huber and John Stephens (2001), for instance, argue that the strength of social democratic ideology in several northern European governments partly explains why those states created and have maintained exceptionally generous welfare policies.

Critics of this approach point to what they see as the underlying motives of ideology and the real explanation for political behavior. The Italian Marxist Antonio Gramsci (1971) argued that the key element we need to understand is **ideological hegemony,** or the ruling class's ability to propagate a set of ideas that justifies and perpetuates its political dominance. For Gramsci, ideology is a means by which the ruling class convinces the population that its rule is natural, justified, or both (see the "Who Rules?" section in this chapter on page 27 for a discussion of the ruling class). Clearly, this ties directly to the "third dimension" of power. Advocates of rational choice models might argue that a particular leader or group adopts a particular ideology because it is in its own self-interest; for

political ideology:
A systematic set of beliefs about how a political system ought to be structured

ideological hegemony: The ruling class's ability to spread a set of ideas justifying and perpetuating its political dominance

example, business owners support an ideology of "free markets" because it maximizes opportunities to make profits. Similarly, advocates of a political culture approach see cultural values as lying behind ideology. In the United States, for instance, vague but deep-seated American values of individualism and individual freedom may explain why Americans are far less willing to support socialist ideologies than are Europeans. The debate between proponents and critics of political ideology as an explanation of political behavior is about whether the political actors' ideological statements should be accepted at face value as explanations of their behavior, or if scholars should dig deeper to look for underlying causes of why those actors support that ideology.

Underlying Structures The third broad approach to explaining political behavior is **structuralism.** Structuralists argue that broader structures in a society at the very least influence and limit, and perhaps even determine, political behavior. These structures can be socioeconomic or political. An early and particularly influential structuralist argument was **Marxism,** which states that economic structures largely determine political behavior. Karl Marx contended that the production process of any society creates distinct **social classes**—groups of people with the same relationship to the means of production. He argued that in modern capitalist society the key classes are the **bourgeoisie,** which owns and controls capital, and the **proletariat,** which owns no capital and must sell its labor to survive. According to Marx, this economic structure explains political behavior: the bourgeoisie uses its economic advantage to control the state in its interest, while the proletariat will eventually recognize and act on its own, opposing interests.

A more recent structuralist theory is **institutionalism**. Institutionalists argue that political institutions are crucial to understanding political behavior. A **political institution** is most commonly defined as a set of rules, norms, or standard operating procedures that is widely recognized and accepted and that structures and constrains individuals' political actions. In short, institutions are the "rules of the game" within which political actors must operate. These rules are often quite formal and widely recognized, such as in the U.S. Constitution.

Other institutions can be informal or even outside government but nonetheless be very important in influencing political behavior. In the United States, George Washington established a long-standing informal institution, the two-term limit on the presidency. After he stepped down at the end of his second term, no other president, no matter how popular, attempted to run for a third term until Franklin Roosevelt in 1940, as the country was coming out of the Great Depression and about to enter World War II. In that context, voters supported his decision and re-elected him, but after his death the country quickly and easily passed a constitutional amendment that created a formal rule limiting a president to two consecutive terms. Informal institutions can be enduring, as the two-term presidency tradition shows. It held for more than 150 years simply because the vast majority of political leaders and citizens believed it should; in that context, no politician dared go against it.

Broadly speaking, two schools of thought exist among institutionalists. **Rational choice institutionalists** follow the assumptions of rational choice theory outlined above. They argue that institutions are the products of the interaction and bargaining of rational actors and, once created, constitute the rules of the game within which rational actors operate, at least until their interests diverge too far from those rules. Barry Weingast (1997), for instance, claimed that for democracies to succeed, major political forces must come to a rational compromise on key political institutions in order to create a system that gives all important political players incentives

structuralism:
Approach to explaining politics that argues that political behavior is at least influenced and limited, and perhaps even determined, by broader structures in a society such as class divisions or enduring institutions

Marxism:
Structuralist argument that says that economic structures largely determine political behavior; the philosophical underpinning of communism

social classes:
In Marxist theory, groups of people with the same relationship to the means of production; more generally, groups of people with similar occupations, wealth, or income

bourgeoisie: The class that owns capital; according to Marxism, the ruling elite in all capitalist societies

proletariat: A term in Marxist theory for the class of free wage laborers who own no capital and must sell their labor to survive; communist parties claim to work on the proletariat's behalf

institutionalism:
An approach to explaining politics that argues that political institutions are crucial to understanding political behavior

political institution:
A set of rules, norms, or standard operating procedures that is widely recognized and accepted by the society and that structures and constrains political actions

rational choice institutionalists:
Institutionalist theorists who follow the assumptions of rational choice theory and argue that institutions are the products of the interaction and bargaining of rational actors

historical institutionalists:
Theorists who believe that institutions explain political behavior and shape individuals' political preferences and their perceptions of their self-interests and that institutions evolve historically in particular countries and change relatively slowly

to remain involved in that system. Institutions that create such incentives will be self-enforcing, thereby creating a stable democratic political system. Weingast applied this argument to several countries, including the United States. He argued that political stability in early U.S. history was due to the Constitution's provision of federalism, a particular separation of powers, and the equal representation of each of the states in the Senate. This gave both North and South effective veto power over major legislation, which enforced compromise and, thereby, stability. The Civil War broke out, in part, because by the 1850s the creation of more nonslave states threatened the South's veto power. This changed context meant that Southern leaders no longer saw the Constitution as serving their interests, so they were willing to secede. Rational choice institutionalists argue that political actors will abide by a particular institution only as long as it continues to serve their joint interests. Therefore, a changed context requires institutions to change accordingly or face dissolution.

Historical institutionalists believe that institutions play an even bigger role in explaining political behavior. They argue that institutions not only limit self-interested political behavior but also influence who is involved in politics and shape individuals' political preferences, thus working in all three dimensions of power. By limiting who is allowed to participate, institutions can determine what a government is capable of accomplishing. Stephan Haggard and Robert Kaufman (1995), for example, argued that two key institutions—a strong executive and a coherent party system—are crucial to explaining which countries in Latin America and East Asia were able to respond positively to economic crises in the 1980s and 1990s and produce not only better economies but stable democracies as well. Beyond limiting who can participate and what can be accomplished, institutions can create political preferences. Because societies value long-standing political institutions, members of a society typically instill belief in those institutions in each succeeding generation. As children go through the process of political socialization, they come to accept and value existing institutions and define their own interests partly in terms of preserving those institutions. Regardless of people's self-interests or cultural values, historical institutionalists argue that the institutions themselves profoundly shape what policies are possible and what political outcomes are likely.

Critics of institutionalism argue that institutions are rarely the actual explanation of political behavior. Skeptics who follow rational choice theory argue that institutions are simply based on rational actions and compromises among elites who will continue to be "constrained" by these only as long as doing so serves their own interests. Scholars who focus on political culture or ideology, on the other hand, suggest that institutions are derived from a society's underlying values and beliefs or a more self-conscious ideology. In either case, the real explanation for political behavior and the shape of the institutions is the underlying values, beliefs, or ideology present in a society.

CONCLUSION

Political scientists look to three sources as explanations of political behavior: rational action, values and beliefs, and structures. Quite often, different scholars use each of these approaches to analyze the same political event. For instance, Chile made one of the smoother and, by most accounts, most successful transitions to democracy in the 1990s. A rational choice theorist might argue that this smooth transition resulted from the strategic interaction of the major political actors, regardless of what they personally believed about democracy. They came to a compromise with the former military regime and with each other around a set of electoral procedures that, given the political context, they thought was better for them than the available nondemocratic alternatives. Therefore, they agreed to act within the democratic "game." A political culture theorist would point to values in Chilean society that favored democracy, values that perhaps derived in part from the European origins of much of the population, as well as the country's past history with democracy. A historical institutionalist, on the other hand, would argue that Chile's prior stable democratic institutions were easy to resurrect because of their past success and that these institutions represented a legacy that many other Latin American countries did not have. So, the question becomes, Which of these theories is most convincing and why, and what evidence can we find to support one or another explanation? This is the primary work of much of political science and the kind of question we will return to frequently in this book. The theories we use are summarized in Table 1.1.

Who Rules?

The second great question in comparative politics is, Who rules? Which individual, group, or groups control power, and how much do they really control? At first glance, the answer may seem obvious. In a democracy, legislators are elected for a set term to make the laws. They rule, after the voters choose them, until the next election. Because of elections, it is the voters who really rule in the long term. In a dictatorship, on the other hand, one individual, one ruling party, or one small group (such as a military junta) rules. This ruling entity has all the power and keeps it as long as it pleases, or at least as long as it is able.

Comparativists, however, question this superficial view. Even in democracies, it can be argued that the voters don't really hold the power and that a small group at the top controls things. Conversely, many argue that dictatorships may not be the monoliths they appear to be in that those officially in charge may have to unofficially share power with others in society in one way or another. Political scientists, in trying to dig beneath the surface of the question, have developed many theories that can be grouped into two broad categories: pluralist theories and elite theories.

Pluralist Theories: Each Group Has Its Voice
Pluralist theories contend that society is divided into various political groups and that power is dispersed among them so that no group has complete or permanent power. This is most obvious in democracies in which different parties capture power via elections. When pluralists look at political groups, however, they look at far more than just parties. They argue that politically organized groups exist in all societies, sometimes formally and legally but at other times informally or illegally. These groups compete for access to and influence over power. Policy is almost always the result of a compromise among groups to some extent, and no single group is able to dominate continuously. Furthermore, over time and on different issues, the power and influence of groups vary. Thus, a group that is particularly successful at gaining power or influencing government on one particular issue will not be as successful on another. No group will ever win all battles. Pluralists clearly tend to think about power in its first dimension; they do not believe that any one group has the ability to exclude another group from the political arena or to influence how another group thinks to the extent necessary to gain permanent power over them.

This pluralist process is less obvious in countries that do not have electoral democracies, but many pluralists argue that their ideas are valid in these cases as well. Even in the Soviet Union under Communist rule, some analysts saw elements of pluralism. They believed that for most of the Soviet period, at least after the death of Joseph Stalin in 1953, the ruling Communist Party had numerous internal factions that were essentially informal political groups. These were based on a

pluralist theory: Explanation of who has power that argues that society is divided into various political groups and that power is dispersed among these groups so that no group has complete or permanent power; contrast to elite theory

person's position in the party and government bureaucracy or on one's economic position, regional loyalty, or personal loyalty to a key leader. For instance, people in the secret police, the KGB, and the military were each a political group, quietly lobbying the official rulers to expand the influence and power of their organizations. Leaders of particular industries, such as the oil industry, could be seen as a group seeking the ruling party's support for greater resources and prestige for their area of the economy. Leaders of a region or city could also act as a group, seeking greater government spending in their area. In all these cases, pluralist politics were hidden behind a facade of iron-clad party rule in which the politburo, the Communist Party's central decision-making elite, made all decisions and all others obeyed. Pluralist analysts of the Soviet Union argue, however, that behind closed doors a great deal of lobbying, coalition building, and power seeking was occurring, not unlike the more public version of such activity that happens in democracies.

Dictatorships in postcolonial countries can also be analyzed via pluralism. On the surface, a military government in Africa looks like one individual or small group holding all power for as long as it is able or desires. Pluralists argue, however, that many of these governments have very limited central control. They rule through **patron-client relationships** in which the top leaders, the patrons, mobilize political support by providing resources to their followers, the clients. The internal politics of this type of rule revolve around the competition of the leaders for access to resources they can pass on to their clients. The top clients are themselves patrons of clients further down the chain. Midlevel clients might decide to shift their loyalty from one patron to another if they don't receive adequate resources, meaning those at the top must continuously work to maintain the support of their clients. In many cases, patrons use resources to mobilize

TYPE	INDIVIDUAL MOTIVATION Understanding what internal factors explain political actions	
Theory or framework	Rational choice	Psychological theory
Assumptions	Political actors bring a set of self-defined preferences, adequate knowledge and ability to pursue those interests, and rationality to the political arena.	Nonrational influences explain political behavior.
Unit of analysis	Individual actors	Group and individual identity and behavior
Methods	Observe outcome of political process; identify actors involved, relative power, and preferences; demonstrate how outcome was result of actors' self-interested interactions.	Explain actors' choices and actions by understanding their personal backgrounds and psychological states.
Critiques	Some difficulty predicting future behavior; hard to explain variation across cases.	Difficult to verify connections between internal state and actions, particularly for groups.

TABLE 1.1

What Explains Political Behavior?

| CULTURE AND IDEOLOGY | | UNDERLYING STRUCTURES | |
| Understanding the effect of values or beliefs | | Understanding how broad structures or forces shape or determine behavior | |
Political culture	**Political ideology**	**Marxism**	**Institutionalism**
A set of widely held attitudes, values, beliefs, and symbols about politics shapes what actors do.	Systematic set of beliefs about how the political system ought to be structured motivates political action.	Economic structures determine political behavior. Production process creates distinct social classes—groups of people with the same relationship to the means of production.	Political institutions are widely recognized and accepted rules, norms, or standard operating procedures that structure and constrain individuals' political actions—the "rules of the game."
Individual actors and groups, political institutions, discourses, and practices	Individual actors and groups	Groups and social classes in particular	Interaction of both formal and informal institutions with groups and individuals
Modernist approach identifies clear attitudes, values, and beliefs within any particular political culture—for example, civic culture or postmaterialist culture. Postmodernist approach holds that cultures do not have fixed and clearly defined values but rather a set of symbols subject to interpretation; focuses primarily on political discourse.	Analyze written and verbal statements of political actors and correlate them with observed behavior.	Conduct historical analysis of economic systems.	Rational choice institutionalists follow rational choice theory; institutions are products of the interactions and bargaining of rational actors. Historical institutionalists examine the historical evolution of institutions to demonstrate how these institutions limit self-interested political behavior and shape individuals' political preferences.
Political culture is not a monolithic, unchanging entity within a given country. Cultural values are not necessarily the cause of political outcomes; the causal relationship may be the other way around. If everything is subject to interpretation, then how can anything be explained or predicted?	Focus on ideology obscures what may be underlying motives, or the real explanation, for political behavior.	Ignores noneconomic motives and ignores groups other than social classes.	Difficult to determine if institutions, rather than self-interest or culture, limit behavior.

patron-client relationships: Top leaders (patrons) mobilize political support by providing resources to their followers (clients) in exchange for political loyalty

elite theory: A theory that all societies are ruled by a small group that has effective control over virtually all power; contrast to pluralist theory

support from others in their own ethnic group, so the main informal groups competing for power are ethnically defined (see chapter 4). Various factions compete for power and access to resources, again behind a facade of unitary and centralized power.

Elite Theory: Concentrated Power While pluralists see competing groups, even in countries that appear to be ruled by dictators, proponents of **elite theory** argue that all societies are ruled by an elite that has effective control over virtually all power. Elite theories usually focus on the second and third dimensions of power to argue that certain elites have perpetual power over ordinary citizens. The longest tradition within elite theory is Marxism, mentioned above. Marx argued that in any society, political power reflects control of the economy. In feudal Europe, for instance, the feudal lord, by virtue of his ownership of land, had power over the peasants, who were dependent on the lord for access to land and thus their survival. The peasants were forced to live on the land of the lord under whom they were born, work that land for their own survival and produce a surplus for the lord, and carry out the lord's will in virtually all things. The lord, by virtue of his economic position, had tremendous political power over them. Similarly, Marx contended that in modern capitalist society, the bourgeoisie and proletariat are the two great social classes. By

Konstantin Chernenko, the last leader of the Soviet Union before economic and political reforms began, waves to other members of the politburo, the Soviet Union's top leadership council. Communist systems seem to be ruled by a small elite, but some pluralist theorists argue that even such dictatorial regimes include an element of pluralism. The men on the podium often represent different factions in the ruling party-state, vying for resources and power behind closed doors.

Credit: AP Photo/Boris Yurchenko

virtue of their ownership of capital, Marx said, the bourgeoisie are the **ruling class,** as the feudal lords were centuries ago. The general population, or proletariat, is forced to sell its labor by working in the bourgeoisie's factories in order to survive and must generally serve the desires of the bourgeoisie. Thus, in *The Communist Manifesto* Marx famously called the modern state "the executive committee of the whole bourgeoisie."

In postcolonial societies, Marxist analysts often argue that at least part of the ruling class is outside the country it rules. With the end of colonialism, a new situation of **neocolonialism** arose. The leaders of the newly independent countries in Africa and Asia benefited politically and economically by helping Western businesses maintain access to their countries' wealth. The new governments came to serve the interests of Western corporations as much as or more than they served their own people. Marxist theorists debate among themselves how much power and autonomy the local elite within a given country has vis-à-vis Western influences, but all agree that internal groups have at most very limited power in relation to the new elite supported by the West.

The Marxist tradition is only one type of elite theory. C. Wright Mills, in *The Power Elite* (1956), argued that the United States was ruled by a set of interlocking elites sitting at the top of economic, political, and military hierarchies. Mills shared with the Marxist tradition an emphasis on a small group controlling all real power, but he did not see the economy as the sole source of this power. He believed that the economic, political, and military spheres, while interlocking, are distinct and that all serve as key elements in the ruling elite. A more recent example of this view was put forward by Charles Lindblom (1977), who referred to the "privileged position of business" in a capitalist society. In his view, government is dependent on business for taxes and the bulk of the population is dependent on business for employment, so business is in a unique position to influence those in power and, therefore, government policy. Lindblom argued that two spheres of power exist in modern democracies: economic and political. The political sphere is subject to democratic control, and the economic sphere is not. Modern democracies, including the United States, are not fully governed by "the people" in any real sense of the word, according to this school of elite theorists, but rather are governed by elites who serve the interests of the owners and managers of capital.

More recently, feminist scholars have also developed elite theories of rule based on the concept of **patriarchy,** or rule by men. They argue that throughout history men have controlled virtually all power. Even though women have gained the right to vote in most countries, men remain the key rulers virtually everywhere. Today this may be caused more by social mores and political discourse than actual law, but men remain in power nonetheless, and the political realm, especially its military aspects, continues to be linked to masculinity. A leader needs to be able to command a military, "take charge," and "act boldly and aggressively"—all activities most societies associate with masculinity. The second and third dimensions of power help preserve male control despite women now having the same formal political rights as men. Men also continue to enjoy greater income and wealth than women and can translate economic status into political power. According to feminist theorists, men thus constitute an elite that continues to enjoy a near monopoly on political power in many societies.

Similarly, some analysts argue that a racial elite exists in some societies in which one race has been able to maintain a hold on power. Historically, this was done via laws that prevented other races from participating in the political process, such as

ruling class: An elite who possess adequate resources to control a regime; in Marxist theory, the class that controls key sources of wealth in a given epoch

neocolonialism: A relationship between postcolonial societies and their former colonizers in which leaders benefit politically and economically by helping outside businesses and states maintain access to the former colonies' wealth and come to serve the interests of the former colonizers and corporations more than they serve their own people

patriarchy: Rule by men

A signpost indicates a "white area" on a beach in South Africa. During apartheid in South Africa and under Jim Crow laws in the United States, such signs of legal racial segregation were common, enforcing white rule. While such legal segregation is a thing of the past, elite theorists who focus on race argue that white socioeconomic and cultural dominance preserve an informal system of white rule in many countries.

Credit: AP Photo

under apartheid in South Africa or the Jim Crow laws of the southern United States. But, as with feminists, analysts of race often argue that one race can maintain dominance through a disproportionate share of wealth or through the preservation of a political discourse in which its attributes are considered to be those most desirable for leadership. Such theorists contend that in the United States, cultural attributes associated with being white, such as personal mannerisms, musical preferences, and accent and dialect of English, are all assumed to be not only "normal" but implicitly superior and are thus expected of those in leadership positions. This gives an inherent advantage to white aspirants for political positions, even when no overt discrimination against others exists.

Pluralists and elite theorists disagree over where power lies. Pluralists tend to see power as dispersed among many groups, and while pluralist theory arose in the context of explaining democracy, it has been applied to nondemocratic societies as well. These societies may be less pluralistic than democracies, but they can still be analyzed as including various groups that either share or have at least some influence over power and government policy. Elite theorists, in contrast, see all societies as controlled by one or more small groups of elites. The most common type of elite theory is based on social class, following from Marx and other nineteenth-century theorists, but other elite groups, such as those based on gender and race, might exist as well.

TABLE 1.2

Who Rules?

	Pluralist theory		Elite theory	
	Society is divided into political groups.		All societies are ruled by an elite with control over virtually all power.	
	Power is dispersed among groups.		Marxism: Political power reflects control of the economy; it is based on the economic power of the bourgeoisie, who owns and controls capital and is the ruling elite in capitalist societies.	
Key arguments	No group has complete or permanent power.		The power elite: Elite consists of military and political elite as well as economic elite.	
	Even authoritarian regimes have important pluralist elements.		Patriarchy: The ruling elite is male; social mores and political discourse keep men in power. The political realm, especially the military, is linked to masculinity.	
			Critical race theorists: The ruling elite is white; assumed superiority of white cultural characteristics keeps whites in power.	

Determining which of these theories best answers the question of who rules requires answering these questions: Who is in power? Who has influence on government decision making? Who benefits from the decisions made? If the answer to all of these questions seems to be one or a select few individuals, then the evidence points to elite theory as more accurate. If various groups seem to have access to power or influence over decision making, or both, then pluralism would seem more accurate. Table 1.2 summarizes these theories, which we investigate throughout this book. The "Where and Why" box on page 34 takes a closer look at how comparativists explore these questions.

PLAN OF THE BOOK

This book takes a thematic approach to exploring the world of comparative politics. Each chapter examines a set of issues by presenting the major theoretical ideas and debates in that area of comparative politics and then examining how those ideas and issues play out in the real world in a set of countries. The rest of Part I looks at a set of key relationships crucial to understanding modern politics. These relationships all involve the modern state (defined fully in chapter 2)—to understand the modern political world, we must first understand how the modern state arose. We then look at the relationship of the state to citizens (chapter 3), group identity (chapter 4), and the market economy (chapter 5). Part II examines the basic institutions of modern politics in both democratic and authoritarian regimes and explores the process of transition from one regime to another. Part III turns to an examination of a set of important policy issues in contemporary politics around the world.

Throughout the book, we draw on a set of eleven countries to illustrate the ideas, debates, institutions, and issues we are examining. Each chapter focuses on a comparison of several of these countries, chosen to illustrate the key ideas

"What explains political behavior?" and "Who rules?" are central questions to all of political science. The particular focus of comparative politics is to ask these questions across countries in an attempt to develop a common understanding of political phenomena in all places and times. The third major question that orients this book is "Where and why?" Where do particular political phenomena occur, and why do they occur where they do and how they do? As noted earlier, comparativists often use single case studies to develop hypotheses that can then be examined comparatively. The comparative method requires picking case studies that are similar in certain ways but different in others to understand the effects of those differences, in the same way that lab scientists control certain variables in order to understand the specific effects of others in which they are interested.

For instance, Sweden is famous for its extensive and expensive welfare state, while the U.S. government spends much less money and attention on providing for people's needs directly via "welfare." Why are these two wealthy democracies so different? Can their differences be explained on the basis of competing rational choices? Did business interests overpower the interests of workers and poor people in the United States, while a large and well-organized labor movement in Sweden overcame a small, weaker business class to produce a more extensive welfare state? Or has the Swedish Socialist Party, which has been dominant over most of the last century, simply been successful at convincing the bulk of the population that its social democratic ideology produces a better society, while Americans' cultural belief in "making it on your own" leads them to reject any form of socialism? Or are the differences because a strong nongovernmental institution, the Landsorganisationen I Sverige (LO), arose in Sweden, uniting virtually all labor unions under one organization that the government came to recognize as a central part of the policy-making process, whereas in the United States the country's more decentralized political institutions resulted in decentralized labor institutions that were not as capable of gaining the government's ear on welfare policy? Comparative politics attempts to resolve this kind of puzzle by examining the various theories of political behavior in light of the evidence found.

We engage in similar comparative efforts when seeking to understand who rules. A case study of the United States, for instance, might argue (as many have) that a corporate elite holds great power in American democracy, perhaps so great that it raises questions of how democratic the system actually is. A Marxist might argue that this is due to the unusually centralized and unequal control of wealth in the United States. A political culture theorist would point instead to American culture's belief in individualism, which leads few to question the leaders of major businesses, who are often depicted as "self-made" individuals whom many citizens admire. An institutionalist, on the other hand, would argue that American political institutions allow corpora tions to have great influence by funding expensive political campaigns and that members of Congress have little incentive to vote in support of their parties and so are more open to pressure from individual lobbyists. A comparativist might compare the United States and several European countries, examining the relative level of corporate influence, the level of wealth concentration, cultural values, and the ability of lobbyists to influence legislators in each country. This study might reveal comparative patterns that suggest, for instance, that corporate influence is highest in countries where wealth is most concentrated, regardless of the type of political system or cultural values. We examine this kind of question throughout the book, highlighting in each chapter some of the best-known examples of comparativists asking where and why questions about the subject matter of that chapter.

and debates in the chapter. The eleven countries include a majority of the most populous countries in the world and provide a representative sample of different kinds of modern political history. They include four wealthy democracies (the United States, Britain, Germany, and Japan), two post-Communist countries (Russia and China), the largest and one of the most enduring democracies in the world (India), the world's only theocracy (Iran), and three examples of countries that have worked to establish democratic systems after lengthy authoritarian regimes (Brazil, Mexico, and Nigeria). In addition, we include a variety of "Mini Cases," brief presentations of key topics in other countries, such as genocide in Rwanda and conflict resolution in Northern Ireland. These countries come from every continent and major region of the world. Our task is to see what we can learn from a comparative examination of politics in this diverse array of settings.

KEY CONCEPTS

authoritarian regime (p. 8)
bourgeoisie (p. 25)
civic culture (p. 21)
civil society (p. 9)
comparative method (p. 14)
comparative politics (p. 10)
comparativists (p. 10)
democracy (p. 8)
elite theory (p. 30)
empirical theory (p. 11)
first dimension of power (p. 10)
historical institutionalists (p. 26)
ideological hegemony (p. 24)
institutionalism (p. 25)
international relations (p. 11)
Marxism (p. 25)
modernists (p. 21)
modernization (p. 7)

most different systems design (p. 14)
most similar systems design (p. 14)
neocolonialism (p. 31)
normative theory (p. 12)
patriarchy (p. 31)
patron-client relationships (p. 30)
pluralist theories (p. 27)
political actor (p. 18)
political culture (p. 20)
political development (p. 7)
political discourse (p. 23)
political economy (p. 10)
political ideology (p. 24)
political institution (p. 26)
political science (p. 10)
political socialization (p. 21)
politics (p. 10)
postmaterialist (p. 22)

postmodernist (p. 23)
proletariat (p. 25)
psychological theories (p. 20)
quantitative statistical techniques (p. 14)
rational choice institutionalists (p. 26)
rational choice theory (p. 19)
research methods (p. 12)
ruling class (p. 31)
second dimension of power (p. 10)
single case study (p. 12)
social classes (p. 25)
structuralism (p. 25)
subcultures (p. 22)
theory (p. 11)
third dimension of power (p. 11)
typology (p. 21)

WORKS CITED

Almond, Gabriel A., and Sidney Verba. 1963. *The Civic Culture: Political Attitudes and Democracy in Five Nations.* Princeton, NJ: Princeton University Press.

———. 1989. *The Civic Culture Revisited.* Newbury Park, CA: Sage.

Bachrach, Peter, and Morton S. Baratz. 1962. "Two Faces of Power." *American Political Science Review* 56 (4): 947–52.

Bratton, Michael, and Nicholas van de Walle. 1997. *Democratic Experiments in Africa: Regime Transitions in Comparative Perspective.* Cambridge, UK: Cambridge University Press.

Collier, Paul, and Anke Hoeffler. 2001. *Greed and Grievance in Civil War*. Washington, DC: World Bank.

Fukuyama, Francis. 1992. *The End of History and the Last Man*. New York: Free Press.

Gramsci, Antonio. 1971. *Selections from the Prison Notebooks of Antonio Gramsci*. Edited and translated by Quintin Hoare and Geoffrey Nowell Smith. New York: International.

Haggard, Stephan, and Robert R. Kaufman. 1995. *The Political Economy of Democratic Transitions*. Princeton, NJ: Princeton University Press.

Huber, Evelyne, and John D. Stephens. 2001. *Development and Crisis of the Welfare State: Parties and Policies in Global Markets*. Chicago: University of Chicago Press.

Inglehart, Ronald. 1971. "The Silent Revolution in Europe: Intergenerational Change in Post-Industrial Societies." *American Political Science Review* 65 (4): 991–1017. doi:10.2307/1953494.

Jacobson, Linda. 2001. "Experts Debate Welfare Reform's Impact on Children." *Education Week* 21 (September 19): 1–8.

Lindblom, Charles E. 1977. *Politics and Markets: The World's Political Economic Systems*. New York: Basic Books.

Lukes, Steven. 1974. *Power: A Radical View*. London: Macmillan

Mills, C. Wright. 1956. *The Power Elite*. New York: Oxford University Press.

Schatzberg, Michael G. 2001. *Political Legitimacy in Middle Africa: Father, Family, Food*. Bloomington: Indiana University Press.

Weingast, Barry R. 1997. "The Political Foundations of Democracy and the Rule of Law." *American Political Science Review* 91 (2): 245–63. doi:10.2307/2952354.

RESOURCES FOR FURTHER STUDY

Blank, Rebecca. 2001. "Declining Caseloads/Increased Work: What Can We Conclude about the Effects of Welfare Reform?" *Economic Policy Review* 7 (2): 25–36.

Dahl, Robert Alan. 1961. *Who Governs? Democracy and Power in an American City*. Yale Studies in Political Science No. 4. New Haven, CT: Yale University Press.

Gaventa, John. 1980. *Power and Powerlessness: Quiescence and Rebellion in an Appalachian Valley*. Urbana: University of Illinois Press.

Katznelson, Ira, and Helen V. Milner, eds. 2002. *Political Science: State of the Discipline*. New York: Norton.

King, Gary, Robert O. Keohane, and Sidney Verba. 1994. *Designing Social Inquiry: Scientific Inference in Qualitative Research*. Princeton, NJ: Princeton University Press.

Landman, Todd. 2003. *Issues and Methods in Comparative Politics: An Introduction*. 2nd ed. New York: Routledge.

Marx, Karl, and Friedrich Engels. 1978. *The Marx-Engels Reader*. Edited by Robert C. Tucker. 2nd ed. New York: Norton.

WEB RESOURCES

CIA World Factbook (https://www.cia.gov/library/publications/the-world-factbook)

Country Statistical Profiles, Organisation for Economic Co-operation and Development (http://stats.oecd.org/Index.aspx?DataSetCode=CSP2010)

Data: The World Bank (http://data.worldbank.org)

Pew Global Attitudes Survey 2010, Pew Research Center (http://pewglobal.org/2010/?cat=survey-reports)

Political Science Data, Comparative Politics at the University of Michigan (http://polisci.lsa.umich.edu/grad/comparative/data.htm)

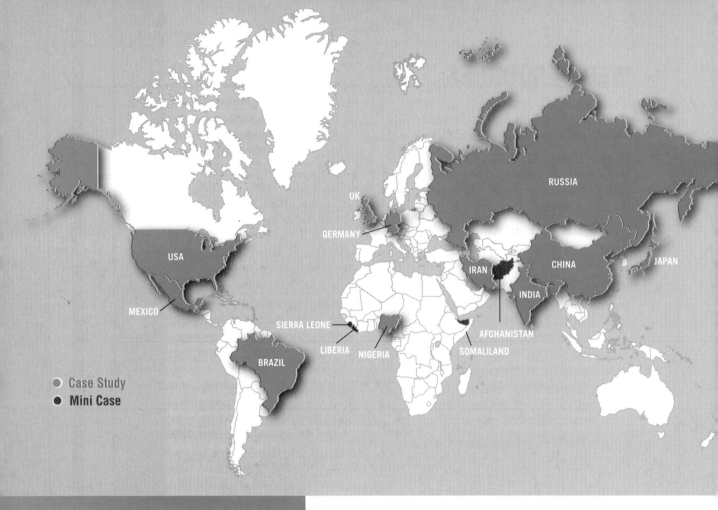

- Case Study
- Mini Case

Who Rules?

- What are the common characteristics of all modern states, and how do these characteristics give their rulers power?
- Do the common characteristics of modern states limit power in any way?

What Explains Political Behavior?

- Why did modern states arise and become universal?

Where and Why?

- Why are some states stronger than others? Why do some states fail completely?

2

THE MODERN STATE

Political development—the origin and development of the modern state—is the main starting point for the study of comparative politics. What is meant by "the modern state"? The answer is not obvious, because although *state* is often used interchangeably with both *country* and *nation,* political scientists use the term in a more specific way. *Country,* the most common term in daily discourse, is not a term used in political science because its meaning is too vague. *Nation,* which we discuss in depth in chapter 4, refers to a group of people who perceive themselves as sharing a sense of belonging, often including connotations of tradition, language, or culture. *State,* on the other hand, does not refer directly to a group of people or their sense of who they are. We say more about the relationship between state and nation later, but for now we will point out that it is perfectly possible to have stateless nations (e.g., Israel prior to 1948 or the Kurds today) and states comprised of more than one nation (e.g., the former Yugoslavia and contemporary Iraq).

For the purpose of political analysis, we need to find a more exact definition of a *state.* One approach is to ask how and when we "see" or contact the state. Purpose-built capitals like Abuja, Nigeria; Brasilia, Brazil; and Washington, D.C., make the state visible because they house a range of state functions in close proximity, including administration, courts, the legislature, and the executive. On some level, these buildings and the people working in them are the "state." Similarly, if you have attended public school, gotten a driver's license, received a traffic ticket, or paid income taxes, you've come into contact with the state, which provides public goods and enforces laws and uses public money in the form of taxes to do so. These observations lead to a very basic definition of the **state** as a set of ongoing institutions that develops and administers laws and generates and implements public policies in a specific territory. The *ongoing* nature of a state's institutions sets it apart from yet another similar term, *government.* Americans use *government* and *state* interchangeably, but "governments" are transient. They occupy and utilize the ongoing apparatus of the state temporarily, typically from one election to the next. Americans often refer to governments at the federal level as *administrations* (e.g., the Obama administration), but the rest of the world uses the word *government* in this context (e.g., the Cameron government of Great Britain).

state: a set of ongoing institutions that develops and administers laws and generates and implements public policies in a specific territory.

Clarifying exactly what the state is can help address that perennial question of political scientists: "Who rules?" Modern states have proven to be an exceptionally powerful and ubiquitous means of ruling over people in the modern era. Any number of groups or individuals, such as dictators, elites, or democratically elected politicians, can rule through the state's institutions. Identifying and understanding the key features of the state helps in analyzing how they rule and how much power they have.

In addition, looking at how much institutional apparatus a particular country has developed and how effectively that apparatus can be deployed (Are people really paying taxes? Are neighborhoods run by drug lords or the police?) can help identify the effective limits of official rule in a particular country. Where such structures are poorly developed, we may conclude that no one rules on a national level, although powerful local groups may effectively rule in place of the nominal state.

Comparativists studying the origins of the modern state are also addressing one of the biggest questions of political behavior: Why did states emerge at all and become so universal? And as always, we seek to answer the "where and why" questions as well: Where did the modern state emerge, and why did it do so at different times in different places? Why did strong state structures develop sooner in some countries and later or not at all in others? A glance at the Country and Concept table on page 61 shows clearly that even within our group of eleven case-study countries, the age and strength of the state varies greatly. These states range in age from over 300 years to just 50, and they include some of the weakest and strongest (the latter identified by a low number on the Failed States Index), as well as some of the most corrupt and least corrupt of all states worldwide.

This brief definition and discussion of the state clearly leave some open questions. As Christopher Pierson said, "We think that we know the state when we see it, but it proves extremely difficult to bring it under some brief but generally acceptable definition" (1996, 5). Like Pierson, though, we believe that political scientists generally agree on a fuller set of shared characteristics that are common among *modern* states. These characteristics help set the state apart from other concepts like those of nation, government, and regime, as well as from earlier forms of political organization.

CHARACTERISTICS OF THE MODERN STATE

territory: An area with clearly defined borders to which a state lays claim

The first characteristic of the modern state is so obvious that you might overlook it. A state must have **territory,** an area with clearly defined borders to which the state lays claim. In fact, borders are one of the places the state is "seen" most clearly, not only by the signs that welcome visitors but also by the customs inspectors and immigration officers who patrol and represent it.

Territory Territories vary enormously, from Russia, the largest geographical state at 6,520,800 square miles, to the seventeen recognized states with territories of less than 200 square miles each. The differences between vast Russia and tiny Tuvalu are significant, but territories and borders allow both to claim the status of state, and both are recognized as such.

A glance at any map of the world suggests there is little room for change in the territories that states control. One look shows no unclaimed territories or great expanses not enclosed by state borders (except Antarctica). Furthermore, many states have inhabited their present borders for so long that we may think of them as being relatively fixed. In truth, the number of states and their borders continue to change frequently. As recently as 2008, Kosovo's independence from Serbia caused

IN CONTEXT

NEW STATES AND THE UNITED NATIONS

Since 1959, the vast majority of new member states in the United Nations (UN) have been admitted after declaring independence. In the 1960s and 1970s, most newly admitted states were former colonies. In the 1990s, most newly admitted states were the result of the breakup of the Soviet Union and other Eastern-bloc countries. New UN members continue to be added in the twenty-first century.

- **1945–1949:** Eighty-one member states admitted.
- **1960–1969:** Forty-two member states admitted.
- **1970–1979:** Twenty-five member states admitted.
- **1980–1989:** Six member states admitted.
- **1990–1999:** Thirty-one member states admitted.
- **2000–2009:** Five member states admitted.

The example of Kosovo reminds us of another important aspect of territoriality: states exist within an international system of other states (see Table 2.1 on level of state recognition). It is not enough for a state to claim a defined territory; other states must also recognize that overall claim, even if they dispute a particular border. Political scientists call internationally recognized states **sovereign.** Essentially, a sovereign state is legally recognized by the family of states as the sole legitimate governing authority within its territory and as the legal equal of other states. This legal recognition is the minimal standard for **external sovereignty,** or sovereignty relative to outside powers. Legal external sovereignty, which entails being given the same vote in world affairs as all other states, is vital for sovereignty.

sovereign: Quality of a state in which it is legally recognized by the family of states as the sole legitimate governing authority within its territory and as the legal equal of other states

external sovereignty: Sovereignty relative to outside powers that is legally recognized in international law

mapmakers to redraw the map of Europe, and in 2011 southern Sudan voted to secede from the rest of that country. These examples are only the most recent in a long history of border changes. Border changes and the creation of new states, as both these examples attest, are often attempts to make states coincide more closely with nations, which are groups with a shared identity that also share or seek to share a territory and government. The lesson of history seems to be that states will continue to change their shapes and borders.

External and Internal Sovereignty In a world of competitive and conflicting states, a state must be able to defend its territory and must not be overly dependent on the resources or decisions of another power. Only in this way can it have real, effective external sovereignty and thus be free of external interference in governing. Invasion, colonialism, and "puppet states" are the most obvious cases of lack of true external sovereignty. Examples include the Japanese-backed and controlled state headed by the Chinese emperor Puyi in Manchukuo (Manchuria) from 1932 to 1945, the collaborationist Vichy government in the unoccupied southern "free zone" of France during World War II, and all colonial states. In all such cases, although some kind of local government apparatus may operate on a day-to-day basis, it is not a sovereign state, because its most crucial decisions are subject to an external authority.

Modern states also strive for **internal sovereignty,** that is, to be the sole authority within a territory capable of making and enforcing laws and policies. They must

internal sovereignty: The sole authority within a territory capable of making and enforcing laws and policies

TABLE 2 .1

The Shifting Borders of Modern States: Not Recognized, Limited Recognition, and Majority Recognition States

NOT RECOGNIZED		
State	Disputed since	Status
Nagorno-Karabakh	1991	Claimed by Azerbaijan.
Somaliland	1991	Claimed by Somalia.
Transnistria	1990	Claimed by Moldova.

LIMITED RECOGNITION		
State	Disputed since	Status
Abkhazia	2008	Recognized only by 4 countries: Russian Federation, Nicaragua, Nauru, Venezuela.
Kosovo	2008	Recognized by 40 countries.
South Ossetia	2008	Recognized only by Russian Federation.
Palestine	1988	Recognized as a proposed state by 96 UN member states.
Turkish Republic of Northern Cyprus (TRNC)	1983	Recognized only by Turkey.
Sahrawi Arab Democratic Republic (SADR)	1976	Recognized by 45 countries as legitimate government of Western Sahara.
Republic of China (Taiwan) (ROC)	1949	Recognized by 23 countries.

MAJORITY RECOGNITION		
State	Disputed since	Status
Czech Republic	1993	Not recognized by Liechtenstein.
Liechtenstein	1993	Not recognized by Czech Republic or Slovakia.
Slovakia	1993	Not recognized by Liechtenstein.
Cyprus	1974	Recognized by all countries except Turkey.
People's Republic of China (PRC)	1949	Not recognized by the Republic of China (Taiwan); the PRC does not accept diplomatic relations with the 22 other UN member states that recognize the ROC.
Israel	1948	Not recognized by Iran or the Sahrawi Arab Democratic Republic (SADR); no diplomatic relations with 34 countries.
North Korea	1948	Not recognized by South Korea.
South Korea	1948	Not recognized by North Korea.

defend their internal sovereignty against domestic groups that challenge it, just as they must defend it externally against possible invasion. Internal challenges typically take the form of a declaration of independence from some part of the state's territory and perhaps even civil war. States rarely are willing to accept such an act of defiance. From the United States in 1861, at the start of the American Civil War, to the former Soviet Republic of Georgia in the 1990s, when the region of South Ossetia tried to break away, most states use all means in their power to preserve their sovereignty over their recognized territories. Even a relatively insignificant challenge will draw the full attention of a state. In Waco, Texas, in 1993, a small religious sect called the Branch Davidians broke various U.S. laws and declared its compound beyond the reach of U.S. authority. Though it was a small and isolated group that most of the country thought was simply "crazy," its direct rejection of U.S. sovereignty ultimately led to high-level government attention. Attorney General Janet Reno was personally involved in the standoff on a daily basis. Even a superpower will react with full force to the smallest threat to its claim to sovereignty.

States try to enforce their sovereignty by claiming, in the words of famous German sociologist Max Weber, a "monopoly on the legitimate use of physical force" (1970). Put simply, the state claims to be the only entity within its territory that has the right to hold a gun to your head and tell you what to do. Some governments claim a virtually unlimited right to use force when and as they choose. At least in theory, and usually in practice, liberal democracies observe strict guidelines under which the use of force is permissible. For example, law enforcement can be called in when a citizen runs a red light or fails to pay taxes, but not when a citizen criticizes government policy. All states, though, insist on the right to use force to ensure their internal as well as external sovereignty. As one political philosopher reportedly said in response to students who complained about the government calling in police during a demonstration, "The difference between fascism and democracy is not whether the police are called, but when."

Sovereignty does not mean, however, that a state is all-powerful. Real internal and external sovereignty varies greatly and depends on many factors. Because the United States is wealthy and controls much territory, its sovereignty results in much greater power than does the sovereignty of Vanuatu, even though both are recognized as legitimate sovereigns over a clear territory. Wealthier states can defend their territories from attack better than poorer and weaker ones, and they can also more effectively ensure that their citizens comply with their laws. Even the United States, though, cannot completely control its borders, as the undocumented immigrants and illegal narcotics crossing its long border with Mexico attest.

Legitimacy The ability to enforce sovereignty more fully comes not only from wealth but also from legitimacy and bureaucracy, which are the final two key characteristics of states. Weber argued that a state claims a "monopoly on the *legitimate* use of physical force [emphasis added]." **Legitimacy** is the recognized right to rule. This right has at least two sides: the claims that states and others make about why they have a right to rule, and the empirical fact of whether their populations accept or at least tolerate this claimed right. All modern states argue at length for a particular normative basis for their legitimacy, and this claim is the basis of the various kinds of regimes in the world today (a subject explored in chapter 3).

Weber described three types of legitimate authority: traditional, charismatic, and rational-legal. **Traditional legitimacy** is the right to rule based on a society's long-standing patterns and practices. The European "divine right of kings" and the blessing of ancestors over the king in many precolonial African societies are examples of this. **Charismatic legitimacy** is the right to rule based on personal virtue, heroism, sanctity, or other extraordinary characteristics. Wildly popular leaders of revolutions, such as Mao Zedong in his early years in power, have charismatic legitimacy; people recognize their authority to rule because they trust and believe these

legitimacy: The recognized right to rule

traditional legitimacy: The right to rule based on a society's long-standing patterns and practices

charismatic legitimacy: The right to rule based on personal virtue, heroism, sanctity, or other extraordinary characteristics

rational-legal legitimacy: The right of leaders to rule based on their selection according to an accepted set of laws, standards, or procedures

individuals to be exceptional. **Rational-legal legitimacy** is the right of leaders who are selected according to an accepted set of laws. Leaders who come to power via electoral processes and rule according to a set of laws, such as a constitution, are the chief examples of this. Weber argued that rational-legal legitimacy distinguishes modern rule from its predecessors, but he recognized that in practice most legitimate authority is a combination of the three types. For example, modern democratically elected leaders may achieve office and rule on the basis of rational-legal processes, but a traditional status or personal charisma may have gained them the electoral victory and may enhance their legitimacy in office.

Legitimacy enhances a state's sovereignty. Modern states often control an overwhelming amount of coercive power, but the use of such power is expensive and difficult. States cannot maintain effective internal sovereignty in a large, modern society solely through the constant use of force or even its threat. Legitimacy, whatever its basis, enhances sovereignty at much lower cost. If most citizens obey the government because they believe it has a right to rule, then little force will be necessary to maintain order. This is an example of the third dimension of power we discussed in chapter 1. For this reason, governments proclaim their legitimacy and spend a great deal of effort trying to convince their citizens of it, especially when their legitimacy is brought into serious question.

bureaucracy: A large set of appointed officials whose function is to implement the laws of the state, as directed by the executive

Bureaucracy Modern **bureaucracy**, meaning a large set of appointed officials whose function is to implement laws, is the final important characteristic of the state. We defined the state at the outset as a set of institutions that develops and administers laws. In contemporary societies, the state plays many complicated roles. It must collect revenue from one source or another and use these resources to shore up its monopoly on legitimacy and the use of force. Typically, as discussed further in chapter 5, modern states spend revenues not only on coercive force but also on ways to strengthen the economy within their territory and provide for the well-being of at least some of their citizens in order to enhance legitimacy. Collecting taxes, as well as paving roads, building schools, and providing retirement pensions to name a few functions of the modern states, all require a bureaucracy. Weber saw bureaucracy as a central part of modern, rational-legal legitimacy, since in theory individuals obtain official positions in a modern bureaucracy via a rational-legal process of appointment and are restricted to certain tasks by a set of laws. Like legitimacy, effective bureaucracy enhances sovereignty. A bureaucracy that efficiently carries out laws, collects taxes, and expends revenues as directed by the central authorities gives the state greater power than it would have otherwise. As we discuss further below, weak legitimacy and weak bureaucracy are two key causes of state weakness in the contemporary world.

From this overview we can expand our notion of the modern state to understand it as a set of ongoing institutions that develops and administers laws and generates and implements public policies in a specific territory. We can see that this definition implies internal sovereignty, and we can add that a state must also maintain its external sovereignty. We can also add that the distinctive features of modern states include performing these activities not only on the basis of a monopoly on the use of force but also through the cultivation of legitimacy, particularly rational-legal legitimacy. Finally, we can add that bureaucracy is an important and effective tool for carrying out these administrative tasks, thereby potentially enhancing legitimacy.

Where modern states overlap with nations, national identity can be a powerful source of legitimacy as well. This is not always the case, however, and most modern states must find other ways to cultivate the allegiance of their inhabitants. They usually do so by attempting to gain legitimacy based on some claim of representation or service to their people, or citizens. The relationship between states and citizens is central to modern politics, and chapter 3 addresses it at length. We explore the contentious relationship among states, nations, and other identity groups more fully in chapter 4.

MINI CASE

Somaliland: Internal versus External Sovereignty

Somaliland is a most interesting recent case of disputed sovereignty. It is a state that has achieved almost unquestioned internal sovereignty, a stable constitutional democracy, and a growing economy. No other state recognizes it, however, so it has no international, legal external sovereignty. This unusual outcome is a result of the collapse of the larger state of Somalia and the international efforts to resolve that country's civil war. Somaliland, the northernmost region of Somalia, originally was a separate colony from the rest of what is now Somalia; it fell under British control, while the rest of the country was an Italian colony. In 1960, the former British colony gained independence for a few days but then quickly agreed to become part of the larger state of Somalia, which had also just gained independence.

When Somali dictator Siad Barre was deposed in 1991, the rebel movement in Somaliland, the Somali National Movement (SNM), declared the region independent within a few months. This was not surprising, given that all of Somalia is deeply divided into rival clans, and Somaliland is no exception. A conference of the elders of all the major clans of Somaliland in 1993 produced a new government that was a civilian administration no longer controlled exclusively by the SNM and its majority Isaaq clan. This government created a parliament modeled after traditional Somali institutions, with representation based on clan membership. In 2001, a referendum approved a new constitution that was fully democratic, with a bicameral legislature: one house is filled by directly elected representatives and the other by clan elders. By 2005, successful democratic elections had been held for president, parliament, and local governments. In June 2010, after two years of repeated delays due to regional insecurity, a second presidential election was held, and an opposition candidate defeated the incumbent president in a three-way race and peacefully took power.

Somaliland's economy has grown substantially, based mainly on exports of livestock to the Middle East and money sent home by Somalis living and working around the world. The government has established much better social services and greater security than exist in the rest of war-wracked Somalia. Yet because it has no official recognition from other governments, Somaliland receives no official aid from other countries, has only one embassy in its capital (that of neighboring Ethiopia), and sends no ambassadors abroad (though it does have unofficial representatives in several foreign capitals, including Washington, D.C.). Unofficially, some Western aid has reached Somaliland via private charities, and the country's leadership has met with representatives of Western countries, including of the United States. But Somaliland remains largely on its own. Most of the world fears that officially recognizing Somaliland's external sovereignty will encourage other regions of Somalia to attempt to break away as well, so recognition of the de facto state, expected eventually by many, awaits resolution of the larger civil war in Somalia.

CASE SUMMARY

Somaliland is an unusually successful African state that has established its effective sovereignty without the support of international legal recognition. It has relied first on internal sovereignty—effectively governing a territory—to give it the strength to protect its borders and thus maintain more or less effective external sovereignty. While it remains in armed disputes with neighboring areas of Somalia, and while the larger state of Somalia still claims it as a province, Somaliland has effectively established a claim to modern statehood with control of territory, de facto (but unrecognized) sovereignty, a reasonable degree of legitimacy, and a functioning bureaucracy. Ironically, it looks far more like a modern state than the official government of neighboring Somalia, which is internationally recognized as a sovereign state but literally controls only a few square blocks of the capital, Mogadishu.

HISTORICAL ORIGINS OF MODERN STATES

Now that we have clarified what a state is, we need to understand the diverse historical origins of modern states, which greatly influence how strong they are as well as their relationships to their citizens and nations. A world of modern states controlling virtually every square inch of territory and every person on the globe may seem natural today, but it is a fairly recent development. The modern state arose first in Europe between the fifteenth and eighteenth centuries. The concept spread via conquest, colonialism, and then independence for former colonies, becoming truly universal only with the independence of most African states in the 1960s.

feudal states: Premodern states in Europe in which power in a territory was divided among multiple and overlapping lords claiming sovereignty

fealty: A relationship between lord and vassal in which the lord gives a vassal the right to rule a piece of land in exchange for political and military loyalty

absolutism: Rule by a single monarch who claims complete, exclusive power and sovereignty over a territory and its people

Modern State in Europe Prior to approximately 1500, Europe consisted of **feudal states,** which were distinct from modern states in several ways. Most importantly, they neither claimed nor had undisputed sovereignty. Feudal rule involved multiple and overlapping sovereignties. At the heart of it was **fealty,** a relationship between lord and vassal in which the lord gave a vassal the right to rule a piece of land known as a fief, including the right to rule and tax the people living on the fief, in exchange for political and military loyalty. This relationship, however, was subject to frequent change. Once a vassal had control of a fief, he could shift his fealty from one lord to another if he was dissatisfied. The system often involved several layers of these relationships, from the highest and most powerful king in a region to the local lord. The loyalty of the peasants—the bulk of the population who had no vassals themselves and had virtually no rights—followed that of their lord. At any given time, each individual was subject to the sovereignty of not only his immediate lord but also at least one higher lord and often others, and that loyalty could and did change. In addition, the Catholic Church claimed a separate and universal religious sovereignty over all and gave religious legitimacy to the kings and lords who recognized church authority.

By the fifteenth century, feudalism was giving way to **absolutism,** rule by a single monarch who claimed complete, exclusive sovereignty over a territory and its people. Absolutist rulers won battles for power among feudal lords by using superior economic and military resources to permanently vanquish their rivals.

Most continued to recognize officially the religious authority of the Catholic Church, but in practice they increasingly proclaimed their undisputed rule within their territories. Scholars debate the extent to which the absolutist state was a truly modern state, but it certainly introduced a number of the modern state's key elements. Perry Anderson (1974), one of the most influential scholars on the subject, argued that the absolutist state included at least rudimentary forms of a standing army and diplomatic service, both of which are crucial for external sovereignty; centralized bureaucracy; systematic taxation; and policies to encourage economic development. It took centuries for these to develop into fully modern forms, however. Legitimacy remained based largely on tradition and heredity, and though most people living in an absolutist state were under a single sovereign, they remained subjects with few legal rights. Because many kingdoms lacked a common language, state officials, both military and civilian, often were not identified as members of the same cultural group as the common people and were thus seen as foreigners appointed by the monarch. Perhaps of greatest importance, the state was not conceived of as a set of ongoing institutions separate from the monarch. Rather, as Louis XIV of France famously declared, "*L'etat, c'est moi*" (I am the state).

Peace of Westphalia: Agreement among European powers in 1648 that codified the idea of states being legal equals that recognized each other's external and internal sovereignty within specified territories and that were prepared to defend that sovereignty

In 1648, the **Peace of Westphalia** codified the idea of states being legal equals that recognized each other's external and internal sovereignty within specified territories and that were prepared to defend that sovereignty and their interests via diplomacy, if possible, or war if necessary. The subsequent survival-of-the-fittest process gradually whittled the number of European states from approximately five hundred in 1500 to about fifty today. Besides reducing the number of states, this competition to actualize and preserve external sovereignty helped further the development of the fully modern state. The states that survived were those that had developed more effective systems of taxation, more efficient bureaucracies, and stronger militaries. Along the way, political leaders realized that a sense of personal loyalty to the state on the part of their subjects (legitimacy) was of great benefit, particularly because these subjects were increasingly required to pay taxes and serve in the military. States therefore began the process of creating nations, expanding public education, and shifting from the use of Latin or French in official circles to the local vernacular so that rulers and ruled could communicate directly, thus adding a new dimension to the rulers' legitimacy. This long process ultimately helped create modern nations, most of which had emerged by the mid-nineteenth century.

Thomas Hobbes, an important early modern British political philosopher, believed that a strong state to which subjects gave their undivided loyalty was essential to prevent the brutality that would inevitably result from anarchy.

Credit: The Granger Collection, New York

The truly modern state emerged as the state came to be seen as separate from an individual ruler. This concept developed in conjunction with that of imposing some limits on a ruler's power. The state as a set of institutions retained its claim to absolute sovereignty, but the powers of individual officials, ultimately including the supreme ruler, were increasingly limited. A political philosophy that came to be known as liberalism, which we discuss in greater depth in chapter 3, provided the theoretical justification and argument for limiting the power of officials to ensure the rights of individuals. The common people were ultimately transformed from subjects into citizens of the state. Bellwether events in this history included the Glorious Revolution in Great Britain in which Parliament forced King James II's resignation, the French Revolution of 1789, and a series of revolutions that established new democratic republics in 1848.

Premodern States Outside Europe Outside Europe, a wide variety of premodern states existed, but none took a fully modern form as we define it. The Chinese Empire ruled a vast territory for centuries but not always from a single, centralized sovereign. Nevertheless, it was perhaps the closest thing to a modern state anywhere in the premodern world (including in Europe). African precolonial kingdoms sometimes ruled large areas as well, but their rule was typically conceived of as extending over people rather than a precisely defined territory, having greater sovereignty closer to the capital and less sovereignty farther away. Virtually all premodern empires included multiple or overlapping layers of sovereignty and did not include a modern sense of citizenship.

The Export of the Modern State Europe exported the modern state to the rest of the world through colonial conquest and began to do so in the Americas as early as the sixteenth century. Colonies in the Americas, Africa, and Asia, however, were not modern states; by definition they lacked sovereignty. Colonial rule in the Americas began with military invasion and the destruction of Native American states and empires. In North America, disease and war decimated local populations, paving the way for extensive European settlement. In South America, larger indigenous populations survived to be subjugated, and one result was substantial mixed-race, or mestizo, populations. In many areas, including Brazil and the southern part of the United States, African slaves were brought in to supplement Native populations and meet labor demands. These demographic patterns ultimately produced today's varied racial patterns across the Americas.

The earliest colonies, such as those in the Americas, were ruled by European absolutist states that were not fully modern themselves. This is not to say that these ruling states did not try to develop some modern methods to administer their distant domains. European monarchs appointed officials to represent them and rule over newly acquired territories, and effective administration ultimately required the appointment of numerous such officials. Yet over time, settlers identified their interests as distinct from and often in opposition to those of the colonizers and their officials, and colonists began to question the legitimacy of rule by distant sovereigns. The first rebellion against colonial rule ultimately produced the United States. Its founders were heavily influenced by European liberalism, and as such, they rejected the notion of an absolute ruler. They instead wrote a constitution that established a sovereign but limited state that carved out a rational-legal basis for its monopoly on the legitimate use of force. This was a major event in the development of both the modern state and liberal democracy.

The second major rebellion came at the hands of black slaves, whose rebellion in Haiti in 1793 led to the first abolition of slavery in the world and, in 1804, to Haitian independence. By the 1820s and 1830s, most of the populations of Central and South America had rebelled as well. As in the United States, the leaders of these rebellions were mostly wealthy, landholding elites. This landed elite often relied on state force to keep peasant and slave labor working on its behalf, so while some early efforts at democracy emerged after independence, most Central and South American states ultimately went through many decades of strongman rule.

Early modern states in the Americas emerged from colonialism, which is a very different context for the birth of a modern state than that of early European states. European states went through several centuries of developing a sense of national identity, which would emerge strongly in most areas by the nineteenth century. In the Americas, the racial divisions produced by colonization, European settlement, and slavery meant that none of the newly independent states had a widely shared sense of national identity. Where slavery continued to exist, as in the United States, citizenship was restricted to the "free" and therefore primarily white (and exclusively male) population. Where significant Native American populations had survived, as in Peru and Guatemala, they continued to be politically excluded and economically marginalized by the primarily white, landholding elite who controlled the new states. This historical context would make the ability of the new states to establish strong national identities difficult and would produce ongoing racial and ethnic problems, explored further in chapter 4.

After most of the first wave of colonies achieved independence, growing economic and military rivalry among Britain, France, and Germany beginning in the mid-nineteenth century spurred a new round of colonization, first in Asia and then in Africa. This time, far fewer European settlers were involved. The vast majority of the populations of these new colonies remained indigenous; they were ruled over by a rather thin layer of European officials. Colonizers effectively destroyed the political power of precolonial indigenous states and empires but did not exterminate the population en masse. This stemmed at least in part from the fact that the indigenous people in these regions had been trading with Europeans for many years and had thus built up some immunity to European diseases. Native Americans did not have that advantage, and countless millions died.

Challenges to this new wave of colonialism, on both the home front and abroad, were quick and numerous. The independence of the first-wave colonies and the end of slavery in the industrialized world raised questions about European subjugation of African and Asian peoples. Colonization in this context had to be justified as bringing "advanced" European civilization and Christianity to "backward" peoples. Education, provided primarily by Christian missionaries, was seen as a key part of this "civilizing" mission. It had a more practical aspect as well: with limited European settlement, colonial rulers needed indigenous individuals to serve in the bureaucracies of the colonial states. These chosen few were educated in colonial languages and customs and became local elites, although European officials remained at the top of the colonial hierarchy and exercised nearly unlimited power. In time, the indigenous elites began to see themselves as equal to the ruling Europeans and chafed at the limits to their political position and economic advancement under colonial rule. They became the key leaders of the movements for independence that emerged in the early twentieth century in Asia and by the mid-twentieth century in Africa. This new elite demanded independence and finally received it after World War II. At that point, modern states covered virtually every square inch of the globe, as Map 2.1 demonstrates.

Though successful at achieving independence, the postcolonial countries faced huge obstacles to consolidating as modern states. Although they enjoyed legal external sovereignty and had inherited at least minimal infrastructure from colonial bureaucracies, legitimacy and internal sovereignty remained problematic for most. The colonial powers had typically established borders with little regard for precolonial political boundaries. Some precolonial states—for example, Siam

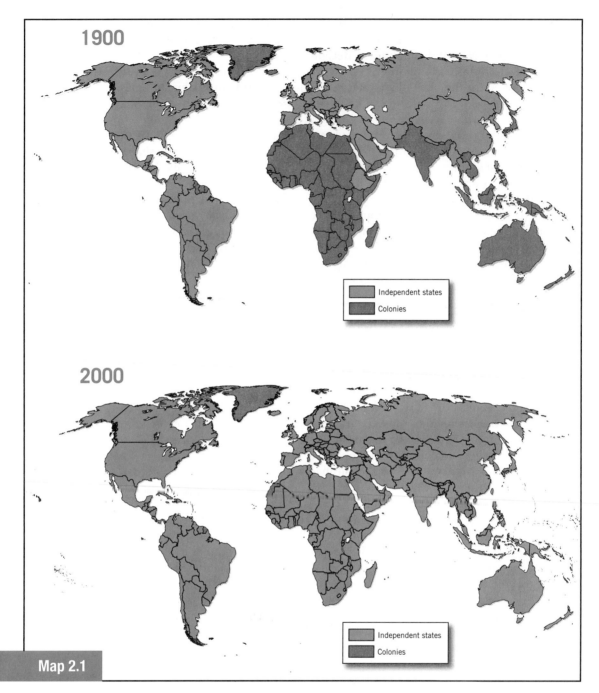

1900

Independent states
Colonies

2000

Independent states
Colonies

Map 2.1

Spread of Modern States

(Thailand), Rwanda, and Burundi—survived with their borders more or less intact, but most did not. This meant that numerous political entities and many distinct religious and linguistic groups were brought together under one colonial state. The nationalist movements that had brought the colonies independence had also created genuine enthusiasm for new nations, but the colonizers had previously tried to inhibit a strong sense of national unity to prevent united action against them. This had the effect of limiting the extent to which a common sense of national identity emerged in the new countries. Political loyalty was often divided among numerous groups, including the remnants of precolonial states. Finally, huge disparities in wealth, education, and access to power between the elite and the majority of the population reduced popular support for the state, and this made the new democracies extremely fragile.

In summary, modern states arose around the world at different times and in very different contexts. Although they shared some common difficulties, such as the need to cultivate a more cohesive national identity as a basis for legitimacy, European and non-European states experienced different timelines for developing both modern states and national identities. A postcolonial state often inherited a minimal bureaucracy and infrastructure that were not necessarily geared toward developing the country's resources, and if this bureaucracy and infrastructure were controlled by local elites, the bulk of the population often perceived them to be of questionable legitimacy.

The results of colonial history for many countries were late development of a modern state and deeply divided loyalties among their citizens that proved problematic for legitimacy, cohesion, and internal sovereignty. Many succumbed to some form of authoritarian rule not long after independence, though democratic movements have emerged more recently. These new states were modern in terms of their most basic characteristics, but most were very weak versions of the modern state model. The differences between strong and weak states, and the causes of state weakness and collapse, are the last subjects we need to address to complete our conceptual overview of the modern state.

STRONG, WEAK, AND FAILED STATES

The modern state as we have defined it is what Weber called an **ideal type,** a model of what the purest version of something might be. Nothing in reality perfectly matches an ideal type; no state indisputably enjoys complete external or internal sovereignty, absolute legitimacy and a monopoly on the use of force, and a completely effective and efficient bureaucracy. Some states, however, are clearly much closer to this ideal than others. States typically use their sovereignty, territory, legitimacy, and bureaucracy to provide what political scientist Robert Rotberg (2004) called "political goods" to their population. Political goods include security; the rule of law; a functioning legal system; and infrastructure such as roads, public education, and health care.

A **weak state** is one that cannot provide adequate political goods to its population. Obviously, knowing exactly what *adequate* means in this definition is not easy, and an absolutely clear-cut distinction cannot be made between strong and weak states. Rather, all states exist on a continuum of relative strength, with no state being perfectly strong in all conceivable categories. States that seem persistently unable to provide adequate security and other essential political goods are demonstrably weaker than those that can and do. As the Country and Concept table (page 61) shows for our case studies, stronger states tend to consume a larger share of economic resources; they are simply economically bigger than weak states. They also are less corrupt, indicating the presence of stronger bureaucracies, and tend to be more legitimate.

A state that is so weak that it loses effective sovereignty over part or all of its territory is known as a **failed state.** Failed states make headlines, for example, Sierra Leone, the Democratic Republic of the Congo, Liberia, Sudan, and Afghanistan. In

ideal type: A term used by Max Weber to denote a model of what the purest version of something might be

weak state: A state that cannot provide adequate political goods to its population

failed state: A state that is so weak that it loses effective sovereignty over part or all of its territory

WHERE AND WHY

Failed and Sustainable States

In response to growing international concern about state failure, the Fund for Peace developed a "Failed States Index" to highlight countries of imminent concern (see Table 2.2). In 2010, the sixth annual index ranked 177 countries on twelve factors in three categories considered essential to state strength: four social indicators (demographic pressures, refugees or internally displaced persons creating humanitarian emergencies, vengeance-seeking group grievance or group paranoia, and chronic, sustained human flight); two economic indicators (uneven economic growth along group lines and sharp/severe economic decline); and six political indicators (criminalization/delegitimization of the state, deterioration of public services, suspension of rule of law/human rights abuses, the operation of a security apparatus as a "state within a state," factionalized elites, and intervention of external political actors). Thirty-seven countries were in the red zone at the top of the list (marked "Alert"), effectively making them failed states based on these factors. Thirteen others were in the green zone at the bottom of the list, marked "Sustainable" (see Table 2.3).

Which states were placed at each end of the list and why? Some patterns are clear: no European, North American, or South American country is on the "Alert" list, and all "Sustainable" states are European except for Australia, New Zealand, and Canada. Twenty-two of the thirty-seven failed states are in Africa, and all but three (Ethiopia, Nepal, and Yemen) were previously colonies. Finally, all of the "Sustainable" states are high-income countries, while none of the failed states are and most are quite low-income. While this information alone is not enough to reach any firm conclusions about where and why strong and weak states emerge, some hypotheses seem plausible. Based on these patterns, one could hypothesize that state failure might be geographically or culturally rooted, but there are also other, equally suggestive patterns. Colonialism and its aftermath may have contributed to ineffectual institutions or produced incentives to develop weak, ineffective governments. The kind of elite accommodation that North, Wallis, and Weingast (2009) argued helped to create states clearly did not occur in colonially imposed and controlled states. Also, postcolonial governing institutions were often not based on negotiated agreements among elites but rather were hastily copied from the departing colonizers. Not having participated seriously in the creation of the new institutions, nationalist elites often did not see themselves as benefitting from them. They therefore changed those institutions, used them for their own purposes, or ignored them. This often meant that postcolonial states did not develop the type of impersonal institutions characteristic of strong modern states. Lange (2009) found that for British colonies, the specific type of colonial rule heavily influenced the strength of state institutions. More directly ruled colonies in which the colonizer had built strong bureaucracies early on (e.g., Mauritius) developed stronger bureaucracies after independence than did colonies where the colonizer had relied on local institutions to rule on its behalf (e.g., Nigeria). The British Empire was by far the most extensive of all colonial empires, and it ruled most colonies with less direct methods. So Lange's findings seem to be a major element providing a general explanation of postcolonial patterns.

Wealth certainly seems to play a role in creating strong states. States need resources to provide security and other political goods. Resources come from taxation, but to have taxation a state must have some viable economic activity. The poorest states simply lack the resources to provide the most basic political goods, regardless of the intentions or administrative competence of their rulers. Wealthy states, in contrast, have the resources to fund the provision of public goods. The political and economic prospects of the elites in those states rise and fall with the health of the domestic economy, so the elites try to pursue policies that strengthen that economy. They have much at stake within the territory of their state and thus seek to improve economic conditions there.

Heavy reliance on external resources, even in relatively wealthy countries, can also result in weak states. Ruling elites in poor, postcolonial states often come to rely on external resources for their survival. This makes the kind of negotiated agreement North, Wallis, and Weingast (2009) portrayed as being the foundation of strong states very difficult to achieve. Elites who control the external resources have no reason to compromise with their domestic rivals, and their rivals, being cut out of all benefits, often rebel violently. During the Cold War, the rivalry between the United States and the Soviet Union led each of the superpowers to back dictators who would support their respective sides in global politics. Both sides provided generous aid to dictators who ruled with little interest in providing services to their people. Mobutu Sese Seko of Zaire (now the Democratic Republic of the Congo), in power from 1965 to 1997, was an example of such a U.S. "client"; Mengistu Haile Mariam of Ethiopia, in power from 1974 to 1991, was an example of a Soviet one. These states both failed a few years after the end of the Cold War because the elimination of the U.S.-Soviet global rivalry meant that neither side was interested in continuing to support the dictators there. Countries with tremendous mineral wealth, such as oil or diamonds, often suffer similar fates, a process dubbed the **resource curse.** A government that can gain enough revenue from mineral extraction alone does not need to worry about the strength of the rest of the economy or the well-being of the rest of the population. If the asset exists in one particular economic enclave, the government simply has to control that area and export the resources to gain revenue in order to survive. Rebel groups likewise recognize that if they can overpower the government, they can seize the country's mineral wealth, a clear incentive to start a war rather than strive for a compromise with those in power.

Comparativists don't all agree on which of these factors is most important, but we look at evidence of state weakness and try to generate testable hypotheses for state failure. Which of these hypotheses seems most persuasive? What kind of evidence would help confirm it or disprove it? What other hypotheses might explain state failure? Comparativists will continue to study what causes state weakness in an effort to help states develop stronger institutions. We do this because the human consequences of state weakness—civil conflict, refugees, and human rights violations—and the consequences for the international system of states are severe.

(continues)

resource curse: Occurs when a state relies on a key resource for almost all of its revenue, allowing it to ignore its citizens and resulting in a weak state

Failed and Sustainable States *(continued)*

TABLE 2.2

Failed States, 2010

Rank and state	Total score
1. Somalia	114.3
2. Chad	113.3
3. Sudan	111.8
4. Zimbabwe	110.2
5. Democratic Republic of Congo	109.9
6. Afghanistan	109.3
7. Iraq	107.3
8. Central African Republic	106.4
9. Guinea	105.0
10. Pakistan	102.5
11. Haiti	101.6
12. Côte d'Ivoire	101.2
13. Kenya	100.7
14. Nigeria	100.2
15. Yemen	100.0
16. Burma/Myanmar	99.4
17. Ethiopia	98.8
18. East Timor	98.2
19. North Korea	97.8
19. Niger	97.8
21. Uganda	97.5
22. Guinea-Bissau	97.2
23. Burundi	96.7
24. Bangladesh	96.1
25. Sri Lanka	95.7
26. Cameroon	95.4
27. Nepal	95.4
28. Malawi	93.6
29. Sierra Leone	93.6
30. Eritrea	93.3
31. Republic of the Congo	92.5
32. Iran	92.2
33. Liberia	91.7
34. Lebanon	90.9
35. Burkina Faso	90.7
36. Uzbekistan	90.5
37. Georgia	90.4

Source: Fund for Peace, 2010, "Failed States Index 2010," www.fundforpeace.org/web/index.php?option=com_content&task=view&id=452&Itemid=900.

TABLE 2.3

Sustainable States, 2010

Rank and state	Total score
165. Iceland	29.8
166. Canada	27.9
167. Netherlands	27.9
168. Luxembourg	27.3
169. Australia	27.3
170. Austria	27.2
171. New Zealand	23.9
172. Denmark	22.9
173. Ireland	22.4
174. Switzerland	21.8
175. Sweden	20.9
176. Finland	19.3
177. Norway	18.7

Source: Fund for Peace, 2010, "Failed States Index 2010," www.fundforpeace.org/web/index.php?option=com_content&task=view&id=452&Itemid=900.

extreme cases, the state collapses totally, as Somalia did in 1991. Since then, the territory comprising Somalia has been divided among competing warlords in the south and Somaliland in the north, which has declared itself a separate country, though with no international recognition (see the Mini Case on Somaliland in this chapter). The total collapse of the Somali state has resulted in two decades of near-total anarchy for much of the population. It became known to many Americans due to the infamous "Black Hawk Down" episode in 1993, in which sixteen U.S. soldiers were killed and dragged through the streets of the capital. State failure, as the cases of Somalia and Afghanistan (see the Mini Case later in this chapter) suggest, can have effects far beyond the state's borders.

Virtually all elements of state strength are interconnected. State weakness causes and is also caused by declines in effective sovereignty, bureaucracy, legitimacy, and even control over territory. If a state lacks the resources to provide basic infrastructure and security, its legitimacy most likely will decline. Lack of resources also may mean civil servants are paid very little, which may lead to corruption and an even further decline in the quality of state services. Corruption in some bureaucracies, such as the military and border patrol, can cause a loss of security and territorial integrity. If the state cannot provide basic services, such as education, citizens will likely find alternative routes to success that may well involve illegal activity (e.g., smuggling) and that undermine sovereignty that much further. If the state does not apply the rule of law impartially, citizens will turn to private means to settle their disputes, undermining the state's monopoly on the legitimate use of force. Continuing patterns of lawless behavior create and reinforce the public perception that the state is weak, so weak states can become caught in a vicious cycle that is difficult to break.

The question of how some strong states managed to emerge has long been a major subject of political history and development. Economists Douglass North and John Wallis and political scientist Barry Weingast recently used a rational-choice institutionalist argument to address this question (2009). They argued that the key issue is the creation of impersonal institutions and organizations. The earliest states were based on elite coalitions created to limit violence among themselves. Power remained very personal, as the state was really just a temporary agreement among competing elites, each of which had control over the means of violence. Because of this, these early states were frequently unstable. Elites abided by the agreements they made with each other in order to gain economic advantages from the absence of warfare and the ability to extract resources from their positions within the state. Eventually, some elites negotiated agreements that recognized impersonal organizations and institutions, such as formal positions within the state, that were separate from the individual leaders. As these developed and functioned credibly, greater specialization was possible, and distinct elites that controlled military, political, economic, and religious power emerged. This required the rule of law among elites. Together with ongoing, impersonal organizations, the rule of law allowed the possibility of a true monopoly over the use of force as individual elites gave up their control of military power. Once established among elites, such impersonal institutions and organizations could expand eventually to the rest of society, typically via the rise of democracy (which we discuss in the next chapter), and a strong modern state was born. The Where and Why box on pages 52–54 examines where and why this process does or does not seem to occur.

The phenomenon of weak states seems to be a growing problem, and part of the explanation lies with relatively recent changes to the international system. Prior to the twentieth century, the weakest states sooner or later faced a hostile invasion; they were the losers in the history of state formation in Europe. The new international system incorporated after World War II fundamentally changed this dynamic. Starting with the League of Nations in 1919 and expanding under the United Nations after 1945, the international system collectively came to an agreement that the hostile takeover of other states was unacceptable. While there have been exceptions, usually based on an inability or unwillingness of great powers to intervene, outright invasion and permanent conquest have become rare. This means that weak states are more likely to survive, at least for longer than they would have a century or two ago. The result can be what Robert Jackson (1990) called **quasi-states:** states that have legal sovereignty and international recognition but lack almost all the domestic attributes of a functioning state. Jackson argued that many postcolonial states, especially those in Africa, the poorest region in the world, are quasi-states.

quasi-states:
States that have legal sovereignty and international recognition but lack almost all the domestic attributes of a functioning modern state

MINI CASE

Afghanistan's Failed State

In 2001, Afghanistan became probably the world's most famous failed state because it served as a refuge for and supporter of al-Qaida leader Osama bin Laden. But its failure as a state long predates the September 11, 2001, attacks on the World Trade Center and the Pentagon. Indeed, its failure figured prominently in the late Cold War era, when the Soviet Union invaded it in 1979 and the United States subsequently supported the country's Islamist *mujahedeen* resistance fighters. Afghanistan serves as a case study of the debilitating interaction between a weak state and self-interested international forces.

The coronation of Ahmad Shah as king in 1747 is generally accepted as the start of a united Afghanistan, though it was far from a modern state at that time. Numerous ethnic groups, all Islamic but practicing different branches of the faith, were united; the Pashtun, Ahmad Shah's group, was the largest. The kingdom relied on local rulers for support, and political loyalty remained focused primarily at the local level as ethnic and religious elders wielded most of the real power. The kingdom fell apart in a succession of battles in 1818, and for the rest of the nineteenth century Afghanistan faced intermittent civil war, as well as increasing British and Russian encroachment. By the end of that

century, much of the country was virtually a British colony. The British helped establish Amir Abdur Rahman Khan as ruler and began a negotiated evacuation in 1880. Abdur Rahman ruled for the last two decades of the nineteenth century and began an ambitious modernization plan that favored Western culture and established the start of a modern state, creating a united army that gained control of virtually all of modern-day Afghanistan. Although Afghanistan's monarchy ruled until 1973, the state remained weak. There was no real national Afghan identity, and most ethnic groups, including the Pashtun, extended into neighboring countries. This meant that people's ethnic loyalty across national borders was often greater than their loyalty to the Afghan state.

Afghanistan also remained susceptible to external powers. The Soviet Union had long been actively involved in the country, but the government that overthrew the king in 1973 began to move away from the Soviet sphere and toward the West. In response, the Soviets invaded in 1979, installing the local Communist Party in power. The Communist government launched a series of land, local government, and educational reforms that struck at the heart of local elder control of society. The response was widespread resistance, which soon took on an Islamic ideology. The *mujahedeen* resistance fighters battled the Soviet army in guerilla warfare throughout the 1980s. Divided along both religious and ethnic lines, the *mujahedeen* still received significant U.S. support. While never able to defeat the Soviets, the resistance nonetheless kept the Communist regime from effectively ruling Afghanistan. They also became a heroic force in the eyes of many Muslims worldwide; young religious fighters from across the Muslim world streamed into Afghanistan to join the fight, including a Saudi by the name of Osama bin Laden.

The reform policies of Mikhail Gorbachev in the Soviet Union led to a Soviet withdrawal and the creation of a *mujahedeen* government in 1989, but the state collapsed into civil war among the various ethnic militias almost immediately. A decade of warfare had left the economy in ruins, encouraging the rise of poppy growing as the only viable alternative for many farmers. As a consequence, Afghanistan became the world's top source of heroin by the 1980s. Warlords arose via control of weaponry and poppy production, and the state collapsed nearly completely.

In the midst of this situation, a new, radical Islamist group emerged among the Pashtun: the Taliban. Supported by external Muslim financing, much of it from individuals in Saudi Arabia (including bin Laden) and Pakistan, the Taliban defeated the divided *mujahedeen* and in 1996 took control of most of the country. The group seemed to care little about the state, instead focusing its policies almost solely on religious concerns of moral purity, religious observance, and gender relations (mostly involving the seclusion of women). Infamously, the group also provided a refuge for bin Laden and his followers.

In retaliation for the September 11 attacks, the United States invaded Afghanistan in late 2001, supporting the northern, non-Pashtun opposition to the Taliban. The United States and the UN helped to create a new democratic government in Afghanistan, which ten years later continues to rely heavily on U.S. and NATO military support. The state has minimally democratic institutions but remains weak, without full control over its territory. The elected president, Hamid Karzai, continues to rely in part on former warlords, who retain considerable local control. Some of their power comes from their continued control of Afghanistan's lucrative poppy production. The rest of the economy has begun to rebound, but poppies remain the largest source of wealth. Corruption has become a growing problem, with Karzai's extended family rumored to be deeply involved in it; the country was rated as the second worst in the world (behind only Somalia) on Transparency International's Corruption Perception Index. And most observers seriously question the legitimacy of both the presidential and parliamentary elections.

The Taliban launched a major offensive to regain territory in 2006. U.S. and NATO forces launched major counteroffensives in 2009 and 2010, though their success remains uncertain as President Barack Obama promised to start reducing troop levels there by 2011. The United States, the UN, and NATO have spent ten years trying to help put a strong and stable state in place, and the process still remains uncertain and far from concluded. International interventions from several sources helped produce the country's total collapse, but similar international forces are having a much harder time rebuilding Afghanistan.

CASE SUMMARY

Afghanistan demonstrates many elements of state weakness. While it became an established state relatively early and was never formally colonized, it also never became a fully modern state. Internal sovereignty was always limited, as local ethnic leaders retained great power vis-à-vis the central government. International forces were soon involved themselves in this mix, and they wreaked havoc, typically choosing sides among the country's competing ethnic factions and warlords. The failure of both Western and Communist modernization efforts in this context helped initially legitimize the

Taliban as an alternative vision of a society, but the Taliban's draconian policies probably undermined that legitimacy quickly. Subsequent NATO and U.S. efforts to establish a modern and democratic state appear to be foundering, as the central government does not seem to be able to rule without continued reliance on warlords, illegal opium production, and growing corruption. All of these continue to weaken an already weak state.

MINI CASE

Sierra Leone and Liberia: Collapsed States

Liberia and Sierra Leone, neighboring states in West Africa, tragically illustrate the worst effects of weak states controlling significant mineral wealth, a phenomenon known as the resource curse. Ironically, both countries began as beacons of hope for liberated slaves. Britain founded Sierra Leone to provide a refuge for liberated slaves captured from slaving vessels, and the United States founded Liberia as a home for former American slaves. Descendants of these slaves became the ruling elite in both countries. Liberia became the first independent postcolonial African state in 1847 with a constitution modeled after the U.S. Constitution but with voting rights restricted to owners of private property. This meant that virtually no indigenous Africans could vote; only the Americo-Liberian elite (as they were called) had political rights. Similarly, Sierra Leone had a colonial elite composed almost exclusively of the "Krio," descendants of freed slaves, until its independence in 1961.

Both countries were heavily dependent on key natural resources from the beginning. The bulk of government revenue in Sierra Leone came from diamond mining, and in Liberia it was derived from iron-mining and rubber plantations owned by the Firestone Tire Company of the United States. Each country was also the recipient of a great deal of aid from its respective former colonial power; during the Cold War Liberia was Africa's single biggest recipient of U.S. foreign aid.

These resources, however, did not produce strong states. In Sierra Leone, six years of

Ellen Johnson-Sirleaf became Liberia's president and Africa's first woman head of state in January 2006. Her inauguration raised the country's hopes that Johnson-Sirleaf would deliver what she promised: a "fundamental break" with its conflict-ridden past. As she prepares to run for reelection in 2011, the country remains at peace, its democracy, though weak, survives, and its economic growth has been healthy, if not spectacular.

Credit: AP Photo/Charles Dharapak

democracy gave way to one-party rule in 1968 under Siaka Stevens, who remained in power until 1985, when he resigned to transfer power to his handpicked successor. Members of the one-party regime used the revenues from diamond mining to support the leaders' own ethnic groups and enrich themselves, while the overall economy, government services, and regime legitimacy declined. Similarly, in Liberia the Americo-Liberian ruling party won every election from 1847 to 1980, becoming the longest continuously ruling political party in world history, and used government resources to enrich the key ruling families while the bulk of the indigenous population was ignored. The legitimacy of both governments declined further as corruption and favoritism toward their supporters destroyed each state's ability to provide the most basic services expected of modern states.

The dramatic downward spiral for both countries began with a military coup in Liberia in 1980, in which the top Americo-Liberian leaders were executed. The new government was led by a twenty-eight-year-old sergeant, Samuel Doe, who shifted power from the Americo-Liberian elite to his own Krahn ethnic group. Doe continued to receive generous U.S. support in spite of holding what all saw as completely fraudulent elections. After enduring a decade of Doe's increasingly brutal and corrupt rule, an exiled former member of his government, Charles Taylor, launched a guerilla war in rural areas inhabited by ethnic groups whom Doe had ignored and repressed. Given the government's near total lack of legitimacy, the uprising spread rapidly. Taylor became the first and worst warlord in west Africa, arming young men who had grievances against the government and allowing them to take whatever spoils of victory they wished. His march to the capital was stopped only by the intervention of forces from other countries, mainly Nigeria. He financed his war by selling timber and other resources on the international market.

In 1991, after he was stopped from taking the Liberian capital, Taylor adjusted his sights and helped finance a guerilla uprising in neighboring Sierra Leone. Once the guerilla forces gained control of Sierra Leone's lucrative diamond mines, Taylor smuggled the diamonds onto the international market to finance the rebellions in both countries. The Sierra Leonean rebellion led to a coup that replaced the one-party regime with a military one. The state was so weak, however, that it ultimately was forced to turn to a private South African company to bring in mercenary forces to regain control of the diamond mines in exchange for the company receiving a share of the mines' profits. At the same time, the government significantly expanded the official armed forces, arming young men in several parts of the country to defend their own home areas against rebels. Many of these armed but poorly trained and paid young soldiers ultimately came to be known as "sobels," soldiers in the government army by day and rebels by night who looted and maimed the civilian population in both roles. After another coup, the military government privately cooperated with the rebels to exploit the country's diamond wealth.

A peace deal was finally brokered in Liberia in 1997, and elections for a new government were held. Charles Taylor, the warlord, was democratically elected as president. Many Liberians reasoned that unless they gave him power, he would continue the war, so it was therefore better to elect him and hope the war would end. Once in power officially, Taylor continued to exploit Liberia's exportable resources and Sierra Leone's diamonds for his own benefit. He also continued to finance the Sierra Leonean rebels, who briefly gained control of the entire country in 1998–1999. Eventually, a regional military force led by Nigeria forced the rebels out of Sierra Leone's capital and set the conditions for a peace process in which the rebels finally gave up their efforts. At about the same time, an anti-Taylor rebel movement invaded Liberia. Taylor continued to smuggle diamonds out of Sierra Leone and timber out of Liberia to finance his government and line his own pockets until 2003, when international sanctions against west African diamonds finally reduced his cash flow and ultimately forced him out of power.

Both countries are now at peace and have fragile, elected governments. Liberia elected the first woman president in African history, Ellen Johnson-Sirleaf, in January 2006. Charles Taylor and several Sierra Leonean rebel leaders are on trial in international tribunals for violations of international human rights laws. Left over from the wars is a legacy of more than 200,000 killed and millions maimed and displaced. Rebel armies used large numbers of child soldiers, meaning that thousands of young boys in both countries grew up in the 1990s with guns in their hands and with looting as a way of life, rather than being schooled and trained for future careers. In addition, both countries remain among the world's poorest. In 2009, Sierra Leone, despite its diamond wealth, was in the third-worst position on the UN's Human Development Index, a measure of overall well-being. On the other hand, corruption in both countries is only moderate, a much better situation than in many African countries. While the future looks much brighter than the past, both countries still have relatively weak states (see Table 2.2 on page 54). They are still being reconstructed to regain some sense of legitimacy and reestablish the basic functions states are supposed to provide: security, infrastructure, social services, and general well-being.

CASE SUMMARY

Liberia and Sierra Leone are classic cases of the resource curse. They were in many ways typical weak African states, products

of unusual but nonetheless colonial rule, with colonially created ruling elites and multi-ethnic populations. Full democracy and legitimacy never existed in either country. Complete state collapse, however, happened largely because both states relied nearly completely on key resources for revenue. This made controlling the state crucial for all elite factions. Controlling key resources allowed governments to stay in power in spite of providing virtually no real political goods to the bulk of the populace. These resources, especially diamonds, gave a huge impetus to rebellions that were not based on alternative ideologies but instead combined ethnic grievances with rebel leaders' desire for economic gain. State failure made recruiting rebel soldiers quite easy, and once rebels captured the key resources, they could finance continued warfare. The importance of the resources became clear when the conflicts finally ended, something that happened only when international forces successfully prevented the continued sale of illegally mined diamonds from both countries.

In the post–Cold War era, the international system and major powers have come to see weak and failed states as a significant problem. Weak states produce corruption and illegal activity. They have porous borders through which all manner of illegal arms, contagious diseases, biological and nuclear weapons, and illegal drugs might pass. They undermine economic growth and political stability, and democracy is difficult or impossible to foster when a state is unable or unwilling to provide at least the basic political goods citizens expect. Somalia since 1991 and Afghanistan prior to the September 11 attacks are only the best-known examples of this worst-case scenario. One of the most important reasons for studying comparative politics is to understand how and why political institutions work effectively to produce strong states that can maintain security, gain real legitimacy, and avoid the humanitarian costs and dangers of state weakness and failure.

CASE STUDIES OF STATE FORMATION

We have chosen eleven countries to illustrate the trends, theories, and debates in comparative politics. We introduce all eleven below by describing the historical development of each state. Nations, citizenship, and political regimes are all examined more fully in the following chapters, but we touch on these issues as well to provide a general political history here.

COUNTRY AND CONCEPT

The Modern State

| Country | Approximate year modern state established | Failed state index, 2010 | | Gov't revenue as % of GDP | Corruption perception index, 2010 (0 = highly corrupt, 10 = highly clean) | Legitimacy (0 = least legitimate, 10 = most legitimate) |
		Rank among 177 countries	Score (12 = lowest risk of state failure, 144 = highest risk of state failure)			
Brazil	1889	119	67.4	35.3%	3.7	5.19
China	1949	62	83.0	18.3%	3.5	6.58
Germany	1871	157	35.4	40.8%	7.9	6.68
India	1947	79	79.2	18.8%	3.3	4.46
Iran	1925	32	92.2	6.1%	2.2	4.72
Japan	1867	164	31.3	27.9%	7.8	5.62
Mexico	1924	96	76.1	9.0%	3.1	3.55
Nigeria	1960	14	100.2	5.6%	2.4	5.56
Russia	1917	80	79.0	34.0%	2.1	2.27
United Kingdom	1707	161	33.9	37.9%	7.6	6.68
United States	1787	158	35.3	28.3%	7.1	6.82

Sources: Failed state data is from the Fund for Peace, 2010. Data on government revenue as percentage of GDP are from the Heritage Foundation's 2010 Index of Economic Freedom, http://www.heritage.org/index/ranking. Data on corruption are from Transparency International, 2010. Data on state legitimacy are from Bruce Gilley, 2006, "The Meaning and Measure of State Legitimacy: Results for 72 Countries," *European Journal of Political Research* 45 (3): 499–525, doi:10.1111/j.1475-6765.2006.00307.x.

These countries represent a diverse set of political and economic situations. Some have been under the same type of government—democratic or authoritarian—for many years; others have seen frequent changes in their governmental systems. Some have been and are democratic; others have struggled to establish democracy. Some are quite wealthy and have achieved high rates of education and health for their populations; others are among the poorest countries on the planet. Together, they provide a full array of the realities of politics in the contemporary world. The Country and Concept table above presents some basic information about our eleven case-study states. The various measures of state strength in the table produce some surprises. Despite Iran's important international role and its moves toward acquiring nuclear weapons, by most measures it is a fairly weak state.

Similarly, the external power of the United States does not translate into its being the strongest state in the world, though it is certainly one of the stronger ones. A measure of legitimacy that includes not just human rights but citizens' perception of the effectiveness of their government suggests that China's government may be more legitimate than many Western observers usually believe. Stronger states tend to have more revenue, though this varies as well because what the state does with its revenue is important as well.

To illustrate the process of state formation, we present our case studies now in the chronological order in which the modern state arose in each country, rather than by region. Most people tend to think of political development as emanating outward from Europe, eventually reaching the former colonies in Asia and Africa. While the modern state certainly arose first in Europe, the order of the case studies below illustrates clearly that some leaders in other areas of the world adopted the modern state form relatively early on; some of our non-Western cases created modern states before some of our European cases.

CASE STUDY

United Kingdom: A Strong, Modern State

- Territory: Consolidated from three nations (England, Wales, and Scotland) by 1707; colonial empire from mid-nineteenth to mid-twentieth century

- Sovereignty: Aided by island status; fully developed by 1707; partially yielded to European Union

- Legitimacy: Traditional legitimacy of monarchy with some limits since thirteenth century; slow transition to liberal and democratic legitimacy since 1688

- Bureaucracy: Industrialization in nineteenth and twentieth century expanded democracy and modern bureaucracy; welfare state since World War II

- State strength: One of the strongest (161 of 177); weakest on "uneven economic development along group lines" and "threat of group violence" (terrorism)

Queen Elizabeth II before delivering her speech at the State Opening of Parliament, in the House of Lords on November 18, 2009. The queen remains the head of state and the key symbol of the United Kingdom's enduring statehood, though she no longer has any real power. Indeed, her speech was written by the elected government of Prime Minister Gordon Brown and handed to her to read. She represents the state and nation, but power resides in the elected Parliament.

Credit: Paul Edwards/WPA Pool/Getty Images

The full union of England and Scotland under the Act of Union of 1707 officially established the Kingdom of Great Britain and marked the start of the modern state. A century later, with the addition of Ireland (a British colony), the

United Kingdom (also called the U.K., Great Britain, or simply Britain) was established. With the independence of the Republic of Ireland, the name was officially changed to the United Kingdom of Great Britain and Northern Ireland in 1927. The origins of the state were laid well before 1707, though. The Norman invasion of 1066 created a new kingdom that initially included part of what is now northern France. The indigenous Anglo-Saxons saw the Norman invaders, who came to constitute the bulk of the nobility of the new kingdom, as foreign oppressors. Over several centuries, however, the cultural and linguistic divisions between conqueror and conquered slowly disappeared, and a new language, English, emerged.

This state expanded over the centuries. The ascension of King Henry VII of the Welsh Tudor family to the throne of England in 1485 began the process of the unification of England and Wales (the western section of the island), which was completed with the Act of Union of 1542. Similarly, Scotland and England were first united under a single crown when James VI of Scotland also became King James I of England. That union finally brought the entire island under a single state, created a single British parliament, and eliminated the separate Scottish and Welsh parliaments. While a distinct Welsh language survived among a small portion of the population, the Scottish tongue died out completely. Both Scotland and Wales came to be primarily English speaking, linguistically uniting the kingdom, though some cultural distinctions remain to this day.

The greatest threat to the monarchy's sovereignty came from religious wars between Protestants and Catholics. After King Henry VIII broke with the Catholic Church and established the Church of England (known as the Anglican Church in the United Kingdom and the Episcopal Church in the United States) in 1534, religious conflicts dominated politics for well over a century. Protestant monarchs, starting with Henry VIII, persecuted Catholics, and when Catholic monarch Mary Tudor (Mary Queen of Scots) regained the throne, she persecuted Protestants. This culminated in a civil war in the 1640s that brought to power a nonroyal, Protestant dictatorship under Oliver Cromwell. The monarchy was restored after about twenty years, only to be removed again, this time peacefully, by Parliament in the so-called Glorious Revolution of 1688. After this, the doctrine of liberalism gained greater prominence, and slowly the two faiths learned to live under the same government. The Glorious Revolution began a long transition in the basis of legitimacy from the traditional monarchy to liberal democracy, which we detail in chapter 3.

Starting in the mid-eighteenth century, Britain became one of the first countries to begin industrializing. By the nineteenth century, rapid economic transformation helped Britain become the most powerful country in the world, enhancing and securing its external sovereignty. British industry and trade dominated the newly independent countries of Latin America and much of Asia. In the 1860s, Britain led the second round of European colonization so that by 1900 it could be said that "the sun never sets on the British Empire." That empire declined after World War II. While Britain helped win the war, it became a distant second power vis-à-vis its ally and former colony, the United States. World War II helped inspire a growing nationalist movement across Asia and Africa that resulted in nearly all British (and other) colonies gaining their independence by the 1960s.

Industrialization expanded the domestic strength of the state as well and helped create its modern bureaucracy, distinct from the monarch and his or her house. Domestically, the sacrifices made to win World War II produced a consensus in favor of a more egalitarian society, leading to the creation shortly after the war of the British welfare state, which provided income support to those in need and government-funded health care for all. Today, Britain's welfare state is less extensive than many in Europe, but it is far more extensive than similar programs in the United States. The state gave up most of its colonial territory but has extended its domestic reach and size (see the Country and Concept table) significantly since World War II.

Starting in the 1960s, the British state slowly yielded some sovereignty to the European Economic Community, which became the European Union (EU) in 1993. The EU requires member states to yield sovereign power over various issues to the larger body and abide by a wide array of EU standards and regulations. In 1999, many members adopted a common currency, the euro, thereby giving up major areas of economic policy to the new European Central Bank. But even as it has participated in various EU programs and policies, Britain has never completely embraced the EU and chose not to adopt the euro, jealously guarding its economic sovereignty. While it has chosen to maintain greater sovereignty than most EU members, Britain has nonetheless yielded its sovereignty in significant areas to the larger body. The EU perhaps represents a new phase in the development of states, one in which states for the first time voluntarily cede elements of sovereignty to a larger body.

CASE SUMMARY

The modern British state developed over centuries of evolution and internal war but was finally fully united in 1707. Industrialization made it the most powerful state in the world by the nineteenth century. While it lost its empire and yielded some sovereignty to the EU in the twentieth century, Britain nonetheless remains a strong, modern state. No one questions its sovereign control of its territory, and it maintains a functioning and legitimate democracy, which rules over an extensive bureaucracy that implements the state's decisions and oversees a fairly extensive welfare state.

CASE STUDY

The United States: A Consciously Crafted State

- Territory: Expanded via purchase, invasion, and war across a continent
- Sovereignty: Established via negotiation among thirteen colonies to create central government; challenged by Civil War over issue of slavery
- Legitimacy: Constitution established liberal state under which democratic rights slowly extended over 200 years to mass of citizenry
- Bureaucracy: Small and corrupt until early twentieth century; progressive reforms created modern form, and modest welfare state added since World War II
- State strength: One of the strongest (159 of 177); weakest on "uneven economic development along group lines"

At first glance, the origin of the United States in a conference that brought together thirteen separate colonies appears most unusual. Few states were so completely created by design rather than by slow historical evolution. Prior to 1776, Britain's thirteen North American colonies were separate entities with significant cultural and political differences. These "united states" declared independence in 1776, but they did not put a national government in place until 1781, and an effective government did not take shape until 1787. A real sense of national unity did not emerge until after the Civil War (1861–1865). Yet while the origin of the U.S. state was unusual, its early trials and tribulations, and questions about its very existence, were similar to those of many other postcolonial states. Its territory changed and expanded, and its sovereignty and legitimacy were severely questioned at times, but it ultimately grew and strengthened into a modern bureaucratic and democratic state.

North America's colonial history was not unlike that of South America, despite primarily British rather than Spanish and Portuguese conquest. The earliest settlers came looking for wealth; others followed looking for freedom to practice their religion, which is not

The signing of the Declaration of Independence in 1776 was a unique event at the time: a state was being created by conscious design rather than emerging from political battles among rival monarchs. It would take much more work to draft a working form of government and a civil war to create a real sense of national unity. Many colonies would follow the example of the United States in later centuries, demanding independence and writing their own constitutions.

Credit: The Granger Collection, New York

to be confused with believing in or practicing freedom of religion. From early on, the economy of the southern colonies was based on large-scale plantation agriculture, which required extensive labor. Because British conquest decimated the Native American population through disease and displacement, this group was not available as a labor force. Indentured servants from Britain were soon augmented by African slaves with no rights and no possibility of gaining freedom. While most northern colonies allowed slavery, their economies did not depend on it.

Acting as representatives of poor and rich alike, the white, wealthy authors of the Declaration of Independence adopted the enlightened views then prevalent among European intellectuals. They envisioned a nation in which "all men are created equal and endowed by their Creator with certain inalienable rights." The five-year war that

followed achieved independence for the American colonies, but the first effort at creating a functioning state in 1781, the Articles of Confederation, fell into disarray within a few years, in part because of a lack of effective sovereignty. The Articles severely curtailed the national government's power, preserving for the separate thirteen states the right to approve all taxes and trade policies. This weakness led to the Second Continental Congress in 1787, which resulted in the writing of the U.S. Constitution, the document on which the state's legitimacy has depended for over two centuries. The Constitution laid out a plan for a stronger, more sovereign central government with powers to establish a coherent national economy and uniform foreign policy. States did retain significant areas of sovereignty, such as responsibility over policing, infrastructure, and education; indeed, all powers not specifically vested in the national government were reserved for the states. This created the first modern form of federalism, a system in which a state's power is divided among more than one level of government.

The Constitution also made clear that the political elite at the time had a very limited concept of "all men are created equal." The Framers certainly meant "men," since women had no political rights, but they did not mean "all." To secure the support of the southern states, slavery was preserved. By counting each slave as two-thirds of a person (but not giving slaves any rights), slave-holding states received more representation in Congress than their number of voters justified.

Under the aegis of white settlers, the United States dramatically expanded its territory at the expense of Native populations and Mexico; industrialization produced a stronger economy; and the population of the new state continued to grow. Each of these events contributed to the establishment of the first mass political parties by the 1830s. The "Jacksonian Revolution" gave all free white men the right to vote, which was a great expansion of political rights, and created the first more or less modern parties: the Democrats in the 1830s and the Republicans in the 1850s.

Immigration and industrialization increased the size and power of the northern states relative to the southern ones, while a growing abolitionist movement questioned the continuing legitimacy of slavery, a position on which the new Republican Party took the strongest stand.

When the country elected Abraham Lincoln as its first Republican president in 1860, Southern leaders no longer recognized the federal government's legitimacy, leading to the Civil War, a four-year, failed effort by the South to preserve a slaveholding society. In the middle of the war, following his abolitionist principles and appealing to support from European powers opposed to slavery, Lincoln signed the Emancipation Proclamation, freeing the slaves. Lacking effective sovereignty over the South, however, the state could not enforce emancipation until the Northern armies definitively defeated the Southern forces and the South surrendered and reentered the Union. African-Americans, however, did not truly achieve full legal citizenship, including the right to vote, for another hundred years with the passage of the Civil Rights and Voting Rights Acts in 1964 and 1965, respectively.

The United States became a global power with the second industrial revolution of the late nineteenth century. Cities grew dramatically, immigrants poured into urban areas to provide labor for rapidly expanding factories, and the country was transformed from a primarily agricultural society into one that was predominantly urban and industrial. This brought demands for changes in the state. The United States had been well known for corruption: political leaders at all levels regularly appointed their supporters to government jobs, often regardless of their qualifications. After a long period of such "machine politics," reformists lobbied for and successfully established a civil service under which most jobs in the government bureaucracy would be permanent and based on some concept of merit, rather than on the whims of the next elected politician. The same reform movement ultimately produced the Federal Reserve Board, which gave control over currency to appointed officials, as well as a 1913 constitutional amendment that created the national income tax, which became the state's primary source of revenue. This helped create the state's modern bureaucracy, which expanded significantly as the government took on additional roles in the twentieth century, especially after World War II.

Further expansion of the state began with the New Deal in the 1930s. After being on the winning side of World War I and fully establishing itself as a superpower, the United States was the first country to feel the effects of the depression that swept the globe after 1929. Newly elected president Franklin Roosevelt envisioned an expanded government that helped to provide jobs and old-age pensions to people in need as part of the effort to bring the country back to economic stability. The New Deal, followed by the Great Society program of the 1960s, which sought to improve health care (Medicare and Medicaid) and reduce poverty (Aid to Families with Dependent Children, or AFDC, and food stamps), increased the size and reach of the U.S. state. Nonetheless, it remained quite a bit smaller than most of its European counterparts, a fact that you can see clearly by comparing the United Kingdom and United States in the "Government Revenue" column in the Country and Concept table on page 61.

These new roles also strengthened the central government vis-à-vis the states. While the formal rules in the Constitution did not change, the central government's ability to fund popular programs run by the states gave it much greater power than it had possessed a century earlier. Federalism continues to divide sovereignty in the United States among the national (or federal) government and the fifty states, a division that tends to be replicated in all sorts of government agencies and functions, making the United States a more decentralized (and critics contend fragmented) state than most wealthy countries. Nonetheless, the state is far more centralized and involved in American lives than it was a century ago.

The United States established its sovereignty in an unusually clear and explicit way, first by making a Declaration of Independence and then by fighting a war to make that independence real. Similarly, its legitimacy is based on a consciously crafted constitution. The new state's sovereignty was tested in the War of 1812 against its former colonizer Britain and again in the Civil War, but it held. The state simultaneously expanded its territory dramatically via invasion of Native American lands, land purchases from European colonial powers, and war with neighboring Mexico. Like the United Kingdom, its modern bureaucracy developed and expanded with industrialization and then the creation of a moderate welfare state. Today, it is the world's leading superpower externally, though internally the strength of its state is high but not the highest in the world (at least according to the Failed States Index). This is due in large part to continuing inequality among the population stemming from the legacy of slavery and territorial expansion via conquest.

CASE STUDY

Japan: Determined Sovereignty

- Territory: Fully consolidated control of island by 1603; colonial empire in Asia in late nineteenth and early twentieth centuries

- Sovereignty: Feudal system with unusually strong center since 1603, with nearly complete isolation until modern state established in 1867

- Legitimacy: Traditional but unusually weak monarchy since 1100s; monarch only symbolic since 1867; liberal democracy since 1950

- Bureaucracy: Developed with industrialization prior to World War II; exceptionally powerful influence on state since World War II

- State strength: One of the strongest (164 of 177); weakest on "mounting demographic pressures" (aging population)

Japan was the first non-Western state to create a fully modern economy. By first isolating itself from Western control and then borrowing Western technology as rapidly as possible, Japan's unusually strong state helped create what was the world's second-largest economy until 2010.

Credit: AP Photo/Shizuo Kambayashi

Japan is one of the few places in the world outside Europe that successfully avoided European colonization. It went on to become the first "non-Western" country to join the ranks of the world's wealthy and most powerful states, creating a new model of capitalism in the process: the developmental state. An island state, Japan has maintained its territorial sovereignty for centuries and had colonial territory of its own in Korea and China for several decades. Japan's modern democracy has achieved a high degree of legitimacy in spite of the fact that it has returned the same party to power for almost all of its history. The developmental state includes an unusually powerful bureaucracy, which the new Japanese ruling party is trying to curb.

Japan reduced its monarchy to a largely symbolic role much earlier than European countries did. As early as the twelfth century, military leaders called shoguns wrested effective power from the emperor, who remained the symbolic source of legitimacy. Japan then suffered a period of "warring states" until Tokugawa Ieyasu fully consolidated control. He claimed the title of shogun in 1603 and consolidated a central state, fully establishing sovereignty over the entire territory. The new state came to be called the Tokugawa Bakufu, or shogunate, and was roughly similar to European feudal states. The ruling Tokugawa family did not hold all power but rather shared it with 260 landlords called *daimyo*. These *daimyo*, however, were not as powerful as most European feudal lords because the central government regularly used its superior military power to extract funds and labor from them, thus limiting their wealth. The third important class in medieval society, the samurai or warriors, were a "landless aristocracy."

Under the Tokugawa Shogunate (1603–1867), Japan virtually isolated itself from outside influence until U.S. warships under the command of Commodore Matthew Perry sailed into the harbor at Edo (present-day Tokyo) in 1853. Perry refused to leave until Japanese officials agreed to undertake trade talks. The officials eventually agreed to a series of unfavorable treaties with the United States, France, and Britain, the closest the country would come to succumbing to Western control until the end of World War II. These agreements produced immediate protests, led by the samurai, against what was seen as undue Western influence. The protests broadened, and by the early 1860s, a samurai alliance had formed in opposition to the shogunate. After a series of battles, the shogunate ceded power in October 1867, establishing what came to be known as the Meiji Restoration, so called because the new government claimed to be restoring the Emperor Meiji to his full powers. In truth, the new government was controlled by the samurai, who eliminated the feudal classes of both the shogun and *daimyo*.

The Meiji government went on to create the first truly modern state in Japan. Though unhappy with the earlier treaties with Western powers, the new government launched a series of modernizations, borrowing openly and heavily from the West, especially Western technology. Successful economic growth and industrialization gave Japan the power to renegotiate its treaties with the Western powers by the end of the nineteenth century, this time on more favorable terms. The new state ultimately included a modern army and navy, the beginnings of compulsory education, and the establishment of a single school to train all government civil servants. Significantly, the new military had nearly complete autonomy, as no form of civilian control existed over it. This military helped Japan gain colonial control over Taiwan in the 1890s and Korea in 1905, briefly creating a Japanese empire. The Meiji government introduced the first written constitution in 1889, formally codifying state institutions, including the first parliament, albeit an extremely weak one. After the death of Emperor Meiji, a period of slightly greater political liberalization emerged under his successor, Emperor Taisho. While the institution of democratic reforms was limited, this period did include the adoption in 1925 of the first universal male suffrage. Economic recession led the military to reverse this liberalization by 1927, however, with General Tanaka Giichi becoming prime minister. While not an actual coup, Tanaka's ascendancy was based on an informal reassertion of military power at the expense of civilian leaders. Military leaders and right-wing parties blamed democracy for the country's economic woes, leading the military to enter politics directly. This ushered in a period of growing Japanese imperialism. The military effectively intimidated all civilian political leaders and pushed the government toward a more aggressive foreign policy. This new approach led to Japan's invasion of China starting in 1931, its alliance with fascist Germany and Italy, and its attack on Pearl Harbor in 1941, which contributed to the entry of the United States into World War II.

This war would end for Japan with the United States dropping atomic bombs on Hiroshima and Nagasaki in August 1945. The Japanese surrender led to the country's full occupation by the United States in the name of the victorious Allies. Under General Douglas MacArthur, the United States completely demilitarized Japanese society and then established a new democratic constitution, written by the occupying Americans, in 1947. The document's provisions prohibited Japan from creating a military or ever engaging in war, although Japan ultimately did create a "self-defense" force that has since become the second most funded military in the world. In addition, the new constitution created a complex electoral system that favored rural over urban areas and helped the Liberal Democratic Party (LDP) maintain electoral control for more than forty years. This single party has won all but two elections since its creation in 1955. In spite of this lack of electoral turnover, liberal democracy has fully replaced monarchy as the basis of the state's legitimacy, though the monarch remains as a symbol of the nation, as in the United Kingdom.

The LDP governments created what came to be known as the "developmental state," a democracy that actively used the government to guide rapid economic growth. The bureaucracy became very powerful under LDP rule, working much more closely with Japanese businesses than did governments in most Western countries. Since 1990, however, Japan's unusually powerful bureaucracy has been rocked by a seeming

inability to restart economic growth and a series of corruption scandals. This led to the LDP's brief ouster from power in 1993–94 and again in 2009. Nonetheless, sixty years after its defeat in World War II, the country remains the third largest economy in the world.

CASE SUMMARY

Japan is unusual among non-Western states, first because it effectively resisted Western colonization under a sovereign but feudal state and secondly because it established a modern state that grew strong enough to allow interaction with the West while resisting incursion. The military ultimately took control of this state, created an empire, expanded industrialization and established a modern bureaucracy, and then lost power at the end of World War II. After five years of occupation, in which Japan's sovereignty was forfeited for the first time in 400 years, Japan reemerged as a sovereign state fully in control of its traditional territory and with a new source of legitimacy: liberal democracy. Its earlier bureaucracy, though, survived the war and became an exceptionally powerful force. Today, despite significant economic problems, it remains one of the strongest states in the world; indeed, it is the strongest of our case studies on the Failed States Index.

CASE STUDY

Germany: The First Modern Welfare State

- Territory: Widespread sense of national identity among German-speaking people, but many states until 1871; boundaries changed with wars until 1990; brief colonial empire prior to World War I
- Sovereignty: Established over much of German-speaking people by 1871; divided by Cold War, 1945–1990
- Legitimacy: Based on nationalism first; failed liberal democracy after World War I

led to Nazi rule; divided state with liberal democratic and communist components until united under democratic constitution in 1990
- Bureaucracy: First modern welfare state starting in late nineteenth century; extensive since World War II
- State strength: One of the strongest (157 of 177); weakest on "vengeance-seeking group grievance" (terrorism threat)

East Berliners stand atop the Berlin Wall in 1989, shortly before it was brought down to reunite the divided German state. Reunification in 1990 meant the elimination of the separate and largely illegitimate East German state, whose territory was absorbed by the much stronger and more legitimate West German state. This was only the most recent change in the boundaries of the German state. Because it lies at the heart of Europe, World Wars I and II and the Cold War had profound influences on what territory the German state controlled.

Credit: AP Photo/Michel Lipchitz

Germany, Europe's largest country, lies at the heart of the Continent. This central position has made it important throughout European history. Indeed, with no clear natural boundaries between German-speaking and neighboring areas, German speakers spread across central Europe in the Middle Ages, resulting in major questions and battles over the extent of German sovereignty and territory. For centuries Germans were split into hundreds of small principalities, duchies, and the like, and political loyalty and identity were primarily local. Adding to this fragmentation, the formation of Protestantism by German monk Martin Luther beginning in 1521 created religious divisions that only exacerbated long-standing political divisions among the German people.

The first stirrings of a united Germany occurred in response to Napoleon's destruction of the Holy Roman Empire. In 1806 Emperor Franz II gave up his title and dissolved the empire under pressure from Napoleon, who had defeated Franz and his allies at the Battle of Austerlitz the previous year. Napoleon then turned much of the former empire's territory into a new "Confederation of the Rhine," a confederation of German client states under Napoleon's "protection." But after Napoleon himself was defeated 1813, the Confederation of the Rhine was dissolved. Thereafter, a new German Confederation arose, but it was only a loose association and not a unified state. Prussia, centered on the city of Berlin, quickly became the economically and militarily dominant member of the confederation. A unified Germany finally emerged under Otto von Bismarck, the chancellor (equivalent of a prime minister) of Prussia. Bismarck came to power in 1862 and set about expanding and uniting Germany under Prussian control. Between 1864 and 1870, he initiated wars with Denmark, Austria-Hungary, and France to conquer lands populated by German speakers that were under "foreign" control. In 1871 a new, united Germany was proclaimed, with the Prussian king named as the German kaiser and Bismarck as the chancellor. This new Germany had a legislature and elections, but virtually all power was in the hands of Kaiser Wilhelm I and Bismarck.

The new German state became actively involved in the economy, pursuing rapid industrialization in an attempt to catch up with the economic might of Britain, at that time Europe's most powerful state. The primary opposition to Bismarck came out of this industrialization in the form of the Social Democratic Party (SDP), founded in 1875, which demanded greater workers' rights and democracy. Bismarck successfully resisted the party's efforts, both by brutal repression when necessary and by creating Europe's first social welfare programs. The latter included health insurance and old-age pensions; administering these programs also expanded the country's bureaucracy.

By 1900 Germany had become an industrial powerhouse with aspirations to become an empire. It colonized what is now Namibia in southern Africa, most of what is now Tanzania in eastern Africa, and parts of Cameroon and Togo in western Africa. Such expansionist behavior contributed to Germany's entry into World War I in 1914. Germany's defeat in "the Great War" ended the country's first united government. As Allied forces moved on Berlin in 1918, the kaiser fled, and the leaders of the SDP proclaimed a democratic republic, the first shift in the basis of legitimacy from nationalism to democracy. But the Weimar Republic survived only fourteen years, with conditions after the war leading to its downfall. Defeat in the war and subsequent reparations to the victorious Allies left the nation devastated. Throughout the 1920s, voters became increasingly disenchanted with "mainstream" politicians, who seemed unable to resolve the country's growing economic crisis. Popular support shifted toward the extreme political groups: the Communists and the Nazis. National Socialist Adolf Hitler became chancellor in 1932 and effectively eliminated democracy a year later (see chapter 3). He went on to create a rigid authoritarian state and launched Germany into World War II in 1939, proclaiming the German state the rightful ruler not only of all German-speaking peoples but of all Europe.

Hitler's defeat in 1945 led to Germany's territorial division. At the end of the war, the victorious Allies (the United States, the United Kingdom, France, and the Soviet Union) each oversaw a separate German occupation zone. While the United States, Britain, and France united their zones under one government, the Soviet Union ultimately refused to allow its sector to rejoin the rest. This zone would become the German Democratic Republic (GDR), better known as East Germany, a communist state so closely controlled by the Soviet Union that its own sovereignty was quite limited. The other three united sectors formed the Federal Republic of Germany (FRG), governed by the Basic Law (the equivalent of a constitution) that took effect in 1949. West Germany, as it came to be known, reemerged as a democratic and industrial powerhouse in Central Europe. It joined France in creating what would become the European Union and created what came to be known as the "social market economy," a distinct form of capitalism (see chapter 5).

Germany and the city of Berlin were to remain divided for nearly thirty years. Not until the fall of communism brought an end to the Cold War in 1989 were the country and city reunited. Nothing signified this more dramatically than the destruction of the Berlin Wall, which had split the German capital since 1961. By 1990 Germany had been reunified under the constitution of the former West Germany. This process was economically and politically difficult, requiring the integration of the much poorer East German population into the unified nation. Once the worst of its growing pains were behind it, a reunited German state led the way in transforming what had been the European Community into the European Union, giving up significant economic sovereignty to the larger body. This transformation culminated with the creation of the euro currency and European Central Bank in 1999.

CASE SUMMARY

The modern German state emerged relatively late in Europe after uniting many of the widely dispersed German-speaking people, and it was defeated and divided during much of the twentieth century. Its sovereignty was questioned and briefly eliminated under occupation, and its territory was divided by the Cold War. Nonetheless, the German state, first under Bismarck and more recently under democratic rule, consciously and effectively created an industrial powerhouse in the heart of Europe that was also the first modern welfare state with an extensive modern bureaucracy. Democracy emerged twice, though disastrously the first time, and was secure and universal throughout Germany after 1990. Today the modern German state is widely considered to be one of the world's strongest, most legitimate, wealthiest, and most stable.

CASE STUDY

Brazil: A Moderately Strong, and Now Legitimate, Modern State

- Territory: Colonial creation; Portuguese half of South America

- Sovereignty: Inherited peacefully at independence; legacy of weak central government vis-à-vis states and local elites

- Legitimacy: Monarchy until 1889; limited democracy thereafter; legacy of military intervention claiming legitimacy based on modernization; now consolidated democracy

- Bureaucracy: Expanded greatly since 1964 under state-guided development; high corruption

- State strength: Moderate (113 of 177); weakest on "uneven development along group lines" and "security apparatus as a state within a state"

Like most countries, Brazil's modern state was the product of European colonial rule. Prior to Portuguese colonization in 1500, its population was relatively small compared to that of many other areas of the Americas. The Portuguese effectively subjugated the indigenous population, and colonial Brazil became a major producer of sugarcane and other agricultural products, farmed largely with African slave labor. Indeed, Brazil had

Brazil's largest city, Sao Paulo, is also one of the largest cities in the world with a population over 11 million. As the hub of South America's largest economy, the city represents the significant industrialization and development over which the Brazilian state has presided in the past half century. Brazil boasts one of the ten largest economies in the world and is a growing player on the world stage as part of the informal "BRICS" (Brazil, Russia, India, China, South Africa) group of midsized powers.

Credit: Keiny Andrade/LatinContent/Getty Images

more slaves than any other colony in the Americas. The economic heart of the colonial economy was the northeastern sugar-producing region, even though Rio de Janeiro in the south became the capital. A Portuguese, landowning elite emerged as the socially and economically dominant force in the colonial society.

In contrast to the Spanish colonies in South America, Brazil gained independence from Portugal as a single country, creating by far the largest territory in South America under one sovereign government. This was partly due to its unusual route to independence. In most of South America in the early nineteenth century, the landowning elite helped lead rebellions against continued Spanish rule, which Spain initially resisted but lacked the power to stop. In contrast, the Portuguese royal family actually fled to Brazil in 1808 to evade Napoleon's conquest of Portugal, taking sanctuary in their American colony. In 1821 King João VI returned to Portugal after regaining his throne, leaving his son, Dom Pedro, in Rio as prince regent to rule on his behalf. A year later, Dom Pedro declared Brazil independent and declared himself emperor, with no real opposition from Portugal. In 1840 his son, Dom Pedro II, became emperor and ruled until 1889.

The new state's economy remained based in northeastern agriculture, using slave labor until the late nineteenth century, when profits from coffee production in the south rivaled those of the decaying sugar industry in the northeast. Brazil was the last remaining slaveholding society in the world, and while coffee growers needed labor, many came to believe that importing wage labor would be easier than maintaining slavery. In addition, growing international and domestic pressure was being applied to end the institution of slavery. Both factors ultimately led to the abolition of slavery in 1888. The same liberal ideas that led some Brazilian elites to oppose slavery also led them to oppose the empire and favor democracy instead. Just a year after the abolition of slavery, civilian and military reformers convinced key military leaders to overthrow the emperor in a bloodless coup, which sent him into exile in Portugal and established a republic.

The leaders of the new republic created Brazil's modern state, drafting a constitution that created a democratic system of government but gave voting rights to literate men only, thus restricting the voting population to 3.5 percent of the citizenry. This widespread official disenfranchisement was due in part to the fact that slavery had been abolished only a year earlier and virtually all the former slaves were illiterate; the literacy restriction effectively deprived former slaves of the right to vote.

Economic influence was shifting to southern urban areas, but political control remained vested in the rural landowning elite. Known as coroneis, or "colonels," these individuals used their socioeconomic dominance to control the votes in their regions in a type of machine politics. Meanwhile, in the growing urban areas, **clientelism**, the exchange of material resources for political support, developed as the key means of mobilizing political support. As more urban dwellers became literate and gained the right to vote, elite politicians gained their support by providing direct benefits to them, such as jobs or government services to their neighborhoods. Clientelism and coronelismo (rule by coroneis) became ways to shore up political power in Brazil's first, partial democracy. Corruption and clientelistic use of bureaucratic jobs as perks for supporters simultaneously bloated and undermined Brazil's young bureaucracy. Such corruption indicated a weak modern state.

One politician to rise out of this system was Getúlio Vargas. After losing a disputed presidential election in 1930, Vargas used his support in the military to launch a coup that brought him to power, ending Brazil's first democratic republic. Vargas overcame the power of the rural coroneis by appealing directly to the growing population of urban poor via populist and nationalist rhetoric and by providing goods and services. He used this support to establish the *Estado Novo*

clientelism: The exchange of material resources for political support

(New State), a quasi-fascist regime that he ruled from 1937 to 1945. During this time, he significantly centralized power in the state. The government created its own steel and oil industries and expanded health and welfare systems to gain popular support and strengthen the state bureaucracy. When the end of World War II brought U.S. and domestic pressure against his state, which too closely resembled those of the discredited fascists of Europe, Vargas was forced to allow a return to democratic rule.

The New (democratic) Republic was plagued by economic problems and political instability. By the early 1960s, the elite and military saw growing militancy on the part of workers as a threat and perhaps the first stage in a communist revolution. In a preemptive strike, the military overthrew the elected government in 1964 with U.S. and considerable upper- and middle-class support. The military ruled until 1985, leading what we will term a "modernizing authoritarian" regime (see chapter 3), which produced very rapid economic growth and industrialization, further expanding the state's size and capabilities. By the late 1970s, growing inequality and a slowdown in economic growth led workers in the expanding industrial cities to organize illegal unions. Despite government efforts to stop them, these unions and followers of liberation theology in the Catholic Church led

a growing movement for democracy, which ultimately forced the military to slowly shift power back to elected officials (see chapter 9). Democratic governments have ruled since, firmly establishing liberal democracy as the basis of legitimacy.

CASE SUMMARY

While maintaining a large sovereign territory since independence, Brazil has faced repeated questions about the state's legitimacy. Various Brazilian leaders have responded by claiming legitimacy on the basis of charismatic appeals, patronage, modernization, and democracy. Brazil's new democracy now seems to be fully established, with a complex party system and quite intense partisan competition in a primarily industrialized economy that is one of the world's largest. This modern state continues to be plagued by high levels of corruption and clientelism, which at times undermine the rule of law and bureaucratic effectiveness, as well as a security apparatus that sometimes seems beyond civilian control and abuses human rights. It is nonetheless a moderately strong modern state, exercising effective control over its territory and people, enjoying democratic legitimacy, and having the largest economy in the Southern Hemisphere.

CASE STUDY

Russia: Strong External Sovereignty with Weak Rule of Law

- Territory: Multinational empire consolidated under tsar; multi-ethnic state now
- Sovereignty: Feudal state with unusually strong monarchy under tsar; modern state established by communist rule; post-communist state weak but getting stronger; continuing challenges to central control from regions
- Legitimacy: Traditional monarchy overthrown by communist revolution; democracy in 1990s; semi-authoritarian regime with strong nationalist appeal
- Bureaucracy: Extremely powerful under Communist rule, controlling economy; post-Communist weakening with growing corruption; perhaps strengthening since 2000

- State strength: Moderately weak (71 of 177); weakest on "uneven economic development," "criminalization of state," and "rule of law"

Our third "European" case, Russia, is actually only partly in Europe. Since its founding, Russian leaders have struggled with how much to identify with Europe and how much with Asia. Russia is the largest single state in the world; its landmass stretches from eastern Europe to the borders of China and Japan. A relatively centralized premodern kingdom emerged in Moscow in the fourteenth century, creating a monarchy that would last until 1917. Ivan IV Vasilyevich (Ivan the Terrible) took the title "tsar" in 1547 and greatly increased the monarchy's power and reach by initiating military campaigns to take over vast swaths of territory to the east and west. By 1660 Russia was the largest country in the world, its rulers having taken control of the previously independent Ukraine and territory stretching far into Asia. The country became a vast, multinational empire in which more than 100 languages were spoken.

The tsar was an absolutist ruler with even greater power than most monarchs in Europe. For example, Russian tsars owned all the land in Russia until 1785, when the gentry were finally allowed to own land. Over the centuries, an expanding bureaucracy emerged to administer the tsar's lands. Nonetheless, the Russian monarchy essentially had the attributes of an early modern absolutist state in terms of effective sovereignty and control over territory, while having only limited state activity and legitimacy.

The tsar faced pressure to reform the government throughout the nineteenth century. Tsar Alexander II gave in to the biggest reform in 1861 by permitting the emancipation of serfs. For centuries, the bulk of the Russian population had lived under the control of the landed nobility and had virtually no rights. Alexander's freeing them was a belated but essential step in the transition to capitalism. Emancipated serfs gained some collective control over their land, thus reducing the

Members of the pro-Kremlin youth movement Nashi rally in support of Vladimir Putin in front of the Kremlin and Saint Basil's Cathedral in Moscow. The new Russian state emerged from the collapse of the Soviet Union in 1991. After a decade as a very weak state, it became significantly stronger under Putin, often to the detriment of democracy. Putin consciously identified himself with the symbols of the Soviet and pre-Communist Russian state, both to project an image of strength and to gain greater legitimacy.

Credit: Shamil Zhumatov/Reuters/Landov

power of the landlords. Rapid industrialization in the late nineteenth century gave freed serfs a reason to move to urban areas, which exploded in size.

Radical movements grew in these newly expanded cities, including groups demanding democracy and a growing Marxist movement. Tsar Alexander III responded initially with repression, but in 1905 he was finally forced to agree to the creation of an elected legislature, the *Duma*. He dissolved the body after only three months, however, changing the electoral laws and spearheading the election of a new, more compliant legislature. Russia's first, very brief experiment with democracy was over.

Not long after, Russia was drawn into World War I, which proved economically disastrous for the country. Because it was still primarily a relatively poor and agricultural society, soldiers were sent to the front ill equipped and hungry, and as conditions worsened, mass desertions occurred. A crisis of legitimacy undermined the state's ability to maintain its territorial integrity and military force.

By the end of the war, the Bolsheviks, a communist group under Vladimir Ilyich Lenin, had gained popularity. The makings of another electoral democracy emerged in February 1917, only to be overtaken by a communist revolution that October. The communists assassinated the tsar and his family, after which many of the non-Russian areas of the empire declared themselves independent. It took the communist movement three years to fully recapture what had been the tsarist empire, more or less preserving prior Russian territory. A new government called the Union of Soviet Socialist Republics (USSR), or the Soviet Union (see chapter 3 for more details), was formed, a brutal but nonetheless modern state. The Communist Party created a dictatorial regime that appeared to create a federal state in which local regions (the soviet republics) had significant power; in truth, all were controlled tightly from Moscow by the Communist Party. A new basis of legitimacy was established in Communist rule, but most analysts believe the Communist regime's real legitimacy was fairly short-lived.

The Communists modernized Russia in a way the tsars had not. At tremendous human cost (estimates range as high as twenty million dead), Lenin's successor, Josef Stalin, rapidly industrialized the country, taking resources and laborers from the countryside as needed. The state took complete control of all economic activity. The secret police dealt with anyone who opposed the state's methods, contributing to the formation of one of the most oppressive police states in history. Yet Stalin also created a superpower, which became the only serious rival to the United States after World War II. After his death, Soviet leaders reduced the degree of terror but maintained centralized control over an increasingly bureaucratic form of communism. The Communist bureaucracy controlled virtually all economic activity and was initially successful at rapid industrialization, but it could not keep pace with the West's economic growth. Recognizing the need for

change, a new leadership under Mikhail Gorbachev began a process of reform in 1985 that eventually resulted in the collapse of the Soviet state.

When elements of the Soviet military who were opposed to some of Gorbachev's reforms attempted a coup in August 1991, Boris Yeltsin, the leader of the Russian part of the Soviet federation and himself a Communist reformer, successfully stood up to the tanks and proclaimed the end of Soviet rule. The military, faced with masses of people in the streets and with the eyes of the world on it, was forced to back down. By December, Gorbachev had agreed to the dissolution of the Soviet state. The old tsarist empire split into fifteen separate states, with Russia the largest by far.

Today Russia remains a very multi-ethnic state, with a federal system of government that gives some power, at least in theory, to the various regions, which are defined loosely along ethnic lines. After the dissolution of the Soviet regime, Russia gained a new claim to legitimacy by proclaiming itself a democracy, and Yeltsin became president. The collapse of Communist rule allowed an electoral democracy to emerge in the 1990s. It was very fragile, however, with rapidly changing political parties, and it appeared for a while that the former Communist Party might return to power by popular election. The state became demonstrably weaker in the 1990s, as powerful mafias and super-rich "oligarchs" controlled most political power and economic wealth. Yeltsin's hand-picked successor, Vladimir Putin, reduced the level of democratic freedoms and simultaneously strengthened the central state in the new millennium. Putin and his handpicked successor, President Dmitry Medvedev, have centralized power in the executive, strengthened the central state vis-à-vis regional governments, reduced crime, and restored order. But they still face a threat to Russia's territorial integrity in Chechnya, where a guerilla movement continues to battle for independence.

CASE SUMMARY

Russia has seen three dramatically different regimes, with a possible fourth emerging in the new millennium. Prior to the 1990s, the country had an exceptionally strong state that controlled most economic activity far more tightly than virtually any modern state today. It also controlled a vast, multinational empire along its borders, one that was lost with the dissolution of the Soviet Union. The smaller but still vast Russian state continues to be plagued by ethnic and national differences, some of which have resulted in violent conflict. The various regimes' claims to legitimacy have been drastically different and have always been challenged. After a period of fairly extreme weakness in the 1990s, the state has become stronger in most areas in the new millennium, though it remains corrupt and has a weak rule of law.

CASE STUDY

Mexico: Challenges to Internal Sovereignty

- Territory: Spanish colonial creation, reduced to half its original size following the Mexican-American War (1846–1848)

- Sovereignty: Achieved in War of Independence (1810–1821); recent challenges by southern guerilla movement and northern drug cartels

- Legitimacy: Nineteenth-century divisions (liberal vs. conservative *caudillos*); revolution followed by twentieth-century semi-authoritarian state; twenty-first-century democracy

- Bureaucracy: Developed with single-party domination over the twentieth century; part of ruling party's clientelistic networks until 2000.

- State strength: Moderately weak (102 of 177); experiences "chronic emigration," and "uneven economic development"; powerful drug cartels

Mexican president Vicente Fox is inaugurated on Friday, December 1, 2000. His victory marked the transition from a semi-authoritarian to a democratic claim to legitimacy for the Mexican state, as the long-ruling Institutional Revolutionary Party (PRI) yielded power for the first time in seventy-five years.

Credit: AP Photo/Dario Lopez-Mills

Like most countries, Mexico's modern state was the product of European colonial rule. Prior to the Spanish conquest, Mexico hosted a series of powerful empires, from the Olmecs, who ruled as far back as 1400 BCE, to the Aztecs, who controlled much of the country when conquistador Hernán Cortés landed his ships on the Yucatan Peninsula in 1519. In colonial times, Spain exploited Mexico for its gold and silver, but most important was the country's large, disciplined population, which provided valuable labor for the colonial regime. Because of this, Mexico did not become an important market for the African slave trade.

Mexico began its history as a sovereign state with the War of Independence (1810–1821), but in the immediate aftermath found itself bitterly divided along regional (north-south) and ideological (liberal vs. conservative) lines. Divisions manifested themselves in the successive military coups that rocked Mexico throughout much of the century, with strongmen (*caudillos*) constantly changing allegiances in support of one side or another. These conflicts resulted in a weak state and a limited capacity to develop a functioning bureaucracy.

The internal rifts also had a negative impact on Mexico's ability to successfully defend its sovereignty, as evidenced by the Mexican-American War (1846–1848) and its immediate aftermath. The terms of the peace, laid out in the Treaty of Guadalupe Hidalgo, called for the sale of territories comprising much of what is now the American southwest to the United States, shrinking Mexican territory to under one-half of its original size.

The chaos of the nineteenth century did eventually end, but at the cost of political freedoms. Porfirio Díaz, a *caudillo* who had mastered the art of consolidating power through bribery and intimidation, founded an authoritarian regime and ruled from 1876 until 1910, marking the longest tenure of any statesman in Mexican history. His rule, termed the *Porfiriato*, based its legitimacy on an ability to deliver political order and unprecedented economic growth. Not unlike some Italians who have claimed that under Mussolini "the trains always run on time," Mexicans have viewed the history of the *Porfiriato* with a degree of national nostalgia at times, despite its oppressive nature.

The Díaz regime's primary supporters were among the upper class and business elite. Its enemies were especially to be found among the peasant class (*campesinos*), who lost land to foreign speculators only to find the state unreceptive to their grievances. When Díaz reneged on a promise to retire in 1910, anti-Diaz forces, especially the rural poor, instigated the Mexican Revolution (1910–1920), which resulted in the regime's collapse. Despite Díaz's resignation in 1911, the revolution soon became a civil war, with various factions turning against the new government of Francisco Madero, each on behalf of diverging regional interests and unique claims to legitimacy. Madero's policies were seen as too tepid, and his efforts at disarming fellow revolutionaries made him enemies, notably the guerrillas led by General Francisco "Pancho" Villa in the north and the peasant armies of Emiliano Zapata in the south.

Ultimately, Villa and Zapata were assassinated, as power was consolidated by an emerging, revolutionary elite, mostly military commanders who had emerged from rural poverty to lead the revolution. The modern Mexican state was established with President Plutarco Elías Calles (1924–1928), who created the longest-ruling political machine in Mexican history, a party that took various names until it settled on Partido Revolucionario Institucional (Institutional Revolutionary Party), or PRI. While the PRI embraced the revolution-era democratic constitution of 1917, in practice it formed a semi-authoritarian system that governed Mexico from 1929 to 2000. The party was able to maintain power through systemic corruption, bribery, and intimidation, as well as clientelism and effective voter mobilization tactics (see chapter 3).

The PRI's legitimacy rested mainly on its association with the values of the Mexican Revolution, especially land reform and the empowerment of the *campesinos*. As the state achieved a new level of stability, Mexico created a functioning bureaucracy that, while corrupt, made important strides in furthering literacy, access to health care, and overall economic development. It used oil wealth and trade with the United States to achieve significant industrialization, transforming Mexico into a middle-income country, though with sharp income and regional inequality.

Starting in the early 1980s, the party moved away from policies that seemed to benefit the rural poor and closer to the precepts of a fully free-market economy, with less government intervention. This led to a fissure within the party and the defection of the left flank under Cuauhtémoc Cárdenas (son of a legendary president who nationalized Mexico's oil industry in 1938). Cárdenas ran for president in the 1988 elections, garnering a significant 30 percent of the vote, though the PRI's candidate still came out ahead with 52 percent. Cárdenas and his supporters claimed electoral fraud, which President Carlos Salinas de Gortari, the PRI's winning candidate, vehemently denied. Despite the denials, the PRI's unending string of questionable electoral victories finally seemed to be taking a toll on its fragile legitimacy.

Mexico transitioned to democracy in 2000 with the election of conservative candidate Vicente Fox of the National Action Party (Partido de Acción Nacional), or PAN. This move from semi-authoritarianism to free democratic competition reflects changing notions of state legitimacy, from one based on providing material benefits to key constituent groups to one of political parties fairly competing to garner broad popular support.

Despite its democratization, Mexico remains plagued by severe economic and regional disparities along with questions over the future strength of the state. First, Mexico has experienced large-scale flight of labor to the United States. This has not only been a source of tension between Mexico and several U.S. states but is also symptomatic of the desperate economic situation faced by millions of Mexicans. In the south, farmers, especially those of indigenous origin, still face economic dislocation. This led in the 1980s to the formation of the Zapatista Army of National Liberation (EZLN). Based in the southern state of Chiapas, the EZLN waged a guerrilla campaign in 1994 in the tradition of Zapata's fighters during the Mexican Revolution, though it has since reverted to more peaceful methods of demonstration.

By far the most critical challenge to Mexican sovereignty today comes in the north, where a war between rival drug cartels led to an average of 10,000 deaths per year between 2007 and 2010. While U.S. consumers have been supporting the border states' manufacturing, or *maquiladora,* economy, America has also been the prime market for the Mexican drug trade. This has raised further questions about the impact and direction of U.S.-Mexican interconnections. Endemic police corruption, lack of alternative economic opportunities, a supply of small arms from north of the border, and a large appetite for drugs there have all led to the degradation of government authority in the northern region. This has called into question the state's ability to keep a monopoly on legitimate violence for the first time since the end of the Mexican Revolution.

CASE SUMMARY

The long-ruling PRI created a modern state that effectively controlled authority and maintained sovereignty for three-quarters of a century. It consciously used an interventionist economic development strategy, funded mainly by oil production, to initiate industrialization. When forced to do so in the 1980s, it adapted to a more open free-market economy that included a great expansion of trade with the United States, its powerful northern neighbor. Economic success amid continuing poverty and declining legitimacy ultimately created a growing movement for democracy, which finally succeeded in peacefully ousting the PRI from power in 2000, changing the basis of the state's legitimacy. Today Mexico faces challenges to its internal sovereignty in the south at the hands of an indigenous guerilla group and, more threateningly, in the north at the hands of drug cartels who seem more powerful than the state's security forces. This important middle-income country has seen significant economic success in the last generation but is plagued by growing questions of internal sovereignty.

CASE STUDY

Iran: Claiming Legitimacy via Theocracy

- Territory: Solidified in nineteenth century; smaller than ancient kingdoms
- Sovereignty: Never formally colonized, though heavily influenced by British and Russian imperialism
- Legitimacy: Traditional monarchy until first modern state; modernizing authoritarian state under shah in twentieth century; Islamic theocracy since 1979
- Bureaucracy: Expanded by shah's modernization policies; expanded social services under Islamic republic; continuing problem of corruption
- State strength: Quite weak (38 of 177); weakest on "uneven economic development," "security apparatus as state within a state," and "elite fragmentation"

An Iranian protester flashes the victory sign during an opposition rally in Tehran on July 9, 2009. Hopes for change to Iran's theocratic government evaporated when incumbent president Mahmoud Ahmadinejad won reelection in June 2009 in what most observers saw as fraudulent elections. The biggest protests since the Iranian revolution of 1979 followed the announcement of the election results, but the state's security apparatus successfully cracked down and the authoritarian regime remains in place.

Credit: AFP/Getty Images

Iran is the modern descendant of the great ancient empire of Persia, and it has been heavily influenced by a series of invasions. The most important of these, by Arabs in the seventh century, brought Islam to the region. The territory of Iran as it is known today, however, was not united under one state until the Safavid invasion of 1501. The Safavids were Turkic-speaking invaders from the north who established the first great Iranian empire of the modern era, which lasted as a united entity until 1722. The power of the Safavids, while seemingly absolute, was actually quite limited. Like many other early modern or feudal states, the shah, as the supreme ruler was known, had to rely on local scribes who could speak and write Persian to administer his state and on militaries loyal to local chieftains to maintain order. The lasting legacy of the Safavid empire was the conversion of 90 percent of the country to the Safavids' own version of Islam, Shia.

After a period of invasions, the Qajar Empire took over in 1794. The Qajar monarchs ruled until 1921, but in the nineteenth century their real power was drastically reduced by Russian and British imperialism. Like China, Iran was never formally colonized, but the government came to be extremely dependent upon and compliant with the Russians and British, granting them very favorable economic terms for key resources such as oil and depending on them for military support when needed. This era also saw the modern, much reduced, borders of Iran clearly demarcated. European imperialism severely compromised Iran's sovereignty and reduced its territory, in spite of never officially colonizing the country.

By the start of the twentieth century, popular discontent with this foreign influence led to street demonstrations from citizens demanding a new constitution. In 1906 the shah allowed the creation of a new democratic state with a real legislature, but it became polarized between social reformers on the one hand and conservatives on the other who wanted to preserve traditional Shiite values. Perhaps more important, the central state still had limited sovereignty over the provinces, which continued to control the bulk of revenue collection and the military. By the end of World War I, Russian (by that point Soviet) and British interests were once again gaining control over the weak and divided Iranian state.

In the midst of this, Colonel Reza Khan led a coup d'etat that overthrew the weakened Qajar dynasty and established what came to be known as the Pahlavi dynasty, ruled first by Reza Shah and then by his son, Mohammed Reza Pahlavi. The Pahlavis created the first truly modern state in Iran. During their rule from 1925 to 1979, they increased the size of the central army tenfold, dramatically expanded the bureaucracy, and gained full control over the provinces. The Pahlavis established a modernizing authoritarian state, modernizing both the state and the economy, increasing agricultural and industrial production, and building tremendous infrastructure, with the government itself directly involved in most of these efforts. They continued to welcome extensive foreign investment, especially in the growing oil sector. They also centralized power in their hands; the elected legislature continued to exist with an elected prime minister at its helm, but its power was greatly reduced. When a left-leaning prime minister, Mohammad Mosaddeq, was elected in 1951 on a platform of taking government control of the foreign-owned oil industry, the shah and his foreign backers saw him as a threat. In 1953 the shah, with active British and U.S. support, overthrew Mosaddeq and established a fully authoritarian state that eliminated all elected offices.

From the start, the 1953 coup was unpopular because many Iranians saw it as foreign inspired. Soon after, the shah launched a series of social and economic reforms to modernize, as he saw it, Iranian society, which expanded the role and reach of the state and its bureaucracy. He staked his claim to legitimacy on these modernizations, which included land reform and secularization; the latter reduced the role of Islamic law. An economic crisis in the late 1970s created growing opposition to his policies, which favored wealthier and urban over poorer and rural sectors of society. The opposition coalesced behind the leadership of an exiled Shiite spiritual leader, Ayatollah Ruhollah Khomeini. Protests spread through the streets and mosques, and local Islamic militias took over entire neighborhoods, leading to a general strike in 1978 and an antigovernment rally of more than two million people in December of that year. Facing this growing opposition, the shah went into what was supposed to be temporary exile in January 1979 but never returned, his legitimacy completely gone. A month later, Khomeini came back from exile and led the creation of the Islamic Republic of Iran, the first theocratic government in the modern era.

The Islamic Republic has gone through phases of greater openness to political debate and greater repression (see chapter 8), but it has endured and remains regionally powerful. While basing its claim to legitimacy firmly in theocracy, it includes limited elements of democratic rule that have had more influence at some times than others. Questions remain, however, about its legitimacy, as seen in the massive street protests against the presidential election outcome in 2009. Its bid to become a nuclear power, or at least to acquire much greater nuclear capabilities, has recently made Iran the center of major global debate.

CASE SUMMARY

The Pahlavis established the first modern Iranian state, expanding its sovereignty internally and externally, and attempted to reduce the influence of Islam. The Ayatollah Khomeini, his followers and successors, have re-Islamized the country but within the confines of a modern (though corrupt) bureaucratic state whose territory and sovereignty are secure but whose legitimacy is less certain. The Islamic regime has also expanded the social services the state provides and, therefore, the size and reach of the bureaucracy, and it has asserted international power and influence via threatened nuclearization.

CASE STUDY

India: Enduring Democracy in a Moderately Weak State

- Territory: Created by British colonial rule, though divided into India and Pakistan at independence
- Sovereignty: Established with independence in 1947; dispute with Pakistan over control of Kashmir region
- Legitimacy: Initially based on nationalist movement; solidified in continuous liberal democracy; secular government questioned by Hindu nationalists and other religious movements
- Bureaucracy: Created by British colonialism; central to economic policy; weakening due to external pressure for reform and growing corruption
- State strength: Moderately weak (87 of 177); weakest on "demographic pressures" and "uneven economic development"

India's parliament, the Lok Sabha, shows the colonial influence on state creation around the world. The Indian state was founded out of the nationalist movement that overthrew British rule but then adopted the British parliamentary system of government. While it is weakened by corruption, has suffered from widespread religious and ethnic tensions, and remains extremely poor despite recent economic gains, India's democratic state has endured for more than six decades, a rare feat in the postcolonial world.

Credit: AP Photo/Lok Sabha TV

As the world's largest democracy, India is one of the few postcolonial countries to maintain democratic rule for nearly all of its history. Arguably, it is also the world's most diverse country, with more than 250 different languages, 5 major religions, and a complex caste system that has crucial political implications. Its independence movement, led by the charismatic Mahatma Gandhi, was the first successful anticolonial effort of the post–World War II era and inspired many other anticolonial leaders to pursue independence.

The territory that is now India, Pakistan, and Bangladesh was once divided among many kingdoms, most of which were Hindu. Muslim invaders created the Moghul Empire in 1526, which dominated most of northern and central India and ruled over a mostly Hindu population, while the south remained under the control of local Hindu kings. As did rulers of other premodern states, both the Hindu kings and Muslim emperors had only loose sovereignty over daily life. At the local level, members of the elite caste, the Brahmin, governed.

Beginning in 1612, the British East India Company established trading centers on India's coast. The company then used its power to eliminate Indian textile and other early industrial production to ensure the export of cheap cotton and other raw materials to feed its factories back in Britain. By the middle of the 1700s, the company had established an informal empire over most of the country, breaking Moghul rule and acting as a government. Like the overseers of other company-controlled colonies, the company ultimately had trouble ruling effectively. The Sepoy Rebellion in the Indian army in 1857 ended company rule, and the British government took direct control of its largest formal colony. As colonizers often did, the British required educated local people to fill the administrative offices of their colonial state. Creating an all-Indian civil service and military and the start of a modern bureaucracy helped create greater unity among the subcontinent's disparate regions, and newly educated Indians filled the offices of these new institutions. Unfortunately for the British, the first stirrings of nationalism would arise from this educated elite.

The Indian National Congress, which eventually became the Congress Party that has ruled India for most of its independent history, was founded by urban elites in 1885. Britain allowed Indian elites some role in internal governance as early as the 1890s. Although its top leadership was primarily Hindu, the Congress operated along democratic and secular principles and claimed to represent all Indians in a society with numerous religious and ethnic divisions. The Congress initially demanded only greater Indian participation in government, but in 1915 Gandhi transformed this single demand into a mass nationalist movement. As the nationalist struggle continued through the 1920s and 1930s under Gandhi's leadership, Hindu nationalists pressed the Congress Party to adopt a more overtly Hindu orientation. On the other end of the spectrum, India's Muslim leaders increasingly felt unrepresented in the organization, and by the end of the 1930s, some Muslim leaders were beginning to demand a separate Muslim state.

The push for independence succeeded after World War II. Muslim leaders, however, demanded and received from the British a separate Muslim state, Pakistan. The simultaneous creation of the two states (against Gandhi's fierce opposition) resulted in the mass migration of millions of citizens, as Hindus moved from what was to be Pakistan into what would become India, and Muslims went in the other direction. At least a million people perished in violence associated with the massive migration, probably the largest in world history.

India thus gained independence under the rule of the Congress Party, with Jawaharlal Nehru, a close associate of Gandhi, as prime minister. The new state was a democratic and federal system, much like that of the United States. Besides economic development, Nehru's other great challenge was the demand for greater recognition by India's diverse ethnic and religious groups. Throughout the 1950s, leaders of local language groups demanded, and some received, states of their own. The legitimacy of the democratic system as a whole was questioned by only a few groups, however, most of which were communist inspired.

After Nehru's death, his daughter, Indira Gandhi (no relation to Mahatma), gained leadership of the Congress Party and the country. She won a crucial 1971 election that broke the power of many local Brahmin elites on whom her father had relied. Gandhi went on to create an increasingly centralized state; in 1975 she declared a "state of emergency" that gave her the power to disband local governments and replace them with those loyal to her. This was the only period since India's independence in which democracy was threatened, and her actions were met with increasing opposition.

Indira Gandhi was assassinated by a member of yet another of India's religious groups, the Sikhs; the assassin was part of a growing movement for an independent Sikh state. While this movement was never successful, it was the first significant example of violent religious-political division since the partition of India and Pakistan. Since then, political battles have increased between Muslims and Hindu nationalists, both of whom reject the official secularism of the national government. Out of this has emerged a renewed Hindu nationalist party that won a national election and formed the government in 1996.

Until the 1990s, India's economic development policies included a role for an active and growing state, including its famous colonially created bureaucracy that over the decades became less efficient and more corrupt. Since the mid-1990s, India has reduced the role of the state in the economy and has achieved much higher growth rates, carving out a major niche in the global economy in areas related to computer services and programming. It remains, however, a country with widespread malnutrition and the largest number of poor people in the world. While presiding over an expanding economy, the current government (again under Congress Party rule but with the country's first non-Hindu prime minister, a Sikh) faces continuing religious tensions, especially vis-à-vis the impoverished Muslim minority, many of whom seem to believe India's democracy is not for them.

Indian territory and sovereignty emerged out of colonial rule and the nationalist movement for independence. Most unusual for postcolonial states, its democracy has survived and seems legitimate in the eyes of the bulk of the population. Its state remains relatively weak, however, with this weakness manifested in continuing corruption, religious tensions, and poverty. India was famed for its strong bureaucracy after independence, but reforms to reduce the bureaucracy's role in economic policy and growing corruption have weakened it. In recent years, the state has presided over a growing economy, and many observers see elements of a potential economic superpower. India increasingly rivals its largest neighbor, China, as an up-and-coming economic power, yet China remains well ahead of India economically and has created an externally strong state through a dramatic process of economic transformation. What it lacks is India's democracy, at least so far.

CASE STUDY

China: Economic Legitimacy over Political Reform

- Territory: Established in ancient empire, though with changing boundaries; Communist rulers annexed disputed territory of Tibet

- Sovereignty: Longest continuous sovereign entity in world history under empire; civil war in early twentieth century until sovereignty fully restored by Communist revolution in 1949 and start of modern state

- Legitimacy: Traditional empire; nationalist government came out of civil war; communist ideology until 1978; modernizing authoritarian state since

- Bureaucracy: Ancient Confucian system of merit; great expansion under Communist rule; growing problem of corruption

- State strength: Moderately weak (57 of 177); weakest on "demographic pressures," "uneven economic development," and "rule of law"

China is the world's most populous country, had the world's fastest growing economy in the 1990s, managed to avoid the recession of 2008–09 entirely, and is widely recognized as the world's "oldest civilization." Although its modern state arose only in 1949 under Communist rule, the Chinese empire was first united in 221 BCE. While several dynasties came to power over the centuries and its exact boundaries shifted somewhat, the empire existed, more or less unified, until 1911. This makes it the longest continuously sovereign political entity in human history.

The empire's demise began in the mid-nineteenth century. While trade with the outside world had long existed, the expanding European imperial powers and the United States began demanding greater access to China in the 1840s. The Opium Wars from 1840 to 1864 between China and Britain were most immediately about Britain's right to sell opium in China but were ultimately about greater European and American access to and control over China. China's war losses resulted in a series of very unequal treaties that gave Western powers access to Chinese markets and trade as well as effective sovereignty over key areas of the country, even though the country was never formally colonized.

A period of extensive Western influence over the Chinese state began, with European powers implementing Western laws in areas they controlled. In reaction to increasing foreign control and economic decline, a series of revolts known as the Taiping Rebellion broke out in the 1850s. The rebellion gained control of a significant share of the country, with a capital based in the city of Nanjing, but was ultimately defeated with the help of European forces that wanted to preserve the favorable treatment they received from the emperor. After 1864 the dynastic government regained control, though with a continuing quasi-colonial European presence.

The restoration of the empire brought relative stability, but only until the end of the century. What many saw as continued excessive foreign domination and economic stagnation produced growing discontent. Sun Yat-sen, an American-educated doctor and revolutionary leader, started a nationalist movement that proclaimed its opposition to the empire and to foreign imperialism. The first stirrings of this movement came in 1905, and by 1911 military uprisings in Shanghai and elsewhere signaled the empire's imminent collapse. On January 1, 1912, the emperor resigned and the Republic of China was established.

The new nationalist government quickly became a dictatorship that couldn't survive the death of its first leader, which ushered in more than a decade of chaos and war. Warlords gained control of various parts of the country as the Chinese state's sovereignty and territorial control crumbled. In the 1920s, the nationalists slowly regained control with the help of an alliance with a new political force, the Chinese Communist Party (CCP). Then the nationalists turned against the Communists after regaining power. Their sovereignty was seriously compromised by reliance on warlords in some areas, the continuous threat of civil war with the CCP, and Japanese invasion. While the nationalists had regained control, they ruled a very weak state.

The CCP, under its new leader, Mao Zedong, moved to the countryside after the nationalists broke the alliance. Starting in the southeast, Mao put together a revolutionary

A sign posted at the entrance of an Internet café in Beijing, China, reads at top, "You should not spread antisocial material on the Internet," and at bottom, "Please come with me because you published materials to harm the unity of the nation." The tension over acceptable Internet activity is just one manifestation of questions about democracy in China's future. The Chinese state has presided over the most successful period of economic growth in human history but has preserved its authoritarian regime. Can an increasingly wealthy and powerful state remain nondemocratic for the long term, in contrast to the pattern of European history?

Credit: AP Photo /Elizabeth Dalziel

movement that began an intermittent civil war with the government. In 1934–35, Mao led the famous Long March, a 6,000-mile trek by party supporters from the southeast part of the country to the northwest, where supporters would be more secure from government attack. The CCP then took effective control of the northwestern section of the country and began creating the prototype of its future Communist regime. The Japanese invasion of 1937 left the country's territory and sovereignty divided, with the CCP controlling the northwest, the nationalists ruling part of the southwest, and Japan occupying the rest. After World War II, the Communist revolution triumphed in 1949, despite U.S. military support for the nationalists, who fled to the island of Taiwan and formed a government there. For many years, the nationalist government of Taiwan claimed to be the sovereign government of China, and the UN recognized it as such until 1972.

Communist rule brought massive changes to China, leading to the creation of the first truly unified modern Chinese state, but at horrific cost. The new government instituted massive land reform programs and campaigns against corruption, opium use, and other socially harmful practices. It also took control of the economy, creating a Soviet-style command economy with a massive bureaucracy, which attempted to industrialize the world's largest agrarian society. The result was the Great Leap Forward, an effort at rapid rural industrialization that led to a famine that killed at least twenty million people. Political purges sent many others to "re-education camps," prison, or execution. The Cultural Revolution from 1966 to 1976 was a period in which Mao mobilized his followers against what he saw as entrenched bureaucrats in his own party and state; his efforts created widespread political uncertainty, repression, and economic and social dislocation.

The Cultural Revolution ended with Mao's death in 1976. Deng Xiaoping, one of Mao's earliest comrades who had been removed from power during the Cultural Revolution, established his supremacy over the party and state in 1979. Deng initiated a series of slow but ultimately sweeping economic reforms that focused on allowing greater market forces in the economy and reducing the direct role of the state. These reforms continue today, a thirty-year process of introducing a market economy that is still not complete. The result has been the fastest economic growth in the world that has moved millions of Chinese out of poverty, spurred a huge exodus from rural areas to cities, and allowed much greater inequality than existed under Mao.

Politically, Deng and his successors have resisted most efforts to achieve greater freedom and democracy. While the state's legitimacy is still officially based on communism, its pursuit of capitalist development has meant its real legitimacy is implicitly based on its ability to modernize the economy and provide wealth. Thus, China is what we will call a modernizing authoritarian regime, which we explain fully in chapter 3. Many observers see a fundamental contradiction between allowing economic freedoms but denying political ones and argue that ultimately the CCP will have to allow much greater political freedom if its economic success is to continue. The most dramatic popular protest for political liberalization occurred in Tiananmen Square in 1989. The demonstrations, initially led by students, began as a demand for greater openness and less corruption within the ruling party, but they ultimately expanded to include demands for more fundamental democratic change. Deng successfully resisted these demands by sending in the army to crush the demonstration, earning the government the opprobrium of much of the world. Since then, the party has presided over a modern state that still has some internal weaknesses but has achieved perhaps the most remarkable economic advance in human history. China has become the second largest economy in the world and a potential economic and political superpower.

CASE SUMMARY

China established its territory and sovereignty centuries ago, though both were severely challenged from the late nineteenth to mid-twentieth centuries. Out of that chaotic period emerged the world's second major communist regime, which created a modern, if often brutal, state. The Communists regained full sovereignty, expanded the state's territory to include the still disputed region of Tibet, and reestablished a strong bureaucracy that came to control the entire economy. The regime's legitimacy was based on communist doctrine, augmented by Mao's initial charisma, but clearly declined over the years. Since Mao's death, the regime has still officially proclaimed communism as its ideology, but in reality the regime now bases its legitimacy on its successful economic policy. While this shift has created a stronger state, it is still plagued by problems of corruption, weak rule of law, and at least some questions about its legitimacy in the absence of any significant political reform.

CASE STUDY

Nigeria: An Extremely Weak State

- Territory: Created by colonial rule out of numerous large and small precolonial systems; divided by civil war, 1967–1970

- Sovereignty: Gained with independence in 1960 but threatened by recent demands for secession; weak internally

- Legitimacy: Nationalist movement divided along ethnic and regional lines; limited legitimacy of postcolonial democratic government; six military coups; weak democracy since 1999

- Bureaucracy: Colonial creation; suffers for extreme levels of corruption fuelled by oil wealth

- State strength: Extremely weak (15 of 177); weakest on "vengeance-seeking group grievances," "uneven economic development," "security apparatus as state within a state," and "elite fragmentation"

Nigerian women occupy an oil terminal, demanding that the oil company provide more jobs. The postcolonial state has seen numerous political changes, but one thing has remained constant since the late 1960s: the overwhelming importance of oil. While oil provides the state with massive revenues, it also has promoted equally massive corruption, which has weakened the state and siphoned benefits from oil production away from the common people. A democracy has emerged over the last decade, but corruption and a lack of local benefits from oil revenues remain problems.

Credit: AP Photo/Saurabh Das

Nigeria, like most African states, is a product of colonialism. It is by far the largest African country in terms of population (approximately one-seventh of all Africans are Nigerians) and a major oil producer, making it an important country to understand both in terms of its impact on the rest of Africa and the world. Approximately 250 languages are spoken within its borders because colonialism amalgamated a huge number of separate societies under one state. Ethnic competition led to a three-year civil war in the 1960s, and today the country is deeply divided along religious lines between Muslims, primarily in the north, and Christians in the south. This has produced serious tensions and occasional violence since the early 1990s. Similarly, grievances among people living near the oil wells in the southeast, who have benefited very little from the region's oil production, have produced significant violence that has at times disrupted oil production and caused global oil prices to rise.

Prior to colonial conquest in the late nineteenth century, the territory that is now Nigeria was home to numerous and varied societies. The northern half was primarily Muslim and ruled by Islamic emirs based in twelve separate city-states. The southern half consisted of many societies, the two biggest of which were the Yoruba and Igbo. The

Yoruba lived in a series of kingdoms, sometimes politically united and sometimes not, though they shared a common language and religion. The Igbo in the southwest also shared a common language and culture but were governed only at the most local level by councils of elders; the group had no kings or chiefs.

The opening of trade with the West started around 1500, and the subsequent rise of extensive slave raiding profoundly altered these societies, especially in the south. Slave raiding devastated the southern region by taking away large numbers of able-bodied young people, primarily men, and causing numerous wars among kingdoms. After the end of slavery in the nineteenth century, however, southerners responded with alacrity to market opportunities by producing palm oil, peanuts, and cocoa for export.

The British conquest of what became Nigeria began around 1870. European powers, increasingly competing with each other economically and politically, collectively decided to carve up the African continent in their own interests. In 1885 they agreed not to go to war over African territory but instead to allow whoever gained military control over a territory to keep it. The "scramble for Africa" ensued. The British united Nigeria as one colony in 1914. In northern Nigeria, they established indirect rule, the form of rule they would use throughout their African empire, which Lange (2009) argued is the basis for many weak postcolonial states. Under indirect rule, the British, in theory, left precolonial kingdoms intact to be ruled through their leaders. In northern Nigeria, this meant ruling through the emirs, who in general accepted British oversight as long as they were left to run their internal affairs mostly as they pleased. In the south, kings and chiefs fulfilled this role where they existed, but in areas such as Igboland, there were no chiefs. The British, therefore, invented them, appointing elders to be chiefs. As in India, British colonialism gave local rulers more power than they had before, in exchange for rulers' acquiescence in implementing unpopular policies such as forced labor and the collection of colonial taxes. This undermined the legitimacy of those who had been precolonial rulers and prevented newly invented rulers from gaining any legitimacy.

As in India, the colonial state required educated natives to help staff bureaucracies that provided essential services. Christian missionaries provided virtually all of the education for many decades. In the south, particularly among the Igbo, Christianity and Western education expanded rapidly; southerners filled most of the positions in the colonial state. The northern emirs, on the other hand, convinced colonial authorities to keep Christian missionaries out in order to preserve Islam, on which their legitimacy was based. This meant that northerners received far less Western education. The north, already poorer than the south, fell behind in educational attainment and subsequent job opportunities. As the colonial state and bureaucracy expanded, especially after World War II, more and more southerners moved north to take up positions as clerks for the government. Their presence would prove explosive after independence.

The educated elite became the leadership of the nationalist movement after World War II. Given the history of divisions in the country, it is no surprise that this movement was split from the start. Northern leaders actually resisted independence for many years, fearing their region would lose out to the more educated southerners who had most of the government jobs. Southerners were split between the Yoruba in the southwest and Igbo in the southeast. The British finally were able to negotiate a new government for an independent Nigeria that would be federal, with three regions corresponding to the three major ethnic groups. Parties formed mainly along regional and ethnic lines, and the government that took power at independence in 1960 was a coalition of one northern and the main southeastern parties.

As in virtually all African countries, the new government was quite fragile. In contrast to their approach in India, the British began introducing the institutions of British-style democracy just a few years before

Nigeria and most of their other African colonies became independent. Nigerians had no prior experience with electoral democracy and little reason to believe that it would be a superior system for them. In response to fraudulent elections and anti-Igbo violence, the army, led primarily by Igbo, overthrew the elected government in January 1966 in the country's first military coup. The new government ended federalism entirely, creating a unified central government. Northerners saw this as an Igbo power grab. A countercoup six months later brought a new, northern-dominated government to power. This new government reestablished federalism, creating twelve states from the three regions in an attempt to reduce regional and ethnic rivalry. The Igbo military leadership refused to accept this new government, and in January 1967 the Igbo declared their region of the country the independent state of Biafra. Not coincidentally, large-scale oil production had just begun, and the oil wells were in the area claimed as Biafra. A three-year civil war ensued that cost the lives of a million people, mostly due to starvation. The central government defeated the separatists in Biafra and reestablished a single state in 1970. Despite promises to return the country to democracy, the military continued to rule until 1979, as rapidly growing oil revenue became a source of equally growing corruption.

After the death of a key leader, the military finally handed power back to civilian, democratic rule in 1979. A fraudulent election in 1983 under the four-year-old democracy was soon reversed by the military, again under northern leadership, beginning a sixteen-year period of military rule under four successive leaders. While all pledged to reduce corruption, in reality, each actively participated in it. Oil revenue, even when world prices were relatively low, overwhelmed all other economic activity and fuelled both corruption and the desire of those in power to stay there. A weak state grew ever weaker and more corrupt. The military maintained control, even as the institutions of government became increasingly ineffective and their popularity plummeted.

In 1999 a new military government finally carried out the country's first free and fair election in twenty years. The newly elected president, former General Olusegun Obasanjo, launched a much publicized drive against corruption, the results of which have been modest. In 2007, his handpicked successor, Umaru Yar'Adua, won an election that most observers saw as fraudulent. Nevertheless, Nigeria's democracy remains intact, with no immediate threat of further military intervention. Yar'Adua's death in 2010 produced momentary concern about the democracy's stability, but Vice President Goodluck Jonathan was duly sworn in as president and went on to win the 2011 presidential election, which was seen as much fairer than the prior one. The democratic government has also faced growing religious tension in the northern states, many of which have adopted Islamic law. Non-Muslims have responded with alarm, and violence has occasionally broken out between Muslim and Christian groups (see chapter 4). In the oil-rich areas of the former Biafra, ethnic militias have demanded greater benefits for their people. Despite its natural resources, the area's residents are among the poorest in the country. In the 1990s, when a nonviolent movement arose among the Ogoni people of the oil-producing region, the military government had the Ogoni leader, poet Ken Saro-Wiwa, executed. More recently, violent ethnic movements have arisen in the same area, and the government has responded with more military force. The violence disrupted oil production and helped drive up world oil prices in 2005 and 2006.

CASE SUMMARY

With the exception of the 1967–1970 civil war, the Nigerian state has maintained its sovereignty and territory, mostly under military rule. It continues to be extremely weak, however. The military's claims to legitimacy always involved promises to end corruption, restore economic growth, and return the country to democracy, but those promises were rarely fulfilled. The democratic government that has been in place since 1999 is a great improvement over previous regimes, but it has had limited success so far in solving the deeply entrenched problems the country faces. While the state's territory is intact, its sovereignty is threatened by ethnic militia, it suffers from widespread corruption that undermines bureaucratic efficiency, and its legitimacy remains an open question. Ironically, the state's weakness results in part from its oil wealth, which has been a huge incentive for corruption.

CONCLUSION

Who Rules?

The modern state is a political form that has been singularly successful. Arising nearly 500 years ago, it has spread to every corner of the globe. In fact, the modern world demands that we all live in states. Strong states can provide the political goods that help improve citizens' lives, though nothing guarantees that they will. Although in the short term, state strength can also be used to oppress the citizenry, many political scientists argue that long-term strength must come from legitimacy and the effective provision of political goods. The characteristics of modern states— territory, sovereignty, legitimacy, and bureaucracy—combine to produce an exceptionally powerful ruling apparatus. In strong states, rulers command military force to prevent foreign attack and domestic rebellion, and they control a set of state organizations than can effectively influence society in myriad ways. When this all works well, it can give ruling elites legitimacy and therefore greater power.

This raises a long-standing question of political theory: What, if anything, limits the rulers of effective modern states? One clear answer is that a ruler's power is limited by how strong a particular state is. The definition and list of characteristics of the modern state are those of an ideal type: no state measures up to it perfectly. Some states are so weak that the real power of their leadership is severely limited. But what can limit power in stronger states? The answer usually involves the creation of impersonal institutions and the rule of law. Both are elements of strong modern states; rule is not based on the individual whim or ability of a particular leader but is embedded in ongoing institutions. These institutions can treat citizens in similar ways (which we explore in greater depth in the next chapter) based on set rules. This in turn can lead citizens to trust the state to act fairly and in the interest of all to the greatest extent possible. The strongest modern states are virtually all democracies, which are based on such notions of treating all citizens equally and limiting what the state can do. Democracy allows citizen participation, which can oversee and limit the state's power further, though none of this is guaranteed. The very impersonal institutions that give modern states their strength can also be a key element in limiting their reach within certain agreed-upon norms. Weaker states are often autocratic (and vice versa) and are both less effective and more repressive than states that are stronger.

What Explains Political Behavior?

We asked at the outset why modern states arose. European history seems to point to the successful combination of military and economic advantage that feudal kings used to gain unrivaled control of a territory. Maintaining that control, however, required the establishment of permanent institutions in the form of an army, a bureaucracy, and a source of continuous revenue through direct taxation. Ruling elites ultimately found it in their interests to create more impersonal and powerful institutions that would allow greater economic growth and, therefore, resources for the state. This is why Marxists often argue that the modern state is dependent on the success of capitalism and always works to enhance capitalist production to gain revenue. Other analysts, though, argue that sustaining the state takes more than just economic and military might; eventually, it requires some degree of acceptance on the part of the subjects. Legitimacy is crucial to state strength in the long run. One source of this legitimacy is a sense of belonging to a nation that the state represents, a subject we return to in greater depth in chapter 4.

Postcolonial states had very different historical origins, based on colonial conquest and carving out of territory rather than agreements among domestic elites and local conquest. With independence, these states took the modern form but not necessarily all of the modern content. They often lacked a strong sense of national unity based on a shared history. The international system, however, demands that they act like states, at least internationally. Their rulers therefore do so, often gaining significant power in the process, even in relatively weak states.

Where and Why?

Not all states are equally successful. Why are some weaker than others, and why do some fail completely? The answers are obviously very complex, but the story usually starts with colonialism. The external creation of a state, as opposed to its emergence from political rivals within a particular territory, often meant that it did not have effective internal sovereignty, even after a nationalist movement led it to legal independence. In centuries past,

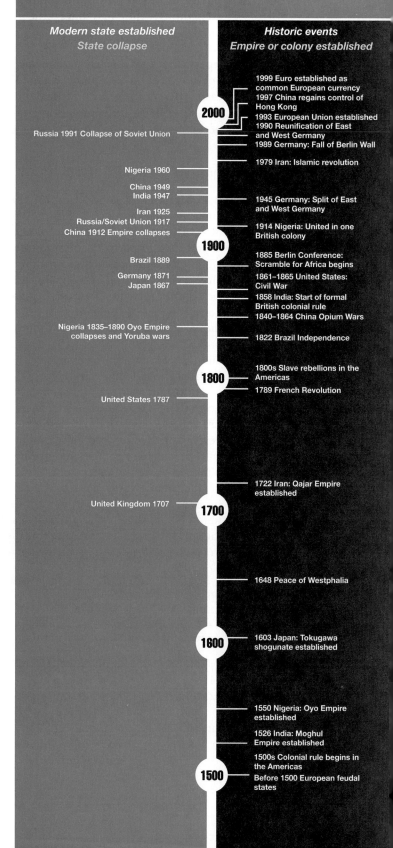

such weak states would have been absorbed by stronger ones, but the current international system makes that virtually unheard of today. Now, weak states can survive as recognized entities, often with significant external financial support, even though they may have little real sovereignty and provide little benefit to their populations. Lack of wealth, or wealth in the form of a resource curse, can also produce very weak states, often in combination with a problematic colonial legacy. The weakest states are prone to collapse, becoming failed states, as violent opponents can challenge the state's monopoly on the use of force with relative ease. This scenario has produced many of the most brutal wars of recent years, including those in Somalia, Liberia, Afghanistan, and the Democratic Republic of the Congo.

Applying Theory to the Study of Modern States

Both Marxist and political culture theorists have long made arguments about how and why states develop. Marxists see them as reflecting the power of the ruling class of a particular epoch. Under capitalism, that ruling class is the bourgeoisie, and the liberal state in particular represents the bourgeoisie's interests. At times, Marxists argue, the state must act against the interests of individual members of the ruling elite in order to rule on behalf of the entire elite and, therefore, may pursue policies against the interests of individual capitalists. This is necessary for the liberal, bourgeois state to remain strong. In postcolonial countries, weaker states reflect the weak, dependent nature of the ruling elite there. Cultural theorists argue that underlying values, in particular a strong sense of nationalism, are crucial to maintaining a strong state, which must be based on some shared sense of legitimacy. Without this, effective sovereignty will always be limited.

In recent years, rational-choice and institutionalist theories have become more prominent. The modern state, these theorists argue, emerged in response to the rational incentives of the emerging international state system, rewarding rulers who developed effective sovereignty, military force, and taxation. Often, this occurred as a process of compromise among elites in a given territory, a process in which some ultimately gave up direct power over military force in exchange for the economic benefits of peace. Once established, strong state institutions tend to reinforce themselves as long as they continue to function for the benefit of the elites whom they were created to serve. As these states demand more from citizens, they develop a rational interest in establishing some type of popular legitimacy, a subject we look at in much greater depth in the next chapter.

KEY CONCEPTS

absolutism (p. 46)
bureaucracy (p. 44)
charismatic legitimacy (p. 43)
clientelism (p. 73)
external sovereignty (p. 41)
failed state (p. 51)
fealty (p. 46)

feudal states (p. 46)
ideal type (p. 51)
internal sovereignty (p. 41)
legitimacy (p. 43)
Peace of Westphalia (p. 47)
quasi-states (p. 56)

rational-legal legitimacy (p. 44)
resource curse (p. 53)
sovereign (p. 41)
state (p. 39)
territory (p. 40)
traditional legitimacy (p. 43)
weak state (p. 51)

WORKS CITED

Anderson, Perry. 1974. *Lineages of the Absolutist State*. London: New Left Books.

Fund for Peace. 2010. "Failed States Index 2010." www.fundforpeace.org/web/index.php?option=com_content&task=view&id=452&Itemid=900.

Jackson, Robert H. 1990. *Quasi-States: Sovereignty, International Relations, and the Third World*. Cambridge Studies in International Relations No. 12. New York: Cambridge University Press.

Lange, Matthew. 2009. *Lineages of Despotism and Development: British Colonialism and State Power*. Chicago: University of Chicago Press.

North, Douglass Cecil, John Joseph Wallis, and Barry R. Weingast. 2009. *Violence and Social Orders: A Conceptual Framework for Interpreting Recorded Human History*. Cambridge, UK: Cambridge University Press.

Pierson, Christopher. 1996. *The Modern State*. New York: Routledge.

Rotberg, Robert I., ed. 2004. *When States Fail: Causes and Consequences*. Princeton, NJ: Princeton University Press.

Weber, Max. 1970. "Politics as Vocation." In *From Max Weber: Essays in Sociology*, edited by H. H. Gaert and C. Wright Mills. London: Routledge and Kegan Paul.

RESOURCES FOR FURTHER STUDY

Jessop, Bob. 1990. *State Theory: Putting Capitalist States in Their Place*. Cambridge, UK: Polity Press.

Levi, Margaret. 2002. "The State of the Study of the State." In *Political Science: State of the Discipline*, edited by Ira Katznelson and Helen V. Milner, 33–55. New York: Norton.

Poggi, Gianfranco. 1990. *The State: Its Nature, Development, and Prospects*. Cambridge, UK: Polity Press.

Tilly, Charles, ed. 1975. *The Formation of National States in Western Europe*. Studies in Political Development No. 8. Princeton, NJ: Princeton University Press.

WEB RESOURCES

Comparative Constitutions Project (http://comparativeconstitutionsproject.org)

Corruption Perceptions Index, Transparency International (www.transparency.org/policy_research/surveys_indices/cpi)

Failed States Index 2010, *Foreign Policy* and *The Fund for Peace* (www.foreignpolicy.com/articles/2010/06/21/2010_failed_states_index_interactive_map_and_rankings)

Index of Economic Freedom, The Heritage Foundation (www.heritage.org/index/ranking)

International Crisis Group (http://www.crisisgroup.org)

Worldwide Governance Indicators, The World Bank (http://info.worldbank.org/governance/wgi/index.asp)

United Nations (www.un.org/en)

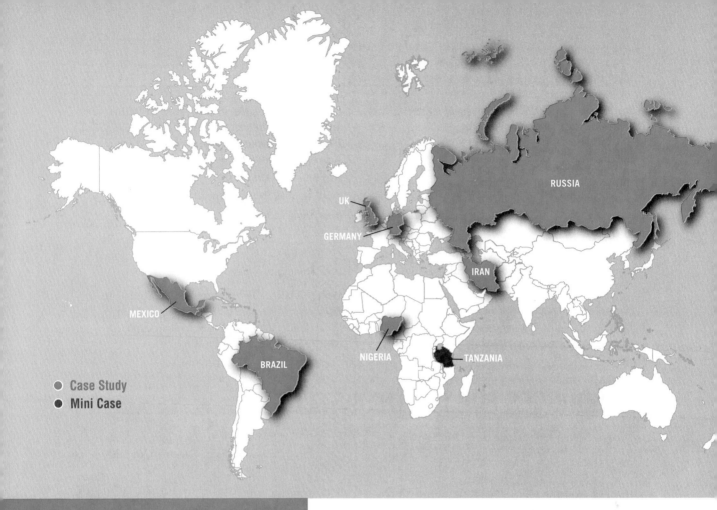

- ● Case Study
- ● Mini Case

Who Rules?

- How do different ideologies balance the rights of citizens with the state's ability to compel obedience?
- On what grounds do different regimes give citizens an opportunity to participate in politics? Who rules where citizens do not seem to have such an opportunity? Can this be justified?

What Explains Political Behavior?

- To what extent does ideology explain how different regimes are organized and justify themselves? What else helps explain how different kinds of regimes actually function?

Where and Why?

- Do our case studies reveal patterns that suggest where different regime types emerge and why?

3
STATES AND CITIZENS

The proper relationship between a state and its people, individually and collectively, is one of the most interesting and debated questions in political science. All successful modern states are able to compel their citizens to obey and to regulate many areas of citizens' lives. No modern state can do this, however, without answering questions about the legitimate boundaries of such compulsion and regulation. Each society must decide how far and under what circumstances the state can compel individuals and groups to obey those in authority, how extensively it can intervene in people's lives, and how and whether some areas of individual and collective life should not be subject to the state's ability to force compliance. States reach widely varying decisions about these issues, from states that claim carefully restricted and circumscribed authority to those that claim virtually unlimited authority to act against their citizens. The Country and Concept table on page 96 demonstrates the wide variety of types of governments and the levels of freedom that states allow their citizens among just our eleven case studies. No matter where it falls on this continuum, however, each state tries to justify the level and extent of compulsion and control it exercises.

In this chapter, we examine various models of the relationship between a state and its people and how states seek to legitimize these models. Each model is embodied in a **regime**, a set of fundamental rules and institutions governing political activity. Regimes are more enduring than governments but less enduring than states. Democratic regimes, for example, may persist through many individual governments. The United States elected its forty-fourth presidential government in 2008, yet its democratic regime has remained intact for over two centuries. Similarly, a modern state may persist though its regime changes from democratic to authoritarian or the other way around. The state—the existence of a bureaucracy, state territory, and so on—is continuous, but its fundamental rules can change. The Country and Concept table shows the great variation around the world in regime stability over the last century, from the single, continuous regimes of the United States and the United Kingdom to the eight regimes Nigeria has seen.

Each regime is based at least partially on a political ideology that is usually explicitly stated and often quite elaborately developed. Political ideologies, at their core, are about answering the question we posed at the outset: What is the appropriate relationship between the state and its people? An ideology's answer to this

regime: A set of fundamental rules and institutions that govern political activity

COUNTRY AND CONCEPT
Modern Regimes

Country	Current regime	Year established	Number of regimes in 20th and 21st centuries	Freedom House score
Brazil	Liberal democracy	1989	5	Free
China	"Communist" modernizing authoritarian	People's Republic, established 1949	3	Not free
Germany	Liberal democracy	Federal Republic of Germany, established 1945; reunited with German Democratic Republic in 1991	4	Free
India	Liberal democracy	Independence, 1947	2	Free
Iran	Theocracy	Islamic Republic, proclaimed 1979	4	Not free
Japan	Liberal democracy	1947	2	Free
Mexico	Liberal democracy	2000 (first free and fair election)	3	Free
Nigeria	Democracy (though with neopatrimonial elements)	1999	8	Partly free
Russia	Semi-authoritarian	Constitution promulgated, 1993	3	Not free
United Kingdom	Liberal democracy	Glorious Revolution, 1688	1	Free
United States	Liberal democracy	1789	1	Free

question influences its answer to the question of "Who rules?" as well; different ideologies assign different amounts of power to those who control the state and give average citizens different amounts of power via the ability to participate in the political process. We will focus on some familiar political ideologies and how they have been used to underpin regimes in various countries. As we discuss each ideology, we stress the way it conceives of the appropriate relationship between a state and the people over whom it claims sovereignty. We also examine the ways in which regimes diverge from their ideological justifications. Explaining how regimes actually operate is one of the biggest "What explains political behavior?" questions in political science. Ideology provides part of that explanation but never all of it. We will also discuss a key "Where and why?" question: Where and why do different kinds of regimes develop?

Before we begin discussing any of this, however, it is helpful to understand a little bit more about the historical development of the "people" over whom modern states claim sovereignty. The basic ideas about how the people stand in relation to the state have changed greatly over time and have evolved in tandem with the modern state described in chapter 2. At the most basic level, a **citizen** is a member of a political community or state. Notice that a citizen is more than an inhabitant within a state's borders. An inhabitant may be a member of a physical community, but a citizen inhabits a political community that places him or her in a relationship with the state. Think of the difference between a resident alien and a citizen: only the latter is a member of the political community. In the modern world, everyone needs to be "from" somewhere. It is almost inconceivable (although it does happen) to be a "man without a country." By this minimal definition, everyone is considered a citizen of some state.

> **citizen:** A member of a political community or state with certain rights and duties

The word *citizen,* however, is much more complex than this simple definition may lead us to believe. Up until about two or three hundred years ago, most Europeans would have thought of themselves as "subjects" of their monarchs, not citizens of states. Most people had little say in their relationship with the state; their side of that relationship consisted primarily of duty and obedience. The very nature of the absolutist state meant that few mechanisms existed to protect subjects and enable them to claim things as their "rights." If the king wanted your land or decided to throw you in jail as a possible conspirator, no court could or would overrule him.

This began to change with the transition to the modern state. As the state was separated from the person of the monarch and its apparatus was modernized, states gained both the ability and the need to make their people more than just subjects. The concept of sovereignty, like the state itself, was divorced from the person of the sovereign, and many European philosophers and political leaders began to toy with the idea that sovereignty could lie with the people as a whole (or some portion, such as male landowners) rather than with a sovereign monarch. This was an important step in the development of the concept of modern citizenship: citizens, unlike subjects, were inhabitants of states that claimed that sovereignty resided with the people. Thus, after the French Revolution overthrew the absolutist *ancien régime,* people addressed one another as "citizen."

The French overthrew their monarch in a series of violent actions, including this march on Versailles in October 1789. The French Revolution abruptly ended their status as "subjects," leading them to celebrate their new status by greeting one another as "citizen."

Credit: The Granger Collection, New York

Citizens are legal subjects of a state, but because modern states represent and act on behalf of the people, they are also, in principle, more than just subjects. Over time, as the modern state developed, people began to associate a complex set of rights with the concept of citizenship. In the mid-twentieth century, the philosopher T. H. Marshall (1963) usefully characterized the rights of citizenship into three areas: civil, political, and social. **Civil rights** are designed to guarantee individual freedom and equal, just, and fair treatment by the state. Examples include the right to equal treatment under the law, habeas corpus, and freedom

> **civil rights:** Those rights that guarantee individual freedom as well as equal, just, and fair treatment by the state

political rights:
Those rights
associated with active
political participation,
for example, to free
association, voting,
and running for office

social rights: Those
rights related to
basic well-being
and socioeconomic
equality

of expression and worship. **Political rights** are those associated with active political participation: the right to vote, form political associations, run for office, or otherwise participate in political activity. **Social rights** are those related to basic well-being and socioeconomic equality. Examples of these rights include the provision of public education, pensions, or national health care. Marshall believed that modern citizenship included basic legal (civil) status in society and protection by the state as well as the right to actively participate in the political process by which a society chooses its leaders and makes policy. He argued that full citizenship also requires enough socioeconomic equality to make the civil and political equality of citizenship meaningful. Modern conceptions of citizenship go beyond just the focus on rights, however; others stress the participatory role of citizens in the political community, the obligations of citizenship, or citizenship as an identity. A citizen, then, is a member of a political community with certain rights, perhaps some obligations to the larger community as well, and ideally (for most theorists) an active participant in that community.

Participation, of course, typically happens in organized groups of one sort or another, what we call civil society. Like citizenship, civil society in Europe developed in conjunction with the modern state. We defined civil society in chapter 1 as the sphere of organized, nonviolent activity between the state and the family or firm. Absolutist states would not have conceived of such a realm of society separate from the state itself, for what would this have meant? If a monarch could dispose of lands and goods, grant monopolies on tax collection, and head the church or at least determine which religion the realm would follow, what could "society" mean apart from that? The rise of religious pluralism and of modern, capitalist economies alongside the modern state meant that there were now areas of social life outside the immediate control of the state, and the gradual evolution of civil and political rights made it possible for individuals to organize themselves into new civil societies for all kinds of purposes, including political action.

The emergence of citizens with rights and of a civil society where they could organize themselves to act politically proved to be mutually reinforcing. As Sidney Tarrow argued in his 1998 book, *Power in Movement,* the ability to share ideas in public spaces such as coffeehouses meant that citizens with minimal rights could organize themselves into groups to demand even more rights. A new and growing civil society and some basic civil rights meant that people could organize to demand expanded suffrage, more political rights, and, eventually, labor and other social rights.

This history should not be romanticized or thought of as a linear movement toward modern, democratic citizenship. Even within the countries that most closely fit this cursory description, it was more often a case of one step forward and two steps back. Change was never inevitable nor always even good. The same changes that gave us the modern state, however, also gave us the modern concept of the citizen and the modern concept of an independent civil society in which citizens could organize collectively for all sorts of purposes, from religious worship to entrepreneurship to political action.

Some argue that a "postnational" citizenship is now emerging as the latest chapter in this history, especially in the European Union (EU) (Lister and Pia 2008). We can see this in several major institutions around the world: the rights of citizenship are embedded in key UN documents, the International Criminal Court in the Hague exists to enforce those rights on behalf of the world community, the EU has a "social charter" that sets standards for treatment of citizens in all EU countries, and most EU members have a common immigration policy that allows their citizens to travel freely within the union as if they were travelling in only one country. In terms of participation, as international organizations such as the World Trade Organization become more important in guiding major policies, citizens are forming international groups to try to influence those policies. Keck and Sikkink (1998) have called this phenomenon "transnational civil society." These new trends are undoubtedly important and likely to grow, but for now almost all citizenship in terms of core rights still resides within the nation-state. Even in the EU, one gains "European" citizenship only via citizenship in a member state. States confer rights, and those vary greatly from one state to another. States also provide legal status for each individual to live in a particular place and to cross international borders.

Today, ideas of citizenship and civil society are connected to regime claims to legitimacy via the concept of "popular sovereignty." Recall that a claim to legitimacy is a key characteristic of modern states: all modern regimes make some claim to legitimacy, and most do so based on representing and speaking on behalf of "the people." Although it is a distinctly European and liberal democratic notion, the idea of popular sovereignty has deeply influenced all subsequent political ideologies. Even dictators claim to be working on behalf of the citizenry. They may claim that they must deny certain rights in the short term to benefit society as a whole in the long term (or, in the case of theocracy, that God has willed certain exceptions to citizens' rights), but they still lay some claim to working toward the well-being of the citizens.

Like the concept of the modern state, the concepts of citizenship, civil society, and popular sovereignty spread globally via colonialism and the international dominance of Europe and the United States. They have become, for better or for worse, modern standards to which states must respond. Marshall's norms of citizenship, for example, are recognized in the United Nations' Universal Declaration of Human Rights, which explicitly recognizes various civil rights, the right to participate in political life, and various social rights such as education. States don't always act in accordance with this declaration and it is not binding, but its very existence suggests that ideologies and states that depart from this model may feel compelled to provide an explanation defending their choices. It may seem that these are very European standards against which to measure global behavior. However, just as the modern European state became a standard that other states needed to respond to in order to be competitive within the international system, modern citizenship and the toleration of civil society have become hallmarks of legitimacy to which regimes and ideologies that question those standards must respond.

In practice, regimes vary enormously in their relationships to both citizen rights and civil society. Virtually no country fully provides all three types of rights described by Marshall, and authoritarian regimes deny that some rights, such as political participation, are even important. Similarly, the manifestation of civil society ranges from flourishing, lively groups of independently organized citizens, like the many interest groups and political movements in the United States or Europe, to highly controlled or actively repressed groups, such as the government-controlled labor union in China. In short, modern citizens and civil society are much like the modern state: modern in the sense of being an ideal type but not in the sense of being universally implemented in contemporary societies. All regimes claim to provide some rights, but the exact details of the relationship between a state and its citizens—the rights and duties of each—vary significantly. By looking at a regime's political ideology, we can learn how it attempts to justify and legitimize its particular relationship with its citizens.

Major Political Ideologies and Regimes

Liberal Democracy

- Individuals are free and autonomous with natural rights.
- Social contract theory: Legitimate governments form when free and independent individuals join in a contract to permit representatives to govern over them.
- Government must preserve the core liberties—life, liberty, and property—possessed by all free individuals.
- Representative democracy: Citizens have direct control, and leaders can be removed.
- Legislature is essential.
- Separation of powers, federalism, and social citizenship supplement, but are not essential to, legitimate government.

Communism

- Based on Marxism.
- Historical materialism: Material (economic) forces are the prime movers of history and politics.
- Ruling class oppresses other classes, based on mode of production: Bourgeoisie rules in capitalist society.
- Liberal democracy is the political and ideological shell that allows capitalism to function, and it serves the interests of the bourgeoisie.
- Social revolution is the transition from one mode of production to another at a time of economic and political crisis.
- Proletariat will lead socialist revolution.
- Socialist society after revolution will be ruled as a dictatorship of the proletariat over other classes; will eventually create classless communist society in which class oppression ends.
- Lenin: Vanguard party can lead socialist revolution in interests of present and future proletariat.
- Vanguard party rules socialist society using democratic centralism and is justified in oppressing classes that oppose it.

Fascism

- Rejects materialism and rationality; "spiritual attitude."
- Organic conception of society: Society is akin to a living organism rather than being a set of disparate groups and individuals.
- The state as head of the corporate body: It is all-embracing, and outside of it no human or spiritual values can exist.
- "Accepts the individual only in so far as his interests coincide with those of the State."
- The state creates the nation, a "higher personality"; intensely nationalistic.
- Supreme leader rules the state.
- Corporatism: State recognizes one entity to lead each group in society (for example, official trade union).

REGIMES, IDEOLOGIES, AND CITIZENS

Not all political ideologies have been embodied in regimes, but every regime has some sort of ideology that attempts to justify its existence in the eyes of its citizens and the world. Regimes are much more than just the legal and institutional embodiments of their ideologies, however. Although all regimes have formal rules and institutions that reflect, at least to some extent, their ideological claims to legitimacy, they also have informal rules and institutions, and these may conflict with their ideological claims. Informal institutions may be more important than official ones; rulers may not actually believe the ideology they proclaim; or the realities of being

Modernizing Authoritarianism

- Not based on a single, consciously elabo-rated ideology but rather on an appeal to a common set of precepts.
- Claim to legitimacy: Government will mod-ernize or "develop" the country.
  - Modernization theory: Postcolonial soci-eties must go through the same process to develop as the West did.
  - Modern elite: Relatively few highly edu-cated people should have power.
  - Technocratic legitimacy: Claim to rule based on knowledge.
  - Development requires national unity.

- Three institutional forms: One-party regimes, military regimes, and personalist regimes.
- Neopatrimonial authority is common.
  - Combines trappings of modern, bureau-cratic states with underlying informal institutions.
  - Constitutions, laws, courts, and bureau-cracies exist, but they really work on the basis of personal favors and patronage.
  - Patron-client relationships are central: Rulers maintain power by distributing patronage; this is more important than formal powers.
  - Politics involves competition among patrons for access to state's resources.

Semi-authoritarianism

- Legitimacy is based on a combination of liberal democratic and modernizing authori-tarian ideologies.
- Allows limited freedoms of expression and association.
- Allows limited political opposition to hold some elected offices but ensures ruling party/leader holds most power.
- Informal institutions are often more impor-tant than formal institutions.
- Contradictions exist between democratic and authoritarian elements.

Theocracy

- Rule is by divine inspiration or divine right.
- God is sovereign, not the people.
- Islamist version:
  - Islamism: Islamic law, as revealed by God to the Prophet Mohammed, can and should provide the basis for government in Muslim communities.
  - *Ijtihad:* The belief that Muslims should read and interpret the original Islamic texts for themselves, not simply fol-low traditional religious leaders and beliefs.
  - *Sharia:* Muslim law should be the law of society for all Muslims.

in power, of trying to govern a complex society, may necessitate ideological modi-fications. As we noted in chapter 2, weak states in particular are characterized by relatively weak formal institutions. In these states, knowing the informal rules and institutions at work may be more important to understanding how their regimes actually function and who rules than knowing the formal institutions embodied in their constitutions.

The major regime types we detail below include some in which the official ide-ology and related formal institutions represent the most important elements of a regime, as well as others in which informal institutions are more important. Even where informal institutions predominate, though, ideologies are important. The

WHERE AND WHY

Authoritarian versus Democratic Rule

One of the biggest questions in comparative politics is why some countries relatively early on developed democratic regimes that have endured for decades or even centuries, while others remained or became authoritarian. Is there something specific about certain kinds of countries that leads to one outcome or the other? Is there a distinct historical process that leads to one or the other? Are some countries likely to remain authoritarian? Why did Britain develop a democracy as early as 1688, while Russia became communist and Germany remained authoritarian, with a brief and unstable exception, until 1945?

A prominent theory for many years relied on political culture. *The Civic Culture,* a famous work of comparative politics published in the 1960s that we mentioned in chapter 1, argued that some countries have cultures that value participation and expression of ideas and tolerate dissent, while others do not. A second long-standing argument was tied to the level of wealth: wealthy countries with large, educated middle classes become democratic; other countries do not. A third approach, and the most influential, was Barrington Moore's *Social Origins of Dictatorship and Democracy* (1966). Moore set out to answer exactly the question we ask above, looking at Britain,

Germany, and Russia, along with several other countries. He provided what many found to be a very convincing structural argument. Influenced by Marxist analysis, it focused on the structure of the transition from agricultural to industrial society. In Britain, for example, the main agricultural economic activity was wool production. British landlords drove peasants off the land and into the cities early on so that their sheep had a place to graze. Sheep husbandry requires little labor, so wool producers did not need many rural laborers and therefore did not need the state to help control their labor force. The displaced, unemployed peasants streamed into the cities and there formed a cheap industrial workforce. Wool producers and traders wanted their freedom from government interference, and subsequently, they supported liberal ideas that argued for a reduction in the power of the king. They were joined by the rising bourgeoisie in industry, whose main source of initial income was the wool trade and who wanted political rights equal to those of the rural aristocracy.

In contrast, in Russia and China the peasantry remained on the land into the modern era, increasingly revolting against modernizing trends that harmed them. These dissatisfied peasants ultimately served as the basis of revolutionary

major political ideologies have defined the terms of the most important political debates of the past century: liberal democracy versus communism versus fascism versus theocracy. (For a description of the major ideologies, see the "Major Political Ideologies and Regimes" box on pages 100–101.) Most regimes have come to power in the name of one or another of the ideologies outlined below, and many have made serious efforts to rule along the lines prescribed by them.

All of the major political ideologies address the key question of the proper relationship between the state and its citizens. While liberal democracy is certainly not universally accepted, it has become powerful enough that all regimes, implicitly or explicitly, must respond to its claims. Authoritarian regimes always at least partially justify themselves by criticizing liberal democracy and showing why their

movements that the communists came to lead. In Germany, on the other hand, agricultural modernization involved grain farming, which required large numbers of laborers. Landlords needed a strong state to help them keep labor on the land and under control. They were joined in their desire for strong government intervention by industrialists, whom the state supported to aid Germany's rapid industrialization. An alliance of the rural elite, rising industrialists, and the state sought to repress workers in the name of rapid modernization, leading down the path to fascism. So Moore concluded that removing the peasantry from the land relatively early and creating an industrial bourgeoisie led to democracy. Where this didn't happen, communist or fascist dictatorships were the result.

A recent addition to this debate partially agrees with Moore but adds several factors. Economist Daron Acemoglu and political scientist James Robinson (2006) used a rational-choice approach to explain where and why democracy emerges. They started by supposing that in a nondemocratic regime, society is divided into two parts: a small ruling elite and the poorer mass of the citizenry. They argued that the mass of the citizenry will demand democracy because they believe it will give them greater power, which they can use to improve their well-being by redistributing income. They will not simply demand redistribution without political change because only institutional change that gives them greater power will ensure their greater well-being in the long term. The ruling elite will only give up power and create democracy when it believes that doing so is essential to prevent severe social unrest or revolution. A move by the elite to create democracy is most likely when (1) civil society is strong, so the masses' demands are well organized and articulated; (2) a crisis in the existing social order occurs; (3) elites' wealth is based on something other than land (here is where Acemoglu and Robinson agreed with Moore: a strong landed aristocracy is unlikely to produce democracy); (4) a strong middle class exists to buffer the effects of the changes on the elite; and (5) inequality is neither so great that it makes the masses' revolt impossible to achieve nor so slight that they do not demand fundamental changes.

While no theory has definitively answered the question of why some countries have established democracies successfully and others have not, sophisticated structural and rational-choice theories have proven more convincing to most comparativists than earlier cultural arguments.

ideologies and regimes are superior at ruling in the interests of the people. Since liberal democracy is central to the ideological debates of the past two centuries, we will turn to it first.

Liberal Democracy

Democracy means different things to different people. It may be difficult for average citizens to define it clearly, but they know it when they see it. We will follow the main convention in comparative politics and use a minimal definition of the term, typically referred to as *liberal democracy*. The two parts of the phrase are stated together so frequently that in many people's minds they have become one. The distinction between the two, however, is important to understanding both the development of liberal democracy and current debates over its expansion around the world, which we discuss in subsequent chapters.

Classical liberalism, the predecessor of liberal democracy, arose in the sixteenth and seventeenth centuries amidst the religious wars in England and the later revolution in France. The key liberal thinkers of the period created a model of political philosophy known as **social contract theory**. Although there are many variations, all social contract theories begin from the premise that legitimate governments are formed when free and independent individuals join in a contract to permit representatives to govern over them in their common interests. The originators of this idea, Thomas Hobbes and John Locke in England and the Baron de Montesquieu and Jean-Jacques Rousseau in France, started from a new and innovative assumption: all citizens should be considered free and equal. They theorized an original "state of nature" in which all men (and they meant men—women weren't included until much later) lived freely and equally with no one ruling over them. They argued that the only government that could be justified was one that men living in such a state of nature would freely choose.

These philosophers did have somewhat different visions of what this state of nature looked like and therefore different reasons for why men would choose to create a government to rule over them. But beginning with Locke, they ultimately came to the same basic conclusion about what such a freely chosen government would look like. Locke argued that in the state of nature, government would only arise if it helped preserve the core liberties of all free men: life, liberty, and property (a phrase Thomas Jefferson later adopted and modified into "life, liberty and the pursuit of happiness" in the Declaration of Independence). This became the central doctrine of liberalism: a regime is only justified if it preserves and protects the core liberties of autonomous, free, and equal individuals. A state can only infringe on these liberties in very particular circumstances, such as when an action is essential for the well-being of all or when a particular citizen has denied others their rights. Preservation of rights is essential and severely limits what governments can do.

Civil Rights and Representative Democracy The classical liberal doctrine on the preservation of rights justifies limited government to enhance individual freedoms, but it says nothing about how a government will come to power or make decisions. Liberals argued that men in a state of nature would desire a government over which they had some direct control, with leaders they could remove from office if they wished as protection against a state overstepping its bounds and trying to destroy basic liberties. The idea of representative democracy was thus born and justified. By voting, citizens would choose the government that would rule over them. Those chosen would be in office for a limited period, with some mechanism for removal if necessary.

With elected representatives, some type of legislature would be essential and central to government. This would be a body in which elected officials would debate and decide the important issues of the day. While kings and courts had long existed in Europe as the executive and judicial branches, liberals argued that the most important branch ought to be the legislative, the body of elected representatives of free and equal citizens. Montesquieu added the idea of separating the main powers of government into distinct branches to divide and thereby further limit power. This doctrine, adopted in the United States but not in the United Kingdom, is not essential to liberal democracy but is rather an extension of the liberal ideal of limited government.

social contract theory: Philosophical approach underlying liberalism that begins from the premise that legitimate governments are formed when free and independent individuals join in a contract to permit representatives to govern over them in their common interests

Who Could Vote and Why For all of their forward thinking about equality and limited government, most classical liberals still conceived of the citizens to which these concepts applied as male property owners only. An important nineteenth-century exception was the English philosopher John Stuart Mill, who made one of the earliest philosophical arguments in favor of women's political rights in his 1870 book *The Subjection of Women,* which he most likely cowrote with his wife. Most liberals, however, argued that while everyone had some basic civil rights, only men who owned property were adequately mature, rational, and independent of the whims of others to be given the right to vote and participate in governing. Classic liberalism answered the "Who rules?" question very clearly, giving power exclusively to a particular slice of the population. Restricting full citizenship to this group also meant that all citizens could be considered equal: different men held different amounts of property and had different abilities, but compared to the rest of society they were roughly similar.

It was not long before groups not initially granted full citizenship, such as men without property, women, and racial minorities, began asking why they weren't considered as free and equal as anybody else. This question produced the largest political struggles of the nineteenth and twentieth centuries in Europe and the United States, struggles to fully democratize liberalism. As citizenship slowly expanded to include more and more groups, real inequality among citizens increasingly began to conflict with the proposition that "all men [and later, all people] are created equal." Reformers started to demand that citizens gain what Marshall called social citizenship: decent living standards so that they could be respected in their communities and fully participate in the rights of citizenship as moral equals. While many would argue this struggle is not yet over in terms of social rights, in formal legal terms in established democracies, all adult citizens are now included in the answer to "Who rules?"

The Birth of Modern Liberal Democracy Social democratic parties emerged in Europe in the late nineteenth century. These parties had originated in Marxist movements, but by the early twentieth century, most had come to accept the basic precepts of liberal democracy, namely that individual rights should be protected and that political change should come via elections. They argued for social rights in order to make the liberal conception of equality not only a formal, legal reality but a social one as well. In their view, the state had to intervene in the economy to provide effective citizenship to all of the population, not just to those with more resources. Social democratic ideology did not create a separate regime, but it became an important variant in the internal debates of liberal democracy (see the "What Is Democracy?" box on page 107).

Modern liberal democratic regimes arose from this history. Leaders in these regimes justify their actions by claiming to preserve and protect core civil and political liberties: freedom from government intervention in private lives (except under clearly defined and limited circumstances), freedom of religious practice, freedom of expression, freedom of association, and the rights to vote and hold office. Citizens in a liberal democracy use these freedoms to create civil society, though civil society's strength, organization, and daily relationship with the state vary from country to country (we discuss this in detail in chapter 7). All liberal democracies are characterized by some system of elections by which voters, now defined almost universally as all adult citizens, choose key members of the government, who serve limited terms and may be removed. Some liberal democracies include other safeguards, such as separation of powers. Some include the provision

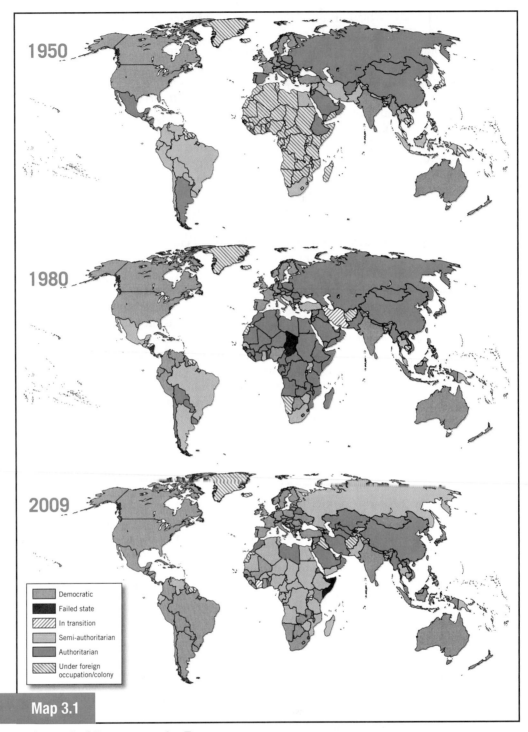

Map 3.1

Spread of Democracy by Era

The idea of democracy that liberalism launched has spread widely, especially in recent years. Between 1950 and 1980, most colonial rule came to an end, but democracy did not spread very far. By 2009, however, many more countries had become democratic, and many authoritarian regimes had become somewhat more open semi-authoritarian regimes that allowed some limited political competition, as we discuss later in this chapter. Only a relative handful of purely authoritarian regimes remain.

Source: Data from Polity IV Project: Political Regime Characteristics and Transitions, 1800–2009, http://www .systemicpeace.org/polity/polity4.htm. The "Polity" variable employed, with the following coding by the authors: democracy (6 to 10); semi-authoritarian, (–5 to 5); authoritarian, (–10 to 6).

What Is Democracy?

Democracy is one of those words that many people find hard to define, yet they know democracy when they see it. The word literally means rule by the *demos,* or the people, but that doesn't tell us very much. In this book, we apply the definition used by most comparativists, often called the "minimal definition." Political scientist Robert Dahl captured the essentials when he coined the concept of "polyarchy." He described a system of government that provides eight key guarantees: freedom of association, freedom of expression, the right to vote, broad citizen eligibility for public office, the right of political leaders to compete for support, alternative sources of information, free and fair elections, and institutions that make government policies depend on votes and other forms of citizen preferences. A system of this nature is generally referred to as **liberal democracy**.

Liberal democracy is certainly not the only form of democracy that democratic theorists have imagined or advocated. Perhaps the best known alternative is **social democracy**, which combines liberal democracy with a much greater provision of social rights of citizenship and typically greater public control of the economy as well. Advocates of social democracy argue that citizen control over the political sphere implies that this control should be extended to the economic sphere, too. They favor public ownership or at least extensive regulation of key sectors of the economy to enhance equal citizenship and the well-being of all. They believe in maintaining a market economy, but one that is regulated in the interests of the greater good of the citizens as a whole. Social democracy advocates also believe that Marshall's third category, social rights, is very important to achieving full democracy. By this reasoning, social programs must be generously funded in an attempt to achieve greater economic equality among all citizens.

Participatory democracy is also a long-standing expansion of liberal democracy. Proponents argue that real democracy must include far more than the minimal list of institutional guarantees associated with Dahl's polyarchy. Real democracy requires direct citizen participation in the decisions that affect their lives. Therefore, advocates of participatory democracy support the decentralization of decision making to local communities to the greatest extent possible, with the goal of direct citizen involvement. Many also support the democratization of the workplace, advocating for worker participation in the key decisions of the companies for which they work. Like social democrats, supporters of participatory democracy believe that real democracy requires citizen control over economic as well as political activity, but they want to see such control directly in the hands of citizens and workers at the local level.

With the spread of democracy around the world in the last thirty years (see chapter 9), an additional kind of democracy has emerged. Many countries over the last two decades have instituted elections that have allowed multiple candidates and parties to compete for power in what had been authoritarian regimes; however, these states have not fully implemented the institutional guarantees listed above for liberal democracy. They hold elections and allow real competition, but liberal rights like equal protection under the law may not be fully in place. Analysts refer to this type of regime as **electoral democracy**. Those who use the term do not advocate for it as a good form of government; rather, they use it to distinguish what they see as partial democracies from fully institutionalized liberal democracies.

participatory democracy: A form of democracy that encourages citizens to participate actively, in many ways beyond voting; usually focused at the local level

liberal democracy: A system of government that provides eight key guarantees, including freedoms to enable citizen participation in the political process and institutions that make government policies depend on votes and other forms of citizen preferences

social democracy: Combines liberal democracy with much greater provision of social rights of citizenship and typically greater public control of the economy

electoral democracy: A political system in which opposition parties are legal and elections take place, but full civil and political rights of liberal democracy are not secure

of extensive government services to attempt to achieve something closer to equal social citizenship. The debate continues, of course, over how much power liberal freedoms actually give to the average citizen vis-à-vis the elite. Marxists, among others, argue that liberal rights to vote and join organizations do not give any real power to the average citizen. They and other elite theorists contend that elites such as major business leaders gain disproportionate influence in any "democracy" and influence government policy in their favor, often against the interests of average citizens, who have no real recourse in spite of the rights liberalism provides.

CASE STUDY

United Kingdom: "Cradle of Democracy"

- First liberal regime
- Gradual but contentious expansion of citizens' rights in nineteenth and early twentieth centuries
- Parliamentary sovereignty
- Constitutional reforms in the new millennium

Many of the most important developments in the history of liberal democracy occurred in the United Kingdom (UK), or England before it became the UK. The core ideas of limiting a sovereign's power and creating what was called a parliament (from the French word *parler,* meaning to talk) arose long before they were codified in the philosophy of Locke and others. The earliest document of importance to this principle was the Magna Carta, signed by King John in 1215. Feudal lords forced the king to sign the document, which restricted his ability to abuse various laws. It included the first implementation of the idea of trial by peers, guaranteed the freedom of the (Catholic) church from monarchical intervention, created an assembly of twenty-five barons (chosen by all the barons of England) to ensure enforcement of the document, and guaranteed nobles the right to be called together to discuss any significant new taxes. Ultimately, all of these rights and guarantees were strictly designed to preserve the dominance of the nobility, but they laid the

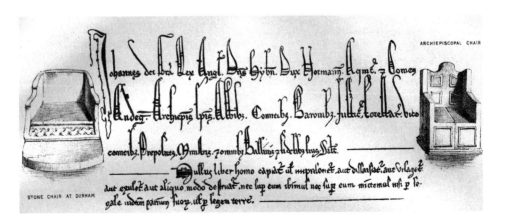

The Magna Carta (Latin for Great Charter), also known as the Great Charter of Freedoms, is considered the first formal limitation on a monarch's power. In 1215, it established the ideas of trial by jury and *habeas corpus* and created the first parliament.

Credit: © Lebrecht Music and Arts Photo Library/Alamy

groundwork for expansion to the broader population centuries later.

For four centuries, the Magna Carta restricted the powers of the English monarchy, but the powers of the sovereign remained strong. King Henry VIII's break with the Catholic Church in 1534, however, ultimately led the English into a civil war in the 1640s that resulted in the beheading of King Charles I. Carried out in the name of gaining control over the monarchy, the war ended in a dictatorship under Oliver Cromwell. Cromwell was eventually overthrown and the monarchy restored, but Locke developed his ideas largely in reaction to the deep religious divisions and violence of the civil war. The Glorious Revolution of 1688 saw Parliament's bloodless removal of King James II from the throne and the installation of a new monarch. The following year, Parliament passed a Bill of Rights that substantially expanded the rights of citizenship. From that point forward, Parliament gained increasing power vis-à-vis the monarchy. This became especially true after the American Revolution, when King George III became increasingly incapacitated and the power of the prime minister—an individual appointed by the king but who worked closely with Parliament—grew significantly.

The growing power of the elected Parliament was significant, but political citizenship was still restricted primarily to men with substantial property holdings, who constituted less than 5 percent of the population. They were the ones who ruled. The nineteenth century saw significant changes to this system, starting with the Reform Act of 1832, which expanded the vote to the growing middle class. Still, the electorate remained all male and grew only to about 7 percent of the population. Political citizenship later expanded to most adult males through the Representation of the People Act of 1867 and the Franchise Act of 1884. A movement for women's suffrage emerged by the mid-nineteenth century, but not until 1918 were all men and women thirty years of age and older given the right to vote, with the age dropping to twenty-one in 1928. None of this expansion of political citizenship occurred easily. Large-scale pressure from civil society, first from the growing middle class in the early nineteenth century, then from the growing working class in the industrializing cities in the latter part of the century, and finally from women, was necessary to achieve each reform. Liberal rights expanded, but only when those without them demanded (vociferously, and sometimes violently) that they be included in full citizenship.

The British model of liberal democracy is unusual, in part because of its history. No equivalent of the American or French Revolution ever occurred to cause a definitive break from monarchy and the establishment of democracy. The development of the liberal democratic regime in Britain was much more gradual. No unified, written British constitution exists, though many of the elements of a constitution—the fundamental rules of how the regime works—are written down in various laws passed by Parliament. In the absence of a single constitution, British democracy is based on the concept of **parliamentary sovereignty,** which holds that Parliament is supreme in all matters. Members can write any law they choose via majority vote. Even without a single constitution, basic liberal rights have long been established in law, though Parliament could change that at any time. Rights are preserved only by a collective consensus that Parliament should not reverse them. This is a great example of a powerful but *informal* political institution, a set of implicit rules and norms that are not violated even though in theory they could be. Political culture theorists would explain this institution by pointing to British cultural values. Institutionalists might suggest that the institution, established primarily in the Bill of Rights of 1689, has served citizens' interests well and therefore is preserved. In any case, the system has continued to operate with only limited change for more than three centuries.

Some of the most significant recent changes to Britain's liberal constitutional order came under the leadership of Tony Blair, who was prime minister from 1997 to 2007. He and his Labour Party allowed the creation of devolution in 1997. This was the granting of

parliamentary sovereignty: Parliament is supreme in all matters; key example is the United Kingdom

some elements of power to newly created parliaments for Scotland and Wales, the two kingdoms integrated into Great Britain centuries earlier. Unlike the constitutionally guaranteed federalist system that grants powers to the states in the United States, devolution was voted on by the British Parliament, which could vote to reverse it. Nonetheless, it was the biggest decentralization of power over government roles like education and social services since the United Kingdom was created. Blair also had Parliament pass a law in 1998 saying that Britain would abide by the European Convention on Human Rights and allow courts to advise Parliament that a particular British law was in violation of the Convention. Unlike in the United States, where the Supreme Court can reverse an act of Congress, a court ruling like this in Britain is only advisory, but it still was a big change to the doctrine of unquestioned parliamentary sovereignty. In 2005, the Blair government created a freestanding Supreme Court as a final court of appeals, a job that had previously been done by the unelected House of Lords in Parliament. The new Supreme Court began hearing cases in October 2009, though it still lacks the power to reverse acts of Parliament that the U.S. Supreme Court has vis-à-vis Congress.

In the twentieth century, Britain's democracy also wrestled with the notion of social rights, for even after civil and political rights were made universal, socioeconomic inequality remained great. After World War II, based on a sense that all citizens had shared the sacrifices necessary to win the war and therefore should share in the rewards, the British government expanded its welfare state extensively. This included the National Health Service, which essentially made access to health care a universal right, plus other universal benefits such as an annual "child allowance" from the government for all parents raising children. In 2010, newly elected prime minister David Cameron questioned the universality of the child allowance, suggesting that only poorer citizens should receive it and instigating a new debate over how much of a social right it should really be.

CASE SUMMARY

Britain's unusual liberal democracy has evolved slowly, and often contentiously, over centuries. Citizenship rights have expanded to include all adult citizens despite the absence of a single, written constitution. Parliamentary sovereignty gives Britain an unusually centralized form of democracy (which we explore in detail in chapter 6) but one that has preserved and expanded basic liberal rights for a very long time. Like all established liberal democracies, Britain continues to debate the concept of how universal social rights should be.

Communism

The first and most influential ideological alternative to liberal democracy was communism, which became the basis for regimes in Russia, China, and a number of other countries. Communism arose from the philosophy of Karl Marx, whose primary works were written between the 1840s and 1880s. Marx, a German, was forced into exile first in France and ultimately in England. He created a philosophy based on what he called **historical materialism**, the assumption that material (economic) forces are the prime movers of history and politics. He believed that to understand politics, one must first understand the economic structure of a society and the economic interests that arise from it. As the material forces in the society—technology, raw materials, and the way they are combined to make goods—change, so too will the political, social, and ideological systems in that society to allow the productive forces to work to their fullest. Feudalism produced all-powerful lords and monarchs, with religious sanction from the church as the chief ideological justification,

historical materialism: The assumption that material forces are the prime movers of history and politics; a key philosophical tenet of Marxism

to keep the peasants in their place producing a surplus for the lords. The shift to capitalism produced liberalism, in which political power was no longer vested in the landed aristocracy but was instead given to all men of property. This allowed the rising bourgeoisie, the owners of capital, to gain political power. Capitalism requires labor that can move from place to place, what is known as **free wage labor** (see chapter 5 for more on capitalism), so the feudal system that required peasants to stay on the land where they were born and work for their lord was abolished, and many peasants were forced off their land to work for a daily wage in cities.

Liberal democracy, according to Marx, is the political and ideological shell that allows capitalism to work and that serves the interests of the bourgeoisie, capitalism's ruling class. When Marx was developing his ideas, only men of property had full political rights in the United Kingdom and many countries. Even where those rights had expanded to others, as in the United States by the 1830s, Marx argued that this was only a charade. He called liberal rights "equal rights for unequal people," arguing that where workers did have the vote and rights of expression, this political participation was virtually meaningless because those with wealth were the only ones with any real power. Civil society, he argued, was a realm dominated by capitalists as well, a sphere created to give capitalists independence from the state and a means by which they could control the state.

Marx saw the transition from one **mode of production** to another, such as from feudalism to capitalism, as a process of **social revolution**. He argued that all modes of production ultimately create contradictions they cannot overcome, leading to revolution. Capitalism, he believed, would be characterized by an ever greater division between the bourgeoisie and the proletariat, workers who must sell their labor for a wage to survive because they own no capital. Marx believed that as more and more wealth and power accrued in the hands of capitalists, the proletariat would become so poor that they would not be able to consume all of capitalism's products, thus creating an economic crisis that would usher in a new era of social revolution. Just as the liberal revolutions had been led by the bourgeoisie and had established liberal democracy, the next revolutions would be communist revolutions led by the proletariat—what Marx called the "specter haunting Europe" in *The Communist Manifesto* (1848/1888). Marx believed this revolution was inevitable and that it was the job of the communist movement to recognize when and where social revolutions were emerging and bring them to fruition to create a new and better society and political system.

The communist society that Marx believed would emerge from these revolutions would abolish class distinctions and collectively own the means of production. All people (or at least men—Marx was no more feminist than most other nineteenth-century philosophers) would be paid the same amount for the same work, and everyone would have to work. This he saw as the first stage of communism, which he also called socialism. He was quite explicit about who would rule during this stage: the **dictatorship of the proletariat**, an absolute rule by workers as a class over all other classes. This dictatorship was not of one man but of the entire class, which would control and ultimately eliminate all other classes. Civil society distinct from this workers' state would no longer be needed. This was justified in Marx's view because all governments, including all liberal democracies, have been class dictatorships: liberal democracies are simply dictatorships of the bourgeoisie. As this socialist society developed, everyone eventually would become equal in the sense of all being part of the proletariat. At that point, the second, higher stage of communism would develop in which no state would be necessary because no class divisions would exist, and all dictatorships would end.

free wage labor: Labor that can move from place to place and is paid based on the time worked; required by capitalism

mode of production: In Marxist theory, the economic system in any given historical era; feudalism and capitalism in the last millennium in Europe

social revolution: In Marxist theory, the transition from one mode of production to another; Marxist understanding of revolution

dictatorship of the proletariat: The first stage of communism in Marxist thought, characterized by absolute rule by workers as a class over all other classes

Marx did not write in detail about what this communist society and its government would look like, in part because he did not believe in prescription and speculation about the future. Philosophically, he believed that communism was both inevitable and the final stage of human historical evolution. Just as political systems and ideologies are the product of economic forces, Marx believed human nature was as well. With class division and exploitation eliminated, he believed that human nature itself would change from being self-interested and greedy under capitalism to being what he viewed as more fully human under communism. This would facilitate the creation of his ultimate and, he believed, inevitable goal of a communist utopia. Critics dispute this utopian goal and therefore the means to achieve it. Liberals reject the notion that any end, whether feasible or not, justifies violating the fundamental rights of any individual or group, as would occur under the dictatorship of the proletariat. They fear instead that a communist state would simply become a dictatorship of an individual or small group over all of society. Postmodern theorists have argued that Marxism, or any theory claiming certainty about the "laws" of human history, inevitably will result in a totalitarian state restricting all freedoms in the name of achieving an unreachable utopia. These themes are illustrated well in the history of communism in Russia.

CASE STUDY

Russia: The First Self-Proclaimed Communist Regime

- Revolution in the "wrong country"
- Vanguard party ruling on behalf of proletariat to come
- Totalitarian regime under Stalin
- Bureaucratic socialism with pluralist battles for resources behind the scenes

Marx thought Russia was not ready for communism, but Vladimir Lenin, above, led a revolution there. He modified Marxist doctrine to adapt it to Russian circumstances and suggested that a vanguard party of committed revolutionaries could lead a precapitalist, agrarian nation into communism.

Credit: AP Photo

Marx was an active revolutionary for most of his life, but he did not live to see a communist revolution succeed. Based on his analysis of capitalism, he believed the revolution would start in the wealthiest and most advanced capitalist societies, such as the United Kingdom, Germany, and France. Russia at the turn of the twentieth century was nothing like these powers. It was what would later be called a third-world country, still primarily rural, with growing multinational investment controlled by foreigners and an unstable and oppressive political system. The liberal, bourgeois revolution, let alone the socialist one, had yet to happen there. In fact, late in his life Marx wrote to Russian revolutionaries, counseling patience and telling them to wait for the revolutions in the wealthier parts of Europe before pursuing their own socialist dreams.

Vladimir Lenin never met Marx; he did, however, read and admire his writings, and by the late nineteenth century, shortly after

Marx's death, Lenin had become a committed communist revolutionary. As Russia writhed in the throes of World War I, a disastrous and unpopular war in Russia, Lenin led his **Bolshevik** forces to victory in the October Revolution of 1917 and created the first self-proclaimed Communist regime. Lenin knew that according to Marx, Russia was not ripe for revolution, so to legitimize his regime, Lenin modified Marx's political theories. He argued that where capitalism had not developed sufficiently to produce the economic crisis and socialist revolution, a committed band of revolutionaries, a **vanguard party**, could still lead a revolution. This party would take power and rule on behalf of the proletariat until the country was fully industrialized and therefore fully proletarian. Socialism, the first stage of communism, would last longer than Marx had envisioned, but the revolution could occur sooner. Lenin also believed that once the revolution succeeded in Russia, the proletariat of the wealthier European countries would see the possibility of a proletarian regime and rise up to create their own. He fully expected the communist revolution to spread quickly across Europe and create a set of socialist regimes that would build communism together.

Once in power, and seeing that the revolution was not going to spread rapidly across Europe, Lenin had to figure out how the Soviet Union would survive as the lone socialist state. Thus, he made the first of many modifications of communist ideology to fit the realities of ruling a modern state. Lenin's regime was led by his Communist Party, which claimed to act on behalf of the present and future proletariat. The dictatorship of the proletariat would, for the time being, be the dictatorship of a single party, which was justified in ruthlessly suppressing all opposition that represented other class interests, especially the nobility and bourgeoisie of prerevolutionary Russia. The party thus became the sole representative of the people, and the regime it created used Lenin's idea of **democratic centralism** as its key organizing principle. In this organization of state power, lower organs of the party and state would vote on issues and individuals to represent them at higher levels; ultimately individuals at the top level would make final, binding decisions. Once these decisions were made, all lower levels were expected to follow orders without question. In practice, those at the top controlled virtually all power, allowing only ideas and people they already had approved to rise through the hierarchy.

The regime consisted of a set of **soviets**, or legislative bodies, which made decisions at all levels. After gaining full control of the prerevolutionary Russian empire and some additional territories, the new regime and state were named the Union of Soviet Socialist Republics (USSR). Officially, the soviet was the decision-making body at each level of the regime, from the village to the province to the national state, but in reality each soviet was tightly controlled by the Communist Party, which was the only legal party to which any politically active person or official had to belong. At the top of the entire system was the **politburo**, the party's chief decision-making organ. This small, mostly male group collectively and secretly selected each new general secretary of the party. The general secretaries were the country's most powerful rulers, and most served in that position until death.

Lenin came to recognize by 1921 that while central state control of the government had merit, similar control of the economy was hurting production, especially in agriculture, the largest sector of the economy. Once again, ideological modification seemed essential. In response, he created the New Economic Policy, under which state control of the economy was partially loosened. Lenin died at a relatively young age only three years later, before seeing this policy and others come to fruition. Most of his policies never would. After a five-year succession struggle, Josef Stalin came to power in 1929, and he radically changed Soviet socialism. Stalin launched a plan to rapidly institute state control of the economy, taking ownership of virtually all land and extracting huge surpluses from agriculture to build industry. The result was the beginning of a rapid industrialization

Bolshevik: Vladimir Lenin's branch of the communist movement in Russia that led the Russian communist revolution

soviets: Legislative bodies in the communist regime of the Soviet Union

vanguard party: Vladimir Lenin's concept of a small party that claims legitimacy to rule based on its understanding of Marxist theory and its ability to represent the interests of the proletariat before they are a majority of the populace

politburo: The chief decision-making organ in a communist party; China's politburo is a key example

democratic centralism: The organization of a ruling party, primarily in communist regimes, in which lower organs of a party and state vote on issues and individuals to represent them at higher levels; the highest level makes final decisions that all must obey

that transformed the Soviet Union from a poor agricultural country to an industrial powerhouse and superpower by World War II. Those who opposed Stalin or his policies were quickly suppressed; estimates of deaths under his rapid industrialization program and political reign range from two to twenty million. He created a **totalitarian regime** that controlled virtually all aspects of society and eliminated all vestiges of civil society.

After Stalin's death in 1953, his successors, Nikita Khrushchev (1956–1964) and Leonid Brezhnev (1964–1982) restored broader party control of the state, reduced aspects of Stalin's reign of terror, and created what became an oppressive but predictable communist system. Political scientists of the time debated extensively over how centralized or pluralist this regime was, and while it certainly was not pluralist in the democratic sense of the term, many observers argued that factions jockeyed for power and influence behind the scenes. It was clearly less totalitarian than it had been under Stalin. By this point, understanding how the regime actually functioned required far more than just understanding the Leninist beliefs on which it was founded. A new subfield of comparative politics emerged called "Kremlinology" in which experts looked for informal signs of who had real power. For instance, which officials were standing or sitting closest to the top leaders indicated who had the most influence at a particular moment. Behind the façade of democratic centralism and the complete absence of public debate, numerous factions, based on which state agency people worked in, where they were from, or simply which top leader they had personal loyalty to, battled to gain resources and power.

With Brezhnev's death, a new generation of leadership emerged in the person of Mikhail Gorbachev (1985–1991). Stalin's policies had rapidly industrialized the economy, but the inefficiencies of central state control had grown over time, and the wealth and productivity of the Soviet Union had declined compared to that of Western countries. To try to increase economic productivity and allow a

totalitarian regime: A regime that controls virtually all aspects of society and eliminates all vestiges of civil society; Germany under Hitler and the Soviet Union under Stalin are key examples

modicum of open political debate, Gorbachev launched new economic and political policies called *perestroika* and *glasnost,* respectively. The implementation of these policies initiated a cycle of events over which Gorbachev eventually lost control. In August 1991, after the military's failed attempt at a coup d'etat that was intended to restore some of the old order, the Soviet Union began to crumble. In December 1991, the Soviet Union officially ceased to exist, and fifteen separate states, including Russia, emerged once the dust had settled. This began the difficult process of transition to democracy in Russia that we explore further in chapter 9.

CASE SUMMARY

For nearly a century, Russia's communist regime, based on the principles of Marx as modified by Lenin, claimed to be working on behalf of the proletariat. Regime members argued, however, that only highly trained and educated communists could use Marxist analysis to serve the proletariat's interests effectively. This claim to legitimacy justified repression of all public dissent; any opposition was automatically liable to be called out as a class-based attempt to reverse the inevitable and morally justifiable movement toward true communism. The regime thus restricted citizenship to those who accepted the party's wisdom and rule; those who opposed the party were traitors to the class that rightfully should rule. Civil society under Communist Party rule was completely eliminated, and the state, led by the party, controlled virtually all aspects of individuals' lives, including where they worked, the clubs and organizations they could belong to, and the prices they paid at the cash register.

The Russian Communist Party set the basic model of communist rule that was copied, with some modifications, in China and elsewhere after World War II. Following Lenin's principles, it justified absolute rule by one tightly controlled party and state control over virtually all economic activity. The system became exceptionally totalitarian and brutal under Stalin but more predictable

REGIMES, IDEOLOGIES, AND CITIZENS   **115**

(though still repressive) under his successors. It successfully created an industrial superpower by World War II, but one that could not ultimately keep pace with capitalist economic growth in the West. Competition with the West eventually necessitated a series of reforms that the Soviet regime lost control of, causing its final collapse. Only China, Cuba, Vietnam, and North Korea still maintain a claim to communism, and only North Korea still maintains the centralized economic system that was at the heart of the effort. Cuba has experimented with limited liberalization of the economy, for example by expanding opportunities for self-employment in 2011. China and Vietnam, as we will see later in the book, have essentially allowed capitalism to emerge and, while still claiming to be communist, are in fact modernizing authoritarian regimes.

Fascism

Fascism was the other major European alternative to liberal democracy in the early to mid-twentieth century. It was self-consciously both antiliberal and anticommunist. Fascist ideology espouses a conception of society being akin to a living organism rather than a set of disparate groups and individuals. The state is central to and dominant within this organic society; it regulates and assures the smooth functioning of the organism, much as the brain does for the body. Italian fascist leader Benito Mussolini, in *Fascism: Doctrine and Institutions* (1933/1968) argued that "the State is all-embracing; outside of it no human or spiritual values can exist. . . . The Fascist State . . . interprets, develops, and potentiates the whole life of a people." He goes on to say that the state creates the nation (that is, the collective identity of the people), which is itself a "higher personality." Fascists are thus intensely nationalistic, but they conceive of the nation as created by and loyal to the state first and foremost. Unlike liberals, who emphasize individual freedom, fascists argue that the individual is and should be subsumed within the state. Mussolini, for example, said the fascist "accepts the individual only in so far as his interests coincide with those of the State, which stands for the conscience and the universal will of man as a historic entity." Thus, the interests of the state are justifiably dominant over both individual citizens and civil society. This state, in turn, is led by one man who becomes the supreme leader and head of the state, which itself is both the head and the spirit of the nation. He is the only one who rules, but he does so on behalf of the entire "body" of society so that it can function properly.

Fascist belief in society as an organic whole leads to the argument that society should not have competing organizations that could potentially work against each other. Fascists reject the liberal notion of civil society as a sphere of voluntary organizations independent of the state. Instead, just one organization, controlled by the state, should represent the interests of each component of society. This idea is known as **corporatism.** In fascist (and some other authoritarian) societies, the state creates one trade union to "represent" all workers, one business association, one farmers' association, one women's association, etc., all tightly controlled by the state.

Fascists also reject Marxists' emphasis on materialism and economic life. Instead, Mussolini calls fascism "a spiritual attitude," describing a fascist life as "serious, austere, religious." Fascists reject much of the rationality that is the basis of all types of Western philosophy, appealing instead to spiritual principles and traditions of a nation as a living organism. Fascist doctrine sees life as a struggle and proclaims a life of action. It views each nation as a unique and historical force that must work

corporatism: Interest group system in which one organization represents each sector of society; originally from the Catholic belief in society as an organic whole; two subtypes are societal and state corporatism

to maximize its power and position in the world, and it accepts war as a part of this struggle for the glorification of the state, the nation, and the leader.

Fascists share the modern conception of citizenship in the sense of a direct relationship between citizens and a state. Like communists, however, they define citizens not as everyone legally in the state's territory but much more narrowly. Only those loyal to the state can be citizens, and even these citizens do not have rights in the liberal sense of the concept. Since they have no existence outside the state, the concept of individual rights preexisting or separate from the state is nonsensical. Citizens are left only with duties, which they fulfill as part of achieving a more complete life. Fascists, like communists, thus justify the complete elimination of civil society, but in contrast to communists, Mussolini openly admitted that the fascist state was and should be totalitarian. Liberals, of course, reject fascism because they start from the premise that the individual exists independently of society and the state. Marxists would accept the elimination of civil society and other restrictions of rights, but not in the name of the organic nation, which they view as detrimental to the real interest of the proletariat on whose behalf they claim to rule.

CASE STUDY

Germany: Rise of the Nazi Party and a Totalitarian State

- Naziism merges fascism and racism
- Nazis elected to office under unstable democracy of Weimar Republic
- State is totalitarian but with internal factions
- Holocaust committed against Jews and various other groups
- Ultimately delegitimizes fascism the world over, but "neofascists" still exist

Fascists believed that the state was preeminent over society, so only one state-sanctioned organization should represent and speak for each group, whether workers, business, or youth. Here, Nazi leader Adolf Hitler poses with a member of the Nazi Youth, an organization the party used to socialize young people into loyalty to the regime.

Credit: © Corbis

Fascists generally glorify the nation, but they do not explicitly proclaim one nation as inherently superior to all others. They also do not define the nation as being of one racial or cultural group. Germany's National Socialists (Nazis) modified the tenets of fascism by adding explicit racism. Under the leadership of Adolf Hitler, they married fascism and racism to claim that not only was the state the embodiment of the nation, but that the German nation, defined in racial terms as "Aryan," was superior to all others and deserved to rule over them.

Germany's economy was in dire straits in the 1920s, due in part to its defeat in World War I and the subsequent peace treaty that forced it to pay massive war reparations. The global Great Depression that started in 1929 made things even worse. Blaming the mainstream parties in power for their increasingly difficult lives, German voters began shifting their allegiance to the "radical" parties: the communists and National Socialists, or Nazis. By the 1932 election, the Nazis had won 37 percent of the vote, the largest percentage of any party. Thus, Adolf Hitler did not grab power via a violent revolution or military coup: he was elected. He had become leader of the Nazi Party in 1920, and his party had competed with others in the very unstable democracy of the Weimar Republic, the regime in Germany from the end of World War I to Hitler's rise to absolute power in 1933.

Following the norms of Weimar's parliamentary democracy (see chapter 6 for an explanation of parliamentary democracy), Hitler became chancellor (the German equivalent of a prime minister), Germany's key leader of the government. Because his party did not have a majority of seats in the Reichstag (the German legislature), he had to invite members of other parties to join his government to form a coalition. Members of the Nationalist Party, the chief mainstream conservative party, sympathized with enough of Hitler's goals to agree to be his partners in government. The Nationalist Party's leaders believed that, despite Hitler's antidemocratic rhetoric and writings, they could use their influence in the government to keep him in check. They were wrong.

The Nazis, while willing to operate within electoral channels temporarily, had no respect for democracy in the long run. Shortly after Hitler became chancellor in early 1933, the Reichstag burned to the ground. Hitler arrested a Communist activist and launched an anti-Communist campaign, claiming that a communist revolution threatened the nation. In reality, it is almost certain that the Nazis themselves burned the Reichstag to initiate their grab for total power. Hitler used the "emergency" to temporarily ban personal liberties, allowing him to arrest Communist members of the Reichstag as well as other opponents. Within months, he had convinced his coalition partners to pass the Enabling Act. ("Convinced" being a nice way of saying coerced, given that the act was passed while the Nazi Party militia surrounded and

entered the Reichstag, intimidating many legislators who had seen what had happened to their Communist colleagues.) This effectively eliminated the Reichstag's legislative powers, and a dictatorship was born. Hitler and his party immediately used this new law to ban all opposition political parties and all trade unions, as the Nazi Party set out to create the totalitarian state that fascist doctrine calls for, including the complete elimination of an autonomous civil society. All German trade unions were replaced with the German Labor Front, and independent youth organizations were eliminated in favor of the National Socialist Youth.

Pluralists, however, argue that even this totalitarian state had factions within it. Some members of the National Socialist Party took the socialist part seriously, favoring government control of the economy to build a stronger nation. Hitler, however, sided with business in the interest of rapid economic growth. Early in June 1934, he had "radical elements" in the party who wanted to institute actual socialism murdered during the "Night of the Long Knives." The regime then sided unequivocally with business, though it interfered in the economy to control prices and wages when it deemed this necessary for the national interest. Large industries worked relatively closely with the Nazis. They initially favored Hitler's elimination of trade unions and later benefited from heavy government investment in infrastructure and military production in the buildup to World War II. Just as was true behind the scenes in the Soviet Union, factions continued to exist within the Nazi regime, with fierce internal battles for power in various ministries. While the regime was as close as any has ever been to being fully totalitarian, factionalism nonetheless continued to exist.

Nazi fascism was combined with racism, aimed primarily at Jews. The regime slowly and systematically implemented anti-Semitic policies, first encouraging boycotts of Jewish businesses and firing Jewish civil servants in 1933, then officially classifying people as Jewish and registering Germany's entire population by race in 1935. Jewish businesses were looted and burned during *Kristallnacht* ("Night of Broken Glass") in November 1937, and shortly thereafter, Jewish citizenship was eliminated and Jews were encouraged to emigrate from Germany to "purify" the state. The Holocaust did not begin in earnest until the start of World War II, when Jews could no longer flee, at least not in large numbers. By the end of the war approximately six million Jews had died at the hands of the Nazis and their allies across Europe. In addition to Jews and political opponents, the systematic killing included the sick and disabled who, according to the Nazis, could not contribute to the national good; homosexuals because they were considered "morally depraved"; members of various faiths other than the official, Nazified, German Evangelical Church (also called the Protestant Reich Church) because such religious faiths were seen as denying the supremacy of fascism and Hitler's control; and "gypsies" (Romanis) because they were seen as impure and flawed.

neofascist:
Description given to parties or political movements that espouse a virulent nationalism, often defined on a cultural or religious basis and opposed to immigrants as threats to national identity

CASE SUMMARY

Fascists came to power in the same era in Germany, Italy, Spain, and Portugal, among other countries. Hitler created Nazi puppet regimes as well in all the countries he conquered. Nazi rule followed the precepts of fascism, denying all individual rights in the name of the strength of the state and the glorification of the nation, defining citizenship in terms of who supported that effort, repressing opponents as necessary, and replacing an autonomous civil society with corporatist control. The Nazis, in contrast to most fascists, added explicit racism, especially vis-à-vis Jews, to their ideological justification.

The horror of Nazi rule, and fascist rule in general, delegitimized fascist ideology the world over. No regime proclaims itself as fascist today. While small fascist political movements and parties exist, none that claims the name has any significant political influence. Many observers, however, argue that fascism, or at least fascist tendencies, continue to threaten democracy in many countries. Parties that espouse a virulent nationalism, often defined on a cultural or religious basis and opposed to immigrants, perceived as threats to the "soul of the nation," are frequently termed **neofascist**. These groups vehemently deny the label, however. The best-known example of neofascism is France's National Front, led by Jean-Marie Le Pen. Le Pen argues that the greatest danger facing France is the immigration of Muslims, mainly from North Africa. He claims that Muslim immigration is destroying the French nation, and he calls for policies that would reward white French women for having more babies and would severely restrict or even eliminate immigration. Shockwaves rippled through France and much of Europe in 2002 when Le Pen came in second in that year's presidential election. Although he ultimately lost in the second round of voting, winning less than 20 percent of the vote, many people were still deeply concerned by his political strength. This concern waned when he won only 4.3 percent of the vote in the 2007 election. In the 2010 regional elections, though, his party surprised the political world once again, gaining almost 12 percent of the vote in the wake of the global financial crisis and growing concern in France over immigration. In early 2011, Marine Le Pen succeeded her father as head of the National Front and was believed to be broadening its popular support. While fascism is dead, it is not clear that neofascism is.

Modernizing Authoritarianism

While no regime currently uses fascism as an acceptable claim to legitimacy, the argument that the needs of the state and nation must take precedence over liberalism's individual rights remains common. Many postcolonial regimes can be termed

REGIMES, IDEOLOGIES, AND CITIZENS 119

modernizing authoritarian: their common claim to legitimacy is that they will modernize or "develop" their countries. These regimes are not all based on a single and consciously elaborated ideology like the other types of regimes in this chapter, but each nonetheless explicitly or implicitly appeals to a common set of precepts. Some have an elaborate ideological justification for their legitimacy; others do not. Many of these states are relatively weak, so the formal institutions based on their claim to legitimacy may reveal less about how they actually rule than their informal institutions. They all, however, share a set of core assumptions that underpin their official claim to legitimacy.

Core Assumptions The first of these assumptions is that development requires the leadership of a "modern elite." In societies with relatively few highly educated people, the assumption is that power should be in the hands of those who understand the modern world and how to advance within it. They should be the ones who rule, at least until their societies are "ready" for democracy.

This assumption is an appeal to **technocratic legitimacy**, a claim to rule based on knowledge that was part of **modernization theory**. This theory of development argued that in order to develop, postcolonial societies needed to go through the same process of modernization that the West had undergone. Modernization theorists argued that the modern elite—a "new type of enterprising men" in the words of Walt Rostow (1960), one of the pioneers of the theory and one of the originators of the American foreign aid program—would lead the development process. Modernization theorists assumed, as we noted in chapter 1, that democracy would develop along with economic development. The leaders of the modernizing authoritarian regimes that emerged, however, recognized the contradiction between arguing that development requires the leadership of an educated elite and assuming that democracy would evolve: the latter does not necessarily produce the former. Postcolonial elites, in particular, believed that in a country in which a large percentage of the population was illiterate, democracy would not necessarily put the "right" people in power. In their eyes, this justified and legitimized truncating democracy and limiting citizens' rights in favor of some form of authoritarian rule led by elites who claimed to have special leadership abilities based on their education.

The second common assumption of modernizing authoritarian regimes is that they can produce the benefits of "development." The word *development* means many things to many people, but in political discourse throughout the postcolonial world since the 1950s, it has meant moving in the direction of creating societies like those found in the West, at least economically, to bring very poor populations closer to the standard of living found in wealthier countries. Rostow saw this economic goal as entering "the age of high mass consumption."

For the poorest countries, this meant transforming poor, overwhelmingly agricultural societies into urbanized, industrialized societies with dramatically higher productivity and wealth. For middle-income countries, such as Brazil, development meant continuing the industrialization that had already started, "deepening" it from relatively low-technology to higher-technology and higher-productivity industries, as well as continuing the overall shift of economic activity and people from countryside to city. All of this required the application of modern science and technology, which the educated and technocratic elite claimed to understand and be able to employ on behalf of the entire country. The goal, and the main justification for authoritarian rule, was development.

Development also required national unity, the third assumption underpinning these regimes. Postcolonial elites argued that achieving the Herculean task

technocratic legitimacy: A claim to rule based on knowledge or expertise

modernization theory: Theory of development that argues that postcolonial societies need to go through the same process that the West underwent in order to develop

of "catching up" to the West necessitated unusual measures. Their countries did not have time to fight internally by engaging in political battles for control of the government or lengthy debates about what policies to pursue. Instead, the modern elite should take control to move the country forward. Debate and democracy had to wait until the "big push" for development was completed, or at least well underway. Some groups in civil society, such as labor unions demanding higher wages or better working conditions, might oppose policies that the elite believed were beneficial. Modernizing elites found such resistance unacceptable because it was not in the interest of development; everyone had to be united to move forward rapidly. They typically tied this appeal for unity to nationalism, pleading that unity was needed to build a more powerful nation in which people could take pride.

All of these assumptions have faced severe criticism. Liberals reject the notion that individual rights must be subsumed in an effort to achieve greater collective ends. They also question the assumption that democracy is necessarily so divisive that effective policymaking cannot occur. Marxists, as noted in chapter 1, argue that modernizing authoritarian regimes really represent neocolonialism. The local ruling class is working in its own interests, not those of the country as a whole and, furthermore, works on behalf of global capitalist forces, which influence policy behind the scenes and against the interests of the poor majority in postcolonial societies. Fascists, on the other hand, would likely be more sympathetic to many of the arguments of modernizing authoritarianism, in that the two doctrines share the notion that national greatness requires restricting individual rights.

Institutional Forms Modernizing authoritarianism has taken three distinct institutional forms: one-party regimes, military regimes, and personalist regimes. While they all share the key assumptions of the general model, each has different origins and somewhat different institutions (or lack thereof). **One-party regimes**, once common in Africa and Asia, were based on a single party gaining power after independence and systematically eliminating all opposition in the name of development and national unity. These regimes eliminated all effective opposition, but some, such as Kenya and Côte d'Ivoire, did achieve notable economic progress.

Military regimes took power via **coups d'etat**, meaning military takeovers of government; they justified elimination of the previous government, whether democratic or not, in terms of modernizing authoritarianism. Often citing prolonged economic stagnation or growing social unrest as their impetus, military leaders argued that they would "clean up the mess" of the prior government and get the country at least started down the road to development before returning it to civilian and democratic rule. Some military regimes were more serious in this intent and more economically successful; others seem to have used the assumptions of modernizing authoritarianism to justify their own hold on power, with little development taking place, as the case of Nigeria illustrates.

Personalist regimes usually arose as a result of either one-party rule or via military coup, but either way a central leader came to dominate. This leader not only eliminated all opposition but also weakened the state's institutions in order to centralize power in his own hands. Mobutu Sese Seko of Zaire (now the Democratic Republic of the Congo) and Ferdinand Marcos of the Philippines were classic examples of this type of leader. Personalist regimes justify their rule by using the assumptions of modernizing authoritarianism, and occasionally the state does see some economic successes. Personalist regimes typically centralize power for the benefit of the leader, however, achieving very little in the way of real development.

one-party regime: A system of government in which a single party gains power, usually after independence in postcolonial states, and systematically eliminates all opposition in the name of development and national unity

military regime: System of government in which military officers control power

coup d'etat: Military takeover of a government

personalist regime: System of government in which a central leader comes to dominate a state, typically not only eliminating all opposition but also weakening the state's institutions to centralize power in his own hands

MINI CASE

Tanzania's One-Party Regime

From the 1960s until the 1980s, the African state of Tanzania was an interesting example of a modernizing authoritarian one-party regime. Julius Nyerere, the president of Tanzania from 1962 to 1985, has been called Africa's "philosopher-king," in part because he was far more self-conscious and explicit in justifying the regime he helped create than most heads of state. He argued that political parties in Western democracies are based primarily on social class divisions and that since Africa had few and minor class divisions, there was no need for opposing parties. He suggested that in Africa, "when a village of a hundred people have sat and talked together until they agreed where a well should be dug they have practised democracy" (1966). He thereby justified a one-party state. His party, the Tanzanian African National Union (TANU), overwhelmingly won the country's first election on the eve of independence, and it didn't take much effort to change the constitution to legally eliminate the opposition.

In addition to his vision of "African democracy," Nyerere also envisioned creating an "African socialism," dubbed *ujamaa* in Swahili. He argued that this would return the country to its precolonial origins but with distinctly modern additions. In line with this, the government took ownership of most major sectors of the economy, but the centerpiece of the effort was the creation of *ujamaa* villages. Nyerere argued that prior to colonial influence, Africans had lived and worked communally and they ought to return to that lifestyle, living together in villages or working on communal farms rather than spread out on their individual farms. This arrangement would also facilitate the provision of more modern social services such as schools, health clinics, and clean water. While Nyerere justified *ujamaa* as a return to precolonial "tradition," it was in fact an example of a modernizing authoritarian regime in action. It distorted precolonial traditions and postcolonial realities against the will of the people in the interests of "development." Nyerere's vision of precolonial Africa was historically inaccurate, and the rural majority had no interest in farming communally or moving into villages. The government first tried to cajole people to form the new villages and then tried incentives. When neither worked, Nyerere turned to force; the state moved millions into new villages and tried to force communal labor. The results were disastrous for agricultural production and the country's economy, though the government was able to improve health care and education, achieving the amazing feat of nearly universal literacy in one of the world's poorest countries.

TANU ruled a one-party regime for thirty years. Nyerere's commitment to village democracy ultimately proved limited; public debate became more and more circumscribed over time. His twin goals of African democracy and African socialism were contradictory. The bulk of the population didn't support Nyerere's vision of African socialism; had they been able to exercise full democratic rights, they would have voted against it. He claimed that both his goals came from African traditions, but when the populace did not accept his vision, he used the modern state to try to force it on them. When they tried to dissent, the ruling party reduced open debate. Throughout TANU's rule, the party did hold parliamentary elections once every five years, allowing two party-approved candidates to compete for each seat. The candidates could not, however, question the ruling party's overall policies. They could and did compete over the question of who would best represent the area, so the elections were fair, if not free.

By 1985, Nyerere realized that his vision had produced a bankrupt country and that the key economic policies would have to change. He resigned the presidency, only the third postcolonial African president ever to do so, rather than implement a reversal of his vision. In the 1990s and following the trend across the continent (see chapter 9), Nyerere argued in favor of opening the country to multiparty democracy, saying the time for one-party rule was over. The country did allow full legal opposition, starting with the election of 1995, but TANU (renamed CCM, Chama Cha Mapinduzi, or Party of the Revolution) continues to rule against only token opposition.

CASE SUMMARY

Nyerere ultimately created a modernizing authoritarian state, restricting dissent and political opposition in the interests of achieving a specific vision of "development." He justified this in creative ways, tying his regime to a vision of precolonial Africa. That vision, however, was historically inaccurate and ignored the profound transformation colonial rule had brought about. Implementing his vision of "African socialism" to develop the country ultimately required eliminating most individual rights and forcing millions to move into "traditional" villages. Ironically, given Nyerere's appeal to tradition, modernizing authoritarian assumptions triumphed over African democracy and traditions.

Modernizing authoritarian regimes arose primarily in postcolonial states, many of which are relatively weak states with weak formal institutions. Informal institutions are therefore often quite important to understanding how these regimes function. Power in weak states becomes quite personalized, and the rule of law is inconsistent at best. These traits can characterize any of the forms of modernizing authoritarian regimes noted above, though they are most likely in personalist regimes. Military and one-party regimes vary more in their level of formal institutionalization. They too can have very weak institutions in which the personal authority of key leaders matters more than the formal organization of power under the party or military as an institution.

Examining some of the weakest states, comparativists studying Africa have suggested that many regimes there are imbued with **neopatrimonial authority**. German sociologist Max Weber (1925/1978) defined "patrimonial" societies as those in which rule is based on reciprocal personal ties and favors, not bureaucratic institutions or formal laws. Many African regimes combine the trappings of modern, bureaucratic states with underlying informal patterns of patrimonial authority that work behind the scenes to determine real power; hence, the term *neopatrimonial*. Constitutions, laws, courts, and bureaucracies all exist, but power really derives mainly from personal loyalty, personal favors, and patronage. Patron-client relations are central in these regimes; gaining state employment, power, and resources requires knowing the right people. Rulers maintain their power by distributing patronage to their followers, who are personally loyal to the rulers. Politics becomes a competition among key patrons for access to the state's resources so that they may distribute those resources to their supporters. Neopatrimonial authority in Africa and elsewhere can exist within military, one-party, or personalist regimes. Indeed, many scholars argue that new democracies in Africa, including our case study of Nigeria, retain many elements of neopatrimonial rule; they may now have the formal institutions of electoral democracy, but power remains based primarily on personal access to the state (now via elections) and distribution of its resources as patronage.

The modernizing authoritarian regime type is different from the other regime types in that both its forms and the extent to which a particular government consciously elaborates the ideology can vary significantly. These regimes do share a

neopatrimonial authority: Power based on a combination of the trappings of modern, bureaucratic states with underlying informal institutions of clientelism that work behind the scenes; most common in Africa

common set of assumptions, at least some of which they use to legitimize their rule. They all make a central claim that democracy, citizens' rights, and civil society must be curtailed to provide development because development requires national unity and democracy would threaten that unity. While their formal institutions are derived from the precepts of modernizing authoritarianism, in many cases informal institutions are at least as important. While many of these regimes have given way to some type of democracy (more or less—see chapter 9) in recent years, their institutional legacy remains strong, and certainly some modernizing authoritarian regimes continue to exist. Our case studies present two military modernizing authoritarian regimes: Brazil, in which formal institutions were relatively strong and the regime really did develop the country significantly, and Nigeria, a military regime that made similar claims to legitimacy but achieved very little in a society characterized by neopatrimonial authority.

CASE STUDY

Brazil: The Bureaucratic Authoritarian State, 1964–1985

- Modernizing, middle-class coup in the face of a "radical" threat
- Bureaucratic-authoritarian state that is a new version of modernizing authoritarian rule
- Ideology: Modernization and anticommunism
- State-led industrialization
- Repressive, but not as severe as many in Latin America at the time

Brazil's military regime was less violent than its infamous neighbors in Chile and Argentina of the same period, but violence was certainly used to repress dissent, and student and worker protests were often targets. In 1968, cavalry charged students gathered to protest the killing of a student by police in Rio de Janeiro.

Credit: AP Photo

Brazil emerged from World War II as a semi-industrialized economy. It had its own version of a quasi-fascist regime, the *Estado Novo* (New State), under Getúlio Vargas in the 1930s and through the war. When fascism became disgraced after the war's end, Brazil returned to being a democracy, but a very unstable one. After the abrupt resignation of President Jânio Quadros, who had been elected in 1960, Vice President João Goulart stepped up to the presidency. Seen by laborers, peasants, and other members of the working poor as sympathetic to their cause, Goulart and his new position of influence emboldened these groups to organize increasing numbers of street protests to claim what they saw as their fair share of the fruits of development. These in turn led to rising concern from business owners, landowners, and other conservatives, who organized their own counterdemonstrations. It was not long before the Brazilian military, with quiet support from the United States, decided that the instability threatened the country's development. Military officials overthrew Goulart in a coup d'etat in 1964.

The Brazilian military came to power at the height of the Cold War, just five years after Fidel Castro had led a communist revolution in Cuba. This meant that anticommunism was an important addition to the common justifications of modernizing authoritarian regimes. Brazilian officials created what Argentine political scientist Guillermo O'Donnell (1979) called a **bureaucratic-authoritarian regime**, a specific version of the modernizing authoritarian regime type. O'Donnell argued that the military came to power to further the economic development model because the continued profitability of Brazil's growing industries was being threatened by workers' demands for a greater share of the rewards. The military regime suppressed independent unions and returned the country to the corporatist model that had been in place during the earlier quasi-fascist regime. It then proceeded to expand industrialization by very consciously making significant government investments in new industries, particularly in heavy industry such as auto manufacturing and airplanes, and industries related to the military. The regime very explicitly claimed legitimacy on the basis of technocratic expertise and anticommunism and brought many talented economists into the government to develop the new economic plan. The result came to be known as the "Brazilian Miracle," a period of particularly rapid economic growth that was at its zenith from 1967 to 1973. Despite this growth, however, much of the population remained mired in poverty.

The Brazilian military government certainly considered repressing its opponents necessary to implement its economic model, though it was less repressive than many Latin American military governments of the time. It allowed elections for a national congress but controlled that body by allowing only two legal parties: one that supported the government and one that was a legal opposition. The opposition, however, was limited in what it was allowed to say, the congress itself had quite limited powers, and the military resorted to electoral tampering to maintain government party control. Ultimate decision making remained with the top military leaders.

By the late 1970s, world oil shocks had contributed to an economic slowdown across the country. Independent unions once again formed, this time in open violation of the law. Strikes became more common and had greater impact than before, given the rapid industrialization of the past two decades; there were now more industrial workers, and their industries were more important to the economy. Trade unions and political activists in the Catholic Church became more active in civil society, playing a key role in starting a movement for democracy that eventually brought Brazil's modernizing authoritarian regime to an end in 1985, when the first civilian president since 1964 took office.

> **CASE SUMMARY**
>
> Brazil's bureaucratic-authoritarian regime was one of the more conscious and committed modernizing authoritarian regimes and emerged in one of the stronger postcolonial states. It elaborated a clear ideological justification for what it did, focusing on the need to further economic development and fight communism. The military leaders saw themselves as a technocratic elite, and they hired civilian technocrats to augment their policy expertise. The elite believed democracy had to be suppressed because it would, at best, slow development and, at worst, lead to a communist takeover. The regime produced a period of rapid economic growth, but as that growth slowed in the late 1970s, regime legitimacy plummeted. The regime was ultimately forced to allow a return to democracy, a process we examine in detail in chapter 9.

bureaucratic-authoritarian regime: A regime characterized by institutionalized rule under a military government with a primary goal of economic development; coined by Guillermo O'Donnell to describe Latin American military regimes in the 1970s

CASE STUDY

Nigeria: Neopatrimonial Military Rule, 1966–1979 and 1983–1999

- Multiple coups justified by claims to restart development and restore democracy
- Weak state and personalist interests in military
- Growing repression and corruption over time
- Neopatrimonial authority throughout

Sani Abacha presided over a dark period (1993–1998) during which his personal interests trumped his stated ideological goals of modernization and development. His unexpected death released Nigeria from military rule and permitted a transition to democracy. This 1998 photo was taken just before rumors about his ill health began circulating through the capital of Abuja.

Credit: Reuters

The Brazilian modernizing authoritarian regime took its ideology and its economic model quite seriously and had formal institutions strong enough to effect significant economic development. Nigeria, on the other hand, suffered through several military regimes whose claims to legitimacy followed the modernizing authoritarian model but who did not always govern in accordance with their rationales. While claiming to use the nation's growing oil wealth to invest in development, military leaders more frequently amassed their own fortunes and spread the state's resources among their favored supporters. Extensive neopatrimonialism has characterized Nigeria through all its regime changes; civilian and military leaders alike use the state to distribute resources to their clients rather than invest in economic development, despite the presence of significant oil reserves. Indeed, oil wealth has allowed for greater patronage and corruption.

Nigeria's first electoral democracy survived six tumultuous years after independence. The country was deeply divided along regional and, therefore, ethnic and religious lines from the outset. The democratic constitution, negotiated with the departing British colonizers, recognized this division by creating three separate regions with significant autonomy from the central government. Corruption among those in power and mutual suspicion among the political leaders of each region produced an increasingly chaotic and, at election time, violent democracy. The northern region controlled the most power in the central government because it was the most populous, a situation that created resentment in the other regions. By 1965, this numerical superiority combined with fraudulent elections to produce a central government that was overwhelmingly controlled by northern officials. This resulted in widespread violence, especially in the western region.

The first of six successful military coups took place in January 1966. A group of mid-level military officers, ethnically Igbo and from the eastern region, attempted to take power; General Johnson Aguiyi-Ironsi, also an Igbo but not part of the rebellion, convinced the democratic government to give him full power. Each of the military governments in Nigeria, starting with Ironsi's, took power claiming that its primary aims were to restore order, end violence and corruption to restart development, and then return the country to a more stable and peaceful democratic rule. The previous civilian government was portrayed as corrupt and incompetent, and the military was touted as a national institution that would serve only as a temporary, "corrective" regime.

General Ironsi saw himself as a nationalist and used the language of modernizing authoritarianism to justify his takeover, which was popular in the southern half of the country. To overcome the regional tensions that had plagued the country since independence, Ironsi eliminated the regional governments entirely and centralized power in the capital. While this may have been a sincere effort at national unity, political and military leaders in the north saw it as an attempt by the Igbo in the east to grab all power. Only six months after Ironsi took over, northern military leaders responded with a countercoup that overthrew Ironsi and killed him.

The military leadership in the east rejected the new government led by General Yakubu Gowon. This resulted in a three-year civil war (see chapter 2). Gowon eventually defeated the rebels and reunited the country, proclaiming a policy of forgiveness for those from the east and reintegration of all citizens into one nation to achieve unity once again. He also promised to restore democratic rule by 1976, after the reconciliation process was complete. His economic policy focused on investing government oil revenues in industry to begin the industrialization process, though corruption and inefficiency plagued the effort. Rapidly growing oil revenues led to parallel growth in corruption in Gowon's regime and a desire to cling to power to continue benefitting from high oil prices. Not long after Gowon announced in 1974 that the country was "not ready" for a return to civilian rule, a new military government overthrew him and proclaimed, once again, that it was dedicated to reducing corruption and restoring democracy.

This regime made some progress on reducing corruption, though not a lot, but it did carry out its pledge to allow democracy, with elections taking place for a new government in 1979.

Nigeria's new democracy, the Second Republic, was short-lived, lasting only four years. At that point, the military once again intervened. When General Muhammadu Buhari took power in 1983, he proclaimed that his regime was in favor of national unity, the elimination of corruption, and the restoration of economic growth ("development"). He launched a major and, at times, brutal campaign against corruption, and he shifted economic policy toward more market-oriented policies with less government involvement, as was demanded by international aid agencies in the 1980s (see chapter 5).

Buhari was overthrown in 1985 by another northerner, General Ibrahim Babangida, who ruled until 1993. Babangida accelerated the shift to a more market-oriented economic policy and promised yet again to restore democracy. After much delay and continuing corruption in the northern-dominated military government, elections were finally held in 1993, but Babangida, unhappy with the winner, annulled them. He instead created a short-lived transitional government, which was overthrown by General Sani Abacha. Abacha led Nigeria into its darkest period, with the most brutal suppression of dissent and the greatest corruption in its history. His regime quickly became a personalist one, and while he still proclaimed the goals of modernizing authoritarianism, in practice he ruled in his personal interests with no coherent development policy in place. His death in 1998 finally allowed a transition to democracy through the Third Republic, which remains in power.

Prior to Abacha, Nigeria's military governments, while certainly corrupt and authoritarian, ruled less harshly than many military regimes. At times, they seemed to take the mandate of modernizing authoritarianism seriously, attempting to unify the country and pursue some sort of development policy.

They all banned political parties and other associations, but prior to Abacha they all allowed a relatively free press to continue to criticize their actions, and some allowed elements of civil society to operate with some autonomy. All relied on the continuing work of the country's civil servants, meaning the government's bureaucrats. Thus, the bureaucratic institutions of the state continued to function, though weakened by growing corruption, under both military and civilian regimes. Under Abacha, when corruption weakened state institutions profoundly, the bureaucracy continued to exist but was so riddled with corruption that it could barely function.

CASE SUMMARY

Nigeria's many military governments ruled over a civilian state. All proclaimed to be working for national unity and development; all argued that after a brief and necessary authoritarian period, in which the country would be put back on the "right track" toward development, democracy would be restored. All, however, ruled over a neopatrimonial system that slowly but systematically undermined the formal institutions of the state and produced virtually no long-term economic growth, making the military's modernizing authoritarian claims of aiding the nation's development sound ever more hollow.

Semi-Authoritarianism

Since the end of the Cold War and the wave of democratizations that followed (see chapter 9), modernizing authoritarian regimes have become far less common. A related but distinct regime type, however, has become more common: **semi-authoritarian regimes**. Comparativist Marina Ottaway coined the term *semi-authoritarianism* to characterize regimes that "allow little real competition for power . . . [but] leave enough political space for political parties and organizations of civil society to form, for an independent press to function to some extent, and for some political debate to take place" (2003, 3). A closely related concept is Andreas Schedler's notion of electoral authoritarianism: "electoral authoritarian regimes play the game of multiparty elections. Yet they violate the liberal-democratic principles of freedom and fairness so profoundly and systematically as to render elections instruments of authoritarian rule rather than 'instruments of democracy'" (2006, 3). We define semi-authoritarian regimes as regimes in which opposition parties are allowed to exist and win some elected offices but the ruling party manipulates electoral rules and processes enough to ensure that it maintains virtually all effective power. Such regimes typically allow some limited freedom of expression as well, but they ensure that this also does not threaten the ruling party's grip on power.

Some scholars have referred to semi-authoritarian regimes as "hybrid regimes" because they seem to combine some democratic and some authoritarian elements. This is clear ideologically: they attempt to legitimize themselves using a combination of democratic and modernizing ideas. Unlike modernizing authoritarian regimes, they proclaim themselves democratic and point to democratic elements to justify this claim, in particular the presence of regularly scheduled elections. In truth, manipulation of the electoral process, limits on basic freedoms, and powerful informal institutions such as patronage limit real competition and ensure the ruling party or leader continues in power. At the same time, semi-authoritarian regimes invoke ideas from modernizing authoritarianism as well, justifying limits on democracy with claims that such limits are essential for national unity and development. This combination means that, as in modernizing authoritarian regimes, informal political institutions and practices are often as or more important in semi-authoritarian regimes than the formal institutions of rule.

semi-authoritarian regime: Type of hybrid regime in which formal opposition and some open political debate exist and elections are held; these processes are so flawed, however, that the regime cannot be considered truly democratic; also called competitive authoritarian and electoral authoritarian

While semi-authoritarian regimes have long existed, as our case study of Mexico demonstrates, they have become far more common in the last twenty years. Indeed, they are probably the most common regime type in the new millennium (Brownlee 2007). This is undoubtedly due in part to the growing international acceptance of liberal democratic norms: in the post–Cold War and postcommunist world, it is no longer legitimate to proclaim a regime as purely authoritarian (of whatever ideology). Growing acceptance and knowledge of democratic norms means that democratic countries are more likely to press regimes to become more democratic and that the regimes' own citizens are more likely to demand democratic changes. Semi-authoritarian institutions—such as minimally competitive elections and a national legislature in which opposition parties are allowed to hold a few seats and, within limits, criticize the ruling party—provide a veneer of democratic legitimacy to regimes that in an earlier era might have been modernizing authoritarian.

This is especially true in regimes that at least initially began some type of transition to democracy. Full reversion to modernizing authoritarianism is unacceptable to the citizenry and the international community, and even the beginning of a transition to democracy usually unleashes popular pressure that the regime can better manage by allowing some limited opposition to exist, rather than repressing it entirely. Our case study of Russia is an example of this path to semi-authoritarian rule (see chapter 9). Authoritarian regimes that successfully avoided any democratization pressure around the end of the Cold War, such as the enduring communist regimes in Cuba and North Korea or some of the monarchies in the Arabian Peninsula, have mostly avoided semi-authoritarian forms of rule, maintaining pure authoritarianism instead. Comparativist Jennifer Gandhi (2008) argued that authoritarian regimes allow the existence of legislatures and limited multiparty elections only when doing so benefits them by co-opting and pacifying oppositional elements within society, especially among competing elites.

Semi-authoritarian regimes inherently contain contradictions between their democratic and authoritarian elements. Even if it is generally true that semi-authoritarian rule prolongs the ruling party's hold on power, the presence of public opposition and elections, however limited, raises the possibility of leadership change. Much current scholarship focuses on when and how this might happen. In most cases, the ruler remains in power, but in about 10 percent of cases, he is forced from office; when the ruler is forced from office, this is done by peaceful—usually electoral—means three-quarters of the time (Schedler 2009, 299). Clearly, greater oppositional strength and organization and some sort of weakening of the existing regime will make such a change more likely. External pressures can also have an effect in this direction. Semi-authoritarian regimes, though, can be stable for a prolonged period; they are not just a regime type that is in transition from one thing to another, as our case study of Mexico demonstrates.

CASE STUDY

Mexico: Semi-Authoritarianism under the PRI

- Mexico: Semi-authoritarian under one party
- Party rule rather than personalist rule
- Complete presidential power for six years; regular elections and orderly succession within ruling party

- Control via labor support, clientelism, electoral fraud, and repression
- Transition to democracy amid growing opposition: 1988–2000

Mexico was home to one of the longest-lasting semi-authoritarian regimes anywhere; one party ruled for seventy-one years but never completely banned opposition. Between 1929 and 2000, Mexico's Institutional Revolution Party, or PRI (Partido Revolucionario Institucional), used control and support of labor, clientelism (the exchange of resources for political support), electoral fraud, and repression to keep key federal and state offices in the hands of a ruling elite. At the same time, the regime allowed and even encouraged the active participation of opposition parties, so long as they did not garner enough votes to pose a significant challenge to the PRI.

The PRI traces its origins to President Plutarco Elías Calles (1924–1928), who used the organization, then called the National Revolutionary Party (PNR), as a vehicle for placing his hand-picked successors in office starting in 1929. The party was a way for Calles to remain influential without running for office again, given the state's commitment to the Revolutionary slogan of "No Reelection." The importance of "No Reelection" largely accounts for the party-centric, rather than personalist, semi-authoritarianism of twentieth-century Mexico.

The PRI's main electoral constituency has been referred to as a three-legged stool comprising laborers, peasants, and bureaucrats, though ideologically the party has always been more like a big tent that includes liberals, radicals, and even conservatives. This broad base increased the PRI's competitive edge and allowed it to poach potential rivals from opposition parties. Pitched battles did take place internally, and many historic presidential administrations emerged as a result of one wing of the party winning over its competition. Such was the case with Lázaro Cárdenas (1934–1940), whose radical faction ended Calles's tenure as party leader and began an era of left-wing reform under a new

Lázaro Cárdenas (1934–1940) was the most important and famous Mexican president during the era of the PRI's semi-authoritarian state. He set the "populist" policy course for the party, helping it to create a sense of legitimacy based on its provision of patronage to core constituencies, especially unionized workers and peasants. His political and economic framework stayed in place, with minor changes, until the 1980s debt crisis forced the PRI to shift to a more open market economy. This was, perhaps, the beginning of the end of the PRI's political dominance.

Credit: Hulton Archive/Getty Images

name: the Party of the Mexican Revolution (PRM), which was renamed the PRI in 1946. For the rest of the PRI's history, power and the presidency shifted from radical to more conservative factions via elections every six years, but the party's control was never in doubt.

During the long period of one-party domination, the president remained the central and most powerful figure within both the republic and the party apparatus. The president appointed the official leader of the PRI's National Executive Committee (CEN), and he could handpick all governors and senators. Despite the precedent set by earlier presidents such as Calles and Cárdenas, who remained influential even after leaving office, the PRI managed a system in which a president would govern unencumbered for one term and then retire from public life altogether. This meant that at the end of every six-year presidential term (called the *sexenio*), a new leader, chosen by his predecessor, would step in and take over the reins of the country.

While this system of orderly succession did forestall the emergence of a personalist regime, it came at great cost: Mexican presidents were known to take advantage of their limited time in office and guaranteed safe retirement to engage in widespread graft, and they encouraged their close associates to do the same. For instance, the campaign committee of former president Carlos Salinas de Gortari (1988–1994) enriched itself following the privatization of a national airline, two banks, and the nation's main telephone provider. In addition, outgoing presidents often escalated government spending at the end of their term to facilitate the election of their successor, which resulted in predictable cycles of inflation at the start of each *sexenio* (see chapter 5).

Despite its many problems, the semi-authoritarian arrangement remained in place thanks in part to robust control of and support from labor, among other groups. Under Cárdenas, labor's relationship with the regime grew to new heights, with the formation of the Mexican Labor Confederation, or CTM (Confederación de Trabajadores de Mexico). Under this corporatist arrangement, the CTM became the overwhelmingly powerful labor union in Mexico and went so far as to organize militias capable of checking the military's power. This close relationship with the regime meant that the CTM, and a similar peasant union, mobilized support for the party in exchange for better working conditions and patronage.

Apart from managing corporatist networks, Mexico's regime reverted to clientelism, which at its most basic level took the form of vote buying. Most of the time, however, clientelist relationships were tied to supporting rural interests. Between the end of the Revolution and the start of World War II,

the state engaged in large-scale land reform. By the 1970s, clientelism was exercised through massive government spending on agricultural development projects By 1975, agriculture-related programs made up 20 percent of public spending. This helped guarantee a loyal rural constituency that to this day remains the electoral backbone of the PRI.

When corporatism and clientelism were not enough to ensure the outcome of a vote—especially in the face of the mobilization capabilities of conservative Catholic activists and leftist students in the universities—the ruling party resorted to electoral fraud. Favorite tactics included stuffing ballot boxes, moving polling locations at the last minute, having supporters vote multiple times, and, if necessary, altering the numbers once the votes had been tallied.

Always concerned about the veneer of democratic legitimacy, semi-authoritarian regimes such as Mexico's prefer to maintain control via clientelism and behind-the-scenes electoral fraud rather than outright violence. If necessary, though, the PRI was not above using force to guarantee its electoral success. The most infamous example of brute force came when the military opened fire on antigovernment student protesters on October 2, 1968—days before the start of the Mexico City Olympics. This became known as the Tlatelolco Massacre, named after the neighborhood in the capital where the killings took place. Aside from being remembered for the dead and injured—with disputed figures ranging from a few dozen to several hundred—Tlatelolco is remembered because the media initially failed to report on the events. When it did, it downplayed their gravity. Though the media was never fully censored in the way one would expect in a fully authoritarian system, self-censorship was commonplace in Mexico, with private media consistently avoiding politically dangerous stories. This stance was due largely to lucrative government advertising and, sometimes, direct bribes of journalists.

These strategies allowed the PRI to win 98 percent of all mayoral and congressional elections between 1946 and 1973. Yet in the late 1980s, opposition parties began to make inroads that could no longer be ignored. Part of this shift was probably due to urbanization and free-market reforms, which made traditional clientelism more difficult to maintain. One party that made inroads was the conservative Partido Acción Nacional (PAN), or National Action Party, which in 1989 became the first party to elect a non-PRI governor. In 1988, Cuauhtémoc Cárdenas (son of former PRI president Lázaro Cárdenas) was part of a left-wing faction that defected from the PRI to form a new party in response to the government's increasingly market-oriented economic policies. Cárdenas ran for president and garnered 30 percent of the vote to the PRI's Carlos Salinas de Gortari's 52 percent (compare this with the 1976 election, in which the PRI trounced the opposition with 98.7 percent). To this day, many believe that Cárdenas, who claimed victory but was denied the presidency, was the actual winner at the polls.

Given the tense political climate that emerged following the closely contested and controversial election, the ruling party was forced to introduce concrete steps toward providing electoral fairness and broader representation in government. It introduced an electoral system for the senate in which each state would hold three seats: two for the winning party and one for second place. This ensured that no fewer than 30 percent of the votes went to the opposition. In the lower house of congress, no party would be allowed to hold more than 315 out of the 500 seats. Also, independent election monitors were added to polling sites, and ballots were numbered to ensure proper counting.

The first free election took place in 1994, and a record 78 percent of eligible voters turned out. During this period of transition to democracy, voters opted for continuity and bureaucratic experience, and they gave the election to Ernesto Zedillo of the PRI. In second place came the PAN, and in last place was Cárdenas and his new Party of the Democratic Revolution, or PRD (Partido de la Revolución Democrática). Although the PRI kept the presidency, the days of one-party rule were numbered. A new, democratic, three-party system emerged in the country, and the PRI would have to compete alongside the others. In 2000, the election of the PAN's Vicente Fox finally broke the PRI's seventy-one year monopoly on the presidency, ushering in a new era in Mexican politics. We examine this transition to democracy in Mexico in detail in chapter 9.

CASE SUMMARY

Though it existed long before the term was coined, the PRI created a classic semi-authoritarian regime. The party's dominance was unquestioned for sixty years. Throughout, however, it held elections for the presidency and the lower house of the legislature that allowed internal elite competition and rotation of power across factions within the party. Opposition parties won a handful of seats but never enough to threaten the regime. This system provided a veneer of democratic legitimacy, and the PRI pursued actual policies that kept many workers and peasants loyal to it for decades. At least implicit, however, was the claim that by maintaining power, the PRI was able to modernize the country; it did in fact achieve significant economic development (see chapter 5). This combination of claims to democratic and modernizing legitimacy under what was really authoritarian rule is the hallmark of semi-authoritarian regimes. Our case study of Russia in chapter 9 will provide a contemporary version of this regime type.

Theocracy

theocracy: Rule by religious authorities

Theocracy is rule by religious authorities. They rule on behalf of God and following His dictates. It's very unlikely that you would have found theocracy included in a textbook on comparative politics thirty years ago, except perhaps as historical background. If it were mentioned at all, it would have been in connection with the "divine right of kings" of medieval and early modern Europe under which the monarchy was thought to represent God on earth, sanctioned as such by the universal Catholic Church. Today, the prime example of theocracy is not Christian but Muslim. Like other kinds of regimes, the Muslim theocracy in Iran is based on a well-elaborated political ideology, but in practice it does not or cannot always adhere perfectly to that ideology. Iran currently is the world's only theocracy, but political movements aimed at achieving similar regimes elsewhere exist throughout the Muslim world. We focus on Islamic theocracy as an ideology and regime type not because it is the only conceivable kind of theocracy but because it is the only contemporary example of a theocratic regime and because theocratic political ideology is an important challenger to liberal democracy today.

The political ideology that has inspired such fear in much of the West and such admiration in some of the Muslim world is typically known as "Islamic fundamentalism," a name that implies a set of ideas that is often quite different from what its adherents actually believe. The word *fundamentalist* implies "traditional" to many people, but nothing could be farther from the truth in this case. "Traditional" Islamic beliefs, as developed over the centuries, hold that religious law ought to be the basis for government, but in practice these precepts were compromised significantly by local cultural traditions and rulers. In many countries in the twentieth century, traditional Muslim religious authorities compromised with modernity and the increasing secularization of the state by, among other things, ignoring the secular and political world as much as possible, withdrawing from politics nearly completely, and allowing effectively secular, modernizing authoritarian regimes to emerge.

Islamism: The belief that Islamic law, as revealed by God to the Prophet Mohammed, can and should provide the basis for government in Muslim communities with little equivocation or compromise

Given this reality, most scholars prefer the term **Islamism** instead of *Islamic fundamentalism*. While it has many variations, Islamism is generally defined as a belief that Islamic law, as revealed by God to the Prophet Mohammed, can and should provide the basis for government in Muslim communities with little equivocation or compromise with more contemporary beliefs. Islamism arose in the nineteenth and twentieth centuries with the goal of "purifying" Muslim society of the creeping influences of the West and secularism that traditional Muslim religious leaders had often been willing to accept. In line with this, most Islamists explicitly reject the Muslim concept of *taqlid,* the acceptance of all past legal and moral edicts of the traditional clergy, and instead embrace *ijtihad,* the belief that Muslims should read and interpret the original Islamic texts for themselves. They base their ideology on their interpretation of the Quran and Sunnah, the two holiest books of Islam, and take as their primary model the original Muslim society and state created by Mohammed. Islamists vary in the degree to which they are willing to compromise with aspects of the contemporary world. Not all, for instance, support stoning as punishment for adultery, but most adhere to a fairly strict belief in Muslim law, **Sharia,** as written in the Quran and Sunnah. Past compromises by traditional clergy are therefore unacceptable.

Sharia: Muslim law

Islamists believe that sovereignty rests with God, so they ultimately reject democracy and its idea of popular sovereignty. Some, however, such as the early Palestinian leader Taqi al-Din al-Nabhani (1905–1978), reserve a place for *shura,* which means "consultation with the people." He believed the Muslim state should be led by a caliph, a supreme religious and political leader, but that the caliph should be acceptable to the population as a whole and be advised by an elected council. Some religious authorities have since used this concept to argue in favor of allowing an ideologically limited civil society, one that stays within the bounds of Islamic practices, ideas, and law. During its less repressive phases, our case study of Iran has been an example of this in practice, though the clerical leadership regularly represses civil society when it makes what the clergy see as unacceptable demands.

Some Islamists, such as the Algerian Islamic Front (FIS), are willing to go a step further and participate in democracy as a means of gaining power. In December 1991, the party won the first round of Algeria's first democratic elections, only to see the second round cancelled and the military take control of the government and subsequently ban the party. Some FIS followers believed that in a true Islamic state, democracy would be eliminated, but they were willing to participate in democratic politics until they were able to create their Islamist regime. Other Islamists, such as Sayyid Qutb, a key early leader of the Egyptian Muslim Brotherhood, reject the notion of democracy altogether, maintaining that any compromise with democracy violates God's sovereignty. More recently, however, the Muslim Brotherhood has taken a path similar to that of the FIS, unofficially participating in Egypt's often fraudulent elections and winning a significant number of legislative seats in the 2005 election.

French political scientist Olivier Roy (2004) and other scholars of Islam have argued that when Islamists gain power, they face a contradiction between their abstract goals and the actual practice of governing. Islam certainly has a long tradition of providing legal structure for many, but by no means all, areas of life. If Islamists gain power, as they have in Iran, they must confront the complexities and political pressures of governing modern states. This requires them to compromise their theologically driven blueprint to govern effectively. The alternative, Roy argued, is a regime like Afghanistan's Taliban government. Roy called the Taliban a **neofundamentalist** group, which he distinguished from an Islamist group. It had no particular plan for how to govern and, in fact, cared little about governing. Followers virtually ignored the state, and many state functions nearly ceased operations while the group ruled in Afghanistan. For example, Afghanistan's foreign policy was essentially run by and through the Pakistani government while the Taliban was in power. The Taliban instead focused only on implementing an extremely rigid vision of Sharia at the local level that concerned itself with how people lived their daily lives. Rule was implemented based purely on theological principles, but this could not really be called *governing* in the modern sense of the word.

As the electoral participation of some groups demonstrates, while all Islamists place great significance on jihad, not all advocate violence. **Jihad** means "struggle," and, although it is not one of the "five pillars" of the faith, it is an important concept in Islam. The Quran identifies three kinds of jihad. The first and most important is the individual's internal struggle to renounce evil and live faithfully by following proper religious practices. The second is the struggle of the individual to right evils and injustice within the *umma*, the Muslim community as a whole. The third and least important is protection, armed and violent if necessary, of the *umma*. The most radical Islamists and neofundamentalists, whom Roy terms *jihadists,* argue that the *umma* is under attack externally from the West and internally via secularization and Westernization. For groups like al-Qaida, this view justifies violent opposition to these forces, both outside and within the *umma*. Furthermore, following *ijtihad,* these individuals reject the traditional teaching that violent jihad should only be carried out on the orders of high religious authorities. They argue instead that individuals, and religiously untrained leaders like Osama bin Laden, can discern for

neofundamentalist: Term for Islamic movements that focus only on implementing an extremely rigid vision of Sharia at the local level that directs how people live their daily lives while ignoring the state; key example is the Taliban in Afghanistan

jihad: Derived from an Arabic word for "struggle" and an important concept in Islam; the Quran identifies three kinds of jihad

umma: The global Muslim community

themselves when and where violent jihad is not only a justifiable option but a moral necessity.

Although Iran's Muslim regime is a recent development and the sole contemporary version of theocracy today is Islamic, theocracy is perhaps the oldest form of government in existence. Like all theocrats, Islamists believe in a government established according to their understanding of God's teaching, giving sovereignty not to "we the people" but rather to God. Followers vary widely in the methods they use to achieve Islamist regimes and in the details of what those regimes would look like. Some include quasi-democratic elements, such as consultation with some sort of legislative body, and some are willing to try to gain power via electoral democracy, give limited rights to citizens, and allow some civil society. All, however, would give great power to religious authorities to interpret and implement God's sovereignty on earth. Critics reject this notion of sovereignty from God, and Marxists famously reject the concept of God altogether. Fascists might have some sympathy with the idea of a strong central ruler governing on behalf of all, but the goal for fascists would not be to follow God's will but to strengthen the nation. Islamist philosophers and ideologues have created many variants of Islamist regimes in the abstract, but only one has gained power and ruled for a sustained period: Iran's revolutionary Islamic government.

CASE STUDY

The Islamic Republic of Iran: Theocratic State, 1979–

- Shi'ite Islam
- Supreme Leader as key ruler
- Tension between theocratic and democratic elements
- Many factions
- Greater repression in recent years

Islam in Iran is unusual in that the vast majority of the country's population and major religious authorities are Shiites, not Sunnis. In the seventh century, Islam split over the succession to the Prophet Mohammed. Those who became Shiite believe the Prophet's son-in-law, Imam Ali, was rightful heir to the leadership of the *umma* and that descendants of Imam Ali remain the only rightful religious authorities. Major Shiite religious authorities are chosen from among his heirs. Sunnis, who constitute approximately 85 percent of the world's Muslims, believe that any religiously educated person of appropriate stature and training can become a major

A poster in Tehran depicting the founder of the Islamic Republic, Ayatollah Ruhollah Khomeini (on the right), and his handpicked successor, Ayatollah Ali Khamenei. They have been the sole "supreme leaders" of the Islamic Republic with the power to veto any law and appoint many key officials throughout the regime. The regime gives the supreme leader such power based on the claim that he is the chief representative of God's sovereignty.

Credit: © imagebroker/Alamy

leader of the *umma*, and they reject the claim that a particular bloodline should rule. Iran and Iraq are two of only four Muslim countries with Shiite majorities; Iran is nearly all Shiite. The Islamic Republic in Iran nonetheless exemplifies the ideology and contradictions of Islamist theocracy more broadly.

Prior to 1979, Iran had a modernizing authoritarian regime under the leadership of the Pahlavi dynasty; father and then son ruled the country from 1925 to 1979. In the 1960s and 1970s, Shah Reza Pahlavi attempted to "modernize" the country via close relations with the West, Westernization of Iranian culture, and industrialization. The dynasty, however, kept whatever benefits came out of this modernization for itself and its close supporters, and domestic opposition mounted. One of the country's major religious leaders, Ayatollah Ruhollah Khomeini, emerged as a major spokesperson and leader of this opposition. At first jailed for his actions and later forced to live in exile in neighboring Iraq, Khomeini was the symbol and by far the most popular leader of the revolution that swept the shah from power in 1978–1979. His Islamist ideals became the basis for the new government.

Khomeini's most original contribution to Islamist doctrine was the concept of the supreme leader. He argued that one leader with enough religious authority and popular support should be the ultimate guide of the Islamic state, with the power to veto any law he deemed as contrary to Sharia. Khomeini also believed, however, in consultation, or *shura*, and so was quite willing to allow the existence of an elected parliament, the Majlis, as long as its laws were subject to the approval of the supreme leader or other major clergy he might deputize to fulfill that function.

An Assembly of Experts wrote the new Iranian constitution, which was ratified by referendum in December 1979. The assembly had been elected, though virtually all politicians opposed to Khomeini had boycotted the election on the grounds that it was rigged. The new constitution established Iran as an Islamic Republic that specifically followed Shiite doctrine and declared God

as sovereign. The position of supreme leader was created, with Khomeini filling that role, and a Guardian Council of twelve clergy was formed. Six members of this council were appointed by the leader and six by the parliament, and the council had the task of examining and approving or vetoing every law the parliament passed. A directly elected president administered the government on a daily basis. Khomeini, in his earlier Islamist writings, had envisioned local Sharia courts as the only judicial system necessary, but upon taking power he quickly realized the benefit of preserving the shah's relatively modern and hierarchical judicial system. This system, however, would henceforth use Sharia as its sole source of law and would be headed at all major levels by clergy. Government ministers, those in charge of the various departments of the government, were appointed by the president but also monitored by clergy in each ministry.

The regime was clearly theocratic from its origin, since supreme religious authorities could ultimately make or unmake any governmental decision. Some democratic elements were allowed, however. Regular elections for president and parliament have been held on schedule since the implementation of the new constitution, a subject discussed in greater detail in chapter 8. Nonetheless, the Guardian Council can disapprove any candidate for office if he is deemed not adequately committed to the goals of the Islamic revolution, and the degree of openness of the elections has varied greatly over time. In the first parliamentary election in 1980, a large number of parties competed and entered parliament, and a "moderate" won the presidency. He claimed commitment to the revolution but also took a practical stance toward modifying Islam to meet the necessities of running a modern state. By 1983 Khomeini forced him and other moderates out of office and banned all but the Islamic Republican Party (IRP), the party supported by most major clergy. By 1986, even the IRP was banned; Khomeini argued that political parties were divisive and in the future all candidates for parliamentary elections would run as independents. Informally, he allowed factions to continue to exist, but the elimination of all parties kept opposition forces repressed in a way that appeared more legitimate.

As real political options narrowed and the power of the Majlis vis-à-vis the Guardian Council declined, elections excited less interest and voter turnout was lower. A decade later, in the late 1990s, elections again became more exciting and popular affairs after the clergy once again allowed a moderate reformer, Mohammad Khatami, to run for president. Following his election, however, the clergy proceeded to frustrate virtually every reform effort he undertook and made sure that a candidate more loyal to them, current president Mahmoud Ahmadinejad, won the election of 2005. Ahmadinejad's rule, which many see as signaling greater military influence over the regime because he and many of his supporters are members of the regime's most loyal militia (the Revolutionary Guard), has become increasingly repressive over time. He was reelected in what most observers believe to have been a fraudulent election in 2009, which was followed by massive street protests, several deaths, and thousands of arrests of regime opponents.

Despite some periods of greater openness, citizen ability to voice opinions and engage in political activity has been quite limited. When allowed, a very active press has emerged, as it did right after the revolution and again in the late 1990s. Whenever this press begins to question the goals of the revolution beyond certain limits, however, religious authorities close it down, and a period of repression sets in. Still, compared to the civil societies of much of the Middle East or that of the shah's regime, civil society and political debate have been relatively open in the Islamic Republic, at least prior to Ahmadinejad's presidency. Intellectual critics and university students have repeatedly spoken out, and they have repeatedly been repressed when they have spoken out too strongly. In 1999, some student leaders began to question a continued commitment to Islam as the key identity

of the state, arguing for democracy and Iranian nationalism instead. Their arrest and the closure of a reformist newspaper sparked demonstrations across Iran's universities in mid-1999, a brutal police response, and then violent student riots. Religious authorities successfully repressed the students but not without losing further legitimacy in the eyes of many. The harsh crackdown on the postelection protests in 2009 almost certainly hurt regime legitimacy even further. The Iranian theocracy limits civil society severely, especially when key religious authorities feel threatened with a potential loss of power. But the country has nonetheless seen growing pressure for change and a more active civil society than was present in many Middle Eastern countries, at least until the "Arab Spring" uprisings of 2011.

CASE SUMMARY

Ayatollah Khomeini helped create the first true theocracy in the modern world. It follows Shiite Islamist principles and includes some democratic elements justified via the concept of *shura*. How much power those democratic elements have had has varied over time. Khomeini's death allowed stronger reformist movements and politicians to emerge in the 1990s, ensconced in the democratic elements of the regime: the presidency and Majlis. Conservative clergy used the religious institutions that the revolution created to frustrate reform and preserve what they saw as the pure path of the Islamist regime. With the ascendancy of Ahmadinejad, religious authorities seem to have decided that they need to control the regime's democratic institutions as well, but pressure for change is clearly mounting. As socioeconomic changes continue and Iranians increasingly use the Internet and other means of communication to access the outside world, theocracy survives, but it seems to rely increasingly on military force to maintain control (see chapter 8). The democratic elements it has allowed to operate in partial form, however, continue to question it and threaten more fundamental change.

CONCLUSION

Who Rules?

All political ideologies involve the question of the proper relationship between individual citizens and the state. Most citizens of established democracies probably consider liberal democracy's insistence on limited state power and citizens' rights, especially the right to participate in politics through voting, as the presumptive norm. Liberal democracy, however, is an outlier in this regard. Communism, fascism, modernizing authoritarianism, semi-authoritarianism, and theocracy all tilt the balance in varying degrees in favor of the state. Each finds some grounds for arguing that government should not rest in the hands of citizens or elected representatives alone. Most ideologies offer some sort of rationale for giving a select group, whether it's the working class, the fascist state itself, or a technocratic or religious elite, more say and limiting the participation of others. In these ideologies, real citizenship is thus restricted to members of the key party, those loyal to the nation, those capable of helping the country achieve development, or those who are part of the faithful. In all these cases, real power is restricted primarily to a small group of elites, whose position of exceptional influence is ideologically justified based on who they are or what they believe. This was true for much of liberalism's history as well, of course, as male property owners were the sole citizens. Despite this history, all long-standing liberal regimes have been democratized over the last century as the formal rights of citizenship have expanded to include all adults.

The question of who rules, though, may be less clear than formal ideological differences suggest. Pluralist theorists have argued that in almost all regimes, even some of the most totalitarian, factions exist. Elites clearly rule, but they do not rule in a fully united manner. They are divided into factions that vie for power, resources, and influence, often behind the facade of a united and repressive regime. And critics of liberal democracy argue that elites often control real power, despite widespread formal rights. Liberal equality of citizenship may exist legally, but it never exists in reality, even where fairly extensive social rights are practiced. In this way, the sharp distinctions between liberalism and its ideological alternatives in terms of who rules may be less distinct in practice than they are in theory.

What Explains Political Behavior?

Ideology offers what regimes hope is a compelling justification for their actions, but regimes rarely abide strictly by their ideologies. Democracies vary in their institutional structures, for instance, and even the most established ones have only relatively recently granted full citizenship rights, including the right to participate, to all adult citizens regardless of gender or race. Similarly, communist regimes modified Marx's ideal of rule by the proletariat in favor of Lenin's concept of rule by the vanguard party. Many modernizing authoritarian regimes have failed to meet their own goals of technocratic government and instead have lapsed into neopatrimonial or other forms of corrupt rule. Sometimes these lapses are based on culture and history. Often, informal institutions and norms tied to culture and history explain more about how a regime actually works than the official ideology does, especially in weak states. In other instances, practical circumstances make leaders choose paths that diverge from their own stated ideology, as when Lenin espoused the New Economic Policy. Similarly, after Mao Zedong's death, reformers in the Chinese Communist Party were able to push for gradual economic liberalization, seeing this as a necessary remedy to the country's frequent agricultural crises and low level of industrialization. The government remains officially communist, but the regime now diverges in many ways from that ideology. Ideology is important to understanding regimes' claims to legitimacy, but understanding how they actually govern requires far more, a subject we investigate further in Part II of this book.

Where and Why?

Comparativists ask why certain ideologies and regime types seem to cluster in certain regions. Most long-established democracies are in Europe and North America, whereas modernizing authoritarian regimes have tended to dominate postcolonial Africa and parts of Asia. Latin America has seen regular regional shifts between predominantly democratic and authoritarian, mostly military, regimes. Some analysts find an explanation in culture, arguing, for instance, that democratic ideas first emerged in the United Kingdom and Europe and so found a more ready home there, or that Islam provides a more ready cultural base for theocracy.

If we look closely, however, we must conclude that other factors are certainly at work as well. After all, fascism as well as democracy had its primary home in Europe, India is one of the world's oldest democracies, and Christianity generated theocracies of a sort in an earlier period in Europe. Moreover, regimes change all over the world: authoritarian and communist regimes have undergone democratization, and Germany, as well as many Latin American cases, reminds us that democracies can collapse into nondemocratic regimes. Our cases above suggest other factors that may be at work. For example, the existence and emergence of an independent and relatively powerful civil society seems to be important to establishing and maintaining democracy. Postcolonial states seem particularly plagued by social and economic problems that favor modernizing authoritarianism. Particular challenges, such as lagging economic development and economic and security crises, may also favor nondemocratic ideologies and regimes that proclaim a particular ability to solve these problems. Much recent scholarship has focused on structural factors that may explain the process by which democracy emerges in certain places and not in others, a theme we explore further in chapter 9.

Applying Theory to the Study of Regimes and Citizens

Understanding regime differences must begin with ideology. On the surface, ideology would seem to be the chief explanation of how regimes function and how they differ from each other, and certainly the ideological bases of regimes' claims to legitimacy are important. Other theories, however, may apply as well. Many analysts over the years have argued that both the regimes and ideologies that emerge in particular places do so because of the broader political cultures of those places. For instance, the first communist dictatorship emerged in Russia in part because of the long-standing authoritarian elements in Russian political culture, bred under centuries of tsarist rule. Marxists, of course, use their structural theory to explain the rise of particular regimes: liberal democracy emerges to serve the interests of the bourgeoisie and foster capitalism; modernizing authoritarian regimes further neocolonialism and the interests of both the budding capitalist elites in postcolonial societies and of the global corporations that invest in places like Brazil.

Institutionalists, on the other hand, would argue that what matters most is not just regimes' ideological blueprints but how well developed and supported the actual formal institutions are and, therefore, how important informal institutions and practices are as well. Understanding how different regime types arise and function is one of the biggest tasks in comparative politics, one for which comparativists have employed virtually all major theoretical approaches.

KEY CONCEPTS

Bolshevik (p. 113)
bureaucratic-authoritarian regime (p. 124)
citizen (p. 97)
civil rights (p. 97)
corporatism (p. 115)
coup d'etat (p. 120)
democratic centralism (p. 113)
dictatorship of the proletariat (p. 111)
electoral democracy (p. 107)
free wage labor (p. 111)
historical materialism (p. 110)
Islamism (p. 132)
jihad (p. 133)

liberal democracy (p. 107)
military regime (p. 120)
mode of production (p. 111)
modernization theory (p. 119)
neofascist (p. 118)
neofundamentalist (p. 133)
neopatrimonial authority (p. 122)
one-party regime (p. 120)
parliamentary sovereignty (p. 109)
participatory democracy (p. 107)
personalist regime (p. 120)
politburo (p. 113)

political rights (p. 98)
regime (p. 95)
semi-authoritarian regime (p. 127)
Sharia (p. 132)
social contract theory (p. 104)
social democracy (p. 107)
social revolution (p. 111)
social rights (p. 98)
soviets (p. 113)
technocratic legitimacy (p. 119)
theocracy (p. 132)
totalitarian regime (p. 114)
umma (p. 133)
vanguard party (p. 113)

WORKS CITED

Acemoglu, Daron, and James A. Robinson. 2006. *Economic Origins of Dictatorship and Democracy.* Cambridge, UK: Cambridge University Press.

Brownlee, Jason. 2007. *Authoritarianism in an Age of Democratization.* Cambridge, UK: Cambridge University Press.

Gandhi, Jennifer. 2008. *Political Institutions under Dictatorship.* Cambridge, UK: Cambridge University Press.

Keck, Margaret E., and Kathryn Sikkink. 1998. *Activists Beyond Borders: Advocacy Networks in International Politics.* Ithaca, NY: Cornell University Press.

Lister, Michael, and Emily Pia. 2008. *Citizenship in Contemporary Europe.* Edinburgh, UK: Edinburgh University Press.

Marshall, T. H. 1963. *Class, Citizenship, and Social Development: Essays.* Chicago: University of Chicago Press.

Marx, Karl, and Friedrich Engels. 1888. *The Communist Manifesto.* Trans. by Samuel Moore with Friedrich Engels. London: William Reeves Bookseller. (Originally as *Manifest der Kommunistischen Partei* in London in 1848.)

Moore, Barrington, Jr. 1966. *Social Origins of Dictatorship and Democracy: Lord and Peasant in the Making of the Modern World.* Boston: Beacon Press.

Mussolini, Benito. 1968. *Fascism: Doctrine and Institutions.* New York: Howard Fertig. (Originally delivered as address to National Cooperative Council, Italy, in 1933.)

Nyerere, Julius K. 1966. *Freedom and Unity: Uhuru Na Umoja; A Selection from Writings and Speeches, 1952–65.* London: Oxford University Press.

O'Donnell, Guillermo A. 1979. *Modernization and Bureaucratic-Authoritarianism: Studies in South American Politics.* Text ed. Berkeley: Institute of International Studies, University of California.

Ottaway, Marina. 2003. *Democracy Challenged: The Rise of Semi-Authoritarianism.* Washington, DC: Carnegie Endowment for International Peace.

Polity IV Project. 2010. "Political Regime Characteristics and Transitions, 1800–2009." http://www.systemicpeace.org/polity/polity4.htm.

Rostow, W. W. 1960. *The Stages of Economic Growth: A Non-Communist Manifesto.* Cambridge, UK: Cambridge University Press.

Roy, Olivier. 2004. *Globalized Islam: The Search for a New Ummah.* CERI Series in Comparative Politics and International Studies. New York: Columbia University Press.

Schedler, Andreas, ed. 2006. *Electoral Authoritarianism: The Dynamics of Unfree Competition.* Boulder, CO: Lynne Rienner.

———. 2009. "The Contingent Power of Authoritarian Elections." In *Democratization by Elections: A New Mode of Transition,* edited by Staffan I. Lindberg, 291–313. Baltimore, MD: Johns Hopkins University Press.

Tarrow, Sidney G. 1998. *Power in Movement: Social Movements and Contentious Politics.* New York: Cambridge University Press.

Weber, Max. 1978. *Economy and Society.* Edited by Guenther Ross and Claus Wittich. Berkeley: University of California Press. (Originally published as *Wirtschaft und Gesellschaft* in Germany in 1925.)

RESOURCES FOR FURTHER STUDY

Dahl, Robert A. 1971. *Polyarchy: Participation and Opposition.* New Haven, CT: Yale University Press.

Esposito, John L. 1997. *Political Islam: Revolution, Radicalism, or Reform?* Boulder, CO: Lynne Rienner.

Held, David. 1996. *Models of Democracy.* 2nd ed. Stanford, CA: Stanford University Press.

Husain, Mir Zohair. 2003. *Global Islamic Politics.* 2nd ed. New York: Longman.

Marx, Karl, and Friedrich Engels. 1978. *The Marx-Engels Reader.* Edited by Robert C. Tucker. 2nd ed. New York: Norton.

McCann, James A., and Jorge I. Domínguez. 1998. "Mexicans React to Electoral Fraud and Political Corruption: An Assessment of Public Opinion and Voting Behavior." *Electoral Studies* 17 (4): 483–503. doi:10.1016/S0261-3794(98)00026-2.

Mill, John Stuart. 1870. *The Subjection of Women.* New York: D. Appleton.

Pitcher, Anne, Mary H. Moran, and Michael Johnston. 2009. "Rethinking Patrimonialism and Neopatrimonialism in Africa." *African Studies Review* 52 (1): 125–56. doi:10.1353/arw.0.0163.

Sargent, Lyman Tower. 1987. *Contemporary Political Ideologies: A Comparative Analysis.* 7th ed. Chicago: Dorsey Press.

Sherman, John W. 2000. "The Mexican 'Miracle' and Its Collapse." In *The Oxford History of Mexico,* edited by Michael C. Meyer and William H. Beezley, 537–68. Oxford, UK: Oxford University Press.

Suchlicki, Jaime. 2008. *Mexico: From Montezuma to the Rise of the PAN.* 3rd ed. Washington, DC: Potomac Books.

WEB RESOURCES

CIRI Human Rights Data Project (http://ciri
.binghamton.edu/index.asp)

Citizenship, Involvement, Democracy Survey
(http://www.uscidsurvey.org)

DataGov, Governance Indicators Database
(www.iadb.org/datagob)

Freedom in the World Survey, Freedom House
(http://www.freedomhouse.org/template.cfm?
page=505)

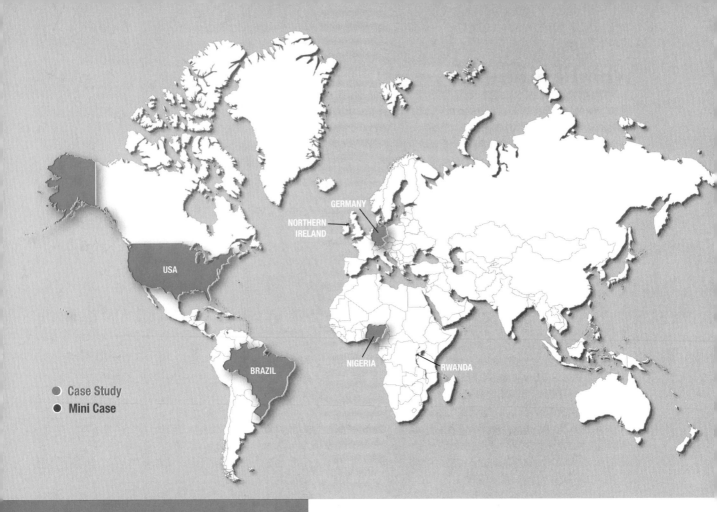

- ● Case Study
- ● Mini Case

Who Rules?

- How does the social construction of identity groups influence who has power in a state?
- How do ethnic, religious, and racial identities affect the type of representation or access to power different groups have?

What Explains Political Behavior?

- How and why do identity groups form and become politically salient?

Where and Why?

- Why does ethnic, religious, or racial diversity lead to violent conflict in some places but not in others?
- What lessons can be learned that might help prevent identity-based conflict in the future?

4
STATES AND IDENTITY

The great political battle of the second half of the twentieth century was
between liberalism and communism, but a dark-horse contender won:
nationalism. Nationalist, ethnic, and religious movements seemed to be the
main beneficiaries of the fall of communism, and they emerged as the greatest challenges to democracy. Since the end of the Cold War, an internationalist Islamist
movement has gained strength in many countries, a number of countries in the
former Soviet sphere have been wracked by ethnically based political battles, and
full-scale genocide has occurred in Bosnia and Rwanda while widespread ethnic
cleansing took place in the Democratic Republic of the Congo and Sudan. From
the battles to create new governments in Iraq and Afghanistan, to the increasingly
tense relations between China and Japan, to secessionist struggles in Chechnya and
ethnic conflict in Kyrgyzstan, "identity politics" have come to the fore.

The political impact of identity is a long-standing concern of comparative politics. Comparativists want to know what explains the current global surge of conflictual political behavior based on nationalist, ethnic, and religious identity. We also
ask how race, ethnicity, and religion influence groups' access to power and how
groups can share power; in other words, how does identity influence "who rules"?
We debate a key "what explains political behavior" question as well: why do these
identities emerge and become politically salient? Finally, we ask the "where and
why" question of why ethnic, religious, or racial fragmentation leads to violence in
some places but not in others.

This chapter examines the most politically important categories of identity
in the modern world—nation, ethnicity, race, and religion. We look at the conceptual debate over the origins of identity groups, the similarities and differences
across the different categories of identity, the political impact of these similarities
and differences, and how these similarities and differences can be the basis of
bloody political battles. The Country and Concept table on pages 144–145 portrays the linguistic, ethnic, racial, and religious diversity in our case study countries as well as the major conflicts that have arisen from that diversity. Our case
studies run the gamut from one of the most ethnically homogeneous societies
in the world, Japan, to two of the most diverse, India and Nigeria. Some have
seen frequent identity-based violent conflicts, while others have had none. What
accounts for these differences?

COUNTRY AND CONCEPT

Ethnicity, Race, and Religion

Country	Major language group	Largest ethnic/racial group, % of population
Brazil	1 major (Portuguese)	White, 53.7%
China	1 major (Mandarin), ~6–12 sublanguages (though categorization is controversial)	Han Chinese, 91.5%
Germany	1 major (German), 7 minor	German, 91.5%
India	1 major linguistic group (Hindi, 41%), with hundreds of other major and minor language groups and dialects	Hindi, 41%
Iran	4 major (Persian, Pashto, Kurdish, and Balochi); more than 80 other varieties	Persian, 51%
Japan	1 major (Japanese)	Japanese, 98.5%
Mexico	1 major (Spanish); several indigenous languages	Spanish, 92.7%
Nigeria	6 major (English, Hausa, Yoruba, Igbo, Fulani, Ibibio); more than 250 total	Hausa and Fulani, 29%
Russia	1 major linguistic group (Russian), with more than 100 other major and minor languages	Russian, 79.8%
United Kingdom	1 (English) with more than 5 others, including Welsh, Gaelic	White British, 92.1%
United States	1 (English), but with 11% of the population speaking Spanish	White alone, 79.96%

Sources: Data are from most recent country census results, the *CIA World Factbook,* and the United Nations. Ethnic fragmentation data from Alberto Alesina, et al. "Fractionalization." *Journal of Economic Growth* 8, no. 2 (2003): 155–94.

* 0 = perfectly homogeneous and 1 = highly fragmented.

Largest religion, % of population	Index of ethnic fractionalization*	Major modern, identity-based conflicts
Roman Catholic (nominal) 73.6%, Protestant 15.4%, Spiritualist 1.3%	0.5408	None
Officially atheist, so percentages unknown. Current estimates are Taoist, Buddhist, and Christian 3–4%; Muslim 1–2%. Actual percentages likely much higher.	0.1538	Uyghur dispute, 1949– Tibetan dispute, 1959–
Protestant 34%, Roman Catholic 34%, Muslim 3.7%	0.1682	Nazi repression of Jews/Holocaust, 1933–1945
Hindu 80.5%, Muslim 13.4%	0.4182	• India/Pakistan partition, 1947–1948 • Kashmir dispute, 1947– • Hindu-Muslim conflicts/riots, 1950– (intermittent) • Sikh independence movement, 1960s–1984
Shiite Muslim 89%, Sunni Muslim 9%	0.6684	Islamic Revolution, 1978–1979
Shinto and/or Buddhist 84%, other 9.8%	0.0119	None
Roman Catholic 76.5%, Protestant 6.3%	0.5418	Chiapas Rebellion, 1994–
Muslim (mostly Sunni) 50%, Christian 40% (largest proportion of Christians, 26%, are Protestant), indigenous beliefs 10%	0.8505	• Biafran civil war, 1967–1970 • Ogoni and related movements, 1993– • Muslim-Christian battles over Sharia, 1999–(intermittent)
Russian Orthodox 15–20%, Muslim 10–15%, other Christian 2%	0.2452	• War of Transniestira, 1990–1992 • Chechen Wars, 1994–1996, 1999–
Church of England 22.2%, all Christian 71.6%	0.1211	Northern Ireland nationalist movement, 1921–1998
Protestant 51.3%, Roman Catholic 23.9%, Mormon 1.7%, Jewish 1.7%, other Christian 1.6%, Buddhist 0.7%, Muslim 0.6%	0.4901	• Civil war with slavery as key issue, 1861–1865 • Urban race riots, 1965–1968

As we noted in chapter 2, states and nations are intimately connected. Internationally, the state is seen as the representative and voice of the nation. Domestically, political leaders can gain legitimacy and power by proclaiming their nationalism and castigating their opponents as "traitors" to the nation. But identities such as ethnicity or race also can serve as foundations of political mobilization and power for subgroups within nation-states. We noted in chapter 3 that groups based on some sense of common identity are only one of many kinds of political groups, but these often have a particularly intense hold on people's loyalties. Few people would risk their lives defending the Sierra Club or the local chamber of commerce, but everyone is expected to do so for their nation, and many would do so for their ethnic or religious group (or groups) as well. The potential for this kind of ultimate political commitment means that states must and do care deeply about identity politics, because mobilization around identity can threaten national unity and even the continued existence of a state. All states seek to develop and gain legitimacy from some sense of identity, but the "wrong" identity can be the gravest threat a state can face.

Many people view loyalty to their nation, ethnic group, or religion as natural, or even divinely ordained, but the intensity and political impact of this loyalty can vary widely across different countries and over time. While group membership of some sort may be "natural" to humans, a particularly intense political loyalty to the nation, ethnic group, or faith clearly is not, given how greatly it varies. The **political saliency**—the political impact and importance—of identity groups is created, not innate. Explaining this process is our first major task.

political saliency:
The degree to which something is of political importance

Ethnic Uzbeks prepare to vote in the city of Osh in Kyrgyzstan in October 2010; in the background are Uzbek homes destroyed in ethnic violence earlier in the year. Ethnic violence between Uzbeks and Kyrgyz broke out in June 2010 in a context of extreme political uncertainty after the Kyrgyz president had been forced into exile and a new government was in the making. Political uncertainty frequently creates fear, which in turn can provoke ethnic violence.

Credit: Victor Drachev/AFP/Getty Images

THE DEBATE OVER IDENTITY

Given the enduring importance of identity to politics, it's not surprising that social scientists have developed several different approaches to understanding how identities are formed and why they become politically salient. Theorists disagree over whether identity politics should be explained by focusing on the elite or society as a whole and whether rational self-interest or political culture is the primary motive force.

The oldest approach to addressing this debate is now commonly called **primordialism**. Primordialism provides the central assumptions of many people's understanding of group origins and differences, and it is implicit in the arguments of many nationalist, ethnic, and racial leaders. The purest primordialists believe exactly what we mentioned above: that identity groups are in some sense "natural" or God given, that they have existed since "time immemorial," and that they can be defined unambiguously by such clear criteria as kinship, language, culture, or phenotype (physical characteristics, including skin color, facial features, and hair). Based on these assumptions, many primordialists see conflict among groups as understandable, and perhaps even inevitable, given their innate differences. Few social scientists see the world in such black-and-white terms, so there are few pure primordialists conducting scholarly work today. However, the approach still holds important popular and political influence.

A more nuanced primordial argument can be based on political culture or political psychology. Because cultural values and beliefs are deeply ingrained, they can be the basis of more or less immutable group identities. Religious tenets understood in this way served as the basis of an influential work by Samuel Huntington entitled *The Clash of Civilizations* (1996/1997). Huntington argued that the world can be divided into seven or eight major "civilizations" based largely on religious identity and that the major wars of the future will occur along the boundaries of these civilizations. Given that the belief systems of many of these civilizations are fundamentally different from those of Western society, Huntington claimed that the West must recognize and address them as possible threats. Psychology, of course, is equally deep-seated. Roger Petersen (2002) argued that emotions like fear, hatred, and resentment can trigger ethnic conflict, typically set off by some structural change such as the abrupt end of communism in Eastern Europe.

The first major challenge to primordialism came from scholars who proposed a theory known as **instrumentalism.** Instrumentalists reject the idea that politically important identity groups originate from the deeply held, enduring characteristics emphasized by primordialists. Instrumentalism is instead a rational-choice theory focused on elites: rational and self-interested elites manipulate symbols and feelings of identity to mobilize a political following. Paul Brass, the first to put this view into words, argued that ethnic groups "are created and transformed by particular elites . . . [and t]his process invariably involves competition and conflict for political power, economic benefits, and social status between competing elite, class and leadership groups" (1991, 25). According to instrumentalists, without elite leadership and context, "primordial" identities have little political relevance, the "cultural givens" won't matter much, and people who possess common cultural traits may not even see themselves as part of a cohesive group.

The most recent and currently dominant approach to understanding identity is **constructivism.** Like primordialism, it is partly based on political culture, but instead of accepting the primordialists' view of cultural identities as unchanging, constructivism uses the postmodern ideas of political culture outlined in chapter 1,

primordialism: A theory of identity that sees identity groups as being in some sense "natural" or God given, as having existed since "time immemorial," and as defined unambiguously by such clear criteria as kinship, language, culture, or phenotype

instrumentalism: A theory of identity politics that argues rational and self-interested elites manipulate symbols and feelings of identity to mobilize a political following

constructivism: A theory of identity group formation that argues identities are created through a complex process usually referred to as social construction emphasizing the shifting interpretation of symbols and stories. It also accepts much of the instrumentalists' focus on the malleability of identity but suggests the process is more complex because elites cannot manipulate identities in any way they please. In this sense, constructivists take a more pluralist and less elite theory approach to understanding identity groups and group conflict. They argue that a complex process, usually referred to as **social construction**, creates identities. Societies collectively "construct" identities as a wide array of actors continually discuss the question of who "we" are.

social construction: Part of constructivist approach to identity, the process through which societies collectively "construct" identities as a wide array of actors continually discuss the question of who "we" are

According to constructivism, this discourse is crucial to defining identities, or "imagined communities" (Anderson 1991). Identity communities are "imagined" in the sense that they exist because people believe they do: people come to see themselves as parts of particular communities based on particular traits. These communities are not immutable, though they typically change relatively slowly. Furthermore, individuals are members of a number of different groups at the same time. Elites can attempt to mobilize people using the discourse and symbols of any one of several identities in a particular time and place, but they cannot create an identity that no one else has imagined; the ongoing social discourse provides the cultural material for and limits on elite manipulation.

This creation of social and cultural boundaries, even where no legal ones exist, is central to the social construction of identity. As a group defines who "we" are, it also creates boundaries that define who "they" are. To take the most obvious example, the concepts and identities of "man" and "woman" could not exist without each other. If humans were a species of only one sex, neither word would exist. The same is true, constructivists argue, for all types of identity, though usually there are more than just two categories.

Afrikaner identity in South Africa, for instance, emerged in the nineteenth century among the descendants of Dutch and French settlers in juxtaposition to both the indigenous black African population and the invasion of British colonists. The social construction of this particular identity inherently included and excluded, and who was included and excluded had crucial consequences for who ruled. When the Nationalist Party took power and instituted apartheid in 1948, it did so in the name of the Afrikaner nation; while Nationalists allowed British citizens full political rights, they kept power closely in Afrikaner hands and denied black South Africans any power whatsoever. Someone perceived as not part of a nation, as black South Africans were, is unlikely to have significant social standing or political influence. Within a nation, if a powerful racial or ethnic group sees itself as superior, other groups may have difficulty asserting significant political power. The very terms by which identities are constructed can influence who has the most power.

Constructivists argue that identities and boundaries are created in part by the interpretation and reinterpretation of symbols and stories. Through families, the media, and the public education system in all countries, individuals develop a sense of identity as they learn the importance and meaning of key symbols and stories. The state always plays an important role in this process. As a government develops and implements educational curricula, it requires that children be taught the "national history," which can include only certain events interpreted in certain ways if the "facts" are to support a specific national identity. Schools may also teach more localized ethnic or racial histories, although these are often more the purview of the family. The end result of this only partly planned and always amorphous process is adherence to certain beliefs, values, symbols, and stories that come to constitute an identity; for example, a flag, a monarch, the struggle for independence, the fight for racial equality, and monuments to fallen heroes.

What about Gender?

Gender is an important identity category that we do not investigate in depth in this chapter. We chose not to focus as much on it because, in contrast to all the other categories, gender has never been the basis of a widespread movement for political autonomy, and it has never threatened the very existence of a state. It has, however, been the basis of very important movements for greater representation and equality. The women's movement has arguably been the most successful political and social movement of the last generation, especially in wealthy and middle-income nations. We examine this movement in detail in chapter 12.

Education and birth control have freed many women from traditional gender roles, allowing them to enter the political and economic spheres far more than at any time in the past. The "third wave" of feminism has demanded greater access to education, which has improved women's economic standing, though in most countries their income still lags behind men's in spite of equal or greater educational achievement. In the last twenty years, the women's movement in postcolonial societies has expanded tremendously as well, as women battle for changes to harmful cultural practices and greater access to birth control, education, and employment opportunities. While perhaps not as successful at changing government policy as in the wealthier areas of the world, the women's movement in poorer countries is nonetheless well on its way to similar results.

Gender does share some clear similarities with other identity categories, but in other ways it is fundamentally different. The demands of women's movements have been broadly similar to those of most racial movements: recognition and representation. And as in the case of race, once basic legal recognition and equality are achieved, women's movements have gone on to demand greater inclusion and integration in politics, the economy, and civil society. On the other hand, because gender always cuts across communities—men and women exist in all communities—it does not serve as the basis of an exclusive communal identity. With a few minor exceptions, no all-women's community has demanded autonomy or its own state.

Gender also has a unique relationship to the other identity categories. While some notions of nationalism can be tied to race (Nazism) or religion (some versions of Islamism), most are not. Gender, on the other hand, is intrinsic in all other categories. As Nira Yuval-Davis and Flora Anthias (1989) have argued, gender symbols and women in general are used to define national, ethnic, religious, and racial boundaries. By having babies, women literally reproduce the community. As the primary child care providers in almost all societies, they also pass on key cultural elements to the next generation. Finally, women serve as symbolic markers of community identity and boundaries. A recent example is the wearing of the Islamic veil, which has become an issue of debate both in Europe and in several Middle Eastern countries (see chapter 12). What women do, how they behave, and where and how they are seen can all be issues of identity. Women's movements, whatever their origins and goals, threaten virtually all other communal identities that rely in part on particular gender roles and symbols to define themselves.

Like most contemporary social scientists, in this text we adopt a primarily constructivist approach, as it seems to combine the best of past theories. It is clear that identities are not fixed, and, as we'll see below, their political saliency varies greatly, both across countries and over time. Elites certainly play an important role in the process of creating and politically mobilizing identity groups, but identities develop over too long a period and are too intensely felt to be subject to complete manipulation. Culture matters, not as a static entity but rather as a set of symbols and stories available for interpretation. Leaders of groups that are excluded from power can interpret the symbols and stories of identity categories to connect them to particular political contexts, to raise passions of various sorts, and, often, to challenge the status quo. State leaders typically work to reinforce a sense of national identity tied to support for the state and to find ways to accommodate other identities without threatening the strength and political legitimacy of the state itself. Conversely, their opponents seek to interpret prevailing symbols and stories in different ways to undermine the political influence of those in power or perhaps even to bring into question the very existence of the state. We examine these processes by looking at each of the major categories of modern identity in turn: nation, ethnicity and religion, and race.

NATIONS AND NATIONALISM

The nation remains a fundamental building block of the global political system. Each state claims to be the sole legitimate representative of a nation, and each nation claims a right to its own state. Despite this, clearly defining the word *nation* is no easy task. Writing over a century ago, French theorist Ernest Renan (1882), after trying to figure out which particular cultural characteristics produced nations in Europe, finally concluded that no single cultural feature was crucial. Instead,

> a nation is a soul, a spiritual principle. Two things, which are really only one, go to make up this soul or spiritual principle. One of these things lies in the past, the other in the present. The one is the possession in common of a rich heritage of memories; and the other is actual agreement, the desire to live together, and the will to continue to make the most of the joint inheritance.

The resemblance of Renan's deduction to contemporary notions of social construction is striking. A nation is an "imagined community," imagined through shared memories. All of those memories beyond the immediate experience of the individuals themselves are shared only because a group has learned to share them, in part through state-sponsored education.

The distinction between a nation and an ethnic group is less clear than that between a nation and a state. The Irish are members of a nation, but when they immigrate to the United States, they become, sooner or later, part of an "ethnic group." The Zulu in South Africa are an ethnic group, but the Palestinians, who are less culturally distinct from their neighbors (or at least from other Arabs) than the Zulu are from neighboring African groups, are generally regarded as a nation. As Renan concluded long ago, no particular set of cultural markers fully distinguishes a nation from an ethnic group. The only clear definition ties back to the state. A **nation** is a group that proclaims itself a nation and has or seeks control of a state. This desire to be a nation and thus to control a national state is **nationalism**. Ethnic groups, on the other hand, do not think of themselves as nations and do not desire to control their own state as much as they want **autonomy** within a larger state.

Perhaps not surprisingly, most nationalist leaders are primordialists: each claims his or her nation has existed since the mists of time as a mighty and proud

nation: A group that proclaims itself a nation and has or seeks control of a state

nationalism: The desire to be a nation and thus to control a national state

autonomy: Ability and right of a group to partially govern itself within a larger state

people. As we saw in chapter 2, however, most scholars see nationalism as a fundamentally modern concept tied in some way to the rise of the modern state and economy. The first European nations, such as France and England, were largely the products of preexisting states. Once nationalism emerged as an idea, though, political and intellectual elites started propagating a sense of national identity long before they controlled their own states, as the development of Germany demonstrates. In former colonies, nationalism emerged as a movement for independence from colonial oppressors. And once the creation of the state is accomplished, the process of developing a national identity continues. As Italian nationalist Massimo d'Azeglio declared shortly after the unification of Italy in the 1860s: "We have made Italy. Now we must make Italians."

A long debate exists over the origins of nationalism. Prior to the 1960s, most scholars were primordialists, assuming and asserting that nations stemmed from ancient cultural entities, just as nationalist leaders claimed. Since then, much historical research has demonstrated that nations are modern entities, though this still leaves much to explain. Probably the most influential scholar, Ernest Gellner (1983), argued that the emergence of nations became necessary as industrialization occurred. Rising industry required a large domestic market, which was facilitated by the rise of modern states, and a large workforce in that territory that was literate in the same language. States therefore created public education systems in a single vernacular language and actively propagated a sense of common identity to serve the needs of industry as well as to strengthen their own legitimacy. Marxist analysts argue that nationalism arose to facilitate capitalism, often in the "periphery" of the capitalist system where leaders needed a sense of national loyalty to gain legitimacy among workers who were hurt by capitalism (Nairn 1977). Benedict Anderson (1991) argued that the rise of printing led to the expansion of a written vernacular around which nationalism developed; the state leveraged this technology in the form of education, mapmaking, and censuses. According to Anderson, the decline of religious authority also contributed to nationalism. Anthony Smith (1998), on the other hand, questioned these modernist claims, arguing instead that nations' ethnic predecessors and the cultures they developed are the original source of most modern nations. Most scholars, though, support the idea that nations are modern entities tied in some way to the development of the modern state.

Nationalism has a complicated relationship with liberal democracy as well. At least until the mid-twentieth century, many nationalists saw themselves as carving democratic nations out of the remnants of feudal or colonial empires. Before "we, the people" can declare ourselves sovereign, "we" must have a sense of "us" as a "people": who is and is not included in "us" defines who has the rights of democratic citizenship. If "we" use particular cultural or physical characteristics to define "us," then we exclude as well as include people in our "nation." In this context, two distinct forms of nationalism have crucial implications. **Cultural nationalism** is national unity based on a common cultural characteristic, and those people who don't share that particular characteristic cannot be included in the nation. This definition poses obvious challenges for democracy, for how can those lacking the "national" characteristic be full citizens with democratic rights? For this reason, most observers see **civic nationalism** as most supportive of democracy. In civic nationalism, the sense of national unity and purpose is based on a set of commonly held political beliefs. Those who share the beliefs are part of the nation.

France and Germany provide a classic comparison of these different kinds of nationalism and their complicated relationship with democracy. The two countries

cultural nationalism:
National unity based on a common cultural characteristic wherein only those people who share that characteristic can be included in the nation

civic nationalism:
A sense of national unity and purpose based on a set of commonly held political beliefs

also illustrate that even what are perceived to be strong and deeply rooted nations were, in fact, constructed, and relatively recently. As Rogers Brubaker (1992) put it, "For two centuries . . . France and Germany have been constructing, elaborating, and furnishing to other states distinctive, even antagonistic, models of nationhood and national self-understanding" (1). He went on to express how these two models illustrate the variation in the relationship between the state and the nation that we outlined above:

> In the French tradition, the nation has been conceived in relation to the institutions and territorial frame of the state. Revolutionary and Republican definitions of nationhood . . . reinforced what was already in the ancient regime an essentially political understanding of nationhood. . . . [T]he German understanding has been *Volk*-centered and differentialist. Since national feeling developed before the nation-state, the German idea of the nation was not originally political. . . . This prepolitical German nation, this nation in search of a state, was conceived not as the bearer of universal political values, but as an organic cultural, linguistic, or racial community. . . . On this understanding, nationhood is an ethnocultural, not a political fact. (1)

These generalizations have regularly been contested within each country, however. French nationalism at first glance seems predominantly civic, but it has strong cultural elements; German nationalism is clearly cultural, but that notion has been continually challenged, especially since the Nazi era. France's absolutist state was instrumental in forging a unified concept of a French nation. The state expanded outward from Paris, incorporating neighboring regions that spoke various languages into a single political unit. The concept of nationalism did not fully enter French political discourse until the Revolution of 1789, long after the state was fully established and quite extensive. This allowed a civic and territorial nationalism to emerge, but French nationalism was culturally **assimilationist** from the start. Regional linguistic and cultural divisions were seen not as the democratic right of separate peoples but rather as unacceptable divisions in the unity of revolutionary and democratic France. This nationalist ideal fully developed under the Third Republic after 1870, when the country's first universal and public education system was created, consciously designed to instill a common version of the French language and a common set of democratic political values. By the end of the nineteenth century, France's citizenship laws were based on *jus soli*, or residence on the state's "soil," thus conferring citizenship on second-generation immigrants.

This primarily civic nationalism did not go without challenge, however. Throughout the nineteenth century, France's political right tried to create a strongly cultural and primordial nationalism that focused on an often quasi-racial definition of the "pure" France that excluded immigrants. The contemporary heir to the movement is the National Front (FN) led by Marine Le Pen. The FN advocates a shift from *jus soli* to *jus sanguinis,* citizenship based on blood rather than residence, a demand that reflects a primordial understanding of the nation. The National Front's efforts to redefine French nationality and citizenship in the direction of *jus sanguinis* have never succeeded, but the party's appeal has been substantial. Our case study of Germany presents quite a distinct picture from neighboring France but nonetheless shows the continuing tension between civic and cultural nationalism.

assimilationist: Characterized by a belief that immigrants or other members of minority cultural communities ought to adopt the culture of the majority population

jus soli: Literally, citizenship dependent on "soil," or residence within the national territory; for example, in France

jus sanguinis: Citizenship based on "blood" ties; for example, in Germany

CASE STUDY

Nationalism in Germany

- Nationalism before the modern state
- Cultural nationalism
- *Jus sanguinis,* until recent reform
- Turkish "guest workers" and continuing debate over who is "German"

German nationalism long predates the modern German state. German speakers migrated widely across central and eastern Europe during the Middle Ages and lived side by side with Slavs and other ethnic groups while retaining their German language and culture. While a "primordial" language and culture existed, however, it took Napoleon's invasion in the early nineteenth century and the influence of the Romantic movement to foment modern German nationalism. Advocates of Romanticism envisioned the nation as an organic whole with a "distinct personality." Intellectual elites shaped German nationalism by defining "Germany" in linguistic and cultural terms that juxtaposed German identity with the identities of the neighboring Slavs in the east and French in the west. The largest German state, Prussia, included large populations of minorities, however, especially Poles. In acknowledgment of this, Prussian reformers tried to develop a state-based sense of nationalism after the defeat of Napoleon in 1815, but this ran counter to the linguistically based German nationalism advocated throughout the rest of the region. German nationalism, Brubaker (1992) argues, has been characterized by a "duality" between a state-based and a cultural nationalism ever since.

As outlined in chapter 2, Otto von Bismarck finally united much of what is now Germany in 1871. Like his contemporaries in France's Third Republic, he tried to use education to create greater cultural homogeneity in the new state, and he wrote citizenship laws that were based partly on *jus soli.* His new *Reich,* however, still included large populations of linguistic minorities and excluded

Until 2000, Germany's *jus sanguinis* definition of citizenship meant that millions of Turkish workers and their German-born children were not citizens. These Turkish parents pose with their daughter, one of the first children born under a recent law that grants citizenship to children born in Germany whose parents have been there at least eight years.

Credit: AP Photo/Jockel Finck

huge numbers of German speakers in Austria and eastern Europe. Continuing emigration of Germans to eastern Europe and immigration of non-Germans into the *Reich* led nationalists, such as the Pan-German League, to demand and get a revision of the citizenship laws in 1913. The new laws reflected the long-standing German cultural conceptualization of the nation by basing citizenship quite strictly on *jus sanguinis,* legally codifying a cultural and primordial understanding of what it meant to be "German."

Nazi ideology developed out of German cultural nationalism but distorted it by marrying it to explicit racism. The nation was thought of not only in cultural, but also racial, terms. The master Aryan race was superior to all others, and Hitler's regime stripped "non-Aryans" of citizenship rights, expelling or exterminating many, especially

Jews. With the end of World War II and the establishment of West Germany, German nationalism remained primarily cultural. The Soviet Union expelled millions of ethnic Germans from Eastern Europe shortly after the war, and by 1950 these émigrés constituted one-sixth of West Germany's population. Germany once again was a nation divided across more than one state. Citizenship continued to reflect the concept of the cultural nation: all ethnic Germans were welcomed into West Germany and automatically granted the rights of citizenship. This open-arms policy was in stark contrast to the treatment of the growing number of non-German immigrants, who rarely gained citizenship no matter how many generations their ancestors had resided in Germany. Access to political power required being part of the German cultural nation.

The debate over who is and should be "German" continues today, especially in the context of growing immigration. The large numbers of Turks who immigrated to Germany in recent decades were initially welcomed to fulfill essential jobs. Following German national self-conception, these immigrants were known as *gastarbeiters,* or "guest workers"; they were to stay as long as employed and then return home. Today more than two million ethnic Turks live in Germany, and many have raised children there. Until recently, however, very few could gain German citizenship because of Germany's *jus sanguinis* law. In 2000, the government finally allowed German-born children of immigrants who had been in the country at least eight years to apply for citizenship, provided they could pass a German language test. As a result, approximately 700,000 former Turkish citizens now have German citizenship. About two-thirds of Turkish residents remain noncitizens, though, despite the fact that many have lived in Germany for decades.

Implementation of and reaction to the new citizenship law has been mixed. Some states have added additional elements to citizenship tests that require applicants to understand various German cultural values as well as the language itself. In 2008, the premier (the equivalent of governor in the United States) in one German state ran what many saw as an anti-immigrant and anti-Turkish reelection campaign, calling for the deportation of noncitizen juvenile delinquents. In 2010, a member of the board of the national bank, Thilo Sarrazin, wrote a book titled *Germany Does Away with Itself* that argued that Germany was becoming literally stupider and culturally weaker due to the presence of too many Muslim immigrants. This touched off a raging debate, and he was forced to resign, but a poll showed that as many as a third of Germans agreed with his sentiments and the book became a best seller. Turks, on the other hand, have become more involved in politics, with a state governor appointing the first German cabinet minister of Turkish descent in 2010. Turkish political activists have also begun demanding the inclusion of Islam in religious education in public schools (in Germany, Christianity is regularly taught in public schools). Providing an avenue for citizenship has clearly not settled the question of how integrated Turkish immigrants will be in Germany.

CASE SUMMARY

The German case shows the underlying complexity of what may seem to be a very stable national identity. Germany long maintained a strictly cultural nationalism that left millions of immigrants and their children without political rights. A 2000 reform finally changed this, though citizenship is far from automatic. Neither civic nor cultural nationalism has become the unquestioned and universal conception of "we," at least not for very long. Political battles between contending visions of the national identity are fought in the realm of citizenship laws, meaning they have a direct bearing on who gains democratic rights and who does not. Nationality is not the only identity that has an important influence on and an ambiguous relationship with democracy, however; ethnicity and religion do as well.

ETHNICITY AND RELIGION

As identity groups in the political sphere, ethnicity and religion share many characteristics. While religion is based on a set of beliefs and ethnicity on a perceived common culture or descent, ethnic and religious groups make similar political demands. Their different markers (beliefs vs. culture) are not terribly important for understanding their political behavior. We turn to ethnicity first and then can apply much of what we learn to religion as well.

Ethnicity and Ethnic Conflict

Now that we have defined and illustrated what a nation is, defining an ethnic group becomes a little easier. An **ethnic group** is a group of people who see themselves as united by one or more cultural attributes or a sense of common history but do not see themselves as a nation seeking their own state. Like a nation and all other identity categories, ethnic identity is imagined: people's perceptions are what matter, not actual attributes or some "objective" interpretation of history. Ethnic groups may be based on very real cultural attributes, such as a common language, but even these are subject to perception and change. In the former Yugoslavia, Serbs, Croats, and Bosnians all spoke closely related versions of what was known as Serbo-Croatian. As ethnic conflict and then war emerged in the early 1990s, each group began claiming it spoke a distinct language—"Serbian," "Croatian," or "Bosnian"—and nationalists in all three groups began to emphasize the minor linguistic differences among them. People think of African "tribes" as modern remnants of ancient, unchanging groups, but the Nigerian case below shows how even there, ethnicity is socially constructed and quite modern. (See the "What's in a Name?" box on page 156 for a fuller discussion of "tribes" in Africa.)

If ethnic groups do not desire to have their own state, what do they want? Their political interests generally revolve around what Charles Taylor (1994) called the **politics of recognition**. All identity groups, including nations, want to be recognized. Ethnic groups usually desire recognition within the confines of a nation-state shared with other ethnic groups. This recognition may take the form of official state support of cultural events, school instruction in the local language, the local language being one of the official languages in which government business is conducted, or explicit inclusion of people and events significant to the ethnic group in the national history curriculum. Where an ethnic group resides primarily in one area of the country, it also may demand some type of regional autonomy, such as a federal system of government in which its leaders can control their own state or province. The issue became so contentious in India in the 1960s that the national government created a commission to examine it. This commission recommended the creation of a number of new states based on linguistic boundaries. For practical reasons, not all of India's hundreds of language areas could receive their own states, but the largest ones did.

In contrast to national identity, ethnicity is not always political. In the United States today, white ethnic identity has very little political content. Irish Americans may be proud of their heritage and identify culturally with Ireland, but few feel any common political interests based on that. This can change, of course: a century ago many Irish Americans felt their identity was tied very strongly to their political interests. A crucial question then is when and why ethnicity becomes politically salient. As instrumentalists point out, leadership can be a key catalyst. Because of the potential intensity of ethnic attachments, they are a tempting resource for

ethnic group: A group of people who see themselves as united by one or more cultural attributes or a sense of common history but do not see themselves as a nation seeking their own state

politics of recognition: The demands for recognition and inclusion that have arisen since the 1960s in racial, religious, ethnic, gender, and other minority or socially marginalized groups

What's in a Name? Tribe, Ethnicity, and Nation

When Westerners think of Africans and Native Americans, they think of "tribes," but no one refers to the Basques in Spain or Scots in Britain as a tribe. Instead they are ethnic groups, linguistic groups, or "nations." We defined a nation as a group of people who have or want their own state. By that definition, Basques and Scots only partially qualify: some of them want their own state, but many simply want greater autonomy within Spain or Britain. In this sense, they are very similar to a good portion of the Zulu in South Africa, who want much the same thing. So why are the Zulu a tribe while the Scots and Basques are not?

The word *tribe* usually conjures up the image of a small, primitive group tied together by a common culture, language, kinship, and system of government based on a chief. People tend to understand tribes in primordialist and negative terms; that is, they are "traditional" groups that have survived into the modern world and therefore cause political problems. As our case study of Nigeria shows, nothing could be further from the truth. Modern African ethnic groups arose in their current form from varying precolonial identities or states during the colonial era. The Kalenjin of Kenya consist of eight separate groups speaking closely related languages that assumed a common ethnic identity only in the 1950s, primarily via a radio program many group members listened to. To call the Kelenjin a "tribe," evoking the word's connotation of a small and primitive group, masks this history and variation.

The real reason *tribe* is associated with Africans and Native Americans is rooted in eighteenth- and nineteenth-century racist assumptions about these people. At least since Julius Caesar, *tribe* has implicitly meant a backward and inferior group of people. Caesar used *tribus* to refer to the "barbarian," blue-eyed blonds he conquered in northern Europe. Later European slavers and colonists used it to classify people they saw as backward and inferior, and the term stuck. For an interesting discussion of the use of *tribe* in Africa, see Chris Lowe's 1997 article "Talking about 'Tribe': Moving from Stereotypes to Analysis" at www.africaaction.org/talking-about-tribe.html. Contemporary scholars of Africa prefer the term *ethnic group* for people in Africa, Europe, or anywhere else who have an identity derived from some cultural characteristic but who are not a nation in the way scholars define that term. Many Native Americans, on the other hand, prefer the term "nation," even though most of them do not seek complete sovereignty from the larger states in which they reside.

ambitious politicians. A leader who can tie ethnic identity to political demands can gain tremendous support.

Constructivists point out, however, that leaders cannot create such an appeal at will. The context is almost always important. If a group believes those in power have discriminated against it economically, socially, or politically, members may see their political interests and ethnic identity as one and the same. Their history, which they may pass from parent to child, is one of discrimination at the hands of the powerful "other." Similarly, if they feel **relative deprivation,** a belief that they are not getting their share relative to others in the society or relative to their own expectations, they may come to see that deprivation in ethnic terms. On the other hand, sometimes relative wealth can lead to ethnic mobilization. If an ethnic group is based in a particular region, as many are, and that region has a valuable resource such as oil, group members may feel that they should receive all or most of the benefits from what they see as "their" resource. The national government, on the other

relative deprivation: A belief that a group or individual is not getting its share of something of value relative to others in the society or relative to group members' own expectations

hand, will see the resource as belonging to the nation as a whole, to be controlled by the central government. This is a central issue in the ethnic and religious divisions in Iraq, because the country's oil reserves are located in both Kurd and Shiite areas but not in Sunni areas. Sunni leaders, not surprisingly, want oil revenue fully controlled by the central government in Baghdad, not by regional governments.

Political or economic uncertainty can also lead to ethnic mobilization. With the fall of communism in Eastern Europe and the former Soviet Union, many people felt great fear about the future. The old institutions had collapsed, and the new ones were untested. In this situation, it is relatively easy for a political leader to mobilize support with an ethnic or nationalist appeal that uses history to suggest that other groups will take advantage of the uncertain situation and try to achieve domination. A classic case is Serbian leader Slobodan Milosevic, who proclaimed sympathy with the Serb minority in Kosovo in a famous speech in 1987, taking upon himself the mantle of Serb nationalism. Croatian and Bosnian Muslim leaders, fearful of Serb domination, soon responded in kind. The eventual result was war and genocide in which the three ethno-religious groups who had lived together relatively peacefully under Communist rule developed increasingly strident cultural nationalism and ultimately dismembered the country.

Government leaders who want to remain in power and preserve peace must respond to such politically mobilized ethnic groups. Indeed, in a country with significant ethnic diversity or ethnic conflict, the government will often seek to preempt ethnic mobilization. One means of doing this, common in authoritarian governments, is simply to ban all public appeals to ethnicity, religion, or other "sectarian" identities. From the 1960s to 1980s, Tanzania's one-party regime had internal elections that were actually competitive, but candidates were strictly forbidden to make any ethnic, regional, or religious appeals when campaigning. Many a military leader has banned not only political parties but all sorts of ethnic groups and clubs as well.

Democracies typically take less draconian measures, trying to create institutions that recognize but limit conflict. Two broad approaches to this are the centripetal and consociational. The **centripetal approach**, championed most strongly by political scientist Donald Horowitz (1985), argues that ethnic conflict can best be resolved by giving political leaders and parties incentives to moderate their demands in order to gain more votes. Particular types of electoral systems can encourage such moderation by requiring winning candidates to gain votes over a broad geographic area. Also, rules for recognition of parties can require them to have representation and leadership across ethnic lines. Our case study of Nigeria is a classic example of this approach.

Consociationalism (Lijphart 1977) doubts the likelihood of moderating ethnic demands via centripetal means and instead assumes and accepts ethnically divided parties, granting each some share of power in the central government. Switzerland, Northern Ireland, and Belgium are examples of this system. Power sharing can be done formally, as in Lebanon where power is divided along religious lines: by agreement of all parties, the president is always a Christian, the prime minister a Sunni Muslim, and the speaker of the parliament a Shiite Muslim. It can also be done more informally. The electoral system, for instance, can be designed to encourage the formation of ethnically based parties. The parties, once elected, can then work out power-sharing arrangements in some type of government of national unity. Typically, each major ethnic party will have, in effect, a veto over major legislation, so all must agree before laws are passed. Consociationalism can be quite stable, but underlying tensions can surface, provoking repeated constitutional crises and government breakdown, as in Belgium since 2007.

Both centripetal and consociational approaches can be combined with federalism (see chapter 6 for more details) as an additional means of limiting ethnic

centripetal approach: A means used by democracies to resolve ethnic conflict by giving political leaders and parties incentives to moderate their demands

consociationalism: A democratic system designed to ease ethnic tensions via recognizing the existence of specific groups and granting some share of power in the central government to each, usually codified in specific legal or constitutional guarantees to each group

tension. Consociationalists argue for creating ethnically homogeneous states or provinces so that central governments can try to shift the focus of ethnic politics from the center to the regional governments. A group may not hold many official positions or much influence in the central government, but members may hold all of the offices in a specific province, whether the government is democratic or authoritarian. Centripetalists, on the other hand, argue for creating ethnically mixed states or provinces to encourage ethnic compromise within each one, moderating tensions. They also hope that subethnic divisions in ethnically homogeneous states or provinces will emerge via local political competition, undermining broader ethnic group loyalty. Federalism with ethnically homogeneous states or provinces has been the most common means of resolving ethnic conflicts in the post–Cold War era.

MINI CASE

Consociationalism in Northern Ireland

The religiously based conflict in Northern Ireland is one of the oldest communal conflicts in the world, but it seems to have been resolved, at least for now, via a consociational system created by the Belfast Agreement of 1998.

The origins of the conflict date back to the British government's seventeenth-century settlement of English and Scottish Protestant plantation owners as a means of securing British colonial rule in Ireland. These landowners oversaw a Gaelic, Catholic population. In the mid- to late nineteenth century, when nationalist movements were widespread across Europe, nationalism emerged in Ireland as well. By the 1920s, the rest of Ireland gained independence as the Republic of Ireland, while the six northern counties gained only devolved government under Protestant control. The nationalist movement, demanding that the northern counties be joined with the Irish Republic, continued its efforts throughout the twentieth century, at times violently and at times peacefully. The late 1960s, as was typical around the world, saw a radicalization of the nationalist movement (also known as "Republicans" because of their desire to be part of the larger Irish Republic). The Provisional Irish Republican Army (commonly referred to as the IRA) instigated a campaign of violence that came to be known simply as "the Troubles." This resulted in the British government sending in troops and reinstituting direct rule from London. The IRA and its political wing, Sinn Fein, became

a major voice of the nationalist movement by the 1980s. This led to radicalization on the part of the unionists (the Protestant majority in Northern Ireland who favored continued union with Britain) and an escalation of violence.

By the 1990s, violence of varying intensity had been ongoing for more than twenty years. British rule favored the Protestants, a relatively wealthy majority. The Catholic minority were far more impoverished and had little real political power. The region, and especially the capital Belfast, was sharply segregated, with sectarian violence claiming lives on both sides. Both unionists and nationalists were divided into moderate and radical factions and parties, with the more radical ones supporting the violence. By the early 1990s, it became clear to both sides that they could not achieve their core aims unilaterally. The IRA came to recognize it could not militarily defeat the British and join the Irish Republic, and the unionists acknowledged they could not continue to rule unilaterally with British backing without paying a steep price in terms of lives, political stability, and economic well-being. This set the stage for a historic agreement creating a consociational solution that, while far from perfect, is holding to date.

The Belfast Agreement of 1998 came about because of the unionists' and nationalists' recognition of their limitations, successful mediation by U.S. Special Envoy George Mitchell, and the impetus of new governments in both Great Britain and Ireland. Under the agreement, Northern Ireland would remain part of Great Britain, and Ireland renounced its long-standing claim to the territory. Government would devolve, however, from direct rule from London to local rule in Northern Ireland based on a consociational system that created a form of power sharing. A new National Assembly would be elected based on a proportional electoral system known as the Single Transferrable Vote (STV), which ensured that nationalists and unionists would have seats in parliament equal to their share of the national vote (see chapter 7 for details on proportional electoral systems). Executive power is shared by a first minister and deputy first minister elected by the National Assembly. They must each win a majority vote of both the nationalist and unionist members of the National Assembly (every member, once elected, must declare him or herself to be officially unionist, nationalist, or other). Cabinet positions are then shared among all parties in the Assembly based on their share of the total seats. In this way, both sides of the sectarian divide must support the government. Given their majority, unionists have so far held the office of first minister, and nationalists have been deputy first ministers. In addition, agreements subsequent to the 1998 agreement have created a new police force. The police previously were controlled by the British government and were seen as very anti-Catholic. Following the principles of consociationalism, recruitment to this new force must be divided evenly between Protestants and Catholics.

Implementation of the agreement was long and fitful. Assembly elections successfully took place in 1998, 2003, and 2007. The executive branch, however, has been harder to put in place. It only existed for a total of nineteen months between 1998 and 2002 and then was suspended entirely from 2002 to 2007. The chief concern contributing to the suspension was disarmament of the IRA. While the nationalist parties were part of the Belfast Agreement, the IRA itself was not. It was up to Sinn Fein, the political party associated with the IRA, to convince the militants to disarm, a process that took longer than anticipated. The main unionist party repeatedly pulled out of the government to protest the failure of IRA disarmament and sporadic continuing violence, leading to the suspension. Finally, the IRA fully disarmed in 2005, and by 2007 a new agreement put the executive in place again. Following the logic of consociationalism, the more radical parties on both sides have gained strength under the new electoral system. While the agreement was negotiated primarily by moderate parties on both sides, which were the biggest parties at the time, by the 2003 election Sinn Fein and the more radical unionist party had become the biggest parties. Sinn Fein had supported the agreement from the start, but the radical unionists had opposed it and continued to until the 2007 agreement, when they finally agreed to participate in the new system. Since 2007, the former radical parties on both sides have shared executive power successfully in the new government.

CASE SUMMARY

Supporters of consociationalism see the successful resolution of the Northern Ireland conflict as a vindication of their argument that deeply divided ethnic or religious conflicts require a political system that recognizes and accepts these divisions and institutionalizes them in some form of power sharing. In contrast, while the violent conflict has ended and a stable government is in place, critics note that sectarian voting has increased on both sides (a moderate party that long championed a compromise and gained votes from both sides has seen its electoral fortunes fall significantly), Belfast remains a deeply segregated city, and opinion polls show little trust across the religious divide. Numerous efforts to forge cross-community relationships in civil society and integrate institutions such as schools have begun, but they have been far from successful so far. Nonetheless, the consociational system, after a decade of difficult implementation, has succeeded in ending the violent conflict and establishing a stable government in which the former antagonists are sharing power peacefully.

METHODS IN CONTEXT

Explaining Ethnic Violence

Identity groups exist everywhere and become politically salient frequently. Fortunately, however, violence based on those identities is less common, which raises the interesting question of why it arises in certain contexts and not in others. Comparativists have put forth numerous theories to answer this question, many of them tied to the construction of identity groups in the first place. Probably the oldest theory, and the one that is most widespread among the general public, is the primordialist argument of "ancient hatreds": some groups of people have grievances dating back centuries, hatreds they pass from one generation to the next, and they will attack each other when they get the chance. This idea ignores the historical variation and modern origins of most ethnic identities, and it fails to explain why violence breaks out at certain times and not others.

A popular alternative to the primordialist argument is a rational-choice explanation based on the **security dilemma**. This is a situation in which two or more groups do not trust one another, and in fact fear one another, and do not believe that institutional constraints will protect them, often because the state is weak or nonexistent. In that context, the fear of being attacked leads people to attack first, believing that doing so is necessary to protect themselves.

A third major approach is instrumentalist: violence occurs when entrepreneurial ethnic elites mobilize their group to violent action. Critics contend this approach, as with instrumentalism generally, gives far too much credence to the idea that the masses can be duped by manipulative elites into engaging in sometimes unspeakable acts of violence.

HYPOTHESIS

Several scholars have taken up this debate in recent years, trying to determine what causes identity groups to turn to violence. They focus on slightly different dependent variables (what they are trying to explain), but all focus on where and why violence breaks out. The best known approach was actually developed by economists (Collier and Hoeffler 2004; Collier, Hoeffler, and Rohner 2009) but has been very influential in political science. These economists sought to explain the outbreak of civil wars. While not all civil wars are based on communal identities, many are—especially, it seems, in the last half century. Paul Collier and his colleagues initially hypothesized that civil war is caused by either greed (desire for material gain via control of key economic resources, such as minerals) or grievance (ethnic or economic disparities). More recently (2009), they hypothesized that the feasibility of civil war is more important than either of the motivational variables, suggesting that where the right opportunity exists, some group of leaders will step forward on the basis of some justification to start a civil war. Implicit in this model is an instrumental view of ethnically based civil war: leaders manipulate the right context to start wars.

Two political scientists have also created theories that try to overcome the weaknesses of past arguments, and their ideas differ radically from the economists' approach. Monica Toft (2003) tried to explain violence in which the state is battling a communally based rebel group (as opposed to two or more nonstate groups battling each other). She hypothesizes that settlement patterns explain ethnic violence: when both a geographically concentrated ethnic group and the state in which it resides view the group's territory as essential and indivisible, violence is much more likely to occur. An ethnic group that is geographically concentrated will have greater capability and legitimacy for demanding sovereignty over its own territory (and thereby becoming a nationalist group in our terms). It also is likely to view its territory as a "homeland" that is essential to its sense of identity, so it will be unwilling to compromise and be more capable of waging war against the

security dilemma: A situation in which two or more groups do not trust one another, and in fact fear one another, and do not believe that institutional constraints will protect them

state. States with more than one potential ethnic conflict, on the other hand, fear the precedent set by the successful secession of any one group and so are likely to view their territory as indivisible and be unwilling to bargain over it.

In contrast, Roger Petersen (2002) combined structural and psychological explanations, hypothesizing that emotions are crucial mechanisms for translating the structural factors that create the possibility of violence into action. He posits three emotions that serve this purpose: fear, hatred, and resentment. Petersen sees these emotions as instrumental, in the sense that they translate a structural situation and prior conceptual understanding of that situation into action. Fear is a response to situations like the security dilemma in which a group's primary motivation is safety. Hatred is a motivation when an opportunity arises for violence against a group that has been frequently attacked in the past. Resentment motivates violence after a sudden change in status hierarchies among ethnic groups. Each logically results in violence against a particular type of group; fear, for instance, targets violence at the group considered the biggest threat, while resentment targets violence at that highest-status group that can be effectively lowered via violence.

RESEARCH AND ANALYSIS

The three sets of scholars trying to explain ethnic violence employed methodologies as distinct as their approaches. The economists, as is nearly universal in their discipline, conducted a statistical analysis of a large data set to test whether greed, grievance, or opportunity best explain the outbreak of civil war. They used a data set that identifies every known civil war from 1960 to 2004 and, using the statistical technique of logit regression, examined the multiple correlations between this dependent variable and a wide array of independent variables: "greed" variables, such as the presence of exportable raw materials that rebels can seize; "grievance" variables, such as ethnic fragmentation and economic inequality; "feasibility" variables, such as the percentage of the population that is young males and the presence of mountainous terrain in which to organize rebellions; and a variety of "control" variables, such as type of regime and overall economic well-being. Their earlier work (Collier and Hoeffler 2004) demonstrated that greed motivated violence much more than grievance: there was no relationship between ethnic fragmentation and the outbreak of war but a significant relationship between the presence of exploitable raw materials to export and civil war. This suggests that "ethnic" civil wars are in fact based on greed, but leaders use communal rhetoric to mobilize support and justify their actions. Their more recent work (Collier, Hoeffler, and Rohner 2009) updated and confirmed these conclusions but added a new finding, that the feasibility of civil war is an even stronger explanatory variable: leaders will start wars, and sometimes justify them in communal terms, when the opportunity arises.

Toft and Petersen both used the comparative method to test their theories. Employing the most similar systems design, they focused on carefully selected cases in the former Soviet Union (Toft 2003) and Eastern Europe (Petersen 2002), allowing them to hold constant a large number of cultural and historical variables for which all the countries in the study are similar. Toft first employed statistical data to demonstrate a correlation globally between the presence of geographically concentrated ethnic groups and ethnic conflict. This correlation supported her hypothesis that conflict occurs where both the state and an ethnic group claim the same key territory. She then examined key case studies to demonstrate the mechanisms of the interactions in greater detail. She showed, for instance, that Russia and Tatarstan avoided conflict because the Tatars' demands were largely economic and therefore divisible. In contrast, a bloody

Explaining Ethnic Violence *(continued)*

conflict broke out between Russia and Chechen rebels because the Chechens demanded an indivisible territory, while the Russian state feared setting a precedent that other geographically concentrated ethnic groups might try to follow and, thus, refused to grant independence. Petersen examined case studies in Eastern Europe over the past century. He first noted that ethnic conflict almost always happens during periods of rapid political change, such as after World War I and after the fall of the communist regimes. He concluded that the two most widely accepted hypotheses in the past—fear based on a security dilemma and "ancient hatreds"—explain little of the ethnic violence in his cases. Instead, he found that resentment is the most common emotional motivation for violence.

QUESTIONS IN CONTEXT

All three approaches can be subject to criticism. Paul Collier and his colleagues (Collier and Hoeffler 2004; Collier, Hoeffler, and Rohner 2009) demonstrated statistically significant relationships among their key variables, but their model as a whole still explains less than a third of the variation in their dependent variable: the outbreak of civil war. As do all statistical techniques, theirs demonstrated correlations, but the authors must assert or assume the mechanisms that connect one variable to another without direct evidence of a connection. This is the case with their implicitly instrumentalist theory of elite manipulation of ethnicity to spur civil war. Comparative case studies can and do look at exactly those mechanisms. They suffer,

Religion as Group Identity

We can apply most of what we have learned about ethnic groups to religious groups as well. A religious group identifies itself as having a particular set of characteristics centered on religious membership or beliefs. When membership alone is the criterion, the group is identified simply by nominal affiliation with the religion, regardless of actual practice or belief. The three major groups in the former Yugoslavia were defined primarily in this manner: Serbs are Orthodox, Croats are Catholic, and Bosniaks are Muslim. As noted above, once tension and conflict began to emerge, leaders in each of the groups started to emphasize cultural distinctions. Ironically, because Communists had ruled the country since World War II, religious belief and practice were very low among all three groups prior to the outbreak of conflict; religious affiliation was a marker of identity based on birth, not a matter of personal faith. As the conflict spread, religious observance increased within all three groups. Once people start shooting at you because of your religion, it starts to loom larger in your consciousness.

One might assume that religious group membership can be more inclusive and flexible than ethnicity, more like civic nationalism than cultural nationalism. Virtually all religions allow conversion to the faith, so while you may not be able to become Chechen, except perhaps through marriage, you can convert to Islam. In practice this may be more difficult than in theory, however, especially where religious identity has become a form of cultural marker and a basis of political

though, from limited ability to consider all variables and all cases. Toft's (2003) and Petersen's (2002) claims are focused on the former communist countries. As our mini case on Rwanda suggests (see pages 168–169), Toft cannot help us understand the genocide in Rwanda, though Petersen's insights might be more helpful. A key criticism of Petersen's theory comes from instrumentalists, who argue that he ignores the crucial role of individual leaders in stirring the emotions at play. Petersen argued, in contrast, that the violence is fairly predictable based on the structural situation, which is translated into action via emotions, regardless of which leaders are involved. Collier and his colleagues would question both authors for their failure to examine cases that did not involve explicit ethnic claims, claiming that these omissions prevented them from realizing that ethnicity might be a rhetorical justification for actions based on opportunity and greed.

With so many variables, it is important to ask, What is the ultimate purpose of this type of research? What do we most need to explain, the outbreak of explicitly ethnic or religious violence or the outbreak of any violence? Is the purpose of our argument simply to explain, or is it to point toward solutions? And which of the studies above provides conclusions on which solutions might be founded? While no theory may yet completely explain why people commit ethnic violence, it is incumbent on social scientists, including comparativists, to try to find explanations, not only to further knowledge but to provide a sound basis on which preventive strategies might be developed.

mobilization that is at least implicitly targeted against other groups. It is unlikely that members of these other groups will want to convert at this point, or be accepted if they did. Conversion is much more likely when the political salience of religious identity is relatively low.

The demands of religiously mobilized groups are comparable to those of ethnic groups: recognition and autonomy. For religious groups, recognition certainly involves the right to practice one's faith openly, but it might also include demands that the state officially recognize the religion in the form of state-sponsored religious holidays or recognize and perhaps fund religious schools. A desire for autonomy could be expressed as a demand for federalism if the religious group lives in a particular region. Within its own state or province, the group could then practice its religion and use the state or provincial government to support it. Demands for autonomy can also take the form of asking that religious leaders and organizations be granted legal control over marriage, death, and other personal matters.

Multiethnic and multireligious states need not be conflictual, though they often are. The wrong context combined with ambitious leaders can produce deep-seated, potentially violent political battles. Authoritarian states often try to avoid such conflict by simply banning any expression of ethnicity or religion, but in the long run this approach is unlikely to work. Some degree of recognition, autonomy, or both is usually essential if a mobilized group is to find its place peacefully inside a larger state. Nigeria provides an interesting case study of the possibility and problems of using political mechanisms to reduce ethnic and religious tension.

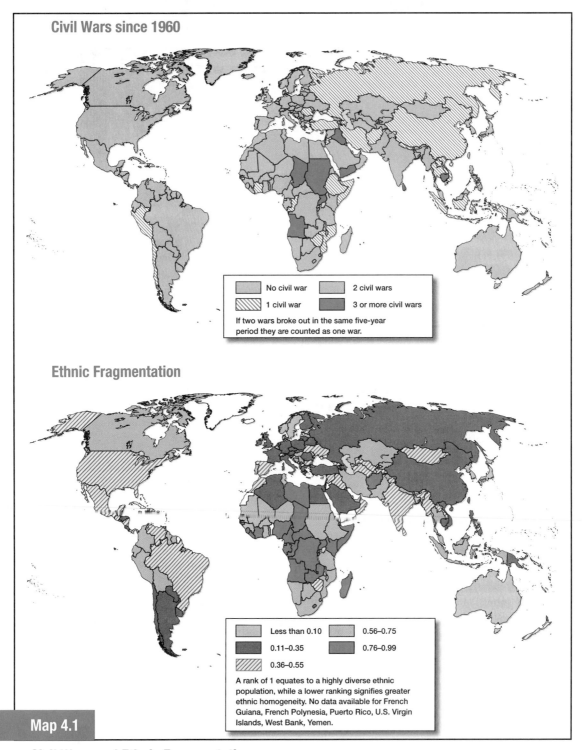

Civil Wars since 1960

	No civil war		2 civil wars
	1 civil war		3 or more civil wars

If two wars broke out in the same five-year period they are counted as one war.

Ethnic Fragmentation

	Less than 0.10		0.56–0.75
	0.11–0.35		0.76–0.99
	0.36–0.55		

A rank of 1 equates to a highly diverse ethnic population, while a lower ranking signifies greater ethnic homogeneity. No data available for French Guiana, French Polynesia, Puerto Rico, U.S. Virgin Islands, West Bank, Yemen.

Map 4.1

Civil Wars and Ethnic Fragmentation

A comparison of the level of ethnic fragmentation and the outbreak of civil wars around the world demonstrates that the relationship between ethnicity and violent conflict is more complicated than people usually assume. While some countries with the highest levels of ethnic fragmentation have suffered from multiple civil wars (such as Congo, Angola, and Nigeria), others have had none (Kenya, Kazakhstan, Canada). As the Methods in Context box on pages 160–163 explains, the task of figuring out when ethnic diversity leads to violence is a complex and ongoing area of political science research.

Source: Civil wars map: Paul Collier, Anke Hoeffler, and Dominic Rohner, "Beyond Greed and Grievance: Feasibility and Civil War," Table 1, *Oxford Economic Papers* 61 (2009): 1–27. Ethnic fragmentation map: Alberto Alesina, et al. "Fractionalization," *Journal of Economic Growth* 8 (2003): 155–194.

CASE STUDY

Nigeria's Strange History of Ethnicity and Religion

- Colonial origins of ethnic identity
- Political power, resource battles, and civil war
- Centripetalism and federalism to manage ethnic conflict
- Shift in political saliency from ethnicity to religion
- Oil and ethnic conflict

Conflict over ethnicity and oil led to an unsuccessful secession attempt by the Igbo and then civil war in 1968. Oil and ethnicity are still a volatile mix in southeastern Nigeria.

Credit: AP Photo/Kurt Strumpf

As outlined briefly in chapter 2, Nigeria is the quintessential colonial creation. People of many languages and faiths were brought together within its boundaries, where approximately 400 languages are now spoken. Three groups emerged as numerically predominant: the Hausa in the north, the Yoruba in the west, and the Igbo in the east. We say "emerged" because that is exactly what happened. While many Nigerians perceive their ethnic identity in primordial terms, those identities were in fact socially constructed primarily in the twentieth century. The Hausa are a Muslim people sharing a common language who were governed in twelve separate city-states by Muslim emirs in the eighteenth and nineteenth centuries. Today they constitute approximately 30 percent of Nigeria's population. The Yoruba shared a common language and a common indigenous religion that later became the basis for Haitian *voodoo* and Brazilian *candomblé*. Like the Hausa, for most of their precolonial history the Yoruba were not politically united. They were instead divided variously among several kingdoms over time, which sometimes lived in peace but suffered prolonged warfare in the late precolonial period. Under colonial rule, most Yoruba converted to Christianity, though a large minority today are Muslim. Yoruba constitute about 20 percent of Nigeria's current population. The Igbo, on the other hand, had no conception of themselves as a people prior to colonial rule. They lived in small, mostly independent villages ruled by councils of elders—a classic **acephalous,** or stateless, society. The word

Igbo first appears in documents in the 1930s. Under colonial rule, members of this group converted to Christianity more quickly and completely than did the Yoruba or Hausa. By independence, they constituted 18 percent of Nigeria's population.

Despite their different origins, all three identities had emerged as ethnic groups by the end of colonial rule. Each came to perceive its collective interests as "tribal," defined by region and language. Indirect rule (described in chapter 2) played a part in this, as colonial chiefs became leaders over what the British, and the Nigerians, increasingly came to see as "tribes." Missionaries and anthropologists were crucial in the recognition of the Igbo and other stateless societies as distinct groups. As they wrote down "tribal histories" that told primordialist stories of ancient and noble traditions and political unity, and transcribed a common "Igbo" language, they codified that language and the Igbo culture.

For all three groups, internal political disagreements faded in the face of their common interests vis-à-vis the colonizer and, increasingly, each other. As members of these groups moved to the growing colonial cities to work, they encountered members of other groups and gained employment and other benefits from members of their own group who had moved to the urban areas before

acephalous society: A stateless society, ruled by very local level government only

them. These migrants began to compete for jobs, with members of each group supporting their own, and patron-client networks like those discussed in chapter 3 emerged. Separate networks developed within the groups, which established the importance of ethnicity to one's material well-being. Those who became Christian were the first to be educated in colonial schools and in the English language, which gave them an advantage in the job market. The Igbo in particular benefited from this; the Hausa, being Muslim and therefore receiving little Christian education, lost out. Military employment, however, required less education than most sectors of the economy, and the Hausa and other northerners found greater success in this arena. Southerners, and especially the Igbo, dominated in education, civil service, and private business, even outside their own region of the country.

The approach of independence in 1960 provided a context for solidifying ethnic and regional identity, and separate nationalist movements emerged in each of the three regions, each led by one of the three major ethnic groups. Budding national leaders mobilized followings on ethnic and regional bases, as instrumentalists would predict. Obafemi Awolowo rallied the Yoruba by creating a cultural organization, the Egbe Omo Oduduwa, or "the descendants of Oduduwa" (the mythical founder of the Yoruba people). Northern leaders used memories of the independent Muslim Sokoto caliphate of the nineteenth century to mobilize support for the Northern People's Congress. There was no comparable Igbo cultural organization, but the National Council of Nigeria and Cameroons, which originated as a broader nationalist party, became a de facto Igbo party led by Nnamdi Azikiwe by the late 1950s. When leaders of the three groups and the British negotiated a federal system of government on the eve of independence, some autonomy was given to each of the three regions. This meant that a coalition of two of the three would be required to form a national government. The northerners, led by the Hausa, shared the country's first independent government with the Igbo; by dint of numbers, the northerners

were the dominant partner. The Yoruba in the west were left in opposition.

The newly independent government was fragile from the start. The three major parties, one representing each ethnic group, consolidated their power over the minorities in their own regions. The minorities, members of Nigeria's over 200 much smaller ethnic groups, resented the political power of the larger groups and began demanding their own regions. By the 1990s, this pressure would result in the Nigerian government creating thirty-six states out of the original three regions. Growing tensions between the central government and the regions, as well as friction among the three major parties, led to a chaotic and violent second election in 1964. The military stepped in with the nation's first coup d'etat in 1966, led mainly by Igbo officers. The new government eliminated federalism, arguing it had caused much of the division and conflict of the prior years. Whatever the military's actual reason for taking power, the Yoruba and Hausa saw the coup and the elimination of federalism as an Igbo effort to grab power. In response, widespread rioting broke out in northern cities. Hausa attacked Igbo working as civil servants and in business, and tens of thousands were killed.

This violence merged with a battle over a new resource, oil, and ultimately escalated to full-scale civil war. A second military coup six months after the first brought a northern military government to power that restored federalism, this time creating twelve states. The division of the three existing regions gave some smaller ethnic groups their own states. It was also an attempt to keep control of oil revenues out of Igbo hands, as oil production in the eastern region was rapidly on the rise. After the second coup and further violence against Igbo in the north, the Igbo military leader of the eastern region declared the independence of a new country, Biafra, in 1967. The effort to create a new nation foundered, however, when non-Igbo minorities in the region did not support the effort. The result was a three-year civil war (1967–1970), ultimately unsuccessful, in which more than a million people perished.

Northerners have ruled Nigeria for most of its history. Under the first two democratic republics (1960–1966 and 1979–1983), their numerical strength gave them electoral victories in voting that was sharply divided along ethnic lines. In the current Third Republic, inaugurated in 1999, leading northern politicians decided to support a southerner, former Yoruba military ruler Olusegun Obasanjo, who ruled with greater support from the north than from his own region from 1999 to 2007. Because of their predominance in the military, northerners also controlled most of the military governments that ruled between the democratic regimes. With each return to democracy, a new constitution was drafted to try to contain ethnoregional conflict through the use of federalism and strict rules governing how political parties could form. The 1979 constitution took an avowedly centripetal approach, requiring all political parties to have representatives in all areas of the country; to win the presidency, a candidate had to win not just the most votes but also at least 25 percent of the vote in two-thirds of the nineteen states. Similar provisions in the 1999 constitution seem to have coincided with less ethnically tense politics at the national level.

The reduction in ethnic tension, however, is due in part to a shift of political saliency from ethnic to religious identity. With the rise of the global Islamist movement, identity politics began to shift subtly in Nigeria. A marginal Muslim sect led by a self-proclaimed prophet emerged in the north and criticized both the government and mainstream Islam. Sect followers, mostly the urban poor and unemployed, engaged in extensive rioting in 1980, Nigeria's first religiously based conflict of any significance. The riots led to growing Muslim-Christian tensions as non-Muslims came to fear that a Muslim government might try to "Islamize" the new capital of Abuja. Religious tension continued to simmer throughout the 1990s, and the country's north-south regional division came to be seen as primarily religious rather than ethnic.

The 1999 constitution gave state governments the right to set their own legal systems. Newly elected governors in several northern states used this provision to rally a religious following by proclaiming Islamic *sharia* as state law. One reason for the popularity of this move was the weakness of the Nigerian state itself. The new government seemed incapable of controlling crime, reviving the economy, or controlling growing ethnic militias in parts of the south. Given this uncertain context, both ethnic and religious identity appealed to many people as possible sources of security. Although in theory *sharia* can apply to only Muslims, and a secular legal system would remain for non-Muslims, Christians were nonetheless mobilized to oppose what they saw as the Islamization of their states. Increasing competition over land among ethnic groups, some Christian and others Muslim, also fuels this conflict. In 2010, a local battle in the ethnically and religiously mixed city of Jos—between a Christian and a Muslim ethnic group who were battling over land, cattle, and local political power—resulted in several hundred deaths, only the latest in a series of clashes in that region.

In the southeastern part of the country, local ethnic movements emerged in the mid-1990s around the issue of benefits from oil. Members of these movements, which contained both peaceful and violent elements, argued that all the oil revenue went to the central government and they were left with environmental devastation and poverty, in spite of living in the oil-rich region. The best known of these movements originated among the Ogoni, who were led by internationally known poet Ken Saro-Wiwa until his execution in 1995. He and his movement successfully linked Ogoni ethnic demands with environmental and oil revenue concerns in a locally powerful movement that the military government ultimately tried to quell by executing Saro-Wiwa and several other leaders. To date, oil revenues remain under the control of the central government, and the situation on the ground remains tense. Violent clashes, mostly involving young men from the Ijaw ethnic group, erupted in 1999 on the day after the newly elected government was sworn in, and in 2002 a group of Ijaw youth took over a ChevronTexaco oil facility to demand better treatment for Ijaw workers. In 2003 several oil producers suspended operations in Nigeria entirely until the country's military regained control of the situation. A 2009 cease-fire temporarily halted the violence, but the government's failure to follow through on reforms quickly enough meant it did not last long. In 2010, the largest violent group, the Movement for the Emancipation of the Niger Delta (MEND), detonated bombs in the capital at Nigeria's celebration of its fiftieth anniversary of independence; this was the first time the oil-fueled ethnic violence had spread beyond the oil-producing region itself.

Among the Yoruba, a separatist movement, the O'odua People's Congress, emerged before the 1999 election in response to the military government, and it continues to attract young urban Yoruba to its sometimes violent activities. Though not focused on oil, the group does advocate Yoruba nationalism and strong federalism.

CASE SUMMARY

A number of lessons can be taken from the history of Nigerian ethnicity and religion. First, although they are socially constructed and usually quite modern, once ethnic and religious divisions are politicized, they become difficult to contain. Both military and civilian governments struggled with these forces, and at times their efforts at control exacerbated the problems rather than ameliorating them. Even seemingly logical solutions, such as creating more state governments and requiring that political parties have some degree of support across the country, had limited success because in the context of economic inequality, relative deprivation, political insecurity, and conflict over oil, political leaders were able to raise ethnic and religious support quite easily. A key problem in Nigeria has been state and local governments' discrimination against "non-indigenes"—people not originally from a particular area and not part of the locally dominant ethnic group—which has made political mobilization of the victims of these policies relatively easy.

Second, the political saliency and focus of different identities can shift relatively quickly. In the 1960s, national political divisions were primarily a three-way split among the major ethnic groups and regions. Thirty years later, the major political division was along a two-way, north-south, Muslim-Christian divide. Ethnicity had not disappeared; it had simply become more localized. In areas of religious conflict over the use of *sharia* as state law, ethnic and religious divisions often overlapped at the local level. In the southeastern oil region, local ethnicity continued to be very powerful, and Yoruba and "Biafran" separatist movements still exist today, ready to gain more followers when the time is right. All of this has posed severe challenges for Nigeria's efforts at democracy. Ethnic conflict was a primary force frustrating the two prior attempts at democracy, and religious and ethnic tensions threaten to undermine the current democracy.

MINI CASE

Rwanda: Trying to Understand Genocide

In 100 days in Rwanda in 1994, thousands of Hutu slaughtered 800,000 of their Tutsi compatriots in the worst genocide since the Holocaust. It's one thing to understand why people adhere to group identities based on some cultural or historical commonalities, or even to understand how ethnically divided civil war might arise, but for most people it's much harder to understand why seemingly "normal" people would violently attack people of another group.

In most cases of genocide, including Rwanda, people had been living together more or less peacefully (though not without resentment and memories of past violence) when, seemingly overnight, large numbers of one group started slaughtering people in a different group. How can we come to terms with such behavior? The most common explanation is the primordial one of "ancient hatreds," yet no situation shows the inaccuracy of the concept of primordial "tribal conflict" better than Rwanda, a precolonial kingdom that survived colonialism with its borders more or less intact. Hutu and Tutsi speak the same language, live in the same communities and neighborhoods, have the same customs, follow the same religions, and have lived for centuries in the same kingdom. Cultural differences between them don't exist. What did exist were several other elements commonly involved in the political mobilization of ethnicity: a potential battle over a key resource (land), a sense of relative deprivation, fear of attack in a situation of extreme political uncertainty, and an elite using a racist ideology to mobilize hatred of the "other."

Tutsis dominated the precolonial kingdom, and Belgian colonial rule reinforced their status by increasing Tutsi power and control. At independence in 1960, a "Hutu revolution" overthrew the Tutsi monarchy and established a Hutu-led government, which would rule until the genocide in 1994. The revolution produced hundreds of thousands of Tutsi refugees, who fled to neighboring countries. An entire generation of Tutsi grew up in neighboring Uganda but were never granted citizenship or full rights there, and they longed to return home. Some launched a successful invasion of the country in 1990. By 1993 a ceasefire had been established, and democratic elections were planned with the goal of establishing a new government of both Hutu and Tutsi. Elements on both sides, however, feared the results. Hutu leaders enjoyed the privileges of power and wanted to maintain them, and some Tutsi rebel leaders seemed unwilling to allow the majority (overwhelmingly Hutu) to rule.

A group of Hutu extremists in the government, some of whom have since been convicted of genocide by United Nations tribunals, began propagating an anti-Tutsi ideology, primarily via radio. They continuously told their followers that the Tutsi were trying to regain complete power, take away Hutu land and power, and kill them. In a very densely populated country dependent on agriculture,

the threat to land ownership was particularly explosive. The Hutu extremists also created private militia of unemployed and desperate young Hutu men, and when the Hutu president's plane was shot down on April 6, 1994, the extremists and their armed militia swung into action. First their military supporters staged a coup. Then barriers went up across streets all over the capital, and the militia began systematically executing "moderate" Hutu who might oppose the genocide (lists of the first to be killed had been prepared in advance), as well as any Tutsi they found. The extremist hate-radio directed much of the effort, telling the militia where Tutsi were hiding and urging them to "chop down the trees." (The stereotype of a Tutsi person is tall and thin; hence the image of cutting down trees.) Members of the militia demanded that other Hutu join them in identifying and killing Tutsi; those who refused would themselves be killed as moderates who could not be trusted. The rest of the world watched in horror but did little to stop the killing. Finally, a Tutsi-led rebellion swept into the capital, took over the country, and stopped the genocide—but not until more than three-quarters of the entire Tutsi population had been killed.

CASE SUMMARY

While crimes of this magnitude are impossible to explain fully, a context of fear and a battle over resources (land) and power, enflamed by irresponsible, hate-mongering leaders, helps us understand how such an event could happen. Many ethnic conflicts have a deep history, but that history does not make violence inevitable. Hutu and Tutsi identities have precolonial origins, but colonial rule increased the tensions between the groups. Battles over control of the newly independent state led to the exile of large numbers of Tutsi, who sought to fight their way back into power thirty years later. Fearing their removal from power and possible retribution, Hutu extremists systematically implemented a "final solution," whipping up Hutu fears to mobilize a fanatical following. Widespread violence is the logical conclusion of any ideology demanding national, racial, or ethnic purity.

RACE

race: A group of people socially defined primarily on the basis of one or more perceived common physical characteristics

While the distinction between ethnic group and nation is relatively clear, the difference between ethnic group and race is much more ambiguous. In a particular context, it may seem obvious, but at a more abstract level, a consistent distinction is difficult to apply systematically. Following Stephen Cornell and Douglas Hartman (2007, 25), we define a **race** as "a group of human beings socially defined on the basis of physical characteristics." Most ethnic identities focus on cultural rather than physical characteristics, though many do see specific physical characteristics as markers of particular groups as well. Most racial groups are distinguished by physical characteristics, though they and others may also perceive cultural distinctions. The distinction between race and ethnicity, then, is not perfect, but this is probably the best we can do.

An interesting example of the interconnectedness of the terms comes from ethnic and racial categorizations in much of Latin America. In many Latin American countries with substantial indigenous populations, such as Guatemala, indigenous people who keep their traditional language, dress, and customs regard themselves as an ethnic group. The dominant groups in society, however, may regard these people in both ethnic and racial terms. This is made clear when a separate term (such as *ladino* in Guatemala) is reserved for persons of indigenous descent who adopt Spanish and no longer maintain indigenous customs. In this case, race and ethnicity are clearly intertwined and depend very much on whose opinion is being asked.

Perhaps more important than the actual definitions of race and ethnicity is the difference in these identities' origins and social construction. Most of the time, ethnicity has its origins at least partially in a group's self-assertion of its identity. While others may try to impose an identity on the group, most ethnic groups represent people who are themselves claiming an identity and the political demands that often go with that claim. Race, in contrast, originates in the imposition of a classification by others. Race in its modern sense began with Europeans' expansion around the globe and their encounter with markedly different peoples. Primarily to justify European domination, European explorers and, later, colonists classified the native populations of the lands they conquered as distinct and inferior races. Embedded within the very classification was an assertion of power (primarily Luke's third dimension of power outlined in chapter 1). This legacy continues today: almost every racial classification system marks current or quite recent differences in power along racial lines. Ethnicity can also represent starkly different positions in a power structure (as many have argued has been the case in Nigeria), but in many cases it does not (as in the case of German Americans or Italian Americans today). Ethnicity and race, then, usually differ in how they are marked (culture vs. physical characteristics), their origins (self-assertion vs. external imposition), and the degree of power differences embedded in their contemporary social construction.

For the concept of race, just as for that of nation and ethnicity, we emphasize perception. Genetically, members of racial groups, such as white and black Americans, have as much in common with each other as they do with members of their own groups: genetic variation is no greater across the two groups than it is within each. Races are constructed by focusing on particular differences, such as skin color, and ignoring the far more numerous similarities. Discussing sex, Sigmund Freud referred to this process as "the narcissism of minor differences," the process by which humans amplify the importance of very minor biological variations, such as X versus Y chromosomes or skin color.

Like all socially constructed categories of identity, racial identity varies across time and space, as the case studies of the United States and Brazil below demonstrate. While racial groups may seem absolutely fixed and "natural" to most people in a particular time and place, they are just as subject to change as national and ethnic identities. This is also true of political mobilization along racial lines. Theoretically, a racial identity need not be political in the sense of being a basis for common political goals, but given the power dynamic inherent in racial classification, a political element nearly always exists. Like ethnicity, whether this leads to political mobilization of a racial group depends on the ability of particular leaders to articulate a common agenda by using the symbols of racial identity and discrimination in a compelling way. A dominant or majority group, such as white Americans, typically will not see itself as pursuing a common political agenda, though members of other races may think otherwise. Groups in a minority or subordinate position are more likely to view their political interests as tied to their racial identity, in part because they face discrimination on that basis.

Politicized racial groups usually desire recognition and representation. Autonomy is a less common goal because racial groups usually do not share a distinct geographical home. Recognition usually means official governmental recognition of the race as a socially important group through such means as inclusion on a census form, the teaching of the group's historical role in the larger national history, and the celebration of its leaders and contribution to the nation's culture. In addition, racial groups desire representation in the sense of full formal and informal participation in their government and society. Thus, racial demands typically do not involve such mechanisms as federalism but instead focus on inclusion in public and private employment, political offices, and the educational system. Frequently, as in the United States, members of minority races may argue that past discrimination justifies some type of preferential system that works relatively rapidly to achieve representation equal to their share of the population. Mechanisms to do this might include numerical targets or goals for hiring, increased funding for training and education, or adjustments to the electoral system that make the election of racial minorities more likely. As the cases of the United States and Brazil show, racial politics can be just as intense as ethnic or national politics, so state leaders often see it as in their interests to respond, or at least appear to respond, to racial demands.

CASE STUDY

Racial Politics in the United States

- Evolving definitions of racial groups
- Legal racial discrimination and boundaries
- The making of "white" America
- Black political responses to discrimination
- Immigration and social construction of new racial categories
- Continuing segregation and inequality
- President Obama and current U.S. racial politics

On the night Barack Obama was elected the first African American president in U.S. history, he stood before a massive crowd in Chicago and said, "If there is anyone out there who still doubts that America is a place where all things are possible; who still wonders if the dream of our founders is alive in our time; who still questions the power of our democracy, tonight is your answer. . . . It's the answer spoken by young and old, rich and poor, Democrat and Republican, black, white, Latino, Asian, Native American, gay, straight, disabled and not disabled. . . ." He claimed a new era had begun. For months, Americans had been debating whether their country was "ready" to elect its first black president. Would doing so mean the end of

President-elect Barack Obama, accompanied by his wife Michelle and Vice President–elect Joe Biden and his wife Jill, take the stage after Obama delivered his victory speech in Chicago, Tuesday night, November 4, 2008. Obama's historic election as the first African American president raised new questions about America's long struggle with racial politics. Would a new postracial era emerge, or did his political repudiation in the 2010 congressional elections signal, in part, a racial backlash against the leadership of a black man?

Credit: AP Photo/Morry Gash

the long national saga of racial animosity and segregation, or was it merely window dressing, the election of a black man who worked hard to appeal to whites and who would govern a country no less racist than before? Further, did his political drubbing two years later in the 2010 congressional elections signal a backlash against the leadership of a black man in America?

Obama's election is but the most recent major event in America's long racial history. While most Americans today see racial categories as self-evident and more or less fixed, nothing could be further from the truth. The three oldest racial categories in the United States are white, black/African American, and Native American. The white-Native conflict reduced Native populations nearly to extinction. The black population, on the other

hand, grew substantially, and the white-black division became the one that had the greatest impact on American political history and national identity. For most of the country's colonial and independent history, this racial division was legally defined to distinguish clearly between black slave and white citizen, and it eventually took the form of the "one drop" rule, which classified anyone with virtually any black heritage as black and therefore as a slave. This rule ensured that the offspring of slave women and white masters remained slaves and thus property. In the immediate aftermath of slavery, legal racial definitions remained important in underpinning the segregationist laws of the Jim Crow era. The famous *Plessy v. Ferguson* case of 1896 codified such postslavery racial definitions by classifying a person as "black" if the individual had one-eighth black ancestry (that is, if one of eight great-grandparents was classified as black). Like the one-drop rule before it, this definition served to keep the black population clearly identified as such and the black-white boundary as distinct as possible.

The black-white division, though, has not been the only racial question in U.S. history. The clear categorization of all European immigrants as white that is so accepted today was by no means automatic. Writing in 1897 in *The Conservation of Races,* and reflecting the racial understanding of his time, the great black intellectual W. E. B. du Bois listed the following races:

> the Slavs of eastern Europe, the Teutons of middle Europe, the English of Great Britain and America, the Romance nations of Southern and Western Europe, the Negroes of Africa and America, the Semitic people of Western Asia and Northern Africa, the Hindoos of Central Asia and the Mongolians of Eastern Asia.

The predominantly Anglo population of the United States in the late nineteenth century shared du Bois's categorization, which meant that immigrants from southern and eastern Europe were not viewed as racial equals. This changed only with the passage of significant time and the slow assimilation across generations of Irish, Italians, Poles, Jews, and others into the white majority. A study of this era and this process is aptly titled *How the Irish Became White* (Ignatiev 1995).

The ultimate success of these groups in claiming a place of equality within the white majority had significant effects. First, most discriminatory practices against them ended over time; by the end of the twentieth century, no discernable differences in socioeconomic standing existed between members of these groups and the larger white population. Second, this assimilation process helped preserve a clear white majority in the country as a whole. Given the huge number of immigrants, had they ultimately been classified into the distinct races listed by du Bois, today

the country would have no clear racial majority. Third, white "ethnics," as they are sometimes called, see themselves as white and American first and "ethnic" only secondarily, if at all. Their ethnic origin may be a source of pride and may influence their culture in various ways, but it has virtually no impact on their political allegiance or behavior.

This is certainly not true, on the other hand, for African Americans and other blacks, whose racial identity has always profoundly affected their political activity. Du Bois (1897) wrote that the "American Negro" (the term he used at the time) suffered from a "double consciousness [in which o]ne ever feels this two-ness—an American, a Negro; two souls, two thoughts, two unreconciled strivings; two warring ideals in one dark body, whose dogged strength alone kept it from being torn asunder." The very history of racial terminology reflects the struggle of descendants of African slaves to assert a positive racial identity. A century ago, *Negro* replaced *colored* as the preferred term; it was an assertion of identity against prior derogatory terms. In the late 1960s, *black* came to replace *Negro* via the "black power" movement, which was an attempt to unite around the most obvious sign of racial character, skin color, and proclaim "black is beautiful." In the 1980s, Jesse Jackson helped popularize *African American,* arguing that his people should have the same status as any other "hyphenated" immigrant group. In the new millennium, even that term has become contested. As unprecedented numbers of black Caribbean and African immigrants have arrived, the question of what term, if any, captures all Americans of African descent is still very much alive. Many Caribbean immigrants do not identify as "African American," while newly arrived Africans, and their American-born children, may be giving a whole new meaning to the term.

Throughout this terminological evolution, African Americans have been united and politically mobilized most successfully by their common experience in the face of discrimination. Until at least the early 1960s, local laws throughout the United States kept most blacks restricted to impoverished ghettoes or isolated rural areas with limited access to social, economic, or political opportunities. They were, at best, second-class citizens. This situation produced two major branches of thinking about their identity, both of which have always involved important political positions and demands. From Frederick Douglass to Martin Luther King Jr. and Jesse Jackson, one strand has focused primarily on proclaiming and demanding racial equality within the existing U.S. political and social system. King's core demands were the rights enshrined in the Declaration of Independence and the U.S. Constitution: a system that actually operates on the precept that "all men are created equal." The legal elements of this effort were achieved with the Civil Rights Act of 1964 and the Voting Rights Act of 1965, finally and permanently granting African Americans the complete rights of citizenship.

These laws did not fully eliminate the effects of past discrimination, however. In the last four decades, the efforts of leaders within the African American community have focused on programs to achieve full social and economic integration that will ensure equal representation of African Americans in the political system, the economy, and civil society. These efforts have included demands for (1) "affirmative action," that is, programs in education, employment, and business that accommodate specific hiring policies directed toward minorities; (2) equal funding for educational opportunities; (3) greater funding for programs to improve conditions for the poor, who are disproportionately black and Hispanic; (4) changes in the electoral system to enhance the possibility that African Americans will be elected into public office; and (5) encouragement of African American voting and other forms of participation in the electoral process.

Running parallel to this first line of defining black identity is the second strand, usually referred to as "black nationalism." Melanye Price (2009) identified four key strands of this ideology: (1) black self-determination in the sense of control over their own community institutions; (2) a clear plan for obtaining and maintaining their own financial, political, and intellectual resources for a self-sustaining community; (3) severing ties with whites that foster ideas of racial inferiority; and (4) a global view of black oppression and liberation. One of the earliest and most extreme manifestations of this was promoted by Caribbean-born activist Marcus Garvey, who popularized the "back to Africa" movement in the early twentieth century. Based on the belief that blacks would never be accepted as full citizens in the United States, he proposed a large-scale immigration to a new, or renewed, homeland in Africa. This was the ultimate demand for autonomy rather than representation.

More recent black nationalists generally do not demand complete segregation from white America but greater black autonomy within it. During the "black power" movement of the 1960s, black power leaders went beyond proclaiming blacks' rightful place in U.S. society by emphasizing that fundamental change in the U.S. socioeconomic system was needed before racial equality could be achieved. Their actions aimed first at creating a more positive self-image among the black community rather than demanding immediate changes in white behavior or attitudes. Groups like the Black Panthers worked to improve the lives of poor blacks in urban areas, provided self-defense training and protection (from the police as well as from criminals), and educated blacks about the glories of their African past, all with little support from or interest by white society at large. Advocates of this approach argued that not until black power was achieved in this way could blacks ultimately force racist whites to move toward racial equality. Survey data from the 1990s showed that only about 15 percent of African Americans could be characterized as adherents of black nationalism, but detailed discussions showed that those who did adhere to it had distinctive political views. They did not trust the American political system to be fair and were more likely to blame the system rather than individual blacks for continuing problems that blacks faced (Price 2009).

Blacks and whites, of course, are not the only racial groups in the United States. The people now called "Asian Americans" and

"Hispanics" have been present since at least the mid-nineteenth century, and Mexicans lived in the Southwest long before it became part of the United States. The terms *Asian American, Hispanic,* and *Latino,* however, are of very recent origin. Immigrants from China, Japan, and other Asian countries, as well as residents of Mexican descent, identified themselves primarily by nationality until the mid-twentieth century. Chinese immigrants, for instance, thought of themselves as Chinese, and later Chinese American, but not as Asian American. A relatively small population and often poor, they had little influence on national politics. Like other immigrants, the Chinese were treated as second-class citizens in many ways, even in areas where their populations were fairly large.

Intellectual and political activists in these minority communities were influenced by the black power movement in the 1960s and began to conceive of themselves and their political demands in new ways. Rather than focusing on their separate countries of origin, leaders began to shift the focus of their identity to their common experiences in the United States. They argued that Chinese, Japanese, Filipino, and other immigrants faced common linguistic and racial hurtles and experiences in the United States, so they coined the term *Asian American* to unite them under one identity. This movement began with a student strike in San Francisco in 1968, as Japanese, Chinese, and Filipino students came together from separate ethnically defined organizations to form a new Asian American Political Alliance. Similarly, leaders of Mexican, Puerto Rican, Dominican, and other South and Central American groups began to use the more overarching *Hispanic* to assert a common identity tied to their common language and experience of discrimination.

Hispanics have been the fastest growing census group in the United States over the past twenty years. They became the largest "minority" group in the country in 2000, and grew by an additional 43 percent by 2010. While most Americans probably think of Hispanic as a racial category, it is legally a linguistic category: Hispanics are defined as Spanish speakers or descendants of Spanish speakers. Officially, these individuals can be of any race. The U.S. census, however, still has not come to reflect accurately the self-perception of Hispanic Americans. In the 2010 census, 53 percent of Hispanics identified themselves racially as white; another 37 percent identified themselves as "some other race," which indicates an unwillingness to accept any of the official U.S. racial categories. After 2000 the Census Bureau tried unsuccessfully to eliminate the category of "some other race" in an attempt to force Hispanics to choose among the existing racial categories, but political pressure by the Hispanic community successfully resisted this effort. A 2005–2006 survey of Hispanics found that fully 51 percent said that "Hispanic/Latino" is a racial category (Latino National Survey). While the construction of the category "Hispanic/Latino"—socially, politically, and legally—is still very fluid, a Hispanic/Latino racial identification may well emerge eventually, becoming the newest addition to the construction of racial categories in the United States. The possible shift from a primarily linguistic to a racial identity reflects in part a shift of focus from a common cultural heritage to a common position in America's racial hierarchy. It is a potential change in the community that Hispanics/Latinos "imagine" themselves to be a part of.

Racial inequality in the United States remains considerable despite the political mobilization of racial groups in recent decades. Table 4.1 shows recent data for education and income for the largest racial groups. As these data make clear, while Asian Americans have achieved, and indeed surpassed, the levels of education and income achieved by whites, African Americans and Hispanics continue to suffer much lower levels of both. And Asian Americans do not graduate from high school in as high a percentage as do whites, indicating something of a divided Asian American population, with many earning college degrees but quite a few not even finishing high school. School segregation actually increased from 1991 to 2004 across all racial categories, and residential segregation remains extensive. While residential segregation has declined since 1970 for African Americans, it has remained high, the highest for any racial group, and has actually increased for Latinos. Asian American residential segregation has also declined and is only moderate, still significant but well below the rates for African Americans and Latinos (Schmidt et al. 2010, 109–120).

Obama's rapid ascent raises new questions about political representation of racial minorities: has their underrepresentation finally started to end, a half century after the Voting Rights Act? It has certainly improved since then, but unevenly; no group is fully represented except whites, who are overrepresented, as the data in Table 4.2 demonstrate. The House in 2011 was notably closer to being representative than the Senate, but even in the House, Hispanics remain significantly underrepresented. African Americans have come close to parity in the House, but had no representation in the Senate, to which only five African Americans have ever been elected—two in the 1870s and three since World War II—and never more than one at a time. Barack Obama was only the second African American senator since 1980. The first was Carol Moseley Braun, also from Illinois. All African American senators have come from three states: Mississippi in the 1870s, and Massachusetts and Illinois since 1960. A broad study by Schmidt et al. (2010) found that while levels of participation and

TABLE 4.1

Racial Disparity in the United States

	White (not Hispanic)	African American	Asian	Hispanic (all racial categories)
Percentage with college degree	30%	17%	50%	13%
Median household income per household member, 2009 ($US)	$30,362	$17,612	$30,719	$14,758

Sources: Income data from the 2009 Census Population Survey, U.S. Census Bureau; education data from "Educational Attainment in the United States: 2007," U.S. Census Bureau, http://www.census.gov/prod/2009pubs/p20-560.pdf.

TABLE 4.2

Racial Representation in Congress

	White (not Hispanic)	African American	Asian	Hispanic (all racial categories)
Percentage of population	74.5%	12.4%	4.4%	15.1%
Political representation in Congress in 2011 (% of House/Senate)	81% / 96%	10% / 0%	3% / 2%	6% / 2%

Sources: Population data from "United States Fact Sheet 2000–2009," U.S. Census Bureau; political representation data from "The United States Congress Quick Facts," ThisNation.com, http://www.thisnation.com/congress-facts.html.

Note: There are 435 total seats in the U.S. House of Representatives and 100 seats in the Senate.

representation have increased significantly for all racial minorities over the last generation, minorities remain outside the main ruling coalitions, and they have been unable to get the policies they most strongly support, such as affirmative action and immigration reform, passed into law in a form they approve of.

In this socioeconomic and political context, then, has the Obama presidency had a major impact? Many African Americans, in particular, claim it has, saying they can now honestly tell their children (or at least their sons) that they can "become whatever they want to be." On the other hand, Obama avoided the most racially contentious issues as much as possible in his campaign, and his election has done nothing to change the data in Table 4.1, at least in the short term. Many celebrated Obama's strong showing among white voters. He won 2 percent more white votes than did the Democratic candidate, John Kerry, in 2004, but his opponent still won 55 percent of white votes overall. Obama, on the other hand, won 95 percent of the African American vote and 67 percent of the Hispanic vote. Obama voters overall were about 60 percent white, compared with 90 percent white for his opponent. Obama also won in the context of a severe recession and a very unpopular incumbent president of the opposite party. Political scientists Michael Lewis-Beck and colleagues created a statistical model based on past elections to predict what we might expect for an opposition victory in that context, and they found that Obama probably would have received about 5 percent more of the vote than he did, were racial bias not a factor. In particular, whites who indicated some degree of racial resentment against blacks were much less likely to vote for Obama than the model predicted. The researchers also noted that the Democratic congressional vote nationwide was several percentage points above Obama's total. Overall, they concluded that Obama's race probably cost him about 5 percentage points of the total vote (Lewis-Beck, Tien, and Nadeau 2010).

Since the election, the virulently anti-Obama "Tea Party" movement has arisen and gained great attention, especially when a few of its members yelled racial and homophobic epithets at black and gay members of Congress during the debate over health care. Surveys of Tea Party members in 2010 showed that whites who strongly supported the movement are significantly more likely to believe that African Americans have received too much attention and that they do not face serious discrimination any more. Also, in the first two years of Obama's presidency, the number of antiblack hate crimes rose sharply.

In the longer term, the Obama presidency, and Obama himself, raise bigger issues about the social construction of race and racial politics in the United States. Many observers have pointed to the growing racial diversity of the country, especially the rapidly growing Hispanic and Asian populations, and the increasing rates of racial intermarriage (something Obama himself symbolizes as the son of a white woman and black man), to argue that the United States may finally move beyond its racial divisions, especially the white-black dichotomy that has defined it for so long. The bulk of intermarriage, though, is occurring within the growing Hispanic community and between Hispanics and members of other groups: black-white levels of intermarriage outside the Hispanic community have risen much more slowly. More generally, the country remains racially segregated in terms of residence, education, and income, especially between whites on the one hand and blacks and Hispanics on the other, and this segregation matters politically. A recent study by Cara Wong (2010) using data from several nationwide surveys showed that whites who identified blacks as part of their "community"—people they felt somehow close to—were significantly more likely to support policies they perceived to favor blacks, such as affirmative action, than whites who did not feel close to African Americans, but only 5 to 27 percent of white Americans (depending on the survey) felt African Americans were part of their community. Similarly, blacks who felt close to whites were less likely to take black nationalist policy stands than those who did not feel close to whites, and between 19 and 64 percent of them felt close to whites. Segregation clearly persists and seems to affect political attitudes across racial groups.

CASE SUMMARY

The election of Barack Obama is clearly an event of great import, the biggest milestone in the fight for racial equality in the United States since the Voting Rights Act of 1965. The debate about whether the United States will overcome the power of inequalities and prejudices built into the country's socially constructed racial system will continue, however. American racial categories were constructed in a way that both reflected and reinforced the divisions of power based first on slavery and then on legal segregation. As segregation and discrimination have become more informal and (some argue) ambiguous, racial identities have as well, now being legally based on self-identification rather than governmental imposition. Immigration has long had an important role to play in the social construction of race in America, and the current era of Hispanic and Asian immigration is no exception.

A crucial question is whether recent immigrant groups, like their European predecessors a century ago, will assimilate into the white majority or remain distinct; the answer will play a major role in how Americans think about race and its political impact over the next century. As in many places around the world, the response of racially subordinate groups has varied from demanding full inclusion to greater autonomy or even separation, but the former has almost always won out over the latter. In our next case study, Brazil, race is socially constructed in quite different ways, resulting in very different racial political dynamics as well.

CASE STUDY

Race in Brazil

- Ambiguous and complex definition of racial categories
- A policy of "whitening" and shifting racial identification
- Claims of a "racial democracy"
- Difficulty of creating a black political movement
- Affirmative action and continued questions of "Who is black?"

A comparison of the United States and Brazil demonstrates in stark terms the variation and importance of racial identity and racial politics in different contexts. Like the United States, Brazil was a major slaveholding society. Indeed, Brazilian slavery was much more extensive and lasted longer: abolition did not occur until 1888, making the country the last in the Americas to outlaw slavery. At the time of abolition, approximately half of Brazil's population was at least partially of African slave descent.

Despite very different conceptions of racial identity and politics, racial discrimination and inequality in Brazil are similar to what is found in the United States. The different conceptions of race, however, have made it much more difficult for a clear black racial consciousness to emerge in Brazil and effectively demand black recognition and representation. Only in the last thirty years has a sustained Afro-Brazilian political movement emerged and achieved some success in altering the country's racial policies.

The black-white dichotomy that characterizes U.S. racial history makes little sense to most Brazilians. Brazil contains literally dozens of informal racial categories and distinctions. Intermarriage between light-skinned and dark-skinned people has been and remains fairly common. More important, Brazil's social construction of race is nearly opposite to that of the United States. Racial identity is constructed not on the basis of descent but on the basis of physical features, with seven major categories from "white" *(branco)* to "black" *(preto)* and numerous minor ones. Throughout the twentieth century, Brazil proclaimed itself a racial democracy because no legal racial segregation had existed there since the end of slavery. Simultaneous with and contradictory to these claims, however, has been an explicit desire to "whiten" the population in a variety of ways.

For many years, Brazilian intellectuals and leaders claimed that Brazilian slavery was more humane than slavery in the United States, although few historians accept this view today. While no more humane, it was certainly different. Slaves in Brazil, working in tropical conditions on plantations, tended to die younger than North American slaves. The system survived for centuries, not by the biological reproduction of slaves but instead by the large-scale importation of new slaves to replace the dead. This meant that defining the children of slaves as slaves was not as economically important as it was in the United States. Combined with the fact that for a long time Portuguese immigrants to Brazil were overwhelmingly male, the result was the early beginnings of a **"pardo,"** or mixed-race, group. The ease of importing slaves also meant Brazilian slaveholders were less opposed than their North American counterparts to slaves buying their freedom. This combination of factors resulted in a significant free population of *pardos* and some blacks by the time of abolition. Since the country was a monarchy until 1889, no one could vote, so the existence of this group also created no immediate political threat to the white elites. Creating a clear "black-white" dichotomy was not as important as it was in the United States, so a multilayered system of racial classification corresponding loosely to Brazil's extensive racial intermarriage emerged instead.

With the declining economic importance of the northeastern plantations in the late

A Brazilian women's group displays the variety of hues that make up Brazil's complex racial system. Brazil never had laws against racial intermarriage, which has long been much more common than in the United States and is reflected in its population. Thus, the question "Who is black?" continues to have no clear answer.

Credit: © Borderlands/Alamy

nineteenth century and international pressure to end the last system of legalized slavery in the New World, Brazil achieved abolition peacefully and nearly simultaneously created a republic. With the growing industrialization of southern cities, many former slaves moved south, especially to Rio de Janeiro. The central government in Rio never imposed legal segregation of the sort found in the United States during the Jim Crow era, but it did pursue the policy of "whitening." This included encouraging and even subsidizing the immigration of European workers and completely banning black immigration. By 1920 half of the industrial workforce was composed of immigrants, and virtually all of them were from southern and eastern Europe. As in the United States, this large-scale immigration of people who came to be defined as "white" kept the black and *pardo* proportion of the

pardo: In Brazil, a mixed-race group

IN CONTEXT

RACE AND ETHNICITY IN LATIN AMERICA

Nearly 50 percent of Brazilians are of African descent, whereas only 1 percent are indigenous. In most Latin American countries, though, identity politics focus on indigenous ethnicity. Survey data on race and ethnicity in Latin America are difficult to interpret, but the following data give some idea of the issues of race, ethnicity, and access to power and resources that concern the region.

- 29 percent (about 150 million people) of the population of Latin America and the Caribbean is of African descent; more than half of these live in Brazil.
- 8 percent (about 40 million people) of the region's population is indigenous and lives in every country except Uruguay.
- 400 indigenous languages are spoken in the region.
- Indigenous people comprise 30 to 50 percent of the populations of Bolivia, Ecuador, Guatemala, and Peru.
- Nearly 25 percent of all Latin American indigenous people live in Mexico, but they comprise only 10 percent of Mexico's population.
- Indigenous people are disproportionately poor; for example, while approximately 66 percent of all Guatemalans are poor, 90 percent of indigenous Guatemalans are.

Source: Mayra Buvinic and Jacqueline Mazza, with Ruthanne Deutsch, ed. *Social Inclusion and Economic Development in Latin America.* Washington, DC: Inter-American Development Bank, 2004.

population smaller than it would have been otherwise.

Whitening in Brazil also included active encouragement of racial intermarriage to "improve" black genetics with white genes, and those few blacks or *pardos* who were able to crawl up the class ladder were also "whitened" in the process. Racial discrimination was milder for those with higher levels of education and wealth, which would come to be the source of the common Brazilian phrase "money whitens." Brazil's white population, facing a country in which at least half of

the population was of slave descent, actively encouraged the creation of intermediate racial categories as buffers between them and poor, uneducated blacks. Even the census was employed for this purpose. Over the years, the Brazilian government actively used it to encourage people to identify with some intermediate category instead of "black" or to deny the existence of race entirely by simply not asking any racial questions at all. The policy worked: the 1890 census recorded 44 percent of the population as "white"; the 1950 census put the figure at 62 percent, with a similar increase in "*pardo*" identification and a reduction in "black" identification. These trends shifted toward the mixed category by 2000, when 42 percent identified as *pardo* and 52 percent as white, but only 5 percent as black.

Brazilian historian and intellectual Gilberto Freyre is credited with coining the term *racial democracy* in the 1930s, arguing that Brazil's racial mixture meant no real racism existed. At the same time, populist president Getúlio Vargas embraced Afro-Brazilian cultural practices such as samba, *carnaval* (Brazilian Mardi Gras), and *condomblé* (a Brazilian descendent of Nigerian Yoruba religion). This meant that African heritage was celebrated as part of the racial democracy and national culture, even as discrimination and efforts to whiten the population continued. Political discrimination, when a democracy existed, was secured by a law requiring voters to be literate, disenfranchising the majority of the black population without imposing legal racial restrictions.

The whitening policy also allowed what was called the "mulatto escape hatch." If education, intermarriage, and a better income could whiten people and improve their social status, why actively try to identify yourself as "black"? For this reason, most poor blacks viewed their difficulties in terms of class, not race, preferring to view themselves as poor, a condition they could escape by winning the lottery or getting money some other way, than as black, a condition they could never change. Bailey (2009), using several surveys from 1995 to 2002, found that most

Brazilians' sense of racial group identity is weak, though they simultaneously recognize racial discrimination as a reality and problem in their society. In this context, political activists had a difficult time constructing and maintaining an Afro-Brazilian identity. In contrast to the United States during the same period, no significant black movement emerged in the 1950s and 1960s. A stronger black movement emerged with the new democracy in the 1990s, but the insistence of most groups in the movement that anyone who is not white should identify as "black" has limited its appeal.

The military government in power from 1964 until 1985 reinforced the policy of denying the importance of race, so when Brazilian social scientists in the 1960s produced the first studies demonstrating the extent of racial inequality, the military banned all studies of racial discrimination and exiled several of the scholars involved. In response, the *Movimento Negro Unificado* (Unified Black Movement) became an active part of the struggle for democracy, but the group's long-term gains remained limited. Beginning in the 1980s, newly elected state governors, especially in the major urban areas like Rio de Janeiro, started to place some blacks in leadership positions and officially began to recognize Afro Brazilians as a group by, for instance, incorporating Afro-Brazilian cultural events in schools. At the national level, however, the major political parties, even those on the left of the political spectrum, continued to focus on class issues and to downplay the importance of race, and very few self-identified blacks were elected to the National Congress.

Brazil is still a racially unequal society. A 2005 United Nations Development Programme (UNDP) study ranked the country overall 73rd in its Human Development Index (a combination of economic well-being, health, and literacy), but the white population alone would have ranked 44th, while the black and *pardo* population together would have ranked 105th. In 2008, 46 of 513 members of the National Congress were identified as being of African descent, but only 17 self-identified as black. One of these, Benedita da Silva, has spent many years trying to create an Afro-Brazilian

caucus in the Congress, an effort that has been successful only in the past few years and then with only a handful of members. Most Brazilian politicians, whatever their background or skin color, still see little political gain from identifying as Afro-Brazilian. Through 2008, only six Afro-Brazilians had ever been appointed cabinet ministers, the first three being Benedita da Silva, soccer great Pelé, and pop musician Gilberto Gil.

The most dramatic change in Brazil's racial policies occurred recently with the government's official endorsement of a quota-based affirmative action program in 2002. Fernando Henrique Cardoso, president from 1995 to 2003, had been one of the pioneers of the study of racial discrimination who was forced into exile during the 1960s. Upon assuming the presidency in 1994, he actively encouraged a rethinking of Brazil's racial policy. This came together with large-scale preparation for the United Nations' 2001 World Conference on Racism to produce the country's biggest debate on race in decades. Those who opposed changing existing policies argued that it is impossible to determine who is truly "black" and therefore deserving of affirmative action; proponents argued that all those who identify as "not white" face discrimination. Affirmative action has mainly occurred within Brazil's universities, where blacks and *pardos* have constituted a tiny fraction of the student body. As universities have implemented racially based admissions policies, they have faced difficult challenges determining who should qualify. Some have used independent panels to assess photos or interview candidates and examine their documents to determine exactly which applicants should qualify for the benefit. In at least one famous case, two brothers received different classifications, one white and the other black (following Brazil's long-standing construction of race based on color, not descent). By 2009, forty-eight public universities and hundreds of (less prestigious in Brazil) private universities had adopted racial quotas, benefitting tens of thousands of students. A study of the state university in Rio de Janeiro, the pioneer of the quota system, found that those admitted under quotas performed equally as well as the general student body, though the numbers coming in under the system were declining (Andrea Cicalò 2008).

Despite evidence of some success, debate over these policies continues. Some observers have argued that affirmative action may actually serve to encourage the creation of a stronger Afro-Brazilian identity and movement, as members of this group come to see themselves as the beneficiaries of such policies (Racusen 2010). Bailey (2009) found that when the possible benefits of affirmative action policies were mentioned in surveys, the percentage of respondents who said they were black increased substantially. Others worry that such policies will further divide the country along racial lines. Many argue that the real problem is class, not race, and some universities now include quotas for graduates of Brazil's relatively poor-quality public schools. The lower house of the national legislature passed a bill in 2009 that mandated quotas of 50 percent for black, *pardo,* and public school graduates in federal universities (so far, they apply in most state universities but are optional for federal ones), but the bill stalled in Brazil's upper house. In mid-2009, a Brazilian court ruled Rio de Janeiro's quota system unconstitutional on the grounds that it is a system of racial discrimination, a decision that was appealed and remains pending. As this debate shows, even with this policy shift, the question "Who is black?" and how the state should respond to past and current racial inequality have not been resolved.

CASE SUMMARY

The social construction of race in Brazil is strikingly different from that in the United States. With the state not needing to demarcate a clear legal line between black and white, either during slavery or after, and with a long history of racial intermarriage, Brazilian racial classifications have been much more fluid and complex than the historical duality between black and white in the United States. Based on this, Brazilians have long argued that their country is a racial democracy and have consciously distanced themselves from the legalized segregation of the United States and South Africa under apartheid. But Brazil's discrimination has been simply different, not less. One of the authors noticed a classified ad in a Brazilian newspaper in the 1980s seeking an office receptionist that said the employer needed a *"moca da boa aparencia"*—literally a "good-looking girl." While that was striking to a postfeminist American, he later found out that the language was coded and really meant a "fair-skinned girl," even more striking to a post–civil rights American.

Indeed, the lack of stark racial divisions and legalized discrimination is a major explanation for the limited black political mobilization in Brazil. Like the United States, Brazil is now engaged in a major debate over affirmative action. While the debate has some familiarity to an American, the difference in how race is socially constructed makes the debate distinct, focusing mainly on Brazil's long-standing question: Who is black?

CONCLUSION

Who Rules?

Identity politics are so common and explosive in part because the very construction of the groups often creates and reflects differences in political power. This is most common in the case of race, but it can be true for ethnic or national differences as well (and certainly for gender and sexual orientation, subjects we examine more closely in chapter 12). As identity categories are created, a sense of superior and inferior status is often embedded within them. European expansion created a white-dominated racial order within many countries and globally. For several centuries, European (white) society, culture, and political systems were seen by those in power as superior; others could gain access to power, if at all, by trying to become "white" (as in the United States and Brazil, in different ways) or at least by adopting and accepting white institutions and norms. The recent economic and political gains of people of color in many countries have altered this trend, though many analysts still see subtle ways in which white norms are held as superior, and in most countries whites remain socioeconomically advantaged in many ways.

As these examples suggest, how a group is defined influences what it may claim in order to gain or enhance its power: anything from specific legal protections like antidiscrimination laws or the right to school their children in a local language to regional autonomy, power-sharing arrangements, or national statehood. In addition, the strength of a group's grievances and the state's response to its demands may determine whether a regionally based ethnic group seeks autonomy or "national" sovereignty. Similarly, actions taken in pursuit of redress of grievances may range from lobbying, voting, and constitutional reform to armed violence and secession. In countries with significant immigration, like the United States and Germany, new immigrants continually raise new issues: their racial or ethnic categorization must be clarified, and the ongoing construction of their categories will influence their place and political power in the broader "nation" they are attempting to join.

What Explains Political Behavior?

Each person belongs to various identity groups, but whether people act politically based on these group memberships depends on a variety of factors. First, the group in question must have a preexisting sense of itself: it must be an "imagined community" with both perceived historic ties and a forward-looking agenda. Second, it must have some felt grievance. This could be a sense of suffering historical discrimination or relative deprivation; a desire to claim a share of some newly important (and enriching) natural resource; or a reaction to a recent change in law, such as passage of a bill requiring all public schools to teach in a dominant national language. Finally, groups seem to need political leadership, elites who can build on and strengthen the identity and link it to the grievance and to appropriate action. This is easier to accomplish if a strongly felt imagined community is already in place. Elites can work with and strengthen a weakly felt sense of identity, as the example of the creation of countries like Germany or Italy out of many smaller regional groups suggests, but the groups must have some shared and accepted basis for this to work, and the elites must have resources to make it work as well.

It is also useful to remember that the political salience of even strongly felt identities can change rather quickly. Nigeria and Sudan are both examples of this. In Nigeria, political conflict has shifted from a primarily ethnic to a primarily religious basis; in Sudan, the change has been in the opposite direction over more or less the same time period. Such changes may have to do with the nature of a conflict and how it overlaps preexisting identities. The case of Nigeria also suggests the influence of globalization on local identity groups: local groups may be influenced by dominant global discourses as they begin to mobilize. Today the resurgence of global Islamism provides a context that enhances the tendency of local groups to see their struggle in religious terms; for most of the twentieth century, in contrast, the dominant global discourse was about nationhood, encouraging local groups that saw themselves as culturally different to cast their struggles in ethnic or nationalist terms. Similarly, the civil rights movement in the United States has served as an inspiration for black movements elsewhere, including in Brazil.

Where and Why?

Identity influences political behavior everywhere. Identity-based political movements have arisen in most countries around the world at one time or another, and every state tries to foster some sense of national identity. Violent identity-based conflict, fortunately, is not as common as nonviolent movements, though there is no shortage of examples to study. Explaining why violence breaks out in certain situations and not others, and what we can do to prevent it, is crucial. Factors that explain the rise of identity movements, such as relative deprivation, can be used to explain the outbreak of violence as well, but that model leaves us with the question of why violence isn't more common than it is. Recent studies have focused on particular aspects of identity-based conflicts that seem to spur violence: irresolvable competing claims to territory perceived by one or more groups as a "homeland" (such as Israel and Palestine, Serbia and Kosovo); fear based on a domestic security dilemma, often in the context of a weak state or rapid political changes (the former Yugoslavia); and resentment based on long-standing feelings of mistreatment and exclusion from power (Rwanda). No single factor will probably ever explain why people seek to harm and kill others simply because they are defined as somehow "different," but we have now developed a fairly convincing list of the various factors that lead identity-based competition to become violent conflict.

The question then is, What can states do to prevent these conflicts? Because identity politics often threaten the very existence of states, governments have to care about the issues involved. The leaders of governments typically want to mobilize a national identity tied to the state, while simultaneously demobilizing all other identities. Sometimes, however, the very effort to create a unifying national identity spawns challenges from ethnic, religious, or other groups. National identities based on specific racial or ethnic groups inherently exclude some as they include others. As the excluded groups are politically mobilized, state leaders must try to find a way either to eliminate that mobilization (the typical authoritarian option) or contain it within the institutional boundaries of the existing political system through federalism or other power-sharing mechanisms (as democracies typically try to do). Power sharing of some type seems essential to keeping identity-based political competition within nonviolent bounds, but this is never easy. Political leaders often try to achieve this while yielding little in the way of real power or resources, as the case of Nigeria has shown over the years, which only causes opponents to demand more. And once a conflict has become violent, reducing tension and rebuilding trust afterward can be particularly difficult. Once mobilized, identity politics can thus be quite explosive.

Applying Theory to the Study of Identity Politics

Comparativists have drawn on many different theoretical approaches to try to understand the dynamics of identity politics. Cultural theories and ideology are of obvious relevance, in that conceptions of identity are often part of particular political cultures and justified by clearly elaborated ideologies such as nationalism. Primordialism often asserts a static conception of a fixed identity as part of an equally static political culture, while the more recent constructivist approach draws on postmodern conceptions of culture. Scholars studying identity-based violence often draw on psychological theory as well, asserting that fear or resentment is crucial to understanding why violence occurs.

Instrumentalists, on the other hand, bring rational-choice theory to bear on identity politics: elites pursue their political and economic interests via the mobilization of identity groups. Instrumentalists' ideas have been extremely influential; virtually all modern arguments about identity politics draw on them in some form, and virtually all theories of how to contain identity-based political conflict implicitly involve rational-actor models as well. Both the centripetal and consociational approaches attempt to design political institutions on the assumption that self-interested leaders of identity groups will respond rationally to these institutions. These models disagree about which institutions will achieve the best outcome because they make different assessments of the probability that political actors will be willing to engage in political mobilization on lines other than identity. Implicit in both approaches is an institutionalist assumption that political institutions matter to shaping political behavior.

Both pluralist and elite theories contend for attention in the study of identity politics as well. Pluralists point to competing groups and the institutions that can encourage or discourage compromise. Elite theorists, on the other hand, see in some identity categories clear systems of dominance that engage Luke's second and third face of power to maintain, for instance, the power of one racial group over others. Ongoing debate demonstrates that no theoretical approach has become dominant in the complex study of identity politics.

KEY CONCEPTS

acephalous society (p. 165)
assimilationist (p. 152)
autonomy (p. 150)
centripetal approach (p. 157)
civic nationalism (p. 151)
consociationalism (p. 157)
constructivism (p. 147)
cultural nationalism (p. 151)

ethnic group (p. 155)
instrumentalism (p. 147)
jus sanguinis (p. 152)
jus soli (p. 152)
nation (p. 150)
nationalism (p. 150)
pardo (p. 179)
political saliency (p. 146)

politics of recognition (p. 155)
primordialism (p. 147)
race (p. 170)
relative deprivation (p. 156)
security dilemma (p. 160)
social construction (p. 148)

WORKS CITED

Alesina, Alberto, Arnaud Devleeschauwer, William Easterly, Sergio Kurlat, and Romain Wacziarg. 2003. "Fractionalization." *Journal of Economic Growth* 8 (2): 155–194.

Anderson, Benedict. 1991. *Imagined Communities: Reflections on the Origin and Spread of Nationalism.* New York: Verso.

Andrea Cicalò, Giuseppe. 2008. "What Do We Know About Quotas? Data and Considerations About the Implementation of the Quota System in the State University of Rio de Janeiro (UERJ)." *Universal Humanist* 65: 262–280. http://www.scielo.unal.edu.co/scielo.php? script=sci_arttext&pid=S0120-48072008 000100012.

Bailey, Stanley R. 2009. *Legacies of Race: Identities, Attitudes, and Politics in Brazil.* Stanford, CA: Stanford University Press.

Brass, Paul R. 1991. *Ethnicity and Nationalism: Theory and Comparison.* Newbury Park, CA: Sage.

Brubaker, Rogers. 1992. *Citizenship and Nationhood in France and Germany.* Cambridge, MA: Harvard University Press.

Collier, Paul, and Anke Hoeffler. 2004. "Greed and Grievance in Civil War." *Oxford Economic Papers* 56 (4): 563–595. doi:10.1093/oep/gpf064.

Collier, Paul, Anke Hoeffler, and Dominic Rohner. 2009. "Beyond Greed and Grievance:

Feasibility and Civil War." *Oxford Economic Papers* 61 (1): 1–27. doi:10.1093/oep/gpn029.

Cornell, Stephen, and Douglas Hartmann. 2007. *Ethnicity and Race: Making Identities in a Changing World.* 2nd ed. Thousand Oaks, CA: Pine Forge Press.

Du Bois, W. E. B. 1897. *The Conservation of Races.* Available at http://www.teaching americanhistory.org/library/index.asp?document=1119.

Gellner, Ernest. 1983. *Nations and Nationalism.* Oxford, UK: Blackwell.

Horowitz, Donald L. 1985. *Ethnic Groups in Conflict.* Berkeley: University of California Press.

Huntington, Samuel P. 1997. *The Clash of Civilizations and the Remaking of World Order.* New York: Touchstone. Originally published 1996 by Simon & Schuster.

Ignatiev, Noel. 1995. *How the Irish Became White.* New York: Routledge.

Latino National Survey. University of Washington Institute for the Study of Ethnicity, Race and Sexuality. http://depts.washington.edu/uwiser/LNS.shtml.

Lewis-Beck, Michael S., Charles Tien, and Richard Nadeau. 2010. "Obama's Missed Landslide: A Racial Cost?" *PS, Political Science & Politics* (January): 69–76. doi:10.1017/S1049096509990618.

Lijphart, Arend. 1977. *Democracy in Plural Societies: A Comparative Exploration.* New Haven, CT: Yale University Press.

Lowe, Chris. 1997. "Talking About 'Tribe': Moving from Stereotypes to Analysis." With Tunde Brimah, Pearl-Alice Marsh, William Minter, and Monde Muyangwa. http://www.africaaction.org/talking-about-tribe.html.

Nairn, Tom. 1977. *The Break-Up of Britain: Crisis and Neo-Nationalism.* London: New Left Books.

Petersen, Roger. 2002. *Understanding Ethnic Violence: Fear, Hatred, and Resentment in Twentieth-Century Eastern Europe.* New York: Cambridge University Press.

Price, Melanye T. 2009. *Dreaming Blackness: Black Nationalism and African American Public Opinion.* New York: New York University Press.

Racusen, Seth. 2010. "Affirmative Action and Identity." In *Brazil's New Racial Politics,* edited by Bernd Reiter and Gladys Mitchell, 89–122. Boulder, CO: Lynne Rienner.

Renan, Ernest. 1882. *What Is a Nation?* http://www.nationalismproject.org/what/renan.htm.

Schmidt, Ronald, Sr., Yvette M. Alex-Assensoh, Andrew L. Aoki, and Rodney E. Hero. 2010. *Newcomers, Outsiders, and Insiders: Immigrants and American Racial Politics in the Early Twenty-first Century.* Ann Arbor: University of Michigan Press.

Smith, Anthony D. 1998. *Nationalism and Modernism.* New York: Routledge.

Taylor, Charles. 1994. "The Politics of Recognition." In *Multiculturalism: Examining the Politics of Recognition,* edited by Amy Gutmann, 25–74. Princeton, NJ: Princeton University Press.

Toft, Monica. 2003. *The Geography of Ethnic Conflict: Identity, Interests, and Territory.* Princeton, NJ: Princeton University Press.

Wong, Cara J. 2010. *Boundaries of Obligation in American Politics: Geographic, National, and Racial Communities.* Cambridge, UK: Cambridge University Press.

Yuval-Davis, Nira, and Flora Anthias, eds. 1989. *Woman-Nation-State.* Consultant editor Jo Campling. Basingstoke, UK: MacMillan.

RESOURCES FOR FURTHER STUDY

Ghai, Yash P., ed. 2000. *Autonomy and Ethnicity: Negotiating Competing Claims in Multi-Ethnic States.* Cambridge, UK: Cambridge University Press.

Hobsbawm, Eric J. 1990. *Nations and Nationalism since 1780: Programme, Myth,* *Reality.* Cambridge, UK: Cambridge University Press.

Hutchinson, John, and Anthony D. Smith, eds. 2000. *Nationalism: Critical Concepts in Political Science,* Vol. IV. New York: Routledge.

Juergensmeyer, Mark. 1993. *The New Cold War? Religious Nationalism Confronts the Secular State.* Berkeley: University of California Press.

Taras, Raymond, and Rajat Ganguly. 2002. *Understanding Ethnic Conflict: The International Dimension.* 2nd ed. New York: Longman.

Van Deburg, William L., ed. 1997. *Modern Black Nationalism: From Marcus Garvey to Louis Farrakhan.* New York: New York University Press.

WEB RESOURCES

Conflict Analysis Resources, Royal Holloway, University of London (www.rhul.ac.uk/economics/research/conflict-analysis/whats_new.html)

Correlates of War (www.correlatesofwar.org)

Data & Research, The World Bank (http://econ.worldbank.org)

Fractionalization Data, The MacroData Guide (www.nsd.uib.no/macrodataguide/set.html?id=16&sub=1)

Research Network on Gender Politics and the State (http://libarts.wsu.edu/polisci/rngs)

The Religion and State Project, Bar Ilan University, Israel (www.religionandstate.org)

United States Institute of Peace (www.usip.org)

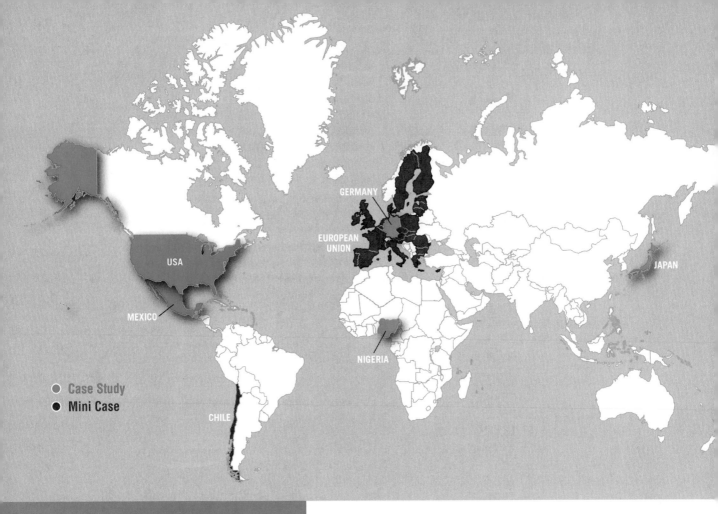

Case Study
Mini Case

Who Rules?

- In what ways do economic policies reflect the relative power of different interest groups in a country?
- How important are globalization and international organizations in determining the economic policies of individual countries?

What Explains Political Behavior?

- Why have some states intervened in the market economy more than others?

Where and Why?

- Why has the most common development policy of the last thirty years—"structural adjustment"—had much greater success in some countries and regions than in others?

GERMANY
EUROPEAN UNION
JAPAN
USA
MEXICO
NIGERIA
CHILE

MEXICO
JAPAN
GERMANY
NIGERIA
USA
EUROPEAN UNION
CHILE

5

STATES AND MARKETS

Barack Obama ran for the U.S. presidency in 2008 with an ambitious agenda for domestic policy: reforming health care, achieving energy independence, fighting global warming, and improving education. As the fall campaign got underway, everything changed. The "Great Recession" began with the bankruptcy of two giant Wall Street banks in the face of a collapsing housing "bubble." The presidential campaign quickly shifted focus, not to future plans for improvement or even to the wars in Iraq and Afghanistan, but to fixing the economy by halting the financial collapse, stemming rapidly rising unemployment, and restarting economic growth. As Bill Clinton's 1992 presidential campaign put it, "It's the economy, stupid!" Political leaders in democracies across the globe rise and fall on the basis of citizens' perceptions of the economy and their own economic well-being. Citizens have come to expect the state to guide the economy to improve their lives, not hurt their bottom lines.

In communist countries such as the Soviet Union and China during the Cold War, governments tried to control virtually all economic activities. While some of these countries initially succeeded at industrialization, as the decades passed, they fell further and further behind the economic productivity of wealthy market economies in the West. Market economies have become nearly universal since the end of the Cold War. In these economies, the state does not control the economy, but a government can and usually does intervene in the economy (to a greater or lesser degree) to try to encourage economic growth and to influence how the benefits of that growth are distributed. Therefore, the relationship between the state and the market and the debates surrounding it are crucial to understanding modern politics virtually everywhere. As the Country and Concept table (page 190) demonstrates, even though virtually all countries are now market economies, they have achieved widely varying levels of economic success. Different histories, positions in the global economy, and economic policies produce dramatically different levels of wealth, economic growth, unemployment, inequality, and poverty.

We can ask questions about how economic policy formulation helps us understand "Who rules?" in a given country, based on who seems to benefit most from particular policies. In this era of globalization, we must also ask about the role of international influences in setting economic policies: perhaps external forces rule more than any particular domestic force, at least in weaker states. We must also ask

COUNTRY AND CONCEPT
States and Markets

Country	Average real GDP growth 1980–2009[1]	Average unemployment, 1980–2008[2]	Average inflation, 1980–2009[1]	Absolute poverty, 2010[3] (% of population below $1.25 per day)	Inequality (GINI Index), 2010[4]
Brazil	2.7	11.5	396.6	5.2	55.0
China	10.0	4.7	5.7	15.9	41.5
Germany	1.7	13.6	2.3	0.01	28.3
India	6.0	5.0	8.1	41.6	36.8
Iran	3.6	10.9*	19.5	< 2.0	38.3
Japan	2.2	5.4	1.2	0.01	24.9
Mexico	2.6	5.4	31.6	4.0	51.6
Nigeria	4.4	N/A	21.1	64.4	42.9
Russia	1.6	13.4	99.7	< 2.0	43.7
United Kingdom	2.1	10.6	4.0	0.01	36.0
United States	2.7	8.3	3.7	0.01	40.8

[1]International Monetary Fund. "World Economic Outlook Database, 2010." http://www.imf.org/external/pubs/ft/weo/2010/02/weodata/index.aspx.

[2]International Labour Organization. http://laborsta.ilo.org/. Data for the unemployment rate, average annual (% of labor force). Reliable unemployment data for Nigeria are not available because of the difficulties of measuring unemployment in an economy characterized by a large informal sector.

[3]Human Development Reports. "Multidimensional Poverty Index." http://hdr.undp.org/en/media/HDR_2010_EN_Table5_reprint.pdf.

[4]Human Development Reports. "Inequality-Adjusted Human Development Index." http://hdr.undp.org/en/media/HDR_2010_EN_Table3_reprint.pdf.

*Average includes only those years from 1990 to 2009.

political behavior questions about why some states and some eras are characterized by greater state intervention in the economy than others, as well as questions about where and why certain economic policies seem to succeed or fail. First, though, we must understand some fundamental economic concepts.

THE MARKET, CAPITALISM, AND THE STATE

market economy: An economic system in which individuals and firms exchange goods and services in a largely unfettered manner

A **market economy** is an economic system in which individuals and firms exchange goods and services in a largely unfettered manner. This includes not only the exchange of finished products but also inputs into the production process, including labor. To most people, this seems like a natural state of affairs, but until fairly recently it was the exception, not the norm. In many preindustrial societies, people subsisted on the fruits of their own labor and engaged in very limited trade. In feudal Europe, most people were legally bound to a particular lord and manor and could not exchange their labor for a wage anywhere they pleased. The creation of the modern market economy required that feudal bonds restricting labor be broken so that most people would become dependent on market exchanges for their survival and so that productivity would increase enough to allow the regular production of a surplus that could be traded. In modern industrial and postindustrial societies, virtually the entire population depends on earning a wage or taking a share of profit via market exchanges.

Capitalism **Capitalism** is not exactly the same thing as a market economy, though the terms are typically used interchangeably (and we do so in this chapter). Rather, capitalism is the combination of a market economy with private property rights. In theory, one can imagine a market economy without individual property rights. For example, collectively owned firms could be free to produce whatever they could for a profit in an unfettered market. Yugoslavia under the communist rule of Jozef Tito attempted but never fully implemented a modified version of such a system in the 1960s and 1970s.

In practice, however, virtually all countries have some form of a capitalist economy today. The degree to which the market is unfettered and the precise nature of private property rights vary widely. There is no absolute law in economics about how "free" market exchanges or private property must be for a capitalist economy to function. The debates over the extent to which the state should intervene to limit and shape market exchanges and property rights are at the core of many of the most important political issues around the globe. The end of the Cold War may have effectively eliminated the communist **command economy**—an economic system in which most prices, property, and production are directly controlled by the state—as a viable political economic model. It by no means ended the debate over what is and ought to be the relationship between the market and the state, however.

Because people tend to see the capitalist market economy as somehow natural, they also see it as existing independently of government. Nothing could be further from the truth. Command economies were ultimately of limited efficiency, but they proved that a state can exist for a long time without a market economy. A market economy, on the other hand, cannot exist without the state. In a situation of anarchy—the absence of a state—the market would be severely limited; without state provision of security, property and contract rights, and money, exchange would be limited to bartering and would require extensive provision of private security forces. Mafias are examples of this kind of capitalism, which arises where states are weak or absent; they provide their own security and enforce their own contracts. While this structure can create some productive economic activity, the costs of private security limit economic growth and create a society in which few would like to live.

Separation of the Economy and the State The rise of the modern state occurred together with the state's separation from direct control of economic activity. Political scientist Robert Bates (2001) used rational choice theory to provide a succinct analysis of how the modern state arose and came to encourage capitalist economic growth. In feudal Europe, political and economic power were fused in the person of a feudal lord. Feudal lords financed their military conquests by raiding wealth wherever they could. They took surplus production from peasants and other forms of wealth from conquered rivals to finance their increasing military and political

capitalism: The combination of a market economy with private property rights

command economy: An economic system in which most prices, property, and production are directly controlled by the state

power. As agricultural productivity increased in early modern Europe, towns and economic activity outside the sphere of agriculture grew rapidly as well. When lords turned to raiding the newly emerging towns in order to gain wealth, however, they found them hard to conquer, in part because towns were easier to defend than castles. More important, much of a town's wealth was mobile. Conquest, or even the threat of conquest, could provoke rapid movement of this wealth out of the town, thus defeating one of the main purposes of the conquest.

The self-interests of kings and business owners led to a historic compromise: in exchange for a share of profits, a king would provide the town with military protection instead of trying to conquer it outright by force. Thus, modern sovereignty and taxation were born. Political and economic power became distinct spheres; the state came to restrict its role in the economy, leaving most productive activity in private hands. The state, nonetheless, still had a crucial role to play; it and business became mutually dependent but separate spheres.

Thus, security was one of the state's essential functions in a market economy, but it was by no means the only one. The various roles the state now plays can be divided into three categories: essential roles, beneficial roles, and politically generated roles.

Essential Roles The essential roles are providing security, establishing and enforcing property and contract rights, and creating and controlling currency. Most essential roles, and many of the beneficial ones as well, involve a state's provision of **public goods**, those goods or services that cannot or will not be provided via the market because their costs are too high or their benefits are too diffuse. National security is an excellent example of a public good. Individual provision of security is extremely expensive, and if any one company could pay for it, the benefits would accrue to everyone in the country anyway, not allowing the company to generate revenue sufficient to cover the costs. The state must provide this service if the market economy is to thrive.

Protection of property and contract rights is also an essential state function in a market economy. Capitalism requires investing now with the expectation of future gains. Some uncertainty is always involved, but if potential investors have no means of ensuring that the future gains will accrue, no one will invest. Property rights protect not only property legally purchased in the market but also future property—the profits of current investment and productive activity. Similarly, profits require honest market exchanges: if a ton of cotton is promised for delivery at a set price, it must actually be delivered at that price. The state, through its legal system, must guarantee both property rights and contracts for this reason. Details of these rights can vary significantly across countries, but some legal guarantee that current and future property and exchanges will be protected is essential to achieving the productivity associated with modern market economies.

The modern state must also provide a currency to facilitate economic exchanges. States did not always print or control currency. Prior to the American Civil War, for instance, private banks printed most currency in the United States (hence the term *banknote*). When the state took over this process and created a uniform currency, exchanges across the entire country were eased. This happened transnationally as thirteen countries adopted the euro as the single currency of the European Union (EU) countries in 2004, greatly expanding exchange across much of the continent. At the same time, the creation and adoption of the euro may be an example of external forces taking on a greater role in national decision making, at least in some of the weaker euro zone countries.

public goods: Those goods or services that cannot or will not be provided via the market because their costs are too high or their benefits are too diffuse

Beneficial Roles Several other roles the state commonly plays in the modern market economy are not absolutely essential, but most analysts consider them beneficial. These include providing infrastructure, education, and health care and correcting market failures. The first three are all examples of public goods. Roads are a classic example of infrastructure as a public good. Private roads can and sometimes do exist, but governments build the bulk of all highway systems. It is simply too costly to build private roads that may only be used by those who build them or pay for access. Public provision of a road network lowers the cost of transporting goods and people, which improves the efficiency and profitability of many sectors of a state's economy.

Similarly, most economists and business leaders see an educated populace as beneficial to economic efficiency. Research has shown that workers who can read, write, and do arithmetic are far more productive than those who cannot. Companies could provide this education themselves, but because education is a lengthy process, because children learn many things more efficiently and effectively than do adults, and because workers can switch jobs and take their company-provided education with them, providing basic education is not a profitable endeavor for most companies and is therefore a nearly universal function of the state.

In most countries, the provision of basic health care is seen in similar terms. Obviously, a healthy workforce is more productive than an unhealthy one, and investment in health is most productive in the early stages of life; the economic benefits of high-quality prenatal and early childhood health care are far greater than the benefits of health care for the elderly. Most countries, therefore, consider basic health care a public good worth providing, and many wealthy countries provide even more than basic care. At the very least, the government aggressively intervenes in the health care market to ensure that such care is provided to all.

Today, vigorous debates about the state's role in providing public goods and services continue in many countries. While virtually all agree that basic education is beneficial and ought to be provided by the state (the United Nations has officially endorsed education as a right for all), that belief still leaves a great deal open to dispute: How much secondary and higher education should the state provide? Should the government pay for all or most of a person's higher education, as is true in most of Europe, or should the individual receiving the benefits of the education pay a substantial share, as in the United States? Health care is even more controversial. While most agree that a healthy workforce enhances a market economy, how to achieve such a healthy population is the subject of nearly constant debate. These issues are analyzed in greater depth in chapter 11.

The fourth beneficial economic function of the modern state is intervention to correct market failure. **Market failure** occurs when markets fail to perform efficiently. The primary justification for a market is efficiency: a well-functioning market maximizes the efficient use of all available resources. Three common causes of market failure are **externalities** (transactions that do not include the full costs of production in the price), imperfect information, and monopolies in which one seller can set prices. Advocates of an unfettered market recognize market failures as something governments should try to correct, but exactly when such intervention is justified and how governments should respond remain controversial.

Market externalities occur when a cost or benefit of the production process is not fully included in the price of the final market transaction, thereby reducing efficiency. Environmental damage is a common externality. If a factory pollutes the air as it makes a product, costs are incurred to the long-term health of local

market failure: Phenomenon that occurs when markets fail to perform efficiently or they fail to perform according to other widely held social values

externality: A cost or benefit of the production process that is not fully included in the price of the final market transaction when the product is sold

residents and to everyone in the case of global climate change. The factory owners, however, do not have to pay any of those costs as they make and sell their products, and the price charged customers doesn't include those costs. The factory will pollute more than it would if it and its customers had to pay the costs of that pollution. Many economists argue, therefore, that the state should intervene either to limit the extent of the pollution or to make the producers and consumers of the product bear its full costs.

Markets can also only maximize efficiency when buyers and sellers know the full costs and benefits of their transactions. Economists call this having "perfect information." In our financially and technologically complex societies, market actors often lack perfect information. The financial collapse that caused the 2008–2009 recession resulted in part from a set of transactions on a mass scale in which consumers and investors did not fully know what they were purchasing. The first breakdown in information came as many Americans purchased homes during the housing boom earlier in the decade. Potential buyers were desperate to purchase before rapidly rising home prices increased further. Some lenders, especially in the "hottest" markets, offered buyers variable-rate mortgages with payments and interest that were low in the short term but that increased dramatically later. Many buyers seemed not to understand fully how high the payments would go or when, and they took on mortgages that stretched their ability to make payments. In addition, many lenders used aggressive (and sometimes even fraudulent) sales techniques to sell these mortgages to uncreditworthy buyers, seeking to earn loan-processing fees and interest in the short term and not caring whether the borrowers would be able to pay back the loans in the long term (a practice known as predatory lending).

The second set of transactions in which buyers lacked perfect information occurred on Wall Street, where major banks sold investments called "mortgage-backed securities" (MBS), which were basically bundles of these high-risk mortgages. The idea was that the MBS investors would buy mortgages from lenders and receive the mortgage payments, taking on the risk that the payments might stop if the borrowers defaulted on their loans. Theoretically, these investments helped to spread out the risks of these high-risk mortgages across many investors. Banks tried to reduce this risk further by selling MBS investors a kind of insurance called credit default swaps (which are part of a broader investment category called derivatives), which would compensate them if the high-risk mortgage holders were to default on their loans. However, the Wall Street banks selling these products and the companies that rate the risks of such products did not fully disclose or did not realize the level of risk in the mortgages, so investors were not aware of the level of risk they were taking on. As early as 2005 and 2006, some analysts were warning that these investments were extremely risky, because the housing market would eventually drop as prices got too high for people to afford to purchase houses. Falling home prices would prevent uncreditworthy borrowers from selling their houses; thus they would go into default on their mortgages. That would stop the flow of mortgage loan payments and cause the values of the MBS that were based on those loans to drop. Once housing prices began to fall significantly in 2008, the most heavily involved Wall Street banks, most notably Lehman Brothers, faced bankruptcy as their investors tried to sell the MBS as quickly as possible but found no buyers, so the prices of those investments collapsed. Even worse, the banks had to pay off those investors who had bought credit default swaps. Bankruptcy ensued for some of the banks, and investors in the United States and around the world (often unknowingly via instruments like pension funds) faced a massive loss of wealth.

The result was the biggest economic downturn since the Great Depression. The market failure embedded in this series of transactions in which buyers of all sorts

Traders on the New York Stock Exchange react to a dramatic drop in the market on Monday, October 6, 2008. The bursting of a housing "bubble" was the chief cause of the financial collapse in the fall of 2008 that created what many call the "Great Recession," the biggest economic crisis since the Great Depression. It began in the United States but spread to virtually every corner of the globe.

Credit: AP Photo/Richard Drew

lacked "perfect information" led to renewed debate over how much government regulation is necessary to ensure that both individual and institutional investors know fully what they are buying in the mortgage and financial markets. Later in this chapter, we discuss the debate over government regulation of the financial sector that the market failure of 2008–2009 set off.

The third common market failure is **monopoly**—the control of the entire supply of a valued good or service by one seller. In a market economy, competition among alternative suppliers is a key incentive for efficiency. Because monopolies eliminate this incentive, the state may intervene to prevent them. It may do so in three ways: by making the monopoly government owned and therefore (in theory) run in the interest of the general public, by regulating the monopoly to ensure that its prices are closer to what they would be in a competitive market, or by forcing the breakup of the monopoly into smaller, competing entities.

Some monopolies are considered **natural monopolies;** these occur in sectors of the economy in which competition would raise costs and reduce efficiency. Where a natural monopoly exists, the state may choose to regulate or take control of it rather than force a breakup. A good example of the different ways in which the state can react to natural monopoly is the history of telephone service. A generation ago, every phone had to be hardwired into a land line, and all calls traveled over wires; this meant that competition would have required more than one company to run wires down the same street. This obviously would have been prohibitively expensive and inefficient. Britain, like many other countries, chose the first option to deal

monopoly: The control of the entire supply of a valued good or service by one economic actor

natural monopoly: The control of the entire supply of valued goods or services by one economic actor in a sector of the economy in which competition would raise costs and reduce efficiency

with this natural monopoly: it created the government-owned British Telephone company. The United States, by contrast, chose to heavily regulate a privately owned monopoly, and all services were provided by "Ma Bell" (as AT&T was nicknamed). By 1984, however, the complacent monopoly was being challenged by new ways to deliver voice and high-speed data transmission that reduced the "natural" quality of its monopoly. A lawsuit led to the breakup of the monopoly, with AT&T spawning several local phone services (in which it retained a minority share) while keeping control of long-distance service. With the advent of satellite and wireless technology, this natural monopoly evaporated; around the world, governments have privatized or deregulated phone services, and consumers now have a choice of providers

Politically Generated Roles Everything discussed to this point, from correction of market failures like monopoly to protection of private property, can be seen as an economically required or at least beneficial function of the state. The final category of state functions in a market economy includes those that are politically generated. Most economists do not see these functions as essential or perhaps even beneficial to creating an efficient market, but states have taken on these roles because a large section of the populace has demanded them through the political process. Karl Polanyi argued in his 1944 book, *The Great Transformation,* that the rise of the modern industrial economy produced political demands to limit what many people saw as the negative effects of the market. This led to what is now termed the modern welfare state. Through the democratic process in European countries and the United States, in particular, citizens demanded protection from the market, and governments began to provide it to a greater or lesser extent. Primary examples of these politically generated state functions are government regulations requiring improved working conditions and the implementation of policies designed to redistribute income.

Because these state interventions are the results of political demands rather than considered essential, they remain very contentious, and policies vary greatly from country to country. In wealthy industrial economies, modern working conditions, including a minimum wage, an eight-hour workday, and workers' health and safety standards, are largely the product of labor union demands. Yet as the case studies at the end of this chapter show, labor policies in wealthy countries vary significantly, particularly in areas such as the length of the workweek, job security, the length of maternity leave, and the amount of paid vacation time that employers are required to give. Countries that have begun industrializing more recently, such as Brazil and China, show even greater variation in these areas. In these countries, labor unions, if they exist at all, are recent creations that have not had the opportunity to successfully champion the same reforms of working conditions that are now taken for granted in countries that industrialized much earlier. Minimum wages may be low or nonexistent, workdays may be as long as twelve hours, and paid vacations are rare. This disparity between wealthier and poorer countries is at the core of the controversies surrounding globalization, a subject we explore below.

Similar controversy and variation exist in income redistribution policies. Typically referred to as "welfare" in the United States (though Social Security, which is not usually seen as "welfare," is also an income redistribution policy), these policies exist to mitigate the effects of unequal income distribution that are generated by the market. Markets generally provide great economic efficiency and growth under the right conditions, but they provide no rules for how wealth is distributed. As social and economic inequality expanded in the late nineteenth and early twentieth centuries, reformers began to demand that the state take action to help those who were gaining little or nothing in the market. For reasons we explore in the case studies at the end of this chapter, the extent to which the early industrializing countries in Europe and the United States ultimately pursued income redistribution and poverty amelioration varied considerably. As with proper and regulated working conditions, income redistribution policies barely exist at all in the poorest countries; the poorest people are left to survive in the market as best they can.

Overall, the symbiotic relationship between the modern state and the market economy provides a means to analyze state interventions in modern economic life. The state must carry out certain roles if capitalism is to survive and thrive. Political leaders know that much of their popularity rests on the ability to generate goods and services, jobs, and government revenue. In the modern economy, states pursue various policies and market interventions beyond those that are the bare essentials for the survival of capitalism. Some of these are widely recognized as beneficial to contemporary economies, though the details of how and how much to pursue them remain controversial. Other policies, however, are generated primarily by political demands emanating from society, especially in democracies. These policies remain the most controversial and vary the most from state to state, as we will see in the case studies at the end of this chapter and in chapters 10 and 11.

KEY ECONOMIC DEBATES

Understanding political economy and the relationship between the state and the market requires the application of both political science and basic economics. Major economic theories lie behind the debates over how governments should intervene in the market. The first, central debate that must be understood is between Keynesian and monetarist theories of when, why, and how the state ought to attempt to guide the economy. Prior to the Great Depression, Western governments engaged in minimal intervention in the economy, and officials believed that the market was best left alone. They acknowledged that during economic downturns, unemployment rose and people suffered, but in the longer term, unemployment lowered wages until labor was cheap enough that businesses started to invest and employ people again, thus creating a new cycle of economic growth. Policy makers believed that during economic downturns, government should do little but provide essential services and wait.

Keynesianism John Maynard Keynes, after whom **Keynesian economic theory** is named, developed a theory that revolutionized economics after watching his native Britain and the rest of the world enter the Great Depression in the 1930s. Keynes argued that the state could, and should, do more to manage economic crises. In an economic downturn like the Great Depression, the main problem was a lack of demand for goods and services, and he believed that through **fiscal policy**, or management of the government budget, government could revive demand and stimulate the economy. He suggested that the government could and should engage in **deficit spending;** that is, it should spend more than it collected in revenue to stimulate demand. To do this, it would borrow money. By creating new programs and hiring people, the government would put that money into people's hands; they in turn would start to buy other goods and services, and the economy would start to rebound. When the economic downturn was over, the government could pay off the

Keynesian theory:
Named for British economist John Maynard Keynes, who argued that governments can reduce the "boom and bust" cycles of capitalism via active fiscal policy, including deficit spending when necessary

fiscal policy:
Government budgetary policy

deficit spending:
Government spending more than is collected in revenue

debt it had taken on while it had been engaging in deficit spending. This would slow demand in the economy if needed, as too much demand too quickly can cause inflation. Keynes believed that in this way the state could manage the economy, smoothing out the cycle of economic expansion and contraction—known as "boom and bust"—that seemed inherent in unchecked capitalism. Done properly, such management might even achieve continuous full employment.

Keynesianism (and the onset of World War II) offered governments a way to help their economies out of the Depression, and most Western governments adopted it either explicitly or implicitly. The power of the economic theory alone, however, was not the only reason Keynesian policies became so popular. Deficit spending, if it could be justified, was very popular with elected politicians because it allowed governments to create new programs to benefit their constituents without having to raise taxes to pay for them. The appeal for politicians facing reelection is obvious. In Europe, Keynesianism also gave social democratic parties economic justification for a significant expansion of social spending and welfare policies after World War II. This political logic led to frequent distortion of pure Keynesian policies— deficit spending continued in many countries even in times of economic growth in contradiction to Keynes's idea that when the economy improved, a government would pay off its debt.

By the 1970s, Keynesian policies came under sustained questioning, first by economists and then in the political arena. Due partly to the quadrupling of oil prices in 1973, most Western countries faced a new economic situation: **stagflation**, meaning simultaneous high inflation and high unemployment. Keynes's prescription of more government borrowing was seen as potentially disastrous in this situation because such action was likely to produce more inflation.

stagflation:
Simultaneous high inflation and high unemployment

Monetarism In this context, an alternative economic theory, known as **monetarist theory,** gained popularity. The core ideas of the theory were developed by American economist Milton Friedman in the 1950s, but they were largely ignored for over a decade. Friedman and other monetarists argued that fiscal policy does not stimulate economic growth. Rather, government borrowing and deficit spending simply "crowd out" private sector borrowing, thus impeding the ability of businesses to invest and potentially reducing long-term growth. The key to economic growth, Friedman argued, is **monetary policy**: the amount of money a government prints and puts into circulation and the basic interest rates the government sets. Inflation, monetarists argue, is caused chiefly by excessive government printing of money, and low growth is due in part to government borrowing. Defeating stagflation and restoring growth would therefore require reducing the amount of money in circulation, raising interest rates, and reducing deficit spending.

monetarist theory:
Economic theory that states only monetary policy can affect economic well-being in capitalist economies; rejects Keynesian policy, arguing instead for a reduced role for government in the economy

monetary policy:
The amount of money a government prints and puts into circulation and the basic interest rates the government sets

Monetarists also argue that every economy has a natural rate of unemployment below which government policy is counterproductive and that a government and a society must accept this, whatever the level is. U.S. president Ronald Reagan and U.K. prime minister Margaret Thatcher each put monetarist policies in place in the early 1980s. The economic boom that followed was seen as a vindication of monetarism, which became the "conventional wisdom" in economic theory, at least until the recession of 2008–2009.

Keynesianism versus Monetarism: An Ongoing Debate The 2008–09 recession and its aftermath led to the most significant debate on economic policy in a generation. As the economy collapsed, most states, including the previously monetarist United States and United Kingdom, turned to Keynesian policy to try to restart economic growth; governments engaged in significant deficit spending to stimulate the economy. Monetarist strictures did not hold in the face of the highest unemployment rates since the Great Depression and the political pressures that such high unemployment produced. The recession also initiated a renewed debate about government regulation, especially of the financial sector. Monetarists believe market failure to be very rare, or even nonexistent. For instance, Alan Greenspan, chairman of the U.S. Federal Reserve for most of the 1980s and 1990s, believed that private competition in the market for investments like mortgage-backed securities and credit default swaps would produce more effective regulation than would government rules. Investors could be counted on not to take on more risk than was prudent, meaning the government would be wasting money if it were constantly watching over their shoulders. Keynesians, on the other hand, believe that market failure is fairly common and therefore are generally willing to accept greater regulation. Many Keynesians believe this to be especially true of the financial sector, since they see it as unusually prone to irrational and inefficient booms and busts. The twentieth-century economic debate firmly underlies the twenty-first-century debate over financial regulation.

Economic Development Debate The monetarist-Keynesian debate also had an influential role in economic policy in the postcolonial world. Keynes was instrumental in the creation after World War II of the International Monetary Fund (IMF) and the World Bank, the two key institutions that helped stabilize the postwar economy and rebuild Europe. By the early 1960s, both also came to play an important role in the economic development of the newly independent countries of Africa and Asia, as well as in Latin America. As the postwar world emerged, economists and policy makers in Latin America, joined by those in a growing list of independent postcolonial states such as India and Pakistan, began to rethink their economic policies. A new field, called "development economics," emerged, the basic premise of which was that the policies that help create stability and growth in already wealthy industrial countries are not appropriate for countries just starting the industrialization process.

One basic assumption of this postwar global economic order was that free trade should be as widespread as possible. The economic argument in favor of this is known as **comparative advantage**. It holds that well-being will be maximized if each country uses its resources to produce whatever it produces relatively efficiently compared to other countries (i.e., it should produce the items that it can produce most efficiently compared to how well other countries produce them, even if it is not the most efficient at anything). It then trades with other countries for goods it does not produce, and all countries gain because they are using their resources as efficiently as possible. What this meant in practical terms was that the poor and agrarian countries of Asia, Africa, and Latin America would, for the foreseeable future, produce primarily agricultural products and raw materials. Their industries, where they existed, were quite new and therefore were not likely to compete successfully against the well-established industrial conglomerates of the wealthy countries. Leaders of these countries and the economists who supported them, however, were not willing to have their countries relegated to being agricultural countries for the foreseeable future.

Development economics, then, came to be about how a state could intervene in the economy to stimulate rapid industrialization and growth. This meshed with the general Keynesian theory that the state could manage capitalism to enhance growth; in "developing countries," this management would simply take somewhat different forms than in industrialized countries. The central policy that developed out of these ideas was **import-substitution industrialization (ISI)**, which stated that a developing nation should protect its new industries by placing restrictions on international trade, thus allowing its new industries to grow until they were strong enough

comparative advantage: Theory of trade that argues that economic efficiency and well-being will be maximized if each country uses its resources to produce whatever it produces relatively well compared to other countries and then trades its own products with other countries for goods it does not produce

import-substitution industrialization (ISI): Development policy popular in the 1950s–1970s that uses trade policy, monetary policy, and currency rates to encourage the creation of new industries to produce goods domestically that the country imported in the past

to compete on the international market. By limiting the number of imported manufactured products or placing tariffs on them, postcolonial governments could encourage domestic and international investment in new industries in their countries. Most postcolonial countries pursued these policies, with the support of Western governments and the World Bank, from the 1950s to the 1970s. In many countries where new industries had not yet begun, governments even took on the role of business owner, creating wholly or partly government-owned industries that supplied the domestic market with key goods.

At first, ISI was relatively successful in creating many new industries throughout middle-income and poorer countries. Countries such as Brazil, Mexico, and Turkey saw very rapid economic growth throughout the 1950s and 1960s. By the 1970s, though, momentum was waning. Protecting industry from competition to get it started perhaps was a good idea initially, but in the long run it resulted in inefficient industries that could not compete on the international market. These industries and their employees put political pressure on postcolonial governments to preserve the protections that they had enjoyed to that point. When oil prices quadrupled in 1973, those postcolonial countries that did not produce their own oil had to pay a lot more for oil and other key imports, but because their industries could not compete globally, the countries could not export enough goods to pay

By the 1980s, ISI was becoming discredited, and neoliberals were advocating that developing countries should instead emulate the East Asian Miracle by promoting export-led growth. This 2006 photo shows the rapidly growing port of Ensenada, Mexico, where Asian exports that California's clogged ports cannot accommodate are offloaded for transport to the United States.

Credit: AP Photo/David Maung

for the imports. These governments were forced to take out international loans to cover the resulting trade imbalance, but in the meantime they changed relatively few policies. When another oil price increase occurred in 1979, many governments that had pursued ISI had to borrow even more money from international lenders. Some reached the brink of bankruptcy, and Mexico's declaration in 1982 that it was unable to meet its international debt obligations began a global "debt crisis," which ushered in a period of new economic policies in postcolonial countries.

The growing problems with ISI were emerging at the same time that economists and policy makers in the West were shifting from Keynesian to monetarist ideas and becoming increasingly skeptical of the ability of governments to manage the market. The World Bank abruptly shifted its development agenda and prescriptions in 1980 and embraced a monetarist-inspired development model now called **neoliberalism**. This shift was partly induced by the great economic success of a handful of East Asian countries that collectively came to be known as the "East Asian Miracle." In contrast to most of the postcolonial world, these rapidly growing countries, most notably South Korea, Taiwan, Singapore, and the city of Hong Kong, either had never adopted ISI or had abandoned it early on in favor of focusing on exporting in sectors in which they were competitive. Their success, especially in light of the problems ISI policies had begun to face, suggested to many policy makers, including those at the World Bank, that a new approach to development was needed.

The neoliberal model that emerged by 1980 shared monetarists' skepticism of the ability of the state to lead economic growth via interventions in the market. Neoliberal economists argued that developing countries were no different from wealthy ones and, as such, they should follow the same basic monetarist policies as wealthy countries. These economists went on to compile a package of policies that came to be known as **structural adjustment programs (SAPs)**. Included in this bundle of programs were directives to end government protection of industries and other restrictions on free trade, **privatize** (sell off) government-owned industries, and reduce fiscal deficits. SAPs required a drastically reduced government that would participate far less in the economy; this would allow comparative advantage and the market to signal how resources should be invested, which would maximize efficiency and economic growth.

The IMF and World Bank imposed this model on much of the postcolonial world. The debt crisis that began in 1982 meant that many postcolonial governments had to ask the IMF for emergency assistance to get them out of what was essentially bankruptcy. Working in tandem, the IMF and World Bank demanded that the governments receiving assistance in the 1980s and 1990s move their policies in a neoliberal direction by implementing SAPs. This was a slow process in many countries; the necessary steps were politically unpopular because they initially resulted in high inflation, increased unemployment, and drastic cuts in government services, including education and health care. The promise was that if a country could endure these transition pains in the short term, the new policies would maximize efficiency and encourage new investment, thus producing economic growth in the long term.

The success of the neoliberal model has been mixed. Supporters point to some striking successes, such as in Chile and several countries in Southeast Asia. While the military government in Chile chose to adopt neoliberal policies of its own volition, other countries, including Malaysia and Thailand, only partly followed the model. In still other countries, especially many in Latin America and Africa, the new policies not only didn't produce growth but actually produced significant economic decline. Supporters of the policies argue that this was because those countries resisted the IMF and World Bank and only partly implemented the SAPs.

neoliberalism: A development theory supporting structural adjustment programs that argues developing countries should reduce the role of government and open themselves to global trade to allow the market to allocate resources to maximize efficiency and thereby economic growth

structural adjustment programs (SAPs): Development programs created by the World Bank and International Monetary Fund beginning in the 1980s; based on neoliberalism

privatize: To sell off government-owned assets to the private sector

The Successes and Failures of SAPs

The neoliberal structural adjustment programs (SAPs) implemented in most postcolonial countries in the 1980s and 1990s had mixed results. Chile, Ghana, and Uganda stand out as relative successes, but many others were far less successful. What explains these differences? The large theoretical and policy debate that arose over this very question pitted those who saw the failure of SAPs in some countries as simply failure of implementation against those who saw fundamental flaws in the model and those who believed that the model was applicable only in certain circumstances.

Most SAPs were implemented at the behest of the IMF and World Bank. To secure essential debt relief, poor countries had to accept the policy requirements that the two institutions imposed. States agreed to make certain policy changes over a period of about three years, and the IMF/World Bank subsequently monitored how those countries followed through on their promises. Often, political leaders only partially fulfilled their obligations, so everything went back to the drawing board. This resulted in very slow and partial implementation of the full set of neoliberal policies as countries went through several rounds of negotiation and implementation with the IMF/World Bank.

One body of critics, including the IMF and World Bank, concluded from this process that the model's limited success was due to failure of political will. Success happened when top political leaders took "ownership" of the ideas, understood their importance, and committed themselves to accomplishing them. In the absence of this, no amount of external arm-twisting would do the job, and partial implementation often made little economic sense.

Other critics contended that the model should have taken political dynamics into account. Lack of implementation, they argued, came not just from lack of understanding and commitment but also from the rational actions of self-interested political leaders in a particular context. This was particularly true in Africa, where neopatrimonial politics meant that leaders' political survival depended on their ability to provide supporters with patronage, something the reforms clearly jeopardized.

Institutionalists pointed to a different flaw in the model. They contended that markets only work well when embedded in strong institutions, such as clear property rights and contracts. The ultimate goal of the neoliberal model is to improve efficiency to encourage investment

Critics counter that the policies themselves were flawed, producing little growth, causing greater unemployment and poverty, and reducing educational opportunity and health care for those most in need. By the new millennium, the neoliberal consensus was shifting, at least somewhat, and critics were proposing significant policy modifications in light of the neoliberal model's limited success and the greater success of countries like China that seemed to pursue alternative models. We discuss this further in chapter 10.

Keynesian economic ideas held sway from the Great Depression through the 1970s, and monetarism has been dominant since. During the economic boom of the 1990s, quite a few governments were able to stick with more or less monetarist policies, and postcolonial governments embraced SAPs as necessary. As economic growth slowed after the turn of the century, however, it became more difficult to adhere to these policies, and they became subject to renewed questioning. Deficit

and thereby future growth. Weak states that have weak institutions, however, will never gain greater investment because investors cannot be certain their investments and future profits will be secure. The initial neoliberal model ignored this essential area entirely and so was successful only where key institutions were already relatively strong.

A fourth group of critics looked at the global economy and argued that the neoliberal model suffered from a *fallacy of composition,* a term used in the study of logic to indicate that just because something is true in one case does not mean it will be true when applied to all cases. In relation to SAPs, it suggests that market-friendly policies designed to attract investment will succeed in some cases, probably the earliest ones and those with other attractions to investors. When the same policies are extended to all countries, however, there will not be enough investment capital available to respond. Furthermore, the earliest success cases will be likely to attract even more investment, leaving the latecomers empty-handed. Even if later or less attractive states pursue the "right" policies, they still may not see the investment necessary to spark economic growth.

A fifth school of critics argued that the neoliberal model undermines the real fundamentals of long-term development: infrastructure and human capital. They contended that states succeed at instigating economic development by providing key political goods that investors will need: infrastructure, especially efficient transportation and communications systems; and human capital, meaning an educated and healthy workforce. SAPs demand fiscal austerity, typically meaning cuts to both. For countries with relatively little of either, these policies proved detrimental to economic growth.

The debate on SAPs has never been fully resolved. Clearly, more than one of these positions can be right simultaneously. The debate, however, did help create a shift in the conventional wisdom about development by the new millennium. While most economists and policy makers still argue in favor of the basics of market-friendly policies like SAPs, they also recognize the importance to developmental success of strong institutions, infrastructure, and human capital. The World Bank, in particular, now has active policies pursuing each of these goals.

spending increased throughout the first decade of the twenty-first century, even in the United States, which arguably had the most monetarist policies of all. The World Bank began to question aspects of the neoliberal development model as well, in particular acknowledging that quality education and health care and strong government institutions are crucial to long-term development everywhere and must be funded accordingly. The bank's policies began to shift in favor of funding these priorities, even though it continued to advocate open trade and a thriving and unfettered market in general as the best ways to create economic growth. The Great Recession of 2008–2009 only raised more questions about economic policy, especially in the wealthiest countries that were hit hardest. While the collapse began in the United States, it had ramifications throughout the world; it was only the most recent example of what many observers saw as a new set of economic concerns emerging over the last two decades: the forces of globalization.

The Role of the State in the Market

Essential Functions of the State

- Providing national and personal security: Failure to do so produces anarchy or the creation of a mafia.
- Protecting property and contract rights: These are essential for investments to produce profits over time.
- Providing a currency: Facilitates widespread exchange.

Beneficial Functions of the State

- Providing public goods: These are goods or services not provided via the market because their costs are too high or their benefits are too diffuse. These include the following:
  - Building infrastructure (e.g., highways, ports)
  - Providing education and health care: Improves labor productivity and is nearly impossible for markets to provide fully.

- Mitigating market failures: intervening when the market fails to allocate resources efficiently.
  - Intervening to correct externalities such as pollution
  - Regulating markets in which buyers have imperfect information
  - Preventing or regulating monopolies: Enhances competition or limits negative effects of natural monopolies.

Politically Generated Functions of the State

- Improving working conditions (e.g., health and safety standards, eight-hour day, minimum wage)
- Redistributing income (e.g., retirement benefits, unemployment compensation, welfare)
- Protecting the environment: Corrects market failures due to externalities.

GLOBALIZATION: A NEW WORLD ORDER OR DÉJÀ VU ALL OVER AGAIN?

There is no doubt that the 2008–2009 recession showed the negative elements of globalization clearly: a financial crisis based squarely in the United States quickly spread around the world. Major European investors had stakes in the high-risk securities that collapsed on Wall Street, causing European banks to face possible bankruptcy and several European governments, most notably Greece, Ireland, and Portugal, to come close to default. Export markets for developing economies like China and India plummeted, and a brief era of economic growth in Africa was nipped in the bud. These global effects all started with average people in places like Arizona and Florida buying homes with risky, variable-rate mortgages.

Globalization has become perhaps the most frequently used, and abused, term in political economy. It first gained prominence in the 1990s, and since then hundreds of books and countless articles have been written about it. It has cultural as well as economic and political implications, but we will focus on the latter two in order to understand its effects on the relationship between the state and the market.

Globalization has many definitions. We can define it as a rapid increase in the flow of economic activity, technology, and communication around the globe. Three key questions have arisen about globalization: (1) Does it represent a brave new world in which the fundamental relationship between the state and the market has changed forever, or is it simply the latest phase in that relationship—something new

globalization: A rapid increase in the flow of cultural symbols, political ideas and movements, economic activity, technology, and communications around the globe

and interesting but not fundamentally different? (2) What caused it in the first place? (3) What can and should be done about it?

A Brave New World? Globalization's earliest adherents saw it as a portent of fundamental change. Japanese scholar Kenichi Ohmae, writing in 1995, argued that globalization would result in the "end of the nation-state." He focused on economic aspects of globalization, but others have broadened this general argument, claiming that the rapid flow of money, goods and services, ideas, and cultural symbols around the globe will eventually make the nation-state irrelevant as such activity will destroy states' ability to manage their economies. Regional, if not global, management will have to fill the role currently played by the state. The flow of ideas and culture will severely weaken national identity, as the Internet in particular will allow people to form identities not linked to territories and their immediate local communities. All of these changes ultimately will require political responses in the form of strengthened international organizations for global governance, and global citizens' organizations will also have to respond to global problems with global political solutions.

Since the initial separation of the economic and political spheres, capital's greatest weapon has been its mobility: business can usually threaten to move if it does not receive adequate treatment from a state. The state, in sharp contrast, is tied to a territory. Ohmae and other prophets of change are right that globalization has significantly increased capital mobility so that businesses can credibly threaten to leave a country much more easily now than they could a generation ago. This mobility has increased capital's power in relation to states. In trying to manage their economies, policy makers must be actively concerned about preserving the investments they have and attracting new ones, and with business able to move relatively easily, states increasingly must compete to attract it.

Similar changes in global finance—the flow of money around the world—also have weakened the state. Most countries now allow their currencies to be traded freely. Electronic communications have made currency transactions nearly instantaneous. For a government trying to pursue sound monetary policies through control of its money supply and interest rates, this new world of global currency flow can be problematic. The collapse of many Southeast Asian economies in 1997 was caused at least in part by currency speculators, traders who purchase a country's currency not to buy goods in that country but simply to try to buy it at a low valuation and sell it later at a higher valuation. When the speculators, led by international financier George Soros, found the Southeast Asian economies were weaker than they had believed, they began to sell the currencies rapidly. This led to a classic market panic in which virtually all international traders sold those currencies, causing immense economic loss and political instability in the region and, ultimately, in developing countries worldwide. States, especially in small and poor countries, must base monetary and fiscal policy not only on domestic concerns but also on how "global markets" might react. Greece learned this lesson in 2010; it faced bankruptcy because the global market thought its debt was too high and therefore charged it extremely high interest rates when the country wished to borrow. Ultimately, the European Union and IMF had to craft a "rescue package" of loans that required Greece to follow "austerity measures" similar to those the IMF imposes on developing countries.

The rapid flow of all sorts of economic transactions across state borders has no doubt shifted the relative power of capital and the state. States do still have an important role to play; however, their power varies significantly. Political scientist Geoffrey Garrett (1998) showed that European countries can maintain policies favoring labor unions and related groups if they provide long-term stability and predictability for business. In poor countries, however, this seems unlikely to work. The kinds of investments now made in Europe mostly involve hiring highly trained labor for which business is willing to pay more to ensure long-term stability. Europe also has the advantage of the EU, a huge and wealthy market in which to sell products. Nigeria, by contrast, has none of these advantages. Investments there are in natural resources and perhaps "light manufacturing," which involves a large amount of cheap, unskilled, and easily replaceable labor. The Nigerian government is in a significantly weaker bargaining position vis-à-vis likely international investors than is, for example, the German government.

In the new millennium, the scholarly consensus has moved away from Ohmae's view of globalization toward a more modest assessment of its effects. Certainly all of the trends described above exist, and most agree that globalization is likely to weaken the nation-state, but few now believe that globalization will destroy it. The state seems to be alive and well in the "global" era. For example, while the 2008–2009 recession severely challenged many governments, they responded with individual economic stimulus packages and had international meetings to coordinate their responses. Some states, notably China, seemed able to respond more swiftly and successfully and recovered much more quickly. Writing in the influential journal *Foreign Affairs,* Roger Altman (2009) declared, "Indeed, globalization itself is reversing. The long-standing wisdom that everyone wins in a single world market has been undermined. Global trade, capital flows, and immigration are declining." While that may be an overstatement made at the height of the crisis, the recession nonetheless showed that states and their economic policies clearly still matter.

In this era of globalization, the fundamental relationship between states and business has not been transformed into something entirely new, but there has been a shift in their relative power. Any state interested in the economic well-being of its populace must negotiate the rapidly expanding global markets as well as possible, bargaining for the best "deal" for its people. Knowing how to do this effectively is not easy, as some of the case studies below illustrate.

Causes of Globalization What factors facilitated this weakening of the state vis-à-vis capital? The causes of globalization are undoubtedly multiple, but two major answers to this question have competed for attention. Determining which of the two answers is correct is crucial to determining what can be done to change globalization, if anything. The first possible answer is that technology is the driving force of globalization. The costs of communication and transportation have dropped dramatically. Air travel, once a luxury good for the elite, is now a common practice for citizens of wealthy countries. Advances in containerization and just-in-time manufacturing have allowed more rapid and efficient shipment of goods. And, as we all know, the personal computer, the mobile phone, and the Internet have created instantaneous global communications capabilities while reducing costs. All of this has allowed businesses to expand across national borders at unprecedented rates.

A second school of thought argues that while technology was necessary for globalization, government policies made globalization a reality. The shift to monetarism and neoliberal economic policies that started around 1980 significantly reduced the role of most governments in regulating economic transactions, especially across their borders. The creation of the World Trade Organization (WTO) accelerated a process, started after World War II, of lowering tariffs on imports and exports. Removing government controls on exchange rates allowed money to travel around the world without limit, seeking the best return at the least risk (a process facilitated by electronic trading systems). In most postcolonial countries, the IMF and World Bank imposed these policies on initially reluctant governments in response to the debt crisis via structural adjustment policies (SAPs). For many years, these two multinational organizations (which were controlled by wealthy governments, which made economic contributions and therefore had voting rights in the organizations) set limits on the economic policies that governments in poor, indebted countries could pursue. While rarely successful at dictating those governments' policies, the IMF and World Bank did heavily influence them toward greater openness to foreign capital.

It is difficult to disentangle technological and policy changes to find a single cause of globalization. If technology is the primary cause, then globalization is inevitable and irreversible. If policies play an important role as well, then globalization may be subject to change. Both technology and policy seem crucial to the ultimate outcome, and they are interrelated. As technological change opened new areas of potential profit for international businesses, the leaders of those businesses became a source of powerful political pressure to liberalize economic policies so that businesses could benefit fully from the new opportunities. Once policy shifted in a more liberal direction, more businesses were able to take advantage of the changes, demand increased for more new technology to facilitate global communications and transportation, and the political pressure in favor of liberalized economic policies expanded that much further. The presence of "foreign" companies became the norm in much of the world, probably blunting the political backlash that might occur otherwise. It is hard to imagine today that controversy would arise in the United States over this issue, as it did when Toyotas and Hondas first entered the mass market in the 1970s or when a Japanese firm briefly purchased Rockefeller Center in the 1980s. People throughout the world have become accustomed to purchasing consumer products from across the globe and working for corporations with headquarters eight time zones away.

Political Responses The expanded global market and capital mobility also raise questions about the level at which political responses to economic problems can and should occur. As we noted above, individual states are still important, as they navigate global markets the best they can via their economic policies. More and more analysts argue, however, that new global problems require global political solutions. An obvious example is the ultimate global environmental problem: climate change. If pollution is an externality that should cause states to intervene in the market to protect the environment, then climate change is a global externality that only global agreement can remedy. Future generations, one way or another, will pay the costs of this externality that businesses and their consumers are not paying today, but no single state, even the largest and wealthiest, can solve the problem alone. Similarly, individual governments acting alone cannot solve the problem of poor states keeping their labor costs low and working conditions poor in an effort to attract foreign investment. Individual governments that change their policies will simply lose out to the competition. A uniform global policy on wages and working conditions, though extremely difficult to achieve, would be needed to reduce this competition.

One example of governments working together to address global problems is the G-20, a working group composed of the finance ministers and central bank governors from the twenty largest economies in the world. This group tried to coordinate a response to the 2008–2009 global financial crisis. In addition, the subsequent crisis in Greece in 2010 required joint action by European Union members and the IMF to arrest the threat it posed to the stability of the EU's common currency, the euro. As the recession eased in 2010, the G-20 agreed tentatively to cut back government budget deficits to avoid more crises like Greece's. This was controversial, as Keynesian theory would suggest that continuing stimulus spending would be prudent with an economy barely out of recession. The G-20 agreement was also vague, communicating little certainty that all governments will carry it out, and it seems to shift back to the antideficit spending advocated by monetarism, a policy that the United States and others pursued in the early 1930s that is now seen as having deepened the Great Depression. The United States under President Obama was slower to reduce deficits than the major European countries, meaning U.S. and European economic policies seemed likely to move in different directions. This division in policy direction made the overall outcome of the global financial crisis uncertain by the end of 2010 and raised questions about whether a new "currency war" might emerge as all major countries desired to lower the value of their currencies to encourage their own exports. This sequence of events demonstrates both the continuing difficulty of global policy coordination in the face of a global crisis and the continuing global debate over economic policy.

Many groups in civil society are not waiting for states to implement globally coordinated policies on their own. Such citizen's groups are actively organizing across borders to put pressure on governments or international bodies such as the UN, the IMF, and the World Bank to enact global measures to address global problems. To the extent that nongovernmental groups are successful, individual states may again be weakened because as citizens focus their political organization and pressure at the international level, they make individual states less relevant. Many core economic problems, including most discussed in this chapter, remain at the national level, however, particularly in large and wealthy countries. So while the state is weakened vis-à-vis capital, it is far from dead. The case studies below show this interplay between state and market and the continuing importance of states in the process.

TABLE 5.1

Economic Overview

Country	GDP per capita[1] 2010	GDP growth[2] 1980–1989	1990–1999	2000–2009	Unemployment[3] 1990–1999	2000–2009
Germany	$35,900	1.95	2.32	0.86	9.06*	9.18
Japan	$34,200	4.37	1.48	0.74	3.06	4.61
Mexico	$13,800	2.29	3.39	1.90	3.86**	3.16
Nigeria	$2,400	0.94	3.07	6.05	N/A	N/A
United States	$47,400	3.03	3.21	1.83	5.75	5.13

[1]CIA World Factbook, Country Comparison: GDP Per Capita, 2010 estimates, https://www.cia.gov/library/publications/the-world-factbook/rankorder/2004rank.html.

[2]The World Bank, Indicators, GDP growth (annual %), http://data.worldbank.org/indicator/NY.GDP.MKTP.KD.ZG.

[3]International Labor Organization, http://laborsta.ilo.org/. Data for the unemployment rate, average annual (% of labor force). Reliable unemployment data for Nigeria are not available because of the difficulties of measuring it in an economy characterized by a large informal sector.

[4]Human Development Report, Multidimensional Poverty Index, http://hdr.undp.org/en/media/HDR_2010_EN_Table5_reprint.pdf.

STATES AND MARKETS AROUND THE WORLD

As with any area of comparative politics, economic policies in the real world do not follow perfectly the various abstract economic models. Many factors not taken into account in economic theories influence government policies. These include broad political ideologies; the relative strengths of particular groups, especially business and labor; and international influences.

To illustrate real-world variation in the relationship of the market to the state, we look at five of our case study countries: three wealthy, industrialized democracies and two developing countries. Table 5.1 provides an overview of key economic data for all five and offers some of the overall story of each country. The market-oriented model in the United States has produced relatively good growth and moderate unemployment and inflation, but relatively high inequality and poverty, compared to those found in the other wealthy countries. Germany's social market economy struggles with low growth and high unemployment, though the country has controlled inflation very well and has far less poverty and inequality than the United States. Japan's developmental state achieved high growth prior to 1990 but has been in crisis since then, with growing unemployment and deflation and modest poverty and inequality. Mexico is a middle-income country that is much poorer than the United States, Germany, or Japan. It has achieved modest economic growth and unemployment and has recently reduced inflation significantly, though it is also one of the most unequal economies in the world. Nigeria, by far the poorest of the five, is dependent on one crucial export, oil, and this single-resource dependency is reflected in Nigeria's erratic growth rates. Nigeria also suffers from relatively high inflation, inequality, and very high poverty.

Inflation, consumer prices[2]			Inequality (GINI index)[4]	Population living below national poverty line[5]
1980–1989	1990–1999	2000–2009	2010	2006
N/A	2.34[†]	1.60	28.3	8.3
2.52	1.23	−0.26	24.9	11.8
69.04	20.42	5.21	51.6	17.6
20.89	30.64	12.23	42.9	34.1
13.50	3.00	2.57	40.8	17.0

[5]This is a relative poverty rate. Data are from UNDP, *The Real Wealth of Nations: Pathways to Human Development*, 2010 Human Development Report, http://hdr.undp.org/en/reports/global/hdr2010/.

*Average does not include data from 1990.

**Average does not include data from 1990 or 1991.

[†]Average does not include data from 1990 or 1991.

CASE STUDY

The United States: The Free-Market Model

- Limited government intervention
- Weak unions
- New Deal and Keynesianism
- Shift to monetarism in early 1980s
- Champion of globalization and free trade
- Origins of Great Recession

The 2008–2009 "Great Recession" that began in the United States shook the foundations of what had been seen as the leading economic model in the world and led the government under newly elected President Barack Obama to engage in the largest Keynesian deficit spending in a generation to stimulate the economy. The United States has long been the greatest exemplar of the free-market, or *laissez-faire,* model of economic development and capitalism. Compared to the governments of most wealthy countries, including Germany and Japan, the U.S. government has taken a hands-off approach to the economy for most of its history. Not until the Great Depression and the New Deal of the 1930s did the government began to attempt to guide the economy to increase growth and employment and to redistribute income to ameliorate poverty. From the New Deal through the 1960s, the government more or less followed Keynesian policies, but by the 1980s, it had shifted toward monetarism, moving back toward its historic reluctance to be involved in the economy. That monetarist focus came into question, though, at the start of the latest major recession.

The modern U.S. economy emerged in the late nineteenth and early twentieth centuries as rapid industrialization transformed the country from a primarily agricultural and rural society into a rapidly growing urban and

The Great Recession began in the housing market as a classic "bubble" burst, ultimately causing a financial crisis felt around the world. Foreclosures were widespread in Michigan, a former industrial stronghold, which saw unemployment grow to well over 20 percent at the height of the recession. The 2010 census found Michigan to be the only state in the union that actually lost population.

Credit: AP Photo/Carlos Osorio

industrial economy. The government's nearly complete lack of involvement in the economy up to that point had to change in response to this transformation. Its initial policies, however, were aimed primarily at ensuring that the market would remain as free as possible. The first time the government took on a major beneficial function other than building infrastructure was in an effort to eliminate or regulate monopoly control of key sectors of the economy, This started with regulation of the railways and then expanded with the landmark Sherman Antitrust Act of 1890, which resulted in the breakup of the Standard Oil monopoly in 1910.

Such regulation might seem "antibusiness," but it did not mean that the government was "pro-labor." The last two decades of the nineteenth century saw the rise not only of potentially monopolistic conglomerates but also of national labor unions. The government opposed the increasingly frequent strikes organized by these unions, the most famous of which were the Haymarket Riots of May 1886 in Chicago. Workers began this strike to demand an eight-hour workday, but within days it included 350,000 people nationwide. On May 4, it ended with a rally during which a bomb killed a police officer and the police killed dozens of unarmed demonstrators. This event helped get May 1 declared "Labor Day" in most countries of the world in honor of workers' struggles for labor rights. (The United States is one of a very few countries that celebrate Labor Day on a different date.)

By the early twentieth century, the U.S. government recognized that it would need to broaden its role in the economy. In 1913, it created both the nation's first central bank, the Federal Reserve (the "Fed"), and the income tax and corporate tax systems. The Fed, modeled after the British and German central banks, was given a monopoly on printing legal currency and charged with regulating the nation's money supply. Unlike central banks in many countries, however, the Fed is an autonomous agency that elected leaders cannot control directly. It was designed that way to ensure its independence from immediate political demands.

IN CONTEXT

CENTRAL BANKS

A central bank or some other monetary authority is a crucial institution of economic policy. Many central banks were started in part to create a unified national currency. In most wealthy countries today, central banks are independent institutions, supposedly free of political influence, that establish currency stability and monetary policy. The U.S. Federal Reserve System was a relative latecomer among monetary authorities, as the time line below demonstrates:

- Bank of England, 1694
- Banque de France, 1800
- Reichsbank (Germany), 1876 (succeeded by Bundesbank in West Germany, 1957)
- Bank of Japan, 1882
- U.S. Federal Reserve System, 1913
- Bank of Canada, 1934
- European Central Bank (EU), 1998

With growing industrialization, the government also recognized that taxes on trade, the primary source of government revenue in the nineteenth century, would no longer suffice. Since industry had come to generate the bulk of the nation's wealth, the federal government began permanently taxing businesses to provide a stronger revenue stream. Although the government began to play a larger role in the economy in this era, it remained focused on ensuring the smooth functioning of a free market by eliminating monopolies, opposing unions, providing a stable monetary system, and gaining government revenue from taxation of private economic activity.

This remained the model of U.S. economic policy until the Great Depression and the New Deal. The Great Depression, which produced 25 percent unemployment at its peak in 1933, shook the foundations of the nation's belief in the free market. During this time of rapidly rising union membership and radical political demands, Franklin Roosevelt won the presidency in 1932 with a promise to alter fundamentally the nation's economic policy. The New Deal was the fruition of this promise, an ambitious program of unprecedented government spending on public works projects that employed large numbers of workers to improve the nation's infrastructure. By 1935, these programs amounted to nearly 7 percent of the country's gross domestic product (GDP). The New Deal also included the first legislation creating a federally mandated eight-hour workday, collective bargaining rights for workers, a minimum wage, protection against unfair labor practices, federal subsidies for farmers, and federal income support for poor single mothers. With government acquiescence, union membership doubled between 1925 and 1941, reaching its peak in the 1960s.

Government social services also expanded, most importantly with the creation of the Social Security system. This began as a program to provide pensions to retired workers but was soon expanded to include pensions for their survivors and assistance for the disabled. Social Security has done more to reduce poverty in the United States than any other government program before or since.

The New Deal era was one of unprecedented growth in government involvement in the economy, in employment creation, and in worker protection, as the government moved to take on more beneficial and politically generated functions. It was a period of more or less Keynesian economic policy in which the government actively worked to improve economic growth and expand employment. The Employment Act of 1946 "declared it the policy of the federal government to maximize employment, production, and purchasing power." After World War II, the United States was by far the world's largest economy and experienced exceptionally rapid growth as the world recovered from the war. The middle class expanded at an unprecedented rate as the economy boomed, infrastructure continued to be built, and returning veterans took advantage of the GI Bill to pursue higher education.

In the 1960s, Lyndon Johnson's administration initiated the "Great Society" to complete the goals of the New Deal. The pillars of this effort were the creation of Medicare,

which is medical insurance for Social Security recipients; Aid to Families with Dependent Children (AFDC), a much-expanded welfare program for poor mothers; and Medicaid, health care for AFDC and other welfare recipients. These programs, along with the earlier Social Security system, helped reduce poverty from 25 percent of the population in 1955 to 11 percent by 1973. However, slower economic growth and waning political support subsequently led the government to reduce the real value of these antipoverty programs, contributing to a rise in the poverty rate to around 14 percent by the 1990s.

Sustained economic growth and Keynesian policies continued through the mid-1960s. By the late 1960s, continued deficit spending caused by involvement in the Vietnam War and by the costs of Great Society programs helped produce rising inflation. The quadrupling of world oil prices in 1973 further slowed economic growth and spurred more inflation, producing "stagflation" by the late 1970s that the government seemed incapable of reversing. Ronald Reagan won the presidency in 1980 on a platform that emphasized the need to reduce the size and scope of government by embracing monetarism's prescriptions for reduced government spending, accepting a "natural rate of unemployment," and freeing the market to restart growth. In short, he hoped to pare back government intervention and limit it as much as possible to the essential functions. President Jimmy Carter had begun some deregulation of industry in the late 1970s, but Reagan expanded this effort substantially, starting with the airline and trucking industries. By successfully defeating an air traffic controllers' strike in 1981, Reagan also reduced the power and reach of unions, whose membership had been declining throughout the 1970s. This trend has continued, with union membership now reduced to about what it was a century ago, although the unionized workforce grew slightly in 2007 for the first time since the 1970s, reaching 12.4 percent by 2009. Reagan also cut spending on social programs and cut taxes to spur economic growth. At the same time, the Federal Reserve embraced monetarist policies, raising interest rates and reining in the money supply to reduce inflation. This combination produced the most severe economic downturn since the Great Depression between 1981 and 1983, but then sustained economic growth reemerged for the rest of the decade. Reagan reversed the Keynesian effort of the New Deal–Great Society period, marking the most dramatic shift in economic policy since the 1930s.

Reagan embraced monetarism, but his tax cuts and high military spending resulted in record budget deficits. President Bill Clinton and Congress finally eliminated these budget deficits in the 1990s. In combination with continued monetarist policies at the Fed, the elimination of these deficits helped spur renewed economic growth. Though Clinton was a Democrat like Johnson and Roosevelt, his economic policies continued the trend begun under Reagan, a Republican. Monetarism continued to be the accepted economic theory, and during the 1980s and 1990s the U.S. government methodically removed most of the restrictive New Deal era regulations on banking. This trend culminated in the Commodity Futures Modernization Act of 2000, which specifically prevented government regulation of derivatives such as credit default swaps (a central feature of the 2008–2009 financial crisis, as described earlier in the chapter). Economists and businesses alike expected these changes to increase efficiency and profitability throughout the banking and financial sectors without creating any undue risk, arguing that modern banking was fundamentally different than it had been during the Great Depression. President George W. Bush continued these monetarist policies after taking office in 2001, although following September 11, 2001, he increased military spending and cut taxes, which returned the nation to the budget deficits characteristic of the 1970s and 1980s.

Except for a brief recession in 1989–1991 and slower growth after 2000, monetarist policies produced substantial economic expansion until 2007. However, they also produced greater inequality and poverty. The GINI Index, an overall measure of inequality, was at about 37 in the United States in the late 1940s. It dropped (meaning greater equality)

to 35 by the late 1960s, but by 1994 it had risen to 42, where it has remained since. As the Country and Concept table (page 190) shows, this is a much higher level of inequality than in other wealthy countries. In the late 1960s, the wealthiest fifth of the U.S. population had 40.6 percent of all income; by 2001, that figure had risen to 49.6 percent. The poorest fifth's share of income, on the other hand, dropped from 5.6 percent to 3.5 percent over the same period.

Although the Great Recession began in 2007, it was not widely apparent until 2008. The Bush administration's first response was a tax rebate to every taxpaying household in hopes that people would spend the money and thereby stimulate the economy. Because the rebate was a tax cut rather than an increase in government spending, the Republican Party supported it even though it was essentially Keynesian: a form of deficit spending to stimulate a sluggish economy. Later in 2008, it became clear that the problem was much bigger than initially realized and that the Bush administration's initial response was inadequate. When the Wall Street firm Lehman Brothers went bankrupt in September 2008, the full-scale financial crisis began. Banks virtually ceased all lending for several months, afraid that any loans they made would not be repaid. At the same time, the country became aware of the magnitude of the slump in housing prices, leading to foreclosures of high-risk mortgages, which in turn caused a rapid drop in the values of investments based on those mortgages. Without access to credit, businesses could not invest and began firing workers. The nation's GDP plunged 8.4 percent in the second half of the year, and unemployment rose from 4.9 to 7.4 percent.

Once it was understood that the crisis was primarily in the housing and financial sectors, the Bush administration proposed unusual interventions. After initially hesitating, Congress supported the administration's proposal to create the Troubled Asset Relief Program (TARP), under which the government agreed to purchase or guarantee bank-owned investments tied to the plummeting housing market in exchange for a substantial share of the banks' stock. The government, in effect, became a substantial owner of a number of American banks. The new Obama administration in 2009 implemented more "bailouts," as they came to be known, this time for the troubled auto industry. It also created a program to assist in the conversion of risky and expensive mortgages into more affordable ones for homeowners in trouble. While the credit market remained very weak until the middle of the year, ultimately credit began to flow again, and the economy began to recover by the end of 2009. In spite of fears that the taxpayers would never get their money back, most major banks and auto companies repaid the government, repurchasing government-owned stock by mid-2010. The Obama administration also pushed through Congress an unprecedented stimulus plan of $787 billion in early 2009 in a clear attempt to use Keynesian policy to "jump-start" the economy.

In late 2010, continued high unemployment led both Congress and the Federal Reserve to take further stimulus measures, while carefully avoiding the term *stimulus* for fear of political backlash from voters worried about the growing deficit. First, the Federal Reserve announced a policy of "quantitative easing," essentially printing new money and using it to buy $600 billion of U.S. Treasury bonds, thus effectively pumping that amount of money into the economy via the banking system. At the end of the year, the Obama administration and Congress compromised on a tax bill that preserved for all taxpayers the so-called "Bush tax cuts," which had been passed a decade earlier, reduced Social Security taxes for 2011, and extended unemployment benefits. The president and Congress paid for all of this by expanding the deficit.

The economic recovery, which saw the stock market rise dramatically from its low point in March 2009, did not provide much relief for the average person. The housing program did stabilize housing prices and slow the rate of foreclosures, though foreclosures continued at an unusually high rate. The stimulus package prevented deep cuts in state governments' budgets and employment levels for 2009. As the stimulus money ran out by 2011, though, states across the country faced the prospect of massive budget cuts, which in turn prompted large protests from groups who would be affected by the cuts. Most importantly, however, overall unemployment continued to worsen throughout the year, hitting 10 percent by December 2009 and dropping only to 9.6 percent a year later. The bailout of the banks, widespread publicity about bank managers' high bonuses in spite of the recession, and the continuing high unemployment rates among average workers left many Americans angry that the government seemed to have saved Wall Street but had ignored "Main Street." This sentiment, combined with continuing high unemployment and growing concern about deficit spending, were among the reasons voters shifted in large numbers from the Democratic to the Republican Party in the 2010 congressional elections. While the administration, Congress, and the Federal Reserve all seemed to agree (at least quietly) that further stimulus was needed in the short term, voters were deeply skeptical of its potential impact on their lives. The newly elected Republicans set out to reduce budget deficits substantially in 2011, locking horns with Democrats who still controlled the Senate and with President Obama; implicitly, this was a classic battle over which economic theory to pursue.

With the worst of the recession over (at least in the financial and housing sectors), the U.S. government turned its attention in 2010 to measures designed to prevent future crises. This debate renewed a focus on financial regulation, a subject often debated before. After the Great Depression, the U.S. government had regulated banks rather strictly, treating commercial banks that people use on a daily basis differently than investment banks on Wall Street. The government limited the activities commercial banks could engage in, while also guaranteeing individual deposits in those banks to prevent future collapses. In the 1990s, however, President Bill Clinton and a Republican-dominated Congress, influenced by monetarist arguments, lifted many of those restrictions, allowing most banks to engage in many different activities. Simultaneously, investment bankers created new kinds of investments that the government regulated only lightly or not at all, including derivatives like the credit default swaps that would be part of the 2008–2009 financial crisis.

In the aftermath of the Great Recession, few economists or policy makers repudiated monetarist policies entirely, but many argued that the crisis had demonstrated the need for more regulation of the financial sector. Some wanted to prevent banks from getting "too big to fail," others wanted to re-create the earlier separation of commercial and investment banks, and still others simply argued that the investment products themselves needed closer government regulation. As is the case when monopolies arise, the state's interest in preserving a healthy and growing capitalist economy may require it to enact policies against the immediate interests of particular capitalists—in this case, major investment banks whose unchecked search for profits seemed to threaten the stability of the system as a whole. In July 2010, Congress passed and President Obama signed the largest financial regulatory bill since World War II. While it did not fully return banks to the pre-1980s regulations or limit their size, it instituted regulation of the derivatives markets; established a council to monitor the largest banks (those considered "too big to fail"); instituted regulations to ensure that if such banks do fail, their stockholders—rather than taxpayers—will pay the costs; and restricted banks from making speculative investments with their own money.

While President Obama pushed through substantially increased government intervention in the economy in response to the financial crisis, he nonetheless embraced the idea of expanding free trade and globalization, as has every president since Reagan. He argued that such policies would maximize efficiency and produce the greatest possible wealth for the United States and the rest of the world. The United States has been a key champion of opening all borders to trade and investment, and U.S. companies have moved thousands of factories and hundreds of thousands of factory jobs out of the country. President Clinton secured approval of the North American Free Trade Agreement (NAFTA), which has

dramatically increased cross-border economic activity among the United States, Mexico, and Canada. Unions, environmentalists, and others have opposed many of these developments, arguing that they are costing the United States jobs and exporting production to countries where workers and the environment are not protected. But official U.S. support of free trade is not universal. Agriculture is the prime example of an economic sector over which the government has maintained protective policies; the United States and the EU continue to protect their farming sectors from low-cost competition from poorer countries in Latin America and Africa.

CASE SUMMARY

The U.S. model of free market growth is an exception, not the norm. Most other governments choose to intervene more substantially in market processes. For a long time, the United States preferred to limit government as much as possible to "essential" functions, as its late creation of the Federal Reserve suggests. It took a half century of union effort to move the U.S. government to adopt more politically generated functions, including regulating working conditions and protecting workers against the economic effects of advancing age and possible disability. The mid-twentieth century saw a period of expanded government involvement in more politically generated roles, starting with the New Deal, but some of those policies have been reversed since the 1980s. Other New Deal–Great Society policies, notably Social Security and Medicare, have proven more popular and durable, despite monetarist demands for reduced government spending. The United States seems to have permanently embraced a somewhat expanded government role in the market, though the government remains far less invasive than the governments of almost all European countries. America's championing of unfettered markets, free trade, and globalization made it a symbol of a new era, but the Great Recession badly damaged that image. Many countries, especially in Europe, blamed the

United States for the crisis that had affected them all, charging that lack of prudent state regulation had caused a massive loss of global wealth, growing unemployment, and even government bankruptcies. Though the recession forced significant cutbacks for financially strapped governments in Europe, many countries still maintain economic systems that include far more extensive state intervention. Germany is one such example.

CASE STUDY

Germany: The Social Market Economy

- Pioneer of social welfare policies
- Monetarist monetary and fiscal policies with generous social services
- Guided capitalism: Close government/ business/labor relationships
- Political consensus on economic policies until late 1990s
- Recent problems: Slowing growth, rising unemployment, growing fiscal deficits
- Liberalizing reforms in the face of globalization

Germany has been a leader in European Union monetary policy, including the creation of the euro and the European Central Bank. Here, the German finance minister unveils the German national euro coin.

Credit: Reuters/Wolfgang Rattay

social market economy: In Germany, a postwar economic system that combines a highly productive market economy with an extensive and generous welfare state, as well as unusually active involvement of both business and labor in economic policy

Over the course of the twentieth century, Germany created a much-admired model of regulated capitalism known as the **social market economy**. This model combined a highly productive market economy that became the world's leading industrial exporter with an extensive and generous welfare state, as well as unusually active involvement of both business and labor associations in setting and implementing economic policy. Productivity, wages, and job security were relatively high, and inequality was relatively low. Germany also led the way in creating the EU and then the euro; the country yielded its control over monetary policy to the new European Central Bank in 1999, which was modeled after Germany's own Bundesbank. Globalization has raised significant questions about the viability of the social market economy, as Germany has faced continuing high unemployment, experienced difficulty financing its generous social welfare benefits, and had trouble maintaining the strict limits on deficit spending

that the euro requires and that Germany itself has long championed. The country pursued several reforms in the new millennium that allowed it to remain one of the world's leading exporters. While it was hit heavily by the recession of 2008–2009, it has recovered more quickly than many other countries. Some analysts were once again talking about a "German miracle" because despite a large drop in GDP, unemployment went up only slightly during the recession. Nonetheless, Germany faces severe budget problems as it tries to continue funding its generous social services in a difficult economic environment.

The modern German economy first developed under Otto von Bismarck in the 1860s and 1870s. Germany was a late industrializer compared to Britain or France. Bismarck set out to build German national strength via economic growth, so he pursued a set of policies that protected industry and produced rapid industrialization and urbanization. This came at the expense of workers, who faced horrific working conditions, social dislocation in the expanding cities, and low wages. These conditions helped produce an active communist movement in Germany, and some followers of this movement created the Social Democratic Party (SDP) in 1875 to work for socialism via nonviolent means. High tariffs protected German industry so it could grow but also resulted in high prices for food and other basic commodities, which further fueled worker unhappiness and the socialist movement.

Bismarck's concern about a socialist threat to his economic program led him to commit the state to some beneficial and politically generated market roles. Starting in 1879, he introduced a series of laws that created extensive (for its time) social policy for workers while simultaneously outlawing socialist parties and labor unions. The new policies included the world's first national health insurance system, accident insurance that was administered and financed by cooperative associations of employers, and old-age and widows' pensions subsidized by the federal government, all developed a half century before similar policies in the United States. Working conditions, on the other hand, did not change. Basically, the program was a conscious effort to continue industrialization via cheap labor while protecting workers from the worst situations they might face.

These social policies slowly expanded after Bismarck left power in 1890. The government also relaxed restrictions on labor unions, which grew as a result. After Germany's loss in World War I and the establishment of the Weimar Republic, social welfare policies expanded still further. The SDP was a prominent force in the Weimar governments of the early 1920s, and its socialist tendencies showed. The government broadened the insurance and pension systems in response to hyperinflation following the war. The influence of labor unions increased rapidly with their increased numbers, and by the mid-1920s, employers had agreed to establish an eight-hour workday, a forty-eight-hour workweek, a system of collective bargaining with unions over wages and other benefits, and binding arbitration to settle disputes. Social expenditures leapt from 19 percent of government spending in 1919 to 40 percent by 1930, and wages rose as employers and unions agreed to mandatory collective bargaining (Crew 1998). In response to rapid inflation, many companies began paying what was termed a "social wage," a wage that was adjusted to account for the costs of supporting a family.

Hitler interrupted this process with his totalitarian state, but after his defeat, the new government of West Germany took up pretty much where things had left off and extended the social welfare system again. The Christian Democratic Union (CDU) under Konrad Adenauer governed West Germany from its first election in 1949 until 1966. Though a "conservative" party, the CDU officially coined the term *social market economy* and fully developed the model. Christian Democrats generally saw protection of workers as part of their Christian ideology. Granted, the SDP often wanted social spending to expand even more rapidly, but both major parties agreed with the basic premises of the system. Not surprisingly, after the SDP became the governing party in 1969, social spending expanded more rapidly than in the past, but the shifts in economic and social policies from one government to the next were not large.

The social market economy created a form of capitalism in which close relationships and interpenetration between the private and public sectors have shaped economic and social policies. The national government passes broad regulatory standards for various sectors of the economy, industries, and professions, but it allows state governments (*Länder*) to work with businesses to formulate detailed implementation plans. The *Länder* work closely with industrial organizations to implement local policies, and industries accept those policies rather willingly because they've had a role in their formulation.

Unions also have a role to play, as the government channels some social programs through unions and religious organizations, which identify and provide money to local beneficiaries. More significantly, unions and employers' associations negotiate binding wage agreements, which all employers in a given sector must follow, and unions are represented on the supervisory boards of all

codetermination: A system in Germany that requires unions to be represented on the supervisory boards of all German firms of more than 2,000 employees

German firms with more than 2,000 employees. This system, known as **codetermination**, was created in 1976 and gives German workers power through their unions to influence employers' policies. One effect was that the unions came to understand what they must do to help achieve the high levels of productivity and product quality for which German firms have become famous. Each business of more than five employees also must have a workers' council. These councils must approve rules regarding working conditions, and many run vocational training programs that have helped make German workers among the most highly skilled in the world. Codetermination creates an element of democracy within the management of business enterprises, though ultimately businesses are still privately owned and must answer to their stockholders as in any other capitalist economy.

This economic model made Germany one of the most successful economies in the world from the end of World War II until the 1980s. No economy is perfect, but Germany enjoyed relatively rapid growth and became one of the world's wealthiest economies with very low unemployment and inflation and exceptionally generous social welfare benefits. It also became one of the world's leading exporters of high-quality manufactured goods. All of this began to change, however, with the end of the Cold War and the acceleration of globalization, as can be seen in Table 5.1 (pages 208–209). Reunification required the economic absorption of much poorer East Germany into the social market economy. Privatization of formerly government-owned industries in East Germany created massive unemployment. West Germans had to fund huge social programs, infrastructure construction and improvement, and job training programs as they worked to integrate the eastern economy into the western. The bill for this was estimated to be about 4 percent of the entire German economy throughout the 1990s (Europa Publications Staff 2007). The biggest single problem resulting from this process was unemployment, which had

hovered around 1 percent for decades in West Germany but hit nearly 12 percent in reunified Germany by 1998 and stayed as high as 9 percent through 2005. After that, it began to drop significantly as the country absorbed more East German workers and collective bargaining with unions changed to give firms more flexibility to reduce wages. In the former East Germany, the unemployment rate was still about 13 percent in 2009.

In addition to pioneering the social market economy, Germany has been a key leader in the European Union. The euro was created in 1999, and the EU members that adopted it were required to allow the new European Central Bank to control their monetary policies (see the following Mini Case on the European Union). The German central bank, the Bundesbank, had restricted German monetary policy to keep inflation low, and the new European bank is charged with doing the same. To be part of the EU, countries must keep their fiscal deficits within strict limits, thus restricting the ability of individual governments to spend on social or other programs unless they can raise the taxes to pay for them. Germany's social policies call for generous benefits to the growing numbers of unemployed, but membership in the EU requires it to maintain strict limits on government spending.

The expenses of reunification and the institution of the euro as a common currency have produced the most significant political discord and electoral shifts in Germany since the end of the Nazi era. In response, Germany voted out the CDU in 1998. That party, led by Helmut Kohl, had championed German reunification whatever the cost. The new SDP government under Gerhard Schröder introduced Agenda 2010, legislation that significantly lowered the protections and benefits the social market economy had provided Germans in the past. Therefore, German voters once again expressed their displeasure in 2005, narrowly but definitively voting Schröder and the SDP out. Voters returned the CDU to power under Germany's first woman chancellor, Angela Merkel, but the election was so close that she had to rule in a grand coalition with the SDP. Merkel then won the 2009 election without requiring the support of the SDP in government, in large part due to her deft handling of the recession, to which Germany responded better than most countries.

The German economy shrank by 5 percent in 2009; this contraction was one of the hardest hits taken in Europe from the Great Recession. The global downturn affected the German financial sector because German banks were heavily invested in some of the risky securities that had caused the financial crisis. The global downturn also caused a nearly 20 percent drop in exports, which had long been the mainstay of German manufacturing. Germany, however, was also one of the first countries to bounce back, starting to grow again slowly in the second half of 2009 and achieving an estimated growth rate of 3.6 percent in 2010. Despite a long history of fiscal austerity, the German government turned to Keynesian stimulus to respond to the recession. It passed a version of the American "cash for clunkers" program that increased automobile sales by 40 percent in 2009, and it passed the biggest stimulus package in Europe. (This was still smaller than the U.S. package; Germany's package was about 1.5 percent of GDP, while the U.S. package was about 2 percent of GDP.) After her reelection, Chancellor Merkel pushed through a tax cut as well. This was aimed at giving families more spending money to stimulate the economy, though many analysts believed that Germans would simply save the money instead. The stimulus plan and tax cut caused the government's budget deficit to soar to 4.5 percent of GDP by 2010, which it must cut to 3 percent by 2013 to abide by EU requirements. As a result, Merkel has proposed billions of euros in spending cuts for 2011, including a 2.5 percent cut in civil servants' pay, to bring the deficit back in line with EU requirements. Remarkably, the recession only raised

unemployment by about one percentage point (from about 8 to 9 percent), a far less dramatic change than most countries saw. Indeed, by the end of 2010, unemployment was at its lowest level since 1992. This was due to reforms made earlier in the decade to allow more flexible bargaining with unions, which we examine in more detail in Chapter 10, as well as growth in exports, Germany's traditional strength.

CASE SUMMARY

Germany's economic model is quite distinct from the free market system of the United States; the difference can be traced all the way back to Germany's initial industrialization. With substantial state leadership by Bismark, Germany's industrialization was more similar to what came to be called developmentalism or import substitution industrialization than the U.S. model. While certainly capitalist, the social market economy includes much more extensive state intervention. In the social market economy's heyday, government, business, and labor organizations worked closely together to guide the economy on a path of growth and near full employment while providing social services far more generous than those available in the United States. Globalization, the EU, and reunification called the model into question by the turn of the twenty-first century, but reforms since then seem to have allowed Germany to start to adapt, with unemployment dropping substantially. Germany's rapid recovery from the Great Recession once again had some analysts proclaiming the "German miracle," while others pointed to continuing high unemployment and growing fiscal deficits to cast doubt on the German economic model's long-term viability. Japan, our next case study, represents a third model of successful capitalism but one that has also struggled in the new globalized era.

MINI CASE

The European Union, Economic Sovereignty, and Globalization

The creation of the European Union (EU), and especially the creation of the European Monetary Union (EMU) and the euro, has raised fundamental questions about globalization and state sovereignty over economic policy. The EU originated in the European Coal and Steel Community of 1952, becoming the more broadly defined European Economic Community (EEC) in 1958. At that point six states, led by West Germany and France, came together with the primary goal of opening their economies to each other and easing trade and investment among them. The EEC, as it was known until 1993, succeeded in substantially reducing barriers to trade among member countries and in effect created an enlarged, multistate market for goods. Member states, however, did not really yield substantial sovereignty because each retained the right to veto any decision of importance; each member state also retained the right to choose what it would and would not agree to. The group expanded to ten members by 1981, fifteen members by 1995 (by which time the group was commonly called the EU), and twenty-seven by 2007 (when twelve mostly eastern European countries joined).

The most ambitious of the original architects of the EEC envisioned it eventually becoming a "United States of Europe," a single state created as member states voluntarily yielded their sovereignty to the larger body over time. While this has never happened, many members have given substantial sovereignty over economic policy to what is now called the European Union. Member states were first required to yield real sovereign decision-making power to the larger body under the Single European Act of 1987. The act limited a single state's veto power in the Council of Ministers and instead expanded a system of qualified majority voting in which 55 to 72 percent (depending on the issue) of the total votes were needed to make policy decisions (with each country's share of the total vote being based on its size). Under this system, not even Germany, the biggest state, can veto decisions; several states must vote together to block a decision, which means that individual states have given up their sovereign right over key economic decisions.

The next and biggest step in the process of states yielding sovereignty was the Maastricht Treaty of 1992, which created the EU and the EMU. This treaty created a common currency—the euro—controlled by a new European Central Bank (ECB). The seventeen states that have so far agreed to participate gave up their ability to control their own monetary policy and agreed to strict limits on their fiscal policy. Given the centrality of monetary and fiscal policy to both Keynesian and monetarist economic management, these states have given up perhaps the most important economic policy tool they have. To "join" the euro, states had to pledge to bring their inflation and interest rates close to the European average and restrict their budget deficits to 3 percent of GDP and their public debt to 60 percent of GDP. Eventually, seventeen states adopted the euro, starting with eleven in 2004. The European Central Bank controls the money supply and therefore monetary policy for these states.

The EU leadership attempted a major expansion of EU sovereignty in 2004 with a proposed European constitution. Despite, or perhaps because of, the successful expansion of EU power before that, the proposed constitution was unpopular in many countries. In 2005, French and Dutch voters rejected the constitution in referenda, effectively killing the proposal. Critics were concerned about giving up greater sovereignty to the EU, especially since many viewed the document as having a "democratic deficit." Despite the existence of the directly elected European Parliament, EU critics argue that the EU is too large to be an effective democracy and that real power continues to lie with the appointed Council of Ministers and European Commission rather than the elected parliament. The constitution would have expanded qualified majority voting, further reducing the veto power of member states and therefore their sovereignty. Following the failure of the constitution, EU members adopted the Treaty of Lisbon in 2007. This treaty subjected more policy areas to majority voting and created a "double-majority" system. The double-majority requires that if an EU-wide policy is to be approved, at least 55 percent of voting member countries must vote in favor of it; furthermore, those countries must represent at least 65 percent of the EU's total population. The Lisbon Treaty was a much watered-down alternative to the fuller yielding of sovereignty that the failed constitution had proposed.

The Great Recession hit the EU and especially the euro extremely hard. Maintaining the limits on debt that were agreed upon when the euro was created has always been hard, even for the healthier economies such as Germany and France. In the economic boom that preceded the crisis, several of the weaker economies in the EU ran up debts and deficits, using the strength of the euro to help them do so. The crisis revealed the problems created by EU control of monetary policy while fiscal policy remained at the national level and member countries' economic strength varied greatly. The crisis also revealed a large split between the wealthier and strong economies, most of which were in the north, and weaker ones in the south. Early in the crisis, the EU tried to coordinate economic responses across members but largely failed to do so. Most member countries passed economic stimulus policies in 2008 and 2009, but their sizes and effects varied.

The full extent of the crisis was only revealed in 2010, when private international creditors began to doubt the weaker states' ability to repay their debts and, therefore, started refusing to buy their government bonds. The worst hit were Greece and Ireland, followed by Portugal and Spain. Usually countries in this situation would, among other things, allow the value of their currencies to drop to encourage exports and restart growth. This was not an option, however, because Greece and Ireland used the euro and the euro's value is tied to the strength of the entire EU rather than that of individual EU members. The value of the euro was dropping but not fast enough to create foreign investment because of the continuing economic strength of the larger countries, especially Germany. Without the ability to lower the value of their currencies, the governments in crisis had to institute severe fiscal policies to reduce their debt, leading to widespread protests, some of which turned violent. Even austerity measures failed to convince international creditors of these countries' economic soundness, and they had to ask for help from the EU and IMF. A bailout package funded by the ECB and IMF was put in place in 2010, first for Greece in May and then for Ireland in November. It gave those countries new funds to back their debt but required continued and more severe fiscal policies to reduce deficits. This led to further and more widespread protests that turned violent in Greece and toppled the government in Ireland by the end of 2010. In September, a day of protests against government spending cuts mobilized tens of thousands across Europe. The success of the bailout packages remained unclear at the end of 2010, though they had given the two countries some breathing room. The agreements to bail out Greece and Ireland were widely unpopular, not only in Greece and Ireland but also in Germany, whose citizens saw themselves as having to pay for the economic mistakes of other countries. In early 2011, the EU agreed to create a permanent fund to support countries in financial crisis in the future, an effort to reassure investors about the long-term stability of the euro. As investors began to fear default in Portugal in early 2011, however, economists debated whether another bailout would be sound policy or if instead Portugal ought to be allowed to write off some of its debts, forcing investors to absorb some of the losses.

For the first time since the creation of the euro, there was open discussion (especially in Greece) of whether continuing to use the common currency was wise. Opponents of the EU have long opposed the fiscal and monetary policies required to join the euro, seeing them as forcing every member country to follow the neoliberal economic orthodoxy that is popular with the IMF and as undermining European social welfare policies. The 2010 crisis reinforced these arguments, calling into question the benefits that a single currency was supposed to provide while requiring even more unpopular fiscal policies. While no serious debate has arisen about abandoning the euro or weakening the EU in other ways, the failure to pass the constitution in 2005 and the crisis in 2010 have certainly brought the benefits of the EU, the largest example of globalization in the world, into greater question.

CASE SUMMARY

The EU is the world's most extensive example of states giving up their individual control over economic policy. By yielding monetary policy to the Union, member states have gained the advantage of functioning in a much larger single market in which virtually anything can flow across national borders without restrictions. The EU took decades to develop, as debate flourished about who would control what policies and how much national sovereignty states and their citizens were willing to give up. The euro seemed to work well until the Great Recession, when stark differences among the member economies and the fact that fiscal policy remains the prerogative of individual states made responding to the global crisis difficult. So far, the wealthier countries and the IMF have funded the weaker countries in order to avoid further collapse and to preserve the strength of the euro. The success or failure of these efforts, and the final verdict of European citizens as to whether the EU is worth the costs, will play a large role in determining whether Europe's experiment with economic integration beyond national borders will expand or contract in the future.

CASE STUDY

Japan: The Developmental State and Its Crisis

- Interventionist policy to industrialize and strengthen the nation
- Weak unions but "lifetime" employment for men at major firms
- Close relations between government bureaucracies and key corporate networks (*keiretsu*)
- Recession and stagnation since 1990 and difficulty of reform
- Globalization undermines some pillars of the developmental state

Japan was the first non-Western society to industrialize successfully and create a fully modern and wealthy economy. This process began under Japan's first modern state, the Meiji regime, which led the country from 1868 until World War II. But the country became fully developed only after World War II, when a distinct model of market-state relations emerged: the developmental state. Though it was interventionist like the German model, the Japanese model arose not from the demands of organized labor and fear of a socialist democratic party but instead from the concerted effort of the government to achieve rapid economic growth and industrialization. The primary purpose of intervention under the Japanese model has been to guide key sectors of the economy to achieve maximum growth, and the developmental state made Japan the second largest economy in the world by the 1980s. Many Americans at the time came to view Japan as a primary threat to U.S. economic hegemony. As Table 5.1 (pages 208–209) shows, however, Japan has experienced persistent economic stagnation since

1990 and has instituted only limited reforms in the face of the vicissitudes of globalization. This has brought the developmental state model into question, both in Japan and around the world.

The Meiji Restoration of 1867 brought to power a fundamentally new state led by the militaristic samurai, who were determined to modernize the country after the humiliation of the country's forced opening to Western trade. The Meiji government focused on creating a strong and prosperous state, defined by its central slogan: "Rich nation, strong army." The government actively intervened in economic activity, directly investing not only in infrastructure but also in key industries. Once the government started an industry, it often sold it to private investors at bargain prices and actively encouraged industrial mergers to create larger and more competitive firms. This produced a very concentrated business class, at the heart of which were the *zaibatsu,* three family-dominated industrial conglomerates that controlled key areas of the economy and had close relations with the government. In contrast to standard practice in capitalist economies, especially the United States, the government helped create business cartels in order to control specific sectors of the economy, and it helped create trade associations in order to coordinate development efforts among firms in the same industry.

World War I was a major boon to the Japanese economy, as wartime demand from the United States greatly increased Japanese exports. This allowed Japan to pursue an early import-substitution industrialization (ISI) policy under which it created even heavier industry than it had before, producing a period of very rapid economic growth, urbanization, and industrialization. After the war, this economic expansion made Japan an attractive place for foreign investment, and by the 1930s, Japanese businesses were asking the government for even more support to create cartels to compete against foreign companies. Meanwhile, the increasingly powerful military was concerned that private capital, both domestic and foreign, was getting too powerful and would pursue its own interests rather than broader national ones. Therefore, it initiated

a system of government licensing of a wide array of economic investments and activities. The government used these licenses to encourage domestic ownership in key sectors, discourage foreign ownership, and encourage all firms to invest in areas it deemed of national interest. A firm that was Japanese owned and was willing to invest in an area that the military-dominated government considered to be of national importance would receive a license to begin operations much more easily than would other firms. This system not only fueled Japan's military machine but also further concentrated ownership of capital.

After World War II, the United States dethroned not only the emperor but also the *zaibatsu.* While the Meiji government saw the conglomerates as part of a deliberate industrialization strategy, the United States objected to them on political and economic grounds. Politically, they were part of the fascist Japanese past and therefore needed to be replaced by a more "democratic" business class. Economically, they were antithetical to healthy competition in a market economy; essentially, they were a market failure, albeit a deliberate one, that had to be corrected. The United States therefore wrote antimonopoly legislation into Japanese law that disbanded the *zaibatsu.* But a shortage of capital for investment forced the United States to allow Japanese banks to own stock in industrial companies and to allow the companies to own stock in each other. The capital shortage also led Japan's ministry of finance to allow twelve key banks to "overlend" money to companies, meaning that the banks were allowed to lend more money than they had and more than other banks were allowed to lend.

By the 1960s, the fully developed result of all this was the *keiretsu:* complex networks of firms that are owned separately but work together closely. Some are direct descendants of the *zaibatsu.* At the center of most *keiretsu* is a major bank, which lends money on favorable terms to its *keiretsu* members and typically sends representatives to work in the firms to which it has lent money to ensure that its loans are being used wisely. Firms in a *keiretsu* own stock in each others' companies and therefore give each other orders for

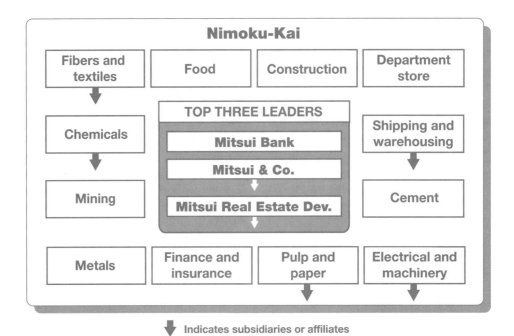

Japan's *keiretsu,* like the Mitsui example shown here, are complex, interlocking, and sometimes vertically integrated industrial conglomerates. They are not technically monopolies, but their highly integrated structures make it difficult for firms outside the *keiretsu* to compete.

products. "Vertical" *keiretsu* like Toyota and Nissan involve a major manufacturer tied to hundreds of favored suppliers. While ownership of capital is not as concentrated as it was under the Meiji regime, the system nonetheless encourages long-term relationships among firms and limits the ability of firms outside the *keiretsu,* including foreign firms, to do business.

What Chalmers Johnson (1982) termed the **developmental state** emerged along with the rise of the *keiretsu.* A developmental state does not seek just to establish the rules of the game for capitalism and encourage overall economic growth. It also consciously seeks to create national strength in particular economic areas, meaning it takes an active and conscious role in the development of specific sectors of the economy. The Japanese government did this via two key bureaucratic agencies, the Ministry of Finance (MOF) and the Ministry of International Trade and Industry (MITI). Until liberalization in the 1970s, the MOF had extensive influence over the banking sector via its control over interest

rates and over the role of banks in the *keiretsu.* The major banks were allowed to overlend to their *keiretsu* members to facilitate industrial investment. The banks could not cover all of these loans, so when a debtor failed to pay, the MOF guaranteed the loan, making the banks (and, in turn, the industrial companies) dependent on MOF goodwill. The MOF also controlled substantial funds via the postal saving system, a state-run system that provided a safe, convenient way for people to deposit their money in savings accounts through the post office. Most Japanese households invested their personal savings in postal savings accounts, and the MOF used these funds to subsidize industries it favored.

MITI influenced industrial policies more specifically through extensive licensing of technology and "administrative guidance," the bureaucracy's practice of informally and successfully suggesting that an industry or firm pursue a particular endeavor. MITI was able to use this informal system to guide industrial growth because of the licensing, financial, and other powers it held over

developmental state: A state that seeks to create national strength by taking an active and conscious role in the development of specific sectors of the economy

business and because of the close relationship that developed among key industries, bureaucracies, and the ruling party. Leaders in all three of these sectors would move from one to the other over the course of their careers; for instance, former bureaucrats frequently became members of parliament.

T. J. Pempel (2000) argued that Japan's development state was fundamentally a "conservative regime" in the sense that it favored business and governing elites over labor. Labor unions in Japan have always been opponents of the ruling party, but they have never been very powerful. This is due in part to what has been termed "lifetime employment" at major Japanese firms. In reality, there is no formal system of lifetime employment; instead, each member of the core, "permanent" workforce has (or at least had) a near guarantee of employment with the same firm. This was made possible in part by the existence of a large, flexible, and mostly female force of part-time workers that firms could hire and fire as market conditions warranted. The full-time male workforce received nearly guaranteed employment and was assured health and retirement benefits via the firm. Therefore, many of them chose to remain loyal to the same firm for life and were uninterested in unionization.

The developmental state created the "Japanese miracle," the sustained growth that made the Japanese economy six times larger in 1975 than it had been in 1950. Japan became the world's second largest economy, and "Japan Inc." was the chief economic rival to the United States in the 1970s and 1980s. As Tables 5.1 (pages 208–209) and 5.2 (page 226) show, Japan has also maintained a relatively low level of inequality and only moderate levels of poverty. This has not, however, been due to an extensive social welfare system. Japan's spending on social welfare is typically the second lowest among wealthy countries, not far above that of the United States, and is well below that of most European welfare states like Germany. Rather, Japan has maintained relative equality via the lifetime employment system and the extensive benefits that large companies provide

workers. Workers at large firms typically get a substantial lump-sum payment upon retirement, and some also receive pensions after that. A governmental social security system exists but is very modest, even compared to the U.S. system. The retirement payment and the fact that many companies pay a substantial share of annual wages via occasional large bonuses have helped make Japan's savings rate one of the highest in the world. This savings helped fuel rapid investment and growth in earlier years, but some economists believe it is now hurting Japan's ability to move out of the recession it has been in since 1993.

Table 5.2 illustrates the sharp difference between the last twenty years in Japan and earlier decades. Economic growth is only a third of what it was in the 1980s, unemployment has increased substantially, and prices are actually falling, a sign of serious economic stagnation or recession. The economic miracle ended in 1990; on the first business day of that year, real estate and stock prices, which had been climbing rapidly, plummeted and the bubble burst. There had been warning signs: productivity growth had been slowing since the 1970s, as had the government's ability to influence the direction of economic activity. Acquiescing to international pressure, the government had slowly begun to reduce its power to control flows of money and financing in the late 1970s. In the 1980s, the system of guaranteeing bank loans led Japanese corporations to take on excessive debt, which they invested in real estate and other unproductive areas. Because of deregulation, the MOF could do little to stop them, and it didn't really try. Simultaneously, the more efficient Japanese companies such as Toyota and Nissan fully entered the age of globalization, investing elsewhere in the world so that instead of exporting cars from Japan, they began building them in the United States and Europe. This reduced Japan's key source of growth: exports. All of this reduced the extent to which *keiretsu* members continued to coordinate their activity, as the corporate structure of the Japanese economy in the 1990s and 2000s moved perceptibly toward

TABLE 5.2

Profile of Japan's Economy, 1970–2009

	1970	1980	1990	2000	2009
GDP growth (annual %)	10.7	2.8	5.2	2.9	−5.2
Social expenditures (total, as % of GDP)	..	10.3	11.2	16.1	22.3 (2007)
Gross national savings (as % of nominal GDP)	..	..	33.2	27.5	24
Share of income or consumption, ratio of richest 20% to poorest 20%	..	..	4.3	3.4	3.4

Sources: Data from World Bank Indicators, OECD, UNDP Human Development Reports.

a more "American" model of vertically integrated, globally active corporations (Lincoln and Shimotani 2009).

All of this meant that when the bubble burst, the government had difficulty responding. It tried both Keynesian and monetarist policies, engaging in deficit spending and lowering official interest rates all the way to zero, but nothing seemed to revive economic growth. A key problem was massive bad bank debt from all the poorly invested loans. Government spending went to paying off the bad loans and keeping alive the banks that had made them. Corporations cut their permanent workforces and shifted to more part-time workers, reducing worker benefits and real wages.

In April 2001, Junichiro Koizumi was swept into power on his promises to reform the system, but he faced entrenched business and bureaucratic interests that were opposed to his efforts. His reforms, intended to dismantle much of the developmental state by reducing regulation and government control over the economy, were only partially successful. Koizumi lowered deficit spending to reduce the size of the government, but, as Keynesian economics would predict, this hurt growth by reducing the demand for goods. After a long battle, he succeeded in privatizing the postal service savings system. Once completed, this privatization will take from the bureaucracy the giant savings system that it used to subsidize favored

industries—a key mechanism of the developmental state.

Global economic growth and Koizumi's partial reforms helped restore positive but slow economic growth from 2003 to 2007, and they also helped rein in the deflation (i.e., a decline in prices) that had plagued Japan for a decade. The global recession of 2008–2009, however, destroyed these modest gains. Japan was hit exceptionally hard by the recession because of its dependence on exports, particularly to the United States. In 2009, the Japanese economy shrank by more than 5 percent, and deflation worsened significantly. The government responded with a Keynesian economic stimulus that increased its already high fiscal deficit and once again reduced interest rates to zero. Modest economic growth returned in late 2009, as it did in much of the world, and continued through 2010. The massive earthquake and tsunami in March 2011, however, would have profound economic effects; it was predicted to be the most costly natural disaster in world history.

The economic crisis produced a seismic political change, as the long-ruling Liberal Democratic Party was swept from power in November 2009. The new government came to office promising to reduce corruption and the bureaucracy's tight control over economic policy (see chapter 7), though its initial reform efforts were met by fierce opposition from entrenched interests. Japanese banks, meanwhile, faced less pressure than banks in the United States or Europe. International financial analysts had long seen Japanese banks as too conservative in their approach, but that meant they were far less exposed to the securities that were at the heart of the 2008 financial collapse. They suffered fewer losses than banks elsewhere and faced less pressure to submit to increased regulation and institute reforms in the aftermath of the recession.

CASE SUMMARY

Postwar Japan created a new model of political economy, called the developmental state, which proved spectacularly successful at transforming the country into a global power and one of the wealthiest countries in the world. Even more than in Germany, the state guided economic growth, encouraging

what a more *laissez-faire* model would see as excessive collaboration among large conglomerates and between them and the government. The mechanisms through which the state achieved this, however, proved to have negative effects when faced with the pressure of globalization in the form of more open financial systems, global investment by Japanese companies, and speculative investment in real estate and stock markets. Given Japan's long-standing stagnation, the global recession affected this country less than it did the United States or Germany, but Japan continues to struggle to adapt its model to the new era. Our next case study, Mexico, is a much poorer, developing economy that illustrates the debate over development policy we outlined earlier, including over the effects of extensive free trade, especially with its large northern neighbor.

MINI CASE

Chile: Early Neoliberal Reformer

Prior to the 1970s, Chile's economic history was similar to that of its Southern Cone peers. It depended heavily on mineral exports developed by foreign investors—first nitrates and then copper—and suffered the vicissitudes associated with primary-product exports. It experimented with ISI, but it was still by no means an industrial economy. In 1970, Chile narrowly elected Salvador Allende, who came to power at the head of a left-wing coalition dedicated to following a "peaceful road to socialism." Allende's government nationalized industries, including American-owned firms; imposed price controls; increased wages; and began land reform. Opposition from the middle and upper classes, as well as from the United States, was swift. Economic chaos ensued. By 1973, strikes, runaway inflation, and shortages had brought the economy to the brink of disaster. On September 11 of that year, the military intervened

in a coup d'etat that left at least 2,000 people dead—the first casualties of a long and brutal military dictatorship under General Augusto Pinochet.

The military turned economic policy over to a group of civilian technocrats who were quickly dubbed the "Chicago Boys." Trained at the University of Chicago, they were devotees of Milton Friedman's monetarist economic policies and sought to modernize the Chilean economy by opening it up fully to the world market and reducing state intervention. They reversed Allende's policies fully, selling Chile's nearly 500 state-owned firms, eliminating subsidies, and forcing Chilean firms to compete with foreign firms. These changes successfully reduced Chile's runaway inflation and promoted growth throughout the 1970s, but ironically, many of the Chilean business owners who had supported the coup lost out in the competition with foreign firms.

Like other poorer countries, Chile's economy shrank tremendously in the aftermath of Mexico's debt crisis in 1982, and nearly one-third of the workforce was unemployed by mid-1983. As a result, General Pinochet brought in new economic advisors who implemented even more radical free-market reforms. GDP growth reached a strong average annual rate of 4.1 percent throughout the 1980s, compared with 2.8 percent in Brazil, 1.1 percent in Mexico, and an 0.3 percent economic decline in Argentina. Unemployment also fell, but wages remained low and poverty high, while many poor Chileans did not have access to the social services like health care that the government had privatized.

In 1988, Pinochet decided to risk a plebiscite on continued military rule. Perhaps he believed that people who were grateful for the renewed economic growth would support him, but a unified opposition including the Socialists and the Christian Democrats, the dominant centrist party, mounted a successful campaign to vote no on continued military rule. After some tense moments, Pinochet accepted the result, paving the way for the election of the Christian Democrat Patricio Aylwin, who assumed office in 1990. Aylwin and his successors all committed themselves to maintaining the basic structure of the free-market economy while espousing various types of social programs to deal with the poverty and inequality left over from the military era. The economic model, though, wasn't completely a free-market one. The state had an active role in developing new export production in areas such as fishing and forestry. The democratic governments also introduced poverty-eradication programs that helped reduce poverty from 39 percent of the population in 1990 to 18 percent in 2006 (Siavelis 2007). Chile continued its commitment to trade liberalization, joining the Latin American MERCOSUR free-trade zone as an associate member in 1996 and concluding free trade agreements with Canada (1996), the United States (2005), China (2005), and Japan (2005).

Chile's free-market economy produced average annual GDP growth of nearly 8 percent throughout much of the 1990s, making it the fastest growing economy in Latin America. Beginning in 1998, the country experienced an economic slowdown and rising unemployment. However, a rise in the price of copper, which still accounts for 40 percent of exports, and consistent macroeconomic policies led to renewed growth in 2003, reaching an estimated 5.8 percent in 2007. Chile entered the global financial crisis in a strong position because rising world copper prices allowed President Michelle Bachelet (the country's first woman president) to build a revenue surplus. The financial crisis of 2008–2009 hit the country hard, producing a 1.5 percent economic decline in 2009, but a quick recovery followed. Although public debt increased, no debt crisis ensued because of the prior surplus. Unemployment peaked at 9.6 percent, up from around 8 percent before the crisis. The biggest recent economic shock was a devastating earthquake in 2010, one of the largest ever recorded. It is estimated to have caused damage equal to 18 percent of the national GDP.

CASE SUMMARY

Chile appears to have created strong financial institutions and the macroeconomic context for strong export-led growth into the future. Chile instituted neoliberal policies by choice rather than having them forced on it by a structural adjustment program, and those policies have combined with selected state support for new exports to achieve exceptionally high growth rates. Lower birth rates and government poverty-reduction programs have also lowered Chile's poverty rate dramatically, but inequality remains as high as elsewhere in Latin America. The challenge now is to use future growth to continue to reduce poverty and income inequality, as Chile attempts to move further along the path toward solidifying its status as a middle-income country.

CASE STUDY

Mexico: From Protectionism to Neoliberalism

- ISI and clientelist policies under the PRI until 1970s, funded by oil exports
- Shift to neoliberalism and SAPs 1980s–1990s
- Repeated economic crises that required further neoliberal reform
- Neoliberalism produced higher growth, higher inequality, and dependence on the United States

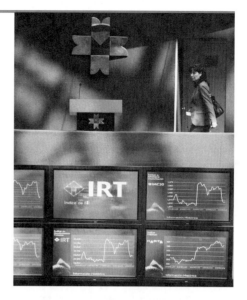

A woman walks by the electronic screen of the Mexican stock market in Mexico City on November 25, 2009. Mexico's economic growth and modernization have helped create institutions like a thriving stock market, but NAFTA has made Mexico heavily dependent on the United States. This dependence resulted in a severe hit during the 2008–2009 Great Recession.

Credit: Omar Torres/AFP/Getty Images

The Mexican economy has gone through several monumental transitions in its modern history—from the late nineteenth-century, pro-business policies of the Porfirio Díaz regime to the postrevolution protectionism of the long-ruling PRI, which dominated the country for most of the twentieth century. A move toward neoliberalism began in the early 1980s, following a massive debt crisis and subsequent IMF-imposed structural adjustment programs. This neoliberal shift is underscored by the fact that Mexico today maintains the highest number of free-market trade agreements of any country in the world, a development that has clearly improved macroeconomic growth but has also led to increased income and regional inequality.

The prerevolutionary era of Porfirio Díaz, known as the Porfiriato (i.e., the "Time of Porfirio"), gave Mexico a glimpse of large-scale economic growth, which remained at about 8 percent between 1884 and 1900. The Díaz regime embraced modernizing authoritarianism, which created vast wealth for the upper crust but left many behind. Existing social class distinctions only became more pronounced with the influx of foreign direct investment, which did not lead to large-scale infrastructural development. The rich simply got richer, while the poor remained poor.

Díaz fell from power in 1911 as a result of the Mexican Revolution. Emerging from the ashes of the revolution was a PRI-led state that followed a model of corporatism and supported the broad, working-class constituency that had inspired the Porfiriato's overthrow. Powerful political figures such as presidents Lázaro Cárdenas (1934–1940) and Luís Echeverría (1970–1976) became associated with a staunch, anti-elite populism. Under these leaders, oil nationalization, land redistribution, and ISI became the touted successes of the radical wing of the PRI.

Such protectionist and clientelistic programs were in large part funded through Petróleos Mexicanos (PEMEX), the company that oversees all of Mexico's oil production. Though it was the world's sixth largest oil producer at its peak, Mexico has seen its reserves decline while haphazard infrastructure development has limited PEMEX's ability to reap the full benefits of its oil fields. Some of the constraints on the oil sector came from the state's appetite for revenue to fund its public programs. In 1976, massive new oil reserves were discovered in the Gulf of Mexico, but the state's disproportionate increase in spending largely cancelled out many of the expected gains.

Things came to a head during the transition between Presidents Echeverría and José López Portillo in 1976, when the Echeverría government allowed the value of the peso to be determined by the currency market rather than set by the government; the peso quickly lost 50 percent of its value. In many ways, the government had no choice but to devalue, since the currency's pricing had lost credibility in the eyes of the market, and capital began to flee. Mexico fell into crisis, and the international community intervened with loans, the first of several such interventions.

Mexico's 1982 debt crisis began with falling oil prices and massive, dollar-denominated debt. The United States pursued its own anti-inflationary policies at home, thus strengthening the dollar and causing the Mexican peso to fall sharply in relation to the U.S. currency. This made it much more expensive for Mexico to pay back its debt, putting the country in a state of near insolvency. As this happened, capital began to flee the country in the billions of dollars. President López Portillo responded by nationalizing Mexico's banks, which remained state controlled until the 1990s. The crisis ushered in what became a global debt crisis, and it put the IMF and U.S. government in a position to demand fundamental changes in economic policy.

The country's steady move toward a neoliberal economic model began in earnest during the presidency of Miguel de la Madrid (1982–1988), who significantly increased the government's reliance on technocrats to run the state. Foreign-educated experts, fully disconnected from the politics of the revolution and the PRI's populist heyday, affected the character of the Mexican state at the ground level. By the time Carlos Salinas de Gortari (1988–1994)—a Harvard-educated technocrat himself—left office, Mexico's commitment to free-market economics was well established and strongly supported by the IMF and U.S. government. The country had joined the General Agreement on Tariffs and Trade (GATT) in 1986 and signed the North American Free Trade Agreement (NAFTA) in 1992. At the macroeconomic level, changes were visible. In the late ISI period (1970–1985), GDP growth averaged 4.5 percent per year in the best-performing Mexican states; this figure dropped to only 2.5 percent during the early free-market period (1985–1992). Studies show, however, that without NAFTA, growth would have been 4 to 5 percent lower by the year 2002. While NAFTA has increased productivity, however, it has had only marginal impact on employment.

The most noticeable effect of NAFTA has been Mexico's shift toward exports, which rose from 25 percent of GDP in 1985 to more than 82 percent in 1998. As the economy became more dependent on trade, however, regional disparities became more pronounced, with northern states most able to exploit their geographic proximity to U.S. markets. The less-developed southern states have lagged behind. In the free-trade economy, traditional and less-developed agriculture meant for local consumption has been displaced by cheap, state-subsidized corn from the United States. This has resulted in billions of dollars in losses to local growers, negatively affecting already impoverished rural communities. Neoliberalism, however, has not ended state spending as a political tool. Toward the end of the twentieth century, currency devaluation and concurrent inflation became staples of the Mexican economy, given the unwritten rule that outgoing presidents would increase social welfare spending in order to increase the popularity of their hand-picked successors. Even Presidents de la Madrid and Salinas did not hesitate to maintain high levels of deficit spending during periods of transition, and this practice brought about yet another catastrophe: the 1994 economic crisis.

The crisis, one of the most serious in Mexican history, was born out of a perfect storm. First, Salinas's social program "Solidarity" ran up the deficit significantly. Second, successor Ernesto Zedillo (1994–2000) allowed the peso to devalue against the dollar, sending the currency on another downward spiral. In addition, a series of political flashpoints—including an insurgency in the south led by the Zapatista Army of National Liberation, the assassination of presidential candidate Luís Donaldo Colosio in Tijuana, and the instigation of democratic competition in 1994—combined to cause investor panic. Only emergency loans from the United States and the International Monetary Fund (IMF) saved Mexico from financial ruin once again.

Today, Mexico continues to depend on the United States, albeit in less dramatic ways. Free trade between the two countries not only gives Mexican manufacturers access to the vast U.S. market, but NAFTA invites companies from all over the world to set up manufacturing plants, or *maquiladoras,* just south of the U.S.-Mexico border to take advantage of inexpensive labor and then export their goods north to the United States tariff-free, providing Mexico with needed foreign direct investment. The dependence on exports to the United States that NAFTA has created meant that the 2008–2009 global recession hit Mexico very hard. Its GDP dropped by 6.5 percent in 2009, though a return to growth was forecast for 2010. The government responded with a stimulus plan that, combined with a drop in revenue caused by the recession,

increased the government budget deficit substantially.

CASE SUMMARY

Mexico's move away from state intervention and toward free-market economics has brought gains, but some structural problems have been exacerbated. One of the most corrosive problems is income inequality. Mexico's GINI index (the measure of disparities between rich and poor) is one of the highest in the world (see Table 5.1).

Mexico represents a classic case of the shift from ISI to neoliberal policies, with all of the benefits and costs that entails. ISI combined with oil revenue to create substantial growth until the 1970s, when growing debt and global economic problems undermined it. Mexico virtually declared bankruptcy and was forced to accept neoliberal policies in exchange for Western (especially U.S.) support. The neoliberal shift culminated with the signing of NAFTA, greatly expanding Mexico's manufactured exports to the United States. This has renewed growth via foreign investment but has also expanded inequality and increased dependence on Mexico's primary export market (accounting for 80 percent of its exports), the United States, leaving it especially vulnerable to global economic shocks like the 2008–2009 recession.

Today Mexico is the fourteenth largest economy in the world, and by 2050 it is predicted to be the sixth largest, ahead of the United Kingdom, Germany, and France. If trade liberalization has created overall growth, however, the country's sharp inequalities have only increased with the emergence of neoliberal policies. In addition, poor governance and endemic corruption have limited the degree to which the population has been able to reap the benefits of a globalized economy.

CASE STUDY

Nigeria: A Weak State, Oil, and Corruption

- Postcolonial, illegitimate state
- State intervention: No local capitalists, state-sanctioned monopolies as part of ISI
- Oil, a weak state, and neopatrimonial rule spur corruption
- Debt crisis and slow and partial shift to SAPs
- Democratic government's recent efforts to reduce debt and corruption

Like almost all African countries, Nigeria was a poor, agricultural country with little industry of any kind when it gained independence in 1960. As much as 98 percent of the population worked in agriculture, producing 65 percent of the country's GDP and 70 percent of its exports. And like the governments of other African states, its new government initially attempted to industrialize via ISI. By the mid-1970s, however, oil production and revenue had overwhelmed all other aspects of the economy and made the government dangerously dependent on the global oil market for political and economic survival. The huge influx of oil revenue and the active involvement of the government in the economy helped create a situation ripe for corruption, and Nigeria ultimately became one of the most corrupt societies and governments

Colonial and independent Nigerian states used marketing boards to reap profits from exports like cocoa, but they failed to reinvest these profits in productive development. Today oil has replaced cocoa as the country's primary revenue generator, but most Nigerians have benefited little from this wealth.

Credit: AP Photo/George Osodi

in the world. Corruption, oil dependence, and mismanagement combined to leave average Nigerians gaining virtually nothing from the country's massive oil wealth. Very little development has occurred under either democratic or military governments, and the country's elite have used oil wealth to enrich themselves and maintain their status among their political and economic clients.

The origins of Nigeria's economic problems, and the troubled relationship between the state and the market, lay in colonial rule. As was true throughout sub-Saharan Africa, colonial rulers in Nigeria allowed only particular economic opportunities to Africans. In Nigeria, peasant farmers were encouraged to produce food and export crops, and these crops became the backbone of an export economy based on cocoa, cotton, peanuts, and palm oil. Nigerians were not allowed any significant opportunity in industry, and foreign businesses controlled what little industry there was. Africans' sole route to economic advancement under colonial rule was education and employment in the colonial government, and in contrast to the situation in most capitalist economies, government employment became a key source of wealth. At independence, the educated elite was primarily employed in government and had virtually no involvement or expertise in private industry. This elite thus saw an expansion of the government's role in the economy as central both to national development and to their own interests. As we noted earlier, development economists at the time agreed with this approach, arguing that in the absence of an indigenous capitalist class, the state could beneficially intervene to initiate the development process.

The earliest manifestation of this model of state intervention in the interests of development came in the agricultural sector with the creation of **marketing boards**. These were government entities with monopoly control over the domestic and international marketing of key crops. Of particular importance were the marketing boards for export crops such as cocoa and cotton. These boards used their monopoly to buy export crops from Nigerian farmers at low prices and then sell them internationally at much higher prices. The difference between the money spent and the money earned became a key source of government revenue, as it was essentially an unofficial but quite substantial tax on farmers. British colonial rulers created this system, and the newly elected independent government continued it. When world prices for key crops were relatively high, the system worked well. When those prices dropped in the late 1960s, however, farmers faced even lower prices, and protests and riots broke out in key agricultural areas.

Despite farmers' opposition to this unofficial tax, modernization theorists would argue that as long as the government used the revenue gained from agricultural exports to make productive investments in industry, its actions were justified. However, this money was not distributed or invested in the most effective or efficient way possible. Nigeria's federal system of government, which included four fairly autonomous regional governments in the 1960s, made effective and efficient distribution of revenues very difficult. The bulk of the revenue from the marketing boards went to the regional governments, and each government used the revenue to build infrastructure and encourage industrialization. In the process, one regional government often duplicated the efforts of another. The marketing board revenues also became an early source of corruption, further undermining efficient investment.

Given the lack of private Nigerian involvement in industry, the government, supported by aid donors and advisors, saw joint government investment with foreign companies as crucial to industrialization. In 1963, private Nigerian investment constituted only 10 percent of large-scale manufacturing, foreign capital controlled 68 percent, and the various governments controlled the remaining 22 percent. By the 1970s, the government had passed laws on "Nigerianization" that required a certain percentage of the investments in key sectors of the economy to come from Nigerian sources, either the government or individual Nigerian investors. Using these

marketing boards: Government entities with monopoly control over the domestic and international marketing of key crops; usually found in Africa

laws and revenue from oil reserves, the government rapidly expanded its investment in large-scale industry during the 1970s. Most of the private Nigerian investors were themselves government officials or political leaders, so participation in the government and politics remained the key source of wealth.

Until the early 1970s, Nigeria's economic story of taxation of agricultural exports and state-led investment in industry was typical of Africa as a whole. Nigeria, however, possessed large oil reserves. In 1961, money from oil exports constituted less than 8 percent of government revenue; by 1974, that number hit 80 percent. Oil production increased steadily after independence, and in the early 1970s, it became subject to Nigerianization along with the rest of the economy. Since then, Nigerian governments have invested virtually nothing in agriculture, which has declined from being the most important sector of the economy to one that continues to employ many people but produces very little. The country depends almost totally on oil exports for its well-being, but both military and democratically elected leaders have frequently misused oil wealth, and huge variations in world oil prices mean the country is at the mercy of a fickle international market.

The biggest economic change came with the quadrupling of world oil prices in 1973. Oil exports went from about 3 percent of the country's total exports at independence to 95 percent in the 1980s and 1990s. This gave the Nigerian government a windfall from which it has yet to recover. The military governments of the 1970s used the oil wealth to invest in large-scale infrastructure projects, borrowing money against future oil revenues to do so. The democratic government elected in 1979 did much the same thing, expanding infrastructure and government employment to purchase political support. When the oil market collapsed in the mid-1980s, the government was unable to pay back its loans and faced bankruptcy. Once again, it became a fairly typical African state, going to the IMF after 1983 to negotiate an SAP. The politically painful reductions in the government's size and activity that the IMF required were more

than even the military governments could bear, and the process of instituting neoliberal policies was long and remains incomplete. Certainly, the government has reduced its involvement in industry (other than oil) and cut its size, but it has still only partially liberalized.

The central role of the state in the economy prior to 1983 combined with huge oil revenues to create a situation ripe for corruption. Nigeria's worst ruler, Sani Abacha, is rumored to have stolen approximately $2 billion in government oil revenue in just five years while he was in power in the 1990s. By 2000, Transparency International ranked Nigeria as the world's most corrupt country. As in other parts of the postcolonial world, state intervention in the economy in the 1960s and 1970s gave government officials and politicians many opportunities to grease palms and stuff their own pockets. Every law that required government approval for some economic activity created a point at which an official could ask for a bribe. In Africa, the fact that government employment was the chief source of wealth contributed to this process. Ambitious young leaders went into government and politics not just to gain political power and to lead but also to make money.

Some analysts argue that Nigerian and other African political cultures encourage corruption. Leaders were long expected to provide for their followers. The colonial government was seen as a source of wealth and resources; it had no other legitimacy in the eyes of the people. A cultural norm arose, then, in which people expected government officials and politicians to provide something for them. Since democratic legitimacy was weak, and military governments had little legitimacy, patron-client links and the provision of resources became nearly the sole means of maintaining political support. Thus, neopatrimonial forms of rule became the norm. Nigerian leaders took bribes and stole from government coffers both to feather their own nests and to provide resources to their supporters, who would reciprocate by granting political support to the leaders. As we argued in chapter 2, weak state institutions are both the cause and the effect of corruption. The illegitimacy of the colonial government and the newness of democracy after independence meant that governmental institutions were weak, so people did not value them and were not interested in fighting to preserve them. Corruption, then, was easy to engage in for those who were interested. The more corruption grew, the less legitimacy state institutions had, and a vicious cycle ensued.

The democratic government that replaced military rule in 1999 came to power with promises to reduce corruption. To that end, the new president initiated a series of anticorruption measures, which included the creation of a special agency to investigate and prosecute corruption cases. An initial target was the return of the billions of dollars that Abacha had stolen, some of which the new government was able to get back from various European banks. In subsequent years, several major politicians in the new government also became targets of court cases. For the first time in Nigeria's history, political leaders faced criminal prosecution for stealing the country's wealth. In the run-up to the election in 2007, however, the anticorruption campaign became more politicized. The president used the anticorruption agency to target and eliminate potential opponents of his party and his hand-picked successor. Still, the overall results of the anticorruption campaign have been positive: Nigeria improved in Transparency International's rankings from a score of 1.2 (dead last) in 2000 to 2.4 (134th out of 178 countries) in 2010. Nigeria remains a very corrupt country, but strides have been made.

The new democratic government used its international support to gain financial aid and debt relief from Western donors, but in turn it was required to make substantial progress in moving its economic policies in a neoliberal direction. By 2003, the government was able to convince Western creditors that the economy was moving in a positive direction. In 2004, half of Nigeria's $36 billion debt was forgiven; by 2006, its overall debt had dropped to only $3.5 billion, less than one-tenth of what it had been two

IN CONTEXT

NIGERIA AS AN OIL EXPORTER

The Country and Concept table allows you to compare Nigeria with two other oil exporters, Iran and Russia, but it is also instructive to compare Nigeria with its partners in the Organization of Petroleum Exporting Countries (OPEC). Nigeria has the largest population and one of the lowest GDPs in OPEC, making it among the poorest countries in the organization. A recent IMF report found that Nigeria and other sub-Saharan African oil exporters face much greater developmental challenges than exporters from other regions, including shorter oil horizons, lower reserves per capita, high oil dependence, and greater infrastructural and human development gaps. All the data below are for 2008–2009.

	Nigeria	OPEC average
Population	149.23 million	47.2 million
Barrels of oil produced per day	2,169,000	2,545,615
Oil exports per capita	$493	$1,642
GDP per capita	$1,118	$21,070
Proven crude oil reserves	36.2 billion barrels	70 billion barrels

Sources: Organization of Petroleum Exporting Countries, *Annual Statistical Bulletin 2009,* http://www.opec.org/opec_web/static_files_project/media/downloads/publications/ASB2009.pdf; World Bank.

years earlier (Gillies 2007, 575). The government also brought inflation under control via tight monetary policy, stabilized government spending and the country's currency, and reduced various tariff barriers. Donors responded not only with debt relief but also with a massive increase in aid, from less than $200 million in 2000 to more than $6 billion in 2005. All this combined with rapidly increasing world oil prices to substantially improve Nigeria's global economic position.

Given Nigeria's long history of development failure, a much longer period of success is needed to fundamentally change people's well-being. Economic growth has been relatively strong—around 5 percent in the new millennium—and non–oil sector growth was an impressive 9 percent from 2003 to 2009, indicating the first significant development outside of the oil sector in decades. The global financial crisis affected Nigeria mainly via the oil sector, which continues to dominate the economy. With oil prices holding up generally and increasing in 2010, however, Nigeria has weathered the crisis relatively well; its 2009 growth rate was 5.6 percent. More than 90 percent of Nigerians still live on less than $2 per day, and the level of corruption—though improved—remains a serious concern. Nonetheless, Nigeria's democratic government has started a process of reversing decades of corruption and ineffective development policy, thus at least slightly improving the country's position.

CASE SUMMARY

At least until the last few years, Nigeria has been a case study of development gone wrong. The largest country in Africa and blessed (or cursed) with abundant oil reserves, it remains one of the world's poorest countries. The development models pursued—both ISI and SAPs—were justified in terms of reigning theories of economic development in their respective eras, but neither led to significant development. Dependence on vacillating oil markets left the government in crisis when oil prices dropped. Weak institutions, political demands, and massive oil wealth when prices were high produced monumental levels of corruption that undermined virtually all development efforts and expanded debt. Neoliberal policies are designed to encourage investment, but they have achieved little success in Nigeria outside the oil sector. In the absence of a strong and coherent set of state institutions and a favorable global economic context, economic blueprints do not produce the expected results, though they are frequently used to justify the politically motivated actions of various leaders. The new millennium has been slightly kinder to Nigeria, however. The new democratic government has somewhat reduced corruption, successfully convinced foreign creditors to forgive debt, and achieved the first real growth outside the oil sector in decades. The global recession has affected the country relatively little because its major connection to the global economy is via the price of oil. Whether this recent and modest success can be translated into lasting gains remains to be seen.

Case Studies in Summary

The five cases and two mini cases in this chapter demonstrate the great variation around the world in the relationship between the state and the market economy. While virtually all countries now have market economies, states intervene and guide them in different ways, with different purposes, and to different effects. And regardless of government polices, vastly different contexts mean the market has vastly different effects in wealthy and poor countries.

The United States has long been the model of a free-market economy with limited state intervention, though as we've seen, even here the state has intervened and expanded over the past century to try to improve economic outcomes and limit negative market effects. Germany's social market economy represents the common European alternative. While there are variations from country to country, most of the wealthier countries of Europe guide and limit the market much more than the United States does, providing much more generous government support to those not "making it" adequately in the market. Like most countries that followed in the wake of the first wave of industrialization that took place in the Netherlands, the United Kingdom, and the United States, Germany and Japan also used state intervention to guide investment into particular sectors. Postcolonial countries industrialized even later, leaving them today with a less secure position in the global market and with greater inequality. Where institutions are reasonably strong, as in Mexico, significant economic development has occurred even though great inequality, poverty, and at times instability persist. In weak states such as Nigeria, weak institutions make implementing any development policy difficult. This is especially true when a weak state possesses oil or other mineral wealth, which distorts economic and political incentives, spurs corruption, and makes development that benefits the bulk of the population even less likely.

CONCLUSION

With the extension of the market economy to nearly every corner of the globe, a universal set of issues exists involving the relationship between the market and the state. The state must perform certain tasks so that the market can function efficiently and in turn produce revenue for the state. The market is likely to generate greater wealth if the state is able to go beyond these essential functions by establishing policies to encourage investment and growth. Political pressure can lead to yet other policies, as organized groups in society demand particular state intervention in the market in their favor. Clear and consistent economic theories of how and why the state should intervene serve as intellectual guides for state actions. However, no government's policies follow these blueprints perfectly, as our case studies have shown.

Who Rules?

Economic policy, more than any other area, is one where we can reasonably expect people to act in their perceived best interests. To the extent that pluralist or rational-actor models explain economic policy, the policies of a given state will reflect who has the most power in that state's political system. For example, Germany's policies, which provide greater protection for those hurt by the market and greater involvement of unions in corporate governance, likely reflect the greater political weight of German workers. On the other hand, business is given a freer hand in the United States, meaning business is probably more powerful there and labor unions weaker. The story, though, may well be more complex than that. Looking at policy outcomes to determine who rules is always difficult. Ideology and beliefs may shift people's perceptions of their own interests: Keynesianism was widely accepted in the 1950s and 1960s, but the economic crises of the 1970s led many to abandon it in favor of monetarism, which itself is under question in the aftermath of the Great Recession. Workers may support free-market policies because they believe they will be better off in the long run, but in the face of prolonged unemployment and lower wages, workers may come to question those policies anew.

While domestic groups of one sort or another are likely the main forces behind economic policy in wealthy and powerful countries, in poorer countries they seem distinctly less able to influence policies. When the socialist party in Chile came to power with promises to share the wealth more equally via greater government intervention, the military carried out a coup, supported by the United States as an anticommunist move, that ushered in a period of rapid growth and investment but repression of labor and wages. In Nigeria, policies that in theory were designed to use the state to enhance national development instead favored the elite, who controlled key government machinery. As a result, the majority of the Nigerian population saw few benefits. In both Mexico and Nigeria, and throughout the post-colonial world, the ideas of development economists in the West have been very influential. Since the debt crisis of the early 1980s, structural adjustment policies imposed by the World Bank and IMF have forced many countries to pursue policies that have had little domestic support. In many such countries, the government's annual budget must receive approval from IMF headquarters in Washington, D.C., before the elected government submits it to parliament for approval. Answering the question "Who rules?" may require looking beyond the confines of a country to the broader international community.

Without question, globalization has challenged all past models of political economy. Whether these models were successful or not in earlier decades, they now face rapidly moving capital that seems to limit their options. Europe has used the EU to try to survive and prosper in this new era, but doing so has required individual nations to adhere to a common set of policies, especially if they wish to be part of the euro zone. The Great Recession put unprecedented strain on this effort, as the EU scrambled to bail out its weakest members. Weaker nations seem to have even less room to maneuver in an era when international forces are increasingly powerful vis-à-vis domestic ones. We return to this subject in chapters 10 and 11, in the final part of the book, where we examine a series of crucial contemporary issues facing the nations of the world and the field of comparative politics.

What Explains Political Behavior?

Our case studies demonstrate a wide array of approaches to and levels of state involvement in the market. Explaining this variation has long been a preoccupation of comparativists. Marxist analysts, whose theories of the dominance of the bourgeoisie are challenged by the existence of extensive welfare states such as Germany's, argue that the elite create policies beneficial to workers to preserve capitalism in the long term, sacrificing the short term interests of particular businesses to preserve the system as a whole. Probably the most widespread explanation, however, is a pluralist one: countries with stronger workers' movements and unions have created the policies these groups favor. This immediately raises the question of why some countries developed stronger unions than others. Analysts comparing the United States with countries in Europe, in particular, have asked why U.S. unions are weaker and why no strong socialist party has emerged in the United States. One common explanation is the "frontier thesis," which cites the option of moving west as an escape valve that allowed workers to flee rather than organize and fight. Another is a racial thesis, which proposes that racial divisions within the American union movement kept it from gaining more strength. Many historians have argued that U.S. business leaders, especially in the south, actively encouraged racial divisions to keep unions weak.

Weak unions are just one example of weak institutions, which institutionalists argue are the key to explaining the economic paths of different countries. They argue that more than just group strength is involved in creating stronger welfare states in some countries than in others. The strength of institutions is also crucial, especially the strength of parties, unions, and business associations. Institutionalists contend that a strong party that supports welfare policies, regardless of how or how much the working class is organized, produces stronger welfare policies. Similarly, unified labor unions and business associations can effectively limit the actions of their individual members, giving the organizations strong bargaining power vis-à-vis the state and each other. Strong business associations can discipline their members to accept policies that the bulk of the association supports but that some individual businesses may not. In contrast, relatively weak unions and business associations in the United States resulted in strikes by local unions, even when national associations opposed them, and in demands by local businesses for lower wages, even when national associations might have agreed to higher ones. On the other hand, the ability of stronger institutions in Germany to discipline their members produced a less confrontational environment that allowed stronger welfare policies to gain support. Strong bureaucratic institutions similarly help explain the rise of the developmental state in Japan, where unions have always been exceptionally weak. Bureaucrats experienced in heavily guiding business in prewar Japan developed a similar system after the U.S. occupation. A state emerged that was dedicated to expanding key businesses in the interests of both the businesses themselves and national economic development.

Where and Why?

Economic theories present abstract models of how economic policies ought to work. Both Keynesian and monetarist ideas have merit on paper, and both have worked better at some times and for some things than at other times and for other things. The context in which the policies are implemented and how well they are implemented make a tremendous difference. We have seen that political demands influence economic policy significantly, especially in wealthier countries with more powerful civil societies. Economic policy is not only about maximizing growth over well-being but also about deciding which values a society holds most strongly and which interest groups are most powerful.

The failure of one set of policies often can lead to a swing in favor of a different set, as was demonstrated by the rise of monetarism after the seeming failure of Keynesianism around the world. Our examination of SAPs in postcolonial societies demonstrates how context matters and how the failure of one idea can lead to the adoption of others. Neoliberal development policies seemed to work somewhat better in middle-income than in poor countries and in countries that freely chose to adopt them rather than being forced to adopt them by the IMF and World Bank. Weak governing institutions also made implementation of such policies ineffective. The disappointing results of the 1980s model led the IMF and World Bank to revise their development policies so as to place greater emphasis on social services to create a healthy labor force, though preserving other elements of neoliberalism. The political, institutional, and social context in which these policies are implemented, however, will undoubtedly influence how well they work in different countries.

Applying Theory to States and Markets

Not surprisingly, economic debates are mostly cast in terms of rational-choice theory, the underlying intellectual paradigm for virtually all modern economics. Markets, when they function properly, maximize efficient resource allocation and therefore productivity and thus generate greater wealth. The key economic debates are over when and why governments should intervene in the market to correct its failings. These are typically cast in rational-choice terms as well, focusing on the situations in which rational action in the market does not maximize efficiency and thereby necessitates government intervention. Other theoretical approaches, however, can help us explain government intervention at least as well as the economic arguments based on rational choice. Both ideology and political culture can have a role to play in understanding why Germany has adopted and is attempting to preserve (see chapter 10) a much more government-guided form of capitalism than that in the United States. Once particular economic institutions are established, historical institutionalist arguments are useful as well to explain why they endure, as groups who benefit from such institutions seek to preserve them and citizens are socialized to accept the institutions' role as legitimate. Finally, pluralist and elite theories regarding who has power can help us explain why certain economic policies are adopted. Such policies reflect the distribution of power in a society, which we can see in their effects. We now turn, in Part II, to an examination of how policies are made, starting in democratic systems.

KEY CONCEPTS

capitalism (p. 191)
codetermination (p. 218)
command economy (p. 191)
comparative advantage (p. 199)
deficit spending (p. 197)
developmental state (p. 224)
externality (p. 193)
fiscal policy (p. 197)
globalization (p. 204)

import-substitution industrialization (ISI) (p. 199)
Keynesian theory (p. 197)
market economy (p. 190)
market failure (p. 193)
marketing boards (p. 233)
monetarist theory (p. 198)
monetary policy (p. 198)
monopoly (p. 195)
natural monopoly (p. 195)

neoliberalism (p. 201)
privatize (p. 201)
public goods (p. 192)
social market economy (p. 216)
stagflation (p. 198)
structural adjustment programs (SAPs) (p. 201)

WORKS CITED

Altman, Roger C. 2009. "Globalization in Retreat." *Foreign Affairs* 88 (4).

Bates, Robert H. 2001. *Prosperity and Violence: The Political Economy of Development.* New York: W. W. Norton.

Crew, David F. 1998. *Germans on Welfare: From Weimar to Hitler.* New York: Oxford University Press.

Europa Publications Staff. 2007. *The Europa World Year Book 2007.* London: Routledge.

Garrett, Geoffrey. 1998. *Partisan Politics in the Global Economy.* Cambridge, UK: Cambridge University Press.

Gillies, Alexandra. 2007. "Obasanjo, the Donor Community and Reform Implementation in Nigeria." *The Round Table* 96 (392): 569–86. doi:10.1080/00358530701625992.

Johnson, Chalmers A. 1982. *MITI and the Japanese Miracle: The Growth of Industrial Policy, 1925–1975.* Stanford, CA: Stanford University Press.

Lincoln, James, and Masahiro Shimotani. 2009. "Whither the *Keiretsu,* Japan's Business Networks? How Were They Structured? What Did They Do? Why Are They Gone?" Working Paper Series, Institute for Research on Labor and Employment, University of California at Berkeley. http://www.escholarship.org/uc/item/00m7d34g.

Ohmae, Kenichi. 1995. *The End of the Nation State: The Rise of Regional Economies.* New York: Simon and Schuster.

Pempel, T. J. 2000. *Regime Shift: Comparative Dynamics of the Japanese Political Economy.* Ithaca, NY: Cornell University Press.

Polanyi, Karl. 1944. *The Great Transformation.* New York: Farrar and Rinehart.

Siavelis, Peter M. 2007. "How New Is Bachelet's Chile?" *Current History* 106 (697): 70–76.

Transparency International. http://www.transparency.org/.

RESOURCES FOR FURTHER STUDY

Friedman, Milton. 1962. *Capitalism and Freedom.* Chicago: University of Chicago Press.

Gilpin, Robert. 2000. *The Challenge of Global Capitalism.* Princeton, NJ: Princeton University Press.

Heilbroner, Robert L. 1985. *The Nature and Logic of Capitalism.* New York: W. W. Norton.

International Monetary Fund. 2007. *Regional Economic Outlook, Sub-Saharan Africa.* Washington, DC: International Monetary Fund. http://www.imf.org/external/pubs/ft/reo/2007/afr/eng/sreo1007.pdf.

Jameson, Kenneth P., and Charles K. Wilber. 1996. *The Political Economy of Development and Underdevelopment.* 6th ed. New York: McGraw Hill.

Keynes, John Maynard. 1935. *The General Theory of Employment, Interest, and Money.* New York: Harcourt Brace.

The Levin Institute, The State University of New York. "Globalization 101: A Student's Guide to Globalization." http://www.globalization101.org/.

Organization of the Petroleum Exporting Countries. 2006. *OPEC Annual Statistical Bulletin 2006.* http://www.opec.org/opec_web/static_files_project/media/downloads/publications/ASB06.pdf.

Rapley, John. 2007. *Understanding Development: Theory and Practice in the Third World.* 3rd ed. Boulder, CO: Lynne Rienner.

Siebert, Horst. 2005. *The German Economy: Beyond the Social Market.* Princeton, NJ: Princeton University Press.

Woo-Cumings, Meredith, ed. 1999. *The Developmental State.* Ithaca, NY: Cornell University Press.

WEB RESOURCES

Human Development Reports, "International Human Development Indicators" (http://hdr.undp.org/en/statistics)

International Labor Organization, "LABORSTA Internet" (http://laborsta.ilo.org)

International Monetary Fund, "World Economic Outlook Database" (http://www.imf.org/external/pubs/ft/weo/2010/02/weodata/index.aspx)

Organisation for Economic Co-operation and Development, "OECD.Stat Extracts" (http://stats.oecd.org/index.aspx)

PART II

Londoners gather in February 2011 to support the nonviolent movement that overthrew Hosni Mubarak's semi-authoritarian regime in Egypt.

Credit: Lewis Whyld/PA Wire URN:10178016 (Press Association via AP Images)

POLITICAL SYSTEMS AND

Chapter	Brazil	China	Germany	India	Iran	Japan	Mexico	Nigeria	Russia	UK	US
6. Governing Institutions in Democracies	●		●	●		●			●	●	●
7. Institutions of Participation			●	●						●	●
8. Authoritarian Institutions		●				●		●			
9. Regime Change	●	●				●	●	●	●		

Country	Current head of state	Type of government	Administrative divisions	Legal system
Brazil	President: Dilma Vana Rousseff	Federal republic	26 states and 1 federal district	Code law
China	President: Hu Jintao Premier: Wen Jiabao	Communist state	23 provinces, 5 autonomous regions, 4 municipalities	Code law
Germany	President: Christian Wulff Chancellor: Angela Merkel	Federal republic	16 states	Code law
India	President: Pratibha Devisingh Patil Prime minister: Manmohan Singh	Federal republic	28 states and 7 union territories	Common law
Iran	Supreme leader: Ali Hoseini-Khamenei President: Mahmoud Ahmadinejad	Theocratic republic	30 provinces	Sharia law
Japan	Emperor: Emperor Akihito Prime minister: Naoto Kan	Constitutional monarchy with parliamentary government	47 prefectures	Code law
Mexico	President: Felipe de Jesús Calderón Hinojosa	Federal republic	31 states and 1 federal district	Code law
Nigeria	President: Goodluck Jonathan	Federal republic	36 states and 1 federal territory	Mix of common and Sharia law
Russia	President: Dmitri Medvedev Premier: Vladimir Putin	Federation	46 oblasts, 21 republics, 4 autonomous okrugs, 9 krays, 2 federal cities, 1 autonomous oblast	Code law
United Kingdom	Queen: Queen Elizabeth II Prime minister: David Cameron	Constitutional monarchy with parliamentary government	England has 34 counties; Northern Ireland has 26 district council areas; Scotland has 32 unitary authorities; Wales has 22 unitary authorities	Common law
United States	President: Barack Obama	Federal republic	50 states and 1 district	Common law

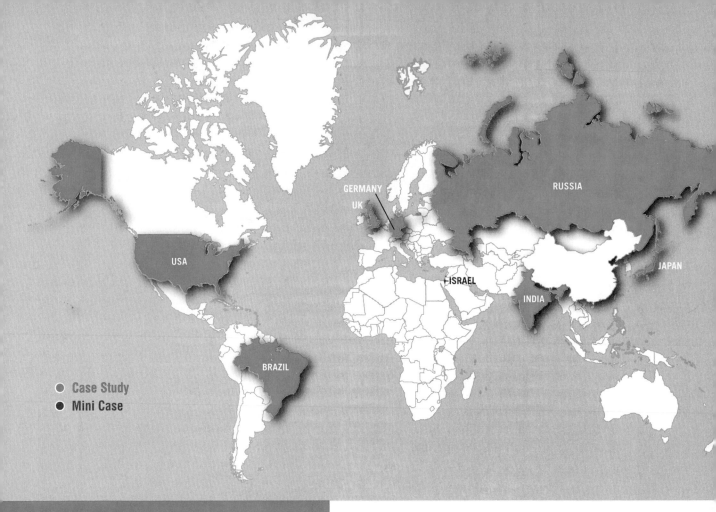

Who Rules?

- A democracy must limit the power of its executives to provide accountability. Which institutional choices best ensure accountability and how?
- How much power should a minority have in a democracy? How do different democracies seek to guarantee that minorities are protected from possible majority tyranny? Do some institutional choices seem to guarantee this better than others?

What Explains Political Behavior?

- Do greater participation and representation of many voices in government result in less effective policymaking?
- How do institutional structures affect how political leaders act?

Where and Why?

- Which variables would be most helpful to explain why an institution that works well in one setting might not work the same way in another?
- Democratic institutions vary around the world. What explains why particular institutions arise in particular countries but not in others?

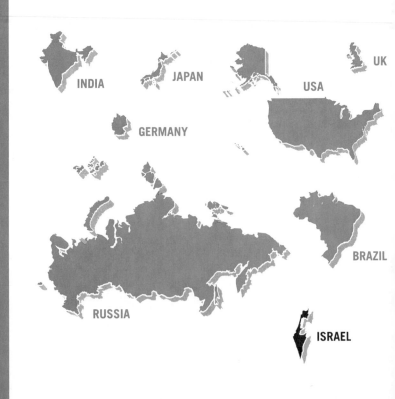

6

GOVERNING INSTITUTIONS IN DEMOCRACIES

Americans are taught from a young age the importance of the three branches of government—executive, legislative, and judicial—and how essential their separate but equal status is for democracy. While these are certainly not the only political institutions that matter to a sophisticated understanding of politics, they are among the most important. Understanding politics, however, requires far more than simply understanding the formal institutions of government. Most modern states, and virtually all democratic ones (the United Kingdom is the major exception), have written constitutions that define the formal powers of their governmental institutions. As we've noted, though, written formal powers do not always translate directly into actual power. The social, cultural, and historical contexts in which formal institutions exist can have significant bearing on how institutions function in practice. On paper, a president in one country may have a similar set of powers as a president in another country, but what each president can achieve in fact might vary greatly between the two specific contexts. The actual power of particular institutions often changes over time as well, as changing socioeconomic and cultural factors give greater resources to one or another institution, or a particular occupant of a formal position helps strengthen or weaken that institution. The first questions we must ask, then, are these: How institutionalized are the various branches of government of a particular state, and to what extent do they function as set out in the constitution that created them?

As we explore the answers to these questions, we can start to answer the other key questions that make the study of institutions important in democracies, which is the focus of this and the next chapter. The first question involves who rules: Do certain institutional arrangements achieve greater **political accountability**, meaning the ability of the citizenry to directly or indirectly control political leaders and institutions?

Argentine political scientist Guillermo O'Donnell (1999) used the terms *vertical* and *horizontal accountability* to analyze the extent to which the power of key state institutions is under democratic control. **Vertical accountability** refers to the ability

political accountability: The ability of the citizenry, directly or indirectly, to control political leaders and institutions

vertical accountability: The ability of individuals and groups in a society to hold state institutions accountable

horizontal accountability: The ability of state institutions to hold one another accountable

of individuals and groups in a society to hold state institutions accountable, whereas **horizontal accountability** refers to the ability of the state's institutions to hold one another accountable. The latter represents indirect control on the part of the citizenry in that particular institutions implicitly act on behalf of the citizenry to limit the power of and thereby control other institutions or leaders. For instance, an elected legislature in a democracy presumably should have enough power vis-à-vis the executive branch to limit what the executive can do, to ask him to justify his actions, and ultimately to punish him if he acts in ways unacceptable to the state's constitution or majority opinion in the country. Similarly, the court system may have the power to rule legislative or executive actions unconstitutional, thus preserving the basic system of government against politicians' attempts to abrogate it.

This chapter focuses on horizontal accountability, as we examine the relative power of governing institutions in relation to each other. We examine vertical accountability in greater detail in the next chapter, looking at institutions of participation and representation.

executive: The branch of government that must exist in all modern states; the chief political power in a state and implements all laws

Note that only one of the basic branches of government, the executive, is essential to a modern state as we defined it in chapter 2. Modern states are sovereign entities that administer territories and people; therefore, an executive power and accompanying bureaucracy are essential to their existence. The **executive** is the chief political power in a state. The position is filled through elections in a democracy and typically is embodied in the single most powerful office in the government, referred to as a president or prime minister in most countries. The modern state, however, also includes a bureaucracy, a large set of lesser officials whose function is to implement the laws of the state, as directed by the executive. We explore both executive powers and modern bureaucracies in this chapter.

The executive is essential, but as the idea of horizontal accountability suggested, a legislature with autonomy from the executive is an important institution of democratization, even if it is not crucial to the modern state itself. Similarly, a judiciary is essential for the state to punish crime and enforce property and contract rights, but it need not have a political role independent of the executive, although it may well be beneficial for democracy if it does. The process of democratization is in part a matter of creating mechanisms through which the power of the executive can be limited. In democratic theory, the **legislature** makes the law, and the **judiciary** interprets it. The power and autonomy of each, however, varies significantly in practice.

legislature: Branch of government that makes the law in a democracy

judiciary: Branch of government that interprets the law and applies it to individual cases

Many political scientists believe that forces in the modern world are strengthening the executive branch. The contemporary state has far more and far more technically sophisticated functions to carry out than in earlier eras, and over the course of the twentieth century, this meant a general upward trend in the size of the bureaucracy that the executive branch leads. Legislators often delegate the more technical decisions implied in particular laws to bureaucrats because the legislators feel they lack the technical competence to make those decisions. All of this gives greater resources and therefore greater power to the executive and the bureaucracy, which makes issues of control of the executive even more paramount. Some political scientists also worry about limiting the role of the judiciary, seeing wealthy democracies in particular as moving increasingly toward a "judicialization" of politics in which courts and judges replace elected officials as key decision makers.

A second crucial "Who rules?" question in democracies is, How much power should be given to the majority that, at least in theory, rules? Democracy implies majority rule, but how much power the majority has over dissident minorities is a fundamental question. Some formal institutions give the representatives of the majority far greater power than do others. The United Kingdom and United States stand in sharp relief on this issue and illustrate the range of available options. As we discuss below, the British parliament has the legal right to pass any legislation it pleases, which gives the majority party tremendous powers. British constitutional and political tradition does limit the exercise of these powers, but few formal limits exist. In contrast, the U.S. Constitution divides and thereby limits power significantly. Even when the same party controls both houses of Congress and the presidency, that party's power is limited by the ability of the Supreme Court to declare laws unconstitutional and by the various powers reserved specifically for state governments. Both countries are democracies, but they address the question of how formal institutions should protect minorities from the will of the majority quite differently, as we demonstrate throughout this chapter.

A key "What explains political behavior?" question is, What is the potential trade-off between popular participation in the government and representation of many viewpoints, on the one hand, and effective governance on the other? If the institutions of a particular regime strongly limit each other and many different groups are represented in the decision-making process, do these factors limit the ability of the government to make effective policy? Comparativist Arend Lijphart (1999) examined this potential trade-off. He suggested that we think of democracies on a continuum from what he termed "majoritarian" to "consensus." **Majoritarian democracies** concentrate power more tightly in a single place and office; they have a single-party executive, executive dominance over the legislature, a single legislative branch, and constitutions that can be easily amended. **Consensus democracies**, in contrast, have multiparty executives called a **coalition government** (in which at least two parties negotiate an agreement to rule together), executive-legislative balance, bicameral legislatures (with two roughly equally powerful houses), and rigid constitutions not easily amended. If a trade-off exists between representation and effective policymaking, majoritarian systems ought to be more effective because they have much more concentrated power with fewer checks on it. They seem likely to produce less horizontal accountability as well, since they have few institutions to check the executive power in the hands of the majority party. Bingham Powell (2000) noted, however, that vertical accountability is likely to be greater in majoritarian systems because voters know exactly who is responsible for government policy. In consensus systems with coalition government and multiple participants in the policy-making process, on the other hand, responsibility is less clear.

Comparativist George Tsebelis (2002) studied limits on effective policymaking as well. He argued that a key distinction among political systems and institutions is the number of veto players they produce. A **veto player** is an individual or collective actor whose agreement is essential for any policy change. Veto players may exist on the basis of institutional positions defined by a constitution or via partisan battles and political support. Tsebelis further argued that the greater the number of veto players and the greater the ideological distance among them, the less likely policy change will be. We will see how both the arrangement of governing institutions (examined in this chapter) and institutions of participation and representation (examined in chapter 7) create veto players in the system. We will examine the trade-offs among horizontal and vertical accountability, representation, and effective policymaking in both chapters.

Examining governing institutions allows us to ask one more classic "What explains political behavior?" question: How do institutional structures influence the behavior of political leaders. Put another way, how valid are institutional theories that

majoritarian democracy: A type of democratic system that concentrates power more tightly in a single-party executive with executive dominance over the legislature, a single legislative branch, and constitutions that can be easily amended

consensus democracy: A democratic system with multiparty executives in a coalition government, executive-legislative balance, bicameral legislatures, and rigid constitutions not easily amended

coalition government: Government in a parliamentary system in which at least two parties negotiate an agreement to rule together

veto player: An individual or collective actor whose agreement is essential for any policy change

COUNTRY AND CONCEPT
Snapshot of Governing Institutions

Country	Executive-legislative system	Judicial system		Federal system	Bureaucracy corruption[1] (scale of 1–10; 10 = least corrupt)
		Type of legal system	Right of judicial review		
Brazil	Presidential	Code law	Yes	Symmetric federalism	3.7
China	NA	Code law	No	Unitary	3.5
Germany	Parliamentary	Code law	Yes	Symmetric federalism	7.9
India	Parliamentary	Common law	Yes	Asymmetric federalism	3.3
Iran	Semipresidential (authoritarian)	Islamic Sharia	No	Unitary	2.2
Japan	Parliamentary	Code law	Yes	Unitary	7.8
Mexico	Presidential	Code law	Yes	Symmetric federalism	3.1
Nigeria	Presidential	Common law and Sharia	Yes	Symmetric federalism	2.4
Russia	Semipresidential	Code law	Yes (but weak)	Asymmetric federalism	2.1
United Kingdom	Parliamentary	Common law	No	Unitary	7.6
United States	Presidential	Common law	Yes	Symmetric federalism	7.1

[1] Transparency International, Corruption Perceptions Index, 2010, http://www.transparency.org/policy_research/surveys_indices/cpi/.

hold that institutions themselves play a crucial role in explaining political behavior? We can also ask some key "Where and why?" questions: Why do certain institutions exist in one democracy and not in another, and why do certain institutions seem to work better in one democracy than another?

The Country and Concept table shows the great variation in our case studies' governing institutions, even among those that are democracies. We begin with the relationship between the executive and legislative branches, which, more than anything else, distinguishes different kinds of democracies. We then examine the roles of the judiciary and the modern bureaucracy and their relationships to the executive and legislative branches. We also look at the question of federalism and the extent to which the overall power of the state is either centralized in national institutions or dispersed among subnational units of government; dispersion can be another means of achieving accountability. We examine these institutions to understand why they exist, what their effects are, and which system, if any, seems most beneficial to democracy.

EXECUTIVES AND LEGISLATURES

The executive is indispensable to any state or regime and fulfills two very important roles. First, as **head of state**, the executive is the official, symbolic representative of a country, authorized to speak on its behalf and represent it, particularly in world affairs. Historically, the head of state was often a monarch, and this continues to be the case in the United Kingdom and Japan. Second, as **head of government**, the executive's task is to implement the nation's laws and policies. The two parts of the executive function may be filled by one individual or two, but both are essential to any regime. Legislatures are less ubiquitous because authoritarian regimes can dispense with them. They are, however, crucial to democratic regimes because a legislature's very democratic function is to debate public policy and pass laws. We discuss the executive and legislature together because the relationship between them distinguishes three classic models of democratic government: parliamentarism, presidentialism, and semipresidentialism.

Parliamentarism: The Westminster Model

If you ask Americans to define democracy, many will start with the "separation of powers." The oldest model of modern democracy, however, does not separate the executive and legislature. Commonly known as the Westminster, or parliamentary, model, it originated in Britain. Lijphart called **parliamentarism** the purest form of his "majoritarian" model in which power is concentrated in one place, creating very few institutional veto players. The fusion of the executive and legislative branches provides for an exceptionally powerful executive. This fusion exists in the office of the **prime minister (PM)** (in Germany, the chancellor), whose relationship to the legislature is the key distinguishing feature of the model. This PM is not only the executive but also a member of the legislature. In fact, he or she is the leader of the majority party or leading coalition party in the legislature. The PM, then, is not elected separately to executive office but rather is named after the legislative election determines the dominant party in parliament. Citizens cast one vote for a party or individual, depending on the electoral system, to represent them in parliament; the majority in parliament then names the prime minister. In practice, when citizens vote for parliament, they know who the PM candidate for each party is, so their vote for their preferred **member of parliament (MP)** or party is indirectly a vote for that party's leader to serve as PM.

Formally, the PM serves at the pleasure of parliament. Should a parliamentary majority lose confidence in the PM, members can cast a **vote of no confidence** that forces the PM to resign. At that point, the leading party in parliament can choose a new leader who will become PM, or the resigning PM will ask the head of state to call new parliamentary elections. Parliamentary systems often do not have fixed terms of office, and while the parliament can oust a prime minister, a PM can similarly dissolve parliament and call for new elections. In Britain, for example, the maximum term allowed between elections is five years, but a PM can call earlier elections to take advantage of an electoral opportunity for his or her party, or the majority party can remove the PM if it loses confidence in her. The latter happened to Britain's formerly powerful PM, Margaret Thatcher, in 1990.

Parliamentary systems separate the two functions of the executive. They have a "nonexecutive head of state," who embodies and represents the country ceremonially.

head of state: The official, symbolic representative of a country, authorized to speak on its behalf and represent it, particularly in world affairs; usually a president or monarch

head of government: The key executive power in a state; usually a president or prime minister

parliamentarism: A term denoting a parliamentary system of democracy in which the executive and legislative branches are fused via parliament's election of the chief executive

prime minister (PM): The head of government in parliamentary and semipresidential systems

member of parliament (MP): An elected member of the legislature in a parliamentary system

vote of no confidence: In parliamentary systems, a vote by parliament to remove a government (the prime minister and cabinet) from power

Figure 6.1

Typical Parliamentary System

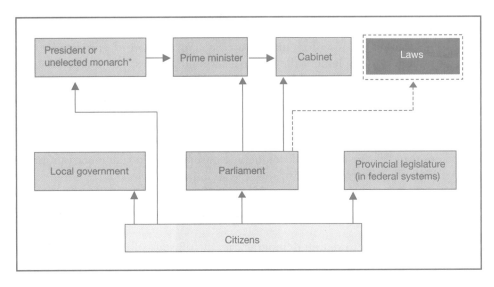

Note: Up arrows indicate elections. Down or horizontal arrows indicate nomination or appointment. Hash-mark arrows indicate which body is responsible for formally passing and signing legislation.

*In this system, the president's only power is nominating a parliamentary leader as prime minister.

Countries lacking a hereditary monarchy (which Britain and Japan still have) typically replace the monarch in this function with an elected head of state who, somewhat confusingly to many Americans, is often called the "president." In most cases, this president's role, like the queen's in Britain, is small and ceremonial. Countries tend to elect esteemed elder statesmen or women who gracefully perform the ceremonial role while leaving all important executive functions to the head of the government, the PM. In some cases, the constitution gives the head of state significant but rarely exercised legal powers, meaning that while "real" power on a day-to-day basis lies with the prime minister, in moments of high tension or conflict, the head of state may intervene. This usually happens only when parliament is unable to choose a PM after a divided election.

When a PM is the leader of the party that holds a majority of the seats in parliament and that party votes regularly as a bloc (as is almost always the case in parliamentary systems), the PM is an extremely powerful executive. Whatever legislation she puts forth is almost automatically passed into law by the legislature. A prime minister is in a somewhat different relationship with parliament if her party does not have a clear majority in parliament. In this situation, the PM will head a coalition government, in which at least two parties negotiate an agreement to rule together. A vote of no confidence is far more likely in a coalition government because if one party in the coalition is unhappy with a PM's policies, it can leave the coalition, causing the coalition to lose its majority. Smaller parties in the coalition often become partisan veto players; the PM must ensure that she has their support before she can get her legislation through parliament, a process that can involve extensive negotiations.

MINI CASE

Coalition Government in Israel's Parliamentary System

Britain's Westminster model is often heralded as a paragon of democratic stability. With the exception of the 2010 election, each parliamentary election in the United Kingdom put one party clearly in charge of the government with a parliamentary majority that voted pretty much in lockstep to pass the government's legislation. The British cabinet is composed of the leaders of the majority party, who publicly support all government legislation as part of their collective responsibility.

Israel presents a very different type of parliamentary system. In a country of numerous ideological, religious, and ethnic divisions, multiple parties compete in each election, and coalitions of parties must band together to form a government. The average government has lasted just twenty-five months. The cabinet is often an ideologically mixed group, and the prime minister must negotiate constantly and often publicly to make policy and keep the government in place.

Israel's parliament, the *Knesset,* functions much like the British or any other: a majority vote is required to elect a prime minister and form a government. *Knesset* elections are held every four years, but they can be called earlier if a government falls. (Or, as in other parliamentary systems, the largely ceremonial president can appoint a new prime minister without holding elections if the prior PM no longer has a parliamentary majority.) The electoral system, called proportional representation (see chapter 7 for further details), encourages the emergence and survival of many, small parties. Any party that receives at least 2 percent of the national vote gets at least one seat in parliament. Most elections feature as many as two dozen parties (the 2009 election included thirty-one), with at least a dozen winning seats in parliament (thirteen parties held seats after the 2009 election). While two or three major parties have always existed, most governments have consisted of one major party,

which provided the prime minister, and at least three others—sometimes as many as six—who also received cabinet seats to ensure their support in parliament.

Until 1977, the Labour Party, the core group who had helped found the country after World War II, won every election and formed the government, though always in a coalition with smaller parties. This provided a degree of stability to the system that, while not as strong, was similar to our case study of India under the Congress Party dominance (see below). In 1977, demographic and ideological changes resulted in a conservative coalition, Likud, winning more seats than Labour and for the first time forming a government. Since the decline of Labour's dominance, Israeli coalition governments have been less stable and secure. In the 1980s, two elections produced results so close that Labour and Likud formed national unity governments, and for a period their leaders took turns being prime minister for two years each. In addition to the major ideological parties on the center-left (Labour) and right (Likud), several much smaller religious parties have always existed. Both major parties have had to form alliances with the religious parties in order to govern, allowing the religious parties to extract promises that government policy would support their particular interests: orthodox religious control of marriage and religious conversion, restrictions on activities during the Sabbath, and state support of orthodox men who want to study the Torah rather than work. While the religious parties have never won a total of more than about 20 percent of the vote, the necessity to include at least some of them in virtually any coalition government has meant they have had influence far beyond their numbers.

Facing increasing instability, the *Knesset* voted in the early 1990s to have the prime minister directly elected instead of come out of parliament; however, he would still need to form a cabinet via gaining a majority vote in parliament. The hope was that a directly elected prime minister would shift the system a little toward a presidential one, encouraging a winner from a major party and reducing the influence of minor parties. In fact, through three elections, the directly elected prime minister was not from the party that won the most seats in parliament, meaning that he had to put together an even more diverse coalition government. After 2001, parliament rescinded the attempt at electoral reform, returning to a pure parliamentary system.

In the 2009 election a centrist party formed a few years earlier won the most seats, twenty-eight. But the conservative Likud, with one seat less, formed the government in coalition with religious parties, an ultra-right nationalist party, and Labour. This isn't the first time a coalition government has been extremely ideologically diverse. In these situations, the prime minister, in this case Binyamin Netanyahu, must negotiate policies continuously to keep the government together. Netanyahu's cabinet includes both ultra-nationalists, who want a much tougher policy vis-à-vis Palestinians and Israeli Arabs, and Labour party leaders, who insist (as their price for joining the government) that Netanyahu continue to pursue the peace process with the Palestinians. Satisfying both these constituencies is a daunting task. Disagreements in the cabinet are regularly leaked to the press; in effect, the prime minister is often publicly negotiating with his coalition partners to pass legislation and preserve his majority. Governmental dissolution and the instability that comes with it often lurk right around the corner.

CASE SUMMARY

Israel, a parliamentary system with many, small parties, demonstrates what critics point to as the weakness of the parliamentary system: government instability. If no party can win a majority, a situation that has always held in Israel, a coalition of parties must come together to form a government. Thus, small parties, which may control only a few seats in parliament but are essential to keeping the government together, hold exceptional power. In Israel, religious parties have regularly had influence well beyond their share of the national vote. Ideologically diverse coalitions have often meant that the prime minister has had to negotiate at length and often publicly over all major policies. In sharp contrast to the majoritarian British system, the Israeli system often makes the prime minister a relatively weak chief executive and makes governments short-lived, creating significant political instability.

The prime minister also appoints the other ministers (what Americans call "secretaries") to the cabinet, but given the close executive relationship with parliament, these individuals cannot be whomever the prime minister pleases. The cabinet, especially in a coalition, serves as a check on the PM. Cabinet ministers must also be MPs, and in a coalition government the prime minister must consult with the other parties in the coalition about the distribution of "portfolios" (cabinet seats). Normally all parties in the coalition, and certainly the biggest ones, get some representation in the cabinet. The cabinet, then, is often the site of the most important negotiations over policy. Whether all cabinet members are from the same party or from different parties in a coalition, once they have agreed to put forth a piece of legislation, it should pass through the legislature quite easily, as the classic case of Britain demonstrates. The case of India, like the mini case of Israel above, shows that how a parliamentary system actually functions depends very much on the historical, social, and cultural contexts in which it operates.

CASE STUDY

Parliamentary Rule in Britain and India

- Power of PM with a party majority versus PM in a coalition government
- Modern PM increasingly "presidential"
- Parliament as "watchdog," even though government legislation always passes
- Efforts to strengthen parliament: committees and resources
- Corruption as source of institutional weakness in parliament

Britain and India illustrate how very similar governing institutions can function dramatically differently in different social and political contexts. As a British colony, India adopted Britain's Westminster model almost completely, with the biggest difference being that India is a federal system. Differences in the party systems and the socioeconomic and cultural contexts of the two countries, however, influence how the model functions in practice.

Britain's prime minister is often called the most powerful democratic executive in the world. The power of the office derives not just from its formal functions but also from the nature of Britain's parties and the strength of British institutions. Like the United States, Britain has two major parties (Labour and Conservative) that alternate in power: one or the other wins a majority of legislative seats in virtually every election. This means that coalition governments are very rare. Unlike parties in the United

Parliamentarians listen to U.S. president Barack Obama deliver a speech at Parliament House in New Delhi on November 8, 2010. India's parliamentary system is modeled closely after Britain's, but the linguistic and religious diversity of Indian society has resulted in a more fragmented party system in recent years, meaning that India's system often operates quite differently than the British model. For over twenty years, India has had coalition governments that require greater compromise than is typical in Britain's Westminster system.

Credit: Jim Young/AFP/Getty Images

States, British parties are highly disciplined in the legislature, meaning that MPs almost always vote in support of their party's position on legislation. This is partly an effect of the parliamentary system itself. Ambitious MPs want to become cabinet ministers, and these positions are controlled by the head of the party; thus, MPs demonstrate loyalty to the party leadership. As head of the majority party, then, the PM can usually get legislation passed with ease. The system has very few veto players of any sort.

The British PM appoints approximately twenty cabinet ministers who run the individual departments of government and whom the PM is supposed to consult before making major decisions. By tradition, the PM's power is checked by the cabinet and the practice of **collective responsibility**, which means that all cabinet members must publicly support all government decisions. A cabinet member who cannot do so is expected to resign. Since cabinet members are themselves senior leaders of the majority party and MPs, collective responsibility constitutes an informal legislative agreement to policies prior to their formal introduction in Parliament.

Many argue that the cabinet's role has declined over the last generation and that PMs have begun to look more presidential. The two most important PMs of the last generation, Conservative Margaret Thatcher (1979–1990) and Labourite Tony Blair (1997–2007), centralized decision making in an inner circle of advisors and paid less attention to input from the cabinet as a whole. This practice reflected both their personalities as strong leaders and their popularity with the voting public. More than most PMs, they became charismatic figures in their own right, and their campaigns looked more like U.S. presidential campaigns, with a great deal more attention paid to the personality and individual attributes of the party leader than is traditional in Britain. As long as these two powerful PMs were so personally popular, they could pursue the policies they desired; their cabinets and parties went along because they also benefited from the popular support showered on the PM. As Thatcher's and Blair's popularity waned, however, both faced increasing resistance, showing that democratic control still exists in the British system. Many observers saw the 2010 election as furthering the "presidentialization" of the British PM. For the first time, the campaign featured American-style televised debates among the three contenders. Nick Clegg, the candidate of the small third party, the Liberal Democrats, performed particularly well, helping his party win enough seats to keep the victorious Conservative Party from winning an outright majority. The Liberal Democrats then forced the Conservatives to form a rare coalition government (the first since World War II) between the two parties.

In Britain, a vote of no confidence is extremely rare. A more common means of removing unpopular PMs who refuse to call a new election early is for the majority party to replace them. When Margaret Thatcher lost popularity in the late 1980s but refused to change her policies or call a new election, Conservative MPs feared their party's future was sinking along with her popularity. They voted to replace her with John Major, who immediately became PM. Britain had a new chief executive without holding a general election, a perfectly legitimate step in a parliamentary system. Similarly, Tony Blair left office without holding an election, albeit on his own terms. He ran for a third term in 2005 (there are no limits on the number of terms MPs or a PM can serve) but promised that he would turn power over during that term to his heir apparent, longtime Chancellor of the Exchequer (equivalent to the U.S. Secretary of the Treasury) Gordon Brown. Blair was losing popularity mainly due to his support of Britain's participation in the war in Iraq, but he gained reelection in part because he pledged to organize a smooth transition to a new leader. Though he seemed reluctant to fulfill this pledge after the election, growing pressure from within his own party led him to retire in mid-2007. Once again, the British chief executive changed hands without a single citizen voting.

collective responsibility: All cabinet members must publicly support all government decisions in a parliamentary system

Given the growing power of the PM, what powers does Parliament have? In Britain's **bicameral legislature,** the lower house, the House of Commons, has virtually all legislative power. The older upper house, the House of Lords, consists of members known as "peers"; these are appointees of the PM and aristocrats who inherited their positions. (In 1999 the Blair government ended the institution of "hereditary peers," allowing only a small minority to remain in office until further reforms.) The only significant power held by the House of Lords for many years was to act as a final court of appeal for individual cases, though only a handful of cases ever reach that point, and the Constitutional Reform Act of 2005 removed even that power, creating a new Supreme Court as the final court of appeal. The newly elected coalition government in 2010 promised to introduce a proposal for an at least partially elected House of Lords. Whether this would result in a more powerful upper house is unclear. The Commons, though, retains considerable power. As noted above, even the most powerful PMs must take account of the views of their party's MPs in the Commons, especially if the PM's popularity is waning.

Parliament also serves an important watchdog function. The PM must attend Parliament weekly for Question Time, a very lively, not fully rehearsed, televised debate among the major politicians of the day. During Question Time, the PM is expected to respond to queries from MPs and defend the government's policies. In addition, MPs from both the ruling and opposition parties have a right to question all cabinet ministers about the activities of their departments, and the cabinet members must respond to these questions personally in Parliament, giving a public airing of issues of concern, large and small. The House of Commons recently took a step that made it a little more like the U.S. Congress when it created more committees that hold hearings on proposed legislation. In the British system, the fate of legislation introduced by the government (the cabinet) is rarely in doubt, but the committees allow

MPs to investigate the implications of proposed laws more thoroughly, and at times the ruling party will allow legislation to be amended if committees identify problems. The prestige of the Commons was damaged severely by a scandal in 2010 in which large numbers of MPs were found to be abusing a housing allowance, purchasing luxury goods and elaborate home repairs with money intended to cover their housing costs while in London. Many MPs subsequently decided not to run for reelection, and the new government promised to introduce legislation allowing constituents to recall their MP between elections.

Even with the recent changes, the British parliament does not modify legislation nearly as much as the U.S. Congress does. Nonetheless, the executive branch must pay attention to the opinions of the majority party MPs, and both houses of Parliament provide a forum for active, and at times closely watched, public debate over major issues. The prime minister's formal powers may allow him to ignore this legislative activity, but his political survival requires that he attend to it closely. Informally, therefore, Parliament remains an important check on even the most powerful PM.

In form, India's parliamentary system differs little from Britain's. As in any parliamentary system, the prime minister and the cabinet are the key executives and decision makers, but India also has an indirectly elected president. Despite few formal differences, the role and power of the Indian prime minister and Parliament are significantly different from the British model. The president's role is similar to that of the British monarch, but it has potentially more political significance. The divergence between the systems is due mainly to differences in the number of parties in the two countries. Like Britain and most parliamentary systems, India's parties are highly disciplined, in the sense that MPs almost always vote with their party. Unlike Britain, India has never had a two-party system but rather has many parties. One party dominated the government for the first forty

bicameral legislature: A legislature that has two houses

years after the nation's independence from Britain, but no party has since enjoyed such a majority. No single party has won a majority of seats in Parliament in the last twenty years, necessitating coalition governments.

In the early days of independence, one-party dominance meant that PMs were far less constrained than their British counterparts. The Indian National Congress (commonly called the Congress) ruled nearly continuously from independence in 1947 until 1989. An opposition coalition won power only once, from 1977 to 1980, over this period. The country's first prime minister, Jawaharlal Nehru (1947–1964), was a hero of the nationalist movement for independence and a deeply popular and respected figure. His cabinet consisted of leaders of the major factions within the ruling party and served as the actual governing body, debating policy as a cabinet is expected to in a parliamentary system. Shortly after his death, his daughter, Indira Gandhi, was selected to lead the Congress and therefore became PM. She desired independence from the faction leaders within the party. With this goal in mind, she achieved much greater centralized control of the Congress and, consequently, the government. Her cabinet ministers were not leaders of major factions in the party but were instead lesser-known MPs loyal only to her, and she ruled on the advice of an inner circle that did not include most of the cabinet. Her son, Rajiv Gandhi, ruled in an even more centralized manner, appointing and dismissing cabinet ministers on average every seven weeks.

The Congress lost its dominant position after 1989 in part because of a corruption scandal that tarnished Rajiv Gandhi's image. Every government since has been a coalition of one large party and a number of smaller ones. This has profoundly changed the role of the PM. He remains the central executive and by far most important leader in the country, but all PMs since 1989 have had to compromise with other parties in order to form a government. Coalition government cabinets have included ministers representing various parties in the coalition who meet to hash out policy in particular areas, a time-consuming

and often fruitless effort. Most PMs since 1989 have had less central control, as they must continually compromise with their coalition partners. Furthermore, if one small party decides to vote against the government, it can call a vote of no confidence and remove the PM entirely. A partial exception to this norm was Narasimha Rao (1991–1996). A Congress PM who ruled with a coalition of other parties, he attempted to centralize power in his personal office, the Prime Minister's Office, while maintaining a coalition government. His rule was plagued by corruption scandals, including allegations that he bribed four MPs of a small party to support his government to maintain his power: Centralization of power in a coalition government had its costs. Rao survived a full five-year term, but the Congress then saw the biggest electoral defeat in its history.

Indian PMs remain quite powerful, but without the ability of any one party to win a majority, coalition government has been essential, and governments have often been unstable. This shift from one-party dominance is clearly seen in the number of PMs India has had: in its first thirty years of independence (1947–1977), the country had only three PMs; in its second thirty years (1977–2007), it had twelve, only three of whom served full terms.

The multiparty context has also given the president somewhat more significance. For the most part, the president's duties are similar to those of the British monarch: to act as official head of state and carry out various official functions "on the advice of the Prime Minister"—in fact, almost always doing what the prime minister says. The president's power to ask a party leader in Parliament to form the next government can sometimes be important in the context of coalition government, however. When a coalition collapses, the president must decide whether to ask a different party to attempt to put together a new coalition or call a general election. He usually follows the advice of the departing PM, but on occasion, if he thinks he has political support, he can make an independent decision.

The rise of coalition government has made small parties who negotiate membership in these coalitions quite important. This, however, has not necessarily meant that Parliament as a whole has become more effective. Indeed, Parliament passes fewer laws now than it did under the dominance of the Congress, and MPs spend far less time there. Parties are more important for their votes in putting together a coalition government than they are for their legislative activity, and most of the 544 MPs are focused more on their states than on the national government. Many of the small parties that are potential members of coalition governments are state-level parties with little support outside a particular state or region, so the political fortunes of many MPs are tied to their role in state-level politics more than they are to the national Parliament. As political malfeasance has increased in India, being an MP has also become a means of gaining access to corruption opportunities. Indian watchdog groups reported that in 2009, nearly a quarter of sitting MPs had been charged with a crime of some sort and, on average, MPs running for reelection in 2009 were 300 percent richer than they had been before the last election in 2004.

The rise of coalition governments has allowed the opposition in Parliament to be more assertive when MPs do focus on legislation. Under the single-party dominance of the Congress, opposition parties were reduced to protests such as walkouts of Parliament. The rise of coalition governments has changed this. As in the United Kingdom, parliamentary committees in India have become stronger. Opposition MPs have also started regularly introducing their own legislation, something relatively rare in parliamentary systems because without some government support, legislation has virtually no chance of being passed. Virtually unheard of in the era of Congress dominance, opposition bills are now quite regular, and some manage to pass with a coalition of small parties supporting them. Similarly, parliamentary debate now more regularly features opposition MPs, who do not stage protests as much as they used to.

CASE SUMMARY

The Westminster model in its purest form is the most centralized form of liberal democratic governing institutions. It is the classic case of Lijphart's majoritarian democracy, having very few veto players. Whether the model operates this way in fact depends, though, on a number of factors. Most important is the number and strength of parties, which we discuss more fully in chapter 7. Britain's case has only two strong parties, so one has ruled unimpeded most of the time. Vertical accountability clearly exists, but horizontal accountability is very limited. The Indian system under Congress dominance was equally majoritarian, and Indira Gandhi's prime ministerial government shows that a powerful PM can undermine even the potential vertical accountability of collective responsibility. Since 1989, however, coalition government in India has substantially increased the potential veto players, adding a degree of consensual democracy. In contrast to Britain, India also has a system of judicial review (see below) in which the Supreme Court can limit parliamentary and executive action to preserve the constitution; the Court has been increasingly assertive in doing so in the last twenty years.

The coalition government elected into office in the United Kingdom in 2010 might enhance the role of Parliament there, as the Liberal Democrats are in a position to assert their interests vis-à-vis the Conservatives, who need their coalition partners to keep their PM in office. A slight, and perhaps temporary, degree of consensual democracy seems to be arising in Britain's majoritarian model as a result. India, on the other hand, may be shifting back toward greater single-party power. The 2009 election did not give the Congress a majority, meaning that a coalition government was still necessary, but the party won more seats than any time since 1989, when the "coalition era" began. It is unclear what these potentially contradictory trends portend, but the governing institutions in both countries seem to be undergoing significant change in the new millennium.

How many parliamentary and presidential countries are there, and where are they located? While parliamentary systems are more common globally, presidential systems historically have dominated in the Americas. Semipresidential systems, which are relatively rare, are concentrated in Eastern Europe and Francophone Africa (see Map 6.1). This pattern suggests that timing and history—especially colonial history—affect countries' institutional choices. As former British colonies throughout the world gained independence after World War II, most adopted the institutions they saw in their colonizer, the "Mother of Parliaments." Former French colonies gained independence after Charles de Gaulle's Fifth Republic established a semipresidential system in France, and many adopted semipresidential constitutions; an example is Côte d'Ivoire. Latin American countries, in contrast, gained their independence much earlier than the British and French colonies (most became independent in the 1820s or so). They had no democratic institutional example to take from their Spanish and Portuguese colonizers, but they did have one from their regional forerunner in achieving independence, the United States. Using it as a model, they wrote presidential constitutions.

Colonialism does not, of course, explain the European patterns, but we can note that as European countries replaced hereditary monarchies with democratic systems, they tended to follow the British idea but also modify it. Most revised and tinkered with their constitutions over time and some even had lapses in democracy, but today most have a modified "Western European" parliamentary system that differs from that of the British by using proportional representation rather than the first-past-the-post electoral system (see chapter 7) to choose the parliament. Recently democratic Eastern European countries have tended to choose one of the two Western European models: parliamentary or semipresidential.

Colonial heritage played an important role in what democratic institutions newly independent countries chose in much of the world. As historical institutionalists have argued, once created, institutions create their own bases of support, both because political leaders who have figured out how to gain power via those institutions are averse to changing them and because political socialization typically reinforces support for existing institutions, especially long-standing ones. Our case study country, Brazil, is one of the rare countries that has had a major debate over whether to retain its long-standing presidential system or shift to a parliamentary one; despite a full-scale national campaign and vociferous national debate, Brazilian voters overwhelmingly chose to preserve what they had long known, the presidential system common to Latin America. Today, as political scientists ponder which institutions are "best" for newly democratic countries, their colonial legacy has become an important part of the debate. Scholars may recommend a particular type of institution as superior for a new democracy, but such fundamental changes are quite rare.

presidentialism:
A term denoting a presidential system of democracy in which the executive and legislature are elected independently and have separate and independent powers

Presidential Systems: The Separation of Powers

Presidentialism needs little introduction for American students, because the most famous and enduring example of this system is the United States. In a presidential system, the roles of head of state and head of government are normally filled by the same person, who is given the title "president." The crucial, defining aspect of a

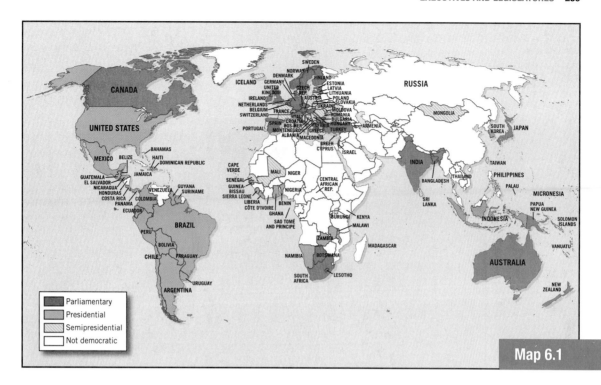

Three Major Types of Electoral Democracy

Source: Freedom House, Electoral Democracies 2010. Modified by the authors.

Note: Countries on the Freedom House list but not included here are as follows: Andorra, Dominica, Maldives, Slovenia, Timor Leste.

presidential system, however, is not this fusion of executive roles. Rather, it is the concept of **separation of powers**. The American founders argued that the functions of the executive and legislative branches should be distinct and separate, and everything about any presidential system reflects this choice, no matter how the particulars of any specific constitution may differ. This means that the executive and legislative branches are elected separately in their own (though possibly concurrent) elections, and the president must be independently and directly (or nearly directly) elected. Regardless of the electoral or party system in place, this institutional feature gives presidential systems an element of consensual democracy: institutional veto players are built into the founding documents of the system.

Presidential election processes can and do vary somewhat; for example, the U.S. president is elected indirectly by the Electoral College, but that institution is bound to follow the popular vote closely. Some countries elect a president by plurality; others use a two-round system to achieve an absolute majority. No matter how the elections are administered, the important thing is that the president's legitimacy as head of state and government derives from an electoral process that legitimizes him or her as the nation's choice. Similarly, the legislature's legitimacy arises from the direct election of the representatives, who should therefore reflect the popular will. Even if the presidency and legislature are controlled by different parties, each is legitimized independently by the electoral process, and creating laws requires the agreement, in some way, of both the president and a majority in the legislature.

Presidents and their legislatures have a hard time interfering with each other's time in office. Presidents serve a fixed term, whether four years, such as in the

separation of powers: Constitutionally explicit division of power among the major branches of government

Figure 6.2

Typical Presidential System

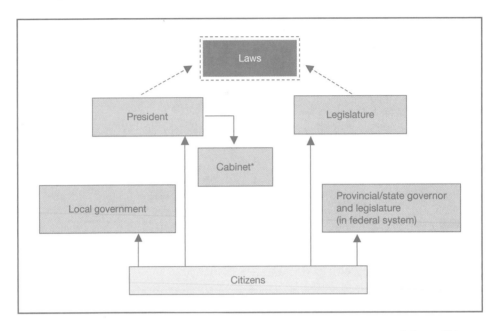

Note: Up arrows indicate elections. Down or horizontal arrows indicate nomination or appointment. Hash-mark arrows indicate which body is responsible for formally passing and signing legislation.

*In most presidential systems, at least one branch of the legislature must approve the president's cabinet members, but cabinet members do not come out of the legislature itself.

United States, Brazil, Chile, and Argentina, or longer, such as six years in Mexico. During that fixed term, it is very difficult for a legislature to remove the president from office. Most countries make provision for some kind of impeachment process, but impeachment requires extraordinary measures and can only be justified in extreme circumstances. Barring this, no matter how much legislators, including members of the president's own party, disagree with the president or question his or her competence or policy, they cannot remove the executive from office. Similarly, legislators also have fixed terms. In a bicameral legislature in a presidential system, terms may be different for each house. In any legislature, elections may be periodic, with only a portion of the legislature being renewed in any particular election. Regardless of the details, a president may not tamper with a legislature's sessions by forcibly shortening or lengthening them.

Finally, the separation of powers is clear in the president's powers of appointment. Although presidents may need the consent of the legislature, they are largely free to appoint their own cabinet ministers or secretaries. They may, and in the case of the United States must, appoint individuals who are not drawn from the legislature. They may also appoint people from any party they wish. Their appointments need not reflect the composition of the legislature in any way; for example, a president whose party is a minority in the legislature does not legally need to include cabinet officers from the majority party. Once appointed and confirmed by the legislature, the officers serve at the president's pleasure, and the legislature can interfere only minimally with their activities. In practice, of course, most presidents try to appoint to their cabinet a group of people more or less representative of the major political factions in their party or the country more broadly, as well as a group that at least somewhat matches the demographic diversity of the country. The separation from the legislature, though, means they only do this loosely and to the extent they think is politically expedient, rather than being required to in order to form a government, as in a parliamentary system. Thus, the cabinet is typically a far less important decision-making body than in a parliamentary system. Also, because members of the legislature are not vying directly for cabinet appointments, the president has less control over them than a PM does, so the legislature becomes a more important and independent decision-making body.

CASE STUDY

Presidentialism in the United States and Brazil

- U.S. president: Weak formal powers but growing informal ones
- Brazilian president: Stronger formal powers but weaker informal ones due to fragmented parties and legislature
- Growing strength of presidency over time in both countries
- Institutionalized veto players in presidential system whose powers vary depending in part on party system

Most countries in the Western Hemisphere have presidential systems, although the socioeconomic and political contexts of these systems vary widely, as the cases of the United States and Brazil show. While the formal rights and duties of each branch of government are different in the two systems, the informal power of the presidency varies even more because the office is set in very different political systems. In the United States, the office of the president was one of the more controversial parts of the Constitution when it was written. Many leaders, most notably Thomas Jefferson, feared that a single executive would inevitably become authoritarian, mimicking the British monarch from which the colonists had just won liberation. These fears might surprise contemporary Americans, for the office as originally designed was far more

Brazil's "worker" president, Luiz Inácio "Lula" da Silva (shown right), was reelected to a second term and was enjoying high popularity ratings in 2008. The first woman president of Brazil was elected in 2010 when Dilma Rousseff (left) succeeded her mentor, Lula.

Credit: Adriano Machado/AFP/Getty Images

modest than what it has become. The president's main powers are (1) approving or vetoing legislation passed by Congress (Congress can override a veto with a two-thirds majority vote); (2) appointing cabinet secretaries and Supreme Court justices, other federal judges, and lower-level political appointees in the bureaucracy, though all such appointments are subject to the Senate's approval; (3) serving as head of state and commander in chief of the armed forces; and (4) entering into treaties and declaring war, again subject to Senate approval.

On their own, these powers are modest by modern standards. The early presidents were certainly important, but they were not the central focus of national politics that the president of the United States has become today. Many of the most well-known presidents are so recognized because they expanded the powers of the office. Ironically, this growth began with Thomas Jefferson, who successfully proclaimed the right of the president to expand the country via the Louisiana Purchase. Starting with Andrew Jackson, the president became the de facto head of his party, giving him greater influence over Congress. In the twentieth century, Franklin Roosevelt created vast new social programs that increased the size and reach of the federal bureaucracy over which the president presides, and as the United States became a world superpower, the president's powers in foreign policy and war correspondingly gained importance as well.

The U.S. president in modern times has become the symbol of the nation, the undisputed leader of his party, and the chief initiator of legislation as well as its chief implementer. The office has retained the symbolic legitimacy of all presidencies as the sole office for which every citizen votes, the embodiment of majority will, even though the individual selected by the Electoral College isn't always the individual who wins the most popular votes, as occurred in the 2000 presidential contest between Al Gore and George W. Bush. While legislation formally starts in Congress, in practice this body looks to the president for major legislative initiatives; as the leader of his party who sits atop a vast technocratic bureaucracy, the president with his cabinet is in a better position politically and technically to formulate complicated legislation. Members of Congress initiate considerable legislation, and they are far more likely to initiate new legislation than are MPs in a parliamentary system, but most legislation of consequence has the support of the president. The president's position as head of his party and chief fund-raiser also gives him great influence over legislators in his party. This is especially true when a president is popular: members of his party want to be closely associated with him and often yield to his desires to gain his support in the next election.

Individual legislators may vie for the president's approval, but the U.S. Congress as a body has substantial powers as well, and it certainly does not always yield to the president. Because legislators are independently elected, Congress jealously guards its autonomy from the executive branch. The U.S. House of Representatives and Senate have perhaps the most extensive and expensive staffs of any legislature in the world. Committees and subcommittees are crucial in investigating, amending, and passing legislation. Individual members have great freedom to introduce legislation compared to members of most national legislatures, and it's entirely possible that individual legislation will become law if it gains the support of the chairs of key committees or subcommittees. Few proposals make it through Congress without significant changes, however; in sharp contrast, in the British parliament, the dominant party typically passes bills as written by the PM and the cabinet. Most observers argue that the U.S. Congress is the most powerful legislature in the world, not only because it legislates on behalf of the most powerful country but because of its autonomy from the executive branch.

One direct result of the separation of powers between two powerful branches of government is "gridlock," or the seeming inability to pass major legislation. This is a constant concern of contemporary American politics. The United States has only two major parties, but these parties are relatively weak; individual legislators are not beholden to party leaders, and they vote as they choose on each piece of legislation. Ideological similarities mean that members of the same party usually vote the same way, but individual members of Congress frequently go against their party's wishes. This alone can occasionally produce gridlock, but stalemates are much more likely when one party controls the presidency and the other controls Congress, a common outcome of the U.S. presidential system. In this case, one of the president's main jobs has become trying to get his legislation passed, either by cajoling members of his own party to support him or by negotiating and compromising with the opposing party in Congress, especially when it is in the majority. The failure of this process produces gridlock.

When not trying to negotiate the maze of political compromise, the U.S. president, as head of the executive branch, oversees a bureaucracy of thousands of people. Most are permanent civil servants, but several hundred at the top of the bureaucratic hierarchy serve at the president's pleasure. This gives the president great influence over the implementation of laws once they pass through Congress and are signed into law. Because no legislation can foresee and include every conceivable detail of implementation in today's increasingly technocratic society, the chief executive is given great latitude to enforce laws. For most of the nation's history, this power has been relatively uncontroversial; under President George W. Bush, however, this executive power became a subject of contention, particularly in regard to issues of national security. Critics charged that a variety of actions taken by Bush in the name of national security were violations of citizens' basic rights to due process and privacy, and they believed that Bush overstepped the president's constitutional authority.

Especially controversial were presidential "signing statements" that President Bush attached to more than 1,000 provisions of legislation he signed into law. The precedent for such signing statements is quite old, but issuing signing statements only became frequent under presidents Reagan and Clinton in the 1980s and 1990s. The strongest of them, "constitutional signing statements," assert the president's authority not to enforce certain aspects of legislation because in his opinion they violate his constitutional powers. President Bush controversially asserted these rights via signing statements on legislation involving torture and treatment of prisoners in the "war on terror." He contended that the legislation unduly restricted his ability to conduct war as commander in chief; his critics argued that Bush's signing statements unconstitutionally and unilaterally revoked parts of legislation he didn't agree with, violating Congress's power to legislate. Despite criticizing Bush's action on the campaign trail, President Obama issued dozens of signing statements early in his presidency, in some cases reversing earlier Bush statements. This is only the latest salvo in a 200-year battle over the power of the U.S. presidency.

The fears of Thomas Jefferson and his followers were partly justified: the presidency of the United States is a very powerful office. On the one hand, the separation of powers in the presidential system, particularly in the context of relatively weak parties in the United States and the separate election of members of Congress, limits what presidents can do. On the other hand, presidents' leadership of their party and control over foreign policy and hundreds of key appointments in the executive branch give them far greater powers than many of the authors of the Constitution envisioned. This divided power in the context of a very old democracy with well-established institutions and only two main parties produces a system that is often seen as slow to make policy, but the system is nonetheless well institutionalized, a crucial context for effective relations among the separate branches in a presidential system.

Presidentialism, however, can look very different when transplanted to different geographic, social, and institutional settings, as the example of Brazil shows. As in most of Latin America, Brazil's democratic regimes have always been presidential. The current system dates to a constitution approved in 1988. Brazil's president has more extensive formal powers than her U.S. counterpart, but a legislature with many weak political parties and the most decentralized federal system in the world make these powers substantially less effective than they appear on paper. Successive presidents have managed to use incentives and growing discipline within the major parties to strengthen the presidency. Their efforts have been generally successful, and recent presidents have been able to govern more effectively than could their predecessors fifteen or twenty years ago.

Unlike in the United States, Brazil's president is directly chosen in a two-round election: if no candidate wins an absolute majority on the first vote, a second vote takes place two weeks later between the top two candidates. Only one presidential candidate has won on the first ballot: Fernando Henrique Cardoso, who won in 1994 and 1998. Originally, the president could serve only 1 five-year term. Constitutional amendments subsequently reduced the term to four years so it would coincide with legislative elections and then allowed one reelection. The last two presidents, Cardoso and Luiz Inácio "Lula" da Silva, both were reelected to second terms. Presidents otherwise have the typical powers of the office in a presidential system: head of state and government, commander in chief of the armed forces, and appointment powers. In Brazil they also have several unusual powers: (1) the authority to issue "provisional decrees" (PDs), which become law for thirty days unless the National Congress approves them permanently; (2) a line-item veto, which allows a president to eliminate individual measures in a bill sent from the National Congress without vetoing the entire law; and (3) a monopoly over initiation of all legislation involving the budget.

The context in which Brazilian presidents must operate is a multiparty system with many fragmented parties. Because of Brazil's electoral system (which we discuss in detail in chapter 9), politicians have little incentive to form broad, inclusive parties to get elected, nor do they have much incentive to follow party leaders once they are in the National Congress. Both houses of Brazil's bicameral legislature, the Chamber of Deputies (the lower house) and the Senate (the upper house), include numerous parties. After the 2010 election, the Chamber of Deputies included twenty-two parties, the biggest of which, the president's party, had only 17 percent of the seats. The only way

for presidents to get their legislation passed is to build coalitions among several parties, which they can do in several ways. In the last few elections, several parties have supported the two major presidential candidates, a result of preelection negotiations regarding sharing power after the election. The president then shares power mainly by appointing members of parties supporting her to the cabinet and other appointed offices. Presidents essentially put together coalition governments like those in parliamentary systems, although the weakness of Brazil's parties means presidents still can have difficulty getting legislators to vote the way the party leadership wants.

Presidents can also use the line-item veto to negotiate with individual legislators to gain their support for particular bills. As in the United States, Brazilian legislators engage in "pork-barrel" politics; that is, they seek to include specific spending projects for their home areas in the national budget. This is the contemporary continuation of a long Brazilian tradition of patronage politics in which elected officials bring home government resources as a primary means of gaining support. The president's line-item veto, however, allows the executive to decide which of these individual items to keep and which to eliminate, so she can exchange approval of a legislator's pet project for the latter's support on a crucial piece of legislation.

The first president directly elected under the 1988 constitution, Fernando Collor, whose party had only 3 percent of the seats in the Chamber of Deputies, used none of these methods to build coalitions. He instead ruled largely through PDs, issuing 150 of them in his first year in office. Often, when one expired, he would simply reissue it the next day, essentially making it last as long as he pleased. Brazil's Supreme Court never ruled against this practice, despite its dubious constitutionality. When he continued to ignore the National Congress and failed to solve Brazil's long-term problem of hyperinflation, however, he lost support; he was ultimately forced to resign over a corruption scandal. Subsequent presidents recognized the need to include the National Congress and used the various negotiation strategies outlined above to pass legislation. In 2001, the Brazilian Congress passed a reform to limit the president's ability to reissue PDs and to discourage their use altogether. Although the law severely limited reissuing PDs the way Collor had done, the use of PDs actually increased. Cardoso doubled the rate of PDs he issued after the law passed, and his successor, President Lula, increased them another 50 percent. The fractiousness of Congress encourages Brazilian presidents to make use of their unilateral power.

Overall, however, the powers of Brazil's president remain limited. Major presidential proposals often fail to pass the National Congress, and of those that do pass, virtually all are modified. Each piece of legislation requires extensive horse trading, not only with party leaders but also with individual legislators looking for favors. Dilma Rousseff, elected to succeed Lula in 2010 and Brazil's first female president, is, like Lula, from the Workers' Party (PT), which is by far the most united and ideologically driven party in the country. Its small share of seats in the National Congress made compromise with other parties a constant part of Lula's governing effort. Although the PT's seats increased slightly in 2010, compromise with coalition partners will still be key for Rousseff. Very slowly the Brazilian presidency and parties are becoming stronger institutions as the possibility of

presidential reelection and limits on PDs give incentives for greater cooperation between the branches of government (see chapter 9 for more details on these recent trends). Governance, though, remains a slow and difficult process in a presidential system with weak and fragmented parties. Brazil's federalism also weakens the power of the presidency, a subject we return to below.

| CASE SUMMARY |

The United States and Brazil both have certain inherent institutionalized veto players, a characteristic they share with all presidential systems. While the president's cabinet need not reflect actual consensus, the bargaining necessary among branches of government, especially when they are controlled by differing parties, adds a degree of consensual democracy. How much this serves as a form of horizontal accountability depends very much on context. As in parliamentary systems, the number and strength of political parties matter; Brazil's fragmented legislature with many, weak parties produces numerous potential veto players. In the U.S. system, the president is more powerful, but again can be strongly checked by a Congress controlled by the opposing party. In both countries, the powers of the presidency have tended to increase, reflecting the continuing concerns about limited executive authority in modern democracies.

Semipresidentialism: The Hybrid Compromise

The third major executive-legislative system is the most recently created. **Semipresidentialism** splits executive power between an elected president and a prime minister. The president is elected directly by the citizens as in a presidential system and serves as the head of state, but she also has significant powers in running the government. The official head of government is the PM, who is the leader of the majority party or coalition in parliament and who appoints the cabinet, as in a parliamentary system, but is himself appointed by the president (with parliamentary approval). Legislation requires the signature of the president, as well as support of the PM as head of the ruling party or coalition in parliament. The parliament can force the cabinet to resign through a vote of no confidence, and the president has the power

semipresidentialism: A term denoting a semipresidential system of democracy in which executive power is divided between a directly elected president and a prime minister elected by a parliament

Figure 6.3

Typical Semipresidential System

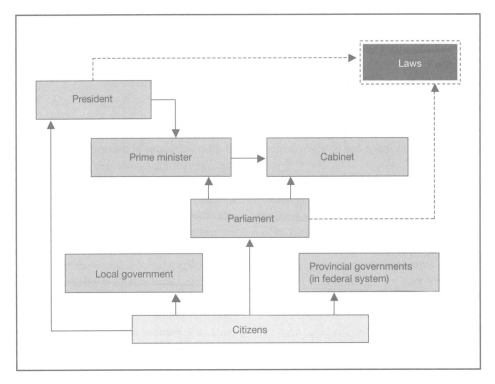

Note: Up arrows indicate elections. Down or horizontal arrows indicate nomination or appointment. Hash-mark arrows indicate which body is responsible for formally passing and signing legislation.

to dissolve parliament and call a new election. The president, however, serves a fixed term; she can therefore force the PM and legislature to run for office anew without threatening her own position, a source of significant power for the office. For a complex arrangement like semipresidentialism to be successful, the powers and duties of the president and PM as dual executives usually must be spelled out clearly in the constitution. For example, the president may be given power over military decisions (as in Sri Lanka) or foreign policy (as in Finland), whereas the prime minister typically concentrates on domestic policies. The specific division of powers varies greatly, however, and is not always clearly delineated.

The semipresidential system originated in France in the 1958 constitution establishing the Fifth Republic. Charles de Gaulle, a World War II hero and undisputed political leader of France at the time, envisioned the presidency as a stabilizing and powerful position, legitimated via national election. He assumed that the same party would win the presidency and a legislative majority. So long as it did, semipresidentialism gave the president, as head of the majority party who also appoints the PM, unparalleled power to govern.

cohabitation: Sharing of power between a president and prime minister from different parties in a semipresidential system

This worked as intended until the 1980s, when for the first time the president was elected from one party and the majority of the legislature from another, a situation the French humorously call **cohabitation**. Under cohabitation, the president must compromise with the legislature by appointing a PM from the majority party in the legislature rather than from his own party. A compromise had to be worked out regarding the specific powers of the president and the PM, since the French constitution did not draw clear boundaries. In practice, the compromise has been that the president possesses power over foreign policy while the PM and the legislature control domestic policy. Critics of semipresidentialism fear that it gives the president too much power in a democracy, but cohabitation clearly limits those powers significantly. If voters elect a majority to the legislature in opposition to the president, dissolving the legislature immediately to call a new election would simply irritate voters; the president may be forced to accept the results and live with cohabitation and the limits it imposes. However, cohabitation can also produce gridlock and inability to legislate effectively, as in a purely presidential system. The semipresidential system, then, produces strong institutional veto players under cohabitation but weaker ones (if any) when the same party controls both the presidency and parliament. Our case study of Russia, however, shows the dangers of having no veto players, as the system aggrandizes power in the presidency, at least in the context of a new democracy with weak institutions across the board.

CASE STUDY

RUSSIA: SEMIPRESIDENTIALISM IN A NEW DEMOCRACY WITH WEAK INSTITUTIONS

- Constitution with very powerful presidency
- Weaker executive-legislative link than in classic semipresidentialism
- Under Putin, even further expansion of presidential powers
- President Medvedev and informal versus formal power

Are two chief executives better than one? Dmitry Medvedev (left) was Vladimir Putin's prime minister and succeeded him as president in 2008. Putin then became Medvedev's prime minister, leading people to ask who was really in charge. As time went on, it became clear that Putin remained the more powerful figure; informal power trumped the formal institutional powers in Russia's semipresidential system.

Credit: AP Photo/Alexander Zemlianichenko

Russia is the largest country in the world with a semipresidential system, and it is certainly one of the most important. Its current government demonstrates the worst fears of the system's loudest critics: that in a regime with weak institutions, a powerful presidency can be dangerous to democracy by allowing one official to achieve overwhelming power. This dominance of the executive is not inherent in all semipresidential systems, as France demonstrates, but Russia is a cautionary case of the problem of a strong presidency in a new democracy with weak institutions.

The Russian constitution adopted in 1993 created a semipresidential system with an exceptionally strong presidency. The president is directly elected to a four-year term, with a maximum of two terms possible. He must be elected by an absolute majority: if no candidate wins a majority in the first election, a second is held between the top two candidates. The president appoints the prime minister with the approval of the parliament,

IN CONTEXT

SEMIPRESIDENTIAL SYSTEMS

Semipresidentialism spread with the wave of democratization in the 1990s. Political scientist Robert Elgie (2005) broadly defined semipresidentialism as any system with an elected president and a prime minister accountable to a parliament, and he classified fifty-three regimes as semipresidentialist systems in 2010. Eight are former colonies of two semipresidential European countries, France and Portugal. Freedom House rated twenty-three semipresidentialist countries "free" in 2010, eighteen as partly free, and twelve as not free.

Region	Number of semipresidential regimes	Free	Partly free	Not free
Africa	19	4	10	5
Americas	2	1	1	0
Asia	4	2	2	0
Europe*	25	16	5	4
Middle East	3	0	0	3

Source: Puddington, Arch. 2010. "Freedom in the World 2010: Erosion of Freedom Intensifies." http://www.freedomhouse.org/.

*Includes nations of the former Soviet Union.

the Duma, but if the Duma votes against the president's candidate for PM three times, it is automatically dissolved and new elections are called. This means that unless the president's opponents in the Duma think they will gain from an election, they will be very hesitant to oppose his nominee. The president also appoints all cabinet members, who do not need approval by the Duma. Neither the PM nor the rest of the cabinet need be members of the Duma, and the vast majority have not been. The Russian system, then, does not link the president and parliament via the PM and cabinet as fully as the original French model. This structure frees the president to appoint anyone he pleases to the cabinet, regardless of which party controls parliament.

Furthermore, the president has direct control over several key ministries (Foreign Affairs, Defense, and Interior) and the Federal Security Service, successor to the KGB; in these areas, his authority bypasses the PM and the cabinet altogether. Perhaps most important, the president can issue decrees that have the force of law and cannot be vetoed by the Duma or challenged in court, which gives him the power to rule without legislative support. A constitutional amendment in 2000 also gave the president the power to appoint and dismiss all governors of Russia's eighty-nine regions (see the section on federalism below), who in turn appoint half of the members of the upper house of parliament. The Duma can vote no confidence in the prime minister but must do so twice to remove him from office. It can also impeach the president by a two-thirds vote, but it has only attempted to do so once, in 1999, and failed.

Russia's two major post-Communist presidents, Boris Yeltsin (1991–2000) and Vladimir Putin (2000–2008), used the powers of the presidency quite differently. Yeltsin, who was elected president while Russia was still part of the Soviet Union, was the hero of the post-Communist revolution. He led the opposition to an attempted Soviet military coup in August 1991, and the success of his opposition movement resulted in the demise of the Soviet Union. He also was the architect of the 1993 constitution. His rule, however, was chaotic. Although he won only 36 percent of the vote in the first-round election in 1996, he did win a majority in the second round. Because he was not a member of any political party, he was unable to marshal strong support for his reforms. For most of his presidency, his chief opposition was the former Communist Party, which had a plurality (but not a majority) of seats in the Duma from 1995 to 2003. Yeltsin fought many battles with a hostile parliament and often enacted law by decree. This course of events came to a head in 1999, when the Communists attempted to impeach him on charges of illegally prosecuting a war against the breakaway region of Chechnya and engaging in corruption. He appointed 7 prime ministers over his tenure and more than 200 different cabinet ministers. His final prime minister was Putin, whom he anointed as his successor as president; Yeltsin actually resigned as president prior to the 2000 election to let Putin run as the incumbent.

Putin, a former KGB agent and leader, would prove to be a much stronger president than Yeltsin ever was, winning 53 percent of the vote in the first-round election in 2000. In the 2003 Duma election, his followers organized a new party, United Russia, which won control of parliament. He had complete control of the Duma for the rest of his presidency: it passed every major bill he submitted. He used his powers of decree and control over the prosecution of corruption to eliminate many of the "oligarchs" who had arisen under Yeltsin and come to control major sectors of the economy, replacing them with his supporters or taking direct state control of some companies. He also severely restricted nongovernment sources of media. After winning the 2004 election with more than 70 percent of the vote, he reformed the constitution to also gain effective control over the country's regional governments and, therefore, the upper house of the legislature as well. Finally, Putin anointed Dmitry Medvedev as his successor, who was duly elected president in May 2008. Putin himself, newly appointed as official head of his ruling party in the Duma, became PM and unofficially remained the chief leader of the country. Observers speculated as to whether Medvedev could use the great formal powers of the presidency to change Putin's policies. While Medvedev made numerous speeches suggesting he would fight corruption and move the country in a more democratic direction, no major policies ensued. As PM, Putin

retained the personal loyalty of the majority of the Duma; no significant policy changes would occur without his support. Having created the vast formal powers of the presidency, Putin showed that his informal powers as the leader who had put virtually the entire political elite into office trumped even the powerful presidency, officially in Medvedev's hands. By 2011, speculation was rife over whether Medvedev would run for a second term or step aside for Putin, who would then be eligible to serve another two terms.

CASE SUMMARY

Putin used the already strong presidency in Russia's semipresidential system to amass great presidential and personal power in Russia's weakly institutionalized regime. His use of appointments, constitutional changes, control of the economy, and restrictions on political freedoms gave him so much unilateral control that most analysts argue Russia is no longer a true democracy but instead is a semi-authoritarian regime, which we examine in detail in chapter 9. The constitution, especially as amended by Putin, gives the president great powers; even if the legislature were controlled by an opposition party, its ability to act as a veto player would be limited, though not altogether absent. The Russian case, then, raises the worst fears about an excessively strong presidency in a semipresidential system that arises in the context of weak institutions in a new democracy. Formally, the system is designed to have elements of both vertical and horizontal accountability, but Putin's exercise of control over the electoral system to create a dominant ruling party with no effective opposition has nearly eliminated both.

Comparing Executive-Legislative Institutions

In comparing parliamentary, presidential, and semipresidential systems, comparativists ask three major questions: Which system is most democratic in the sense of providing greatest accountability? Which system is most effective at making public policy? Which system provides the greatest political stability for a democratic regime?

All three systems provide vertical accountability in that major leaders are subject to electoral sanction by voters. The question is, How frequent and effective is this vertical accountability? Also, how much horizontal accountability exists? Lijphart (1999) argued that the more majoritarian systems provide less representation because power is so concentrated; on the other hand, concentration of power could well make policymaking easier. More consensual systems tend to be just the opposite: the distribution of power among major parties and institutions makes more robust horizontal accountability, often based on the presence of veto players, but may threaten effective policymaking.

In theory, the Westminster system, the most purely majoritarian system, is extremely democratic because it makes the legislature, the elected body of the people, supreme. In practice, the question of accountability is far more complex. First, much depends on the electoral system used to select the legislature. In multiparty systems, parliamentarism may be more consensual, promoting negotiation, coalition building, and representation of a wide range of views in the cabinet. As we describe more fully in chapter 7, however, a majoritarian electoral system such as Britain's that produces a "supermajority" for one party obviates this advantage: the PM may be an unusually powerful executive because he or she is guaranteed a legislative majority as long as the majority party supports his or her leadership. This, Powell (2000) argued, can provide greater vertical accountability: at election time citizens know whom to hold responsible for government policy. Some critics also argue that the modern world, particularly given the rise of television and other media and the growing importance of national security, has strengthened the hand of the PM. Campaigns have become more personalized and focused on the party leader who will become PM rather than on the party as an institution, and security issues tend to require more secrecy and private consultation and less discussion with party members or with the parliament in general. If this is true, then prime ministers are similar to presidents—presidents who always have a legislative majority. Thus, some critics say that parliamentary systems vest too much power in the hands of a single individual, thereby threatening representative government. These critics advocate instead the separation of powers characteristic of presidentialism.

Presidentialism, despite the directly elected president, seems to have greater horizontal accountability because of the separation of powers. The independent legislature can limit the president's prerogatives on a regular basis, and the individual elected members of the legislature are likely to have more influence on policymaking than under a parliamentary system. Given a particular partisan division in the legislature, some members can become individual veto players. Again, how true this is depends in part on the nature of parties, which we discuss in the next chapter. A presidential system with strong parties that vote in lockstep and in which the president's party has a majority in the legislature will function much like a parliamentary system. On the other hand, a presidential system with weaker parties (as in the United States) or with a divided government (with the presidency and legislature controlled by different parties) provides for much greater horizontal accountability, though perhaps at the expense of effective policymaking. In these cases, what Americans call "gridlock" can set in.

Making public policy effectively in a democracy always requires compromise. A parliamentary system in which the PM's party controls a majority of the legislature is most effective at making policy precisely for the same reason critics say it is less democratic: there are no institutional constraints on the ruling party's actions. This allows it to decide what policies it wishes to pursue and make them law relatively quickly, compromising very little with opponents. Of course, the ruling party's members will ultimately face voters' judgment, but in the short term they face no formal constraints. Many observers contend this explains why PM Margaret Thatcher in the United Kingdom changed economic policies in a monetarist direction so much more successfully than did U.S. president Ronald Reagan, elected at about the same time and with a very similar ideology. Thatcher had a majority in Parliament who passed her proposals more or less without question, while Republican Reagan spent much of his term with a Democratic majority in Congress with whom he had to compromise. In a parliamentary system with a coalition government, policymaking requires more compromises, but the multiparty cabinet with representatives of all parties in the coalition serves as forum within which discussions over compromises take place. If cabinet negotiations are successful, legislation is then very likely to pass parliament.

In a review of the political science literature on this question, David Samuels (2007) concluded that overall, presidential systems are less likely to change the status quo via legislation, and when they do, change will take longer and be more expensive than in parliamentary systems. In semipresidential systems, much depends on whether the president, PM, and parliamentary majority are from the same party. If so, little compromise will likely be necessary. If one or more are from different parties, compromise is more essential and successful policymaking less likely. This, of course, makes short-term horizontal accountability stronger.

The biggest debate in recent years among comparativists examining these institutions has been over whether one system is more stable than another. This became a source of hot debate in the 1990s, as formerly communist or authoritarian countries in Eastern Europe, Latin America, and Africa considered what institutional arrangements would best serve their nascent democracies. Political scientist Juan Linz (1990) initiated the debate, arguing that presidentialism has many potential disadvantages. He saw the separation of powers as leading to what he called "dual legitimacy." Since both the legislature and the executive are independently and directly elected, each has legitimacy. Linz thought that since neither had a higher claim to legitimacy, there could be no democratic resolution of conflicts between them. He also argued that the direct election of the president could lead to chief executives with a "winner take-all" mentality who would overemphasize their national mandate and be less willing to compromise; in this sense, he saw them as tending to be more majoritarian than consensual. Majoritarian electoral systems (see chapter 7) and presidential systems in highly divided societies are particularly problematic in this regard. In addition, direct election of the president could increase the chances of a political renegade or destabilizing outsider being elected. Moreover, because the executive is separate from the legislature, a president has little incentive to consider the composition of the legislature or to reflect the divisions of the popular vote in the composition of the cabinet. Linz believed all of these factors could foster an antidemocratic, domineering presidential style that threatens accountability and legitimacy. Lastly, Linz claimed that presidentialism is too inflexible: fixed terms mean that any serious problem for which a president might need to be removed—or even a president's death in office—could provoke a political crisis (as indeed happened in Nigeria in 2010).

Following Linz, most scholarship has found that presidentialism is likely to be more crisis-prone and threatening to the survival of a new democracy than is parliamentarism (Samuels 2007). This is much more likely to be true, however, in a multiparty system, especially if the president does not have a working majority in the legislature. The smaller the size of the president's party in the legislature, the greater the likelihood of regime collapse in presidential regimes (Samuels 2007). Similarly, greater fragmentation of the legislature among different parties makes regime collapse more likely in presidential systems. All of these concerns are relatively muted in a more established democracy in which regime collapse does not seem to be a real possibility. In those cases, the fixed terms of the presidential system, some argue, provide greater continuity and stability, especially compared to some of the more fragmented parliamentary systems with many parties, as in Italy in the past or Israel still. Fixed terms can also be an advantage since they provide a timeline for the development of policy and accomplishment of objectives that allows legislators and the executive to think in the long term rather than worrying about the imminent fall of the government. All of these factors, supporters argue, allow presidentialism to achieve effective governance while simultaneously maintaining accountability.

Defenders of presidentialism have agreed with Linz's point about the potential for such problems to arise in a presidential democracy. They argue, however, that whether these factors become problems or not depends on a great many other variables unrelated to presidentialism per se. Moreover, it has proven very difficult to disentangle failures of presidentialism from these other variables. Parliamentary systems do have a better numerical track record of democratic stability, but how much of this can be attributed to the institutions? Skeptics note that since almost all presidential systems have been in Latin America, regional or cultural factors rather than presidentialism may be the problem. On the other hand, the number of stable parliamentary democracies is high in part because of Britain's many small, relatively homogeneous island former colonies having chosen parliamentarism. So, which is more important to stability: a parliament or a small, socially homogeneous population? In the end, Linz's critics argue that presidential institutions themselves are not the problem. After extensive quantitative analysis, political scientist Jose Antonio Cheibub concluded that the society, not the institution, is the problem. Presidential systems "tend to exist is societies where democracies of any type are likely to be unstable" (2007, 3).

Semipresidentialism, with its combination of a parliament and president, seems more difficult to analyze. Are its effects more like those of a parliamentary or presidential system? On the one hand, Linz argued semipresidentialism poses the dangers of the strong presidency—dual legitimacy and unwillingness to compromise. On the other hand, the PM's dependence on parliament means that her cabinet will, if necessary, reflect a coalition of parties in a fractionalized system (as many new democracies are), and the president's power to disband the legislature and call new elections allows a degree of flexibility not found in pure presidential systems. While Linz initially argued that semipresidentialism is most similar to presidentialism, later research has not found the problems Linz identified (Schleiter and Morgan-Jones 2009). While the specific powers of the president in different semipresidential systems are important (powers that override the legislature should be avoided), overall the empirical research does not suggest that these systems as a whole are any less stable than parliamentary systems, even under cohabitation. Empirical research also suggests that voters in semipresidential systems are quite capable of assigning responsibility for policies to particular officials, in spite of the dual executive, making accountability clear. Finally, research also shows that semipresidential systems seem just as capable at making policy decisions as other systems, though again, this outcome depends on the specific powers of the president.

Executive-legislative institutions are at the heart of the biggest debates over how well democracies represent and govern their citizens. The effects of different institutional arrangements often appear reasonably clear in the abstract, but in practice the social, cultural, and political contexts, as well as details of how an individual system operates, make analysis much more complex. This complexity means that debates over democracies' varying effectiveness will continue to be a major subject of research in comparative politics for some time to come.

JUDICIARY

The judiciary is the least studied branch of government in comparative politics, which is unfortunate since it is becoming more important in many countries. On a daily basis, the job of the judiciary is to enforce a state's laws. Its more important political role, however, is to interpret those laws, especially the constitution. Most democracies have some version of **judicial review**, the right of the judiciary to decide whether a specific law contradicts a country's constitution. This authority, vested in unelected judges, makes the court that holds it a veto player in the political system. It is clearly a potential means to limit majority rule and achieve horizontal accountability, but it also raises a fundamental question: Why should unelected officials have such power? How much power they actually have, though, depends not just on formal rules but on the strength of the judiciary as an institution. New democracies have often had to build new judicial institutions, and the weakness of these has become a major concern in comparative politics. In this section, we discuss judicial review and its relationship to democracy, the judicialization of politics, and the question of judicial independence and institutional strength.

Judicial Review and the "Judicialization" of Politics

Two legal systems, common law and code law, emerged in modern Europe and spread to most of the world via colonialism (see Map 6.2). **Common law** developed in the United Kingdom and was adopted in most former British colonies, including the United States (it is sometimes referred to as Anglo-American law). Under common law, judges base decisions not only on their understanding of the written law but also on their understanding of past court cases. When a judge finds a law ambiguous, he or she can write a ruling that tries to clarify it, and subsequent judges are obliged to use this ruling as precedent in deciding similar cases. This is known as the principle of *stare decisis*.

Code law is most closely associated with the French emperor Napoleon Bonaparte, who codified it in what became known as the Napoleonic Code. (It is also known as Continental, or civil, law.) Under code law, which has its origins in ancient Roman law and was spread in modern Europe via Napoleon's conquests, judges may only follow the law as written, interpreting it as little as necessary to fit the case. Past decisions are irrelevant, as each judge must look only to the existing law. Like common law, code law spread globally via colonialism, especially to former French, Spanish, and Portuguese colonies.

The two systems logically led to different kinds of judicial review. Common-law countries, such as the United States, usually have decentralized judicial review: the same courts that handle everyday criminal cases can also rule on constitutional issues and can do so at any level. If a constitutional question begins in a lower court, it can be appealed upward, ultimately to the highest court. Code-law countries

judicial review: The right of the judiciary to decide whether a specific law contradicts a country's constitution

common law: Legal system originating in Britain in which judges base decisions not only on their understanding of the written law but also on their understanding of past court cases; in contrast to code law

stare decisis: Literally, "let the decision stand"; in common law, the practice of accepting the precedent of previous similar cases

code law: Legal system originating in ancient Roman law and modified by Napoleon Bonaparte in France in which judges may only follow the law as written and must ignore past decisions; in contrast to common law

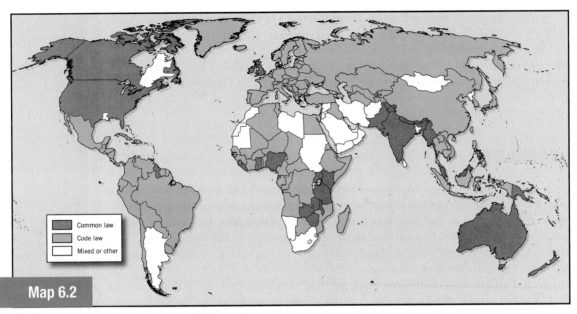

Map 6.2

Code- versus Common-Law Countries

usually have centralized judicial review: a special court handles constitutional questions. Another important distinction between these types of judicial review is the question of who can initiate cases. Most common-law systems, including that of the United States, have concrete judicial review: only someone who has actually been negatively affected by the law in question can initiate a case. Most code-law systems have abstract judicial review; certain public officials or major political groups can call on the courts to make a constitutional ruling even before the law is fully in effect. The length of appointments to whatever court handles judicial review is also important. Some countries have lifetime appointments; others limit judges' terms.

The fundamental question about judicial review in a democracy is why judges, who are typically not elected and therefore not subject to vertical accountability, should be allowed to make decisions with major political consequences. Proponents argue that the difference in democratic legitimacy between judges and elected officials is one of degree, not kind, and it may well be far less sharply defined than often assumed. First, legislatures and executives are never perfectly representative or accountable, so the difference between them and the judiciary may be less than it first appears. Second, the judiciary's horizontal accountability to executives and legislatures can be seen as an indirect source of democratic accountability. Judges are typically appointed by elected officials, so their stands on issues reflect the ideas of those officials and, consequently, the ideas of the majority of the populace who put those officials into office. Robert Dahl, one of the foremost scholars of democracy, argued in a widely read 1957 article that U.S. Supreme Court justices are part of political coalitions just as elected officials are and that they reflect the same political divisions that divide elected officials. The greater the consensus among elected officials, the greater the likelihood that appointed courts will come to reflect that, both in their composition and their decisions. This means that they are less likely to act as veto players in the policy-making process. Advocates of judicial review also argue that even if the judiciary is an imperfect democratic institution, it plays several crucial roles. It provides a check on executive and legislative power, and it is itself a mechanism of horizontal accountability.

Taylor (2008), however, argued that the judiciary can also serve as a veto point, rather than veto player. For instance, while courts themselves may not act directly as veto players in the policy-making process, other political actors can use the judicial system to conduct their policy battles, making the judicial venue a veto point.

In the United States, many argue as well that judicial review exists to protect minority rights that might be trampled by a legislature or executive acting on majority opinion. In practice, however, most studies have shown that courts are more likely to rule in favor of those in power than on behalf of marginalized or oppressed minorities. And Stuart Chinn (2006) has argued that under some circumstances, the judiciary can support *majority* beliefs that might otherwise go unheard. Chinn contends that in a two-party system, parties shy away from issues that provoke strong minority reactions, even if the majority moderately favors action on the issue. For instance, suppose that most citizens favor abortion rights but don't feel strongly about them, while a more vocal minority strongly opposes abortion. Neither political party will gain an electoral advantage by acting on abortion rights, because it won't be a decisive vote getter among the majority but it will strongly antagonize the minority. In a case in which neither party acts on an issue, a court's ruling may do what the executive and legislative branches will not.

However one answers the questions raised by judicial review, it is certainly becoming more widespread, a process that Tate and Vallinder called the "judicialization" of politics. They argued that judicialization is "one of the most significant trends in late-twentieth and early-twenty-first-century government" (1995, 5). There are exceptions: the United Kingdom is one of the few democracies in the world that has no system of judicial review; and Japan has judicial review, but the highest court rarely had the temerity to rule against the long-dominant ruling party that appointed all of the judges. When large numbers of authoritarian governments adopted new constitutions in their move toward democracy in the 1980s and 1990s, these constitutions included some type of judicial review, although the strength and importance of these systems vary just as they do in older democracies.

Judicial Independence and Institutional Strength

Under any legal system, new or old, the judiciary must constitute a strong institution if it is to carry out its function properly in a system of horizontal accountability. Judicial review only matters in practice to the extent the key courts are willing and able to act independently of the other branches of government. This requires **judicial independence**, the belief and ability of judges to decide cases as they think appropriate, regardless of what other people, and especially politically powerful officials or institutions, desire. Judicial systems that lack independence are weak institutions in which corruption is common; judges may accept bribes to decide cases in a particular way or refuse to rule against powerful individuals. This can affect everyday criminal and civil cases as well as constitutional questions. No particular formal procedure or power guarantees judicial independence, though Ferejohn and Pasquino (2003) found that the distinct constitutional courts common in code-law countries are particularly independent and effective.

What undoubtedly matters most to judicial independence, though, is informal factors that help make formal independence real in practice. Any number of factors can influence how much courts can actually practice the official powers granted them. Ferejohn, Rosenbluth, and Shipan (2007) argued that political fragmentation is key: countries with more fragmented political systems provide more political space for the judiciary to act independently. For instance, a presidential system's

judicial independence: The belief and ability of judges to decide cases as they think appropriate, regardless of what other people, and especially politically powerful officials or institutions, desire

division of the executive and legislature raises the possibility of a divided government in which the judiciary may feel it can act more independently because the other branches disagree with one another. A parliamentary system with many parties that requires a coalition government can create a similar context for judicial independence. Judicial independence is less likely when greater consensus exists in government, as courts do not feel they have the power to counter a strong majority consensus among elected officials.

A study of post-Communist countries found that even where judicial review is well established in the constitution, high courts use it rarely and warily, in part because they lack legitimacy and therefore do not believe themselves to be strong enough to withstand pressure from more powerful officials. Given that the judiciary lacks both military and financial resources, legitimacy is crucial to its institutional strength; without widespread support and acceptance on the part of other officials and the general populace, the judiciary has little power. James Gibson, Gregory Caldeira, and Vanessa Baird (1998) found that judiciaries typically gain legitimacy only over time as the populace comes to understand their role more fully and is satisfied with key court decisions. As we will see in the case study of Germany and Brazil and in chapter 9, the institutional strength of the judiciary in new democracies, and therefore judicial independence, is often a problem.

CASE STUDY

The Judiciary: Germany and Brazil

- Code law: Special constitutional courts and abstract judicial review
- Growing judicialization
- Judicial system as veto point
- Different levels of judicial institutionalization and legitimacy

Germany and Brazil illustrate the role of judicial review, the judicialization of politics, and the problem of judicial independence in even well-established democracies. Both countries use code law and therefore have multiple court systems in addition to a specialized constitutional court. Germany's court system has three branches. The Special Constitutional Court, called simply the Constitutional Court, is the country's highest court and handles constitutional issues exclusively. The Federal High Court is the final court of appeal for all criminal and civil cases. The administrative court system includes labor, social security, and finance courts that deal exclusively with these areas of law. Because Germany has a federal system,

the separate states (*Lander*) have their own courts as well.

The Constitutional Court is the main court of political interest and is widely considered one of the most powerful courts in the world. The two houses of Germany's parliament together choose the sixteen members of the court, who serve single, twelve-year terms. The court is divided into two "senates," each of which hears particular kinds of cases. Both senates have the right of judicial review, but unlike courts in common-law countries, each senate can hear cases not only from individuals who think a law is unconstitutional (referred to as "constitutional complaints") but also from particular political institutions, which can seek a constitutional ruling before a law is implemented (called "abstract judicial review"). The federal government, one-third of the legislators in the lower house of parliament, or *Lander* governments can bring a law directly to the Constitutional Court for judicial review. If the court finds a law violates the constitution, it can declare that law invalid, send it back to

Germany's sixteen-member Constitutional Court is widely considered one of the most powerful in the world. The Court meets in Karlsruhe in southern Germany, a deliberate choice meant to emphasize its independence by keeping it separate from other national institutions based in the capital of Berlin. For greater efficiency, it is divided into "senates" like the one shown here, which hear cases separately.

Credit: Michael Latz/AFP/Getty Images

parliament (at the federal or *Land* level) for a particular revision to make it constitutional, or rule that it must be interpreted in a particular way to fit the constitution.

Most observers argue that Germany has seen a significant judicialization of its political process. Because both common citizens and key political groups can take a constitutional question directly to it, the Constitutional Court is overworked. Its caseload increased dramatically in the 1980s and 1990s, and the great majority of cases these days are constitutional complaints by individual citizens. While only about 2 percent of these cases have been successful, they represent an important constitutional right to German citizens. In contrast to the U.S. Supreme Court, the German Constitutional Court (and most courts in code-law countries, including Brazil) must consider all cases brought before it. As the number of cases has risen, the Court

has adjusted its procedures to cope. To that end, three-judge panels rule on most cases, and as long as each panel unanimously rules against a complainant (saying the individual's rights were not violated), the case does not have to go to the full Court.

Requests for abstract judicial review have been more successful and more politically important. Scholars have calculated that from 1951 to 1990, the Constitutional Court dealt with about 40 percent of all "key decisions" in parliament and invalidated about 5 percent of all federal laws (Landfried 1995, 113). This process is at the heart of the judicialization of German politics. Taking a question to the Court has become a fairly regular move of last resort for opposition politicians; about two-thirds of all cases of abstract judicial review have been brought to the court by either the opposition in the federal parliament at the time or a *Land* government controlled by an opposition party. In a parliamentary system with strong party discipline like Germany's, opposition parties rarely win legislative fights, so they instead try to use the strong provisions for abstract judicial review as an alternative means of policymaking. Inclusion of the Court has become so common that the majority party now uses it as well, asking the Court to rule on laws that the party would like to pass but that are politically unpopular. If the law is written the right way, the majority party can get the Court to rule a particular way, and then the party can blame the Court for the unpopular decision that the party in fact wanted.

Germany unquestionably has one of the world's strongest states with strong institutions. Even in this context, though, the question of judicial independence arises. The Constitutional Court long had one of the highest approval ratings of any political institution in the country; however, after a couple of controversial decisions in the mid-1990s involving reunification with East Germany and abortion, public approval dropped precipitously. A recent study by Georg Vanberg (2005) argued that in spite of Germany's strong institutions, the Court itself thinks strategically in making its decisions. Vanberg argued that to enhance its institutional strength, the German high court wants to ensure its decisions are obeyed. Using rational actor analysis, he concluded that since Parliament is unlikely to defy or reverse a court ruling through new legislation if public opinion strongly supports the Court's decision, the court is more likely to overrule other branches of government when the judges believe public opinion is on their side. Even in Germany, with one of the strongest constitutional courts in the world, the judiciary's institutional strength and therefore independence depends in part on its popular legitimacy. Vanberg argued, therefore, that judicial review fits within the broad norms of democracy: the Court actually follows popular opinion more often than not, even though its members are not elected.

Brazil's relatively young democracy does not have one of the world's strongest judicial systems, but the judiciary has nonetheless achieved what many courts have not: a degree of judicial independence that has curbed executive and legislative power. Independence, however, has not necessarily brought legitimacy or effectiveness, and many observers argue that it has harmed policymaking while encouraging growing judicialization of the political process.

Judicial independence, judicial review in a code-law system, and moderate institutionalization have combined to produce Brazil's unusual situation. Judicial independence was enshrined in Brazil's 1988 constitution, which outlined in detail a complex judicial system with constitutional protection for its autonomy in most personnel, budgetary, administrative, and disciplinary areas. The system is headed by the Supreme Federal Tribunal (STF), the equivalent of the U.S. Supreme Court, which hears constitutional cases. Under the STF is the Supreme Justice Tribunal, the court of final appeal for nonconstitutional cases. Judges to these highest courts are appointed by the president with approval of the Senate (the upper house of the legislature).

Judges in the two levels of federal courts below these are appointed by the judiciary itself based on criteria of merit. Most serve life terms up to seventy years of age. As is typical in code-law countries, in addition to these constitutional and criminal courts, separate codes (and courts) exist for labor disputes, military issues, and elections. This system is replicated in large part within each state of Brazil's federal system, resulting in a total of approximately 16,900 judges in hundreds of separate courts.

Initially, Brazil's top judges seemed hesitant to use their independence vis-à-vis the president; for example, they permitted Fernando Collor to rule via the dubious use of emergency decrees. By 1992, though, the STF had gained confidence, and its rulings helped lead to Collor's impeachment on corruption charges, a watershed event in the four-year-old democracy. The top courts have since ruled against a number of major political leaders on both constitutional questions and corruption charges, including during a massive corruption scandal involving several close aides of President Lula da

Silva. Oliveira (2005) found that STF justices decided cases most frequently based on values of professionalism and expansion of the court's role vis-à-vis the other branches of the government; they were rarely submissive to political demands from elected leaders. This independence enhances horizontal accountability vis-à-vis the executive, but it has also left few restraints on the judiciary. Carlos Santiso (2003) argued that while Brazil's judiciary serves an important function in horizontal accountability, its own lack of vertical accountability has become a major problem. Virtually all observers view the judiciary as slow, inefficient, and corrupt. Scandals involving judges have sometimes gone unpunished, many courts have a backlog of cases stretching out for years, and Brazilian judges are some of the most highly paid in the world. All of this has meant that "public contempt for the judiciary has reached unprecedented levels" (177).

Part of the problem with the huge number of cases is the system of code law and judicial review established in the constitution. Constitutional cases can come to the STF either on appeal from lower courts or directly from key political actors, including most government agencies, national business or labor organizations, state governments, and political parties. Without *stare decisis*, lower courts ignore precedent and higher court rulings; therefore, cases that would be resolved according to principle in a common-law country still require trial in Brazil. The STF processes as many as 100,000 cases per year, probably the highest number in the world. It even has a drive-up window for lawyers to file cases! Political leaders and groups have taken advantage of this situation by increasingly judicializing Brazilian political issues. If they cannot win in a state legislature or at the federal level, they take a case to court, making a constitutional argument if possible. They can start at a lower court and work their way up the system, or they can go directly to the STF, which gives them the right to "jump the queue." Cases on appeal from lower courts must then wait. Just initiating a case can often bring significant publicity to a group's pet cause. Taylor (2008) found this tactic to be particularly common in policy areas in which there are concentrated costs to particular groups; they are very likely to make a constitutional challenge to try to protect themselves, even after losing the legislative battle. Brazil's independent judiciary has at times ruled in their favor and against major policy reforms, creating a powerful veto point in Brazil's already fragmented system.

Judicial independence has also made it difficult to clean up corruption or reform the parts of the system that almost everyone agrees aren't working. Brazil has long been one of the most unequal societies in the world, and Brazilians widely believe that all branches of the government favor the wealthy over the poor. Stories abound of wealthy people bribing judges to ensure court decisions go their way. Aside from outright corruption, the courts are widely seen as partial and subjective: the poor are more likely to be brought to court, more likely to be convicted, and more likely to be sentenced to long terms in Brazil's overcrowded and often violent prisons. So while Brazil's top court has become an important player in the national policy-making process, and a venue for other actors to pursue their policy goals, the judiciary as a whole remains only moderately institutionalized, and its continuing problems seem likely to limit its legitimacy.

Judicial leaders have successfully fought against reforms of this system since its creation in the 1988 constitution. In December 2004, to reduce the number of cases in the courts, the legislature passed some minimal reforms that legalize *stare decisis* for STF decisions if two-thirds of the judges vote to make a particular ruling binding on other courts. The legislature also created a National Judicial Council composed of both top judges and nominees outside the judiciary to oversee the budget and administration of the courts. While this reform is still in its early stages of implementation, it represents a clear effort to bring some horizontal accountability to bear to resolve the worst problems created by judicial independence without accountability and institutionalization.

CASE SUMMARY

The German and Brazilian cases demonstrate how similar formal institutions can function quite differently in different settings. Code law and abstract judicial review put tremendous strain on the court systems in both countries, particularly at the top, and encourage the judicialization of politics. The stronger overall institutional setting of Germany seems to be able to offset some of the problems Brazil faces. Some would argue that the German Constitutional Court is too involved in politics, but none question its integrity. Judicial independence has been an important achievement in Brazil's relatively young democracy and has helped the country start to resolve the corruption found throughout the state, but it has not helped eliminate corruption within the judiciary itself. In both countries, the top court has at times acted as a veto player, providing a strong element of horizontal accountability. The judicialization of politics occurs in both, though, as the court serves as a veto point where other actors—typically government bureaucracies or opposition parties—can limit or reverse policy decisions that had majority legislative support. This raises the classic question of whether too many and too strong "checks and balances" (horizontal accountability) excessively limit governments' ability to govern. An additional arena in which this question emerges is the modern bureaucracy, to which we now turn.

BUREAUCRACY

Chapter 2 identified a bureaucracy as one of the key characteristics of a modern state. All states have an executive branch that includes a bureaucracy of some sort. The ideal modern bureaucracy, as originally envisioned by one of the founders of modern social science, Max Weber, would consist of officials appointed on the basis of merit and expertise who would implement policies lawfully, treat all citizens equally according to the relevant laws, and be held accountable by the elected head of the executive branch. This ideal is an important component in the full development of an effective modern state; as we noted in chapter 2, a state (whatever type of regime it has) will have greater capacity to rule its territory and people if it has an effective bureaucracy. A bureaucracy in this modern sense is also a key component of liberal democracy, as it recruits officials according to merit and administers policies according to law, treats citizens equally, and insulates bureaucratic officials from the personal and political desires of top leaders. On the other hand, bureaucracy can be a threat to democracy, so bureaucrats themselves must be held accountable. Who will prevent them from abusing their independence and autonomy? Because they are not elected, vertical accountability does not exist, meaning that horizontal accountability is very important.

Bureaucracy can limit the executive in a number of ways even as it enhances a state's capacity. Prior to modern reforms, state positions in most societies were based on political patronage: leaders appointed all officials to suit the leaders' interests. (China was a major exception—Confucian ideas of merit in that country go back millennia.) Professionalization involved recruitment based on merit and a reduction of political patronage. It also came to mean that bureaucratic officials held technical expertise, on which political leaders often have to rely to make decisions in an increasingly complex world. Knowledge and expertise are key sources of bureaucrats' independent power. Modern bureaucracies developed into formal, hierarchical organizations in which career advancement, at least ideally, was based on performance and personal capability rather than on political connections.

Bureaucratic professionalization keeps the bureaucracy at least partially insulated from the whims of political leaders, but it raises the question of how the political leadership will hold the bureaucracy accountable. This fundamental problem can be understood as a **principal-agent problem**. The principal (the elected or appointed political leadership in the executive or legislative branches) assigns an agent (the bureaucrat) a task to carry out as the principal instructs; the problem is how the principal makes sure the agent carries out the task as assigned. Bureaucratic agents might well have strong incentives to deviate from their assigned tasks. Rational-choice theorists argue that bureaucrats, however professional, are as self-interested and rational as any other actors. Bureaucrats' preferences are usually to expand their sphere of influence and the size of their organization to enhance their own prestige and salary. This can expand the size of the bureaucracy, create inefficiencies, and distort the principals' purposes. Self-interest can also lead to corruption, if bureaucrats exchange favorable treatment of political leaders or ordinary citizens for favors.

Numerous solutions to this problem have emerged over the years. In every state the political leadership of the executive branch selects a certain number of **political appointees** to head the bureaucracy. These appointees serve at the pleasure of the president or prime minister and, among other things, are assigned the task of overseeing their respective segments of the bureaucracy. Different countries allow different numbers of political appointees: the United States typically allows six or eight for each significant department in the federal government, whereas two is more typical for each ministry in the United Kingdom. (The United States uses the term *department* to designate the major agencies of the government, whereas most of the world uses *ministry* to mean the same thing, harkening back to the religious influence on the early modern state.)

Political appointees' power over professional bureaucrats is limited by the legal means through which the latter are hired and paid and earn career advancement; bureaucrats, however, must answer to political appointees within those legal limits. In democracies, legislators can write laws that are as specific as possible to limit bureaucrats' discretion. Whether they choose to do so, though, depends on a number of factors, including whether they have the ability to write detailed legislation in that particular policy area and whether they trust current and future bureaucrats to implement the policy as the legislators' intend. **Legislative oversight** is another key means of horizontal accountability; members of the legislature, usually in key committees, oversee the working of the bureaucracy by interviewing key leaders, examining budgets, and assessing how successfully a particular agency has carried out its mandate. Often, citizens use the judicial system to try to achieve accountability by taking individual officials or entire agencies to court, arguing that they have either failed to carry out their duties or have done so unlawfully.

None of these efforts to influence the bureaucracy work perfectly, in large part because principals never know exactly what their agents within a bureaucracy are doing, especially as technocratic knowledge becomes more and more important. For most of the twentieth century, governments relied heavily on professional socialization to maintain standards. They recruited people who had been trained to abide by key professional norms of neutrality and legality, and they believed they could count on most of these recruits to behave in the general "public" interest in alignment with their training. Some states, such as France

principal-agent problem: A problem in which a principal hires an agent to perform a task but the agent's self-interest does not necessarily align with the principal's, so the agent may not carry out the task as assigned

political appointees: Officials who serve at the pleasure of the president or prime minister and, among other things, are assigned the task of overseeing their respective segments of the bureaucracy

legislative oversight: Members of the legislature, usually in key committees, oversee the working of the bureaucracy

METHODS IN CONTEXT
When Do Politicians Constrain Bureaucrats, and When Do They Not?

In theory, democracies ought to control independent bureaucracies enough to ensure that they accurately and fairly implement the policies that elected officials pass into law. Political scientists have long noted, however, that sometimes legislators pass laws that give bureaucrats great discretion and other times they pass much more specific laws that limit that discretion. Given the apparent importance of controlling bureaucracy in a modern democracy, when and why do politicians try to do something about it, and when do they seem to ignore it?

Comparativists studied this question in parliamentary systems, mostly in Europe, and in the U.S. presidential system, but no studies lent themselves to the development of broad theories that could be applied to legislation in any democratic political system. Comparativists John Huber and Charles Shipan (2002) argued that the parliamentary case studies have been unable to generate testable hypotheses about which approaches really work best and fail to adequately address the question of whether politicians try to write more precise legislation to limit bureaucratic discretion. On the other hand, because the U.S. studies focus entirely on the U.S. system, they have been unable to aid in the development of general theories that can be applied in different political systems. For instance, battles between Congress and the executive, especially when controlled by different parties, are important in determining the level of detail Congress writes into laws. (When the two branches are divided, Congress writes more detailed laws, presumably not trusting implementation under a president of the opposite party.) In parliamentary systems, however, the executive and legislative branches are fused, making this finding irrelevant.

HYPOTHESIS

Huber and Shipan (2002) set out to develop a theory that could explain, in any democratic political system with a well-developed modern bureaucracy, when politicians will try to write legislation that limits bureaucratic discretion and when they will give bureaucrats more room to interpret the law. Using rational-choice theory, Huber and Shipan developed a set of hypotheses based on individual rational action. As do all rational-choice theorists, they make several assumptions from which they trace the logic of politicians' and bureaucrats' behavior. These assumptions include the following: both politicians and bureaucrats have policy preferences, and they often disagree; bureaucrats are more knowledgeable about the policy area and likely outcomes of legislation than are the politicians; legislators vary in their ability to write detailed laws that constrain bureaucrats; writing detailed laws is costly in time and resources; and in most systems some other means of influencing policy outcomes besides the legislature exist, such as the court system where various actors can seek remedies to bad implementation. Huber and Shipan developed several hypotheses from those assumptions: (1) the greater the policy conflict between politicians and bureaucrats (the more their preferences differ), the more detailed the laws will be; (2) the more legislative capacity the politicians have, the more detailed the laws will be; (3) the more politicians can rely on nonlegislative means (such as courts) to achieve their policy objectives, the less detailed the laws will be; and (4) in presidential systems, the more conflict between the two legislative houses, the less detailed the laws will be.

RESEARCH AND ANALYSIS

Huber and Shipan (2002) tested these hypotheses by gathering data for all relevant variables and applying the statistical technique of regression analysis, which allows the estimation of the simultaneous effects of all independent variables on the dependent variable (detailed laws). They did this separately for parliamentary systems around the world and for U.S. states. Since the

United States is the only national presidential system among the well-developed and long-established democracies studied, the inclusion of U.S. states provided comparative data on many presidential systems (fifty for comparison). In both the parliamentary and presidential analyses, Huber and Shipan examined just one kind of policy (Medicaid in the U.S. states) to control for the fact that some kinds of policy lend themselves to more detailed laws than others.

A key problem with any statistical analysis is determining how to measure the variables in question. The dependent variable in this case was how much discretion the laws give bureaucrats; that is, how detailed the laws are. How can thousands of laws in a couple dozen countries and fifty states be read and objectively compared on this measure? Huber and Shipan's answer: Simply measure the length (number of words) of the laws—longer laws presumably are more detailed than shorter ones. For the independent variables, similar problems existed. To measure policy conflict, they needed to know the preferences of both politicians and bureaucrats. While politicians have publicly stated preferences, bureaucrats typically do not. Other research, however, showed that bureaucrats rarely go against the wishes of the executives directly above them in the cabinet, so Huber and Shipan used partisan differences as a proxy measurement for policy conflict: for the U.S. presidential system, they used divided government—the legislature and governorship controlled by different parties; for parliamentary systems, they used the presence of coalition governments on the assumption that parties in the coalition but not in the party of the PM will disagree more on policy.

Measuring legislative capacity has similar problems: How can one measure legislators' ability to write detailed laws? In the United States, Huber and Shipan used legislators' pay as a proxy for capacity (in many U.S. states, legislators are only paid to be part-time, so the researchers assumed that higher pay rates meant legislators were closer to legislating full-time and that more capable people were attracted to the legislature). In parliamentary systems, given that the key decisions are made in the cabinet and not the parliament itself, the researchers used the turnover rate of cabinet members; Huber and Shipan's assumption was that the longer cabinet members are in place, the more knowledgeable they are about their policy area. After Huber and Shipan carefully defined all of their measurements, their statistical results strongly confirmed most of their hypotheses: politicians weigh the costs of writing more detailed legislation against the benefits, considering how likely those in control of the executive branch are to disagree with them, how far apart they are in terms of policy preferences, etc. The researchers' findings apply to both parliamentary and presidential systems: policy conflict, legislative capacity, and the presence of nonlegislative means to affect policy (as these variables were measured) influence the length of laws in the predicted directions. The implications of this study are that the context of the broader political system and institutions (rather than the internal strength of the bureaucracy itself, as is often asserted) profoundly affects how much discretion bureaucrats have to influence policy outcomes.

QUESTIONS IN CONTEXT

Huber and Shipan's results are impressive, but they rest heavily on the assumptions the researchers made about the behavior and preferences of both politicians and bureaucrats. The validity of the findings also depends on how well their variable-measurement techniques accurately reflect the underlying concepts being tested. Look back at both the assumptions and measurements in this study: Are they convincing? Can you think of ways in which they might not be accurate, thereby raising questions about the research results?

and Japan, went so far as to recruit almost exclusively from one high-profile educational institution so that government bureaucrats garnered great prestige and professional status.

Rational-choice theorists, however, argued that training could not overcome the inherent incentives in the bureaucracy and self-interest. Following this line of argument, the **New Public Management (NPM)** movement arose. The movement first emerged in the United States and United Kingdom in the 1980s and was associated with President Ronald Reagan and Prime Minister Margaret Thatcher. NPM advocates contended that inherent inefficiencies meant that the public bureaucracy required radical reforms to make it operate more like a market-based organization. Reforms included privatizing many government services so that they would be provided by the market, creating competition among agencies and subagencies within the bureaucracy to simulate a market, focusing on customer satisfaction (via client surveys, among other things), and flattening administrative hierarchies to encourage more team-based activity and creativity. The ideas of NPM became widely popular and were implemented in many wealthy democracies, though to varying degrees. Some countries, such as the United Kingdom and New Zealand, cut the size of their bureaucracies extensively via NPM, while others, including Germany and Japan, implemented it slowly and partially. In those countries that adopted it more extensively, NPM reduced the size of government significantly, though debate continues as to whether it improved bureaucratic performance in general; in other countries, its effect was far less despite much discussion of the new approach.

Critics have argued that NPM focuses too much on citizens as clients or consumers of services rather than as citizens. Put another way, NPM defines the public interest as the aggregation of individual interests rather than a common set of values arrived at through democratic dialogue and processes. Critics call for NPM to be replaced with what they term a **New Public Service (NPS),** which would focus on serving the public, which would be organized in networks of groups interested in a particular policy area. They do not want to return to the older notion of a purely hierarchical bureaucracy but also do not support the rational choice-based NPM and its emphasis on market-based solutions. Instead, NPS supporters believe bureaucracy can facilitate a more participatory and democratic process of determining regulations and service provision that fits local community needs (Denhardt and Denhardt 2001). While this concept has not been as influential as NPM, it was part of the "New Labour" approach to reform under PM Tony Blair (1997–2007) in the United Kingdom (Bevir 2010). The debate between supporters of NPM and NPS has taken place within the confines of states with well-institutionalized bureaucracies; where bureaucracies are less institutionalized, other and often more important debates arise.

Where the state and its institutions are generally weak, reform requires not only making the bureaucracy more efficient but also strengthening it as an institution. When bureaucratic rules and norms are extremely weak, corruption and massive inefficiency are likely (O'Dwyer 2006). Political elites may be able to use a weak bureaucracy to pursue personal or financial interests of their own, citizens may be able to gain favors from the state via bribery, and bureaucrats themselves may steal from the state. Corruption exists in all societies (see Map 6.3) and infects all bureaucracies, but the extent and type vary from state to state and regime to regime. O'Dwyer's (2006) study of new democracies in Eastern Europe found that where political party competition is strong but institutions are weak,

New Public Management (NPM): Theory of reform of bureaucracies that argues for the privatizing of many government services, creating competition among agencies to simulate a market, focusing on customer satisfaction, and flattening administrative hierarchies

New Public Service (NPS): Theory of reform of bureaucracies that argues for a more participatory and democratic process of determining regulations and service provision that fits local community needs; it relies on bureaucracy interacting with networks of citizens interested in a particular policy area

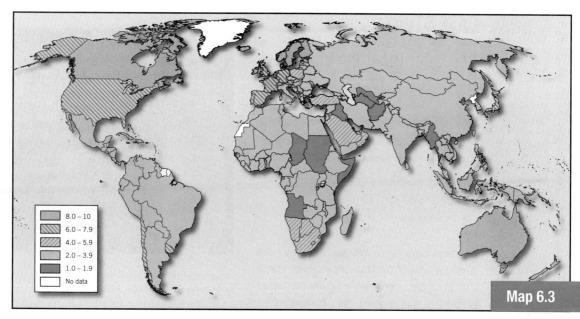

Map 6.3

Annual Corruption Scores, 2010

Countries' 2010 scores on the Corruption Perceptions Index, in which 10 equals the least corruption and 1 the most. The Index is constructed by surveying business leaders and others who work in each country, asking them how much corruption they perceive. In the most corrupt countries, bureaucratic rules are rarely followed, producing less equality under law and less efficiency in government.

Source: Transparency International Corruption Perceptions Index Scores, 2010, http://www.transparency.org/policy_research/surveys_indices/cpi/.

parties use patronage to compete. In these cases, parties create "runaway states" in which the size of the bureaucracy expands rapidly but the state's capacity does not improve.

Bribery and rent seeking are two other primary types of corruption in bureaucracies. In the least institutionalized bureaucracies, citizens often have to bribe officials to get them to carry out the functions they are mandated to do. The principals—the political leadership—may not be interested in encouraging the bureaucracy to function effectively because they benefit from their own ability to purchase favors from bureaucrats. Alternatively, they may simply have lost all ability to control their agents in the bureaucracy, often because of very low bureaucratic salaries. To supplement low salaries, officials seek bribes before they will carry out the most menial functions, such as issuing a driver's license, providing basic medicine, or building a school. **Rent seeking** is the gaining of an advantage in a market without engaging in equally productive activity; it usually involves using government regulations to one's own benefit. In weakly institutionalized bureaucracies, for example, businesses may be able to bribe officials to grant them exclusive monopolies over certain sectors of the economy or exclusive rights to import certain items, thereby reaping huge profits for little effort. The case studies of Japan and India demonstrate both the power and limits of bureaucracy and the complex issues that arise when bureaucracy weakens.

rent seeking: Gaining an advantage in a market without engaging in equally productive activity; usually involves using government regulations for one's own benefit

CASE STUDY

Bureaucratic Control and Corruption: Japan and India

- Historical legacies of strong bureaucracies
- Key bureaucratic role in major economic policies: the developmental state and ISI
- Corruption via increasing political influence in democratic setting
- Frustrated reform efforts

Japanese Prime Minister Naoto Kan speaks at a news conference in Tokyo on January 4, 2011. His party, which swept the long-ruling party out of power in 2009, promised to reform Japan's powerful and corrupt bureaucracy. Early in his government, though, following through with significant reform remained difficult.

Credit: Kim Kyung-Hoon/Reuters/Landov

All states have bureaucracies, but they have played a greater political role in some states than in others. Japan and India are two cases justifiably well known for bureaucracies that played pivotal roles in their early economic and political development. They both emerged from World War II with unusually strong bureaucratic organizations: Japan's was almost the sole surviving institution from its prewar government, and India's developed out of British colonial rule. Both countries' bureaucracies were intimately involved in setting economic policy, in particular from the 1950s to the 1970s. Unfortunately, they have both also been weakened by corruption over the last twenty years that arguably has had a negative impact on economic well-being and the legitimacy of the countries' democratic governments more broadly.

The sweeping victory of the Democratic Party of Japan (DPJ) in 2009 (see chapter 7 for details) over the long-ruling Liberal Democratic Party (LDP) was the most important electoral outcome in Japan since World War II. One of the DPJ's major campaign promises was to reform the entrenched bureaucracy, seen by many Japanese as a source of unaccountable power that was preventing necessary political and economic reforms. The Japanese economy boomed for four decades after the war, thanks in part to Japan's long-standing tradition of a highly professionalized, elite bureaucracy that worked with business and elected leaders to create the famed "developmental state" (see chapter 5). Fears that the bureaucracy was becoming too powerful and a source of too much corruption, though, were realized when the political system was shaken by revelations of the "Recruit scandal" in 1988. Numerous scandals involving both bureaucrats and politicians have occurred since, but the power of the bureaucracy has been trimmed only partially.

The Japanese bureaucracy was the only major political institution to survive the post–World War II U.S. occupation largely intact. This gave it a tremendous advantage vis-à-vis other institutions in the new democracy. As in France, Japan's top bureaucrats are recruited primarily from one place: the Faculty of Law at the University of Tokyo. From the 1950s through the 1970s, the unwritten rule was that the top graduates of that school would enter the elite corps of the bureaucracy to begin their ascent to the top. The fifteen ministries were very hierarchically organized and insulated from external pressure. As a "class" moved up the bureaucratic ladder, those passed over for promotion would take early retirement. By the time the group reached the top rung, one of their number would be appointed to a top post, and the rest would retire to leave him as the sole senior manager.

Early retirement and limited political oversight were facilitated by the common practice of **amakudari**, or the "descent from heaven," and rigid **iron triangles** among business, politicians, and key bureaucrats. Under *amakudari*, retiring civil servants gained lucrative positions in the businesses they previously regulated. Among other things, this gave bureaucrats an incentive to maintain favorable conditions for and relations with key corporations in their regulatory area. The term *iron triangle* was coined in reference to the United States, but the phenomenon is even stronger in Japan. Key bureaucrats, business leaders, and politicians cooperate to set policy to their mutual interest. In a classic example of the type of corruption Michael Johnston (2005) termed the "influence market," businesses give generous contributions to top politicians; in exchange, the politicians secure favorable treatment from key bureaucrats; and bureaucrats grant the favors because they will eventually be working in the businesses themselves.

The power of Japan's bureaucracy was unusual for a democracy: it controlled the key information and expertise needed to guide the growing economy and was a source of highly prestigious employment. The prime minister only made two or three political appointments in each ministry, for a total of fewer than fifty appointments (as compared to several hundred that a U.S. president makes), giving him little executive oversight. Combined with little legislative oversight due to the iron triangles, the bureaucracy was left with great power vis-à-vis the other branches in Japan's democracy. At the height of its power, most major legislative initiatives began not with the prime minister or the legislature but rather in the relevant bureaucracy. Interestingly, this power did not result in the further growth of the bureaucracy. Though it retained great regulatory powers in the economy, the number of officials as a percentage of all employment was and remains the lowest among wealthy democracies,

undoubtedly in part because of bureaucrats' ability to gain lucrative posts upon early retirement.

Admirers of the developmental state argued that this centralized and powerful bureaucracy played a positive role in Japan's economic success. Lack of oversight and the incentives of the iron triangle and *amakudari*, however, let corruption get out of control, provoking major scandals. Such scandals had long occurred in Japanese politics, but while most Japanese knew that corruption was fairly common, they thought it did not affect the top echelons. Major scandals in the 1980s and 1990s destroyed that belief and led to fundamental changes in the electoral system (see chapter 7). Combined with the economic stagnation of the 1990s, the scandals also diminished the prestige of the bureaucracy in general. At the height of the bureaucracy's power in the 1960s, forty-three top university graduates competed for each top bureaucratic position; by the 1990s only eleven did (Pempel 2000, 160). Business stagnation made *amakudari* more difficult, and the prestige of the bureaucracy plummeted.

Changes to Japan's bureaucratic system have long been proposed but have seldom succeeded. The 1993 electoral reforms, a direct response to the worst scandals, seem to have had limited effect on the role of money in the election process (see chapter 7). The ideas of NPM filtered in from the United States and United Kingdom but also had relatively little impact. Neither Japanese bureaucrats nor politicians had significant interest in reforming a system from which they all benefited, and given the small size of Japan's bureaucracy, some of NPM's analysis clearly did not fit the Japanese case. During the 1980s, Japan did privatize a few state-owned companies, including the railway system. A reformist prime minister, Junichiro Koizumi, entered office in 2001 with bold proposals for reform, but few became law (see chapter 5). Australian political scientist Aurelia Mulgan (2002) argued that the bureaucracy's continued power prevented acceptance of many of Koizumi's reforms, and some of the reforms he did pass were

amakudari: In Japan, the "descent from heaven," in which senior bureaucrats get positions in the industries they formerly regulated

iron triangle: Three-sided cooperative interaction among bureaucrats, legislators, and business leaders in a particular sector that serves the interest of all involved but keeps others out of the policy-making process

favored by particular sectors of the bureaucracy, especially the Ministry of Finance.

Longtime Japan analyst Karel van Wolferen (2010) argued that the DPJ government that came to power in 2009 has implemented by far the most serious reform effort so far. Its key leader wanted to fundamentally reduce the power of the bureaucracy vis-à-vis the PM and cabinet by building up the strength of elected offices and decentralizing government to the local level. Before and after winning the election in 2009, major DPJ leaders faced corruption charges, and some were forced from office. Van Wolferen suggested that the public prosecutor's office worked in tandem with sympathetic journalists to pursue scandal accusations against those who threatened the power of entrenched interests in the bureaucracy. Whether or not this analysis is accurate, the scandals severely weakened the new government. In mid-2010, the PM in office for less than a year was forced out. A new DPJ leader with a strong reformist reputation replaced him, but scandals and instability meant that the new government that came to power promising sweeping reforms accomplished little in its first year and saw its popularity plummet. It then faced the unprecedented crisis of the 2011 earthquake and tsunami, which understandably halted all other policy initiatives.

The relative power of the bureaucracy today remains much disputed. A number of scholars disagree with Mulgan (2002), arguing that the position of the bureaucracy has been significantly reduced as Japanese policymaking has become more pluralistic over the past decade. While van Wolferen (2010) still sees the old power system as well entrenched, political scientists Frances Rosenbluth and Michael Thies (2010) argue that fundamental changes are underway. Green (2010) argues as well that the DPJ's policies that centralize control over the budget in the PM's office are an important reform that will reduce the bureaucracy's power. The bureaucracy remains more powerful than in most wealthy democracies, but globalization and deregulation have reduced its control of the economy (see chapter 5). In addition, it has become more internally divided, allowing more voices within and without to have an effect on key questions in Japanese politics. Even if reforms do not work, this trend seems to point in the direction of at least somewhat greater accountability.

In the case of India, accountability is only one thing critics point to as needing improvement. The bureaucracy in any postcolonial developing state like India faces many demands. It not only implements state policies and helps mold economic growth, similar to the bureaucracy in the Japanese model, but also it is often assigned the task of furthering "development" and helping to end poverty. It is also asked to serve as a link between the highly educated, literate officials of the central state and the mostly poor, illiterate, rural populace. India's bureaucracy has certainly been assigned all of these roles at one time or another. Its evolution and current status is heavily influenced by the country's development efforts, from import-substitution industrialization (ISI) and central state planning in the 1950s–1970s to neoliberal reform since the 1990s. It expanded dramatically under ISI, taking on numerous developmental tasks, but since the 1990s it has been asked to reduce its role in line with neoliberal policies to do less but do it more efficiently. The combination of development policy and the pressures of political competition have produced corruption, which seems to be an endemic problem today. Indeed, although India has become a "hot" new economy, growing rapidly and emerging as a leader in a number of fields such as software development (see chapter 10), most business leaders note that one of the biggest problems facing expanded economic growth is an inefficient and corrupt bureaucracy.

As in all postcolonial states, India's bureaucracy developed first under colonial rule, in this case from the British-created Indian Civil Service (ICS). Initially staffed only by British colonial officials, the ICS was nearly half Indian by the time of Indian independence. The British called it the "steel frame" of their Indian colonial empire, and they saw it as the crucial link between themselves and the majority of the population. As in all colonies, the civil service not only implemented laws but also acted as the eyes and ears of the colonial state, keeping order over the often "restless natives." At independence, the ICS lost nearly half its staff when the British officers nearly all went home and most Muslim officers migrated to the newly formed Pakistan. It subsequently was renamed the Indian Administrative Service (IAS), and many of the nationalist leaders who had criticized the ICS as a key component of colonial oppression embraced the IAS as a crucial element of their new state.

The IAS kept virtually all of its colonial organization, recruitment, and training structures in place, with the obvious exception of the body now being composed only of Indians. It was designed to provide an elite cadre of bureaucratic officials who would link the elements of India's diverse federal system. Its members are recruited nationally from top universities through an extensive examination process, trained for their service for more than a year, and then assigned to a state. They typically spend their careers working in that state, though they are rotated to the central government in Delhi, the national capital, occasionally. In this way, a nationally recruited bureaucracy with knowledge of the central government works in and for the state governments, providing a bureaucratic bridge between the two levels of government that few federal systems have. The extensive recruitment and training were designed to produce a group of officials with a common understanding and professional norms who could integrate the country's administration. Below the elite IAS, India has more than twenty national civil service groups, and each state has its own as well; these add up to a huge bureaucracy that the IAS is supposed to integrate and to some extent coordinate.

India's bureaucracy has been profoundly influenced by the country's evolving development policies, which it is supposed to implement. The government of the first prime minister, Jawaharlal Nehru, pursued a version of ISI with unusually extensive state involvement. Central development planning was seen as essential, with the state creating specific targets for growth in various sectors and often initiating specific projects to achieve them. The bureaucracy was tasked with implementing all of these projects. As with most ISI efforts, Nehru's plan involved the creation of state-owned enterprises, often via nationalization of private entities such as major banks. The bureaucracy expanded accordingly: the public sector accounted for 10 percent of GDP in 1960 but 27 percent by 1987, where it has remained, more or less, ever since. Virtually all economic undertakings required some sort of government permit, available only from the bureaucracy. The system's critics came to refer to it as the "license raj." Beginning in 1991, this model began to shift toward the neoliberal economic development model. That model called for a reduced and more efficient bureaucracy, which freed business from unnecessary regulation and tried to strengthen the rule of law via an uncorrupt and competent administration. India's bureaucracy has certainly not fulfilled that role completely. While it has not expanded significantly since the late 1980s, it hasn't shrunk significantly either, and the level of corruption has changed little.

Corruption has long been a problem in India, and it got much worse over the years, at least until recently. From the colonial era on, most Indians would tell you that you often had to pay a small bribe to get something accomplished at a government office. That kind of petty corruption, however, was just that: small and limited. By the 1970s and 1980s, it had become much more serious and extensive. Several factors explain this transformation. First, the ISI and development planning model of the first three decades after independence put bureaucrats in key positions from which to demand bribes. As the state regulated more economic activity, more people had to get licenses for what they wanted to do. Each license and each form that required a stamp of approval held the potential for a bribe. Second, civil servants' wages declined over the years, giving them an incentive to look for other sources of income. The IAS, in particular, had been a service of great prestige, with some of the highest wages in the country, and it attracted the best university graduates who were trained to be professionals in their field and were well paid to uphold those standards. Then civil service wages at all levels were effectively frozen for thirty years, lowering their real purchasing power dramatically. By the 1980s, even the IAS was no longer a very high-prestige career; the most ambitious people pursued careers in the private sector, and those in the civil service increasingly took bribes to supplement their income.

The most important impetus to large-scale corruption, however, was politicization of the bureaucracy. As political competition increased in India's democracy, politicians at all levels wanted bureaucrats to grant favors to them and their constituents, and bureaucrats who refused often found themselves transferred to an unpleasant assignment in a remote village. This type of political pressure on the bureaucracy began in earnest under Prime Minister Indira Gandhi in the late 1960s and 1970s, and it continued and expanded under her son Rajiv in the 1980s. Increased party competition after the demise of the Congress Party's domination in 1989 (see chapter 7) only exacerbated the problem. As political leaders were increasingly able to have bureaucrats moved, the latter often had little choice but to yield to politicians' demands. The result, especially combined with declining bureaucratic wages, was an ever weaker civil service. Corruption exploded at the top of the political system in the late 1980s and 1990s and helped end two governments over allegations of involvement by the PM in large-scale bribery and kickback schemes. In 2010, a new and perhaps the largest scandal erupted over irregular granting of mobile phone licenses, resulting in the arrest of a cabinet minister, the suspicious death of his close aide, and paralysis in the government. These were only the most dramatic examples of a growing and continuing problem throughout the civil service and political system.

Influenced in part by NPM and aid donors' growing concern over corruption, India has pursued numerous civil service reform efforts over the years. These have included the creation of various government watchdog agencies, some decentralization efforts, and an attempt to strengthen elected local governments to take over some of the functions of the bureaucracy. None of these has been wholly successful. The bureaucracy, its critics contend, remains an overly hierarchical organization, is more concerned about procedures than outcome, and continues its long-standing participation in corruption. The number of public scandals over corruption has certainly increased over the years, publicized by an increasingly assertive media and provoking growing public concern. Increased scrutiny perhaps makes it more difficult for politicians and civil servants to do just as they please. These efforts are having some effect. In 1998, Transparency International, a global anticorruption nongovernmental agency, ranked India 66 out of 85 countries in terms of corruption with a score on its corruption perceptions index of 2.9 (with 10 being the best). By 2010, India was number 87 out of 178, a much higher ranking relative to others, with a score of 3.3. While the change is not dramatic, it does indicate progress.

Bureaucracy in poor and developing societies ought to fulfill all the roles that it does in any other state. However, it also is asked to take on the additional roles of ending poverty and linking the government elite to the poor populace. As the Indian case demonstrates, bureaucracies have been heavily influenced by the shifting models of development policy over the years. India is not unusual in seeing more corruption come from ISI and greater political competition: somewhat weak postcolonial bureaucratic institutions become much weaker in the face of strong incentives for corruption on the part of civil servants, political leaders, and ordinary citizens. The neoliberal model,

WHERE AND WHY

Explaining Corruption

Political corruption—the illegal use of political office for personal or political gain—is universal, but its extent varies widely from one society to another and over time. The United States in the nineteenth century was widely known for its corruption. Today, it remains more corrupt than many European countries but is far less corrupt than most of the rest of the world. What explains the differing levels of corruption across different eras and countries? Political scientists have used the full array of theories to try to explain this.

Many have looked at political culture, arguing that corruption is greater where societies lack shared values about the importance of the public sphere, instead placing personal, family, or kin interests above those of the society as a whole. Others have noted that greater corruption is found in postcolonial societies; they contend that the lack of legitimacy of a postcolonial state that has no firm roots in the society leads citizens to believe one should gain whatever one can from the public sphere. Nigerian sociologist Peter Ekeh (1975) argued that in Africa, two "publics" exist: a more "primordial public," which includes ethnic, religious, and community identities in which people feel reciprocal moral responsibility toward one another, and an amoral "civic public" involving the state, toward which people feel no obligation and therefore take from freely.

Michael Johnston, one of the foremost scholars of corruption, used a structural approach in his 2005 book, *Syndromes of Corruption: Wealth, Power, and Democracy*, to argue that the type and extent of corruption vary systematically with the type of state and regime. In wealthy, established democracies,

the primary type of corruption is what he terms "influence markets," in which corporations use access to politicians, usually via generous contributions to campaigns and parties, to gain preferential access to and treatment from key economic bureaucracies. In democracies in which the overall level of institutionalization is weaker, typically in middle-income countries, political competition is both more intense and the outcome less certain. In these countries, "elite cartels" emerge in which key political and business leaders form networks to gain control of the government and systematically use it to their joint political and financial benefit.

In middle-income countries that have recently become democracies, institutions are even weaker and political competition more intense, uncertain, and personal. Under these conditions, "oligarchs and clans" form whose members scramble for spoils in the system. This situation is likely to arise where a recent economic liberalization has occurred, such as in Russia, one of Johnston's primary examples. In the least institutionalized (and often poorest) states with personalized or neopatrimonial rule, corruption often takes the form of the "Official Mogul," a strongman who uses the resources of the state as he pleases to favor his political allies and punish his enemies.

The extent of the problem and the possible remedies for corruption vary, Johnston argued, across these four types of countries, though corruption is an important issue in all of them. Where it exists, even in modest proportions, it undermines the capacity of the state and the democratic ideal of equal citizenship, two areas in which the modern bureaucracy is crucial.

to the extent that it has reduced the role of the bureaucracy in the economy, is likely to improve the situation, as it has in India, but only very slowly; the wheels of bureaucracy, whichever way they spin, spin slowly.

CASE SUMMARY

As technocratic expertise becomes ever more important, major economic and social forces have pushed both wealthy and developing countries in the direction of enhanced bureaucratic autonomy and power. This process can give rise to corruption, especially in countries with a historical legacy of strong bureaucracy such as Japan and India. Reform efforts to create greater horizontal accountability have been difficult to put into effect, even though models like NPM and NPS have long been available to draw on. Even where formal controls exist, corruption is an ever-present threat. The dynamics of the principal-agent problem are exacerbated by corruption, as agents accept payments from outsiders and act against principals' instructions. Corruption, though, can also involve the principals (in the persons of elected officials) purchasing agents' loyalty, shifting bureaucrats from doing the bidding of the law as enacted by the legislature to doing the bidding of individual legislators instead. Where corruption becomes widespread, no amount of formal reform seems likely to work until corruption itself is tackled.

FEDERALISM

So far, we have only considered governmental institutions at the national level. In every country, of course, they exist at lower levels as well, though their role and autonomy vis-à-vis the national government vary widely. The most important distinction is between unitary and federal systems. In **unitary systems** the central government has sole constitutional sovereignty and power, whereas in **federal systems** the central government shares constitutional sovereignty and power with subunits, such as states, provinces, or regions. Local governments exist in unitary systems, but they derive their powers from the central government, which can alter them as it pleases. In federal systems, some subnational governments have constitutionally derived powers separate from the central government that can only be changed via change to the constitution itself, which generally is difficult to effect.

The first modern federal system was the Dutch Republic of the United Provinces in what is now the Netherlands, but the best-known early example is the United States. Both states originally were contiguous units within larger empires that declared independence and banded together. In the case of the United States, separate and sovereign states—the original thirteen British colonies—came together to form a federation only after a looser union, a confederation, failed to produce a viable central state. Political scientist William Riker (1964) provided a now classic rational-choice explanation of how American federalism emerged, arguing that it resulted from a bargain among self-interested leaders of separate states who were motivated primarily by military concerns—protecting themselves from external threat.

Australia and Switzerland are other examples of federalism that arose from separate states that came together to form a new state. Most modern federations, however, came about in exactly the opposite way: through states trying to remain together, often after colonial rule, as our case study of India below demonstrates. In some cases, such as India, federations arose via democracy and implicit bargaining between regional elites and the central government. In other cases, such as Russia, authoritarian rulers imposed federalism to help them rule a vast, heterogeneous

unitary systems: Political systems in which the central government has sole constitutional sovereignty and power; in contrast to a federal system

federal systems: Political systems in which a state's power is legally and constitutionally divided among more than one level of government; in contrast to a unitary system

territory. As the Russian case study below indicates, imposed federalism seldom provides the stability or strong institutions of negotiated federalism.

Why Countries Adopt Federalism

While federal systems are a minority of the world's governments, they include most of its geographically largest countries. As the Country and Concepts table for this chapter (page 248) shows, among our case studies, all of the larger countries except China are federal systems. This is not accidental. Larger countries tend to adopt federal systems in part to provide some level of government closer to the populace than the national government. Providing a relatively local form of government in a large state is one of the primary purposes of federalism, but there are at least two others.

A second purpose is to limit the power of the majority by decentralizing and dividing governmental power. Federal systems usually have bicameral legislatures, with the second (usually referred to as the upper) house representing the interests of the states or provinces. They also have some sort of judicial review to settle disputes between the levels of government. Both institutions limit the power of the executive and the majority controlling the lower (and always more powerful) house of the legislature. Federal systems, then, typically institutionalize several veto players that do not exist in unitary systems.

Finally, as we mentioned in chapter 4, federalism is often a means to protect the interests of religious or ethnic minorities and create subnational governing structures to serve them. States use this federal solution when minorities are geographically concentrated in particular regions. When regional minority communities feel threatened by other groups' control of the national government, a federal system that creates separate states or provinces with clear ethnic or religious majorities can ease concerns. This explains why some relatively small states have chosen federal systems. One such state is Belgium, created in 1830 as a buffer against potential French expansion. Federalism there is combined with consociationalism: the national cabinet and many other appointments must be split 50–50 between the two major language groups, the Flemish and Walloons; separate elections and parties exist for each group; and governments are virtually always a coalition of the two largest parties from each side. Despite its prolonged existence as a nation-state, regionalism in Belgium has always remained strong and seems to be increasing. In 2010, a Flemish nationalist party that calls for Flemish independence won an unprecedented 30 percent of the Flemish vote to become the largest party in the Belgian parliament.

IN CONTEXT

FEDERALISM

Federalism is an unusual institutional choice: only twenty-six countries have a federal system. Those twenty-six, however, account for over 40 percent of the world's population. In addition,

- seven are among the world's ten geographically largest countries, and six are among the world's ten largest countries by population.
- seven of the world's ten largest electoral democracies by area are federal, as are five of the ten largest democracies by population.
- federal countries average 0.55 on an index of ethnic fractionalization, where 0 is perfect homogeneity and 1 is highly fragmented; the world average is 0.48.
- five federal countries are geographically fragmented, composed of two or more islands or of a peninsula and at least one island.

Source: Based on data from Forum of Federations 2011 (http://www.forumfed.org/), Fearon 2003, and Freedom House 2007 (http://www.freedomhouse.org/).

Federalism and Accountability A key determinant of the extent to which federalism limits majority power and provides accountability is the relative power and autonomy of the national and subnational governments. These factors, in turn, depend on the specific powers set out for each level of government in the constitution, the resources each level of government controls, and the composition and relative strength of the upper house in the legislature. The constitutions of all federal systems lay out the powers of both the central government and the states or provinces. Military, foreign, and monetary policies are always placed under the authority of the national level, as they are essential to the sovereignty of the modern state and a modern economy. States or provinces typically have power over education, transportation, and sometimes social services (at least partially). In more decentralized systems like the United States and Brazil, states also have separate judicial systems that handle most criminal law.

The real power of each level of government, however, depends not only on formal powers ordained by the constitution but also on the resources it has. Two key questions, and areas of political combat, in any federal system are how much each level of government can collect in taxes and how much it can spend. The power of taxation is particularly important, as it gives subnational units autonomy from the central government they would not have were they wholly dependent on the central government for their revenue. In the most centralized unitary states, such as the United Kingdom and Ireland, the central government collects more than three-quarters of total government revenue; in the least centralized, such as Germany and Switzerland, the central government collects less than a third. Similarly, the central government in some unitary systems is responsible for around 60 percent of all expenditures, whereas in decentralized federal systems it is responsible for as little as 30 percent.

During the twentieth century, revenue collection in federations became more centralized, reflecting the growing power of national governments over state or provincial ones. Alberto Diaz-Cayeros (2006) argued that in Latin America, this resulted from a bargain between national and regional elites. Regional elites would only give up their taxing powers in exchange for either guaranteed political support from the center or a guaranteed share of revenue. Political guarantees came in the form of national parties limiting or completely preventing political competitors from challenging incumbents. In Mexico, the long-ruling party in the semi-authoritarian state, the PRI, served this function, and tax collection became much more centralized, creating one of the most centralized federations in the world. In other cases, national governments guaranteed states a share of revenue and expenditure, often in national constitutions, to get regional elites to give up some of their taxing power.

The upper and weaker house of the legislature in a federal system is usually designed to represent the state or provincial governments, while the lower and more powerful house represents individual voters. The upper house's power and composition help determine the extent to which federalism limits majority rule, and its powers can be quite sweeping, as in the case of the U.S. Senate, which must approve all legislation. Alternatively, its powers can be much more limited, as in Germany's Bundesrat, which can only delay bills unless they directly relate to the *Lander.* Because states or provinces are typically of different sizes, smaller ones are often overrepresented in the upper house. In the U.S. Senate, every state has two seats: in 2010, the twenty least populous states had just over 10 percent of the U.S. population but elected 40 percent of the senators; the most populous state, California, had about 15 percent of the national population but elected only two senators. Given that Senate legislation requires the approval of 60 percent of the body on important issues, the representatives of just over 10 percent of the population can stop legislation, an unusually severe restriction on majority rule. The ratio of representation of the smallest states to the largest in the U.S. Senate is about 66 to 1. The same ratio in the German Bundesrat is only 13 to 1; this ratio, combined with the weaker powers of the Bundesrat, shows clearly that German federalism does not restrict majority rule nearly as much as American federalism does.

Federalism and Minority Rights

Most federal systems today exist in heterogeneous societies; part of their purpose is to give some local autonomy to ethnic or religious minorities. While all of the issues outlined above apply to these federal systems, other factors also come into play in preserving ethnic minority autonomy. The United States is an example of a **symmetrical federal system**: all states have the same relationship with and rights in relation to the national government. In contrast, many federal systems in ethnically divided societies are **asymmetrical**: some states or provinces have special rights or powers that others do not. These special relationships are often negotiated individually between the leaders of a particular group and the central government, sometimes at the end of a civil war or under the threat of civil war or secession (complete separation from the country). A recent comparative study concluded that federal systems on the whole help to accommodate ethnic and religious divisions, resulting in less conflict than occurs in unitary systems with heterogeneous populations. However, the study also found that federal systems work best where there has not been a history of severe repression of one group over another; in such cases, even the best designed federal institutions may not be able to overcome the tensions and lack of trust between a particular regionally based group and the central government (Amoretti and Bermeo 2004).

symmetrical federal system: A federal system in which all subnational governments (states or provinces) have the same relationship with and rights in relation to the national government

asymmetrical federal system: A federal system in which different subnational governments (states or provinces) have distinct relationships with and rights in relation to the national government

Recent Trends in Federalism

In recent years, the once sharp division between federal and unitary systems has been blurring. The most decentralized federal systems have become somewhat more centralized as these federal governments have used their revenue power and constitutional authority to override state prerogatives in areas such as civil rights, education, and even the drinking age. (Since the 1980s, the U.S. federal government has enforced the mandatory minimum drinking age of twenty-one by denying transportation funding to states that refuse to abide by it; therefore, all states comply.) In unitary systems, such as the United Kingdom, some decentralization has taken place. This process is often termed **devolution** because it devolves power from the center to the regions or subnational units. A British parliamentary report commented that devolution differs from federalism because parliamentary sovereignty means that devolution of power is reversible. The "devolved" institutions in Scotland, Wales, and Northern Ireland also remain subordinate to the British parliament. Interestingly, Britain is an example of "asymmetrical devolution," since each region has its own set of devolved responsibilities and there is no common pattern (Leeke, Sear, and Gay 2003). In France on the other hand, which had one of the most centrally controlled unitary systems, new regional governments with limited powers were created in the 1980s in a symmetrical devolution.

devolution: Partial decentralization of power from central government to subunits such as states or provinces, with subunits' power being dependent on central government and reversible

All governments, both democratic and authoritarian, struggle with how much power to give subnational units of government and how much to retain in the center. In a democracy, this tension has crucial implications for the power of the majority and the preservation of minority rights, as the case studies of Brazil, India, and Russia below demonstrate.

CASE STUDY

Federalism: Brazil, India, and Russia

- Centralized versus decentralized federalism

- Importance of revenue control

- Importance of political context: parties in India, semi-authoritarian rule in Russia

- Problem of weak institutions and lack of democracy: Russia

Russian troops guard a checkpoint in the center of Grozny, the capital of Chechnya. Federalism in Russia has long been used to diffuse ethnic tensions. After the collapse of the Soviet Union, it mostly worked. In Chechnya, however, a war for independence broke out, and the Russian army brutally crushed the rebellion. Since then, Russian ruler Vladimir Putin has greatly centralized power, reducing federalism to little more than a shell, as it was under Soviet rule.

Credit: AP Photo/Shakh Aivazov

Brazil, India, and Russia provide us with three distinct models of federalism: each represents differing degrees of centralization, symmetry, and institutionalization. Together, they demonstrate that how federalism works in practice depends more on political context and control over government revenue than on the formal powers granted in constitutions. Brazil is a case of exceptional decentralization that stringently limits what the majority in control of the national government can achieve; critics argue that the system was so decentralized that it harmed effective governance, at least until reforms were made in the 1990s. India, in contrast, is a much more centralized federal system in which the center, especially under the continuous rule of a dominant party, controls state governments rather tightly. Also in contrast to Brazil, India is an example of an asymmetrical federal system that arose in part to ameliorate and contain the effects of linguistic and religious diversity. Russian federalism is also asymmetrical, is formally centralized, and exists in part to contain ethnic differences, but it shows the limitations of federalism if federal institutions are weak and democracy threatened or eliminated.

Like the United States, Brazil is a case of decentralized, symmetric federalism. The power of states, and of their governors in particular, can severely limit national policy-making, though the balance between central and subnational power has ebbed and flowed over time. Brazil's overall federal structure also is similar to that of the United States, with Brazil having twenty-six states, each with an elected governor and legislature. Federalism in the country dates back to the era of Portuguese colonialism, and it has never been based on ethnic or racial divisions. Rather, the Portuguese divided their vast and lightly populated South American colony into separate units, each under the informal control of local landowning elites, while the emperor maintained central control. At independence, local elites reacted against the empire's centralization by creating a very decentralized federal system and giving themselves great power at the local level, including constitutional guarantees to collect certain taxes. Although they never completely abandoned federalism, Brazil's authoritarian regimes (1930–1945 and 1964–1985) did recentralize control, whereas each new democracy, including the current one established under the 1988 constitution, reasserted local control via decentralized federalism. In contrast to other Latin American federations, state elites in Brazil never agreed to give up their taxing power, a key explanation for Brazil's exceptionally decentralized federal system today. Even under military rule, state governors were powerful enough to limit the degree of centralization.

The constitution of 1988 spells out the powers of the states in great detail. They are guaranteed a share of national tax revenue, continued taxing powers, control over their own state banks, and very little oversight from the federal government. The upper house in the federal legislature, the Senate, is composed of three senators from each state. Given the exceptionally unequal populations of the states, each vote for a senator in the least populous state is worth 144 votes in the most populous, a ratio more than double the disparity in the U.S. Senate. As in the United States, the Senate must pass all legislation, meaning that senators representing 13 percent of the population can block any legislation. Even the lower house, the Chamber of Deputies, favors the less populous states, because no state's delegation can be smaller than eight seats or larger than seventy. Since the population differences between the most populous and least populous states are much greater than this, the lower house does not provide equal representation for each citizen, as it does in most federal systems. Among other things, the power this provides the smaller and poorer states has resulted in their receiving far more than their per capita share of national revenue; the wealthier states have agreed to allow this to occur as long as they can maintain their own taxing powers.

The greatest powers, however, are reserved for state governors. Brazilian politics have long revolved around the use of patronage to build a political following, and much of that patronage is in the hands of state governors. National political parties have always been quite weak, in part due to Brazil's electoral system (see chapter 9); in reality, they are collections of separate state parties controlled via patronage by governors and other local elites. Members of the Chamber of Deputies, and even senators, aspire to be governors or mayors of large cities in their home states, as these positions have more influence and power than the national legislature. This structure emerged at the end of Brazil's military regime in reaction to the centralization of the authoritarian period, understandably, and it makes central policy-making extremely difficult.

Brazil's primary problem in the 1990s—massive inflation and debt—was connected to the power and influence of these state governors. Much of this debt was held by banks owned and controlled by the twenty-six states, and governors used these banks as sources of patronage. They also had the power to force the federal government to bail out the banks if they got into financial difficulty. Thus, by the mid-1990s, Brazil's states were facing bankruptcy because of their irresponsible spending.

President Fernando Cardoso negotiated the following agreement with the governors: the federal government would bail out the states in exchange for the states agreeing to privatize the state banks. Cardoso also was able to shift some spending to the states and increase federal tax revenue. He combined these reforms with a constitutional amendment that allows both the president and all governors to be reelected. Previously, like officials in most of Latin America, Brazil's executives could only serve one term, so governors used their one term to gain as much patronage from the state's resources as they could. The possibility of reelection gave them a longer-term stake in successful reform and allowed them to run for reelection in support of the widely popular Cardoso. After reelection, Cardoso succeeded in passing the Law of Fiscal Responsibility in 2000, which limits the amount states can spend on salaries and employees (a key form of patronage) and prevents the federal government from bailing out the states in the future, effectively limiting governors' resources for patronage. Aaron Schneider portrayed the law as "the culmination of the long process of forming a new federal arrangement" (2007, 486), using fiscal rules to substantially increase the power of the national government vis-à-vis the states. These changes helped produce an improved fiscal position for the Brazilian government as a whole, with far less debt than in the past, to the benefit of Brazil's economic growth. Brazilian federalism remains one of the most decentralized in the world, but over the past decade the pendulum has shifted noticeably back in the direction of centralization, facilitating more coherent policymaking at the national level.

As in Brazil, the origins of India's federalism lie in the colonial era. The British colonial government put modern India together from literally hundreds of separate states, ruling some areas directly and others via various agreements with hundreds of local rulers. After independence, the new constitution recognized various categories of states and "union territories" with various powers. While most states today have the same basic powers, the central government has bargained with regional groups to create new states to enhance regional loyalty to the center. This has meant giving certain states greater autonomy and power than others. The designers of India's constitution specifically said they were not creating states along linguistic or ethnic lines, but over time that is primarily what has happened. A major commission in the 1950s led to the creation of new states drawn mostly along linguistic lines. In the northeast, six new states were eventually created along ethnic lines as well, and each of these has greater power and autonomy than the other states, including the freedom to respect local customary law and religious practices. (One of these states, Sikkim, was a separate country that India successfully added to its territory after agreeing to allot it a distinct set of powers as a state.)

India's constitution created an unusually centralized system of federalism. States do not write their own constitutions; each is under the authority of the same central constitution, which includes a parliamentary government with a chief minister who is the state-level equivalent of prime minister. The national government, however, has the right to create, eliminate, or change state boundaries as it pleases. It can also declare President's Rule in a particular state, under which the state government is dismissed and the prime minister in effect governs the state directly until he or she calls a new state election. President's Rule was to be implemented only in cases of severe emergency, such as a political crisis in the state, but has been used for political gain. The constitution also sets out clear lists of responsibilities and taxation powers for the national and state governments: states control issues such as public order, health, agriculture, and land rights. The national government has the greatest taxation ability, as the states' only significant taxing ability is a sales tax on goods. The power of the purse, which has expanded over time, has given the central government great control over the policies of the states. In 1955–1956, Indian states could finance an average of 69 percent of their expenditures, with the rest coming from the national government; by 2000–2001, this was down to 49 percent (Rao and Singh 2005, 172). An upper house, the Rajya Sabha, exists to represent states but has very limited power in that it has no significant effect on legislation or the composition of the national government.

The extent to which this centralized constitutional arrangement has limited majority rule has varied over time, depending mainly on the party system. When the Indian National Congress (INC) was the sole dominant party and controlled the national government between 1947 and 1977, it had tremendous power. Prior to 1967, it controlled virtually all state governments, so they generally did the bidding of the central government, making federalism extremely weak. Once greater political competition at the state level emerged in the 1970s, prime ministers Indira (1966–1977; 1980–1984) and Rajiv (1984–1989) Gandhi used President's Rule for partisan purposes: they would have the president declare President's Rule in states controlled by opposition parties and then call and win new state elections. As we detail in chapter 7, since 1989 India's ethnically based federalism has helped create a number of state-level parties, especially in the south. These parties dominate the politics in their states but have little influence or support elsewhere. Since 1989, India's national governments have always been coalitions between a major national party and several state-level parties. The state parties have used this situation to bargain with the national parties for greater state autonomy, protecting their states' interests vis-à-vis the majority party better than either the upper house or other elements of the Indian constitution have. Thus, perhaps, state governments are beginning to achieve some degree of institutional autonomy, and horizontal accountability may be increasing vis-à-vis national institutions.

Despite the centralization of the system, India's federalism has managed to keep most ethnic and linguistic conflict within democratic bounds. Atul Kohli (2004), one of the foremost scholars of Indian politics, argued that India has used federalism to contain conflict when national leaders have been willing to compromise with regional groups and political institutions were strong. In the 1950s and 1960s, Prime Minister Jawaharlal Nehru used the creation of states to appease movements, such as the Tamils in the south, who demanded greater autonomy for their linguistic groups. In the 1970s and 1980s, prime ministers Indira and Rajiv Gandhi were less willing to compromise with regional forces, partly because they had less national political support. Since 1989, coalition governments and a 1994 ruling by India's Supreme Court have limited the ability of prime ministers to declare President's Rule or pursue other centralizing activities in respect to states.

Although they have weakened over the past several decades, India's major political institutions remain strong enough for political leaders to make compromises that mean something. If state leaders can successfully bargain for certain powers, they have state institutions under their control that can make more or less effective use of those powers. Therefore, it is reasonable for them to assume that central authorities will adhere to the bargain struck, in contrast with our last case, Russia.

Russian federalism dates back to the expanding Russian Empire, but its more recent antecedent is federalism under the Soviet Union. Officially, the Soviets created the largest federal system in the world, consisting of fifteen separate soviet "republics,"

of which Russia itself was only one; numerous smaller divisions also existed within the Russian Republic. Soviet federalism was elaborate, but absolute control by the Communist Party gave the republics and smaller political units no real autonomy. Local rulers, appointed by the central party, were able to run their governments more or less as personal fiefdoms, but they could not challenge or question central authority if a conflict between the center and the region arose. Federalism in any real sense cannot exist in an authoritarian system as centrally controlled as Soviet communism. The collapse of the Soviet Union resulted in the separation of the fifteen republics into fifteen sovereign countries. The Russian Republic became a federation, though new and weak institutions have made it relatively ineffective in terms of horizontal accountability vis-à-vis the center and effective governance.

Ethnic nationalism was a major challenge to post-Soviet Russia. The Soviet creation of federal units that it justified as "ethnic" homelands led leaders of many ethnic groups to demand various degrees of autonomy from Moscow after the Soviet Union collapsed. Most serious was Chechnya's demand for independence. Chechnya has long been a sore spot for Russia. Stalin forcibly removed its mainly Muslim population to Siberia in the 1950s, and its demands for independence have led to two wars between Russia and Chechen rebels. Today, it remains under Russian rule through the control of a Russian-backed government with little popular support and continued rebel opposition. While Chechnya was the only conflict to produce widespread violence, similar tensions across the former Soviet Union resulted in repeated efforts to amend federalism to recognize local, ethnically defined governments while preserving the Russian Federation as a whole. The Russian constitution of 1993 created an asymmetrical federal system with eighty-nine subnational units ranging in size from republics to two federal cities (Moscow and Saint Petersburg). The status of *republic* is given to areas deemed ethnically non-Russian. The boundaries of republics, however, are arbitrary. At the time the constitution was adopted, the titular ethnic group constituted a majority of the population in only seven of the twenty-one republics. For example, in 2002 Karelians were only 9 percent of the population of the Karelia republic, Udmurts were 29 percent of the population of Udmurtia, and Khakas constituted 12 percent of Khakassia. Republics do have noticeably more power than other federal units, including more power over state property and trade. The constitution, however, gives by far the greatest powers to the central government, reserving only a handful of powers for joint national-local control, and no powers are reserved exclusively for subnational governments. The central government also has the greatest taxation powers: in 2001 it collected 85 percent of all revenue.

While the Russian constitution seems to have created a highly centralized system, its operation in practice in the 1990s has been termed "legal chaos" (Graney 2009, 205). Between 1993 and 1998, demands from various republics and other subnational units led President Boris Yeltsin to sign separate bilateral treaties with more than half of the country's eighty-nine subnational governments. In the case of Tatarstan, the republic gained the power to make separate treaties with foreign powers. Tatarstan essentially could pursue its own foreign policy, especially in economic areas, as long as it did not conflict with Russian foreign policy. While the laws of each of the federal units are supposed to comply with the national constitution, a recent study found that more than half violate that rule, some quite intentionally. Given that until 2004 each republic was governed by an elected president and elected legislatures, Kathryn Stoner-Weiss (2004) argued that these local officials "[are] the undisputed boss of any given region." Yeltsin attempted to overcome these centrifugal tendencies by creating the position of "presidential representative" to be the "eyes and ears" of the Russian president in each of the eighty-nine federal units. He left the powers of these representatives rather vague, however, and

many representatives became active in local corruption while doing little to assert greater central authority.

Vladimir Putin, Yeltsin's successor, came to power with a goal of centralizing power in Russia. One of his first acts was to reorganize the presidential representatives, establishing just seven of them in superdistricts that together covered all the federal units. The legitimacy of these new representatives, who seem to be a new layer of government in Russia's federalism that is not in the constitution, has been questioned by many. Nonetheless, they have succeeded bringing republic and other subnational laws more in line with the national constitution. In 2004, Putin introduced a second round of reforms that allowed him to appoint governors and up to half of the upper house of parliament, thereby further centralizing what was already a centralized system of federalism. These reforms were part of his effort to transform Russia from a weak democracy to a semi-authoritarian state in which he and his allies had an effective monopoly on power. In terms of actual power, Putin effectively eliminated the substance of federalism in Russia.

Russia's long history with federalism has been fraught with difficulty. Federalism under the chaotic democracy of the 1990s was institutionally weak and fragmented by an extreme asymmetry based on Yeltsin's individual deals with the republics and other subnational regions, but it was federalism nonetheless. As we noted earlier, it's difficult to have real federalism without democracy; even the semi-authoritarian rule of the sort Putin created requires enough centralization that any significant federalism is a threat that the ruling elite will seek to eliminate.

CASE SUMMARY

Federalism should include a number of institutionalized veto players, limiting majoritarian democracy and adding an element of horizontal accountability, as subunits limit the power of the central government and vice versa. Our three examples here demonstrate that the extent to which this is true varies greatly and does not always depend on formal rules. Brazil and India are models of unusually decentralized and centralized systems, respectively. In Brazil, state governments and leaders were so powerful, at least until recent reforms, that they made national governing difficult. In India, by contrast, Congress domination and constitutional rules favoring the center made states quite weak. The party system in India, however, has had a role in decentralizing that power, as Congress has become dependent on state-level parties to stay in power. The evolution of Indian federalism is an example of the bargaining relationship inherent in all federal systems; how much accountability exists and who can check whom more depends on past bargains between governing units and their leaders. Russia, indeed, shows the extreme case, that of a central authority able to eliminate virtually all real elements of federal autonomy. This case shows that federalism at its core is a liberal system: to function at all, it must allow some autonomy from central authority.

CONCLUSION

Who Rules?

Political institutions clearly have an impact on who has the most power in a society and how they can exercise it. In strong institutions, the formal rules matter because on the whole they are obeyed. Rational-choice institutionalists argue that formal rules create a set of incentives that political actors respond to, incentives that can produce greater compromise or greater conflict in the political system as a whole.

A crucial question for a democracy is how the executive power of the state can be effectively limited and kept within democratic norms. The first and most obvious answer is to subject the executive to vertical accountability via elections of some sort, directly or indirectly. That leaves great variation though, focused mostly on horizontal accountability between elections: Does one set of governing institutions systematically hold executive power more accountable than other types of institutions? The answer in most cases depends not just on the formal governing institutions but on the broader political context in which they operate. The Westminster model seems to provide the weakest horizontal check on executive power, but only when the PM leads a cohesive majority party in Parliament. And it arguably provides the clearest vertical accountability: voters know exactly who is responsible for government policy. Coalition governments, as India has had since 1989 and the United Kingdom since 2010, provide a nearly constant check on the PM, as he or she must secure coalition partners' agreement to make any significant policy. The judiciary in most democracies is specifically tasked with horizontal accountability via judicial review, but we've seen that courts must assert their independence carefully, given their lack of democratic legitimation via elections and lack of other resources on which to base their power. Japan and India show us that even when the elected executive is held accountable, an entrenched bureaucracy may wield great and unelected power and successfully resist reforms to democratize it.

Besides accountability, the other great question in liberal democracy is how to protect minority rights. Accountability is to the majority, which can and often does trample the liberal rights of minorities. Does one set of institutions help preserve minority rights better than others? Most Americans would immediately think of the Supreme Court as fulfilling this role, but political science research indicates that the judiciary upholds the interests of the dominant majority at least as often as it does the minority, and that is likely to be even more true when the judiciary as an institution is relatively weak.

More consensual democracies in which a variety of viewpoints are represented within the major governing institutions and compromise is required to make decisions would seem to enhance minority rights. One form of this is federalism, which is often designed specifically to protect ethnic and regional minorities. How well this works depends on how much real power—determined not only by formal rules but by control of revenues—a federal system provides the national and regional governments. Again, the broader political context matters. For example, the strength of federalism in India has varied mainly due to variation in the party system. One dominant party controlling virtually all levels of government, as in India's first twenty years of modern statehood or in Russia now, eviscerates federalism nearly completely. State-level parties that champion local interests, on the other hand, as in India today, strengthen federalism notably, presumably to the benefit of local minorities represented by those parties and state governments.

What Explains Political Behavior?

What can the study of governing institutions tell us about political behavior? Are institutionalist theories correct that institutional arrangements and incentives explain political behavior better than cultural, ideological, or economic factors? While we can't definitively answer this question, our case studies give us some insights into how institutions shape leaders' actions. Most importantly, we see a common pattern of leaders fighting to strengthen institutions in which they hold positions of power. As institutionalist theorists have argued, institutions create incentives for their own preservation and expansion. Prime ministers in the United Kingdom and elsewhere attempt to augment their power and public persona, appearing more presidential over time. Presidents in the United States and Brazil, regardless of their formal powers, try to enact measures that strengthen the office of the president, from the "unitary executive" theories of the Bush administration to President Cardoso's efforts to gain presidential control of Brazil's decentralized federalism. Judicial leaders attempt to assert the autonomy of their courts, and bureaucrats fight to maintain and strengthen their influence vis-à-vis elected officials.

A second behavioral question comparativists ask examines the potential trade-off we've discussed at length between representation and effective policymaking. Do some institutions provide more of one or the other, and does a clear optimum balance between them exist? Lijphart's consensual and majoritarian democratic models directly address this question. Majoritarian systems like the Westminster model, as well as tightly controlled policymaking such as under Japan's developmental state at the height of its bureaucracy's power, ought to provide more effective policymaking at the expense of some immediate representation. Institutions that provide more horizontal accountability and require greater consensus, such as the U.S. presidential system with weak parties and federalism, seem likely to slow down the policy-making process, perhaps bringing it to a stop altogether. The classic comparison of Britain's Margaret Thatcher and America's Ronald Reagan implementing similar ideologies at very different speeds demonstrates this contrast well. Lijphart, though, argued that overall consensual models legislate nearly as effectively as majoritarian systems but add much greater representation. While Lijphart favored that balance, the debate is far from concluded. Political context matters here as well: the number and strength of political parties in office will affect how the institutions operate, as Indian history demonstrates, a subject we will examine in detail in the next chapter.

Where and Why?

Looking comparatively, we can ask why the same institutions seem to work better in certain places than in others and why particular countries come to adopt particular institutions in the first place. Our cases suggest that wholesale change of institutions is difficult and extremely unusual. Countries seem prone to follow what they know, as the examples of Britain's former colonies suggest. It is rare for a country to decide, as France did in 1958, that a complete change of structures is in order, but countries transitioning to democracy face this choice as they write new constitutions. Brazil is our only case study that seriously debated switching major institutions (from presidential to parliamentary), and it ultimately rejected the change. This data strongly suggest that cultural and historical institutional theories best explain the continuity of institutions. Deeply held values, socialized into the population over time, tend to preserve existing institutions unless they prove exceptionally dysfunctional. And as we noted above, institutions create incentives for their own survival, making large-scale change extremely rare.

More common is tinkering to improve a system at the margins: borrowing anticorruption policies to improve the bureaucracy's functioning, for instance, or delegating more authority to regions within a unitary system. Political leaders and political scientists regularly look at institutions comparatively, trying to understand why a particular type of institution works better in one place than another. No clear answer is obvious, though certainly social, political, and ethnic contexts matter greatly. A society that is deeply divided by certain issues, such as ethnic difference and past conflicts, is likely to benefit most from a more consensual set of institutions that requires compromise at every step of the way. A majoritarian system or powerful single office like a presidency is likely to breed distrust, as no political actor in the system is willing to trust the others with such great power. This indeed is exactly the situation in which federalism is so often prescribed, to diffuse power from the center. How well this approach works, though, depends on the broader context as well; excessive fragmentation across political parties and local governments may make policymaking nearly impossible or even threaten the continued viability of the state as a whole.

A crucial element in understanding what system works where is the overall strength of institutions themselves, of whatever type. The older and the stronger they are, the more they are likely to socialize the populace into accepting them, provide incentives for political leaders to want to preserve them, and give those leaders time to figure out how to make them work effectively. Newer and weaker institutions in new democracies, which we examine in detail in chapter 9, provide a more difficult context in which institutional failure can be quite common, regardless of what particular institutions are in place.

Applying Theory to Governing Institutions

The entire study of democratic institutions assumes a certain position in the theoretical debate between pluralists and elite theorists over who rules. If elite rule is secure and unchallenged, then the exact nature of the governing institutions won't matter to things like representation and participation. The debate is about the extent to which pluralism is right and how institutions can assist in ensuring that it remains an accurate depiction of the dispersion of political power in a democracy. It is also about the trade-off between elite power, which might be more effective at making policy, and more dispersed power, which, while slowing down the policy-making process, provides greater representation.

The debates in this chapter also assume that institutions matter to political behavior. To some extent, institutionalist theories must be important. Beyond that, however, much debate occurs. The bulk of recent political science research in these areas has been explicitly or implicitly informed by rational-choice theory, including rational-choice institutionalism. Political actors, many arguments assert, act rationally within an institutional context; understanding the effects of institutions requires understanding the incentives they provide to these rational actors. Historical institutionalists, however, are also influential. Despite the elegant logic of rational-choice arguments, fundamental institutional change is quite rare. Most of the time, in spite of whatever shortcomings analysts might see, political institutions that are well established survive. Political science research might suggest modest modifications, which occasionally are implemented, but more fundamental change is rare. As historical institutionalists argue, institutions create their own support, both from leaders whose positions and power derive from the institutions and from the citizens' acceptance of the institutions as legitimate, despite their possible shortcomings. We turn next to institutions of participation and representation, which, while also enduring, are subject to somewhat more frequent change.

KEY CONCEPTS

amakudari (p. 287)
asymmetrical federal system (p 295)
bicameral legislature (p. 255)
coalition government (p. 247)
code law (p. 273)
cohabitation (p. 266)
collective responsibility (p. 254)
common law (p. 273)
consensus democracy (p. 247)
devolution (p. 295)
executive (p. 246)
federal systems (p. 292)
head of government (p. 249)
head of state (p. 249)
horizontal accountability (p. 246)

iron triangles (p. 287)
judicial independence (p. 275)
judicial review (p. 273)
judiciary (p. 246)
legislative oversight (p. 281)
legislature (p. 246)
majoritarian democracy (p. 247)
member of parliament (MP) (p. 249)
New Public Management (NPM) (p. 284)
New Public Service (NPS) (p. 284)
parliamentarism (p. 249)
political accountability (p. 245)

political appointees (p. 281)
presidentialism (p. 258)
prime minister (PM) (p. 249)
principal-agent problem (p. 281)
rent seeking (p. 285)
semipresidentialism (p. 265)
separation of powers (p. 259)
stare decisis (p. 273)
symmetrical federal system (p. 295)
unitary systems (p. 292)
vertical accountability (p. 245)
veto player (p. 247)
vote of no confidence (p. 249)

WORKS CITED

Amoretti, Ugo M., and Nancy Gina Bermeo, eds. 2004. *Federalism and Territorial Cleavages.* Baltimore, MD: Johns Hopkins University Press.

Bevir, Mark. 2010. *Democratic Governance.* Princeton, NJ: Princeton University Press.

Cheibub, Jose Antonio. 2007. *Presidentialism, Parliamentarism, and Democracy.* New York: Cambridge University Press.

Chinn, Stuart. 2006. "Democracy-Promoting Judicial Review in a Two-Party System: Dealing with Second-Order Preferences." *Polity* 38 (4): 478–500. doi:10.1057/palgrave.polity.2300071.

Dahl, Robert. 1957. "Decision-Making in a Democracy: The Supreme Court as a National Policy-Maker." *Journal of Public Law* 6: 279–94.

Denhardt, Robert B., and Janet V. Denhardt. 2001. "The New Public Service: Putting Democracy First." *National Civic Review* 90 (4): 391–400.

Diaz-Cayeros, Alberto. 2006. *Federalism, Fiscal Authority, and Centralization in Latin America.* Cambridge, UK: Cambridge University Press.

Ekeh, Peter P. 1975. "Colonialism and the Two Publics in Africa: A Theoretical Statement." *Comparative Studies in Society and History* 17 (1): 91–112. doi: 10.1017/S0010417500007659.

Elgie, Robert. 2005. "A Fresh Look at Semipresidentialism: Variations on a Theme." *Journal of Democracy* 16 (3): 98–112.

Fearon, James. 2003. "Ethnic and Cultural Diversity by Country." *Journal of Economic Growth* 8 (2): 195–222. doi:10.1023/A:1024419522867.

Ferejohn, John, and Pasquale Pasquino. 2003. "Rule of Democracy and Rule of Law." In *Democracy and the Rule of Law,* edited by Jose Maria Maravall and Adam Przeworski, 242–60. Cambridge, UK: Cambridge University Press.

Ferejohn, John, Frances Rosenbluth, and Charles Shipan. 2007. "Comparative Judicial Politics." In *The Oxford Handbook of Comparative Politics,* edited by Carles Boix and Susan Carol Stokes, 727–51. Oxford, UK: Oxford University Press.

Forum of Federations. 2011. http://www.forumfed.org/.

Freedom House. 2007. Democracies. http://www.freedomhouse.org/.

Gibson, James L., Gregory A. Caldeira, and Vanessa A. Baird. 1998. "On the Legitimacy of National High Courts." *American Political Science Review* 92 (2): 343–58.

Graney, Katherine E. 2009. "Ethnicity and Identity." In *Understanding Contemporary Russia,* edited by Michael Bressler, 191–220. Boulder, CO: Lynne Rienner.

Green, Michael J. 2010. "Japan's Confused Revolution." *The Washington Quarterly* 33 (1): 3–19. doi:10.1080/01636600903418637.

Huber, John D., and Charles R. Shipan. 2002. *Deliberate Discretion? The Institutional Foundations of Bureaucratic Autonomy.* Cambridge, UK: Cambridge University Press.

Johnston, Michael. 2005. *Syndromes of Corruption: Wealth, Power, and Democracy.* New York: Cambridge University Press.

Kohli, Atul. 2004. "India: Federalism and the Accommodation of Ethnic Nationalism." In *Federalism and Territorial Cleavages,* edited by Ugo M. Amoretti and Nancy G. Bermeo, 281–300. Baltimore, MD: Johns Hopkins University Press.

Landfried, Christine. 1995. "Germany." In *The Global Expansion of Judicial Power,* edited by C. Neal Tate and Torbjörn Vallinder, 307–24. New York: New York University Press.

Leeke, Matthew, Chris Sear, and Oonagh Gay. 2003. *An Introduction to Devolution in the UK.* Research Paper 03/84, 17 November. House of Commons Library. http://www.parliament.uk/documents/commons/lib/research/rp2003/rp03–084.pdf.

Lijphart, Arend. 1999. *Patterns of Democracy: Government Forms and Performance in Thirty-six Countries.* New Haven, CT: Yale University Press.

Linz, Juan Jose. 1990. "The Perils of Presidentialism." *Journal of Democracy* 1 (1): 51–69. doi:10.1353/jod.1990.0011.

Mulgan, Aurelia George. 2002. *Japan's Failed Revolution: Koizumi and the Politics of Economic Reform.* Canberra, Australia: Asia Pacific Press.

O'Donnell, Guillermo. 1999. "Horizontal Accountability in New Democracies." In *The Self-Restraining State: Power and Accountability in New Democracies,* edited by Andreas Schedler, Larry Diamond, and Marc F. Plattner, 29–52. Boulder, CO: Lynne Rienner.

O'Dwyer, Conor. 2006. *Runaway State-Building: Patronage Politics and Democratic Development.* Baltimore, MD: Johns Hopkins University Press.

Oliveira, Vanessa Elias de Dados. 2005. "The Judiciary and Privatizations in Brazil: Is There a Judicialization of Politics? [Judiciario e privatizacoes no Brasil: Existe uma judicializacao da politica?]." *Dados* 48(3): 559–87.

Pempel, T. J. 2000. *Regime Shift: Comparative Dynamics of the Japanese Political Economy.* Ithaca, NY: Cornell University Press.

Powell, G. Bingham, Jr. 2000. *Elections as Instruments of Democracy: Majoritarian and Proportional Visions.* New Haven, CT: Yale University Press.

Puddington, Arch. 2010. "Freedom in the World 2010: Erosion of Freedom Intensifies." http://www.freedomhouse.org/.

Rao, M. Govinda, and Nirvikar Singh. 2005. *The Political Economy of Federalism in India.* Oxford, UK: Oxford University Press.

Riker, William. 1964. *Federalism: Origin, Operation, Significance.* Boston: Little, Brown.

Rosenbluth, Frances McCall, and Michael F. Thies. 2010. *Japan Transformed: Political Change and Economic Restructuring.* Princeton, NJ: Princeton University Press.

Samuels, David. 2007. "Separation of Powers." In *The Oxford Handbook of Comparative Politics,* edited by Carles Boix and Susan Carol Stokes, 703–26. Oxford, UK: Oxford University Press.

Santiso, Carlos. 2003. "Economic Reform and Judicial Governance in Brazil: Balancing Independence with Accountability." *Democratization* 10 (4): 161–80. doi:10.1080/135103403123312 94077.

Schleiter, Petra, and Edward Morgan-Jones. 2009. "Review Article: Citizens, Presidents and Assemblies: The Study of Semi-Presidentialism beyond Duverger and Linz." *British Journal of Political Science* 39:871–92. doi:10.1017/S0007123409990159.

Schneider, Aaron. 2007. "Governance Reform and Institutional Change in Brazil: Federalism and Tax." *Commonwealth & Comparative Politics* 45 (4): 475–98. doi:10.1080/14662040701659928.

Stoner-Weiss, Kathryn. 2004. "Russia: Managing Territorial Cleavages under Dual Transitions." In *Federalism and Territorial Cleavages,* edited by Ugo M. Amoretti and Nancy G. Bermeo, 301–26. Baltimore, MD: Johns Hopkins University Press.

Tate, C. Neal, and Torbjörn Vallinder. 1995. *The Global Expansion of Judicial Power.* New York: New York University Press.

Taylor, Matthew M. 2008. *Judging Policy: Courts and Policy Reform in Democratic Brazil.* Stanford, CA: Stanford University Press.

Transparency International. 2010. "Corruption Perceptions Index." http://www.transparency.org/policy_research/surveys_indices/cpi/.

Tsebelis, George. 2002. *Veto Players: How Political Institutions Work.* Princeton, NJ: Princeton University Press.

Van Wolferen, Karel. 2010. "Japan's Stumbling Revolution." *The Asia-Pacific Journal* 15–2-10 (April 12). http://japanfocus.org/-Karel_van-Wolferen/3341.

Vanberg, Georg. 2005. *The Politics of Constitutional Review in Germany.* Cambridge, UK: Cambridge University Press.

RESOURCES FOR FURTHER STUDY

Cappelletti, Mauro, Paul J. Kollmer, and Joanne M. Olson. 1989. *The Judicial Process in Comparative Perspective.* Oxford, UK: Clarendon Press.

Frederickson, H. George, and Kevin B. Smith. 2003. *The Public Administration Theory Primer.* Boulder, CO: Westview Press.

Graber, Mark A. 2005. "Constructing Judicial Review." *Annual Review of Political Science* 8: 425–51. doi:10.1146/annurev.polisci.8.082103.104905.

Herron, Erik S., and Kirk A. Randazzo. 2003. "The Relationship between Independence and Judicial Review in Post-Communist Courts." *Journal of Politics* 65 (2): 422–38. doi:10.1111/1468–2508.t01–3–00007.

Mainwaring, Scott, and Matthew Soberg Shugart, eds. 1997. *Presidentialism and Democracy in Latin America.* New York: Cambridge University Press.

WEB RESOURCES

Binghamton University, "The Institutions and Elections Project" (http://www2.binghamton.edu/political-science/institutions-and-elections-project.html)

International Institute for Democracy and Electoral Assistance, "Democracy and Development" (http://www.idea.int/development/index.cfm)

Melton, James, Stephen Meserve, and Daniel Pemstein, "Unified Democracy Scores" (http://www.unified-democracy-scores.org/index.html)

Transparency International, "Surveys and Indices" (http://www.transparency.org/policy_research/surveys_indices/)

University of Bern, "Comparative Political Data Sets" (http://www.ipw.unibe.ch/content/team/klaus_armingeon/comparative_political_data_sets/index_ger.html)

○ Case Study
● Mini Case

Who Rules?

- Do some types of institutions in democracies provide better overall representation of and influence for average citizens?
- How do institutions affect the representation of ethnic, gender, religious, and other groups?

What Explains Political Behavior?

- Why do people join political parties and participate in other kinds of political activity?
- How do different types of institutions affect political leaders' behavior?

Where and Why?

- Are there clear patterns of when and where particular types of formal institutions (party and electoral systems) develop?

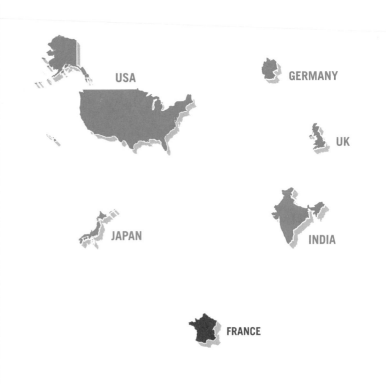

7

INSTITUTIONS OF PARTICIPATION AND REPRESENTATION IN DEMOCRACIES

This chapter examines the institutions that shape political participation and interest representation in democracies. Virtually all regimes allow some degree of participation and representation, if only to shore up their own legitimacy or at least the appearance of it. Regimes differ dramatically, however, in the degree to which they seek to control and limit participation and representation. Democratic regimes all claim to value and promote widespread participation and representation, but they differ significantly in regard to the "best" ways to promote citizen involvement and fair and accurate representation of interests. In general, democratic regimes face the problem of stimulating and channeling participation and representation, whereas authoritarian regimes are more interested in constraining or co-opting them. Because participation and representation are vital to and hallmarks of democratic regimes, we discuss the relevant institutions in these regimes first. In chapter 8, we examine and compare the same kinds of institutions in authoritarian regimes.

One of the first questions that immediately comes to mind is, Why do people participate in politics in the first place? This is one facet of the broader question: What explains political behavior? We might imagine that the answers would be obvious: people want to have power or influence, to make a contribution to their community and nation, or to gain recognition and status. While all this is undoubtedly true for some political activists, rational-actor theorists long ago explained that for most people most of the time, there is no rational reason to participate in political activity, including voting, because most people cannot influence the outcome of the process to any significant degree. Expending time or money to work toward any political goal is irrational, given the huge number of citizens and the correspondingly small impact of each individual. This is an obvious problem in a democracy, and it is exacerbated by the fact that members of the elite, with their much greater direct access to key decision makers, have a greater incentive to participate and thus seem more likely to influence policy in their favor. Without any ameliorating circumstances, all of these factors would suggest that elite theory is correct: "democracies" are really elite controlled.

Democratic institutions need to help citizens overcome this **collective action problem**: individuals are unwilling to engage in a particular activity because of their rational belief that their individual actions will have little or no effect, yet when they all fail to act, all suffer adverse consequences (in the case of participation in democracy, losing control to the elite). If individuals participate in politics, they may be able to benefit collectively, but it is irrational for each individual to participate in the first place because his or her individual impact will be negligible. The net effect of this problem is less political participation by and fewer political benefits to citizens than would be possible with greater participation. Understanding to what extent

collective action problem: Individuals being unwilling to engage in a particular activity because of their rational belief that their individual actions will have little or no effect, yet collectively suffering adverse consequences when all fail to act

Here, members of the German Green Party demand greater use of solar and other alternative fuel sources. The party grew out of Germany's environmental movement, going from social movement to interest group to political party. It was part of the governing coalition from 1998 to 2005.

Credit: AP Photo/Sven Kaestner

institutions overcome this problem is crucial to understanding how democratic any particular system is. Part of institutions' role is their influence on political leaders' behavior: What incentives do particular institutional arrangements give leaders to act in a certain way in the political system? Do these incentives encourage leaders to promote more participation and representation, or less?

Participation and representation clearly have major implications for answering "Who rules?" as well. Any democratic system worthy of the name ought to translate greater participation into greater power and influence, however imperfectly. All democracies elect people to represent citizens, but they differ widely in how those people are elected and which citizens' voices are represented more fully. Different electoral systems have different principles of representation behind them and different effects on accountability. We can demonstrate this by examining how well the systems represent those who seem likely to have less power in the society at large, such as women or racial or ethnic minorities. Given that these groups typically have fewer economic resources, do some systems of representation and participation allow such groups to have greater influence than do other systems? Elite theorists,

COUNTRY AND CONCEPT

Parties, Elections, and Civil Society

Country	Electoral system	Party system	Number of significant parties in legislature[1]	Interest-group system
Brazil	Open-list PR	Multiple	7	Pluralist
China	NA	One	1	State corporatist
Germany	Mixed PR	Two and a half	5	Neocorporatist
India	FPTP	Multiple	4 (in addition to dozens of minor parties)	Pluralist
Iran	FPTP	None	0[2]	Weak
Japan	Mixed PR	Multiple	3	Pluralist
Mexico	Mixed PR	Multiple	3	Neocorporatist
Nigeria	FPTP	Dominant	3[3]	Weak
Russia	Closed-list PR	Dominant	4	Weak
United Kingdom	FPTP	Two	3	Pluralist
United States	FPTP	Two	2	Pluralist

[1]Data on number of parties in legislatures are from *Political Handbook of the World, 2007* (Washington, DC: CQ Press, 2007).

[2]Although political parties are permitted under the constitution, none were recognized following the formal dissolution of the government-sponsored Islamic Republican Party in June 1987, despite Tehran's announcement in October 1988 that such groups would thenceforth be welcomed if they "demonstrated commitment to the Islamic system."

[3]Parties winning a significant number of seats in parliament in the 2007 elections and running viable presidential candidates in 2011 elections.

again, argue that modern electoral democracies in reality give limited power to those in more marginalized positions; elites dominate the national discourse, control major institutions including the media, and influence voters more than voters influence who is in office. If true, this allocation of influence obviously undermines vertical accountability, a crucial element of democracy.

As always, comparativists also ask "Where and why?" questions. We will see that democracies vary greatly in terms of the three key institutions of representation and participation: elections, parties, and civil society. A glance at the Country and Concept table shows variation among our case study countries across all the institutions we will define and examine in this chapter. Can we explain these patterns? If certain types of institutions can better represent people than others, where and why have they developed, and can they be replicated elsewhere to the betterment of democracy overall? We now turn to an examination of each of these three institutions, formal and informal, that structure and constrain participation and representation in modern democracies.

FORMAL INSTITUTIONS: THE ELECTORAL SYSTEM

electoral systems:
Formal, legal mechanisms that translate votes into control over political offices and shares of political power

Electoral systems are formal, legal mechanisms that translate votes into control over political offices and shares of political power. Different electoral systems provide distinct incentives to individual voters and can even influence voter turnout. They also influence political parties' respective strengths and numbers, so they are crucial to understanding how individual parties function and what constraints on and opportunities for citizen participation they provide. Electoral rules and practices shape political participation by prescribing who votes, when, and by what mechanisms. They are also a means of representation, because while all types of regimes have executives and bureaucracies, electoral systems are a hallmark of democratic regimes. A truly democratic electoral system enfranchises a large portion of the population and permits a variety of choices.

In almost all elections, enfranchised citizens vote for people who will represent them rather than voting directly on policy. This raises a key issue in all electoral systems: How are votes aggregated and counted? Countries express quite different perspectives on what "good" representation looks like when they make this basic decision. One common choice is to represent people geographically; a country divides its territory into geographic units, and each unit elects one or more representatives. This system assumes that citizens can best be represented via their membership in geographically defined communities. In contrast, some countries elect their legislatures nationally or in very large districts. This system assumes that what's important is representing beliefs espoused by the parties or individual candidates voters choose, rather than regional interests. In rare cases, democratic countries choose to represent specific groups within society rather than or in addition to geographic districts or parties. After an ethnic conflict, for instance, a country may decide it needs to ensure special representation for ethnic minorities. Several countries have also legally reserved seats in parliament specifically for women to ensure that they are represented.

Thinking about the dramatically different options available can lead us to ponder interesting normative questions about good representation. On what basis do we wish to be represented, and with whom do we share our most important political interests or views? Each electoral system discussed below answers these questions differently. The answers affect participation as well, making these decisions crucial in any democracy.

In addition, electoral institutions often have important effects on governance. Their impact on the party composition of legislatures and the relationship between ruling legislative and executive parties mean that they interact with other institutions to affect the stability and effectiveness of a government. Familiar examples of gridlock in American politics or the legendary instability of Italian parliamentary regimes after World War II illustrate this dynamic. Such problems do not result from presidential or parliamentary institutions per se but rather from the ways in which these institutions interact with the electoral system. Systems that encourage many, fragmented parties provide representation of diverse views in the legislature, but they may make effective government difficult because of the instability of coalition governments in parliamentary systems or the gridlock of different parties controlling the executive and legislative branches in presidential systems.

Single-Member Districts: "First-Past-the-Post" and Majoritarian Voting

Americans borrowed the idea of the **single-member district (SMD)** from Great Britain. In both countries, each geographic district elects a single representative. Whoever gets the most votes—a **plurality**—becomes the district representative. In a race with multiple contestants, the winner can be elected with a relatively low percentage of the vote total: 30 percent or so is not uncommon. This system is often called **"first-past-the-post" (FPTP)** because, as in a horse race, the single winner merely needs to edge out the next closest competitor. Some countries modify this system by requiring the winner to gain an absolute majority of the votes rather than a plurality. In majoritarian systems, if no candidate wins an absolute majority (50 percent plus one), a second election takes place between the top two candidates to produce a winner with a majority of the popular vote. Because SMD systems produce one winner per district, they tend to be part of and support the majoritarian model of democracy; a single-party government is more likely to result, and each voter has "his" representative to hold accountable for government actions. Minority voices, however, are less likely to be represented.

Single-member districts can give constituents a strong sense of identification with their representative. Even if you didn't vote for your representative and you disagree with him or her, that representative is still expected to work for you (as U.S. representatives often do by solving Social Security problems for constituents or writing letters of nomination to service academies). Your most vital needs and interests are assumed to have been aggregated into those of your district. This may explain why most Americans famously dislike Congress but love their own representatives. They may feel the member is "from" their district or constituency and therefore understands them and their needs.

In other ways, however, FPTP may not be good for representation and participation. First, many votes are "wasted," especially in systems with more than two viable parties. Perhaps only 30 or 35 percent of voters actually favored the winner, so the votes of the majority of the voters were arguably wasted, because their preferences and views may not be represented at all. It is a winner-take-all system in which the winner does not necessarily reflect the preferences of the majority of the people. This may be one reason why voter participation tends to be lower in countries with FPTP than elsewhere. Voters—especially those who prefer minor parties—may have less incentive to overcome the collective action problem and may therefore find voting a waste of time.

single-member district (SMD): Electoral system in which each geographic district elects a single representative to a legislature

plurality: The receipt of the most votes, but not necessarily a majority

"first-past-the post" (FPTP): Electoral system in which individual candidates are elected in single-member districts; the candidate with the plurality of votes wins

TABLE 7.1

Results of the 2005 United Kingdom Parliamentary Election

Party	Total votes	% of votes	% of seats	Number of seats
Labour	9,562,122	35.3	55.2	356
Conservative	8,772,598	32.3	30.7	198
Liberal Democrat	5,981,874	22.1	9.6	62

Source: http://news.bbc.co.uk/2/hi/uk_news/politics/vote_2005/constituencies/default.stm.

Second, this problem can be compounded by the under- or overrepresentation of particular parties. Consider a case in which a third party wins a significant share of the votes in many districts but a plurality in only one or two. The party would win a lot of votes but get only a couple of seats in the legislature. Conversely, if a large number of candidates from a particular party win by a very small plurality in their districts, that party's vote in the legislature will be inflated. The number of its representatives will suggest an overwhelming national consensus, when in fact the party may not have even won a majority of the vote nationwide. Table 7.1 gives an example from Great Britain's 2005 election, in which the two major parties won similar vote shares but very different numbers of seats. Does this constitute a good representation of the voting public? According to proponents of FPTP, it does, but others argue that the voice of a large segment of the electorate is ignored. On the other hand, this supermajority may promote efficient, stable policymaking by allowing decisive legislative action. This is one reason some proponents prefer FPTP, despite its wasted votes, to the primary alternative, proportional representation.

Proportional Representation

proportional representation (PR): Electoral system in which seats in a legislature are apportioned on a purely proportional basis, giving each party the share of seats that matches its share of the total vote

Proportional representation (PR) differs from FPTP in almost every conceivable way. In PR, representatives are chosen nationally or in large electoral districts with multiple representatives for each district. Thus, either a national legislature is simply divided on a purely proportional basis, or multiple representatives for large districts are allocated proportionally according to the vote in each district. So, for instance, a party that gains 25 percent of the national vote receives a quarter (or very nearly a quarter) of the seats in the legislature. There usually is some sort of cutoff, though; in most PR systems, a party must cross a minimal electoral threshold—for example, 3 or 5 percent of the vote—to gain representation in parliament. Any parties that cross that threshold can be certain that they will be represented. As Table 7.2 demonstrates for the 2010 Swedish parliamentary elections, a PR system translates each party's share of the votes into almost exactly the same share of legislative seats (in stark contrast to the FPTP system, as a quick comparison of Tables 7.1 and 7.2 shows). PR systems tend to be part of and support consensus models of democracy; multiple voices via multiple parties are likely to be represented in the legislature, and coalition government is a common outcome.

If voters are not choosing among individuals running for a single seat, whom or what are they voting for, and who ends up in the legislature? The answer reflects a

	TABLE 7.2

Results of Sweden's 2010 Parliamentary Election

Parties and coalitions	Votes %	Total seats %
Swedish Social Democratic Party (*Arbetarepartiet-Socialdemokraterna*)	30.7	32.09
Moderate Party (*Moderata Samlingspartiet*)	30.1	30.65
Centre Party (*Centerpartiet*)	6.6	6.59
Liberal People's Party (*Folkpartiet Liberalerna*)	7.1	6.68
Christian Democrats (*Kristdemokraterna*)	5.6	5.29
Left Party (*Vänsterpartiet*)	5.6	5.29
Green Party (*Miljöpartiet de Gröna*)	7.3	7.16
Sweden Democrats (*Sverigedemokraterna*)	5.7	5.73

Source: Election Resources, http://electionresources.org/se/riksdag.php?election=2010.

very different view of representation from FPTP, because in PR systems, the voter is usually voting for a party, not an individual. In **closed-list proportional representation** (the version of PR most dissimilar to FPTP), each party presents a ranked list of candidates for all the seats in the legislature. Voters can see the list and know who the "top" candidates are, but when they vote, they actually vote for the party. If party X gets ten seats in the legislature, then the top ten candidates on the party list occupy those seats.

Another variant of PR is called **open-list proportional representation**. In this version, voters are presented with a list and may actually mark the ballot for the particular candidate of their choice. When the votes are counted, each party receives a number of seats based on the total number of votes cast for all candidates from that party. Those seats are then awarded to the top individual vote getters within the party.

PR assumes that voters primarily want the ideas and values they share to be represented. Voters, in theory, feel they are represented by the party they support and its actions in the legislature, regardless of the geographic origins of individual legislators. This has some obvious advantages over FPTP. First, there are very few wasted votes, because even very small parties can gain some seats. To the extent that voters feel represented by a party, they can be assured that someone in the legislature is there to give voice to their views—although realistically, smaller parties can usually only impact policy significantly when they act in coalition with larger parties. Second, perhaps because fewer votes are wasted, participation rates in PR countries are higher, as Figure 7.1 shows. Proponents of PR argue that elections under PR systems are therefore more democratic and more broadly representative, since larger percentages of voters participate. PR systems also tend to elect women and members of ethnic or racial minorities more frequently than FPTP systems do, as party leaders often feel compelled (and in some countries are required by law) to include women or minority candidates on their party lists.

Of course, the PR system has its critics, who point to the "indirect" nature of PR elections: voters don't really choose individual representatives, even in an open-list

closed-list proportional representation: Electoral system in which each party presents a ranked list of candidates, voters vote for the party rather than for individual candidates, and each party awards the seats it wins to the candidates on its list in rank order

open-list proportional representation: Electoral system in which multiple candidates run in each district, voters vote for the individual candidate of their choice, and the candidates with the most votes in the party get the seats the party wins

Figure 7.1

What Affects Turnout?

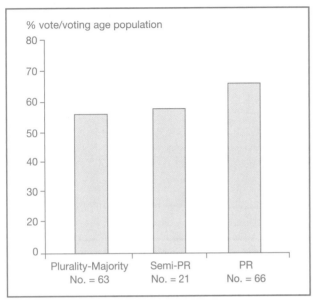

Source: International Institute for Democracy and Electoral Assistance, "What Affects Turnout?" Figure 25, www.idea.int/vt/survey/voter_turnout8.cfm.

Note: No. = number of elections

system. In large, multimember districts, the individual voter does not know that a certain person is "his" or "her" unique representative. And in a closed-list system, party officials are the ultimate arbiters of a candidate's fate because they assign the ranking. Because of this, legislators are less likely to open local offices and focus on issues of local concern (Shugart 2005). In addition, while representation of a broad range of parties in a legislature can be seen as a plus, opponents argue that in practice it often becomes a negative. Small parties, as noted above, often have little voice unless they join coalitions, but small extremist parties can gain inordinate power if they are able to negotiate key roles in ruling coalitions, as our Mini Case on Israel in chapter 6 demonstrated. Coalitions can be hard to form in such a fragmented environment, and where they do form, they may be unstable. PR, therefore, is often criticized as leading to governmental instability and ineffective, fragmented policymaking.

Mixed, or Semiproportional, Systems

mixed, or semiproportional, representation system: An electoral system that combines single-member district representation with overall proportionality in allocation of legislative seats to parties; Germany is a key example

Given the plusses and minuses of FPTP and PR, it is not surprising that some countries, including our case studies Germany and Japan, have chosen to combine the two. The resulting hybrid is called a **mixed,** or **semiproportional, representation system**. A semiproportional system combines single-member district representation with overall proportionality. Voters cast two ballots: one for a representative from their district, with the winner being the individual who gains a plurality, and a second for a party list.

Under the compensatory mixed system in Germany, the legislature is composed by first awarding seats to all the district representatives, after which the party lists are used to add members until each party gets seats equal to approximately its proportionate share of the party list vote. So, for example, a very small party that crosses the 5 percent threshold required to enter parliament might send one or two representatives from its list to the legislature even though none of its candidates for individual district seats were elected. On the other hand, a large party that narrowly sweeps quite a few seats might gain no more from its list when proportional representation is factored in. At the end of the day, the party composition of the legislature looks much as it would have if it had been chosen based strictly on PR, but each district is also guaranteed its own, individual representative, as in a single-member FPTP system. In Japan, the noncompensatory mixed system reserves separate seats for representatives from the individual districts and from the party vote. Parties get whatever the two seat totals happen to be, making Japan's system far less proportional than Germany's.

Women in Power

On January 4, 2007, Rep. Nancy Pelosi, a Democrat from California, became the first woman to be elected Speaker of the U.S. House of Representatives. Her election came only about six weeks shy of the eighty-fifth anniversary of the passage of the Nineteenth Amendment (February 22, 1922), which gave women in the United States the right to vote. Americans are used to considering themselves progressive when it comes to women's rights, but one reason the first election of a woman Speaker took so long was that not many women are found at high levels of government in the United States. In 2010, only 16.8 percent of representatives and 15 percent of senators were women.

Those numbers put the United States slightly below the global average percentage of female elected representatives in national legislatures, which in 2010 was about 19 percent. Americans can take heart at being close to the average, but the country lags well behind twenty-four countries in which women comprise 30 percent or more of lower- or single-house legislatures and another forty-five countries where they account for 20 percent. What explains these disparities in how many women achieve power at the national level?

An initial hypothesis might come out of political culture, because regional breakdowns seem to suggest that it plays a role. The famously progressive Scandinavians elect the most women (42.1 percent); followed by the Americas (22.7 percent); Europe, excluding Scandinavia (20.1 percent); Asia (18.6 percent); sub-Saharan Africa (18.3 percent); the Pacific (13.2 percent); and the Arab states (9.2 percent). These figures might be interpreted to suggest that countries with longer histories of feminism and more secular societies are culturally more receptive to electing women. When we look at particular cases, however, we can ask whether this pattern holds up. For example, why does the United States elect fewer women than Bolivia, Ecuador, or Costa Rica—all countries that enfranchised women later than the United States and have arguably less "feminist" cultures?

An alternative and persuasive hypothesis is that the election of women is a case in which institutions matter. Overall, PR systems are more conducive to electing women than are SMD systems. Of the more than sixty countries that were above the world average for females in elected national legislatures in 2007, only eight used a first-past-the-post electoral system. Thirty-seven FPTP countries elected less than the average percentage of women legislators. More evidence to support this hypothesis comes from countries that use semiproportional, or mixed, electoral systems. Data from Germany and New Zealand in the mid-1990s, for example, show that the percentage of women elected from single-member districts was around the U.S. average, whereas the percentage elected from PR lists was closer to Scandinavian levels.

Why would PR systems be more conducive to electing women? First, the more often women are nominated, the more they win. Since PR systems require parties to submit lists of candidates, more women are nominated. Second, a party may be under some inherent pressure to include at least some women on its list, since an all-male (or even overwhelmingly male) list would invite voter scrutiny and possibly a negative reaction. Finally, a quota system (a national requirement that parties run a certain percentage of women candidates) is easier to implement in a PR system than in a single-member district system, especially one as decentralized as that found in the United States. When a country uses a quota to increase the number of women nominated, more are elected. In fact, one reason the regional average for the Americas is higher than the U.S. average is that a number of Central and South American countries adopted PR systems, quotas for women, or both when they returned to democracy in the 1990s after periods of military rule. Increased representation of women may not be an intended effect of a PR system, but it is an example of how institutional choices can matter to political outcomes.

Source: Inter-Parliamentary Union, "Women in National Parliaments," World Classification Table, http://www .ipu.org/wmn-e/classif.htm. Based on figures for lower or single house.

Mixed systems share some of the advantages of FPTP and PR systems. Because there are fewer wasted votes, participation rates tend to be slightly higher, as in PR (see Figure 7.1), yet citizens are also guaranteed a personal representative to whom they can appeal. In addition, the single-district component of semiproportional systems tends to reinforce the dominance of a couple of large parties that find it easier to win a significant number of individual seats. Small parties also form and are represented, but the dominance of a couple of major parties facilitates coalition formation and stability.

Other Systems

single, nontransferable vote (SNTV) system: Electoral system in which multiple seats exist in each legislative district but each voter only votes for one candidate; Japan prior to 1993 was a key example

alternative-vote (AV) system: Single-member district electoral system in which voters rank all candidates rather than voting for just one

While the three systems noted above are by far the most common, a couple of others exist as well. Until 1994, Japan had a **single, nontransferable vote (SNTV) system**. This system has large, multimember districts, but each voter votes for only one candidate. The candidates who receive the most votes win. Each party, therefore, runs several candidates in each district, and the winning candidates often receive only 15 to 20 percent of the votes in their district. This system encourages campaigns to adopt a local focus; candidates have to have a clear and often focused electoral base to win enough votes to get one of the seats, but they do not need to appeal broadly to a majority of the district's voters.

A referendum in the United Kingdom in May 2011 asked citizens if they wished to switch to an **alternative-vote (AV) system**. AV is an SMD system in which voters rank all candidates rather than voting for just one. When the ballots are counted, the first-place votes for the candidate with the least votes in a district are reallocated to those voters' second-choice candidates. This continues until one candidate has

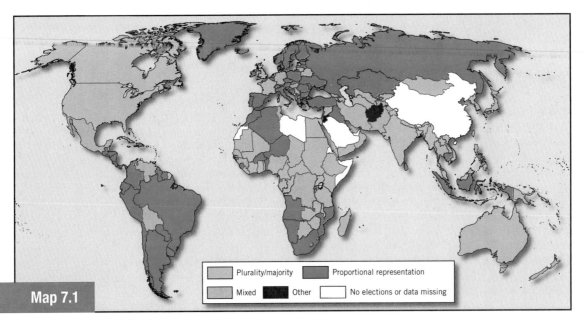

Map 7.1

World Electoral Systems

The influence of colonization and region are clear in the distribution of electoral systems around the world. Former British and French colonies tend to have pluralist systems, while the rest of continental Europe and its former colonies tend to have proportional systems.

Source: International Institute for Democracy and Electoral Assistance, http://www.idea.int/esd/world.cfm. Modified by the authors.

gained a majority of the votes for the district. This system provides a single representative for each district who has the legitimacy of having won a majority of the votes, and it wastes fewer votes than does FPTP in a multiparty context. It is likely to achieve greater proportionality than FPTP but certainly not as much as a simple PR system. Critics have also contended that AV's complexity would make it difficult for voters to understand, thereby lowering its legitimacy in their eyes.

Summary

Single-member district systems give preference to representation based on geography, as opposed to the representation based on ideology that proportional representation systems favor. Geographical representation means that citizens can know specifically who "their" representative is and hold him or her accountable at election time. PR systems, on the other hand, represent ideological divisions in society. Given the importance of ideological beliefs in influencing how people vote in modern democracies, PR systems may represent important social divisions more effectively than SMD systems do. PR systems, however, do not give citizens a specific person who is "their own" representative. Mixed and alternative systems fall in between the SMD and PR models. The type of representation is only one of the trade-offs that the choice of electoral system entails. An electoral system can also have an important impact on two other formal institutions: political parties and party systems.

FORMAL INSTITUTIONS: POLITICAL PARTIES AND PARTY SYSTEMS

American political scientist E. E. Schattschneider wrote that "modern democracy is unthinkable save in terms of the parties" (1942/2009, 1). Political parties are associations that seek to formally control government. In democracies, parties seek to control the government via elections and are limited in what they can do once they gain control. They bring together many individual citizens and a number of discrete interests into a coalition of broadly shared interests that potentially helps to overcome the collective action problem. The number of parties and their relative institutional strength constitute a **party system**. Parties perform important functions in any democracy, such as mobilizing citizens to participate in the political process, recruiting and training political elites, clarifying and simplifying voter choices, organizing governments, and providing strong opposition to the current government. Political scientists compare parties and party systems based on their ideologies, internal organization, and the number of parties in a system. These differences have important implications for where and how citizens can participate in a political system and the extent to which diverse interests are represented in a legislature.

party system: The number of parties and each one's relative institutional strength

Political Parties

Party organizations and their relationships to their members vary widely. Many parties in Europe began in the nineteenth century as **cadre parties,** collections of political elites who chose candidates and mobilized voters to support them. They had small memberships and often started among elected politicians who restricted membership to themselves and their closest elite supporters. One of the foremost

cadre parties: Parties that have a small membership of political elites who choose candidates and mobilize voters to support them; in contrast to mass parties

scholars of parties, French political scientist Maurice Duverger (1969), argued that with the universal franchise and full-scale industrialization, cadre parties became **mass parties** that recruited as many members as possible who participated actively in the party organization and expected to have some influence over it.

mass parties: Parties that recruit as many members as possible who expect to have some control over their party and from whom the parties gain financial support, labor, and votes; in contrast to cadre parties

All parties in democracies must mobilize citizens to support them, so how do they overcome the classic collective action problem of convincing the average citizen to participate? Most people would answer that citizens join parties because they agree with their ideas; in other words, citizens join parties for ideological reasons. This is often the case, but it is certainly not the only reason. People also join parties to gain direct material benefits. The party machines in early twentieth-century U.S. cities, for example, offered preferential treatment to party members when allocating jobs or awarding business contracts with city governments. Most political scientists argue that material incentives for joining a party are more typical in new democracies in which parties are relatively weak and in relatively poor economies that lack economic alternatives. In postindustrial wealthy democracies, ideological reasons for joining a party are the most common. Joining a party can also come almost automatically from being a member of a particular group, as in the case of ethnically or religiously divided societies in which each group has its own party, or in the case of the Labour Party in Britain, which most union members automatically join via their union membership. Party membership itself can become a source of identification for particular families; new voters join and support the party their families "have always supported" without necessarily making a conscious choice.

The size of its membership and the reasons citizens join it are important in determining a party's relative institutional strength or weakness. The relationships among party members, political candidates, and campaign resources (mainly money) are also essential. Parties that have internal mechanisms through which registered members select candidates are likely to be stronger than those that select candidates via external processes, such as primaries in the United States. Candidates who are chosen by party members in an internal process like that used in Britain are likely to be very loyal to the interests and demands of the party members who formally select them and who provide the bulk of their campaign resources. Also, legislators from such a party are more likely to vote as a block in support of official party positions. In contrast, candidates in the United States raise most of their own campaign funds and gain their party's nomination via a primary election that is open to all registered voters in the party (or, in some states, to all voters regardless of party), not just formal party members who have paid dues and attended meetings. This means that candidates in the United States are much more independent of party leaders' demands, so they can act more independently once in office. U.S. parties are less unified and weaker than many of their European counterparts for this reason. A parliamentary system in which top party leaders can aspire to become cabinet members also strengthens parties, as MPs follow their party leaders' wishes in the hope of being selected for the cabinet.

When most people think of parties and their differences, though, the first thing that comes to mind is ideology. Klaus von Beyme (1985) created the classic categorization of European parties based on their origins and ideologies. The most important of these categories are liberal, conservative, socialist/social democratic, communist, christian democratic, right-wing extremist, and the ecology movement. These party types reflect the social and economic changes that characterized nineteenth-century Europe. For example, conservative parties originated as cadre parties that were interested in defending the traditions and economic status of the landed elite against the liberals, who pressed for expanded rights for the bourgeoisie and the growth of market economies. Socialists and communists, meanwhile, tried to create mass parties to represent the interests of the emerging, but as yet disenfranchised, working class. The box on page 322 explains each of von Beyme's categories in more detail.

In the last twenty years, however, political scientists have noted a new trend: the decline of partisan loyalty toward the traditional parties that competed to govern wealthy democracies throughout the twentieth century. Russell Dalton and others proposed a sociological explanation: the decline in traditional social divisions based on class and religion, the rise of widespread access to education, and the growing importance of the media have combined to produce a marked drop in membership in and loyalty to political parties since the 1950s and especially since the 1980s (Dalton and Wattenberg 2000). Declining partisanship has resulted in lower voter turnout in most countries; increased electoral volatility in that voters switch parties more frequently from one election to the next; more single-issue voting, especially on such postmaterialist issues as the environment or abortion; more new parties successfully entering the political arena; and greater focus on the personality of individual candidates rather than on parties and policy platforms.

Parties have responded by changing how they conduct campaigns and how they relate to their members. In almost all countries, parties today have fewer members than in the past, though in many cases the members who remain have been given a greater role in choosing candidates and setting policies (Scarrow, Webb, and Farrell 2000). The ideological differences among parties have also tended to narrow over time, as parties can no longer rely on a core of committed partisan voters and must instead try to attract the growing number of uncommitted voters; these are mostly highly educated individuals who tend to be in the ideological center. Many parties have therefore become what are termed "catch-all" parties. Overall, fragmentation and individualization of the electorate have weakened parties as institutions. Parties remain important legislatively, but they no longer represent core groups as clearly. Dalton and others argue that this trend weakens democracy.

Political scientists Mark Blyth and Richard Katz (2005) took this argument one step further, creating an elite theory of contemporary parties. Using a political economy argument, they suggested that formerly catch-all parties are now becoming what they term "cartel parties." Catch-all parties, they argued, attracted voters by offering more and more aid and services to them, justifying their actions in part by pointing to Keynesian economic theory's advocacy of extensive state intervention in the economy and the provision of social services (see chapter 5). By the late twentieth century, however, this strategy was meeting fiscal constraints, in part created by globalization. Governments were no longer able to expand social benefits continuously, so parties could no longer simply offer more to attract voters. They instead accepted monetarist theories and sold those to the electorate, lowering expectations about what was possible. At the same time, changes in media made individual party members and activists increasingly irrelevant; elections were won and lost based on access to large amounts of money for successful media campaigns. Mobilizing party members based on ideological passion and commitment was no longer necessary. Competition came to be about "managerial competence" rather than ideological differences or promises of benefits. In effect, major parties formed a cartel to maintain power, using media and money to persuade voters to support them without offering significant policy plans or changes; all major parties implicitly came to agree on preserving the status quo. The only innovative policy alternatives in this context come from minor parties, which is perhaps one reason why their share of votes is increasing in most countries. FPTP systems that keep minor parties out of power, then, would seem to be the most elitist under this theory.

Von Beyme's Categorization of Political Parties

CONSERVATIVES arose in the nineteenth century to represent the landed aristocracy and other rural supporters who opposed economic reform and industrialization. They favor a strong state, nationalism, and preservation of the status quo. In the late twentieth century they increasingly accepted free-market ideas, coming closer to the ideology of the Republican Party in the United States.

CHRISTIAN DEMOCRATS emerged in the nineteenth century to represent Catholics in predominantly Protestant countries, but the parties now appeal to Protestants as well. Their Christian ideologies led to a centrist position between socialists and conservatives on social welfare, combined with very conservative positions on social and moral issues.

LIBERALS emerged in eighteenth- and nineteenth-century Europe to represent the growing bourgeoisie, who were interested in expanding their political rights vis-à-vis the aristocracy and in creating a largely unfettered market and limited social programs. These are the parties of classic liberalism described in chapter 3. Von Beyme classified both major U.S. parties as liberal.

SOCIALISTS/SOCIAL DEMOCRATS emerged in the nineteenth century from the working class and championed political rights for workers, improved working conditions, and expanded social welfare programs. Most socialists became social democrats and remained committed to electoral democracy, in contrast to the communists.

COMMUNISTS split off from the socialists after World War I to align themselves with the Soviet Union. They participated in elections only as a means to power. After the expected global communist revolution failed to materialize, "Eurocommunism" emerged in the 1970s. This ideology retained the goal of eventually achieving a communist society but held that communists in the meantime should work within the electoral system to gain power and expand social welfare policies. They often did this in alliance with socialist parties.

RIGHT-WING EXTREMISTS include European nationalist parties that began to emerge in the 1980s. They believe in a strong state, articulate an ideology based on the concept of "national character," and want to severely limit immigration and instill "traditional values."

ECOLOGY MOVEMENT parties such as the German Greens are left-wing parties (see the German Case Study in this chapter). They emerged from the environmental social movement of the 1970s to try to gain representation for environmental issues in the legislature. They often support socialist parties but have a stronger environmental commitment that extends even to protecting the environment at the expense of economic growth or jobs, which socialists typically are unwilling to sacrifice.

Before these recent changes, the European ideologies that arose in the nineteenth and early twentieth centuries influenced parties throughout the world, though each country has its own variations, including parties based on social divisions and ideas other than those derived in Europe. In Latin America, as in Europe, cadre parties emerged in the nineteenth century that pitted some type of conservative party favoring the landholding elite against liberals favoring reforms in the interest of industry and urbanization. Later, socialist parties emerged as well. With industrialization, parties expanded their mass membership to some extent, though in many countries they remained rather weak due in part to authoritarian (usually military) interruptions to the democratic process. Military governments banned or severely limited the freedom of political parties and eliminated elections, at least for a while. Parties had to reemerge and rebuild whenever democracy was restored.

Populism developed in the mid-twentieth century as a distinct and powerful movement and ideological basis for parties in much of Latin America. Populists proclaimed a vaguely socialist ideology that promised direct government aid to poor people and gained support from urban workers. They also, however, were often close to the military and championed a strong sense of nationalism and a strong state, at times undermining democracy altogether in the name of state strength. Their policies were often based on a form of clientelism—populist rulers rewarded urban supporters with government services and infrastructure—rather than a systematic shift toward a more socialist society. Material incentives, then, remained an important reason to support populist parties, which in many countries have been and continue to be weak.

Parties emerged as part of the nationalist movements in Asia and in Africa during colonial rule. These were mass parties from the start but often remained very weak, in part because they were so new. In addition, their only ideology was anti-colonialism because their members did not agree on much else. Many, in reality, were collections of disparate leaders, each with a following based on patronage and ethnic identity. Their deep factional divisions were therefore based not so much on ideology as on personality or identity. After independence, many of these parties fragmented, inviting military intervention. Alternatively, one faction would gain control, create a one-party state, and eliminate democracy. Either outcome eliminated real party competition by destroying or emasculating most parties. These parties would eventually reemerge in the 1990s as very weak institutions in new democracies, a subject we turn to in chapter 9.

Party Systems

Individual parties exist in party systems, which are categorized by the number of parties and their relative strength. By definition, democratic party systems include at least two parties, but there is variation beyond that. At one extreme is the **dominant-party system**, in which multiple parties exist but the same party wins every election and governs continuously. In this system, free and (more or less) fair elections take place following the electoral rules of the country, but one party is popular enough to win every election. In South Africa, for instance, the African National Congress (ANC), Nelson Mandela's party that led the struggle for liberation from the racist apartheid regime, has won all four elections easily. (It garnered just less than 66 percent of the vote in the 2009 election.) Numerous opposition parties exist, and they have some seats in the legislature and are allowed to compete openly in the elections, but the ANC remains overwhelmingly popular. The line can be thin between a dominant-party system and a semi-authoritarian regime; in the latter, a dominant party maintains power not only via its popularity but also via manipulation of the electoral system, control of government resources, and intimidation of other parties. We explore semi-authoritarianism in detail in chapter 8.

In a **two-party system**, only two parties are able to garner enough votes to win an election, though more may compete. The United Kingdom and United States both have two-party systems. In the nineteenth century in the United Kingdom, the Conservatives and the Liberals vied for control, and one or the other always won. With the rise of labor unions, the Labour Party emerged and eventually became stronger than the Liberal Party. Since the 1920s, the Labour Party and the Conservative Party

populism: A broad and charismatic appeal to poor people on the part of a leader to solve their problems directly via governmental largess; most common in Latin America in the early to mid-twentieth century

dominant-party system: Party system in which multiple parties exist but the same one wins every election and governs continuously

two-party system: Party system in which only two parties are able to garner enough votes to win an election, though more may compete; the United Kingdom and United States are key examples

METHODS IN CONTEXT

What's the Trouble with Political Parties?

The trend of major parties losing the support of a portion of the electorate is widespread across wealthy democracies, regardless of the type of governing institutions, party systems, or electoral systems in those countries. Parties that routinely shared the vast majority of voters' loyalty in the 1950s have seen their shares of the vote decrease and their memberships decline. At the same time, voters switch parties more frequently, and new parties have arisen in the last twenty years. Two schools of thought have emerged about what is happening and where it will lead. One school sees a fundamental partisan dealignment, as voters and parties disconnect, probably for the long term. Another school, more optimistically perhaps, sees a less permanent realignment; voters' preferences have changed and the traditional parties haven't kept up, but as they change or as new parties emerge, voters and parties will once again come into alignment and a new period of partisan stability will emerge. Determining which of these assessments is more accurate is crucial to determining what democracies in wealthy countries will be like in the future.

HYPOTHESIS

Such a broad trend presents a rich field for comparative politics research. The dependent variable (the thing we want to explain) is the major parties' declining share of the vote. Scholars have hypothesized about numerous independent variables that might explain this trend, some of which we mentioned in the text above. Those who see a realignment happening point to evidence of changes in voters' preferences. Inglehart's (1971) theory of postmaterialism (see chapter 1) is perhaps the most widely accepted

explanation of such a realignment: the traditional economic divisions on which parties were based are no longer as important to voters. Others have argued that economic concerns are still important but that in postindustrial service economies and the age of globalization, those interests no longer fall neatly on either side of the "left-right" divide that has long separated major parties (Iversen and Wren 1998; Rodrik 1997). Following the arguments of Blyth and Katz, other scholars have used data from party manifestos and parties' policy positions to show that the ideological differences between parties are narrowing (Budge, Robertson, and Hearl 1987; Caul and Gray 2000).

Those supporting the dealignment school point to evidence of deeper sociological changes that they fear are permanently delinking parties and voters. Major parties used to serve two key functions: educating voters about political issues, and simplifying choices for voters. As voters have become more educated and media outlets have multiplied, they no longer need parties to educate them. The media changes have also prompted parties to campaign increasingly via national media rather than by mobilization of grassroots membership, and this has made it less important for them to maintain their membership base (Dalton and Wattenberg 2000). We are faced, then, with two sets of hypotheses trying to explain the growing delinking of voters and traditional parties, and the evidence suggests that all of these independent variables are moving in the direction theorized.

RESEARCH AND ANALYSIS

Anne Wren and Kenneth McElwain (2007) used regression analysis to try to answer the question of which theory of declining party influence is most important, as all the trends seem to be moving in the same direction. (Regression is a statistical technique that analyzes the effects of multiple independent variables on a dependent variable, taking the effects of all independent variables into account simultaneously.) In this instance, the key dependent variable used by Wren and McElwain is the share of the vote in each election from 1960 to 2002 that was received by parties that existed prior to 1960 (i.e., the old, traditional parties). The researchers included a total of eleven independent variables, the most important of which were (a) the number of new parties in each election; (b) electoral volatility, which is a measure of the number of voters who switch parties from one election to the next; and (c) voter turnout. Each of these independent variables was assessed to determine if trends go in a particular direction by decade.

As is often the case, the results are somewhat ambiguous. On the one hand, all the variables together explain 97 percent of the change in the dependent variable. This is an unusually strong finding in political science, but the specifics still leave uncertainty as to what is happening. The entry of new parties has the largest impact on the older parties' share of the vote, which can be interpreted as supporting realignment; voters' preferences are shifting, and new parties are emerging in response. Electoral volatility also has a greater impact on older parties than on newer ones, again indicating that the older parties are losing votes to newer ones rather than to other older parties. Declining turnout also affects the major parties more than new parties, and Wren and McElwain suggested that this finding supports the dealignment theory by showing that

older parties are no longer able to mobilize grassroots supporters adequately. Because some variables point to realignment and others to dealignment, the authors suggested that further research is necessary but noted that a close look at electoral volatility may be helpful. If realignment is occurring, then volatility should eventually drop as voters settle into new, stable patterns. The researchers examined the rate of increase in volatility since 1960 and found that it had been steady across the decades; volatility has been increasing, and there are no signs that it will slow. They cautiously concluded that dealignment is more likely to be occurring than realignment, though even this sophisticated statistical analysis cannot support that conclusion definitively.

QUESTIONS IN CONTEXT

Because the key variables are easily quantifiable, electoral studies lend themselves to statistical analysis, but even Wren and McElwain's rather sophisticated regression analysis did not produce definitive results. Two key questions in any statistical analysis are whether the variables actually measure the underlying concepts they are intended to measure and how the results are interpreted. As Wren and McElwain noted for electoral volatility, interpretation is not always obvious. Look back at their variables mentioned above: Do they measure the concepts they are intended to? Wren and McElwain also depended entirely on voting results for their data. Are there other research methods or types of data that might help us understand better why voters are changing how they vote?

have been the only two parties able to win a majority in a national election. In the United States, no third party has had significant representation in government since the Republicans first emerged in the 1850s. Third parties, such as Ross Perot's Reform Party during the presidential campaigns of the 1990s, arise to compete in particular elections, but they never survive more than two elections as a political force of any significance.

In the oddly named **two-and-a-half-party system,** two large parties win the most votes, but typically neither gains a majority. Thus, a third party (the "half" party) must join one of the major parties to form a legislative majority. The classic case, at least until recently, is Germany. In addition, an unusual 2010 election in the United Kingdom made Britain's system look like a two-and-a-half-party system for the first time ever. The Conservatives failed to win a majority, so they had to form a coalition government with the Liberal Democrats.

Finally, **multiparty systems** are those in which more than two parties could potentially win a national election and govern. Some of these, such as Italy, are similar to the two-and-a-half-party system in that two of the parties are quite large; one of the large parties almost always wins the most votes, but neither is able to win a majority. This requires the large parties to form coalitions with one or more of several smaller parties in order to govern. In still other multiparty systems, three or four relatively equal parties regularly contend for power, with a legislative majority always requiring a coalition of at least two parties.

How and why did these different systems emerge and change over time in different countries? The explanations offered have usually been either sociological or institutional. Sociological explanations posit that a party system reflects the society in which it emerges. Parties arise to represent the various interests of self-conscious groups in particular societies. In nineteenth-century Europe, two major conflicts emerged: an economic one between capital and labor and a religious one either between Protestants and Catholics or between church supporters and more secular voters. The economic conflict became universal as industrialization expanded. All countries eventually had some sort of party defending business interests (usually called "liberal") and a socialist or social democratic party championing workers' concerns. Religious divisions, on the other hand, existed in some places but not everywhere. For instance, Germany has a Christian Democratic Party and France does not because Catholics were a self-conscious minority in nineteenth-century Germany; overwhelmingly Catholic France did not need a Catholic party, but the German Catholic minority did. Where economic and religious divisions were politically salient, multiparty systems emerged; where only the economic division was important, two-party systems emerged.

Institutionalists, on the other hand, argue that the broader institutional setting, especially a country's electoral system, greatly shapes both the number and strength of parties. Political leaders will respond rationally to the institutional constraints they face by creating the types of parties that will help them gain power in the system in which they operate. One classic institutionalist argument is known as **Duverger's Law,** named after Maurice Duverger. He contended that the logic of electoral competition in SMD electoral systems results in the survival of only two parties in the long term. Multiple parties are unlikely to survive because all political parties must gain a plurality (or a majority if required) in a particular district to win that district's legislative seat. The successful parties will be those whose members realize that their parties must have very broad appeal. Relying on a small, ideologically committed core group will yield no legislative seats. Over time, ambitious politicians realize that the way to electoral victory is through the already established major parties rather than the creation of a third one.

two-and-a-half-party system: Party system in which two large parties win the most votes but typically neither gains a majority; a third party (the "half" party) must join one of the major parties to form a legislative majority; Germany is key example

multiparty systems: Party systems in which more than two parties could potentially win a national election and govern

Duverger's Law: Institutionalist argument by French political scientist Maurice Duverger that FPTP electoral systems will produce two major parties, eliminating smaller parties

In contrast, PR systems create an incentive for small, focused parties to emerge. The German environmental movement was able to create a successful Green Party because even with a narrow focus, the party could get enough votes to cross the minimum threshold and gain seats in parliament. Conversely, the United Kingdom does not have a strong Green Party because such a party cannot compete for a meaningful number of seats with the Labour Party and the Conservatives. As mentioned above, semiproportional systems tend to produce a couple of dominant parties, which usually win the SMD seats, but also allow for the emergence of smaller parties in the proportional voting.

The debate between sociological and institutional theories of party systems creates something of a "chicken and egg" question: Did political leaders create electoral systems to match the number and kinds of parties they led, or did the electoral systems provide incentives to create particular kinds of parties? The logic in both directions seems strong. In a society with multiple viable parties, party leaders seem likely to favor a proportional system if given the opportunity to choose. No one or two parties are dominant, so all would fear they would lose out in a SMD electoral system. Conversely, in a two-party system like that in the United Kingdom in the late nineteenth century, the two dominant parties would logically favor creating or preserving an SMD system, which strongly favors them over newer and smaller rivals. Carles Boix (2007) presented a historical analysis to try to bring the two approaches together. He argued that in almost all of Europe, parties began as cadre parties—one liberal and one conservative—among the elite, with tiny electorates in SMD systems. Where religious divisions grew, religiously based parties challenged and sometimes split the two established parties. With the rise of the working class and its enfranchisement in the late nineteenth century, socialist parties emerged as well. Where SMD systems were well entrenched, such as in the United Kingdom, the socialists tended to displace one of the prior parties, and the two-party system survived. Where religious divisions had already split the two parties, or in newer democracies in the early twentieth century that did not have well-institutionalized electoral systems, the socialists and other smaller parties successfully demanded a proportional system. The number of PR systems rose rapidly in the late nineteenth and early twentieth centuries, and electoral system changes have been rare ever since. Boix's history suggests that sociological and institutional forces influenced each other at particular historical points to create the systems of the twentieth century, which then remained relatively stable until the late-century decline of partisanship discussed above.

MINI CASE

France and the Shift toward a Two-Party System

Maurice Duverger's native France provides a classic example of Duverger's Law at work, though the country's two-round system and multiparty heritage has meant that even there the law has not worked perfectly. Political instability plagued France's Third (1871–1940) and Fourth (1946–1958) Republics. Both suffered from constantly changing governing coalitions that each typically lasted only a few months. The country under both regimes was deeply divided along ideological lines. Every election put numerous parties into parliament, producing unstable coalition governments. A crisis at the end of the Fourth Republic led to the creation in 1958 of the Fifth Republic, whose semipresidential system was designed to end the instability. The Fifth Republic has been successful in this regard, though not only because of the semi-presidential system—a new electoral system has also had a significant impact.

The prior republics had PR systems, which facilitated the election of numerous parties into parliament. The constitution of the Fifth Republic created not only a strong presidency but also a two-round, majoritarian electoral system. For both legislative and presidential elections (after 1962), a first-round election is open to all registered parties. The country is divided into single-member legislative districts similar to FPTP systems. If a candidate for a legislative district (or nationally for the presidency) wins a majority of the votes in the first round, he or she is duly elected. If not, a run-off election is held two weeks later between the top two candidates in the first round, producing a majority winner. This allows all of France's numerous parties to contest the first-round election. In each district in which a second round takes place, the losing parties usually support the candidate who is ideologically closest to them.

This system resulted in the creation of two "families" of ideologically similar parties, one on the left and one on the right, which are pledged to support each other in the second-round elections. In some cases, if they know a particular candidate is very strong in a particular district, other candidates within a party family might agree not to contest the first round to ensure the stronger candidate's victory. By the 1970s, each party family consisted of two significant parties, the Communists and the Socialists on the left and the Gaullists (political descendants of the Fifth Republic's founder, Charles de Gaulle) and Centrists on the right. Within each family, the two major parties were almost equally represented in the National Assembly, thus producing four major parties.

The first shift away from this came in the 1980s and 1990s. The Communists became less popular, and the Socialists won the presidency for the first time in 1981. By 1988, the Socialists held nearly 90 percent of the seats won by the left as a whole. They still governed in a coalition with the Communists but were overwhelmingly dominant in that relationship. On the right, the two main parties survived longer, but once the Gaullist Jacques Chirac became president in 1995, his movement also became dominant, gaining nearly 90 percent of the seats controlled by the right. By 2007, the two largest parties, the Socialists on the left and the Gaullists on the right, controlled 88 percent of the seats in the National Assembly, compared to only 56 percent in 1973.

CASE SUMMARY

France's two-round electoral system has allowed numerous smaller parties to survive, though their share of real power has declined substantially. Smaller parties use the first round to gain the support of their ideologically committed followers, often as a form of protest vote against the two major parties. The most notable recent example was the far-right (most say racist), anti-immigrant National Front, whose presidential candidate shocked the country and the world by coming in second in the first round of the 2002 presidential election. (He won only 18 percent of the vote in the second round.)

Indeed, the major-party families have seen their share of the vote in the first round of legislative elections decline over time as more people vote for small parties outside the mainstream. The logic of the majoritarian system, however, has meant that the two largest parties have come to control the lion's share of the legislative seats and have the only viable presidential candidates. While the smaller parties continue to exist and gain some legislative seats, Duverger's Law has worked in his own country; the shift from PR to a majoritarian system has come close to producing a two-party system. This has provided much greater political stability than France had under earlier regimes, but some would argue that it has diminished real representation of the country's ideologically diverse citizenry.

Summary

Parties and party systems have important implications for democratic rule. Duverger's model of the mass party has long been viewed as the most democratic, with its large membership base that has an active voice in party policies and candidate selection. Recent trends suggest that the strength of the long-standing mass parties is declining in most countries. Parties may have less need than before for active members and be more focused on lowering citizen expectations and keeping themselves in power than on pursuing an ideological agenda. Does it matter whether citizens are more involved in the daily workings of the party, or is citizen approval or disapproval of party actions via the ballot box enough? Elite theorists point to declining partisan loyalty and grassroots activity as signs of growing elite control of modern democracies. Pluralists counter that ultimately voters still have the power to decide which party is in power.

The number of parties in a party system influences the type of parties that exist, the choices voters have, and the stability of governments. SMD tends to encourage two-party systems rather than the multiparty systems that are more likely under PR. In two-party systems, citizens must compromise with others within large parties before they elect representatives, rather than electing a representative of a relatively small and ideologically narrower party who will then compromise with representatives of other parties after being elected. The former system may produce less diverse viewpoints in the legislature, but it also means that two (or relatively few) broad parties will govern, probably making governing easier and perhaps making policy more coherent. Multiparty systems, on the other hand, give more formal voice to diverse opinions in the legislature but can produce unstable coalition governments. How is this trade-off best made?

CIVIL SOCIETY

A great deal of participation and interest representation occurs in civil society, which is the sphere of organized citizen activity between the state and the individual family or firm that we discussed in chapter 3. As that chapter delineated, civil society arose in Europe with capitalism, industrialization, and democracy. Business associations, farmers' groups, and trade unions were the most important initial components of it. Civil society and the organizations within it provide a space and mechanisms that citizens can use to influence government. That makes civil society an important component of participation and representation in a democracy. As with parties, we ask questions about how well organizations in civil society enhance democracy: Are their internal rules democratic? Do they represent their constituents accurately? Do they gain undue influence? Do they have beliefs and foster policies that enhance democracy or harm it?

These questions often seem harder to answer for civil society organizations than for political parties. Our definition of civil society above is a very broad one. It includes every conceivable organized activity that is not focused on individual self-interest and is not controlled by the government. Do all of these necessarily enhance democratic participation and representation? Does a parent-teacher organization or a local Little League matter to democracy? More troubling, does the Ku Klux Klan (KKK)? Is it a viable member of civil society? The KKK is clearly an organized group of citizens that provides a venue for participatory activities that could certainly be political in the sense of trying to influence governmental policy. Its core

TIMELINE

Political Institutions

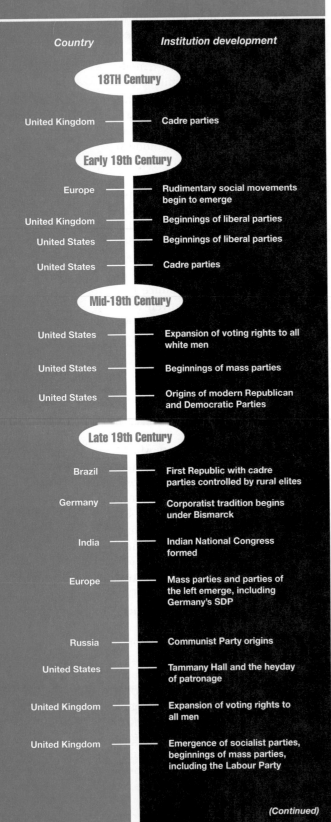

Country	Institution development
18TH Century	
United Kingdom	Cadre parties
Early 19th Century	
Europe	Rudimentary social movements begin to emerge
United Kingdom	Beginnings of liberal parties
United States	Beginnings of liberal parties
United States	Cadre parties
Mid-19th Century	
United States	Expansion of voting rights to all white men
United States	Beginnings of mass parties
United States	Origins of modern Republican and Democratic Parties
Late 19th Century	
Brazil	First Republic with cadre parties controlled by rural elites
Germany	Corporatist tradition begins under Bismarck
India	Indian National Congress formed
Europe	Mass parties and parties of the left emerge, including Germany's SDP
Russia	Communist Party origins
United States	Tammany Hall and the heyday of patronage
United Kingdom	Expansion of voting rights to all men
United Kingdom	Emergence of socialist parties, beginnings of mass parties, including the Labour Party

(Continued)

beliefs, however, violate the basic tenets of liberal democracy, so we could liken it to a political party that espouses openly racist policies or that runs candidates for office on a platform that questions whether democracy should continue (as the Islamic Front did in Algeria in the early 1990s). The beliefs of civil society organizations may well matter to how we assess their impact on democracy.

Their internal structure and the reasons their members join them can matter as well. These issues come up, in particular, with organizations focused on propagating ethnic or religious ideologies. Often, though certainly not always, membership in one of these organizations requires being born into the broader group that it represents. Ethnic and religious organizations are therefore very different from groups in which individual citizens choose to come together based on a shared concern. Ethnic and religious groups also often view any internal dissent as a threat to the broader group, resulting in an undemocratic internal organizational structure. As more and more different kinds of countries become democratic, more and more varied types of civil society organizations arise, making these questions increasingly important.

In most long-standing democracies, though, the term *civil society* typically connotes interest groups. These associations of individuals attempt to influence government, and most claim to represent clearly defined interests that their members share, such as protecting the environment, advancing civil rights, or representing various industries. They are formally organized, though their degree of institutionalization varies widely. They also are often regulated by the government and have to follow certain rules and procedures if they wish to be recognized as legitimate. Well-institutionalized interest groups are visible, have relatively large and active memberships, and have a significant voice on the issues in which they are interested. Less-institutionalized groups are less effective, and their legitimacy as representatives on various issues is often questioned. Similar to parties, interest groups bring together like-minded individuals to achieve a goal, but interest groups do not seek formal political power. If they are effective in carrying out their functions, a particular political system becomes more responsive and inclusive. Political scientists therefore investigate the internal organization of interest groups, the resources at their disposal, their overall institutional strength, and their relationships to the governments they try to influence.

Modern interest groups emerged in the nineteenth century alongside mass electoral democracy. In Europe, this was also a period of rapid industrialization, and labor unions and business associations quickly became the most important interest groups. Associations representing the dwindling farming community also emerged to champion its concerns. Labor, business, and agriculture became the key "sectoral" categories of interest groups; that is, they represented the three key sectors of the economy. As the bulk of the citizenry became more involved in the political process, other interest groups emerged as well, including groups focused on expanding participation rights for women and racial minorities. In postcolonial countries, similar groups emerged. In Latin America, unions and business associations arose with the beginning of industrialization in the late nineteenth century. In Asia and Africa, trade unions developed under colonial rule as colonial subjects began to work for wages and started to organize. Unions became important in the nationalist struggles for independence in most countries.

Government–Interest Group Interaction: Two Models

No matter their origin or cause, the formal and informal relationships that interest groups have with government are crucial to how they operate and how effective they can be. The two major democratic models of government–interest group interaction are known as "corporatist" and "pluralist."

Interest-Group Pluralism We used the word *pluralist* in chapter 1 to describe one of the major theories that attempts to answer the question "Who rules?"; here, however, **interest-group pluralism** means a system in which many groups exist to represent particular interests and the government remains officially neutral among them. Under a pluralist system in this sense, many groups may exist to represent the same broad "interest," and all can try to gain influence. The government, at least in theory, is neutral and does not give preferential access and power to any one group to allow it to be the official representative of a particular interest. The Unites States is the primary model of this pluralist system. The Chamber of Commerce exists to represent business interests, but so does the National Association of Manufacturers, the National Realtors Association, and myriad other groups. Washington, D.C., contains literally thousands of interest groups, sometimes dozens organized around the same issue, all vying for influence over decision makers. This is repeated, on a smaller scale, in all fifty state capitals. The government of the day may listen more to one than another of these groups on a particular issue, but no official and enduring preference or access is given to one over others. Even when one large organization speaks on behalf of most of a sector of society—such as the AFL-CIO for labor—it is a loose confederation of groups whose individual organizational members can and do ignore positions and policies of the national confederation if they choose to do so. Alternative groups have the right to organize as best they can. Figure 7.2 depicts this often confusing system, with multiple groups interacting directly with the government as well as forming various loose affiliations (such as the AFL-CIO) that also interact with the government.

interest-group pluralism: Interest-group system in which many groups exist to represent particular interests and the government remains officially neutral among them; the United States is a key example

Early 20th Century

Brazil	Populist political leaders and parties
China	Origins of Chinese Communist Party
Germany	Origins of National Socialist (Nazi) Party
Japan	Taisho Democracy with electoral competition, 1912–1926
Russia	Russian Revolution; Soviet Communist Party becomes ruling party
United Kingdom	Labour replaces Liberals as second major party
United States	Progressive movement (social movements such as temperance, women's suffrage); early interest groups such as Sierra Club, League of Women Voters

Mid-20th century

Brazil	New Republic; rapid industrialization and expansion of labor unions
Brazil	Military rule and state corporatism with limited party competition, 1964–1985
Germany	New social movements, including Greens, antinuclear, women's movements
Germany	Electoral system created
India	Mass nationalist parties and independence
Iran	Competitive elections; Mossaddeq elected prime minister in 1951, later overthrown
Japan	Electoral system created
Japan	Origins of Japan's LDP
Nigeria	Mass nationalist parties and independence
United States	New social movements, including civil rights, antiwar, women's; new interest groups arise, including NOW, EarthFirst!, PETA

(Continued)

Corporatism The major alternative to interest-group pluralism is corporatism. Unlike pluralism, which exists only in democracies, corporatism has more democratic (societal or neocorporatist) and less democratic (state corporatist) variants. We discuss the latter in chapter 8. **Neocorporatism**, also known as societal corporatism, is most common in northern Europe, where strong **peak associations** bring together numerous local groups to represent the major interests in society and government works closely with them to develop policy, but no legal restrictions exist to prevent other groups from arising. Figure 7.2 depicts this more hierarchical system, in which government tends to interact with fewer, larger, and more highly institutionalized peak associations than under pluralism. Germany is a key example, examined in greater detail in the case study below. In a neocorporatist system, peak associations maintain their unity and institutional strength via internal mechanisms that ensure local organizations will abide by the decisions of the national body. By negotiating binding agreements with them, the state in effect recognizes the peak associations as the official representatives of their sectors. Unlike **state corporatism,** however, no individuals or groups are required to belong to these associations, and they maintain internal systems of democratic control. Dissatisfied members may try to change the association's policies or found alternative organizations, but most do not pursue the latter option because membership in the main body provides direct access to government.

Pluralism and Neocorporatism Compared Both pluralist and neocorporatist models have strengths and weaknesses. Pluralism allows greater local control and participation because any individual or group is free to start a new organization. However, many national organizations have limited control over their local affiliates, so local members can work internally to move their local organization in whatever direction they wish. Because the state does not officially recognize any one group, there are

FIGURE 7.2

Contrasting Models of State-Interest Group Interaction

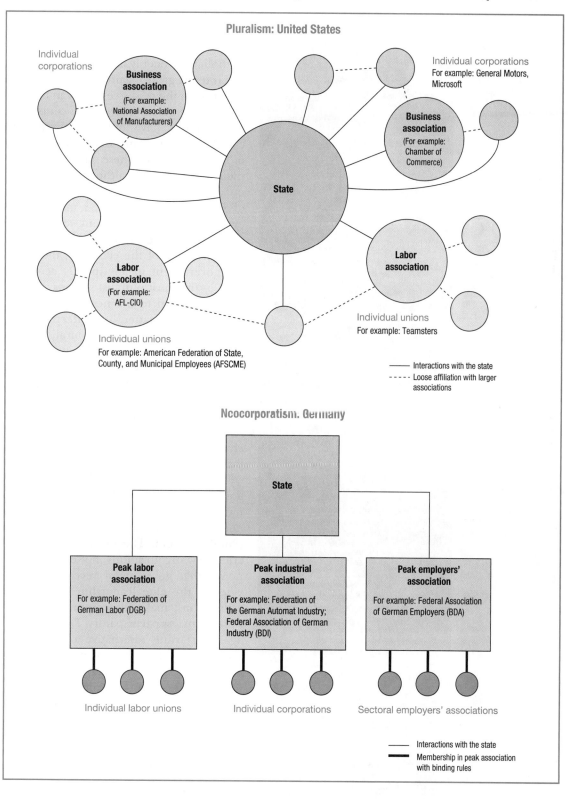

Pluralism: United States

Individual corporations

Business association
(For example: National Association of Manufacturers)

Individual corporations
For example: General Motors, Microsoft

Business association
(For example: Chamber of Commerce)

State

Labor association
(For example: AFL-CIO)

Labor association

Individual unions
For example: Teamsters

Individual unions

For example: American Federation of State, County, and Municipal Employees (AFSCME)

——— Interactions with the state
- - - - Loose affiliation with larger associations

Neocorporatism: Germany

State

Peak labor association

For example: Federation of German Labor (DGB)

Peak industrial association

For example: Federation of the German Automat Industry; Federal Association of German Industry (BDI)

Peak employers' association

For example: Federal Association of German Employers (BDA)

Individual labor unions

Individual corporations

Sectoral employers' associations

——— Interactions with the state
▬▬▬ Membership in peak association with binding rules

Late 20th/early 21st century

Brazil	Transition to multiparty democracy, 1985–1989
Brazil	Presidential victory of strong, programmatic party, the PT, in 2002
China	Emergence of very limited civil society under state corporatism
Germany	Reunification of East and West Germany, rise of Green Party, and expansion of number of parties from three to five
India	Rise of religious parties
India	End of Congress Party dominance, replaced by coalition governments from 1989 onward
India	Rise of lower-caste movements and parties
Iran	Elections, some with parties, under Islamic Republic, from 1980 onward
Japan	Electoral reform from SNTV to semiproportional system in 1993; watershed defeat of long-ruling LDP in 2009
Nigeria	Transition to multiparty democracy in 1999, though with seriously flawed elections; rise of dominant party, the PDP, by 2007
Russia	Fall of communism and birth of new parties, 1991
Russia	Reduction of party competition under Putin from 2000 onward; shift from mixed to PR electoral system in 2005
United Kingdom	Continued dominance of centrist, mass parties; first coalition government in sixty years after 2010 election
United States	Continued dominance of centrist, mass parties; growing electoral volatility from one party to the other

fewer incentives for large organizations to maintain unity. This decentralization may limit the institutional strength and overall power of organizations in national politics. France is well-known for its weak labor unions, for instance, in part because its two largest unions (one communist and one Catholic) are deeply divided over ideology.

Interest groups gain power vis-à-vis the state due to the resources they can bring to bear on the government. More centralized organizations have more resources and can legitimately claim to speak on behalf of more citizens. These factors increase their potential clout, although critics point out that no government treats each kind of group equally, at least in a market economy. Following the argument we laid out in chapter 5, business interests are crucial for the well-being of the economy; therefore, the government in any market economy, even in the most pluralist systems, will pay more attention to business interests than to others, no matter how effectively others organize. Critics of the pluralist model contend that business is still favored while other groups are weakened by their own divisions. They suggest that such groups would be better off under neocorporatism, in which they would be united in large, strong organizations that have a better change of countering the always strong influence of business.

Because neocorporatist associations are so large and united, they typically have more direct influence on government than does any single national association in a pluralist system. The disincentives to creating new organizations, however, and the power that government recognition provides to the elite leadership of the peak associations, make neocorporatist associations seem less participatory. The incentives against starting alternative organizations are so strong that the vast majority of relevant constituents conclude that it is wiser to participate within the confines of already established entities than to start new ones, no matter how dissatisfied they may be. A crucial question in these systems, then, is the degree of democratic control *within* the peak associations. If an institution has strong mechanisms of internal democracy, such as open elections for leadership positions and constituent participation in setting organizational policies, its leaders can legitimately claim to represent members' views. If the institution does not, it may have significant access to government and subsequent influence, but it may not really represent its members' views democratically.

Social Movements

Established interest groups also may not change quickly enough to reflect changes in even the most pluralist of interest group systems. Well-established institutions provide powerful means for participation and representation, but because they are deeply entrenched, they tend to change relatively slowly. When citizens perceive formal institutions as providing inadequate representation or opportunities for political participation, they may choose to participate in groups or activities outside of them. Such informal participation often occurs through **social movements**. Like interest groups, these are part of civil society, but unlike them, social movements have a loosely defined organizational structure and represent people who have been outside the bounds of formal institutions, seek major socioeconomic or political changes to the status quo, or employ noninstitutional forms of collective action.

Perhaps the best-known social movement in recent history is the American civil rights movement of the 1950s and 1960s. In the 1960s, social movements aiming to change women's status, protect the environment, and oppose war arose throughout Western democracies. These movements brought a new generation of activists into politics, changed significant elements of Western societies, and fundamentally altered the way citizens have engaged in politics ever since. Sometimes social movements generate formal interest groups, but rarely does an interest group or broader movement become a political party. An exception is the European "green" movement, which eventually produced Green Parties with representation in a number of European legislatures

What we now call social movements arose at least a century ago, but as noted above, they have become much more common since the 1960s. In that decade in much of the Western world, growing numbers of citizens, particularly young "baby boomers," came to feel that their governments, political parties, and interest groups were not providing adequate forms of participation or representation of their interests. All major political institutions, inside and outside of government, were viewed as organs through which the elite ruled exclusively. Established interest groups were overwhelmingly controlled by white men. In response, new social movements arose among those challenging the status quo, including racial minorities, women, antiwar activists, and environmentalists. These groups have since been joined by many others, such as the antiglobalization movement that proclaimed itself to the world in 1999 in protests and riots in Seattle and the Tea Party movement that arose in the United States in 2009 in opposition to health care reform and what it saw as a broader encroachment of government on personal freedoms and the Constitution.

Social movements are distinct from interest groups in that they are more informal, pursue participation outside the bounds of formal institutions, and tend not to have single and officially recognized leaders. Leaders may emerge, as Martin Luther King Jr. did in the civil rights movement, but they neither lead nor speak for a single unified organization that controls the entire movement. Others may propose other courses of action, as Malcolm X did during the civil rights movement. Yet these informal, uncoordinated social movements, and the underlying social changes they represent, have profoundly changed Western societies. Women entered public life

neocorporatism: Also called societal corporatism; corporatism that evolves historically and voluntarily rather than being mandated by the state; Germany is a key example

peak associations: Organizations that bring together all interest groups in a particular sector to influence and negotiate agreements with the state; in the United States, an example is the AFL-CIO

state corporatism: Corporatism mandated by the state; common in fascist regimes

social movements: Part of civil society; they have a loosely defined organizational structure and represent people who have been outside formal institutions, seek major socioeconomic or political changes, or employ noninstitutional forms of collective action to a degree never before seen. Minorities united to get many segregationist and discriminatory policies overturned and were able to enter public life to a much greater degree. Today, environmental concerns are on national political agendas everywhere, and in the age of global climate change, environmentalists are putting it on the agendas of international political, social, and corporate institutions.

Most of these examples are generally seen as pursuing a "progressive" agenda, meaning an agenda of social change based on new ideas favored by those who consider themselves "on the left" of the political spectrum, usually in the name of the less powerful members of society. The rise of the Tea Party, however, demonstrates that social movements can come from the conservative side of the political spectrum as well. The Tea Party possesses all of the elements of a social movement: loose organization and leadership, opposition to what its members see as the status quo in both political parties and established interest groups, self-perception of its members as outsiders, and demands for fundamental change. It is a conservative movement, though, in the sense that it calls for a return to an earlier era (based in what its members see as the original meaning of the U.S. Constitution). Such a return would mean a rollback of many major policies of the last half century.

Evolution of Social Movements
As social movements have succeeded, sometimes they have changed. Some of their members have founded or joined formal interest groups, such as the National Organization of Women, or even political parties, such as the German Greens. When successful social movements cross over into the sphere of formal institutions, new social movement groups often emerge to replace them with new and more challenging agendas. In the environmental movement, for example, the institutionalization of groups like Friends of the Earth as interest groups has left the role of social movement open to new challengers like EarthFirst!

Social Movements and Democratic Participation
Some political scientists see social movements as symptomatic of the problems that have come to be associated with participation and representation in wealthy democracies in the last two decades. Robert Putnam, for example, decried a decline in **social capital**, that is, social networks and norms of reciprocity. He saw social capital as crucial to democracy and economic growth. Developed in the context of Italy and later applied to the United States in a widely read article and book, both titled *Bowling Alone* (2000), Putnam's argument was that even apparently "nonpolitical" organizations in civil society create social networks and mutual trust among members, which can be used for political action. The demise of traditional membership-based organizations such as local parent-teacher associations and, yes, bowling leagues, undermines the ability of citizens to trust and cooperate with one another, in turn hindering their ability to engage in collective action in a democracy. Most research in this vein has focused on the United States, but scholars note that since the 1970s, public opinion polls throughout Europe, North America, and Japan have shown a decline in levels of trust in government, political parties, and virtually all other political institutions. The extent to which this is true varies across countries, but the trend is similar virtually everywhere.

Many theorists have argued that mass communication—television, the Internet, portable cellular devices, and social networking technology—has had a role in reducing social capital and trust in political institutions such as parties. Others,

social capital: Social networks and norms of reciprocity that are important for a strong civil society

though, question this. While Putnam (2000) and Dalton (Dalton and Wattenberg 2000) faulted mass media for undermining civil society, Pippa Norris (2002) reached less dire conclusions. Using different data sets and dividing countries on the basis of wealth, she concluded that while party membership has declined in wealthier countries overall, and that this decline is tied to the presence of television in particular, it is questionable whether representation and parties as institutions are weakening. In countries without mass communication, building effective and representative parties by necessity depends on face-to-face communication and campaigning, which is not easy. Communication (and therefore representation) improves in countries with nearly universal access to television, telephones, and the Internet. The use of social-networking technology in the recent political mobilization in Iran, Egypt, and Tunisia, among other places, has also led analysts to argue that the new technology may actually enhance participation rather than harm it.

Moreover, while levels of trust have declined, involvement in political activities has not. It has, however, shifted to new and different organizations and forms, including social movements; in other words, political involvement has morphed into new and important, but sometimes informal, forms of participation. Nicholas Lemann (1996), for instance, countered Putnam's thesis in *Bowling Alone* with the aptly titled article "Kicking in Groups," in which he highlighted increasing participation in youth soccer organizations. Citizens may participate in these new groups and perhaps influence government successfully, but they move relatively quickly among different issues and movements and may not develop strong ties with any particular group. The U.S. organization MoveOn! is an example; members are connected mainly via the Internet, and communication is almost exclusively via e-mail. Such a relatively new communications medium encourages electronic letter writing and petitions, phone call campaigns, and local demonstrations, despite the absence of formal local branches with official membership lists or regular meetings. Given her findings, Norris questioned whether the changes she and others have observed are undermining democracy.

As is often the case in comparative politics, there are no certain answers about trends and what they mean. Nonetheless, the questions raised are profound. All agree that, in wealthy democracies at least, the ways in which people participate in local community groups and larger political institutions are changing significantly and that trust in political institutions has declined markedly. What effect does this have on the health of democracy? How much participation must take place and in what forms if a democracy is to thrive? What kinds of institutional connections must exist between the political elite and the citizenry for the former to represent the interests of the latter? How much involvement and influence do average members need in political organizations—whether interest groups or parties—to ensure that those institutions represent their members well? Do new, less formal, and less stable forms of participation adequately replace mass-membership organizations such as trade unions and the mass-membership parties common in the early and mid-1900s? Keep these questions in mind as we examine participation and representation in five of our case study countries below.

PATRON-CLIENT RELATIONSHIPS

Another type of informal participation is undoubtedly the most widespread: patron-client relationships, meaning the direct provision of material support to individual voters in exchange for their support. Like all informal participation, patron-client relationships are most important where formal institutions are weakest or most restrictive. This means that patron-client relationships are usually most important in authoritarian regimes, but they certainly exist in democracies and are quite important in some, as the following case studies on Japan and India demonstrate. Patron-client relationships sound undemocratic, or at least threatening to democracy. In the absence of other effective means of participation and representation, however, forming a relationship with a patron may be the best option available for having a voice and getting government help.

This form of participation is most common in a set of fairly clear contexts. Weak formal institutions are almost always part of this context, but are rarely the only aspect. Poverty and/or inequality are frequently associated with extensive use of patron-client relationships as well. Poor people are more likely to need and accept material inducement in exchange for their political support, and a large income gap between patrons and their potential clients gives the patrons plenty of resources to pass out as "gifts" to clients. Some analysts also argue that political culture and norms play a role in this: societies in which gift giving and reciprocity between the elite and the average citizen are long-standing traditions are more likely to accept and practice these norms in the political arena. Patron-client relationships are particularly important in much of Africa. Extreme poverty and inequality in the context of weak government institutions that are characterized by extensive corruption mean that average citizens participate mostly by following a key patron. The patron's clients provide him (or, much more rarely, her) with political support, including votes, in exchange for material help when the patron needs it. Even political parties are really just vehicles for key patrons to contest elections; when a patron changes parties, his clients move with him. Loyalty to the patron, not the party, is key. There is clearly an element of domination and inequality involved in patron-client relationships. But in a context in which formal institutions do not provide the means for average citizens to overcome collective action problems and achieve meaningful participation and representation, becoming a client of a powerful patron may be the most beneficial form of participation available.

It is important to remember as well that patronage and patron-client relations played an important part in the early growth of many political parties and party machines in countries we now consider quite democratic, including the United States. Material inducements are certainly one of the reasons people join and support political parties, as we noted above. Our case studies show that many, if not all, countries have or used to have some elements of patron-clientelism. In newly democratizing countries, patronage networks may carry over from non-democratic to democratic regimes. Will they weaken with time and succumb to anticorruption measures, as they seem to have done in more established democracies? This is one of the comparative historical questions that political scientists try to answer.

CASE STUDIES IN PARTICIPATION AND REPRESENTATION

We now turn to an examination of participation and representation in several of the established democracies among our case studies. This will allow us to examine the interaction and overall effect of the electoral system, parties and the party system, civil society, and patron-client relationships on citizens' ability to participate and be represented. It will illustrate as well the questions and trade-offs addressed above.

CASE STUDY

The United Kingdom and the United States: FPTP and Pluralist Systems in Different Contexts

- FPTP and pluralism in parliamentary and presidential systems
- Declining social capital and support for traditional parties and interest groups
- Third-party survival versus continued two-party dominance
- Electoral changes: AV in Britain? Internet-based campaigning in the United States?

Given their historical relationship, the United Kingdom and the United States share many political traits, including their FPTP electoral system and pluralist interest-group system. These systems operate in very different contexts, though: a parliamentary system in Britain and a presidential system in the United States. As Duverger's Law would predict, the electoral system in both countries has produced a two-party system, but Britain may be shifting to a two-and-a-half-party system, while in the United States the two parties are very well entrenched. Both countries also have pluralist interest-group systems, but interest groups function quite distinctly in the two countries, focusing their efforts more heavily on the executive in Britain and on Congress in the United States. Both countries have also seen all the trends of declining partisan loyalty that have characterized wealthy democracies more broadly, though recent trends in the United States suggest that greater ideological differences between the parties may be promoting renewed party loyalty.

The 2010 parliamentary election in Britain produced the first coalition government since World War II, as neither of the two major parties managed to win a majority of the seats in the legislature. This result necessitated a coalition between the Conservatives, who won the most seats, and the Liberal Democrats, the perennial third party. The election marked, perhaps, the culmination of a long transformation of Britain's party system.

British parties began centuries ago as cadre parties within parliament, divided primarily over how much power they thought should be reserved for the long-ruling aristocracy. As the reforms of the nineteenth century (see chapter 3) expanded the franchise, the two major parties, the Conservatives and Liberals, slowly built mass parties to incorporate and appeal to the growing number of (male) voters. In 1900, a new party was founded by trade unions and socialist societies: the Labour Party. Throughout the world, parties formed or evolved to represent workers as industrialization expanded, but only in Britain did labor unions actually create their own party. By the 1920s, Labour had replaced the Liberals as the second major party and had led its first government. The Liberals survived as a third party, but until the 1970s they received a small fraction of the vote and only a handful of seats in parliament. In terms of seats and votes, the United Kingdom for all intents and purposes had a two-party system. As we demonstrated in the discussion of the 2005 election earlier in this chapter, the FPTP system in Britain usually translated slim vote pluralities into significant parliamentary seat majorities, ensuring that one of the two dominant parties could form a single-party government.

As elsewhere in Europe, the major parties' share of the vote in Britain started to decline in the 1980s. When leftist members of the Labour Party moved into leadership positions in 1981, more moderate leaders quit the party and formed the Social Democrats. They shared the "third-party" vote with the much older Liberals for one election, then ran in an alliance with them, and finally merged into one party, the Liberal Democrats. Since 1974, when the Liberals secured 19 percent

TABLE 7.3

British National Election Results, 2010

Party	Total votes	% of votes	% of seats	Seats
Labour	8,609,527	29.0	40	258
Conservative	10,726,614	36.1	47	307
Liberal Democrat	6,836,824	23.0	9	57

Source: BBC, http://news.bbc.co.uk/2/shared/election2010/results/.

of the vote (but only 2 percent of the seats in parliament), the third party has won between 15 and 25 percent of the vote but always a much smaller share of seats, thanks to the FPTP electoral system. In 2010, neither major party was very popular in the context of the Great Recession. The British election was generally seen as the most "presidential" ever, in terms of focusing on the party leaders rather than the parties as a whole. Among other things, it featured, for the first time, live televised debates among the three candidates for prime minister. In the first of these, Liberal Democrat leader Nick Clegg performed well, and the party's popularity grew. With the incumbent Labour PM Gordon Brown extremely unpopular, pundits began to speculate that Labour might even finish third for the first time in eighty years. That did not happen, but the electoral results (see Table 7.3) denied the Conservatives a majority of seats, setting up the coalition government. The Liberal Democrats' vote share actually dropped slightly, but Labour's bigger decline and the distribution of seats in the FPTP system produced the coalition government. The thirty-year slide of support for the two major parties finally went far enough to deny either party a parliamentary majority, even given the effects of FPTP.

The internal organization of British parties has evolved over the years as the parties' electoral fortunes have shifted. Perhaps ironically, the major parties have tried to increase the role of formal members in their activities and decisions while the actual

number of members has plummeted. Britain has no primary system like the one in the United States. Parties select their MP candidates for each constituency and present them to voters. Like most European parties, the Conservatives began as a cadre party in parliament, and MPs long controlled most real decision making within the party, including choosing the party's leader. That changed after their 1997 electoral defeat, when the new party leader proposed direct election of the leader by all dues-paying party members. Candidates for individual seats are selected by dues-paying members in each constituency but are subject to approval from national headquarters.

The Labour Party's initial organization was most unusual, having been created by unions rather than out of Parliament. The party had no individual members, only members via unions or socialist societies. Union members were automatically a part of Labour, whatever their individual party preference. Party policy is officially set by an annual conference, and the party is run on a daily basis by a National Executive Committee (NEC). Initially, unions controlled 90 percent of the voting power in the party, but since the 1960s that has been trimmed substantially. This was due first to pressure from new social movements whose activists wanted greater voice in the party and more recently to party leaders (particularly Tony Blair) wanting to distance the party from the declining labor unions. The party leader is now elected via an equal weighting of the vote of (a) paid-up individual members, (b) union members (who now must identify themselves as party members, rather than being automatically members based on their union membership), and (c) party MPs. Similarly, unions now only control half the votes at the annual convention, with individual members representing the other half. Like candidates from the Conservative Party, Labour candidates for parliamentary seats are chosen by local constituency members but are vetted by the NEC. The practical effect of these reforms has been to reduce the influence of the unions vis-à-vis local activists and even more so the top leaders, who can appeal directly to members for support and often do. The long history of internal reform has been dramatic for the party. The ascendancy of social movement activists in the 1970s and 1980s pulled the party toward the left. In response, PM Tony Blair championed the reforms of the 1990s not only to democratize the party and get himself elected leader but also to move the party toward the center of the political spectrum and away from its socialist roots. He did this in a (successful) effort to gain electoral support from middle-class voters, effecting a transformation of the party into what he called "New Labour."

The United Kingdom and the United States both have pluralist interest-group systems. Of thirty-six long-established democracies, they rank third and fourth, respectively, on Lijphart's "index of interest-group pluralism"; Canada and Greece rank one and two (Lijphart 1999, 177). The traditional economic sectors in Britain have long been somewhat more centralized than those in the United States, with each represented by one major peak association: the Confederation of British Industry (CBI) for business and the Trades Union Congress (TUC) for labor. Until the 1970s, these organizations had somewhat greater control over their members than is true in most pluralist systems. Indeed, in the 1960s and 1970s, Labour Party governments created quasi-corporatist arrangements in which the party consulted regularly and formally with both groups in an attempt to set wages and other economic policies. The limited ability of the groups to control their members, though, resulted in widespread strikes in the 1970s, culminating in the "winter of discontent" in 1978–79. This resulted in Margaret Thatcher quickly leading the Conservatives in ousting Labour from power, and the Conservatives ruled for over a decade thereafter.

Thatcher immediately ended the corporatist arrangements and largely shunned not only the TUC but also the CBI, preferring the advice and support of various conservative think tanks and ideological pressure groups.

Because decision making in Britain's parliamentary system is centralized in the Cabinet, interest groups focus much more on lobbying the executive than the parliament. Indeed, they lobby MPs primarily as a conduit to gain access to Cabinet members. How much influence particular groups have, then, depends very much on which party is in power. As Thatcher demonstrated, the party in power can effectively shift various groups' level of access and influence. Of course, all groups still have other means of influencing policy, such as petitioning, gaining media attention, contributing to campaigns, etc. British civil society has seen the same evolution that we noted earlier throughout Western societies: a decline in the support of traditional interest groups and the rise of new social movements. Environmental, women's, antinuclear, and racial groups became important in the struggle for reorganization of the Labour Party in particular. The number of such groups has exploded since the 1960s. At the same time, the TUC in particular has declined as its membership base has contracted. This was spurred by Thatcher's aggressive anti-union policies in the 1980s, which made organizing and striking much more difficult.

The Liberal Democrats' insistence that changing the electoral system should be put to a referendum portends significant changes in British politics. The FPTP system in the United Kingdom has long been particularly disproportional because a third party has always survived. Since the 1970s, the Liberal Democrats have won a significant percentage of the vote, but that vote has been spread widely across the country, giving the party a tiny share of seats in Parliament. Some smaller parties win one or two seats as well, including nationalist parties in Scotland, Wales, and Northern Ireland. The British have long studied and debated changing the FPTP system. Indeed, they have instituted various systems for other elections, most prominently a closed-list PR system for elections to the European Union Parliament, making British voters unusually aware of alternatives. The Liberal Democrats (and the Liberals before them) have long called

U.S. President Barack Obama delivers his State of the Union Address on Tuesday, January 25, 2011, in front of Vice President Joe Biden (left) and newly elected House Speaker John Boehner (right). Republicans took control of the House of Representatives in the 2010 midterm elections, while Democrats clung to a majority in the Senate. The two parties have completely dominated American electoral politics since 1860, but Congress provides many avenues for interest groups to gain access to the legislative process.

Credit: AP Photo/Pablo Martinez Monsivais

for a PR system, but they compromised with the Conservatives to join the governing coalition, agreeing to a referendum on instituting an AV system instead. AV ought to encourage voters to vote first for a smaller party if they prefer and second for one of the major parties, knowing that if their preferred party doesn't win, their vote won't be "wasted" but will be transferred to their second choice. This should reverse FPTP's disincentive to voters interested in smaller parties. British voters, however, preferred to keep the FPTP system, soundly defeating the 2011 referendum that would have switched to the AV system.

Americans complain frequently about "gridlock" and partisan division, the seemingly inherent inability of the two parties and the various governing institutions to pass laws to solve problems. This gridlock, however, reflects the exceptionally participatory nature of the American institutions of participation

and representation, even if many citizens fail to take advantage of the opportunities the system provides. The FPTP system and decentralization have resulted in two broad catch-all parties that are relatively weak in terms of internal party discipline, though some argue that the two parties have become stronger in recent decades. Americans vote more frequently and for more offices than just about any citizens in the world. They typically have the opportunity to elect people to anywhere from six to twelve offices and judgeships at each of three subnational levels of government—municipal, county, and state—plus five national offices. In contrast, British voters typically elect one local representative, one MP, and one EU MP, and that's it. Yet ironically, the United States also has among the world's lowest voter turnout rates.

The U.S. Constitution is silent on the details of an electoral system. The president was to be elected by an electoral college, not directly by the populace. The Senate originally was appointed by state governments to represent their interests. This left only the House of Representatives to be elected directly by the people. The individual states had the task of designing their own electoral systems. Following the British model, almost all adopted a FPTP system with single-member districts. As suffrage was expanded over the decades, voter turnout initially increased accordingly.

Electoral districts for congressional and state legislative seats must be very close in size so that equal weight is given to each vote. State legislatures, however, are left to determine the exact boundaries of these districts, including those for Congress. The standard practice has become to draw the lines to provide a reasonably clear majority for one party in each district, with the total such districts for each party more or less matching its share of the voters in that state. This approach helps protect incumbents of both parties. A constitutional amendment in 1920 determined that U.S. senators were to be popularly elected, resulting in senators having electoral districts whose boundaries are fixed, regardless of population (i.e., the state boundaries). This results in overrepresentation of small states and underrepresentation of large ones, which is reflected in the electoral college as well.

Most Americans probably think of the current two-party system as a permanent fixture that is as much a part of the U.S. political system as the Constitution and the three branches of government. In fact, the Democratic and Republican parties did not coalesce until the election of Abraham Lincoln in 1860, and they, as well as the two-party system, have evolved significantly since then even though the two parties remain in place. The earliest parties were cadre parties that emerged as factions in the first few Congresses. One of these, the Jeffersonian Republicans, led by the "Virginia dynasty" of Thomas Jefferson, James Madison, and James Monroe, created what was really a dominant-party system from 1800 to 1824. This faction controlled the presidency throughout this period and in the early 1820s controlled 187 of 213 seats in the House and 44 of 48 seats in the Senate.

Andrew Jackson and Martin Van Buren, both of whom would serve as president, founded what would become known as the Democratic Party in the 1820s. As the franchise expanded to include all white men regardless of property ownership, members of Jackson and Van Buren's faction recognized the need for a party to organize and register more voters, so they created the first party based on mass membership and appeal. Their opponents responded in kind, creating the Whig Party. This ushered in the first real two-party system, from Jackson's election in 1828 to Lincoln's in 1860. The new mass parties greatly increased participation at the polls; turnout among the adult white male electorate increased from just over 25 percent in 1824 to 56 percent in 1828 and to almost 80 percent by 1840. A new party, the Republicans, emerged as the party of abolition in the 1850s. Victory in the Civil War ushered in a long period of Republican dominance at the national level, and only three Democrats would win the presidency between 1860 and 1932.

The election of 1932 proved another decisive turning point, as Franklin Delano

IN CONTEXT

FPTP

- In 2010, fifty countries used "first-past-the-post" rules for their legislative elections.
- These countries included the Bahamas, Canada, Jamaica, Kenya, Malaysia, Yemen, and Zambia.
- The vast majority of countries using FPTP are former British colonies.
- In 2010, no country in continental Europe used FPTP.

Source: International Institute for Democracy and Electoral Assistance, Table of Electoral Systems Worldwide, http://www.idea.int/esd/world.cfm.

Roosevelt forged a New Deal coalition that made the Democrats politically dominant until the election of Ronald Reagan in 1980. Starting in the 1960s, the New Deal coalition came under increasing strain from sharp ideological differences between Northern liberals and younger members in the antiwar and civil rights movements, on the one hand, and white Southern Democrats on the other, with civil rights as the major dividing line. By the 1990s, this conflict had resulted in a wholesale shift of Southern political loyalty from the Democrats to the Republicans, producing the current era of sharper partisan differences.

In a wealthy society such as the United States, party loyalty is based primarily on ideology. The early parties, however, were based not just on ideology but also on the material benefits of patronage. Until the early twentieth century, most government employees served at the will of elected leaders. When power changed hands at any level of government, a bureaucratic purge took place; the incumbent's appointees were removed, and the new victor's people were placed in office. In the late nineteenth century, urban politicians mobilized and politically controlled large numbers of new immigrants through what came to be known as political machines. These large, patronage-based parties provided jobs and public services to new citizens and voters in exchange for their loyalty.

Along with suffrage and the political parties, candidate selection has also evolved over time. Originally, party caucuses that consisted of existing officeholders, such as members of Congress and state legislators, selected a party's candidates. The elitism of this system came under fire in the Jacksonian era, and the major parties shifted to a convention system. The patronage machines gained great influence in the convention system by the late nineteenth century, and it was often said that candidates were selected in "smoke-filled back rooms." Reformers of the Progressive era reacted against this by creating the direct primary in which all voters who were registered in a party would select the party's candidates by direct vote. This has since produced the era of the long primary contest, especially at the presidential level, which is unique to the United States. Candidates spend months—or even more than a year—campaigning for their party's presidential nomination.

Even with these reforms, party leaders still maintained significant influence over candidate selection. They controlled the selection of a majority of the delegates sent to conventions, and rules allowed these delegates to switch their votes. A series of reforms in the Democratic Party starting in the late 1960s weakened the influence of party leaders and, consequently, the delegates they selected. As this last institutionalized influence the national party leadership had over candidate selection came to an end, the nomination came to depend entirely on winning the popular vote in the primaries. National party organizations have lost virtually all direct control over the process. Instead, they have come to play a supporting role by providing candidates with services during campaigns and by spending their own money for part of the campaigns, even if they do not directly control who the candidates are or what they say. Candidate selection has slowly become more participatory, but at the expense of weakening the parties as coherent organizations. In the era of party machines, parties were the main means through which Americans participated in politics, and loyalty to them was

fierce. Primary elections, independent funding of candidates, and mass communication have weakened the role of parties, and much political participation currently takes place in civil society instead. European parties, with no primary system, remain significantly stronger, whichever electoral system is used.

The party system in the United States has been an unusually enduring two-party system for well over a century. While third parties occasionally arise and win as much as 20 percent of the vote, since 1860 none has survived more than two electoral cycles. Over the last century, this has been partly due to the primary system. Long elections—first for each party's nomination and then for the general election—and lack of public funding of campaigns give advantages to candidates who have organizational and financial resources. Each state has its own system of determining who qualifies for a spot on the ballot, meaning that new parties must navigate fifty such systems to run a national campaign for president, a feat very few have achieved. While regional and racial differences have long existed and might in another system serve as the basis of alternative parties, one of the two major parties has always been able to capture those voting blocs in the United States. Examples include the Democrats capturing the votes of African Americans and the Republicans capturing the votes of white Southerners. No long-term third party, such as the Liberal Democrats in the United Kingdom, has been able to survive in the United States.

Ideological shifts since the 1960s, though, may be strengthening parties in the United States. Every American is familiar with the lament that national politics have become "too partisan," with the major party leaders seemingly disagreeing on everything. This is often contrasted to an earlier era of bipartisan respect and cooperation. Political science research shows that greater ideological division along party lines has indeed arisen, but also that it is a return to long-standing partisan differences in the United States. The relative bipartisanship of the New Deal consensus after World War II was an anomaly in U.S. history. Matthew Levendusky (2009) used voter surveys to argue that a process of "sorting" has occurred. Ideological and partisan divisions among elites have aligned more (Democrats have become more consistently liberal, and Republicans more consistently conservative), and voters have followed the elites to more ideologically divided positions. This has made partisan differences clearer and party loyalty stronger. While parties may be weaker organizationally than they once were, greater ideological clarity has created stronger bonds between parties and their core voters. Levendusky traced this back to the reforms in the Democratic Party in the 1960s and the impact of Ronald Reagan on the Republicans in the 1980s. Frances Lee (2009), however, argued that this growing ideological division does not fully explain the partisan divisions and gridlock in Congress. Looking at the Senate, where the requirement of 60 votes to pass major legislation creates a significant veto player, Lee analyzed roll-call votes to argue that party members have a joint electoral interest in opposing one another, even when they do not disagree ideologically. This is especially true when parties can block an opposing president's goals and control the congressional agenda to assert their electoral message. American gridlock, he argued, extends well beyond the growing ideological divisions in the country as a whole.

The election of Barack Obama in 2008 was seen as a watershed in a number of ways, not only because he was the first African American elected president (see chapter 4 on the racial impact of his election). His campaign and its results suggested a potential shift in American campaigns and electoral divisions, though subsequent events suggest that the old order may not be changing as much as initially thought. Obama's campaign was uniquely successful at mobilizing supporters, especially young people and first-time voters. This occurred primarily via the most sophisticated online campaign and organizing ever undertaken, in terms of both the amount of money contributed and the number of people who volunteered in the

campaign. The election results showed this as well: voter turnout went up significantly for the first time in decades, especially among those groups who tend to vote less. Obama won or came close to winning in some key states, such as Virginia and North Carolina, that had long been bastions of Republican support, suggesting a possible shift in partisan alignments. Obama's subsequent decline in popularity and the Republicans' sweeping victory in the 2010 congressional elections, however, raised questions about all of this. The Tea Party emerged as an unusual new social movement, a conservative one critical of Obama's policies. Whether this showed a partisan shift back to the Republicans in the longer term, or was just a reaction to the severe economic downturn that began as Obama took office, is uncertain. The 2012 election will help political scientists understand whether a fundamental shift is taking place or a period of growing electoral volatility is underway.

The pluralist system of interest groups in the United States has been the venue of much political participation, especially since the early twentieth century, though concerns about declining social capital have been on the rise since the 1980s. The United States has long been perceived as a country of joiners and associations. The French social commentator Alexis de Tocqueville famously observed in the 1830s, "Americans of all ages, all stations in life, and all types of dispositions are forever forming associations. . . . [A]t the head of any new undertaking, where in France you would find the government or in England some territorial magnate, in the United States you are sure to find an association" (1835–40/1969, 513). Political scientist Theda Skocpol (2003) has meticulously documented the extent of what she termed "translocal but locally rooted membership associations" from the early nineteenth to the mid-twentieth century. These local groups and clubs involved citizens in meetings, social gatherings, and community betterment. Over time, many formed state-level and national associations. Reflecting the society of the time, these were gender segregated and exclusively white affairs, though they often included members from across religious and class divisions. Whereas many did not have specific political agendas, some certainly did, notably temperance organizations, women's organizations, and anti-slavery societies. They all actively pursued local community improvements that included working with government at various levels.

Modern interest groups with political agendas arose in the Progressive era, as partisan loyalty began to decline. Disenchantment with the corruption of party politics led activists to create organizations independent of parties. These new groups engaged in a new activity called lobbying, in which they spoke directly to legislators to influence how they voted. They also began working directly with the newly created civil service to influence the executive branch of government. In many ways, these large membership associations were like many others that had come before, but they behaved differently, focusing explicitly on particular political issues and having as one of their primary purposes direct influence over government. Thus began the modern era of the pluralist interest-group system in the United States, with literally thousands of groups free to organize when and how they pleased.

Skocpol argued that this system of mass-membership organizations began to change, starting in the mid-twentieth century, into what she calls "managed advocacy" groups. Groups now rely on members for financial support and for direct political support via occasional phone calls, e-mails, or presence at rallies. But they no longer have active local branches that bring members together on a regular basis. According to Skocpol, this shift has harmed the country's social capital, as citizens no longer work actively together in face-to-face situations. Other scholars, however, have looked at the same trends and questioned Skocpol's concerns, pointing out that some types of political activity have held steady or even increased. Americans also volunteer more than ever before and join small groups such as self-help groups

at higher rates than in the past. New forms of activities have arisen to replace, at least in part, those that have declined. The open question is whether these new forms of activity are as effective at facilitating participation and representation and building social capital as those of the past.

American interest groups have multiple entry points into the political process, though the central focus in the presidential system is Congress, where individual members on key committees can have a major impact on legislation (in sharp contrast to Britain's Parliament). If they cannot get their ideas approved via legislation, interest groups may try getting approval in the courts, or vice versa. The United States arguably provides more points of entry into the system than almost any other country. In combination with the country's relatively weak parties, which leave legislators free to vote how they please, so many points of entry make its political system one in which organized citizens can actively attempt to influence the political process on an almost daily basis, not just during elections.

CASE SUMMARY

Comparing the United Kingdom and the United States shows as clearly as anything can how governing institutions, electoral systems, party systems, and interest-group systems are interrelated. The two countries share a common history and culture (many analyses speak of "Anglo-American" values and institutions), but the differing governing institutions of the two countries make these commonalities function quite distinctly. The American presidential system with its weaker parties allows interest groups greater access to various levels of decision making, whereas in Britain's parliamentary system they concentrate on the executive branch. Both countries have seen the common Western patterns of declining partisan identification (though this has perhaps begun to change in the United States recently), declining traditional interest groups, and rising social movements. These trends have raised significant questions about social capital. In the United Kingdom, though, the survival of a viable third party has produced a coalition government and the briefly raised possibility of fundamental change to the electoral (and therefore party) system, while in the United States the two parties continue to capture an increasingly divided and distrusting electorate.

CASE STUDY

Germany: Two-and-a-Half-Party System and Neocorporatism under Threat

- Stable two-and-half-party and neocorporatist system: 1949–1970s
- Social changes undermining bases of support: declining trade unions and peak associations, new social movements, secularization
- Weakening support for major parties and rising support for minor parties: the end of the two-and-a-half-party system?

In the 2005 election, the two major parties in Germany split the electorate nearly perfectly but gained only 70 percent of the vote, which was their lowest combined total ever. After weeks of tense negotiations, the two parties, for only the second time since World War II, joined forces to create a "grand coalition" to govern over what seemed to be a divided and increasingly alienated citizenry. Four years later, the two parties again engaged in electoral battle, this time in the midst of the fallout of the global financial crisis. Their combined share of the vote dropped to another new low, as three smaller parties all significantly increased their vote totals. This time, the party of incumbent Chancellor Angela Merkel was able to forge a coalition with one of the smaller parties to avoid a grand coalition. But the decline in the fortunes of the long-dominant major parties was clear, as were its causes: the declining significance of long-standing class and religious divisions in Europe and the partial unraveling of Germany's neocorporatist system.

Coleaders of Germany's leftist party *Die Linke* (The Left), Oskar Lafontaine (left) and Gregor Gysi, at a campaign rally in 2009. *Die Linke* arose when Lafontaine left the SPD because it had moved too far to the center. It is one of three smaller parties that now regularly gain seats in the German parliament. The rise of these new parties raises questions about whether Germany's "two-and-a-half-party" system is shifting toward a multiparty system.

Credit: John MacDougall/AFP/Getty Images

Germany's democracy long provided an example of a two-and-a-half-party system with relatively strong political parties; an unusual, mixed electoral system; and a neocorporatist interest-group system. For much of its history, many political scientists saw the country as a model of effective policymaking in a democratic context. In recent decades, however, unusually strong social movements inspired by seemingly alienated citizens and by the economic effects of globalization have raised serious questions about both the effectiveness of the German model and the adequacy of its institutions of participation and representation. Indeed, analysts have come to question whether both the two-and-a-half-party system and neocorporatism will survive.

The instability of Germany's first democracy, the Weimar Republic (1918–1933), profoundly influenced the post–World War II system the Allies helped create in West Germany. Parties were central to the new democracy and were explicitly recognized and regulated in the Basic Law, West Germany's constitution. The major parties that eventually developed were the Christian Democratic Union/Christian Social Union (CDU/CSU), a primarily northern and Protestant group (CDU) combined with a primarily Catholic group based in Bavaria in the south (CSU), and the Social Democratic Party (SPD), which had been the dominant party prior to the Nazi era and which reemerged after the war. The third or "half" party is the liberal Free Democrat Party (FDP), which lies ideologically between the two major parties. The mixed PR system adopted in the Basic Law encouraged the rise of this party system, but so did other factors. The conservative nationalists of the Weimar era were completely discredited by their association with Hitler, so no other conservative parties arose to challenge the CDU/CSU on the right. The Basic Law limited free association by insisting that all parties had to support democracy to prevent the rise of a new Nazi Party or any other nondemocratic party. In the mid-1950s, the government took two smaller parties—a "radical right" party and the Communist Party—to the Constitutional Court, arguing that since neither believed in democracy they should be banned. The Court agreed and ruled that both should be dissolved. The German electoral system was also the first semiproportional one, with a requirement subsequently added of a 5 percent minimum share of the national vote for a party to win seats in parliament.

Initially, the CDU/CSU under Konrad Adenauer was the dominant party, ruling continuously from 1949 to 1969, usually with the support of the FDP. Then the SPD moderated its ideology in 1959, giving up the official goal of nationalizing industry and creating a truly socialist economy and accepting the basic parameters of Germany's social market economy (described in chapter 5). This shift helped increase its electoral appeal, and by 1969 it had become the biggest party, forming a government with the FDP. Since that time, power has shifted back and forth between the two major parties, almost always in coalition with the FDP or, more recently, with the Green Party. The SPD's moderation and the willingness of the CDU/CSU to support the social market economy significantly reduced the ideological differences between the two major parties. They increasingly became catch-all parties, competing for the most votes via expanded government programs but having limited ideological differences.

At the same time, German neocorporatism reached its zenith. The German Trade Union Federation claims to represent 85 percent of the unionized workforce. Via codetermination (see chapter 5) in the social market economy, its members constitute close to half of the board members of Germany's 482 largest firms. Business is represented by three organizations: the BDA represents the largest industrial groups, the BDI represents other large and medium-sized firms, and the DIHT represents small businesses. From the 1950s through the 1970s, these three organizations worked closely with the major political parties and the government at each level to set wages and social policies. Most MPs on key committees were members of one of these three key interest groups, and many had worked professionally for them before entering politics. SPD MPs often had strong union backgrounds, and CDU/CSU MPs had business connections, though labor and business associations had members in and maintained close contact with both parties, especially the party in power at any particular time.

Political scientists and policy makers saw this model of stability and neocorporatism as a great success into the 1970s. Underlying it, however, were trends that would raise serious questions about key aspects of the system. Popular discontent with the "New Germany" started to emerge in West Germany in the 1950s and became quite apparent by the late 1960s. The country was rocked by a student movement that was opposed to the Vietnam War and German rearmament and that advocated a more neutral stand in the Cold War. Members of the movement also criticized what they saw as a growing consumer culture, which they characterized as an inhumane society focused solely on economic growth and consumption. Growing unemployment affected would-be middle-class college students and working-class young adults alike. All of this discontent culminated in widespread protests in 1968, which the CDU/CSU government, with SPD support, effectively and forcefully put down. The demise of this movement led young political activists to pursue several different paths. Some tried to reenter the SPD and reform the party from within with the goal of shifting it further to the left. Others turned to violence, creating a series of small terrorist organizations that were responsible for a number of bombings in the early 1970s before the state ultimately defeated them.

Some activists from the middle class formed what came to be known as "civil action groups." These were small, local groups of usually not more than thirty people that were focused on petitioning local government to better people's lives in a variety of areas, such as building new schools or cleaning up pollution. Members continued to engage politically, but they were no longer willing to participate only through the major interest group associations or the major parties. By 1979, 1.5 million Germans were participating in at least 50,000 such groups. In the mid-1970s, some of the groups that focused primarily on the environment came together to form a national association to push environmental issues at the national level. This new movement, along with growing women's and antinuclear movements, was a key pillar of the "new social movements" in Germany. As in the United States, the feminist movement emerged out of the student movement of the 1960s, as women demanded more access to education, employment, and power. A strong antinuclear movement grew in the 1970s in opposition to U.S. plans to base nuclear weapons on German soil and plans by the German government to increase the country's dependence on nuclear energy.

These new social movements trusted neither major party. By 1980, the Green Party had evolved out of these groups, and in 1983,

it became the first new party since 1949 to break the 5 percent barrier and gain seats in Parliament, reducing SPD support in particular. After falling below 5 percent in the next election, the Greens rebounded, gaining more than 7 percent in 1994 and entering into government in 1998 with the SPD, creating what came to be called the "Red-Green Alliance" (*Red* referring to socialism), which ruled until 2005. The semiproportional system allowed the environmental movement to become a successful political party, though the activists who were most critical of the system were not necessarily happy with this outcome. This is an example of a classic trade-off between pure principles and compromise in the name of gaining influence or power.

The other major shift in the German party system came with the reunification with East Germany in 1990. The East German Communist state had a one-party regime, of course. A host of new parties emerged as this regime collapsed. The West German electoral system covered the entire reunited country, and initially, the major parties in the west reached out and worked with like-minded parties in the east to gain support there. Ultimately, they absorbed the eastern parties. The CDU/CSU was initially the most popular party in the east because its leader, incumbent chancellor Helmut Kohl, had championed German unity after the fall of the Berlin Wall and promised to transfer large sums of money from west to east to improve the eastern economy. Continuing high unemployment and low incomes in the east, however, slowly eroded his support; as a result, the SPD did well in the east in the 1998 and 2002 elections.

The former ruling Communist Party recreated itself as the Party of Social Democracy (PDS) and positioned itself ideologically to the left of the SPD to champion in particular the poorer and heavily unemployed Germans in the east. Its association with the country's Communist past resulted in it gaining only 2.4 percent of the party vote in the first joint election in 1990, but it slowly expanded its appeal, winning 21 percent of the eastern vote by 1998. In 2007, it merged with some former members of the SPD who were unhappy that their party had supported economic reforms that reduced social services (see chapter 5). It thus became the Left Party, with Oskar Lofantaine, a former SPD party leader and finance minister, as its new leader.

At the same time that the new social movements, new parties, and reunification were altering the landscape of party politics, economic problems were threatening neocorporatism. The neocorporatist model in West Germany developed in the 1950s and reached its zenith in the 1970s after labor unions gained new power from a series of strikes, the union-aligned SPD took control of the government, and the codetermination laws were enacted. The ability of the peak associations of business and labor to enforce collective wage agreements was key to the operation of this model. In the 1980s, these key associations began to weaken as globalization began to increase unemployment. To encourage more employment, government and employers agreed to reduce the work week to thirty-five hours in 1984, and in exchange the unions allowed greater flexibility in setting working conditions within firms. As control of working conditions became more localized, local unions had less reason to obey the dictates of the peak associations, thus weakening the associations' ability to speak on the behalf of all workers.

These trends accelerated in the 1990s as global competition heated up. Facing rising costs from exporters elsewhere in the world, smaller businesses began leaving the employers' association, which meant that central agreements covered fewer businesses. Some business leaders began to campaign openly for a shift to a more neoliberal economic model. The decline of traditional manufacturing, meanwhile, caused union membership to plummet by four million during the decade. The peak associations for both business and labor were speaking for and able to enforce central agreements on a shrinking share of the private sector, and this further weakened neocorporatism.

Politicians responded by distancing themselves from these associations. The long tradition of SPD politicians coming from the unions and CDU/CSU politicians coming from

business associations and churches changed drastically. Far fewer members of Parliament from both parties were members of or worked in the key associations, and more of them developed career paths as professional politicians, staying in elected office rather than returning to work for the interest groups. In the face of these changes and continuing high unemployment, neither the CDU/CSU government prior to 1998 nor the SPD/Green government from 1998 to 2005 was able to negotiate new binding agreements with business and labor for fundamental reforms in the face of globalization. Both governments ultimately tried to impose these reforms unilaterally, without the support of the peak associations, and both failed to get them fully implemented and therefore lost power. In 2003, the SPD/Green government did enact a major reform of the welfare system (see chapter 11) aimed at reducing its costs, a change that their supporters opposed.

The SPD government's attempt to reform the economy and welfare system in the new millennium alienated its traditional "left" and working-class voters while failing to attract more pro-free-market voters. The result was the closely divided 2005 election that resulted in the grand coalition government. The new chancellor, Angela Merkel, was the leader of the CDU; she was also the first woman and first East German to lead the country. The 2009 election saw a continuation of the same trends, but this time in favor of the CDU/CSU. The major parties' share of the total vote dropped to an all-time low of 57 percent (see Table 7.4), but the SPD's share dropped much more, allowing Merkel to form a new government in coalition with the FDP. As Table 7.4 shows, the vote share of all three minor parties increased, with each surpassing 10 percent. Union members mostly still supported the SPD and religious voters supported the CDU/CSU, but economic changes and secularization meant there were fewer voters in both categories. Social changes had therefore caused the decline of the two major parties' core bases of support (Zettl 2010).

Ironically, German voters were fairly content with how the government had handled

TABLE 7.4

German General Election Results, 1998–2009

Party	1998		2002		2005		2009	
	% votes	Seats (of 622)	% votes	Seats	% votes	Seats	% votes	Seats
CDU/CSU	35	245	39	190	35	226	34	239
SPD	41	298	39	251	34	222	23	146
FDP	6	43	7	47	10	61	15	93
Left	0	0	0	0	9	54	12	76
Green	7	47	9	55	8	51	11	68

Source: Election Resources, http://electionresources.org/de/.

the 2008–2009 financial crisis. At the time of the election in late 2009, Germany seemed to have weathered the storm better than most countries, though subsequent policies to help bail out bankrupt Greece and preserve the euro system caused a large drop in Germans' support for Merkel's government. The longer-term trends, however, seem to be the most important. Globalization and European unification have weakened Germany's neocorporatist system, weakening labor unions in particular as well as the union and business associations' ties with the major parties. Other social changes, such as the rise of new social movements and the decline of religious observance, have also eroded the major parties' bases of support, following the trends Dalton and others (e.g., Dalton and Wattenberg 2000) have noted for Western democracies generally. In Germany's semiproportional electoral system, the result has been growing support for three small parties. This trend has been strong enough that Green, Hough, Miskimmon, and Timmins (2008) argued that Germany's "two-and-a-half-party" system has fundamentally changed to a multiparty system similar to what Italy used to have, with two large parties vying for control but always requiring the support of at least one of several minor parties to form coalition governments. This system could reduce Germany's famed political stability.

CASE SUMMARY

Germany has faced the same long-term trends of declining support for major parties and interest groups that are common to other Western democracies. Germany's semiproportional electoral system has allowed these changes to result in the rise of significant new parties that influence elections. As in Britain, these trends produced an unusual coalition government, though the CDU/CSU subsequently won enough seats to return to Germany's typical coalition of one major and one minor party. Germany's neocorporatist interest-group system has also come into question, as declining support for and power of the peak associations have made the corporatist institutions ever more difficult to maintain. In this sense, a pluralist system is more flexible because the decline of particular organizations does not necessitate a change in the institutions themselves, as no particular groups are given greater official access to the government. Despite its substantial differences with the United Kingdom and United States, however, Germany's experiences again raise questions about the ability of any major party to govern effectively with broad national support.

CASE STUDY

Japan: From Dominant-Party to Two-Party System?

- SNTV, dominant party system, and factional politics

- Economic crisis, corruption, and electoral reform: Birth of a mixed electoral system

- Electoral reform effects: Birth of a two-party system?

- Weak civil society, but signs of growing strength

Japanese Prime Minister Naoto Kan (right) and former secretary-general of the Democratic Party of Japan Ichiro Ozawa shake hands prior to their party presidency debates in September 2010. Ozawa, despite being the chief architect of the party's sweeping 2009 election victory, was forced out of the party in February 2011 because of charges of campaign finance irregularities.

Credit: Everett Kennedy Brown/EPA/Landov

On August 30, 2009, the Democratic Party of Japan (DPJ) swept into power, winning 308 of the 480 seats in the lower and more powerful house of the Diet, Japan's parliament. It unseated the Liberal Democratic Party (LDP) that had ruled nearly continuously since 1955. Despite subsequent problems that the DPJ encountered in governing effectively, many analysts see the 2009 election as the dawning of a new era in Japan. The election was also, though, the outcome of an electoral reform fifteen years earlier that had transformed Japan's electoral and party systems, spawning new parties and new political strategies. This fifteen-year history provides a textbook example of Duverger's Law at work, as a new electoral system seems likely to transform Japan slowly but surely into a two-party system. Japanese democracy has had a rather weak civil society and limited participation, though that may be changing as well. Since the government liberalized its regulations over civil society, many new groups seem to be springing up and demanding greater voice in the policy-making process. Arguably since the crisis of the early 1990s, participation is increasing, but effective policymaking may be declining. The various governments seem unable to solve the fundamental economic problems facing the country, and the 2011 earthquake and tsunami created even more profound problems.

The LDP dominated Japanese politics from the first election in 1955. Despite its name, it was a conservative party that supported the interests of business and economic growth, with state intervention as necessary, to rebuild a strong nation and economy. Its creation was in part an effort to establish a strong anticommunist party, and it had active U.S. support. The party guided the creation of Japan's phenomenally successful development model, which we outlined in chapter 5, winning a majority of the legislative seats in every election to the Diet from 1955 to 1993 and always gaining a plurality (though after 1963, rarely a majority) of the national vote, until its stunning loss in 2009. Its great economic success until 1990 allowed it to provide benefits to large segments of the population, including the rapidly growing urban middle class. It was a relatively weak party in terms of internal organization, with strong factions and weak central leadership, but the electoral system allowed those factions to share power and keep the party from splitting.

Japan's unusual SNTV electoral system prior to 1993 was crucial to the LDP's success.

Like all plurality systems, SNTV gave the winning party a larger share of seats in the legislature than its share of actual votes. So even as the LDP's popularity declined, it maintained majority control of the Diet and therefore the government. In addition, district lines were drawn to favor rural areas, giving those areas greater weight in the electoral system than their numbers of voters warranted. Some rural districts had a four-to-one advantage over urban districts, meaning each rural vote was equal to four urban votes. This intentional gerrymandering was meant to provide strong rural support for the conservative, anticommunist LDP.

The multimember districts under SNTV allowed several factions within the dominant party to run candidates and potentially win seats in each district. Most campaigns were mainly battles among the LDP factions rather than between the LDP and other parties. LDP factions were based not on ideology but rather on the loyal, patron-client networks that emerged within the party for campaign purposes. In each district, a winning party had to run several candidates who would draw votes from different groups of voters so as not to dilute the support of each individual candidate. To gain the resources to compete not only against other parties but also against other candidates in the LDP, potential candidates would become loyal members of a faction. Each faction was led by a patron, who was a leading national party (and often government) official who provided campaign funds. To make sure no single candidate became too popular and took too many votes away from the party's other candidates in the same district, each candidate also developed a local voter-mobilization machine, called *koenkai,* which consisted of area notables and leaders of important local groups who could deliver votes. A candidate then promised the factional leader that he could use his *koenkai* to deliver a certain percentage of the vote in a district if the patron would provide campaign financing. As a result of this networking, five major factions emerged in the LDP in the 1950s, with each based around personal loyalty to key leaders. Over time,

IN CONTEXT

SNTV

- The SNTV voting system used in Japan prior to 1993 is one of the world's rarest electoral systems.
- Currently, only three countries use SNTV: Afghanistan, Jordan, and Vanuatu.
- SNTV systems have the lowest average turnout of any electoral system: just 54 percent.
- SNTV encourages better representation of minority parties and independent candidates than do simple FPTP systems because SNTV elects multiple candidates in the same district.

Source: International Institute for Democracy and Electoral Assistance, Table of Electoral Systems Worldwide, http://www.idea.int/esd/world.cfm.

these factions became informally institutionalized, complete with leadership battles for succession. Locally, *koenkai* were often informally institutionalized as well, and an entire local machine could transfer its loyalty from a retiring candidate to a new one, sometimes the original candidate's son. As in any other dominant-party system, several small opposition parties continued to exist, but they never threatened the LDP's grip on power.

The 1990 economic crisis outlined in chapter 5 inspired a reform of the electoral system that had long been discussed but was previously blocked by LDP leaders. It didn't help the LDP that the crisis came on the heels of growing corruption scandals within the party. Patronage politics of the type practiced within the LDP require a great deal of money. Quite simply, loyalty is based on rewards. These rewards took the form of governmental largesse such as infrastructure improvements (and awarding the associated construction contracts to local supporters). Although this sort of behavior is common in many countries, Japanese politicians were also expected to attend local events, such as the weddings and funerals of their supporters, and provide generous gifts. Japanese elections, not surprisingly, soon became the most expensive in the world, in spite of the fact that candidates were not allowed to advertise on television and the length of campaigns was strictly limited. Candidates required huge amounts of money for patronage, money that came from the patrons in their factions. These patrons, in turn, gained these huge sums via corrupt deals that provided kickbacks from large businesses in exchange for government contracts or exemptions from the developmental state's strict regulations. As the economy and therefore the popularity of the LDP began to slip, citizens and the media began to question this system, leading to the revelations of major corruption we discussed in chapter 6. The economic crisis was the final straw. Perceiving imminent electoral disaster, several major LDP leaders left the party in 1993 to form new opposition parties, though these did not differ ideologically from the LDP. Some formed a coalition government after the 1993 election that would briefly exclude the LDP from power for the first time since its founding.

In response to popular outrage at the corruption scandals and economic disaster, the new government passed a fundamental reform of the electoral system, creating a mixed system in which 300 seats in the Diet would be elected in single-member districts and 180 would be elected via closed-list PR. A crucial difference between this new system and Germany's is that Japan's is noncompensatory, meaning that the SMD and PR votes are completely separate (though candidates can simultaneously run in both elections). Because there are far more SMD than PR seats, the system overall is more majoritarian than proportional. This is reinforced by the practice of both major parties awarding PR seats to candidates who perform well but do not win SMD seats. This gives candidates an incentive to campaign hard in an SMD election even if they have little chance of winning; they may perform well enough to gain a Diet seat via the PR list. Reformers believed this new system would reduce the role of money (and therefore corruption) in the electoral system, limit the power of the LDP, and lead to the emergence of a two-party system.

They were initially frustrated by the pace of change; indeed, they reduced the number of PR seats from 200 to 180 in 1996 to make the system more majoritarian. Table 7.5 demonstrates, however, the power of Duverger's Law. Over the five elections since the reform, the two largest parties' share of both votes and parliamentary seats has risen, mainly due to the SMD seats. The difference between votes and seats in the SMD results demonstrates once again the disproportionality of the SMD system. At the district level, the trend is toward two candidates per district (from an average of 2.96 candidates per district in 1996 to 2.41 in 2003), and increasingly those contests are between the two largest parties (Reed 2005, 283). While both the LDP and DPJ have governed via coalition governments with one small party, they have nonetheless established themselves as the clearly dominant two parties of the new system.

The new electoral system initially led to more parties, not fewer. After decades of relative stability in the party system, uncertainty led to many new parties being created and dissolved as politicians jockeyed for position in response to the incentives of the new system. The first major opposition party that formed to try to challenge the LDP under the new rules was the New Frontier Party (NFP), a coalition of several smaller parties. Its failure to dislodge the long-ruling party in the 1996 election led it to split and eventually disband. By the 2000 election, the DPJ had replaced the NFP as the primary opposition until its victory in 2009. Smaller parties survive, partly as a result of the PR seats, but their share of both votes and seats has declined steadily.

The LDP managed to survive as the ruling party until 2009 via several means. Probably most important was the emergence in 2001 of Junichiro Koizumi, the first person to win the presidency of the LDP, and therefore the right to become prime minister, without the support of any of the major party faction leaders. He instead appealed directly to the local voting members of the party, advocating a reformist agenda that attempted to solve the decade-old economic crisis. This successful effort led to his victories in

TABLE 7.5

Japan's House of Representatives Election Results, 1996–2009

	1996			2003			2009		
	% of total vote	% of SDM seats	% of PR seats	% of total vote	% of SDM seats	% of PR seats	% of total vote	% of SDM seats	% of PR seats
Liberal Democratic Party	35.7	56.3	35.0	39.4	56.0	38.3	32.7	21.3	30.5
Democratic Party of Japan	13.3	5.7	17.5	37.0	35.0	40.0	44.9	73.7	48.3
Other parties	51.0*	38.0	47.5	23.6	9.0	21.7	22.4	5.0	21.2

Source: Election Resources, http://electionresources.org/jp/.

*The New Frontier Party came in second to the LDP, with 28 percent of the vote.

the parliamentary elections of 2003 and 2005, the latter being one of the LDP's biggest election victories. Koizumi ran populist national campaigns much more like a presidential campaign in the United States than anything seen before in Japan. As required by party rules, he resigned as president of the LDP and, subsequently, as prime minister in 2006, though he remained quite popular.

More structural changes, however, helped the LDP remain in power until the DPJ sweep in 2009. The LDP and opposition parties have become more centrally controlled in response to the electoral reform. A reformed system of leadership selection that included local-level party branches as well as MPs helped Koizumi win the LDP presidency. With the advent of the closed-list PR system, party endorsement became more important, enhancing the party leaders' influence over local politicians in all parties. The combined effect of the rise of Koizumi and the end of multimember districts greatly reduced the power of factions within the LDP. Politicians still have and use their *koenkai* to campaign and raise funds, but their share of total campaign expenditures has dropped relative to central party money, and the overall cost of campaigns has declined as well (Carlson 2007). LDP incumbents were able to use their

influence in the party and *koenkai* to continue winning elections in many cases, but the old system became much less important under the new rules. Kabashima and Steel (2010) found that *koenkai* became less important from the voters' perspective as well; they increasingly shifted their attention during campaigns from local leaders to national media and the prime ministerial candidates.

The DPJ swept into power in August 2009 largely because of the collapse of the LDP. The three LDP PMs after Koizumi each lasted less than a year in office. The 2008–2009 global financial crisis caused a significant drop in Japanese income, after nearly two decades of stagnation. Voters saw the LDP as unable to move the country out of the crisis. The DPJ campaigned on a platform of reducing the power of the bureaucracy (see chapter 6), improving social welfare policy, and distancing the country from the United States. Opinion polls suggest, however, that voters supported the DPJ mainly because they wanted change, not because they fully believed in the DPJ's policy plans. The issue on which the voters gave the DPJ their strongest support, though, was the party's promise to "change the relationship between politicians and bureaucrats" (Green 2010, 8). Once in power, the new PM wavered on some important policies, including moving the major U.S. military base on Okinawa. The DPJ was also hurt by scandals surrounding its secretary general and chief strategist, Ichiro Ozawa, who was eventually forced to resign from the party. The government's popularity plummeted throughout 2010, leading the PM to resign in June. Its popularity took another hit with what many saw as a lackluster response to the earthquake and tsunami of early 2011. Despite these problems, the election of the DPJ signaled the dramatic changes wrought by the new electoral system put in place fifteen years earlier.

Japan's civil society has always been considered rather weak by political scientists. Business was certainly very well represented and served during the period of LDP dominance. Most major business interests were represented in the *Keidanren*, a single organization closely associated with and supported by the ruling party in a neocorporatist manner. At least as important, though, were the connections among key bureaucrats, major political leaders, and individual businesses. A major business interest, a relevant bureaucratic agency, and key members of the Diet would form an iron triangle, a three-sided cooperative interaction that served the interests of all involved but kept others out of the policy-making process. Iron triangles exist in many countries, but Japan was particularly well known for them. They allowed privileged business interests, especially the large conglomerates known as *keiretsu* (see chapter 5), personal access to and influence over governmental decisions, but they excluded other interests. In addition, they fuelled the corruption that Japan would become famous for in the 1980s and 1990s. As globalization arose, larger businesses became increasingly active in global trade and therefore needed less from the government in terms of special favors and regulations. Accordingly, they reduced their unquestioned support of the LDP, a factor that led to the LDP splits in the early 1990s. Even with all of these changes, however, business remains the organized interest with the greatest access to and influence over the central government.

Japan's rate of unionization has always been lower than that found in most of Europe and, as in other wealthy nations, has declined in the face of globalization since the 1980s. Two major union organizations existed until their merger in 1989. The larger of the two, which represented public sector workers, was fiercely critical of the LDP and was long the backbone of the largest opposition party, the Japan Socialist Party. As union membership declined and workers prospered during Japan's economic miracle, support for the "left" withered, leading to the merger of the two labor associations. The group actually fielded its own candidates in the first elections after the merger, arguing that no major party could defend workers adequately. By the mid-1990s, though, its members increasingly supported the LDP or the DPJ. Throughout this process, unions never gained great influence over government policy.

In addition to unions, Japan has a pluralist interest-group system, but it is tightly regulated by the bureaucracy. To gain legal status, organizations in civil society must have the approval of a relevant ministry, and the government has used these regulations to limit the scope of interest groups. Many environmental, women's, senior citizens', and religious groups exist, as in other pluralist systems (more than 400,000 were legally recognized in the late 1990s), but the vast majority are local and have few professional staff and little expertise or influence. Political scientist Robert Pekkanen (2006) characterized Japan's interest groups as having "members without advocates." In the United States, nearly 40 percent of all research reported in major newspapers comes from civil society organizations; in Japan, only about 5 percent does. Instead, the government itself is the major source of reported research.

This civil society weakness, however, may be changing. In 1999, the government passed a law creating a Non-Profit Organizations (NPOs) legal category. This significantly liberalized the regulations on civil society organizations and provided tax breaks for financial support to many of them. More than

30,000 NPOs were officially recognized by 2007 (Ogawa 2009, 2). The new law gives civil society organizations much greater autonomy from the government and the ruling party. The LDP supported the law, in part, because the traditional campaign machines were not delivering votes as easily as they used to and the party saw NPOs as possible new bases of electoral support. Whether NPOs' new status gives Japan's civil society significantly greater autonomy and influence is yet to be determined. The majority of the new NPOs focus on social welfare, especially on care for the elderly and adult education, and these issues do not much involve directly "political" activity. Ogawa (2009) contended that the government's practice of actively encouraging volunteerism via NPOs is part of a broader neoliberal agenda of reducing the size of the state overall. NPOs, supported by unpaid volunteers, provide social services so that the state no longer needs to. Furthermore, volunteerism is encouraged in particular areas that are supportive of the state's needs but not in others that could be seen as oppositional or threatening. Greater volunteer activity is certainly occurring, and with it presumably social capital is increasing, but whether this is creating a stronger civil society to represent Japanese citizens in the political realm is less clear.

CASE SUMMARY

The 1994 electoral reform in Japan was one of the biggest systemic changes in established democracies of the last generation. While change has been slow, it is clearly having a profound impact on Japanese elections, parties, and the government in power. The trends suggest that participation is increasing; an opposition party has won power, coalition governments have become common, and civil society seems to be on the rise. As in our other case studies in this chapter, it is not clear that this trend has improved the ability of the government to formulate effective policies in the face of economic crisis. Japan's reforms, though, may provide an example of a successful change to an electoral system that has enhanced participation and representation.

CASE STUDY

India: From Dominant-Party to Multiparty Democracy

- Dominant-party system and factional battles, 1947–1977

- Expanded civil society: language, caste, and religion

- Fragmentation of political parties and decline of the dominant party

- Shift to two-party systems in individual states, producing multiparty system and coalition government nationwide

India is regularly heralded as "the world's largest democracy," which it certainly is. It is also a fascinating case study of democracy in a poor, exceptionally heterogeneous, post-colonial society. Critics initially argued that it was only partially democratic, with severe limits on real political alternatives or effective participation. The growth of multiple parties and coalition governments in recent years, along with the rise of interest groups and social movements representing the poorest segments of society, now suggest greater participation and representation. For three decades after independence, India had a dominant-party system similar to Japan's. The ruling party used broad-based support in an FPTP electoral system to win every election from 1947 to 1977. Starting in 1967, however, when the dominant party first lost a handful of state elections, the logic of FPTP combined with the sociological reality of a diverse India to produce two-party competition between a national and a state-based party within many states. At the national level, this ultimately produced a multiparty system that has been characterized by coalition governments since 1989. And as in most postcolonial societies, the most politically influential groups in civil society are not business and labor, as they are in more industrialized societies, but instead identity-based groups.

The Indian National Congress (commonly called the "Congress") led India to independence and became the country's dominant, ruling party. With a secular and social-democratic ideology, the Congress under the charismatic leadership of the Mahatma Gandhi, Jawaharlal Nehru, Indira Gandhi (Nehru's daughter), and her son Rajiv Gandhi dominated Indian politics for four decades. Nehru served as prime minister until his death and was succeeded two years later by his daughter, who led the country from 1966 to 1984 (except for 1977–1980); she in turn was succeeded by her son, Rajiv, from 1984 to 1989. To achieve this dominance, Congress became a very broad-based party. While proclaiming a transformative ideology of social democracy, its electoral success actually rested on long-established hierarchies based on caste and wealth. It mobilized support primarily via local Brahmin elites, many of them landowners, who effectively controlled the votes of millions of local peasants. Because India uses an FPTP electoral system (adopted from its British colonizers), Congress never had to win an outright majority of the vote to control a majority of seats in parliament. In the first two decades, it polled between 45 and 47 percent of the national votes, and that number dropped to around 40 percent in later years.

As in any dominant-party system, the most important political battles were among factions within the ruling party. Like the LDP in Japan, Congress was a giant patronage machine, sharing the benefits of government in exchange for rural support via the local Brahmin elite, who became increasingly corrupt over time and less willing to follow dictates from the center. This was particularly true after Nehru's death, when his daughter Indira tried to assert her own authority over the party. Before the 1971 election, the party split when she broke with the traditional elites, demanding greater loyalty to her and the central party leadership. After the split, Indira Gandhi launched the largest political campaign in Indian history with the slogan *garibi hatao* ("abolish poverty"), trying to appeal directly to the poor peasantry with promises of improved programs. Their support gave her a massive victory. After the election, she centralized control of the party in an attempt to control factional battles, a course of action that local elites increasingly resented. Facing questions in court about the legitimacy of her election and growing resistance from powerful local Brahmin, she declared emergency rule in 1974, suspended most civil rights, threw political opponents in jail, and essentially ruled as a dictator for three years. This has been the only interruption in India's democracy since independence. When forced to return to democracy three years later, Indira lost the election badly, resulting in Congress losing power for the first time since independence.

Opposition to Congress initially came from two ideological alternatives: communism and Hindu nationalism. The Communist Party of India (CPI) has existed since independence but split in two in the 1960s, with one faction supporting the Soviet Union and the other supporting communist China (the CPI(M)). The latter became the stronger party and controlled two state governments for many years. It sometimes agreed to be part of a Congress-led coalition government and maintained a steady share of parliamentary seats until a precipitous drop in 2009. **Hindu nationalism** dates back to the late nineteenth century. As Congress became stronger and fully secular, Hindu nationalists called for a Hindu conception of the Indian nation, one based on the three pillars of geographical unity of all of India, racial descent from Aryan ancestors, and a common culture with Hindu roots. In the 1980s, the Bharatiya Janata Party (BJP) emerged as the primary Hindu nationalist party, with its greatest strength in

Hindu nationalism: In India, a movement to define the country as primarily Hindu; the founding ideology of the BJP party

the northern, Hindi-speaking region of the country, where both Hinduism and caste identities are strongest.

The first opposition victories over Congress came at the state level in 1967, at the hands of communist parties as well as several local state-level parties. The latter would mushroom over the course of the 1970s and 1980s. In many states, elections became essentially two-party races between Congress and a local, state-level party that championed that state's interests. With the rise of the BJP in the 1980s and 1990s, the Hindu nationalists came to compete with state-level parties, especially in the north, to the exclusion of Congress. What emerged, then, starting with the 1989 election, was a national system with two major national parties and numerous smaller parties, mostly at the state level. Each state party that competed against a national party successfully at the state level sent a handful of MPs to the national parliament. In the process, the total number of parties has exploded, from only 50 in 1952 to 342 in 2009 (Hasan 2010, 245).

Every election since 1989 has resulted in a coalition government since neither of the major parties has been able to win a majority of parliamentary seats. An anti-Congress coalition ruled briefly from 1989 to 1991. Then Congress won enough of the vote to form its first coalition government; it ruled from 1991 to 1996 and again from 2004 to the present. Its opponents, led by the BJP, ruled in coalition governments from 1996 to 2004. By the late 1990s, as political leaders realized coalitions were essential, they began forming them before elections, led by a national party and supported by numerous state-level allies, so that elections came to be contests among two major alliances and one or two smaller ones. Electoral losses were the result not only of receiving fewer votes but also of parties' shifting alliances. The alliances were based more on practical considerations, such as geographic interests and striking deals with the national parties, than on ideological affinities among coalition partners. Throughout this process, the two major parties' combined share of the vote

declined and local parties' share increased (though this trend was reversed somewhat with Congress's sweeping victory in 2009).

These fundamental political changes played themselves out at the same time major changes in other types of political participation were taking place. As in most postcolonial, primarily rural countries, the most important groups in Indian civil society are not trade unions and business associations. Both certainly exist, but they are relatively weak. The unionized workforce is a very small percentage of the population. Both unions and businesses depended on access to the sole ruling party as the only real way to influence government, because threatening to shift support to the opposition is not a credible option in a dominant-party system in which no viable opposition exists. A movement among farmers who benefitted from India's famed "Green Revolution" focused on immediate economic concerns like crop prices. While these class-based groups certainly mattered, they were ultimately overshadowed in civil society by groups championing ethnic, religious, or caste interests. These new groups came out of and appealed to the poor, rural majority but ultimately have come to speak for many urban citizens as well. Numerous movements arose around ethnic identity, based primarily on language. This was particularly true in the non-Hindi-speaking south of the country, where groups demanded greater recognition and autonomy in India's federal system. In the end, a major government commission created additional states, drawn largely along linguistic lines, to appease these groups (see chapter 6).

Religion-based movements proved much more explosive. The best known of these was an initiative for Sikh independence in the state of Punjab on the border with Pakistan. Much of this movement took the form of a Sikh political party, the Akali Dal, which successfully sought the creation of a separate Punjab state as a Sikh homeland. Elements of the movement, however, wanted the Punjab to become a separate Sikh country, as Pakistan is for Muslims. These elements used the Sikh Golden Temple in the Punjabi

Two boys, members of India's *dalit* (formerly known as "untouchable") caste, return home from private school. India's constitution outlawed untouchability, but the *dalit* community has had to organize its own interest groups and parties to demand improved treatment. While large numbers are still poor, increasing numbers of *dalits* are now able to gain access to an education and become professionals.

Credit: Reuters/Stringer India

capital of Chandigarh as a base from which they conducted terrorist campaigns against those they viewed as opponents, in particular Hindu nationalists. In 1984, Indira Gandhi ordered the military to invade the Golden Temple, militarily defeating the Sikh movement. A Sikh bodyguard assassinated her in retaliation a few months later.

The largest and most recently active religious movement remains Hindu nationalism. While its main pillars do not refer to religion as such, they assert a national identity tied to what the movement's followers see as the Hindu cultural heritage of all Indians. This position is vociferously opposed by Muslims and Sikhs. The primary organization of this Hindu nationalist movement is the Rashtriya Swayamsevak Sangh (RSS), founded in 1925. It became a militaristic—many say neofascist—organization that trained young men for nationalist struggle, rejecting

Gandhi's nonviolence and his mobilization of the lower castes. From the start, its primary supporters were educated, middle-class Brahmins, particularly in the northern regions of the country. After being fairly quiescent during the period of Congress dominance, the RSS reemerged strongly in the 1980s and founded the BJP. Its greatest cause became the destruction of a mosque and construction of a Hindu temple in its place in the northern city of Ayodhya. The mosque was built centuries ago on the site of the mythical birthplace of Lord Rama, one of Hinduism's most important deities. By 1990, the RSS had begun a march to the site with thousands of followers to destroy the mosque and begin building the temple. The government militarily repulsed the march, leading to violence across northern India in which hundreds of Hindus and Muslims died. Another march in 1992 was also put down, but only after RSS supporters had invaded the site and destroyed the mosque. The site remains in that condition to this day. Occasional violent conflicts between Hindus and Muslims have occurred ever since, as religion has replaced language as the most volatile basis of political divisions in India. In October 2010, a state High Court ruled that the site would be shared among two Hindu groups and one Muslim group, but the Muslim group vowed an appeal to the Indian Supreme Court.

The most common elements of Indian civil society, however, have been based on caste. The Indian caste system is an exceptionally complex social hierarchy that has changed dramatically over the past century. At an abstract level, virtually the entire society is divided into four large *varna,* or castes; in reality, there are literally thousands of subcastes at the local level with more specific identities. Traditionally, most of the distinctions among castes were based on occupation, with certain castes performing certain types of work. Along with these economic distinctions came strict social practices, such as not eating dinner with, drinking from the same well as, or marrying a member of a caste beneath you. At the bottom of this hierarchy were the so-called untouchables, now known as *dalits.*

The introduction of technological change, increased access to education, and urbanization have changed the economic basis for caste divisions markedly. Brahmin landlords no longer control land as completely and thoroughly as they once did, many of the lower-caste occupations no longer exist, and growing numbers of people of all castes have moved to cities, taking up new occupations at various levels of education and compensation. Nonetheless, caste remains very important. A 1999 survey found that 42 percent of Brahmins worked in "white-collar" professional positions or owned large businesses, as opposed to only 17 percent of middle castes and 10 percent of *dalits.* Conversely, less than 4 percent of Brahmins worked as agricultural laborers, as opposed to 35 percent of *dalits.*

Although the Indian constitution legally banned "untouchability" at independence, the data show that *dalits'* position in society remains rather poor. Electoral politics led them to organize to fight for their interests. These associations started in the colonial period, developed rapidly after independence, and have expanded further since the 1980s. Starting in the 1950s, the government has pursued what Americans would call an "affirmative action" program (Indians refer to it as "positive discrimination") for *dalits,* which gives them preferential access to education and government employment to create a small minority of educated and wealthier members of those castes. Those individuals typically have become the leaders of the *dalit* associations, using the resources and knowledge they have gained to help others. They have also successfully championed the reservation of parliamentary seats exclusively for *dalits* and "Other Backward Castes and Tribes"; these seats now constitute 120 of the nearly 600 seats in Parliament. In several northern states in the 1990s, a party led by and championing *dalits* became the BJP's chief rival and won several state elections. Developing these caste associations has involved shifting the social construction of caste identity. Traditionally, specific caste identities were very localized, and people mainly thought of themselves in relation to other local castes above and below them. Leaders of caste associations have helped create a more "horizontal" understanding of caste, forging common identities among similar castes with different names in different locales. These movements created a new type of interest group based on caste identity to which parties had to respond if they wanted to win elections.

The mobilization of caste, ethnic, and religious groups, combined with growing corruption scandals and the unpopularity of the neoliberal economic model that the government adopted in the mid-1980s, led to Congress's electoral defeat in 1989. The BJP rapidly gained popularity in the early 1990s because of the Ayodhya cause and the unpopularity among the higher castes of caste-based affirmative action programs. Hindu nationalist ideology, however, proved to have limited appeal outside the northern region. In the mid-1990s, moderate elements in the BJP gained power within the party and modified some of its most extreme nationalist stances, including on Ayodhya, in an effort to gain wider popular support. The revised party platform also appealed to lower castes by promising more extensive social benefits. These positions helped the BJP win the 1996 election, when it formed a coalition government with numerous regional parties that remained in power until 2004.

CASE SUMMARY

Institutionalists would expect India's FPTP electoral system to create a two-party system. In India, however, great social and cultural diversity, a federal system, and FPTP have combined to produce numerous state-level two-party systems (following Duverger's Law). These forces have collectively created a multiparty national system, with two large national parties competing for power at the head of multiparty coalitions. Both institutional and sociological theories are essential to understand this evolution. Both major parties have lost support to the growing numbers of regional and state-level parties. In the 1977 election, the first one that Congress lost, the Congress and its primary national opponent together received 75 percent of the national vote. In the last three elections, the two major parties combined received less than half the total votes, and the myriad regional parties totaled about 29 percent (Hasan 2010, 245). This history is partly explained by the expansion of civil society, as excluded groups have organized and begun demanding greater access and participation. Unfortunately, some of these demands have taken violent forms, from some communist movements in the 1960s to the religious violence of the last decade. Much political organizing, however, has taken place within the nonviolent framework of India's electoral system.

India provides a case study of an electoral system in a very different context from the wealthy, Western democracies. Combined with a federal system and ethnic and religious diversity, FPTP has followed Duverger's Law, but only at the local level. As in the United States, federalism in India has helped decentralize the party system and has produced weak parties, while diversity has created many parties. A pluralist interest-group system also looks quite different in a country where the most important divisions are based not on industrialization but on region, ethnicity, caste, and religion. While often corrupt and sometimes violent, the Indian system has nonetheless persevered as a democratic system, keeping interest groups and parties mostly operating within institutionalized bounds. It has also been a system in which participation and representation have expanded over the decades.

CONCLUSION

Citizen participation and representation are at the heart of democracy, which ideally gives each citizen equal voice and power. The reality, of course, is that no set of institutions can translate participation into representation and power in a way that treats everyone perfectly equally. Different electoral, party, and interest-group systems channel participation and provide representation in different ways. These institutions also interact with the governing institutions we outlined in chapter 6, creating yet more variation as we seek to understand who rules and what affects political behavior.

Who Rules?

The most fundamental question about institutions of participation and representation is which system, if any, facilitates greater participation and better representation. Those systems that are more open to diverse organizations and viewpoints seem to create greater participation: multiparty systems, PR electoral systems, and pluralist interest-group systems. These seem to allow the greatest variety of voices to be heard within official halls of power. Whether they provide greater representation, however, depends on whether representation means only giving a set of people a voice or actually giving them influence. If the latter is a concern, then some would argue that a neocorporatist interest-group system that is based on stronger interest groups is better. While such a system limits the ability of internal dissenters to form their own groups, it arguably provides the greatest influence for members as a whole by collectively representing them with one voice and one strong organization. Similarly, fewer and larger parties may provide less representation but more influence for the party (and its constituents), which is able to hold more power than would be true in a multiparty system.

This discussion raises the trade-off that Powell (2000) discerned between opportunities for participation and representation on the one hand and accountability on the other. Institutions that allow much representation of diverse interests often make it more difficult for citizens to know exactly whom to hold accountable for government action. More majoritarian systems, with a single ruling party at any given time, arguably provide less representation of diverse voices but make accountability more clear. Similarly, institutions of participation and representation influence the trade-off we discussed in chapter 6 between participation and effective governance. PR electoral systems that allow numerous, small parties to gain legislative representation arguably allow more distinct viewpoints to be expressed, but the party coalitions that are then necessary to govern are often difficult to form and prove unstable.

Different institutions affect the representation and participation of marginalized groups even more than they do average citizens. Ethnic or racial minorities and women are often unrepresented in large, catch-all parties or interest groups controlled primarily by the dominant groups in a society. One of the most robust findings in comparative politics is that PR systems provide greater representation of women in parliament. India provides an example of going even further to ensure representation of minorities, reserving a specific share of legislative seats for them. While India does this on the basis of caste, several countries do it for women as well (see chapter 12). Such laws implicitly assume that members of these groups can only be truly represented if members of their own groups are their official representatives. An SMD system without reservations, such as in the United States or the United Kingdom, assumes that people will vote for whomever they wish to represent them, regardless of the individual's own characteristics. In a two-party system, though, the choices are limited and disproportionately exclude women and racial or ethnic minorities.

The ultimate "Who rules?" question goes back to the classic debate between pluralist and elite theorists, Do modern democracies really provide government in which average citizens have effective power, or do elites' abilities to gain direct access to decision makers, shape the political agenda, and influence (or control) key institutions mean that they really rule? In the elite model, voters occasionally get a limited choice among a handful of alternatives, all of them led by elites and all typically within a relatively narrow set of ideological debates. Declining partisan loyalty and social capital in recent decades simply strengthens these trends of elite control. Pluralists counter that institutions can and do make a difference in who is represented and in how much meaningful participation average citizens, and especially more marginalized citizens, can have. And, regardless of institutional differences, liberal democracies ultimately provide all voters with the ability to organize and sanction leaders via the ballot box.

What Explains Political Behavior?

Despite what has long been viewed as the fundamental irrationality of participating in politics—that is, the collective action problem—millions of citizens do so. Why? The answers are many. Clearly, ideological belief in how their government should operate is a major factor, but it certainly is not the only one. Material incentives are more common than most people think; joining a political party can provide connections and opportunities that further individuals' personal interests as well as their ideological predispositions. This is especially true in poorer societies with fewer and less-institutionalized economic opportunities. And for some, participation is almost automatic with membership in a particular group, as we saw in the case of union members in Britain's Labour Party. This is often the case in ethnically divided societies as well, where one's birth into a particular ethnic group pretty much determines which ethnically based party one will support.

While all democratic institutions can overcome the collective action problem to some extent, how they do so depends on what incentives they provide leaders in the political system. Duverger's Law is one of the most powerful findings in political science: following the logic of rational-choice theory, the electoral system's rules send powerful signals to party leaders about how many parties will likely be viable. This then heavily influences the opportunities for individual participation and the array of political parties. Similarly, an established neocorporatist system gives few incentives to start new interest groups but gives powerful incentives to become a leader in those already recognized. This again affects the type of political opportunities available to average citizens.

Where and Why?

Comparativists seek to understand how different systems interact and work in different social contexts in part to provide a menu of useful choices for countries thinking about ways to improve their democracies. Such a fundamental choice, however, arises rarely, usually only when a new democracy is being created. We examine this subject in chapter 9. Most of the time, countries use the systems they have inherited, either from a founding moment such as the writing of the U.S. Constitution or, in the majority of countries that are former colonies, from their colonial masters. This institutional continuity is a major answer to the question of why particular institutions exist in particular countries. Taking a step further back, however, rational-choice, institutionalist, and political-culture theorists all have explanations of why particular institutions originated in particular places. Rational-choice theorists see electoral rules as determining how many parties will emerge, or conversely see a society with a set number of parties and argue that those parties will negotiate rationally to choose a particular electoral system to maximize their chances of gaining power. Historical institutionalists, cultural theorists, and sociological theorists look at long-standing ideas and practices in a particular society to explain the system that emerged in that society. In postcolonial societies, colonial history has a powerful influence on that development. The case study of India illustrates how sociological and cultural influences can combine with the rational-choice logic of FPTP to produce a particular type of party system that is unique to that country.

Applying Theory to Institutions of Participation and Representation

As the discussion of where and why institutions emerge suggests, rational-choice, institutionalist, and cultural theories contend for dominance in the study of participation and representation. Formal rules, such as those embedded in electoral systems, provide clear incentives for rational, self-interested political actors. Most theorists assume that these actors seek to maximize their power and behave accordingly within the confines of the electoral system in any particular country. Cultural and institutionalist theorists, however, point out that the systems themselves often develop from prior institutions or express cultural values. In this chapter, we also introduced a new category of theory, called sociological theory, which argues that political phenomena such as political parties reflect broader social divisions. As religious belief declines, union membership declines, or ethnic identity intensifies, parties and civil society will reflect these shifts. Understanding political actors' rational responses to institutional incentives alone does not allow us to explain major shifts in political behavior. Cultural theorists note that some political behavior, such as actively participating in civil society, reflects underlying cultural values, such as how deferential average people believe they should be toward elites. Fully understanding the complex area of political participation and representation seems to require a rich combination of theoretical approaches.

While this chapter has focused exclusively on democratic systems, the same institutional questions face authoritarian regimes, though their leaders make very different choices as they try not to enhance but to discourage active participation. Still, many of them use (and abuse) institutions of participation and representation to try to have some sense of democratic legitimacy. We turn to these regimes in the next chapter.

KEY CONCEPTS

alternative-vote (AV) system (p. 318)
cadre parties (p. 319)
closed-list proportional representation (p. 315)
collective action problem (p. 310)
dominant-party system (p. 323)
Duverger's Law (p. 326)
electoral systems (p. 312)
"first-past-the-post" (FPTP) electoral system (p. 313)
Hindu nationalism (p. 358)

interest-group pluralism (p. 331)
mass parties (p. 320)
mixed, or semiproportional, representation system (p. 316)
multiparty systems (p. 326)
neocorporatism (societal corporatism) (p. 335)
open-list proportional representation (p. 315)
party system (p. 319)
peak associations (p. 335)
plurality (p. 313)

populism (p. 323)
proportional representation (PR) (p. 314)
single, nontransferable vote (SNTV) (p. 318)
single-member district (SMD) (p. 313)
social capital (p. 336)
social movements (p. 335)
state corporatism (p. 335)
two-and-a-half-party system (p. 326)
two-party system (p. 323)

WORKS CITED

Blyth, Mark, and Richard Katz. 2005. "From Catch-all Politics to Cartelisation: The Political Economy of the Cartel Party." *West European Politics* 28 (1): 33–60. doi:10.1080/0140238042 000297080.

Boix, Carles. 2007. "The Emergence of Parties and Party Systems." In *The Oxford Handbook of Comparative Politics,* edited by Carles Boix and Susan Carol Stokes. Oxford, UK: Oxford University Press.

Budge, Ian, David Robertson, and Derek Hearl, eds. 1987. *Ideology, Strategy and Party Change: Spatial Analyses of Post-War Election Programmes in 19 Democracies.* Cambridge, UK: Cambridge University Press.

Carlson, Matthew. 2007. *Money Politics in Japan: New Rules, Old Practices.* Boulder, CO: Lynne Rienner.

Caul, Miki L., and Mark M. Gray. 2000. "From Platform Declarations to Policy Outcomes:

Changing Party Profiles and Partisan Influence over Policy." In *Parties without Partisans: Political Change in Advanced Industrial Democracies,* edited by Russell J. Dalton and Martin P. Wattenberg, 208–37. New York: Oxford University Press.

Dalton, Russell J., and Martin P. Wattenberg. 2000. *Parties without Partisans: Political Change in Advanced Industrial Democracies.* New York: Oxford University Press.

de Tocqueville, Alexis. 1969. *Democracy in America.* Garden City, NY: Doubleday Anchor. (Originally published in two volumes in 1835 and 1840, respectively, in London by Saunders and Otley.)

Duverger, Maurice. 1969. *Political Parties, Their Organization and Activity in the Modern State.* London: Methuen.

Green, Michael J. 2010. "Japan's Confused Revolution." *The Washington Quarterly* (33) 1: 3–19. doi:10.1080/01636600903418637.

Green, Simon, Dan Hough, Alister Miskimmon, and Graham Timmins. 2008. *The Politics of the New Germany.* New York: Routledge.

Hasan, Zoya. 2010. "Political Parties in India." In *The Oxford Companion to Politics in India,* edited by Niraja Gopal Jayal and Pratap Bhanu Mehta. Oxford, UK: Oxford University Press.

Inglehart, Ronald. 1971. "The Silent Revolution in Europe: Intergenerational Change in Post-Industrial Societies." *American Political Science Review* 65 (4): 991–1017. doi:10.1017/S0003055406392568.

Iversen, Torben, and Anne Wren. 1998. "Equality, Employment, and Budgetary Restraint: The Trilemma of the Service Economy." *World Politics* 50 (4): 507–46.

Kabashima, Ikuo, and Gill Steel. 2010. *Changing Politics in Japan.* Ithaca, NY: Cornell University Press.

Lee, Frances E. 2009. *Beyond Ideology: Politics, Principles, and Partisanship in the U.S. Senate.* Chicago: University of Chicago Press.

Lemann, Nicholas. 1996. "Kicking in Groups." *The Atlantic Monthly* 277 (4): 22–26.

Levendusky, Matthew. 2009. *The Partisan Sort: How Liberals Became Democrats and Conservatives*

Became Republicans. Chicago: University of Chicago Press.

Lijphart, Arend. 1999. *Patterns of Democracy: Government Forms and Performance in Thirty-six Countries.* New Haven, CT: Yale University Press.

Norris, Pippa. 2002. *Democratic Phoenix: Reinventing Political Activism.* New York: Cambridge University Press.

Ogawa, Akihiro. 2009. *The Failure of Civil Society? The Third Sector and the State in Contemporary Japan.* Albany, NY: SUNY Press.

Pekkanen, Robert. 2006. *Japan's Dual Civil Society: Members Without Advocates.* Stanford, CA: Stanford University Press.

Powell, G. Bingham. 2000. *Elections as Instruments of Democracy: Majoritarian and Proportional Visions.* New Haven, CT: Yale University Press.

Putnam, Robert D. 2000. *Bowling Alone: The Collapse and Revival of American Community.* New York: Simon and Schuster.

Reed, Steven R. 2005. "Japan: Haltingly Toward a Two-Party System." In *The Politics of Electoral Systems,* edited by Michael Gallagher and Paul Mitchell, 277–94. Oxford, UK: Oxford University Press.

Rodrik, Dani. 1997. *Has Globalization Gone Too Far?* Washington, DC: Institute for International Economics.

Scarrow, Susan E., Paul Webb, and David M. Farrell. 2000. "From Social Integration to Electoral Contestation: The Changing Distribution of Power within Political Parties." In *Parties without Partisans: Political Change in Advanced Industrial Democracies,* edited by Russell J. Dalton and Martin P. Wattenberg, 129–53. New York: Oxford University Press.

Schattschneider, Elmer Eric. 2009. *Party Government.* 3rd ed. New Brunswick, NJ: Transaction. (Originally published 1942 in New York by Holt, Rinehart and Winston.)

Shugart, Matthew Soberg. 2005. "Comparative Electoral Systems Research: The Maturation of a Field and New Challenges Ahead." In *The Politics of Electoral Systems,* edited by Michael Gallagher and Paul Mitchell, 22–55. Oxford, UK: Oxford University Press.

Skocpol, Theda. 2003. *Diminished Democracy: From Membership to Management in American Civic Life.* Norman: University of Oklahoma Press.

von Beyme, Klaus. 1985. *Political Parties in Western Democracies.* Aldershot, UK: Gower.

Wren, Anne, and Kenneth M. McElwain. 2007. "Voters and Parties." In *The Oxford Handbook of Comparative Politics,* edited by Carles Boix

and Susan Carol Stokes, 555–81. Oxford, UK: Oxford University Press.

Zettl, Christian. 2010. *The German Federal Elections of 2009: The (Ultimate) Downfall of the German Volksparteien?* Paper prepared for the PSA Conference. Newcastle-upon-Tyne, UK: Political Studies Association. Available at http://www.psa.ac.uk/journals/pdf/5/2010/961_418.pdf.

RESOURCES FOR FURTHER STUDY

Aldrich, John H. 1995. *Why Parties? The Origin and Transformation of Political Parties in America.* Chicago: University of Chicago Press.

Pharr, Susan J., and Robert D. Putnam, eds. 2000. *Disaffected Democracies: What's Troubling the Trilateral Countries?* Princeton, NJ: Princeton University Press.

Putnam, Robert D, ed. 2002. *Democracies in Flux: The Evolution of Social Capital in Contemporary Society.* New York: Oxford University Press.

Rosenbluth, Frances McCall, and Michael F. Thies. 2010. *Japan Transformed: Political Change and Economic Restructuring.* Princeton, NJ: Princeton University Press.

Thomas, Clive S. 2001. *Political Parties and Interest Groups: Shaping Democratic Governance.* Boulder, CO: Lynne Rienner.

Ware, Alan. 1996. *Political Parties and Party Systems.* New York: Oxford University Press.

WEB RESOURCES

Consortium for Elections and Political Process Strengthening (CEPPS), "Election Guide" (http://www.electionguide.org/reports.php)

Constituency-Level Elections Archive Project, "Constituency-Level Elections Archive" (http://www.electiondataarchive.org)

Golder, Matt, "Democratic Electoral Systems around the World, 1946–2000" (http://home pages.nyu.edu/~mrg217/elections.html)

Hyde, Susan, and Nikolay Marinov, "National Elections Across Democracy and Autocracy" (http://hyde.research.yale.edu/nelda/#/)

Inter-Parliamentary Union, "PARLINE Database on National Parliaments" (http://www.ipu.org/parline-e/parlinesearch.asp)

University of California, San Diego, "Database of Electoral Systems and the Personal Vote" (http://polisci2.ucsd.edu/jwjohnson/espv.htm)

University of California, San Diego, "Lijphart Elections Archive" (http://libraries.ucsd.edu/locations/sshl/data-gov-info-gis/ssds/guides/lij/)

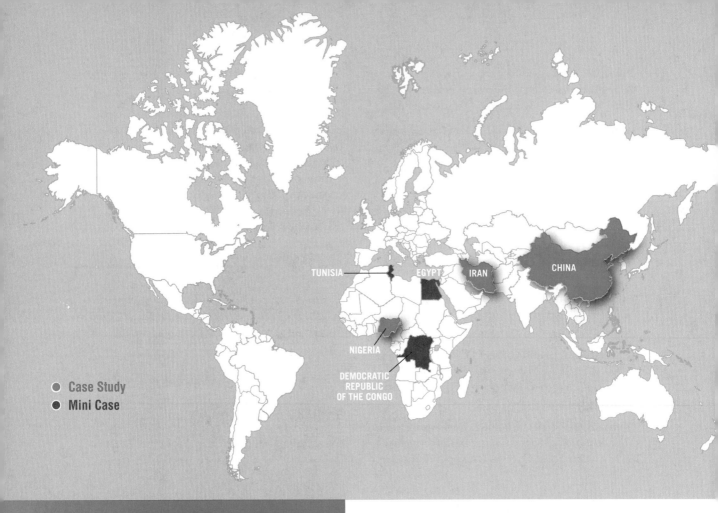

Who Rules?

• Some authoritarian regimes disperse power more widely than others. How can comparativists determine "who rules" and what limits executive power in an authoritarian regime?

What Explains Political Behavior?

• Authoritarian regimes come in several different subtypes: military, one-party, theocratic, personalist, and semi-authoritarian. In what ways do differences across these subtypes explain differences in leaders' actions, levels of repression, and types of popular participation?

• Why are patron-client networks so prevalent and important in authoritarian regimes? In what types of authoritarian regimes do they seem most important, and what might explain this?

Where and Why?

• Some authoritarian regimes allow at least some institutionalized limits on rulers' power. What explains where and why this happens, or doesn't happen?

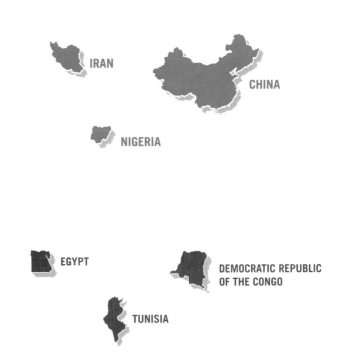

8

AUTHORITARIAN INSTITUTIONS

The spread of democracy in the aftermath of the Cold War led some to believe that democratic rule was irreversible and would eventually become universal; dictators were historical relics, soon to be relegated to the "dustbin of history." Many Eastern European and African societies that threw off or at least severely challenged their authoritarian regimes, however, ended up creating new ones, albeit less repressive than their predecessors. Semi-authoritarian regimes, in which some opposition and participation were allowed but a key ruler or party firmly held onto power, via nondemocratic means when necessary, became more common. In other cases, especially in the Middle East, the winds of democratic change did not blow strongly enough to seriously challenge long-standing authoritarian regimes until the sudden outburst of popular opposition in 2011. Therefore, abandoning the study of authoritarian regimes at the end of the Cold War was clearly premature, and in the new millennium comparativists have taken renewed interest in the subject. Authoritarian regimes have long outnumbered democracies. Indeed, only two of our case studies, the United States and the United Kingdom, have not had authoritarian regimes in the modern era. In both of these cases, "democracy" emerged very early and for many years was based on an extremely limited franchise; it was really democracy only for wealthy white men with no political rights for the majority of the citizenry. The Country and Concept table on page 371 shows how common and how varied authoritarian regimes are, just within our ten case studies.

The answer to the question "Who rules?" seems like it ought to be particularly obvious in authoritarian regimes: the dictator does. In fact, discerning who really has power and how much power they have is not always obvious. In chapter 3, we noted that in modernizing authoritarian regimes, neither ideology nor formal institutions necessarily explain who rules or how a particular regime functions. Authoritarian regimes tend to arise in relatively weak states, either via a violent takeover or via the successful nonviolent elimination of formal democratic institutions (often in a postcolonial context). Weak states, as we know, have weak formal institutions, and therefore informal institutions and processes are more important.

This makes determining who really rules—who has how much power—particularly difficult.

The prevalence of important informal institutions in authoritarian regimes also makes explaining political behavior challenging. In chapter 3 we outlined several subtypes of authoritarian regimes based on their origins and formal institutions: one-party, military, personalist, theocratic, and semi-authoritarian. These subtypes clearly have somewhat different governing institutions, but given that formal institutions in authoritarian regimes tend to be weak, how much does this really explain? Are one-party regimes as a group different in distinctive ways from military regimes? Does one subtype always provide greater levels of institutionalized limits on executive power? Is one subtype always more repressive? It is clear as well that patron-client relationships and networks are important in virtually all authoritarian regimes. Why is this the case, and does this also vary across the subtypes of authoritarian regimes? These are key political behavior questions that we examine in this chapter.

While formal institutions tend to be weak in authoritarian regimes, they are not universally so. Some regimes clearly have stronger formal institutions, including things like legislatures and judiciaries that limit rulers' powers at least to a small extent. Where and why do regimes with stronger formal institutions occur? If a dictator comes to power via a military coup, for instance, or inherits absolute power from his father in a personalist regime, why would he ever yield any of that power to other institutions? Trying to explain variations in institutionalized limits on power is a classic "Where and why?" question that we examine in this chapter as well.

Zimbabwean president Robert Mugabe addresses the crowd at the celebration of the thirtieth anniversary of the country's independence in April 2010. Mugabe, a nationalist hero who was originally elected to office, rules over one of the more repressive and corrupt authoritarian regimes. In the last decade, he has been forced to allow an opposition to exist, and he has had to share power with it in a "grand coalition" since 2008. He continues to use his control of the security apparatus and key resources, however, to thwart further moves toward democracy.

Credit: Aaron Ufumeli/EPA/Landov

A key difference among the various types of authoritarian regimes that will help us to answer all these questions is the regimes' level of **institutionalization**. By this we mean how much government processes and procedures are established, predictable, and routinized. In the least-institutionalized personalist regimes, decisions truly can be made and implemented at the whim of the dictator. In other authoritarian regimes, the leader's power is still extensive, but it is somewhat curtailed by institutionalized checks. For example, the Brazilian military regime institutionalized a rotating presidency, with each branch of the military designating a president for an established term. Communist regimes have politburos and other mechanisms of high-level party consultation that may force some discussion and consensus building, at least among the party elites.

institutionalization: The degree to which government processes and procedures are established, predictable, and routinized

COUNTRY AND CONCEPT

Authoritarian Rule

Country	20th-century authoritarian rule since independence (years)	Regime type	Number of supreme leaders	Average length of leader's rule (years)	Cause of regime demise
Brazil	1930–1945	Modernizing authoritarian	1	15	Democratization
	1964–1985	Military	5	4	Democratization
China*	1927–1949	Modernizing authoritarian	1	22	Revolution
	1949–	Communist/modernizing authoritarian	4	14.5	NA
Germany	1871–1918	Modernizing authoritarian	2	23	War loss
	1933–1945	Fascist	1	12	War loss
India	None	—	—	—	—
Iran	1921–1979	Modernizing authoritarian	2	27	Revolution
	1979–	Theocratic	2	16	NA
Japan	1867–1945	Modernizing authoritarian	3	26	War loss
Mexico	1924–2000	Modernizing authoritarian	15	4.5	Democratization
Nigeria	1966–1979	Military	4	3	Democratization
	1983–1998	Military	3	5	Democratization
Russia	1917–1991	Communist	7	10	Democratization
	2000–	Semi-authoritarian	1	11	NA
United Kingdom	None	—	—	—	—
United States	None	—	—	—	—

*China's republic (1912–1927) never consolidated an effective state.

All modern states, including those with authoritarian regimes, have executive branches and bureaucracies and provide some sort of judiciary, though how much the judiciary is independent of the executive is a major question. Some authoritarian regimes also develop institutions such as legislatures and even hold elections to provide some degree, however small, of citizen participation, though not enough to threaten the power of the key rulers. We therefore examine the same sets of institutions in this chapter that we did in chapters 6 and 7 for democracies, but the distinct context and logic of authoritarian regimes require somewhat different foci and theoretical lenses to understand those institutions and how well they work, or don't.

GOVERNING INSTITUTIONS IN AUTHORITARIAN REGIMES

supreme leader: Individual who wields executive power with few formal limits in an authoritarian regime; in the Islamic Republic of Iran, the formal title of the top ruling cleric

Virtually all authoritarian regimes recognize one supreme leader, even if he leads a larger ruling group, such as the politburo in a communist system or the ruling junta in a military government. This **supreme leader** typically wields executive power with few formal limits. He is likely to consult with other top leaders and may be chosen by them, but he nonetheless contends with few of the constraints on power that apply to an executive in a democratic regime. In some regimes, the top leaders each informally control an important source of power, an institution, or a faction within the government, and the supreme leader must make sure that he has sufficient support from these other leaders before he makes major decisions. For example, in a military regime, the supreme leader may consult informally with the leader of each branch of the military before making an important policy decision. In some more personalist regimes, even these informal limits often do not exist. Government in these cases (for example, in Haiti under Jean-Claude "Baby Doc" Duvalier from 1971 to 1986) becomes erratic, reflecting little more than the whims of the supreme leader.

All supreme leaders rule through some combination of repression, co-optation, and efforts at legitimation. Repression is the popular image that pops into people's minds when they think of dictators, but it is an expensive means of rule. Even the most ruthless dictator needs to find other means by which to ensure citizens' loyalties. Co-optation via material inducements and official positions (which often go hand in hand with corruption), particularly of key elites who could be potential rivals, is the most obvious alternative means of securing support. Most regimes also expend resources to try to instill loyalty in the citizenry to secure some actual legitimacy; if citizens believe in the regime, they will obey it without the costs of repression or co-optation. Communist parties use their well-developed ideology for this purpose to a greater extent than do most authoritarian regimes, but virtually all authoritarian regimes do so in some way. This is a topic we will examine in more detail in the next section.

Security is certainly all regimes' top priority, and this is especially true for authoritarian regimes, which often lack legitimacy. All types of authoritarian regimes, not just military ones, spend generously on military security, typically aimed more at internal than external threats. The loyalty of the military is, of course, crucial. One-party states either incorporate key military leaders into the party leadership or make sure that loyal party leaders have control of the military, or both. For example, after the 1979 revolution that overthrew Anastasio Somoza's personalist regime in Nicaragua, the new Sandinista regime insisted that the military (which replaced the Somoza-created National Guard) remain under the control of the Sandinista army that had fought the revolution. The head of the army, Humberto Ortega, was not only a prominent Sandinista but was also the brother of Sandinista president Daniel Ortega. In personalist regimes, leaders often place close supporters, even family members, in key positions in charge of the country's security apparatus, including the military and police. In ethnically divided societies, they often place people of their own ethnic group, or even from their own hometown, within the security apparatus to ensure its loyalty. For instance, Saddam Hussein in Iraq put not only his fellow Sunni Arabs but also people from his home village in positions of authority in his extensive security apparatus. Personalist leaders also frequently create entirely new security organizations. Unable to rely on the loyalty of the existing military, they create personal, elite security forces that are loyal only to the executive, as both Hosni Mubarak did in Egypt and Muammar Gaddafi did in Libya. If a president has access to enough resources, his personal security force might be better paid and armed than the national army.

Many authoritarian rulers also create vast networks of spies, both civilian and military, whose job it is to gather intelligence on who is opposed to the regime. Security forces can then sweep in to arrest opposition members, throw them into detention without the benefit of a trial, or even execute them. Ronald Wintrobe (1998) used a rational-choice approach to argue that all authoritarian leaders face what he termed the **dictator's dilemma**: because of the repression they practice, they lack accurate information on how much political support they actually have. Repression breeds fear, which in turn breeds misinformation; the greater the repression, the greater the dictator's dilemma. Uncertain of their position, dictators try to co-opt potential rivals by purchasing their loyalty. They can never be certain, however, of how much they need to spend to purchase the loyalty they require, so they tend to overspend, lavishing resources on key sectors from which they believe threats may emanate. Thus, some groups are extremely well provided for by the regime. Various elements in the military often receive such attention, because all states must ensure a loyal military to survive. This is especially true in military regimes that came to power via coups d'etat themselves. They are acutely aware that they themselves may be overthrown by the military, so they work to prevent this. In ethnically divided societies, dictators may lavish resources on their own ethnic group to maintain what they believe to be their core base of support. In a number of African authoritarian regimes in the 1970s and 1980s, you could tell who was in power by how well paved the roads were in different regions of the country. The current dictator would build infrastructure such as roads, schools, and hospitals mainly in his own home area. As you drove from one region to another, you could literally see who ruled by the immediate and extreme change in the quality of the roads.

Another means of co-opting potential opponents is the creation of formal institutions such as legislatures and single ruling parties that provide lucrative government positions and access to patronage that dictators can use as payoffs. Jennifer Gandhi (2008) argued that these institutions are more than just mechanisms of co-optation; they can actually provide a space in which policy compromise can occur. Legislatures, and especially multiple parties (albeit in a semi-authoritarian regime in which the ruling party always maintains power), provide arenas in which policy compromises are possible. As Gandhi stated, "Within these institutions, leaders or religious organizations, business and labor associations, and various other groups can express demands that do not appear as acts of public resistance to the regime. The dictator, in turn, uses legislatures and parties as a way to control dissent and to make concessions while appearing to be magnanimous rather than weak" (137). Gandhi demonstrated that regimes with legislatures and parties spend less money on the military and have greater respect for human rights,

dictator's dilemma: An authoritarian ruler's repression creates fear, which then breeds uncertainty about how much support the ruler has; in response, the ruler spends more resources than is rational to co-opt the opposition

both of which are classic demands of opposition forces. This finding indicates that policy compromise is greater in authoritarian regimes with these formal institutions than in those without them.

Our case study of Brazil, discussed in chapter 3, is an example of this dynamic. The military (in power from 1964 to 1985) re-created an elected legislature, limiting participation to two parties: one officially supporting the regime and one officially opposed. The opposition, however, was severely restricted in what it was allowed to say or do in the legislature, whose powers were fairly nominal in any case. Nevertheless, the legislature served as a forum in which the opposition party could voice its views and the government could respond via policy changes. Many one-party

WHERE AND WHY

Institutional Limits on Dictators' Rule

Authoritarian regimes vary widely in terms of the presence and strength of their formal institutions. In some of the most personalist regimes, like Idi Amin's tyrannical regime in Uganda in the 1970s, the dictator eliminates virtually all institutions and rules on the basis of his often ruthless and paranoid whim. In others, elaborate institutions place some limits on what the supreme leader can do and provide a level of predictability that can reduce conflict and repression. Where and why do such institutions arise in authoritarian regimes, and why aren't they present everywhere?

As with any big question in comparative politics, a number of answers have been offered over the years. Given that supreme leaders are so important and powerful in authoritarian regimes, scholars have understandably focused on them individually. Psychological theorists have examined the historical record to study the personality types of major authoritarian leaders such as Hitler, Stalin, and Mao, arguing that each supreme leader's individual personality comes to be reflected in the regime itself. They try to discern why some leaders are more ruthless and arbitrary than others. Other scholars note that different types of authoritarian regimes are likely to result in different levels of institutionalization. A military that itself has strong institutionalized norms, such as the Brazilian military that created the bureaucratic-authoritarian regime we outlined in chapter 3, is

a hierarchical organization with a strong sense of identity and purpose. In this type of regime, the strength of the military as an institution is reflected in a relatively institutionalized form of military rule. Similarly, Communist parties might seem to be natural breeding grounds for more-institutionalized regimes. They often exist underground before taking power and have highly structured organizations, including politburos, committees, and cells, in addition to consultative and decision-making mechanisms.

Both political culture theorists and historical institutionalists look to broader societal factors and history to explain where and why institutions emerge. An authoritarian regime in a country with some historical experience with democracy may well be more likely to adopt or re-create some limited formal institutions like a legislature and perhaps limited opposition parties. Citizens are accustomed to these institutions, and the regime leaders would therefore likely believe they can gain legitimacy by at least appearing to adhere to these institutional norms. The benefits to the supreme leader of allowing some limitation to his rule in these cases would likely be greater than in a country with little or no cultural or institutional history of democracy.

Focusing solely on the emergence of institutionalized ruling parties, Jason Brownlee (2007) used a historical-institutionalist account

states in Africa preserved a legislature as well, though such bodies consisted only of members of the ruling party. In Kenya in the 1960s and early 1970s, legislators were able to voice limited criticisms of the government, work on behalf of their constituents to gain resources for their home areas, and use their access to government to gain direct benefits for themselves and their closest associates via corruption. The parliament clearly served as a mechanism of co-optation and, occasionally, of limited policy discussion. When MPs criticized the dictator too much, though, they faced repression: several sitting MPs were detained and tortured in the mid-1970s when their criticisms of the regime became too strident, and the most popular member of their group was assassinated.

that does not rely on prior history or culture. Examining four carefully chosen cases, he showed that ruling parties emerge at a particular decisive moment when the regime is formed. If the supreme leader and his supporters are successful at repressing and co-opting rival elites, they can form a strong ruling party that can mobilize popular support and marginalize would-be opponents. Once created, ruling parties gain institutional strength from the incentives they provide; politicians benefit from being inside them rather than fighting them from the outside. If well established early in the regime, such parties are likely to endure and enhance the prospects that the regime as a whole will endure as well.

Rejecting older theories, Jennifer Gandhi (2008) presented a rational-choice institutionalist argument for where and why dictators allow the creation of legislatures and parties. She argued, as we noted above, that these formal institutions serve not only to co-opt opposition but to create a political space in which limited policy compromises can take place. By giving the opposition access to and even limited influence over government, legislatures and limited opposition parties give regime opponents incentives to work within the system rather than to seek its overthrow. Rational and successful dictators, she argued, will understand what institutional concessions they must make to the opposition, depending on their own and the opposition's strength. Where the opposition is united, she demonstrated, formal institutions are more likely to arise. Where the regime controls extensive mineral wealth, giving it resources for greater patronage, institutions are less likely. Furthermore, Gandhi showed that institutions arise more frequently in civilian dictatorships than in either monarchies or military regimes. The latter, she argued, have independent power bases—the monarchy in its family and perhaps traditional legitimacy and the military in the strength and professionalization of that institution itself—that provide them greater power vis-à-vis the opposition and therefore less need for legislatures or opposition parties.

As is always the case, no single theory explains this important where and why question perfectly. Gandhi demonstrated with sophisticated statistical techniques that her theory predicted correctly more than half of the cases of institutional creation in authoritarian regimes since World War II, but her theory by no means explained all of them. Other factors such as historical background, culture, and at times the personality of a supreme leader who is in a position to indulge his whims undoubtedly can all play a role in a full explanation. For now, however, Gandhi's theory seems to have explained it more systematically than prior theories.

As the Kenyan case demonstrates, how well formal institutions serve their purposes of co-optation and policy compromise depends not only on their existence but also on their level of institutionalization. Prior to the mid-1970s, Kenyan MPs had immunity from arrest or prosecution on the basis of their actions or statements in parliament, a policy known as parliamentary immunity. For the first decade of Kenya's one-party state, President Jomo Kenyatta, the founding leader and dictator of Kenya, respected parliamentary immunity. When he abrogated it in the 1970s, parliament's strength and importance were severely weakened. Its institutional strength did not recover until the advent of multiparty competition in the early 1990s.

Institutionalization requires institutions to function more or less as they are legally designed to do over an extended period of time. Both historical and rational-choice institutionalists argue that as institutions continue to function, they gain strength; actors become socialized into their functions and, rational-choice theorists argue, self-interested politicians will abide by institutional rules as long as they believe they can benefit from them. Formal institutions like legislatures can expand political leaders' time horizons as they come to believe that they will have some influence over policy and access to resources via the institution. They will be more likely to accept the compromise of working within the institution rather than make more fundamental demands for reform, to which the dictator would respond with repression. Compromise that reduces conflict and probably lengthens the life of the regime comes from this process of institutionalization.

Some authoritarian regimes also allow for a degree of rule of law and autonomy for the judiciary, though this is always limited. Typically, judicial autonomy is permitted only in nonpolitical cases. Providing the political good of basic personal security to citizens who do not oppose the regime allows the regime to gain a degree of legitimacy. Allowing this type of limited judicial autonomy can also allow top leaders to gain an understanding of how effectively their state functions on the ground. Citizens can go to court to attempt to get local government to carry out its functions properly, revealing to leaders potential local problems. In all of these cases, though, regime leaders do not allow the rule of law to limit them in any fundamental way. Politically, they are more likely to use the judicial system to imprison their opponents or worse, reserving the right to remove judges as necessary to ensure that the executive's will is done. And in many authoritarian regimes, the judiciary becomes quite corrupt as well. Regime leaders and other influential and wealthy people often bribe judges to rule in their favor; once this begins, more and more people recognize what "justice" actually requires and corruption expands. The regime may formally preserve the rule of law, but in practice, justice is based on wealth, power, and influence.

All states, regardless of regime type, require a bureaucracy, and all leaders face the principal-agent problem we identified in chapter 6 as they try to ensure that the bureaucracy follows their orders. Judicial autonomy of the limited type we described above can help with this, as court cases alert leaders to bureaucratic failures. In an authoritarian regime, though, the question is how strong and independent a bureaucracy the supreme leader wants. A less-institutionalized bureaucracy, while not serving citizens' interests well, may have distinct advantages to the leader in the form of corruption opportunities that it offers regime supporters. Bureaucratic positions at various levels provide opportunities for corruption. The top leaders can thus maintain loyalty by allowing officials to use their positions to their own benefit, weakening the institutions of the state but rewarding the loyalty of potential rivals. If this behavior is institutionalized, it can become somewhat predictable: lesser officials will remain loyal because they believe they can rise to higher and more rewarding positions, which can lead to somewhat predictable career paths

GOVERNING INSTITUTIONS IN AUTHORITARIAN REGIMES

within key institutions. In more personalist regimes, a similar process takes place but in a less institutionalized manner. The key leader alone puts people in positions of power in the state or party bureaucracy. He may well change these frequently to ensure that no official has too much connection with or influence over any one organization because that could ultimately threaten the supreme ruler by creating an alternative power base for a potential rival. Our mini case of Zaire demonstrates this strategy.

MINI CASE

The "Politics of Survival" in Mobutu's Zaire

Zaire (now the Democratic Republic of the Congo) under the dictatorship of Gen. Mobutu Sese Seko (1965–1997) was a classic case of a corrupt, personalist regime in a weak state. Mobutu came to power via a military coup and created the formal structures of a one-party state, but his rule was very personalist. All power and all major decisions went through him, and personal loyalty and patronage were the key elements of political power. The state he took over had collapsed shortly after independence into a four-way civil war that became a significant episode in the Cold War in the early 1960s, ultimately involving the United States, Belgium, the Soviet Union, and China. With U.S. support, his coup and subsequent regime managed to pull the country together again but never did create strong institutions or a strong state. In fact, over time his regime severely weakened virtually all state institutions by following the logic of what political scientist Joel Migdal (1988) termed "the politics of survival."

On the surface, personalist leaders like Mobutu appear all-powerful. In reality, these authoritarian leaders of weak states have limited power because they preside over weak institutions that can accomplish relatively little. One might think that this would lead them to try to strengthen those institutions to tighten their own grip on power. While this can happen, Migdal (1988) pointed out that doing so can be extremely risky for the dictator; indeed, more often than not, a dictator in a weak state is driven to weaken rather than strengthen his country's institutions.

Strong institutions are certainly sources of power but not necessarily for the supreme leader. He cannot directly control all of a state's institutions but must instead, like any national leader, rely on subordinates. Those subordinates who lead state agencies directly may well be the primary beneficiaries of the power that derives from strengthened institutions. An agency that can solve people's problems or provide valuable resources gains political support for those directly in charge of the agency, not only or even necessarily for the supreme leader. Therefore, subordinates in charge of such agencies can easily become political rivals of the leader. Migdal (1988) argued that this is why leaders of weak states often engage in practices that undermine the possibility of creating stronger institutions. Such practices include frequently shuffling subordinates so that none of them become entrenched in any one position, appointing people who are personally loyal to the leader but who may have little competence for the positions in question, and harassing subordinates by, for example, incarcerating them temporarily on trumped-up charges.

Mobutu was a master of this kind of politics. He ruled first and foremost by patronage, creating a regime that many referred to as a "kleptocracy," or rule by theft. He was personally corrupt, amassing an alleged $5 billion over his three decades in power, and he allowed anyone he appointed to office to do the same. A government appointment was a license to steal whatever resources to which one's position gave access. Over time, he increasingly appointed people who were personally loyal to him as well, especially in the all-important military. He even created several competing security agencies, the most important of which was a personal presidential guard staffed almost entirely with people from or near his home village. He shuffled cabinet members on a regular basis, and if he got angry with a cabinet minister, he was known to remove that individual from the cabinet, put him or her in jail, and then release him or her a few months or years later to return to the cabinet. A famous such case involved Nguza Karl-i-Bond. He was foreign minister and then head of the ruling party in the mid-1970s, but after being mentioned as a possible successor to Mobutu he was accused of treason in 1977, imprisoned, and tortured. A year later, Mobutu forgave him and restored him to the prominent office of state commissioner. Then in 1981, Nguza fled into exile in Belgium, denounced Mobutu for his corruption and brutality, and even testified against him before the U.S. Congress. In 1986, however, Mobutu once again forgave him, and Nguza returned to Zaire to a hero's welcome; shortly afterward he was named

to the prestigious position of ambassador to Washington, D.C. Examples like this ensured that no one was secure in any position for too long and proved to all that Mobutu could take people from a top position to prison and back again in the blink of an eye.

CASE SUMMARY

"The politics of survival" (along with generous Western support during the Cold War) kept Mobutu in power for three decades but weakened all institutions in Zaire. Even basic infrastructure declined as the state's resources and capabilities collapsed. When Mobutu's neighbor and ally, Rwandan president Juvénal Habyarimana, was facing an armed insurrection in the early 1990s, Mobutu is alleged to have told him, "Your problem is you built roads. They are coming down those roads to get you." Mobutu did not make that mistake: Zaire's road network deteriorated to almost nothing under his rule. Nonetheless, rebel forces supported by the governments of Burundi, Uganda, and Rwanda (now composed of the rebels who overthrew Habyarimana) eventually forced the aging Mobutu out of power at the point of a gun.

Especially in cases where a single leader controls appointment to high offices and changes personnel frequently to protect his power, authoritarian regimes are plagued by the question of succession. Electoral democracies provide a means of changing leadership on a regular basis; authoritarian regimes have no such procedure readily at hand. This means that each regime must create its own system for choosing new leaders. Again, the degree of institutionalization matters greatly. Communist regimes, for instance, generally choose new leaders from among key contenders within the politburo. While the exact process is usually hidden from the general public, both regime leaders and citizens know that should a leader die, resign, or be forced from office, a pool of successors is available and top party leaders will collectively choose one from among their own. The Country and Concept table on page 371 illustrates the institutionalization of succession in the Soviet regime; it had seven different leaders, while many other authoritarian regimes had only one and thus failed to survive their founder's demise.

Less-institutionalized regimes typically have no succession system. Personalist leaders often rule for life or until they are forced out of office. Many will groom a successor as they age, all the while working to make sure that the potential successor does not become a threat before the time to pass the baton arrives. In the most personalist regimes, the leader grooms his own son to be his successor. The Somoza dynasty in Nicaragua (1936–1979) began with Anastasio senior, who was succeeded by his son Luis, who in turn was succeeded by his brother (and head of the only military, the National Guard), another Anastasio. This was also the case in the regimes of "Papa Doc" (1957–1971) and "Baby Doc" Duvalier (1971–1986) in Haiti. Baby Doc was only nineteen years old when his father died and he became head of state. Should a personalist ruler die without clearly identifying a successor, a battle among key elites can emerge that can cause the regime to crumble, often resulting in a military coup (or, in the past, external invasion) to reestablish order. Sometimes, as in the case of Nigeria, the death of a personalist ruler can be the opportunity for democracy to emerge anew. These various outcomes demonstrate that the lack of a succession process creates significant uncertainty and potential instability in less institutionalized authoritarian regimes.

Summary

Some authoritarian regimes do have modest institutionalized limits on executive power, but this is almost always a matter of very limited horizontal accountability among the elites and the institutions they lead. For example, institutionalization may require a supreme leader to gain some degree of elite consensus before making major decisions. In the somewhat more open semi-authoritarian regimes, legal opposition and a legislature are allowed, but power is kept firmly in the hands of the key rulers. This can also provide some level of predictability in the political system: key policy changes may have some opposition input, and the rise of new leadership develops out of an opaque but at least vaguely understood process. None of this, however, means that average citizens have real representation or more than token opportunities for participation. Vertical accountability, the ability of the citizenry to hold leaders directly accountable, is extremely limited. We will take up this subject again after examining three cases of governing institutions in authoritarian regimes.

CASE STUDY

China: From Communist to Modernizing Authoritarian Rule

- Institutionalizing one-party rule and succession
- Reduced power of the supreme leader
- Growing rule of law without democracy
- Some judicial autonomy to overcome dictator's dilemma
- Corruption as a key problem

In October 2007, the Chinese Communist Party (CCP) held the biggest event on its calendar, the Party Congress, which happens once every five years. The elected congress publicly ratifies major policies and officially

Chinese vice president Xi Jinping visits a car factory in Changchun. At the 2007 Party Congress, Xi became the heir apparent to succeed Hu Jintao as president. He has since been given several major positions in the party, state, and military commission, signaling that at the Party Congress in 2012 Xi will become the new supreme leader.

Credit: Ju Peng/Xinhua/Landov

elects its top leaders, which the current leadership has already chosen. Analysts watch closely what happens at this event, and they look especially at any changes in the top leadership to try to understand the direction the country may be going. What they see, at least on the surface, is uniformity, with nearly unanimous votes on every issue and leader. But no one knows what goes on behind closed doors. The united face shown to the public is the product of months of jockeying among key leaders to get their people into top positions. Nonetheless, an opaque but somewhat predictable succession process has emerged over time. When Hu Jintao, the supreme party leader, completes the second of his two five-year terms in 2012, Xi Jinping will almost certainly succeed him. This orchestrated changing of the guard has added a level of regularity to China's political process that didn't exist under the regime's founder, Mao Zedong.

China's communist regime has been in power since 1949 but has changed profoundly since Mao's death in 1976. Although it remains a one-party state under the unquestioned leadership of the CCP, more institutionalized rule has produced greater predictability within state institutions and the beginnings of what could become the rule of law. Though communist in name, in practice China has become a modernizing authoritarian regime by successfully encouraging capitalist development while maintaining a firm one-party hold on political power. This transition has allowed slightly more political participation in the system, which has led some observers to wonder if it is on the way to becoming semi-authoritarian or even democratic.

This is a far cry from the early days of the regime. Communist rule under Mao developed into a full-blown personality cult by the late 1960s. Mao's rule, especially during the Cultural Revolution (1966–1976), undermined most institutions. The party, state bureaucracy, and other institutions still existed, but the regime was increasingly personalist and obedient to the whims of the aging Mao.

The era is perhaps best captured by Chen Jo-hsi's short stories (1978), in which a young boy causes his parents great fear because he utters the phrase "Chairman Mao is a rotten egg." His parents also keep comic books with images of Mao away from the boy, because should he draw in them and accidentally deface a picture of Mao, the family would be in serious political trouble. These may sound like exaggerated tales written to make a point, but the threat of being seen as unpatriotic for even the most innocuous of actions was very real.

Upon Mao's death, the new leader Deng Xiaoping (1978–1989) joined others in trying to reestablish order and stable governing institutions under the authority of the CCP. The leaders seem to have deliberately set out to create a more institutionalized system of rule. These reforms were embodied in a new constitution in 1982, which was significantly amended in 1999. Among other things, the 1982 constitution abolished the position of party chairman, the position Mao had held and abused. Authority remains vested first and foremost in the ruling party, however, which fuses executive and legislative functions. As Figure 8.1 shows, each key governing institution has a parallel party institution. The National Party Congress is the official decision-making body of the party, and the National People's Congress is the equivalent of the legislature. Both institutions are ostensibly elected by provincial and local bodies, but in reality the higher organs choose virtually all the candidates or at least ensure that only candidates loyal to the ruling party are elected. For all of this, both institutions still have very limited power. They include several thousand members and meet only occasionally (annually for the legislature and every five years for the Party Congress), doing little more than ratifying the decisions of the party elite. Real power lies in the party's Politburo and even more so in the smaller Politburo Standing Committee (PSC). The State Council and its Standing Committee are in effect the cabinet that actually runs the government, overseen by the Politburo and PSC.

Figure 8.1

China's Governing Institutions

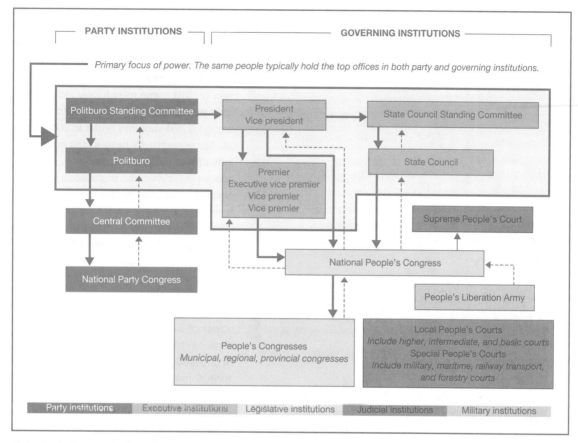

Note: Dashed arrows indicate formal selection process or direction of authority. Bold arrows indicate actual selection process or direction of authority.

Like all communist regimes, China struggles with the relationship between the party and state institutions. Under Mao, membership in the top parallel institutions was nearly identical; today, overlapping membership continues but is by no means universal. The regime under recent leaders has tried to distinguish between the governing role of the State Council and the political oversight role of the Politburo and the PSC. The ultimate authority of the party organs and their top leadership, however, remains unchallenged. There has always been one paramount leader, though he does not rule alone. While the workings of the Politburo and the PSC are secret, all reports suggest that today a great deal of open discussion occurs within these highest organs of power. For instance, Deng shared formal powers with key colleagues. He was chair of the crucial Central Military Commission (CMC) that was in charge of the military, but he allowed allies to serve as general secretary of the party and as premier, the head of the State Council. More recently, top executive authority again has been fused in the hands of one individual: Hu Jintao is not only president but also general secretary of the party and chair of the CMC.

IN CONTEXT

THE DECLINE OF COMMUNISM

Number of one-party communist states in 1975: 16

Albania	North Korea
Bulgaria	Poland
China	Romania
Cuba	South Yemen (People's
Czechoslovakia	Democratic Republic of
East Germany	Yemen)
Hungary	Soviet Union
Laos	Vietnam
Mongolia	Yugoslavia

Number of one-party communist states in 2011: 5

China (in name only)	North Korea
Cuba	Vietnam (in name only)
Laos	

Source: http://en.wikipedia.org/wiki/Single-party_state#Former_single-party_states and http://en.wikipedia.org/wiki/List_of_Communist_States.

Greater institutionalization has also become apparent in leadership succession, which is the perennial problem of authoritarian regimes. Upon Mao's death in 1976, a two-year battle among factions ensued that created a period of great uncertainty. Ultimately, Deng and his allies emerged victorious, launching China on its current path of opening its economy to the world and reforming its institutions while preserving CCP rule. Deng anointed Jiang Zemin as his successor and systematically began transferring power to him in 1989, starting with the chairmanship of the CMC. In 2003, the transfer of power became regularized as Jiang chose Hu as his successor and duly appointed him to all three key executive positions (general secretary, chair of the CMC, and president). Jiang became known as the "core of the third generation" of the leadership, and Hu is now the "core of the fourth generation." Generational change, indeed, has been a hallmark of recent Party Congresses: the Central Committee elected at each Party Congress now routinely includes about 60 percent new members, with each Party Congress seeing a significant shift toward younger and more highly educated members (Shambaugh 2008, 153). The 2007 Party Congress seems to have anointed Xi Jinping as the next heir apparent, electing him to the PSC. Xi became vice president in 2008 and vice chairman of the military commission in 2010; these roles further indicate that he is the agreed-upon successor to become president and supreme leader in 2012. All in all, China seems to have institutionalized a form of leadership succession that, while still opaque to outsiders, promises some predictability and stability. The new leader now "emerges" among key contenders within the PSC and other top institutions and, once agreed upon, is formally anointed by the leadership. Thus, a smooth transition is signaled some time in advance of the formal handing over of full power.

Though the top leader has the fused power of all three important executive positions, he still does not rule alone. Indeed, Jing Huang (2008) went so far as to argue that the institutionalized collective leadership makes the concept of "supreme leader" of little importance in contemporary China, though many observers still see Hu as at least "first among equals." Chinese politics has always been characterized by internal factionalism. Essentially, the only reason Mao and Deng had greater power than current leaders was because of the respect they received as two of the revolutionary founders of the regime. Jiang and Hu do not command that kind of respect and therefore must negotiate with other key leaders to gain support for their leadership and policies. With Hu's elevation to the top leadership, two major factions have emerged: those with backgrounds in the party's youth league, through which Hu rose and who are supported by leaders from inland and poorer regions who back Hu, and those from the wealthier, coastal areas, collectively known as the "Shanghai gang" (Li and White 2006). The two factions have split power very evenly since 2007 in terms of membership in the top decision-making organs. Li Cheng (2010) saw the factional balance serving as an informal system of checks and balances on the top rulers as they limit each other's power and, therefore, the power of the supreme leader. The succession of Hu to replace Jiang and, assuming nothing changes, Xi (a member of the Shanghai faction) to replace Hu in 2012 may also be establishing a norm of shifting the leadership between the factions on a regular basis. Such factional battles occasionally spill over into the larger legislative bodies; while the National People's Congress has never opposed the top leadership, since the early 1990s it has occasionally had some open debate, particularly within regional group meetings. Perhaps the best example of this was a debate over the controversial Three Gorges Dam, which was condemned by many environmentalists but seen as essential by the leadership for China's future energy needs. While the Congress approved it, out of a total of nearly 3,000 members an unprecedented 77 members voted against it and 664 abstained.

In addition to the party leadership, the military has always been a crucial faction in Chinese politics. Both Mao and Deng retained great military loyalty because of their personal roles during the revolution. Even Deng, however, had to appease the armed forces at times. For example, the army refused to allow Deng to appoint one of his allies, Zhao Ziyang, to head the CMC in the mid-1980s. Then when the top commander in Beijing refused to use his troops to disperse the student demonstrators in Tiananmen Square in June 1989, Deng had to call a meeting of all seven regional commanders and persuade the other six to back the move before the army would act. After that, Deng initiated major reforms of the military, which Jiang continued. These have significantly professionalized the officer corps as well as improved its funding, reflecting China's rapidly growing strategic position in the world. The army remains an important faction behind the scenes, but for the moment the top leadership under Jiang and now Hu seem to have institutionalized effective civilian control over it, at least barring another crisis such as Tiananmen.

The judiciary has also seen significant institutionalization in the past two decades. Under Mao, virtually no criminal justice system existed; criminal and political opponents were identified by Maoist loyalists and subject to local "people's courts." Little in the way of codified law existed, and what law did exist was not followed with any regularity. Significant changes have occurred since 1980 as part of the general post-Mao reform process and the expansion of a market economy, though the Chinese legal system still does not include the basic rights familiar to Western citizens. A key institution in China is the Procurator, which serves all levels of the court system. The Procurator combines the roles of prosecuting and defense attorney. He or she decides if a case should go to trial and provides the court with the relevant evidence. If a case does go to trial, conviction is almost certain. A defendant can appeal a case to a higher level of court but may do so only once. Trials are now supposed to be open to the public, and most are, but the government still prevents the public from attending high-profile political cases. Civil law has been liberalized more extensively than criminal law, as the government has had to start the process of protecting private property rights and contracts to attract foreign investment. A 1989 reform of administrative law greatly increased the ability of citizens to take local government agencies to court for not doing their job properly. An average of 100,000 such cases are filed annually, with a success rate estimated at 15 to 20 percent (Ginsburg 2008). A broad survey found rapidly growing use of and trust in courts among Chinese citizens in the new millennium, especially for handling civil disputes (Landry 2008).

While the legal rights now in place are not fully implemented, Chinese law has made significant reforms in the direction of providing the basic legal framework that capitalism requires, and the regime has been able to use that legal framework to improve local government performance without threatening party control overall. It has helped the central government to gather information on what is happening in local government, partially overcoming the dictator's dilemma that all authoritarian regimes face. The Supreme People's Court, the country's highest court, has the right to interpret the law and the constitution but not to overturn decisions of the National Congress. As always, the party remains supreme over all, including the judiciary.

China has significantly institutionalized its regime while maintaining ruling party control, but the government is certainly still willing to use repression when necessary. Crackdowns against human rights activists and others became particularly severe leading up to the 2008 Olympics in Beijing. The government significantly increased security and restrictions in Tibet, a region whose populace desires greater autonomy or independence, after 500 monks protested continued Chinese rule. A similar response met protests by ethnic Uyghurs demanding greater freedoms and social services. The government has also fought a long-standing battle to limit access to the Internet to prevent citizens from posting or reading material that is too critical of the regime. In 2010, Google decided to quit operating in China because of what the company saw as excessive restrictions on its search engine, as well as repeated cyberattacks on its computers that the company blamed on government agents. The government's response was to introduce a new law demanding that companies cooperate even more fully with the regime's efforts to limit information. Fearing a public reaction to the 2011 uprisings in the Middle East, the government cracked down again on journalists, dissidents, and an internationally known artist and censored Internet sites related to the uprising, including all references to the word *jasmine* because of the "Jasmine Revolution" in Tunisia. In 2009, the international NGO Reporters without Borders ranked China number 168 out of 175 countries on press freedom, down from the previous year.

One of the biggest threats to the CCP does not come from protesters or dissidents but from within: corruption. With the rise of a market economy that is now parallel with and increasingly replacing the state sector, opportunities for corruption have multiplied rapidly. State and party officials are in positions to receive bribes because of their control over regulation of financial services, key licenses for business activities, land use rights, infrastructure contracts, and government procurement. A new practice since the 1990s is *maiguan maiguan,* the buying and selling of government positions, especially at the local level in less-developed regions. In an extreme case, 265 local politicians in Heilongjiang Province, including the governor, were involved in the sale of government positions. The execution of Zheng Xiaoyu in 2008 for taking bribes to approve often dangerous medicines, and accusations that same year that schools destroyed in the 7.8-magnitude earthquake in Sichuan Province were shoddily constructed because local officials took bribes, have focused popular and global attention on corruption. But the problem is more pervasive than these high-profile examples illustrate. Between October 1997 and September 2002, an average of 6,000 senior local officials were prosecuted annually for corruption (Pei 2007).

The party's Central Commission for Discipline Inspection is charged with ferreting out corruption within the party itself. In a five-year period from 1987 to 1992, it investigated nearly a million cases of corruption within the party and expelled more than 150,000 members. The odds of being convicted of corruption are not great, however. While 130,000 to 190,000 party members have been disciplined since 1982, only 6 percent have been prosecuted, and only half of those have been convicted. As a result, the risks of prosecution remain low compared to the rewards of corruption (Pei 2007). The central leadership clearly recognizes that corruption is undermining the governing institutions it has built up since the 1970s. Nonetheless, as always, the top leadership itself is beyond accountability, even though rumors of massive corruption among family members of the top elite are rampant. While these incidents have never been aired publicly or prosecuted, the widespread belief that corruption reaches the highest levels of government can only encourage those at lower levels to continue to participate in it themselves. It may well be the most serious institutional problem the regime faces.

Modern China has transformed itself from a communist regime with strong personalist overtones under Mao into a modernizing authoritarian regime that has substantially institutionalized its rule. In the process, it has become much more stable and predictable,

though it continues to use repression when necessary and faces a grave threat from corruption. Rising corruption, though, demonstrates that expending resources to co-opt potential opposition is an important survival strategy for the Chinese regime, just as it is for most authoritarian regimes. Despite these continuing problems, the regime has presided over the fastest growing economy in the world and has found a solution to one of the chief problems of authoritarian rule: succession. The level and effect of participation, and the prospects of eventual democratization, remain controversial questions that we explore later in the chapter.

CASE STUDY

Iran: Theocracy or Military Dictatorship?

- Supreme Leader created as top position after Islamic Revolution
- Formal institutions combine theocratic and quasi-democratic elements
- Theocratic institutions always have more power than quasi-democratic ones and repress reform movements when necessary
- Patronage via Islamic foundations helps regime stay in power
- Growing power of Revolutionary Guard raises specter of informal transition to military regime

Ayatollah Ali Khamenei speaks in front of a portrait of the Islamic Republic of Iran's founding leader, Ayatollah Ruhollah Khomeini. Khamenei succeeded Khomeini upon the latter's death in 1989. Succession is often difficult in authoritarian regimes, but Iran's constitution gives clerical authorities the clear right and ability to choose a successor for the position of supreme leader.

Credit: Raheb Homavandi/Reuters/Landov

In February 2010, U.S. Secretary of State Hillary Clinton claimed that Iran was becoming a military dictatorship. Officially, Iran is a theocracy that has some potentially democratic elements, though the latter have been kept tightly in check. The growing strength of a military unit created after the revolution—the Revolutionary Guard—has raised the question of whether this theocracy is indeed becoming a military regime in practice, though it retains

the theocratic and quasi-democratic formal institutions built into its constitution. The triumph of the Ayatollah Khomeini in 1979 in toppling the U.S.-supported regime of the shah of Iran, and the subsequent Iranian hostage crisis that helped push U.S. president Jimmy Carter from office, were singular events in modern history. They ushered in the world's first modern theocracy—a new type of regime that the West greatly feared. Radical Islam had emerged as a new force in world politics. As reformist elements tried to use the quasi-democratic institutions of the regime to move away from purely authoritarian rule, conservative clerics and the Revolutionary Guard turned increasingly to repression, strengthening the Guard relative to other institutions and raising the possibility of a more purely military regime emerging.

The Islamic Republic of Iran created a unique set of political institutions that are based on the theocratic principles we outlined in chapter 3, but with significant participatory elements. The regime mixes appointed and elected offices to maintain the central control of the leading clergy while allowing some voice to other political forces, though usually within strict limits. Figure 8.2 provides an overview of these institutions, which are discussed in detail below. During its more open phases, Iran has come close to becoming a semi-authoritarian regime but has not quite moved into that category because the appointed clergy ultimately maintain legal power to do as they please. Elected officials are allowed to pass laws and voice some public criticism, but the authority of the Shiite clergy is final. So despite its unique institutions, the Iranian government rules like many other authoritarian regimes, through a combination of repression and co-optation but with a greater than usual effort to gain legitimacy. Also like other authoritarian regimes, it has and will again face the problem of the succession of its supreme leader. Similar to China, it also faces a question of whether it will become more democratic in the foreseeable future, as there is significant domestic pressure in that direction.

Khomeini's contribution to Islamic political thought is the position of supreme leader, which is always filled by a respected member of the clergy. With one decree, Khomeini created the single most important position in the Iranian government; it bestows upon one individual the role of both legal and spiritual guide of the country. First occupied by Khomeini himself and then (since Khomeini's death in 1989) by Ayatollah Ali Khamenei, the office has the power to appoint the heads of all the armed forces, the head of the judiciary, six of the twelve members of the all important Guardian Council, and the leaders of Friday prayers at mosques. These powers mean that very little of significance can occur in Iran without at least the supreme leader's tacit consent. An Assembly of Experts composed entirely of clergy but that is popularly elected by citizens appoints the supreme leader and at least theoretically has the right to remove him, though so far it seems that the position has a lifetime term of office.

The supreme leader shares executive power with a directly elected president in a theocratic version of a semipresidential system. The supreme leader has broader powers than the president and is the legal head of state. The position is loosely equivalent to that of president in France (though with far more powers in reality, given the lack of real democracy in Iran). The elected president appoints a cabinet, which the parliament must approve and can remove, and runs the daily affairs of government. The president is selected via a majoritarian election, so if one candidate does not win more than 50 percent of the vote in the initial election, a runoff is held between the top two candidates. The winner can serve two four-year terms, which the last three presidents have done.

As in other semipresidential systems, laws must be passed by the parliament and approved by the president. The Iranian system, however, strictly limits the freedom of these elected offices. The Guardian Council, consisting of six clergy appointed by the supreme leader and six lay leaders nominated by the head of the judiciary and approved by parliament, must also agree to all legislation. Given that all of its members are either appointed directly by the supreme leader or nominated by his appointed judiciary, the Council of Guardians is a bastion of conservatism and clerical authority that preserves the theological underpinnings of the regime and the will of the supreme leader. It also must approve all candidates for elections at all levels and has repeatedly

Figure 8.2

Iran's Governing Institutions

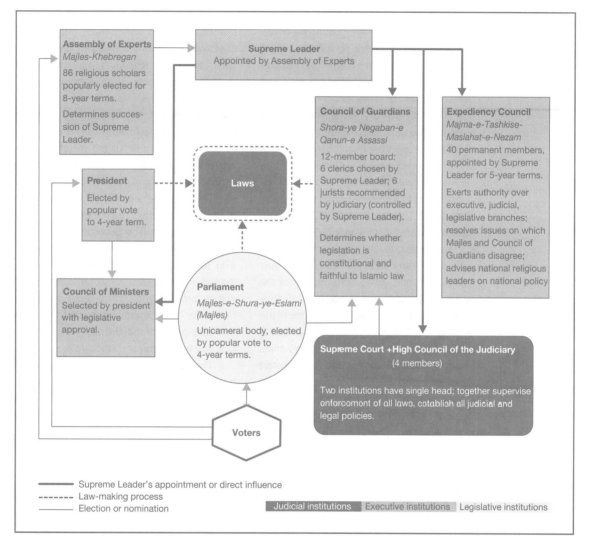

Assembly of Experts
Majles-Khebregan

86 religious scholars popularly elected for 8-year terms.

Determines succession of Supreme Leader.

Supreme Leader
Appointed by Assembly of Experts

Council of Guardians
Shora-ye Negaban-e Qanun-e Assassi

12-member board: 6 clerics chosen by Supreme Leader; 6 jurists recommended by judiciary (controlled by Supreme Leader).

Determines whether legislation is constitutional and faithful to Islamic law

Expediency Council
Majma-e-Tashkise-Maslahat-e-Nezam

40 permanent members, appointed by Supreme Leader for 5-year terms.

Exerts authority over executive, judicial, legislative branches; resolves issues on which Majles and Council of Guardians disagree; advises national religious leaders on national policy

President

Elected by popular vote to 4-year term.

Laws

Council of Ministers

Selected by president with legislative approval.

Parliament
Majles-e-Shura-ye-Eslami (Majles)

Unicameral body, elected by popular vote to 4-year terms.

Supreme Court +High Council of the Judiciary
(4 members)

Two institutions have single head; together supervise enforcement of all laws, establish all judicial and legal policies.

Voters

———— Supreme Leader's appointment or direct influence
-------- Law-making process
———— Election or nomination

Judicial institutions   Executive institutions   Legislative institutions

Note: Bold arrows indicate strength of actual authority of supreme leader.

banned candidates it has deemed unacceptable for president, parliament, and local government councils. A second body, the Expediency Council, was added via constitutional amendment in 1989 to be an advisory body to the supreme leader. It has the power to resolve disputes between parliament and the Guardian Council, and its rulings are final. The supreme leader appoints all of its members, so it is an additional way for him to make sure that the elected

president and the elected officials in parliament do not pass laws of which he does not approve.

The dual executive has control over the bureaucracy, judiciary, and armed forces. Like many authoritarian systems, Iran has more than one army. The Revolutionary Guard was formed as the armed wing of the revolution. Khomeini maintained it after the revolution because he didn't trust the regular national army, which was an institution of the prior regime. The Revolutionary Guard has become a politically and militarily important organization. Along with the regular army, it successfully defended the revolutionary government in the Iran-Iraq War (1980–1988) and has since developed large commercial interests as well. Its members constitute a major political force, out of which emerged the current president Mahmoud Ahmadinejad. The clerical leadership takes good care of the large and ideologically loyal Revolutionary Guard in return for its continued loyalty—its annual budget is larger than those of all but a handful of government ministries.

Many analysts believe that the Revolutionary Guard has emerged since 2005 as the most powerful network of officials in the government and that it is militarizing the regime. Shortly after its creation, the Guard created a part-time civilian militia, the Basij, that is now three million men strong. The mission of the Basij is to defend the revolution against internal enemies. After the Guard's success in the Iraq-Iran War, the government encouraged it to fund itself by starting its own companies to help rebuild the country. This was the start of an expanding business empire controlled by the Guard, which now includes the largest contractor in the country and numerous other companies in many fields, as well as rumored large-scale smuggling of illegal products into the country. Hen-Tov and Gonzalez (2010, 21) estimated that the Guard's business empire now constitutes at least 25 percent of Iran's national economy. The Guard began to play a more direct political role after 1997, when a reformist won the presidency and later reformist candidates took control of the elected legislature. The supreme leader and his allies, who were opposed to the reformists, turned to nonelected institutions, including the Revolutionary Guard, to thwart the reform movement's policies. The Guardian Council turned against the reformers, banning many of them from running in the 2004 legislative elections. This ushered in a major election victory for conservative forces, and one-third of the new parliament's members were former Guard members. By the 2005 election, former Guard member Mahmoud Ahmadinejad won

the presidency, and two-thirds of the people he appointed to his cabinet were also former Guard members. The Guard and especially its Basij militia finally and most infamously led the attacks against the street protesters after the disputed June 2009 presidential election, effectively repressing the largest demonstrations since the revolution and preserving the fraudulent reelection of Ahmadinejad. In this context, analysts have begun to see the regime as increasingly controlled not by the Guard as a monolithic entity but by a network of current and former Guard members who operate in elected and appointed positions to enhance their control over the country.

The supreme leader appoints the head of the judiciary, who in turn appoints all of the judges under him. The Guardian and Expediency Councils perform functions somewhat akin to judicial review in democracies, but the judiciary's role is strictly that of interpreter and enforcer of the Islamic legal code, the Sharia, for criminal and civil cases. Other than nominating half of the Guardian Council, the judiciary has no major political role.

The Iranian bureaucracy has expanded by as much as 50 percent under the theocratic regime. Because of Iran's massive oil revenue, government spending is a majority of the country's economy. The president is in charge of this large bureaucracy and appoints cabinet ministers to oversee it. He also appoints the heads of various government agencies. Parliament must approve cabinet ministers. The supreme leader, of course, can and does exercise informal influence over both political and high-level technocratic appointments to the bureaucracy, thus further limiting the president's prerogatives. Throughout, the supreme leader has far greater powers, informally if not formally, than the elected president. President Ahmadinejad has used his control of the bureaucracy to remove many previously appointed officials and insert personnel who are loyal to him, with many of them being former Revolutionary Guard members.

The importance of the supreme leader and his de facto life term leaves Iran with one of the classic problems of authoritarian rule:

succession. Khomeini's popularity and power were based not only on the traditional legitimacy he enjoyed as a Grand Ayatollah, one of a handful of the highest religious authorities in Shiite Islam, but also on his charismatic legitimacy as the leader of the revolution and spokesperson for the "masses" against the hated regime of the shah. Khomeini and most other major political actors in the country did not believe that any single person could fully replace him as the supreme leader, so to avert a potential crisis, Khomeini appointed a council to review and revise the constitution before his death. The constitutional amendments enacted by this council somewhat reduced the power of the state's religious authorities, but more importantly, they eliminated the requirement that the supreme leader come from only among the Grand Ayatollahs. This allowed a politically astute candidate, then-president Ali Khamenei, to be selected as the new supreme leader. He was only a midlevel cleric and in fact was raised overnight to the rank of Ayatollah (still below Grand Ayatollah) in an effort to give him greater religious authority. In reality, Khomeini and his advisors decided on political expediency, appointing someone who understood politics rather than an icon of religious authority. The other Grand Ayatollahs did not fight Khamenei's ascendance because they had become increasingly disillusioned with the regime; while initially in favor of the revolution, most had taken an increasingly traditionalist position during the 1980s, divorcing themselves from active politics. Lack of clerical support raised questions about Khamanei's legitimacy as supreme leader, which was one of the factors that led him to strengthen the power of the Revolutionary Guard, a military force loyal to him.

In contrast to the absolute authority of the supreme leader, the autonomy and strength of the parliament (the *majlis*) and the parties that compete to win election to it are severely circumscribed by multiple appointed positions and councils. The constitution gives the *majlis* significant power in the absence of interference from the Guardian and Expediency Councils. No legislation may be enacted unless it is passed by the *majlis*, and the *majlis* can also amend legislation. In addition, the *majlis* has approval authority over cabinet nominees and half the nominees to the Guardian Council, and it can investigate the executive's implementation of the law. It has used these powers repeatedly, exposing corruption in the bureaucracy and refusing to approve some of Ahmadinejad's initial cabinet nominees because they were seen as incompetent. The power of the appointed clerics, however, always lurks behind the actions of the *majlis*. When the clerics disapprove of significant legislation, they don't hesitate to use their power to veto it and ultimately rewrite it in the Expediency Council. When the reformists gained control of the presidency and the *majlis* in 2000, the Guardian Council vetoed virtually all their significant reform legislation.

The Iranian regime, like virtually all authoritarian regimes, also uses patronage to maintain its control. Government and quasi-governmental foundations (called *bonyads*) have become key venues through which the nation's oil wealth is shared with regime supporters. For instance, the revolutionary regime established Islamic foundations to provide aid to the populace during and immediately after the revolution. Facing international pressure to adopt neoliberal economic policies, the government has privatized formerly government-controlled economic activities by giving these activities to foundations led by regime supporters. The foundations themselves often receive government funding, and some engage in commercial activity as well. One of the largest, the Imam Charity Committee, receives private donations in addition to the fourth-largest share of the government's annual budget. It is controlled by conservative supporters of the clergy, who use it to mobilize poor voters in favor of conservative candidates. The Revolutionary Guard also controls one of the largest *bonyads,* which provides income support of various kinds to millions of people, giving the Guard its own independent basis for patronage. Some of these foundations and their leaders engage in outright corruption as well, stealing oil revenues and accepting bribes in return for access to key officials.

CASE SUMMARY

Iran's formal system of government combines theocratic institutions with quasi-democratic elected ones that are intended to provide some space for participation and for popular voices to be heard. The constitution, though, ensures that the supreme leader and the institutions he directly controls can dominate when they need to. In the 1990s, the regime allowed reformist politicians who wanted to reduce strict adherence to Islam to gain elected office, but then it effectively blocked them from enacting significant changes. By 2005, the conservative clerical leadership and the increasingly powerful Revolutionary Guard had regained control, and they have not given it up since. The Guard, which is distinct from and better funded than the national army, was intended to defend the ideals of the revolution from external and internal enemies. As the supreme leader became more dependent on the Guard in the new millennium, its power grew, leading some to see the regime as slowly, via informal means, making a transition from a theocracy to a military dictatorship. Major societal demands for greater democracy, however repressed, remain below the surface still. For now, Iran's formal institutions remain what they have always been, though the informal networks of former Revolutionary Guards may be surreptitiously gaining control of them.

CASE STUDY

Nigeria: Weakening Institutions under Military Rule

- Rationale of "return to democracy" but no legislature or parties
- Initially preserved institutions but increasingly personalist
- Increasing repression
- Oil wealth and federalism as patronage

Gen. Sani Abacha, Nigeria's most corrupt and brutal military leader, was in power from 1993 until his death in 1998. He used his control of the military to prevent a transition to democracy, despite widespread popular support for it. A transition finally happened shortly after his unexpected death.

Credit: Reuters

Nigeria's military ruled the country for a total of twenty-nine years, under seven military dictators, at various times since independence in 1960. This history of recurring military intervention is outlined in the timeline on page 391. Nigerian military rule relied on a combination of repression, massive patronage, and attempts to gain legitimacy by promising a "return to democracy." Although some observers saw military rule as beneficial in the 1960s, coercion became more common as the economy declined, and the military regimes became more personalist. In the 1980s and 1990s, three successive leaders from the same regional military group consolidated their control over the government and its all-important oil revenues and used these revenues to engage in massive corruption and patronage to maintain their power. As this continued, Nigerian institutions grew weaker so that by the 1990s the country was recognized as one of the most corrupt in the world.

Every Nigerian military government eliminated the country's legislature entirely; none attempted to use a legislature with even limited power to gain increased legitimacy. Instead, the military governments created executive councils to rule by decree. The top leader took the title of president, head, or chairman, and the councils went under various names, such as the Supreme Military Council (1967–1975 and 1983–1985) or the Armed Forces Ruling Council (1985–1993). Under the first long-serving leader, Gen. Yakubu "Jack" Dan-Yumma Gowon (1967–1975), the council was somewhat consensual. As the military governments became more personalized over the years, however, the councils became mere rubber stamps for the key leaders. Military governments typically appointed a mix of military and civilian leaders as cabinet ministers, and civilian elites in business, academia, and politics repeatedly proved themselves willing to work with a military government in exchange for the perks and power that came with cabinet positions. Military leaders used these positions to co-opt both military and civilian elites to ensure their loyalty, and not surprisingly, as oil revenues and corruption grew over the years, these positions became more lucrative and coveted. Each of the military regimes used such rewards as patronage to buy off at least some of its potential civilian opposition as well as to ensure the loyalty of key military personnel.

While the legislature was the only branch of government the military banned outright, it also severely weakened the judiciary, bureaucracy, and state governments. Many observers believe the Gowon government actually increased the power of the bureaucracy initially, in that the elimination of elected officials ended the tense relationship between elected politicians and career civil servants that is inherent in a democracy. As was typical for the era, and in keeping with

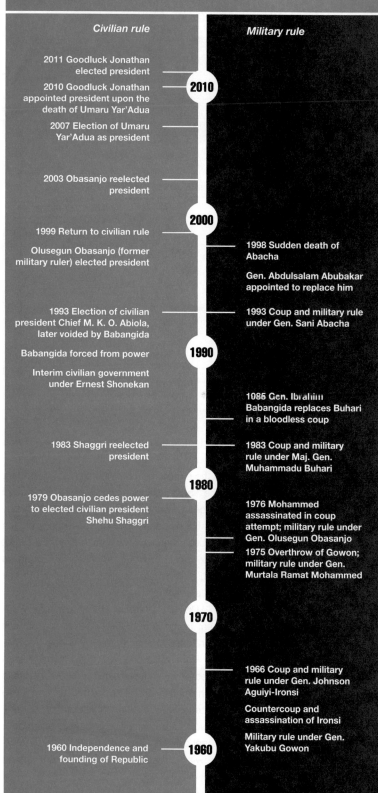

TIMELINE
History of Military Intervention in Nigeria

Civilian rule   *Military rule*

2011 Goodluck Jonathan elected president

2010 Goodluck Jonathan appointed president upon the death of Umaru Yar'Adua — **2010**

2007 Election of Umaru Yar'Adua as president

2003 Obasanjo reelected president

2000

1999 Return to civilian rule

1998 Sudden death of Abacha

Olusegun Obasanjo (former military ruler) elected president

Gen. Abdulsalam Abubakar appointed to replace him

1993 Election of civilian president Chief M. K. O. Abiola, later voided by Babangida

1993 Coup and military rule under Gen. Sani Abacha

Babangida forced from power

1990

Interim civilian government under Ernest Shonekan

1985 Gen. Ibrahim Babangida replaces Buhari in a bloodless coup

1983 Shaggri reelected president

1983 Coup and military rule under Maj. Gen. Muhammadu Buhari

1980

1979 Obasanjo cedes power to elected civilian president Shehu Shaggri

1976 Mohammed assassinated in coup attempt; military rule under Gen. Olusegun Obasanjo

1975 Overthrow of Gowon; military rule under Gen. Murtala Ramat Mohammed

1970

1966 Coup and military rule under Gen. Johnson Aguiyi-Ironsi

Countercoup and assassination of Ironsi

1960 Independence and founding of Republic — **1960**

Military rule under Gen. Yakubu Gowon

IN CONTEXT

AUTHORITARIAN RULE IN SUB-SAHARAN AFRICA (SSA), 1970–2010

Number of SSA countries with one-party regimes				
1970	1980	1990	2000	2010
16	27	28	2	1

Number of SSA countries with military regimes				
1970	1980	1990	2000	2010
9	15	13	4	2

Level of freedom in SSA countries		
Freedom rating	1976	2010
Free	3	9
Partly free	16	23
Not free	25	16

Sources: Freedom House (2010); African Elections Database, http://africanelections.tripod.com/electoral_democracies.html.

modernizing authoritarian rule, the Gowon government expanded the role of the state in the economy in the name of development. The "indigenization" decree of 1972 required Nigerian ownership of most business investment, thus opening up lucrative opportunities for both the civilian and military elites. Direct state ownership of enterprises expanded as well, giving more power and influence to key civil servants.

Up until Ibrahim Babangida's government in the late 1980s, top bureaucrats still maintained their permanent, professional status. Babangida changed this, however, with a decree that allowed the top civil servants in each ministry to be appointed by and leave office with the cabinet ministers. This sharply reduced the distinction between top professional civil servants and political appointees. Growing corruption, as leaders throughout the system stole oil revenues, severely weakened the bureaucracy as an institution. As corruption became rife throughout the government, civil servants no longer worked on the basis of clear rules and hierarchy. Instead, they increasingly gave jobs to their own clients, family, and friends; stole government funds for themselves; and engaged in nongovernmental businesses. All of this made clear bureaucratic control of the civil service impossible. Orders were not followed, functions were not properly carried out, and the bureaucracy lost all respect from the citizens, who had to bribe civil servants to get anything done.

Nigeria's military governments did not eliminate the judiciary either, but as with the bureaucracy, they severely weakened it. Civilian courts continued to exist, but military decrees were beyond any court's jurisdiction. Each military regime became more assertive than the one before in limiting individual rights, ignoring or undermining the courts, and repressing potential opposition. The first military leader, Gen. Johnson Thomas Umunnakwe Aguiyi-Ironsi (January–July 1966) declared that he wanted Nigeria to continue operating in a way that was "as normal as possible," so his and Gowon's government interfered relatively little in daily governmental activities, including the judiciary. The later military governments, however, were another story. The Muhammadu Buhari government issued a series of decrees in 1984 and 1985 that severely undermined the judiciary, and military governments from that point on had the power to appoint judges. This was still to be done with the advice and consent of a panel of judicial leaders, but the Supreme Military Council had ultimate appointment powers, and it could remove judges as well. The Buhari and Babangida governments (1983–1985 and 1985–1993, respectively) rewarded compliant judges by promoting them and punished uncooperative judges by removing or at least not promoting them. In this environment, it is no surprise that the courts did not challenge the military regimes. Sani Abacha (1993–1998) went even further, entirely eliminating the jurisdictions of many courts, eliminating habeas corpus, and arresting hundreds of political opponents in 1994–1995.

Despite its control of the judiciary, the military created separate military tribunals to try opposition politicians, coup plotters (Babangida faced coup attempts from disgruntled soldiers in 1985 and 1990), and leaders of local resistance movements such as the Ogoni movement discussed in chapter 4. With a weakened judiciary, individual rights had little protection. The Buhari government, in particular, took draconian measures against opponents. Coming into office with a claim of wanting to "clean up" the corruption of the elected leaders of Nigeria's Second Republic (1979–1983), Buhari used tribunals to try people accused of corruption. The accused had little ability to defend themselves and often faced the death penalty. We mentioned the most famous case in chapter 4: the 1995 execution of poet and political activist Ken Saro-Wiwa. Saro-Wiwa was leader of the Movement for the Survival of the Ogoni People (MOSOP). This organization campaigned peacefully for the right of the Ogoni, who live in the oil-producing area of the country, to benefit more from the oil. Abacha, who was by far the most brutal of Nigeria's rulers, accused Saro-Wiwa and several other MOSOP leaders of killing several Ogoni traditional elders, a charge that all independent observers believe to be false. Saro-Wiwa and the others faced a military tribunal with no public access to the trial and were convicted and summarily executed. These deaths produced the greatest international outrage and protest a Nigerian government has ever faced, including the withdrawal of U.S. ambassadors and those from major European nations, as well as the removal of Nigeria from the British Commonwealth, a group of former British colonies. Despite this, Abacha's government would continue its rule for another three years until his sudden death in 1998.

Nigeria's military rulers used federalism to reward supporters, divide potential opposition, and manage ethnic political competition, all while centralizing control of federal institutions. In 1967, General Gowon replaced the three existing political regions with twelve states—six in the north and six in the south—in an effort to reduce the conflict that the division of the country into three large regions had caused (see chapter 4). This strategy worked to reduce conflict following the civil war (1967–1970), but it also began the process of centralization of power. The federal government became more powerful, and the new state governments were far less powerful than the governments of the larger regions had been prior to 1966. This shift of power to the central state was driven in part by rapidly rising oil revenues as world oil prices quadrupled in the early 1970s. The Gowon government used these revenues to fund the states, dividing the revenues more equally than they had been divided before but nonetheless providing a growing percentage of all the revenues that states received. This strategy strengthened the central government's power in Nigeria's federalist system.

Division into ever smaller states continued: Gowon added seven new states in the 1970s; General Babangida increased the total to thirty by 1991; and Abacha created six more, for a total of thirty-six, by 1998. State creation became a mechanism of patronage to reward supporters and divide opponents. Each new state required its own state government, which allowed for the local hiring of civil servants and for plum political positions to go to local government loyalists. State governors, who were military men, became famous for their corruption, using their state's share of oil revenue to feather their own nests and reward their own clients. In the southwest, where opposition to Abacha was strong, he created new states to divide his opponents, successfully pitting those who benefited from the creation of a new state against their would-be allies in neighboring areas. Throughout, Nigeria maintained a symmetrical federal system, but one run by the military with power increasingly centralized in the military's hands.

CASE SUMMARY

Nigerian military governments began as relatively institutionalized regimes with a proclaimed goal of restoring democracy while preserving much of the daily functioning of the prior civilian government. Despite a rationale of returning to democracy soon, they made no attempt to create a legislature or allow political parties. Without these institutions, the military regimes became increasingly repressive, personalized, and less institutionalized. Speaking of the military dictator Ibrahim Babangida (1985–1993), Larry Diamond, one of the leading experts on Nigerian politics, said:

> Babangida degraded every institution he touched, and his fellow ruling officers followed his lead. Indeed, one of the most important legacies of Babangida's rule—with his lavish dispensation of cash, cars, contracts and kickbacks to the officer corps, as well as his license to use political appointments for personal accumulation—was the degradation of the military's own professionalism and institutional integrity, so that it increasingly became, like the politicians, a set of political actors, patrimonial ties, and factional alliances seeking after power, patronage, and wealth; another political party, but with an official monopoly on arms (1997, 471).

As oil wealth grew rapidly starting in the early 1970s, corruption grew, giving military leaders an incentive to stay in power and a huge source of money for patronage. They used federalism as a form of patronage and increasingly undermined the institutional strength and autonomy of the judiciary and bureaucracy.

ELECTIONS, PARTIES, AND CIVIL SOCIETY IN AUTHORITARIAN REGIMES

Elections, parties, and civil society are important to democracies in part because they help to overcome the collective action dilemma: they encourage participation and channel and promote democratic representation. It should not come as a great shock that authoritarian regimes are not particularly interested in overcoming the collective action problem. In fact, they often go to great extremes to suppress any groups that might attempt to organize because they see such groups as a threat. Many authoritarian regimes nonetheless create institutions that at least superficially resemble elections, parties, and interest groups, but these differ greatly from their more democratic counterparts, often in both form and function.

As we noted above, supreme leaders cannot rule by repression alone. They must care about gaining the support of potentially rival elites and, ideally, some legitimacy from the general populace. Many authoritarian regimes, both more and less institutionalized, use elaborate public displays of support to try to gain this legitimacy, a form of often forced political participation. For example, they hold massive independence day celebrations, complete with throngs of cheering supporters and displays of military might to show their popularity and power. Participants typically have little choice but to participate, and doing so can often be of material benefit. When Mexico's Partido Revolucionario Institucional (PRI) ruled as a semi-authoritarian regime, supporters would be trucked in from the countryside to rallies in the cities, where they would enjoy free food, drink, and entertainment. Referring to authoritarian regimes in Africa, Achille Mbembe (1992) called such huge but empty displays of regime support the "banality of power." In the most extreme cases of personalist rule, such public demonstrations become a **personality cult** that constantly glorifies the ruler and attempts to turn his every utterance into not only government fiat but also divine wisdom. Personality cults have arisen in an array of regimes, from communist North Korea under "Great Leader" Kim Il-Sung to Zaire under Western-supporting dictator Mobutu Sese Seko to "President for Life" Saparmurat Niyazov in post-Soviet Turkmenistan. Regimes with more elaborate ideological justification for their rule, such as communist and theocratic regimes, also make extensive use of their founding ideologies to try to gain popular legitimacy, as the case of Iran below demonstrates.

Beyond these demonstrations of massive support, most authoritarian regimes encourage carefully monitored and limited political participation. Most now hold elections of some type and typically allow some opposition parties to participate. Elections in one-party regimes have long existed as well. Communist regimes usually allow direct elections only at the most local level. The general electorate may get to participate in local block, neighborhood, or town elections, but then those representatives elect the next layer of representatives above them and so on up to the national parliamentary level. In addition, although nonparty candidates may be permitted at the local level, all candidates typically have to be cleared by the Communist Party before they can run. Such an electoral system is consistent with the ideological perspective of communism because it permits popular participation while also preserving the guiding role of the Communist Party, the only legitimate representative of the people.

More common now are semi-authoritarian regimes in which a ruling party wins major elections easily, with some opposition parties winning a small share of power. The ruling party creates the system to ensure its continued rule. The more sophisticated and institutionalized systems do not usually require outright voter fraud for the ruling party to remain in power, though ruling parties will certainly engage in that too if necessary. Usually, the type of electoral system (typically a majoritarian one that favors the already large ruling party), gerrymandering constituency boundaries, vote buying, controlling access to the media, restricting civil liberties, using government resources for partisan purposes, and even jailing opponents serve to keep the opposition under control. In Kenya in the 1990s, government civil servants openly campaigned for the ruling party during work hours, candidates handed potential voters gifts of cash or food, and opposition party rallies were often denied permits and harassed by police when they did happen. In Rwanda's 2010 presidential election, three opposition candidates ended up in jail by election day, allowing President Paul Kagame (in power since the genocide in 1994) to win 93 percent of the vote. In Mexico under the PRI's long rule, the government systematically spent money before each election to purchase political support in areas where the PRI needed votes (Magaloni 2006).

Given that authoritarian rulers can hold power without any opposition or elections at all, an obvious question is why they bother creating these systems. A longstanding answer has been that such systems serve as a facade of democratic legitimacy, both domestically and internationally. The ascendancy of liberal democracy in the post–Cold War era makes this more important than it was earlier. Recently, scholars have come to believe that elections in authoritarian regimes serve other purposes as well. As we discussed above, Jennifer Gandhi (2008) argued that both legislatures and multiple parties co-opt the opposition and provide a space for some policy compromise. Using our case study of Mexico under the PRI as an example, Beatriz Magaloni (2006) argued that in addition to co-opting opposition within the system, elections provided the ruling party with information on who opposed it

personality cult: Phenomenon that occurs in the most extreme cases of personalist rule in which followers constantly glorify the ruler and attempt to turn his every utterance into not only government fiat but also divine wisdom (helping to overcome the dictator's dilemma of lack of information), allowed power sharing among leaders within the ruling party, and deterred opponents by showing (via large election victories) the ruling party's ability to mobilize support. She suggested that elections in semi-authoritarian regimes typically indicate real mass support, which is often created via government largesse and vote buying. Furthermore, she claimed that support is crucial to the long-term survival of semi-authoritarian regimes. They need to hold elections to demonstrate to elite opponents that the ruling party continues to enjoy significant support, thereby discouraging those opponents from openly challenging the system. Authoritarian elections, then, do not threaten the regime but provide it with several clear benefits. The danger always exists, of course, that somehow the opposition will find a way to actually gain power. This is rare, and when it happens, the ruling party may openly "steal" the election via voter fraud to remain in power. This happened in Kenya in December 2007, setting off two months of ethnically based violence that killed 1,500 and displaced hundreds of thousands. In certain circumstances, however, such elections can be part of a transition from an authoritarian to a democratic regime. This is a subject we explore in the next chapter.

Authoritarian elections are coupled with very limited party systems. Most important and strongest is always the ruling party, whether in a one-party or semi-authoritarian system. Jason Brownlee (2007) argued that strong ruling parties emerge early in an authoritarian regime if the supreme leader is able to repress and co-opt potential opposition to create an elite coalition within the party. If he is unable to do this, a weak ruling party (or none at all) will develop, and the regime will be less stable and more likely to be overthrown. Indeed, Barbara Geddes (1999) demonstrated statistically that since World War II, single-party authoritarian regimes have lasted much longer than either military or personalist regimes (she did not classify semi-authoritarian regimes separately). The ruling party is nearly always a vehicle for access to goods and jobs and thus a key mechanism for large-scale patronage. In Alfredo Stroessner's Paraguay, for instance, membership in the ruling Colorado Party was compulsory for government employees, and nearly a quarter of the population belonged to it. Mexico's PRI politicians operated on the basis of patronage, and those in rural regions in particular understood that votes for the PRI meant the potential to receive some benefits for their communities. Similarly, membership in the Communist Party is usually a prerequisite for many types of jobs in any communist regime. Communist parties also promote political socialization of young people through party youth organizations so that they will have an ideological reason to become members. Moreover, in communist regimes the party serves as an ideological watchdog for the leaders. Party cells exist in all government agencies, communities, and major organizations, such as state-run companies. Their task in part is to ensure conformity with the party leadership's dictates. While ruling parties in semi-authoritarian regimes do not fulfill all of these socialization and watchdog functions, they nonetheless provide real incentives that keep potential opponents within the system.

Ironically, one-party systems tend to weaken the ruling party as an institution because the lack of a competitive electoral environment gives parties no incentive to build institutional strength. The only meaningful participation and competition takes place within the ruling party; therefore, all politically significant factions in society and their leaders must become part of the ruling party. Such parties often show their weaknesses when forced to compete with opponents in anything close to a competitive electoral system. The fate of the Soviet and Eastern European Communist parties after democratization amply demonstrates their underlying weakness, in that most were able to gain only very small shares of votes in the first competitive elections. In postcolonial one-party systems, parties were often even weaker. They became empty institutional shells within which factions competed for power because of legal proscriptions on any alternative parties, but they had little unified purpose or identity. This may be another explanation of the rise and seeming durability of semi-authoritarian regimes: a little competition can make the ruling party stronger than it would be in a one-party system. The PRI in Mexico and the Kuomintang (KMT; or Guomindang, GMD) in Taiwan are examples of ruling parties in semi-authoritarian states that survived the transition to democracy and remain major players.

Because what little participation that can occur must go through approved regime channels, civil society in authoritarian regimes is extremely circumscribed and repressed. Indeed, often it hardly exists at all. Communist regimes such as the Soviet Union and China at their height were totalitarian, as North Korea remains today. Totalitarian regimes completely eliminate civil society; the ruling party "represents" all interests that it believes deserve representation. Trade unions or youth or women's groups often nominally exist in communist countries, but these "mass organizations" are always part of the Communist Party, as they are today in Cuba. They cannot be said to be truly part of civil society, which by definition is autonomous from the state.

Similarly, noncommunist regimes often use state corporatism to control interest groups. Remember that corporatism is the idea that each component (or interest) in society should be represented by one officially sanctioned organization. When a government legally mandates this, it is referred to as state corporatism because the state controls the interest groups and chooses the ones it wishes to recognize. A recent example was Mexico for most of the twentieth century under the PRI. The PRI claimed it was a revolutionary party representing the poor, and as such, it recognized and included within the party structure a single labor organization, a single peasant association, and a single association for "popular groups"—small businesses, women's interests, and various others. These groups were to represent their constituents within the party. Over time, however, these groups became increasingly corrupt and controlled by the elite at the top of the party hierarchy. The workers' organization, in particular, was very powerful within the party, and real wages rose in the economy for most of the PRI's long rule, even though the union did not publicly represent any workers' interests that contradicted official party policies.

The emergence of social movements within authoritarian regimes is often one of the first signs of a democratic opening. In Latin America in the 1970s, labor-based social movements outside the confines of the official corporatist unions began challenging the status quo and ultimately forced authoritarian regimes to move toward redemocratization. Other social movements arose as well. Brazil, for instance, has active gay rights, Afro-Brazilian, and women's movements, many of which originated during the military regime. As the case of Mexico shows, however, most of Latin America also has a legacy of state corporatism under authoritarian rule in the twentieth century. This weakened the major interest groups and undermined their claim to legitimate representation of their constituents. The return to democracy in most of these countries over the last twenty years has allowed some of these groups to regain institutional strength and legitimacy and has allowed new groups to emerge. Neocorporatist systems, however, remain fairly common.

In most of Asia and Africa, unions and other major interest groups arose with and were part of nationalist movements for independence. After independence, however, authoritarian regimes emasculated these organizations, often creating state corporatist systems in their place in which the official interest groups were extremely weak institutions with little autonomy from government or ruling-party control. With the spread of more electoral democracy since the end of the Cold War, interest groups and civil society more broadly have reemerged in most of these countries, but they face a legacy of extreme weakness.

With civil society very weak and parties and elections mainly aimed at ensuring elite cohesion and regime survival, patron-client relations are often the primary means through which average citizens can participate in politics in authoritarian regimes. The weaker the formal institutions, the more this is likely to be true. Strong ruling parties and small but accepted opposition parties in semi-authoritarian regimes provide some means of participation. In more personalist regimes, or regimes in which parties are weak institutions that command little loyalty, even these avenues are mostly cut off. By attaching themselves to a powerful patron, citizens can gain access to some resources or power or at least have influence over some area of government. Such influence would occur behind closed doors, of course, as authoritarian regimes severely limit public debate. As the patron gains power and position in the system, the clients gain also through special privileges and access to resources.

Such patron-client relationships are the primary means of political participation in virtually all sub-Saharan African countries. While myriad formal institutions exist, most citizens participate by attaching themselves to a patron. In Kenya's authoritarian regime (1963–1992), the long-time ruling party consisted of ethnically and regionally based factions that were headed by major patrons. The system allowed very limited public political debate, so political leaders gained support by directing government resources toward their home areas and providing individual support to their myriad clients. Clients got jobs in government or influence in local politics by attaching themselves to patrons who could offer them these benefits.

In the absence of other effective means of participation and representation, following a patron may be the best available option. A patron can represent a client's most immediate interests vis-à-vis the government. The problems in this type of system, though, are numerous. First, its informality means that no client is ever guaranteed anything. Each individual has a unique and largely private relationship with a patron, who will try to maintain the client's loyalty in the long term but who will not respond to every demand. Clients have no recourse unless an alternative patron is available. This is sometimes the case, but transferring loyalty is never easy or quick. Second, clientelism discourages citizens from organizing on the basis of collective interests. As long as citizens believe that following a personal patron is the most effective route to obtaining what they need from government, they have little incentive to organize collectively to change the government and its policies more broadly. This is especially true in authoritarian regimes that violently repress any significant organized political activity.

Summary

Participation in authoritarian regimes is extremely limited. More-institutionalized regimes have allowed some formal participation, including elections with limited choices. With the spread of semi-authoritarian regimes in the last two decades, tightly controlled elections have become more common. Their main purpose, however, is elite cohesion and regime support. Citizens are rarely content with these limited choices in the long term because they give voters little real influence. Less-institutionalized regimes typically grant little or no opportunities for participation. This means that parties and interest groups do not really serve the same functions they do in democracies, in which real political participation and competition exist.

Given this, many citizens "participate" on a daily basis simply to survive and prosper individually through the use of patron-client networks. This allows the leadership of a regime to use co-optation to maintain adequate support, or at least prevent outright rebellion.

Rebellion, however, can and does happen. Social movements often arise in these situations outside the limited formal boundaries of legal participation. Larger movements for change that bring an entire regime into question also can emerge and produce fundamental regime change, a subject we examine in the next chapter. But first, we need a better understanding of how participation happens in actual authoritarian regimes in our case study countries.

MINI CASE

Egypt and Tunisia: The Unraveling of Semi-Authoritarian Regimes

As 2011 began, the world watched as seemingly out of nowhere tens of thousands of Tunisians took to the streets, successfully demanding the ouster of the country's long-ruling president, Zine Ben Ali, in what came to be known as the "Jasmine Revolution." As this revolt unfolded, Egyptians began flooding the main square in Cairo, successfully demanding the ouster of even-longer-ruling president Hosni Mubarak. After less than three weeks of protests, Mubarak resigned, the military took control of the government, and it appointed a commission to revise the constitution and plan democratic elections for later in the year. These dramatic stories show what can happen when a semi-authoritarian regime loses control over the process of allowing but severely limiting political participation.

Ben Ali and Mubarak both came to power in the 1980s with sweeping promises of political reforms and democratization of their countries. Initially, both leaders freed political prisoners, and Ben Ali negotiated an agreement with the opposition to allow electoral competition. He also promised not to serve more than two full terms as president. Mubarak's predecessor, Anwar Sadat, had allowed very restricted multiparty competition starting in 1976, and Mubarak continued this. Many observers saw Ben Ali's proposed changes as a real move toward democracy,

but he ultimately clung to power as had his predecessor. Similarly, despite allowing some minor opening of the political system, Mubarak ruled under an "emergency law" after coming into office in 1981. This allowed him to rule by decree when necessary. Both leaders created classic semi-authoritarian states. Both used legalization of the opposition and parliamentary elections to co-opt much of the potential opposition, convincing important segments of the political and business elite to cooperate with the system rather than publicly oppose it.

Upon coming to power in 1981, Mubarak preserved the opening that his predecessor had begun. Parliamentary elections with token opposition took place every five years, with the ruling party typically winning at least 80 percent of the seats. The electoral rules allowed candidates to run as independents, providing a means for candidates to run even if they did not secure a nomination from the ruling party. When independent candidates won, as they occasionally did, the vast majority simply rejoined the ruling party, giving it well over 90 percent of the parliamentary seats most of the time. Facing growing pressure from a relatively independent judiciary, Mubarak amended the electoral system in 2000 to allow judges to preside over polling places. While this improved the integrity of the actual voting, the judges had no power beyond the polling places; the voter intimidation, media bias, and vote buying that constituted Egyptian elections continued unabated. Egyptians came to see the legal opposition parties as little more than sycophants of the ruling party. The only real opposition came from the banned Muslim Brotherhood, an Islamist movement that claims to be nonviolent and willing to work within a democratic system. In 2005, Mubarak finally allowed some of its candidates to run as independents, though he required them not to officially use the Brotherhood's name (even though they were widely known to be its supporters). They won over 20 percent of the seats in parliament. Over the next five years, the independent Brotherhood parliamentarians were a vocal but constantly harassed legislative minority. In 2010, however, the regime reversed course, fraudulently preventing the Brotherhood's candidates from winning in what was the least free-and-fair parliamentary election since 1995. That same year, Mubarak finally allowed competition for the presidency, but the rules on who could be nominated were so restrictive that only two minor candidates stood against him and Mubarak won nearly 90 percent of the vote.

Throughout, Mubarak's real power rested in the ruling party, the military, and the secret police. He had served in the military and long maintained its loyalty, largely by allowing the military itself to become a major economic actor. It is one of the largest commercial conglomerates in the country, producing everything from military hardware to household appliances and running major tourist resorts. However, he increasingly built up a secret police force that was independent of the military and personally loyal to him. The ruling party provided a means to co-opt the elite, providing them with seats in parliament and thereby access to key government officials. A reform movement of business leaders arose within the party centered around Mubarak's son, Gamal, the heir apparent. As the government was increasingly forced to open the economy to international trade following conventional neoliberal policies, these younger entrepreneurs became increasingly important, but perceptions of them as exceptionally corrupt made them very unpopular. After Mubarak's overthrow, the new military government quickly initiated corruption investigations against some of these business leaders, including members of Mubarak's family.

Ben Ali's regime in Tunisia was, if anything, more politically restrictive than Mubarak's. After his initial promise to open the system to opposition, he quickly banned the Islamist Renaissance Party, which was by far the most popular party in the country. Like Mubarak, Ben Ali maintained control not only via the military but via a separate police force that was personally loyal to him. Reforms did allow secular opposition parties to win legislative seats starting in 1994, and these parties increased their share of seats in parliament in each election through 2009, when they won 15 percent of the vote and held 43 of the 214 seats. These results, however, were largely due to an unwritten agreement between the regime and the very weak secular parties, which gave them a share of power in exchange for their acceptance of the regime's banning the much more popular Renaissance Party (Sadiki 2002). Despite these severe limitations, little real popular opposition to Ben Ali emerged over two full decades of rule. This was mainly due to his successful economic policies. Tunisia became a developmental model for the region, with rapid growth, burgeoning export and tourist sectors, and close economic ties with the European Union. Under Ben Ali, per capita income increased substantially, gender equality was much greater than in most of the region, and a growing middle class emerged. Despite opening the economy to greater international trade, however, Ben Ali managed to keep most business and labor interests tied to the government and therefore politically quiescent (Bellin 2002). Other than the banned Islamist movement, opposition came only from students, academics, and some journalists. Those who spoke openly were quickly expelled from the country.

In December 2010, a university-educated Tunisian street vendor committed suicide via self-immolation because he was distraught over his inability to support an extended family of eight via the only job he could get, which was far beneath his level of education. While economic growth had remained relatively good even through the 2008–09 global recession, Tunisian unemployment had risen into double digits. At about the same time as the dramatic suicide, which sent shockwaves through the country, a U.S. diplomatic cable released by WikiLeaks gave a frank portrait of the lavish lifestyle and corruption of the president's family and suggested that the United States privately thought it would soon be time for a political change in Tunisia. Calls for demonstrations spread via social media such as Facebook and Twitter, led mainly by unemployed, college-educated young people. The protests started in mid-December and continued nearly daily into mid-January. After initially resisting and calling in the police to shoot protesters, Ben Ali was forced to resign and go into exile, reportedly at the urging of the military, who refused to turn its guns on its own people. One of Ben Ali's close associates took power and appointed a new cabinet with some opposition figures, but this wasn't enough for the people in the streets, and the Jasmine Revolution continued. Ultimately, a cabinet of entirely new figures, mostly from the opposition, came into office as a transitional government. Ben Ali's assets were frozen, and his party was banned. Elections for a constituent assembly to write a new constitution were scheduled for later in 2011.

Al Jazeera, the largest independent media outlet in the Middle East, covered the Tunisian protests extensively from the start. This was in sharp contrast to major Western media, who paid no attention until just before the fall of Ben Ali. Al Jazeera beamed its reports not only across Tunisia but throughout the Arab world, and Egyptians were watching. Having recently gone through the fraudulent 2010 elections and facing growing inflation, young Egyptians used Facebook and Twitter to call for protests on January 25, 2011, to demand Mubarak's ouster. The response was overwhelming; tens of thousands poured into Cairo's central square. The

military rolled in tanks to keep order, but it did not prevent the protest and was even cheered by the protesters. After initial hesitation, the Muslim Brotherhood joined the protests, as did older secular opposition leaders, but the initiative was clearly with the younger professionals who had started the movement. Mubarak responded by firing his cabinet and announcing that neither he nor his son would run in the upcoming presidential election. The new prime minister, though, was one of his closest supporters, and the cabinet remained firmly in the hands of the ruling party, so the protests continued. The regime then sent police and civilian supporters into the streets to attack the demonstrators, while the military remained present but neutral. After two days of international condemnation, the violence abruptly ended, and the protesters returned to the square. The new prime minister called a meeting with about fifty opposition leaders, including older politicians, the Muslim Brotherhood leaders, and the young professionals who had started the protests, but no agreement emerged on a transition to a new government.

The protests continued and Mubarak clung to office, but the military had seen enough. Its major stakes in the economy gave it a strong interest in restoring stability, so it forced Mubarak's resignation, appointed a prime minister to run the government who had the support of the protesters, and created a commission to draft a democratic constitution under which new elections would be held later in the year. The commission proposed nine amendments to the constitution. While the youthful leaders of the revolt did not think that went nearly far enough, the military, members of the former ruling party, and the Muslim Brotherhood supported the changes, which won an overwhelming majority in a popular referendum. While the referendum was hailed as the best election in Egypt's history, some observers still saw it "free, but not fair," in that the Muslim Brotherhood and ruling party members were alleged to have intimidated opposition voters. Growing unrest under military rule produced widespread strikes for better working conditions and political changes, and opposition leaders charged that the military continued to detain and torture its political opponents. Nonetheless, parliamentary and presidential elections seemed firmly set for later in the year.

CASE SUMMARY

Semi-authoritarian regimes allow some restricted participation in an effort to co-opt their opponents. Opposition movements typically use this limited openness to push for more influence. In response, regimes often crack down, restoring greater repression as necessary to maintain their rule. This dynamic has characterized both Tunisia and Egypt since the 1980s. Tunisia's greater economic success allowed it to co-opt potential opposition more successfully, resulting in less-dramatic crackdowns, but freedom always remained very restricted. Economic success, however, produced the very middle class whose younger and unemployed members eventually led the Jasmine Revolution. A couple of dramatic catalysts, spread by the new social media that governments around the world are having trouble controlling (per the case studies of China and Iran in this chapter), brought massive numbers of people into the streets for an Arab version of the "color revolutions" that began in Ukraine earlier in the decade. Media quickly spread the protests to Egypt as well. In both cases, the regimes attempted to use their own police forces to repress the demonstrators. But the national militaries in both countries, driven by concerns about their own image as well as the major incentives they had to maintain long-term stability, remained neutral or moved against the old order. Major protests subsequently broke out in Yemen, Bahrain, Libya, and Syria as Arabs in other authoritarian regimes demanded similar changes. These very different regimes, however, produced distinct scenarios, including the transformation of Libya's protest into a bloody civil war and the successful repression of Bahrain's protests. Semi-authoritarian regimes can at times co-opt opposition successfully, but their limited legitimacy in the face of sudden political or economic shocks can cause them to lose control seemingly overnight, though that alone does not guarantee that a democratic regime will replace them. If they can maintain control of the repressive apparatus, even massive protests may not be enough to topple them.

CASE STUDY

China: Growing Participation but Not Democracy or Semi-Authoritarian Rule

- Increasingly institutionalized one-party rule
- *Guanxi* personal networks under communism and modernizing authoritarianism
- Changing party membership: Technocrats, entrepreneurs, and lawyers
- Competitive local elections help overcome dictator's dilemma
- Growing local protests, labor unrest, online activism, and NGOs

China's Communist regime under Mao included ritualistic "participation" by the public in the form of token elections, but it also initiated spurts of greater participation in an attempt to, as Mao saw it, overcome the inertia of bureaucratic control of his "revolution." After each of these periods, the government would again clamp down on participation because the uninstitutionalized participation was difficult to control and sometimes resulted in unwanted criticism of the government. The best-known of these periods were

Young people gather in a Beijing neighborhood during the Cultural Revolution in the 1960s to read a letter they have written to Mao, promising to be personally loyal and faithful to him. Such displays of personal loyalty sometimes superseded party rule under Mao's personality cult.

Credit: Rue des Archives/The Granger Collection, New York

the Hundred Flowers Campaign in the 1950s and the Great Proletarian Cultural Revolution in the 1960s–1970s. During the latter campaign, Mao encouraged young people and students to interrogate the party and government leadership. Mobilized "red" brigades spread across the country, uncovering "traitors" to the revolution who were sent to work camps or put to death. While this was clearly a form of political participation, it was one without any institutionalization or limits, other than absolute loyalty to Mao. The newly empowered young people in the red brigades often went beyond party control to attack teachers, neighbors, and even party officials. Many human rights abuses resulted, and countless lives were ruined. After Mao's death, the government was left to bring this spiraling mobilization under control.

For the average citizen, however, influencing government during Mao's era was much more informal and individual. CCP membership was the essential and only formal route into the political process beyond the most local level. Party membership was

also the sole road ambitious citizens could travel to political, social, or economic success. Yet fewer than 10 percent of citizens were party members, which meant that most people who wanted to influence the government had to do so in informal ways. With the complete ban on any independent organizations, citizens had little ability to demand changes in government policy or to petition the government about local issues on which the populace in freer countries typically lobby their governments. Individuals could only hope to gain a personal benefit or perhaps influence the way a policy was implemented locally.

As with most authoritarian regimes, patron-client linkages were crucial to this process. In China, networks of personal supporters, including but not exclusively family, are known as ***guanxi***. Before, during, and since the Mao era, the Chinese have used their *guanxi* to survive and attempt to prosper. At the height of the communist system, the state controlled virtually the entire economy, including the allocation of jobs, houses, and

guanxi: In China, networks of personal supporters, including but not exclusively family, that are important for economic and political survival and advancement

other services. Appearing loyal to the regime was crucial to one's success in the system, but *guanxi* helped a great deal as well. Relatives and friends in the system could help get you a better job or apartment or keep you out of trouble with local authorities. Working the system in this way was essential to many people's survival. For the more ambitious, participation included becoming a member of and taking an active role in the local CCP apparatus in addition to using *guanxi* to help career advancement.

The rapid expansion of the market economy has forced the regime to open up the system of participation and representation at least slightly, making some political accommodations in terms of who can participate and how. This has involved co-opting new elites, allowing semicompetitive elections at the local level, and implementing elements of state corporatism to manage relations with the still limited civil society. One change has been a loosening in the Communist Party itself as it moves away from reliance on ideological and revolutionary credentials and toward more inclusion of people from many backgrounds who bring valuable skills and knowledge to the party. Throughout the communist era, a debate raged over the role of "reds" and "experts." On one side were leaders, usually including Mao, who argued that those properly committed to revolutionary ideals (that is, loyal to Mao and the CCP) and from the proper "revolutionary classes" (the peasantry and proletariat) should constitute the core of the party and be given preference in participation. On the other side of this argument were those who favored party membership and participation for experts— that is, intellectuals, scientists, and engineers who, presumably, could help modernize the country. Since the country's opening to the world market, the CCP has shifted significantly in the direction of the experts. Farmers' and workers' share of party membership dropped from 63 percent in 1994 to 44 percent in 2003. Large numbers of scientists, engineers, and other intellectuals have joined the party, including many among the new

fourth generation of the top party leadership. By 1997, technocrats made up about three-quarters of top Chinese leaders, a share that has since shrunk as they have been replaced by the two newest additions: lawyers and entrepreneurs. In 2001, the party leadership decided to allow private entrepreneurs into the party—the ultimate irony, including successful capitalists in a Communist Party (Dickson 2003). By 2004, surveys showed that a third of Chinese entrepreneurs were party members (Li 2010, 180–82).

While these changes have undoubtedly increased the pool of experts who are available for making decisions, the political implications of the changes are not clear. Given the development of liberalism in the West, we might expect that allowing intellectuals and especially entrepreneurs to enter the political system would expand democracy; the bourgeoisie, after all, was the class that helped create liberalism in Europe. Market economies, in precisely this way, are supposed to help produce and sustain liberal democracy. Political scientist Bruce Dickson (2003), however, surveyed China's new entrepreneurs and found that their political attitudes do not suggest they will help create greater democracy. In fact, they share the concerns of other party officials about limiting participation to within the elite to maintain stability. The CCP so far seems to have opened up the party to the intellectual and business elite without risking its continued control.

Some observers see changes in the electoral laws as another attempt at co-opting potential opposition; others see it as the first real step in the direction of democracy. Over the course of the 1980s, the government revised the electoral law several times, first creating and then expanding the potential competitiveness of elections to rural village committees and township and county legislatures. Following typically Communist practices, China long had direct elections for these positions but with only one party-approved candidate for each position. By the early 1990s, a new system was in place. Now most local elections to both state and party offices can be subject to competition. Candidates can be nominated by the party, other local organizations, or any group of ten citizens. The party, however, maintains great control, including final approval of those nominated. In theory, this system can allow a level of local criticism and participation, fulfilling at the local level Jennifer Gandhi's (2008) argument that a legislature can provide a space in which policy compromise is possible and helping to overcome the dictator's dilemma.

Studies have shown that how this system actually works in practice varies greatly because local officials often severely limit the level of competition to ensure their own positions. Overall, however, most scholars see local elections as expanding participation and political openness. Hundreds of thousands of candidates have lost village elections since 1999, and 48 percent of elected village officials are not Communist Party members (Landry, Davis, and Wang 2010, 766). One survey in the late 1990s found that more than half of voters had attended a campaign event and nearly 20 percent had participated in nominating a candidate (Shi 2006, 365). Electoral turnout has varied widely but in some places has been as high as 30 percent, a higher turnout than in most local elections in the United States. A survey of one rural area found significantly higher voter turnout in competitive elections than in those with only one candidate (Landry, Davis, and Wang 2010). A survey in Beijing found increasing participation in and acceptance of the legitimacy of local elections during the 1990s (O'Brien 2006, 389). In rural areas, voters have often used the elections to remove unpopular or unresponsive local officials. Several studies have shown that directly elected members of village committees are more responsive to villagers' concerns than are nonelected officials and that they more fairly allocate land, which is probably the most important task of village government (Kennedy 2010, 235).

Along with greater openness in local elections have come the problems that plague new democracies elsewhere: corruption,

kinship-based politics, and sexism. Candidates in some village elections have engaged in vote buying, handing out gifts in exchange for votes and spending large sums to do so. The candidates earn a return on this investment via corrupt land deals after they take office. Local village politics are often divided not by policy questions but by competition among local kinship groups for political control. And local elections have actually reduced the number of women in rural village committees, from 15 percent among party-appointed committees to less than 1 percent for elected ones. Even limited democracy allows local social mores and customs to have full expression in the political process, for better or for worse.

Under full Communist rule, the party completely controlled all interest groups. The All-China Federation of Trade Unions (ACFTU), for instance, was the sole legal union organization, with mandatory branches in any enterprise with more than 100 employees. The rapid expansion of private enterprises has made it difficult for the party to maintain its monopoly on union organization, but the ACFTU remains tightly controlled by and supportive of the government. A revised labor law enacted in 2008 made arbitration and court cases by workers easier. The number of such cases more than doubled, and in the most industrialized regions the system is overwhelmed with cases. Lee and Friedman (2009) argued that, as in other countries around the world, the opening of the economy to globalization has reduced workers' ability to secure the growing rights that the government has formally granted them. Forty percent of urban workers are part-time, casual, or temporary employees who have great difficulty demanding better treatment; nearly half of them report not receiving wages on time. In 2010, however, several major strikes erupted, most notably at Honda and Toyota plants. As the Chinese economy rebounded, it became clear that its seemingly endless stream of cheap labor was running out: employers were starting to face labor shortages, and wages were rising in some areas, giving some workers the economic strength to strike and demand more. At the Honda plant in Foshan, workers unsuccessfully demanded the right to form their own independent union, something that is still illegal in China. Even white-collar workers joined the fray, as bank tellers who had been downsized by state-owned banks began to protest at bank branches, in spite of the fact that they had little legal recourse because they were employees of state-owned companies.

Citizens at all levels of society have become less dependent on the state, which in turn has less control over them. These increasingly independent citizens have taken the initiative to form various NGOs (nongovernmental organizations), which are focused mostly on local, material grievances such as housing or working conditions. To control these organizations, the government has created a registration system under which NGOs must gain official state approval. Moreover, the state approves only one organization of a particular type in each administrative area, in effect beginning a system of state corporatism. The state has also created its own organizations for the policy issues in which it is particularly interested; these are referred to by the Orwellian name Government Organized Non-governmental Organizations (GONGOs). An example is the China Family Planning Association, created to support China's one-child-per-family policy. Despite the restrictions the government puts on them, NGOs and interest groups have at times influenced the direction of government policy independently. Local branches of the ACFTU have successfully supported workers' strikes on a number of occasions, and the national organization helped to get a five-day workweek approved. Lu Yiyi (Lu 2009) studied NGOs providing social services in several cities and found that despite financial and informational dependence on the state, Chinese NGOs can achieve a degree of autonomy, in part through their personal relationships with local bureaucrats, who can protect them from the more draconian demands of state policies. Indeed, she found

that government-initiated NGOs actually achieve greater autonomy than citizen-initiated ones. Both are often limited, though, by their own internal management practices, and therefore autonomy may not produce effective services for their clientele. NGOs, of course, cannot voice any significant political criticisms of the regime as a whole.

The Chinese media, though tightly controlled, has expanded dramatically in the past generation. In the aftermath of economic reform, media outlets are mostly private and must be profitable. Commercialization has driven them to provide more popular content than the earlier government-controlled media. Government restrictions remain, however, and have tightened in some areas, especially in regard to the Internet. While criticisms of local officials' malfeasance are tolerated, political criticism of the regime is strictly prohibited. The biggest venue for criticism of the regime has been the Internet, and the government has created the so-called "Great Firewall of China" to prevent Internet users from accessing information on sensitive topics. The regime employs tens of thousands of cyberpolice and sophisticated security programs to constantly monitor Internet use. Nonetheless, Chinese "netizens" have created active online communities and techniques to evade censorship. The latter include new Chinese-language characters that can make it past filtering systems, Web sites based on foreign servers, and meetings held in secret chat rooms. Online activism has become a major source of criticism of the regime, most dramatically with the "Charter 08" that called for democracy (Yang 2009). In response to the 2011 Internet-fuelled uprising in the Middle East, the Chinese government clamped down even more tightly on Internet use, censoring all references to the events taking place halfway around the world. Those found violating Internet use rules are severely punished, often with long detentions. So while a private media now exists in China, its content remains tightly regulated, and it is a less important element of civil society in China than in democratic societies.

Even though elections and civil society now offer opportunities for greater participation than in the past, pressure for more changes and informal opposition still exist. The most open and vocal of these movements have been successfully repressed by the government over the years. The most familiar case is perhaps the Tiananmen Square protest in 1989. It began in response to the death of Hu Yaobang, a popular party leader seen as a key champion of political reform who had recently been ousted from the party leadership. What started as a few hundred students gathered in protest mushroomed within a week to daily protests by 200,000 students. Among their demands were calls for the government to reevaluate Hu's career, free jailed intellectual dissidents, publicly account for party leaders' finances, permit freedom of the press, and provide greater funding for education (note that they did not demand full democracy with competitive national elections, as is often asserted). The government eventually agreed to negotiate with the students but gave little ground. With student interest waning and many returning to class, a group of 3,000 began a hunger strike as a final effort to make their demands heard. This action garnered massive public support, as more than a million Beijing residents turned out to support the hunger strikers. Those who had undertaken the hunger strike finally got some minor concessions from the government and, facing serious health consequences, decided to end the hunger strike. That night, the government declared martial law in the city and tried to bring in the army. At least a million citizens, including many workers, poured into the streets and erected barricades to prevent the army from entering, but by June 4, the army had successfully moved into Tiananmen Square. In the middle of the night it opened fire on the remaining student dissidents, killing between 1,000 and 3,000 students and civilians (sources vary considerably on this total; many estimate it as much higher). The military action sparked worldwide outrage and condemnation, and there were calls to break off trade and negotiations with China to protest its violations of human rights.

More recently, the government cracked down on Falun Gong, a religious sect founded in 1997. It was legally registered as a religious organization, but in April 1999 the group organized a silent march of 10,000 followers in Beijing to protest a government article critical of the movement. After that, the government banned the organization and has since jailed thousands of its supporters. Large-scale protests in the outlying regions of Tibet and Xinjiang in 2008 met similar repression.

This history of repression has successfully eliminated most large-scale protests for the time being, but many local protests continue. According to Tony Saich, "Hardly a day goes by in China without some workers' demonstration over layoffs or unpaid wages, farmers' unrest over land issues or excessive taxes, or go-slows or stoppages being reported" (2001, 185). As this quotation suggests, the vast majority of these continuing protests are not political but rather are in regard to local economic grievances. Reports abound of rural residents protesting and at times rioting over abuses committed by a local official. These protests are typically against the imposition of illegal taxes and are designed to draw the attention of higher officials whom local citizens believe will right the wrong. In addition, a number of illegal local unions are said to exist and actively support strikes in the private sector. Students and other urban dwellers also protest occasionally to attempt to change local laws or remove abusive local officials.

Cai (2010) examined over 250 local protests and found that they achieved a significant degree of success in getting governments to change policies. Most protests were against local governments, so a key organizational tool for protesters and petitioners is to get the ear of the central government via the media or dramatic acts like large-scale street protests. The central government is often more willing to make concessions to the protesters than local government because the central authorities are more concerned about the overall legitimacy of the system. If protests are large, can connect several issues of abuse at the local level, and can use the media to gain attention, they can succeed in changing policy. An additional successful technique is to use individuals' *guanxi* networks; if a protest leader has a personal connection with higher authority, he or she can often use that to gain the central government's attention. Overall, Cai concluded that social groups in China are similar in many ways to social movements elsewhere; where they can amass their forces and use media exposure well, they can overcome opposition from local governments to force change. Success depends, of course, on the cost to the government of making the change; making demands whose costs are too high often leads to repression.

How far and how fast all of the political reforms will go is probably the major question that political scientists looking at China ask. Teresa Wright (2010) used a political economy approach to argue that the regime has been more successful than many assume at maintaining its legitimacy. China's economic policy, while creating much greater inequality than in the past, has nonetheless favored many segments of society. First and foremost, the regime has earned the support of budding entrepreneurs and professionals, who have gained great wealth due to the government's policies. In addition, workers in the private sector, and even workers in the declining state-owned sector who still have some social welfare protections from the state, fear that they would be worse off if the ruling party were no longer in power. A 2006 survey found that Chinese citizens have very high levels of trust in the central government (over 90 percent) to manage the society well but that they have much lower levels of faith in local government due to their direct experiences with it (Fewsmith 2008). David Shambaugh (2008) examined the ruling party itself as an institution and cautiously concluded that its pragmatic approach to reform has

allowed it to survive reasonably well. While he hesitated to predict the future, he concluded that stability and continued one-party rule with a continuing pattern of slow reform were more likely than not.

CASE SUMMARY

China has evolved from a classic communist regime into one that is modernizing authoritarian. As it has done so, it has adjusted its communist system of forced participation in a way that helps to legitimize the regime. The opening of the market economy has forced the party to allow greater participation, though it has done so in a way that has kept demands for fundamental reform effectively repressed. The co-opting of key elites into the ruling party, the creation of state corporatist regulation of civil society, and the use of repression when necessary have kept large-scale protest to a minimum since Tiananmen Square in 1989. Locally, reforms have been haphazard and only partially implemented, though the best evidence suggests that they have been expanded over time. Semicompetitive elections have allowed some real participation at the local levels of government but nothing on a larger scale.

All of this suggests that China may be evolving in the direction of a semi-authoritarian regime but that it is clearly not there yet. China's regime has not allowed even token partisan opposition to date. Democracy advocates within China and around the world hope that the initial expansion of participation will ultimately yield greater pressure toward real democratic reform, though that seems a long way off at this point. This is a characteristic that China shares with Iran, our next case study. Both countries have been ruled by charismatic leaders who were surrounded by a personality cult and who saw no reason to allow dissent, even if they allowed discussion and debate to a limited degree. And each country has drawn scrutiny from the rest of the world for human rights abuses and incidents of corruption throughout its government.

CASE STUDY

Iran: From Participation and Reform to Renewed Repression

- Participation via presidential and legislative elections
- Pattern of reformers gaining power and conservatives repressing them
- Weak civil society but growing until post-2005 crackdown
- 2009 election crisis perhaps the end of reform

On June 12, 2009, Iran's President Mahmoud Ahmadinejad faced reelection. Early on, he was predicted to win easily against two not particularly strong reformist candidates. Student, human rights, and women's groups, however, decided to back the reformist candidates rather than boycotting the elections as they did in 2005 (Boroumand 2009). Ahmadinejad fared poorly in a televised debate, deriding his opponents on personal grounds and claiming that the economy was doing much better than it actually was, both of which enraged voters. Suddenly, his opponents and their supporters believed he was vulnerable. Interest in the election skyrocketed, and predictions shifted to possible opposition victory. The morning after the elections, the government announced the results with only two-thirds of the votes counted, claiming the president had won with 62 percent of the vote. It quickly became clear that this couldn't possibly be the case. The number two candidate, reformist Mir-Hossein Mousavi, called on his supporters to take to the streets in peaceful protest, and within a day more than one million people marched through the streets of Tehran in the largest demonstration since the 1979 revolution. After weeks of demonstrations, the government finally and effectively cracked down, arresting as many as 5,000 protesters, putting over 100 on televised trials on what seemed like trumped up charges, and allegedly torturing and raping some in prison. Ahmadinejad's victory was upheld,

but only via the greatest use of repression in decades, and it incurred widespread international condemnation of both the election and the repressive aftermath.

These dramatic events were perhaps the culmination of a long battle between, on the one hand, conservative supporters of the regime who wished to preserve the power of the clergy and Revolutionary Guard and, on the other, reformist elements that wanted to strengthen the quasi-democratic institutions, reduce the role of Islamic law, and more fully open the society to the world. Citizens demanding change have put reformers into office off and on over the history of the Islamic Republic, most notably during the Khatami presidency (1997–2005). The supreme leader and his allies, however, effectively blocked reformers' efforts and forced them out of office via Ahmadinejad's first election in 2005. The tension between the theocratic and quasi-democratic elements of the regime have existed from the start and risen over time, culminating in the 2009 "Green Movement" that followed the election. Its repression seemed to signal the end, at least for the moment, of effective participation by reformists and mark the growing power of the Revolutionary Guard discussed earlier.

Majlis elections in Iran are majoritarian in single-member districts, with a runoff if the top winner in the first round does not get more than 50 percent. They are held regularly, once every four years, and while none has been truly free and fair by democratic standards, the Guardian Council at times has allowed significant competition. The Council is pivotal to the process because of its power to ban any and all candidates it deems unsuitable based on their perceived loyalty (or, rather, lack thereof) to the ideals of the Islamic Republic. A pattern has emerged in which the Guardian Council cracks down on the next election after any *majlis* election in which reformist candidates win a significant

Smoke billows from a burning car during a demonstration in Tehran in 2009. The "Green Revolution" arose to protest the fraudulent reelection of President Ahmedinejad, but the regime successfully repressed the protesters, arresting thousands and sentencing hundreds to prison.

Credit: AFP/Getty Images

share of seats. So when reformers won quite a few seats in 1988, the council banned many of those victors in 1992 and 1996. In the 1997 presidential election, Mohammad Khatami, a reformist cleric who emerged as a spokesperson for change, won a sweeping victory that many observers saw as the start of a major liberalization of the political system. Until 2000, there were too many conservatives in the parliament, however, for him to get any major reforms passed. In the 2000 *majlis* election, the Guardian Council did not prevent reformist candidates from running because of Khatami's popularity, and reformists won an overwhelming victory, clinching 80 percent of the vote. The new *majlis* passed major reforms involving greater freedoms of expression, women's rights, human rights in general, and market-oriented economic policies. The Guardian Council, however, vetoed many of these, arguing that they violated Sharia. By the 2004 *majlis* election, Khatami's failure to institute major reforms had hurt his popularity, and the Guardian Council once again felt

it was safe to clamp down. Thousands of reformist candidates were banned from the election, leading most to boycott it. Conservatives won the election, but turnout dropped from nearly 70 percent to 50 percent.

Political parties are weak institutions in contemporary Iran, but given the severe restrictions on the power of elective offices, this is understandable. The prerevolutionary regime of the shah was modernizing authoritarian and rarely allowed significant participation, so the country has no major history of political parties. And despite the Islamic constitution's guarantee of a right to form parties, Khomeini banned them in 1987, claiming they produced unnecessary divisions. Reformist president Khatami successfully legalized parties again in 1998, which helped make the 2000 *majlis* election the most open and competitive since the revolution. Khatami's reformist supporters coalesced into a party called the Khordad Front that won the huge victory that year. The party brought together several newly formed parties, most of which were formed around the leadership of a well-known reformer. Its opposition consisted of similar coalitions of supporters of Khomeini's original revolutionary ideals and of the continued dominance of the clerical establishment.

Like political parties, civil society is not particularly strong in Iran, but the period of reformist ascendancy—especially 1997 to 2004—saw an explosion of such activity when government restrictions were temporarily relaxed. Of particular note were media, women's, and student groups. Whenever the government has allowed it, the media has expanded rapidly in Iran. Leading up to the 2000 *majlis* election, many newspapers emerged, and an exceptionally open political debate occurred. Since that time, religious authorities have again repressed newspapers, closing them down for criticizing the government too harshly and drastically reducing public debate. Civil society groups once again emerged in the 2009 protests until met with overwhelming repression.

Women have become an important organized force over the last decade. Ironically, in terms of women's position in society, the Islamic regime may well have been more "modernizing" than the earlier modernizing authoritarian regime of the shah. Women now constitute 62 percent of university students, and a birth control policy has lowered childbearing and population growth rates dramatically. Conservative clergy have resisted changes to laws regarding divorce, clothing, and other issues associated with religious observance, but they have allowed significant socioeconomic changes in women's lives. These changes have fostered the growth of women's organizations calling for even further change, a topic we explore in chapter 12. All major politicians now court the women's vote during elections.

Intellectual critics and university students have repeatedly spoken out against the government and have repeatedly been repressed when they have spoken out too strongly. This came to a head in 1999, when some student leaders began to question continued commitment to Islam as the key identity of the state, arguing for democracy and Iranian nationalism instead. Their arrest and the simultaneous closure of a reformist newspaper resulted in demonstrations across Iran's universities, a brutal police response, and violent student riots. Religious authorities successfully repressed the students but not without losing further legitimacy. Whenever the government has allowed it, civil society groups such as students, women, and the media have quickly emerged and voiced their complaints against the government, but they have faced government repression when those complaints have gone too far in the eyes of religious authorities.

The Green Movement that emerged in response to the fraudulent 2009 election showed both the strength and weakness of Iran's incipient civil society. It brought at least a million people onto the streets of Tehran and reached beyond its middle-class base, but it did not have much effect in the countryside. Though initiated in response to an appeal from the losing candidate, it had no clear formal organization. A decentralized organizing system using Twitter and Facebook became the main means of communication, aided by public statements and occasional public appearances by Moussavi and other reformist leaders. Protests continued for weeks, but the government successfully repressed them in spite of widespread international condemnation. While most of those convicted of crimes during the protests have been released, others are serving long prison sentences, and two were executed. The top leaders were not arrested but have been effectively silenced. Moussavi called off a planned march on the first anniversary of the disputed election, saying he feared more bloodshed. The government successfully prevented planned demonstrations in support of the 2011 uprisings in Tunisia and Egypt, even though the Iranian government itself supported the overthrow of the Tunisian and Egyptian governments. It feared that such demonstrations would lead to calls for similar changes at home. Reformers continue to communicate online and desire change, but two years after the huge demonstrations, the reform movement seems effectively

IN CONTEXT

IRAN AND THE MIDDLE EAST

In spite of its reputation as a "pariah state" in much of the West, Iran was about average in its region in terms of the level of freedom and social well-being enjoyed by its population, at least until the controversial 2009 election and its aftermath moved the country in a less democratic direction.

	Iran	Middle East average*
Freedom House civil liberties score	6	5
Freedom House political rights score	6	6
Democracy Index 2008	2.83	3.54
Democracy Index 2010	1.94	3.43
Human Development Index 2010	0.702	0.59
Literacy rate	77	82

Source: Data are from Freedom House (2010); CIA World Factbook; and Democracy Index 2010 (Economist Intelligence Unit), http://www.eiu.com/public/thankyou_download.aspx?activity=reg&campaignid=demo2010.

*Averages exclude North Africa. For Human Development Index, use "Arab States."

crushed, at least until some new opening (most likely via a split within the regime) allows some political space for action.

Given the weak formal institutions of participation and the government's repeated repression of them, it is not surprising that patron-client networks are a crucial form of political activity as well as a key means used by the ruling elite to co-opt people to gain their support. Patron-client factions long predate the Islamic regime in Iran, and the regime has done little to eliminate them. Indeed, many scholars argue that such factions are essential to the regime's continued rule. The ruling elite consists of numerous patrons, formally in one government position or another or well placed in the leadership of a foundation and informally leading a large number of clients who provide them with political support. These factions are crucial venues through which political participation occurs. Indeed, President Khatami's reforms in the late 1990s and early 2000s were aimed in part at strengthening civil society to weaken the patron-client networks that clerics and their supporters use as tools of co-optation. Under President Ahmadinejad, factions and networks of former Revolutionary Guards have expanded their power and position within the government dramatically, and they probably now represent the strongest elements in Iranian politics.

Ideological factions exist as well, overlapping and at times crossing the existing factional divisions that are based on clientelism. David Menashri, an Israeli expert on Iran, argued that shortly after Khomeini's death, three significant factions emerged among both clergy and secular politicians (2001). Conservatives supported adherence to pure Islamist ideals in terms of personal life and moral values and opposed interaction with the West, but they generally supported a market economy and private property. Radicals agreed with conservatives on religious and moral purity, but they supported Khomeini's revolutionary rhetoric in favor of significant state intervention in the economy, which was the economic policy the regime followed for most of the 1980s. Pragmatists, the third faction, were willing to moderate Islamic purity and open up more to the West as well as move in the direction of a market economy; these were the core of the reformists who supported President Khatami. President Ahmadinejad is now the chief radical, trying to enforce Islamic purity in social and cultural areas, but coupling that with populist economic policies that were initially popular with the impoverished and still win him support from some. These divisions are not always stable; various groups have shifted alliances over the years in factional battles that were based on clientelist ties as well as various ideological disagreements.

The era of more open political competition and discussion and efforts at significant reforms of the theocratic regime definitively ended with the election of President Ahmadinejad. (Most Americans know him for his international defense of Iran's nuclear program and his questioning of the fact that the Holocaust occurred.) Domestic, not international, issues dominated the campaign, and Ahmadinejad won the 2005 election with the support of a coalition of social conservatives and the poor, to whom he appealed with a populist campaign that promised more jobs, housing, and social spending. His radical positions quickly revealed significant internal contradictions. For instance, social conservatives in the *majlis* have rejected some of his economic policies, such as using more oil money to fund social programs for the poor. On the other hand, despite his socially conservative rhetoric, Ahmedinejad has limited his reversal of earlier social reforms, knowing that his youthful supporters would likely rebel if he reimposed too many social restrictions. He has banned "Western and indecent music" from state-owned media but has only partially restored restrictions on women's attire and other policies that social conservatives favor. His very loud support for the continuation of Iran's nuclear program and his generally anti-Western and anti-U.S. rhetoric appeals to both halves of his coalition, which perhaps explains why he has been so vocal on these positions. Substantial domestic policy changes may well alienate one or another part of his coalition, but they can all unite behind him in support of his nationalistic rhetoric on the international stage. Ahmedinejad's loss of popularity, though, is probably due mainly to his poor management of the economy, which has declined under his rule, even before the global recession of 2008–09.

CASE SUMMARY

Iran is the only fully developed Islamic theocratic regime in the world today. This gives it an unusual ideological justification and, at least initially, gave it revolutionary and ideological legitimacy. After three decades, however, the regime shows attributes of many other authoritarian regimes in that it rules via repression, co-optation, and efforts at legitimation. The clerical elite and their secular supporters in virtually all key positions have proven themselves willing to repress opponents who step beyond what they are willing to tolerate. The 2009 crisis badly damaged the legitimacy of Iran's quasi-democratic institutions and raised questions about the future of any real participation or representation. Ahmadinejad's cementing of his power and placing of his fellow Revolutionary Guard members (or former members) in many positions of influence raise the specter that neither theocracy nor democracy will survive in the long term. Instead, military rule, at least behind the scenes, seems entirely possible. On the other hand, journalistic reports suggest that underneath the regime's strength lies a population that is much more cynical and quietly critical than they were before the 2009 crisis (Anderson 2010; Yong and Slackman 2010). While the population lacks organizational strength or a public voice in the face of severe repression, it may be waiting for an opening to reemerge even more forcefully.

CASE STUDY

Nigeria: Declining Participation amid Increasingly Personalist Rule

- Little formal participation: No legislature or political parties, except during transitions to democracy

- Civil society and media initially allowed to operate openly as a means to overcome dictator's dilemma

- Growing personalist rule and repression of civil society
- Growing corruption and patron-client relationships as sole means of participation
- Growing ethnic sentiment

Each time a Nigerian military ruler has taken power, he has claimed that he would remain in power only briefly and restore democracy soon. Perhaps for this reason, Nigerian military leaders have never allowed even limited elections or the establishment of legislatures to enhance their legitimacy. They have, however, allowed some political participation as part of a seemingly unending, Sisyphean process of "returning to democracy." While all of the country's military rulers promised a return to a democratic regime, nearly all delayed taking action on this promise for as long as possible. Actual transitions to democratic rule

occurred only in 1979 and 1999. One of the primary ways the military tried to gain legitimacy was to create elaborate processes for writing new constitutions to prepare for a new democracy. Constituent assemblies were created in which politicians and leading members of civil society participated, and new procedures and electoral rules were drafted. The most open political activity took place within these assemblies, as old political alignments based on region and ethnicity informally emerged in the form of factions. While none of this fully fulfilled the functions that Jennifer Gandhi (2008) laid out for legislatures in authoritarian regimes, they did provide occasional space for actual political participation.

In the process of preparing for a return to democracy, the military government would eventually have to allow political parties to reemerge, officially register, and begin campaigning. Olusegun Obasanjo's (1976–1979) government allowed this in the late 1970s,

A crowd demonstrates in 1995 against military dictator Sani Abacha's refusal to allow a real process of democratization to end military rule. Abacha was the most brutal and corrupt of Nigeria's military rulers. His 1998 death finally led to the end of military rule and a democratic transition.

Credit: AP Photo/Peter Obe

following the particular rules for party registration set down by the new constitution to try to ensure that the government had national appeal. Babangida (in 1989–1993) and Abacha (in 1995) interfered more elaborately in the process of party creation. Babangida rejected all thirteen parties that sought registration and instead created two and wrote their platforms himself. Abacha allowed five parties to be officially registered, but all of them were pledged to support him for the presidency. Such parties were aimed not at participating in the current regime but at being part of the alleged new democratic regime whenever it emerged. They provided little real opportunity to voice opposition to the military regimes themselves.

Civil society fared better under Nigerian military rule than did political parties. The military governments of the 1970s interfered relatively little with civil society. By and large, labor unions and professional associations continued to operate as they had before, though this was in part because they did not challenge the regimes. The press also was unusually free for an authoritarian regime. All of this gave the military rulers some means of overcoming the dictator's dilemma because it allowed them to gather information on what people actually thought of their rule. The governments of the 1980s and 1990s, however, increasingly repressed civil society. When medical doctors went on strike to protest their working conditions and to express their general opposition to the government in 1984–1985, the Buhari government responded by banning all associations. Babangida reversed this when he came to power in an attempt to gain some initial legitimacy, but he quickly changed course when the organizations he had legalized came out in opposition to him. For example, the Nigerian Bar Association opposed the use of military tribunals, preventive detention, and other restrictions on the rule of law and human rights, and the Nigerian Union of Journalists defended its colleagues who had been jailed and detained in crackdowns on the press in the late 1980s and early 1990s. Both met with repression by the regime.

Setting himself up for further criticism, Babangida began a structural adjustment program in 1986 that harmed far more Nigerians than it helped and increased poverty substantially, despite the country's massive oil wealth. Growing levels of poverty and unemployment fueled protests against the policies themselves and the military government more generally. These were led by the Nigerian Labor Congress and the country's national student association. Abacha's even greater brutality and corruption inspired greater opposition, as several major democracy movements coalesced to oppose him. We examine these movements in greater detail in chapter 9.

Ethnic and religious associations also grew substantially in the 1990s. Nigerians increasingly saw the military rulers of the 1980s and 1990s (all of whom were Muslims from the north and associated with the Kaduna mafia, a group of military men named after the northern city in which many of the members maintained homes) as centralizing political power in the hands of one ethno-regional and religious group. Christians in the southern part of the country voiced strong opposition to Babangida's 1989 decision to have Nigeria join an international group called the Organization of the Islamic Conference (OIC). In religiously mixed areas, violent conflicts broke out in several cities in the late 1980s and early 1990s as tensions rose. As discussed in chapter 4, new and more fundamentalist Islamic movements began to emerge in the northern region. Ken Saro-Wiwa and MOSOP became the best known ethnically based movement, but many others arose as well.

Nigerian political scientist Julius Ihonvbere argued in the mid-1990s that Abacha's crackdown on all efforts to establish democracy led many political activists to resort to ethnic political mobilization, producing "more than at any other time in Nigeria's history, a hardening of regional positions" (1994, 218). This legacy of growing religious and ethnic sentiment and organizations, some of which became violent, is one of the major obstacles to stability of Nigeria's young democracy.

CASE SUMMARY

Nigeria's military regimes became increasingly centralized, repressive, and corrupt over time. While those of the 1970s allowed civil society to survive more or less intact, later rulers centralized power in their own hands and eliminated virtually all institutionalized channels of dissent. Predictably, corruption became a way of life in such personalized regimes of weak institutions, and patron-client networks became the main form of political participation and economic survival. Nigerian political scientist Julius Ihonvbere reported that by the early 1990s, it was "impossible to survive or make progress in the country without (1) belonging to a particular religion; (2) having connections with top military officers, their spouses, or traditional rulers; (3) coming from particular sections of the country; and (4) getting involved directly in one form of corruption or another" (1994, 1). Civil society, rather than being a means of participation and influence within the authoritarian regime, focused solely on fundamental regime change as part of the democratization movement that was sweeping Africa in the 1990s. The questions we take up in the next chapter are whether and how a new democracy can emerge from such a regime and, if so, what will be its prospects and problems.

CONCLUSION

One of the subjects of chapter 9 is the "third wave" of democratization that began to sweep the world in the mid-1970s and accelerated in the 1990s. By the dawn of the new millennium, however, it was clear that while democracy had expanded, authoritarianism was not about to disappear entirely. Since the end of the Cold War, semi-authoritarian rule has expanded, and more "closed" authoritarian rule that allows no formal opposition has been on the wane (with China clearly being the world's biggest exception to the trend). The differences between fully authoritarian and semi-authoritarian rule, though, aren't as great as they might at first appear. Understanding the often opaque political dynamics of authoritarian regimes will continue to be a concern for comparative politics for the foreseeable future.

Who Rules?

On the face of it, dictators seem to control virtually everything in authoritarian regimes. The executive would seem to be all-powerful. As we've seen, though, this is often not the case, which makes figuring out who rules rather difficult. The key question is not just what formal institutions exist but how institutionalized they are. Ultimately, in authoritarian regimes the supreme leader or a small coterie of leaders (such as a politburo) has final authority to decide as they will. Ruling by fiat and repression alone, however, is both difficult and expensive. Holding a gun to every citizen's head, as well as maintaining the unquestioned loyalty of those holding the guns, is not easy. All regimes, therefore, seek to gain some sort of legitimacy or at least to buy support via co-optation. A means to achieve both legitimacy and support is to limit the supreme leader's power in order to give others, especially key elites, some influence. Institutionalized and therefore predictable governing and limited participatory institutions can accomplish this. Examining those institutions and how strong they are can thus be a key means to understanding who really rules and how much influence they have. Even in the most personalist regimes with little institutionalization, patron-client relationships are important for co-opting opposition. More powerful individuals control more patronage, and on the other side, some clients are more powerful and thus more likely to have their requests attended to than others. Patronage networks may provide an entrée to the state in otherwise closed regimes, but they create a situation in which some politicians and some citizens are more equal than others. Comparativists attempt the difficult task of understanding these informal networks and relationships to determine who rules in countries where institutions matter little.

What Explains Political Behavior?

Comparativists have long catalogued authoritarian regimes into various subtypes, several of which we discussed in chapter 3 and again in this chapter. It's clear, however, that certain commonalities exist in all authoritarian regimes. For instance, all dictators face the dictator's dilemma, though they attempt to solve it in different ways. All dictators also rule through some combination of repression, co-optation, and attempts at legitimation, but again in differing ways and amounts. Some of this variation is systematic across subtypes: different subtypes display consistent and distinct behavior. Regimes that come to power on the basis of a strong single party, often following a revolution or via a coup by a well-institutionalized military, tend to circumscribe the leader's actions from the start. One-party and theocratic regimes usually have more elaborate ideological justifications for their rule, which usually (though not always) limit leaders as well. Participation varies also by subtype. One-party and of course semi-authoritarian regimes provide opportunities for greater participation via formal institutions. Military regimes are less likely to do so, as political participation and open dissent are foreign to professional military culture. Following the logic of the dictator's dilemma, regimes that allow less participation are likely to require more repression and co-optation. Military regimes seem likely to use repression, given their inherent control of force. Personalist regimes that have weak institutions across the board focus mostly on co-optation via patronage, using repression as well but often in less institutionalized and therefore less effective ways. Such a personalist regime might have, for example, multiple and competing military agencies that are informally loyal to individual leaders rather than to the regime as a whole. The splits within the military in response to the 2011 uprising in Libya show the possible effects of this aspect of personalist rule.

Personalist regimes are also where patron-client relationships are most prominent. Certainly these relationships are universal in authoritarian regimes, but the unusually weak institutions of personalist regimes logically make patron-client relationships more important. As we noted earlier, such relationships become the primary means of political participation and influence where formal institutions are weakest. Patron-client relationships are important in virtually all authoritarian regimes, however, because patronage is a pillar of authoritarian rule that serves as a key means of co-optation, on which all authoritarian regimes rely to varying degrees. The importance of patron-client relationships can vary over time in individual regimes as well, as repression becomes more or less costly or institutionalization becomes more or less dangerous for the supreme leader. While patron-client relationships are important in all politics, they are systematically more important in authoritarian regimes than in democracies. This is because of dictators' greater need for co-optation and, in almost all cases, their weaker legitimacy.

Where and Why?

Most authoritarian regimes, whatever their specific type, attempt to create some institutions, but the types of institutions and their strength vary greatly. This variation has been the subject of extensive political science research in recent years. Earlier scholars focused on cultural or historical-institutional explanations, such as the theory that regimes in countries with prior institutional experience tend to preserve long-standing institutions or re-create institutions they have had previously. More recent scholarship has focused on the dictator's dilemma. Institutions can serve as a means of providing patronage to potential rivals, but in addition, legislatures and parties can be mechanisms to allow some limited criticism of the regime and allow citizens to engage in policy compromise; in these ways they can enhance regime legitimacy. Jennifer Gandhi (2008) argued that dictators are rational actors who will create such institutions when they need them, in situations where they are weak. Institutions are therefore more likely to exist in civilian regimes than in military regimes or monarchies because the latter have other sources of strength.

Beyond the mere existence of such institutions, though, is their institutional strength. All regimes have executives and bureaucracies, but personalist regimes in particular seem to have weakly developed institutions that place little restraint on the leader and his cohort and have little ability to create predictable lines of succession. In contrast, regimes that originate in the military or in a political party, whether communist or not, often seem to create more durable and somewhat more predictable institutions. On the other hand, the case of Nigeria demonstrates that not all military governments further institutionalization. Institutionalization varies greatly across countries and over time and forms very different regime traits and levels of stability and predictability, as the contrasting cases of China and Nigeria show clearly.

Applying Theory to the Study of Authoritarian Regimes

The earliest theoretical approaches to understanding authoritarian regimes focused mainly on individual leaders or national cultures. Individual leaders are clearly crucial in such regimes, so scholars used psychological theories to assess them and their backgrounds and to understand their personal influences and motivations. These studies yielded an understanding of why famous dictators such as Adolf Hitler or Mao Zedong behaved as they did. Other scholars, looking beyond the individual, used political culture theories to argue why such regimes emerged in the first place and how they operated. Authoritarian regimes emerged in countries with political cultures that had authoritarian traits such as lack of interpersonal trust, lack of belief in core democratic principles, lack of popular interest in participation in politics, or a popular desire to follow a perceived "strong" leader. These regimes' institutions were shaped by cultures and historical practices as well. For example, the lack of any lengthy democratic experience in postcolonial Africa created regimes that eliminated virtually all democratic trappings.

More recently, scholars have used rational-actor or historical-institutionalist models to understand authoritarian regimes. Dictators face a common set of governing problems known as the dictator's dilemma. To overcome these problems, they engage in a combination of repression, co-optation, and institutionalization. This action pattern, rational-actor theorists argue, is determined by the dictators' rational responses to their conditions, the most important of which are their strengths relative to potential opponents and the resources at their disposal. Historical institutionalists agree with much of this, but assert that the creation of key institutions, such as strong ruling parties, happens at particular historical junctures and heavily influences regime strength and longevity; institutions cannot be created at any time the dictator comes to believe he needs them. As with many arguments in comparative politics, institutionalist theories are at the forefront of the debate today but have not definitively proven their case. We turn next to another set of difficult questions about regimes: why and how they change from one type to another via military coup, revolution, or democratization.

KEY CONCEPTS

dictator's dilemma (p. 373)   institutionalization (p. 371)   supreme leader (p. 372)
guanxi (p. 403)   personality cult (p. 395)

WORKS CITED

Anderson, Jon Lee. 2010. "After the Crackdown." *The New Yorker,* August 19. http://www.newyorker.com/reporting/2010/08/16/100816fa_fact_anderson/.

Bellin, Eva Rana. 2002. *Stalled Democracy: Capital, Labor, and the Paradox of State-Sponsored Development.* Ithaca: Cornell University Press.

Boroumand, Ladan. 2009. "Civil Society's Choice." *Journal of Democracy* 20 (4): 16–20. http://www.journalofdemocracy.org/articles/gratis/Boroumand-20-4.pdf.

Brownlee, Jason. 2007. *Authoritarianism in an Age of Democratization.* Cambridge, UK: Cambridge University Press.

Cai, Yongshun. 2010. *Collective Resistance in China: Why Popular Protests Succeed or Fail.* Stanford, CA: Stanford University Press.

Chen, Jo-hsi. 1978. *The Execution of Mayor Yin and Other Stories from the Great Proletarian Cultural Revolution.* Bloomington: Indiana University Press.

Diamond, Larry, 1997. "Postscript and Postmortem." In *Transition without End: Nigerian Politics and Civil Society under Babangida,* edited by Larry Diamond, Anthony Kirk-Greene, and Oyeleye Oyediran, 465–84. Boulder, CO: Lynne Rienner.

Dickson, Bruce J. 2003. *Red Capitalists in China: The Party, Private Entrepreneurs, and Prospects for Political Change.* New York: Cambridge University Press.

Fewsmith, Joseph. 2008. "Staying in Power: What Does the Chinese Communist Party Have to Do?" In *China's Changing Political Landscape: Prospects for Democracy,* edited by Cheng Li, 212–28. Washington, DC: Brookings Institution Press.

Gandhi, Jennifer. 2008. *Political Institutions under Dictatorship.* Cambridge, UK: Cambridge University Press.

Geddes, Barbara. 1999. "What Do We Know about Democratization after Twenty Years?" *Annual Review of Political Science* 2: 115–44. doi:10.1146/annurev.polisci.2.1.115.

Ginsburg, Tom. 2008. "Administrative Law and the Judicial Control of Agents in Authoritarian Regimes." In *Rule by Law: The Politics of Courts in Authoritarian Regimes,* edited by Tom Ginsburg and Tamir Moustafa, 58–72. Cambridge, UK: Cambridge University Press.

Hen-Tov, Elliot, and Nathan Gonzalez. 2010. "The Militarization of Post-Khomeini Iran: Praetorianism 2.0." *The Washington Quarterly* 34 (1): 45–59. doi:10.1080/0163660X.2011.534962.

Huang, Jing. 2008. "Institutionalization of Political Succession: Progress and Implications." In *China's Changing Political Landscape*, edited by Cheng Li, 80–97. Washington DC: The Brookings Institution Press.

Ihonvbere, Julius Omozuanvbo. 1994. *Nigeria: The Politics of Adjustment and Democracy*. New Brunswick, NJ: Transaction.

Kennedy, John James. 2010. "Rural China: Reform and Resistance." In *Politics in China: An Introduction*, edited by William A. Joseph, 225–49. Oxford, UK: Oxford University Press.

Landry, Pierre. 2008. "The Institutional Diffusion of Courts in China: Evidence from Survey Data." In *Rule by Law: The Politics of Courts in Authoritarian Regimes*, edited by Tom Ginsburg and Tamir Moustafa, 207–34. Cambridge, UK: Cambridge University Press.

Landry, Pierre F., Deborah Davis, and Shiru Wang. 2010. "Elections in Rural China: Competition without Parties." *Comparative Political Studies* 43 (6): 763–90. doi:10.1177/0010414009359392.

Lee, Ching Kwan, and Eli Friedman. 2009. "The Labor Movement." *Journal of Democracy* 20 (3): 21–24.

Li, Cheng. 2010. "China's Communist Party-State: The Structure and Dynamics of Power." In *Politics in China: An Introduction*, edited by William A. Joseph, 165–91. Oxford, UK: Oxford University Press.

Li, Cheng, and Lynn White. 2006. "The Sixteenth Central Committee of the Chinese Communist Party: Emerging Patterns of Power Sharing." In *China's Deep Reform: Domestic Politics in Transition*, edited by Lowell Dittmer and Guoli Liu, 81–118. Lanham, MD: Rowman and Littlefield.

Lu, Yiyi. 2009. *Non-Governmental Organizations in China: The Rise of Dependent Autonomy*. New York: Routledge.

Magaloni, Beatriz. 2006. *Voting for Autocracy: Hegemonic Party Survival and Its Demise in Mexico*. Cambridge, UK: Cambridge University Press.

Mbembe, Achille. 1992. "Provisional Notes on the Postcolony." *Africa: Journal of the International African Institute* 62 (1): 3–37. doi:10.2307/1160062.

Menashri, David. 2001. *Post-Revolutionary Politics in Iran: Religion, Society, and Power*. London: Frank Cass.

Migdal, Joel S. 1988. *Strong Societies and Weak States: State-Society Relations and State Capabilities in the Third World*. Princeton, NJ: Princeton University Press.

O'Brien, Kevin J. 2006. "Villagers, Elections, and Citizenship in Contemporary China." In *China's Deep Reform: Domestic Politics in Transition*, edited by Lowell Dittmer and Guoli Liu, 381–404. Lanham, MD: Rowman and Littlefield.

Pei, Minxin. 2007. *Corruption Threatens China's Future* (Policy Brief 55). Washington, DC. Available at http://carnegieendowment .org/files/pb55_pei_china_corruption_ final.pdf.

Sadiki, Larbi. 2002. "Political Liberalization in Bin Ali's Tunisia: Facade Democracy." *Democratization* 9 (4): 122–41. doi:10.1080/714000286.

Saich, Tony. 2001. *Governance and Politics of China*. New York: Palgrave.

Shambaugh, David. 2008. *China's Communist Party: Atrophy and Adaptation*. Washington, DC: Woodrow Wilson Center Press.

Shi, Tianjian. 2006. "Village Committee Elections in China: Institutionalist Tactics for Democracy." In *China's Deep Reform: Domestic Politics in Transition*, edited by Lowell Dittmer and Guoli Liu, 353–80. Lanham, MD: Rowman and Littlefield.

Wintrobe, Ronald. 1998. *The Political Economy of Dictatorship*. Cambridge, UK: Cambridge University Press.

Wright, Teresa. 2010. *Accepting Authoritarianism: State-Society Relations in China's Reform Era*. Stanford, CA: Stanford University Press.

Yang, Guobin. 2009. "Online Activism." *Journal of Democracy* 20 (3): 33–36. doi:10.1353/ jod.0.0094.

Yong, Will, and Michael Slackman. 2010. "Across Iran, Anger Lies Behind Face of Calm." *The New York Times*, June 12. http:// www.nytimes.com/2010/06/12/world/ middleeast/12iran.html.

RESOURCES FOR FURTHER STUDY

Clapham, Christopher S. 1982. *Private Patronage and Public Power: Political Clientelism in the Modern State.* New York: St. Martin's Press.

Clapham, Christopher S., and George D. E. Philip, eds. 1985. *The Political Dilemmas of Military Regimes.* Totowa, NJ: Barnes and Noble.

Mbembe, Achille. 2001. *On the Postcolony.* Berkeley: University of California Press.

McFaul, Michael. 2005. "Chinese Dreams, Persian Realities." *Journal of Democracy* 16 (4): 74–82. doi:10.1353/jod.2005.0068.

WEB RESOURCES

Quality of Government Institute, University of Gothenburg, 2010, "The QoG Data" [Quality of Government Dataset] (http://www.qog.pol.gu.se/data/data_1.htm)

World Bank, 2010, Database of Political Institutions 2010 (http://go.worldbank.org/2EAGGLRZ40/)

World Justice Project, 2010, "Rule of Law Index" (http://www.worldjusticeproject.org/rule-of-law-index/)

World Values Survey, 2009 (http://www.worldvaluessurvey.org/)

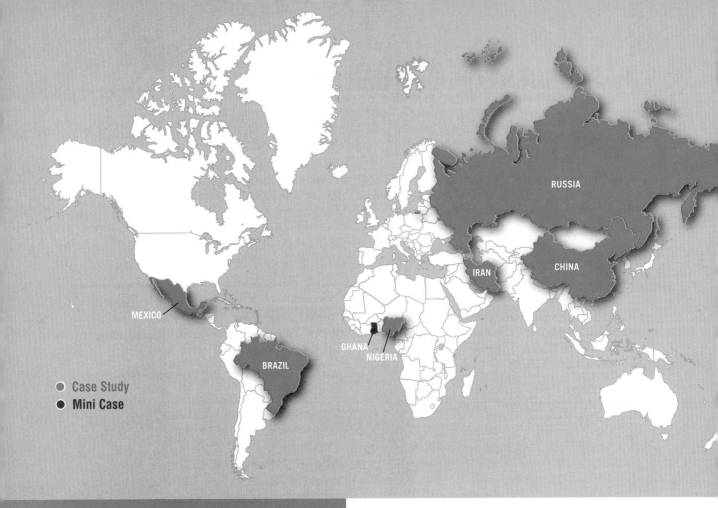

- **Case Study**
- **Mini Case**

Who Rules?

- Revolutions require massive support from a mobilized populace. What do the regimes that result from revolutions tell us about how much power the average citizen has in and after revolution?
- How can civilians maintain effective control over the military? When the military takes power, does it rule alone, or do civilians have any part in ruling as well?

What Explains Political Behavior?

- What best explains why some new democracies survive to move toward consolidation while others revert to authoritarianism?
- Why do revolutions occur? What motivates leaders and followers, and what determines whether they succeed or fail?

Where and Why?

- Why does the military intervene in politics in certain countries and not in others?
- Does democracy's long-term well-being require a certain type of society, culture, or economy, or can it happen anywhere?

9

REGIME CHANGE

Fundamental political change has long been one of the primary interests of comparative politics. Major changes are dramatic events, long remembered in the country in which they occur and sometimes around the world. People rise up, peacefully protesting or even taking up arms to force governments to give up power, and new regimes are established with promises of a better world. Comparativists understand this as regime change, the process through which one regime is transformed into another. The last three chapters have examined political institutions in different kinds of regimes. We now examine how countries go from one type of regime to another and how that process influences the institutions and behavior of the new regime.

The end of the Cold War raised high expectations for positive political changes in the world. Francis Fukuyama (1992) termed the new era "the end of history" because he believed that the great political differences that had defined the twentieth century—the different ideologies and regimes we outlined in chapter 3—had ended for good. The new world he envisioned would be uniformly democratic and based on market economies. Many comparativists questioned Fukuyama's thesis from the start, but the terrorist attacks of September 11, 2001, definitively ended the "end of history." The 1990s were certainly a period of significant institutional and regime change, but that change was neither uniformly toward democracy nor the first of its kind. Comparativists have long studied regime change. Since the 1980s, we have focused primarily on what Samuel Huntington (1991) called the "third wave" of democratization. Earlier, however, the main focus was on military coups d'etat and social revolutions. All three remain important, as the Country and Concept table on page 424 illustrates. While democratization has been the most widespread type of regime change in the last two decades, successful or attempted military coups occurred in recent years in Guinea and Madagascar, the so-called "color revolutions" occurred in several former Soviet states, and even more recently political revolutions swept Tunisia and Egypt.

The study of regime change raises several fundamental questions in comparative politics. We ask what effects revolutions have on who rules: Do revolutionary regimes really rule on behalf of the people they claim to represent, and do those people in fact have a voice in ruling themselves? How can civilians, who are

COUNTRY AND CONCEPT

Regime Change and Outcome

Country	Date	Type of regime change (20th century)	Outcome: type of regime	Length of new regime (years)
Brazil	1930	Military coup	Neofascist	15
	1945	Democratization	Democracy	19
	1964	Military coup	Bureaucratic-authoritarian	21
	1985	Democratization	Democracy	23+
China	1911	Revolution from above	State collapse/warlord rule	16
	1949	Revolution from below	Communist	48+
Germany	1918	Democratization	Democracy	15
	1933	Fascist putsch	Fascist	12
	1950	Democratization	Democracy	57+
	1990	Democratization (end of East German state)	Democracy (expanded)	NA
India	1947	Democratization (end of colonial rule)	Democracy	60+
Iran	1921	Military coup	Modernizing authoritarian	58
	1979	Revolution from below	Theocratic	28+
Japan	1950	Democratization	Democracy	57+
Mexico	1910	Revolution	State collapse/successive *caudillos*	10
	1920	Election	Semi-authoritarian	74
	1994	Democratization	Democracy	12+
Nigeria	1960	Democratization (end of colonial rule)	Democracy	6
	1966	Military coup	Personalist	13
	1979	Democratization	Democracy	4
	1983	Military coup	Personalist	16
	1999	Democratization	Democracy	8+
Russia	1917	Revolution from below	Communist	74
	1991	Democratization	Democracy	9
			Semi-authoritarian	7+
United Kingdom	None	NA	NA	NA
United States	None	NA	NA	NA

supposed to rule in all democratic and many authoritarian regimes, keep the military under their control? When the military does take charge of a regime via a coup, does it rule alone, or are civilians involved as well? Does the military as a whole rule or only certain elements within it? Explaining the regime changes themselves raises a set of classic "What explains political behavior?" questions as well: Why does democratization succeed or fail? Why do revolutions occur? What motivates their leaders, and what explains their success or failure? Finally, there are many "Where and why?" questions related to regime change. Why do military coups happen in some countries and not in others? And can democracy survive in any country or in only certain types of countries, and why? We address all of these questions in our examination of regime change, starting with the historically most common type: military coups d'etat.

THE MILITARY IN POLITICS: COUPS D'ETAT

Military force is central to the modern state. All states must have a military and maintain effective control over it to maintain sovereignty. Americans generally view the military as an organization that is firmly under civilian control and that should stay out of politics. In reality, no military is completely apolitical. When President Barack Obama and various members of Congress made clear that they sought to allow gays and lesbians to serve openly in the military, thus ending the "Don't Ask, Don't Tell" policy, they discovered a divided military leadership, with some favoring the move and others fiercely resisting it. When congressional committees consider the U.S. defense budget, they hold hearings and listen to the advice of top military leaders, among others. These are both examples of the military engaging in political activity. The key is that a regime with effective control over the military, whether democratic or authoritarian, keeps such activities within strict limits: the military does not go beyond the bounds set by the civilian leadership. When it does, a constitutional or political crisis can arise. We now examine the most flagrant military intervention in politics, the coup d'etat, in which the military forcibly removes the existing regime and establishes a new one.

When American students are asked why the military does not stage a coup in the United States, the first answer is usually that the Constitution prevents it. The elected president is commander in chief, and the military must obey him. But given that the Constitution is a piece of paper and the president is one unarmed person, whereas the U.S. military is arguably the most powerful force on the planet, there must be more to it. And there is. A civilian regime, whether democratic or authoritarian, goes to great lengths to ensure that the military is loyal to the regime's ideals and institutions. The primary means it uses to do this is the inculcation of appropriate values in the military leadership, either professional values specific to the military or more general values that are supportive of the regime and that reflect the broader political culture. Well-established democracies train military leaders carefully in military academies, such as West Point in the United States or Britain's Sandhurst, in an attempt to instill professional values that portray the military as a prestigious and important profession with core values that must be maintained, including nonintervention in political affairs. Since military officers and enlisted personnel come out of society as a whole, a strong system of political socialization that ingrains democratic norms of respect for the major political institutions helps to build and maintain democratic legitimacy among those military personnel as well as among the population at large. Communist systems attempt to achieve the same ends via direct Communist Party involvement in the military, mandatory party membership for the military leadership, and, like democracies, a reliance on political socialization in the broader society.

Less institutionalized authoritarian regimes often lack these types of generally effective and systematic mechanisms. Instead, they rely on the creation of multiple military institutions (as mentioned in chapter 8), so that no single one becomes too powerful, or on informal ties of loyalty such as ethnic affiliations between the ruler and military personnel. Many African personalist rulers created a well-equipped and well-paid presidential guard from the same ethnic group or region as the president, which then was personally loyal to the president as an individual patron. The job of this presidential guard was, in part, to protect the president from his own army.

WHERE AND WHY

Coups in Africa: Colonialism or Contagion?

All of the major explanations for military coups could apply to Africa, but the following map suggests other possibilities as well. What trends do you see in terms of where coups have happened most frequently?

Clearly, colonial background and region could have a role to play. Political scientists have long noted the tendency of former British colonies to have more stable and democratic regimes (see "Where and Why: Parliaments and Presidents" in chapter 6). The pattern in Africa suggests that the same could be true for military coups. Former British colonies have clearly had far fewer coups than other African countries. But colonial rule was rather regional as well. West Africa consists of former French colonies and three British colonies, and it is the region that has had the most coups. A total of forty-two out of the eighty-five successful coups on the continent from independence to 2000 occurred in west Africa, and the British colonies there have had numerous coups just like the French colonies. Perhaps a regional explanation accounts for the pattern. Political scientists have long noted "contagion" effects, meaning that when a country of a particular type or in a particular region does something, other countries of the same type or in the same region often follow. A contagion may have swept west Africa but never spread as far as southern Africa. What could explain this? There are several possibilities that a researcher could investigate. Does west Africa have distinct cultural differences? Did it go through a different process of decolonization that increased the likelihood of coups? Did it have distinct postcolonial political institutions that made coups more likely? (The last two questions, of course, lead back to colonial rule.) These are the kinds of questions that comparativists try to answer to disentangle patterns of political behavior.

Africa scholar Chris Allen (1995) argued that military coups in Africa in the 1960s and 1970s (when most of them occurred) happened in states in which the "clientelist crisis" that resulted from decolonization could not be resolved effectively by civilian elites. He argued that African political parties mobilized voters via clientelism in the elections before and right after independence, as we discussed in chapter 7. The parties that won the first elections gained enormous advantages by gaining control of state expenditures to use as patronage; those who lost used whatever means they could to battle against the incumbent advantage.

Why Do Military Coups Happen?

Military coups occur when all efforts to keep the military loyal to (or at least under the control of) the regime fail or are overridden by other concerns among military leaders. Three major schools of thought attempt to explain why coups happen. In the 1960s, when coups became quite common in postcolonial countries, the dominant explanation focused not on the military itself but instead on the societies in which the coups occurred. Samuel Huntington, focusing on the weakness of institutions, contended that "the most important causes of military intervention in politics are not military . . . but the political and institutional structure of the society" (1968, 194). Samuel Finer, in his classic 1962 work *The Man on Horseback*, made

The losers appealed more strongly to ethnic loyalty and used violence as necessary and helpful to try to regain power. Politics became an unregulated "spoils" game of growing ethnic divisions, corruption, and violence. Some leaders managed to avoid the worst of this by creating a very centralized, authoritarian, one-party regime with a powerful central ruler who limited political competition (Tanzania and Kenya are classic examples). Regimes that could not achieve this spiraled into crisis, with military coups as a common result (our case study of Nigeria is a prime example of this pattern). This plausible explanation, though, still leaves unanswered the question that our map raises: Why did these unregulated crises occur so much more frequently in some regions of Africa than in others?

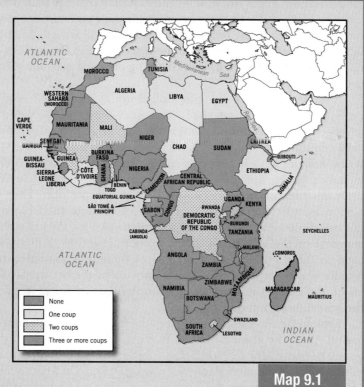

Map 9.1

Coups in Africa

Source: Peter J. Schraeder, *African Politics and Society: A Mosaic in Transformation,* 2nd ed., New York: Thomas/Wadsworth, 2004, 203.

a political-culture argument: countries with political cultures that do not highly value nonmilitary means of transferring power and civil society are more prone to coups. Weak institutions and corrupt rule under early postcolonial leaders created political instability and often violence. The military, these theorists argued, intervened to restore order when civilian leaders had weakened the civilian regime via corrupt and incompetent rule. Most of these early students of military coups, including Huntington, were modernization theorists who argued that the military, with its training and hierarchical organization, was one of the few modern institutions in postcolonial societies. They believed that the military could rule in the national interest, reestablishing order and restarting development. This thinking was in line with the theories of modernizing authoritarianism prominent at the time (see chapter 3).

More recently, John Clark (2006) argued that political legitimacy is especially important to explaining coups in semi-authoritarian regimes. In particular, he argued that these regimes require some degree of democratic legitimacy. Their leaders cannot simply rely on external support to avoid coups (as many authoritarian regimes in Africa did during the Cold War) or on using patronage to buy military support (because spending too much on the military, especially via corrupt means, will undermine regime legitimacy). Therefore, building regime legitimacy by moving in the direction of greater provision of basic rights and better economic growth is more important in semi-authoritarian regimes than it is in purely authoritarian ones. Loss of legitimacy in semi-authoritarian regimes, then, is the most likely cause of a coup because potential coup makers will see it as an opportunity to strike. While not sharing modernization theorists' belief in the positive aspects of military rule, Clark does share their understanding of coups as coming from failures of civilian leadership.

A second school of thought looked not at society but within military organizations themselves. These theorists argued that a military engages in a coup to advance its own institutional interests, such as getting larger budgets, higher pay, better equipment, and better tasks to perform (Huntington 1964, Janowitz 1964). When military leaders perceive civilian rulers as not adequately considering the military's needs, they may intervene, not in the national interest or because of prior misrule, but rather to improve their own position. They may also instigate a coup in response to what they perceive as unjustified civilian intervention in military matters, such as the appointment of top officers without the military's approval or the assignment of inappropriate duties. Military leaders may see a coup in these situations as a defense of their professional status vis-à-vis civilian leaders who are trying to get the military to engage in unprofessional behavior. In effect, the military is just another group clamoring for power and position within the government, but one with guns.

Samuel Decalo was the pioneer of the third major explanation of coups. Focusing on Africa, he argued that the first two schools of thought misunderstood the nature of many African (and perhaps other postcolonial) militaries and therefore misunderstood the motivations for coups. The typical African military, he said, was "a coterie of distinct armed camps owing primary clientelist allegiance to a handful of mutually competitive officers of different ranks seething with a variety of corporate, ethnic and personal grievances" (1976, 14–15). He believed that prior theorists mistakenly viewed the military as a united and professional body concerned with either national interests or its own interests. Instead, he saw African armies as riven with the same regional, ethnic, and personal divisions that characterize neopatrimonial rule in general. Decalo argued that most coups occurred because particular military leaders wanted to gain power for their own interests, those of their ethnic group or region, or those of their faction within the military. Coups were about gaining a greater share of power and resources for the coup leaders and their clients, not about the interests of society as a whole or even "the military" as an institution.

The three schools of thought on the causes of military intervention derive from the following major theoretical strands in political science: political culture, institutionalism, modernization, rational-choice theory, and neopatrimonialism. As our case studies below demonstrate, it is often very difficult to discern which theory best explains a particular coup. Military leaders invariably claim that they intervened to save the nation from corruption and incompetence and, as always in modernizing authoritarian states, to provide unity to pursue an effective development policy. The leaders portray the military as a modern and national institution that intervenes only out of necessity. But their subsequent rule often betrays them as having other motives, though knowing definitively why they intervened is still difficult because motives for intervention and subsequent actions are not always connected.

What Are the Results of Coups?

Whatever the reasons behind coups, different kinds of militaries and different kinds of coups tend to produce different kinds of military regimes. The factor that is probably of greatest importance in determining the kind of military regime is the institutional strength of the military itself, as we noted in chapter 8. A military that maintains a strongly hierarchical organization is less likely to produce a coup that is driven by individual or sectional interests, as in Africa. Rather, an institutionalized military might instigate a coup to try to create order out of political chaos or a coup that is in the narrow interests of the military as an institution. The military regime resulting from the coup is likely to be relatively institutionalized, predictable, and stable, if not necessarily legitimate. In addition, a coup carried out primarily in the interests of the military as an institution is likely to result in a shift of governmental resources toward military spending, which usually has deleterious economic effects on the society as a whole. A more personal coup is likely to produce a more personalist regime that is far less institutionalized than the other regime options and is more subject to countercoups or so-called palace coups in the future.

CASE STUDY

Comparing Coups: Brazil and Nigeria

- Different levels of institutionalization in the military lead to different types of military regimes
- Societal versus military versus personal explanations for coups are difficult to untangle

Brazil and Nigeria provide stark contrasts in the contexts of their coups, the natures of their militaries, and their postcoup regimes. They both demonstrate, however, the difficulty of explaining military coups. Political scientists have used both societal and institutional (within the military) arguments to explain Brazil's 1964 coup, which ushered in a bureaucratic-authoritarian state, a crucial milestone in the country's political and economic development. The Brazilian military has been involved in politics since the founding of the republic in 1889. It was instrumental in the governments of the first decade and emerged again as central under the neofascist Estado Novo in the

Gen. Ernesto Geisel is shown here being sworn in as Brazilian president in 1974. Geisel was the third president in Brazil's highly institutionalized military regime. His government began the slow liberalization process that eventually led to a return to democracy in 1989.

Credit: AP Photo/AJB, Evandro Texeira

1930s. Even during the country's democratic periods, the military has been politically influential. Elected officials regularly consult with military leaders on a variety of policy issues, especially those touching on Brazil's rather broad concept of national security. When they believed the national well-being was at stake, military leaders were quite willing to get involved in politics privately, at least until the consolidation of Brazil's new democracy in the 1990s.

With U.S. assistance, the Brazilian military created an elite military academy after World War II. This was the Escola Superior de Guerra (ESG), or Superior War College, which came to play an influential role in the Brazilian military and elite politics in general. Its faculty developed what came to be known as the National Security Doctrine in the 1950s. This doctrine was then taught to students, who were not only high-ranking military officers but also selected senior civilian officials. Essentially, it envisioned national security as including not just protection from foreign

aggression but also economic development and prevention of domestic insurrection. At the height of the Cold War, the ESG military intellectuals saw domestic communist insurrection as much more of a threat than external aggression from another state. They also argued that strong economic development was essential to national security, as it would provide the economic basis on which overall national strength would depend. They came to distinguish between "national" policies, meaning their own doctrine of what was essential for national well-being, and "government" policies, meaning the policies of the particular government of the day. Ultimately, the ESG's National Security Doctrine laid the intellectual roots for the 1964 coup and subsequent military regime.

In 1961, President Jânio Quadros abruptly resigned and was succeeded by his vice president, João Goulart. From the start, elements of the military opposed Goulart. He was a leftist who seemed intent on instituting such major reforms in Brazil's very unequal society as strengthening labor unions, pursuing land redistribution, and providing greater benefits to the urban working classes. Goulart clashed with both the military elite and the National Congress, which was controlled by more conservative politicians. Some military officers tried unsuccessfully to prevent him from taking office in the first place, but others retained their loyalty to the legal institution of presidential succession. Then, as Goulart failed to get his policies passed through the National Congress and faced growing opposition within the military, he became more populist. He requested, but did not receive, extraordinary powers from the National Congress to enact his reforms. To gain greater military loyalty, he replaced several senior officers who opposed him with others who were more supportive, thus dividing the military itself. Finally, in March 1964, he dramatically called for fundamental reforms that the conservative elite, both civilian and military, opposed. When junior navy officers revolted against their superiors, demanding the right to unionize, Goulart supported them.

The night after Goulart proclaimed his support for the naval officers, the military moved to take over the reins of government in a largely bloodless coup it dubbed the "Revolution." The regime it subsequently created was strongly institutionalized and based heavily on the National Security Doctrine. It did attempt to keep a veneer of civilian rule by preserving most of the prior constitution, but it also issued Institutional Acts, which gave the military president the power to overrule the legislature and revoked many basic rights. Eventually, the party system was restricted to two tightly controlled parties, one that supported the regime and one that was allowed to oppose it within strict limits. When popular opposition from students, workers, and the rural poor arose, the military leadership did not hesitate to use force against them. Brazil's military government may have been far less brutal than many in Latin America at the time, but it nonetheless jailed and killed opponents when necessary.

Several explanations for the 1964 coup have been put forward. The best known is Guillermo O'Donnell's concept of the bureaucratic-authoritarian state. O'Donnell (1979) argued that the coup came about because of economic contradictions that the democratic government could not resolve. If capitalist industrialization was to continue, it required a repressive government to force it on an increasingly restless population. Brazil's economic development model could advance no further than the industrialization that had occurred up to that point. Populism, the dominant way of mobilizing support in Brazil's democracy, had produced a growing working class that demanded a greater share of the benefits of economic growth, and the elite realized that this would reduce the resources available for further investment. Further development would require the "deepening" of industrialization via investment in heavier industry, and that in turn would require a repression of wages. An elected government could not achieve a repression of working-class wages, so the military stepped in, under the auspices of its National Security Doctrine, to take the necessary steps.

IN CONTEXT

MILITARY COUPS IN LATIN AMERICA BY DECADE

Brazil's military coups and regimes (1930–1945 and 1964–1985) were part of a broader trend of coups and military rule in the region.

Of the thirty-three countries in the region,

- eight had a military coup in the 1930s.
- four had a military coup in the 1940s.
- seven had a military coup in the 1950s.
- five had a military coup in the 1960s.
- seven had a military coup in the 1970s.
- three had a military coup in the 1980s.
- four had a military coup in the 1990s.
- two had a military coup in the 2000s.

Source: Political Handbook of the World 2011. Washington, DC: CQ Press, 2011.

Other analysts, however, have noted that the coup itself was caused just as much by Goulart's direct threat to the military hierarchy. By removing military officers who opposed him, and especially by supporting junior officers who wanted to unionize, Goulart was interfering with the autonomy of the military itself, or so a number of officers believed. Riordan Roett, another prominent scholar of Brazil, contended that the military remained divided over Goulart's economic policies but ultimately united in opposition to him because of what the leadership perceived as his threatening behavior toward both the autonomy of the military and the National Congress (1978). It is entirely possible, of course, that these two sets of factors (economic pressures plus threats to the autonomy of the military and the National Congress) dovetailed, coming together to give the military the incentive and justification to intervene and set Brazilian politics on a fundamentally different course.

IN CONTEXT

MILITARY COUPS IN AFRICA BY DECADE

Nigeria's history of military coups and regimes from the 1960s into the 1990s was part of Africa's continuing pattern of coups and military rule in the region. Coups in the first decade of the twenty-first century were down 43 percent from the average of twenty-one coups per decade from the 1960s to the 1990s.

Of the fifty countries in the region, there were

- one military coup in the 1950s.
- twenty-three military coups in the 1960s.
- twenty-four military coups in the 1970s.
- eighteen military coups in the 1980s.
- nineteen military coups in the 1990s.
- nine military coups in the 2000s.

Source: George K. Kieh and Pita O. Agbese. *The Military and Politics in Africa: From Engagement to Democratic and Constitutional Control.* Aldershot: Ashgate, 2002. Updated by the authors.

Nigeria's military is very different from Brazil's because it is far weaker as an institution. Nevertheless, Nigeria's history of regime changes once again demonstrates the difficulty of understanding the motives for military coups. The country has had six successful coups (see the timeline in chapter 8) and at least two failed coup attempts. Without exception, each of the military leaders came to power promising to serve only in a "corrective" capacity to end corruption, restore order, and revive the economy before handing power back to elected civilians. In reality, the military ruled for two very long periods (1966–1979 and 1983–1999) under multiple leaders and returned the country to democratic rule only after much domestic and international pressure, as we detail later in this chapter. Analysts have identified both societal and individual motives behind the actions of Nigeria's military. We focus here

primarily on two of the six coups, those that overthrew democratic governments.

The first two military interventions happened six months apart in 1966. Nigeria's First Republic, its initial postcolonial democracy, had very weak institutions and grew increasingly chaotic from independence in 1960 until 1966. The democratic government and subsequent military governments were riven by increasingly intense ethnic rivalries. Numerical advantage gave the northern region control of the government at independence, in coalition with the main party of the eastern region. The government manipulated the 1964 national election and the 1965 election in the western region to ensure victory for itself and its allies. The situation in the western region became violent, as westerners felt the northern-dominated national government had stolen control of their regional government. By late 1965, the national government had lost effective control of the western region, and general lawlessness was spreading throughout the country.

In January 1966, five army majors led a rebellion in an attempt to overthrow what they saw as an illegitimate national government. The coup attempt was only partially successful, but it led the head of the army, Gen. Johnson T. U. Aguiyi-Ironsi, to step in as the new national leader. Both he and four of the five majors who attempted the coup were ethnic Igbos from the eastern region, and in carrying out the coup, they killed several important northern and western political and military figures but no eastern ones. Ironsi abolished all parties and ethnic associations, and he soon declared the end of Nigeria's fractured federalism, instead creating a unitary state in an attempt to bring the nation together. Many analysts viewed Ironsi as genuinely interested in national well-being, but northerners saw the coup and Ironsi's elimination of federalism as an attempt by the eastern, Igbo military elite to centralize all power for themselves. Certainly, easterners appeared to be at the core of the new regime.

Six months later, the northerners responded with a countercoup that brought Army

Chief of Staff Yakubu Gowon to power. Gowon himself was from the Middle Belt in the center of the country and therefore technically not part of any of the major ethnic regions. He was backed, however, by northern military leaders who were intent on removing what they saw as an "Igbo" government. Gowon re-created a federal system, with twelve states replacing the former three regions, and restored the regional power sharing represented by federalism. Eastern military leaders rebelled, proclaiming themselves the leaders of the independent Republic of Biafra. A three-year civil war ensued. Gowon received much credit for successfully ending the conflict and helping reconcile the nation afterward. As all of Nigeria's military leaders would do, he had from the start promised a return to democracy. By the mid-1970s, however, he and the military governors of the states were seen as increasingly corrupt, stealing from Nigeria's rapidly growing oil revenues and continually delaying the promised return to democracy. Ultimately, he was overthrown by other northerners who attempted to reduce corruption and did return the country to democracy in 1979.

That democracy would last until 1983, and in many ways, the events of that year can be seen as a repeat of those of 1965, though without the same ethnic conflict. The Second Republic government that was elected in 1979 and reelected in 1983 was again dominated by officials from the northern part of the country, and by 1983 it was both corrupt and malfeasant. Nigeria's economy was declining as the level of corruption seemed to be skyrocketing. Consequently, the 1983 election in which incumbent president Shehu Shagari was reelected was widely seen as fraudulent, though neither as fraudulent nor as violent as the 1964 and 1965 elections.

The coup weeks later came with little opposition. At first glance, one could say that the coup leaders were motivated by the weakness and chaos of the civilian government and provoked by the weakness of political institutions. William Graf, a leading scholar of the era, argued differently (1988). In contrast to 1966, the coup leaders were not junior officers but rather the top military officials in the country, primarily from the north. This means that the coup was not ethnically motivated, in that both the perpetrators and the main victims were northerners. Graf went on to say that instead, the main motivation for the coup was the desire of top officers to maintain their access to government resources and preserve the social status quo. He suggested that the top military officers took control because they saw the corruption of the civilian elite as excessive. These officers believed that corruption threatened to provoke an uprising within the military and perhaps within the broader society. Indeed, rumors did abound that junior officers, with a more radical interest in fundamentally changing the Nigerian regime, were about to stage a coup.

The new regime under Gen. Muhammadu Buhari waged a harsh "War Against Indiscipline" in which many civilian political elites were convicted on fraud charges. By 1985, the northern military elite saw Buhari's campaign as pressing too hard and removing essential leadership from all levels of government, and another countercoup brought Army Chief of Staff Gen. Ibrahim Babangida to power. Power remained, however, in northern hands, among what Nigerians refer to as the "Kaduna mafia" (see chapter 8).

Nigeria's two coups that directly overthrew democratic rule can be explained by societal factors, which include the weakness of prior political institutions and increasing political and economic chaos. In both cases, the argument goes that the military stepped in to restore order in a situation in which stable democracy no longer really existed. However, the leaders of the coups had other motives, and both faced subsequent countercoups. These brought to power northern military leaders who ruled for extended periods during which corruption grew and institutions weakened, as we discussed in chapter 8. Personal, ethnic, and regional interests in gaining power and resources seem at least as likely an explanation of the coups as the political problems the military allegedly stepped in to resolve.

In both Brazil and Nigeria, understanding the precise motives for coups is difficult because while all coup leaders claim to intervene in the national interest, the subsequent governments, especially in the case of Nigeria, belie those intentions. Therefore, motives other than protecting the national interest seem at least equally plausible. The biggest difference between the two countries, as we argued in chapter 8, is the level of institutionalization of their militaries. Brazil's more institutionalized military entered politics with a clear ideology and was a strong enough institution to implement its vision, for better or worse, and it preserved some very limited civilian political participation in the process. Nigeria's far less institutionalized military reflected the country's ethnic and class conflicts, and it ruled in a far less institutionalized manner that ultimately undermined Nigeria's political institutions. It also engaged in at least as much corruption as the civilian officials it overthrew.

REVOLUTION

Military coups change governments and often regimes, while revolutions change the entire social order. Revolutions are rare and profound events that mark major turning points in the life of not only the countries in which they occur but often world history. On the continent of Africa alone there have been more than eighty military coups since 1960, whereas only a handful of revolutions have occurred anywhere in the world.

As with so many terms in political science, scholars have debated endlessly how to define *revolution*. The important point for our purposes is to distinguish revolutions from other forms of regime change. We therefore define a **revolution** as a relatively rapid transformation of the political system and social structure; it results from the overthrow of the prior regime by mass participation in extra-legal political action that is often, but not always, violent. The major revolutions in the modern era have happened in France (1789), Russia (1917), China (1911–1949), Cuba (1959), Nicaragua (1979), Iran (1979), and the Eastern European satellite states of the Soviet Union—Bulgaria, Czechoslovakia, East Germany, Hungary, Poland, and Romania (1989–1990). More recently, the regime changes in Tunisia and Egypt have often been referred to as revolutions. Whether they are or not, though, will depend on their long-term outcomes. They clearly included widespread popular participation in extra-legal activity, some violence, and major regime change. Whether they will fundamentally change the social structure of the countries, though, remains uncertain.

revolution: A relatively rapid transformation of the political system and social structure that results from the overthrow of the prior regime by mass participation in extra-legal political action, which is often (but not always) violent

Types of Revolution

Political scientists distinguish among revolutions in several ways. One way is to classify them by the ideologies that inspire them: the liberal revolution of France, the communist revolutions of Russia and China, and the Islamic revolution of Iran. These ideological differences would seem to be crucial, yet most scholars of revolution argue just the opposite, that the ideological motivations and pronouncements of key leaders do not explain very much about revolutions. Typically, only the top leadership thoroughly understands and believes in the ideology in whose name the revolution is fought. Many participants have other motivations for joining the revolution, and specific political circumstances must exist for revolutions to succeed.

Ideology helps more to explain the outcomes of revolutions in that the subsequent regimes, as we discussed in chapter 3, arise out of the ideological commitments of the revolutionary leadership. However, ideology usually does not tell us much about why the revolutions happened in the first place.

A common way that scholars distinguish among revolutions is to classify them as either **revolutions from above** or **revolutions from below**. The classic revolutions before the 1980s are the main cases on which theories of revolution are based, and these are all revolutions from below; that is, in each the mass uprising of the populace to overthrow the government was a central part of the process. Some scholars argue that the revolutions to end communism in Eastern Europe, in contrast, were primarily revolutions from above (Sanderson 2005). The end of communism was certainly a revolution in the sense that the fundamental social and economic structures of societies were transformed from communist to capitalist. Political changes were equally dramatic, though they varied more widely. Some countries created fully democratic regimes while others created new forms of authoritarian rule, though none of the new regimes were communist. While popular pressure was certainly involved in the process, communism fell in most countries primarily because the political elite within the system abandoned it, choosing instead to create new systems. The outcomes were often negotiated among political elites, each with the backing of a segment of the populace. In contrast to revolutions from below, massive and violent uprisings usually did not occur and were not necessary, and except for the ill-fated Soviet coup attempt of August 1991, the old regime was not able to strike back violently against the revolutionary forces. These revolutions from above happened relatively peacefully and quickly. Several of them also produced liberal democracy, an outcome that no revolution from below has yet to achieve. We explore Russia's transition to democracy (and its more recent movement to semi-authoritarian rule) in the section below on democratization.

revolutions from above: Revolutions in which the outcomes are negotiated among political elites, each with the backing of a segment of the populace

revolutions from below: Revolutions in which a mass uprising of the populace to overthrow the government plays a central role

Why Do Revolutions Happen?

As with military coups, comparativists have developed several theories to explain why revolutions occur and their likely outcomes. These theories focus on the economic structure of the old regime, psychological theories of motivation to revolt, the resources and organization of the revolutionary movements, the structure and weakness of the old state institutions, and the process of modernization. The first theorist of revolution in the modern era was probably Karl Marx. As we explained briefly in chapter 3, Marx believed that social revolution was the necessary transition from one mode of production and society to another and that the most important transition would be from capitalism to communism. Therefore, he thought the major revolutions of the future would be communist and would happen first in the wealthiest, most advanced capitalist countries. Events would show that he was clearly wrong about where, and therefore why, revolutions would occur. Most major revolutions from below since Marx's death have been communist inspired, but they have not happened in wealthy capitalist societies or democracies. Instead they have occurred in relatively poor countries with authoritarian regimes, most notably in Russia and China. On the other hand, most revolutions from above have not been inspired by communism but instead by the desire to put an end to communism.

More recent scholars have used some of Marx's concepts to try to explain contemporary revolution, but they have focused mainly on the economic structure in rural areas and its effects on peasant farmers. Jeffery Paige, for instance, argued that sharecropping, a particular type of agrarian economic system, tended to produce

Was the American Revolution Really a Revolution?

The careful reader might note that we did not include the United States in our list of countries where major revolutions have occurred. This may come as a surprise to American students who are accustomed to thinking of the "American Revolution" as a pivotal historical event. It certainly was that, but whether it was a revolution in the sense that comparativists use the term has been subject to extensive debate among political scientists and historians. Barrington Moore (1966) argued that the real revolution in the United States was the Civil War, which ended slavery as an economic system and established the dominance of industrial capitalism. In the slaveholding states in particular, this was the conflict that was the true social revolution. The crux of the debate is about whether the American war for independence and the founding of a new republic fundamentally transformed not just political institutions but society as a whole. It was clearly the first nationalist war to throw off the yoke of colonial rule. It also clearly established an unprecedented republic based on liberal ideals that was a crucial milepost on the long road to liberal democracy (though many of its ideals, such as the assertion that "All men are created equal," were far from perfectly implemented). But was it a true revolution?

Our definition of the term *revolution* follows conventional usage, which includes not just political change but also fundamental social change. Scholars have long argued that the American War of Independence did not really do this. It was led primarily by the colonial elite, who did not envision or implement a major redistribution of wealth. Granted, they eliminated British rule and created a new republic based on the republican ideal of equality of all citizens, but they defined citizens very consciously and deliberately as white male property owners. Wealth was actually distributed less equally after the war than it had been before, and, arguably, slavery was more entrenched (Wood 1992). Not only was slavery codified in the Constitution ratified in 1787, but it enjoyed a period of great expansion for several more decades. Indeed, the Constitution as a whole can be seen in part as an effort to limit the effects of egalitarianism in that it created a powerful Supreme Court to protect individual rights (including, of course, property rights) from majority tyranny, an indirectly elected Senate to represent state governments rather than citizens, and an indirectly elected president with the power to veto laws passed by the directly elected House of Representatives.

The chief opponent of this view is historian Gordon Wood, who put forth his arguments in his 1992 Pulitzer Prize–winning book, *The Radicalism of the American Revolution.* Wood argued that the American Revolution "was as radical and as revolutionary as any in history"

peasant involvement in revolution, whereas other economic systems produced more conservative peasant political participation (1975). Others have focused on motivations for participation in revolution from the perspective of social-psychological theories, which examine individual feelings. James Davies (1962) argued that revolution occurs at periods of rising expectations: people don't revolt when they are at their lowest point but rather when things have started to get better and they want more. Ted Robert Gurr (1970) contended that relative deprivation explains revolution because people revolt when they feel deprived relative to what they believe they deserve. All these theories focus on the motivations of the populace to participate.

(5). Though he readily conceded most of the points mentioned above, he argued that the egalitarian ideals of republicanism created not just a political but also a social and cultural revolution during and after the war. Republican thought did not deny the existence of all forms of superiority but instead argued that superiority should not come from birth but from talent and reason. Some men (women were not included) would rise to the top as leaders of the new society based on their abilities, their hard work, and the willingness of others to elect them to positions of leadership. These individuals would have to be not only white men but also property owners who had the independence to speak and act on their convictions. Government was thereby to serve the public interest in a way that a monarchy never did or could.

This egalitarian ideal spread throughout society, Wood contended, leading to further questions about the prerogatives of rank and privilege. He noted numerous changes to social and cultural norms, such as pressure to end many private clubs, the taking of the titles "Mr." and "Mrs." that were previously reserved for the landed gentry, and the shift from reserving the front pews in churches for select families in perpetuity to selling rights to those pews to the highest bidders. As the latter suggests, the revolution caused commerce to expand rapidly as well; wealth became even more unequally distributed, but many new men gained it. This revolution of ideas and in the way men treated other men helped to create a new society never before seen in which inherited status was considered illegitimate and leadership and high status were to be based solely on merit and election.

In the long term, the American Revolution clearly had a profound effect, especially due to its notion of equal citizenship. As Wood rightly noted, its ramifications went far beyond what its original Founders intended. But most of the political and social elite before the War of Independence remained in that position after the war, with the biggest exception being the significant number of Loyalists who emigrated either to Canada or Britain. As for the grand ideals of equality, they applied only within the very restricted realm of white, male property owners for another generation. As Crane Brinton (1965) noted in his classic study of revolutions, the American Revolution (which he included as one of his cases) is also quite peculiar in its evolution and result: no reign of terror occurred, as is so common in revolutions, and an authoritarian state did not ultimately result. This isn't to say that it's a bad thing that these events didn't happen, but their absence, along with the other points above, raises questions about whether the first war of independence against European colonialism was also a revolution.

A later school of thought puts forth the idea that while motivation is important, it alone cannot explain why some revolutions are successful while others are not. Adequate resources in the hands of revolutionary groups or a weak and therefore vulnerable state, or both, are also necessary conditions for successful revolutions. Charles Tilly (1978) suggested that the directly political dimension of a potentially revolutionary situation is important because not only must there be grievances against the old regime, but also an organization must arise to mobilize those grievances into a mass movement with sufficient resources to challenge the regime. Theda Skocpol (1979) noted that a crucial ingredient for successful revolutions is a state in crisis, often one that has been weakened by international events. She

terrorism:
Political violence targeted at civilian noncombatants

What about Terrorism?

Revolutions and coups bring to mind an image of armed men taking over a state, perhaps killing innocent civilians in the process. A more contemporary image of politically instigated violence is terrorism. An important question in the new millennium is the difference, if any, between revolution and terrorism. Is a revolutionary a terrorist and vice versa? Is terrorist just a new term for a revolutionary? Both revolution and terrorism can be forms of what is today termed **political violence**, the use of violence by nonstate actors for political ends. We include the term nonstate in this definition simply to distinguish political violence from war or other violent efforts by states to secure their sovereignty or expand their power. We make no assumption or argument here about the ethical superiority or justification of political violence over war or vice versa, but we think it is useful to distinguish them analytically.

Despite the fact that they both involve political violence, revolutions and terrorism have fundamental differences. The most important distinction is between ends and means. Successful revolutions result in a fundamental transformation of a society. They are usually violent, but not always. Their end, or goal, distinguishes them from other types of political movements or political violence. **Terrorism**, on the other hand, is a means. It can be defined quite simply as political violence targeted at civilian noncombatants. Some revolutionaries have certainly used terrorism and some terrorists have been revolutionaries, but not all.

Revolutionaries by definition seek to overthrow an existing state. On the other hand, leading scholar of terrorism Martha Crenshaw (1981) long ago noted that terrorists usually have different purposes. The most common goal of an act of terrorism is to influence a broader audience, not the actual target of the violence. Revolutionaries aim at the state and attempt to overthrow it. Terrorists generally try to avoid the state and make no effort to overthrow it; they typically engage in acts of terrorism, whatever their long-term political goals, to inflict violence without directly confronting the state.

Some terrorists may indeed pursue revolutionary aims, but many do not. Since 2001, the primary form of terrorism in the news is connected with radical Islamists, but many political groups, such as the Irish Republican Army (IRA) in Northern Ireland, have engaged in terrorism

political violence:
The use of violence by nonstate actors for political ends

pointed to the effects of World War I on Russia as an example. A revolution can only happen where a state faces a severe crisis and lacks the resources to respond and where a mass uprising is in process. This conjunction of events, she argued, explains the major revolutions of the past as well as the infrequent outbreak of revolutions today and their continued unlikelihood in the future.

A long-standing school of thought argues that revolutions are part of the modernization process. Samuel Huntingon (1968) saw them as being most likely to occur after some level of economic development has raised popular expectations and political demands, but state institutions have not developed adequately to respond to them. Steven Pincus (2007) argued more narrowly that state modernization is the key: revolutions are most likely when the old regime is attempting to modernize the state, which brings new groups into contact with the state and expands the state's activities. If, in this process, it becomes apparent that the state may lack a full monopoly on the use of violence, revolutionary leaders will try to take advantage of the situation. Modernization theories clearly suggest that revolutions are a product of particular historical processes, which could explain their declining frequency in

with nationalist, secessionist, or other quite secular aims that involve neither religious zealotry nor social revolution. Indeed, it is debatable how revolutionary the goals of al-Qaida and related groups are. They certainly seem to seek the establishment of a new type of society, though it is unclear how much they wish to take over existing states. Much of their ideology centers on the purification of the Islamic *umma,* the broad, transnational Muslim religious community. Some groups, such as the Taliban in Afghanistan, seem willing to mostly ignore the state rather than build a new one once they have destroyed the old. This is in marked contrast to social revolutionaries, whose primary aim after the revolution typically is to build a new state. When an Islamist extremist attacks a Western target, it is often not completely clear whether he or she seeks to undermine the existing social order (in Western or Islamic countries), to force the West (especially the United States) to change its foreign policy, or to encourage religious reform within existing Islamic societies. The aims of such an extremist may or may not be "revolutionary" in the sense of how the term is used in comparative politics.

Comparativists and others have used a wide array of theories to try to explain terrorism and particularly the motivation behind it. This debate draws on many of the ideas used previously to explain revolutions or social movements (see chapter 7). Scholars have argued that motivation for terrorism comes from psychological sources, relative deprivation or other types of alienation, structural inequalities, charismatic leaders, or ideological (including religious) beliefs. Others note that, like revolutions or social movements, terrorism requires resources and political opportunities to actually happen, regardless of individual motivations.

Terrorism, a concept that has been around for two hundred years, has become a "hot" new topic in international politics, but methods of understanding it have largely been based on long-standing theories in comparative politics. This reasoning, as well as the clear distinction between terrorism as a means and revolution as an end, leads many scholars to think of both revolution and terrorism in the context of regime change rather than as forms of political violence, regardless of their ultimate goals.

the last several decades. Revolutions may also be less frequent in the future because in the past they overthrew authoritarian regimes; the spread of democracy since the 1970s may mean that revolutions will be much less likely.

What Are the Results of Revolution?

Aside from some of the former communist countries of Eastern Europe, the general outcome of revolution has been fairly consistent: authoritarian rule. Postrevolutionary governments have taken various forms, based in part on the ideological beliefs of their revolutionary leaders, but none has become an enduring democracy directly after the revolution. This was true even in France where many of the revolution's leaders were liberals.

Scholars account for these outcomes by pointing out the extremely difficult political circumstances facing postrevolutionary governments. The entire regime and social structure has been overthrown, so new ones must be created. Massive violence outside the control of the state is at the heart of most revolutions, and any new regime must re-create the state's monopoly on the use of force. Postrevolutionary societies are almost by definition deeply divided along ideological lines; the new leadership is committed to a particular ideological blueprint of what the new regime and society should look like, while many followers do not fully share this commitment. All of these factors lead postrevolutionary leaders to brook little dissent and to view almost any opposition as a threat to the revolution. As our cases below demonstrate, the immediate postrevolutionary situation often includes a diversity of viewpoints, but those who do not share the vision of the key leadership are quickly eliminated, and with them go the prospects for democracy, at least in the short to medium term.

The exceptions to this rule are some of the postcommunist revolutions that were revolutions from above (for example, those that occurred in the Czech Republic, Hungary, and Poland). These led to countries becoming electoral democracies. The complete collapse of communism in the early 1990s led to a widespread perception in Eastern Europe that communist regimes were illegitimate; thus, postrevolutionary divisions in these cases were not nearly as great as in classic revolutions. The populaces were also not as mobilized, and the revolutions from above were largely nonviolent. All of these elements made the compromises necessary for democracy more possible, though the failure to establish democracy in some of the postcommunist countries, including parts of Yugoslavia, Romania, and the Central Asian republics, indicates that a democratic outcome was by no means guaranteed (Sanderson 2005).

CASE STUDY

Revolution: China and Iran

- Multifaceted but similar causes of revolution
- Relative deprivation and a weakened state in both cases
- More united political organization produces more unified postrevolutionary regime in China

While political scientists have long debated the causes of revolutions, looking at actual revolutions suggests that they cannot be explained by any single factor. Several factors came together simultaneously to create the conditions for revolution in our case studies, and this perhaps explains why revolutions have been such rare events. The outcomes of these revolutions were similar in that they produced authoritarian regimes, but these regimes are quite distinct because they are based on the differing ideologies of the revolutionary leaders.

The revolution in China in 1949 resulted from a combination of a sense of relative deprivation on the part of the peasant majority, the creation of a political organization (the Communist Party) that could mobilize popular discontent, and an extremely weak state. The first Chinese revolution, which was largely a revolution from above, occurred in 1911 when the ancient empire finally fell (see chapter 2 for more details on this period). Since the Opium Wars of the mid-nineteenth century, the Chinese empire had been in decline. The peasantry, which constituted the great majority of the population, had long-standing grievances and a tradition of revolting against local landlords and other elites who became too repressive. During the late nineteenth and early twentieth centuries, though, the peasantry faced greater impoverishment than usual as the empire declined and lost control of much of its territory to

Japanese and Western interests. A younger generation of elites increasingly questioned the traditions of and justifications for the old empire, given its inability to modernize Chinese society or reverse the country's decline. In the first decade of the twentieth century, the Empress Dowager Cixi tried to respond to this growing disenchantment and rebellion with reforms. These included the creation of the first consultative assembly, which was a quasi-legislature, and the elimination of the Confucian system of government employment that was mostly restricted to the elite. Reformers, however, wanted far more radical change, and many wholly rejected Confucian traditions and argued for a Western and liberal society. Young military leaders in the provinces shared these sentiments and were the local leaders of the 1911 rebellion that created Sun Yat-sen's nationalist Republic of China.

The new republic failed to establish a democracy or hold the country together; regional warlords took over provinces and preyed on the local population while battling each other for territory. The plight of the peasantry only got worse. Chiang Kai-shek managed to reunite the country in 1927, but under a repressive authoritarian regime. A new generation of people educated in the post-Confucian era still clamored for change inspired by Western models, not only liberal ones but also communist. Members of the same young, educated elite who had championed nationalism and liberalism were the initial adherents of communism, with support from the newly established Soviet Union. The Communist Party became the principle military and political rival to the Nationalists in the 1920s. During the famous Long March (1934–1935), Mao Zedong gained control of the party and began implementing his major revision of Marxist revolutionary doctrine by focusing on the peasantry as a potentially revolutionary group.

At the end of the Long March, the Communists established themselves in Yenan in northern China, creating in effect a separate state from that of the Nationalists in Beijing. They began implementing their new society,

This 1934 photo shows Chou En Lai, one of Mao Zedong's chief lieutenants who helped lead the Long March of 1934–1935. This event contributed to the victory of Mao's Communist Party in China's revolution in 1949. Chou, like Mao's successor Deng Xiaoping, came to represent "moderates" in the revolutionary government, often working against some of Mao's more radical policies.

Credit: AP Photo

including moderate land redistribution, careful distribution of consumer goods to ensure the survival of as many people as possible in difficult circumstances, and reduction of the usurious interest rates that peasants paid to landlords. For the first time in a century, a significant segment of rural Chinese society saw their situation in life at least stabilize, if not improve, and they became the backbone of Communist Party support. Mao also built up the party in Yenan, welcoming intellectuals, elites, and peasants. It became the central authority in the "liberated" territory, an early version of the state he would create after 1949. The Communists' guerrilla tactics also proved effective against the Japanese occupiers during World War II and popular with the Chinese public, giving the Communists the mantle of defenders of the beleaguered nation.

After World War II, the final phase of the revolution broke out: a four-year civil war that the Communists won based on expanding support from the peasantry and use of effective guerrilla tactics against better-armed, Western-supported Nationalist forces. Communist victory ushered in a new state that completely changed Chinese society; a full social revolution from below had occurred. And like other such revolutions, it resulted in an authoritarian state. Those who had supported the revolution but were not Communists, and even Communists who argued for alternatives to Mao's preferred policies, were quickly eliminated, making the People's Republic of China a full-scale dictatorship.

The 1949 revolution certainly was based on grievances among the peasantry, including their disillusionment at seeing the 1911 revolution from above make their lives worse instead of better. But success also required political resources—a mechanism through which local peasant grievances and revolts could be channeled into a broader movement—and the Communist Party became that mechanism. It successfully overthrew a regime that had been weak from its inception in 1911 and had been weakened further by its humiliation at the hands of the Japanese in World War II. Deprivation, state weakness, and political mobilization had to combine to produce the Chinese revolution.

The Iranian revolution of 1979 that created the Islamic Republic was in stark contrast to the Chinese Communist revolution in terms of ideology, but it emerged from roughly similar circumstances. A sense of relative deprivation among many segments of the population despite a growing economy, a state weakened by at least the perception of a loss of international (especially U.S.) support, and a religious movement whose leader had become the symbol of revolution combined to produce Iran's revolution. The movement, though symbolically led by the Ayatollah Khomeini, was not united under one organization like the Chinese Communist Party. After the revolution, therefore, numerous groups with differing ideologies competed for power. Khomeini and his religious followers simply proved to be the most popular and were able to outmaneuver other groups to assume complete control during the first year of the new government.

The shah of Iran's government had seemed to be a classic case of a modernizing authoritarian regime during the 1960s and 1970s. The shah consciously sought to modernize society through his "White Revolution" by encouraging foreign investment, greater mechanization of agriculture, access to higher education, and secularism. Iran seemed to be taking its place among the modern nations of the world. The shah's policies, however, did not benefit everyone equally. Instead they favored larger over smaller enterprises, foreign over domestic investors, and urban over rural interests. Therefore, while economic growth and personal incomes rose noticeably on average, what the poor saw was the elite's conspicuous consumption, which they compared to their own very meager gains. In rural areas, peasant farmers and nomadic pastoralists often lost land and income, and these trends accelerated after the 1973 quadrupling of world oil prices. This event brought Iran a glut of wealth but skewed its distribution even further toward the elite. It also caused significant inflation, which eroded the purchasing power of the poor. The elite who benefited became increasingly conspicuous consumers and thus became a target of resentment for the rest of society. Modernization of agriculture drove rural migrants to the cities, and there they joined the long-standing *bazaari* groups (petty traders in Iran's traditional bazaars). *Bazaaris* felt threatened by modernization as well, as the shah encouraged Western shops and banks to open in Iran to cater to the growing urban middle class, thus reducing the *bazaaris'* market opportunities (Clawson and Rubin 2005).

The *bazaaris* and recent urban migrants, along with students and workers, became key supporters of the revolution. Opposition to the shah had survived underground ever since the brief political liberalization under Mohammad Mosaddeq in the early 1950s (see chapter 2). Despite brutal and often effective repression at the hands of the shah's secret police, two guerrilla groups survived: the Fedayin and the Mujahedin. By the 1970s, both groups were divided along ideological lines among nationalists who wanted greater democracy, Marxists, and religious groups. While students gave much of their support to Marxists, the *bazaaris* saw their trade as part of Islamic traditional practice and tended to support religious leaders. Secular intellectuals wrote anonymous letters and circulated pamphlets calling for the overthrow of the shah. The Islamic clergy, the *ulema,* opposed the shah's Westernization policies as a threat to Islam. Exiled radical cleric Ayatollah Khomeini increasingly became the chief symbol of opposition to the regime, and even though the opposition groups supported varying ideologies, they all united in opposition to the shah.

A perception that the shah's regime was weak was a crucial element in igniting the actual revolution. U.S. president Jimmy Carter enunciated a new foreign policy based on human rights and noted the shah's regime as one that did not adequately protect such rights. While Carter nonetheless continued to support the shah, the mere mention of U.S. criticism was enough to make some opposition leaders believe that the United States would not support the shah if the people rose up against him. The United States had supported the regime for decades, including the regime's crushing of an attempt at greater freedoms under Mosaddeq in the 1950s, so even the hint of U.S. willingness to consider regime change inspired the opposition to act. In January 1978, the government wrote a newspaper article attacking Khomeini. The following day, theology students responded by organizing a large demonstration in the holy city of Qom. The shah's police responded with violence, and at least seventy people were killed. The religious opposition, joined by students and the *bazaaris*, then used the traditional mourning gatherings for those killed to organize greater demonstrations, and the government could not disrupt these proceedings due to religious strictures. By September 1978, a demonstration of more than a million people took place in Tehran, and the shah once again reacted with the use of force: more than 500 people were killed. The government declared martial law shortly afterward, shutting down universities and newspapers. This only led to greater opposition as the urban working class joined the movement by organizing strikes, including one in the country's crucial oil sector.

By December, the shah had tried to respond to the rising revolt by replacing his prime minister with one seen as more sympathetic to reforms, but this change was not nearly enough to satisfy the growing opposition. In January 1979, the new prime minister managed to get the shah to leave office "temporarily" and began dismantling his hated secret police. The opposition, though, demanded Khomeini's return from exile, a demand the government continued to resist until finally giving in on February 1. Khomeini immediately declared one of his supporters the "real Prime Minister," a claim the government rejected. The guerrilla groups and students mobilized their followers to invade prisons, police stations, and military bases on February 10 and 11 to take them over in the name of the revolution. After two bloody days in which hundreds more people were killed, the revolutionaries succeeded in gaining power.

Unlike the Chinese revolution, however, no single political organization had control of the movement. Khomeini was the charismatic and symbolic leader but one who also pledged to work with other forces, starting with his appointment of a secular prime minister and support for a secular president. The revolutionary forces that came to power included religious groups that followed Khomeini, secular liberal nationalists who argued for democracy, and Marxists of various sorts. Over the course of the first year, Khomeini systematically put his supporters in charge of key institutions and called for an early referendum on the creation of an Islamic republic. The population overwhelming approved this move, and the new constitution discussed in chapter 8 was put in place. Over the next few years, Khomeini and his religious supporters increasingly repressed the other factions of the revolutionary movement to take firm control and create Iran's authoritarian theocracy.

CASE SUMMARY

The revolutions in China and Iran both came out of societies in which a sense of relative deprivation was widespread and the state had been noticeably weakened. The Chinese people had seen massive social dislocation and economic decline for at least fifty years prior to the revolution, while Iranians had witnessed a growing economy that precipitated growing inequality. Both felt a sense of deprivation relative to what they thought they deserved. Both states were weakened and appeared vulnerable, though in China's case the decline of the state was much more severe and included full-scale collapse and civil war. The political organization that took advantage of the revolutionary opportunity in China was much more united and organized than the mix of forces that overthrew the shah, resulting in a more united, but also more ruthless, postrevolutionary regime in China.

DEMOCRATIZATION

In 1972, Freedom House, a nongovernmental organization (NGO) that analyzes the level of political and civil rights in countries around the world, classified forty-four countries as "free," meaning that they are functioning liberal democracies. In 1990, the number of "free" countries rose to sixty-one, and in 2009 it had grown to eighty-nine. The third wave of democratization (the first two waves having followed each of the world wars) was a dramatic process. It included the "People Power" movement that overthrew the corrupt and brutal Philippine dictator Ferdinand Marcos, the fall of the Berlin Wall, and the election of Nelson Mandela in South Africa. It seemed that the world's people were arising en masse to demand democratic rights. Without a doubt, democracy expanded, but the image of global mass rebellion overwhelming dictators and establishing lasting democracy was, alas, overly simplistic. Furthermore, in the new millennium, progress has slowed or even been reversed. Freedom House measured an overall drop in global levels of freedom for the fourth consecutive year in 2010; this represents the longest period of continuous decline in the forty-year history of its index. Comparativists have tried to understand the expansion of democracy and its more recent stagnation by asking why countries become democratic, how they become democratic, what obstacles they face, how democratic they are, how likely they are to stay democratic, and how they can become more democratic.

Prior to the third wave, all but a handful of democracies were wealthy, Western countries. In the 1950s and 1960s, political scientists understandably followed the ideas of modernization, arguing that democracy could be sustained only in certain types of modern societies. Seymour Martin Lipset (1959) famously argued that democracies arise only in countries with reasonably wealthy economies and a large middle class that is educated and has its basic needs securely met. According to Lipset, these factors lead to a situation in which political competition is not too intense and in which compromise, an essential component of democracy, is easier. In *The Civic Culture* (1963, 1989), Gabriel Almond and Sidney Verba argued that democracy can thrive only in countries that have democratic political cultures (what they called "civic cultures") that value participation and whose citizens are willing to defer to elected leaders so that these leaders can govern while in office (see chapter 1). Other scholars argued that political developments must occur in a particular sequence. For instance, a strong state and sense of national identity must emerge before a democracy can do so.

The Third Wave of Democracy

The third wave wreaked intellectual havoc on modernization theories as democracy began breaking out in all the "wrong" places. First southern European and then Latin American military dictatorships became democratic. Then the end of the Cold War unleashed a new round of democracy creation, first in the former communist countries of Eastern Europe and then in Africa and parts of Asia. These were countries that were far too poor, that still faced questions about the strength of their state and national identity, and that seemed not to have democratic cultures, yet here they were writing constitutions, holding elections, and establishing democracies. Almost out of necessity, a new approach to the study of democratization emerged. Influenced by rational-choice theory, a new generation of democratization theorists argued that democracy could emerge in any country if the major political elites came to see it as a set of institutions that could serve their interests, whether they or their followers actually believed in democratic principles or not. Well-institutionalized democracy provides all major political actors with a degree of participation, protection from the worst forms of repression, and the possibility that they can gain power at some point. These features led self-interested political leaders to create democracies in countries that comparativists previously had seen as bound to be autocratic for years to come.

Basing their ideas mainly on the experiences of southern Europe and Latin America, democratization theorists argued that understanding elite dynamics and negotiations in times of crisis was crucial to explaining this new process of **transition to democracy**. They defined this as a regime change typically involving a negotiated process that removes an authoritarian regime and concludes with the founding election of a new, democratic regime. When an authoritarian regime faced a severe crisis of some sort—economic downturn or succession were common crises out of which democracy could emerge—its leadership would split internally into **hardliners** and **softliners.** The former would believe in repressing any opposition and preserving the status quo, while the latter would be willing to consider compromising with opponents as a means to survive the crisis. Simultaneously, the crisis would produce a surge in the activity of civil society, typically led by unions, religious authorities, or middle-class professionals who demanded fundamental political reforms. Civil society subsequently would often divide between **radicals**, who would want immediate and complete democratization, and **moderates**, who would be willing to compromise with the authoritarian government to make some gains. A successful transition to democracy would be most likely if the softliners in the regime and the moderates in civil society could each gain the upper hand over their internal opponents and then negotiate with each other to establish new rules of the game. Some form of democracy, though often with limits, would become a compromise on which both sides could agree (Huntington 1991).

Most theorists believe that the ideal process of transition to democracy would involve a **pact**, meaning an explicit agreement among the most important political actors in the regime and those in civil society to establish a new form of government. A pact would usually be preceded by **political liberalization**, or the opening of the political system to greater participation. This would include legalizing opposition parties, lifting restrictions on the media, and guaranteeing basic human rights. The pact would ideally produce a new democratic constitution and be followed by a **founding election**. This would be the first democratic election in many years (or ever) and would mark the completion of the transition. Most theorists argue that the regime and civil society would have to be of roughly equal strength for the transition process to produce a democracy. If the regime, and

transition to democracy: A regime change typically involving a negotiated process that removes an authoritarian regime and concludes with a founding election of a new, democratic regime

hardliners: Leaders of an authoritarian regime who believe in repressing any opposition and preserving the status quo when faced with a demand for political liberalization or democratization

softliners: Leaders of an authoritarian regime who are willing to consider compromising with opponents as a means to survive demands for democratization

radicals: Leaders of democracy movements who wish to achieve immediate and complete democracy and are unwilling to compromise with the existing regime

moderates: Leaders of democracy movements who are willing to compromise with the authoritarian regime to gain partial democracy

pact: In a transition to democracy, a conscious agreement among the most important political actors in the authoritarian regime and those in civil society to establish a new form of government

political liberalization: The opening of the political system to greater participation; typically before a transition to democracy

founding election: The first democratic election in many years (or ever), marking the completion of a transition to democracy

democratic consolidation: The widespread acceptance of democracy as the permanent form of political activity; all significant political elites and their followers accept democratic rules and are confident everyone else does as well

electoral democracies: Political systems in which opposition parties are legal and elections take place, but full civil and political rights of liberal democracy are not secure

democratic deepening: Improvement in the quality of democracy, including the extent of participation, the rule of law, and vertical and horizontal accountability

delegative democracies: Democracies in which free and fair elections take place but neither vertical nor horizontal accountability is strong enough to prevent the emergence of elected executives with nearly unlimited power

especially the hardliners within it, were very strong, it would control the process, and any democracy that resulted from the transition would have significant limitations. In Chile, for instance, the military under dictator Augusto Pinochet wrote a democratic constitution that reserved seats in the Senate and control of the central bank for the army. On the other hand, if civil society, especially its more radical elements, were too strong, it would demand full democratization with no protection for members of the old regime, and the resulting hardliner backlash would crush the nascent democratization.

New Democracies: Resilient or Not?

Once the transition is complete, the obvious question is whether the democracy will last. Transition theorists developed the concept of **democratic consolidation** to aid in consideration of this question, but much dispute over the definition and utility of the concept has arisen. Intuitively, democratic consolidation is simply the idea that democracy has become widely accepted as the permanent form of political activity in a particular country. It has become "the only game in town," and all significant political elites and their followers accept democratic rules and are confident that everyone else does as well. This is important, because democracy requires faith that in the future, any significant party or group might gain power via an election. If some major political actors do not believe that, they might be tempted to use nondemocratic means to gain power in the present, fearing that their opponents will not give them a chance to win via free and fair elections in the future.

Knowing when a country has reached the point of democratic consolidation, however, is quite difficult because it is difficult to know whether all the actors in the country have accepted democracy unquestionably. Samuel Huntington (1991) argued that a country must pass the "two-turnover test" before we can consider it a consolidated democracy: one party must win the founding election, and then a different party must win a later election and replace the first party. Only then, he stated, can it be known for certain that consolidation is complete. By this strict standard, West Germany did not become a consolidated democracy until 1969, India did not qualify until 1980, Japan did not qualify until 1993, and neither South Africa nor Mexico qualify yet today.

Transition theorists looked for evidence of democratic consolidation because they feared democratic breakdown, that is, the return to authoritarian rule. Relatively few countries that have completed a transition to democracy, however, have reverted to full-scale authoritarian rule. Some have become what are often termed **electoral democracies**: democracies that hold reasonably free and fair elections but do not abide by the full array of liberal rights and the rule of law. With these trends in mind, theorists have examined **democratic deepening**—that is, improvement in the quality of democracy, including the extent of participation, the rule of law, and vertical and horizontal accountability. In addition, Guillermo O'Donnell (1994) argued that many Latin American regimes are **delegative democracies** in which free and fair elections take place but neither vertical nor horizontal accountability is strong enough to prevent the emergence of elected executives with nearly unlimited power. Another common trend has been the ultimate transition to semi-authoritarian regimes in countries that had transitioned to democracy. Such regimes allow formal opposition, some open political debate, and elections, but these processes are so flawed that the regimes cannot be considered democratic in any real sense.

These disappointing results of the third wave have led to renewed debate about both transitions to and the sustainability of democracy. Scholars have tried to explain the weaknesses in new democracies by looking at the effects of rapid economic reform, weak civil society, and weak political institutions, as well as by reviving modernization theory's emphasis on economic development and political culture. A major quantitative study covering 135 countries from 1950 to 1990 found that while wealthy countries are no more likely to become democracies than poor countries, democracies in wealthier countries, once established, are much more likely to survive. According to the authors, "democracy is almost certain to survive in countries with per capita incomes above $4,000" (Przeworski et al. 2000, 273). Economic development, they argued, does not produce more transitions, but it does produce more sustainable and consolidated democracies once transitions happen. Others, however, have criticized the findings of this study; they have demonstrated that the data show that economic development improves the chances of a democratic transition happening, though not by a lot, and that prior to 1950, economic development made a transition to democracy much more likely (Boix and Stokes 2003).

Cultural norms have also reemerged as a focus of research on what makes consolidated democracy more likely. Most scholars have assumed that ethnic fragmentation is likely to harm the chances of democracy; following the lessons of the school of sequential political development, they argue that ethnically divided societies have a weaker sense of national unity. Such divisions often become bitter political competitions for control of the state that threaten to go beyond democratic norms and institutions. A study by Steven Fish and Robin Brooks (2004) across approximately 160 countries found no correlation between ethnic diversity and the strength of democracy, however. Ronald Inglehart and Christian Welzel (2005) argued that while clearly stated citizen support for democracy does not seem to be associated with democratic transitions or consolidation, what they call "self-expression values" that emphasize "freedom, tolerance of diversity, and participation" are highly correlated with democracy. In their model, economic development leads to rising self-expression values, which in turn lead to both support and successful demands for greater democracy. Others, however, have criticized some of these findings as well (see Methods in Context box).

Transition theorists have long worried that if democracy does not produce favorable policy outcomes quickly, a populace with limited attachment to core democratic values will reject democracy altogether rather than blame the particular party or individual in power. Many postcolonial countries going through transitions to democracy simultaneously go through neoliberal economic reform, which in the short term often causes economic decline before it brings benefits. Adam Przeworski (1991) contended that in such cases, governments are well advised to pursue economic reform as quickly and thoroughly as possible rather than slowly and partially, because getting through the worst of the economic crisis quickly means less chance that the populace will blame democracy and start supporting nondemocratic alternatives. In her 2003 book *Ordinary People in Extraordinary Times*, however, Nancy Bermeo examined the hypothesis that popular disenchantment undermines democracy, looking at the breakdown of democracy in Europe before World War II and in Latin America in the 1960s. She found that in these cases, the populace as a whole did not reject democracy but key elites did reject it in times of economic crisis. The military in Latin America, for instance, feared economic instability and put an end to democracy without widespread popular support for their action.

Weak political institutions and civil society can also lead to democratic breakdown and the rise of semi-authoritarian regimes. The transition process in sub-Saharan Africa has not fit the model derived from Latin America and southern Europe very well because African countries possess much weaker institutions and civil societies. Africa's neopatrimonial regimes systematically weakened almost all

Does Modernization Cause Democracy?

Scholars of transitions to democracy during and after the third wave rejected modernization theory's argument that only certain societies could become consolidated democracies. They argued instead that elite compromise could produce democracy in any type of society and that democracy, once created, could imbue society with the values necessary to sustain it. The recent slowing down, or even faltering, of the third wave has brought modernization theory back to the fore. Are democratic transitions and sustained democracy likely to occur only in modernized societies?

HYPOTHESIS

Early modernization theorists (Almond and Verba 1963; Lipset 1959) noted a simple correlation between the presence of economic wealth or a civic culture and democratic governments, and they hypothesized that democracy required a society with one or both of these key characteristics. Transition theorists of the third wave engaged in comparative case studies to demonstrate common patterns of elite compromise between authoritarian regimes and leaders of democratic movements that produced transitions to democracy; they hypothesized that elite compromise could produce democracy anywhere (O'Donnell and Schmitter 1986; Huntington 1991). In the past decade, new research using new data and statistical techniques has reexamined the modernization thesis. This research has found support for some elements of the thesis, though not without controversy, especially over how key concepts are measured. The core hypotheses for each school of thought have not changed, but the techniques to measure them have become much more sophisticated, as we discuss below.

RESEARCH AND ANALYSIS

Adam Przeworski and his colleagues (2000) examined a data set of 141 countries from 1950 to 1990, classifying each country's regime for each year as either democratic or authoritarian. They defined a regime as democratic if it holds elections for its top offices and has more than one party and if those parties alternate in taking power. Using a statistical technique called probit, they examined the ability of socioeconomic development, which they measured as per capita income, to predict both whether a country had a democratic regime and whether it would transition to democracy. They found a strong statistical relationship between development and the sustainability of democracy (in wealthy countries, democracies once established are almost guaranteed to survive) but a very weak one between development and the likelihood that a country would have a transition to democracy. They concluded that in terms of predicting transitions, "modernization theory appears to have little, if any, explanatory power" (Przeworski et al. 2000, 137).

Carles Boix and Susan Stokes (2003) challenged these findings, rerunning the same statistical tests on the data but dividing the data by income level and including international factors as control variables. They found that development and transitions to democracy were unrelated at the highest level of income, skewing the overall results. They argued also that during the Cold War, Soviet-influenced states were so tightly controlled they would not have been able to transition to democracy regardless of other factors. Oil wealth, they added, also prevents transitions because authoritarian regimes can use oil money to buy off opposition. Removing these groups of countries from the data, Boix and Stokes showed that for the rest of the countries, development *does* make a transition to democracy more likely. Finally, they extended the data set back to 1850 and showed that prior to World War II, development strongly increased the likelihood of a transition. They concluded that for the countries that the theory focuses on—poor and middle-income countries that are not in some unusual international situation (under Soviet control or oil-rich)—development does indeed make transitions to democracy more likely.

Hadenius and Teorell (2005) criticized Przeworski and his colleagues (2000) for how they measured democracy, arguing that instead of simply drawing a line between "democracy" and "authoritarian" regimes, they should have measured degrees of democracy using Freedom House's seven-point scale. Using this, Hadenius and Teorell found that development increases democracy not only in the completely "free" countries (full-fledged democracies) but also in the "partially free" countries, a category that includes many semi-authoritarian regimes and regimes in transition. They concluded that development does influence the level of democracy in all but the most autocratic regimes. Ultimately, the answer to the question of whether or not development causes democracy seems to depend on how and when one measures democracy and what countries one includes in the study.

A similar debate arose among those examining the effects of culture. Ronald Inglehart and Christian Welzel (2005) used data from the World Values Survey, a global survey of citizen beliefs conducted every few years since the 1980s, to examine the effect of what they call "emancipative values" on democracy. They attempted to measure what they termed "effective democracy," based on a combination of Freedom House scores and a measure of corruption. They argued that Freedom House scores primarily measure formal democratic rights rather than whether such rights operate in practice. They also argued that corruption is a measure of "elite integrity," meaning the extent to which elites follow the rule of law, and is therefore a measure of the degree to which formal rights are actually put in practice. Using a measure of democracy based on these two sets of data (the Freedom House scores and measures of corruption), they showed that even controlling for earlier experience with democracy and prior economic development, countries with higher emancipative values in the early 1990s were much more likely to have stronger democracies after 2002.

Hadenius and Teorell (2005), however, criticized Inglehart and Welzel's work, arguing that their measure of effective democracy combined a measure of democracy (Freedom House scores) with an unrelated measure of corruption that has no clear relationship to democracy. Using only the Freedom House measures, Hadenius and Teorell found no relationship between emancipative values and later levels of democracy. Welzel and Inglehart (2006) countered this, using data from slightly different years and showing that the cultural values still explained democracy, even using only the Freedom House scores. Once again, how scholars measured democracy and the exact timing of the data collected influenced their findings.

QUESTIONS IN CONTEXT

Inglehart and Welzel's book *Modernization, Cultural Change, and Democracy* (2005) provided probably the most comprehensive analysis of the modernization debate to date, combining measures over time of socioeconomic development, cultural values, and democracy. We have much more convincing evidence than scholars could provide decades ago that modernization is connected to the sustainability of democracy and perhaps to its creation. Still, how much of this evidence one accepts depends on one's understanding of what democracy is and therefore how it can most accurately be measured. Is democracy something that you either have or don't, according to the strict tests like those of Przeworski and his colleagues, or can it be measured along a spectrum, with countries being more or less democratic? How much time should elapse between the measure of development or culture and observing its effects on the likelihood of democratic transition: one year, five years, twenty? These are questions to ask yourself as you assess the merits of this theoretical and methodological debate. Ultimately, they are not statistical but conceptual questions.

political institutions prior to the arrival of the third wave in the early 1990s, when severe economic crises of the 1980s as well as the end of the Cold War produced a wave of democratization efforts across the continent. The old authoritarian governments often did split, as transition theory suggests, but typically not between hardliners and softliners but instead between patrons leading competing ethnic groups. Continued poverty means that citizens depend on this patronage for much of their well-being, and clientelism remains a primary form of political participation. Holding an open election does not substantially change this situation.

Many new groups arose in civil society and demanded greater democratization, but in countries with miniscule middle classes, these groups had limited resources and leadership. This made it difficult for such groups to hold governments accountable. Civil society groups in Africa are based around a small, elite leadership that is dependent on external funding from foreign-aid programs. Because they do not need to rely on their own members for resources, the level of internal democracy and connections with ordinary citizens found in these organizations is often quite limited. In Latin America, where democracy has generally been more institutionalized and has a longer history, civil society often has stronger roots in society and does not face these problems to the same extent as in Africa.

Michael Bratton and Nicholas van de Walle (1997) put forth the argument that African neopatrimonial regimes have a distinct logic of transition. During and after a formal "transition," political competition remains primarily about securing access to government to gain resources, except that now this is done via elections rather than by way of military coups. Pacts almost never happen because parties are little more than temporary vehicles for shifting coalitions of patrons trying to gain power, and parties neither have sufficient ideological disagreements nor are stable enough to provide the credible commitments that pacts require. In the absence of pacts, incumbents typically do not liberalize their regimes completely, instead holding elections that are only partially free and fair. More often than not, they win those elections, and even when the opposition wins, it also often uses the reins of power in undemocratic ways. In the absence of a clear agreement over a new constitution and new institutions, whichever group is currently in power has access to important authoritarian means of staying there. The result is often the rise of semi-authoritarian regimes. Freedom House ratings reflect this: six African regimes were rated as "free" and eighteen as "not free" in 2010, but twenty-two were "partly free," the designation given to a majority of semi-authoritarian regimes.

Not only weak institutions but also inappropriate ones can harm new democracies and create semi-authoritarian regimes. New democracies are often deeply divided societies, either ideologically or ethnically. The "perils of presidentialism" (see chapter 6) that Juan Linz (1990) identified are, he argued, particularly important in new democracies. Presidential systems, he suggested, lead to "winner-take-all" mentalities as parties compete for the presidency, and this makes compromise unlikely and often produces policy deadlock whenever each party captures one branch of government. Linz and others believe that parliamentary systems are more likely to survive in new democracies because they allow for coalition governments. Following Arendt Lijphart's consociational theory (1969), many comparativists argue that because new democracies are often deeply divided and competing elites do not fully trust one another or the new democratic institutions, power-sharing mechanisms are likely to help preserve democracy.

Others disagree with all of these arguments, suggesting instead that presidential systems can provide both democratic legitimacy and stability by having a single head of state directly elected by a majority of the nation. Advocates of this stance point out the stability of many Latin American democracies, virtually all of which have presidential systems. Kapstein and Converse (2008) found that democratic breakdown is slightly more likely to occur in parliamentary systems. They argued that the issue of whether a new democracy is presidential or parliamentary is less important than how effective the limits on the executive are. A study by Steven Fish (2006) supported this argument. It used a new set of data that measured the strength of the legislative branch to show that a strong legislature is the most important institutional ingredient in maintaining democracy, regardless of the kind of political system in place.

The spread of semi-authoritarian regimes has led scholars to focus on them specifically, asking whether and when these regimes might give way to greater democracy. Most believe that the quantity and quality of elections is important to the likelihood of further democratization. Lindberg (2009) argued that in Africa, a new model of "democratization by elections" has emerged and that even in semi-authoritarian regimes, the holding of elections expands democratic freedoms. Even quite limited elections allow the opposition to win some share of power—a significant share of legislative seats for instance—making further democratization more likely. Regimes that allow such elections give dissidents within the ruling party incentives to defect to the opposition because doing so is a viable means of

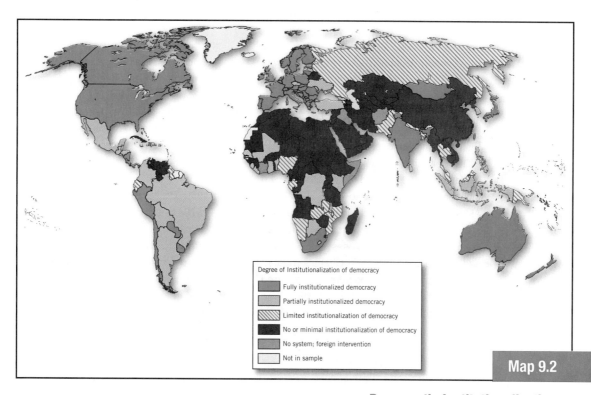

Map 9.2

Democratic Institutionalization

Note: The map shows Polity IV institutionalized democracy scores for 2006 on the Freedom House scale. The Polity IV institutionalized democracy score measures the degree of institutionalization of democracy within a state, with 10 being the highest degree of institutionalization and 0 being the lowest. Democracy is conceived as three essential, interdependent elements. First is the presence of institutions and procedures through which citizens can effectively express preferences for alternative policies and leaders. Second is the existence of institutionalized constraints on the exercise of power by the executive. Third is the guarantee of civil liberties to all citizens in their daily lives and in acts of political participation. Other aspects of plural democracy, such as the rule of law, systems of checks and balances, and freedom of the press, are means to, or specific manifestations of, these general principles. Polity IV institutionalized democracy scores do not include coded data on civil liberties.

maintaining a political career, which in turn encourages splits in the ruling party. Just this type of situation helped produce greater democracy in our case study of Mexico, for instance. Similarly, a real chance at some share of power encourages opposition coalitions, as does a majoritarian electoral system. Opposition fragmentation is likely to keep the incumbent regime in place because a coalition is often essential for any real chance at electoral victory and regime change. When political leaders think an opposition coalition has a real chance to win, they become more likely to join it themselves, thus further strengthening its chances until a "tipping point" is reached at which a large opposition coalition emerges to win an election in spite of the incumbent's manipulation of the system. Opposition protest around elections has also been found to be an effective tool for increasing the chances of democratic outcomes. All of this suggests that in semi-authoritarian regimes, opposition parties ought to take part in even rigged elections so that they can coalesce as parties as much as possible and thereby pressure the incumbent regime via both their electoral participation and their protests of electoral irregularities.

MINI CASE

Ghana, an African Democratic Success Story

In January 2009, after having run in three presidential elections, John Atta Mills was sworn in as president of the nation of Ghana in west Africa. He won the national vote, in Ghana's fifth election since restoring democracy in 1992, by less than one-half of 1 percent. His party, the National Democratic Congress (NDC), fell three seats short of a majority in parliament, but it worked out an alliance with independent candidates to reach a majority. Although the losing party threatened a lawsuit over the results, it ultimately accepted the outcome of Ghana's closest election ever, and for the second time in Ghana's modern history, power was peacefully transferred from one party to another in the still-young democracy. In contrast to our case study of Nigeria and many other African countries, democracy is functioning well in Ghana. Freedom House gave it a rating of 3 (2 is the best possible and 14 the worst) in 2010, declaring it fully "free." The Failed States Index in 2009 rated it as the second strongest state in sub-Saharan Africa. As Ghanaian political scientist E. Gyimah-Boadi (2009) remarked, "These exceptional events have confirmed Ghana's place as a beacon of hope for democracy in Africa" (138).

Nothing in Ghana's past would have made most political scientists predict its democratic success. Indeed, a number of factors suggest it to be a rather inauspicious place to launch a democracy. Since independence in 1957, it suffered through a one-party regime (1960–66), four military regimes (1966–69, 1972–79, 1981–92), and two brief and failed prior attempts at democracy (1969–72, 1979–81). Ghana's economy in the 1970s was one of the worst on the continent. While it has improved notably since the 1980s, Ghana took until 2000 to reach the same per capita income level it had in 1960. It is still a poor country, with a per capita income of only $450 in 2008. Economically and politically, Ghana seemed to be one of the least likely places to have a democratic success story. So what happened to produce a successful democracy there, and why?

As the third wave of democratization washed over Africa, Ghanaian president Jerry Rawlings, a charismatic and fairly popular ruler who gained power in a military coup in 1981, agreed to allow multiparty competition based on a new constitution that he and his aides wrote. It created a presidential system with a single-member district (SMD) electoral system, but gave the president great powers of appointment at both the national and local levels. Rawlings won the presidency in 1992, and the main opposition parties, charging electoral fraud, boycotted the parliamentary elections a few weeks later, giving Rawlings's NDC the vast majority of parliamentary seats. Domestic and international electoral observers saw significant fraud, and many feared an only partial move toward real democracy. Rawlings and his party won the next election, held on schedule in 1996. This time, the election was much cleaner, and the opposition participated fully. Rawlings and the NDC stayed in power, but the opposition won a large share of parliamentary seats. In 2000, Rawlings was constitutionally barred from running for a third term. Despite rumors that he would either attempt to change the constitution to allow a third term or run his wife in his place, he agreed to step down, but he handpicked Mills as his successor and actively campaigned for him. Rawlings's popularity, however, did not transfer fully to his successor. The main opposition party, the National People's Party (NPP), won the presidency and gained a majority in parliament by allying with smaller parties. The NPP and the new president, John Kufuor, handily won reelection in 2004 amidst a growing economy. In 2008, Kufuor duly bowed out at the end of his second four-year term, and his successor lost to Mills in the too-close-to-call 2008 contest as the NDC regained both the presidency and a narrow majority in parliament.

Ghana's democracy is certainly not without its problems. The exceptionally strong presidency that Rawlings's constitution created allows the president vast powers of appointment, which all presidents, most notably Kufuor (2000–08), have used to cement political loyalty to themselves. In contrast to most presidential systems, cabinet members can simultaneously sit in parliament, and the cabinet size can vary. Presidents have therefore expanded their cabinets, appointing MPs to lucrative and prestigious cabinet positions to maintain their loyalty. Under Kufuor, nearly half of the ruling party's MPs were in cabinet positions. Similarly, the president appoints

one-third of local government council members and the heads of the councils, thus allowing him to provide patronage to up-and-coming politicians at the local level. All of this has made parliament relatively weak vis-à-vis the presidency, and it has arguably gotten weaker in the last decade. As Gyimah-Boadi noted, "While Ghana may have successfully made the transition from quasimilitary authoritarian rule to pluralistic democracy under the Fourth Republic, it is still struggling to make a clean break with neopatrimonialism" (2009, 147). One result is a continuing and perhaps growing problem with corruption. The Kufuor presidency was known for lavish spending that the parliament did not fully control and for refusing to remove officials who were charged with being or rumored to be corrupt. Ghana's 2009 ranking in Transparency International's Corruption Perception Index was 3.9, or position 69 out of 180 countries. While Ghana is one of the less corrupt countries in sub-Saharan Africa, this score still represents a significant corruption problem.

Nonetheless, the remarkable success of Ghana's democratization cries out for explanation. No cultural indicators strongly attest to a culture that is favorable to democracy. While its populace is somewhat more educated than the African average, and AfroBarometer (2005, 2008) surveys have found somewhat greater support for democracy in Ghana than the African average, neither Ghanaian education levels nor Ghanaian support for democracy is exceptionally high. While the economy certainly improved until the 2008–09 Great Recession, the country remains relatively poor. Its greatest success was cutting its poverty rate in half since the early 1990s, though over one-quarter of the population remains poor. These recent data don't fully explain why Ghana's democracy strengthened in the 1990s instead of weakening to the point where the country would revert to the semi-authoritarian rule so common to third-wave transitions. Therefore, the modernization thesis cannot fully explain Ghana.

Lindsay Whitfield (2009) argued that growing trust among Ghanaian political elites and strong parties are the keys to Ghana's democratic stability. After the contentious founding election in 1992, a commission was set up to bring the opposing political leaders together to discuss what electoral rules they would use in the future. With the support of external aid, the leaders helped strengthen the national election commission, and this process helped the opposing leaders gain some additional trust in each other and in the political process in general. The fairness of the 1996 election reinforced this trust. Ghana's party system is most unusual in Africa. Since a division in the nationalist movement prior to independence, the country's politics have been divided into what are called two main "traditions." These are loosely grouped ideological alternatives, one rhetorically more centrist and the other more leftist. Each tradition, however, also has an ethnic base in a particular region of the country. In every recurrence of electoral competition in the country's history, these two traditions, going under different party names, have reemerged. Combined with the SMD electoral system, the vague but nonetheless well-known ideological images of the two major parties has served as a basis for them to reach out to voters beyond their ethnic bases. Surveys show that Ghanaians have significantly greater party loyalty than most African voters do, in large part because of their identification with one or the other of these two long-standing political traditions. The SMD system has helped the two parties attract a growing share of the total vote, limiting the smaller parties to a shrinking and now tiny share of the electorate. Because they can appeal to voters on a basis other than just ethnicity (in contrast

to parties in a number of other African countries such as Nigeria and Kenya), the logic of the SMD system has been able to function in Ghana. Both parties increasingly appeal to "swing voters" outside their ethnic regions of core support, and elections are decided on the basis of whose appeals to these voters are more successful in a given campaign. Thus far, this has led to regular alternation of parties in power. The existence of two distinct and strong political traditions sets Ghana apart from most of Africa much more clearly than any economic or cultural factors.

CASE SUMMARY

Ghana is not the only case of a successful democracy in Africa (Benin, Botswana, and South Africa are other clear examples), but it is one of the most striking. Nothing in its history led scholars to predict a more successful transition here than elsewhere on the continent. Ghana has nonetheless succeeded admirably, probably mainly due to the presence of enduring "political traditions" that provide a basis for the creation of relatively strong political parties. Ghana nonetheless faces more hurdles on the road to full democratic consolidation. Neopatrimonial means of mobilizing political support continues, and horizontal accountability remains weak. It is perhaps justified to conclude that Ghana is what we termed in chapter 3 an "electoral democracy," with free and fair elections and real competition but continued limits on political participation. Democratic deepening remains an incomplete process but one that seems entirely feasible given the country's remarkable success to date.

The 1990s were the halcyon days of democratization, when it seemed that democracy was spreading to nearly every corner of the globe. It has certainly spread significantly, with most Latin American countries making apparently long-term transformations toward consolidated democracy. Some Asian and African countries, as the mini case on Ghana demonstrates, have also made successful transitions. In many other cases, though, initial transitions have produced at best electoral democracies and, more often, semi-authoritarian regimes. The struggle for further democracy continues in many of these countries, though a number of countries (such as Egypt until 2011) demonstrate that such regimes can endure for a very long time. Comparativists continue to describe and try to explain this ever-changing process, the most common type of regime change today. Our case studies of Brazil, Mexico, Russia, and Nigeria demonstrate the diverging processes and outcomes of the "transition era."

CASE STUDY

Brazil: Model Transition and the Question of Democratic Deepening

- Slowly evolving transition ending in pact and new constitution
- Rise of new type of party representing workers: the PT
- Weak but slowly strengthening political parties
- Continuing corruption but growing accountability
- Continuing problem of weak and unequal rule of law
- Clear consolidation but less complete democratic deepening

A key element of any transition to democracy is successfully convincing the military to give up its formal and most of its informal political power. Many observers believe that Brazil's democracy had achieved this by the beginning of the new millennium. While Brazil still boasts a large and relatively powerful military, the civilian leadership seems to have firm control over it to a greater extent than at any time in the country's history.

Credit: AP Photo/Eraldo Peres

Brazil has long been one of the world's most unequal societies. From the *coronelismo* of the late nineteenth century to the populism of the more industrialized mid-twentieth century, Brazil's elite has kept the masses under its control. Given this, January 1, 2003, was not your average day for poor Brazilians. On that day, they celebrated the inauguration of President Luiz "Lula" Inácio da Silva, a trade-union leader who grew up in poverty with a fourth-grade education. The inauguration of the leader of the social democratic Workers Party (PT) seemed to herald the fruition of Brazil's new democracy. His party, born out of the workers' struggle to gain the right to form their own unions and end military rule, was a new type of political organization in the country's history. It had been created from the bottom up rather than from the top down.

Early in his presidency, however, Lula disappointed many of his most ardent supporters by compromising on key economic issues, following mostly neoliberal policies that supported stable growth and a generally beneficial business climate. These policies were partly the result of a need to compromise with the many other political forces and parties in Brazil's fractious political system. Yet Lula comfortably won reelection in 2006, and the popularity of his government's innovative social welfare program (see chapter 11) and rapid economic growth (see chapter 10) gave him approval ratings of 75 percent in 2010. This prompted U.S. President Barack Obama to call him "the most popular politician in the world." Lula's popularity led to a debate in Brazil about amending the constitution to allow him to run for a third term (Brazil's constitution, like the American one, limits a president to two 4-year terms). Lula rejected that effort, however, which many

IN CONTEXT

FREEDOM IN BRAZIL AND LATIN AMERICA

In 1990, Brazil's Freedom House Civil Liberties score was 3, compared to the Latin America average of 2.73; its Political Rights Score was 2, compared to the Latin America average of 2.42.

In 2010, Brazil's Freedom House Civil Liberties score was 2, compared to the Latin America average of 2.44; its Political Rights Score was 2, compared to the Latin America average of 2.26.

saw as a sign of a further maturing of Brazil's democracy after twenty years.

Brazil's democracy is certainly thriving, but weak political institutions have long plagued the country, raising questions about democratic deepening, accountability, and the rule of law. The latest research indicates growing institutional strength in key areas, however. Whatever the state of Brazil today, its transition to democracy stands as one of the models of the process. A long and gradual transition, beginning in 1974 and not fully ending until 1989, eased the country from military rule into democracy. Despite contentious moments along the way, the result was a new constitution and electoral democracy that has stood for twenty years; six presidential elections have put five presidents in power from three different parties. By the basic measures of free and fair elections, free association and expression, and electoral turnover, Brazil is a consolidated democracy, and it achieved the status of "free" in Freedom House's rankings in 1986 after the first indirect election of the president. It dropped to "partly free" from 1993 to 2003, however, because its score in the "Civil Liberties" category fell, due mainly to rampant and nearly unchecked police brutality. Since 2003, the country has once again achieved the status of "free," though problems of the rule of law and weak institutions remain.

Brazil's liberalization began in 1974 when a new military president allowed greater political rights within the limited electoral system under the military regime. The official opposition party (the only one allowed) dramatically increased its share of the vote in legislative elections that year, undermining the status of the official ruling party. This inspired greater pressure for change, but while the military presidents in the 1970s favored some liberalization, they did not support democratization. The modest political opening, however, just led to greater demands for real democracy. Some business leaders began calling for political reform, as did some leaders of the Catholic Church who were part of the liberation theology movement, which used church teaching to argue for greater justice for the poor. Then in 1978–1979, large strikes broke out in the industrial heartland of São Paulo; illegal unions rejected the complacency of the military's official unions and the corporatist system that had long guided Brazilian unionism. These massive strikes won workers the right to form their own unions and then their own party, the PT.

In response to growing demands for further liberalization, the military allowed direct elections for state governors in 1982. The opposition's victory in the largest states demonstrated the increasing popularity of democracy. Shortly afterward, the military announced that it would allow a civilian to be elected president in 1985, but only indirectly; he would be elected by the National Congress. The PT and other groups in the democracy movement responded with a massive "Diretas já!" ("Direct elections now!") campaign, which mobilized hundreds of thousands of people in street protests to demand full democratization. Military leaders soon recognized the overwhelming popular opposition to their rule and agreed to a pact that gave birth to full democracy. According to this pact, the National Congress and the indirectly elected president who would be put in office in 1985 would write a new constitution; this would stipulate direct elections for all offices in 1989.

The 1988 constitution created the presidential system we outlined in chapter 6. Brazil was unusual in that it had a full public debate about whether to switch to a parliamentary system or stick with a presidential one. The Constituent Assembly that wrote the constitution favored a parliamentary system, but the president and the military favored preserving the presidential one. In the end, they compromised and adopted a constitution that was initially presidential but promised a national referendum in 1993 on which system to adopt permanently. The referendum engendered a rare (for anywhere in the world) public debate over the merits of each system, complete with often misleading campaign ads. In the end, voters supported the presidential system by a large margin.

The most interesting and controversial element of Brazil's new democratic constitution was the electoral system that has helped produce the extremely fragmented party system we mentioned in chapter 6. Brazil uses an open-list PR electoral system for the Chamber of Deputies, which is the lower and more powerful house of the National Congress. Each state is an electoral district that has a number of seats based on its population, with a minimum of eight seats and maximum of seventy. *Open-list* means that the individual candidates are listed on the ballot and voters can vote either for the party or an individual candidate. Within each district, a party gets a number of seats that is proportional to its total share of the vote, and then the individual candidates from that party who get the most votes get those seats.

This system gives candidates an incentive to garner as many individual votes as possible to place them as high as possible among their party's candidates. It provides no incentive for candidates within the same party to cooperate with each other. It doesn't matter whether candidates gain many votes within a particular area of a state or have more widespread but shallow support across that state as long as their total number of votes is as high as possible. Given the long-standing role of patronage in Brazilian politics and the decentralized federal system (as described in chapter 6) in which state governors are very influential, candidates understandably focus

almost exclusively on local issues. Most are really representatives of particular areas or particular social groups in somewhat larger areas such as major cities, rather than party stalwarts. They are dependent on their own ability to mobilize supporters in their home areas and perhaps on important local leaders such as major city mayors and state governors.

The obvious result of this electoral system is weak parties. In fact, parties were so weak that between 1989 and 1995, one-third of legislators switched parties while in office. Their party affiliation was a matter of convenience rather than an indication of ideological commitment. A national party organization has virtually no means of controlling who runs on its ticket; rather, a party is dependent on the ability of locally popular candidates to garner votes that add to the party's total tally in a state. With the exception of a few major parties, most parties (like most candidates) are really local. They represent one region or sometimes are just vehicles in a region for a particular local candidate. The electoral system has no minimum threshold of votes a party must get to gain representation in the chamber, so a locally popular candidate with a tiny fraction of the national total may well end up in office. And, yes, this produces many parties in the legislature. There were twenty-two after the 2010 election, though these were grouped into two broad coalitions: one supporting Lula and the PT (which won a majority of seats—311 of 513) and one opposing them.

In addition, party leaders in the legislature have few means of influencing legislators' votes once they are in office. This is in part because the long-term career goals of most of these legislators are to win the more important local executive positions, such as mayor of a significant city or state governor. These positions ultimately have more clout in Brazil's system than do individual members of the legislature, another reason legislators focus on local issues.

The degree and effect of this party weakness has been the subject of significant debate among scholars of Brazil. Initial assumptions in the early 1990s were that such weak parties inhibited the system's ability to pass coherent legislation, especially in the all-important area of economic reform. The economic reform efforts of the first directly elected president, Fernando Collor, a member of a tiny local party who ruled mainly via the president's power to issue provisional decrees (see chapter 6), were unsuccessful and unpopular. Brazil's classic problem of inflation remained out of control, supporting the argument that the political system was dysfunctional.

Research by Brazilian scholars Argelina Figueiredo and Fernando Limongi (2000), however, demonstrated that Brazil's parties were stronger than previously believed. Figueiredo and Limongi's evidence showed that legislators voted with their parties to a higher degree than had been assumed, suggesting that party leaders were able to marshal their troops in favor of their preferred policies. More recent research (Santos 2008; Hagopian et al. 2009) suggested that legislators are increasingly voting as a bloc, that party switching has dropped to half of what it was in the early 1990s, and that electoral volatility (voters switching parties from one election to the next) is down. And though they are quite vague, the major Brazilian parties do have distinct ideological positions. They can loosely be grouped into "right," "center," and "left" parties (with several in each category). In recent elections, ideologically similar parties have formed coalitions to support the most popular candidates. The popularity of the last two presidents, Fernando Henrique Cardoso and Lula, has undoubtedly helped spur coalitions since parties want to support a winner if possible.

Some scholars have questioned the argument that Brazilian parties are gaining strength, suggesting that final votes in the National Congress are not terribly important because many presidential proposals never make it that far. (Presidents often drop them for lack of support from among the fractious coalitions). Political scientist Barry Ames (2001) suggested that legislators' votes on controversial issues are explained not by the influence of the party leaders but instead by the characteristics and needs of constituents and the ability of legislators to gain patronage and resources for their home areas in exchange for their votes. Frances Hagopian and her colleagues (2009), however, used a rational-choice analysis of politicians' incentives to argue that over time, changes in economic policies have made patronage less important and party loyalty more important. Cardoso's economic reforms in the 1990s substantially reduced the size and role of the government, drying up many of the sources of "pork" (both government spending and government jobs) that individual members of Congress used to get elected. This, Hagopian and her colleagues argued, has made politicians more dependent on parties' "brands" to secure office, which in turn has led them to support their party leadership more faithfully in legislative votes, stick to one party for longer, and campaign on the party's platform. It seems increasingly clear that as weak as Brazilian parties were in the first few years of the new democracy, they have since gained some strength, even if they remain weak compared to parties in older democracies.

Another reason for somewhat stronger parties in recent years is the presence of the PT. Forged in the massive strikes of 1978–1979, the PT was a different kind of party from the start. From its first election in 1982, it refused to play by the rules of "politics as usual" in Brazil, insisting instead that it would recognize only those candidates whom it vetted and approved as supporting its ideology. Because of its scathing critique of the corruption of the Brazilian political elite, it refused to cooperate before or after any election with any other party, even others on "the left." It also refused to use patronage to gain political support. Its long-time leader, Lula, is a union leader who campaigned wearing blue jeans and using the working-class vernacular. He and the party, with their socialist policies and symbols, represented a grassroots critique of the entire Brazilian political elite.

The party's discipline and ultimate success in becoming very influential by the 1990s led other parties to become somewhat more disciplined in imitation. Lula ran for president and came in second in the elections of 1989, 1994, and 1998, finally winning the presidency in 2002. In the end, the PT did have to make some compromises to win. To reassure the upper and middle classes, the business sector, and even some workers who feared a president who was "uneducated," Lula donned suits when campaigning and improved his speech to sound more formal and educated. The PT dropped its opposition to forming coalitions, a crucial factor in Lula's eventual election. Yet while the PT ultimately compromised, it remains one of the more disciplined parties in the country, and most observers argue that it has positively impacted the institutional strength of its major competitors.

Lula's government was not without its faults, however. Despite its official stance against the same old–same old of Brazil's political system, it nonetheless was plagued by corruption, another continuing problem for Brazil's democracy. The country's patronage politics and weak institutions made it a bastion of corruption throughout the twentieth century, so much so that Transparency International's 1995 Corruption Perception Index gave it a score of 2.7 out of 10 (with 10 being the least corrupt), ranking it 37 out of 41 countries surveyed. By 2009, it had improved notably to a score of 3.7 and a rank of 75 out of 180 countries. While improved, this number still represents a significant corruption problem. The good news is that high-level corruption has been exposed and some officials involved in it have been forced from office. Cleanup began in 1992 with the impeachment and resignation of the first elected president, Collor, after he was accused of embezzling $23 million. It was the first time a Brazilian president had ever been constitutionally removed from office. This policy of nonpreferential treatment continued under Cardoso's presidency, when members of the National Congress who had been caught discussing taking bribes to support changing the constitution to allow presidential reelection were forced to resign. The most recent major scandals were under Lula; it seems the PT's compromises to win election led it into the corruption morass of Brazilian politics. Several leading party members were forced to resign as a result, and Lula publicly apologized for corrupt campaign finance practices. Heading into the 2010 elections, scandal once again rocked the party, as Lula's chief of staff was forced to resign after being accused of influence peddling. This briefly threatened the election of Lula's successor as president. These cases demonstrate the continuing problem of corruption in Brazil, but they also illustrate the first major steps toward holding officials accountable for their actions.

The most recent major step in Brazil's maturing democracy was the October 2010 election, in which Lula's handpicked successor retained the PT's grip on the presidency. Though she can't claim anywhere near Lula's level of charisma, new President Dilma Rousseff, Brazil's first female head of state, benefitted from Lula's enormous popularity and the economic success of the PT government's policies. As in the two prior elections, the chief opposition was a center-right coalition of parties led by the same candidate Lula defeated in 2002. Though Rouseff fell shy of the 50 percent mark in the first round of voting, she handily won the runoff three weeks later with over 56 percent of the vote. A sixth free and fair election, along with Lula's insistence that he would step down after his constitutional limit of two terms in spite of his popularity, were additional signs of a securely consolidated democracy.

While few political scientists question the consolidation of Brazil's democracy, many question its quality and degree of democratic deepening. Frances Hagopian (2005), in a major review of the quality of Brazil's democracy, argued that it has improved over time. The electoral system and the existence of multiple parties mean that citizens' views are represented relatively accurately. The system's effects on vertical accountability are ambiguous, however; the large, multimember electoral districts make direct connections between citizens and particular legislators tenuous. Informally, though, the system encourages legislators to focus on their home areas, and this does enhance accountability. Stronger parties with clearer ideological positions also enhance accountability, as voters have clearer choices in the ballot box.

Horizontal accountability has increased as major politicians have been forced out of office for inappropriate behavior and the legislature has gained powers to investigate the executive that have helped expose corruption. Although the country's supreme court has increasingly ruled against the other branches, the weakest element of Brazil's democracy is almost certainly the rule of law. Brazil's gross social inequality has long meant that the police treat citizens of different classes differently, and law enforcement, which is decentralized to the state level, regularly abuses the rights of the poor. Brazil's courts are famous for favoring the wealthy who can afford the best legal help, the wheels of justice turn exceptionally slowly in the country's overwhelmed judicial system (see chapter 6), and the prisons are reportedly full of prisoner abuse. So while Brazil's democracy increasingly represents citizens and the latter can hold politicians accountable in certain areas, equality before the law is far from being realized.

Brazil's civil society was instrumental in the initial transition process to democracy and remains quite active. Despite this, democratic deepening and participation remain a concern among observers. The country's exceptional social inequality, many argue, affects participation in the same way that it affects the rule of law: the poor, who are often black, are left out. Once again, the PT has been innovative in trying to overcome this problem. Starting in the city of Porto Alegre under a PT government, the party has instituted a "participatory budgeting" (PB) system in which citizens in neighborhoods meet to set their priorities for the annual government budget. These groups elect representatives who meet at higher levels to produce a set of budget proposals for the city's officials to consider and enact. The system gives local citizens a voice and serves as a means of higher-level participation for more active citizens, who typically are members of local social movements or NGOs. Most observers credit the PB process with providing an avenue for greater participation for the poor. It is an innovative institutional design that may foster increased local participation in Brazil's democracy (Avritzer 2009).

CASE SUMMARY

Brazil's still-young democracy is an example of a successful transition and consolidation. The transition itself is considered a model due to its relatively smooth and gradual process. The institutions created in the 1988 constitution satisfied the various interests involved, although they perhaps did not create the most coherent political system imaginable. The electoral system provides few incentives for strong parties to emerge, and the unusually decentralized federalism limits central power. Nonetheless, and in part because of these features, the power of the executive has been reduced from what it was during Brazil's earlier democratic regimes. The military is firmly under civilian control, and these days no one expects any significant intervention from that quarter. Accountability and even party strength seem to be rising, though weak institutions and corruption remain serious problems. Participation is undoubtedly greater than at any time in Brazil's history, and the prominence of the PT has allowed poorer citizens more access to government than ever before. This is not to say that problems do not remain. Continuing inequality affects the quality of democracy, especially the rule of law. Effective governance continues to be hampered by a system that includes twenty-two rather weak parties in the National Congress. But compared to many of the third wave of democracies, including Russia, Brazil stands as a relative success case.

CASE STUDY

Mexico: Transition from a Semi-Authoritarian Regime

- Modernization lays backdrop for democracy: rural-urban migration
- Elite split within ruling party creates three-party system
- Reforms of electoral system to solidify free and fair elections
- Growth of civil society that demands democratic changes
- Continuing problems of a weak state: corruption and drug-cartel violence

Mexican president Felipe Calderón (2006–) holds a newspaper announcing his electoral victory in September 2006. He is the second president elected since Mexico's transition to democratic rule, but the fact that both have come from the same party makes some observers question whether the country has fully achieved democratic consolidation.

Credit: Henry Romero/Reuters/Landov

On July 30, 2006, Andrés Manuel López Obrador, the center-left candidate of the Party of the Democratic Revolution (PRD), spoke before hundreds of thousands of supporters in Mexico City's main square, the Zócalo. Less than one month prior, one of the closest elections in Mexican history had been held, and Felipe Calderón of the center-right National Action Party (PAN) had been declared president by a margin of one-half of 1 percent. In his speech, López Obrador called on his partisans to stage a sit-in at the Zócalo as they awaited a ruling by the Federal Election Tribunal over the veracity of the vote. López Obrador dramatically told the crowd that without the proper channels of democracy, only "submission or violence" remained as viable alternatives for his movement.

Ultimately, the Tribunal held Calderón to be the legitimate victor, but the summer of 2006 was a difficult test for Mexico's young democracy. Between the years 1929 and 2000, the PRI's semi-authoritarian regime (see chapter 3) made one-party rule a fact of life in Mexico, and this had been the only post-PRI election ever held. The contention surrounding Calderón's victory now threatened to plunge the country into disarray. But this result never materialized, as the majority of the public soon turned its back on López Obrador, preferring to accept the official results as declared by Mexico's democratic institutions.

So how did Mexico become a bona fide democracy? The spark of change was lit in 1988 by Cuauhtémoc Cárdenas, a PRI insider who revolted and eventually formed the PRD as an opposition party. Son of the legendary president Lázaro Cárdenas, who famously nationalized the country's oil industry in the 1930s, Cuauhtémoc was heir to his father's political reputation and thus was able to galvanize the radical left and more nationalist segments within the PRI to join his cause of reforming the party. The was the first significant split in the long-dominant ruling party in decades.

Facing resistance within the establishment, Cárdenas finally broke away to run for president under the National Democratic Front (Frente Democrático Nacional), a left-wing coalition that included satellite parties that had previously left the PRI. The 1988 election became among the most contested in modern Mexican history, with PRI candidate Carlos Salinas de Gortari officially garnering around 50 percent of the vote, Cárdenas 31 percent, and conservative PAN candidate Manuel Clouthier 17 percent. Cárdenas denounced the election as a fraud and claimed to be the legitimate victor of the 1988 vote—something millions of Mexicans believe to this day. Adding intrigue to controversy, Clouthier was killed in an automobile accident in 1989, an event that aroused widespread suspicion that Salinas was somehow involved. Given the dark reputation of the PRI, it ultimately didn't matter whether either of these claims was true—the PRI was morally bankrupt and severely lacking in credibility.

Several important developments took place following the 1988 vote that put Mexico on the road to democracy. First, constitutional changes gave birth to the IFE (Instituto Federal Electoral, or Federal Electoral Institute) and the TRIFE (Tribunal Federal Electoral, or Federal Electoral Tribunal). The IFE was established as an independent body tasked with administering federal elections, while the TRIFE was a subsidiary of the judiciary tasked with resolving electoral disputes. (It was the TRIFE that ultimately validated Calderón's victory in 2006.) Second, the media shed many of its self-imposed limits on expression. Newspapers and television stations began taking an increasingly fair approach to political coverage, exposing the country's leaders to criticism and even ridicule. Third, Cárdenas formed the PRD in 1989 as a permanent home for disaffected PRI activists who sought both further democracy and a greater commitment to the radical heritage the PRI had once claimed. The PRD helped turn Mexico into the three-party system it is today. Finally, the long-established but previously weak opposition party, the PAN, also became an increasingly powerful force. As a Christian democratic party, the PAN began to attract a larger following, and for the first time since its founding in 1939, it won a statewide office. With the PAN victory of U.S.-born Ernesto Ruffo Appel as governor of Baja California in 1989, the PRI no longer held an electoral monopoly. Other aspects of the constitution changed little; the country preserved its presidential and federal system of government, which included a single, six-year term for the presidency. The changes in the 1990s made these institutions function

closer to the way they were supposed to on paper, rather than being controlled completely by the PRI as they had been under the semi-authoritarian regime.

By the time of the 1994 election, political contestation was open enough that President Ernesto Zedillo is now considered to be the first democratically elected president of Mexico. Yet the question remains as to why Mexico democratized when it did. While modernization theorists might have expected Mexico to democratize as early as the 1950s, Sebastian Garrido de Sierra (2011) argued that three factors combined to delay democratization until well into the 1990s. First, prior to the electoral reform laws of 1996, Mexican elites did not have viable avenues to defect and form an opposition. Second, urbanization moved Mexicans away from the reach of the PRI's rural clientelistic networks and into areas where mobilization was more easily achieved. Last but not least, Cárdenas's historic split from the leadership of the PRI created the necessary impetus for opposition.

Even after Zedillo was duly elected, his administration was not free of controversy. Unlike past candidates, he ran for office only following the death of Luis Donaldo Colosio, the successor that Salinas had originally handpicked. Colosio was brutally gunned down while campaigning in Tijuana, prompting Salinas to choose Zedillo, then Colosio's campaign manager, to replace him. While a lone gunman was captured after the murder, conspiracy theories sprang up over the question of who, if anyone, had ordered the killing. Some suspected Zedillo, while others, including Colosio's own father, laid the blame on Salinas himself (Pérez Silva 2004). Although Zedillo won on the basis of his moderate tone and technocratic legitimacy, Colosio's murder reinforced the view that the highest political circles in the country were criminal in nature.

Although the PRI held its first openly contested primary in 2000, its monopoly over the presidency had finally reached its limit. Change came with the election of conservative Vicente Fox Quesada, a member of the PAN. Fox, a former president of Coca-Cola of Mexico and governor of Guanajuato, won with around 43 percent of the vote, as opposed to PRI candidate Francisco Labastida's 36 percent and Cuauhtémoc Cárdenas's less than 17 percent.

The election of Vicente Fox brought wild, unrealistic hopes about what democracy would mean for Mexico, and Fox himself did little to tamp down expectations. At one point, he infamously claimed that as president he would resolve the government's dispute with Zapatista rebels in the south "in fifteen minutes." This was one of many election promises that fell short of their mark, as Mexico experienced increasing inequality, greater criminal violence, and general political gridlock, making the Fox presidency among the least popular in recent Mexican history.

Yet the Fox presidency was not without its milestones. With a new party in power, the country would now be able to openly confront the crimes that had marked the PRI's seventy-one-year rule. The most serious charges against the former government revolved around the repression and marginalization of student political movements during the 1960s and 70s, which at times involved imprisonment, disappearances, torture, and even murder. The most visible and infamous act of this so-called "*guerra sucia*" (dirty war) was the Tlatelolco massacre of 1968, which reportedly led to hundreds of deaths.

Since the 1970s, civil society actors like the Eureka! Committee (Comité ¡Eureka!) have fought to shed light on the crimes perpetrated by the state. In 2000, with the PRI out of power, former president Luis Echeverría was charged with the crime of genocide over the killings at Tlatelolco (during which he had served as secretary of the interior) as well as the Corpus Christi massacre of 1971, in which 10,000 peaceful demonstrators were attacked by plainclothes policemen, resulting in 25 student deaths and hundreds of injuries. The genocide charge laid on Echeverría was largely tactical, since the crime of murder carried a statute of limitations that would have expired. Following several court motions, however, Echeverría was cleared of any culpability in 2009. Despite the failure to bring

any high-level officials to justice, the process of airing grievances helped bring some healing to the country as it continued to move beyond its semi-authoritarian past.

Mexican democracy is still in its infancy. The country has not yet passed Huntington's "two-turnover test," meaning that the country has not had two different parties elected peacefully to power in consecutive fashion. And while Freedom House has classified the country as "free," its scores for political rights (2) and civil liberties (3) leave much room for improvement (one would expect a score of 1 on both counts in a fully fledged democracy). Adding to the ambivalence are the problems associated with weakened and nontransparent labor unions and occasional harassment of civil society organizations. Worse still, state institutions have begun to fail in the north amid drug violence, and corruption is still endemic throughout the country. All of these challenges do not mean that Mexico's democracy is under imminent threat. Perhaps most indicative of Mexico's democratic consolidation was the swing in public opinion against López Obrador and his open denunciation of the electoral process in 2006; the people by and large supported the state's mechanisms for determining a winner. The PRI has itself reformed significantly, and it remains a viable electoral force at the local level. Following the 2010 gubernatorial elections, in which the PRI won in several states, experts predicted that 2012 would be the likely year for the PRI's return to power—this time, as an opposition party winning a democratic election (Cattan 2010).

CASE SUMMARY

Mexico has completed a transition to democracy that few doubt. Consolidation, in the sense of all major actors (save the drug cartels) accepting the democratic process as "the only game in town," seems well established and perhaps will soon be verified by another electoral turnover. Modernization certainly may have provided the backdrop that helped this democracy come into being, but specific political changes within the elite in the 1980s and 1990s were necessary to make it happen when it did. This democracy, though, is plagued by the problems of a still-weak state, the most important of which are endemic corruption and drug-related violence that seem beyond the state's ability (or desire) to stop. Gaining democratic control over these problems will likely be essential to the long-term health of Mexicans' hard-won democracy.

CASE STUDY

Russia: Transition to a Semi-Authoritarian Regime

- Transition with weak institutions, starting with constitutional crisis
- Strong presidency
- Weak legislature and parties
- Patronage from oil wealth to build dominant party and undermine real competition

As Russian president Boris Yeltsin climbed atop a tank in Moscow to stop a coup attempt in August 1991, it seemed that freedom was on the rise in Russia. The coup was the last-gasp effort of hardliners in the old Communist regime of the Soviet Union. The reforms of Soviet president Mikhail Gorbachev in the late 1980s had significantly opened the

Boris Yeltsin (left) stands on a tank on August 19, 1991, as the Soviet military attempts a coup d'etat to reverse the reforms initiated by the last Soviet leader, Mikhail Gorbachev. Yeltsin's actions helped convince military leaders to reverse course, which led to the peaceful dissolution of the Soviet Union on December 31, 1991, and the birth of an independent Russia.

Credit: AP Photo

Soviet political system and economy, but demands for far greater reforms were in the air. With Gorbachev on vacation, elements in the military tried to roll the tanks into Moscow to restore the old system and prevent the reconfiguration of the Soviet Union as a smaller, more decentralized federation. Popular and international opposition, led by Yeltsin, forced the military to back down. By December, the Soviet Union was dissolved. Fifteen new countries emerged, with Russia being by far the biggest and most important, and each was expected to transition to democracy. The world's number-two superpower appeared to be starting an unprecedented transition from a Communist regime to one that was democratic and capitalist.

Russia's transition, however, has not been to democracy but instead to semi-authoritarian rule. In 1991–1992, Freedom House gave the country's political rights and civil liberties each a score of 3 on its 7-point scale, defining the country as "partially free." These scores deteriorated slowly over the next decade to 5, the low end of the "partially free" category. In 2005, Russia's political rights score slipped to 6, marking it as "not free," where it has stayed. This slide from moving toward democracy to moving away from it is a result of weak institutions, an exceptionally strong presidency, and the perverse effects of Russia's abundant natural resources. The full effects of this shift to semi-authoritarian rule would be clear only after Vladimir Putin, Russia's second president, consolidated his rule in the first few years of the new millennium.

Gorbachev's most dramatic reform was ending the Communist Party's claim to absolute power in February 1990. This was followed in March by Russia's legislative elections for the Congress of People's Deputies. At the time, Russia was still just one of fifteen constituent republics of the Soviet Union, and this was the first election to include non-Communist candidates since the Communist revolution. A year later, Boris Yeltsin was elected to the new position of Russian president, only two months before the coup attempt. With the dissolution of the Soviet Union, the provincial Russian institutions became those of the newly independent state. Yeltsin was the elected president, and the Supreme Soviet, which had been the working body of the Congress of People's Deputies, became the legislature but one that still had a Communist Party majority. This would lead to what would become a long-term battle between Yeltsin and his legislature.

Yeltsin initially used what came to be known as "shock therapy" to free prices from government control overnight and create the rudiments of a market economy. Within six months of starting the effort, however, political pressures forced him to compromise, resulting in a hodgepodge of policies that included some shock therapy and other more gradual approaches that slowed or limited the full transition to a market economy. He claimed that the benefits of the new capitalist economy would be widespread, but the immediate effect was a dramatic increase in prices that left Russians with little means of support; especially hard-hit were those who relied on government pensions for their livelihoods. Rapid privatization of the government-owned economy came about via distributing vouchers to all citizens, who could then use them to purchase shares in formerly government-owned companies. But widespread poverty among average citizens gave them an incentive to sell their shares to the companies' managers instead. More often than not, the formerly Communist factory managers became the owners of the newly privatized businesses. To the average worker, it looked like not much had changed, until the owners had to fire much of the bloated workforce to compete in the new market economy. The economy shrank 14.5 percent, and inflation ballooned to more than 1,500 percent in 1992. Unemployment tripled from 1992 to 1998. A few spectacularly successful businessmen, especially in Russia's huge oil sector, emerged to control vast swaths of the economy. Key allies of Yeltsin, they formed a group that came to be known as the "Family" and in effect ran the economy and the government.

The early years of an independent Russia were as chaotic and difficult politically as they were economically. Yeltsin chose early on not to hold elections to create a legislature with a more democratic mandate, because he feared that the unpopularity of his economic reforms would produce a legislature even more opposed to him. Faced with an increasingly hostile parliament, he ruled primarily by decree. In lieu of revising the constitution, he proposed the creation of the semipresidential system with an exceptionally strong presidency that we outlined in chapter 6. The legislature refused to ratify his ideas, leading him to disband it in September 1993. Legislators barricaded themselves in the parliament building, determined not to leave and voting to impeach Yeltsin. After a weeklong standoff, Yeltsin called in the army to lay siege to the parliament building, forcibly ending the Soviet-era parliament. He subsequently held a referendum on the constitution, which passed by a narrow margin, and an election for a new legislature. In spite of these successes, Yeltsin continued to face opposition to many of his reforms in the newly elected Duma (parliament) and frequently had to use his powers of decree to govern in the absence of legislative support. Citizens also blamed him for the unpopular, brutal, and ineffective war in the breakaway region of Chechnya. He narrowly won reelection in 1996, but neither his popularity nor the economy ever fully recovered.

A primary reason Yeltsin and his policies lacked support in the legislature was that he refused to join a political party, trying instead to appear "above" partisan politics. His refusal to participate, in addition to the very weak powers of the Duma, resulted in the creation of weak parties. Some observers at the time saw a strong presidency and a weak legislature as ensuring stability while Russian democracy "matured," but most now recognize this institutional arrangement as a flaw that undermined democracy. The mixed electoral system (similar to Germany's) in the 1993 constitution was part of the problem. Half the Duma's seats were elected via closed-list proportional representation (PR) and the other half via single-member districts. Unlike in Germany, few parties could

compete effectively in both types of elections; the few national parties won most of the PR seats, and independent candidates with no party affiliation but strong local bases of support won many of the SMD seats. The system operated more as two separate electoral systems than as a unified mixed system. Also, because the legislature was so weak, party loyalty among both the elite and the citizenry was low. Power resided overwhelmingly in the executive branch, and until Vladimir Putin joined a party in October 2007, the chief executive remained distanced from parties. Therefore, parties were of limited consequence except as often-temporary vehicles to gain election. They rose and fell with the popularity and shifting allegiances of major politicians.

Only seven of the thirteen parties in the first elected parliament in 1993 also had seats in the second parliament, elected in 1995. That parliament included seventeen parties, only five of which returned after the 1999 election. The 1999 parliament included fourteen parties, only six of which survived into the parliament that was elected in 2003, which included twelve parties or coalitions, none of which were new. While some of these changes were in name only or were the result of the creation of new parties via the merger or the splitting of old ones, this trend nonetheless shows the lack of durability of Russian parties as institutions. Ironically, the biggest exception is the Communist Party, which has the clearest ideology and is reputed to include 500,000 members. It has endured as a significant voice throughout Russia's tumultuous post-Communist history and was the largest party in the Duma from 1995 to 1999. To date, it is also the largest force in the Duma not allied with the executive.

Political scientists Hans Oversloot and Ruben Verheul (2006) argued that the most important party in Russia is the "party of power, the party that those around the president create to win as many seats as they can in the *duma,* insuring support for the president's proposals." This party has changed from one election to the next; it was called Russia's Choice in 1993, Our Home Is Russia in 1995,

Unity in 1999, and United Russia since 2003. Putin chose to help foster his party of power, United Russia, to a degree Yeltsin never did. He used his greater popularity (throughout his eight years in office, his popular approval ratings rarely dipped below 70 percent) and his control over patronage fueled by rising oil revenue to ensure that United Russia won handily. Since 2003, United Russia has easily dominated the Duma with a two-thirds majority, meaning the Duma has rubber-stamped everything Putin has proposed. As of 2008, United Russia also controlled all regional legislatures, and seventy-eight of the eighty-three regional governors were party members. Oversloot and Verheul noted that the presence of these parties of power reverses the democratic relationship between party and state. Rather than a party gaining control of the state via an election to the legislature, those in charge of the executive branch of the state create a party to win an election and gain control of the legislature.

Putin, anointed as Yeltsin's successor in 1999, was duly elected in 2000 and then reelected with more than 70 percent of the vote in 2004. He significantly centralized power in the executive and eliminated most vestiges of real democracy. In addition to increasing the powers of the presidency vis-à-vis the regions, he harassed and closed down most independent media, undermined independent civil society groups with new regulations, and broke the informal power of the oligarchs who had arisen under Yeltsin. Many of these oligarchs quietly agreed to support Putin in exchange for his allowing them to continue their business practices. Others, including a major media magnate and the owner of Yukos, a huge oil company, tried to resist his power. Their economic empires were systematically destroyed; Putin shut down the media and, in the case of Yukos, used charges of corruption to arrest the oligarch and seize his assets. Putin replaced Yeltsin's "family" with a group of former agents of the Federal Security Bureau (FSB), the successor to the KGB where he had spent most of his career. Members of this group sit in key ministries and agencies throughout the executive branch, have been appointed as governors, and control many important companies (Hesli 2007).

Putin also changed the electoral system. Under the mixed electoral system, his most significant opposition came from independent MPs elected in the single-member districts. He first put a 5 percent threshold on the PR seats, requiring parties to get that percentage of the national vote to gain seats in parliament. Then he had parliament change the electoral system altogether to a purely closed-list PR system to eliminate independent candidates entirely. More recently, he passed a law increasing the threshold for representation from 5 to 7 percent to eliminate more small parties. Combined with stricter laws on what parties must do to be officially registered, these changes reduced the number of parties from forty in 2003 to fourteen in 2008. If real electoral competition existed, this could be seen as enhancing democracy, since fewer and larger parties give voters clearer and more credible options. But in the context of Putin building his party of power, repressing civil society and the media, and using oil wealth as patronage to buy off opponents, the drop in the number of parties was simply part of a broader process of centralizing control. Early on, Putin also claimed he wanted to streamline the vast government bureaucracy. In fact, he expanded it, mainly as a means to buy off potential opposition. Until the 2008–09 economic crisis, rising oil prices gave vastly expanded revenues to the government, which under Putin had reasserted control over most natural resources. Putin used government takeovers of major natural resource companies and the revenue they generated to reward loyal supporters with major positions in companies and in government. He created large advisory bodies, often termed "parallel parliaments," which he filled with supporters who thus gained income and access to power. Patronage, as well as changes to the formal institutions of government, was crucial to Putin's centralization of power.

In October 2007, Putin officially joined the United Russia Party, his party of power.

Constitutionally barred from running for a third term as president, he announced he would be a candidate for prime minister. He also handpicked Dmitry Medvedev, a relatively obscure bureaucrat without a major political following, to succeed him as president. While some observers speculated that Medvedev had a stronger commitment to the rule of law than Putin, little has changed during his presidency. Medvedev carries out the official duties of president, including meeting with foreign heads of state, but Prime Minister Putin clearly remains the dominant political figure, controlling both Medvedev and parliament.

By 2010, the main debates over Russia's semi-authoritarian rule were how personalist it was becoming and what Putin's future plans were. Leon Aron (2009) reported a 2008 estimate that Putin's political allies head the boards of companies that together constitute 40 percent of the national economy. He saw a "sultanistic" rule developing that merges political power and control of wealth in the hands of a small elite around Putin. Reuter and Remington (2009), on the other hand, argued that Putin's party, United Russia, is creating a dominant-party system. Using a rational-choice approach, they saw the growing strength of the party as a compromise between Putin and regional elites to maintain themselves in power at lower political costs than they had incurred under the more chaotic party system of the 1990s. If true, this could represent a more institutionalized form of semi-authoritarian rule, eventually detached from Putin himself. In the meantime, though, Putin continues to be the clearly dominant force in Russian politics, and much speculation has focused on whether Medvedev would "choose" not to run in the 2012 presidential election, allowing Putin to run again and start a new two-term presidency. Part of this speculation is based on Putin's support of an extension of each presidential term from four to six years, meaning that if he were to be elected in 2012, he could rule until 2024. The only significant threat to his power has been

the effect of economic decline on his popularity. The global economic crisis of 2008–09 caused a significant economic downturn in Russia, but by 2010 the economy was starting to grow a little again. At the height of the crisis in 2009, some local protests against the government occurred but were easily put down, and Putin's longer-term popularity and control now seem secure.

CASE SUMMARY

Putin's rule fully transformed Russia from a weak but fledgling democracy to a semi-authoritarian regime. Political scientist Steven Fish (2005), one of the foremost experts on Russia, argued that this has occurred because of a weak legislature, limited economic reform, and a dependence on oil. Yeltsin and his supporters chose to establish a weak legislature to enable a strong presidency; the result has been the weak parties and the dynamics described above. Limited economic reform and massive oil production led to large-scale corruption. Putin justified his actions against the oligarchs and reduction in civil liberties in terms of building a strong state and reducing corruption, though the evidence suggests that he has achieved relatively little to that end. The worst elements of the weak state—widespread mafia activity in Moscow that characterized the mid-1990s—have been reduced, but overall corruption remains a problem. Transparency International gave Russia a score of 2.4 (out of 10, with 10 being least corrupt) in its 1999 Corruption Perceptions Index and a 2.2 in 2009, meaning that corruption had gotten slightly worse after a decade of Putin's rule. Oil revenues also mean the government can limit economic reform because rising oil prices allow it to co-opt potential opposition in civil society and the political class by controlling who can engage in business and how. Weak institutions in the context of abundant resources and limited reform have turned a transition to democracy into a transition to semi-authoritarian rule.

CASE STUDY

Nigeria: Neopatrimonial Transition

- Country's most enduring democracy
- New dominant party system?
- Tension over regional, ethnic, and religious political rivalries
- Weak parties and electoral system
- Strengthened judiciary, limits on presidential power, and civilian control of the military
- Continued problem of corruption, though improving

Nigeria's three presidents since the return of democracy in 1999: Olusegun Obasanjo (left; 1999–2007), Umaru Yar'Adua (right; 2007–2010), and Goodluck Jonathan (center; 2010–), stand together in 2007. When Obasanjo was prevented from running for a third term, he handpicked Yar'Adua as his successor. Yar'Adua's death in office in 2010 elevated Jonathan, who consolidated power and won the 2011 election. Elections marred by widespread irregularities and the continued rule of the same party since the transition have raised serious questions about the quality and sustainability of Nigeria's democracy.

Credit: AP Photo/George Osodi

Nigeria held its fourth consecutive multiparty election and inaugurated a third elected president in April 2011. Just four years earlier, the presidency had changed hands via election for the first time in the country's history, though the same party has won every election since the democratic transition in 1999. Domestic and international observers saw the 2007 election as deeply flawed, neither free nor fair; the prior president's party and his handpicked successor won an overwhelming victory at all levels of government, and each of three successive national elections (1999, 2003, 2007) was further from democratic norms than the one before. Given that history, the fact that the 2011 election was deemed to be improved over 2007 gave some hope that the deterioration of Nigeria's young democracy might be reversing. Throughout, Freedom House has rated Nigeria as "partially free," with scores of 4 or 5 out of 7 for both political rights and civil liberties during most years. Though the latest election seemed hopeful, a dominant-party system appeared to be emerging that limited democratic competition, and corruption remained a serious problem.

The election of 1999 marked Nigeria's third attempt to return to democratic rule. The military had allowed elections in 1979. These created the Second Republic, which ended in a military coup in 1983 (see chapter 8) amidst

claims that elected leaders had expanded corruption and stolen the election. A second transition attempt occurred in 1993, when military ruler Gen. Ibrahim Babangida allowed a carefully controlled election in which only two parties, both created by him, were allowed to run. The party he did not favor won, so he annulled the election. This decision not only plunged Nigeria into its darkest period under Gen. Sani Abacha, but it also gave rise to a vociferous democracy movement. The 1999 democratic constitution was modeled almost exactly after the 1979 one and created a presidential system with an FPTP electoral system very similar to that of the United States. As in much of Africa, democratic transition in Nigeria began with grassroots protests. The country's first human rights group, the Civil Liberties Organization, emerged in 1987. By 1991, a number of new human rights groups formed an umbrella organization, the Campaign for Democracy (CD), which became Nigeria's first large-scale civil society movement for democracy.

IN CONTEXT

FREEDOM IN AFRICA

In 1990, Nigeria's Freedom House Civil Liberties score was 5, compared to the Africa average of 5.06; its Political Rights Score was 5, compared to the Africa average of 5.56.

In 2010, Nigeria's Freedom House Civil Liberties score was 4, compared to the Africa average of 4.28; its Political Rights Score was 5, compared to the Africa average of 4.65.

This movement put pressure on Babangida to complete his "long transition program," started in 1985, and finally led to an election in 1993. Babangida's annulment of that election and the subsequent jailing of the rightful winner, Moshood Abiola, produced outrage in Nigeria and around the world.

The annulment of that long-awaited election motivated many new groups to join the democracy effort; in 1994, they formed a new umbrella group, the National Democratic Coalition (NADECO), which included former politicians, union members, students, and human rights campaigners of the CD. NADECO's breadth allowed it to bring even greater pressure to bear on Nigeria's military government. In its first campaign, "Babangida Must Go," it demanded that Babandiga be replaced by Abiola, the rightful winner of the election. Babangida did go, but he only gave up power to a handpicked "caretaker" government, which was overthrown by Abacha a few months later. While amassing a fortune from corrupt control of oil revenue, Abacha severely repressed the democracy movement. Most NADECO leaders ended up in jail, and (as discussed in chapter 4) the Ogoni leader Ken Saro-Wiwa and eight others were hanged in 1995.

Although Abacha claimed in 1995 that he was initiating a transition to democracy, this promise was a sham from the start. The five parties he allowed to register for what was to be the first election all proclaimed loyalty to him and only him. The real transition began only after his death in 1998. His successor recognized how discredited the military had become under Abacha's rule and immediately agreed to a transition and elections. The subsequent elections in 1999 were far from perfect, but most observers deemed them minimally adequate to start Nigeria's new democracy. The military elite of the Kaduna mafia put together what became the ruling party, the People's Democratic Party (PDP), and chose the military dictator who had shepherded the 1979 transition, Gen. Olusegun Obasanjo, as its presidential candidate. Obasanjo was credited with having revived democracy in 1979 and having actively opposed Abacha, spending part of the 1990s in jail. He also had become something of an elder statesman in Africa, with wide international respect. Further, in Nigeria's ethnically and religiously divided society, he benefited from being a Yoruba from the southwest. The long dominance of northerners under military rule and the annulment of the election of Abiola, a Yoruba, led all Nigerians to recognize that it was time for a president from the country's southern region.

So the Kaduna mafia, a group of Muslim military leaders from the north that has controlled most of Nigeria's governments, picked a southerner whom it trusted and who was a former general himself as its candidate. He faced only one opponent, another Yoruba, though his party faced two major opposition parties in the legislative races. Ironically, Obasanjo won handily in most of the country but not in his home area among the Yoruba, who saw him as having sold out to northern military interests. By the 2003 election, Obasanjo and his party won more easily than in 1999. The only significant opposition came from a party led by northern leaders who were unhappy with Obasanjo. Its presidential candidate was Muhammadu Buhari, the military dictator from 1983 to 1985, who had a reputation for being a devout Muslim and uncorrupt. He and Obasanjo's handpicked successor, Yar'Adua, were the two major presidential candidates in 2007 as well. Yar'Adua won 72 percent of the vote, and the PDP won a similar majority in the legislature. Though many parties existed, by 2007 only two had a real shot at gaining power, and the ruling party scored an overwhelming victory, though partly via fraudulent means. As the 2011 election approached, the PDP continued to be dominant, with the most closely watched campaign being the primary election for the party's presidential nomination. In the legislative election, however, the party actually lost some seats, though it retained a slim majority overall. Its presidential candidate, incumbent president Goodluck Jonathan, won as well, defeating his major opponent, Buhari, who ran and lost for the third time. This time, the ruling party's victory was significantly smaller than in 2007. Until 2011, it seemed that the country was moving toward a dominant-party system in which the PDP would rule without any serious competition; the closer 2011 election left this outcome less certain.

Political parties in Nigeria are not strong institutions with loyal supporters based on party ideology and symbols; instead they are based mainly on the support of key Big Men and their use of patronage. The neopatrimonialism that characterized military rule has continued under the new democracy. In 1999, a rule that required parties to gain the support of 5 percent of the voters in three-quarters of the states resulted in there being only three parties on the ballot. By 2003, the Supreme Court had invalidated this limit, and dozens of parties registered, "but most parties consisted primarily of the office staff at the national headquarters . . . and were typically centered on a Big Man who was funding the operations and running for president" (Kew 2004, 147). By 2010, sixty-two parties were officially registered, though only a handful were of widespread significance and the ruling PDP remained dominant.

Elections are institutionally weak as well. Former U.S. president Jimmy Carter was so upset by what he saw as electoral fraud in 1999 that he refused to endorse the results as legitimate, though ultimately his organization and other international election observers decided to accept the elections as minimally adequate, in part out of fear that not doing so would encourage yet another military coup.

In 2003, the elections were free and fair in about one-third of Nigeria's states, "dubious" in another third, and completely fraudulent in the final third (Kew 2004). By 2007, observers for Human Rights Watch reported that "the elections were marred by extraordinary displays of rigging and the intimidation of voters in many areas throughout Nigeria" (Rawlence and Albin-Lackey 2007, 497). In quite a few states, no elections took place at all: officials simply made up results in favor of the ruling party. Incumbent governors won in most states, whether they were members of the PDP or the opposition ANPP. Voter turnout was grossly inflated in many states in which the ruling party won, and observers saw officials openly stuffing ballot boxes in a number of cases.

After assuming the presidency in 2010, Jonathan promised to improve the electoral process and appointed a well-known democracy advocate and scholar to head the electoral commission; this individual is credited with having improved the process significantly. The legislative election in 2011 actually had to be postponed a week because of logistical difficulties, but once it took place, followed by presidential and state government elections in succeeding weeks, most observers credited the electoral commission with having substantially improved the credibility of the elections. Sporadic violence, long a part of Nigerian elections, continued to be a problem however. In the northern state of Madiguri, a radical Islamist sect set off bombs shortly before the election, and rebels in the oil-producing delta region also used violence to disrupt the process.

While institutions of participation are extremely weak, Nigeria's experiment with democracy has produced some examples of institutionalization that have seemed to strengthen democracy. Civilian control of the military has been key. Military leaders of the Kaduna mafia backed Obasanjo for president in 1999 because they assumed that they could control him after he took office. In a number of areas, they were proven wrong. After becoming president, he quickly removed those northern generals most actively engaged in politics and replaced them with less politically active and more southern officers. Presidents Yar'Adua and Jonathan also replaced military leaders without a military backlash, and when Yar-Adua's prolonged illness left him incapacitated and the country's government very uncertain for nearly three months, rumors of military intervention were rife but the armed forces remained in their barracks. While it is difficult to make predictions, given Nigeria's history of military coups, the Third Republic seems to have established civilian control over the military, a first in Nigerian history. Indeed, some observers believe that the reason elections have become so hotly contested and fraudulent is that the stakes are so high. No one expects military intervention, so election is the sole means of gaining political power. The growing presence of former military rulers as presidential candidates suggests the same conclusion.

A second institution that has been strengthened is the Supreme Court. The new constitution created a National Judicial Council that has helped insulate the judiciary from pressures from elected officials. The Supreme Court has made several important rulings over questions of federalism that have long been of importance in Nigeria. In the area of federal versus state control over oil revenues, the Supreme Court ruled in some key cases in favor of the oil-producing states and in other cases in favor of the federal government, indicating a certain degree of autonomy from political pressure from either side. On the eve of the 2007 presidential election, it also ruled that Obasanjo's estranged vice president, whom the president had tried to prevent from running, could stand in the election. While this created havoc in terms of the ballots, since his name was not on them, the Court's ruling against an important issue for the sitting president was nonetheless another indication of its autonomy. After the faulty election, the courts also ruled several gubernatorial victories invalid and required new elections. But in December 2008, a deeply divided high court narrowly ruled that Yar'Adua's presidential victory was

legitimate, a conclusion doubted by virtually all impartial observers. The opposition candidates, though, chose to accept the ruling, preventing a more prolonged crisis for the country's still fragile democracy.

Perhaps the two most important tests of institutional strength for Nigerian democracy went against incumbent presidents, indicating some degree of institutionalization of limits on personal rule. The first came when President Obasanjo launched a major campaign to revoke the two-term limit for the presidency. Amending the constitution to allow Obasanjo a third term required Senate approval. Reportedly, he and his supporters were even trying to bribe senators to vote in favor of the amendment with offers as high as $750,000. It became crystal clear, though, that the population overwhelmingly opposed the move, and the Senate voted it down despite all the pressure and inducements Obasanjo brought to bear. Some observers also argue that many of the elite quietly opposed Obasanjo as well. In a patronage-based system with oil revenue available, the presidency is very powerful and very lucrative. The political elite want that office to rotate rather than be monopolized for too long by any one individual so that other leaders and other groups have a chance to gain its benefits. The result, in any case, was the preservation of an institutionalized limit on one individual's time in office, despite the power and wealth at his disposal.

The second major institutional challenge began in 2009, when President Yar'Adua became gravely ill and left the country for treatment in Saudi Arabia. A president can indicate by letter to the legislature that he is incapacitated and must temporarily turn over his powers to his vice president, but Yar'Adua refused to do this. Led by his wife, his closest aides refused to let any Nigerians see him and released no information about his health. For two months, the country was without even an acting president. Amid growing domestic and international pressure to clarify this situation, Yar'Adua gave a radio interview in which he said in a weak voice that he hoped to return to work soon. The National Assembly took that as a public statement that he was incapacitated and appointed Vice President Jonathan as acting president. Once again, the sitting president and his closest aides were rebuffed in an illegitimate attempt to retain power. A couple of months later, after returning to Nigeria, Yar'Adua finally died, and Jonathan assumed the full powers of the presidency.

Establishing a stable federal order in Nigeria has long been a contentious process, and it continues to be under the new democracy. The biggest issue is control of revenue from the oil that is located in a handful of southeastern states. Not surprisingly, these states argue that they should receive a larger share of the revenue generated from resources within their borders, while the federal government and other states argue exactly the opposite. The current formula gives 13 percent of all such revenue to the state of origin, meaning that the oil states receive far more money than states without oil. Nonetheless, their leaders demand more, and their people remain among the poorest in the country, in large part because of still massive corruption in the oil-producing states. The ethnic movements we discussed in chapter 4 arose and continue because of the population's failure to gain much from the oil in their land. In recent years, unfortunately, some of these armed movements have become armed gangs for hire to the highest bidder. Not infrequently, they act as armed thugs for politicians in the oil-producing states and serve as the violent wing of campaign teams. Most shockingly, at the nation's celebration of the fiftieth anniversary of its independence, bombs exploded in the capital, killing at least sixteen people. The Movement for the Emancipation of the Niger Delta (MEND) took credit before and after the attacks; it was the first time the violence from the oil-producing region had hit the capital, and the event was deeply embarrassing for President Jonathan, who hails from that region himself.

The Sharia controversy we described in chapter 4 is also part of the federalism question in Nigeria. The 1999 constitution allows states to set their own legal codes within national law, and Nigeria has long allowed dual civil law codes based on religion. The twelve northern states that have implemented Sharia have expanded its use to criminal law as well, setting off confrontations with Christian minorities in several of these states and opposition from the south in general. Long-standing northern and Muslim control of national politics has left southerners and Christians fearful of any further Islamic movements. And because of federalism, each state's version of Sharia is slightly different; some states apply some Muslim laws to non-Muslims and other states don't, while some include the harshest penalties such as stoning and others don't. So far, national courts have neither revoked states' rights to implement Sharia nor insisted on a uniform version of Sharia across all states.

Ethnic and regional political rivalries continue to dominate Nigerian democracy. The informal understanding in 1999 that the presidency should alternate between a northerner and a southerner (hence from Obasanjo to Yar'Adua) became an official policy of the ruling party. Yar'Adua's death and Jonathan's ascension to the presidency inadvertently violated this principle in that Yar'Adua only completed part of his term and was replaced by Jonathan, a southerner. Initially, party leaders resisted the idea that Jonathan would be allowed to run for a full term of office in 2011. After extensive behind-the-scenes campaigning, which allegedly included funneling oil money to key governors to gain their support, the ruling party allowed him to stand for office, effectively ending the policy of alternating the presidency between north and south. Jonathan faced serious primary challenges within the party, though, from several major northern leaders. These included the former military dictator Babangida, who is one of the wealthiest men in the country, and Obasanjo's former vice president, Abubakar Atiku. Northerners felt strongly that they have a right to see a northern leader returned to office to complete what they presumed would be Yar'Adua's two terms in office; Buhari, the major opposition candidate, gained support because of this. Residents of Jonathan's homeland in the oil-producing southeastern region, however, feel just as strongly that he deserves to continue as president.

All of these institutional problems in Nigeria are related to the overall weakness of the state. The country continues to be one of the more corrupt in the world, though it has made improvements. Transparency International's 1999 Corruption Perception Index ranked Nigeria number 98 of 99 countries surveyed, with a score of 1.6 on a 10-point scale (with 10 being least corrupt). In 2010, it was number 130 of 180 countries, with a score of 2.5. While Nigeria's ranking is still far below average, the numbers are nonetheless showing an improvement. This is due in part to an anticorruption drive Obasanjo launched that received great praise in its early years. Unfortunately, it seems that before both the 2003 and 2007 elections, Obasanjo and his party were willing to use their anticorruption efforts for political purposes, targeting charges at their opponents while protecting their supporters. Yar'Adua achieved little progress in fighting corruption while in office. Jonathan appointed a new head of the Central Bank who won praise for removing some corrupt officials, but how much change the new president would really achieve, and how much change he wanted, remained unclear. Continued corruption has made all state institutions weak, harmed the ability of the electoral commission to conduct proper elections, prevented people in the oil-producing states from benefiting from their oil, and led

northerners to turn to Sharia in the hope that it will be less corrupt and more just than secular courts.

CASE SUMMARY

The Nigerian case demonstrates the potential to establish democracy in a poor country, as well as the severe problems that can arise when politics are based on patronage. The competition for office becomes all-consuming and often violent, undermining democratic norms of the "free and fair" choice of candidates. Corruption continues throughout the country with only slight improvement, weakening all state institutions and popular faith in democracy. Yet the fragile democratic regime in Nigeria seems to have brought the military under control, and a coup seems less likely than at any time since the first one occurred in 1966. A few other key institutions—term limits and judicial independence—have been strengthened as well. In 2011, even the much criticized electoral process seemed to be improving at least slightly. Advocates of democracy in countries like Nigeria hope that these institutional gains will be the basis for further improvement and the slow establishment of a consolidated and relatively high-quality democracy, though that seems quite far off in Nigeria's case. Indeed, if the PDP continues to dominate, the regime may become a clear example of a minimally democratic but dominant-party system. In the meantime, widespread poverty, ethnic and religious tensions, and failure to gain real improvements from the country's massive oil wealth continue to plague the country.

CONCLUSION

Regime change is the high drama of comparative politics. Many of our most iconic political images are of regime change, from the "shot heard round the world" in 1776 to Boris Yeltsin standing atop a Soviet tank in 1991 to Nelson Mandela taking the oath of office in 1994. They are images of popular and charismatic leaders backed by the mobilized masses demanding a better world. There can also be less positive images, though, like that of a general seizing power as tanks roll into the capital. Of course, when examined systematically, regime change is more complex and less clearly positive or negative than it is often portrayed. It involves the destruction of an old regime (and sometimes a state) that is already weak followed by the attempt to create a new one. No matter how it is carried out or by whom, regime change is no simple process.

Who Rules?

At least in theory, democratization produces regimes in which citizens rule. How true that is, of course, depends on the nature and effectiveness of the particular democratic institutions, a subject we investigated in depth in chapters 6 and 7. Revolutions and military coups also raise questions about who rules. A seemingly united revolutionary front can often hide a disparate set of groups, past grievances, and future agendas. This makes building a new regime with strong institutions particularly fraught with troubles and unlikely to have a democratic outcome. Revolutionary leaders almost always impose their own vision on society, at least initially, and demobilize popular participation in the new regime. All revolutions from below have ultimately resulted in authoritarian regimes of some sort. Revolutions from above, on the other hand, have been characterized by less mass mobilization, less deep social divisions, and less violence, and they seem to have a better chance of producing democratic rule. As is so often the case in politics, those who fight for change do not necessarily get what they seek.

The military always presents a problem in politics. Civilian regimes, from communist to democratic, have to worry about the possibility that those holding the guns will use them against the civilian order, regardless of what the constitution says. Institutionalizing norms of professionalism and loyalty to the civilian regime is crucial to keeping the soldiers in their barracks. When push comes to shove, the military holds the guns on which the state and regime rely. But militaries, even highly institutionalized ones, are not designed to rule. Every military regime relies on civilian support to some extent, especially within the state itself. Military rulers need and want an effective modern state as much as civilian rulers do, so they rely on state bureaucrats to carry out their rule. In some instances, such as under Brazil's bureaucratic-authoritarian regime, the military relies even more on civilians, inviting those who are sympathetic to it to actively participate in governing, even at the highest levels. Military rulers do keep a tight rein, however, on how much influence civilians have and how far they can wander from military mandates.

What Explains Political Behavior?

Regime change raises some of the biggest political behavior questions in comparative politics. The third wave of democratization has been dramatic, but only some of the new democracies have moved toward consolidation; others have become semi-authoritarian regimes. Consolidating a new democracy is an extremely challenging process. Major political groups often do not trust one another or the new and untried democratic institutions they have created, but democracy requires trust in both in the long run. Partly for this reason, comparativists for years believed that democracy would only survive in very specific kinds of countries. That position was challenged by the "transition" paradigm, which argued that democracy could survive anywhere. More careful recent scholarship suggests that while democracy can arise anywhere, its chances of survival are definitely higher in favorable cultural or economic contexts. The process can be easily undermined by institutional breakdowns of all sorts. An increasingly common result of these breakdowns, especially in the former Soviet Union and much of Africa, seems to be semi-authoritarian regimes, whose future will have a major impact on the future of democracy around the world.

Revolutions are much rarer and more dramatic events, the stuff of which world history is made. Due to their rarity, a particular set of circumstances must account for them, but it is not always easy to figure what those circumstances are. A weakened old regime and state seem essential, as strong states can resist revolution no matter how many people are involved. A strong revolutionary organization that unites and mobilizes people's grievances also seems vital. Revolutions are known by their leaders' ideologies, but that does not always explain the motivations of the masses supporting them. The masses are often motivated by the failure of the old regime as well as a sense of relative deprivation, whether due to declining economic circumstances or rising expectations that have not been met.

Where and Why?

Military coups are the most common and quickest form of regime change. When civilian efforts to socialize and thereby control the military fail, troops seize the capital for a variety of reasons. These can range from the military's sense that the nation needs to be "rescued," to the military's own interests as an organization, to the more particular interests of individual leaders or groups within the military. The explanation for any particular coup may include more than one of these reasons. Which explanation is most useful often depends on the nature of the military itself, especially its degree of institutionalization. Less institutionalized militaries, such as in Nigeria, usually produce more personalist coups and subsequent regimes. More institutionalized militaries, such as in Brazil, typically intervene as an organization, whether for their own interests or due to their sense of the "national interest." In those cases, a more institutionalized military regime is the likely result, though that does not guarantee that the military will govern better or less ruthlessly than more personalist military regimes.

Applying Theory to Regime Change

Regime change is such a large and important topic that virtually all major theories of comparative politics have been used to explain it. Political-culture theorists long argued that attributes of particular cultures set the stage for particular kinds of regime change. Traditions of rebellion make revolution easier, and an absence of democratic norms makes military coups more likely and democracy less likely. Ideology clearly has a role to play in explaining revolutions, or at least in explaining the revolutionary leaders' motivations, but it is of limited help in explaining mass involvement. Transition-to-democracy theorists argue that neither culture nor ideology is particularly important in understanding when a transition will occur. Influenced by rational-choice theory, they argue that transitions take place when political elites see the acceptance of democratic institutions to be in their rational self-interest. This usually occurs when moderate elements in the old regime recognize reform as being essential to their survival and moderate elements in the mass democratic movement are willing to negotiate an institutional arrangement that is acceptable to all. Mass mobilization for democracy is important in almost all cases, but only as a background condition that spurs elites to shift their perceptions of what is in their own interests. When the interests of the masses and the elites align, a democracy can result. Whether the new democracy can be consolidated and survive, however, is another matter.

While the first transition theorists seemed to believe that new democracies would survive as long as all major elites continue to view the institutions of democracy as operating to their collective benefit, modernization theorists have responded, with growing evidence, that either culture or a structural condition—such as economic development—is necessary to preserve democracy in the long run. Modernization theorists address all three types of regime change. They explain revolutions and military coups as particular conjunctures in the modernization process, and they assert that stable democracy is likely only in more fully modernized societies. The often chaotic process of regime change, however, continues to limit comparativists' predictive powers. Some cases, such as our mini case of Ghana, defy the odds, producing democracy where theorists would least expect it. The study of regime change, always difficult to predict, will undoubtedly continue.

Comparative politics today focuses much more on democratization than on military coups or revolutions. We suggest, however, that the latter two types of regime change remain important topics of investigation. Military coups have certainly continued to occur in this era of democratization; a coup took place in Niger (not to be confused with Nigeria) in February 2010. Coups occur less frequently than in the past, however, and studying revolutions teaches us much about how people are mobilized into political activity of all types. While the dramatic regime changes in Egypt and Tunisia in 2011 may not qualify as revolutions by the standard comparative politics definition, they may represent a new paradigm of profound political change that scholars might eventually embrace as a distinct category of revolution. Further evolution of events on the ground and scholarly analysis are necessary to allow us to understand the full implications of these recent examples of regime change.

KEY CONCEPTS

delegative democracies (p. 446)

democratic consolidation (p. 446)

democratic deepening (p. 446)

electoral democracies (p. 446)

founding election (p. 446)

hardliners (p. 445)

moderates (p. 445)

pact (p. 445)

political liberalization (p. 446)

political violence (p. 438)

radicals (p. 445)

revolution (p. 434)

revolutions from above (p. 435)

revolutions from below (p. 435)

softliners (p. 445)

terrorism (p. 438)

transition to democracy (p. 445)

WORKS CITED

AfroBarometer. 2005. "Sustained Support for Democracy in Ghana" (Briefing Paper No. 18). http://www.afrobarometer.org/.

AfroBarometer. 2008. "Popular Attitudes to Democracy in Ghana" (Briefing Paper No. 51). http://www.afrobarometer.org/.

Allen, Chris. 1995. "Understanding African Politics." *Review of African Political Economy* 22 (65): 301–20.

Almond, Gabriel A., and Sidney Verba. 1963. *The Civic Culture: Political Attitudes and Democracy in Five Nations.* Princeton, NJ: Princeton University Press.

———. 1989. *The Civic Culture Revisited.* Newbury Park, CA: Sage.

Ames, Barry. 2001. *The Deadlock of Democracy in Brazil.* Ann Arbor: University of Michigan Press.

Aron, Leon. 2009. "The Merger of Power and Property." *Journal of Democracy* 20 (2): 66–68. doi:10.1353/jod.0.0086.

Avritzer, Leonardo. 2009. *Participatory Institutions in Democratic Brazil.* Baltimore: Johns Hopkins University Press; Washington, DC: Woodrow Wilson Center Press.

Bermeo, Nancy Gina. 2003. *Ordinary People in Extraordinary Times: The Citizenry and the Breakdown of Democracy.* Princeton, NJ: Princeton University Press.

Boix, Carles, and Susan Carol Stokes. 2003. "Endogenous Democratization." *World Politics* 55 (4): 517–49. doi:10.1353/wp.2003.0019.

Bratton, Michael, and Nicholas van de Walle. 1997. *Democratic Experiments in Africa: Regime Transitions in Comparative Perspective.* New York: Cambridge University Press.

Brinton, Crane. 1965. *The Anatomy of Revolution.* New York: Vintage Books.

Cattan, Nacha. 2010. "Drug Violence Mars Mexico Election," *Christian Science Monitor* July 5. http://www.csmonitor.com/World/Americas/2010/0705/Drug-violence-mars-Mexico-election/.

Clark, John F. 2006. "Armed Arbiters: When Does the Military Step into the Electoral Arena?," In *Electoral Authoritarianism: The Dynamics of Unfair Competition,* edited by Andreas Schedler, 130–48. Boulder, CO: Lynne Rienner.

Clawson, Patrick, and Michael Rubin. 2005. *Eternal Iran: Continuity and Chaos.* New York: Palgrave MacMillan.

Crenshaw, Martha. 1981. "The Causes of Terrorism." *Comparative Politics* 13 (4): 379–99.

Davies, James C. 1962. "Toward a Theory of Revolution." *American Sociological Review* 27 (1): 5–19.

Decalo, Samuel. 1976. *Coups and Army Rule in Africa.* New Haven, CT: Yale University Press.

Figueiredo, Argelina Cheibub, and Fernando Limongi. 2000. "Presidential Power, Legislative Organization, and Party Behavior in Brazil." *Comparative Politics* 32 (2): 151–70.

Finer, Samuel E. 1962. *The Man on Horseback: The Role of the Military in Politics.* New York: Praeger.

Fish, M. Steven. 2005. *Democracy Derailed in Russia: The Failure of Open Politics.* New York: Cambridge University Press.

———. 2006. "Stronger Legislatures, Stronger Democracies." *Journal of Democracy* 17 (1): 5–20. doi:10.1353/jod.2006.0008.

Fish, M. Steven, and Robin S. Brooks. 2004. "Does Diversity Hurt Democracy?" *Journal of Democracy* 15 (1): 154–66. doi:10.1353/jod.2004.0009.

Freedom House. "Freedom in the World." http://www.freedomhouse.org/template.cfm?page=15.

Fukuyama, Francis. 1992. *The End of History and the Last Man.* New York: Free Press.

Garrido de Sierra, Sebastián. 2011. "Eroded Unity and Clientele Migration: An Alternative Explanation of Mexico's Democratic Transition." Paper presented at the annual meeting of the Midwest Political Science Association, Chicago, March–April.

Graf, William. 1988. *The Nigerian State: Political Economy, State Class, and Political System in the Post-Colonial Era.* London: J. Currey; Portsmouth, NH: Heinemann.

Gurr, Ted Robert. 1970. *Why Men Rebel.* Princeton, NJ: Princeton University Press.

Gyimah-Boadi, E. 2009. "Another Step Forward for Ghana." *Journal of Democracy* 20 (2): 138–52. doi:10.1353/jod.0.0065.

Hadenius, Axel, and Jan Teorell. 2005. "Cultural and Economic Prerequisites of Democracy: Reassessing Recent Evidence." *Studies in Comparative International Development* 39 (4): 87–106.

Hagopian, Frances. 2005. "Chile and Brazil." In *Assessing the Quality of Democracy,* edited by Larry Diamond and Leonardo Morlino, 123–62. Baltimore: Johns Hopkins University Press.

Hagopian, Frances, Carlos Vervasoni, and Juan Andres Moraes. 2009. "From Patronage to Program: The Emergence of Party-Oriented Legislators in Brazil." *Comparative Political Studies* 42 (3): 360–91.

Hesli, Vicki L. 2007. *Government and Politics in Russia and the Post-Soviet Region.* Boston: Houghton Mifflin.

Huntington, Samuel P. 1964. *The Soldier and the State: The Theory and Politics of Civil-Military Relations.* New York: Random House.

———. 1968. *Political Order in Changing Societies.* New Haven, CT: Yale University Press.

———. 1991 *The Third Wave: Democratization in the Late Twentieth Century.* Norman: University of Oklahoma Press.

Inglehart, Ronald, and Christian Welzel. 2003. "Political Culture and Democracy: Analyzing Cross-Level Linkages." *Comparative Politics* 36 (1): 61–79.

———. 2005. *Modernization, Cultural Change, and Democracy: The Human Development Sequence.* New York: Cambridge University Press.

Janowitz, Morris. 1964. *The Military in the Political Development of New Nations: An Essay in Comparative Analysis.* Chicago: University of Chicago Press.

Kapstein, Ethan B., and Nathan Converse. 2008. "Why Democracies Fail." *Journal of Democracy* 19 (4): 57–68. doi:10.1353/jod.0.0031.

Kew, Darren. 2004. "The 2003 Elections: Hardly Credible, but Acceptable." In *Crafting the New Nigeria,* edited by Robert I. Rotberg, 139–73. Boulder, CO: Lynne Rienner.

Kieh, George Klay, and Pita Ogaba Agbese. 2002. *The Military and Politics in Africa: From Engagement to Democratic and Constitutional Control.* Aldershot, UK: Ashgate.

Lijphart, Arendt. 1969. "Consociational Democracy." *World Politics* 21: 207–25.

Lindberg, Staffan I. 2009. "The Power of Elections in Africa Revisited." In *Democratization by Elections: A New Mode of Transition,* edited by Staffan I. Lindberg, 25–46. Baltimore: Johns Hopkins University Press.

Linz, Juan. 1990. "The Perils of Presidentialism." *Journal of Democracy* 1 (1): 51–69. doi:10.1353/jod.1990.0011.

Lipset, Seymour Martin. 1959. "Some Social Requisites of Democracy: Economic Development and Political Legitimacy." *American Political Science Review* 53 (1): 69–105. doi:10.2307/1951731.

Moore, Barrington. 1966. *Social Origins of Dictatorship and Democracy: Lord and Peasant in the Making of the Modern World.* Boston: Beacon Press.

O'Donnell, Guillermo A. 1979. *Modernization and Bureaucratic-Authoritarianism: Studies in South American Politics.* Berkeley: Institute of International Studies, University of California Press.

———. 1994. "Delegative Democracy." *Journal of Democracy* 5 (1): 55–69.

O'Donnell, Guillermo A., and Phillipe Schmitter. 1986. *Transitions from Authoritarian Rule: Tentative Conclusions about Uncertain Democracies.* Baltimore: Johns Hopkins University Press.

Oversloot, Hans, and Ruben Verheul. 2006. "Managing Democracy: Political Parties and the State in Russia." *Journal of Communist Studies and Transition Politics* 22 (3): 383–405. doi:10.1080/13523270600855795.

Paige, Jeffery M. 1975. *Agrarian Revolution: Social Movements and Export Agriculture in the Underdeveloped World.* New York: Free Press.

Pérez Silva, Ciro. 2004. "Colosio Fernández dirige sospechas contra Salinas." *La Jornada,* February 11. http://www.jornada.unam.mx/2004/02/11/008n1pol.php.

Pincus, Steven. 2007. "Rethinking Revolutions: A Neo-Tocquevillian Perspective." In *The Oxford*

Handbook of Comparative Politics, edited by Carles Boix and Susan Carol Stokes, 397–415. Oxford, UK: Oxford University Press.

Przeworski, Adam. 1991. *Democracy and the Market: Political and Economic Reforms in Eastern Europe and Latin America.* Cambridge, UK: Cambridge University Press.

Przeworski, Adam, Michael E. Alvarez, José Antonio Cheibub, and Fernando Limongi. 2000. *Democracy and Development: Political Institutions and Well-Being in the World, 1950–1990.* Cambridge, UK: Cambridge University Press.

Rawlence, Ben, and Chris Albin-Lackey. 2007. "Briefing: Nigeria's 2007 General Elections; Democracy in Retreat." *African Affairs* 106 (424): 497–506. doi:10.1093/afraf/adm039.

Reuter, Ora John, and Thomas F. Remington. 2009. "Dominant Party Regimes and the Commitment Problem: The Case of United Russia." *Comparative Political Studies* 42 (4): 501–26. doi:10.1177/0010414008327426.

Roett, Riordan. 1978. *Brazil: Politics in a Patrimonial Society.* rev. ed. New York: Praeger.

Sanderson, Stephen K. 2005. *Revolutions: A Worldwide Introduction to Political and Social Change.* Boulder, CO: Paradigm.

Santos, Fabiano. 2008. "Brazilian Democracy and the Power of 'Old' Theories of Party Competition." *Brazilian Political Science Review* 2 (1): 57–76. http://www.bpsr.org.br/english/arquivos/BPSR_v2_n3_jun2008_03.pdf.

Skocpol, Theda. 1979. *States and Social Revolutions: A Comparative Analysis of France, Russia, and China.* New York: Cambridge University Press.

Tilly, Charles. 1978. *From Mobilization to Revolution.* New York: McGraw-Hill.

Welzel, Christian, and Ronald Inglehart. 2006. "Emancipative Values and Democracy: Response to Hadenius and Teorell." *Studies in Comparative International Development* 41 (3): 74–94. doi:10.1007/BF02686237.

Whitfield, Lindsay. 2009. "'Change for a Better Ghana': Party Competition, Institutionalization and Alternation in Ghana's 2008 Elections." *African Affairs* 108 (433): 621–41. doi:10.1093/afraf/adp056.

Wood, Gordon. 1992. *The Radicalism of the American Revolution.* New York: Knopf.

RESOURCES FOR FURTHER STUDY

Ackerman, Peter, and Jack Duvall. 2000. *A Force More Powerful: A Century of Nonviolent Conflict.* New York: St Martin's Press.

Casper, Gretchen. 1995. *Fragile Democracies: The Legacies of Authoritarian Rule.* Pittsburgh, PA: University of Pittsburgh Press.

Dahl, Robert. 1971. *Polyarchy: Participation and Opposition.* New Haven, CT: Yale University Press.

Diamond, Larry, and Leonardo Morlino. 2005. *Assessing the Quality of Democracy.* Baltimore: Johns Hopkins University Press.

El Diario. 2010. "¿Qué quieren de nosotros?" September 18. http://bit.ly/96ILN9.

Haggard, Stephan, and Robert R. Kaufman. 1995. *The Political Economy of Democratic Transitions.* Princeton, NJ: Princeton University Press.

Levitsky, Steve, and Lucan Way. 2002. "Elections without Democracy: The Rise of Competitive Authoritarianism." *Journal of Democracy* 13 (2): 51–65. doi:10.1353/jod.2002.0026.

Morgenstern, Scott, and Benito Nacif, eds. 2002. *Legislative Politics in Latin America.* New York: Cambridge University Press.

O'Donnell, Guillermo. 1999. "Horizontal Accountability in New Democracies." In *The Self-Restraining State: Power and Accountability in New Democracies,* edited by Andreas Schedler,

Larry Diamond, and Marc F. Plattner, 29–51. London: Lynne Rienner.

Pinkney, Robert. 2003. *Democracy in the Third World*. Boulder, CO: Lynne Rienner.

Reynolds, Andrew. 2002. *The Architecture of Democracy: Constitutional Design, Conflict Management, and Democracy*. New York: Oxford University Press.

Schedler, Andreas. 2006. *Electoral Authoritarianism: The Dynamics of Unfree Competition*. Boulder, CO: Lynne Rienner.

Webb, Paul, and Stephen White, eds. 2007. *Party Politics in New Democracies*. Oxford, UK: Oxford University Press.

Wegren, Stephen K., and Dale R. Herspring, eds. 2010. *After Putin's Russia: Past Imperfect, Future Uncertain*. New York: Rowman and Littlefield.

Zakaria, Fareed. 2003. *The Future of Freedom: Illiberal Democracy at Home and Abroad*. New York: W. W. Norton.

WEB RESOURCES

Bueno de Mesquita, Bruce, Alastair Smith, Randolph Severson, and James Morrow, "The Logic of Political Survival Data Source" (http://www.nyu.edu/gsas/dept/politics/data/bdm2s2/Logic.htm)

Global Integrity, 2009, "Global Integrity Index" (http://report.globalintegrity.org/globalIndex.cfm)

Melton, James, Stephen Meserve, and Daniel Pemstein, 2011, "Unified Democracy Scores" (http://www.unified-democracy-scores.org/)

Polity IV Project, 2011, "Political Regime Characteristics and Transitions, 1800–2009" (http://www.systemicpeace.org/polity/polity4.htm)

PART III

Former Army National Guard Lt. Dan Choi, an Arabic-speaking specialist and West Point alumnus, was dismissed from the New York National Guard under the "Don't Ask, Don't Tell" policy after he came out on the *Rachel Maddow Show* on MSNBC in 2009. Choi became the focal point of the successful effort to repeal the policy that prevented gays and lesbians from serving openly in the U.S. military.

Credit: AP Photo/Damian Dovarganes

ISSUES AND POLICIES

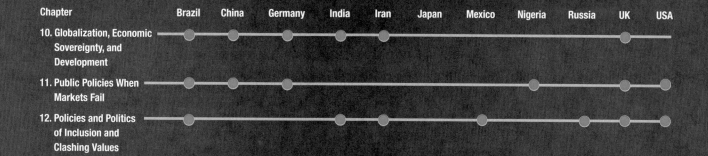

Chapter	Brazil	China	Germany	India	Iran	Japan	Mexico	Nigeria	Russia	UK	USA
10. Globalization, Economic Sovereignty, and Development	●	●	●	●	●					●	
11. Public Policies When Markets Fail	●	●	●					●		●	●
12. Policies and Politics of Inclusion and Clashing Values	●		●		●	●	●		●	●	●

Country	GDP distribution by sector (percent of total)*			Forest area change (thousands of sq. kilo.)[†]	Internet users (per 100 people)[§]
	Agriculture	Industry	Services		
Brazil	6.1	25.4	68.5	−423.3	37.5
China	10.3	46.3	43.4	401.5	22.5
Germany	0.8	26.6	67.8	3.4	75.5
India	16.1	28.6	55.3	37.6	4.5
Iran	25.0	31.0	45.0	0.0	32.0
Japan	1.6	21.9	76.5	−0.8	75.2
Mexico	4.3	32.9	62.8	−6.3	22.2
Nigeria	32.5	33.8	33.7	−61.5	15.9
Russia	4.7	32.9	62.4	1.6	31.9
United Kingdom	0.9	22.0	77.1	2.3	76.0
United States	1.2	21.9	76.9	44.4	75.9

*CIA World Factbook, http://www.cia.gov/.

[†]UN *Human Development Report* data from the latest year available.

[§]*Human Development Report*, 2009, http://hdrstats.undp.org/en/indicators/54.html.

● Case Study
● Mini Case

Who Rules?

- Do states continue to have effective economic sovereignty, or does globalization force them to adopt certain economic policies?

What Explains Political Behavior?

- What explains the ability of states to pursue successful development policies in the context of globalization?
- In what ways has globalization affected states' ability to respond effectively to economic crises?

Where and Why?

- Why has Asia seen such dramatic economic success while Africa remains the poorest region in the world?
- Why have some countries moved to liberalize their economies in the face of globalization more than others?

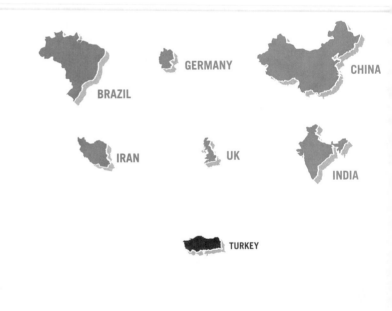

10

GLOBALIZATION, ECONOMIC SOVEREIGNTY, AND DEVELOPMENT

The two biggest economic crises since the Great Depression began a decade apart, in 1997 and 2007. Both involved financial crises that started in largely unregulated financial markets in one part of the globe and then spread rapidly, affecting countries around the world. Both showed the potential negative effects of globalization and the limits it can put on individual states' ability to control their economies. The first crisis started when the government of Thailand was forced to "float" its currency, the baht. The Thai economy had been booming, along with those of the rest of the countries that were part of what was known as the "East Asian Miracle." International capital poured into Thailand, factories opened, and the real estate market soared. Much of this activity, however, went through unregulated banks in a relatively weak state, which may be why international investors began to doubt the stability and long-term prospects of the Thai economy, although this is still up for debate among economists. The famous venture capitalist, George Soros, was one of the first to sell his Thai currency, and as more investors sold, the Thai government no longer could afford to trade dollars for the baht at the set value. Running out of money, the government had to adjust the rate downward, lowering the baht's value against the dollar and other currencies. To beat the odds, investors sold their currencies rapidly, getting out of the currency market the way people get out of a stock market when they think it's about to crash. As investors pulled out, real estate prices and company profits collapsed. Economies that had been booming went into steep decline, and unemployment soared. The economic contagion spread rapidly from Thailand to Indonesia, Malaysia, the Philippines, and South Korea and later to other developing economies like Brazil and Russia.

The second crisis started in the booming U.S. housing market and the financial market in mortgage-backed securities and derivatives that was tied to it

Spaniards stand in line at a government job center in April 2009. Spanish unemployment neared 20 percent at the height of the global recession. The recession, which began in the U.S. housing market, spread across the globe via financial interconnections, hitting many European countries particularly hard and bringing into question the continued viability of the euro as a currency for the EU.

Credit: Sergio Perez/Reuters/Landov

(see chapter 5). Beginning in the heart of the world's largest economy, it spread even more rapidly, hitting hardest in countries whose banks were heavily exposed to the market in U.S. mortgage-backed securities. In contrast to the East Asian crisis, in the Great Recession of 2008–09, the wealthy economies declined the most and had the hardest time recovering, while the rapidly developing economies of China, India, and Brazil fell less and recovered sooner. In both cases, though, the crises spread rapidly through the global financial system, leaving individual states scrambling to respond effectively and raising questions about their economic sovereignty.

Globalization has clearly raised major questions about economic policy in both wealthy and poorer countries. As we discussed in chapter 5, the biggest of these are the "Who rules?" questions related to whether or not the state still matters. Are states still sovereign over their economies? Does globalization force different regimes and societies with different values to follow the same economic policies that are dictated by the need to attract global capital? Modern states, whatever the regime type, are expected to guide economic growth; even the most venal want leverage over the economy so they can benefit from it. Economic growth provides revenue to a state and legitimacy to a regime. How does globalization affect states' abilities to gain these benefits? Globalization also raises key "What explains political behavior?" questions. What explains whether a particular set of policies can steer an economy beneficially, and what explains which states are able to adopt these policies? Does the rapid flow of capital and goods around the globe impede these efforts? Finally, we can ask the "Where and why?" questions of why some regions (such as Asia) are so much more successful than others (such as Africa) and why some governments have pursued neoliberal policies more fully than others.

One thing is certain: globalization has helped produce dramatically different levels of economic development around the world. The "Country and Concept" table below demonstrates this for our case study countries. First, it shows the level of industrialization among our case study countries, demonstrating that the wealthiest are now accurately termed "postindustrial." It also shows key aspects of globalization: **foreign direct investment (FDI)**, foreign investment in directly productive activity; **trade**, exports and imports of goods and services; and **international capital flows**, the movement of money across national borders. In most countries, all three areas show marked increases. The greatest increases, though, are in the final column, portfolio investment equity, which is a measure of international capital flows. These have expanded dramatically in almost all countries. The virtual elimination of barriers to moving money across borders and improvement in global communications have resulted in more than $1 trillion crossing international borders daily.

foreign direct investment (FDI): Investment from abroad in productive activity in another country

trade: The flow of goods and services across national borders

international capital flows: Movements of capital in the form of money across international borders

COUNTRY AND CONCEPT

Globalization, Economic Sovereignty, and Development

Country	Industry as percentage of GDP[1]		Net foreign direct investment (FDI) inflows as percentage of GDP[2]		Exports of goods and services as percentage of GDP		Imports of goods and services as percentage of GDP		Portfolio investment equity as percentage of GDP	
	1995	2009	1995	2009	1995	2009	1995	2009	1995	2009
Brazil	36.7	25	0.63	1.65	9.5	11	9	11	0.36	2.36
China	47.2	46	4.92	1.57	20.9	27	19	22	0.00	0.56
Germany	32.1	26	0.48	1.18	23.5	41	23	36	0.48	0.35
India	28.1	28	0.60	2.64	12.2	21	12	25	0.45	1.61
Iran	34.2	44.6*	0.02	0.91	13.1	39***	13	39****	0.00	—
Japan	34.4	28**	0.00	0.23	7.8	13	8	12	0.96	0.25
Mexico	27.9	35	3.32	1.60	30.4	28	28	29	0.18	0.48
Nigeria	46.7	56.8***	3.84	3.34	42.2	36	42	27	0.00	0.30
Russia	37	33	0.52	2.98	25.9	28	26	20	0.01	0.27
United Kingdom	32	21	1.88	1.14	28.8	28	28	30	0.70	3.52
United States	26.3	21***	0.79	0.95	12.3	11	12	14	0.22	1.14

* 2006

** 2008

*** 2005

**** 2006

1 Data on Industry as percentage of GDP are from the World Resources Institute.

2 Data on Stock of FDI, Imports and Exports of Goods and Services as a percentage of GDP, and Portfolio Investment Equity are from the World Bank.

All areas of global economic activity have expanded, and most areas of activity have shifted toward some of the faster growing developing countries. This chapter examines the impact of these trends on both economic well-being and states' abilities to respond effectively and maintain their economic sovereignty. We turn first to the wealthy countries. For them, the biggest issues are how to respond to the movement of manufacturing out of their countries and whether they can continue to maintain the level of social spending their citizens have come to expect, especially in Europe.

WEALTHY COUNTRIES: GLOBALIZATION AND ECONOMIC SOVEREIGNTY

In the first globalization debate in the wealthy countries of Europe, North America, and Australasia (Australia, New Zealand, and Japan), the situation was not referred to as "globalization," a word that had not yet come into vogue in the 1970s. It was about "deindustrialization," especially in the United States. The countries that had long been known as "advanced industrial democracies" discovered that they were rapidly losing their industry; their economies were making a transition to "postindustrial" society in which the service sector, high-technology endeavors, and research and design were replacing manufacturing as the core of the economy. In retrospect, this was the start of a wave of globalization that began in earnest in the 1970s.

As transportation and communication improved and liberal trade policies allowed industries to take advantage of lower production costs in developing countries, corporations began moving manufacturing plants out of wealthy countries and exporting products back to their home markets. Hundreds of thousands of workers, long reliant on relatively well-paying and secure jobs in such industries as automobile manufacturing and steel, faced unemployment and bleak prospects. Not only did they lose their jobs, but other positions in the same field were not available. Entire sectors shrank and moved overseas. Workers had to seek retraining in newly emerging fields or take lower-paying, unskilled positions in sectors such as retail, where they often had to work multiple jobs for longer hours. Managers, meanwhile, reaped increasing salaries as their companies profited and expanded. The result in many countries has been growing inequality.

The abstract logic of globalization's effects on wealthy countries, then, seems pretty clear. As capital becomes more mobile and can flow around the globe, even wealthy governments must do what they can to attract it. They must maintain macroeconomic stability by keeping inflation low, which requires restraining government spending and the money supply (following the monetarist principles we outlined in chapter 5). They must keep corporate taxes low so that businesses will want to invest, but if taxes are low, then spending must be low as well, meaning that social welfare programs also have to be restrained. They must ensure that labor is flexible and relatively compliant and do what they can to keep labor unions from making too many demands, because rigid contracts and rules that guarantee jobs or benefits for long periods discourage investment. And, of course, they must keep tariffs and other barriers to the entry and exit of capital at a minimum.

According to this perspective, which Colin Hay (2004) called **hyperglobalization**, globalization tends to produce a **convergence** among the policies of wealthy countries. The distinctions among liberal market economies (e.g., the United

hyperglobalization: Thesis that globalization is so powerful, it will overwhelm the power of nation-states, forcing convergence of economic policies

convergence: Argument that globalization will force similar economic and social policies across all countries

States), European welfare states (e.g., Germany), and developmentalist states (e.g., Japan), as well as partisan differences over economic policy within each country, tend to disappear as all of these governments, regardless of their past economic models or current ideological disposition, are forced to conform to the logic of attracting global capital. In the last decade, however, growing numbers of scholars have questioned this argument, noting that while changes are certainly occurring in the general direction Hay predicted, they are not happening very rapidly and are strikingly different in different countries. Empirical studies generally show differences in taxation, welfare spending, union power, and overall levels of inequality.

For this reason, many comparativists use institutionalist arguments to suggest that, at least for wealthy countries, national economic sovereignty will continue to exist: countries can and are choosing unique means to respond to globalization's demands. While most agree that the forces of globalization apply pressure in the direction that the hyperglobalization theory suggests, many also believe that long-established political and economic institutions in specific countries heavily influence how these countries can and will respond, with different effects on their long-term economic well-being.

Varieties of Capitalism Approach

The most influential school of thought that questions hyperglobalization is known as the **varieties of capitalism** approach. It focuses primarily on business firms and how they are governed in terms of their interactions with government, each other, workers, and sources of finance such as banks and stock markets. Proponents of this approach distinguish between two broad types of economies among wealthy capitalist countries: liberal market economies (LMEs) and coordinated market economies (CMEs).

Liberal Market Economies (LMEs)

Liberal market economies (LMEs), such as the United States and the United Kingdom, rely more heavily on market relationships, meaning that firms interact with other firms and secure sources of finance through purely market-based transactions. They know little about each others' inner workings, which leads them to focus primarily on short-term profits to enhance stock prices, a key source of finance. Such firms' relationship to workers is also primarily via open markets: rates of unionization are low and labor laws are flexible, allowing firms to hire and fire employees with ease. The government's role in such economies is relatively minimal and is focused simply on ensuring that market relationships function properly through, for instance, fairly stringent antimonopoly laws and rules governing stock exchanges that guarantee that all buyers are privy to the same information.

Coordinated Market Economies (CMEs)

Coordinated market economies (CMEs) by contrast, involve more conscious coordination among firms, financiers, unions, and government. Many firms and banks hold large amounts of stock in each other's operations, which gives them inside information on how the others operate. This, in turn, encourages firms to coordinate their activities and establish long-term relationships in terms of finance and buying inputs. Firms are able to focus on longer-term initiatives because financiers have inside information about the

varieties of capitalism: School of thought analyzing wealthy market economies that focuses primarily on business firms and how they are governed; divides such economies into LMEs and CMEs and argues that globalization will not produce convergence between them

liberal market economies (LMEs): In the varieties of capitalism approach, countries that rely heavily on market relationships to govern economic activity; the United States and United Kingdom are key examples

coordinated market economies (CMEs): In the varieties of capitalism approach, capitalist economies in which firms, financiers, unions, and government consciously coordinate their actions via interlocking ownership and participation; Germany and Japan are key examples

Figure 10.1

Globalization's Effects on Economic Policies: Two Views

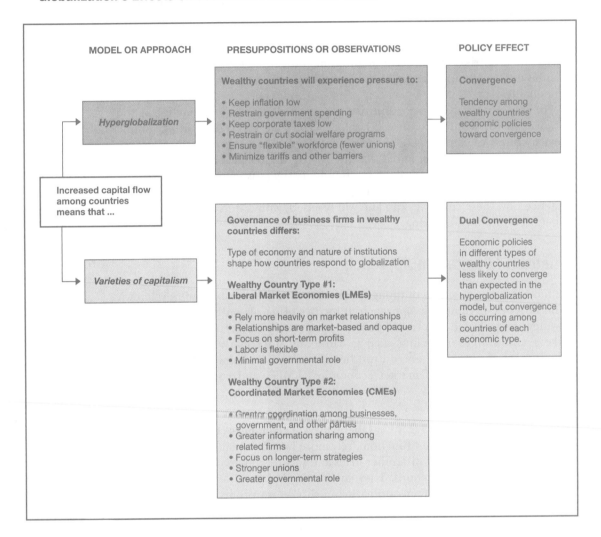

comparative institutional advantage: Idea in the varieties of capitalism school of thought that different kinds of capitalist systems have different institutional advantages that they usually will try to maintain, resulting in different responses to external economic pressures

potential for long-term gains. CMEs tend to have stronger unions and higher levels of unionization, and worker training is focused within sectors of the economy and within related firms. The government is involved in negotiating agreements among firms and between firms and unions, and it allows or even encourages the close relationships that might be termed "insider trading" or quasi-monopoly situations in an LME. Germany is a prime example of a CME. Japan's developmentalist state is usually classified as a CME as well, though with a smaller role for unions than is found in European CMEs.

LMEs and CMEs: Responses to Globalization Peter Hall and David Soskice (2001), who created the varieties of capitalism approach, coined the term **comparative institutional advantage**, as opposed to the standard comparative (economic) advantage, to help explain how these different kinds of economies respond to the pressures of globalization. They argued that the various institutionalized relationships in each kind of economy are complementary: the institutions work together to provide greater benefits than any single institution could alone. It is difficult, they argued, to change one particular institution, such as corporate finance, without changing many others. Consequently, firms have interests in maintaining the institutions in which they operate, and they will be reluctant to change them in response to globalization. Firms in CMEs benefit from the various institutions that help them coordinate their activities, train their workers, and secure the services of employees over the long term. A more rigid labor market that does not make it as easy for workers to move from firm to firm, for instance, complements a training system in which firms invest in educating their workers for specific tasks. If workers could quickly move from job to job, the firms would lose the benefits of their training investment. In LMEs, by contrast, more flexible labor markets give firms little incentive to train employees. Workers and the public education system therefore invest in more general skills that workers can transfer from firm to firm, meaning that firms don't have to invest directly in employee training.

The comparative institutional advantage of LMEs is in their flexible market relationships. In response to globalization, they tend to strengthen market mechanisms even more. Governments work to decrease union influence, provide broad-based education for an ever more flexible workforce, and increase the variety and efficiency of open-market sources of finance such as stock markets. LMEs, advocates argue, are more adept at making radical innovations in response to new opportunities. Management and workers all have few reasons for caution, as their long-term futures are not tied to a specific firm.

The comparative institutional advantage of CMEs is in their ability to adjust but maintain their coordination mechanisms in response to globalization. Firms do not abandon countries with CMEs because doing so would cause them to give up the institutional advantages they have there, advantages in which they have long invested. CMEs are better at marginal innovation than at radical innovation because they can and must coordinate activities across a number of firms and sectors, including training workers in specific skills. Management and workers have incentives to make marginal changes to improve the performance of the firms in which they have a long-term interest. CMEs tend to be more innovative in older industries, such as pharmaceuticals, than in newer industries, such as high-tech sectors. Indeed, firms in CMEs tend to transfer their branches that engage in more radical innovations to LMEs, where they benefit from the comparative institutional advantages that LMEs offer.

The varieties of capitalism approach has implications for contemporary welfare policies as well. Convergence theorists argue that governments will have to cut social spending as they cut taxes to attract global capital, whereas scholars using the varieties of capitalism approach argue that in CMEs, business often supports social spending. Much of this social spending provides workers with security in the form of pensions, health care, and disability benefits, which helps workers stay with a particular firm without fear of losing their jobs. Spending on industry- or even firm-specific job training also benefits firms in CMEs. These scholars argue that since large businesses in CMEs benefit from social spending, they do not insist on reducing it. Rather, they tolerate higher taxes and spending to help secure a highly trained and productive workforce. LMEs, on the other hand, operate much as convergence theorists speculate they "should." Greater labor market flexibility does not provide the same incentives found in CMEs, and firms are less willing to tolerate the high taxes necessary to maintain high spending, so social spending drops more precipitously in the face of globalization.

How, then, have these different economies responded to the pressures of globalization? Is convergence in fact happening, despite the differences in types of advanced capitalist systems? Hall and Gingerich (2009) examined the varieties of capitalism concept with a series of extensive statistical tests. They found that the patterns outlined by the approach do hold up empirically. Each type of economy (LME and CME) can be discerned by a set of complementary practices across a variety of statistical measures. Comparative institutional advantage holds up under scrutiny as well, in the sense that countries that more closely conform to one of the two models have achieved higher growth rates. Countries with more mixed systems, and therefore less reinforcing comparative institutional advantages, have grown more slowly. Across a variety of measures, most wealthy economies in the new millennium are moving in the direction the forces of globalization would suggest: protection of labor is down, social spending is down, and flexibility has increased. Hall and Gingerich found, though, that the differences between LMEs and CMEs persist; while both types of economies have moved in the same direction, CMEs remain quite distinct from LMEs in terms of their policies. The differences remain important even in the face of globalization.

Summary

The logic of globalization seems clear. Capital's greater mobility ought to give it greater power vis-à-vis immobile states and less-mobile workers. Virtually all scholars agree that this has happened to some extent over the past thirty to forty years, but the changes may not have been and are not now as dramatic as initially asserted. The institutional, ideological, and cultural legacies of different models of state-market interaction in wealthy capitalist countries have not disappeared entirely. Unionization, taxation, social spending, and coordination efforts among businesses, unions, and governments continue to a noticeably greater extent in some countries than in others. Two paradigmatic examples in the varieties of capitalism debate are two of our own case studies, the United Kingdom and Germany. The United Kingdom demonstrates how an LME responds by instituting more "market-friendly" policies in the face of crises, aided by its majoritarian parliamentary system that makes enacting large policy changes relatively easy. Germany, in contrast, demonstrates that despite noticeable reform in the direction of an LME, a CME model still seems to be viable and can respond effectively to even the most severe crises.

CASE STUDY

United Kingdom: Radical Reform in a Liberal Market Economy

- Two major reforms in direction predicted by LME model
- Reduced power of trade unions and privatization of state-owned companies in 1980s
- Less substantial reduction in social spending

- Hard hit by global financial crisis, responding first with stimulus and then with severe reduction in government spending to reduce debt
- Majoritarian parliamentary system facilitated dramatic economic reforms

The United Kingdom and the United States are the classic examples of LMEs for scholars using the varieties of capitalism approach. Prior to the 1980s, however, the United Kingdom had exceptionally large and active trade unions, and since World War II, the country has had a far more extensive welfare state than the United States. While its social spending is below that of most European countries, it is well above that of the United States. Twice in the last generation, the United Kingdom has pursued some of the most radical economic reforms of any major Western country, first in the 1980s under Prime Minister Margaret Thatcher and again beginning in 2010 under newly elected Prime Minister David Cameron. Thatcher's government profoundly reduced the role of the state in key areas via privatization of state assets, and it reduced the power of unions, as the varieties of capitalism approach would predict an LME would do in the face of globalization. Thatcher did not significantly reduce overall social spending, however. Cameron's more recent efforts zeroed in on spending and the budget deficit, introducing dramatic reductions to both, again as would be expected in an LME facing a severe financial crisis.

The 1970s were a period of unparalleled economic crisis in the United Kingdom. Rising oil prices and global recession hit the country particularly hard, reducing growth and increasing inflation. Both Conservative and Labour governments tried but failed to improve the economy. As inflation grew, union demands that wage increases keep up became a key problem, as wage increases would simply fuel more inflation. About half of the British labor force belonged to a union, an unusually high level even by European standards. The government tried voluntary agreements like those common in a corporatist system to get unions to restrain their demands and thereby slow inflation. Unfortunately, the peak labor association, the Trade Unions Congress (TUC), did not have the power over its members that unions in corporatist systems do, and local unions repeatedly ignored the voluntary restraints negotiated by the TUC leadership. In an LME such as the United Kingdom, neither

A protester in front of the British parliament on the day in March 2010 when the new British PM, David Cameron, delivered his budget, which included what many saw as "draconian" cuts to public employment and social services. The Conservative–Liberal Democrat coalition government argued that the cuts were essential to reduce the budget deficit produced by the 2008–2009 global recession.

Credit: © Andy Rain/epa/Corbis

unions nor businesses have a history of or an incentive to negotiate lasting agreements to moderate wage increases, so the result was a growing number of strikes. These culminated in the "winter of discontent" in 1978–1979, when the Labour government lost control and massive strikes occurred.

Out of this crisis rose a new manifestation of the Conservative Party, which Margaret Thatcher led to victory in the 1979 election. She won on promises of implementing a completely new approach to economic policy, unions, and the welfare state, very much along the same lines as the approach adopted by Ronald Reagan, who was elected U.S. president a year later. Her first target was the power of unions, which she sought to reduce to create a more flexible labor force in line with the LME model. Over her first five-year term, Thatcher passed legislation that made it far more difficult for unions to strike, culminating in a standoff with the National Mineworkers Union in 1984–1985 over a strike against the state-owned coal companies. Thatcher ultimately defeated the union, which gave up its strike after gaining virtually nothing. This symbolized the end of an era of union strength in the United Kingdom. The number of strikes dropped dramatically, and by 1995, union membership had dropped from half of all employees when Thatcher was elected to only a third of all employees. As the LME model suggests, when facing global economic pressure, LMEs look to reduce labor costs and increase flexibility to compete more effectively. This is precisely what Thatcher did.

The second area of major reform under Thatcher was privatization of state-owned assets. Since World War II, the British state, especially under Labour governments, had taken ownership of numerous large companies, including utilities, mining companies, auto manufacturers, and airlines. Many of these were far from profitable when Thatcher took power. She began selling off the state-owned companies to private investors—a process that continued through the 1990s—ultimately privatizing 120 corporations. Some became profitable private-sector companies; others simply went bankrupt. One immediate effect was increased unemployment as the unprofitable companies laid off workers in large numbers; unemployment rose from an average of 4.2 percent in the late 1970s to 9.5 percent in the 1980s (Huber and Stephens 2001, A11).

Thatcher's most popular policy was not privatization of state-owned companies but rather the sale of state-owned housing. After World War II, the British government had dedicated itself to building public housing for the working class. By the 1970s, the vast majority of the working class—typically union and Labour Party members—paid subsidized rents to live in publicly owned houses or apartments. Thatcher sold more than a million housing units, mostly single-family homes, mostly to the current tenants. This created a dramatically expanded class of homeowners who were no longer tenants of the state. Most political analysts argued that it also transformed many of these individuals from Labour voters into Conservative voters and helped Thatcher win two unprecedented landslide reelections.

Prime Minister Thatcher was less successful at reforming monetary and fiscal policy. She came to power a committed monetarist, advocating a reduced government with lower budget deficits and tight monetary policy to eliminate inflation. Like all monetarists, she put greater priority on macroeconomic stability than on achieving full employment, the long-term goal of the Keynesian consensus that had dominated British economic policy in earlier decades. In the early 1980s, her government successfully reduced inflation by reducing the money supply and budget deficit. This deepened the ongoing recession but made clear that fighting inflation was Thatcher's top priority. The government relaxed monetary policy starting in 1986, however, to generate greater economic growth, producing inflation of 10 percent by 1990. Thatcher also shifted the source of taxation, reducing individual and corporate income taxes and compensating by raising Britain's national sales tax (the value-added tax, or VAT). The net result was an increased tax burden on lower-income groups and a lower burden on the wealthy.

Thatcher's inability to reduce the overall size of the government's budget was due in no small part to her failure to reduce social spending. After her election, she set out to radically reform Britain's welfare state, which centered on what the British call "social security," government payments to the poor, unemployed, disabled, and others who are unable to make a minimally adequate income in the market. Her biggest reform was to reduce the real value of social security payments and insist that the unemployed seek work while collecting social security. She also proposed dramatic changes to Britain's universal health system, the National Health Service (NHS), but the system's popularity prevented her from implementing most of these proposals. She was only able to instill some market-type mechanisms within the NHS, not fundamentally change the system as a whole (see chapter 11). In the end, her only revolutionary change to Britain's welfare system was the dramatic reduction in public housing. Later, the Labour government under Tony Blair (1997–2007) actually instituted the first work requirement for welfare benefits, and the new coalition government led by the Conservatives in 2010 increased these requirements, ultimately fulfilling some of Thatcher's long-held goals.

Despite the fact that social spending did not drop, inequality increased more in Britain under Thatcher than in any other wealthy country: the share of the population living on less than half of the average national income increased from 9 to 25 percent under Thatcher and has since dropped only slightly (Ginsburg 2001, 186). Regional inequality increased a great deal as well. Many of the unprofitable state-owned companies and older manufacturing firms were in the northern half of the country. Deindustrialization combined with Thatcher's reforms to hurt that region severely, causing increased unemployment and poverty, while the southern part of the country, especially London, became one of the wealthiest regions in Europe. The later Labour governments succeeded in reducing overall inequality slightly but did not change regional inequality at all.

Thatcher's reforms reshaped the British economy by making it a purer LME. The reforms were particularly dramatic not only because of the crisis the country faced at the time but also because the British parliamentary system allows a government great power in reorienting policy. The comparison with Ronald Reagan in the United States is interesting in this regard. Elected at around the same time and holding the same ideas as Thatcher, Reagan was not able to make nearly as sweeping reforms. While he pursued a similarly successful monetary policy to defeat inflation and reduced the power of unions (though not as significantly as Thatcher), Reagan instituted no changes as substantial as Thatcher's privatization. The U.S. presidential system, in which an independent Congress is often controlled by the opposition party, combined with a federal system that reserves considerable power for the states, limited what Reagan could accomplish.

Subsequent British governments have not fundamentally changed Thatcher's policies. The Labour government under Tony Blair (1997–2007) and Gordon Brown (2007–2010) took its most dramatic action immediately after coming into office: it gave autonomy to the Bank of England to set monetary policy, much as the Federal Reserve does in the United States. In the past, the PM and the cabinet had controlled monetary policy, so giving the bank autonomy clearly signaled to the world that the new Labour government would value macroeconomic stability at least as much as its Conservative predecessors. The Labour government presided over a period of unprecedented economic well-being from 1997 to 2007, until the financial crisis of 2008–2009. GDP growth, averaging 2.6 percent annually, was well above that of other European countries; inflation averaged only 1.5 percent; the deficit was kept low; and Britain was the favored location for foreign investment in Europe (Faucher-King and Le Galès 2010). After 2002, the government invested more heavily in education and job training in a successful effort to lower the unemployment rate, which dropped to only 5.5 percent. A successful anti-child-poverty policy removed over one million children from poverty between 2005 and 2007, though overall inequality was reduced only slightly. Labour, however, did not reverse the policies that had weakened trade unions or the basic monetarist orientation of British macroeconomic policy, thus preserving the fundamentals of the British LME.

The exceptional British economic success up to 2007 was based in part on growing financial, stock, and real estate markets, all of which were heavily hit by the global financial crisis. The economy shrank nearly 5 percent in 2009, and unemployment hit 8 percent (up from 4.5 percent a couple of years earlier). As in most Western economies, sluggish growth resumed in 2010, though unemployment dropped only slightly. Gordon Brown's Labour government initially responded similarly to the U.S. government, first with large infusions of cash to ailing banks and then with a stimulus program that dramatically increased the government deficit. The failure of these measures to have a significant short-term effect led to a Labour rout in the May 2010 election, which brought an unusual Conservative-led coalition government to power (see chapter 7). The new government quickly reversed course on economic policy, arguing that the government's growing debt threatened to undermine Britain's financial standing in the global economy, as was happening to both Greece and Ireland. The government's first budget introduced in October 2010 instituted draconian cuts in spending, averaging 19 percent. Ultimately, nearly half a million public employees would be fired due to these cuts. The government also raised the retirement age, required those on long-term unemployment benefits to seek work actively, and capped those benefits at one year. Protests erupted several times after the announcement of the new budget, primarily among university students reacting against major tuition increases. The only sectors spared the ax were the National Health Service (see chapter 11) and primary and secondary education. The new policies clearly followed the standard path of an LME facing a globalization-induced crisis in that they reduced the size of the government to restore financial order and encourage renewed business investment. Britain's majoritarian parliamentary system allowed the new government to pursue these policies with little compromise, making them among the most dramatic responses to growing deficits anywhere in the world.

CASE SUMMARY

Faced with crises induced by global economic forces, British economic policy responded in a manner predicted by the LME model. First, Britain reduced the power of unions and privatized many state assets, and then it cut government spending and debt to encourage new investment. Thatcher's reforms resulted in a more flexible labor market with more competitive wages in which a higher percentage of employees worked at part-time jobs and far fewer were unionized. Britain's corporate ownership system, like that of the United States, remained dominated by large pension and insurance funds that were interested in short-term profitability. This strategy is typical of an LME, and with a more flexible labor market, it allowed British companies to enter new markets aggressively and relatively successfully. The initial result was a booming economy accompanied by growing inequality, but one that was highly exposed to the very global markets most severely affected by the financial crisis of 2008–09, which hit the country hard and forced a change in government and another round of dramatic economic policy reform. While Britain remains a highly competitive LME that has reformed to succeed in the globalization era, its prospects are uncertain as it tries to recover from the downside of its success: exposure to the global crisis.

CASE STUDY

Germany: Struggling to Reform a Coordinated Market Economy

- Moving in the direction of an LME, but still a CME
- Greatest changes in corporate finance
- Reduced role for neocorporatist wage agreements, creating greater labor market flexibility

- Reforms modest due to high number of veto players in the political system
- Relatively successful response to global financial crisis
- Continuing problems of large debt and aging population

By the late 1990s, political pundits had shifted away from portraying the German social market economy as a singular success story of "high everything"—high productivity, high-quality goods, high wages, high taxes, high benefits—and toward portraying it as the "sick man of Europe" that was unable to reform in the face of new economic realities. Following the hyperglobalization thesis, they argued that Germany needed to change its economic model to prosper under globalization. Scholars using the varieties of capitalism approach question this conventional wisdom, however. To them, Germany is a classic case of a CME whose institutions, though modified, continue to function to its comparative institutional advantage. They argue that Germany has changed relatively little in the face of globalization and that it won't need to. It was particularly hard-hit by the 2008–09 recession, in part because of changes to the CME model, especially in the financial sector. But its ability to rebound relatively quickly and to keep unemployment from increasing substantially indicated to many scholars that reforms had made the German model flexible enough to withstand the latest shocks from globalization. While having modified its policies in the direction of an LME, Germany still maintains a distinctively CME model that has weathered the latest crisis relatively well, though other crises loom ahead.

What seems beyond dispute is that German policies are moving in the direction of an LME model; the question is how much fundamental change is occurring. Cox (2002) argued that most reforms have been "tinkering" rather than "transformative," but Streeck (2009) suggested that the cumulative changes across an array of economic sectors demonstrate that fundamental changes are in process. Streeck argued, though, that those changes are not caused by globalization nor will they lead to Germany's transformation into an LME. Instead, Streeck argued that the changes are primarily due to internal contradictions and tensions within the vaunted German model itself and that they will cause Germany to evolve in the direction of liberalization; they will, however, replicate neither

The German stock index on September 18, 2008, as the global recession hit. Deregulated German banks became much more exposed to global markets in the new millennium, including the mortgage-backed securities and derivatives based on the U.S. housing market, whose collapse caused the recession. Germany was hit heavily by the recession but was the quickest European economy to rebound.

Credit: AP Photo/Michael Probst

the old CME nor an LME. The international market perhaps provided greater opportunity for these changes to occur, but was not the driving force. Streeck pointed to changes to (1) corporate finance; (2) collective bargaining between employers and unions, which threatens to undermine the corporatist agreements that have kept wages high and labor unrest minimal; and (3) Germany's elaborate social welfare programs in response to chronic deficits. These factors have combined to significantly liberalize Germany's CME, though they have not completely transformed it.

Globalization has had its biggest impact in Germany's corporate finance system. While German practices have certainly not adhered completely to the LME model, German businesses have taken advantage of globalization in ways that have altered the coordination within Germany's CME. With the rise of new global financial opportunities, large German businesses and the German government have pushed for financial reform, including legal reforms to open the stock market up to global investors and the listing of German firms on global markets. Manufacturers have looked to these changes as providing new sources of finance, and banks see them as new areas of profit. The net effect from 1996 to 2002 was a reduction of over 50 percent in the share of firms' capital that was controlled by the banks that lent them money (Streeck 2009, 80). German firms instead rely increasingly on sales of stock to global investors as a primary means of obtaining financing. This means that German firms, like firms in LMEs, have had to become more concerned about anonymous shareholders' short-term interests in profits. Codetermination, unions' participation in corporate management (see chapter 5), still exists, but it has been reduced significantly due to increased concern for shareholders' short-term returns.

For banks, globalization provided new profit opportunities but exposure to high risk as well. Starting in the late 1980s and accelerating rapidly in the new millennium, German banks began investing heavily in securities and other tradable assets, including mortgage-backed securities and derivatives based on the risky U.S. mortgages that were the source of the 2008–2009 recession. Until 2007, these investments provided significant profits, but the banks suffered severe losses when the bubble burst in 2008. The German government responded by creating a fund that troubled banks could voluntarily draw on, as well as essentially nationalizing the banks in the worst trouble. The government subsequently passed legislation in 2009 that tightened up regulations to limit the practices that had gotten the banks into trouble in the first place and to increase the assets that banks were required to keep on hand in case of a crisis (Hardie and Howarth 2009).

Globalization has also affected wages and collective bargaining between employers and unions in Germany, though key elements of neocorporatism (see chapter 5) remain and have helped Germany weather the Great Recession relatively well. Germany's neocorporatist model was always

based on peak associations of employers and unions being able to make and stick to wage agreements. These agreements kept wages high while providing stability and predictability. Globalization, though, has created divisions among German companies. The largest have invested significantly outside of Germany, including in the rest of the European Union. In key sectors, notably pharmaceuticals, the most successful firms have noted the institutional advantages of LMEs such as the United States and the United Kingdom and have relocated (or sold) their more innovative components to those economies, leaving the less innovative areas, such as chemicals and metal working, in Germany. In doing so, they have created globally linked production processes that are very sensitive to disruption. Because of this, they have become more willing to agree to high wages to avoid strikes or lockouts. Smaller businesses, which lack international investment and are often in direct competition with manufacturers in other countries, cannot afford these higher wages, and they increasingly ignore agreements set between unions and the largest employers. Unions respond with more strikes at the local level against the smaller firms. The result has been a fragmentation of the neocorporatist agreements that used to govern wages. In 1995, 53 percent of all workplaces had wage agreements negotiated by industry-wide collective bargaining; by 2006 this had dropped to 37 percent, due in part to a decline in the number of businesses that were members of the major business associations that negotiated the agreements (Streeck and Hassel 2003, 112; Streeck 2009, 39). Greater flexibility has also allowed firms to increase their use of temporary workers, who are not covered by any agreements and therefore have little job security. These trends coincided with the steep decline in membership in employers' associations and unions that we discussed in chapter 7.

High unemployment has long been the Achilles' heel of the German economy (see Figure 10.2). Unemployment dropped

Figure 10.2

Employment Growth and Unemployment Rates in Germany, 1997–2010

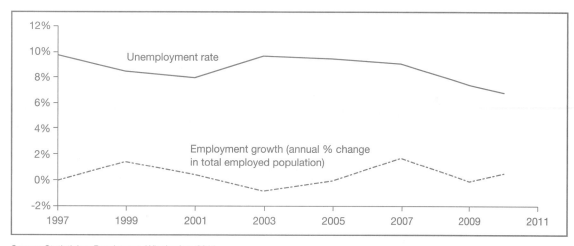

Source: Statistiches Bundesamt, Wiesbaden, 2011.

substantially in the first decade of the new millennium, from a high of nearly 12 percent in the late 1990s to below 8 percent just before the recession in 2008, though that level still poses a long-term problem. The recession itself only increased unemployment by 1 percent, a phenomenon that some analysts dubbed a new "German miracle." The greater flexibility in bargaining conditions at the level of the individual firm had a role in this success. Businesses were able to lower real wages throughout the decade of the 2000s, which facilitated the rise in employment. When the recession hit, the social market economy tradition of working cooperatively with unions allowed many employers to negotiate with their unions to accept cuts in wages and hours to avoid layoffs, keeping unemployment limited. The government gave incentives for this with its *Kurzarbeit* program, which subsidizes agreements that retain workers. Since the turn of the century, the German labor market, like many in Europe, has become more flexible. That has meant lower wages for many workers and less secure collective bargaining agreements,

but the greater flexibility has probably helped Germany adjust to the forces of globalization, especially in the recession.

One problem plaguing almost all wealthy countries is low population growth and aging populations mean that fewer workers must pay for the social welfare benefits of more retirees. In Germany, the problem is particularly acute. German governments came face-to-face with the reality of this problem in the early 1980s. From then through the late 1990s, they enacted reforms to the country's extensive welfare system to ease financial constraints (see chapter 11). While these efforts did reduce spending increases from what they might have been, they were not enough to reduce Germany's relatively high public debt, which went from about 40 percent of GDP in 1994 to over 60 percent in 2006 (Streeck 2009, 69). Similarly, tax reforms that favored business were gradually enacted. From 1985 to 1995, corporate taxes' share of all taxes was cut in half, with most of the revenue loss compensated for by increases in payroll taxes on workers (Daly 2001, 88). In the first decade of the new

IN CONTEXT

GOVERNMENT AND GROWTH IN THE EU

The government in Germany and in the EU as a whole consistently takes in a larger share of economic production as taxes than does the United States (see chart A). Many economists predict that this will hurt economic growth. Chart B, however, shows that the EU grew faster than the United States at the dawn of the new millennium, though the United States started to recover from the Great Recession sooner.

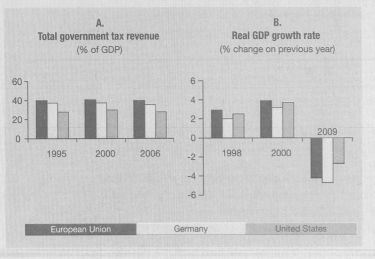

Source: All data are from OECD and EUROSTAT.

(meaning most laws) must pass the upper house as well as the lower house. Thus, the system has a large number of veto players who can stop proposals. As early as the mid-1990s, Germany's third party, the liberal FDP, was calling for fundamental reforms of the economic system. These were opposed by one or the other of the major parties, as well as by unions and even some business interests that were content to preserve the status quo. Opponents were able to use one house or the other, as well as Germany's strong civil society, to resist radical reforms.

> **CASE SUMMARY**

In its core activity of high-quality manufacturing, Germany's CME seems to be holding its own in a globalizing world, though analysts forecast different long-term trends. Germany has reformed its economic model in the direction of greater liberalization in both finance and labor, but most elements of the CME remain in place, though with reduced overall effects on the economy. Reforms reduced wages and workers' bargaining positions and reduced social welfare benefits somewhat, but they arguably helped Germany survive the Great Recession with only limited impact on employment. Both the Christian Democratic government of Helmut Kohl (1982–1998) and the Social Democratic government of Gerhard Schröder (1998–2005) attempted for years to forge agreements on pensions, unemployment, and tax reform, but neither government was successful, and both ultimately instituted unilateral moves to achieve some reform. Germany's political system has enough veto players that negotiated agreements have become nearly

millennium, corporate taxes fell a further 22 percent, while personal income taxes dropped only 1.5 percent, thus shifting the burden even further from business to individuals. The combined result has been some increase in inequality in the new millennium, which we discuss further in Chapter 11.

A number of analysts have noted that the relatively slow pace of reform in the German system is partly due to the nature of the country's political institutions. Germany's bicameral legislature and federal system give unusually strong powers to the legislature's upper house (not unlike the powers of the U.S. Senate), which has often been controlled by opposition parties. Any law that affects the state governments

impossible. Most analysts now believe that the next challenge for the German government will be complying with membership in the European Monetary Union (EMU), which requires it to reduce its fiscal deficit to half of what it was in 2010. Germany willingly took on this problem, as it championed the EMU, but reducing wages and taxes while caring for an aging population is complicated by global pressures.

DEVELOPMENT AND GLOBALIZATION

Globalization has clearly affected the ways in which wealthy and powerful states guide their economies. While most political scientists no longer subscribe to the hyperglobalization thesis that the state is now irrelevant, virtually all recognize that states have had to alter their economic and social policies in response to pressures from rapidly expanding global market forces. If this is true for even the relatively powerful and wealthy states, could the hyperglobalization thesis apply to much poorer and less powerful states? Have they in effect lost economic sovereignty to the global market, or do its effects vary among them as well?

The world's relatively poor and powerless states are almost all postcolonial. Their economic and social policies, and debates about them, have long involved the goal of "development." Officially, their governing regimes seek to achieve economic growth to improve the lives of their people through industrialization and other forms of economic diversification. A key part of the debate over development, of course, has been not only about how to achieve growth but also about how the benefits of that growth should be distributed to relieve poverty. The development debate we outlined in chapter 5—from import-substitution industrialization (ISI) to structural adjustment programs (SAP)—long preceded the contemporary globalization debate, but both address the same key question: How can states in developing countries use economic policies to help them navigate the global economy in ways that are most beneficial to their people? A key question in this debate is not economic but political: What types of regimes are most willing to and capable of pursuing beneficial policies? The long-standing debates over economic and political development are now intertwined with the globalization debate as the countries in question are increasingly subject to the vicissitudes of the global market.

What Role Should the State Play in Development? At the heart of these debates is the role that the state can and should play in the development process, including vis-à-vis global markets. The reigning conventional wisdom is that the state should allow the market to operate more or less unfettered, following the logic of comparative advantage. Regardless of local circumstances, a free market maximizes the efficiency with which resources are used and therefore improves economic well-being overall. This is the core of the argument supporting the neoliberal development model and SAPs.

Since the early 1990s, however, scholars and practitioners have been raising a growing number of questions about this model. The World Bank, in particular, has articulated an agenda of "good governance," arguing that states need to have more of a role in reform than the neoliberal model allows. Focusing on the alleviation of poverty, the World Bank argues that states need greater capacity to achieve key goals. First, they need to effectively and efficiently provide the key requisites for capitalist development that we outlined in chapter 5: security, property rights, contract enforcement, and infrastructure. Second, they need to enhance human capital and development potential via providing essential health and education services to the poor. Virtually all major Western development agencies continue to support the basic principle that states should not distort markets (as they did under ISI), but many now believe that the state does have a role to play in simultaneously attracting capital and alleviating poverty.

Critics of neoliberal development policies, even in their newer form, which includes a focus on improving institutions and social services, have long contended that they benefit the wealthy and international business at the expense of the poor majority and that they leave developing countries more dependent on wealthy countries and foreign investment. Supporters of neoliberalism, on the other hand, have long argued that no coherent alternative development theory or set of policies exists. Various NGOs in both developed and developing countries promote local-level alternatives that focus on improving the economic conditions and viability of the poor majority. These alternatives include alternative agricultural strategies that focus on local food production and microfinance that provides very small loans to poor business people. Much of the thinking behind these kinds of alternative policies is influenced by the idea of **sustainable development**, which holds that development must be environmentally sustainable and not excessively dependent on uncertain foreign sources of aid or investment. While these policies (especially microfinance, most famously in Bangladesh, where its premier champion and pioneer, Mohamed Yunus, won the 2006 Nobel Peace Prize for his work) have achieved some successes in improving the lives of poor people around the world, they have not come together in a form that constitutes a credible national-level development policy.

A recent addition to the debate comes out of Latin America, where economists and governments have increasingly questioned the neoliberal model, which has produced only moderate growth in the region. Brazilian economist Luiz Carlos Bresser-Pereira (2009) called for a "new developmentalism." Focusing on our case study country Brazil, he argued that the neoliberal model has failed to produce significant growth but rejected the idea of returning to a closed economy or the deficit spending that characterized the ISI era. Bresser-Pereira supported the notions that governments should not run large fiscal deficits to provide social services they cannot afford and that export-led growth (rather than ISI focused on imports and the domestic market) is essential. He argued that the conventional neoliberal model, however, has defeated inflation and reduced government deficits only via very high interest rates and an overvalued currency, both of which slow growth. Instead of these policies, he calls for more moderate interest rates to stimulate growth and increased government regulation of exchange rates to reduce the value of Latin American currencies, thereby encouraging exports and domestic investment. Recently elected governments led by "leftist" political parties have implemented some of these policies in a number of Latin American countries. Interestingly, these policies are similar to those that China has pursued for much of the last decade as its growth has exploded.

Why Have Globalization's Effects Varied?
While the debate over the best policies continues, one thing is clear: the effects of globalization have varied dramatically by region. Virtually all governments have opened their economies to the global market

sustainable development: Economic development that can continue over the long term because it is not environmentally unsound or excessively dependent on uncertain foreign sources of support

over the past generation, but the results have not been consistent. While Asia, and especially China, has narrowed the gap between it and the developed countries, Latin American and Africa have fallen further behind relative to the wealthy countries. (Latin America's GDP per capita was 35 percent of the developed world's in 1980 but only 25 percent in 2002; for Africa, the numbers were 10 percent in 1980 and only 6 percent in 2002.) With the exception of China and a few other rapidly growing economies, the overall story is one of growing inequality as certain countries and regions benefit much more than others from globalization (Ocampo and Vos 2008).

Table 10.1 compares each region's Economic Globalization Index score—a measure of economies' interactions with the global economy—to growth rates and poverty rates since 1981. Poverty has dropped everywhere, though not by much in Africa and Latin America. Economic growth and poverty reduction vary dramatically by region, but the connection to globalization is unclear. East Asia, which grew by far the fastest and reduced poverty the most, had significantly higher globalization levels than other regions (except Western Europe) in 1981, but the gap has narrowed considerably. Greater globalization in the other regions, though, has not produced greater growth or poverty reduction. The question is, What has caused these trends, and what can be done to improve the effects of globalization in the countries that are falling behind?

The View from East and Southeast Asia

Any discussion of globalization and development today must start in East and Southeast Asia. The Asian economic miracle has been the primary development success story of the last generation, especially in the four original East Asian "Tigers"—Taiwan, South Korea, Hong Kong, and Singapore—and, more recently, in China. The Tigers have all become wealthy industrialized countries, and as they initiated

	Economic Globalization Index[1]			Growth of GDP per capita (%/year)			Extreme poverty (% of population living on less than $1/day)		
	1983	1993	2004	1980–84	1990–94	2000–04	1981	1993	2004
Sub-Saharan Africa	0.034	0.080	0.123	−1.2	−2.0	1.5	42.3	45.5	41.1
Latin America	0.094	0.103	0.123	−0.8	1.7	0.8	10.8	8.4	8.6
South Asia	0.009	0.133	0.146	3.2	2.8	3.7	49.6	36.9	30.8
East Asia	0.113	0.112	0.138	5.7	7.7	6.5	57.7	25.2	9.1
Western Europe	0.139	0.142	0.160	NA	NA	NA	NA	NA	NA

TABLE 10.1

Economic Globalization Index

Source: Round (2010).

[1]Composite of openness to trade, foreign direct investment, portfolio investment, and remittances.

Hyundai automobiles await export to South Africa. South Korea's phenomenal economic growth has been based on exports, making some of the country's biggest companies into household names around the world. The economic success of South Korea and the other Asian Tigers was a major reason global development agencies shifted their support from ISI to EOG in the 1980s.

Credit: AP Photo/Ahn Young-joon

export-oriented growth (EOG): Development policy based on encouraging economic growth via exports of goods and services, usually starting with light manufacturing such as textiles

the process of industrialization, inequality actually dropped. This is the only place in the world where that has happened. A famous comparison is between South Korea and Ghana in West Africa. Upon Ghana's independence in 1957, it and South Korea had nearly identical per capita incomes and economies. Both were poor and mostly agricultural. Today, however, South Korea is a member of the OECD (Organisation for Economic Co-operation and Development), the club of the world's wealthiest countries. It had a per capita gross national income (GNI) of $19,830 in 2008, compared to Ghana's GNI of $1,190.

The Asian story (or at least interpretations of it) has served as the model for development policy throughout the world, especially before the 1997–1998 financial crisis. Asia's success was clearly based on **export-oriented growth (EOG)**, development policy based on encouraging economic growth via exports of goods and services, usually starting with light manufactures such as textiles. This was in contrast to the ISI policies that were popular prior to the 1980s. The neoliberal model was in part a reaction to the success of the four original Tigers. Their spectacular growth based on exports stood in sharp contrast to the growing problems that ISI began facing in the 1970s. Neoliberal economists argued that if exports produced success, then all countries should open up to the market, pursue their comparative advantages, and export as much as they could.

The original SAP efforts based on neoliberalism assumed that success in Asia was founded on getting the state out of the way of the market and allowing comparative advantage to work its magic. Further research clearly showed that this was not always the case in the successful East Asian cases. Hong Kong, while still under British colonial rule, certainly followed a laissez-faire policy of minimal governmental intervention, probably the most minimal on the planet. The other three Tigers, however, did not.

In 1993, the World Bank published a major study, *The East Asian Miracle*, that distilled this research into a series of lessons learned that could be applied to policy elsewhere in the world. This study showed that the state had a greater role in the economic successes in East Asia than originally had been assumed. Taiwan and South Korea especially had developmental states similar to Japan's that guided industrialization. They used carefully targeted credit and subsidies and provided some protection to create new industries that could compete on the world market. These states guided investment into areas of comparative advantage, rather than simply allowing the market to send signals. However, they followed neoliberal recommendations on fiscal and monetary policy, keeping inflation low and their currencies stable and realistically valued vis-à-vis others, thus encouraging investment and exports. They began with ISI policies but shifted their focus to EOG very early on (in the 1950s and 1960s). Their successes were also based on the fact that their high-quality education systems had produced a highly literate and therefore productive workforce.

The 1993 study went on to suggest that a key component of all these success stories was a strong state, one in which economic bureaucracies were insulated from short-term political pressures so that they could pursue solid, long-term policies. A strong state was necessary to make the often painful transition from ISI to EOG early on, as well as to guide subsequent industrialization along channels that enhanced rather than diminished comparative advantage. This revised understanding of the East Asian miracle helped lead the World Bank and other development experts to recognize that the state still has a role to play in effective development.

Rapid growth almost always produces greater inequality, as some people get much richer and others are left behind. Growth in the early success stories such as South Korea and Taiwan, however, was combined with reduced inequality. This was largely due to earlier policies that supported rural areas; reforms gave peasant farmers more equal access to land, universal education, and good infrastructure, facilitating their participation in economic growth. Labor-intensive manufacturing such as textiles also helped reduce inequality, as it employed large numbers of people at relatively equal wages. In contrast to the first "Tigers," China has seen a more typical pattern of growing inequality accompanying rapid growth. The growth has been so great, though, that it has reduced poverty in spite of expanding inequality. Overall, the Asian experience is one of very rapid growth-induced poverty reduction combined with moderately growing inequality. Despite the latter, it is a very positive story (Nissanke and Thorbecke 2010).

The 1997–1998 financial crisis shook the foundations of the original East Asian model. The massive loss of wealth in the region ultimately brought down the government of long-time Indonesian dictator Suharto and threatened the political stability of other countries as well. The crisis originated in and centered on the "Little Tigers" of Thailand, Indonesia, Malaysia, and the Philippines—rapidly growing countries whose industrialization followed behind that of the original four Tigers and who remain middle-income countries today. Their impressive economies were booming in the 1990s, and they were generally seen as following the successful model of the original Tigers until the crisis erupted. They suffered a severe recession as a result of the crisis, though a decade later, they had recovered and were growing substantially again (at rates varying from a low of about 5 percent in Thailand to a high of more than 7 percent in Indonesia). This growth was slowed by the 2008–2009 global financial crisis, though like virtually all developing countries, the Tigers were hit less hard by the recession than were wealthy countries.

In spite of this recovery, the Asian crisis and response to it profoundly affected the globalization and development debate. The International Monetary Fund (IMF), whose job it is to help resolve such crises, blamed lax financial regulation by the governments involved. The crisis revealed that the developmental states' regulation of the financial sector in particular was very weak. Banks took on unsecured international loans and lent money for dubious investments, often to companies with which they had close, even familial, ties. When the crisis hit, the banks rapidly sank into bankruptcy since their creditors could not repay them and, in turn, they could not repay their own international loans. Neoclassical economists argued that in spite of East Asia's rapid success, the state's role was not as beneficial as had been assumed. Many began to argue that economic growth would have been even more rapid without state credit and subsidies to key industries. Neoclassicists began calling for states to provide regulations needed to protect against financial and corporate malfeasance but not to attempt to "guide" the market.

Critics of globalization argued that the problem was unfettered global currency markets. Exchange rates that were pegged to the dollar before the crisis had seemed to guarantee investors a high rate of return in the booming regional economies, so money had poured into these countries from around the globe, causing a massive "bubble" in their stock and real estate markets. When the bubble burst, investors sold rapidly, causing a market panic that had no basis in the strength of the actual economies. The problem, critics argued, was rapid flow of investment in and out of countries that were open to the global economy. This suggested the need for mechanisms to slow down the speed at which these transactions could occur and to guide investors into longer-term investments rather than short-term currency speculation.

Despite this raging debate, neither global nor domestic policies in the region have changed substantially. Critics' calls for a reform of the IMF and mechanisms to slow down unfettered currency exchanges petered out after a couple of years of debate, with no major changes enacted. The Little Tigers have recovered well but have mostly kept their exchange rates pegged to the dollar. The biggest changes enacted by the Little Tigers have been regulating their financial sectors more strongly to put them more in line with international standards and allowing greater international investment in their banking sectors. Both changes, it is hoped, will prevent another crisis like the one that shook these countries at the end of the twentieth century. Since the crisis, China has emerged as unquestionably the leading economic powerhouse of the region, and while it was not heavily affected by the crisis itself, it has become a major market for the Little Tigers' exports (MacIntyre, Pempel, and Ravenhill 2008). The Little Tigers clearly remained substantially exposed to the global market, since the 2008–2009 global financial crisis dropped their growth rates from 5–7 percent down to as low as 1 percent in some cases. Only Indonesia, backed by oil production, maintained a relatively healthy growth rate through the crisis.

East Asian development, including our case study of China below, is the current reigning model of success. Initially misunderstood as a model of development based on an unfettered market, the "East Asian miracle" subsequently was shown to be based on careful state intervention to enhance comparative advantage and encourage exports. These policies required a relatively strong state that could engage in sound macroeconomic policies and make investments that fostered long-term growth in spite of short-term political pressures. All the states in the region began the development process under authoritarian regimes, but several have since made transitions to democracy and continue to thrive economically. The region has arguably benefitted more from globalization than any other, especially in the post-colonial world. While the leading countries' exposure to global economic forces caused them to feel the effects of the 1997–1998 and 2008–2009 crises, they nonetheless have achieved substantial overall economic growth and poverty reduction via engagement with the world market.

The View from Latin America

The Asian experience and model have had implications for development policy throughout the world. The major Latin American countries have faced many of the same issues, though with distinctly different outcomes. The neoliberal model and the IMF have probably influenced Latin America more than any other region. The debt crisis that began in Mexico in August 1982 and quickly spread to Brazil and Argentina paved the way for the first implementation of SAPs, and the 1980s became known as the "lost decade" in Latin America because of the severe economic downturn that followed the debt crisis. Countries initiated market-oriented reforms at different rates, but all implemented such reforms eventually. Chile was the regional model of neoliberal reform, having begun the process under the dictator Augusto Pinochet prior to and without IMF insistence. Its economic success and later return to democracy became a model for neoliberal reformers in the region. Some countries, notably Brazil and Argentina, experimented with "heterodox" reforms in the 1980s and early 1990s by combining elements of the neoliberal model with continued state controls in key areas. All of these efforts, however, were ultimately unsuccessful. By the mid-1990s, most Latin American countries had engaged in extensive privatization of state-owned activities, reduction of trade barriers, and fiscal restraint.

The economic and political effects of these reforms have varied. Overall economic growth recovered in the early 1990s but slid again in the late 1990s and early 2000s. By 2004, however, it had recovered to healthy rates of more than 5 percent in most years. The global financial crisis resulted in an economic contraction of nearly 3 percent per capita in 2009, but the region rebounded relatively quickly and experienced 4.5 percent per capita growth in 2010. The region has tremendous trade with and investment from the United States, and during some years, its overall foreign capital inflow has surpassed East Asia's. It has been plagued, though, with repeated financial crises. The first major crisis since the full implementation of neoliberal reforms happened in Mexico in 1994 and required a major inflow of cash from the U.S. government. Brazil's currency and stock markets were hit by the contagion from East Asia in 1998, though not as severely as Asia itself. Argentina, which had the highest growth in the region in the 1990s, experienced a spectacular financial crash in 2001–2002. Like Thailand, it had pegged the value of its currency to the U.S. dollar, but investors no longer believed the Argentine peso was worth that much. In 2002, the Argentine economy shrank by more than 10 percent, and the country went through four presidents within a few weeks as economic crisis produced political chaos.

The 2008–2009 global financial crisis is thus only the latest in a long string. Most regional governments were able to respond with stimulus packages to limit the crisis's effects, in part because they entered it with fiscal surpluses (in sharp contrast to most of Europe and the United States). Indeed, by the end of 2010, the biggest effect of the crisis in the region was what many saw as an excessive inflow of capital, as investors sought to benefit from the relatively high interest rates and returns on stocks in the region. This pushed up currency values, which threatened to reduce the competitiveness of the regions' exports. While the region has seemed to respond well to the crisis, the response of global financial markets might actually choke off renewed growth (United Nations 2010).

High, but at times unstable, growth has not produced major changes in levels of poverty or inequality. Latin America has long been the most unequal region in the world, due in part to unequal distribution of land dating back to the colonial era. Improved growth and export levels under the neoliberal model have not changed this. The lives of many of the poor, then, have not improved substantially in spite of better economic growth, investment, exports, and employment.

Not surprisingly, this has helped cause a political backlash. Citizens in Argentina, Bolivia, Ecuador, Brazil, and Venezuela have elected leftist critics of neoliberal

The focus on the state in the Asian miracle debates raises a classic question of comparative politics: Do democracies or dictatorships produce better economic development? All four original Tigers achieved their early growth under authoritarian regimes, in marked contrast to the relative economic stagnation in Asia's democratic giant, India. In the 1990s, the two largest Tigers—Taiwan and South Korea—made relatively smooth transitions to democracies, which continue to function today. Pundits and policy makers used this as evidence to argue that newly developing countries could not "afford" democracy, meaning that less wealthy countries need authoritarian rule to guide successful development. Pushing democracy on a poor country, this argument goes, will produce neither a healthy democracy nor economic development. The more modest success and high levels of corruption of the Little Tigers brought this argument into question, however. There, as well as across Africa, authoritarian rulers seemed far less capable of guiding beneficial development. Comparativists have engaged in extensive research to try to resolve this important question.

HYPOTHESIS

We can easily generate a number of hypotheses about why democracy does or does not increase economic growth (the common measure of "development"). Those arguing that democracy enhances growth focus mostly on accountability, stability, and the protection of the rule of law. They hold that democracies provide greater popular accountability, so citizens will demand that their governments pursue beneficial economic policies. Political leaders who fail to do so will be removed, so in the long run, democracies will produce greater growth. Regarding stability, while changes of governmental leaders are frequent in democracies, they are quite predictable as long as a democracy continues to function properly. Therefore, changes in leadership will not threaten the ability of investors to predict future returns, and the investment that is the basis of growth will continue to flow. Finally, proponents of the idea that democracy enhances economic growth argue that democracies better protect the rule of law, including the property rights and contracts that are essential elements of capitalist growth (see chapter 5). Again, this enhances the prospects of growth-inducing investment. In contrast, dictatorships are less accountable, are more prone to unpredictable instability like coups d'etat or revolutions, and do not protect the rule of law from the whims of the ruling elite.

Opponents of this view hypothesize that democracy impedes growth because democratic governments must follow political demands that favor consumption over investment and because democracy is inherently less stable. Long-term economic growth depends on investment, which can only happen if some of society's resources are not consumed. There is therefore a direct trade-off between investment and consumption. Democracies, this school of thought argues, have to bow to the will of the citizens, and citizens typically want more consumption now and are unwilling to invest and wait for future benefits, thus slowing growth. This is especially true in poorer societies, critics believe, where more impoverished people understandably demand consumption now. For instance, labor unions will likely have greater clout in a democracy and demand higher wages, taking money away from capitalists who would invest it in future growth. Furthermore, in democracies with weak institutions and weak political parties, these demands translate into political systems based on patronage, in which political leaders have an incentive to control as many resources as possible. Patronage has the effect of expanding the role of the state, as political leaders distribute resources to their followers in return for their support. To make the case that democracies are less stable, critics point to polarized democracies that experience frequent and major swings in who is in power and therefore in economic policies (such as corporate tax rates). This, critics argue, creates uncertainty for investors, who want to have some reasonable expectation of long-term returns. Dictatorships, the argument goes, can resist pressure for greater consumption by repressing citizens' demands and can follow more consistent policies over time. While perhaps repressive, dictatorships can achieve higher growth, as the East Asian "Tigers" demonstrate.

RESEARCH AND ANALYSIS

In the new millennium, two major quantitative statistical analyses and one major comparative case study analysis have tried to determine which of these hypotheses is correct. Przeworski, Alvarez, Cheibub, and Limongi (2000) and Yi Feng (2003) have undertaken analyses of the relationship between regime type and economic growth, using elaborate statistical techniques to take into account numerous economic factors that influence growth in an effort to isolate the independent effect of regime type. Przeworski et al. divided all countries in the world into the categories of democracy or dictatorship (based on their having multiparty elections and changes in their heads of state). Feng, rather than making an either-or classification, used two measures to gauge how democratic a country is, with each measure ranging from most democratic to most authoritarian.

Przeworski, Alvarez, Cheibub, and Limongi looked at economic growth using standard economic growth models in each group of countries. They demonstrated overall that democracies and dictatorships achieve the same levels of growth. Given that democracies tend to be wealthier and that poor democracies are thought to be particularly likely to harm growth, they also divided their sample into two groups, above and below $3,000 per capita GDP. Even after doing this, they still found no difference in growth levels between democracies and dictatorships. They did find, however, that while growth is the same in higher-income countries, it comes from different sources. Wealthy dictatorships use labor less efficiently and pay less for it, giving workers a lower share of total income. Wealthy democracies, on the other hand, use labor more efficiently and pay more for it, giving workers higher incomes.

Feng used economic-modeling techniques to look at the effects of democracy, political stability, and policy uncertainty on economic growth. He found, like Przeworski, Alvarez, Cheibub, and Limongi, that democracy has little effect on growth one way or the other but that this is due to two contradictory results. The direct effect of the level of democracy on growth is slightly negative (i.e., democracy harms growth), but democracy enhances growth indirectly by creating greater political stability. Overall, the two results more or less cancel each other out. Both studies found that regime change impacts growth negatively, at least in the short term, while democratic changes of government via elections have no impact on growth.

Do Democracies or Dictatorships Produce Better Development? *(continued)*

Atul Kohli (2004) examined a slightly different question using the comparative method, but he came to conclusions about democracy indirectly. He examined the question of why some states have been more successful at facilitating industrialization (and therefore economic growth) than others. Using a most-different-systems design, he examined four major postcolonial societies that have had different levels of success at industrializing: South Korea (one of the East Asian Tigers), India, Brazil, and Nigeria. He concluded that a certain type of state, what he called a "cohesive-capitalist" state, is the most successful industrializer, with South Korea being an example. This kind of state is based on a narrow ruling coalition that focuses consistently on maximizing growth over a long period, working closely with business interests to do so and repressing other interests (particularly labor) when necessary. The least successful is a neopatrimonial state in which resources are used for consumption and distribution as a means of maintaining political power; our case study of Nigeria is an example of this type of state. In between are "fragmented-multiclass states," which have reasonably strong institutions but must respond to broad coalitions of interests and therefore do not pursue industrialization policies as consistently over time; our case studies India and Brazil are examples of "fragmented-multiclass states." As Kohli noted, it is difficult to imagine how a democracy could be a cohesive-capitalist state, while fragmented-multiclass states may well be democratic and neopatrimonial states could be democratic. Ultimately, his analysis suggested that stable democracies in the postcolonial world are likely to be middling performers, neither the most nor the least successful. Interestingly, Przeworski, Alvarez, Cheibub, and Limongi came to a similar conclusion, noting that virtually all cases of extremely high growth (over 7 percent per year) and extremely low growth (less than 1 percent

reforms in the new millennium, creating what many have called "Latin America's Left Turn" (Cameron and Hershberg 2010). These new governing parties and coalitions have implemented policies that, while not rejecting all of neoliberalism, have significantly modified it. Some, such as Argentina and Brazil, have preserved the major macroeconomic foundations of neoliberalism but have attempted to implement greater social programs aimed at the poor. Others, most famously Hugo Chavez in Venezuela, have intervened in the economy in ways that more seriously challenge the market model, including by heavily subsidizing certain sectors, such as food and fuel, and nationalizing some key industries, especially minerals. Neoliberal economists and policy makers watching these political shifts feared that this "left turn" would undermine what they see as the gains of neoliberalism, including fiscal austerity and controlled inflation. In fact, through 2007, the "leftist" governments as a whole had achieved slightly higher growth rates than other Latin American governments, and they had actually produced slight fiscal surpluses in contrast to modest deficits elsewhere in the region. The leftist governments did have higher inflation rates, but the difference was small (Moreno-Brid and Paunovic 2010). New

per year) have been dictatorships. Democracies are all in between these extremes.

QUESTIONS IN CONTEXT

The chief conclusion we can come to from these analyses is that neither democracies nor dictatorships are inherently more likely to achieve greater economic development. Different statistical analyses have come to the same conclusion on this point. What seems more likely is that specific characteristics of certain democracies or dictatorships have more effect on economic development than simply the regime type itself. Major and unexpected political instability does harm growth, at least in the short term, so any regime that produces unpredictable change is likely to experience problems. Both democracies and dictatorships with weak institutions that lead to patronage-based political mobilization seem to experience low growth as well. Przeworski, Alvarez, Cheibub, and Limongi (2000) noted that at the lowest income levels, dictatorships and democracies look economically identical, concluding that "poverty appears to leave no room for politics" (178). The poorest societies have very weak states and institutions that affect all regimes equally and negatively. The other clear conclusions are that dictatorships vary more in terms of their economic outcomes and that democracies are neither the most nor the least successful. Kohli's comparative analysis provided one explanation of why that would be the case. What else might we use from our understanding of comparative politics to explain this conclusion and to explain which societies have the specific kinds of democracies or dictatorships that foster greater economic development? Furthermore, what kinds of democratic institutions might foster democracies that enhance economic development rather than harm it? Ultimately, is greater economic development worth the repression inherent in authoritarian rule?

social policies and strong fiscal policies were fuelled in part by high prices in the new millennium for major primary exports from the region, especially oil and other minerals. This raised questions about the sustainability of such policies. The 2008–2009 financial crisis, though, did not result in long-term setbacks to the region, including among the new leftist governments.

The major countries of Latin America are newly industrialized, middle-income countries, similar to those of Southeast Asia. But they have not benefited as fully from globalization. They did not start with the land reform policies, high literacy rates, and relative equality of the most successful Asian Tigers, and they were much slower to make the transition from ISI. As a result of the severe debt crisis, the countries in the region adopted the neoliberal model more fully than anywhere else but with mixed success. In part because of its limited success, the region has produced what most see as the most viable modification of the neoliberal model to date in some of the new leftist governments, including in our case study of Brazil. The region's future success, or lack thereof, will have an important effect on the broader debate over globalization and development.

MINI CASE

Turkey: A Middle Eastern "Tiger"?

Ask comparativists to list the world's most rapidly industrializing, export-oriented economies, and they are likely to name a number of countries in East Asia, South Asia, and Latin America but not in the Middle East. Except for a handful of oil-rich countries like Saudi Arabia, the Middle East has not seen the development success stories of some other regions. The country that clearly comes closest is Turkey, whose economy has expanded rapidly in the new millennium. How much this country teaches us about the rest of the region, though, is uncertain. Turkey's position between the Middle East and the European Union (EU) and its close relationship with the EU put it in an unusual position that other countries in the Middle East may have difficulty emulating.

Turkey has benefited from a number of favorable conditions that set it apart from surrounding states. For instance, despite setbacks and limitations, Turkey experienced an early version of developmentalism and the early creation of a formally democratic regime beginning in the 1920s. By the 1960s, it was undertaking ISI and industrial deepening very similar to that taking place in Latin America and with similar results of moderate industrialization and growth, high inflation, and growing inequality. Like Latin America, it faced growing pressure to liberalize in the 1970s and 1980s, and it negotiated five structural adjustment programs with the IMF. After the military government that began the liberalization restored democracy in the late 1980s, the government's commitment to further liberalization waned. Turkey's weak political parties, governing in multiparty parliamentary coalitions throughout the 1990s, mobilized support mainly via populist policies and patronage (like many Latin American parties in earlier decades). These policies led to growing fiscal deficits and international debt. Following IMF advice, the country also opened up its financial sector and currency to the world market before undertaking fundamental banking reforms. Combined with growing debt, this led to financial crises and recessions in 1994, 1998–1999 (tied to the Asian crisis), and 2001. The 2001 crisis was by far the most severe and produced both more fundamental economic reforms and the election of a new and very different ruling party.

The coalition government that was in power during the crisis agreed to a new IMF program, hired a Turkish national from the IMF to run it, and began a fundamental reform of the banking sector to eliminate weak banks and better regulate the survivors. Despite this significant response, the 2002 election saw the coalition lose power to the Justice and Development Party (JDP), which won a sweeping victory that allowed it to govern alone. The JDP was the first party with a parliamentary majority in Turkey in a long time. Best known as an Islamic party challenging the long-standing strict secularism of the Turkish state (see chapter 12), the JDP also championed the economic reforms begun by its predecessor. Over its first term in office, real incomes increased by 35 percent, exports and imports soared, and inflation was reduced from 45 percent (down from a high of 120 percent in 1994) to single digits. Prior liberalization had already started trade expansion, especially with the EU, which had signed a Customs Union with Turkey in 1996 allowing free flow of manufactured goods across the Turkish border. Most of Turkey's exports came to be manufactured goods, with the EU as the primary market. The Great Recession of 2008–2009 hit Turkey exceptionally hard, partly because its growth was so heavily tied to Europe. As a result, the government, trying to preserve fiscal restraint, delayed instituting an economic stimulus plan. In 2009, the GDP dropped nearly 5 percent, and unemployment increased from under 10 percent to 14 percent. By 2010, however, the economy was again growing at an estimated rate of

7.5 percent. Like other developing economies, Turkey faced a rapid inflow of foreign currency in search of high returns, which increased the value of its currency significantly. By 2011, rising inflation and debt raised questions about whether Turkey's boom could continue indefinitely.

Turkey's impressive gains have been heavily tied to Europe, to which its exports increased by 300 percent from 1996 to 2006. In 2005, Turkey formally began "accession talks" with the EU, the first step in becoming a member. Part of the government's commitment to fiscal discipline has been motivated by the goal of achieving EU membership, and by 2010, Turkey was closer to meeting the euro deficit and debt targets than most EU members were. Membership, though, remains a long way off. Turkey is a large economy with a still significant agricultural sector. European powers fear a flood of agricultural products and migrant workers if Turkey were to join the European Union, and many Europeans question whether heavily Islamic Turkey should ever be a member of Christian and secular "Europe," even if the economic concerns are resolved. In recent years, Turkish citizens, frustrated by the slow pace of accession, have become less supportive of EU membership and increasingly look to the rest of the Middle East for economic opportunities. The country's trade since 2006 has shifted noticeably from Europe toward the rest of the Middle East, Russia, and China.

CASE SUMMARY

While Turkey has long been one of the stronger economies in the Middle East, it has emerged in the new millennium as the only Middle Eastern country that is close to achieving the status of "rapidly industrializing." Lacking oil wealth (and therefore the oil curse), it has liberalized trade and benefitted from its close proximity to Europe. Liberalization brought the same initial problems, especially in the financial sector, that occurred in many countries. A severe crisis in 2001, though, provoked fundamental economic reforms that seem to have put the country on a path of stronger growth and rising incomes. Higher incomes have caused Turkey to import more than it exports, and rapid growth has more recently attracted inflows of foreign capital seeking short-term high returns; both of these circumstances could be problems in the long term. Turkey has relied on its ties to Europe to fuel much of its growth but now seems to be shifting to markets elsewhere, which may help sustain its growth as well as benefit other Middle Eastern economies. Whether this change will occur and what long-term impact it will have on the economic potential of other Middle Eastern countries remain open questions.

The View from Africa

Africa continues to be the home of primarily poor countries. Of 169 countries on the United Nations's Human Development Index in 2010, 23 of the bottom 25 are African. The continent has become the poster child of economic failure in the age of globalization and the subject of growing attention from global development agencies, charitable foundations, and even rock stars. Africa suffered the same debt crisis in the 1980s that afflicted Latin America and was also, in turn, subject to neoliberal reform. The neopatrimonial regimes of Africa, however, did not implement these reforms as thoroughly as did many Latin American countries. Because government employment was a chief source of patronage, cutting government services was a politically costly policy. Most African regimes were forced to do so to some extent to secure Western aid, but reform proceeded much more slowly than it did in Latin America.

WHERE AND WHY

Asian Miracle Versus African Malaise

The spectacular economic success occurring in East Asia and the continuing stagnation and poverty of sub-Saharan Africa raise a classic "Where and why?" question: Why has East Asia been so successful while Africa has not? The facts are indisputable. From 1970 to 2000, sub-Saharan Africa's per capita GDP actually declined 0.2 percent per year, while East Asia's rose 5.7 percent per year. In the new millennium before the global financial crisis, Africa's growth improved, but it still paled in comparison to East Asia's growth rate. Different growth rates have resulted in huge differences in overall wealth. In the 1960s, East Asia's GDP per capita was only 63 percent greater than Africa's, but by the early 1990s, it was more than 500 percent greater. What explains this startling disparity?

The potential answers can be grouped into four broad categories: culture, policies, background conditions, and institutions. Many early development theorists of the modernization school believed that cultural values influenced development. Ironically, in the 1950s, many believed "Confucian values" in Asia prohibited successful development. More recent cultural theorists now argue exactly the opposite, seeing Asian values as helping capitalism grow. In contrast, African values of tolerance for corruption and ethnic identification are seen as potentially harming development. The shift in evaluation of Asian values, though, demonstrates the problem with cultural theories of development. Indeed, at one time, many analysts thought predominantly Catholic countries would not develop as much as others, a position that few hold today given the great economic success of countries like Spain and Chile.

The neoliberal development model argues that governments' policies explain development success or failure. Advocates credit the early opening of East Asian countries to the market economy, which encouraged exports and investment, as the chief determinant of the region's success. African countries after independence, on the other hand, practiced ISI policies that restricted market access. They attempted to encourage industrial investment but did so at the expense of harming Africa's key export sector, agriculture. Extensive government regulation and intervention heavily taxed the agricultural sector to provide investment and lower food prices for urban centers. The result was inefficient investment and continued reliance on a narrow range of exports. Weak export production led African governments to take on increasing debt, which they couldn't pay back when productivity did not increase. There may be a light at the end of the tunnel, however: African policies have certainly become more market-friendly in the past two decades. Perhaps the noticeable African growth in the new millennium is at long last a result of this, though Africa is still not growing as fast as most East or even Southeast Asian countries.

Other analysts, such as Jeffrey Sachs, the former head of the UN's Millennium Development Program, argue that various background conditions limit African growth. These analysts suggest that such background conditions explain why improved policies have yet to achieve as much success as they have in Asia or Latin America. Sachs (2005) pointed to geography, disease, and climate as key issues. Low population densities, few good ports, long distances between major consumer markets, many landlocked countries, and the ravages of tropical diseases all reduce Africa's growth potential in the absence of major foreign assistance. Africa at independence also lagged behind Asia in human capital, that is, the education and health levels of its people. Numerous economists have shown that Asia's relatively high levels of literacy are key to its economic success.

What are called "neighborhood effects" might help explain the difference as well. Using what is called the "flying geese" model, Teru-tomo Ozawa (2010) argued that East Asian success is largely due to the presence of an already rapidly growing industrial power in the neighborhood: Japan. In the 1960s, Japan became the "lead goose," helping those in its wake to fly faster. After its initial success at exporting labor-intensive products to the United States, Japanese capital began outsourcing this type of production to nearby countries, starting with South Korea. As the first Tigers expanded in these sectors and began investing in higher-value production processes, they outsourced the low-end, labor-intensive production to the "Little Tigers" and, ultimately, to China. These subsequent developers exported both to the United States and to the growing markets in Japan, South Korea, and Taiwan. Each goose rode the tailwind of the one in front of it. Each had to maintain proper policies that encouraged investment and provided infrastructure and an educated workforce, but being in the neighborhood helped tremendously. For some, especially South Korea and Taiwan, their location at a Cold War crossroads was also beneficial; they received massive levels of U.S. aid in the 1950s and 1960s—far greater in real terms than almost any country receives today. All of these factors potentially explain why good policies have made a much greater difference in Asia than in Africa.

The fourth and most recent explanation takes an institutionalist approach. Institutionalists in both comparative politics and economics argue that strong, market-friendly institutions are the chief cause of Asian success and that their absence in Africa explains the region's general level of stagnation. The core of the Asian developmental state model is strong economic institutions, such as key government bureaucracies, which encourage high levels of investment. And even though Asian success cases include noticeable amounts of corruption, this corruption tends to occur at the top and be market-friendly; top government leaders benefit from kickbacks from successful capitalists in exchange for favorable government policies. In Africa, institutionalists argue, corruption harms investment and markets by exacting benefits at all levels and distributing them via vast patron-client networks. The level of corruption is generally higher, and its constant presence continually drains resources from investment. Patron-client networks are themselves a response to very high levels of risk, both political and economic. For the poor, rain-fed agriculture remains an extremely risky way to survive, and they use patrons in times of emergency to reduce their risk of completely losing their livelihoods. Patrons in positions of power in turn search for sources of patronage, stealing government resources rather than investing in infrastructure and education. Lack of infrastructure and the political instability associated with Africa's neopatrimonial forms of rule make large-scale capitalist investment risky as well. African states thus do not build better infrastructure, and key institutions do not function according to clear rules. This heightens risk for both domestic and international investors, further limiting growth even when policies improve.

The striking difference between Asia and Africa cries out for explanation. Comparativists have suggested many plausible ones, outlined above. No single theory has, so far, proven definitive. How might we as analysts go about sorting through these theories and finding evidence to show which is right and why?

By the millennium, though, most African countries had finally implemented significant reforms. In doing so, they typically cut spending on the poor, meaning the rural majority who had the least political clout to protest effectively. African political leaders preserved as much as possible the patronage positions available to wealthier and urban political supporters (Van de Walle 2001). Simultaneously, many of these states were making transitions to democratic or at least semi-authoritarian regimes. With political divisions across Africa based mainly on ethnicity, region, religion, and patronage rather than on class or ideology, democratization did not substantially affect reform efforts. Neither democratic nor semi-authoritarian regimes have been more or less likely to implement neoliberal reforms than their authoritarian predecessors.

The effects of (often partial) neoliberal reforms have been even less impressive in Africa than in other regions. The debate over whether this outcome is the result of the nature of the reforms themselves or the fact that African governments have only partially implemented them continues. In any case, economic growth in Africa throughout the 1980s and 1990s remained sluggish at best and was often negative in per capita terms. By the beginning of the new millennium, Africa's economic decline meant that its share of global trade and investment had fallen substantially. In sharp contrast, its share of foreign aid increased, and it became the largest aid recipient of any region in the world. Aid declined substantially in the 1990s after the end of the Cold War, but it doubled on a per capita basis between 1998 and 2005 as the world's attention became more focused on the problems of African poverty.

Despite negotiating debt agreements and reform measures with the IMF and other Western donors, African countries continued to have problems because lack of economic growth made it impossible for many to pay off past debts. By 2005, a growing movement had convinced Western governments that Africa needed relief from its debt burden, most of which had been contracted and stolen by dictators during the 1970s and 1980s. This effort led the World Bank and IMF to create the Heavily Indebted Poor Country (HIPC) initiative, which began forgiving the debt of poor (mostly African) countries in exchange for new economic reforms (following pragmatic neoliberalism). In 2005, the G-8, an organization comprised of the world's eight largest economies, agreed to accelerate this process by fully relieving in a matter of a few years the past debt of the countries that had completed the HIPC process. By 2007, this effort had substantially reduced Africa's overall debt. The result was a modest decline in African poverty levels, from 47 percent of the population living on less than $1 per day in 1990 to 41 percent in 2004. While this was positive news, Africa remains the world's poorest continent. Neoliberal reform, while perhaps starting to show results very recently, has yet to produce a substantial African success story like Chile in Latin America or the Little Tigers in Asia.

Africa's continued poverty has inspired a host of theories and policy debates about what to do to alleviate the situation. In the new millennium, a vigorous debate about how to end poverty ignited passions and ideas to an extent not seen in decades in development circles. The United Nations launched the **Millennium Development Goals (MDGs)**, a set of targets to reduce poverty and hunger, improve education and health, improve the status of women, and achieve environmental sustainability, all fueled by a call for a large increase in aid. Economist Jeffrey Sachs (2005), the chief intellectual architect of the effort, called for a massive inflow of aid, arguing that a large enough volume targeted the right way could end African poverty in our lifetime. He even created his own nonprofit foundation, the Millennium Promise, which has established "millennium villages" in several African countries to demonstrate how his vision can work. But critics such as William Easterly (2006) and Dambisa Moyo (2009) have pointed to the fact that Africa has a long history as the

Millennium Development Goals (MDGs): Targets established by the United Nations to reduce poverty and hunger, improve education and health, improve the status of women, and achieve environmental sustainability

world's largest aid recipient and yet has failed to achieve substantial development. Easterly argued that the result of misguided efforts such as Sachs's will be that "the rich have markets" while "the poor have bureaucrats." The former, he suggested, is the only way to achieve growth; the latter will waste and distort resources and leave Africans more impoverished and dependent on Western support. Moyo pointed to microfinance and the global bond markets as better means to achieve development than continued dependence on aid.

In both Africa and the Middle East, a special concern is the blessing (or curse; see chapter 2) of natural resource wealth, especially oil. Resource wealth ought to provide a government with the resources to build roads, schools, health clinics, and communications networks to foster economic development. Unfortunately, it often does just the opposite by creating incentives for massive corruption and bad economic policy. In the most resource-rich states, the government gains all the revenue it needs by exporting natural resources, and that revenue can be a source of large-scale corruption because it can be used for political patronage. This means the government of a resource-rich country doesn't need to bother with much general taxation of the economy and that it therefore has little incentive to try to improve the economy outside the key natural resource sector. This is most true for large oil producers. A perennial problem, even for the wealthiest states in the Middle East, is economic diversification. Oil wealth often allows these states to ignore other kinds of economic development, as well as demands from citizens for political change. Our case study of Iran demonstrates the problems and prospects such oil wealth provides.

In the new millennium, some analysts, including a number of African leaders, began to talk of an "African Renaissance." Overall economic growth improved significantly, averaging nearly 5 percent from 2000 to 2007. Much of this was fuelled, however, by rising prices for Africa's raw materials, especially oil. The democratic transitions of the 1990s were successful in some countries as well, and most measures of the region's political institutions indicated notable improvement. African countries, led by South Africa, attempted to build on this by creating the New Partnership for Africa's Development (NEPAD). Under NEPAD, delegations of leaders and experts from within the continent have begun monitoring each others' practices in an attempt to enhance stable macroeconomic policies and build stronger institutions. The global financial crisis did not hit Africa as hard as it did elsewhere, in part because of Africa's limited integration into the global economy. Growth slowed in 2009 to 1.6 percent, but if one doesn't count South Africa, which is by far the biggest and most globally integrated African economy, growth was a much higher 3.7 percent. It rebounded to 4.5 percent in 2010 and is expected to top 5 percent in 2011. Clearly, some notable improvement has occurred, undoubtedly due to a combination of improved economic policies, stronger governing institutions, and high commodity prices. Whether improvement can be sustained over the long term, as in other regions, will determine whether Africa can finally begin to see the benefits of globalization.

Summary

Globalization and development clearly show large regional variations in their impact. East and Southeast Asia, in spite of the financial crisis of 1997–1998, have been globalization success stories, achieving rapid growth that quickly reduced poverty levels. China, one of our case studies, is the latest and most dramatic entrant into this Asian success story. Latin American governments have pursued neoliberal reform more fully than Asian governments and have achieved substantial growth in recent years, though nothing compared to Asia. Continuing inequality in Latin America has also meant that poverty has not declined very much despite significant growth. Africa, at least until recently, showed few signs of development and had actually been disengaged from the global economy, except as an aid recipient and a producer of raw materials.

In all regions, global market forces have shaped and limited governments' economic policies, but governments have nonetheless had some room to maneuver. Malaysia rejected the IMF's proposed recovery plan after the 1997 Asian financial crisis and has done quite well since. China, as we will see below, has also succeeded without full adoption of the unfettered market model, though it has adopted most of it. Several of Latin America's democracies, including Brazil, have elected governments that are questioning and modifying the neoliberal model, while African governments (until recently) limited reforms in the interest of their own political well-being. This mixed record of achievement has led development theorists and policy makers to adjust the original neoliberal model that championed hyperglobalization, modifying it to re-create a role for the state. We examine the detailed contours of these trends in the following case studies.

CASE STUDY

China: An Emerging Powerhouse

- Modernizing authoritarian state gradually expanding its market economy
- World's greatest economic growth and poverty reduction
- Incentives for productivity and strengthening institutions
- Expanding private sector but continued role for state-owned industries
- Growing inequality, social welfare policies, and labor unrest
- Successful response to global financial crisis and expanded role in the world economy

China's economic development has been unparalleled since the country's initial entrance into the world market. Its economy has taken more people out of poverty faster than any other in history. Since economic reforms began shifting the country away from the communist-planned economy in 1978, the population in absolute poverty (living on less than $1 per day) has dropped from about 60 percent to 10 percent, and

Chinese torchbearer Luan Xiuju in May 2008 in Hainan province was part of the massive lead-up to the Beijing Summer Olympics. In many ways, the games were China's "coming of age" on the global stage. Rapid economic growth since the 1970s has been heavily based on integration into the global economy, has made China a major world power, and has helped the country remove more people from poverty faster than any other country in history.

Credit: Imaginechina via AP Images

GDP per capita has increased sixfold. Economic growth has averaged between 8 and 10 percent for thirty years and went above

10 percent in 2005–2007. (Exact data on long-term economic growth in China are disputed due to faulty data collection. The official figure for 1978–1998 was 9.7 percent per year, but the World Bank estimates the actual figure at 8.4 percent.) China even weathered the global financial crisis of 2008–2009 exceptionally well, experiencing reduced growth but no actual recession; growth rebounded quickly in spite of China's dependence on exports to Western markets that were all in severe recession. Indeed, by mid-2011, the country's main economic concern was rising inflation caused by economic growth that many observers saw as too fast. China's development path, while certainly not identical to that of the earlier East Asian Tigers, nonetheless shares some of its key elements: a strong authoritarian state that guided policy via gradual opening to the world, pursuit of EOG after a long period of internal focus, and the benefits of being in the East Asian region.

China's reforms emerged gradually, starting in 1978. The process continues, and remains incomplete, thirty-five years later. The first reforms were focused inward and on agriculture. Deng Xiaoping's first major economic changes were designed to give producers in state-owned endeavors an incentive to produce more efficiently. The "household responsibility system" converted many of China's collective farms into family-leased and operated enterprises in which families could dispose of their surplus production on the open market. In six years (1978–1984), virtually all farming households had converted to this system, agricultural production was growing at an unprecedented rate of 7 percent per year, and per capita rural incomes increased by more than 50 percent. Shortly thereafter, the government signed contracts with state-owned enterprises (SOEs) that allowed the SOEs to sell their surplus production (after meeting state quotas) and retain part of the profits to reinvest in their plants. In rural areas, Town and Village Enterprises (TVEs), mostly owned by local governments, were given even greater freedom to produce what they could for a

profit. Their production rose fivefold between 1983 and 1988 (Qian 2006, 235–37).

At the same time, the government gradually began to open to the market, domestically and internationally. It created a "dual-track" market system in 1984 under which SOEs continued to sell their products at official state prices up to their official state production quota but were free to sell their surplus at whatever market price they could get. Prior to reform, the government had set all retail prices. By 1985, 34 percent of retail commodities were sold on the open market, and that number had risen to 95 percent by 1999. Internationally, starting in 1980 the state created "special economic zones" (SEZs), which were allowed to engage in external trade. Throughout the 1990s, the government gradually but systematically lowered tariffs on imports and loosened restrictions on companies' rights to both import and export, a process that culminated in China's joining the World Trade Organization (WTO) in 2001. The result has been an explosion of international trade for the country: it increased fivefold between 1996 and 2005, with three-quarters of that expansion occurring after China joined the WTO (Qin 2007, 721).

The market had opened up to a large degree before China legally institutionalized private property. While private property, often in the form of foreign investment, existed in the SEZs more or less from the start, the SOEs and TVEs that increasingly produced for the market remained largely government owned until 1995. By then, the private sector had grown so quickly that the SOEs represented a rapidly shrinking share of the total economy. In 1995, the government announced the start of privatization, selling off the vast majority of SOEs to private investors. The process resulted in the laying off of at least twenty million workers from 1995 to 1997, but the fact that the growing economy was able to employ many of these individuals while the government was able to create a pension system for the unemployed meant that the layoffs did not cause widespread unrest (Qian 2006, 243; Frazier 2010). A decade later, the private sector constituted 70 percent of the economy and the state-owned sector only 30 percent, with the latter mostly in utilities and natural resource production. The move to private property culminated in a 1999 amendment to the constitution that recognized private enterprises as being on an equal footing with state-owned ones and then a 2001 invitation to private business leaders to join the Chinese Communist Party (CCP). It's not clear, however, that the government intends to eliminate SOEs entirely. They remain important players in major sectors of the economy such as energy and steel. Indeed, in 2009, in the midst of the global financial crisis, SOEs' share of the economy actually increased slightly for the first time in a generation. The government's large stimulus package that helped the economy rebound quickly was channeled largely into infrastructure built mainly by SOEs. Government-owned energy companies have aggressively sought out contracts to extract raw materials, especially oil, around the world. The government seems to view direct control over key economic sectors, especially energy, to be an important continuing part of its development model, at least for some time to come.

The role of the state in creating institutionalized incentives for greater efficiency and production has been crucial to China's economic success. Change began with fiscal decentralization early in the reform period. Local governments controlled many SOEs and what became TVEs under the command economy. By giving these businesses the right to keep a larger share of the revenue their enterprises earned, the central government gave them a strong incentive to produce beyond their state-mandated quotas. A recent World Bank study (Winters and Yusuf 2007) argued that the institutionalization of Chinese Communist Party (CCP) rule that we delineated in chapter 8 was also essential. Local officials and would-be entrepreneurs needed to trust that the central government would follow through on its commitments to allow profits to stay within local enterprises and continue support for the growing market. Given the history of Mao's capricious rule, it was not obvious at the dawn

of Deng Xiaoping's era that the government would stick to its new commitments. The CCP gained credibility by institutionalizing its rule, assuring local party leaders and government officials that they would be promoted based on clear criteria tied in part to the success of their local enterprises and economies. As the system worked successfully over the first decade, it gained greater credibility. When China invited increasing foreign investment in the 1990s, greater institutionalization led investors to believe that continued political stability was likely. At the same time, the government began large-scale spending on infrastructure expansion and improvements, facilitating and showing its financial commitment to both domestic and foreign private investment.

China's economic success, measured in terms of economic growth, per capita income, and poverty reduction, is spectacular. This does not mean, however, that no problems exist. China faces growing global pressure, especially from the United States, to revalue its currency, the renminbi. It tied the value of the renminbi to the U.S. dollar early in the reform process and has periodically raised its value relative to the dollar, but the state has never allowed the currency's value to be determined solely by the market. This and a large amount of foreign currency from exports allowed China to weather the Asian financial crisis in 1997–1998 and the global crisis a decade later relatively easily. The government came under renewed pressure to raise the value of its currency during the global financial crisis, especially in 2010 as Chinese growth took off again while U.S. and European growth remained sluggish. U.S. and European governments wanted China to allow the value of its currency to rise to make Western exports more affordable for Chinese companies and consumers. The government responded with very slight revaluations in 2010 and promises to do more in 2011, promises similar to those they have made in the past and not fully implemented.

Domestically, China has experienced what most countries in the early stages of rapid industrialization experience: growing inequality. This is in marked contrast to several of the East Asian Tigers, notably South Korea and Taiwan, which simultaneously grew and became more equal. Inequality within rural areas, within urban areas, between urban and rural areas, and between provinces has grown substantially over the past thirty years. China's overall inequality as measured by the GINI Index is now slightly higher than that of the United States, which represents a sharp increase in inequality since the communist era. Since the early 1990s, the urban-rural gap has grown considerably as foreign investment and manufacturing in coastal cities have exploded. Even though virtually all households have gained from the expanding economy, the wealthiest 20 percent in both rural and urban areas have gained far more than their poorer neighbors, and the booming coastal regions have become much wealthier than the distant interior provinces, which remain largely rural and poor. One result has been the massive migration to the coastal cities of workers in search of jobs, and while the state has long tried to regulate this movement, it has been only partially successful. Privatization and migration from the countryside have produced considerable urban unemployment in recent years.

Under Jiang Zemin, the government recognized these problems and officially shifted focus from maximizing growth to providing greater social services to improve the lives of the least fortunate. In response to rising unemployment, especially from the privatized SOEs, it initiated new social welfare policies, mainly in the form of pensions for unemployed and retired workers. These expanded greatly starting in the mid-1990s and covered nearly half the workforce a decade later. Pensions provided a way to try to keep social and political peace by providing income to workers who were dislocated by the massive economic changes. The actual benefits provided by pensions varied greatly from one city and region to the next, though, because each area was allowed to establish its own system. Government support for many workers was designed to limit worker protests; it also acted as a source of

funding that often corrupt local officials could use for their own purposes (Frazier 2010). In 2010, the government passed a comprehensive Social Insurance Law that is designed to guarantee all citizens a right to a pension, medical insurance, employment injury insurance, unemployment insurance, and maternity insurance—a policy that will undoubtedly take years to implement fully.

The government also revised the national labor law in 2008 to respond to growing worker unrest. The new law gave full-time workers rights to longer and more secure contracts and streamlined the arbitration process through which workers could demand better wages and working conditions. It stopped short, though, of allowing workers to form their own unions, preserving the monopoly of the official union in the country's state corporatist system. These changes backfired in many ways. Passage of the new law gave workers greater awareness of their rights, and cases flooded the courts. The number of cases doubled in 2008 and has remained high ever since, creating a huge backlog. By 2010, the fastest-growing cities were facing a growing shortage of cheap labor, as the country's endless migration from rural areas finally appeared to be slowing. Worker protests and strikes expanded dramatically in mid-2010, most notably with a strike at a major Honda automobile plant where workers demanded the right to form their own union. While the government successfully resisted that demand, wages did increase in some places, and the tight labor market continues. Despite conscious government policies to ameliorate the worst effects of the economic transformation on Chinese workers, growing labor unrest seems likely to remain a problem for the foreseeable future.

The global financial crisis of 2008–2009 seemed mainly to augment China's role in the world. Like other "emerging markets," China recovered from the crisis much more quickly than the United States and Europe. It surpassed Japan in 2010 to become the second-largest economy in the world. While growth slowed to 8.7 percent (still a very high rate compared to world averages), it rebounded in 2010 to 9.1 percent. Part of this success is credited to the government's very large stimulus program in 2009, which invested heavily in infrastructure, including renewable energy and improved road and rail networks. The crisis caused a brief period of deflation, but by late 2010, economic growth had produced inflation anew. Indeed, the government became concerned that growth was too rapid and promoting inflation, so it raised interest rates in late 2010 to attempt to slow growth and inflation. At this time, the United States was still trying to stimulate its economy to reignite growth. The problems of rapid growth—potential "asset bubbles" (such as high real estate prices) that could pop, rising inflation, and growing government debt—remained China's major concerns, while other major economies were still focused on recovering from the recession.

CASE SUMMARY

China's growth has been phenomenal. Opening itself to market forces has created the largest increase in wealth and decrease in poverty the world has ever seen. Growth did not result, however, from a rapid conversion to the neoliberal economic model. China chose a more gradual approach, slowly increasing incentives for public and private entrepreneurs to engage in production for a growing market. An increasingly institutionalized state provided investors with assurances that they would be able to keep their profits. The state also invested in expanding public infrastructure and continued the Communist Party's policy of educating the populace. As in most of the East Asian Tigers, an increasingly strong state guided China's export-oriented growth. The country also benefited from its massive size and population, which gave it a huge labor force to draw upon and a vast domestic market to attract investors. Being in East Asia helped as well, since Japan, Hong Kong (which Britain returned to China in 1997), and Taiwan are major investors in mainland China and significant buyers of Chinese exports. A strong state pursued wise policies, navigating the shoals of globalization exceptionally well, even through the two biggest financial crises since the Great Depression. But it did so in unusually favorable circumstances. China certainly faces problems in the future that could slow its growth or create political instability, notably growing inequality, worker unrest, and massive environmental problems (which we examine in chapter 11).

India is the latest challenger to China as a rapidly industrializing economy. While India has not grown as quickly as China, in the new millennium it has become a very "hot" economy, and, in contrast to China, it has done so under a democratic regime.

CASE STUDY

India: Development and Democracy

- ISI and a closed economy until about 1980

- State intervention shifted to pro-business reforms in the 1980s

- Gradual but continual neoliberal reforms by a democratic government since 1991

- Rapid growth and poverty reduction, but growing inequality

- Globalization of Indian business, especially technology

- Still the largest population in poverty and the most malnutrition in the world

In a reversal of the typical pattern of globalization, India's giant software company, Infosys, invested $250 million in 2007 to purchase a Polish call center, whose staff can speak and work with clients in half a dozen European languages. Infosys also owns call centers in Mexico and China to serve regional clients in their languages. Bangalore, site of Infosys's headquarters, has become a major global hub for information technology, especially software development and call centers. Infosys is the high-visibility element of India's recent broader success in dealing with globalization; the country's overall economic growth rate surpassed 7 percent in 2003 and 9 percent in 2005, averaging a very strong 6.4 percent from 1996 to 2009. Indeed, Infosys is not unique; in 2006–2007, Indian companies spent nearly $13 billion buying companies elsewhere in the world. Widely seen to be "on the move," India has become an increasingly important player in world economic affairs and the second Asian giant to rise via globalization. Yet it is also home to the largest number of poor people in the world, with nearly one-quarter of its population being undernourished. India's development and continuing problems stem from a significant 1991 policy shift toward engagement in the global economy, though its success is based on foundations laid much earlier. As with other developing economies, the 2008–2009 global recession did not hit India nearly as hard as it did wealthier countries. India's growth slowed briefly but rebounded to more than 7 percent by 2010, as longer-term trends seemed to continue undiminished. India's improved growth and gradual but continuous economic liberalization demonstrate the possibilities and perils of economic reforms achieved by a democracy.

During its first three decades of independence, India pursued a classic policy of planned ISI, with self-proclaimed "socialist" goals. While the economy was based on the market, it was highly regulated, both internally and externally. A number of major industrial sectors were reserved exclusively for government investment and control. Doing business required so many governmental forms and licenses that the system came to be known as the "permit, license, quota Raj." The extensive regulations were based on the idea that

The headquarters of Infosys in Bangalore, India. The company has become a major transnational corporation and now outsources work to Eastern Europe and Mexico, among other places. India's economic policies have successfully encouraged massive growth in software and related services since the 1990s. These are centered in Bangalore, South Asia's version of Silicon Valley. Simultaneously, India is home to the largest number of poor and malnourished people in the world.

Credit: Wikipedia Commons/Amit

the government should guide the economy in the national interest and reflected standard development theory in the ISI period. But the regulations also provided numerous sources of patronage for the dominant Congress Party and its supporters. The program certainly produced substantial, albeit inefficient, industrial investment. Then in the 1960s, the Green Revolution, with considerable public investment, dramatically increased agricultural production, especially of key grains for food consumption. While progress was made, growth remained sluggish, rarely surpassing about 3 percent per year. This led some observers to refer to a "Hindu rate of growth" that would never exceed about 3.5 percent—a cultural argument to explain limited economic success.

Political dynamics in India's democracy affected economic policies in a major way in the 1970s and 1980s. Indira Gandhi's break with the Brahmin leaders of the old Congress in 1969 (see chapter 7) and her appeal to the poor with the rallying cry of *"Garibi hatao!"* ("End poverty now!") led her to enact populist economic policies. In the 1970s, her government lowered public investment and increased fiscal deficits by refusing to raise taxes while simultaneously expanding government subsidies to various groups, all in a bid to maintain her political support. Growth was lower under her rule than it had been earlier, with little reduction in the country's level of poverty. Her fall from power in 1977 ushered in a period of increased political competition, which drove a change in policy beginning with her return to power in 1980. Increased competition and the failure of populism forced the Congress governments in the 1980s to shift economic gears.

Many observers trace India's current high level of growth to the 1991 liberalization of the economy, but comparativist Atul Kohli (2004, 2007), a leading expert on India, argued that this success is based on earlier changes that were only partially liberal. Around 1980, elites within the ruling party and bureaucracy, influenced in part by the shift in global development thinking at the time, came to the conclusion that development policies needed to be much more pro-business to achieve economic growth. Indira Gandhi appointed these individuals to key committees that developed a pro-production set of policies. The new government sharply curtailed limits on the size of private business and the sectors in which it could invest, reduced business taxes, liberalized the stock market, and passed laws to limit the ability of unions to strike. It also initially liberalized import restrictions, but domestic business opposition to having to compete with imports forced a reversal within a couple of years. Government also made new public investments in infrastructure, funding these mainly by deficit spending.

The result of this policy shift was a doubling of growth rates in the 1980s to about 5.5 percent. Kohli argues that while these policies only partially followed the new neoliberal development model being pushed by the World Bank and IMF in the 1980s, they were very pro–domestic business. In a modest and gradual way, these policies paralleled those of the pro-business interventionist states of East Asia, especially targeted policies designed to encourage growth in the computer sector (Evans 1995). India's democracy did not allow the government to pursue pro-business policies too thoroughly or at the complete expense of the poor majority of voters, but it nonetheless put economic policy in the hands of a group of pro-business elites, who were able to guide policy to favor business over the poor in the interest of increasing growth.

More dramatic liberalization began in 1991 in response to economic crisis and opened the country much more to globalization. The growth of the 1980s had been partly fueled by debt, both public and private. The end of the Cold War and the first Iraq war of 1990–1991 left India close to bankrupt, and it had to go hat in hand to the IMF to secure emergency funding. The coalition government (led by the Congress) that came to power in 1991 used the emergency to justify greater liberalization. The pro-business policies of the 1980s expanded, and the government implemented new policies to lower restrictions on imports, foreign exchange, and foreign investment. It also promised to reduce the size of the public sector and the fiscal deficit, privatize state-owned companies, and reform labor laws to further favor business. While these measures helped secure IMF support and were initially received favorably by the population, once the immediate crisis was over, opposition emerged. Like those of the early 1980s, these policies had been initiated by technocrats in the key ministries. While the ruling party supported the policies, it made little effort to sell them to the populace as a whole. Farmers feared a reduction in their governmental subsidies, government bureaucrats resisted the reduction in their power that a more open market would entail, and advocates for the poor feared that the needy would fare even worse in a more open market. Business groups divided over the reforms. Older businesses in what was called the "Bombay Club" opposed opening to the global market, fearing that they wouldn't be able to compete, whereas new businesses in the engineering and computing sectors, which were interested in exporting, formed a new association that favored liberalization. The latter were joined by a still small but rapidly growing urban middle class who held jobs in trading sectors such as computer software. Business associations developed much closer relationships with key government economic policy makers, those associations increasingly competed against one another for the government's attention in India's pluralist interest group system, and business owners themselves entered politics via parliamentary elections (Sinha 2010). The result of these political forces in India's democracy has been significant but partial reform that continues to unfold.

On the economic front, the reforms of the early 1990s did not really change growth rates. After the economy recovered from the 1991 crisis, growth resumed at about the same 6 percent rate of the 1980s. The composition of growth, though, changed substantially (Kohli 2007). To reduce the fiscal deficit, the government had curtailed public investment, while the reforms encouraged greater private investment, both domestic and international. To date, the greatest growth has come not in manufacturing but rather in services, including computing services. In 2007, India had two-thirds of the global market in offshore information technology services. Foreign direct investment increased from under $10 billion annually in the 1990s to about $90 billion in 2008, and trade went from 15 percent of the economy in 1990 to 40 percent by 2008.

Compared to the most open economies of the world, India remains only partially globalized. Tariffs on imports were still at about 30 percent and only about one-quarter of the economy was involved in trade at the beginning of the new millennium (Kohli 2007, 105). By 2006, tariffs had dropped to 22 percent but remained among the highest in the world. Nonetheless, compared to prior decades, the country has opened a great deal. The promised reforms of drastically reducing government's role by privatizing state-owned companies (including banks) and reforming labor laws never happened. Reform has

been significant, albeit gradual, due in part to the politically contentious effects of those changes. The country certainly felt the global recession of 2008–2009, though growth remained above 5 percent and rebounded to over 7 percent by 2010. The government responded, as did most governments, with a Keynesian-style stimulus plan in early 2009 that invested heavily in infrastructure (long seen as a weak spot by domestic and international analysts) and that significantly increased deficit spending. Renewed growth by 2010 produced increased inflation and growing concern about the burgeoning government deficit. Indian growth and inflation were high enough that the central bank began raising interest rates in 2010 to combat inflation. This was in stark contrast to the policies of more heavily affected countries in the West that continued to face very low growth and, in some cases, fears of deflation.

Despite India's impressive growth record since 1980, poverty remains a serious problem, and inequality has grown. This is not to say that growth has not significantly lowered poverty, which stood at more than 50 percent in the 1970s, dropped to around 40 percent in the 1980s, and then dropped to 28 percent by 2005. Since the onset of the 1991 liberalization, sixty million people have moved out of poverty, although India still has the largest number of poor people in the world. Forty-three percent of children under age five were malnourished in 2000, 68 percent of adults were literate in 2008 (up from 48 percent in 1990), and 53 out of every 1,000 babies died in infancy (down from 94 in 1990) (Adams 2002; World Bank 1993; Kapur 2010).

A great deal of progress has occurred, but much remains to be done. Many of the poor remain in the agricultural sector. After rapid growth during the Green Revolution in the 1960s, agriculture has grown at a much slower rate than the rest of the economy since liberalization. It has also been regionally concentrated. The highly productive areas, notably the Punjab state on the Pakistani border, have seen tremendous growth in agriculture, while other states have stagnated. The same pattern appears for overall growth and poverty. A few states have grown very rapidly and reduced poverty quite significantly, even as several others have seen little change. Some, most notably Kerala, have experienced only moderate growth but have invested heavily in social services, achieving very high literacy rates, low population growth, and high-quality health care. While these states have not seen the same growth as the wealthier states, their residents live better than most Indians because of committed public investments (Adams 2002).

CASE SUMMARY

India's recent opening to the global market has made it a major player in key sectors such as software and other technology services, but the agricultural sector has stagnated. Reforms have reversed decades of ISI policies and heavy government intervention in the economy that produced much slower growth. New economic activity has

been regionally uneven, however, so high levels of poverty remain in poorer areas and overall inequality is increasing. By favoring domestic business in ways that loosely emulate the East Asian development model and then opening further to global markets, the Indian government has helped produce an expanding economy that increased income per capita from $355 in 1990 to $585 in 2005 while reducing overall poverty substantially. The surprisingly strong reelection of Prime Minister Singh and the coalition government led by the Congress in 2009 suggested that Indian citizens were relatively happy with the direction their country was headed as it navigated globalization. The new government promised a continuation of economic reforms toward greater liberalization, though in India's democracy, these reforms are likely to continue in a gradual manner and to face regular questioning by sectors of society that see themselves as losing out in the process.

CASE STUDY

Brazil: Does Globalization Allow a Different Path?

- Prolonged ISI followed by "heterodox" policies
- Defeat of inflation via neoliberal policies in the 1990s
- Leftist government and greater social spending since 2002
- Core dilemma: Can a government pursue neoliberal policies and reduce poverty?
- Modest success at both neoliberalism and poverty reduction by 2010

When working-class hero "Lula" and his Workers Party (PT) won the 2002 presidential election in Brazil, the poor celebrated it as the victory of one of their own who promised to provide them with a better life, while the rich worried that the economy would be ruined.

Both have been proved partially wrong. Lula was one of the first of the new "leftist" leaders in South America and was seen as friendlier to continued market-oriented policies than more "radical" leaders such as Hugo Chavez of Venezuela. Lula's presidency has not reversed the core of Brazil's economic policy, which has been primarily neoliberal since the early 1990s. The new government did, however, institute major new social programs aimed at poverty reduction, and by its second term had achieved faster economic growth. Together, these resulted in Lula at least partially realizing his promises to substantially reduce poverty. After years of floundering in the 1980s and 1990s, Brazil has navigated the shoals of globalization more effectively in recent years. Brazil's success made Lula the most popular president in the country's history as he handed off power to his hand-picked successor in January 2011.

Brazil's twentieth-century economic history is similar to Mexico's (see chapter 5). Brazil went through a prolonged period of ISI that was one of the more successful in the world until the 1982 debt crisis, when it began a long, slow, and painful transition to neoliberal policies. Under the neofascist Estado Novo (1937–1945), the first state-owned companies were created, and the state invested heavily in the infrastructure needed by industry. The Estado Novo also controlled labor unions via state corporatism, keeping workers' wages low to attract investment. The military coup in 1964 produced a modernizing authoritarian regime that intensified ISI, rapidly expanded the state's involvement in the economy by creating more state-owned companies in heavy industry, built more infrastructure, and repressed unions further. The results from 1967 to 1973 came to be known as the "Brazilian Miracle," during which the economy grew at a rate of 9 to 10 percent per year, one of the fastest growth rates in the world. This completed the country's transition from an agricultural to an industrial economy, but it also produced much greater inequality. The southeastern states and cities, especially São Paulo and Rio de Janeiro, received the bulk of investment and grew rapidly. The rural populace migrated to these two cities in huge numbers. At one point, São Paulo was growing by more than half a million people a year. This left the northern part of the country and the interior depopulated and even poorer. Within the booming cities, however, inequality was also increasing.

By the onset of the 1982 debt crisis, Brazil had become the world's biggest debtor. It negotiated several agreements over the next decade with the United States and the major banks to which it owed money. These agreements reduced some of the debt in exchange for promises of policy changes in line with the neoliberal model advocated by the IMF. With the transition to democracy underway in the 1980s, however, change to the state's role in

Brazilian president Luiz Inácio "Lula" da Silva holds a sign reading, "Food: A Privilege for the Few." Elected on a platform of reversing social inequalities, Lula started programs to that end but also had to maintain orthodox macroeconomic policies to reassure global markets that their capital was safe in Brazil. His critics saw his policies as contradictory. Lula's election raised questions about how much the electorate of a middle-income country can change economic direction in the face of globalization.

Credit: AP Photo/Andre Luiz Mello-File

the economy was relatively slow. High inflation remained a major concern as well. Some efforts at privatizing industry and reducing the size of the government were made, but with limited success. Until the early 1990s, Brazil followed a mix of policies—often termed "heterodox" because they followed no clear economic model—that had only modest success in reorienting the economy.

In 1992, the impeachment and resignation of Brazil's first directly elected president, Fernando Collor, brought the short-lived government of President Itamar Franco to power. More importantly, it brought Fernando Henrique Cardoso to power as finance minister. Cardoso and a team of economists created what came to be called the "*Real* Plan" to

IN CONTEXT

BRAZILIAN ECONOMIC GROWTH

Before 1980, the Brazilian economic miracle produced higher economic growth rates than in much of the world. Since then, however, Brazil has struggled in comparison to the wealthy countries, as has Latin America as a whole.

Per Capita GDP Growth Rates (average annual percentages)

	Wealthy countries (OECD members)	Latin America	Brazil
1950–1979	3.3	2.3	3.9
1980–1989	2.3	−0.3	1.0
1990–1999	3.04	1.34	0.82
2000–2006	3.01	1.49	1.47

Source: Luiz Carlos Bresser-Pereira. 2009. *Developing Brazil: Overcoming the Failure of the Washington Consensus.* Boulder, CO: Lynne Rienner, 30. © 2009 by Lynne Rienner Publishers, Inc. Used with permission of the publisher.

battle inflation. The key components of this plan were greater fiscal discipline via increased taxes and reduced spending; a tighter monetary policy via high interest rates; and a new currency (named the *real*), which was loosely tied to the value of the U.S. dollar. The plan followed orthodox neoliberal economic theory, which holds that inflation is caused by some combination of loose fiscal and monetary policy. The *Real* Plan was spectacularly successful. Inflation fell from more than 50 percent per month in June 1994 to less than 3 percent by the end of the year. Annual inflation went from 2,407 percent in 1994 to 11 percent in 1996. The Plan's success helped Cardoso get elected president in 1994 and thus continue his economic reforms. Due to the effects of the Asian financial crisis of 1998, however, Brazil had to accept a bailout package from the IMF that came with stringent demands for fiscal

reform. In the mid-1990s, economic growth had hit 5 percent, but the crisis reduced it to nearly zero in 1998–1999.

By 2002, Cardoso's economic policies were widely unpopular, despite his success at ending inflation eight years earlier. The country had shifted a major share of its economy from public to private ownership, expanded exports dramatically, and finally beaten inflation and severe fiscal problems. Greater opening to the world economy, however, produced a greater concentration of assets in both the industrial and large-scale agricultural sectors, as well as greater output. Profits increased relative to wages, and unemployment increased from less than 5 percent in the 1980s to nearly 10 percent twenty years later. More efficient private industry replaced less efficient SOEs; the latter had employed more people but produced less (Baer 2008, 369–80). The Workers' Party (PT) had long championed a move toward a more socialist economic policy, though PT leaders often left that policy vaguely defined. During the 2002 presidential campaign, domestic and international business leaders feared a PT government, so investment slowed and foreign capital dried up in anticipation of what might come. To ease these concerns, the PT wrote a manifesto stating that "social development," focused on reducing poverty and inequality, was crucial to the party but that it would be coupled with orthodox economic policies to keep inflation low and the government budget in surplus. Despite these reassurances, business remained uncertain after Lula's election.

In part to convince such skeptics, Lula appointed a well-known orthodox economist as finance minister, and he pledged that the government would actually surpass the IMF's goal for a low budget deficit via more efficient tax collection and continuing limits on government spending (the 1998 IMF package had forced the government to reduce the budget deficit). To maintain international business confidence, he kept interest rates high and the budget deficit low. High interest rates, however, forced the government to pay more on its existing debt, leaving it little money to spend on Lula's new social programs.

A leading scholar of the Brazilian economy, Werner Baer, argued that Lula's government faced a "core dilemma": "the pursuit of a macroeconomic policy orthodox enough to win the approval of the international financial community and the achievement of a greater socioeconomic equality" (2008, 167). Lula tried to do these two things sequentially by first securing economic stability and business confidence and then focusing on social programs. Baer suggested, however, that a fundamental incompatibility would persist: Brazil's orthodox policies to ensure international investor confidence in an open economy would prevent large amounts of social spending on the poor. Lula's first term (2003–2006) seemed to bear this prediction out, but his second term (2007–2010) saw substantial gains for the working class and poor, as the government achieved both new social programs (see chapter 11) and increased growth and employment.

Lula's government disappointed many of his most ardent followers in its first term. Ironically, the election of the "socialist" PT initially pleased international business far more than it did the urban or rural working class, as foreign investment into the country remained strong and inflation was kept in check. Real wages in the industrial cities, the heart of his electoral support, remained stagnant through 2006, and unemployment only dropped from 11 to 9 percent by 2005 (Baer 2008, 161–64). In Lula's second term, however, unemployment dropped from 9 percent to under 6 percent by 2010, poverty was cut roughly in half by 2007, and the GINI coefficient dropped from about 58 to 55, indicating modestly greater equality.

As in most "emerging markets," the Global Recession did not hit Brazil as hard as it did wealthier countries. The robust growth rate of 5 to 6 percent in the two years before the recession plummeted to 0.2 percent in 2009 but rebounded strongly to 7.5 percent in 2010, accompanied by a substantial decline in unemployment. Lula's government responded to the recession with a strong stimulus package that focused on building infrastructure, and it seemed to work. Indeed,

by the end of 2010, when Lula left the presidency and his handpicked successor Dilma Rousseff (the country's first woman president) succeeded him, the main economic concern was the possibility of an "overheated" economy—one growing so fast that inflation was already over 5 percent. Inflation was in part due to better interest rates in Brazil (and most other emerging markets) than in wealthier countries, which caused capital to flow in from around the world, thus raising the value of Brazil's currency. Investors, searching for better returns than they could get in the sluggish economies of the United States and Europe, found them in Brazil and similar countries. While this investment boosted short-term growth, it threatened to harm Brazil's exports and raised inflation.

CASE SUMMARY

Lula came to power as one of a new wave of "leftist" leaders elected across Latin America, with promises to challenge the neoliberal economic orthodoxy. He was, however, one of the more moderate members of this group. He promised to change priorities, which for him meant not reversing the opening to the global market so much as substantially redistributing its rewards to the poor. While he initiated commendable social programs (see chapter 11), maintaining international investor confidence required economic policies that initially gave him few resources to redistribute. Investment and exports increased, but overall economic growth over his first term averaged only 3.35 percent. His second term was much improved, with growth over 4 percent, even with the recession. Growth combined with greatly expanded social programs to reduce poverty substantially, but 12.7 percent of Brazil's population still lived on less than $2 per day in 2007. As Lula handed power and continued PT rule to Rousseff, the biggest economic concern was a reflection of Brazil's economic strength: a rising currency and consequent fears of inflation due to rapidly inflowing capital. Rising currency could be a long-term problem as the country becomes a major exporter of another product that will bring in large amounts of foreign investment: oil. In 2007, Brazil announced that it had discovered a large offshore oil field that, when fully developed in twenty-five years, will make it one of the top five oil exporters in the world. This could certainly be good news (and Lula heralded it as such) because oil could eventually provide the revenue needed to address the country's remaining social problems. Oil, though, is often a very mixed blessing, as our case study of Iran demonstrates.

CASE STUDY

Iran: Struggling with the Blessings of Oil

- Oil is chief connection to global economy and a key source of government revenue
- Economic policies similar to ISI, until partial and temporary move toward neoliberal policies by reformist governments, 1997–2005
- Oil revenue used to provide regime supporters with wide array of subsidies
- Global financial crisis forces some reduction in subsidies
- Future continues to depend on global oil prices

When most Americans think of Iran, they think of its Islamist regime, U.S. sanctions against it, and its attempts to attain nuclear weapons. Economically, though, oil production and exportation is the country's most important global role. Oil wealth provides the vast majority of the country's exports and the state's revenue, and the leadership uses the latter to enhance its legitimacy. But these revenues have not necessarily encouraged wise use of resources. The Islamist regime uses oil revenue, channeled through Islamist charities and its own paramilitary groups, to provide a wide array of subsidies to the population. Thus, the government continues to control a major swath of the economy. Reformist governments in the late 1990s and early 2000s made some strides toward reducing the role of government and improving efficiency, but the current government under President Mahmoud Ahmadinejad has partially reversed that. The country continues to rely heavily on the often fickle world oil market.

Iran's unusual theocratic regime has not shielded it from the impact of globalization and the problems it brings to middle-income countries, but the revolution and oil have heavily influenced Iran's specific trajectory. The revolutionary government nationalized many economic assets in 1980. Many large private companies, including banks, became SOEs, and property confiscated from the shah's family and close associates funded Islamic foundations (*bonyads*), which became a key part of revolutionary rule. The eight-year Iran-Iraq War in the 1980s pummeled the economy, which shrank nearly 1.3 percent per capita per year over the decade. The 1990s saw some improvement, with per capita growth of nearly 2 percent per year, but this was accompanied by annual inflation of more than 20 percent and growing unemployment, which reached 16 percent by 2000. The end of the war did help the poverty rate drop dramatically, however, from 36 percent in 1985 to less than 15 percent in 1992 (Saeidi 2001, 231). Throughout both decades, the country remained critically dependent on oil, which accounted for more than 80 percent of exports and anywhere from one-third to two-thirds of government revenue, depending on world oil prices.

The heavily state-controlled economy resembled the ISI policies of decades earlier in other middle-income countries. The Iranian government, though, intervened more extensively than did governments in many other countries. Government-controlled banks set interest rates uniformly, trade barriers were high, and the government set multiple foreign exchange rates. The latter served to subsidize the SOEs and *bonyads*, which had access to the more favorable rates. As we noted in chapter 8, the government budget provided large subsidies to the *bonyads* and to the SOEs as well, and lack of fiscal discipline played a major role in the high rates of inflation. Government subsidies and protection gave SOEs little incentive to operate efficiently: their losses from 1994 to 1999 equaled nearly 3 percent of the country's GDP (Alizadeh 2003, 273). The growing power of the Revolutionary Guard under President Mahmoud Ahmadinejad (2005–) has meant that it and its affiliates have gained ownership of a significant share of the economy. The subsidies channeled through the *bonyads* and the Revolutionary Guard constituted 27 percent of the economy in 2008–2009; they essentially channel oil revenue to regime supporters to maintain their loyalty.

Facing growing economic problems, in the late 1990s the government under reformist President Mohammad Khatami attempted the first significant liberalization of the economy, a belated response to global trends and pressures. Iran's theocratic government even took advice from the bastion of Western economic imperialism, the IMF, in setting new policies. The most dramatic reforms were announced in 2000 in the Third Five-Year Development Plan. This plan included the implementation of a unified and floating exchange rate, the sale of some government-controlled banks to the private sector (the government gave up controlling interest rates in the mid-1990s), and reduction of import and export barriers. All these policies were designed to open the economy to greater global activity. The plan also called for significant privatization of SOEs and the creation of an Oil Stabilization Fund (OSF), which would take in oil revenue when prices were high and spend it when prices dropped. Neither of these reforms worked as envisioned. Privatization of SOEs has been slow and partial, in part due to fear of increasing already high unemployment. The government has also already used some of the OSF to, among other things, continue

An Iranian man refuels his car in Tehran. The Iranian government long relied on heavy subsidies to consumers, including on gasoline, to maintain support. The global recession forced President Ahmedinejad to reduce many subsidies, and gas prices quadrupled. The regime's successful clampdown on all protests, though, resulted in little public uproar over the changes.

Credit: Ahmad/Xinhua/Landov

subsidizing *bonyads* (Amuzegar 2005). Overall, the reforms increased growth in the new millennium to around 5 percent per year and reduced inflation to less than 15 percent, but unemployment and poverty levels remained largely unchanged. These partially successful reforms may have prompted the backlash that brought President Ahmadinejad and more populist economic policies to power in 2005.

Economic growth, fuelled by rising oil prices, reached nearly 8 percent before the global financial crisis. While the direct effects of the crisis were relatively slight in economically isolated Iran, the country was nonetheless heavily affected by declining world oil prices. Oil export revenue fell 24 percent in 2009, and overall growth dropped to only 1.5 percent. Unemployment is officially estimated to be in the teens most years, but many analysts believe that it is much higher, perhaps as high as 30 percent. The economic slowdown did bring inflation down substantially, but it remained at about 15 percent during the crisis, and the government budget went from surplus to deficit. Rising oil prices in late 2010 undoubtedly fed more revenue to the government, highlighting its continued dependence on a fickle global market. In response to the crisis, President Ahmedinejad, in spite of his rhetoric in favor of continuing subsidies, began to cut them; his hand was forced by the rapidly growing budget deficit. Past efforts to reduce subsidies had led to widespread protests and reversals of the cuts, but in late 2010, the government allowed gasoline prices to quadruple. This move was met with little visible protest, perhaps because of the severe crackdown on protests after the 2009 election (see chapter 8). How long the regime's legitimacy can survive more extensive cuts to the popular subsidies provided by oil revenue is an open question. How severe the cuts will have to be will depend almost entirely on the global price of oil.

Even with these reforms, Iran's chief interaction with the global economy remains its oil exports, which still account for about 80 percent of exports. This means that Iran's overall economic well-being remains tightly wedded to fluctuations in the global oil market. In fact, its economic growth has been more closely related to oil revenue since the Islamic revolution than it was under the shah (Karshenas and Hakimian 2005). The 1980s, when the country fought a war and faced a declining world price for oil, were economically disastrous. The late 1990s and the new millennium have been better, but primarily because of the high price of oil. Oil revenue is also of great political importance; it is still the key source of patronage on which the regime depends to fund the various Islamic foundations that are crucial pillars of regime support.

CASE SUMMARY

Despite its massive oil revenue, Iran's theocracy has faced many of the same challenges that other middle-income countries in a global economy have navigated. Its attempt at state control of major assets resulted in inefficiency, inflation, and unemployment, though the regime has successfully lowered poverty levels. Khatami's attempt to enact more market-oriented reforms by moving in a slightly neoliberal direction was only partially successful, both in terms of changing policy and improving the economy. Subsequently, Ahmadinejad was elected president in 2005 on a pledge to reduce corruption and redistribute resources to the poor. These policies were a return to the revolution's promise of social justice, and they made Ahmadinejad's rise not unlike Lula's rise to power in Brazil. Ahmadinejad's first two years in office saw significantly increased public spending, buoyed by rapidly rising oil prices. It also saw higher inflation, however, and the lives of the poor were not changed much. The global financial crisis resulted in a temporary drop in oil prices, sending the Iranian government's budget into a tailspin that finally forced the government to begin to remove some subsidies. Political supporters of the regime in the *bonyads* and Revolutionary Guards, however, continue to control a large share of the economy, and reducing their role will be politically difficult. Throughout the upheavals of revolution, expanding state control, and partial liberalization, Iran has remained as dependent on oil as it was under the shah, and that dependence seems likely to hinder further reform.

CONCLUSION

Who Rules?

Globalization has certainly changed the context in which sovereign states, whether rich or poor, make economic policy. The increasingly open global economy pushes rich and poor states away from the use of time-honored economic policies that had limited the market, such as taxes, tariffs, and exchange rate control. In addition, states are under increasing pressure to pursue policies that will keep inflation and state spending low and labor flexible.

As our case studies suggest, however, states have not all responded to globalization in the same way. Economic sovereignty, while clearly reduced, still exists. Among the wealthy countries, LMEs have intensified their openness to the market to varying degrees, whereas CMEs have moved in that direction much more slowly while preserving some aspects of their distinct model. Poorer countries are much more susceptible to the vicissitudes of the global market, as the repeated financial crises in these countries suggest, but these states are not powerless. They can play an important role in creating a context that fosters growth, and human development, and effective responses to crises. Recent experience suggests that, within some parameters set by the global market, they respond differently based on their own political histories, cultures, and institutions.

What Explains Political Behavior?

Why have some states been more successful in the era of globalization than others? A key explanation is wealth. Despite challenges, wealthy countries have benefitted more from globalization than they have been hurt by it. The gap between the wealthiest and the poorest has increased, and the varieties of capitalism paradigm shows that wealthy countries continue to enjoy a significant degree of autonomy in how far they go in the direction driven by the forces of global capitalism. Poorer countries have virtually all moved in the general direction of economic liberalization, but whether this has been a blessing is not always clear. While pursuit of export-oriented growth in East Asia has generated strong growth and reduced poverty, the East Asian model is based on strong state intervention in ways that favor rather than hamper exports. Neoliberal policies elsewhere have not always reduced poverty and have sometimes led to repeated financial crises. One clear difference is in the strength of the state. States with relatively strong institutions that are insulated from immediate political pressures seem to be able to create sound and sustained macroeconomic policies that make them more likely to prosper under globalization.

The global financial crisis of 2008–2009 was only the latest in a series of economic crises in the era of globalization. Each has shaken the foundation of one or another economic development model and has raised questions about who weathers a crisis best and why. The latest crisis has shown perhaps more clearly than ever the force of the global market in limiting states' responses to crises. The crisis produced rapidly rising debt in several European countries, which ultimately were forced to seek bailouts from the EU and IMF. Initial stimulus packages in many countries gave way to fiscal austerity to appease international markets. The Asian crisis a decade earlier hit developing countries the hardest, but the more recent crisis left them stronger. The degree to which different countries are affected by a particular crisis depends in large part in how they are integrated into the global economy and what the exact origin of the crisis is.

Where and Why?

Globalization has produced widely diverging results in different regions of the world. The wealthy countries have clearly benefitted the most, but the most successful Asian countries have benefitted tremendously as well, with some (e.g., South Korea) effectively joining the ranks of "the wealthy." The starkest contrast, however, is between Asian success and African malaise. Numerous possible answers arise for this difference, and in all likelihood, a combination of them is necessary for a full explanation. It seems clear, given Asian history, that culture is not likely to be the answer. Geography, resource endowment, institutional strength, and government policies all have a role to play. While some of these factors, (e.g., geography) cannot be overcome, others, at least in theory, can be. Perhaps Africa's recent economic upturn is in part an indicator of African governments' improved policies and institutions. Economic liberalization is very difficult, both economically and politically. The relatively strong, insulated states of East Asia were able to pursue it earlier and more selectively, on their own terms and to their benefit. Latin American and especially African states are not as strong and politically insulated, and powerful domestic forces there resist the short-term costs of what may be beneficial long-term economic policies. Even with great international pressure (such as during the 1980s debt crisis), domestic political factors play a large role in determining how much liberalization occurs and how effective it is.

Applying Theory to Globalization and Development

The oldest school of thought for understanding economic policy and development success is undoubtedly the cultural approach. According to this school of thought, different regions of the world were believed to be wealthier because of the nature of their cultures. Northern Europe and the United States were endowed with what Max Weber called "the Protestant work ethic," which championed hard work, productivity, and economic success. China and India were characterized by "Confucian" and "Hindu" culture, respectively, both of which ostensibly led to fatalistic acceptance of the status quo and therefore little economic growth. The rise of southern Europe, China, and India has raised major doubts about cultural theories. In their place, most political scientists have tended to accept the rational-choice paradigm of mainstream neoclassical economics, which states that certain fundamental economic laws, based on rational behavior, explain why some market economies produce more wealth than others. The political task of any state is to understand these laws and institute a set of policies that works with them rather than against them. Attempts to do more or act differently will ultimately be counterproductive. This is the theoretical underpinning of the neoliberal model, which has clearly worked in some places but not everywhere, and does not seem to be essential everywhere.

The most recent theoretical turn is to institutions. Among wealthy countries, institutional differences embedded in the distinction between LMEs and CMEs explain why different countries need not follow exactly the same path in response to globalization and economic crises. Among poorer countries, the strength of institutions seems to explain much about why certain states can and do pursue more sound economic policies that encourage greater growth while also protecting their people from the worst effects of globalization. While institutions certainly do not explain everything, after two decades of studying globalization and its effects, they seem to play a very important role. They are also important in helping us understand how states pursue important policies in the face of market failure, a subject to which we turn next.

KEY CONCEPTS

comparative institutional advantage (p. 490)
convergence (p. 488)
coordinated market economies (CMEs) (p. 489)
export-oriented growth (EOG) (p. 504)

foreign direct investment (FDI) (p. 487)
hyperglobalization (p. 488)
international capital flows (p. 487)
liberal market economies (LMEs) (p. 489)

Millennium Development Goals (MDGs) (p. 516)
sustainable development (p. 502)
trade (p. 487)
varieties of capitalism approach (p. 489)

WORKS CITED

Adams, John. 2002. "India's Economic Growth: How Fast? How Wide? How Deep?" *India Review* 1 (2): 1–28.

Alizadeh, Parvin. 2003. "Iran's Quandary: Economic Reforms and the 'Structural Trap.'" *Brown Journal of World Affairs* 9 (2): 267–81.

Amuzegar, Jahangir. 2005. "Iran's Third Development Plan: An Appraisal." *Middle East Policy* 12 (3): 46–63. doi:10.1111/j.1061-1924.2005.00212.x.

Baer, Werner. 2008. *The Brazilian Economy: Growth and Development.* 6th ed. Boulder, CO: Lynne Rienner.

Bresser-Pereira, Luiz Carlos. 2009. *Developing Brazil: Overcoming the Failure of the Washington Consensus.* Boulder, CO: Lynne Rienner.

Cameron, Maxwell A., and Eric Hershberg, eds. 2010. *Latin America's Left Turns: Politics, Policies and Trajectories of Change.* Boulder, CO: Lynne Rienner.

Cox, Robert Henry. 2002. "Reforming the German Welfare State: Why Germany Is Slower Than Its Neighbors." *German Policy Studies* 2 (1): 174–96.

Daly, Mary. 2001. "Globalization and the Bismarckian Welfare States." In *Globalization and European Welfare States: Challenges and Change*, edited by Robert Sykes, Bruno Palier, and Pauline M. Prior (with Jo Campling), 79–102. New York: Palgrave.

Easterly, William. 2006. *The White Man's Burden: Why the West's Efforts to Aid the Rest Have Done So Much Ill and So Little Good.* New York: Penguin Press.

Evans, Peter B. 1995. *Embedded Autonomy: States and Industrial Transformation.* Princeton, NJ: Princeton University Press.

Faucher-King, Florence, and Patrick Le Galès. 2010. *The New Labour Experiment: Change and Reform under Blair and Brown.* Stanford, CA: Stanford University Press.

Feng, Yi. 2003. *Democracy, Governance, and Economic Performance: Theory and Evidence.* Cambridge, MA: MIT Press.

Frazier, Mark. 2010. *Socialist Insecurity: Pensions and the Politics of Uneven Development in China.* Ithaca, NY: Cornell University Press.

Ginsburg, Norman. 2001. "Globalization and the Liberal Welfare States." In *Globalization and European Welfare States: Challenges and Change*, edited by Robert Sykes, Bruno Palier, and Pauline M. Prior (with Jo Campling), 173–92. New York: Palgrave.

Hall, Peter, and Daniel Gingerich. 2009. "Varieties of Capitalism and Institutional Complementarities in the Political Economy: An Empirical Analysis." *British Journal of Political Science* 39 (3): 449–82. doi:10.1017/S0007123409000672.

Hall, Peter Andrew, and David W. Soskice, eds. 2001. *Varieties of Capitalism: The Institutional*

Foundations of Comparative Advantage. Oxford, UK: Oxford University Press.

Hardie, Iain, and David Howarth. 2009. "*Die Krise* but Not *La Crise?* The Financial Crisis and the Transformation of German and French Banking Systems." *JCMS: Journal of Common Market Studies* 47 (5): 1017–39. doi:10.1111/j.1468-5965.2009.02033.x.

Hay, Colin. 2004. "Common Trajectories, Variable Paces, Divergent Outcomes: Models of European Capitalism under Conditions of Complex Economic Interdependence." *Review of International Political Economy* 11 (2): 231–62. doi:10.1080/09692290420001672796.

Huber, Evelyn, and John Stephens. 2001. *Development and Crisis of the Welfare State: Parties and Policies in Global Markets.* Chicago: University of Chicago Press.

Kapur, Devesh. 2010. "The Political Economy of the State." In *The Oxford Companion to Politics in India*, edited by Niraja Gopal Jayal and Pratap Bhanu Mehta, 443–58. Oxford, UK: Oxford University Press.

Karshenas, Massoud, and Hassan Hakimian. 2005. "Oil, Economic Diversification, and the Democratic Process in Iran." *Iranian Studies* 38 (1): 67–90. doi:10.1080/0021086042000336546.

Kohli, Atul. 2004. *State-Directed Development: Political Power and Industrialization in the Global Periphery.* Cambridge, UK: Cambridge University Press.

———. 2007. "State, Business, and Economic Growth in India." *Studies in Comparative International Development* 42 (1–2): 87–114. doi:10.1007/s12116-007-9001-9.

MacIntyre, Andrew, T. J. Pempel, and John Ravenhill, eds. 2008. *Crisis as Catalyst: Asia's Dynamic Political Economy.* Ithaca, NY: Cornell University Press.

Moreno-Brid, Juan Carlos, and Igor Paunovic. 2010. "Macroeconomic Policies of the New Left: Rhetoric and Reality." In *Latin America's Left Turns: Politics, Policies, and Trajectories of Change*, edited by Maxwell A. Cameron and Eric Hershberg, 193–232. Boulder, CO: Lynne Rienner.

Moyo, Dambisa. 2009. *Dead Aid: Why Aid Is Not Working and How There Is a Better Way for Africa.* New York: Farrar, Straus and Giroux.

Nissanke, Machiko, and Erik Thorbecke, eds. 2010. *The Poor under Globalization in Asia, Latin America, and Africa.* Oxford, UK: Oxford University Press.

Ocampo, José Antonio, and Rob Vos, eds. 2008. *Uneven Economic Development.* London: Zed Books.

Ozawa, Terutomo. 2010. "Asia's Labour-driven Growth, Flying Geese Style: Types of Trade, FDI, and Institutions Matter for the Poor." In *The Poor under Globalization in Asia, Latin America, and Africa*, edited by Machiko Nissanke and Erik Thorbecke, 87–115. Oxford, UK: Oxford University Press.

Przeworski, Adam, Michael Alvarez, Jose Cheibub, and Fernando Limongi. 2000. *Democracy and Development.* Cambridge, UK: Cambridge University Press.

Qian, Yingyi. 2006. "The Process of China's Market Transition, 1978–1998: The Evolutionary, Historical, and Comparative Perspectives." In *China's Deep Reform: Domestic Politics in Transition*, edited by Lowell Dittmer and Guoili Liu, 229–50. Lanham, MD: Rowman and Littlefield.

Qin, Julia. 2007. "Trade, Investment, and Beyond: The Impact of WTO Accession on China's Legal System." *China Quarterly* 191: 720–41.

Round, Jeffrey. 2010. "Globalization, Growth, Inequality, and Poverty in Africa: A Macroeconomic Perspective." In *The Poor under Globalization in Asia, Latin America, and Africa*, edited by M. Nissanke and E. Thorbecke, 327–67. Oxford, UK: Oxford University Press.

Sachs, Jeffrey D. 2005. *The End of Poverty: Economic Possibilities for Our Time.* New York: Penguin Books.

Saeidi, Ali A. 2001. "Charismatic Political Authority and Populist Economics in Post-Revolutionary Iran." *Third World Quarterly* 22 (2): 219–36. doi:10.1080/01436590120037045.

Sinha, Aseema. 2010. "Business and Politics in Changing India: Continuities, Transformations, and Patterns." In *The Oxford Companion to Politics in India*, edited by Niraja Gopal Jayal and Pratap Bhanu Mehta, 459–76. Oxford, UK: Oxford University Press.

Streeck, Wolfgang. 2009. *Re-Forming Capitalism: Institutional Change in the German Political Economy*. Oxford, UK: Oxford University Press.

Streeck, Wolfgang, and Anke Hassel. 2003. "The Crumbling Pillars of Social Partnership." *West European Politics* 26 (4): 101–24. doi:10.1080/01402380312331280708.

United Nations: Economic Commission for Latin America and the Caribbean (ECLAC). 2010. *Preliminary Overview of the Economies of Latin America and the Caribbean 2010*. http://

www.eclac.org/cgi-bin/getProd.asp?xml=/publicaciones/xml/4/41974/P41974.xml.

Van de Walle, Nicolas. 2001. *African Economies and the Politics of Permanent Crisis, 1979–1999*. Cambridge, UK: Cambridge University Press.

Winters, L. Alan, and Shahid Yusuf, eds. 2007. *Dancing with Giants: China, India, and the Global Economy*. Washington, DC: World Bank.

World Bank. 1993. *The East Asian Miracle: Economic Growth and Public Policy*. New York: Oxford University Press.

RESOURCES FOR FURTHER STUDY

Ferreira, Francisco H. G., and Michael Walton. 2005. *Equity and Development*. Washington, DC: World Bank.

Garrett, Geoffrey. 1998. *Partisan Politics in the Global Economy*. Cambridge, UK: Cambridge University Press.

Haggard, Stephan, and Robert R. Kaufman. 1995. *The Political Economy of Democratic Transitions*. Princeton, NJ: Princeton University Press.

Jha, Prem Shankar. 2002. *The Perilous Road to the Market: The Political Economy of Reform in Russia, India, and China*. London: Pluto Press.

Jones, R. J. Barry. 2000. *The World Turned Upside Down? Globalization and the Future of the State*. Manchester, UK: Manchester University Press.

Kohli, Atul, Chung-in Moon, and Georg Sørensen, eds. 2003. *States, Markets, and Just Growth: Development in the Twenty-First Century*. New York: United Nations University Press.

Rothstein, Bo, and Sven Steinmo, eds. 2002. *Restructuring the Welfare State: Political Institutions and Policy Change*. New York: Palgrave Macmillan.

Sykes, Robert, Bruno Palier, and Pauline M. Prior (with Jo Campling), eds. 2001. *Globalization and European Welfare States: Challenges and Change*. New York: Palgrave.

WEB RESOURCES

CountryWatch (http://www.countrywatch.com/)

European Commission, "Eurostat: Your Key to European Statistics" (http://epp.eurostat.ec.europa.eu/)

KOF Index of Globalization (http://globalization.kof.ethz.ch/). Based on data from Dreher, Axel. 2006. "Does Globalization Affect Growth? Evidence from a New Index of Globalization. *Applied Economics* 38 (10): 1091–110; updated in Dreher, Axel, Noel Gaston, and Pim Martens. 2008. *Measuring Globalisation: Gauging Its Consequences*. New York: Springer.

Luxembourg Income Study (http://www.lisproject.org/)

Organisation for Economic Co-Operation and Development (OECD), "OECD. StatExtracts" (http://stats.oecd.org/index.aspx)

UN Millennium Project, "Millennium Villages: A New Approach to Fighting Poverty" (http://www.unmillenniumproject.org/mv/mv_closer.htm)

United Nations University World Institute for Development Economics Research, "World Income Inequality Database" (http://www.wider.unu.edu/research/Database/)

World Bank, "Economic Policy and External Debt" (http://data.worldbank.org/topic/economic-policy-and-external-debt/)

Who Rules?

- What do policy outcomes tell us about who has effective representation and power in a political system?

What Explains Political Behavior?

- Why do states intervene in the market via social, health, and environmental policies?
- Why have many governments pursued significant reforms to welfare states in the era of globalization?
- Why have states found it so difficult to reform health policy and control costs?

Where and Why?

- Why have extensive welfare states developed in certain countries and not in others?
- Where and why did more effective welfare and health systems emerge, and can the most effective ones be replicated in other countries?

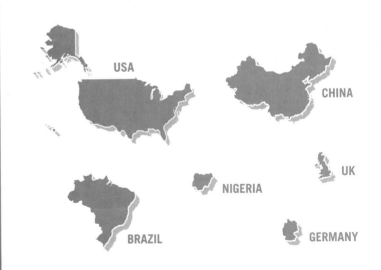

11

PUBLIC POLICIES WHEN MARKETS FAIL

Welfare, Health, and the Environment

As globalization expands the market economy, the issues raised in chapters 5 and 10 about the relationship between the state and the market loom ever larger. States must continue to provide the essential public goods that allow capitalism and the market to operate: security, property rights, contract enforcement, and some basic infrastructure. Chapter 10 showed that the current debate is over how else governments ought to intervene in the market in an effort to maximize the well-being of the citizenry. This chapter addresses three key areas that have long been subjects of debate in virtually every country: welfare, health care, and the environment. The common thread among them is the call for government to intervene in response to market failure.

We defined market failure in chapter 5: economists say markets fail when they fail to maximize efficiency, most commonly because of externalities, monopolies, or imperfect information. In this chapter, we think of market failure in these terms but add a more general understanding that markets fail when they fail to perform according to other widely held social values. As we noted in chapter 5 and explore in depth below, environmental damage is a classic example of a market failure to allocate resources efficiently. In other ways, though, markets fail because they don't achieve the results a society might collectively desire. For instance, markets do not lead to a particular distribution of wealth. They do not necessarily reduce inequality or end poverty, even though the elimination or at least alleviation of both is often a widely held social value. Governments develop what Americans typically call "welfare" policies in part to respond to market failures to distribute wealth in socially acceptable ways that reduce poverty, inequality, or both.

Markets respond to individuals or companies with resources (money or commodities) that can be exchanged for other resources, and because poor people have fewer resources they receive less from the unfettered market. Economists speak of

COUNTRY AND CONCEPT

Welfare, Health, and the Environment

Country	Welfare system	Life expectancy	Infant mortality (deaths per 1,000 births)	Health care system
Brazil	Liberal	73	18	NHS, plus much private financing and some private insurance
China	Liberal welfare state emerging: social insurance for pensions and unemployment; means-tested programs for others in urban areas	74	18	NHI emerging, plus much private financing and some private insurance
Germany	Christian democratic	80	4	NHI
India	Minimal: small means-tested programs, such as food subsidies and rural employment	64	52	NHS, plus much private insurance, direct financing, and NGO provision of health services
Iran	Mixed: social insurance for retirees; state-funded means-tested programs; Islamic charity via *bonyads* (Islamic foundations)	72	27	NHI
Japan	Employment-based, with additional means-tested government programs	83	3	NHI
Mexico	Liberal welfare state	76	15	NHS, plus much private insurance and direct financing
Nigeria	None	49	96	NHS, plus much private financing and NGO provision of health services
Russia	Social insurance for pensions; other benefits targeted to particular groups (in kind until 2007, cash since)	68	9	NHI
United Kingdom	Liberal	80	5	NHS
United States	Liberal	78	7	Market-based insurance

Sources: Life expectancy and infant mortality data are from WHO. Health care spending data are from OECD and WHO for most recent year available; see http://www.oecd.org/document/16/0,3343,en_2649_34631_2085200_1_1_1_1,00.html and http://www.who.int/whosis/data/Search.jsp?indicators=[Indicator].[HSR].Members. Per capita total expenditures on health care data are from *World Health Statistics 2010*. CO_2 Emissions data are from *UN Millennium Development Goals Indicators*; original source is International Energy Agency, CO_2 *Emissions from Fuel Combustion,* 2006 ed. (Paris: IEA); available at http://data.iea.org/ieastore/default.asp.

Public expenditure on health (% of total expenditure on health)	Per capita total expenditures on health (int'l dollars, PPP)	Annual CO_2 emissions (million metric tons of CO_2)	Global share of CO_2 emissions (%)
42	837	368	1.26
45	233	6,583	22.3
77	3,588	788	2.7
26	109	1,612	5.5
47	689	496	1.7
82	2,696	1,255	4.28
45	819	471	1.6
25	131	95	0.32
64	797	1,537	5.24
82	2,992	540	1.84
46	7,285	5,838	19.9

"effective demand" in a market, meaning demand backed with money. There is often very little effective demand for food during a famine in a very poor country; government and international intervention in the form of emergency food aid is justified because of the social value of keeping people from starving to death. Similarly, poor, uninsured individuals who are very sick may have no effective demand for health care, so the market will provide none, but government might choose to intervene to restore their health based on a value of preserving and extending life for all citizens regardless of their relative wealth.

Government interventions of this type raise a host of interesting questions because they pit various groups of citizens against each other. The policy outcomes often tell us much about the classic "Who rules?" question: Who is better represented and, thus, has power? They also raise major "What explains political behavior?" questions focused on why government intervenes in the first place in these areas. In recent years, governments in all wealthy countries have reformed welfare policies substantially and tried, with limited success, to reform health care policies as well. So another political behavior question is, Why have these trends been so widespread over the past twenty to thirty years, and why have some states been more successful than others at achieving reforms? Finally, policy questions raise the obvious "Where and why?" questions: Why have states chosen different policy options? And which work better and why?

The Country and Concept table shows the great variation in these policy areas across our case study countries. Welfare systems vary from quite extensive to non-existent, with dramatically different effects on the level of poverty. Key health care indicators like life expectancy and infant mortality vary dramatically as well. The wealthy countries achieve roughly similar health outcomes but at very different costs, while poor countries' health fares far worse. Looking at the most important environmental concern, carbon dioxide emissions that cause global warming, our case studies include the two biggest polluters in the world—the United States and China—and others that, while likely to suffer the effects of global warming, are only a miniscule part of the problem. The case studies will allow us to examine these policy options and outcomes in widely varying circumstances.

"WELFARE": SOCIAL POLICY IN COMPARATIVE PERSPECTIVE

social policy: Policy focused on reducing poverty and income inequality and stabilizing individual or family income

Most Americans think of welfare as a government handout to poor people. Being "on welfare" is something virtually all Americans want to avoid, as a certain moral opprobrium seems to go with it. Partly because of this, and partly because different countries relieve poverty in different ways, political scientists and other scholars of public policy prefer the term **social policy** to welfare. Social policy's primary goals are to reduce poverty and income inequality and to stabilize individual or family income. Most people view a market that leaves people in abject poverty, unable to meet their most basic needs, as violating important values. Similarly, when market distribution produces inequality that goes beyond some particular point (the acceptable level varies widely from one individual and society to another), many people argue that it should be reversed. Markets also inherently produce instability: in the absence of government intervention, capitalism tends to be associated with boom and bust cycles, as John Maynard Keynes argued. This instability can create severe economic insecurity, especially due to unemployment. Reducing this insecurity has been one of the main impetuses behind modern welfare states.

Various philosophical and practical reasons justify social policies. On purely humanitarian grounds, citizens and governments might wish to alleviate the suffering of the poor. States might also be concerned about social and political stability: high endemic poverty rates and temporary economic instability often are seen as threats to the status quo, including a state's legitimacy, and poverty is associated with higher levels of crime almost everywhere. Some Keynesians argue as well that policies to reduce poverty and stabilize incomes are economically beneficial for society as a whole because they help increase purchasing power, which stimulates market demand.

Opponents of social policy disagree, criticizing it primarily for producing perverse incentives. Markets maximize efficiency in part by inducing people to be productive by working for wages, salaries, or profits. Neoliberal opponents of social policy argue that providing income or other resources for people whether they are working or not gives them a disincentive to work, which leads to underutilization of productive labor. This reduces efficiency and productivity, and ultimately, overall wealth. Critics also argue that financing social policy via taxes discourages work and productivity because higher tax rates reduce incentives to work and make a profit.

In liberal democracies, the debate over social policy also has implications for citizenship. According to liberalism, citizens are supposed to be equal, autonomous individuals, yet in a market economy, citizens are never truly socioeconomically equal. As we saw in chapter 3, T. H. Marshall (1963) argued that social rights are the third pillar of citizenship because without some degree of socioeconomic equality, citizens cannot be political equals. Following this line of thought, when the market fails to create an adequate degree of equality, governments should intervene to preserve equal citizenship, even if doing so may conflict with the other element of liberal citizenship: autonomy. In all market economies, market participation is the primary means of achieving economic autonomy. The founders of liberalism believed only male property owners could be citizens because they were the only ones truly autonomous; women and nonproperty owners were too economically dependent on others to act effectively as autonomous citizens. All liberal democracies have modified this position, but the fundamental concern remains. Many citizens view those who participate in the market—whether by owning capital or working for a wage—as autonomous citizens.

Welfare policies that provide income from nonmarket sources can then be seen as problematic. Traditional liberals argue that social policy undermines equal and autonomous citizenship by creating two classes of citizens: those who earn their income in the market and those who depend on the government (funded by the rest of the citizens). This argument typically makes an exception for family membership: an adult who depends on other family members who participate in the market is implicitly granted full autonomy and citizenship. Social democrats argue, to the contrary, that citizens should be granted full autonomy regardless of their source of income and that social policies that keep income inequality and poverty below certain levels are essential to preserving truly equal citizenship. Different kinds of welfare states are in part based on different values in this debate.

Types of Social Policy

Whatever their justification, social policies can be categorized into four distinct types: universal entitlements, social insurance, means-tested public assistance, and tax expenditures. **Universal entitlements** are benefits that governments provide to all citizens more or less equally, usually funded through general taxation. The only

universal entitlements: Benefits that governments provide to all citizens more or less equally, usually funded through general taxation; in the United States, public education is an example

major example in the United States is public education. Education is an indirect component of social policy because a greater level of education tends to reduce the chances a person will end up in poverty. All communities in the United States must provide access to public education for all school-age residents without exception, making it a universal benefit. Many European countries provide child or family allowances as universal entitlements: all families with children receive a cash benefit to help raise the children, and this allowance increases with the number of children and sometimes is adjusted slightly for household income. Universal entitlements by nature do not raise questions about equal and autonomous citizenship, even when individual citizens may choose not to take advantage of them. No one questions the equal citizenship of public versus private school graduates in the United States or those who do not have children and therefore don't get child allowances in the Netherlands. Critics, on the other hand, argue that universal entitlements are wasteful because much of the money goes to relatively wealthy people who do not necessarily need the benefits.

social insurance: Provides benefits to categories of people who have contributed to a (usually mandatory) public insurance fund; typically used to provide retirement pensions

Social insurance provides benefits to categories of people who have contributed to a (usually mandatory) public insurance fund. The prime examples in the United States are Social Security, disability benefits, and unemployment insurance. In most cases, workers and their employers contribute to the funds while people are employed. Workers can then benefit from the fund when they need it: after retirement, when temporarily unemployed, or when disabled. Because only those who contribute can gain benefits, fewer questions arise about the beneficiaries deserving their benefits, even though there is usually only a very general relationship between the size of one's contribution and the amount of one's benefit. The average American retiree, for instance, earns substantially more in Social Security benefits than the total of his lifetime contributions with interest, but that gap has never raised questions of equal citizenship. (This may change, however, as the number of retirees increases in coming years.) In addition, by covering entire large groups of people—all workers or the spouses of all workers—social insurance is not seen as undermining equal citizenship because it covers things nearly everyone expects (retirement) or hopes to avoid (unemployment).

means-tested public assistance: Social programs that provide benefits to individuals who fall below a specific income level; TANF is an example in the United States

Means-tested public assistance is what most Americans think of as "welfare." The Supplemental Nutrition Assistance Program (SNAP; also commonly known as "food stamps"), subsidized public housing, and Temporary Assistance to Needy Families (TANF) are examples in the United States. These are programs that individuals qualify for when they fall below a specific income level. Some countries impose additional requirements for public assistance, such as work requirements or time limits, but income level is the defining characteristic. Means-tested programs target assistance at the poor in contrast to the broader distribution of universal entitlements or social insurance, so they are the most economically efficient means of poverty relief. Their disadvantage, though, is their impact on recipients' status as equal and autonomous citizens. Because only those below a certain income level can benefit, and benefits are typically financed from general taxation, recipients may be seen as somehow less deserving or not fully equal with other citizens who are paying taxes and not receiving benefits. When people believe—even erroneously, as our case study of the United States shows—that recipients of means-tested assistance receive it continuously or at least for very long periods, their perception is reinforced that the recipients are somehow less deserving or not fully equal and autonomous citizens.

tax expenditures: Targeted tax breaks for specific groups of citizens or activities designed to achieve social policy goals

All three types of social policy discussed so far involve direct government spending. **Tax expenditures,** targeted tax breaks for specific groups of citizens or activities, do not appear to be quite the same, and until recently they were not included as part of social policy. To most people, tax breaks—not collecting taxes from someone—seems different from government spending. The net effect of the two, however, is quite similar. When the government selectively lowers the tax someone would otherwise pay, it is increasing that person's disposable income. A tax break for a particular activity, such as purchasing a home or investing in a retirement pension, subsidizes particular activities that the government presumably believes to be socially beneficial. So a tax break for low-income people with children has the same effect as the same amount of social spending targeted at that group. By giving tax breaks for employees' and employers' contributions to health insurance and retirement pensions, the U.S. government is subsidizing those activities.

Tax expenditures are an important part of social policy, especially in the United States, as our case study below demonstrates. Their precise effect depends on at whom and for what they are targeted. They can be restricted to lower-income people or provided much more widely, with different effects on reducing poverty and inequality. In the United States, for instance, the Earned Income Tax Credit (EITC) aimed at lower-income families has become one of the largest poverty-reduction programs in the country, larger in fact than TANF, the program most Americans think of as "welfare." The tax deduction for interest paid on home mortgages, on the other hand, subsidizes all but the most expensive home purchases; it is a social policy designed to encourage home ownership (presumably improving standards of living and economic security) that provides greater benefits to the middle and upper classes than to the poor.

Different types of social programs are often associated with particular kinds of benefits or groups of recipients. Workers are often covered by social insurance, for instance, while public housing is typically means tested. What is true for tax expenditures, however, is true for all types of social programs; in theory, any of them could be used for any type of benefit. For instance, unemployment insurance is fairly restricted in the United States, benefiting only long-term employees and usually for only six to nine months after a worker becomes unemployed; elsewhere, similar programs are more extensive and less distinct from what Americans call "welfare." Preschool is a universal entitlement in France but is means tested via the Head Start program in the United States. Retirement benefits also could be means tested so that when older people no longer earn a market-based income, only those below a certain income level would qualify for benefits. Indeed, this has been one policy suggested in the United States as a way to reduce the long-term cost of the Social Security program. This would target retirement benefits more efficiently at reducing poverty but might raise questions of equal citizenship common to means-tested programs, questions that retirees currently don't face.

Types of Welfare States

Governments combine social programs in different ways and with different levels of generosity, creating distinctive **welfare states**. The Country and Concept table (page 540) gives some idea of the wide variety of combinations states use, especially in poor and middle-income countries. Evelyne Huber and John Stephens (2001), modifying the pioneering work of Gøsta Esping-Andersen (1990), classified wealthy countries into three main types of welfare states: social democratic, Christian democratic, and liberal. **Social democratic welfare states** strongly emphasize universal entitlements to achieve greater social equality and promote equal citizenship. Governments typically provide numerous universal entitlements in a wide array of areas, including paid maternity leave, preschool, child allowances, basic retirement pensions, and job training. They use high rates of general taxation to fund their

welfare states:
Distinct systems of social policies that arose after World War II in wealthy market economies, including social democratic welfare states, Christian democratic welfare states, and liberal welfare states

social democratic welfare states:
States whose social policies strongly emphasize universal entitlements to achieve greater social equality and promote equal citizenship; Sweden is prime example

generous social benefits and, at their most generous, transfer more income from the wealthy to the poor (taxing the wealthy more and giving equal universal entitlements to all) than do the other types of welfare states. Social insurance programs, such as employment-based retirement pensions, also exist, but these usually supplement the universal entitlements that are available to all. The primary examples of social democratic welfare states are the Scandinavian countries.

MINI CASE

Sweden's Welfare State

Sweden's generous, redistributive social welfare state is a long-standing model of "the middle way" between capitalism and socialism. The Swedish Social Democratic Party was in power continuously from 1932 to 2006, except for two brief periods. The Party instituted the first elements of a welfare state in the 1920s. From the start, it established basic services such as unemployment benefits and retirement pensions as universal social rights of citizenship, in part to gain the support of the important Agrarian Party in the 1930s, when the country still had a large farming population opposed to tying benefits to wage employment. In the late 1950s, the party added extra benefits above and beyond the flat-rate universal ones. These additional benefits were tied to earnings and replaced as much as 90 percent of workers' wages when they were unemployed, disabled, or retired. In the 1970s, the Social Democratic government expanded services designed to induce women into the workforce and support them once they are employed, including the world's most generous maternity leave and sick leave policies.

The state then combined these benefits with very high tax rates on income (60 percent of the economy at their peak in the 1970s), but it used low corporate tax rates to encourage large-scale investment in export industries while maintaining one of the most open trade policies in the world. At its height in the 1970s, Sweden was the world's second wealthiest country, with robust growth, strong export levels by brand-name companies such as Volvo, virtually no unemployment, and the

world's most generous social services. Even after reforms in the 1990s, Sweden's social services and taxes remain among the world's highest. Unemployment benefits still cover about 80 percent of wages and have virtually no time limit. The universal family allowance in 2001 was $138 per child up to sixteen years of age (higher for children with special needs), and parental leave provides sixteen months of paid leave at any time during the first eight years of a child's life at 80 percent of full salary. Parents get ten paid "contact days" per year to spend time in their children's schools as volunteers, up to sixty days of benefits per year to care for sick children, and a daycare system that enrolls 75 percent of preschoolers, with more than 80 percent of the cost funded by the state (Olsen 2007, 147–51). To pay for this, government revenue remains more than half of the entire economy (compared to a little more than a third for the United States). In addition, more than 30 percent of all employees work in the public sector.

Sweden's model faced a crisis in the early 1990s. Declining industry and growing outsourcing of business combined with the bursting of a housing bubble (not unlike conditions in the United States in 2008) and demographic changes to increase unemployment, inflation, and the government's debt. When the Social Democrats lost the 1991 election, the newly elected Moderate Party government passed what was seen at the time as the most sweeping tax reform in the Western world, with the top rate on income tax dropping from 80 to 50 percent and the marginal rate on corporate taxes from 57 to 30 percent (Huber and Stephens 2001, 242). The strong incentive in favor of domestic investment was eliminated, which encouraged Swedish corporations to enter the global market more fully. Even with these changes, government finances were still in dire straits by the mid-1990s.

Returning to power in 1994, the Social Democrats negotiated a series of reforms. These included the creation of a new index that tied retirement pensions to levels of unemployment and economic growth and divided financing of pensions equally between employer and employee (previously, employers paid for virtually all of the benefit). Similarly, the government reduced unemployment benefits from 90 to 80 percent of income. Unions successfully resisted an attempt to impose a three-year limit on such benefits (nine months is typical in the United States).

These were seen as unprecedented changes to Sweden's social welfare system, but it remains one of the world's most generous. Prior to the 2008–2009 recession, global economic growth and these policy changes had restored Sweden's growth to normal levels. While the size and scope of the government had shrunk, inequality had increased only slightly, and that increase was due mainly to rising incomes among the rich rather than falling incomes among the poor. Poverty remained very low. Unemployment dropped as well, to about 8 percent, but remains one of the country's biggest problems. The global recession hit the country hard because it relies heavily on exports; its economy declined by nearly 5 percent in 2009 and barely grew in 2010, though forecasts were for higher growth in 2011 and most analysts believed it was recovering as well or better than most of Europe. The government's success helped the ruling Moderate Party win reelection in late 2010, the first time a party other than the Social Democrats had been reelected in over 80 years.

CASE SUMMARY

Sweden's welfare state is one of the most generous and was once one of the most successful in the world. The country's recovery from the 1990s crisis was impressive. The generous social democratic welfare state was trimmed but retained its essential elements, and renewed growth raised overall incomes and lowered unemployment, though unemployment remains one of the country's ongoing concerns. Sweden's voters have consistently supported this extensive welfare state, indicating a widely held set of values that supports extensive government intervention to reduce poverty, inequality, and economic insecurity. The country's reliance on universal entitlements means extensive social policies do not seem to raise significant questions about equal citizenship.

Christian democratic welfare states primarily emphasize income stabilization to mitigate the effects of market-induced income insecurity. Their most common type of social program, therefore, is social insurance, which is designed to provide a relatively high percentage of a family's income when its market-based source of income is disrupted through unemployment, disability, or something similar. Benefits are usually tied to contributions to social insurance plans, and financing is mainly through employer and employee payroll taxes rather than general taxation. This means that redistribution is not as broad as under social democratic welfare states. Most Christian democratic welfare states also feature corporatist models of economic governance; that is, social insurance programs tend to be administered by and through sectoral-based organizations such as unions though under the state's guidance. We explore a prime example of such a state, Germany, in detail below.

Christian democratic welfare states: States whose social policies are based on the nuclear family with a male breadwinner, designed primarily to achieve income stabilization to mitigate the effects of market-induced income insecurity; Germany is key example

WHERE AND WHY

The Development of Welfare States

Why have three types of welfare states arisen in different wealthy, industrialized countries? Comparativists have come up with numerous cultural, institutional, and structural (both economic and political) arguments to explain the origins of welfare states. An early economic theory is known as the "logic of industrialism" approach. It argues that as societies get wealthier, they can afford to care for their remaining poor; it further argues that as industrialization grows, groups harmed by it, such as the unemployed and the elderly, will organize to demand protection (Willemsky 1975). Peter Katzenstein (1985) proposed a different economic theory: openness to international trade led to greater welfare spending to ameliorate the increased uncertainty brought on by trade. This is the opposite of the convergence theory discussed in chapter 10, which argued that globalization decreased spending. These theories may explain in general why welfare states arose and expanded over time, but they are not very helpful in explaining why distinct types of welfare states emerged.

Cultural arguments have looked at differences in long-standing values among wealthy countries to explain the variation among welfare states. Anglo-American countries, they argue, have stronger liberal traditions emphasizing the importance of the individual and individual autonomy, which causes them to be more reluctant to engage in extensive government spending to help people via policy. Numerous surveys have shown, for instance, that despite upward social mobility being about the same in the United States and Europe, Americans are much more likely than Europeans to believe that people can work their way out of poverty if they really want to (Alesina and Glaeser 2004, 11–12).

Other experts argue that religious beliefs influence welfare states: countries more influenced by Protestantism, especially Calvinism, see wealth as morally superior and have less sympathy for the poor, whereas countries with more Catholics are more generous due to their belief in preserving social and family stability. And a final cultural explanation focused on the United States argues that racial divisions explain the country's particularly small welfare state. Surveys show that people (not only Americans) are less sympathetic to those of different races, and in the United States many whites perceive the poor as being primarily black or Hispanic. As a result, Americans are relatively unwilling to support policies to assist the poor. Two Harvard economists, Alberto Alesina and Edward Glaeser (2004), recently argued this was part of the explanation for the striking difference between generosity of social spending in the United States and Europe. Yet while cultural explanations may help explain why some states are more generous than others, they still don't fully explain the rise of different kinds of welfare states.

Huber and Stephens (2001) combined a structural argument focusing on the political organization of social classes with an institutionalist argument to explain the rise of distinct types of welfare states, as well as their relative levels of generosity. They argued that welfare states primarily reflect the strength and political orientation of the working and lower-middle classes. In countries where the working classes were able to organize into strong labor unions and powerful social democratic parties that were able to hold office for a long period of time, social democratic welfare states emerged. Countries with more Catholics that had stronger Christian democratic parties that appealed successfully to working and lower-middle classes saw the emergence of Christian democratic welfare states. Where the working classes were not strong enough to organize to gain political power, liberal welfare states emerged. Following their party ideologies, social democratic parties instituted welfare states with far-ranging social services, including ones that facilitated greater redistribution of wealth and the entry of women into the workforce. Christian democratic welfare states followed Catholic belief in decentralizing welfare payments to the local community and emphasizing social and family stability rather than resource redistribution and women's participation in the workplace. Liberal welfare states believed in minimal support only for those deserving poor who were truly unable to work.

Huber and Stephens (2001) then went on to combine this argument with an institutionalist argument that regimes with fewer veto players developed more extensive welfare states. Federal systems, for instance, tend to produce less extensive social policies, as do presidential systems. These authors also argued that once created, the welfare state tends to be self-perpetuating: both recipients and the middle-class bureaucrats who staff the social service agencies have an interest in preserving the institutions as they exist. Other institutionalists have argued that state bureaucracies themselves created the welfare state. Hugh Heclo (1974) contended that the central ideas for and differences between the Swedish and British welfare states were developed by bureaucrats first and were later championed by political leaders. Huber and Stephens rejected this argument based on extensive quantitative analysis, but they agreed that once created (by parties and unions mobilizing the lower classes), the institutions tend to be self-perpetuating.

The study by Huber and Stephens is an impressive analysis of how and why the three types of welfare states arose, but the debate will continue. Cultural theorists might well argue that underlying values (Catholicism, solidarity) allowed the social democratic or Christian democratic parties to organize the lower classes in a way that is most unlikely in Anglo-American culture with its individualist orientation. Race theorists will continue to argue that the exceptionally low levels of social spending in the United States reflect racial divisions. An interesting question is whether rising racial and religious diversity in much of Europe will have the same effect over time.

Recently, a new school of thought has emerged questioning the continued existence of three distinct welfare states (Garfinkel, Rainwater, and Smeeding 2010; Alber and Gilbert, 2010). Looking at new measures of social policy, which include the effects of taxation and mandatory private spending (such as government regulations that require employers to provide retirement pensions), they argued that the level of social spending is not as different across the three models of the welfare state as has been suggested. While Sweden spends generously on universal programs, for instance, it also has high taxes on consumption (e.g., sales tax), so some of the spending on the poor comes back to the government when the poor spend that money. The United States, on the other hand, has very low social spending but much higher tax expenditures targeted at low-income people. Including all of these effects in the data shows that while Sweden still has more generous social policy overall, the difference between it and the United States is much narrower than previously assumed, though the emphasis on different kinds of programs remains. The debate over the nature, evolution, and future of different welfare states seems far from over.

TABLE 11.1

Comparison of Welfare State Outcomes

Year	Social expenditure (% of GDP)			GDP growth (%)		
	1980	1995	2006	1979–1989	1995–1997	2003–2006
Social democratic welfare states	22.2	28.1	25.4	2.3	3.3	2.82
Christian democratic welfare states	20.6	23.6	26.0	1.8	1.7	1.79
Liberal welfare states	15.2	17.8	17.6	2.1	4.1	3.37

Source: World Bank, http://data.worldbank.org/indicator/SL.TLF.CACT.FE.ZS?order=wbapi_data_value_2006+wbapi_data_value&sort=asc.

liberal welfare states: States whose social policies focus on ensuring that all who can do so gain their income in the market; more concerned with preserving individual autonomy than with reducing poverty or inequality; the United States is key example

Liberal welfare states focus on ensuring that all who can work and gain their income in the market do so; these states are more concerned with preserving individual autonomy via market participation than with reducing poverty or inequality. They emphasize means-tested public assistance more than the other types of welfare states, targeting very specific groups of recipients for benefits. A great deal of government effort often goes into assessing who is truly deserving of support, which usually boils down to determining who is unable to work for a wage as opposed to who is unwilling. The emphasis on ensuring that only the poor and truly deserving receive benefits often means that some poor people don't receive benefits, and the desire to provide incentives for people to work can mean that social benefits for the poor still do not raise them above the poverty level. But not all programs are means tested in these countries; retirement benefits are typically provided via social insurance. The United States, which we turn to below, is a prime example of this type of welfare state; the United States also emphasizes tax expenditures more than any other wealthy country.

Comparing Welfare States The different types of welfare states have created significantly different societies in terms of how much of the national income passes through government coffers and how much is redistributed from the rich to the poor. Tables 11.1 and 11.2 provide data comparing the three types of welfare states.

TABLE 11.2

Social Expenditure, in Percentage of GDP, 2007

	Gross public social expenditure	Net publicly mandated social expenditure
Social democratic welfare states	28.6	23.13
Christian democratic welfare states	29.86	26.78
Liberal welfare states	19.55	19.45

Source: OECD (2011).

	Unemployment (% of civilian labor force)			Women's labor force participation (% of women in labor force)		
1980–1989	1995–1998	2003–2006	1980	1994	2006
4.6	8.1	6.05	69.3	72.2	60
7.1	8.5	7.33	47.2	58.2	50.5
10.2	8.1	5.40	53.8	63	57

Social democratic welfare states used to take the biggest share of the national economy as government revenue to provide extensive social services, reflected in their high social expenditures. In recent years, however, the Christian democratic systems have spent more as the costs of their extensive income-maintenance programs for the unemployed and elderly have risen rapidly. The liberal welfare states spend significantly less, though as Table 11.2 shows, when we compare gross (meaning just government expenditures) and net (taking into account taxes recipients of social expenditures pay back to the government) we see the difference in net expenditures isn't quite as large. In spite of globalization, social expenditures in all three systems have continued to climb, fuelled mostly by expenditures on the growing elderly population.

The extensive social policies of the social democratic and Christian democratic welfare states did not lower the rate of economic growth significantly at their height in the 1980s, though liberal welfare states seem to be growing faster recently. Similarly, more generous welfare states actually achieved lower levels of unemployment until recent years. These economic data suggest that while states have been able to maintain different levels of social policy in the face of globalization, the more generous ones may be paying a price in recent years in terms of economic growth and employment.

Figure 11.1 shows that all three types of welfare states distribute enough income to lower poverty substantially, but the reductions are greatest in social democratic states, followed by Christian democratic states; the liberal welfare states achieve far less poverty reduction and therefore tolerate much more poverty and inequality among their citizens. Note, however, that poverty has only gone down in Christian Democratic states, and inequality has increased at least slightly in all three types of welfare states. Table 11.1 demonstrates differences as well in terms of gender inequality, at least as measured by participation in the paid labor force. Social democratic welfare states facilitated greater female participation via such policies as universal child allowances, paid maternity leave, and subsidized preschool. Liberal welfare states, with their emphasis on work, achieve higher female participation rates than do Christian democratic states, which built their welfare state around the male breadwinner.

FIGURE 11.1

Poverty and Inequality in Welfare States

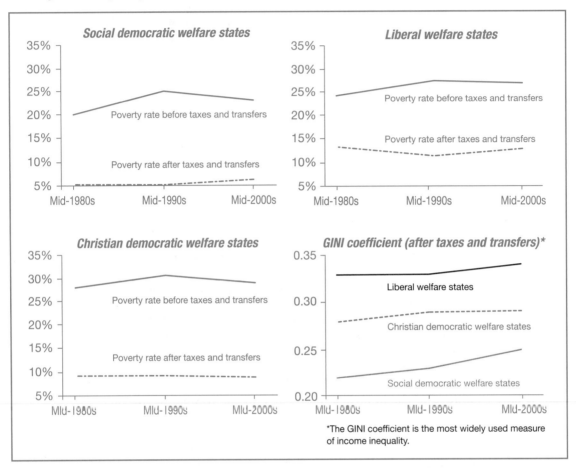

Source: OECD StatExtracts, http://stats.oecd.org/Index.aspx. Calculated using the classifications of the three welfare states (liberal welfare state, Christian democratic welfare state, social democratic welfare state) as defined in Evelyne Huber and John D. Stephens, *Development and Crisis of the Welfare State* (Chicago: University of Chicago Press, 2001).

Welfare States and Globalization All welfare states have been under pressure to reform in the age of globalization. As we suggested in chapter 10, though, few countries have fundamentally altered their social policies. The aggregate data, however, hide the reforms that have been occurring. Pressure on social expenditures comes primarily from demographic changes in wealthy countries: as populations age, fewer workers must somehow pay the benefits for larger dependent populations, particularly the elderly and, in Europe, the growing number of unemployed. While only a few countries have fundamentally changed policies (as the United Kingdom did under Prime Minister Margaret Thatcher in the 1980s), most have reduced benefits to some extent, and these changes have focused mainly on reducing the costs of the programs. Governments have raised the minimum age at which people can retire, reduced the length of unemployment or other benefits and the percentage of salary that is replaced, changed the indexing of benefits relative to inflation to lower the real value of those benefits, raised employee contributions to social insurance programs, and removed guarantees of set benefits so that governments can reduce them in the future if necessary (Bonoli, George, and Taylor-Gooby 2000).

These changes contradicted the most common understanding of welfare state reform. Institutionalist theorists (Pierson 1996) argued that the welfare state created institutions and their beneficiaries, which then constituted powerful coalitions blocking reform. Advocates of hyperglobalization, in contrast, saw globalization as demanding radical reform. The result of this conflict, it seemed, would either be an absence of reform and growing economic crisis in European welfare states, on the one hand, or globalization overwhelming the resistance and forcing Christian democratic and social democratic welfare states to become more like liberal welfare states, on the other hand. Neither of these extremes seems to have happened.

Silja Häusermann (2010), focusing specifically on Christian democratic welfare states, argued they have been able to achieve significant reforms without completely changing their fundamental nature because of the shift to postindustrial society that globalization has helped bring about. The rise of service workers, greater use of part-time workers to achieve greater labor flexibility, and growing female participation in the workforce combined to create new groups of workers who were not benefitting fully from the Christian democratic welfare state, which emphasizes income stability for unionized male breadwinners in older industries. Reforming politicians of both conservative and social democratic parties have been able to put together new coalitions of support by combining different reforms into one package. They have reduced benefits to older, unionized, male workers while providing new benefits, like more flexible pension coverage and greater child care, to the mostly female workers in service industries. The result, Häusermann argued, has been substantial reform but not complete reversal or retrenchment to the point of shifting to a liberal welfare state model. Globalization has, in a sense, forced change, but change has been filtered through shifting political institutions and coalitions.

Poorer Countries and Social Policy

In poorer countries, neoliberal development strategies, bolstered now by the spectacular success of China, have long focused on achieving high economic growth as the best means of reducing poverty. The limited success of neoliberal strategies in other regions, however, led to the reemergence of social policy as an important issue in developing countries in the 1990s, especially in Latin America. Older social programs in Latin America were almost all social insurance systems benefitting only workers in the formal sector of the economy, disproportionately in the public sector. These workers are in fact a relatively well-off group in Latin America; the truly poor are in the informal sector (e.g., workers in small enterprises not recognized by the government, street vendors, and day laborers) and agriculture in which employment is not formally recorded. To reach these truly poor, a number of governments adopted **conditional cash transfer (CCT)** programs, which provide cash grants to the poor in exchange for these families sending their children to school and to health clinics. These programs, pioneered in our case study of Brazil, are means tested and target the poorest households to gain the maximum impact with very limited resources. Results have been mixed, and most programs remain relatively modest in scope. They nonetheless constitute a new development in social policy that in the best of the programs (including Brazil and Mexico) has noticeably reduced poverty (Diaz-Cayeros and Magaloni 2009). The case studies below demonstrate in greater detail the struggle governments have faced in trying to finance social policies in an era of globalization and shifting demographics.

conditional cash transfer (CCT): Programs that provide cash grants to the poor and in exchange require particular beneficial behavior from the poor, such as children's attendance at school and visits to health clinics

CASE STUDY

Germany: Reforming the Christian Democratic Welfare State

- Pioneer of social insurance for income stability
- Growing pressure from unemployment and aging population
- Long effort at reform since 1980s
- Major reform of unemployment insurance starting in 2003
- Moving toward a liberal welfare state?

Otto von Bismarck pioneered social insurance, beginning the first programs of this kind in Germany in 1883. Most of the country's modern Christian democratic welfare state was not put into place until 1949, but it still relies primarily on social insurance to provide the bulk of benefits. Programs are paid for mainly by roughly equal employer and employee contributions. Following Germany's corporatist model, the system is run by nongovernmental organizations overseen by employer and employee associations, with the state providing the legal framework and regulations. In the golden era during which the economy was growing rapidly and achieving close to full employment, the system provided relatively generous benefits and was self-financing. Structural changes, including reunification of West and East Germany, a lower rate of economic growth,

Demonstrators in Berlin in November 2005 protest the Hartz IV reforms, the most significant change to the German welfare state since World War II. Despite the protests, the coalition government passed the reform, justifying it in part by the need to be globally competitive. In the long term, it will reduce both the amount and length of unemployment/welfare benefits, moving Germany's Christian democratic welfare state some distance toward a more liberal welfare state model.

Credit: Sean Gallup/Getty Images

higher unemployment, and an aging population have since brought severe financial constraints to the system, producing seemingly continuous reform efforts since the early 1980s. Both the Christian Democratic Union (CDU) and Social Democratic Party (SDP), however, continue to vary only marginally on their policy choices; before 2003, reforms by governments of both major parties only slightly reduced the generosity of the system. That year, both parties supported a more fundamental change to unemployment benefits, which many argue is moving the system toward a liberal welfare state, though the other pillars of the system remain largely unchanged and social spending remains unusually high (Siebert 2005).

Prior to these recent reforms, the core social insurance system provided nearly complete income replacement in case of illness, at least 60 percent of an unemployed worker's salary for up to thirty-two months, and a retirement pension that averaged 70 percent of wages. These benefits continue to constitute the great majority of German social spending. Those unemployed for periods longer than three years who had worked at least a year at some point gained unemployment assistance at about 53 percent of their most recent salary, adjusted for family and other available support, with no time limit, which was funded by general taxation. Those who had not worked a full year still received social assistance, a means-tested system that indefinitely provided a level of support to individuals to keep them above the poverty line. Originally, the system assumed a male breadwinner would support his wife and children, with wives gaining benefits only through their spouses. As women entered the workforce, they supported reforms to make the system less focused on male breadwinners. In 1986, child benefits were added, including direct payments to and tax breaks for parents and government-paid contributions into social insurance for unemployed parents so that they could care for any children three years of age or younger. In the 1970s, maternity benefits of fourteen weeks that covered the full income of many women were added,

and more recently, up to three years of unpaid parental leave have been made available.

An aging population and growing unemployment imposed financial constraints. The reform debate began in 1982 with the conservative CDU government under Helmut Kohl. It focused on strengthening support for the family via child benefits and reducing social spending somewhat by increasing employer and employee contributions. Social spending dropped from a high of more than 31 percent of GDP in 1975 to 28 percent in 1989. Then German reunification in 1990 dramatically increased the costs of the system: unemployment rates skyrocketed in the former East Germany as the economy transitioned from a communist to a capitalist system, and massive transfers of funds from the former West Germany were essential to pay social insurance benefits to these workers. By the mid-1990s, social spending had exceeded its previous high of twenty years earlier.

The CDU government and then the leftist SDP/Green government after 1998 responded to this financial pressure with additional proposals. While the SDP criticized the CDU government in the 1990s for making the system less generous, once in power the Social Democrats produced even more substantial reforms. In 2003, the SDP/Green government passed what became known as the Hartz reforms, part of a broader effort to modernize the economy known as "Agenda 2010." The most controversial part, which came to be known as "Hartz IV," fundamentally changed a key element of Germany's welfare state. Rather than allowing workers to collect full unemployment insurance (set as a percentage of a worker's wage) indefinitely, a time limit of twelve months (later increased to twenty-four months for older workers) was placed on it, after which a worker would be placed on "Unemployment Benefit II," which was set at a fixed level (not connected to past earnings). Germany in effect switched the "welfare" system for the long-term unemployed from a social insurance system of income stability to a means-tested benefit paid in part by general taxation, like that typical of a liberal welfare state. The reform

IN CONTEXT

THE GERMAN WELFARE STATE

Germany devotes an unusually large share of its economy to social spending, though not as much as Sweden. Both countries spend more and transfer more income to the poor than does the United States.

	Germany	Sweden	U.S.
Gross public social expenditures in 2007 (% of GDP)	28.4	32.1	17.4
Net (after taxes) publicly mandated social expenditures in 2007 (% of GDP)	27.2	26.0	18.9
Mean social transfers (% of pretax household income)	25.1	44.5	11.7
Poverty rate (pre-tax and transfer) in mid-2000s (% of population)	33.6	26.7	26.3
Poverty rate (post-tax and transfer) in mid-2000s (% of population)	11.0	5.3	17.1

Sources: Mean Social Transfers: Alesina and Glaeser (2004, 31); Public Social Expenditure: OECD (2011); OECD, "Income Distribution and Poverty," http://www.oecd.org/document/2/0,3343,en_2649_33933_45043394_1_1_1_1,00.html

upper house of parliament, however, forcing the government to search for a compromise on the issue. Unemployed workers are also now required to accept jobs at only 80 percent of their prior wage levels, rather than being allowed to wait for positions equivalent to their previous ones (Vail 2004). Similarly, retirement pension generosity was reduced, from an original level in the 1980s of 70 percent of retirees' wages to what will eventually be only about 45 percent. After years of effort, a fundamental reform of the German welfare state was enacted, though by 2010, it was seriously challenged in both the Court and the legislature.

CASE SUMMARY

The primary goal of the Christian democratic welfare state in Germany was to ensure income stability throughout a person's life. Once securely in the workforce, or dependent on someone who was, citizens could count on relative stability for as long as needed, at a minimum of half of their prior salary. This system was far more generous than those of liberal welfare states but transferred less income from the wealthy to the poor than did social democratic welfare states. As male unemployment mounted in the 1990s, women increasingly entered the workforce, and globalization put pressure on companies to shift to more flexible and part-time workers, the German welfare system came under increasing pressure. Lack of workers meant the insurance on which the system was based was underfunded, and growing numbers of part-time and female workers were left out.

Facing financial constraints as the population aged and unemployment remained near 10 percent, the government, even under the Social Democrats, had to modify the system. The generosity of retirement benefits has dropped, and the unemployment system now provides income stability for only two years. Implicit in this policy is the assumption common to liberal welfare states that everyone who wants to can find employment in a reasonable amount of time. Permanent support continues to exist but only at a level just

sparked massive protests, but the government refused to back down. Opposition to Hartz IV was one of the main reasons several leading "leftists" in the SDP split off to form a new party before the 2005 election, which in turn was a key reason the SDP lost the election and was forced to share power with the CDU (see chapter 7).

In 2010, Germany's Constitutional Court ruled the benefit level was beneath what was necessary for the dignity of the unemployed and their full participation in the society (in essence, calling for Marshall's "social rights," which we discussed in chapter 3). The Court, however, did not mandate a clear level for the benefit, and the CDU government responded by proposing only a very modest increase. The proposal met fierce opposition in the

above the poverty line. On the other hand, in response to the changing demographics of the labor force, the government expanded participation in the system to include more women, part-time workers, and the self-employed. In the long run, the hope is that these changes will reduce overall social spending, which in 2003 was at 27 percent of gross domestic product (GDP), well above the Organisation for Economic Co-operation and Development's (OECD) average of 21 percent. The cost of these changes, though, is growing inequality and poverty; from the mid-1990s to the mid-2000s, the German poverty rate

increased to 11 percent, going from below to above the OECD average.

The new system makes Germany's Christian democratic welfare state notably more similar to a liberal welfare state, as a comparison with the United States will demonstrate. While more similar than they used to be, however, the two systems remain distinct. The In Context box provides data on the ability of each system to reduce poverty from what the market alone would produce, showing that clear differences remain between Christian democratic Germany, the liberal United States, and social democratic Sweden.

CASE STUDY

The United States: Reforming the Liberal Welfare State

- Emphasis on means-tested programs and tax expenditures
- New Deal: Social Security retirement system—most effective antipoverty program
- Great Society: 1960s expansion of means-tested programs; reduced poverty but this trend later reversed
- 1996 welfare reform: End of entitlement for poor—less welfare and more work
- How big is the U.S. welfare state? Social spending versus tax expenditures
- Highest level of poverty and inequality among wealthy countries

The In Context box on page 556 shows that based on income earned in the market alone, the United States has a smaller percentage of people in poverty than Germany or Sweden, but taxes and government social programs lower the poverty rate by only about 7 percentage points in the United States compared to 20 or more in the European cases. The end result is much less poverty in Germany and Sweden than in the American liberal welfare state. Aside from Social Security, the large

social insurance system for the elderly, most U.S. social programs are means tested or tax expenditures and are restricted to certain categories of recipients. The United States only legislated unpaid parental leave in the 1990s, and it is one of only three countries in the world (the other two are Papua New Guinea and Swaziland) that guarantee no national paid maternity leave. Most European states heavily subsidize child care, in contrast to the small U.S. means-tested Head Start program and tax deductions for child care. Since 1996, poor people can still receive some income support for a maximum of five years, but they no longer have a legal entitlement to it beyond that unless they are disabled. The Earned Income Tax Credit (EITC), a tax expenditure program, is now larger than Temporary Assistance to Needy Families (TANF), the main means-tested spending program. The federal system also sets only minimum standards and allows state governments significant flexibility in implementing the main social programs, so benefits vary widely across states.

The United States was a pioneer in one type of social policy, its sole universal entitlement program: public education. It invested

Children attend a Head Start program in Hillsboro, Oregon. Publicly funded prekindergarten programs have expanded rapidly in recent years in the United States, funded mostly by state governments. The country's liberal welfare state provides only limited free or subsidized preschool, in contrast to the much more generous funding of these programs in most European welfare states.

Credit: AP Photo/Greg Wahl-Stephens

heavily starting in the nineteenth century, and by 1930, it had by far the highest rates of secondary school enrollment in the world. In 1970, it still had one of the highest rates. The early lead, in terms of both enrollments and test scores in core subjects, however, dissipated in the last quarter of the twentieth century. By the new millennium, the United States was closer to the middle of the pack among wealthy nations. Other types of social policy in the United States began in the Great Depression as part of President Franklin D. Roosevelt's New Deal policies. The Social Security Act of 1935 established the system and remains the country's primary social program. The most important manifestation of this program is the Social Security system of retirement pensions. This social insurance program is similar to Germany's but is administered by the federal government, not by nongovernmental organizations. Pensions are tied to individuals' previous earnings and are financed by mandatory employer and employee contributions. Social Security is the country's most successful antipoverty program, and while not as generous as most European pension systems, it nonetheless dramatically reduced poverty among the elderly. By 2000, Social Security alone reduced inequality in the United States by nearly 7 percent, far more than any other social policy. Combined with Medicare, the health care plan for the elderly (see the Health Policy section below), it reduced American inequality by nearly 10 percent. (In contrast, "public assistance"—what most Americans think of as "welfare"—reduced American inequality by only 0.4 percent.) Prior to Social

Security, the elderly had constituted the country's largest group in poverty, but now this group has one of the lowest rates of poverty, less than 10 percent in 2005. The Social Security Act also created Aid to Dependent Children (ADC), a program that provided cash grants to poor households with children present but no resident male breadwinner.

President Lyndon Johnson's War on Poverty in the 1960s produced the second major expansion of American social policy. During the unprecedented post–World War II economic boom and on the heels of the civil rights movement, the nation came to recognize that many nonelderly individuals remained in poverty. The War on Poverty augmented Social Security with Medicare, a health insurance program for the elderly. In addition, Aid to Families with Dependent Children (AFDC, the descendant of ADC) became an entitlement, with each state legally obligated to indefinitely provide a minimum level of support, primarily to single mothers with resident children. Medicaid was created to fund health services for AFDC recipients, and the Food Stamps program provided vouchers for food purchases by poor families. By 1975, the poverty rate hit a low of about 12 percent of the population, half of what it had been in 1960.

For all of this, the programs were not widely accepted. Whereas Social Security was regarded as an earned benefit, AFDC was controversial from the outset. Critics argued that its structure of indefinite, per child payments to families headed by women created perverse incentives for the poor to divorce or have children out of wedlock, have more children, and become dependent on government payments. Benefit levels also varied widely from state to state, with some states providing as much as five times what others did. In spite of the concerns of permanent "welfare dependence" and incentives to have more children, in reality, half of AFDC recipients received benefits for fewer than four years, and the average household size of recipients dropped from 4.0 in 1969 to 2.9 in 1992, meaning an average of only 1.9 children per mother, below the national average

of about 2.1 (Cammisa 1998, 10–17). Nonetheless, the perception of a perverse incentive structure persisted.

Reform proposals began as early as the late 1960s under President Richard Nixon, but they grew significantly in the 1980s under President Ronald Reagan. Reagan's 1980 campaign was based in part on fundamentally changing the welfare system, though with a Democratic-controlled Congress, he never succeeded in changing social policy substantially. Indeed, when faced with a financial crisis in Social Security, Reagan led a bipartisan effort to increase the mandatory payroll tax to the system to restore solvency without substantially cutting benefits. Reagan did help pass a law that allowed state governments greater flexibility in implementing AFDC, including permitting them to demand that recipients work, a condition for receiving aid with which many states began experimenting.

President Bill Clinton got elected as a "New Democrat" in 1992 on a platform that included a promise to "end welfare as we know it," and when the Republicans swept into control of Congress in 1994, they made a similar pledge, setting the stage for major reform. Two years later, Congress, with Republican support and mostly Democratic opposition, passed and President Clinton signed the most important reform of social policy since the 1960s. The legislation ended AFDC as an entitlement to poor, single mothers and replaced it with a new program, Temporary Assistance for Needy Families (TANF). TANF eliminated the bias against households with fathers, limited recipients to two years of continuous benefits and five years over a lifetime, required virtually all able-bodied recipients to work to keep their benefits, and allowed them to keep a significant share of those benefits after they began working.

The creation of TANF changed social policy to a greater degree than reforms in almost any other country. Supporters believed it would reduce welfare dependence, encourage individuals to work, and lower poverty. Critics claimed it meted out harsh punishment to the poor, who would be cut off without the possibility of finding work that would lead them out of poverty. Numerous studies of the program's effects have been carried out without definitive conclusions. Part of the problem is that many factors besides social policy, the most important being overall economic growth, affect poverty and employment rates. TANF was introduced during a period of rapid economic growth. Poverty and the number of AFDC recipients actually had started falling two years before TANF was enacted because of strong growth, so it is difficult to judge TANF's impact.

What is clear is that the number of people receiving benefits via AFDC and now TANF fell sharply, from a monthly average of more than five million households in 1994 to fewer than two million by 2005. Most of those leaving the rolls gained employment in the year they left the program, but only a minority worked the entire year. Most still work at part-time, low-paying jobs with no long-term job security or hope for advancement. Overall incomes among poor households increased through 2000, though the poverty rate dropped only slightly (Grogger and Karoly 2005; Slack et al. 2007). Since 2000, as economic growth has slowed, TANF rolls have continued to shrink, though the number of recipients working has also started to fall and poverty levels have risen slightly. The recession of 2008–2009 increased the official U.S. measure of poverty (different from and lower than the internationally recognized rate in the In Context above) by 1 percent, to 14.3 percent of all Americans, and TANF roles increased for the first time (by about 8 percent) since the 1996 reform. Overall, since the reform, the percentage of poor single mothers (the main beneficiaries of the program) receiving AFDC/TANF and not working dropped by about half (from over 40 to about 20 percent) by 2009, and the percentage working and not receiving welfare doubled (from about a quarter to nearly half). More troubling, though, the percentage of poor single mothers neither working nor receiving welfare also doubled (from about 15 to nearly 35 percent) (Lower-Basch 2011). Welfare reform seems to have moved many poor people away from dependence on the government, but it has neither substantially improved their overall well-being nor reduced the nation's poverty rate, which remains by far the highest among wealthy countries.

At the same time that the program most Americans think of as "welfare" was fundamentally reformed and shrank drastically, other income-support policies expanded. The EITC, a major tax expenditure that aims to benefit the "working poor," was the fastest-growing social program in the country from 1990 to 2009. By 2009, the U.S. government spent four times more on EITC than TANF. Congress passed a major expansion of it shortly before the 1996 welfare reform, raising the amount of the benefit and expanding eligibility to include families with income at 175 percent of the official poverty level. Much of the United States's social expenditures, then, go not to raise people out of poverty but to supplement the incomes of those slightly above poverty. Similarly, the funding and number of recipients of food stamps or Supplemental Nutrition Assistance Program (SNAP) benefits fell during the 1990s but increased substantially in the first decade of the new millennium.

These contradictory trends in American welfare policy mirror debates over how generous the country's social policy really is. For decades, analysts mainly compared government social spending and found the United States lagging far behind just about all European countries: in 2007, U.S. spending was 17.4 percent of national income compared with 22.4 percent on average for the OECD (the world's wealthy countries). If you include the effects of taxation of benefits and tax expenditure, though, the U.S. figure rises to 18.9 percent compared with an OECD average of 20.2 percent (OECD 2011). If you go one step further and include government-mandated private social expenditures, the gap would be even narrower. Taking into account all of these factors, Christopher Howard (2007) argued that the American welfare state is much more extensive than commonly assumed but is still not very effective at reducing poverty or inequality. It channels a lot of money toward education and tax expenditures, which benefit far more people than just the poor, and the high cost of health care (see U.S. case study on health policy below) means that a large share of its social spending goes to Medicaid and Medicare rather than to increasing poor people's income.

CASE SUMMARY

The American liberal welfare state has accepted entitlement to permanent benefits only for the elderly and the disabled. All other spending programs are means tested, and the most important, TANF, is strictly limited in terms of how long people can use it and what they must do (work at whatever job is available) to get it. Indeed, tax expenditures have come to constitute a much bigger share of overall social policy than the standard "welfare" programs. Both creating and reforming social policy take place in the United States only at times of unusual crisis or consensus: the Great Depression, the tumultuous 1960s, and the politically volatile 1990s. The decentralized American system, with its weak political parties, means that major changes can occur only in unusual circumstances. The American federal system also means that social policy on the ground, in terms of who benefits and how much, varies greatly from state to state. The United States tolerates much higher levels of poverty and inequality than other wealthy countries in exchange for encouraging participation in the workforce at whatever level of remuneration possible.

In poorer countries, like Brazil, the poor have long been left pretty much on their own to survive, or not, in the market. Only relatively recently have middle-income countries like Brazil begun to think seriously about social policy to alleviate at least some of their extensive poverty.

CASE STUDY

Brazil: Starting a Welfare State in a Developing Economy

- Social insurance only for privileged formal-sector workers
- Expansion of pensions funded by general taxation to eliminate poverty among the elderly
- Bolsa Família, a pioneer CCT program
- Social right to income enacted but not implemented
- Substantial reduction in poverty and inequality

At his first presidential inauguration in 2002, former metalworker Luiz "Lula" Inácio da Silva famously declared, "If, by the end of my term of office, every Brazilian has food to eat three times a day, I shall have fulfilled my mission in life" (Hall 2006, 690). When he handed power to his hand-picked successor in 2010, there were still hungry Brazilians, but the nation's poverty rate had dropped from nearly 49 percent to under 29 percent, and inequality had declined by 17 percent, one of the most impressive drops in history.

Despite being the largest economy in South America and one of the fastest growing in recent years, Brazil has long been home to great poverty and inequality. In the last two decades, however, the country expanded its pension system for the elderly and created Latin America's first CCT program, which ultimately reached over a quarter of the population, representing a new and important effort at alleviating poverty. As it has industrialized, the country has faced the same set of social policy options as wealthier states, but it has done so with far fewer resources and less effective bureaucratic

A Brazilian family, recipients of the Bolsa Família program, watch President Lula da Silva on television. The Bolsa Família program has become the largest social program of its kind in Latin America. Along with rapid economic growth, the program has helped move millions out of poverty and reduced Brazil's high levels of inequality.

Credit: Vanderlei Almeida/AFP/Getty Images

institutions to implement policy. In this context, it is moving in the direction of creating a liberal welfare state focused primarily on means-tested programs in practice, in spite of lofty language in the constitution and recent legislation that suggests it will provide universal benefits.

For most of the country's history, Brazilian economic policy focused on achieving growth, while it became one of the most unequal societies in the world. Its populist tradition meant most assistance to the poor came from government or private in-kind contributions, such as food baskets. Populist politicians also helped the poor through programs like housing projects to gain political support. As in many countries, the first systematic government social policy focused on the elderly. The pension system implemented early in the twentieth century was expanded significantly after the adoption of the 1988 democratic constitution. Until the 1990s, the pension system covered a small percentage of the population: civil servants, whose pensions were paid for by the government, and formal-sector private employees, whose pensions came from mandatory contributions. This left out the large share of the population that works in the informal sector: most agricultural

workers and those in unofficial and quasi-legal businesses that are not officially recognized and don't pay taxes. The new constitution established a right to a minimum income for all elderly people. In response, the government expanded existing pension programs and created new ones for those elderly not already covered. The major new policies are financed primarily via general taxation rather than employee contributions. One program covers anyone over a certain age who can prove past employment in the agricultural sector. The other offers means-tested benefits to any elderly person in a household with a monthly income less than one-half the minimum wage. Both provide a set benefit equivalent to the national minimum wage. While slightly less than half the population contributes to the pension system, 90 percent of the elderly now receive benefits from the combined programs, an unusually high number for Latin America. The result has been a near elimination of poverty among the elderly (Lavinas 2006, 110).

The biggest criticism of this pension system is its inequality. The contributory and civil service systems still constituted more than 90 percent of all benefits in 2002, and half of the recipients were in the top 10 percent of households in terms of wealth. The new systems expanded rapidly, but they remained quite limited in terms of total resources, which is part of the reason Lula's first and largest reform was to the pension system for civil servants. He and his advisors argued that the generous benefits went to mostly middle-class civil servants (a small proportion of the population) and that reducing the program's cost would free up resources for the poor. He was eventually able to get the National Congress to pass a reform that increased the retirement age, required middle-income civil servants to contribute to their pension system, and reduced the generosity of the pensions. In the long run, these changes are predicted to save the government a great deal of money.

Lula's pledge to end hunger led to the creation of his signature program, Bolsa Família (Family Grant), early in his first term. The program consolidated and expanded several programs from the 1990s to provide food and cash grants through various channels. It targeted poor and "very poor" households in the exceptionally poor northeastern region, with those in the very poor group receiving larger grants. The largest single component of Bolsa Família is Bolsa Escola (School Grant), which provides grants to poor parents who guarantee they will send their children to school and utilize children's health services. Local social service councils were created to oversee implementation of the program, an attempt to reduce corrupt and political selection of recipient households. Anthony Hall (2006) reported that these measures have been successful where implemented, but the councils only function in two-thirds of municipalities. In the rest, the mayor's office is typically involved in recipient selection, with benefits often going to the mayor's political supporters. Both the World Bank and the Inter-American Development Bank support Bolsa Família, providing about one-quarter of its funding. Overall, it has been relatively successful, reaching forty-six million people by 2010, about one-quarter of the population, and tripling the average benefit (Baer 2008, 402; World Bank 2010). By the 2010 presidential election to choose Lula's successor, the program was so popular that both major candidates pledged to expand it.

Despite the program's success, criticisms and concerns have certainly arisen. Some fear that it will create a "culture of dependency" because there are no time limits on how long people can receive benefits. On the other hand, some critics argue that far more expansive policies are needed, including transferring assets (especially land) to the poor and providing guaranteed and universal benefits. In fact, a leader of Lula's Workers' Party (PT) led a successful effort to have Brazil's National Congress pass a law in January 2004 that provides a universal entitlement to a minimum income for all residents. The law, however, allows the government to implement it by focusing first on the neediest and includes no time limit by which this new social right must be implemented (Lavinas 2006). Bolsa Família and expanded pensions for the elderly remain the only programs aimed at achieving greater incomes for the poor. Brazil's robust economic growth has helped these programs to achieve unusual poverty reduction over the past decade, but the universal right to a minimum income is some distance from realization.

CASE SUMMARY

Bolsa Família, the largest antipoverty program in Latin America, is a major innovation in the development of the welfare state in that region and in developing countries in general; thirteen Latin American countries had CCT programs in place by 2009. The World Bank and other international financial institutions (IFIs) have come to support means-tested and carefully targeted social programs, which they see as alleviating the poverty that continues in the region despite (or, some argue, because of) the implementation of neoliberal economic reforms. Bolsa Família has substantially reduced poverty and inequality, though in a context of strong economic growth. How well the program can battle poverty in the face of slower growth remains to be seen.

Summary

Social policy emerged as countries industrialized and became relatively wealthy; poverty was no longer the norm. Many citizens came to see the continued presence of poor people as unacceptable. For the poorest countries, such as Nigeria, poverty remains the norm, and no real social policy exists (save social insurance for a tiny fraction of workers, mostly in the public sector). Citizens of middle-income countries like Brazil, however, are beginning to ask the same questions as citizens of wealthy countries: How can social policy help reduce poverty?

In part because dependence on government support has implications for democratic citizenship, governments in wealthy countries have made different choices about how and how far to pursue poverty alleviation via government programs, creating distinct types of welfare states. Some mainly use universal entitlements to provide extensive and largely equal benefits to all, emphasizing values of equality, while others use means testing to target assistance only at the poorest, reflecting values about the importance of ensuring as many people as possible are "making it on their own" in the market economy. The different welfare states reflect these differences in values, as well as differences in moral assessments of those who require assistance.

Our next area of government intervention, health care, is characterized by greater value consensus around the world about the importance of extensive government involvement, though exceptions do exist to this consensus, especially in the United States.

HEALTH CARE AND HEALTH POLICY

Much of the world has adopted the idea that health care is a social right of all citizens regardless of their position in the market. Wealthy countries have the resources to make market interventions in an attempt to realize this concept, but most others lack the resources to make it a reality. A few countries, including the United States, do not embrace health as a social right but nonetheless claim the provision of the best health care possible to the largest number of people as a legitimate political and social goal.

Health Care and Market Failure

Social values are not the only reason for policy intervention in health care markets, however. Market failure takes distinct forms in health care that are based on specific characteristics of the health care market. The key problems are very high risk and poor consumer information, and both produce inefficiency and misallocation of resources. High risk is the biggest factor driving the dynamics of the health care market and government intervention in it. People will do almost anything—pay any price or undergo any procedure—to restore their health when it is seriously threatened. On the other hand, healthy people don't need much medical care beyond annual checkups and preventative care. So demand for health care in a pure market is episodic: most individuals demand little health care except when sick, and then they demand a great deal. Those who lack the resources to pay for care when sick may face severe harm or even death. Insurance is the typical solution to high-risk markets. It spreads risks across many people so that the healthy subsidize the sick and in turn are subsidized when they face illness. Paying smaller, regular premiums more or less fixes the cost for each individual in the insurance pool, so catastrophic illness does not mean catastrophic bills. This principle also is true of homeowner's or auto insurance. Government or private companies can provide insurance as long as a relatively large group of people with diverse risks pool their resources to cover emergencies as necessary.

Although insurance is a potential market-based solution to high risk, it creates its own potential market failure: **moral hazard**. Moral hazard occurs when parties to a transaction behave differently than they otherwise would because they believe they won't have to pay the full costs of their actions. In health insurance, this results

moral hazard: Occurs when parties to a transaction behave in a particular way because they believe they will not have to pay the full costs of their actions

from the gap between paying a fixed premium for health care and the costs of the care itself. If insurance covers the full cost of the care, the individual has no incentive to economize in its use because her costs (the insurance premium) will not change as a direct consequence of her greater use. Moreover, many insurance systems pay medical providers for each procedure, giving providers an incentive to oversupply procedures just as the patient has an incentive to overuse them. The obvious results are excessive (and perhaps unnecessary) medical procedures and rising costs. Governments intervene in health care in part to attempt to limit the effects of the moral hazard inherent in an insurance system.

Another market failure, poor information, compounds the problem of overuse. Patients generally rely on medical professionals to know what procedures or drugs are needed to get well. Concerned about getting well, even most highly educated patients will readily agree to their doctor's recommended treatment, especially if they are insured and face relatively little direct cost. Transactions are unlikely to be efficient because the lack of information compounds the likelihood of unnecessary procedures. In addition, a completely unregulated market with poor information can produce the iconic image of nineteenth-century American medical quackery, the "snake-oil salesman," a charlatan selling false remedies to desperate people. To avoid this, virtually all governments regulate both pharmaceuticals and medical practitioners.

Health Care Systems

Wealthy countries have developed three distinct types of health care systems to address these problems. These have served as models for poorer countries as well, though these countries are severely limited by lack of resources. The earliest and still most common system in wealthy countries is **national health insurance (NHI)**. In an NHI system, the government mandates that virtually all citizens have insurance. NHI countries typically allow and encourage multiple, private insurance providers, while the government provides access to insurance to the self-employed or unemployed who do not have access via family members. Since the government mandates the insurance, it also regulates the system, setting or at least limiting premiums and payments to medical providers. In many NHI systems, access to health care is not specific to a particular employer, so workers can keep their insurance when they switch jobs. Germany pioneered this system in the late nineteenth century and continues to use it today, as do many other European countries and Japan. Few poor countries attempt to implement NHI because many of their citizens simply cannot afford insurance, although some do use a limited form of it for wealthier segments of the population, such as civil servants or employees of large corporations.

A **national health system (NHS)** is the second most common type of health care system in wealthy countries and the most common type worldwide. Frequently called a **single-payer system**, NHS is a government-financed and managed system. The government creates a system into which all citizens pay, either through a separate insurance payment (like Medicare in the United States, but for everyone) or via general taxation. The classic example of this type of system is in the United Kingdom, which established its NHS after World War II. In most NHS countries, the majority of medical professionals gain their income directly from the government, which implicitly controls the cost of medical care via payments for procedures, equipment, and drugs. Most poor countries have an NHS through which the government provides most medical care via hospitals and local clinics and in which

national health insurance (NHI): A health care system in which the government mandates that virtually all citizens must have insurance

national health system (NHS)/ single-payer system: A government-financed and managed health care system into which all citizens pay, either through a separate insurance payment or via general taxation, and through which they gain medical care

doctors are direct government employees. With limited resources, however, clinics and doctors are few, and many people lack access to or must wait long periods for what is often low-quality care.

market-based private insurance system: Health care system that relies on private insurance for the bulk of the population

The third system, a **market-based private insurance system**, is the least common. Although NHI and NHS countries typically permit some private insurance as a supplement for those who can afford it (and, indeed, private insurance is usually the chief means of securing health care for the rich in resource-starved poor countries), the United States, Turkey, and Mexico are the only OECD countries that rely on private insurance for the bulk of their health care. In the United States, citizens typically gain insurance through their employment, and medical care is provided mostly by for-profit entities such as private clinics and hospitals and self-employed doctors. A variety of government programs might exist in market-based systems to cover specific groups without private insurance, such as the poor, noncitizens, the unemployed, and the self-employed. Market-based systems, though, do not guarantee access to health care to all citizens, and even in the wealthiest of these countries, a sizeable minority lacks any insurance.

Common Problems

Almost all countries face a common set of problems regardless of the system they choose. The most evident of these are rising costs (especially in wealthy countries), lack of access to care, and growing public health concerns. Because of the need to contain costs, all countries and systems make decisions about how to ration care: who will get it, when, and how much.

Controlling Costs
Wealthier countries are perhaps most concerned with cost, because as wealth increases, health care costs rise faster than other costs. This is because wealthier people demand more and better care, and improved but often expensive technology emerges to help provide that care. Wealthier countries also have relatively low birth rates and high life expectancies, so the proportion of the population that is elderly increases over time and needs more health care. In 2009, health expenditures in OECD countries varied from a high of 16 percent of GDP in the United States to a low of 5.7 percent in Turkey, with an average of 8.9 percent. Furthermore, from 1997 to 2007, expenditures grew at an annual average of 4.1 percent, well above overall economic growth. People in almost all wealthy countries use more and more of their income for health care, regardless of the system in place.

Wealthy countries choose several means to try to control costs depending on their health care systems, though some methods can be used by any system. A key factor is the size of insurance pools. Larger and more diverse pools of people lower costs because a larger number of healthy people (especially young adults) cover the costs of those (often the elderly) who use health care more heavily, thereby lowering premiums for everyone. NHS and NHI systems that group most or all of a country's citizens into one insurance pool gain a cost-saving advantage. In market-based systems, on the other hand, the risk pools are much smaller (usually the employees of a particular company), so costs tend to be higher. Governments in these countries spend less tax revenue on health care than countries with other systems, but society as a whole may spend more on health care overall via private insurance premiums and direct fees. The United States, which depends heavily on private insurance and has very low government expenditures on health care, has by far the highest overall health costs, both in terms of dollars spent per capita and as a share of GDP (compare the wealthy countries in the Country and Concept table on page 540).

Other cost-saving measures focus on limiting the effects of moral hazard and can be used under any system. For example, paying doctors on a capitation, or per patient, basis rather than for each procedure prescribed creates an incentive to limit unnecessary procedures. Critics, however, argue that this gives providers an incentive to underprescribe, which endangers patients' well-being. A second strategy, "gatekeepers," also may be used to limit patients' demands for expensive treatments. Typically, a general practitioner serves as a gatekeeper who must give approval before patients can consult specialists in order to limit unnecessary trips to expensive specialists and procedures. Health maintenance organizations (HMOs) in the United States used both capitation and gatekeepers extensively in the 1990s to try to lower health care costs. A third approach is to require patients to make copayments, small fees that cover part of the cost of each service. Copayments change patients' incentives by making them pay more out of pocket for using health care rather than just pay fixed monthly insurance premiums or taxes.

IN CONTEXT

HEALTH CARE IN WEALTHY COUNTRIES, 2009

Different health care systems in our case study countries have significant differences. Costs, in particular, vary dramatically, while outcomes are similar. Access to doctors, hospitals, and technology depends on how each country chooses to spend its health budget.

	Germany	UK	US	OECD average
Costs				
Health care expenditures per capita ($)	3,588	2,982	7,290	2,984
Health care expenditures per GDP (%)	10.4	8.4	16	8.9
Public share of total health expenditures (%)	76.8	82.6	46.5	73
Physicians' remuneration (ratio to average wage)	3.3	4.2	3.7	—
Outcomes				
Life expectancy at birth (years)	80	79.5	78.1	79.1
Infant mortality rates (per 1,000)	3.9	4.8	6.7	3.9
Childhood measles vaccination rate	—	86.2	92.3	92
Access				
Practicing physicians (per 1,000 pop.)	3.5	2.5	2.4	3.1
Acute care hospital beds (per 1,000 pop.)	5.7	2.6	2.7	3.8
Access to specialists (% waiting longer than two months for appointment)	20	33	10	—

Source: OECD (2009); Access to specialists: Commonwealth Fund (2008).

METHODS IN CONTEXT

Can Democracy Make You Healthier?

The Methods in Context in chapter 10 examined the relationship between democracy and development measured simply in terms of GDP growth. Numerous scholars of development, however, have argued that economic growth is not the only or even the most important element of development (Sen 1999). They argue that overall quality of life should be the real definition of "development" and that health is a crucial element of quality of life. For political scientists, this raises the obvious question of whether regime type has an effect on a society's overall health: Can democracy produce better health? The answer may seem obvious, in that it seems likely that citizens will want better health if possible and so will demand it in a democracy; elected leaders will then spend more on health, resulting in a healthier population. Dictatorships, on the other hand, can resist popular pressure more easily and thus seem more likely to spend money elsewhere. The picture might be more complicated, however. Greater overall economic well-being is one factor that produces better health, so if dictatorships produce faster economic growth, they might improve health more. Similarly, if democracies are less effective and efficient at providing public health services, then increased spending might not improve health. Can we sort out whether democracy really does improve health?

HYPOTHESIS

Comparativist James McGuire examined this issue in great depth in a recent study (2010). He tested a wide range of hypotheses regarding improved health, including the effects of democracy. A long-standing debate in the study of health is whether economic growth alone is all that is needed to improve health or whether providing greater health-related social services is also necessary. McGuire hypothesized that greater social spending results in greater access to basic health services and greater overall health. Furthermore, he hypothesized that democracy produces greater social spending because, as noted above, citizens demand it and elected officials respond accordingly. He also noted, however, that democracy allows freedom of expression and debate, which may not only add pressure for greater social spending but also improve citizens' education about how to access health services and how to make healthier lifestyle choices. McGuire divided his hypotheses on democracy, then, into short-term and long-term, arguing that citizens' demands for greater social spending can have an effect in the short term, but producing a more educated citizenry requires democracy to be in place for longer. He thus hypothesized that in addition to increasing social spending, democracy, especially in the long term, will improve citizens' use of social services as well as their overall health.

RESEARCH AND ANALYSIS

McGuire combined a large statistical analysis of these hypotheses with a careful examination of eight case studies, four in Latin America and four in Asia. The statistical analysis was based on a dataset of 105 developing countries that included measurements of health, wealth, social spending, and access to health-related services for 1990 and data from Polity IV on the presence of democracy in each country, both short-term (1980–1990) and long-term (1900–1990). As is common in the field of health, he used infant mortality to measure overall health. (Infant mortality is widely accepted as the single best measurement of a society's health because across all cultures people want to keep their infants alive and will do whatever is in their power to do so.) Using regression analysis, McGuire examined simultaneously the relationships among these many variables.

His statistical analysis confirmed the importance of overall wealth to reducing infant mortality but showed this is much stronger over the long term than over a shorter period; economic growth does not improve health in the short term. McGuire also confirmed the surprising but not unusual finding that social spending itself does not directly improve health. Social spending does, however, improve access to health services, which in turn reduces infant mortality. Surprisingly, having a democracy, short-term or long-term, does not increase social spending. Long-term democracy, on the other hand, is correlated with better access to health services and lower infant mortality. What most analysts had seen as the strongest argument for democracy—citizens' demands for greater social spending—was not confirmed by the data analysis, but the long-term effects of democracy brought about by greater freedom of expression, citizen expectations, education, and health-related choices were important in reducing infant mortality.

Examining the eight case studies in detail to interpret and explain these results further, McGuire found that a key to improving health is the provision of basic health services aimed at poor people. Neither economic growth alone nor general government social spending guarantees that this will be achieved; even short-term democracy does not guarantee it. While citizens do demand better health care, wealthier citizens tend to be more influential and focus more on curative than basic, preventative care, even though the latter is more important for overall health. Longer-term democratic experience does help reduce infant mortality, McGuire argued, because over the long term, citizens begin to think of public services as a right that they expect from government and use when provided, and freedom of expression exposes problems with the health care system that governments then try to improve. Longer-term democracy also provides poorer citizens more opportunity to organize and demand the services they need. Even during periods of authoritarian rule, if a country has had prior sustained experience with democracy, it provides better basic health services, as McGuire's case study of Chile demonstrated. He noted that very rapid growth, as occurred in Taiwan and South Korea, can improve health dramatically, but so can relatively inexpensive provision of basic services even with much lower economic growth, as demonstrated by Chile and Costa Rica. Long-term democracy helps ensure that those services exist and people use them.

QUESTIONS IN CONTEXT

McGuire's impressive study not only provided some interesting findings for political science; it also has clear policy implications. He suggested that while rapid economic growth can improve health, achieving such growth is difficult; providing inexpensive basic health services seems likely to be much easier to implement. In spite of McGuire's impressive results, though, no study definitively resolves all debates on the subject. That his data focused primarily on a key year—1990—may have skewed the results, as is always possible in quantitative models. While McGuire found strong relationships among the key variables, some are stronger than others. His case studies were selected in part based on the availability of information on the countries; other case studies might lead to different conclusions. While he included a number of important variables, perhaps others could be included as well. What other variables could be added to a future study that might help explain the relationship between democracy and health more fully?

If kept to moderate amounts, copayments can theoretically discourage unnecessary or frivolous procedures; if set too high, however, they may discourage poorer patients from getting medically necessary care.

Clearly a trade-off exists between cost containment and achieving a healthy population. Meeting all demands for health care instantly might produce the healthiest possible population, but it would be prohibitively expensive and would aggravate moral hazard. No government ever does this; instead, all choose to ration health care in some way, though many people may not perceive it as rationing. NHS countries can control costs most directly simply by limiting the overall health care budget, the payments to medical providers, purchases of new equipment, and/or drug prices. The result can be relatively low-cost but sometimes limited care. Limits most typically take the form of patients waiting for certain procedures rather than getting them on demand. An NHS country must ration care by setting priorities on which services to provide more quickly and which, such as elective surgery, to delay. Waiting lines are longer in systems, including Britain's, that simply have fewer doctors per capita, another cost-saving measure. NHI countries can set insurance premiums and medical payments as well; they usually don't do so as universally as NHS countries, though Germany has experimented with greater regulation in recent years. Some countries, including the United States (the only wealthy country in this category), provide insurance only to a segment of the population, who thereby have access to fairly extensive care; those without insurance have very limited or no access to care. This is another way to ration.

The data in the In Context box (page 567) suggest that the form of rationing does not make a substantial difference to achieving a healthy population among wealthy countries. Those with the lowest costs, such as Britain, do not have significantly lower health outcomes overall, measured in terms of key data such as infant mortality or life expectancy. For poorer countries, where the main problem is not cost containment but availability of resources, lower costs do seem related to lower-quality health as the Country and Concept table (pages 540–541) shows.

Access to Health Care Access is a much greater problem than rising costs for the very poorest countries, where limited resources mean much smaller numbers of doctors, hospitals, and clinics per capita. Even though individuals may be nominally covered by a government health plan, they cannot access health care if facilities and providers are not available, and the poorest countries cannot afford to expand their health care networks. While many have NHS systems, as the Country and Concept table demonstrates, most health care funding still comes from private financing, often direct payments to providers without even the benefit of insurance. As a result of limited access and costs too high for the poor majority, preventable and easily treatable diseases continue to shorten life spans and cause debilitation and loss of income and productivity in much of the world.

Public Health The third major common problem is public health concerns. These are common to all countries but vary greatly. In the poorest countries, access to enough food and clean water remains a public health issue. Without access to clean water, populations continue to be plagued by a variety of contagious diseases. Further, malnourishment exacerbates the effects of water-borne contagions as immune systems are weak and resistance low. The health effects in terms of core indicators such as infant mortality and life expectancy are clear in the Country and Concept table (page 540): compare the data for wealthy countries such as the United States, the United Kingdom, or Japan with poorer countries such as India or Nigeria.

The wealthiest countries face a different kind of malnutrition: obesity. The highest rates of obesity in the OECD are in the United States and Mexico and now include more than 30 percent of the population. Obesity rates are rising in almost all wealthy countries: food is relatively inexpensive compared to our incomes, so we overconsume it.

Other public health issues resulting from affluence—alcohol and tobacco consumption—have seen positive change recently. Rates of alcohol use in the OECD declined by 13 percent from 1980 to 2007, while rates of tobacco use declined by about 20 percent from 1995 to 2007. Active public health education programs, along with legal limits and higher taxes on alcohol and tobacco consumption, reaped impressive results in many wealthy countries. Unfortunately, alcohol and tobacco consumption rates are increasing in many poorer countries, as their populations become wealthier and as alcohol and tobacco producers actively market in developing countries to compensate for shrinking consumption in their traditional markets.

Finally, globalization has produced a new set of public health concerns that cross borders as physical interaction among populations increases. These include the expansion of sexually transmitted diseases (especially HIV/AIDS) and insect-borne diseases such as Lyme disease, West Nile virus, and malaria. Increased importation and exportation of products and international travel have also led to the global spread of such conditions as salmonella, foot-and-mouth disease, and SARS. The spread of diseases to new populations lowers overall well-being and raises health care costs. Contagious disease is best dealt with via preventative measures such as education campaigns, infrastructure projects, free condoms, and control of insect populations, all of which are public goods and therefore inherently government responsibilities. With increasing globalization, what happens in one country increasingly affects others, meaning that health care policy makers in one country might be well advised to assist the citizens of other countries as well as their own.

CASE STUDY

Germany: Pioneer of Modern Health Policy

- NHI system with universal coverage but high costs

- Reforms to lower costs via incentives

- Reforms to maintain equity of access

- Continuing debate of equity versus cost control

As noted earlier, Germany's Otto von Bismarck created the first modern, national health insurance system as part of his effort to use social policies to calm labor unrest and weaken worker sympathy for communist movements and demands for democracy. The 1883 Sickness Insurance Act created the world's first modern health insurance program, the system

that Germany still uses. Germany's NHI system is corporatist in both organization and management and relies heavily on professional and patient associations to implement it under the overall regulation of the state. It provides very generous benefits, including dental, hospital, and preventative care and even rehabilitative health spa treatments, primarily through a network of sickness funds financed by payroll taxes shared by employers and employees. Cost control has been a major issue (though less so than in the United States) and has prompted a series of reforms introducing limits on overall costs, increased competition within the system, and a shift of the cost to users. As the previous In Context feature (page 567)

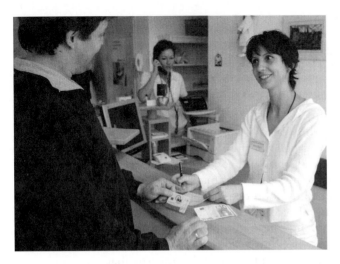

A patient pays his €10 (about $14) copay at a dentist's office in Bremen, Germany. While dental benefits have long been standard in Germany's NHI system, modest copays for many services have become a means of cutting down costs in recent years.

Credit: AP Photo/Joerg Sarbach

shows, Germany has achieved average to above-average health outcomes as compared to other wealthy countries, but it has done so at above-average costs.

The sickness funds are nonprofit organizations run by boards of employers and employees. They are connected to employer, profession, or locale and are autonomous from the government in setting most of their policies and prices, though the services they must offer are uniform across the country. They negotiate services and payments with regional physician associations; doctors who wish to participate in the system (about 95 percent of them do) must be members of their regional association and abide by the negotiated agreements. All but the wealthiest Germans must belong to a sickness fund; in this way, Germany has long achieved universal coverage. The unemployed must belong to a fund as well, the costs of which are covered by federal and local governments, and by law these individuals must receive the same benefits as other members. The wealthiest individuals may opt out of the system and purchase private insurance, though about two-thirds of them choose to join a sickness fund anyway. More than 90 percent of the population uses the sickness fund system.

Residents can also purchase supplemental insurance to give them greater choice in where and how they are treated, and about 10 percent of members do so (Adolino and Blake 2001, 225; Green and Irvine 2001, 57).

Employment determined which fund a German belonged to until a 1997 reform allowed Germans to choose their sickness fund and change it annually, introducing competition among funds. This reduced the number of sickness funds from 1,200 in 1985 to under 200 by 2010, as competition has pushed most out of the market (Green and Irvine 2001, 57; *The Economist* 2010). Nonetheless, German patients have exceptional levels of choice among sickness funds and, once they've selected a fund, among doctors. The German system has not traditionally had gatekeepers, and patients are free to go to any physician in any specialty. Some sickness funds have been allowed to experiment with using general practitioners as gatekeepers or creating networks of providers like HMOs in the United States, but few have done so.

Despite nearly universal coverage, equity has been a continuous concern, especially for the Social Democratic Party. Some sickness funds have unusually high numbers of poor and unhealthy members or are in regions with unusually poor and unhealthy populations, meaning their costs are well above the national average. A 1992 reform attempted to resolve this by creating a compensation system in which money is transferred from wealthier sickness funds to poorer ones. As costs have risen in recent years, relatively young, healthy, and wealthy people have increasingly opted out of the system altogether, taking the lowest-cost members out of the sickness funds and thereby raising premiums for everyone else. This becomes a particular burden in already poor funds. Reforms in 2007 for the first time mandated that all citizens have insurance, but the wealthy can still purchase private insurance instead of joining a sickness fund. The SDP argued for eliminating the option of purchasing private insurance to provide greater equity by forcing all citizens to join a sickness fund, but Chancellor Angela

Merkel's Christian Democratic Party did not support the proposal.

Cost containment has long been a major issue in the German system. The key relationship in the system is between the sickness funds and the regional associations of physicians who negotiate agreements as to how the physicians will be paid. In the early twentieth century, physicians were paid on a capitation basis, but a 1950s reform demanded by doctors allowed a shift to fee-for-service payments. This led to the first spurt of cost increases and the first major reform of the system in 1977, which established a classic corporatist solution: national negotiations among the sickness funds, physicians' associations, and the government to set targets for annual expenditure growth. The targets were tied to increases in wage levels so that, in theory, health care costs would rise no faster than wages. By 1986, players recognized that the negotiated targets were not adequately constraining costs, so a further reform introduced a cap on expenditures. Each year, sickness funds and physicians' associations negotiate a binding cap (with government intervention if they cannot agree) on cost increases tied to general wage increases of the people in each sickness fund. Each sickness fund pays the physicians' association a lump sum based on the cap multiplied by the number of patients the association serves, giving the doctors an incentive to police their own expenditures. As a result, German health care costs rose much more slowly in the 1980s than those in many countries, including the United States. Reforms in 1989 and 1993 went further, extending the expenditure cap system from physicians to hospitals and pharmaceuticals and doubling many patient copayments. The 1997 reform allowing patients to choose which sickness fund to join has created much greater competition, presumably lowering costs as well as creating larger pools in each fund since the number of funds has dropped by three-quarters in twenty years.

Despite these reforms, cost remains a major concern for Germans in the new century. An aging population and expensive technological innovations continue to increase the cost of health care. Germany's extraordinarily high number of doctors and hospital beds per capita (see the In Context box, page 567) give patients tremendous choice and moderate wait time for treatment, but they also cost a great deal. A reform in 2004 increased copayments again and shifted a greater share of total costs onto contributions from employers and employees, and another reform in 2007 more fundamentally changed health care financing by creating a single nationwide premium schedule tied to workers' incomes. The new national fund distributes the premiums plus general tax revenue to sickness funds on a per capita basis, adjusting for the wealth and health of the membership of each fund. Individual sickness funds can give rebates to their members if they can provide services at a cost lower than what they receive from the national fund, or they can charge members additional premiums if necessary. This policy is designed to encourage efficiency as the funds compete for members.

In the face of massive budget deficits due to the global recession, Angela Merkel's Christian Democrat–Free Democrat coalition government passed yet another controversial reform in November 2010. It raised the insurance premiums from 14.9 to 15.5 percent of wages, with most of the increase paid for by employees. More controversially, it allowed future increases by insurance funds that will be paid fully by employees and can be flat fees, rather than a percentage of income; future increases will therefore hit poorer Germans more than wealthier ones. To try to control rising drug costs, the 2010 reform also required pharmaceutical companies to negotiate prices with insurance funds for new drugs; failure to do so will result in the government setting prices. The reforms proved extremely controversial, with the Social Democratic opposition arguing that they imposed virtually all additional costs on workers and did little to bring down overall health costs. Merkel's health minister, a member of the liberal Free Democrat Party, on the other hand, wanted an even more radical change to a completely flat-fee system. Overall, the long series of reforms has meant that patients' share of immediate costs has more than doubled since 1991, providers have new incentives to economize on the number and type of procedures they prescribe, and growing reports suggest some patients are not receiving services in order to keep costs down (Gerlinger 2010).

CASE SUMMARY

Germany has long been a model of the NHI system, but it continues to struggle with higher-than-average costs. Bismarck established it before physicians were a major political force in German politics, so they provided little effective opposition to the state intervening in their market. Decades later, as they became a political force of some influence, the system was modified to their

benefit, putting pressure on costs. Reform efforts remained within the corporatist tradition and the German Christian democratic welfare state until the most recent reforms, which have fundamentally altered financing by creating a uniform national premium schedule and shifting costs onto workers. Germany, like all wealthy countries, will continue to struggle with a health care sector that consumes an ever larger share of national income, though Germans have a system that achieves unusually high levels of care coupled with widespread patient choice and universal coverage. This is in sharp contrast to the United Kingdom's NHS, which controls costs quite effectively but, as the In Context box demonstrates, does so by limiting access more than in the United States or Germany.

CASE STUDY

United Kingdom: Reforming the NHS

- Pioneer of NHS: Universal coverage, funded by general taxes, nearly free at point of service

- Relatively low costs but less access than other wealthy countries

- Rising costs have led to reforms since 1990 to increase competition and efficiency

- 2011 reform the most significant since World War II

In early 2011, Conservative prime minister David Cameron introduced legislation in Parliament that was heralded as the biggest change to British health care since the creation of the NHS after World War II. Like Germany, the United Kingdom was a pioneer of health care, creating the earliest and most universal NHS based on four key principles: universal services, comprehensive services, free to the patient, and financed by general tax revenue. With minor exceptions, the NHS has worked that way ever since, though both

Conservative and Labour governments have made significant reforms in the last twenty years. Britain achieves health outcomes that are about average for wealthy countries at lower-than-average costs. As the In Context box (page 567) shows, it accomplishes this in part by having fewer doctors and hospital beds and, most importantly, by rationing nonemergency care via long waits. The 2008–2009 recession, which hit Britain particularly hard, was one of the reasons the Conservative-LDP coalition government introduced a sweeping plan to create incentives to improve efficiency and lower costs further.

The NHS traditionally functioned like one giant managed care system: it signed contracts with general practitioners (GPs) in each region of the country to deliver primary services to patients. Each region served as one large insurance pool, with an average of about half a million patients. GPs are paid on a combination of fee-for-service and capitation basis, while British patients sign up with the GP of their choice, usually in their neighborhood, who provides basic care and functions as a gatekeeper, referring them to a specialist or hospital as needed. The NHS regional and district health authorities receive national government revenue to provide hospital and specialist services, and most services (except for some pharmaceuticals) are free to the patient at the point of service, having been paid for by general taxes. Waiting times for seeing GPs are very low, but waiting times for specialists and nonemergency hospital stays are among the world's highest.

No one can opt out of the NHS since it's funded by general taxes, but patients can purchase private supplemental insurance that allows them to see private doctors and get hospital services without the long waits of the public system. As Britons have grown wealthier and, like citizens in all wealthy countries, have demanded more health care, a growing number supplement NHS coverage with private insurance. Patients can use the NHS for routine illnesses and private insurance for procedures that have long waiting lines in the NHS.

Britain has been less concerned with rising costs than other wealthy countries, at least until recently. While costs have risen substantially, they remain below average. The NHS allows the national government to control costs directly: it simply sets the annual overall budget, thereby limiting the system to a certain expenditure level. This has resulted in Britain spending far less than most wealthy countries on health care; in the mid-1990s, it spent barely half what the United States did as a share of its GDP. As part of reform efforts to improve the system, the Labour government (1997–2010) significantly increased health care spending, resulting in Britain partially closing the gap in terms of money spent and doctors available, as reflected in the In Context table (page 567). Despite the UK's ability to control costs, health care reform has been a major political issue since the 1980s. The NHS has always been and remains very popular with British citizens, but there are those unhappy with the long wait times for certain procedures and lower-quality care, both by-products of cost-control structures.

Prime Minister David Cameron (center) and Health Secretary Andrew Lansley (left) meet doctors and other medical personnel in January 2011 as part of their effort to popularize their sweeping reform proposals for the National Health Service. The proposals promise to be the biggest changes to the NHS since its creation. Initial reaction to them from both medical personnel and the general public was overwhelmingly negative.

Credit: Oli Scarff/PA Wire URN:10118215 (Press Association via AP Images)

The NHS as originally structured had no internal incentives for efficiency. The Conservative government under Margaret Thatcher initiated a reform in 1990 that introduced elements of competition to increase efficiency. The idea was never popular, but Thatcher used her majority in Britain's parliamentary system to pass the reform anyway. It created large purchasers and sellers of health care. GPs with large practices (5,000 patients or more) were given their own budget by the NHS, which they used to purchase specialist and hospital services for their patients. Those who negotiated better deals would be likely to get more patients and earn more money. Similarly, hospitals gained the ability to manage their own affairs. Rather than being run by the regional health authorities, hospitals would sell their services to GPs. Hospitals were still public entities but could increase their revenue by providing the best services at the lowest cost.

The results of this bold experiment were mixed. Wait times did drop and there were signs of improved efficiency, but the benefits mainly went to patients of the GPs with the largest practices in the wealthiest areas. The Conservative government also kept overall funding low, so improvements in wait times and quality of care were not dramatic. Indeed, unhappiness with the state of the NHS was one reason the Labour Party under Tony Blair swept into office in 1997. Labour campaigned on a platform of reversing the market-based incentives. In reality, in a series of reforms starting in 2000, the Labour government modified rather than eliminated the new system. The main reform was to strengthen regional associations, which would purchase services for patients. This kept an element of competition but eliminated the different deals GPs in the same area provided their patients. By 2005, the new associations managed 75 percent of the NHS's total spending. The Blair government also increased funding to hire more doctors and reduce wait times in hospitals, raising costs substantially.

Cameron's 2011 reforms reversed course again, moving even further in the direction of competition than Thatcher's policies two decades earlier. The sweeping Conservative/LDP proposal would hand 80 percent of the NHS budget to GPs, who will form local consortia to purchase services for their patients. They would be free to use that tax money to purchase services from NHS or private hospitals and specialists. NHS hospitals would become independent units, required to break even via selling their services to the GP consortia. Those that lose money would be sold to private operators or closed. The goal is to use competition to spur greater efficiency; the government was intent on reducing the NHS budget by 4 percent per year (far less than its more draconian overall budget cuts—see chapter 10). Immediate reaction to the proposals was overwhelmingly negative. Initial polls showed two-thirds of doctors opposed the reforms, and only one-quarter thought they would improve patient care. Many were concerned that the GPs would not know how to manage the new consortia and would ultimately contract that work out to (most likely American) private companies to purchase care for them. Elimination of the regional authorities would cut about 25,000 jobs, though many of those employees seem likely

to be hired by the new GP consortia. Others feared that the reform would ultimately allow a full privatization of the system and that it would create inequities, as patients in healthier and wealthier areas would ultimately obtain better care. The fierce opposition led Carmeron to make the very unusual move of modifying the proposal before sending it to parliament because he feared even his own party wouldn't support it. The modified plan returned some government regulation to the system and delayed full implementation of the competition between public and private services providers such as hospitals.

CASE SUMMARY

In contrast to corporatist and federal Germany, Britain's NHS is a unitary and centralized system of health care. It has always been one of the country's most popular government programs, and it has allowed the government to keep costs relatively low, but at the expense of quality and timeliness of service, or so its critics claim. Britain's parliamentary system has allowed recent governments of both parties to enact significant reforms more easily than either Germany or the United States. These reforms have focused on reorganization to encourage improved efficiency and quality of service. The Labour government coupled this with sharply increased spending to provide Britons with health care quality closer to that of other European countries. In contrast, the successor Conservative/LDP government proposed sweeping reforms to increase competition and the role of the private sector and to drive costs down. Even with this reform, however, British health care will continue to be funded by general taxation and be free or nearly so at the point of service. The United States, in contrast, remains the only wealthy system in the world with a primarily private health system that, as the In Context box (page 567) shows, achieves slightly below-average outcomes at much higher than average costs.

CASE STUDY

U.S. Health Policy: Trials and Tribulations of the Market Model

- Highest costs in the world and average health outcomes

- Employer-based system created by market, not government

- Government programs only for particular categories of citizens: the elderly and the poorest

- 2010 reform to expand coverage and perhaps bring down costs

- Continued aversion to government creation of a universal system

President Barack Obama signs the health care reform bill on March 23, 2010. The reform, the biggest since the creation of Medicare and Medicaid in 1965, promises to increase insurance coverage to 95 percent of Americans while reducing costs. Even after its passage and initial steps of implementation, the public was evenly divided on its benefits, and opponents were challenging it in the courts and in voting booths.

Credit: AP Photo/Charles Dharapak

On March 23, 2010, President Barack Obama signed the largest reform of the market-based health care system in the United States at least since the creation of Medicare and Medicaid in 1965. Its chief goals were to expand insurance coverage to 95 percent of the population and reduce overall costs, primarily by the government's (1) mandating that nearly all citizens get insurance; (2) helping to create statewide markets for those without employment-based insurance so they could purchase insurance at reasonable prices, with subsidies as needed; and (3) increasing regulation of private insurers. The national debate over the reform was long and exceptionally divisive. Opponents on the right argued it represented an unprecedented expansion of government into the lives of citizens, while opponents on the left argued that failure to create a true NHS would mean the country would achieve neither universal coverage nor significant cost control. Even a year after it was signed, only about half of the public supported the plan.

The United States spends more on health care—both as a dollar amount and as a share of its total economy—than any other country in the world. In 2009, health spending hit an all-time high of 17.6 percent of the entire economy. The data in the In Context box (page 567) suggest these large expenditures produce health outcomes comparable to, albeit slightly below, those in other wealthy countries. The United States possesses considerably more medical technology than most countries, but this has not produced better health. High and rising costs have led to the term *crisis* being associated with United States health care policy at least since the early 1970s. Since the inception of the private insurance system in the mid-twentieth century, proposals have existed for creating a national, universal system similar to those in other wealthy countries, but not until 2010 was something approaching those systems put in place, and even then it was continuously challenged.

More than 60 percent of the U.S. population is covered by employment-based private insurance, with another 25 percent or so covered by government programs for particular categories of people. The remaining 15 percent or so have no health insurance and rely on their own resources or free care from mobile clinics, community outreach programs, or hospital emergency rooms, which are required by law to provide aid to anyone who walks in, though many do not. The uninsured have very limited access to care. Most are near poverty but are not recipients of government welfare benefits, work part-time jobs that do not provide insurance benefits, or are self-employed. They are the primary intended beneficiaries of the 2010 reform.

The American private insurance system became widespread during World War II, when wage freezes prevented employers from using higher wages to attract employees; instead, they competed by offering more generous health benefits. After the war, the government encouraged this system via tax incentives: health benefits are not taxable income. The system gives advantages to large employers and their employees because each employer negotiates insurance rates as a company; larger companies have bigger risk pools and therefore can get lower premiums and better coverage. The authors of this textbook, for instance, had the best health coverage of their lives when they were very low paid teaching assistants in graduate school. Their salaries were near the poverty level, but because they taught at a state university, they were state employees and received the generous benefits a very large employer (the entire state government) provided. Now, they have much higher salaries working at a small liberal arts college but not nearly as generous health benefits from an employer of only about 500 employees.

Extensive U.S. government health programs only began in 1965 with the creation of Medicare and Medicaid. Medicare provides health insurance to retirees who receive Social Security (the disabled were later added as recipients as well), and Medicaid is a means-tested program that provides coverage to most recipients of the country's primary social program (now TANF). In 1997 the State Children's Health Insurance Program (SCHIP) was created to provide insurance for poor or low-income children. The combination of SCHIP and an expansion of Medicaid coverage reduced the percentage of low-income children who were uninsured from 22.3 percent in 1997 to 14.9 percent in

2005 (CBO 2007, 8). Prior to the 2010 reform, Congress passed a major expansion of SCHIP in 2009. Overall, even before the 2010 reform, government spending on health was more than 40 percent of total health spending (though that remains the second lowest level in the OECD). Most of this spending went to the expensive Medicare program for the elderly, who utilize more health care than other groups. Health costs became a serious political issue in the 1970s, but it was in the 1980s that costs rose at alarming rates, reaching an annual inflation rate of nearly 20 percent by the end of the decade. This led even large corporations to start demanding some type of intervention to bring costs under control, and health care reform became a major issue in the 1992 presidential campaign. After his election, President Bill Clinton proposed a plan that would have set up funds similar to Germany's sickness funds across the country and encouraged them to compete for clients among employers. Coverage would be mandatory and could travel with the employee from one job to the next, and those not employed would be covered by various federal programs and still be part of the funds. Facing fierce opposition from the insurance industry, the reform never passed Congress, though SCHIP did emerge three years later as a result of the raucous political debate.

In the absence of national policy reform, employers (the primary purchasers of insurance packages) began reforming the existing system to lower costs via a rapid switch from fee-for-service insurance to HMOs and related groups, which try to hold costs down by capitation and gatekeeper rules. The share of privately insured Americans in fee-for-service plans dropped from 70 percent in 1988 to 14 percent in 1998. As a result, annual cost increases dropped from 18 percent in 1990 to less than 4 percent by 1996, removing health care costs as a significant political concern as the country entered the new millennium (Graig 1999, 22–35). The ability of managed care to keep costs under control seems to be limited, however; while costs as a share of national income actually shrank slightly from 1993 to 1998, from 13.7 to 13.5 percent, by 2006 they had risen to 17.2 percent. In the 2008 presidential election, rising costs had once again put health care on the national political agenda.

Obama entered office with a promise, strongly supported by his party, which controlled both houses of Congress, to achieve universal health insurance coverage. Labor unions had long championed a "single-payer system," essentially an NHS. This radical reform, however, did not have majority support even within the Democratic Party, and it was vigorously opposed by the private insurance industry and Republicans. Many Democrats wanted instead to create what came to be called a "public option," which would be one health insurance choice available to individuals. The public option could be realized by opening up any of three programs to the broader public: the federal government's insurance plan for its own employees, Medicare, or Medicaid. Obama's initial proposal included a public option that would be open only to those not insured through their employers, preserving all existing private insurance as is. Ultimately, even this limited public option proved to be one of the most controversial elements of the plan and was eliminated.

The health reform that Obama and Congress adopted is projected to provide coverage eventually for about 95 percent of the population (up from the current 85 percent). It does this by mandating that all people but exceptional "hardship" cases must obtain health insurance of some sort and providing subsidies to premiums for low-income people. By 2014, it will create insurance "exchanges" in each state that will be available to all those who don't have insurance through their employers. Private insurance companies will offer plans in these exchanges that must meet certain minimum federal standards of service coverage. The exchanges will be available to the uninsured in each state, creating large pools intended to be attractive to insurance companies and allowing the uninsured to obtain much cheaper coverage than they each could individually. Medium and large employers will have to offer minimal health insurance to their employees; those that don't will pay a fine that will help pay for the subsidies for the uninsured. The reform also includes substantial regulation of insurance companies, preventing them from denying insurance to those with preexisting medical conditions or revoking it from the already ill, restrictions to which the insurance industry readily agreed in exchange for access to an additional 10 percent of the population (the uninsured) as clients in the new exchanges. To make sure young and healthy people obtain insurance and thereby improve the overall insurance pool, the reform also allowed young adults to remain on their parents' insurance until age twenty-six.

The reform is intended to control costs first by forcing nearly everyone, including young and healthy people who are often uninsured, to pay into the system. This will create larger and more diverse pools that should reduce average costs. By reducing the number of uninsured people, the plan should also reduce the very expensive but unnecessary use of hospital emergency rooms on which the uninsured have long relied as their primary health care option. Insurance regulations will also restrict administrative and advertising costs to a set percentage of insurance premiums to help keep costs down. The most expensive insurance plans, dubbed "Cadillac plans," will eventually be taxed to discourage excessive use of the health system. In the longer run, the reform also creates a panel that will study and recommend "best practices" for broader implementation to keep costs down.

While opponents claimed that the government couldn't afford the new health plan, the Congressional Budget Office estimated it will actually save the government money over a decade. What is less clear is whether the cost controls will be adequate to reduce the very high U.S. health costs (private and public) to any significant degree. The plan was designed to have minimal effect on the already insured (other than lower costs, fewer restrictions on access, and higher taxes on the wealthiest population). Judith Feder and Donald Moran (2007), however, argued that until political leaders accept the fact that universal coverage combined with cost containment will require greater limits on the already insured, no fundamental reform will be possible. The implementation of the Obama plan over the next decade will determine whether or not they were right.

CASE SUMMARY

The American political system's openness and weak parties have made significant health care reform difficult. Obama and Democrats in Congress finally passed a substantial reform in 2010 but one that does not shift very far from the free-market model. The most fundamental change is the mandate that virtually all Americans obtain coverage, a mandate that opponents view as unconstitutional and immediately began opposing in the courts. Many analysts point to American political culture as an explanation for why the country has been so opposed to a universal health care system: Americans generally distrust "big government" and anything that can be labeled "socialist," making major government interventions in the economy relatively rare. Employer-based health insurance emerged as an industry initiative in the labor market during World War II, and the insurance industry has been a powerful voice in preserving the market-based system ever since. Medicare, Medicaid, and SCHIP have expanded coverage, though they have not achieved the universal coverage found in other wealthy countries. They also have done little to rein in costs, which remain by far the highest in the world. The great question of the next decade is whether the 2010 reform can finally bring costs down closer to the level in other wealthy nations or whether more fundamental reforms will be necessary.

Summary

Like social policy, distinct health care models have arisen in wealthy countries, providing different levels of government involvement in trying to ensure all citizens have access to adequate health care. No society can afford to provide every type of care instantly to everyone who demands it. Within this limit, the "bottom line" of any health care system is, presumably, to produce the healthiest possible population at the lowest possible cost. Based on this formula, both NHI and NHS systems seem to fare better than purely market-based ones, probably because of the unique aspects of the health care market we discussed above. All wealthy countries, though, face a common set of problems, regardless of what type of system they have: rising costs due to an aging population and demand for more and better care, perverse incentives for both consumers and producers of health care that make it difficult to maximize efficiency, and growing public health problems associated with wealth such as obesity and heart disease. These structural problems have made health care reform a particularly divisive political issue, bringing down governments or realigning legislative majorities in all three of our case studies. Poor countries are in a starkly different situation: their biggest problems are lack of resources for health care of whatever type and the presence of massive public health problems associated with poverty, such as high infant mortality and preventable communicable diseases such as measles. Some of these public health problems arise from environmental problems, a subject to which we now turn.

ENVIRONMENTAL PROBLEMS AND POLICY

Global warming (climate change) is only the latest and largest environmental problem confronting governments around the world. The modern environmental movement and environmental policies developed in the 1960s and 1970s. Some environmental activism, however, especially that for preservation of natural spaces, started much earlier. Environmental problems became a significant policy issue later than either health care or welfare, perhaps in part because the environment, in contrast to the other two, is a classic postmaterialist concern. Environmental preservation tends to become a more widespread social value as wealth rises and material interests are met. Early industrializers in Europe and the United States weren't very concerned about environmental degradation until the 1960s, when people began to look at the effects of long-term pollution from the new context of economic security. Today, increasing wealth and security in some more recently industrialized countries also seems to be stimulating interest in clean air, water, and other environmental concerns. Globalization simply has added a new dimension to the problem.

The Environment and Market Failure

Environmental damage is also an exceptionally clear case of market failure in the form of externalities. No form of pollution is without cost. When a factory pollutes a river with sewage, people downstream get sick and need costly health care while fish and other aquatic life die, raising the cost of fishing and reducing ecosystem diversity. Vehicle exhaust produces cancer-causing smog that results in millions of dollars of health care costs annually, and most people consider clean air and water beneficial, so they pay an implicit cost any time it is fouled. Polluters rarely pay the cost of their own pollution in an unfettered market: most commodities cost less than they would if their true costs, including environmental costs, were internalized in the production process. The market therefore devotes more resources to those undervalued products than it ought, creating inefficiency. Meanwhile, other people bear the costs of the pollution produced, a classic externality.

Many environmental goods are inherently public and often free. Unregulated use of free goods like air, water, or public land can lead to the **tragedy of the commons**. This is an old idea. If free public grazing land exists in a farming area, all farmers will use it to graze their herds, and none will have an incentive to preserve it for future use; collectively, they will likely overgraze the land and destroy it so that they all lose out in the end. In wealthy industrial countries, a more current example is clean air, a completely "common" good we all breathe and pollute. Without a collective effort to limit use and abuse, no individual has the incentive or ability to preserve it, so it's likely to be overused and perhaps ultimately depleted. The free market grossly undervalues (at zero cost) a valuable public good.

National governments have been grappling with market interventions to compensate for environmental externalities, trying to avoid the tragedy of the commons, for most of the last hundred years. Recently, globalization has raised new, international challenges in this process. Globalization has spread not only industrialization but also environmental damage. Industrialization always increases the pollution of previously agrarian societies. In addition, many observers fear that the dynamics of global competition will produce a "race to the bottom," as countries use lax environmental rules to attract foreign capital. Many argue that wealthy countries are not only outsourcing factories and jobs but pollution as well. For example, the

tragedy of the commons: No individual has the incentive or ability to preserve a common, shared good that is free, so without collective effort, it is likely to be overused and perhaps ultimately destroyed

quality of the air and water around Pittsburgh has dramatically improved as the city's steel industry has declined, while China, now the world's largest steel producer, faces a rapidly growing pollution problem. Opponents of the race-to-the-bottom thesis argue that as globalization helps produce wealth, it will help lower pollution because wealth and environmental concerns seem to increase in tandem. Whichever argument proves more accurate in the long term, rapidly industrializing countries now face dramatically expanding environmental problems. This is clearest in Asia, as our case study of China shows.

Also tied to globalization are what many term "third-generation" environmental problems: these problems are global and therefore require global responses. Air and water pollution have always crossed borders, but this new concern is distinct. The source of the pollution matters little because the effects are truly global. The major example is global climate change. Burning fossil fuels—full of previously trapped carbon—has pumped excess carbon into the atmosphere. Virtually all scientists now agree that this has increased the entire planet's ambient temperature by an estimated 0.7°C (1.3°F) since the dawn of the industrial age in the nineteenth century, and the pace is accelerating. The 2007 *United Nations Human Development Report* (UNHDR) focused on climate change, recommending that the world endeavor to keep the temperature increase in the twenty-first century to no more than 2°C (UNDP 2007, 7). Current projections, if no changes are made, go as high as a 5°C rise (UNDP 2007, 3, 7). This may not sound like much, especially if you live where the winters are long and cold, but it is greater than the change from the last ice age to our present climate. The effects would be catastrophic: rising sea levels would flood coastal areas around the world, and severe drought would afflict many areas, especially in the tropics, which are already relatively poor.

Developing countries have long struggled to achieve sustainable development: economic development that can continue over the long term. Development always involves increased use of resources, but if nonrenewable resources are being used quickly, development won't be sustainable. As demand for food and land increases, for instance, farmers and ranchers clear forested areas throughout the tropics. This gives them nutrient-rich soil on which to grow crops and graze cattle, as well as valuable wood to sell on the global market, but tropical rainforest soils are thin and are quickly depleted when put to agricultural use. After a few years, new land must be cleared as the old is exhausted. The result is rapidly disappearing forests and development that is unsustainable in the long run. Deforestation also increases global warming because trees absorb and retain carbon. Farmers' and ranchers' rational response to growing global demand for agricultural products, then, has created unsustainable development and more global warming. Globalization-induced pollution of air and water and rapid use of nonrenewable resources make the goal of sustainable development ever more challenging for many poor countries.

Risk and Uncertainty

Most analysts agree that environmental damage is an externality that must be addressed, but a vociferous debate thrives on the uncertainty nearly always present in environmental issues. Scientists can rarely tell us exactly what a particular form or amount of pollution will do. As with health problems, the best we can do is predict *likely* outcomes. The top climate scientists in the world won the Nobel Peace Prize for their 2007 Intergovernmental Panel on Climate Change Report, but even their most certain predictions were termed "very likely" (90 percent certainty) or "likely" (66 percent certainty) outcomes of climate change. Similarly, we know that air pollution causes lung cancer, but we can't predict with absolute certainty how many cases it will cause, let alone which individuals will be affected. Environmental policy everywhere has to be based on **risk assessment** and **risk management**. Risk assessment tells us what the risks of damaging outcomes are, and risk management is policy used to keep those risks to acceptable levels. The costs of reducing risks must be weighed against the potential (but always uncertain) benefits.

Much of the debate, of course, is over what level of risk is "acceptable." In recent years, the European Union (EU) and its member states have employed the **precautionary principle**, which emphasizes risk avoidance even when the science predicting the risk is uncertain. This principle lies behind the EU ban on genetically modified organisms (GMOs) in food. With limited scientific evidence on whether GMOs are harmful or benign, the EU errs on the side of caution, banning them until the science is clarified. The United States, especially under the administration of George W. Bush, erred more toward reducing the costs of environmental fixes. For example, the United States currently allows extensive use of GMOs in the absence of greater scientific evidence of harm. This difference became a dispute that the United States took to the World Trade Organization (WTO) for resolution in 2010. The United States argued, and the WTO agreed, that the EU's ban on imports of GMO-based food was against international trade rules. The EU, however, can continue to insist on labeling GMO-based products so consumers can choose to buy them or not, a practice the United States still considers a form of illegitimate discrimination against American agricultural exports.

How do governments respond when they decide that environmental damage is an unacceptable risk? Several approaches exist. The oldest is known as **command and control policies**, which involve direct government regulation. These were the first type of policies most wealthy countries enacted in the 1970s. Based on assessments of health and other risks, a government simply sets a level of pollution no one is allowed to surpass, or requires companies to pay a penalty if they do. Businesses must reduce production or find ways to produce the same goods with less pollution. At least in the short term, this policy is likely to raise production costs partially through internalizing the costs of pollution control. Command and control policies also require governments to set very specific limits on many pollutants from many sources and to inspect possible polluters to ensure they are following the regulations. Both of these tasks are expensive, leading many analysts to argue for what they see as more efficient means of pollution control in the form of incentive systems.

The best-known incentive system is the **cap and trade system**, in which a government sets an overall limit on how much of a pollutant is acceptable from an entire industry and issues vouchers to each company that give it the right to a certain number of units of pollution. The individual companies are then free to trade these vouchers. Companies that face high costs to reduce their pollution levels will be interested in buying additional pollution rights, while those who can more cheaply invest in new and cleaner technology will sell their rights. In theory, pollution is reduced in the most efficient way possible and at the least cost. Government agencies must still determine the overall cap on pollution, but the market allocates that pollution.

Critics point out that cap and trade can result in high levels of pollution at particular sources. If you live downriver from the factory that purchased a large number of pollution rights, your water will be particularly polluted, while the water in other locations gets cleaner. This problem can be corrected by setting a maximum allowable level of pollution rights for any single source, limiting the market in pollution rights to ensure people in particular spots do not pay the costs for the rest of the country's cleaner air and water. Simply taxing pollution directly is another way

risk assessment: Analysis of what the risks of damaging outcomes are in a particular situation

risk management: Policy used to keep risks to acceptable levels

precautionary principle: A policy that emphasizes risk avoidance even when the science predicting a risk is uncertain

command and control policies: Pollution control system in which a government directly regulates the specific amount of pollution each polluting entity is allowed

cap and trade system: Market-based pollution control system in which the government sets an overall limit on how much of a pollutant is acceptable and issues vouchers to pollute to each company, which companies are then free to trade

to provide an incentive to reduce it without dictating specific levels from specific sources. Both cap and trade and taxation systems require the government to set an overall cap or tax at a level that will reduce pollution by the desired amount. While perhaps less complicated than specifying pollution levels from each source, this is still a complex and uncertain task.

Tax or cap and trade systems attempt to set a direct cost on pollution, forcing polluters to internalize an externality. A similar goal is embedded in policies to control use of what otherwise could be free goods, such as public land and the minerals under it, to avoid the tragedy of the commons. User fees on public land exist to limit use of it for ranching and other activities so that the overuse inherent in free public goods does not occur. Similarly, governments can charge for access to minerals, including oil. Given that minerals and fossil fuels are nonrenewable, their depletion contains an intergenerational externality: future generations will pay the price of finding alternatives to the finite resources current generations use. Many economists argue that this justifies government intervention to tax mineral extraction, raising the internal cost of mineral production. In practice, many governments, including the United States, pursue exactly the opposite strategy, subsidizing mineral exploration and development in order to maximize production and lower consumer costs in the present. Cheaper minerals and fuels spur economic growth, which all legitimate states strive to achieve. Oil production, in particular, is also seen as a matter of national security, as each state tries to reduce its dependence on other states for this most crucial of commodities. Subsidizing this activity, however, encourages rather than discourages the tragedy of the commons in nonrenewable resources.

Climate Change The complexity of environmental regulation is magnified at the international level, but the policy options are similar. Global warming became a well-known concern in the 1980s, but the first significant international effort to respond to it was signed at the major international environmental conference in Rio de Janeiro in 1992, and this was only a voluntary agreement for countries to adopt goals of reducing their carbon output. Growing scientific consensus and continued negotiations led to the signing of the Kyoto Protocol in 1997, which included mandated targets for developed countries: they would reduce their carbon emissions by an average of 5 percent below their 1990 levels by 2012. U.S. president Bill Clinton signed the protocol but never submitted it to the Senate for ratification, knowing it would fail. His successor, President George W. Bush, repudiated it entirely.

President Obama reengaged the United States in the international effort to achieve a treaty reducing the "greenhouse gases" that cause global warming. His administration became active in the lead-up to the climate conference in Copenhagen in 2009, which was to produce a new treaty to replace Kyoto. Once again, a treaty that included all countries—including the two biggest producers of greenhouse gases, China and the United States—failed to materialize. In its place, and in part via Obama's personal intervention, a nonbinding accord was produced in which countries pledged to adopt voluntary measures that would keep twenty-first-century warming to no more than the targeted 2°C. In fact, the International Energy Agency examined the promises the individual countries made and concluded that following them would likely produce a temperature rise of 3.5°C; only the most dramatic and least likely policy changes would result in meeting the 2°C target. Following up on Copenhagen, a meeting a year later in Cancún produced a very modest accord in which wealthy countries agreed to fund programs to mitigate the worst effects of climate change in poor countries and to pay poor countries to prevent deforestation, but a comprehensive treaty was once again delayed until "next year."

Much of the controversy over climate change is a battle between developed and developing countries. As Map 11.1 shows, wealthy and a few rapidly industrializing countries account for the vast majority of CO_2 emissions. Wealthy, industrialized countries have been producing significant amounts of greenhouse gases since industrialization began two centuries ago. Because these gases do not dissipate, wealthy countries have produced the vast majority of the total greenhouse gases to date. The United States alone is estimated to account for nearly 30 percent of the total since 1840 (UNDP 2007, 40). The large, rapidly industrializing countries, however, are quickly catching up in terms of their annual output of greenhouse gases; China overtook the United States as the single largest annual contributor in 2007. Still, the developing countries, led by China, argue that the wealthier countries will long remain the main source of the total excess carbon in the atmosphere and can afford the costs of reducing their emissions. Moreover, denying countries now industrializing the right to pollute will doom them to inferior status forever. The wealthy countries remain by far the heaviest emitters of greenhouse gases per capita: China and India produce a lot because they have so many people, but each Chinese or Indian citizen produces a small fraction of what the average American does. The developed countries, especially the United States, argue that mandatory limits must apply to all to be fair and effective. Inarguably, someone must pay the costs of this ultimate externality of industrialization; the political and normative debates are over who it will and should be.

No international consensus exists on exactly which policy mechanisms should be used to reduce greenhouse gases. The United National Development Programme (UNDP) 2007 report on climate change attempted to push the debate forward by suggesting that the world adopt a carbon tax or a cap and trade system to reduce emissions. The EU had already instituted its own cap and trade system, which operates as one market across all EU members, as a means of complying with the Kyoto

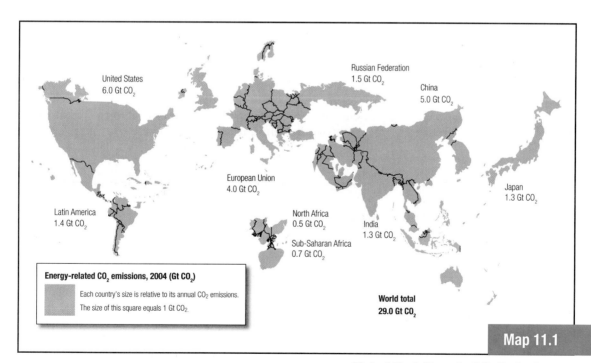

Energy-related CO_2 emissions, 2004 (Gt CO_2)

Each country's size is relative to its annual CO_2 emissions. The size of this square equals 1 Gt CO_2.

United States 6.0 Gt CO_2

Russian Federation 1.5 Gt CO_2

China 5.0 Gt CO_2

European Union 4.0 Gt CO_2

Japan 1.3 Gt CO_2

Latin America 1.4 Gt CO_2

North Africa 0.5 Gt CO_2

India 1.3 Gt CO_2

Sub-Saharan Africa 0.7 Gt CO_2

World total 29.0 Gt CO_2

Map 11.1

Global Variations in CO_2 Emissions

Source: United Nations Human Development Report, 2007/2008.

Protocol. While it has been plagued by controversies, including charges that it was too generous because it ended its initial three-year trial period with surplus emissions rights (that no one needed), it is nonetheless estimated to have reduced emissions at participating facilities (utilities, factories, etc.) by 2 to 5 percent (Ellerman et al. 2010). Kyoto also allows companies and countries to gain emission credits by investing in projects that reduce emissions elsewhere in the world. Because many factories in the developing world use older technology, it's cheaper to reduce emissions in developing areas than in Europe. Given that global climate change is just that—global—it doesn't matter where emissions are reduced. A rapidly growing market has emerged that now includes several thousand emissions reduction projects globally, with over half of them located in China. The EU system has created the beginning of what could become a truly global market for greenhouse gas emissions, if a comprehensive agreement to cap them globally is eventually reached.

In the meantime, however, leaders of Europe's energy intensive industries complain that they cannot compete internationally because they face carbon constraints that their competitors elsewhere, including in the United States and China, do not. Analysts worry that a logical response to this in the longer term will be to move industrial production from countries with carbon limits to countries without limits, which could actually increase overall carbon emissions because the products of those industries would be shipped back to their consumer markets. Without a truly universal system, existing cap and trade systems could make things worse rather than better.

Of the three policy areas we discuss in this chapter, the environment is the easiest area in which to justify government intervention in markets. Environmental damage is clearly an externality that should be internalized for efficient allocation of resources and long-term sustainability. This has become particularly clear and urgent in the face of global climate change, which threatens to wreak havoc on the lives of millions in the relatively near future. A number of clear policy choices exist as well. Their implementation, however, has been limited and slow. Different policies internalize costs in different ways, resulting in different people paying those costs. Both within individual countries and on a global scale, individual polluters and national governments strive to minimize the costs they will have to pay. Our three case studies of three large countries that are crucial to the debate—the United States, China, and Nigeria—illustrate the conflicts well.

CASE STUDY

The United States: Pioneer That Lost Its Way?

- Early policies to protect land and animals
- 1970s pioneer on air, water, endangered species, and ozone
- Reagan era slowdown and reversal
- Opposition to binding treaty on global climate change
- Limited success by Obama despite initiatives on climate change and energy
- Overall success at reducing air and

water pollution, but not on preserving endangered species, reducing energy consumption, and mitigating climate change

April 22, 1970, the first Earth Day, marked the coming of age of the environmental movement in the United States. The now annual event emerged out of the fervor of the 1960s and represented a strikingly broad consensus in the country: environmental problems were important, and the government should do something about them. From 1965 to 1970, the number of people saying the quality of their air and water was a serious issue went from less than a third of the population to nearly three-quarters. In May 1969, only 1 percent of people mentioned pollution as one of the "most important" problems facing the country, but by May 1971 that number had risen to 25 percent (Layzer 2006, 33). A decade of rapid expansion of the government's role in protecting the environment made the United States a pioneer in the field. The decentralized U.S. political system and shifting ideological trends in the country, however, meant that further progress was mixed. Indeed, by the twenty-first century, the United States had become one of the chief obstacles to a comprehensive, binding treaty to reduce the greenhouse gases that cause global warming. The country had gone from environmental policy pioneer to environmental policy problem.

The major U.S. environmental policy that predates 1970 was the protection of public lands for recreational and ecological purposes, from the creation of the national park system in the early 1900s to the preservation of pristine wilderness areas where no development is allowed starting in 1964. Landmark legislation of the early 1970s included the creation of the Environmental Protection Agency (EPA), the Clean Air Act (1970), the Clean Water Act (1972), and the Endangered Species Act (1973). The decade ended with legislation dramatically expanding protected land, with the addition of 102 million acres in Alaska. In one area, this leadership continued in the 1980s, as President Ronald Reagan, generally an opponent of environmental policy, helped champion the Montreal Protocol of 1987, which eliminated the use of ozone-depleting chemicals. It is projected to restore the ozone layer to its pre-1980 level by the middle of the twenty-first century. These were all command and control policies, setting specific regulations for allowable levels of pollution from individual sources and protecting specific species and plots of land. Coming from a broad bipartisan consensus, they

By far the most terrifying film you will ever see.

Former U.S. vice president Al Gore at the 2006 premier of his movie, *An Inconvenient Truth,* in Hong Kong. Gore and the Intergovernmental Panel on Climate Change (IPCC) jointly won the Nobel Peace Prize for their advocacy of solutions to global climate change, including the Kyoto Protocol, which the United States refused to ratify.

Credit: Paul Yeung/Reuters/Landov

established the United States as a pioneer in environmental protection, generally seen as being well ahead of most European countries.

Reagan's election in 1980 began a reversal of this environmental trend. His neoliberal economic ideology led him to argue for a reduced government role in the environment. With environmental protection still relatively popular, he did not try to reverse the legislation of the 1970s; instead, he significantly reduced funding to the EPA and other environmental agencies, and he appointed opponents of government intervention to key environmental posts. These officials rewrote regulations to reduce their impact on business. By mid-decade, Congress began resisting some of these policies. The most significant congressional reversal was the Superfund Act (1986), which required that thousands of toxic waste sites be cleaned up over several decades. A later milestone was a major amendment to the Clean Air Act in 1990, which for the first time included a cap and trade system focused on one particular pollutant: sulfur dioxide, a key ingredient in acid rain. The system has significantly reduced this pollutant nationwide, at an estimated cost of only half what a similar reduction under the older command and control model would have incurred (Freeman 2006, 206).

The 1980s also saw the emergence of a new element in U.S. environmental activism in the form of the **environmental justice movement.** It began in 1982, in Warren County, the poorest county in North Carolina, in which 65 percent of residents were African-American (three times the state average). Buoyed by EPA approval, a waste disposal company proposed locating a toxic waste facility in the county. The residents organized demonstrations, and the environmental justice movement began. Focused on environmental damage in particular locales, members initially argued that poor and, especially, black or Hispanic neighborhoods are much more likely to be sites for polluting industries and toxic waste depositories. The movement has grown significantly since, and it laid out a clear set of principles at a major conference in 1991. While research results depend on how the researchers define "neighborhood" or "community," it seems that across the United States, black and Hispanic citizens are more likely to live in areas where air and water pollution exceed legal limits and where toxic chemicals are produced or stored (Ringquist 2006).

Bill Clinton's election in 1992 with noted environmentalist Al Gore as his vice president gave environmental advocates hope that the policies of the Reagan/Bush years would be reversed. By the end of the decade, however, environmentalists had mixed assessments of the Clinton administration, noting some significant successes but also major failings. A key issue was global warming. Both Republican and Democratic presidents had agreed to voluntary reductions in greenhouse gas emissions, but they continued to resist mandatory targets, including the Kyoto Protocol. President George W. Bush repudiated the treaty entirely and pursued an energy policy that provided greater incentives for fossil fuel exploration and development. The United States is estimated to spend about $100 billion per year—half the world's total—on fossil fuel subsidies, encouraging rapid use and therefore depletion of these nonrenewable resources

and promoting global climate change (Hempel 2006, 305).

Once again, Barack Obama's election as president in 2008 gave environmentalists renewed hope. The new president came to office having pledged to enact fundamentally new energy and climate change policies. Obama committed his administration to full involvement in negotiating a replacement for the failed Kyoto Protocol. The United States was active in negotiations leading to the December 2009 international meeting in Copenhagen, which Obama and others hoped would finally produce a binding climate change agreement. Obama personally helped negotiate the rather weak resolution that emerged from Copenhagen after a binding treaty once again failed to gain support. Domestically, the administration proposed and the House of Representatives passed legislation to create a cap and trade system to reduce greenhouse gases by 17 percent by 2020 and over 80 percent by midcentury, but Republican (and some Democratic) opposition in the Senate blocked the measure. Environmentalists criticized Obama for not pushing harder to get the legislation passed. Congress did pass, with Obama's support, a bill to raise average automobile gas mileage considerably, though the levels projected for 2016 still lie far below China's or Europe's. The failed effort to pass climate change legislation led the administration to pursue EPA regulation of greenhouse gases, which the agency in 2009 ruled substantially harmed health and therefore could be regulated legally under the Clean Air Act. That Act, however, requires reduced emissions only on new and renovated utilities, so the EPA's long-term impact is uncertain, and it faces fierce opposition from Republicans in Congress.

Despite what environmentalists see as setbacks, U.S. policy has produced a much cleaner environment, though not all areas have seen success. The greatest success has been with air pollution. Since the first Earth Day in 1970, production of the six key ingredients of air pollution has dropped by 60 percent in spite of significant population growth and even greater economic growth.

environmental justice movement: A movement focused on exposing and fighting against racial and class inequalities in exposure to pollution, started in the United States in 1982

The only exceptions were a slight increase in nitrous oxide (a secondary ingredient in acid rain) and carbon dioxide, the key greenhouse gas. Acid rain, regulated by a cap and trade system, has dropped substantially as well. Surveys of water quality at the turn of the century indicated that 61 percent of rivers and 55 percent of lakes met acceptable standards for clean water, though destruction of wetlands by development continues at about 58,000 acres per year. By 2004, the Superfund Act had cleaned up, or was in the process of cleaning up, 61 percent of the "National Priorities" list of toxic waste sites (Kraft and Vig 2006, 21–24; Yarett 2010). On the other hand, the number of species on the endangered list has quadrupled, energy use per person has not changed and is much higher than that in most other wealthy countries, and the average amount of garbage per person has increased 38 percent despite a quintupling of recycling.

CASE SUMMARY

Environmental policy success in the United States seems to require a broad popular consensus. The American political system provides numerous opportunities for interest groups to influence policymaking. The nature of Congress, especially the Senate, makes it particularly easy for groups to get legislation vetoed. Rational-choice scholars have noted that environmental legislation often provides diffuse benefits to many people and high costs for a few (typically businesses), and the latter are often able and highly motivated to block such legislation. Environmental legislation succeeds only at times of generally high concern among the broader public, which leads legislators to override the veto efforts of a few key players. As a result, U.S. policy has a stop-and-go character, with occasional great advances followed by periods of reversal or stagnation. Some legislation, such as fossil fuels subsidies, works in reverse: it provides huge benefits to particular actors and diffuse costs (via taxes to pay the subsidies) to the general population. These types of policies have endured in the U.S. system despite what most economists see as their clear encouragement of externalities and therefore inefficiency and environmental damage. The U.S. political system produced both the pioneering legislation of a generation ago and the limits on action more recently, especially regarding global climate change.

CASE STUDY

China: Searching for Sustainable Development

- Rapid economic growth produces massive environmental problems
- Increased emphasis on environmental policy since 2002
- Incentives for local governments to prioritize economic growth over environmental protection
- Environmental NGOs increasingly pressure government
- Major pledges to reduce greenhouse gases but resistance to binding international accords

As the 2008 Summer Olympics approached, commentators around the world began to question whether Beijing could really host the games adequately, not because of a lack of infrastructure or resources but because of the quality of the air the athletes would be breathing. Global concern was certainly not misplaced. In 2007, China was home to sixteen of the twenty most polluted cities in the world. Even after the government instituted a policy to remove half of Beijing's 3.3 million vehicles from highways, banned 300,000 aging vehicles found to be especially heavy

A long-distance race participant wears a mask to protect himself from the smog as he runs past the new National Stadium built for the 2008 Summer Olympics in Beijing. China's rapid industrialization has produced dramatic environmental problems, including several of the most polluted cities in the world. Chinese authorities took numerous measures, such as banning some vehicles and shutting down factories, to clean the air for the Olympics.

Credit: Guang Niu/Getty Images

polluters, encouraged commuters to return to using the bicycles once so ubiquitous across the country, opened three new subway lines, and set up numerous new bus lines, some athletes still bowed out of competition in China, citing fears of asthma attacks and physical stress (Associated Press 2008a, 2008b).

Since 2002, however, the "fourth generation" of Chinese leadership has made a significant commitment to environmental protection, exemplified by the 2008 elevation of the main environmental protection agency to a full cabinet ministry and the adoption of the eleventh Five-Year Plan for Environmental Protection, which, among other things, doubled funding for the environment. The Chinese government has passed an impressive array of environmental laws and signed numerous international environmental treaties, but protecting the environment still is in conflict with the country's rapid economic growth, and the laws are weakly enforced at the local level.

China's environmental degradation and problems are breathtaking, no pun intended. Besides urban air pollution, 30 percent of the nation's water is unfit for human or agricultural use, almost 90 percent of the country's grasslands and forests are suffering degradation, and the Yellow River now dries up before it reaches the ocean, becoming an open sewer (Morton 2006, 64–65; Ho and Vermeer 2006). Severe soil erosion and desertification have doubled since the 1970s and are degrading an area the size of New Jersey each year (Economy 2010, 66). Sandstorms from the deserts have become common in Beijing, with a particularly severe one in 2006 dumping 400,000 tons of sand on the city and much more around the world. The result of all of this is skyrocketing health problems: air pollution is estimated to cause 400,000 deaths per year, and cancer rates increased by 30 percent over the past 30 years. To meet its soaring energy needs, the government is building the infamous Three Gorges Dam on the Yangtze River, the largest project of its kind in human history. While it will reduce China's dependence on coal for electricity, helping to clean the air, the dam forcibly displaced 1.27 million people, and the reservoir it has created has inundated both agricultural and pristine forest land.

The communist government under Mao put little priority on environmental concerns. Marxist ideology favored production over all else, and the country's rigid communist political system allowed no environmental movement to emerge as it did in other countries in the 1960s and 1970s. Environmental issues were included explicitly in the earliest legal reforms that were part of Deng Xiaoping's opening of the Chinese economic system in 1979, when the government amended the constitution to include environmental protection as one of its explicit duties. A number of laws specifying protections of and standards for such things as air and water quality were enacted over the 1980s and 1990s. This culminated in 2008 when the State Environmental Protection Agency (SEPA) was raised to ministerial rank and renamed the Ministry of Environment Protection (MEP).

The MEP is the key agency governing environmental protection in China, and while it has had energetic leaders and been a bureaucratic advocate for the environment, it has had limited ability to enforce China's environmental laws. It is dependent on Environmental Protection Bureaus (EPBs) controlled by local governments for most of its funding and staff. Local government leaders are rewarded in China's system primarily for their ability to further rapid economic growth, so they have had virtually no incentive to slow growth in favor of protecting the environment. Consequently, most have not taken MEP concerns seriously, and many divert much of the funding for environmental efforts to corrupt purposes or simply to other governmental tasks they consider more important. Consequently, the effectiveness of environmental policies varies greatly. In some major cities, such as Shanghai and Guangzhou, leaders have become more committed to environmental concerns, in part due to pressure by strong environmental NGOs (see below) and because they have the resources to fund better policies. Shanghai, for instance, has committed 3 percent of its GDP to environmental protection, more than double the national average (Chan, Lee, and Chan 2008, 297; Economy 2010, 123). Even the doubling of China's national environmental budget falls well below the 2 percent of GDP that most scholars see as essential for it to reverse its most severe environmental problems (Wu 2009). While the greater emphasis on and funding for the environment since 2008 seems promising, it has not been accompanied by greater central authority for the MEP or necessary changes to local officials' incentives, though the 2011–2015 economic plan might finally change that.

Most early environmental policies were command and control, though in the last decade SEPA/MEP has begun to experiment with market-based policies as well. The two major command and control policies have long been fining excessive polluting from individual sources, such as factories, and requiring environmental impact assessments (EIAs) for new industrial projects. The fines, however, are quite small, so even when the laws are enforced, many firms find it cost-effective to pay the fines and keep polluting. The local EPBs often collude in this because they gain their revenue from the fines, so

if they really succeeded at reducing pollution, their revenue would decline. In this context, the EIAs had little effect for many years, though recent trends suggest that may be changing. From 1995 to 2005, SEPA approved all but two new industrial projects. In 2005 it began a highly publicized process of rejecting greater numbers of projects and insisting that all relevant projects actually produce an EIA prior to approval. In what came to be known as "environmental storms," SEPA suspended 30 projects in early 2005, and by August 2008 it had rejected over 400 more. The global recession, though, seems to have partially reversed this. To expedite construction projects that were part of the government's successful economic stimulus plan, the MEP created a "green passage" policy that gave quick approval to 150 major projects; provincial authorities radically reduced the time they took to approve EIAs as well (Johnson 2008, 97–99; Wu 2009, 280; Economy 2010, 78).

An initial market-based experiment was SEPA's 2006 introduction of the concept of a "green GDP" in several major cities, in which an estimate for the cost of environmental damage is subtracted from the cities' annual GDP increase. The intent was to introduce a measure by which local government officials could be held accountable: the central government could use this measure, instead of simple GDP growth, as the chief means of evaluating local officials' performance. The data showed that environmental damage cost 3 percent of the cities' total GDP, though many were skeptical of these results; earlier, the World Bank had estimated pollution costs at 8 to 12 percent of GDP. SEPA initially announced that it would expand this green GDP to the entire country the following year, but local governments successfully resisted the plan, and there has been no follow-through on the experiment (Johnson 2008, 95–97). SEPA has also experimented with some taxes, such as the "chopsticks tax" on wood products to slow deforestation and taxes on yachts and luxury cars that consume a lot of fuel. Most of its efforts, however, remain command and control, and given that the MEP is charged with monitoring the pollution level of 300,000 factories and other pollution sources, and has only a few hundred employees directly working for it, it faces a daunting task.

Concern about the environment among Chinese citizens was evident as far back as the 1970s, but it has taken an organized form only since the mid-1990s, as the government has allowed some NGOs to function. The first two environmental NGOs were created in 1994 and 1996, and by 2008 more than 3,500 were officially registered with the government. Most are urban based, and as many as half are student organizations. This trend is reflected in local protests as well: in 2005 there were 51,000 environmental protests across the country, an increase of 30 percent over the previous year. The government often tolerates environmental NGOs and local-level protests, because top officials see them as pushing recalcitrant local officials to enforce environmental policies better while doing little harm on the national level. Indeed, the government has started its own environmental government-organized nongovernmental organizations (GONGOs) as well. If NGOs criticize the broader policies too severely, though, the government is certainly willing to crack down, including by jailing leaders and trying them for crimes against the state. In May 2007, students used cellular phones to mobilize between 7,000 and 20,000 people to protest construction of a petrochemical plant. The authorities stopped the construction but also attempted to publicly discredit the organizers of the protest, which seems to have been larger than they were willing to accommodate (Chan, Lee, and Chan 2008).

Internationally, China is best known for its successful opposition to any mandatory limits on production of greenhouse gases for developing countries. It has ratified the great bulk of international treaties but jealously guards its sovereignty, implementing only those with which it agrees. Despite being one of the main obstacles to a binding agreement at the Copenhagen negotiations on climate change, the Chinese government committed itself to cut its carbon intensity—carbon dioxide emissions per unit of GDP—by 40 to 45 percent by 2020. As part of this effort, it

has achieved greater energy efficiency over the past several years. Its automobile gas mileage standards already surpass those of the United States, and it has pledged to adopt standards that will surpass European ones by 2015. It nearly met the goal of a 20 percent reduction in energy intensity set in the five-year plan that ended in 2011. The MEP's final report on that plan also noted that it had reduced pollutants in surface water by 32 percent and sulfur dioxide emissions by 19 percent. It nonetheless called the overall environmental situation "very grave" (Johnson 2011). The new plan for 2011–2015 sets a goal of reducing carbon intensity by 17 percent, which puts China on pace to achieve its Copenhagen goals (though on the low end). Part of this is to be achieved by reducing economic growth from what has typically been around 10 percent per year to 7 percent per year. Analysts hope that this reduced growth target will give local officials incentives to act more favorably toward environmental concerns. The country has also become an active participant in the global carbon market, becoming the biggest seller of carbon credits to the rest of the world (India is second). In the meantime, China's environmental problems impact other countries as well. Its pollution has had major effects in neighboring countries, including Myanmar and North and South Korea, and lesser effects as far away as California.

CASE SUMMARY

China's rapid industrialization and massive size have made it one of the largest polluters in the world, though on a per capita basis it remains a modest one. After decades of nearly complete neglect of environmental protection, the fourth generation of leadership has significantly raised the official emphasis on doing better. Its efforts are supported by a rapidly growing network of local and national environmental groups, but while progress has clearly been made, the fundamental conflict between rapid economic growth and environmental protection remains unresolved. The MEP has become stronger but is still relatively weak vis-à-vis essential local governments. Fundamental changes of direction, such as the idea of the green GDP or changing key performance incentives for local officials, continue to be resisted. As the largest producer of greenhouse gases and with a rapidly growing economy, China's environmental policies have become crucial not only to its own well-being but to that of the planet as a whole.

CASE STUDY

Nigeria and Oil: A Question of Environmental Justice and Sustainable Development

- Massive oil production externalities in the form of pollution
- Question of environmental justice: local population pays the costs and receives few benefits
- Peaceful and violent reactions threaten oil production at times
- Weak state, revenue-sharing in federal system, and corruption are key problems
- Recent possible improvements under democratic government

Flaring gas is much more common in Nigeria's oil fields than in most oil facilities around the world. This is just one of many environmental problems caused by oil production in the Niger Delta in southeastern Nigeria.

Credit: Chris Hondros/Getty Images

The Niger Delta in southeastern Nigeria is the world's third largest wetland and its largest freshwater mangrove swamp. It is also a major oil-producing region, supplying 40 percent of U.S. oil imports. Demand for fuel wood and extensive desertification in the north, mainly caused by deforestation of nearly one million acres per year, are among the numerous environmental concerns Nigeria faces, but the best known issue, and one with global implications, is the impact of oil production. Oil production not only causes serious environmental damage to a fragile ecosystem but has also generated local responses, including the rise of ethnic militias and the kidnapping of Western oil workers. Inhabitants of the region receive very few benefits from the oil drawn from their homeland but pay most of the environmental costs. Their protests raise profound questions about environmental justice and sustainable development, both locally and globally, in the context of a weak state with little effective environmental policy.

A 2006 UN development report clearly catalogs oil's negative environmental impact in Nigeria (UNDP 2006). The region is dotted with nearly 1,500 oil wells, about 4,000 miles of oil pipelines, and 4 refineries. To ease transportation through the large wetlands, oil companies have dredged numerous canals, depositing dredge material on the banks. Both the oil wells and the canals have severely hurt the local fishing industry by disrupting the fragile freshwater ecology, in some cases allowing saltwater to enter. With most of the pipelines above ground, oil spills are more common than in most oil-producing areas; nearly 7,000 occurred between 1976 and 2001, though the annual rate of spillage dropped slightly from 2001 to 2004. Still, estimates suggest as much oil is spilled annually in Nigeria as was spilled by the disastrous Exxon *Valdez* oil spill in Alaska in 1989. A May 2010 spill spewed out a million gallons in a week before ExxonMobil stopped it. Spills are caused not only by human and equipment failures but also by sabotage. The desperately poor people of the region frequently break into the pipelines to gain access, in particular, to refined gasoline to sell on Nigeria's active black market. Between 10 and 15 percent of daily production is lost to illegal "bunkering," the stealing of oil and gas.

Gas flaring is an element of oil production everywhere, but Nigeria is second only to Russia in the amount of gas flared annually, even though the practice has been illegal there since 1984. Natural gas is found wherever oil is, but given the expense and difficulty of storing and transporting it, if it cannot be piped to consumers immediately, it is often burnt off at the well. The poverty in West Africa means there are few paying customers for natural gas, so an estimated 75 percent of Nigeria's gas is flared, costing the country $2.5 billion annually in potential lost revenue. Gas flaring causes significant air pollution, which surpasses national and international standards in the region in spite of its poverty and lack of industry. Acid rain is also a problem. Given its poverty, Nigeria produces relatively little greenhouse gas, but gas flaring from oil wells represents a major component of Nigeria's greenhouse contribution.

The environmental damage caused by oil production in the Niger Delta is a massive set of external costs not factored into the price of the Nigerian oil purchased on the global market. In the absence of effective environmental policies either to control the pollution or internalize its cost, local people pay the price. Nigeria's exceptionally weak and corrupt state, unfortunately, has virtually no environmental policy. An excerpt from the 2006 UNDP report sums up the situation well:

The oil companies, particularly Shell Petroleum, have operated for over 30 years without appreciable control or environmental regulation to guide their activities. The Federal Environmental Protection Agency did not come into being until 1988, and all the environmental quality standards on emissions and effluent discharge, and the laws requiring an environmental impact assessment for every major project, did not come into effect until the early 1990s. By that time, the Niger Delta environment had suffered much damage at the hands of the oil companies. Even now, it is doubtful whether the Government's environmental monitoring agencies can adequately control the activities of the oil companies. (81)

Even with new environmental laws in place since the 1990s, Nigeria's corruption-riddled government rarely enforces them effectively—or wants to. Oil companies, for instance, are supposed to compensate individuals harmed by oil spills, and an elaborate set of compensation benefits exists in law. In practice, local people often receive less than they are due, and redressing the problem requires going to court, something impoverished local people do not have the resources to do (Ikporukpo 2004). Shell, the largest producer in Nigeria, established a "corporate social responsibility" program in 1997 through which it provides local benefits such as new schools and funding for health programs. None of this, however, reverses or even ameliorates the environmental damages oil production causes.

Niger Delta inhabitants do not believe they are benefiting as much as they should from oil wealth. As Nigerian scholar Chris Ikporukpo (2004) pointed out, they have raised a question of environmental justice: most of the benefits of oil go to global oil consumers and recipients of government revenues elsewhere in Nigeria, while Delta inhabitants absorb the environmental costs. In Nigeria's ethnically divided political system, the sense of injustice aligns with ethnic divisions. Local leaders have mobilized people in opposition to the oil companies and the central government by arguing that their ethnic group has been discriminated against. The most famous example is the Movement for the Survival of the Ogoni People (MOSOP) led by the poet Ken Saro-Wiwa. MOSOP published an Ogoni Bill of Rights in 1990, claiming that $30 billion of oil wealth had been pumped out of Ogoni land and that the Ogoni had received virtually nothing in return, had no representation in the federal government, and had been left with land that had become an "ecological disaster." The military government in the 1990s responded brutally to this effort, ultimately hanging Saro-Wiwa and eight other Ogoni leaders in 1995 to international condemnation.

Since the destruction of the mostly peaceful MOSOP, numerous violent movements have arisen. They have initiated armed attacks on oil company workers, oil installations, and government soldiers. This has included kidnapping and holding for ransom Western oil company employees, as many as 200 in 2007. Sabotage of oil installations and safety concerns for workers have at times lowered Nigerian production, with a noticeable impact on world prices. Ethnic militias have also turned on each other, fighting for control of land that may contain oil or might generate compensation claims for oil spills. With the return to multiparty elections in 1999, local politicians unaffiliated with the ethnic movements have hired and used members of some of the militias for their own partisan purposes, harassing and intimidating political opponents during campaigns. After the elections, they often end their patronage of the militia groups, leaving the latter to hire themselves out to the next bidder. In a weak state that cannot provide a strong sense of security, such militias for hire often arise, whatever their original purpose might have been. Shell has hired militants in recent years to act as its security force to protect oil installations. This

has neutralized some of the violence against Shell but has provided income to militants, who use it partly to buy more weapons and terrorize the local population.

The federal government has repeatedly used military force, both under the military government and the democratic regime since 1999, to oppose the ethnic militias. As the conflict simply grew in response, President Yar'Adua in 2008 appointed a commission to examine policy options. It recommended and the government agreed in 2009 to an amnesty for all Delta militants. This substantially reduced violence in the region, though not completely. Indeed, in 2010, the main violent group, the Movement for the Emancipation of the Niger Delta (MEND), struck outside the Delta itself for the first time, setting off bombs in the capital, Abuja, that killed a dozen people at the celebrations of the fiftieth anniversary of Nigeria's independence. The amnesty has improved the situation, but the grievances and at least some violence remain.

The grievances of the local inhabitants focus on not only environmental problems directly but also on the disbursement of oil revenues the government collects. In all federal systems, tensions arise over what share of revenue from natural resources each level of government should receive. Nigerian law originally gave only about half of all oil revenue to the federal government, but when world prices rose dramatically in the early 1970s, the military government declared all natural resource wealth to be the property of the central government and increased its share of the revenue generated from it. By the 1990s, states in the Niger Delta received only 3 percent of total revenue. The new democratic constitution improved this significantly, guaranteeing states 13 percent of oil revenue, a position they have maintained since, though many local leaders call for at least 25 percent. Even with the rise in funds to states, the local population often does not see much benefit. Corrupt state officials steal much of the revenue before it reaches the citizens.

Over a period of many years, the federal government has created various development agencies that it claims are meant to meet the development needs of people in the Delta. Under the military governments, these were fraught with corruption and led by people from outside the region. The last of them, the Oil Mineral Producing Areas Development Commission (OMPADEC), was established in 1992. It received a total of $135 million in oil revenue to repair environmental problems and enhance development in oil-producing regions. When the democratic government came to power in 1999, it disbanded OMPADEC after discovering that the agency had given construction contracts to numerous firms that had stolen the money, that the organization was deeply in debt, and that it had completed virtually no actual work (Ikporukpo 2004, 335–37). The new government replaced OMPADEC with the Niger Delta Development Commission (NDDC). After several years, NDDC appears to have made some progress. It has partnered with the main Nigerian antipoverty organization to train Delta youths with job skills and in 2008 was under new management about which observers felt hopeful, though formal results are still uncertain. The Nigerian press has also accused it of some corruption, and its failure to follow through on a major road-building project in the region led a government ministry to take it over directly.

CASE SUMMARY

Nigeria and its oil are a case of severe environmental problems in the context of a weak state that cannot or will not intervene. Local people, mostly impoverished, absorb the bulk of the externalities of oil production, even as the benefits go to others in Nigeria who make use of oil revenue in the form of government services, corruption, and new roadways and who export the oil to consumers worldwide. The political response has been, in a sense, an environmental justice movement with motivations similar to those in the United States. In Nigeria, however, the movement has faced a weak and, until recently, military state, and as a result it has taken an ethnic and sometimes violent form. The return of democracy did not fundamentally change the situation for another decade. It improved revenue sharing in Nigeria's federal system, but that revenue still has not reached many of the people who actually pay the cost of oil production, and until 2009, the main response to the violence was ineffective government military campaigns. The 2009 amnesty and what observers hope will be better development efforts in the region portend possible improvements, though that outcome is far from certain. The Nigerian case demonstrates some of the worst possibilities of environmental externalities in the absence of effective state intervention.

Summary

Pollution is a classic example of market failure, and it has now gone global. In an attempt to internalize the external costs of pollution, governments initially intervened by imposing specific limits on pollution to create cleaner air, water, and land. More recently, market-based policies have emerged that promise to achieve similar results at lower costs. With intervention, the costs of various production processes shift, with some people bearing those costs and others benefiting, which leads to major political battles in every country. Climate change is only the latest, and biggest, of these environmental battles. It has the added problem, and perhaps potential benefit, of being truly global, requiring a global solution that has little to do with locale. But it raises the same question as all environmental issues: Who will pay the costs of internalizing major externalities?

CONCLUSION

This chapter has examined three areas in which most states choose to intervene in markets: social welfare, health care, and the environment. The common element across all three is an economic and political justification based on market failures. Examining the policy similarities and differences across the three issue areas and across our case studies can tell us much about who rules, why some common trends appear, and what explains the variations.

Who Rules?

The outcomes of policy battles can tell us much about "Who rules?" Policy outcomes reflect the relative strength of various groups in a given political system. More extensive welfare states, especially prior to the 1990s in Europe, clearly reflect the greater power of workers and unions in those countries, in contrast to the United States. European countries for the most part have at least slightly reduced welfare benefits in recent decades, though, suggesting that power is declining relative to other forces, domestic and international. Less interventionist social welfare, health, and environmental policies in the United States suggest that business interests, who usually oppose intervention in all three areas, are stronger there. In poorer countries, the poor who would benefit most from social welfare and health care interventions seem to lack significant power, as those countries pursue few such policies, either because the governments are not interested or because they lack the resources. Either of these causes demonstrates the relative powerlessness of the world's poorest people. Innovative Brazilian social policies, though, suggest that in a democratic setting, it is possible for the poor to overcome these problems at least partially and gain greater benefits.

Environmental policies, which usually involve exceptionally clear costs and benefits for various groups, perhaps demonstrate relative power most clearly. Self-interested actors, whoever they are, are likely to resist paying the costs of environmental improvement, at least until a broader consensus emerges that change is essential for all to survive. Regarding most environmental issues, including especially climate change, the least powerful player in the game is probably future generations, who lack any political clout now. They may well end up paying the greatest costs for internalizing externalities in the long run.

What Explains Political Behavior?

State intervention in each of the three policy areas has its own rationale, but in all three, market failure of some sort offers a reason for the state to modify pure market outcomes. States don't seem to intervene just on the economic basis of recognition of market failures, however. Market failures, such as the externalities associated with pollution, long predate state intervention. Normative and political motivations also need to be present for a state to implement new policies in these areas. For instance, the Great Depression in the United States helped bring the value of reducing poverty to the fore and led to the birth of the welfare state, while in Britain it was the post–World War II consensus on rebuilding a new and more equitable society that produced social and health policy. Similarly, wealthy industrial countries have led the way in environmental intervention, reflecting a classic postmaterialist value. Middle-income and rapidly industrializing countries may be attempting to join the bandwagon, but in the very poorest countries, it is difficult to argue convincingly that resources are something to be conserved rather than depleted to meet immediate human needs.

Forces that counter the market are necessary because market participants who are gaining income and wealth will usually oppose intervention proposals, which threaten their market position. Markets create what can be powerful veto players, which can only be overcome via collective action and/or consensus on the part of broader and usually more diffuse actors who believe they will benefit from intervention. Globalization, too, has had an impact on policies in all countries. If hyper-globalization theorists are correct, then wealthy states will converge toward more market-based policies, and poorer countries, rather than choosing among models, will be forced to do the same. We can't know yet whether this will happen fully. For now, our cases show a persistence of diverse models but a trend toward at least limited reform in the direction of a more liberal welfare state. Across all three types of welfare states, workers and the poor have seen social policy benefits reduced, work requirements and limits on access to social assistance increased, and their contributions to social insurance systems also increased.

Reform in health policy seems to be more difficult. Not only globalization but also simply increasing wealth and an aging population have put pressure on health policy that makes reform both more urgent and more difficult. While significant changes occurred after about 2005 in our case study countries, they do not represent wholesale shifts from the long-standing systems in each country. Health care systems create their own institutionalized interests that resist change, from medical practitioners' support of the NHS in the United Kingdom and NHI in Germany to the American insurance industry's successful resistance to changes that threaten its market position. Health care, perhaps because it affects everyone, including relatively wealthy and powerful players, seems particularly difficult to reform.

Where and Why?

In general, wealth seems to raise the prospect that countries can and will act effectively on value consensus in these three policy areas. Wealth alone does not explain, however, the significant variation among wealthy countries. Social and institutional structures provide important clues to timing and implementation of policies. For example, many European countries concerned about gaining the support of workers implemented welfare policies in advance of the United States and United Kingdom, where labor was not as well organized. Parliamentary democracies also seem to be able to implement policies in a more holistic and cohesive fashion than the divided powers and many veto points allowed in, for example, the United States. This cuts both ways, of course: the United Kingdom's parliamentary democracy has not only created major interventionist policies like the NHS but also made some of the most dramatic reforms of both welfare and health policies, most recently the 2010 and 2011 proposals of PM David Cameron. As Huber and Stephens (2001) demonstrated, variations in the types of welfare state and reform of them seem to be explained most successfully by a combination of considering who are the relatively powerful groups in each society and what are the political institutions within which they must act. Huber and Stephens explained why, for instance, Sweden developed such a more extensive welfare state than did the United States, as well as the degree to which each has been subject to reform.

Judging which set of policies is most "successful" in each of the three issue areas must in part be based on normative values, especially in social policy. If reducing poverty is the key goal, social democratic welfare states seem to be best; if ensuring people are employed is most important, though, a liberal welfare state may seem to be better. In health policy, what is "best" may be a little clearer. If the key criterion is gaining the most health at the least cost, it seems clear that market-based systems fare poorly, and well-established economic arguments explain why. Judging which is better between the NHS and NHI models, however, depends more on values. The NHS seems to be able to keep costs lower, but the NHI provides better services and choice. Judging environmental policy success also depends on values: How much do we value clean air and water? How much do we value the well-being of future generations versus that of ourselves right now? In terms of economic theory, environmental policy seems the easiest area in which to justify government intervention, but how much and how it should be done depend very much on larger value questions, including about who should pay how much of the costs and when.

Often, poorer countries simply lack the resources to intervene effectively in any of these areas. They face quite a different set of problems: rather than creating mechanisms for appropriate distribution, they may first need to find the resources (doctors, clinics, clean water) before they can worry about equitable distribution. Similarly, they wish to develop largely along the lines of the already wealthy countries, and doing so has in the past required sacrificing the environment in the short term. If wealthy countries were able to damage the environment, including by emitting greenhouse gases, and reap the benefits, why, they ask, should they be denied?

When resources and social consensus permit, poorer countries may look at the wealthier countries to see whether there are practical models to be followed. Would they be better off with command and control or cap and trade policies? NHI or NHS? As more countries develop policies in these areas, they will no doubt examine the effectiveness of earlier models and ask whether their own social and institutional conditions would allow them to replicate these policies. Most policy instruments, such as social insurance, command and control, or cap and trade, can in theory be used by anyone, but a country's particular institutional structure and the relationship between the state and important social groups may make it more feasible to adopt and implement a particular set of policies. While models may be replicated, they cannot be lifted wholesale from one country and dropped in another. Wealth levels, political institutions, and cultural values all play important roles in determining if a particular model can be used elsewhere.

Finally, truly global health and environmental problems, especially, may require new types of global policy solutions. States may increasingly have to interact with one another to hammer out effective and feasible policy solutions to problems, implementing these solutions across borders. The normative, political, and economic issues associated with working out such new global policies will be significant, as the example of climate change suggests, but global problems will increasingly demand states' attention in the twenty-first century.

Applying Theory to Public Policy

Many major political science theories have helped us analyze and understand social, health, and environmental policy. The most widespread explanation of why some governments intervene more extensively than others is implicitly pluralist: in some countries, poorer groups have organized better and have more power, and policy reflects this. On the other hand, elite theorists might argue that the effects of globalization show that the elite are likely to reverse these gains in the long run. Institutional theories are prominent in explaining variations in where and why certain policies emerge. Institutional histories, perhaps tied to cultural values as well, help us understand why more interventionist welfare states exist in some places and not in others. Institutions also create veto players that can be particularly powerful at blocking policy change, toward either more or less intervention. Germany's federal system and less centralized parliament, for instance, seems to make policy change there more incremental than in the more centralized United Kingdom, where policy changes have been dramatic at times.

Political ideology can matter as well, as it can achieve a consensus in favor of certain policies that, if strong enough, can overcome powerful veto players. Rational-choice theory is probably clearest in environmental policy, where costs and benefits are most clearly distributed across players in the process, who in turn respond rationally to defend their interests. Where some of them can constitute themselves as powerful veto players, they can hamstring environmental policies that the scientific community argues would be beneficial in the long run and that even significant segments of the public may support. Many observers see this to be the case regarding climate change policy within most countries as well as on a global scale.

KEY CONCEPTS

cap and trade system (p. 583)
Christian democratic welfare states (p. 547)
command and control policies (p. 583)
conditional cash transfer (CCT) (p. 553)
environmental justice movement (p. 588)
liberal welfare states (p. 550)

market-based private insurance system (p. 566)
means-tested public assistance (p. 544)
moral hazard (p. 564)
national health insurance (NHI) (p. 565)
national health system (NHS) (p. 565)
precautionary principle (p. 583)
risk assessment (p. 583)

risk management (p. 583)
single-payer system (p. 565)
social democratic welfare states (p. 545)
social insurance (p. 544)
social policy (p. 542)
tax expenditures (p. 544)
tragedy of the commons (p. 581)
universal entitlements (p. 543)
welfare states (p. 545)

WORKS CITED

Adolino, Jessica R., and Charles H. Blake. 2001. *Comparing Public Policies: Issues and Choices in Six Industrialized Countries.* Washington, DC: CQ Press.

Alber, Jens, and Neil Gilbert, eds. 2010. *United in Diversity? Comparing Social Models in Europe and America.* Oxford, UK: Oxford University Press.

Alesina, Alberto, and Edward L. Glaeser. 2004. *Fighting Poverty in the US and Europe: A World of Difference.* Oxford, UK: Oxford University Press.

Associated Press. 2008a. "Beijing to Take Half of All Government Cars off the Road." *USA*

Today, June 23. http://www.usatoday.com/news/world/environment/2008-06-23-china-cars_N.htm.

Associated Press. 2008b. "Beijing Traffic Cut to Help Clear Air for Olympics." *CNN/IBNLive.com,* July 21. http://ibnlive.in.com/news/beijing-traffic-cut-to-help-clear-air-for-olympics/69238-2.html.

Baer, Werner. 2008. *The Brazilian Economy: Growth and Development.* 6th ed. Boulder, CO: Lynne Rienner.

Bonoli, Giuliano, Vic George, and Peter Taylor-Gooby. 2000. *European Welfare Futures: Towards a Theory of Retrenchment.* Cambridge, UK, and Malden, MA: Polity Press and Blackwell.

Cammisa, Anne Marie. 1998. *From Rhetoric to Reform? Welfare Policy in American Politics.* Boulder, CO: Westview Press.

CBO (Congressional Budget Office). 2007. *The State Children's Health Insurance Program.* Washington, DC: Government Printing Office.

Chan, Gerald, Pak K. Lee, and Lai-Ha Chan. 2008. "China's Environmental Governance: The Domestic-International Nexus." *Third World Quarterly* 29 (2): 291–314. doi:10.1080/01436590701806863.

Commonwealth Fund. 2008. Commonwealth Fund International Health Policy Survey of Sicker Adults. http://www.commonwealthfund.org/Content/Surveys/2008/2008-Commonwealth-Fund-International-Health-Policy-Survey-of-Sicker-Adults.aspx.

Díaz-Cayeros, Alberto, and Beatriz Magaloni. 2009. "Aiding Latin America's Poor." *Journal of Democracy* 20 (4): 36–49.

The Economist. "Dr. Rösler's Difficult Prescription: The Hard Case of Reforming German Health Care." April 29, 2010. http://www.economist.com/node/16015443?story_id=16015443.

Economy, Elizabeth C. 2010. *The River Runs Black: The Environmental Challenge to China's Future.* 2nd ed. Ithaca, NY: Cornell University Press.

Ellerman, A. Denny, Frank J. Convery, and Christian de Perthius. 2010. *Pricing Carbon: The European Union Emissions Trading Scheme.* Cambridge, UK: Cambridge University Press.

Esping-Andersen, Gøsta. 1990. *The Three Worlds of Welfare Capitalism.* Princeton, NJ: Princeton University Press.

Feder, Judith, and Donald W. Moran. 2007. "Cost Containment and the Politics of Health Care Reform." In *Restoring Fiscal Sanity 2007: The Health Spending Challenge,* edited by Alice M. Rivlin and Joseph R. Antos. Washington, DC: Brookings Institution Press.

Freeman, A. Myrick, III. 2006. "Economics, Incentives, and Environmental Policy." In *Environmental Policy: New Directions for the Twenty-First*

Century, 6th ed., edited by Norman J. Vig and Michael E. Kraft, 193–214. Washington, DC: CQ Press.

Garfinkel, Irwin, Lee Rainwater, and Timothy Smeeding. 2010. *Wealth and Welfare States: Is America a Laggard or Leader?* Oxford, UK: Oxford University Press.

Gerlinger, Thomas. 2010. "Health Care Reform in Germany." *German Policy Studies/Politikfeldanalyse* 6 (1): 107–42.

Graig, Laurene A. 1999. *Health of Nations: An International Perspective on U.S. Health Care Reform.* 3rd ed. Washington, DC: CQ Press.

Green, David G., and Benedict Irvine. 2001. *Health Care in France and Germany: Lessons for the UK.* London: Institute for the Study of Civil Society.

Grogger, Jeffrey, and Lynn A. Karoly. 2005. *Welfare Reform: Effects of a Decade of Change.* Cambridge, MA: Harvard University Press.

Hall, Anthony. 2006. "From Fome Zero to Bolsa Família: Social Policies and Poverty Alleviation under Lula." *Journal of Latin American Studies* 38 (4): 689–709.

Häusermann, Silja. 2010. *The Politics of Welfare State Reform in Continental Europe. Modernization in Hard Times.* Cambridge, UK: Cambridge University Press.

Heclo, Hugh. 1974. *Modern Social Politics in Britain and Sweden: From Relief to Income Maintenance.* New Haven, CT: Yale University Press.

Hempel, Lamont C. 2006. "Climate Policy on the Installment Plan." In *Environmental Policy: New Directions for the Twenty-First Century,* 6th ed., edited by Norman J. Vig and Michael E. Kraft, 288–331. Washington, DC: CQ Press.

Ho, Peter, and Eduard B. Vermeer. 2006. "China's Limits to Growth? The Difference Between Absolute, Relative, and Precautionary Limits." *Development and Change* 37 (1): 255–71. doi:10.1111/j.0012-155X.2006.00477.x.

Howard, Christopher. 2007. *The Welfare State Nobody Knows: Debunking Myths about U.S. Social Policy.* Princeton, NJ: Princeton University Press.

Huber, Evelyne, and John D. Stephens. 2001. *Development and Crisis of the Welfare State: Parties and Policies in Global Markets.* Chicago: University of Chicago Press.

Ikporukpo, Chris O. 2004. "Petroleum, Fiscal Federalism and Environmental Justice in Nigeria." *Space and Polity* 8 (3): 321–54. doi:10.1080/1356257042000309643.

Johnson, Ian. 2011. "China Faces 'Very Grave' Environmental Situation, Officials Say." *New York Times,* June 3.

Johnson, Thomas R. 2008. "New Opportunities, Same Constraints: Environmental Protection and China's New Development Path." *Politics* 28 (2): 93–102. doi:10.1111/j.1467-9256.2008.00316.x.

Katzenstein, Peter J. 1985. *Small States in World Markets: Industrial Policy in Europe.* Ithaca, NY: Cornell University Press.

Kraft, Michael E., and Norman J. Vig. 2006. "Environmental Policy from the 1970s to the Twenty-First Century." In *Environmental Policy: New Directions for the Twenty-First Century,* 6th ed., edited by Norman J. Vig and Michael E. Kraft, 1–33. Washington, DC: CQ Press.

Lavinas, Lena. 2006. "From Means-Test Schemes to Basic Income in Brazil: Exceptionality and Paradox." *International Social Security Review* 59 (3): 103–25. doi:10.1111/j.1468-246X.2006.00249.x.

Layzer, Judith A. 2006. *The Environmental Case: Translating Values into Policy.* 2nd ed. Washington, DC: CQ Press.

Lower-Basch, Elizabeth. 2011. "Cash Assistance since Welfare Reform." *TANF Policy Brief,* January 21. Washington, DC: CLASP. http://www.clasp.org/admin/site/publications/files/CashAssistance.pdf.

Marshall, T. H. 1963. *Class, Citizenship, and Social Development: Essays.* Chicago: University of Chicago Press.

McGuire, James W. 2010. *Wealth, Health, and Democracy in East Asia and Latin America.* Cambridge, UK: Cambridge University Press.

Morton, Katherine. 2006. "Surviving an Environmental Crisis: Can China Adapt?" *Brown Journal of World Affairs* 13 (1): 63–75.

OECD (Organisation for Economic Co-operation and Development). 2008. *OECD Factbook 2008: Economic, Environmental, and Social Statistics.* Rev. ed. Paris: OECD.

———. 2009. "Health at a Glance 2009." http://www.oecd.org/document/14/0,3343,en_2649_33929_16502667_1_1_1_37407,00.html.

———. 2011. "Social Expenditure Database." http://www.oecd.org/document/9/0,3746,en_2649_33933_38141385_1_1_1_1,00.html.

Olsen, Gregg M. 2007. "Toward Global Welfare State Convergence? Family Policy and Health Care in Sweden, Canada, and the United States." *Journal of Sociology and Social Welfare* 34 (2): 143–64.

Pierson, Paul. 1996. "The New Politics of the Welfare State." *World Politics* 48 (2): 143–79. doi:10.1353/wp.1996.0004.

Ringquist, Evan. J. 2006. "Environmental Justice: Normative Concerns, Empirical Evidence, and Government Action." In *Environmental Policy: New Directions for the Twenty-First Century,* 6th ed., edited by Norman J. Vig and Michael E. Kraft, 239–63. Washington, DC: CQ Press.

Sen, Amartya. 1999. *Development as Freedom.* New York: Knopf.

Siebert, Horst. 2005. *The German Economy: Beyond the Social Market.* Princeton, NJ: Princeton University Press.

Slack, Kristin Shook, Katherine A. Magnuson, Lawrence M. Berger, Joan Yoo, Rebekah Levine Coley, Rachel Dunifon, Amy Dworsky, et al. 2007. "Family Economic Well-Being Following the 1996 Welfare Reform: Trend Data from Five Nonexperimental Panel Studies." *Children and Youth Services Review* 29 (6): 698–720.

Smeeding, Timothy. 2005. "Government Programs and Social Outcomes: The United States in Comparative Perspective." Luxembourg Income Study Working Paper Series, Working Paper No. 426. http://www.lisproject.org/publications/liswps/426.pdf.

UNDP (United Nations Development Programme). 2006. *Niger Delta Human Development Report.* Abjua, Nigeria: UNDP Nigeria.

———. 2007. *Human Development Report 2007/2008: Fighting Climate Change; Human Solidarity in a Divided World.* New York: Palgrave

Macmillan. Available at http://hdr.undp.org/en/reports/global/hdr2007-8/.

Vail, Mark I. 2004. "The Myth of the Frozen Welfare State and the Dynamics of Contemporary French and German Social-Protection Reform." *French Politics* 2 (2): 151–83.

Willemsky, Harold L. 1975. *The Welfare State and Equality: Structural and Ideological Roots of Public Expenditures.* Berkeley: University of California Press.

World Bank. 2010. Lifting Families Out of Poverty in Brazil—Bolsa Familia Program. http://web.worldbank.org/WBSITE/EXTERNAL/COUNTRIES/LACEXT/BRAZILEXTN/0,,contentMDK:20754490~menuPK:2024799~pagePK:141137~piPK:141127~theSitePK:322341,00.html.

Wu, Joshua Su-Ya. 2009. "The State of China's Environmental Governance After the 17th Party Congress." *East Asia* 26 (4): 265–84. doi:10.1007/s12140-009-9089-9.

Yarett, Ian. 2010. "Has Anything Gotten Better Since That First Earth Day?" *Newsweek*, April 26, p. 56.

RESOURCES FOR FURTHER STUDY

Brady, David. 2009. *Rich Democracies, Poor People: How Politics Explain Poverty.* Oxford, UK: Oxford University Press.

Donaldson, Cam, and Karen Gerard. 2005. *Economics of Health Care Financing: The Visible Hand.* New York: Palgrave Macmillan.

Goodin, Robert E., Bruce Headey, Ruud Muffels, and Henk-Jan Dirven. 1999. *The Real Worlds of Welfare Capitalism.* Cambridge, UK: Cambridge University Press.

Jacobs, Lawrence R., and Theda Skocpol. 2010. *Health Care Reform and American Politics: What Everyone Needs to Know.* Oxford, UK: Oxford University Press.

———. 2011. "Society at a Glance 2011—OECD Social Indicators." http://www.oecd.org/document/40/0,3746,en_2649_37419_47507368_1_1_1_37419,00.html.

Schreuder, Yda. 2009. *The Corporate Greenhouse: Climate Change Policy in a Globalizing World.* New York: Zed Books.

WEB RESOURCES

American Human Development Project, "The Measure of America 2010–2011: Mapping Risks and Resilience" (http://www.measureofamerica.org/the-measure-of-america-2010-2011-book/)

Council on Environmental Quality, U.S. Department of Energy, "Environmental Quality Statistics: Section 11—Global Environment" (http://ceq.hss.doe.gov/nepa/reports/statistics/global.html)

OECD (Organisation for Economic Co-operation and Development) (http://www.oecd.org/)

United Nations Statistics Division, "Environment" (http://unstats.un.org/unsd/environment/default.htm)

U.S. Census Bureau, 2011, "The 2011 Statistical Abstract: International Statistics" (http://www.census.gov/compendia/statab/cats/international_statistics.html)

World Health Organization, "Global Health Observatory" (http://www.who.int/gho/en/)

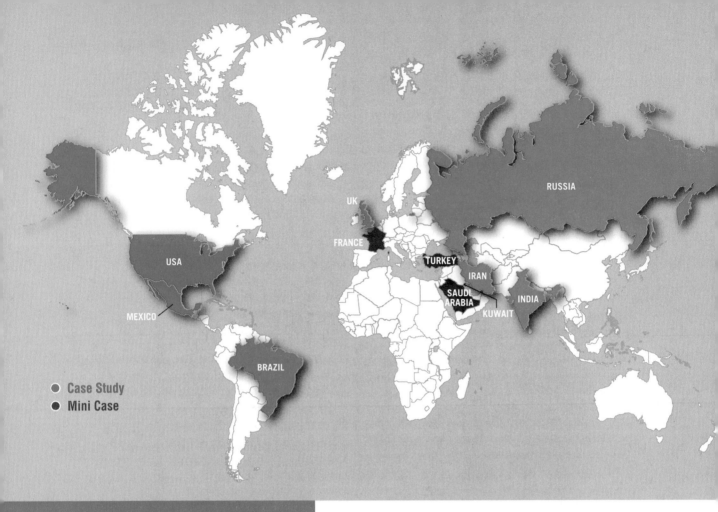

- Case Study
- Mini Case

Who Rules?

- When values and identities such as religion and gender clash, what does the outcome tell us about who rules?

What Explains Political Behavior?

- How do culture and institutions shape the particular demands of identity groups?
- What role does globalization play in increasing group demands for recognition and inclusion?

Where and Why?

- What might explain why different types of secularism have developed in different countries?
- How have differences in secularism affected religious conflict and state responses to challenges from religious groups for inclusion?

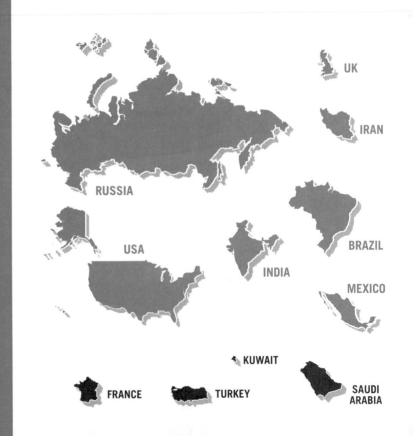

12

POLICIES AND POLITICS OF INCLUSION AND CLASHING VALUES

O ver the past fifty years, numerous groups have demanded greater inclusion in their societies and in the political process, raising a host of new policy issues. These groups include the ethnic, racial, and religious groups we discussed in chapter 4 as well as groups demanding changes to policies toward gender and sexual orientation. In many countries, these have been part of the new social movements we mentioned in chapter 7. The demands of these movements have raised fundamental questions about equal citizenship and how to reconcile clashing moral values. States throughout the world have created new policies to try to address these concerns, and globalization has meant that even states with very little open political space or only weak demands for change have nonetheless felt pressure to address at least some of these issues.

These battles raise a number of new questions in comparative politics. First, what can the policy outcomes of these debates tell us about who rules? Who seems to have most power in these policy areas? A key "What explains political behavior?" question is, How do the theories we've discussed throughout the book help us explain why groups make the demands they do and why governments respond as they do to those demands? We can also ask "Where and why?" questions about why different types of policies, such as different versions of secularism, are adopted in different places and how those differences affect states' responses to demands from religious groups. Variation in these policy areas is certainly great, as the Country and Concept table demonstrates for our case studies. Levels of religiosity, gender equality, and acceptance of homosexuality vary widely across just our eleven cases, producing distinct dynamics that we explore throughout the chapter.

COUNTRY AND CONCEPT

Policies and Politics of Inclusion and Clashing Values

| Country | RELIGION | | GENDER | |
	Freedom of religion constitutionally guaranteed?*	% of respondents who say, "I am a religious person" [†]	Gender Empowerment Measure (GEM) value (higher scores = less gender disparity) [‡]	Gender-related Development Index (GDI) value[§] (higher scores = less gender disparity)
Brazil	Yes.	88.0	0.504	0.810
China	Yes, but very little actual freedom of religion exists, and the government tries to control religious institutions and practice.	21.8	0.533	0.770
Germany	Yes, but some small religious groups have lodged complaints about discrimination.	42.9	0.852	0.939
India	Yes, but minority Muslim and Christian populations complain of discrimination.	77.9	—	0.594
Iran	No. Islam declared official religion.	83.7	0.331	0.770
Japan	Yes. Religious corporations monitored by Ministry of Education in wake of Aum Shinrikyo attacks.	24.2	0.567	0.945
Mexico	Yes, but restrictions on role of churches, such as no religious schools, no clergy can serve in public office, and no property ownership.	75.4	0.629	0.847
Nigeria	Yes, but in practice many parts of Nigeria under Sharia.	—	—	0.499
Russia	Yes, but only certain religions afforded full legal status.	73.6	0.556	0.816
United Kingdom	No constitution, but customary legal protection against religious discrimination.	48.7	0.790	0.943
United States	Yes.	72.1	0.767	0.942

* Information is from the International Coalition for Religious Freedom, http://www.religiousfreedom.com/.

[†] World Values Survey data, http://www.worldvaluessurvey.org/.

[‡] GEM, the UN's Gender Empowerment Measure, is a composite indicator that captures gender inequality in three key areas: political participation and decision-making power, as measured by women's and men's percentage shares of parliamentary seats; economic participation and decision-making power, as measured by two indicators—women's and men's percentage shares of positions as legislators, senior officials, and managers and women's and men's percentage shares of professional and technical positions; and power over economic resources, as measured by women's and men's estimated earned income (Purchasing Power Parity in U.S. dollars, or PPP US$). See UN *Human Development Report 2009*, Table K, http://hdr.undp.org/en/media/HDR_2009_EN_Table_K.pdf.

[§] GDI, the UN's Gender Development Index, is a composite index that measures human development in the same dimensions as the Human Development Index (HDI) while adjusting for gender inequality in those basic dimensions. These dimensions are a long and healthy life, access to

GENDER		SEXUALITY		
Ratio of estimated female to male earned income**	Ratio of female to male adult literacy	Laws against homosexuality; extent of rights or extent of punishment††	% of respondents who say that "homosexuality is never justifiable"‡‡	% of respondents who say that "homosexuality is always justifiable"‡‡
0.60	1.00	No. Limited same-sex unions. Some constitutional and de facto rights.	31.8	9.6
0.68	0.91	No. No same-sex unions.	78.1	1.5
0.59	1.00	No. Registered partnership exists as well as some laws against discrimination. Some states have constitutional protections.	10.5	27.1
0.32	0.65	No. Same-sex intercourse decriminalized in 2009; no laws allowing or prohibiting same-sex marriage and widespread reports that such marriages occur.	63.7	9.3
0.32	0.87	Yes, punishable by prison term or possibly death.	82.3	1.3
0.45	1.00	No. Some laws against discrimination exist.	24.2	9.1
0.42	0.77	No. Same-sex marriage allowed in the Federal District. Some laws against discrimination exist.	34.4	13.4
0.42	0.77	Yes, in areas governed by Sharia, punishable by death.	—	—
0.64	1.00	No. Some laws against discrimination exist.	66.4	4.5
0.67	1.00	No. Civil partnership and laws against discrimination exist. Adoption possible.	20.3	21.7
0.62	1.00	No. Some discrimination laws and some form of union or marriage permitted in some states.	32.5	14.8

knowledge, and a decent standard of living. These basic dimensions are measured separately for females and males in the GDI by life expectancy at birth; adult literacy and combined gross enrollment in primary, secondary, and tertiary level education; and estimated earned income per capita in PPP US$, respectively. See UN *Human Development Report 2009*, Table J, http://hdr.undp.org/en/media/HDR_2009_EN_Table_J.pdf.

** Data are from UN *Human Development Report 2009*, http://hdrstats.undp.org/en/indicators/130.html.

†† Data are from Daniel Ottosson, LGBT World Legal Wrap Up Survey, May 2010. Available at http://old.ilga.org/Statehomophobia/ILGA_State_Sponsored_Homophobia_2010.pdf. See also http://www.ilga.org/statehomophobia/LGBcriminallaws-Daniel_Ottoson.pdf.

‡‡ Response to World Values Survey Question: "Please tell me for each of the following statements whether you think it can always be justified, never be justified, or something in between?"

THE DEBATE OVER INCLUSION AND GROUP RIGHTS

The policy debates that these questions raise return us to issues we examined in prior chapters. Chapter 4 argued that identity-based groups desire some combination of recognition, autonomy, representation, and participation. In this chapter, we add improved social status to this list. The groups that have made these demands do so in part to achieve what we examined in chapter 3—equal citizenship—and they see better social status as part of that. Their demands for inclusion raise questions about what equal citizenship should look like. Formally or informally excluding particular groups of citizens from the political sphere threatens this fundamental democratic value. Including them, however, can cause clashes with other groups with equally strong and opposing values. While few people or governments question the legitimacy of equal treatment of all citizens regardless of ethnic or racial identity, doing the same for women, homosexuals, or transgender individuals often conflicts with deeply held religious beliefs or long-standing cultural practices. Even when the principle of equal citizenship is not questioned, major controversies arise over what the state must and can do to help ensure equal status and even what "equal treatment" means.

The Demands of Identity Groups The first demand identity groups usually make is for recognition. They want the state and the rest of society to recognize them as distinct with particular sets of legitimate concerns. They usually seek legal rights at least equal to (or perhaps greater than) those of other citizens. While the last vestige of legalized racial discrimination was eliminated with the end of apartheid in South Africa in 1994, legal discrimination against women, especially in areas of property ownership and family law, remains fairly common, and legal discrimination against homosexuals is the norm in most of the world.

Members of ethnic or religious groups also sometimes seek autonomy to control their own affairs, either in a particular region where they are in the majority or over areas of their lives influenced by cultural traditions or religious beliefs, such as family law and property rights.

A third demand that virtually all groups make is for representation and participation, essentially the right to participate fully in the political process. This is initially a simple legal matter of ensuring basic political rights, but it often becomes more complicated and controversial as groups question whether they are truly being allowed to participate on an equal footing with other citizens and whether institutional changes are necessary for them to achieve that equality.

A final demand that we add in this chapter is the demand for better social status. Virtually all groups that mobilize to make demands for inclusion on the basis of identity begin in a socially marginalized position: they are typically poorer and less educated than the average citizen and may be socially segregated as well. Harkening back to T. H. Marshall's (1963) ideas of the social rights of citizenship (see chapter 3), they argue that they need better education and economic positions and greater respect from and acceptance in society as a whole. How to achieve those improvements has proven quite controversial in many countries.

Equal citizenship is not the only value involved in policies of inclusion. Demands for inclusion often produce confrontations among competing values. Historically, demands for racial or ethnic equality gave rise to such conflicts: many white supporters of apartheid in South Africa and Jim Crow laws in the southern United States believed that racial mixing would threaten the well-being of society as a whole. In the contemporary world, most such conflicts are between religious or cultural beliefs, on the one hand, and claims for equality across genders or sexual orientations on the other. Recent controversies over gay marriage are just the latest in a long history of clashes of deeply held values.

Politics of Inclusion and the Modern State

The questions these policies raise are so profound and so central to liberal democracy that numerous political philosophers have developed arguments in recent years centered on which policies of inclusion should be pursued and why. Most of this debate has taken place in the context of democratic theory: normative theories about how democracy ought to work. It has clear implications, though, for any modern state, since all modern states grapple with the demands of mobilized groups asking for greater inclusion in the political process. At the heart of the debate is the question of individual versus group rights. Liberal democracy in its classic formulation is based on individual rights and the equal treatment of all citizens. As we saw in chapter 3, it took the better part of two centuries to implement this idea in basic legal terms before getting to the contemporary debates liberal regimes face over what true inclusion means.

Arguments for Group Rights Some theorists argue, however, that individual rights, no matter how fully respected, will never allow full inclusion of culturally distinct or socially marginalized groups. Social or cultural differences mean that legal equality alone cannot facilitate real inclusion for these groups. More must be done, usually in the form of rights for or preferential policies that target the distinct needs and weak social position of particular groups. Theorists making these arguments support policies of several types: (1) recognizing and actively supporting the preservation of distinct cultures, (2) granting some degree of governing autonomy to particular groups, (3) reforming representative institutions such as electoral systems and political parties to enhance or guarantee participation and office holding for members of particular groups, and (4) actively intervening to improve the socioeconomic status of distinct groups, usually via government intervention in the market. Opponents argue that such "special" group rights or preferences undermine the norm of equal citizenship, serve to perpetuate a group's distinct and therefore unequal position, and threaten the common identity and bonds on which citizenship and national identity must be based.

Two of the most prominent advocates of group rights and preferences are political theorists Will Kymlicka (1995) and Iris Marion Young (2000). Both argued from within the tradition of liberal democratic theory, but they suggested that in certain circumstances group rights are not only justified but are essential to achieve full inclusion of all citizens. Kymlicka argued that minority cultures must be recognized and granted certain collective rights because the individual autonomy on which liberal democracy is based entails freedom to choose among various options in life, and those options can only be understood within the context of a particular culture. Culture gives individuals the means to understand the world and their role in it, providing them with the means to choose how to act and what to believe. For this reason, among others, people deeply value their cultures and are justified in doing so.

Kymlicka contended that collective rights for minority cultures are justified "to limit the economic or political power exercised by the larger society over the group, to ensure that the resources and institutions on which the minority depends are not vulnerable to majority decisions" (1995, 7). This is particularly true for minority groups that are part of preexisting cultures incorporated into larger states, such as Native Americans in the United States; these groups not only deserve protection within the larger society but also, if they wish, merit some degree of autonomy to preserve their culture. Even for immigrants and other minority groups, though, Kymlicka favored cultural support and protection, arguing that most people find it very difficult to fully cross cultural barriers and so, without recognition and protection of their distinct cultures, they will not be able to participate completely in the larger society and make the choices on which democratic citizenship depends.

Kymlicka and coauthor Wayne Norman (2000) argued for **multicultural integration** rather than assimilation. The latter, as practiced in the United States and elsewhere, has the goal of eventually integrating immigrants' cultures into the larger culture of the whole society. Conversely, multicultural integration

> does not have the intent or expectation of eliminating other cultural differences between subgroups in the state. Rather, it accepts that ethnocultural identities matter to citizens, will endure over time, and must be recognized and accommodated within [political] institutions. The hope is that citizens from different backgrounds can all recognize themselves, and feel at home, within such institutions. (14)

Kymlicka and Norman drew inspiration from the **communitarian** philosophical tradition, which argues that humans are inherently social and political animals and therefore can only function well in strongly bonded communities. Public policy, therefore, should not be neutral toward communities but should actively work to strengthen them, including cultural ones. Similarly, communitarians argue that liberals fail to recognize that citizens are bearers not only of rights but also of responsibilities to the larger community on which they depend. Some communitarians have been accused of being willing to forsake some individual rights, especially freedom of expression and gender equality, in favor of strengthening communities. Kymlicka and Norman, though, were clear that only cultural practices that do not violate fundamental liberal rights should be allowed and encouraged via multicultural integration.

Young (2000) offered a different approach to justifying group rights, although she focused not on identity and culture but rather on what she termed "structural social groups," or groups of people who share a structural position and therefore similar experience in social and political institutions. A structural position can be based on economic position, physical attributes, or a variety of other factors. Structural groups can therefore overlap with cultural groups but are not the same thing. She argued that collective rights or preferences for such groups are justified in the interests of justice and greater democracy. Democracy, she suggested, should have as one of its primary goals the seeking of justice. Achieving this requires a democratic debate that includes all important perspectives on relevant issues. This is a form of what is termed **deliberative democracy**, that is, democracy that asks citizens not only to assume their rights and minimally participate through voting but also to engage actively in democratic discussion in the effort to build a better society.

Deliberative democracy, Young argued, is enhanced and justice is more likely to be attained when all important social perspectives are included in the discussion. She further argued that groups in structurally marginalized positions are typically not included unless governments intervene to ensure that they are. Her goal was inclusive democracy:

multicultural integration: Accepts that ethnocultural identities matter to citizens, will endure over time, and must be recognized and accommodated within political institutions; in contrast to assimilation

communitarianism: Philosophical tradition supporting the argument that humans are inherently social and political animals and thus can only function well in strongly bonded communities

deliberative democracy: Democracy that asks citizens not only to assume their rights and minimally participate through voting but also to engage actively in democratic discussion in the effort to build a better society

> Inclusion ought not to mean simply the formal and abstract equality of all members of the polity of citizens. It means explicitly acknowledging social differentiations and divisions and encouraging differently situated groups to give voice to their needs, interests, and perspectives. (2000, 119)

Young's version of deliberative democracy draws on feminist theory. Modern feminism began philosophically to examine women and their structurally marginalized position but over time came to recognize that other groups were in similar structurally marginalized positions. Feminists concluded that policy needed to take those positions into account for true equality to be achieved. Not only legal equality but the recognition of and appropriate response to differences across groups are essential.

Young's position leads her to favor adjusting political discussion and debate to recognize and value the forms of communication that marginalized groups, such as women or speakers of different languages, are often more comfortable using. She also suggested that if a history of discrimination or current practices prevent members of marginalized social groups from being elected or appointed representatives in political institutions, some reform to ensure that they can enter such positions is warranted. This could take the form of rules for how parties select candidates, reserved legislative seats for particular groups, reserved positions on appointed boards for particular groups, or the drawing of electoral districts to increase the likelihood that members of particular groups will be elected.

Arguments against Group Rights Critics of group rights make several arguments in response to Kymlicka, Young, and others. The classic liberal position is that only individuals can have rights and all individuals should have them equally. This implies support for government policies of nondiscrimination, but it does not justify giving any rights or preferences to members of particular groups who would then receive treatment different from what other citizens get. Once legal equality is achieved, individuals are and should be free to pursue political participation as they desire and are able. The state should not intervene in any way in response to either cultural or social differences, which, even if acknowledged to exist, are beyond the state's rightful purview.

Indeed, proponents of civic nationalism (see chapter 4) fear that group rights will undermine political stability and democracy, both of which, they argue, require a common identity, a shared set of values, or both. Nationalism underlies the development of the modern state and of democracy, and each state is given international legitimacy as a representative of "a people." A sense of commonality, then, is essential to domestic and international legitimacy for all states. Civic nationalists see group rights and preferences as divisive and fear that acknowledging and accommodating them will preserve differences rather than encourage commonality. This in turn will ultimately undermine political stability and make democratic discussion difficult because of a lack of common values.

A third, but similar, strand of criticism of group rights comes from proponents of deliberative democracy who suggest that the goal of democratic discussion should not be the representation of particular interests and bargaining among them but instead should be the achievement of a collectively defined common good. Giving special rights or preferences to particular groups will encourage them to pursue their own interests, and others will respond in kind, diverting attention from the common good.

Finally, all liberal theorists ask, To what extent can and should group rights be supported if those groups pursue goals contrary to a state's liberal ideals? Should a religious group that explicitly opposes equal rights for men and women not only be allowed to participate in the political process but be given specific preferences?

These theoretical arguments lie behind the many concrete policy debates that face contemporary states. These debates take different forms in different societies, depending on which groups have demanded inclusion, how they have done so, and the nature of the regime. While many of the overtly political goals of representation and participation seem relevant only in democracies, even leaders in authoritarian regimes face pressure to include women and members of various religious or ethnic groups in positions of authority. We examine the most controversial contemporary debates in this chapter, those involving religion, gender, and sexual orientation.

RELIGION: RECOGNITION, AUTONOMY, AND THE SECULAR STATE

Religion is both the oldest and, in a sense, newest basis for questions of inclusion and clashing values. As we noted in chapter 3, religious divisions within Christianity in early modern Europe led to civil wars and the emergence of liberalism. Eventually, secular states became universal in Western societies, which, at least in theory, relocated religion into the private sphere. The secular state reached its zenith after World War II and the onset of independence of numerous secular states across Africa and Asia. In the past generation, however, and with renewed emphasis since the terrorist attacks of September 11, 2001, religion has again become a major issue in both Western and postcolonial societies. As we noted in chapter 4, religious groups typically seek recognition and autonomy, though individual members of those groups may also seek to participate in politics and achieve greater social status, ambitions which they may feel have been hindered by society's lack of respect for their religious beliefs.

The vast majority of the world's states are officially secular, with most of the exceptions being in the Middle East. Secularism, however, takes many different forms in principle, and its implementation does not always match those principles. The key relationship is between the state and organized religious groups such as churches and religious associations. In liberal democracies, few question the right of citizens to practice any religion they choose in the private sphere (with the possible exception of religious practices that break other kinds of laws, such as those against drug use or polygamy). Religious groups may organize, build houses of worship, and do charitable work as they desire. Controversies arise over what role, if any, the state should play in this process and what role, if any, the religious groups should play in secular politics and policy.

The Different Forms of Secularism

Several approaches to secularism exist today. The version most familiar to Americans views the state as neutral about, and not opposed to, religion: the state does not actively support religious activities such as religious schools or charitable work, but it does not oppose them either. Religious perspectives in secular politics are treated the same as any other perspectives, with the state (at least in theory) being a neutral arbiter that does not choose sides in the debate. This form of secularism stems from the earliest days of the United States, when thirteen colonies with different predominant branches of Christianity (in many cases, officially recognized by the individual colonial governments) had to find a way to live together. They believed that the example of the English civil war just over a century earlier illustrated the price paid by a state that was not neutral. Recent controversies in the United States have therefore involved actions that seem to question this neutrality, such as posting the Ten Commandments in courtrooms or public school classrooms, or requiring children to pray in school or learn about creationism in addition to or instead of the theory of evolution. Other controversies implicate the state in actively supporting religion, such as government funding for religious groups' charitable work; abstinence programs in classrooms in lieu of sex education courses; or incentives for individuals to marry rather than have sexual relations, and possibly children, out of wedlock.

A more absolute version of secularism developed in societies whose political origins lay in a battle to separate the state from a single, dominant religion. France, Turkey, and our case study of Mexico are all examples of this. The French and Mexican revolutions and the establishment of the modern state in Turkey after the demise of the Ottoman Empire each involved the creation of a secular republic independent of the politically powerful Catholic Church in France and Mexico and the Islamic caliphate in Turkey. The result was what the French call *laïcité,* a secularism advocating that religion should play no part in the public realm. The state is not neutral toward religions but rather is actively opposed to religion having any role in the public sphere. Private religious practice remains acceptable, as long as it is kept private. Religious references in political discourse, while not illegal in most cases, are nonetheless considered inappropriate by most political elites. In practice, not all of these societies have enforced this doctrine strictly: in France, for instance, the state supports many Catholic schools as long as they follow central state educational guidelines. Controversies arise in this type of secularism when a religious group seeks a public role for its religious beliefs, as the case of Islamic girls wearing veils in France and Turkey demonstrates.

MINI CASE

Islamic Head Scarves in France and Turkey

France and Turkey share a similar version of secularism: a strict version that separates religion and state, with religion viewed as a private matter to be kept out of the public sphere as much as possible. France is at least nominally largely Christian, but it is home to the largest Muslim population in Europe, most of whom are immigrants from North Africa. The population of Turkey is nearly all Muslim. Both countries have faced considerable controversy over young women wearing Islamic head scarves to school. The issue aroused such passion in part because each state's sense of national identity includes its particular conception of secularism; any questioning of it threatens national identity itself. A 2004 law in France

attempted to resolve the controversy but has not laid it to rest, while in Turkey, the issue briefly threatened to bring down the government of the day.

The French concept of secularism, or *laïcité,* became law in 1905 after a century of controversy over the public role of the Catholic Church. The law represented a triumph of the secular Republic over the church, and it seemed to resolve religious tensions. Then in October 1989, the principal of a junior high school in a Paris suburb expelled three Muslim girls for wearing the *hijab,* the Muslim head scarf, in school. This immediately became a major national controversy that pitted defenders of *laïcité* and feminists, who viewed the head scarf as a form of oppression, against defenders of religious freedom and multicultural understanding. The case was initially resolved in about a week, with the girls allowed to wear their head scarves to school as long as they took them off in class. Ten days later, though, the girls demanded the right to wear them in class as well, reigniting the firestorm. The government determined that religious symbols could be worn in schools unless "by their nature . . . or by their ostentatious or protesting character . . . [they] disturb the order or normal functioning of public services" (Fetzer and Soper 2005, 79). In effect, the national government left the wearing of head scarves to local schools to decide on a case-by-case basis.

As a consequence, dozens of Muslim girls were expelled from school and denied a public education. The few Muslim families that could afford lawyers filed lawsuits, which led to a clarification of the ruling in 1997: simply wearing the head scarf was not "ostentatious," and a school had to present a clear justification for each individual case of expelling a girl from school. The debate continued into the new millennium, arising more vociferously whenever a particularly dramatic case occurred and intertwining with France's broader debate about the place of Muslims in France, assimilation versus cultural and religious distinctiveness, and French national identity.

In 2003 Conservative president Jacques Chirac finally appointed a commission on *laïcité* that recommended completely banning the wearing of all "conspicuous religious symbols" in schools. After heated debate, the French parliament passed a law to this effect in 2004, and since then, more Muslim girls have been banned from school for wearing the *hijab*. Critics contend that the law is an anti-Muslim attack on religious freedom, since students have long worn small crosses and yarmulkes to school without incident. Supporters argue that the law is essential to the preservation of a secular republic under the threat of encroaching Islamist ideology and to the preservation of French gender equality. French Muslims themselves are divided over the issue. A tiny fraction of them

wear head scarves regardless of the law. They split almost evenly in opinion polls for and against the 2004 ban.

More recently, the *burqa,* the full-body and full-face covering worn by some Muslim women, has become controversial. France's President Sarkozy appointed a parliamentary commission to investigate the matter, which issued a report in early 2010 recommending a complete ban on the *burqa* in public places because it saw the garb as contradicting the French ideals of *laïcité,* equality between the sexes, and *fraternité.* By the end of 2010, both houses of parliament had passed the ban, and the Constitutional Court upheld it as constitutional, allowing an exception only for places of worship. Most Muslims argued against the ban, saying it would further marginalize them from mainstream French life. Critics also noted that fewer than 2,000 women in the entire country regularly wear the *burqa*; they suggested that the campaign was more about political leaders appealing to nationalist sentiments to gain political support, and "Islamophobia," than it was about an actual policy problem. This move came as several other European countries passed similar bans, the Swiss passed a referendum banning the building of mosques with minarets, and the United States vociferously debated whether to allow the opening of an Islamic education center and mosque near the former World Trade Center site in New York City. Debates about the role of Muslims in Western societies are clearly far from over.

In Turkey, as in France, secularism is tied deeply to national identity. Kemal Atatürk founded the modern Turkish state after World War I based on an explicit campaign to modernize and Westernize the country, in part by eliminating the role of Islam in the former seat of the Muslim caliphate and Ottoman Empire. The secular elite ran the country's bureaucracy, judiciary, and military. Whenever Muslim parties, which opposed Westernization and called for Turkey to recognize its place in the Muslim Middle East, gained too much power, they were banned or the military carried out a coup to reorganize the government entirely. The Muslim head scarf on women, though, was not banned in universities and government offices until 1981, and the ban wasn't regularly enforced until after the highly secular military forced an Islamist government out of power in 1998.

The first Islamic party to lead the government came to power in 1995 in a coalition government. It was banned after two years in office and its leaders arrested, but a new Islamic party, the Justice and Development Party (JDP), arose in 2001, led by the popular, charismatic mayor of Istanbul, Tayyip Erdoğan. In contrast to past parties, the JDP modified the call for an end to Westernization. While preserving its embrace of Islamic principles on social issues, it also supported globalization, economic modernization tied to the West, and Turkey's application to join the EU. This garnered it greater support than prior Islamic parties, and it won the 2002 election with 34 percent of the vote, by far the largest share in Turkey's multiparty system. It has been the ruling party since, winning the 2007 election with 47 percent of the vote, and Erdoğan has served as prime minister since 2002.

Over half of Turkish women are estimated to wear some sort of head covering regularly, though head scarves are banned on university campuses and in government offices (meaning no public employees can wear them). The JDP came to power promising to allow them to be worn more widely, including in universities, but it did not pass legislation to that effect in its first five years in power. The president, Ahmet Necdet Sezer, was a strong secularist from another party and promised to veto a lifting of the ban, and the Constitutional Court ruled in favor of preserving the ban in 2005.

The election of a JDP leader, Abdullah Gül, as president in 2007 changed the equation. Indeed, one of the biggest controversies in that presidential election was the fact that Gül's wife wears a head scarf (as do Erdoğan's wife and daughters). With a JDP president, Erdoğan passed a law in February 2008 that lifted the ban on Muslim head scarves in public universities, with JDP members promising the ban on them in

all public offices would be lifted soon. The secular elite reacted swiftly. Millions of secularists held pro-ban demonstrations, and the Constitutional Court ruled in June 2008 that the new law was unconstitutional. The public prosecutor filed a case asking the Constitutional Court to ban the JDP and seventy of its top leaders for violating Turkey's secular principles, in part because of the party's effort to lift the head scarf ban. In 2009, however, the Court ruled in favor of the party, and it remained in power.

After winning a referendum in 2010 to amend the constitution, the JDP government felt it had the political strength to reverse the head scarf ban. While it has not done so via the parliament, it simply stated that it would support university students who wanted to wear the head scarf. Without government enforcement of the ban, universities across the country began to allow women to wear the veil on campus. The constitutional referendum included a restructuring of the Constitutional Court, which prevented it from ruling against the ban once more, at least for the time being.

CASE SUMMARY

Because American conceptions of secularism involve neutrality on the part of the state but not restrictions on the public display of religion, Americans often find it odd that a simple head scarf would provoke a major political crisis on two continents. The huge controversy over locating an Islamic center near the site of the former World Trade Center, though, should give Americans some feel for the powerful emotions that can be unleashed by religious symbols. French and Turkish secularism, and more importantly, nationalism, have long envisioned a strictly secular public sphere. This is a vision that rising Islamic sentiment is challenging. Both states have reacted by restricting women's ability to wear clothing that symbolizes their Islamic faith, though by 2011 Turkey was moving toward fewer restrictions while France was moving toward more. As we noted in chapter 4, what women do and wear can become symbolic markers of national identity. This clearly seems to be the case, and the source of long and fraught debate, regarding head scarves in France and Turkey. A similar debate emerged after the 2011 "Jasmine revolution" in Tunisia. The long-banned Islamist party quickly emerged as a powerful political force, and women increasingly donned head scarves in what had been the most secular Arab state, raising concerns among secularists that the revolution would result in a religious "takeover" of government.

A third variant of secularism sees the state as neutral among but willing to support religions that it recognizes as important elements in civil society. Our case study of Germany is the classic model of this type. Following its corporatist tradition, Germany since the end of World War II has officially recognized various Judeo-Christian faiths, the leaders of which register with the government to gain recognition. The state even collects a tax on their behalf to help fund them, and they help administer some of Germany's extensive welfare programs. Controversies in this type of secular state involve deciding which religious groups gain recognition and how they have to be organized to do so. Most Sunni Islamic sects, for instance, are nonhierarchical, which means that each mosque is independent. This has raised questions in Germany about if and how the state should recognize Muslim groups the way it has Judeo-Christian ones. (Several pilot programs have been instituted in recent years to address this situation.) As with the other models, states do not always implement this type of secularism fully. Indonesia, which is 90 percent Muslim, officially allows freedom of religion and the state legally recognizes Islam, Catholicism, Protestantism, Hinduism, and Buddhism. In 2008, however, the government yielded to pressure from Islamists to ban a small Islamic sect known as Ahmadiyah, which does not believe Mohammed was the last prophet, a central tenet of mainstream Islam.

The primary models of secularism arose first in Europe and North America, but most postcolonial states are also officially secular, while making various accommodations for religions. On the whole, perhaps the biggest difference between African and Asian states, in particular, and European states is that the former are much more religious, as the Country and Concept table (pages 606–607) indicates for most of our case study countries. As in the United States, religious expression in the public sphere is widely accepted. Most African states have Christian majorities, and while many of them do not officially discriminate against Muslims, political leaders nonetheless openly practice Christianity and make religious references in public discourse. Similar patterns exist in majority Muslim states. Some of these make no pretence of being secular. In Saudi Arabia, for example, the regime's legitimacy is tied closely to its support of Islam, and key clerics play important roles in establishing laws on personal behavior that follow their interpretation of Sharia. In contrast, a number of other majority Muslim states, such as Syria, maintain a strict secularism, especially vis-à-vis Islamist groups that are the most powerful domestic threats to these regimes.

Challenges to the Secular State

Religious groups worldwide have challenged the secular state in all its forms. In seeking recognition and autonomy, they are typically interested in gaining official status in countries where that is important, including the teaching of their religion in public schools, establishing and gaining support for their own parochial schools, gaining legal recognition of their religious holidays, using religious symbols and

WHERE AND WHY

Explaining Policy Differences toward Muslims in Europe

Increasing Muslim immigration to Europe has made the place of Islam in these primarily secular and historically Christian societies a major issue in policy circles and in comparative politics. Islam now constitutes the third largest religion in Europe after Catholicism and Protestantism, and as Muslims have settled in the region, their demands for the right to build mosques that look like the mosques in the countries they came from, to establish Muslim schools, to have women wear veils in public, to have their religious holidays as official holidays, and to have their religious teachings included in secular school curricula have echoed across the continent. European states have responded in various ways, and political scientists have developed a spectrum of theories to explain this variation in policy response. Joel Fetzer and Christopher Soper (2005) outlined several of these.

Some explanations have focused primarily on Muslim groups themselves, using social movement theories to explain success or failure in getting policies adopted. Resource mobilization theory argues that the success of any social movement depends on how many financial and organizational resources it has. Muslim groups, these theorists suggest, are often decentralized and financially weak, meaning that most have had limited success at convincing European states to change their policies. Those that are somewhat wealthier and more hierarchically organized have been more successful. A second social movement theory argues that the political opportunity structures best explain success. For instance, German immigration laws mean far fewer Muslims have gained citizenship than in Britain, so British Muslims have the opportunity via citizenship to have greater influence. Similarly, the more centralized political system and parties in France mean Muslims have had to focus on national-level politics, whereas in Britain local government is a more important political arena and Muslims have been able to win some policy battles at the local level.

Other scholars look at the state itself, rather than at Muslim groups, to explain response to Muslim demands. One focus has been on ideology. In France the core ideological concept of *laïcité* has meant that the state has been unwilling to support Muslim schools or allow Muslim symbols and teachings in public schools, as any such move would violate the core principle of the secular state. Fetzer and Soper (2005) argued that the most important explanation of all, however, is the legacy of past church-state relations. Germany's formal recognition of several religious groups has led Muslims there to ask for the same, to become part of the system, and to organize themselves in a manner that allows the German state to work with them. Germany's long-standing church-state relationships have shaped not only the government's response to the Muslims but also what Muslim groups have requested. Similarly, the presence of the official Church of England and the tradition of teaching religion in both religious and secular schools have meant that Britain has been willing to include the study of Islam in its secular school curriculum and has been more willing to fund Muslim schools than has France.

As is often the case, more than one theory presents a plausible explanation of why states enact the policies they do. Combining several often results in the fullest explanation. The ideas developed for studying responses to Muslims in Europe might also be useful for explaining other states' responses and policies toward religious groups and their demands, beyond Europe and involving religious groups other than Muslims.

ideas in the public sphere, and being allowed to practice their own religious law in personal and family matters. Some of these simply require the state to include a new religious group in policies it already pursues toward other religious groups. Other groups, though, ask for more. They ask that the state be less secular in one way or another or that it set policies preferential to their religion over others.

All of these demands have provoked debates in various countries in recent years. We investigate some of them in three quite distinct case studies of secular states grappling with religious demands: the United Kingdom, India, and Mexico.

CASE STUDY

United Kingdom: Religious Challenge to Multiculturalism

- Multiculturalism as official policy goal expanded from race to religion
- Postcolonial immigration diversified Britain
- Shifting identity among immigrants and their children from ethnic and racial to religious
- Fight to gain Islamic schools and state funding of them, parallel to Christian schools
- Antiterrorism laws seen as attack on Muslims; softened under Prime Minister Cameron
- Continued segregation and discrimination breed some sympathy for extremist Islam among a minority of British Muslims

London is without question one of the most racially, culturally, and religiously diverse places on Earth. After centuries of relative homogeneity, since World War II and decolonization Britain has been the recipient of large-scale immigration from its former colonies in the Caribbean, South Asia, and Africa. The 1960s gave witness to Conservative member of Parliament (MP) Enoch Powell's thinly veiled racist call for the end of immigration to preserve the white Briton heritage and well-being, on the one hand, and the adoption of an official policy of **multiculturalism,** on the other. Britain's multiculturalism policy

encouraged cultural groups to create their own organizational structures, to safeguard their customs and religious practices as they saw fit, and to introduce an awareness of and celebration for Britain's cultural pluralism into the state education system. (Fetzer and Soper 2005, 30)

Until very recently, however, this policy was focused almost exclusively on race and culture, not religion. Antidiscrimination laws on the basis of race became national policy in the 1960s, but not until December 2003 did the government make discrimination on the basis of religion illegal. Since the 1980s, British Muslims have increasingly sought inclusion as a religious group, and their goals have included recognition, support, and some degree of autonomy. They have sought greater inclusion of their religion in school curricula, funding for their own schools, and rights to practice their faith publicly without discrimination.

Britain's unusual immigration history produced the challenges it faces today in dealing with religious diversity. From 1948 to 1962, citizens of the Commonwealth (the former British colonies) could immigrate to Britain and automatically gain rights equal to those of British citizens. At first it was mostly young men who immigrated to work in Britain's labor-short, postwar economy with the intent of saving money and returning home. Starting in 1962, British immigration policy made it much more difficult for Commonwealth citizens to immigrate, based

multiculturalism: The belief that different cultures in a society ought to be respected; in the United Kingdom, the policy governing how the state treats racial and religious minorities

Crowds of children await Queen Elizabeth II on a street in London's East End. Immigration has made the city probably the most culturally and racially diverse in the world, raising major questions about what it means to be a Briton. This debate has been especially acute around the question of religion, focusing on the role and demands of Britain's large Muslim minority.

Credit: Tim Graham/Getty Images

on explicit fears that too many nonwhite immigrants were arriving. This change in policy dramatically reduced the arrival of new migrant workers, but the migrants already in the country retained all of their rights, including the right to bring their families to join them, which actually led to higher numbers of immigrants than before 1962. For the first time, Britain was host to a number of immigrants from their former colonies who were complete families and who intended to stay. By far the largest number of these came from South Asia, and many of them were Muslim.

Muslims now represent about 5 percent of Britain's population and have founded more than 1,000 mosques and many educational associations. Some of these institutions receive funding from Muslim countries such as Saudi Arabia and Libya and may therefore follow the theological teachings of those countries, but not all do. Muslims remain socially and economically marginalized in several ways, however. They constitute about 12 percent of the nation's prison population,

even though they are only 5 percent of the overall population. Residential segregation continues to predominate in most British cities, and Bangladeshis and Pakistanis, who constitute three-quarters of Britain's Muslims, are the poorest demographic group in the country. Their children also perform more poorly in school than other groups.

Britain's policy of multiculturalism originally focused on race. The 1976 Race Relations Act created the Commission on Racial Equality (CRE), whose job it was to improve race relations and battle racial discrimination. By the 1980s, a "black" political movement had grown that attempted to group all people who were not white under one political and racial umbrella to gain greater political strength. While championed by prominent political activists, the common identity was only visibly popular among people of Caribbean descent. It was far less clear whether many Africans and South Asians accepted "black" as their personal identity, and by the end of the decade, it became increasingly evident that most Muslims did not. The event that made clear to all that religion, not race, was becoming the most important identity for Britain's Muslims was the controversy over Salman Rushdie's novel *The Satanic Verses.* Rushdie is a British, Pakistani novelist who was already well-known in literary circles when he published his controversial novel in 1988. Many religious Muslims of various sects were offended by the novel's portrayal of the Prophet Mohammed and his family, and Iran's Shiite Ayatollah Ruhollah Khomeini, among other leaders, issued a *fatwa* condemning Rushdie. Large-scale protests broke out across Britain, and numerous Muslim organizations united to demand that the book be banned. This produced a major political backlash in the name of free speech that a large number of non-Muslim blacks readily joined. Many Muslims concluded from the experience that their interests diverged from those of the black community, even though virtually all British Muslims are also racial minorities.

Muslim organizations were well established long before the Rushdie affair, however: the first umbrella organization, the Union of Muslim Organizations, began in the 1970s, and the Council of Mosques was established in the 1980s. The political prominence of such organizations grew substantially in the 1990s, as Muslims came to identify with their religion more than with their ethnicity or race. Yet this did not mean that most of them supported an Islamist ideology that questioned the legitimacy of the secular state. To the contrary, most of Britain's Muslims follow the Hanafi school of Sunni Islam, which respects the *ulema* (clerics) and Sharia (Islamic law) but also the sovereignty of the secular state. These Muslims practice their religion, including its laws, within the confines of the secular state. Nonetheless, surveys show that British Muslims are more closely identified with their religion than Muslims in much of the rest of Europe: 80 percent think of themselves as Muslims first and British second and are worried about the decline of religious values in Britain. On the other hand, they generally have a favorable view of their government and are actually more trusting of it than British Christians (Allen and Wike 2009, 155–56; Maxwell 2010). Individually, Muslims are very active politically. Most are British citizens, and in Britain immigrants from the Commonwealth have the right to vote. Indeed, Muslims are registered to vote and vote at higher percentages than white Britons. Given that most Muslims live in urban areas (40 percent in London alone), many have been elected to local urban offices. Four Muslims also are now MPs, all from the Labour Party, though that number is less than 1 percent of the Parliament, far below full representation for 5 percent of the population.

Participation, however, has not produced complete satisfaction of all their demands. Muslim associations seek recognition and the right to religious equality. A key area of dispute has been education. The Church of England (also called the Anglican Church in the United Kingdom or the Episcopal Church in the United States) is by law the country's official church and faith. This means relatively little now, but it has left an important institutional legacy in church-state relations. The British education system, even in public schools, includes religious instruction. Historically, this meant the teaching of Anglican beliefs. As Britain became more secular in the twentieth century, however, religious instruction increasingly came to be a nondenominational, vague Christian message that focused more on basic moral beliefs than on doctrine. The Anglican Church runs many schools, especially at the primary level, and it receives state funding to do so, with the requirement that these schools must teach the same national curriculum as public schools. Muslim parents placed their children in these highly regarded church schools, but they increasingly resented the Christian elements of the education. Since the 1980s, the government has encouraged local school authorities to include religious instruction that reflects the school's community. This has meant including Islamic instruction in areas with heavy Muslim populations, though this process has been long and slow, requiring significant agitation by Muslims at the local level. Local *ulema* have been actively involved in urging and assisting schools to incorporate Islamic education (Fetzer and Soper 2005).

The heavily secular nature of British education, however, has become a growing concern to many Muslims, who responded by creating a movement to found separate Muslim schools. The movement began in the 1970s, and by 2007 there were 126 Islamic schools across the country (Fetzer and Soper 2005, 44). In the late 1980s, a few of these started petitioning the government for funding parallel to that received by Christian and Jewish schools. This met with resistance from secularists, who sided with Muslims on the need for parity but wanted to achieve it by ending funding for all religious schools. After initial government resistance, the Labour Party government elected in 1997 changed course, officially approving the United Kingdom's first state funding for Muslim schools; by 2007, eight schools had been funded. These institutions must comply with the established national curriculum just like all other religious schools. In 2010, a controversy arose when the BBC reported that over 40 Saudi-funded Muslim schools not recognized by the state were teaching a curriculum from Saudi Arabia, including material deemed to be anti-Semitic ("*Panorama*" 2010).

Like all religious groups, British Muslim organizations have worked to achieve government recognition in various areas of everyday life. They were less successful in areas other than education until quite recently. Despite the clear rise of religion as an identity of importance, especially among Muslims, British multicultural policy continued to focus only on race and culture, reflecting Britain's increasingly secular society. (Nominal Christians are so secular that most estimates suggest there are more religiously observant Muslims than religiously observant Anglicans in Britain today.) This is reflected in the fact that not until the 2001 census were people asked what their religious affiliation, if any, was; prior to that, estimates of Muslims and

Hindus were based on the census's racial and ethnic information. Discrimination in employment on the basis of religion was made illegal in 2003, and then only because EU provisions required this legislation. In October 2007, the CRE, which had become an important source of information and policy on multiculturalism, merged with commissions on gender and disability to became the Equality and Human Rights Commission, with a mandate to work "to eliminate discrimination, reduce inequality, protect human rights and to build good relations" on the basis of not only race, gender, and disability but also "age, sexual orientation and religion or belief, as well as human rights" (Local Government Improvement and Development 2011).

This new recognition of religion as an important category for inclusive citizenship comes in the shadow of the September 11, 2001, attacks on the World Trade Center and the Pentagon in the United States and the July 7, 2005, London subway bombings carried out by British-born Muslims. Responding to both, the Labour government enacted Terrorism Acts in 2001, 2005, and 2006 that give the state much greater latitude to investigate and detain, without charges, citizens or foreigners suspected of being or assisting terrorists. The most controversial of these is the 2006 law, which allowed detention for twenty-eight days without charges being filed and made such activities as publishing terrorist materials and training terrorists illegal. Many British Muslims felt threatened by these new laws. Indeed, between September 2001 and September 2004, 664 people had been held in detention without being charged or given a trial, almost all of them Muslim (Modood 2006, 46–47). The Conservative–Liberal Democrat government that came to power in 2010 modified the antiterrorism laws in 2011, reducing detention to the previous fourteen-day maximum and softening other restrictions as well.

The terrorist bombings and debate over Islamic schools have brought to the fore new questions regarding Britain's official "multiculturalism." Critics contend they reinforce segregation rather than integration by encouraging ethnic and religious groups to focus on their distinct identities more than they otherwise would. Critics point to the Netherlands, which has reversed what was a strongly stated multicultural policy. Some see the British terrorism laws as a significant retreat from the policy, and Prime Minister Cameron (2010–) has questioned whether multiculturalism as a policy goal should continue at all. Meer and Modood (2009), however, argued that these debates and pressures do not represent a wholesale repudiation of the policy but a rethinking of it. The debate over how multicultural British policy should be seems likely to continue.

CASE SUMMARY

Since the 1980s British Muslims have become a significant political force. They have used Britain's multiculturalism policy, which long ignored recognition on the basis of religion, to include Islam in school curricula and to gain state funding for some Muslim schools. Individually, many have become active participants in the political process as well. Nonetheless, British Muslims remain overrepresented in prisons, poorer, less educated, and residentially segregated. In this context, a minority of young Muslim Britons have become alienated and attracted to more radical versions of Islam, a problem that will continue to challenge the British government as it attempts, belatedly, to recognize and work to include Muslims as full citizens. Without a doubt some British Muslims are sympathetic to al-Qaida and other similar Islamist extremist organizations; the perpetrators of the 2005 subway bombings were almost all native-born British Muslims, not immigrants. Yet the great majority of British Muslims believe in nonviolent versions of Islam, and they condemn terrorism even as they protest Britain's participation in the invasions of Afghanistan and Iraq. They are both British and Muslim, a relatively new and complex identity category that British society still struggles to understand, accept, and accommodate.

CASE STUDY

India: Secularism in a Religious and Religiously Plural Society

- Three competing versions of secularism
- Ambiguity between granting religious groups autonomy and working toward uniform laws
- Growing Hindu-Muslim disputes and tensions
- Central importance of personal law and women's rights
- Debates over who speaks for the Muslim community

On February 27, 2002, a train full of Hindus returning from a pilgrimage to a disputed Hindu temple unexpectedly stopped in a small town in Gujarat, a western state in India and the birthplace of Mahatma Gandhi. A Muslim mob set the train on fire, killing fifty-eight passengers. In response, Hindu nationalists called for a massive protest, which the state government supported. The protest quickly became a rampage against Muslims and their businesses; as many as 2,000 Muslims were killed and 150,000 displaced, and for three days the police did nothing to stop the violence.

This was only part of the most recent round of major religious violence in India, the world's largest and officially secular democracy. Religious divisions led to the partition of

India and Pakistan at independence, which left India with a population that is more than 80 percent Hindu but that has numerous religious minorities, including a Muslim minority that is about 13 percent of the population. After partition, religion was not a major division in India's secular democracy for two decades, but since the 1970s it has become an increasingly important issue and has led to significant conflicts. India has seen major debates over what exactly secularism should mean, especially in the area of personal law governing marriage, divorce, and inheritance, and these debates have pitted the idea of equal citizenship for all individuals against the idea of community rights to practice a religion and observe specific religious laws.

British colonial rule had to deal with India's religious diversity from its earliest days. To avoid conflict, the British mostly allowed religious leaders of various groups to implement their own laws locally, and in the nineteenth century the colonizer helped codify religious laws into written and more uniform codes. As Britain accepted the idea of Indian independence and the nationalist movement took center stage, the issue of religious divisions grew. The Congress, the main nationalist movement of Mahatma Gandhi and Jawaharlal Nehru, believed itself to be democratic and secular, and it rejected the claims of the Muslim League for special status for Muslims based on their religious identity and community. This ultimately led to the partition of India and the creation of Pakistan. As Indian leaders debated the country's new constitution in the 1940s, with partition emerging as a clear threat, most recognized that religious divisions could be explosive in the new country. All major leaders in the Congress agreed that some sort of secular state was essential, but various ideas of what secularism entailed arose and continue to be debated today.

Three ideas of secularism have competed throughout India's history: the state as modernizer working to reduce the influence of all religions, the state as neutral arbiter among religions, and the state as protector of religious minorities against the Hindu

Bodies of Hindu pilgrims are laid out in Gandhinagar, capital of the state of Gujarat, on September 23, 2002, victims of anti-Hindu violence. This was part of a new round of Hindu-Muslim violence, a recurring problem in India, especially since the early 1990s. Both the rise of the Hindu nationalist party, BJP, and the growing global Islamist movement have raised religious tensions that have long simmered in India's secular but religiously pluralist state.

Credit: Amit Dave/Reuters/Landov

majority. Much of the top leadership of the nationalist movement, the educated elite, saw religion as backward and standing in the way of modernization. Nehru, India's first prime minister and scion of its leading political family, was a self-defined agnostic. For him and much of his cohort, secularism meant that the state worked to reduce the influence of religion in public life, encouraging instead an equal and secular citizenship and national identity. Most recognized, however, the reality that the country was very religiously observant and religiously diverse.

Ultimately, the constitutional statutes regarding the place of religion in the operation of the state were based on the idea of equal respect for all religions. In Hindi, the term used for secularism literally means "religious neutrality." The Indian state, then, in a fashion similar to that of the United States, is supposed to be a neutral arbiter among faiths. For the most part, religious organizations were left the authority to mind their own affairs, though within limits. Article 26 of the country's constitution "provides freedom to manage religious affairs, subject to public order, morality and health," and Article 25

> provides for freedom of conscience and free profession, practice and propagation of religion subject to public order, morality, and health. It confers on the state the right to regulate or restrict any economic, financial, political, or other secular activity which may be associated with religious practice. (Rao 2006, 53–54)

These clauses seem to grant religious groups some autonomy to practice their faiths but also grant the state the ability to limit these practices when it deems necessary, an ambiguous stance that has led to decades of dispute.

Not surprisingly, these principles have been put into practice in varying ways over the years in different states in India's federal system. The state does not allow religious education in publicly financed schools, but it does allow and even aids religious schools that have religious curricula. Given the decentralized nature of both Hinduism and Islam, the government has also intervened at times to facilitate interactions among religious organizations or has informally recognized certain groups as representing these religions. The southern state of Tamil Nadu, for instance, helps administer Hindu temples and their large endowments, with prominent members of the government on the boards of directors of the temples as well. These temples own half a million acres of prime agricultural land and manage great wealth, making the happiness of their membership politically important.

Personal law came to be the most controversial religious question in India, especially involving Muslims. Uncertainty over Islamic law led to the creation of the All India Muslim Personal Law Board (AIMPLB) in 1973 to oversee the implementation of Sharia in personal law. By the 1980s, it had established itself as the unofficial voice of the Muslim community on personal law, but its position soon came into dispute. In 2000 it issued what it hoped would be a definitive treatise giving a detailed version of proper Sharia personal law, but that failed to quell growing questions about the Board's position. Critics within the Muslim community argued that the Board had become beholden to the Deobandi version of Sunni Islam and therefore did not represent the larger community (Jones 2010). By 2005 the Board had split, and two additional boards had been created, the All India Shia (Shiite) Personal Law Board and the All India Muslim Women's Personal Law Board, the latter an Islamic feminist effort to interpret Sharia in ways that support expanded rights for women. As in other cases where the state recognizes and gives autonomy to a religious group, who is the official arbiter of the group's traditions and beliefs is an important and often contested question.

The constitution's ambiguous position of granting autonomy to religious groups to follow their own personal law while simultaneously promising to work toward an eventual "uniform civil code" applicable to all is at the heart of growing legal disputes. The first battleground in this area was Hindu law. At independence, a debate was already underway over a Hindu Code Bill that would reform Hindu law to outlaw polygamy for Hindus and grant women greater rights to divorce and inheritance. Opposition was significant and focused especially on enforcing monogamy, sanctioning divorce, and giving women equal rights to property (even though the constitution prohibited discrimination on the basis of sex). A compromise bill passed in 1955 finally gave limited rights to women but still excluded agricultural land, the most important form of wealth in the country, from the laws allowing women to inherit. While only a partial victory for women's rights, the 1955 act nonetheless established the principle that Hindu law was subject to secular legal principles. Secular legal principles did not, however, govern Muslim law, leaving a disjointed legal framework that remains to this day (Harel-Shalev 2009).

The biggest battle over personal law and religion occurred in 1986. Shah Bano, a seventy-three-year-old Muslim woman divorced from her husband of more than fifty years, went to court to seek financial support from him because a law in the criminal code, which applies to all citizens regardless of religion, requires husbands to provide for their former wives as a means of preventing vagrancy. Under Muslim law, however, a husband is not usually obligated to support his wife for more than three months after divorce. The case went all the way to the Supreme Court, which ruled that the state's criminal code overrides Muslim personal law and, therefore, Shah Bano's husband had to support her. This seemingly innocuous personal case led to large-scale protest and intense political drama. The AIM-PLB launched a campaign against the ruling that included a demonstration of half a million people in Bombay, numerous conferences attended by tens of thousands of people, and even a 35,000-strong women's protest. In response, secular liberals and women's movements launched counterdemonstrations and demanded further reforms directed toward fulfilling the constitution's promise of a uniform civil code.

The case pitted individual equal rights of citizenship directly against communal rights of religious law and practice. After some hesitation, the Congress Party government chose the latter side, introducing the Muslim Women's (Protection of Rights on Divorce) Bill in Parliament in February 1986. The vociferous debate, framed mainly in terms of the rights of a religious minority versus universal equal rights, was closely watched across the country; few MPs raised questions of gender equity. The bill passed, making an exception for Muslims to the criminal code's requirement for maintenance after divorce. The communal rights of the religious minority had won out. Ironically, in the new millennium, courts have interpreted its provisions in ways that favor Muslim women, giving them greater benefits after divorce (Basu 2008).

The Shah Bano case also occurred in the context of rising religiously inspired participation in electoral politics. Although a small minority, Muslims in India participate actively in party politics. Where they constitute a sizable group, they often support a Muslim-identified party such as the Muslim League, a re-creation of the party that helped create Pakistan; this strategy works where Muslims make up around a third of the electorate. Where they are a smaller minority, they choose a secular party they hope will support their interests, though such parties are usually dominated by Hindu politicians. While it was dominant, the ruling Congress Party received the most Muslim votes, which partly explains its support for the Muslim Women's Bill. Since the Congress's decline in the late 1980s, Muslims also have supported state-level and ethnic parties.

Growing Muslim movements are in part a reaction to the growth of Hindu nationalism and its party, the Bharatiya Janata Party (BJP) (see chapter 7), which was the ruling party from 1999 to 2004. The BJP's ideology, *Hindutva,* is based on a claim that Hinduism lies at the core of Indian national history and identity. Most Hindu nationalists do not claim that Muslims have no rights in India, but they do argue that Muslims and others must recognize the cultural influence and centrality of Hinduism to true Indian nationalism. The party actively opposes what it sees as "appeasement" of Muslims and other religious minorities and instead calls for a uniform civil code and the end of quotas reserving educational and civil service positions for Muslims or other minorities (an Indian form of affirmative action). Hindu nationalists reject official secularism, arguing it is a Western import of little relevance to deeply religious India and that it has been used as an excuse to pander to religious minorities and thereby divide the nation: "According to the BJP, India will emerge as a strong nation only when it becomes a cohesive *Hindu Rashtra,* a Hindu nation-state" (Rao 2006, 76). They favor assimilation rather than recognition and support of minority rights. At the state level, BJP governments have actively worked to rewrite Indian textbooks to remove what they see as bias in favor of the Muslim role in the country's history. In Gujarat, the party actively used the 2002 anti-Muslim violence as a means to gain electoral support (Spodek 2010). While in power at the national level, however, the party moderated its views substantially and did not pursue the uniform civil code. Despite this partial moderation, the Hindu nationalists have caused significant fear and opposition among Muslims.

Since the start of the U.S.-led war in Afghanistan, fears of Islamic militancy have risen in India. The disputed northern region of Kashmir has long been a flashpoint. The Kashmiri movement was originally a regionally based movement for autonomy or independence from both India and Pakistan, rejecting both Hindu and Muslim domination. India's continued refusal to allow a referendum on Kashmir's independence, however, has led the movement in an increasingly religious direction, with active support of neighboring Pakistan. Terrorist bombs that destroyed a Mumbai hotel and killed hundreds in 2008 raised tensions further, though in response, Muslims led a major demonstration in the city against terrorism. Howard Spodek (2010) argued that while violent Muslim militancy certainly exists in India, it is unlikely to achieve a widespread following; India's democracy continues to allow Muslim participation, and its economic success is reducing the young, unemployed population that is typically subject to militant recruitment. A potentially violent conflict was avoided when an appeals court ruling in 2010 divided ownership of the disputed temple site in Ayodhya (from which the Hindu pilgrims were returning when attacked in 2002) between Hindus and Muslims and no major reaction occurred.

In early 2011, the country's Supreme Court stayed the appeals court ruling, however, pending its own decision.

CASE SUMMARY

India's battle over secularism and the role of religion raises the classic questions about equal citizenship and clashing values that have arisen in the West, but it does so in very different circumstances. Faced with a religious and religiously divided population, the founders of India's democracy agreed to a secular state but defined that state as a neutral arbiter among religions rather than as a supporter or opponent of any particular religion. Recognizing religious groups' autonomy to follow their own laws, however, has pitted communal rights against individual rights of equal citizenship. The state has come to treat Hindus and Muslims differently in this arena, granting much greater autonomy to the Muslim minority. Much of this debate has involved, as is so often the case, questions about women's rights within the religious community. Despite the goals of the country's first leaders, the state's official secular stance does not seem to be reducing the role of religion. Indeed, religious movements seem stronger now than at any time since independence. These movements among Hindu and Muslim groups (as well as other small religious groups such as Sikhs) have raised serious challenges to Indian secularism, the survival of which some see as threatened.

CASE STUDY

Mexico: Anticlericalism in a Catholic Country

- Nineteenth-century political battles over role of the church

- Revolution established principle of separation of church and state

- Ambiguity between state as neutral arbiter versus *laicismo*

- Democracy tolerates public role of religion somewhat more

- *Laicismo* nonetheless seems fully established

Mexico is a predominantly Christian country, with over 90 percent of its population self-described as Catholic. Despite the over-whelming influence of the church, however, the country has a long-running tradition of French-style *laïcité,* or *laicismo* in Span-ish, meaning secular society. The Mexican state under the seventy-one-year rule of the PRI always maintained an uneasy rela-tionship with the Catholic Church, in large part owing to the anticlerical tradition of the party's radical wing, which itself had roots in nineteenth-century battles over the influence of the church. While Mexico's presidency is now in the hands of a traditionally pro-Cath-olic conservative party, the Party of National Action (PAN), the story of Mexico serves as an important example of a highly religious society that has grappled with movements for strict church-state separation.

Anticlericalism in Mexico originated in large part from the *laïcité* that emerged out of the French Revolution. The Mexican War of Independence of 1810 was led by an alliance of convenience between liberal activists and conservatives. Although the conservatives were essentially pro-monarchy, they had seen their mother country, Spain, overrun by Napo-leon's armies and were essentially forced to seek independence from French-ruled Spain. This liberal-conservative division colored many of the subsequent political battles, which in the nineteenth century took the form of several armed conflicts and coups d'état.

For liberals, the church became a pre-ferred target, as it represented the connec-tion to the elite of the old (colonial) regime, much as it had to French revolutionaries just decades prior. In the 1830s, Vice President Valentín Gómez Farías (acting as the chief executive under the largely absentee presi-dent, General Antonio López de Santa Anna) began a series of reforms, which included the secularization of education; the breaking of financial ties with the church; and, most alarmingly to the conservatives, the expro-priation of church land. Santa Anna returned to the capital and overthrew his own vice president in a coup. He then reversed much of Farías's liberal agenda. But the seesawing between moderate sentiments and radical secularism would continue for decades.

A Mexican woman attends an Ash Wednesday service in Mexico City. Mexico has long had a complicated relationship with the Catholic Church. While the overwhelming majority of Mexicans are Catholic and fairly religious, the state since the revolution has been secular and usually anticlerical, having policies similar to the French *laïcité.*

Credit: Sara Escobar/LatinContent/Getty Images

In 1859, radical liberals launched a successful attack against the conservative government and pushed to marginalize the church in several ways. They nationalized church property and sold it at auction; closed down monasteries; and created a civil service system to infringe on the church's traditional role of cataloguing births, marriages, and deaths. The new government thus estab-lished a clear separation between church and state, which remains a pillar of the Mexican political system. By the time of the Mexican Revolution of 1910, anticlericalism ran strong among the commanders, many of whom viewed religion as an oppressive instrument of elite landowners. The aftermath of the Mexican Revolution, when the victors took over the state, only sparked further distrust between church and state.

The 1917 Constitution helped set in place many of the radical views that emerged from the Revolution. Like the Indian consti-tution, Mexico's constitution portrays an ambiguous vision of secularism. Early on, the Constitution employs the kind of secular language found in the First Amendment of the U.S. constitution, in that "Congress may not dictate laws that establish or prohibit any religion" (Article 3, 1917 Constitution). But later the document is more reminiscent of the French and Turkish models of *laïcité*. It mentions "the historic principle of the separation of the state and the churches" (Article 130), and goes on to state that "ministers of cults [i.e., priests] will not be able to carry out public duties. As citizens, they will have the right to vote, but not to be voted in" (Article 130, Sec. D). In addition, clergy were banned from holding public religious services, publishing religious literature, or opposing "the laws of the country or its institutions" (Article 130, Sec. E).

By the time the postrevolutionary regime consolidated power under Plutarco Elías Calles (president 1924–1928), divisions between the radical victors of the revolution and the church had only intensified. In 1926, in response to political attacks from conservatives, Calles deported around 200 members of the clergy, closed all religious schools, and halted all religious services. Christians in Jalisco and Michoacan rebelled, inspiring other forms of resistance around the country and igniting the Cristero War (1926–1929). It is against this backdrop of state-led anticlericalism that the PAN was founded in 1939. The PAN, which took the presidency in 2000 in the first transfer of power away from the PRI in seventy-one years, became associated with conservative values and has traditionally been seen as closer than the PRI to the church.

In conjunction with the move toward democratization in the 1990s, the Mexican state began to embrace a more tolerant stance toward religion in general, though the principles of staunch secularism remain part of the debate. The late public intellectual Carlos Monsiváis (cited in Campos Jiménez 2009) wrote that without *laicismo*, the Mexican state would not be "viable," since the protection of religious minorities, including Protestants, remained central to the duties of any Mexican government. In many ways, the inheritors of the tradition of *laicismo* are members of the Party of the Democratic Revolution (PRD), which since its founding in 1989 has attracted many disaffected radical PRI members. In

Mexico City, where abortion is legal in the first twelve weeks of pregnancy, the PRD has been dominant since the late 1990s. In 2009 the party was the driving force behind the legalization of gay marriage in the capital. The Catholic Church fought these reforms, but the Supreme Court ruled abortion to be a matter for the states to decide and the gay marriage law to be constitutional. In the conservative state of Guanajuato, the Church has tried to push for the public funding of Catholic education, and as of early 2011, the state government had decided to delegate that decision to the federal Congress.

Despite the strong influence of the Catholic Church, Mexicans have become accustomed to the lay state. For example, a survey conducted by a progressive Catholic organization found that 91 percent of Catholic Mexicans were in favor of access to contraception and 96 percent felt that access should be provided free of charge by the government— positions inconsistent with traditional Church doctrine. Even the PAN, whose founding came about in part as a result of the PRI's anti-Catholic oppression of the past, has been coy about taking on church-state separation directly. Both PAN presidents since 2000— Vicente Fox and Felipe Calderón—have not ventured far in their criticism of *laicismo*, though Calderón has openly discussed his faith. Instead, the PAN has focused the bulk of its agenda on economic policies and issues related to security and corruption.

CASE SUMMARY

Mexico's long-standing anticlericalism is unusual, but it is reminiscent of Turkey and France, with whom it shares a history of a political founding based in part on opposition to an established religion. While Mexicans by and large remain religious people, the church has not played the role it has in many Latin American countries. In the nineteenth century, as was true in much of Europe, divisions between conservatives supporting the church and liberals wanting to reduce its power were central to national politics. The revolution established *laicismo* as the law of the land. The church and its supporters have at times battled to regain a greater role for the church, and in the context of the new democracy the state has become more tolerant of religion. Nonetheless, *laicismo* appears to be firmly planted in Mexico, at least for the foreseeable future.

Summary

Secularism has long been seen a part of modernity and therefore the modern state. In reality, however, religion continues to play a prominent role in many parts of the world. Officially secular states find it nearly impossible to be truly neutral among religions, and religious minorities argue the state should not be completely neutral but instead should work to protect their threatened interests. Doing so in the name of cultural respect raises fundamental questions about values, often pitting individual rights as understood by liberals against group rights aimed at cultural preservation. These debates have affected Western states, many of which seemed headed toward complete secularization just a decade or two ago, as well as more religious postcolonial states and societies. Religion and religious divisions, it seems, are becoming more, not less, relevant to modern politics. As is so often the case, these battles about the place of religion and religious values centrally involve the role of women and women's rights, a subject to which we now turn.

GENDER: THE CONTINUING STRUGGLE FOR EQUAL SOCIAL STATUS, REPRESENTATION, AND PARTICIPATION

The women's movement and changes in women's position, activity, and status have been the most dramatic social and political revolution of the last generation, especially in wealthy countries. The number of women in the workforce in wealthy countries, in professional positions, and in higher education has skyrocketed since the 1960s. Jeane Kirkpatrick wrote in the early 1970s in her classic study of the United States, *Political Woman:*

> Half a century after the ratification of the nineteenth amendment, no woman has been nominated to be president or vice president, no woman has served on the Supreme Court. Today, there is no woman in the cabinet, no woman in the Senate, no woman serving as governor of a major state, no woman mayor of a major city, no woman in the top leadership of either major party. (1974, 3)

With the exception of presidential nomination by a major party (and Hillary Rodham Clinton came close in 2008), all that has changed. While women still make up a small percentage of each of the offices Kirkpatrick mentions, they are present in noticeable numbers, and many other countries outstrip the United States in percentage of women in high offices.

The contemporary women's movement in the West emerged from the tumultuous 1960s. Initially, women's rights and feminism were seen as exclusively Western concerns of little relevance to the rest of the world, especially the poorest countries. In many postcolonial countries, though, the women's movement has expanded greatly since the 1980s, often in conjunction with the democratization process we discussed in chapter 9. This expansion was marked by major United Nations conferences on women in 1985 in Nairobi, Kenya, and in 1995 in Beijing, China. Women in many postcolonial societies struggle to gain equal legal status with men in areas of family law, a victory now mostly won in wealthier countries. Also, like women in wealthier countries, they demand greater social status and a more extensive role in the political process.

The women's movement and feminist theory have raised fundamental political questions. We noted in a text box in chapter 4 that gender is a distinct identity category in part because women themselves often are used as markers of identity. Particular notions of gender roles frequently help define what it means to be a member of a particular nation, ethnic group, race, or religion, so when women challenge traditional gender roles, they implicitly challenge the validity of other identity groups to which they belong. Women who demand recognition of gender as a distinct category of concern have thus come into conflict not only with nationalists in the West but also with postcolonial nationalists who demanded national unity to throw off colonial rule, male revolutionary leaders who demanded unity to achieve the revolution, and leaders of racial or ethnic groups who demanded unity to overcome oppression. Women's movements and feminist theory have threatened all other groups at one time or another.

Differing Feminist Agendas As they challenged other groups in many societies, feminists also debated among themselves what their full agenda ought to be. Liberal feminists focus on gaining equal rights with men as their main goal, and they tend not to challenge social or political norms beyond that, accepting existing political and economic systems but demanding equal treatment within them. Many feminist theorists, though, demand more than just equal treatment in legal, political, and economic contexts. Most have come to believe that major social and political institutions need to change if women are to make full use of legal equality. Carole Pateman (1988), for instance, questioned the terms of equal citizenship itself, contending that citizenship as typically conceived is inherently male and patriarchal, with its greatest expression being military service. She argues for a new conception of citizenship that values women's lived experience—one that places motherhood, for instance, on the same moral level as military service. Women in racial or ethnic minorities and in the Global South, on the other hand, have criticized the global women's movement as being too focused on concerns exclusive to white women in wealthy countries, arguing successfully over the last two decades for an expansion of feminist theory and political demands to recognize the distinct needs of women of color and poor women.

Still other feminists point to more practical concerns: key aspects of welfare states such as access to health care and to contraception in particular and affordable child care have been recognized as essential to women achieving full political and economic participation. Even where broad equality has been achieved, much of society, including many young women, still assumes that women will (and should) be the primary caregivers for children, and this responsibility impacts their economic and political lives. Studies show that even in families where women work (though still often do not earn) as much as men, they continue to provide the bulk of child care and unpaid household labor, creating what has come to be known in the United States as the "second shift." In response, feminist activists increasingly are calling for a change in social assumptions, perceptions, attitudes, and discourses as essential to full realization of the equity that is now legally theirs in many countries.

Objectives and Outcomes

Shifting the Boundaries of the Public and Private Spheres Women's demands for inclusion have raised a fundamental question about what is and ought to be "public" and "private." Most political debate is restricted to what is deemed public, with private matters left to the individual, family, and religious institutions. Each society defines for itself, however, what is public and what is private, and the women's movement has successfully pressured many societies to redefine these boundaries to make formerly private concerns into public ones. In most societies, including those in the West, men's treatment of their wives was a private concern: verbal, physical, and sexual abuse, as long as it did not go as far as murder (and sometimes even when it did), was typically ignored and considered a private, family matter. The women's movement has changed this in many societies by arguing that abusive relationships within the private sphere of the family violate fundamental rights and impede women's ability to participate fully in the public sphere. Women's demands continue to question and at times shift the public/private boundary in many societies, especially in areas of legal status and relationships within families.

Social, Legal, and Economic Status In many societies, women have gained recognition as a group with legitimate concerns and basic political rights equal to men; they are allowed to vote and, at least in theory, hold elective office. Their social and legal status, however, is less uniformly equal to men's. Women's groups worldwide have sought greater access for women to education and participation in the labor force at all levels, and while women have not achieved full parity, they have made tremendous gains in a wide variety of societies. While many people in the West have an image of Western women as having achieved nearly equal status with men

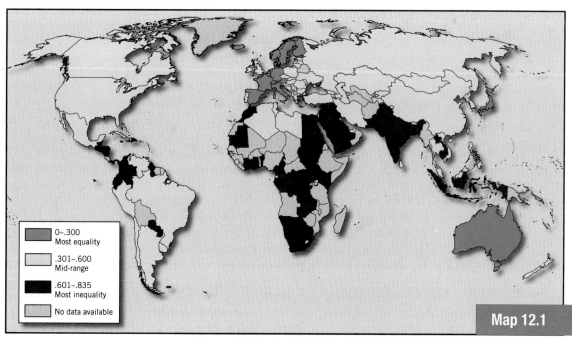

0–.300
Most equality

.301–.600
Mid-range

.601–.835
Most inequality

No data available

Map 12.1

Gender Inequality

Source: Gender Inequality Index 2008, International Human Development Indicators, United Nations Development Programme.

even as women in postcolonial countries continue to be mired in oppression, in many postcolonial countries, this image no longer applies. The gender gap in educational access and attainment has narrowed substantially in most Latin American and African countries and in some Asian ones as well over the last two decades, although, as is true everywhere, professional status and labor force participation rates lag behind education. The Country and Concept table (pages 606–607) provides several measures of gender equality for our case study countries, showing that some postcolonial societies are not that much more unequal in gender terms than are wealthier countries, while Map 12.1 displays gender inequality rankings around the world. Note that much of Latin America, for instance, is in the same broad mid-range as the United States.

Concerns about achieving greater social and economic status have led women to demand reproductive rights and state support for childbearing and child rearing. Because women bear children and in all societies continue to do the bulk of child rearing, improvement in these areas is essential to improving their social status. Women's movements have successfully championed the spread of access to contraception in much of the world, and birth rates have fallen significantly in most countries over the last generation. Legalized abortion remains a controversial subject, with women successfully leading efforts in many societies to support it even as moral objections, often from other women, keep it illegal in quite a few others and disputed in most. Women in approximately sixty countries currently have access to legalized abortion.

Women, especially in wealthier countries, have also demanded greater state support for childbearing and child rearing to facilitate their participation in the labor force while allowing them to have children. Support has included paid and unpaid maternity leave, paid and unpaid paternity leave (for fathers to help with child rearing), and access to affordable and high-quality child care. State responses to these demands have broadly mirrored the types of welfare states outlined in chapter 11. Social democratic welfare states provide more generous maternity leave and greater access to child care, and women's labor force participation is highest in these societies. Christian democratic welfare states are generous, but their ruling philosophy remains based primarily on the male-head-of-household model, and these societies have lower labor force participation rates for women. Liberal welfare states, though providing relatively ungenerous benefits, are in the middle on women's labor force participation, reflecting the emphasis of these states on work for wages.

A key target of women's groups worldwide has been the achievement of legal status equal to that of men in areas of family law, including rights in regard to custody of children, land ownership, and inheritance of family property. These gains have been achieved in virtually all wealthy countries but not in all postcolonial countries. In many of the latter, women still face various legal inequities vis-à-vis men that prevent them from independently owning land or inheriting property; in some cases, women are even restricted from having independent access to banking and travel. And while virtually all countries have active women's movements working toward these goals, women in most developing societies remain poorer and less educated, on average, than in wealthier countries, so their movements lack the resources that have helped wealthier women achieve many gains.

Women in the poorest countries, though, often have powerful potential allies in international development agencies and nongovernmental organizations (NGOs), which have come to recognize that women, especially in rural areas, play a crucial role in development. Educating and employing women has been shown to lead to dramatic increases in use of contraception and reduced birth rates, and helping women obtain better incomes demonstrably improves the education and health of children, as women on average are more willing to spend their income in those areas than are men. Development agencies and NGOs therefore support efforts to educate women and improve their legal status as part of a broader development effort; a primary form of this in recent years has been microfinance loans to women to start their own small businesses. As with the broader women's movement, external efforts such as these have raised numerous debates. Women activists in postcolonial societies often argue that Western development agencies and NGOs, however sympathetic to the cause they might be, do not fully understand the perspectives or needs of the women they are trying to help. Donor agencies' and NGOs' priorities can distort domestic groups' goals because the latter must follow the direction of those providing them with financial support. That said, it is nonetheless clear that the women's movement has expanded globally over the last generation, and that numerous aid agencies and NGOs are actively working to champion what they perceive to be women's interests.

MINI CASE

Women in Saudi Arabia and Kuwait

Women's rights to equal citizenship remain in dispute in many countries around the world, though in no area are the disputes and gender disparity greater than in the countries in the Persian Gulf region. The restrictions on women's rights are not necessarily of long standing; in many cases, they arose with the expansion of oil wealth and Islamist movements in the last few decades. Prior to the rise of oil wealth, greater variation in the treatment of women was common in the region. Saudi Arabia and Kuwait are two countries that have seen repeated struggles over the issue of women's rights. Despite their many similarities and official adherence to Islamic law, the status of women in the two countries is different, though in ways that would not be predicted from the history of women's inclusion in citizenship in the West.

Both of these Persian Gulf kingdoms base their laws on Islam, but each interprets that law somewhat differently. The two countries share laws regarding women's rights in marriage, divorce, and inheritance that give men much greater freedom than women. They differ, however, in that Saudi law effectively defines women as legal minors, who have virtually no adult rights. This means that they are not allowed to travel, work, study, marry, receive medical treatment, legalize a

contract, or testify in court without the permission or accompaniment of a close male relative, usually a father or husband. Women exist legally under what is known as "male guardianship" at all times. In addition, Saudi Arabia has created a system that critics have dubbed "sexual apartheid," complete gender segregation in all public facilities. Universities, most offices, shopping malls, restaurants, and other such places are strictly segregated by sex. In recent years, women-only shopping malls and hotels have been built. In contrast, Kuwaiti women have greater freedom on a day-to-day basis. While they do not have full freedoms in the area of marriage and divorce, they are allowed to drive, travel, and dress as they please. Sex segregation has not been nearly as consistent, though it is growing. A rising Islamist group in the Kuwaiti parliament successfully pushed to resegregate public universities in 2003, which had been integrated since the 1970s.

In both countries, however, women have become increasingly prominent in the economic and educational arenas. As in Iran (see our case study in this chapter), women now form a majority in both countries' higher education systems. In Kuwait there are two-and-a-half times more women than men in higher education, in Saudi Arabia one-and-a-half times more. This does not necessarily translate into higher income however. First, in these oil-rich states, a college education is not always necessary for a high income: men often simply go to work in business after secondary school. Second, Islamic versions of the "glass ceiling" exist that limit women's advancement. In Saudi Arabia, in particular, it is illegal for women to work in any position in which they will come into regular contact with unrelated men. This leaves them working more heavily in the public sector, as teachers of girls, and out of sight of the general public. Saudi women who work earn only 16 percent of the income of working Saudi men; in contrast, Kuwaiti women earn 35 percent what Kuwaiti men do. In 2006 women constituted 42 percent of the Kuwaiti workforce, making the country the highest-ranking Arab state in this respect.

While some women seem willing to live with these restrictions, both countries certainly have budding women's movements. Saudi Arabia's women's movement is still having difficulty getting legal recognition for its organizations. Nonetheless, in November 1990, forty-five Saudi women shocked the nation by driving through the streets of the capital. In Kuwait, in contrast, an active women's movement emerged in the 1960s and, among other things, successfully resisted the imposition of wearing of the *burqa,* the full-body Islamic covering common in the region. In urban Kuwait, wearing the *burqa* has long been the exception rather than the rule. This is in sharp contrast to Saudi Arabia, where it remains the norm and is legally enforced by "morality police" who have virtually unlimited power to harass or arrest women who show any body part in public.

In Kuwait, the main goal of the women's movements since the 1970s has been gaining the right to vote. Kuwait's parliament has greater power than most in the region; the emir still must approve its laws, but he tries to support the parliamentary majority whenever possible to maintain his popularity. A major women's push for the right to vote failed in 1999, but a renewed effort succeeded in

2005. In the 2007 parliamentary elections, Kuwaiti women voted and ran for office for the first time. They constituted a majority of the electorate and helped put an opposition coalition into power (though one that included a conservative Islamic party, so the new government did not expand women's rights further). In 2009, four women were elected to Kuwait's parliament, and a total of three women have been appointed to cabinet positions since 2000. In contrast and in spite of the fact that Saudi Arabia has also had a woman appointed to the cabinet, the most immediate focus of the much smaller and weaker Saudi women's movement is on gaining the right to drive. In 2008, a major Saudi cleric argued that under certain circumstances, women driving would not violate Islamic law, raising women's hopes that the law might change in the not too distant future. Many observers speculate that the aging king is also sympathetic to greater freedoms for women, though he hasn't said so publicly. In 2011, the battle over gender roles seemed to heat up, in part in response to the "Arab Spring" uprisings. Women activists used Facebook and Twitter to demand the right to drive, and in May one of the effort's leaders was arrested for publicly driving.

CASE SUMMARY

The image of a woman fully clad in black is one of the first that comes to the minds of many Westerners when they think of the Persian Gulf or of the Middle East in general. That image has some validity, especially in Saudi Arabia. Kuwait, however, is only one of several examples of Middle Eastern countries where that image is inaccurate. While women have not achieved the Western feminist goal of fully equal citizenship anywhere in the region, they are much closer in some countries than in others. Even in Saudi Arabia, one of the most restrictive states in terms of women's rights, women have made economic and educational gains within sexual apartheid, and a budding women's movement is demanding more.

Political Representation Women's movements have also focused on improving the representation and participation of women in the political process, even in countries that are not fully democratic. As we noted in chapter 7 (see Where and Why: Women in Power), proportional representation (PR) electoral systems tend to produce higher numbers of women representatives, as do multimember district systems. Scholars use the term "descriptive representation" to indicate representation by people who look like you and have similar life experiences. Jane Mansbridge (2000) argued that such representation is particularly important when social inequality results in particular groups of citizens not trusting their elected representatives who hail from a different group, when communication among members of different groups might be difficult, and when unforeseen issues arise between elections. For instance, gender inequality may make many women not trust or feel comfortable communicating honestly with their male representatives. Furthermore, when a new issue arises that did not exist at the time of the last election, citizens may want representatives from their social group who have had similar experiences to make decisions that will reflect their perspectives. For all these reasons, women's movements have worked to improve the percentage of women in political office. Many countries have women's groups whose primary purpose is to train and fund women candidates.

While women have definitely gained ground in parliaments around the world, they remain just over 19 percent of the total members of parliament worldwide (see Map 12.2). As with the overall gender inequality shown in Map 12.1, parliamentary representation varies widely but not systematically by region; a number of postcolonial states have higher percentages of female representatives than do the United States or some European countries. The relatively slow process of change has led women's movements in many countries to champion the creation of quotas for women's legislative participation. These take three forms: (1) political parties, in closed-list PR systems in which they create a list of candidates, voluntarily impose their own internal quota for women on their list; (2) laws require that women constitute a certain percentage of all parties' candidates; or (3) laws reserve a certain number of legislative seats for women, elected in a separate vote from the rest of the legislature. Quotas are typically set at anywhere from 25 to 50 percent of the total seats or candidates. While only 10 states had any type of quota before 1980 and 12 more had adopted them by 1990, over 100 had them by 2010. The last twenty years have seen an explosion of quotas for women's representation, though the majority of these have been voluntarily adopted within parties.

Krook (2009) argued that quotas are implemented most successfully where they fit with other major political institutions; if they contradict other aspects of the political system, they are unlikely to have a major impact. Because party quotas are for the number of candidates, they do not guarantee women a particular number of legislative seats; how well the rest of the political system supports women's candidates is therefore important. Aili Mari Tripp and Alice Kang (2008) concluded from a large statistical analysis of quota use all over the world that quotas, especially reserved seats and voluntary party quotas, and use of PR electoral systems have a greater effect on the number of women in legislatures than economic development, religion, or other commonly used explanations for why women do or do not gain seats.

The success of quotas, especially those mandated by law (more typical in Asia and Africa than in Europe), raises major questions for democratic theories of inclusion that are similar to debates over affirmative action (see chapter 4). Does requiring that women represent a certain percentage of candidates or MPs violate the liberal principles of equal citizenship, or is it a necessary measure to enhance those principles in the face of long-standing social pressures and norms that have kept women out of political office?

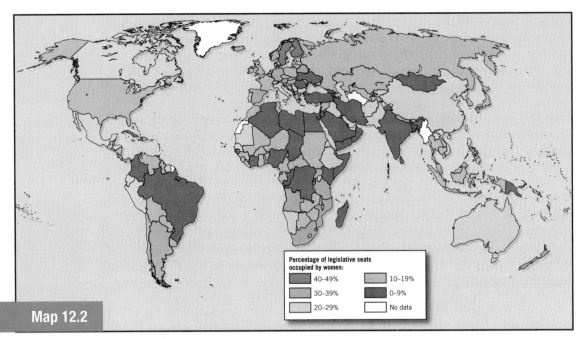

Map 12.2

Women in Legislative Seats Worldwide

Source: Inter-Parliamentary Union's Women in National Parliaments, http://www.ipu.org/wmn-e/classif.htm.

Note: Percentages are for lower and single houses only. Data for upper houses, where available, can be found at the source Web site above. South Africa's estimate does not include the thirty-six special rotating delegates appointed on an ad hoc basis; all percentages given are therefore calculated on the basis of the fifty-four permanent seats.

Even in countries where women have achieved substantial gains, they have not achieved full parity with men. Nowhere are women fully equal with men in terms of professional status, wages, or political representation. We examine these issues in two countries that have faced significant changes in the last twenty years, countries that most people do not think of as having important women's movements: Russia and Iran. These countries demonstrate the ubiquity of the global women's movement and the questions it has raised.

CASE STUDY

Russia: Women through Social and Political Transformation

- Soviet era: Social status relatively good but no political participation

- Transition to market economy lowered women's employment and wages

- Transition to democracy lowered number of women in legislature

- Resurgence of traditional attitudes about gender roles

- Active women's movement in 1990s curtailed by Putin's semi-authoritarian rule

Russian women, like Russian men, have lived through dramatic and at times traumatic social, economic, and political change since the end of the Cold War. The state and regime they grew up under imploded, an older state (Russia) was re-created, the state's social and economic systems were transformed almost entirely, and a new regime (some would argue two regimes) emerged. The Soviet Union left an unusual legacy for women's role in society. Soviet women were heavily involved in the labor force and highly educated before their contemporaries in the West or postcolonial societies, and the Soviet Union at times attempted to counter traditional cultural norms about gender roles, though with mixed results. Yet Soviet women had no history of autonomous political action, in spite of some formal "representation" in the centralized Soviet political system. In the new Russia, women have nearly complete legal rights in all areas, but in practice these are often not enforced. They continue to face cultural and social constraints to their full participation in society and politics, but they remain nearly equal to men in their participation in the economy and superior to men in their educational achievement. Neither of these achievements, however, has translated into equal wages and incomes. A growing women's movement emerged in the 1990s, but Vladimir Putin's elimination of much of Russia's autonomous civil society severely curtailed it after 2000.

Even as the Soviet Union claimed to favor full gender equality, this was always ideologically subordinated to the needs of the proletarian revolution, and in practical terms it was secondary to the needs of building a stronger state and economy. Early Soviet laws gave women more freedoms than most societies at the time. For example, by the 1920s, women had gained the right to marry whom they wanted and divorce when they wanted, own their own property separately from their husbands, inherit property, keep their own surnames after marriage, refuse to move with their husbands, and have abortions paid for by the state. As Josef Stalin created a more centralized dictatorship in the 1930s, he declared the "woman question" closed and women to be completely "liberated." Facing a falling birth rate, he made abortions illegal to encourage more children but also encouraged women to expand their participation in the labor force because of a labor shortage. By the 1960s, women's participation rate in

Feminists celebrate International Women's Day in Moscow in 2006. The banner reads "Flowers—today, shackles—every day?" Like women in many countries, Russian women achieve at higher levels than men in the educational system but still command significantly lower wages, and they continue to provide the bulk of household labor and child rearing.

Credit: Nataliya Kolesnikova/AFP/Getty Images

the labor force was nearly equal to men's, abortion was again legal and widely available, and women were rapidly catching up to men in the educational system.

The state continued to face a demographic dilemma, which only grew worse after the end of communism: it encouraged women to participate in the labor force to increase production, but at the same time Russian women were having fewer babies. To counter this, the Soviet government instituted generous and widely available child care as early as the 1920s and later added generous maternity leave: a total of 112 days at full pay. Economic reform in the late 1980s under Mikhail Gorbachev, the Soviet Union's last Communist leader, led to the first recognized official unemployment policy under the Soviet system. With fewer workers needed and the birth rate continuing to fall, the communist state in its last years shifted to a more traditional attitude. In the words of Gorbachev:

> Over the years . . . we failed to pay attention to women's specific rights and needs arising from their role as mother and home-maker, and their indispensable educational function as regards children. . . . Women no longer have enough time to perform their everyday duties at home—housework, the upbringing of children and the creation of a good family atmosphere. . . . We are now holding heated debates . . . about the question of what we should do to make it possible for women to return to their purely womanly mission. (quoted in Racioppi and See 1995, 824)

This would be a harbinger of things to come in terms of cultural attitudes, though not of actual shifts in the work done by women.

The transition to a market economy after the dissolution of the Soviet state produced dramatic economic decline for most of the 1990s. Men and women alike suffered from this, but most observers see women as having lost more. Women's full legal rights were preserved in the new 1993 constitution, but economic and cultural change nonetheless harmed women's position. Women continued to equal men in their participation rates in employment, and both suffered unemployment at about the same rates as the communist economy transitioned to a market-based system. Women, however, faced much longer periods of unemployment than men, who gained new jobs more quickly. In the early 2000s, as the economy began to rebound, men and women benefited about equally in terms of gaining new jobs. Women's wages, however, have always been and remain below men's: they were on average 70 percent of men's at the end of the communist era, and by 2009 this number had dropped to 65 percent despite women's higher education levels. Women receive lower wages and are in less prestigious positions even in fields in which they predominate, such as education and public service. The biggest cause of the wage gap, though, is the shift of women out of high-paying sectors, such as finance and industry, since the end of the Soviet era (Roschin and Zubarevich 2005, 7–17). A 2010 UN report found that 71 percent of all professionally employed women were working in sectors in which the average wage was lower than the national average, as compared to only 51 percent of men (Baskakova and Soboleva 2010).

The transition to a market economy has unquestionably affected other aspects of women's working and personal lives. Women increasingly end up in part-time employment, which further lowers their income relative to that of men. They are also overrepresented among Russia's poor, in part due to the large numbers of impoverished and elderly widows, as Russian women's life expectancy is thirteen years longer than men's (seventy-two versus fifty-nine years), one of the largest gaps in the world. (The reasons for this gap are the subject of much debate; the factors include much higher male rates of tuberculosis, industrial accidents, suicide, and alcohol and drug abuse.) Women, in contrast, seem to suffer more from psychological problems.

The Soviet system of state-sponsored preschools shrank dramatically as funding dried up in the 1990s, causing attendance to drop as well. In the late Soviet era, as many as 84 percent of children three years of age and older were in child care institutions; by 2000, that number had fallen to only 47 percent. Families, including extended families, have been forced to make up the difference. The Soviet Union's relatively generous maternity leave policies were preserved and even extended, and a "parental leave" for either parent was instituted as well, to be used until a child reaches eighteen months of age, though it only provided $17 per month in the 1990s, when the poverty level was about $200 (Teplova 2007).

By 2007, the Russian government was once again concerned about low birth rates, so it began offering financial rewards to mothers of second and third (and more) children. Welfare benefits were widespread but provided very little income, forcing most women to continue working at least part-time. Like women in the United States and elsewhere, Russian women continue to work the second shift as well. In the mid-1990s, they were employed an average of thirty-eight hours per week, compared to forty-three hours for men, but women also did an average of thirty hours per week of household chores and child care, whereas men did only fourteen hours per week (Roschin and Zubarevich 2005, 20).

Russian women did not sit idly by in the face of these challenges. An active women's movement arose in the early 1990s, supported by Western donors interested in developing Russia's new civil society. The Soviet Union had allowed only official and therefore state-controlled women's organizations to exist, so no autonomous civil society groups had been permitted until the reforms of the late 1980s. New women's organizations mushroomed in the early 1990s, with 300 registered by 1994 and 2,000 by the end of the decade. Many of these were small and poorly funded groups that did not survive long, but a few became important centers for gathering information and publicizing issues of concern to women. The most prominent of these groups began under the leadership of highly educated, professional women. Not all automatically adopted all aspects of Western feminism, though their emphasis on better working conditions, welfare support for women, and greater political representation were familiar to feminists worldwide. A division emerged within the movement between those who had been members of the official state-sponsored organizations of the Soviet era and focused on making practical gains in women's immediate well-being, and self-consciously feminist groups that were critical of the former Soviet organizations and sought extensive changes in social and cultural attitudes toward women. Other women's groups focused on broader issues such as the environment or peace, particularly in opposition to the war in the Russian province of Chechnya. While the women's movement gained strength in the early 1990s, by the end of the decade, internal divisions and a lack of resources had noticeably weakened it. Under President Putin it declined further,

as did most autonomous organizations in Russian civil society (Racioppi and See 1995).

Even at its height in the 1990s, the movement had limited success placing women in decision-making positions. The powerless Soviet legislature had a quota that ensured one-third of its members were women. This quota was eliminated at the time of the first competitive election for the Russian (as opposed to Soviet) parliament in 1990, resulting in only 5.4 percent of its members being women. The successor to the official Soviet women's organization, the Union of Women of Russia, formed a political party, Women of Russia, to contest the 1993 legislative elections. The party succeeded in raising women's numbers in the lower house of parliament, gaining 8 percent of the seats, and women overall constituted 13.6 percent of all members (higher than in the United States at the time), a significant accomplishment given the context. By the next election in 1995, however, many women were disillusioned with the party's failure to provide any concrete benefits, and it failed to gain the 5 percent of votes necessary to be allotted seats in the parliament. The total representation of women in that parliament fell to 10 percent, with a further decline to less than 8 percent in the 1999 election. This trend was reversed in elections in the new millennium: by 2011 (in the far less powerful legislature) 14 percent of the members of the lower house were female, tying Russia for eightieth place with Zambia on a global list (Inter-Parliamentary Union 2011).

Despite possessing full legal rights, Russian women continue to face attitudinal barriers to full participation in society. Social attitudes about women's roles seem to have become more traditional since the end of Communist rule. While a majority of both men and women expect women to work for a wage and accept women's participation in the paid workforce, and a majority of women want a fulfilling career, a majority of both genders also think that the man should be the primary breadwinner in the family. A 2002 study found the persistence of many traditional stereotypes of ideal male characteristics: strength, intelligence, and the provision of material security; ideal female characteristics were appearance, loving children, and housekeeping skills (White 2005, 431). These attitudes are apparently reflected in the economy as well: women have reported discrimination in hiring by men who prefer them to stay in the home, as well as incidents in which they were forced by employers to sign contracts promising not to get married or have children because businesses fear having to pay maternity leave.

CASE SUMMARY

While the new Russian state has preserved full legal rights and fairly extensive benefits for women, including maternity leave, it has done little to counter the underlying attitudes and norms that continue to limit the progress of women. Both President Boris Yeltsin and President Putin established government agencies ostensibly meant to improve the

status of women, but neither accomplished much. Overall, the state provides little support for ending discrimination against women. A recent United Nations report summed up the situation:

> There have been two distinct phases of policy formulation and implementation [about women's issues in Russia]. The first stage, in the 1990s, gave an appearance of activity, but tended to be limited to words. . . . [In] the second phase, dating from the turn of the Millennium, the state has given up both declarations and actions. Gender issues have effectively dropped out of the Government's socioeconomic priorities. (Bobylev 2005, 60)

Putin's crackdown on women's organizations along with the rest of civil society and his complete control of the legislature suggests that little will change in the foreseeable future.

CASE STUDY

Iran: Social Gains, Political and Cultural Restrictions, and Islamic Feminism

- Contradiction between social and economic gains and restrictive laws
- Female majority at all levels of education and growing inroads of women in employment
- Women's movement strongest when reformist elements were in power
- Women's movement mixes secular and Islamic women
- Active women's participation in the 2009 antiregime protests
- Greater legal restrictions under Ahmadinejad

In 2003, Iranian human rights lawyer and feminist activist Shirin Ebadi won the Nobel

Peace Prize amidst great adulation from much of the world but condemnation from the Iranian government. Three years later, a large group planned a demonstration in Tehran to protest discrimination against women. Police arrived and broke up the demonstrators before they really got started, arresting forty-two women and twenty-eight men. These actions launched a new wave of women's activity against laws they felt were discriminatory under the Islamic Republic. In response, the government under conservative President Mahmoud Ahmadinejad began a new crackdown in 2007 on public morality, especially women's public appearance. "Chastity police" arrested hundreds and harassed thousands of Iranians, mostly

Women featured prominently in the 2009 Iranian election and its aftermath. Here, women supporters of reformist candidate Mir Hossein Mousavi rally on election night as part of the "Green Movement." After the election, the movement put millions of people, including women, in the streets protesting what they and most of the world saw as fraudulent election results. The Iranian regime, though, successfully repressed the movement and subsequently clamped down on reformists of all types.

Credit: AP Photo/Ben Curtis

women, for not abiding by a particular interpretation of Islamic teachings about what women can do and how they can appear in public. This is only the latest battle in a long-standing dispute over women's rights in Iran. While the Iranian government certainly does not treat women equally in cultural and political areas, it has nonetheless allowed and often even encouraged significant social and economic gains. This has created a contradiction, as educated and employed women demand greater equality and the government continues to deny it. The women's movement leading this effort includes not only secular feminists opposed to the Islamic regime but also Islamic feminists who argue for an interpretation of Shiite Islamic teachings that grants greater gender equality than the Islamic Republic so far will accept.

Under the shah's modernization program of the 1960s and 1970s, women were encouraged to reject their traditional roles and appearance in order to "modernize" along Western lines. The effort had a much more significant effect in urban than rural areas. Like the rest of the shah's policies, however, it increasingly came to be seen as imposed by a dictator doing the West's bidding, and women were active participants in the 1978–1979 revolution that created the Islamic Republic. The political forces that brought down the shah included groups with disparate ideologies united in their opposition to the old regime (see chapter 9). Women were active in virtually all of these groups: secularized women in the secular forces of students, professionals, and traders and religious women in the Islamist groups. The revolutionary process itself, regardless of ideology, gave women an active role (though not as leaders) that brought them into the political arena in unprecedented numbers.

As the Islamist clerics under the Ayatollah Khomeini consolidated their power in 1979–1980, one of their first acts was to reverse the shah's Family Protection Law, which had Westernized much of the country's family law. The new regime eliminated women's right to divorce while giving men nearly an unlimited right to leave their wives; required women to wear the *hijab,* the Islamic veil, in public; forced women out of the legal profession and restricted them from several other professions; banned contraception; and segregated the education system. Many secular and Islamist women who had been active in the revolution felt betrayed and protested these changes, including hundreds of thousands who took to the streets in March 1979 to protest mandatory veiling, but their protests proved fruitless.

During the 1980s most of the social gains women had made since the 1960s were at least partially reversed: women's employment levels dropped, their political participation was minimal (only 4 women out of 270 MPs were elected to the first parliament after the revolution), and without access to contraception they bore more children. At the same time, the Iran-Iraq War (1980–1988) pushed women into the public sphere in other areas, as they performed much of the volunteer work the war required. The absence of men also gave women an opportunity to enter school at all levels to an unprecedented degree, which the government encouraged as part of a large literacy campaign. Indeed, gender segregation of schools increased girls' enrollment, as conservative parents were more willing to send their daughters to all-female schools. Any critical political activity was still severely repressed, however, especially in light of the war, but women found new paths to enter the public arena and education system.

With the war over, the government set out to improve the country's weak economy by pursuing an economic liberalization program throughout the early 1990s. Yet the various restrictions put on women's economic roles after the revolution came into direct conflict with economic growth. Spurred by a renewed women's movement and facing economic necessity, the government partially reversed various laws restricting the advancement of women. Over the course of the decade, most restrictions on what women could study and where they could work were eliminated, and the government reintroduced and actively supported contraception to reduce the birth rate and mandated maternity leave. Women were also allowed to reenter the legal profession in any position except that of courtroom judge. Fertility rates dropped, women advanced through the educational system, female literacy increased dramatically, more women chose not to marry, and the age of women's first marriage increased (Bahramitash and Kazemipour 2006).

By the new millennium, the results of these actions were quite significant. From the revolution to 2002, women's life expectancy increased from fifty-eight to seventy-two years, their illiteracy rate fell from 69 to 31 percent, the percentage of women still single in their early twenties increased from 21 to 54 percent, their fertility rate dropped from an average of 6.5 live births to 2.7, the gap between men and women in age of marriage and level of education dropped dramatically, and starting in 2000, women surpassed men to become the majority of entering university students (Bahramitash and Kazemipour 2006). By 2008, women were a majority of students in all university fields except engineering. They had become so prominent in medical education that the government passed a regulation that medical fields had to have a student body that included at least 30 percent of each gender to ensure a place for men.

Among other outcomes of these social changes, Iran's divorce rate skyrocketed in the new millennium, tripling from 2000 to 2010—this despite laws making divorce extremely difficult for women. One in seven marriages now ends in divorce. Women frequently waive their right to financial support under Islamic law in order to gain their husband's agreement to divorce. Anthropologist Pardis Mahdavi (2009) studied sexual relationships in contemporary Iran and reported she never met a woman who was "happily married" but did find very high levels of extramarital affairs, instigated by both wives and husbands.

As these dramatic social and economic changes were taking place, an active women's movement reemerged that involved both secular and Islamic feminists. The latter asserted their right to interpret the holy texts (*ijtihad*) and argued that Islam actually emphasizes gender equality. They used the Prophet Mohammad's wives and daughters as examples of women actively involved in the public sphere. They argued that

> true Islam . . . combined equality of opportunity for men and women to develop their talents and capacities and to participate in all aspects of social life, because it acknowledged women's maternal instinct and their essential role within the family. (Paidar 1995, 241)

These feminists rejected what they saw as Western society's sexual objectification of women and the individualistic assumptions of much Western feminism, but they nonetheless argued for a place of equality within Iran's Islamic society.

As the broader reform movement grew in the 1990s (see chapter 8), the women's movement became even more active. This was clear in the growing role of women's NGOs. Although only an estimated twenty NGOs were operating in Iran in 2005, they were very active in providing services and education for women, especially in urban areas (Alaedini and Razavi 2005, 69). Women also have started numerous publications whenever press restrictions are partially eased, the best known of which has been *Zanan* (*Women*), which became a major forum for both secular and Islamist women to present their arguments. Inspired in part by Shirin Ebadi's Nobel Prize, the women's movement proclaimed itself publicly at its first major demonstration at Tehran University in 2005, demanding constitutional changes to end gender discrimination. Despite police harassment, some 5,000 women managed to attend. Subsequently, the movement began a campaign to collect a million signatures on a petition demanding the constitutional changes (Hoodfar and Sadeghi 2009).

IN CONTEXT

WOMEN IN IRAN AND THE MIDDLE EAST

Improvements in the status of women in Iran since the late 1980s have made it roughly equal with the average of other Middle Eastern states on a variety of measures of women's well-being and equality, below average on political representation, but well ahead of the regional average in reduced fertility rate and women's education.

	Gender Inequality Index (2008)	Gender-empowerment measure (2010)	Fertility rate (births per woman, 2010–2015)	Ratio of female to male income (2009)	Percentage female adult literacy rate (2007)	Percentage female population with at least secondary education (2010)	Percentage female seats in parliament (2008)
Iran	0.674	0.331	1.7	0.32	77.2	39	2.8
Rest of Middle East	0.699	0.430	2.6	0.30	75.5	27	8.7

Source: United Nations Development Report 2007/2008 and 2009/2010, http://hdr.undp.org/en/statistics/data and UNDP Gender Indices, http://hdr.undp.org/en/statistics/indices/gdi_gem/.

Despite severe cultural and legal restrictions on women, the Islamic constitution gave them full rights to participate in politics, except for being barred from holding the office of the president. Prior to 1991, only women who were clearly identified as Islamists had been elected to the parliament. In that year's election, secular women activists were added to their ranks, and women's numbers peaked in the 1996 election at fourteen MPs, who formed the first women's caucus in the parliament. From the start of the Islamic Republic, most of the small number of women MPs worked actively in support of achieving greater equality for women. In the area of family law, women were granted slightly more rights to divorce, including the indexing of the traditional payment a man must make to his wife when divorcing her to take inflation into account, and greater rights over guardianship of children, which came with child allowances from the government. Such legal victories, though, have remained relatively few and minor. In defiance of the restriction on being president, forty-two women submitted their names as candidates in 2009, but the Guardian Council, which must approve all candidates, rejected them all.

The height of the reformist movement under President Mohammad Khatami (1997–2005) saw relatively limited legal changes beyond those already mentioned, but the government reduced the severity of the cultural restrictions on women's public actions. It did not enforce the rules about veiling and public segregation of the sexes with the zeal of earlier or subsequent governments. As we noted in chapter 8, the Islamic Republic has a long history of the clerical elite allowing reform efforts to expand and then clamping down on them when they go beyond what the conservative clerics find acceptable.

The election of President Ahmadinejad ended the Khatami-led reform effort. While Iranian women made unprecedented social and economic gains after 1988, they achieved much less in the way of legal equality and cultural freedom. Ahmadinejad's renewed efforts to restrict women and segregate them in public has included not only the crackdown since 2007 but also banning numerous women's (and other dissident) publications and Web sites and expanding the gender segregation of public amenities, including buses, taxis, and even telephone booths. In 2007–2008, more than one city built women-only parks behind high walls within which women could enjoy being outside and exercise without being veiled.

This crackdown, however, did not eliminate the women's movement. A women's coalition formed during the 2009 campaign and demanded to know each presidential candidate's position on key women's issues, a level of engagement women had not achieved before in presidential elections. Women were also very active participants in the massive protests that followed the rigged elections. Tahmasebi-Birgani (2010), a participant in the demonstrations, argued that both secular and Islamist women were involved not only to demand democracy but to demand greater gender equality, as they now see the two as inseparable. Nonetheless, and perhaps in response, the government passed a bill in early 2010 further restricting women's rights in divorce cases.

CASE SUMMARY

Economic needs and the women's movement to date have combined to achieve significant social, educational, and economic gains for women, though success has been far less in the legal, political, and cultural spheres. These changes have had a profound effect on Iranian families in terms of frequency and age of marriage, number of children, and frequency of divorce. An active women's movement continues. The movement is not only secular but also Islamic and tries to use powerful religious symbols and ideas to reinterpret women's place in the Islamic Republic. The 2009 protests in which it actively participated and the government's response to those protests, however, show that women have much still to achieve.

Summary

The women's movement has fundamentally questioned and challenged conventional liberal notions of modern citizenship as well as all other forms of identity. It has been the most successful domestic and international social movement of the last half century, changing mores and policies in many countries. While it has arguably achieved the greatest success in wealthy democracies, its effects have been felt everywhere, as our case studies demonstrate.

Our case studies and much other evidence point to a broad trend of women achieving great gains in the educational sphere that have translated only partially into gains in the economic sphere. While women are working for wages far more frequently than they used to in virtually every country, they work for less money and in less prestigious positions than men. Similarly, while they have made substantial gains in political power in many countries, especially in parts of Europe, they are nowhere equal to men in the political sphere. These continued shortcomings raise fundamental questions about whether our understanding of citizenship, common social attitudes, and major institutions have to change before women will achieve equal citizenship in its broadest conception. In addition to raising all these questions, the feminist movement has been intimately connected with the rise of the "gay rights movement," to which we now turn.

SEXUAL ORIENTATION: ASSIMILATION OR LIBERATION?

What is commonly known as the "gay rights movement," the demand for inclusion in full citizenship for people of all sexual orientations, challenges social norms at least as much or more than the women's movement with which it is interrelated. The movement for equality based on sexual orientation faces a unique set of challenges compared to the other movements discussed in this chapter and chapter 4. Its primary demand has been for public recognition; once this is achieved, other demands include full legal equality and open representation and participation in the political process. Recognition is especially central to the movement because homosexual activity has been hidden through most of human history. Homosexuals are able to hide their identity in a way women or minorities typically cannot. Throughout history and around the world, people have engaged in homosexual activity but have hidden it because of social and political discrimination and criminalization. In this context, being publicly recognized and "coming out" as gay or lesbian is the first crucial political act and demand. Literal recognition, in the sense of no longer having to hide, is essential.

Who Is Included in the Movement A major debate within the gay rights movement has long been how to identify the group(s) and whom to include. The matter of definition is not simple. Indeed, the term *homosexual* itself first appeared in print only in 1869. Prior to that, most people were well aware of the fact that individuals of the same sex had sexual relations, but this was thought of as a practice, not as a category of people. Given the strong social and financial pressure to marry in virtually all societies, much homosexual activity took place and continues to take place among individuals married to members of the opposite sex. Only in the last century have people come to think of themselves as homosexuals and, more recently, as "gay" or "lesbian."

But even with this social construction of an identity category, the name and exact boundaries of the group and movement have shifted over time. Originally referred to as "homosexual," by the late 1960s the group had adopted the term "gay and lesbian" in some countries, in part because "homosexual" had been a term used by psychiatrists to classify the practice as a mental disorder. By the 1980s, though, it was becoming clear that not all people who were not heterosexual identified themselves as gay or lesbian. Sex research has long shown that sexual preferences do not fit into absolute categories but rather extend along a continuum, from sole preference for the opposite sex on one end and for the same sex on the other and a range of variation in between. Eventually, the categories "bisexual" and "transgender," the latter meaning people who do not identify clearly with either major gender, were added to produce "lesbian, gay, bisexual, and transgender" (LGBT), the most common current designation in the United States. Recently, some activists and theorists have adopted the word *queer*, formerly considered derogatory, as an affirmative term to include the entire LGBT group or sometimes as an addition to the label, as in LGBTQ.

Assimilationist versus Liberationist Approach

In addition to these definitional debates, the LGBT community has debated the terms on which they should try to gain inclusion. Like the women's movement, members are divided over the extent to which they should simply seek equal rights within the existing system or seek to transform the norms of the system. Those who favor an assimilationist approach seek equal civil and political rights but generally are willing to adopt the cultural norms of mainstream, heterosexual society: for instance, they favor same-sex marriage, the expansion of a heterosexual institution to include them. The **liberationist approach**, on the other hand, seeks to transform sexual and gender norms, not simply to gain equal rights with heterosexuals but also to liberate everyone to express whatever sexual orientation and gender identity they wish; the goal is to gain social acceptance and respect for all regardless of their conformity to preexisting norms or institutions. Those favoring a liberationist approach question the importance of same-sex marriage because they question the entire idea of marriage as a patriarchal, heterosexual institution that they would like the freedom to move beyond. They certainly favor equal rights, but they seek much greater change than that, calling for a new "sexual citizenship" (Bell and Binnie 2000).

In terms of rights, members of the LGBT group are unusual in the sense that they secured basic political rights as individuals long before civil rights; that is, as individuals they could vote or run for office like any other citizen, as long as they kept their sexual orientation private. As a group, though, they were unwelcome until quite recently in all societies. They could not proclaim their identity publicly in most countries because of laws criminalizing their behavior. Repeal of such laws therefore became one of the movement's first priorities. Beyond decriminalization of their behavior, they have worked for passage of antidiscrimination laws that prevent government, employers, educators, and adoption agencies from discriminating on the basis of sexual orientation. Those who favor same-sex marriage do so in part because they see the right to marry as part of equal civil rights since in all societies, marital status comes with legal benefits of some sort, usually involving taxation, inheritance, employment benefits, and control over major health decisions. The movement's political success remains greater than its success in the area

liberationist approach: Branch of the LGBT movement that seeks to transform sexual and gender norms so that all may gain social acceptance and respect regardless of their conformity to preexisting norms or institutions

of civil rights in a number of countries. While active gay rights movements engage in the political process in wealthy democracies without restraint, in most countries they have still not achieved equal civil rights in terms of antidiscrimination laws, marriage, and related areas.

State Responses to the LGBT Movement

States have responded to these movements in various ways, as Map 12.3 demonstrates. Some have not only decriminalized homosexual activity but have legalized same-sex marriage; others have severe penalties for any homosexual activity. In most countries, homosexual activity is no longer criminal, though it is still socially ostracized in various ways. On the whole, the movements have clearly been more active and influential in wealthier countries. In well-established democracies, LGBT movements have been able to use their political rights to demand full civil rights but with only partial success. The biggest issue of recent years has been same-sex marriage. A handful of states have granted complete rights to marry, starting with the Netherlands in 2001 and subsequently Argentina, Belgium, Canada, Iceland, Norway, Portugal, South Africa, Spain, and Sweden. Proponents of same-sex marriage argue it is a matter of equal civil rights for all. Opponents disagree based on religious beliefs or on the argument that heterosexual marriage is a key building block of social order and should be preserved as such. In contrast to many of the debates over inclusion, in this case those arguing for the status quo do so on the basis of preserving particular group rights (for heterosexual marriages), while those seeking change argue for treating all individuals equally.

A number of states have legalized domestic partnerships or civil unions of various types that grant many but not all the rights of marriage. When first enacted, civil unions in France became surprisingly popular with heterosexual couples even though they were intended primarily for gay and lesbian couples; given France's strict divorce laws, many straight couples preferred a civil union to marriage. Today in France, two civil unions occur for every three marriages, and the vast majority of those unions are heterosexual.

Fewer postcolonial societies have active LGBT movements. Higher levels of religiosity and cultural traditions in many of these societies mean greater social opposition to public proclamation of homosexuality, as the Country and Concept table (pages 606–607) demonstrates for our case study countries. In a number of countries, however, active gay rights movements do exist. Indeed, South Africa became the first country in the world to include sexual orientation in its constitution as a category protected from discrimination. In 2005, a South African court interpreted this to apply to marriage, making it also one of the first countries to legalize gay marriage. Fledgling LGBT movements elsewhere in Africa, such as in Zimbabwe and Uganda, however, face much greater popular and legal resistance, and in many African and Middle Eastern countries, homosexual activity remains explicitly illegal. However, one of our two case studies, Brazil, is an example of a postcolonial society with an active LGBT movement that has had some notable policy successes. We compare it with the United States, the country that has been at the forefront of the LGBT movement for a generation now, though the U.S. government has not responded with pro-LGBT policies as quickly as a number of other governments around the world.

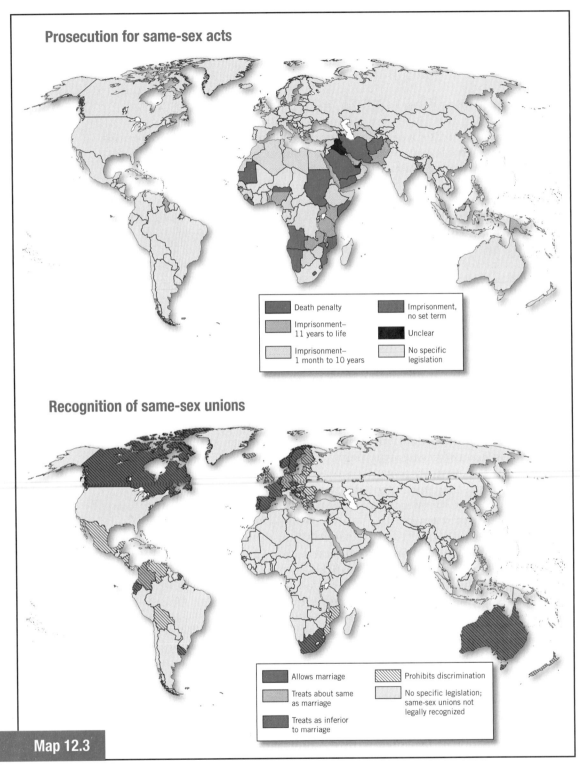

Prosecution for same-sex acts

Death penalty

Imprisonment—
11 years to life

Imprisonment—
1 month to 10 years

Imprisonment,
no set term

Unclear

No specific
legislation

Recognition of same-sex unions

Allows marriage

Treats about same
as marriage

Treats as inferior
to marriage

Prohibits discrimination

No specific legislation;
same-sex unions not
legally recognized

Map 12.3

Gay Rights

Source: International Lesbian, Gay, Bisexual, Trans and Intersex Association, May 2010.

CASE STUDY

The United States: Birthplace of a Movement but Limited Policy Change

- Early movement very small and assimilationist
- Stonewall riots create expanded movement in 1969
- Full political rights and action but limited policy success
- Success mostly via courts rather than legislation
- Key battles remain employment discrimination and same-sex marriage

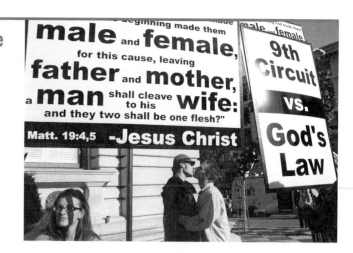

Two men kiss in front of opponents of same-sex marriage in San Francisco, California, in December 2010. After California voters changed the constitution to ban same-sex marriage, the 9th U.S. Circuit Court of Appeals overturned the ban. Both sides expect the case to end up before the U.S. Supreme Court.

Credit: Justin Sullivan/Getty Images

The modern gay rights movement was born in New York City in 1969 at the famous Stonewall riots. New York police raided a popular gay bar, the Stonewall Inn, on June 28, setting off five days of sometimes violent defense of the bar and attacks on the police. While a small gay rights movement had existed since the 1950s, the Stonewall event led to its rapid expansion across the country and then around the world. The movement has had greater success at the state and local level than at the national level in the American federal system, resulting in a patchwork of laws and rights across the country. This limited success has been due in part to the growth of an equally active anti–gay rights movement centered in conservative religious groups, with greater strength in some areas of the country than in others.

The first gay rights movement was the Mattachine Society, founded in Los Angeles in 1951. Known as the "homophile" movement, its main goals were to unify homosexuals, raise their and others' consciousness of their existence and numbers, and lessen discrimination against them. The movement quickly divided over assimilationist versus liberationist strategies, with the former becoming dominant through the 1960s. While branches opened in a number of major cities and the movement won a couple of important

court cases on discrimination in employment, it remained a small effort. William Eskridge described the effects of Stonewall on this fledgling movement:

> Literally overnight, the Stonewall riots transformed the homophile movement of several dozen homosexuals into a *gay liberation movement* populated by thousands of lesbians, gay men, and bisexuals who formed hundreds of organizations demanding radical changes. (1999, 99)

A month after Stonewall, the Gay Liberation Front was formed. Soon thereafter a more assimilationist Gay Activist Alliance emerged, once again reflecting division in the movement.

By the 1980s, this social movement had grown exponentially, with the assimilationist forces forming several major interest groups, including the Human Rights Campaign (HRC), the National Gay and Lesbian Task Force (NGLTF), and the Lambda Defense and Legal Education Fund. These and other groups lobbied Congress and state legislatures for legal changes, pursued court cases, and funded gay candidates for office as well as straight candidates who supported their cause. The HIV/AIDS crisis, which primarily affected the gay male population in its early years, gave new impetus to a more social movement orientation among activists. Believing that neither the government nor the mainstream gay rights groups were adequately addressing the epidemic, new groups emerged and demanded greater attention as well as greater freedom to express their sexuality publicly. The best known of the HIV/AIDS groups was the AIDS Coalition to Unleash Power (ACT UP), formed in 1987. It and other groups fought for greater funding for AIDS research and drugs and initiated the practice of occasional marches on Washington, D.C., the first of which was held in 1979, to demand broader gay rights in general. ACT UP also sought to recruit racial minority members, whose absence from the broader movement (similar to their absence from the early women's movement) had been notable and a source of criticism and weakness.

The LGBT movement, both the assimilationist and liberationist strands, has become a significant component of American civil society and political activity, as has opposition to it. The movement has successfully elected a growing number of openly LGBT candidates to office at all levels of the American political system. In an extensive quantitative and qualitative study of descriptive representation of the LGBT community at the state level, Haider-Markel (2010) found that LGBT candidates are just as likely to get elected as straight candidates but that they choose their electoral districts carefully, only running in districts with constituents who are likely to be sympathetic to them. He also found that a higher percentage of LGBT state legislators made it more likely that "gay rights" legislation would be initiated and passed, though the LGBT legislators themselves were not always the chief sponsors of the legislation. Often, they instead played a role they termed "educating" straight legislators about the importance of LGBT issues. The most important factor in passage of gay rights legislation, however, was not the

number of LBGT legislators but the general attitudes of the states' voters toward gay rights issues, leading Haider-Markel to recommend that the movement continue to focus on changing broad societal attitudes.

Members' success in establishing themselves as a political force to be reckoned with, however, has not been matched with complete success in achieving their policy objectives. Legal battles have become a major area of policy action because a central issue is civil rights and the American judicial system is a major arena of policy making. The pre-Stonewall movement focused narrowly on particular cases of egregious discrimination, winning some lower-court verdicts whose reach was relatively narrow. Police harassment of gay bars, for instance, continued unabated, using sodomy and other laws as legal justification. The first Supreme Court decision of note ruled in favor of the Mattachine Society's right to transmit its magazine through the mail; the U.S. Post Office had banned its distribution via the mail on the grounds of obscenity, even though it was simply a news magazine addressing gay issues.

LGBT legal activists believed the Supreme Court had set the stage for a federal repeal of all sodomy laws in the 1965 *Griswold v. Connecticut* decision, which legalized the use of contraception by married adults on the grounds of a "right to privacy" implicit in the Constitution (a right later used to legalize abortion in *Roe v. Wade*). In 1986, the Court heard *Bowers v. Hardwick,* in which a Georgia man had been arrested in his own bedroom for having sex with another man. In a 5–4 decision, the Supreme Court ruled that the right to privacy did not apply, in part because no long-standing tradition of respecting privacy in the case of homosexual relations existed, in contrast to the case for married couples. Finally, in the 2003 case of *Lawrence v. Texas,* the Court ruled 6–3 that sodomy laws were unconstitutional for violating the right to due process, explicitly reversing its 1986 decision.

Another area of success, after a protracted battle, is the right of members of the LGBT community to serve openly in the military. When President Bill Clinton came to office, the movement thought—based on statements made during his campaign—that it had a champion for its concerns, and he was the first president to meet with leadership from the major groups in the White House. Nonetheless, facing nearly certain opposition from Congress and from the military, Clinton chose not to insist that the military allow gay men and women to serve openly. Instead, in 1993 Clinton created the "don't ask, don't tell" policy under which the military no longer inquired about sexual orientation but gay soldiers could not reveal their orientation. Discharges based on sexual orientation continued under the policy, totaling over 17,000 before its repeal. In September 2010, a federal judge in California ruled that the policy violated the Equal Protection and First Amendment rights of service members. At the same time, the U.S. military leadership, after an extensive survey of its members, concluded that allowing gays and lesbians to serve openly would not jeopardize military readiness and therefore national security. With a court ruling against "don't ask, don't tell" and the military undermining the main argument in its favor—national security—Congress passed, and on December 22, 2010, President Obama signed, a bill that repealed the law. Gays and lesbians would be allowed to serve openly from that point on.

Other legislative and legal battles have not been as successful. While twenty-one states have laws protecting against employment discrimination on the basis of sexual orientation and another twelve on the basis of gender identity, the federal government has never passed a law prohibiting private sector discrimination nationwide, even though federal employees themselves have this protection. Legislators first introduced such legislation in 1974. Currently titled the Employment Non-Discrimination Act (ENDA), the bill has continuously been introduced and been passed in the House of Representatives but has fallen short in the Senate. Its latest version includes protection not only on the basis of sexual orientation but also gender

identity, thus including transgendered people, who are already protected in some states.

The biggest current issue in the United States and much of the wealthy world is legalization of same-sex marriage. The mainstream, assimilationist organizations in the American movement have fought for this right in terms of American civil rights laws, arguing that restricting marriage to a man and woman discriminates against homosexual individuals. The LGBT movement has successfully convinced numerous urban municipalities and (as of 2011) nine states (Hawaii, California, New Jersey, Nevada, Illinois, Maine, Oregon, Wisconsin, and Washington) to legalize some type of domestic partnership or civil union to give same-sex couples most of the rights of married couples. The first court case to question a state's refusal to grant a same-sex couple a marriage license was in 1993 in Hawaii, but it ultimately resulted in the state passing a constitutional amendment banning same-sex marriage and passing a law allowing civil unions. The case produced a nationwide campaign against same-sex marriage, which led to twenty-nine state laws and constitutional amendments explicitly restricting marriage to a union between a man and a woman and a federal law, the Defense of Marriage Act (DOMA), passed by Congress and signed by President Clinton in 1996, doing the same. On the other hand, Vermont was the first state to legalize same-sex civil unions in 2000; Massachusetts became the first state to allow gay marriage in May 2004; and by 2011, five other states (Vermont, Connecticut, New Hampshire, Iowa, and New York) and the District of Columbia had followed suit. Similar efforts narrowly failed in 2010 and 2011 in Maryland. The movement's efforts, therefore, have succeeded only in a handful of states and have produced a backlash in many others.

But the battle over same-sex marriage is far from over. In California, a state court ruled in 2008 that a law banning same-sex marriage violated the state constitution, temporarily legalizing gay marriage in the state. That November, however, voters passed a referendum, Proposition 8, that overrode the court and restored the ban. A lawsuit against Proposition 8 was then filed in a federal court, which ruled in August 2010 that the proposition violated the federal constitution's Equal Protection clause, a ruling that all expect to be heard by the U.S. Supreme Court. In Massachusetts, a federal judge ruled that the national Defense of Marriage Act was unconstitutional, and in February 2011, President Obama directed the Department of Justice to stop defending the act in court. Congressional opponents of same-sex marriage vowed to try to pass a bill forcing the executive to continue defending the law, but its chances of passage were uncertain.

> [!NOTE]
> CASE SUMMARY

The United States was the birthplace of the LGBT movement and continues to have one of the most active movements in the world. Strong opposition from Christian conservatives, a stronger political force in the United States than in other wealthy countries, and the decentralized, federal system have resulted in the movement achieving only partial success, however. While it has clearly gained recognition as a legitimate interest group in American politics, it has only partially succeeded at changing policies, mainly via litigation. Though successful at ending criminalization of homosexual conduct and discrimination in the military, the movement has achieved only partial success in ending employment discrimination and restriction on same-sex marriage. These battles, however, are far from over. Opinion polls show the nation divided on the issue of same-sex marriage in particular, though with a large generational gap: younger Americans are much more supportive than older ones, giving the movement hope that change will come eventually.

CASE STUDY

Brazil: LGBT Rights in a New Democracy

- Large and active gay rights movement
- Decriminalization of homosexual behavior in nineteenth century
- Divisions over identity categories and who is in the movement
- Active engagement of movement in legislative process
- Rights for same-sex couples nearly the same as for heterosexual couples, though neither civil unions nor marriages legally recognized
- Harassment of gays in society still a common problem

In 2006, São Paulo, Brazil's largest city, hosted the biggest gay pride parade in world history, and it remains the biggest annual LGBT gathering on the planet. Although Brazil is the world's largest predominantly Catholic country, it has a long history and reputation of being relatively open about sexuality in general. It has long had a well-established LGBT community, but it only developed an open political movement with the start of the transition to democracy in the late 1970s. Like the movement in the United States, the Brazilian movement went through years of controversy over how to define itself. It has succeeded in getting policies that are more inclusive of LGBT rights than most states, especially in comparison to most postcolonial states, but its aims are by no means completely met. The movement continues to work to achieve policies to eliminate discrimination on the basis of sexual orientation, to establish same-sex marriage or at least civil unions, and to reduce violence against members of the LGBT community.

The first explicit Brazilian gay rights group, Grupo Somos (We Are Group), formed in São Paulo in 1979. It was preceded in the 1960s by mostly apolitical homophile groups not unlike those in the United States before Stonewall. Grupo Somos emerged at the same time that major pressure on the military regime for political opening of the country began (see chapter 9). By the early 1980s, about twenty LGBT groups existed, but many of these did not survive more than a few years and were plagued by divisions over the inclusion of lesbians and transvestites. Both of the latter formed separate organizations at various points: lesbians in the 1980s and transvestites in the 1990s. Until 1992, the major annual meeting of the movement was called the Brazilian Meeting of Homosexuals; in 1993, this became the Brazilian Meeting of Lesbians and Homosexuals; in 1998, the Brazilian Meeting of Lesbians, Gays, and Transgenders. Finally in 2005, the Brazilian Association of Lesbians, Gays, and Transvestites was founded, bringing all the major groups under one umbrella. (In Brazil the movement is known usually by the label GLT rather than LGBT, and *T* includes the active transvestite community but not a "transgender"-identified group, a category not widely accepted there.)

The movement's growth, despite its divisions, has been impressive and was initially helped and inspired by the post-Stonewall movement in the United States and Europe. It also benefited from the political opening in the early 1980s as the country began the transition to democracy. The leadership of the union-based Workers' Party (PT) (see chapter 9) rhetorically embraced gay rights activists and their cause at the first party convention in 1981, though opposition from some Catholic activists in the party continued. The AIDS crisis first hurt and then strengthened the movement in the 1980s. Initially, AIDS hit the gay male population the hardest, as it did in the United States. As awareness grew, however, infection rates among gay men dropped significantly. Simultaneously, and partly as a result of active pressure from the movement, Brazil developed an AIDS prevention and treatment policy, which became a global model of success. Many AIDS NGOs with ties to the gay rights movement arose in the 1980s. By the 1990s, the World Bank and other international donors were funding

São Paulo's tenth annual Gay, Lesbian, Bisexual, and Transgender parade was held in 2007. The city hosts the world's largest LGBT parade, drawing over three million participants and spectators. Brazil has one of the most active LGBT movements in the postcolonial world, and pushed by the movement, the country now supports numerous benefits for homosexual couples though it has not legalized civil unions or gay marriage.

Credit: Daniel Kfouri/AFP/Getty Images

some GLT groups that were helping to implement the National AIDS Program. In 2006, Juan Marsiaj noted that "the size and diversity of the Brazilian GLT movement make it the largest and one of the strongest of its kind in Latin America" (172).

In 1823, Brazil became one of the first countries in the world to eliminate antisodomy laws. While homosexual activity is not illegal, the law only partially enforces antidiscrimination. The gay rights movement worked hard to get "sexual orientation" included in the 1988 constitution's antidiscrimination clause but was unsuccessful. A national antidiscrimination law focusing on discrimination by commercial enterprises and government offices passed the National Congress in 2000. By 2003, three states and more than seventy municipalities, including the country's two largest cities, had passed some type of antidiscrimination law.

Attempts to legalize civil unions and same-sex marriage have not been as successful, and current efforts focus primarily on establishing civil unions. In contrast to the United States, the federal government controls marriage law in Brazil. The PT introduced a bill in the National Congress in 1995 to legalize civil unions nationwide, but it has languished there ever since. Court cases have expanded the rights of same-sex couples, however, in a number of important ways. The Constitution's antidiscrimination clause does not list "sexual orientation" specifically but does mention "and other forms of discrimination." Using this clause, the federal high court ruled in 1998 that a gay man deserved to inherit the property of his partner of seven years. The court went on to rule in 2000 that same-sex partners in a "stable union" should be treated as married couples in the social security and public pension systems. In the most important of these cases, the state government of Rio Grande do Sul legalized civil unions after a case on the issue was argued in the state court in 2004. In 2008, the movement's hopes increased further when President Luiz Inácio "Lula" da Silva of the PT said publicly he would do all he could to see that a hate crimes law against homophobia and a civil union law were enacted. While neither of these had been achieved by 2011, in 2010 the government did announce that same-sex couples would receive the same retirement pension, health insurance, and income tax benefits as married couples. Harassment of gay citizens, though, remains a major concern and common occurrence, and Congress still has not passed a law criminalizing such behavior.

Despite achieving only partial success, Brazil's GLT community has actively engaged in the legislative process, focusing more attention on that arena than the movement has in the United States. Much of the activity has taken place within the PT, which became the governing party in 2002. In 1992, a gay and lesbian group was officially formed within the party to pressure elected members to support GLT causes. Over the next decade, it grew to the point where it was hosting annual national meetings, though ultimately it fell apart due to internal divisions. Nevertheless, it helped spur PT legislation in numerous state and local governments, but it continues to face opposition from PT members with strong traditionalist ties to the Catholic Church. In June 2003, GLT activists in the National Congress convinced the lower house to convene a National Seminar on Affirmative Politics and Rights of the Gay, Lesbian, Bisexual, Travesti (transvestite), and Transsexual Community. The seminar brought together legislators, bureaucratic officials, and GLT activists to discuss civil rights issues, and out of it grew the Parliamentary Front for Freedom of Sexual Expression, whose eighty-five members convinced the PT government to create and fund a program explicitly aimed at combating homophobia nationwide.

CASE SUMMARY

The GLT community in Brazil enjoys significantly greater rights than it did during the 1980s and more than those allowed to LGBT communities in many countries. Arguably, it has been at least as successful as the U.S. movement that helped inspire it. The transition to democracy, which emphasized expanded rights for all, even though "sexual orientation" was explicitly rejected for inclusion in the new constitution, established a political context in which Brazilian policy has shifted significantly. While the state has not yet legalized civil unions, let alone same-sex marriage, Brazilian same-sex couples in practice have rights nearly equal to those of married couples in many important social and policy areas, and they certainly have these rights more uniformly throughout the country than do same-sex couples in the United States. In terms of recognition, the first and most important goal of the LGBT movement, Brazil has achieved a great deal. The GLT community is widely known and celebrated, especially via São Paulo's gargantuan gay pride parade. Opposition from both traditionalist Catholic and evangelical Protestant movements continues, but all indications are that the Brazilian political system has expanded its definition of equal citizenship to include GLT members in such a way as to effect permanent change.

Summary

The LGBT movement has raised, if anything, more profound challenges to conventional social mores and institutions than the women's movement. Sexual orientation is unique as an identity category due to the ability of homosexual and bisexual individuals to "hide" their identity relatively easily. This has meant that as individuals they have long had basic political rights that women, racial, and other minorities often had to fight for. As a group, however, they were repressed and forced to hide until quite recently. They remain the group least frequently given recognition, respect, and rights by states around the world. Like feminists, gay rights activists raise fundamental questions about core institutions such as marriage, not only who ought to be included but also how it should be defined and whether it should exist. Some simply want inclusion in existing institutions, but others want more fundamental institutional and attitudinal changes. Our case studies are two countries that have had unusually active movements, yet their policies continue to allow certain areas of discrimination based on sexual orientation. This is in part because the goals of the movement conflict with deeply held values based on cultural or religious traditions that accept group membership and behavior only within the bounds of heterosexual practice. In this sense, the LGBT movement raises the same questions about citizenship and inclusion that we have discussed throughout this chapter.

CONCLUSION

Identity groups always pose challenges to the modern state. As we saw in chapter 4, under some circumstances ethnicity, race, or religion can challenge the very conception of a nation. At other times, religion, like gender and sexuality, poses a different kind of challenge to modern states as they address issues of inclusiveness and equal citizenship. In liberal democracies, such challenges cut to the heart of one of the defining characteristics of the regime. Demands for inclusive citizenship can also raise challenges when they clash with the demands of other identity groups. States must then resolve the question of which groups' demands to meet. This can be particularly difficult when, for instance, women or gays demand individual civil rights in the name of equality, while a religious, ethnic, or other minority group claims a conflicting right to respect for its cultural practices. This is a difficult challenge for democracies that pride themselves on respecting minority rights and cultural pluralism but also wish to promote individual equality.

Who Rules?

The outcomes of protracted and intense political battles always reveal something about who rules in a particular political system. Policy outcomes, at least in part, reflect the relative power of different political forces. In the political disputes we examined in this chapter, a dominant group protecting the status quo exists in almost all cases. Lack of identity-based conflict may indeed reflect nearly complete domination by that group, as the "second face of power" (see chapter 1) would suggest. Where questions about the inclusion of minority or marginalized identity groups have become politically salient, those groups have at least gained a modicum of power in the system, enough to raise their demands. In these societies, they publicly assert their shared identity and make further political demands. Their success, as with the success of the women's movement in wealthier countries, demonstrates growing power; continuing limitations on their demands equally demonstrate limits on their power. On that basis, women, especially in wealthier countries, seem to have achieved greater power than LGBT groups. The power of religious minorities varies more around the world; Muslim traditionalists in India seem to have enough power to keep control over personal law, an important issue to them, while Muslims in France have met with far less success in their ability to assert their religious identity publicly.

What Explains Political Behavior?

As the comparison of Muslims in India and in France suggests, culture and institutions can play an important role in explaining what demands are raised, how they are raised, and how successful they are. As our cases suggest, many factors are at work in this process. First, it is important to recognize that the demands of similar groups in different countries are not always the same. Cultural context, at least in the short term, can have an important role in explaining these differences. For instance, our cases show that not all women's groups have adopted Western feminist demands or rationales for women's rights. Islamic women's groups and others throughout the non-Western world have developed their own sets of demands, which only partially overlap those of European and North American women's movements. Thus, states are responding to different sets of demands from the start.

Second, the institutional context in which identity groups make demands also matters. A group may deem it pointless to demand greater inclusion in formal political institutions if the context is one in which those institutions ultimately have little decision-making power. As examples from the former communist countries suggest, numerical inclusion in formal decision-making institutions does not ensure equality or recognition of rights for women and other identity groups. Institutions matter in another way as well. They create the avenues through which groups approach the state, sometimes shaping groups' demands. Does a group approach the state at the local or national level? Through protests, votes, or lawsuits? On which particular issues? All of these questions are deeply affected by the institutional context, as cases from gay rights in the United States to Muslim rights in the United Kingdom suggest.

Finally, many aspects of the groups themselves play a key role in their success or failure in gaining their preferred policy outcomes. Most important, a critical mass of people must recognize themselves as part of a group with common interests vis-à-vis the state. These interests may be communal rights, as they often are for religious minorities, but they may also be individual rights of access and equal citizenship. Whatever their goals, a shared sense of identity allows members of these groups to form a social movement or interest group. At that point, their ability to mobilize resources, to frame a persuasive argument, and to exploit political opportunities can be crucial to their success. As several of our examples suggest, from religious Muslims in Turkey to LGBT groups in the United States, their mobilization may also encourage the countermobilization of groups with conflicting values. Struggles for recognition, whether they involve demands for equal citizenship or communal rights or both, are usually protracted and difficult.

More and more groups throughout the world appear to be demanding inclusion, recognition, and individual or communal rights, suggesting that aspects of globalization may be playing a role. Cultural and ideological aspects of globalization seem to be particularly important, starting with the rhetorical dominance of liberal democracy. As we've stressed throughout the book, the dominance of democratic discourse makes it important for virtually all states to justify their actions in terms of citizenship, and this provides an opening and a basis on which groups can demand inclusion and recognition. In addition, although many formally democratic states still only imperfectly respect civil liberties and freedoms, they do allow more space for civil society on the whole than do their authoritarian counterparts or predecessors. Thus the wave of democratization in the 1990s has opened political space for identity groups around the world. Indeed, women's movements and other identity-based movements were part of the social movement cohort that helped push the tide of democratization forward in the first place.

Globalization also has given more impetus to the construction of identity movements around the world, whether via globalized examples and inspiration or via assertions of local identity against the forces of global homogenization. As the European examples in the section on religion show, the movement of people across borders and especially postcolonial immigration has raised questions about inclusiveness and the definition of citizenship in long-established democracies. Media also certainly play a role, as news of identity group mobilizations in one place travels quickly and may spark similar organizing elsewhere. For this reason, people often speak of a wave of "global feminisms" of different types beginning in the 1970s. Although groups throughout the world developed feminist goals and tactics to suit their particular circumstances, news and ideas from other countries encouraged women everywhere to organize for their own agendas.

Where and Why?

While numerous "Where and why?" questions arise when examining the politics of inclusion, religious differences among groups raise particularly clear ones. Most modern states at least proclaim that they are secular, but the type of secularism varies. Why? History clearly plays a crucial role here. Different forms of secularism arose to try to resolve different kinds of religious problems. American secularism—a state that is neutral among religions—followed the British model, intent on limiting the political impact of religious conflicts, originally between Protestants and Catholics. French *laïcité*, on the other hand, arose in states whose birth included a strong effort to distance the public realm from one powerful religious institution, such as the Catholic Church. Once different types of secularism are well established, they influence the contours of future religious conflicts. Not only do states typically respond to demands from new religious groups via the terms of their long-established form of secularism, but the different forms of secularism influence the demands new religious groups make, as the differences among Muslim demands and states' responses in the United Kingdom, France, and Germany demonstrate.

Applying Theory to the Policies and Politics of Inclusion and Conflicting Values

We have already seen how cultural and institutional theories are important in understanding both demands for inclusion and states' responses to them. Cultural and institutional legacies profoundly influence how societies and states respond to demands for inclusion from newly mobilized identity groups as well as the nature of the demands themselves. Asserting new demands in terms of existing cultural values and institutional practices usually makes it likely the larger society will be more sympathetic: LGBT demands for same-sex marriage are cast in terms of equal individual rights in the United States, and Muslim demands for inclusion in the educational system are cast in terms of multiculturalism in Britain. Meanwhile, German Muslims attempt to create clearer hierarchical organizations to demand state recognition and support similar to that long granted to Christian churches.

Rational-choice theories, as we saw in chapter 4, can also be relevant to identity politics. Indeed, rational-choice theorists would point out that political actors' rational assessment of how to pursue their preferences most effectively can be seen as they respond logically to existing institutional constraints. This same type of argument can be applied to how identities are asserted in the first place: India's political system has long accommodated identity groups of various sorts via creating specific institutional arrangements with each (as its asymmetrical federal system demonstrates—see chapter 6), so traditionalist Muslim leaders defend their political and social position vis-à-vis both the state and challenges from within the Muslim community by negotiating an institutionalized system of autonomy that gives them control over key elements of personal law. They assert that this autonomy preserves Muslim identity itself in a context of ever-present Hindu dominance.

The trend toward greater mobilization around issues of identity is strong right now, but as always in comparative politics, we cannot assume that what is true today will be true tomorrow. We do believe that identity will continue to be a key challenge to the politics of nation-states, and particularly liberal democracies, and these challenges are likely to arise in other places if more countries expand their openness to global ideas and increase the scope of their civil societies. In the future, however, new conflicts and new political trends will arise, and students of comparative politics will be challenged to document and explain the patterns, sources, and outcomes of future political conflicts.

KEY CONCEPTS

communitarianism
    (p. 610)
deliberative democracy
    (p. 610)

liberationist approach
    (p. 646)
multicultural integration
    (p. 610)

multiculturalism (p. 618)

WORKS CITED

Alaedini, Pooya, and Mohamad Reza Razavi. 2005. "Women's Participation and Employment in Iran: A Critical Examination." *Critique: Critical Middle Eastern Studies* 14 (1): 57–73.

Allen, Jodie T., and Richard Wike. 2009. "How Europe and Its Muslim Populations See Each Other." In *Muslims in Western Politics*, edited by Abdulkader H. Sinno, 137–60. Bloomington: Indiana University Press.

Bahramitash, Roksana, and Shahla Kazemi-pour. 2006. "Myths and Realities of the Impact of Islam on Women: Changing Marital Status in Iran." *Critique: Critical Middle Eastern Studies* 15 (2): 111–28.

Baskakova, Marina E., and Irina V. Soboleva. 2010. "Promoting Gender Equality and Empowerment of Women." In *National Human Development Report in the Russian Federation 2010: Millennium Development Goals in Russia; Looking into the Future,* edited by Sergeĭ Nikolaevich Bobylev, 48–62. Moscow, Russia: United Nations Development Programme. http://www.undp.ru/nhdr2010/National_Human_Development_Report_in_the_RF_2010_ENG.pdf.

Basu, Srimati. 2008. "Separate and Unequal: Muslim Women and Un-uniform Family Law in India." *International Feminist Journal of Politics* 10 (4): 495–517. doi:10.1080/14616740802393890.

Bell, David, and Jon Binnie. 2000. *The Sexual Citizen: Queer Politics and Beyond.* Cambridge, UK, and Malden, MA: Polity Press and Blackwell.

Bobylev, Sergeĭ Nikolaevich. 2005. *Human Development Report 2005—Russian Federation: Russia in 2015; Development Goals and Policy Priorities.* Moscow, Russia: United Nations Development Programme.

Campos Jiménez, Laura. 2009. "Carlos Monsiváis: El estado laico y sus malquerientes" [blog post]. *Bi-National Magazine,* January 7. http://binationalmagazine.com/bin/editoriales.cgi?ID=238&q=1.

Equality and Human Rights Commission (UK). "About Us." http://www.equalityhumanrights.com/about-us/.

Eskridge, William N., Jr. 1999. *Gaylaw: Challenging the Apartheid of the Closet.* Cambridge, MA: Harvard University Press.

Fetzer, Joel S., and J. Christopher Soper. 2005. *Muslims and the State in Britain, France, and Germany.* Cambridge, UK: Cambridge University Press.

Haider-Markel, Donald P. 2010. *Out and Running: Gay and Lesbian Candidates, Elections, and Policy Representation.* Washington, DC: Georgetown University Press.

Harel-Shalev, Ayelet. 2009. "The Problematic Nature of Religious Autonomy to Minorities in Democracies—The Case of India's Muslims." *Democratization* 16 (6):1261–81. doi:10.1080/13510340903271860.

Hoodfar, Homa, and Fatemeh Sadeghi. 2009. "Against All Odds: The Women's Movement in the Islamic Republic of Iran." *Development* 52 (2): 215–23. doi:10.1057/dev.2009.19.

Inter-Parliamentary Union. 2011. *Women in National Parliaments.* http://www.ipu.org/wmn-e/classif.htm.

Jones, Justin. 2010. "'Signs of Churning': Muslim Personal Law and Public Contestation in Twenty-first Century India." *Modern Asian Studies* 44 (1): 175–200. doi:10.1017/S0026749X09990114.

Kirkpatrick, Jeane J. 1974. *Political Woman.* New York: Basic Books.

Krook, Mona Lena. 2009. *Quotas for Women in Politics: Gender and Candidate Selection Reform Worldwide.* New York: Oxford University Press.

Kymlicka, Will. 1995. *Multicultural Citizenship: A Liberal Theory of Minority Rights.* Oxford, UK: Clarendon Press.

Kymlicka, Will, and Wayne Norman, eds. 2000. *Citizenship in Diverse Societies.* Oxford, UK: Oxford University Press.

Local Government Improvement and Development. 2011. "Equality and Human Rights Commission." http://www.idea.gov.uk/idk/core/page.do?pageId=9277949.

Mahdavi, Pardis. 2009. *Passionate Uprisings: Iran's Sexual Revolution.* Stanford, CA: Stanford University Press.

Mansbridge, Jane. 2000. "What Does a Representative Do? Descriptive Representation in Communicative Settings of Distrust, Uncrystallized Interests, and Historically Denigrated Status." In *Citizenship in Diverse Societies,* edited by Will Kymlicka and Wayne Norman, 99–123. Oxford, UK: Oxford University Press.

Marshall, T. H. 1963. *Class, Citizenship, and Social Development: Essays.* Chicago: University of Chicago Press.

Marsiaj, Juan P. 2006. "Social Movements and Political Parties: Gays, Lesbians, and *Travestis* and the Struggle for Inclusion in Brazil." *Canadian Journal of Latin American and Caribbean Studies* 31 (62): 167–98.

Maxwell, Rahsaan. 2010. "Trust in Government Among British Muslims: The Importance of Migration Status." *Political Behavior* 32 (1): 89–109. doi:10.1007/s11109-009-9093-1.

Meer, Nasar, and Tariq Modood. 2009. "The Multicultural State We're In: Muslims, 'Multiculture,' and the 'Civic Re-balancing' of British Multiculturalism." *Political Studies* 57 (3): 473–97. doi:10.1111/j.1467-9248.2008.00745.x.

Modood, Tariq. 2006. "British Muslims and the Politics of Multiculturalism." In *Multiculturalism, Muslims, and Citizenship: A European Approach,* edited by Tariq Modood, Ann Triandafyllidou, and Ricard Zapata-Barrero, 37–56. New York: Routledge.

Paidar, Parvin. 1995. *Women and the Political Process in Twentieth-Century Iran.* Cambridge, UK: Cambridge University Press.

"*Panorama* Finds Anti-Semitic Texts in Schools."2010. BBC, November 22. http://www.bbc.co.uk/news/uk-11808658/.

Pateman, Carole. 1988. *The Sexual Contract.* Stanford, CA: Stanford University Press.

Racioppi, Linda, and Katherine O'Sullivan See. 1995. "Organizing Women before and after the Fall: Women's Politics in the Soviet Union and Post-Soviet Russia." *Signs* 20 (4): 818–50.

Rao, Badrinath. 2006. "The Variant Meanings of Secularism in India: Notes Toward Conceptual Clarifications." *Journal of Church and State* 48 (1): 47–81. doi:10.1093/jcs/48.1.47.

Roschin, S. Yu, and N. V. Zubarevich. 2005. "Gender Equality and Extension of Women Rights in Russia in the Context of Millennium Development Goals." Moscow, Russia: United Nations Development Programme. http://www.undp.ru/Gender_MDG_eng.pdf.

Spodek, Howard. 2010. "In the *Hindutva* Laboratory: Pogroms and Politics in Gujarat, 2002." *Modern Asian Studies* 44 (2): 349–99. doi:10.1017/S0026749X08003612.

Tahmasebi-Birgani, Victoria. 2010. "Green Women of Iran: The Role of the Women's Movement During and After Iran's Presidential Election of 2009." *Constellations* 17 (1): 78–86. doi:10.1111/j.1467-8675.2009.00576.x.

Teplova, Tatyana. 2007. "Welfare State Transformation, Childcare, and Women's Work in Russia." *Social Politics* 14 (3): 284–322. doi:10.1093/sp/jxm016.

Tripp, Aili Mari, and Alice Kang. 2008. "The Global Impact of Quotas: On the Fast Track to Increased Female Legislative Representation." *Comparative Political Studies* 41 (3): 338–61. doi:10.1177/0010414006297342.

White, Anne. 2005. "Gender Roles in Contemporary Russia: Attitudes and Expectations among Women Students." *Europe-Asia Studies* 57 (3): 429–55. doi:10.1080/09668130500073449.

Young, Iris Marion. 2000. *Inclusion and Democracy.* Oxford, UK: Oxford University Press.

RESOURCES FOR FURTHER STUDY

Hunter, Shireen T., ed. 2002. *Islam, Europe's Second Religion: The New Social, Cultural and Political Landscape.* Westport, CT: Praeger.

Lovenduski, Joni, ed. 2005. *State Feminism and Political Representation.* Cambridge, UK: Cambridge University Press.

Mazur, Amy G. 2002. *Theorizing Feminist Policy.* Oxford, UK: Oxford University Press.

Parekh, Bhikhu C. 2000. *Rethinking Multiculturalism: Cultural Diversity and Political Theory.* Cambridge, MA: Harvard University Press.

Sinno, Abdulkader H., ed. 2009. *Muslims in Western Politics.* Bloomington: Indiana University Press.

WEB RESOURCES

Center for American Women and Politics (http://www.cawp.rutgers.edu/fast_facts/index.php)

International Lesbian, Gay, Bisexual, Trans and Intersex Association, 2010, "Lesbian and Gay Rights in the World" (http://ilga.org/ilga/en/article/1161/)

Quota Project, "Global Database of Quotas for Women" (http://www.quotaproject.org/)

Servicemembers Legal Defense Network, 2008 (http://www.sldn.org/templates/index.html)

UNDP Human Development Report, "Gender Inequality Index" (http://hdr.undp.org/en/statistics/gii/)

World Values Survey (http://www.worldvaluessurvey.org/)

Glossary

absolutism   Rule by a single monarch who claims complete, exclusive power and sovereignty over a territory and its people (chapter 2)

acephalous society   Stateless; ruled by very local level government only (chapter 4)

alternative-vote (AV) system   Single-member district electoral system in which voters rank all candidates rather than voting for just one; if no candidate wins a majority of first-place votes, the first-place votes of the candidate with the fewest such votes are reallocated to those voters' second-choice candidates; this continues through list of candidates with the fewest first-place votes until a candidate has a majority (chapter 7)

amakudari   In Japan, the "descent from heaven," in which senior bureaucrats get positions in the industries they formerly regulated (chapter 6)

assimilationist   Someone who believes immigrants or other members of minority cultural communities ought to adopt the culture of the majority population (chapter 4)

assymetrical federal system   Division of constitutionally assigned power to national and subnational governments, with different subnational governments (states or provinces) having distinct relationships with and rights in relation to the national government (chapter 6)

authoritarian regime   A regime lacking democratic characteristics, ruled by a single leader or small group of leaders (chapter 1)

autonomy   Ability and right of a minority group to partially govern itself within a larger state (chapter 4)

bicameral legislature   A legislature that has two houses (chapter 6)

Bolshevik   Vladimir Lenin's branch of the communist movement in Russia that led the Russian communist revolution (chapter 3)

bourgeoisie   The class that owns capital; according to Marxism, the ruling elite in all capitalist societies (chapter 1)

bureaucracy   A large set of appointed officials whose function is to implement the laws of the state, as directed by the executive (chapter 2)

bureaucratic-authoritarian regime   A regime characterized by institutionalized rule under a military government with a primary goal of economic development; coined by Guillermo O'Donnell to describe Latin American military regimes in the 1970s (chapter 3)

cadre parties   Parties that have a small membership of political elites who choose candidates and mobilize voters to support them; in contrast to mass parties (chapter 7)

cap and trade system   Market-based pollution control system in which the government sets an overall limit on how much of a pollutant is acceptable from an entire industry or country and issues vouchers to pollute to each company; individual companies are then free to trade these vouchers (chapter 11)

capitalism The combination of a market economy with private property rights (chapter 5)

centripetal approach A means used by democracies to resolve ethnic conflict by giving political leaders and parties incentives to moderate their demands (chapter 4)

charismatic legitimacy The right to rule based on personal virtue, heroism, sanctity, or other extraordinary characteristics; one of Max Weber's three versions of legitimacy (chapter 2)

Christian democratic welfare states States whose social policies are based on the nuclear family with male breadwinner, designed primarily to achieve income stabilization to mitigate the effects of market-induced income insecurity; Germany is key example (chapter 11)

citizen A member of a political community or state with certain rights and duties (chapter 3)

civic culture Political culture in which citizens hold values and beliefs that support democracy, including active participation in politics but also enough deference to the leadership to let it govern effectively (chapter 1)

civic nationalism A sense of national unity and purpose based on a set of commonly held political beliefs (chapter 4)

civil rights The first of T. H. Marshall's rights of citizenship, those rights that guarantee individual freedom as well as equal, just, and fair treatment by the state (chapter 3)

civil society The sphere of organized, nonviolent activity by groups smaller and less inclusive than the state or government, but larger than the family or individual firm (chapter 1)

clientelism The exchange of material resources for political support (chapter 2)

closed-list proportional representation Electoral system in which each party presents a ranked list of candidates for all the seats in the legislature; voters can see the list and know who the "top" candidates are, but they vote for the party, and each party is awarded legislative seats based on their percentage of the total vote and awards those seats to the candidates on its list in the order in which they are listed (chapter 7)

coalition government Government in a parliamentary system in which at least two parties negotiate an agreement to rule together (chapter 6)

code law Legal system originating in ancient Roman law and modified by Napoleon Bonaparte in France, in which judges may only follow the law as written, interpreting it as little as necessary to fit the case; past decisions are irrelevant, as each judge must look only to the existing law; in contrast to common law (chapter 6)

codetermination In Germany unions are represented on the supervisory boards of all firms of more than 2,000 employees (chapter 5)

cohabitation Sharing of power between a president and prime minister from different parties in a semipresidential system (chapter 6)

collective action problem The unwillingness of individuals to undertake political action because of the rational belief that their individual action will have little or no effect; a problem democratic regimes must overcome via parties and interest groups (chapter 7)

collective responsibility All cabinet members must publicly support all government decisions in a parliamentary system (chapter 6)

command and control policies Pollution control system in which a government directly regulates the specific amount of pollution each polluting entity is allowed (chapter 11)

command economy An economic system in which most prices, property, and production are directly controlled by the state (chapter 5)

common law Legal system originating in Britain in which judges base decisions not only on their understanding of the written law but also on their understanding of past court cases; in contrast to code law (chapter 6)

communitarianism Philosophical tradition supporting the argument that humans are inherently social and political animals and thus can only function well in strongly bonded communities (chapter 12)

comparative advantage Theory of trade that argues that economic efficiency and well-being will be maximized if each country uses its resources to produce whatever it produces relatively well compared to other countries and then trades what it has produced with other countries for goods it does not produce (chapter 5)

comparative institutional advantage Idea in the "varieties of capitalism" school of thought that argues that different kinds of capitalist systems have different institutional advantages that they usually will try to maintain, resulting in different responses to external economic pressures (chapter 10)

comparative method   The means by which scholars try to mimic laboratory conditions by careful selection of cases (chapter 1)

comparative politics   One of the major subfields of political science, in which the primary focus is on comparing power and decision making across countries (chapter 1)

comparativists   Political scientists who study comparative politics (chapter 1)

conditional cash transfer (CCT)   Programs that provide cash grants to the poor and in exchange require particular beneficial behavior from the poor, such as children's attendance at school and visits to health clinics (chapter 11)

consensus democracy   A democratic system with multiparty executives in a coalition government, executive-legislative balance, a bicameral legislature, and a rigid constitution not easily amended (chapter 6)

consociationalism   A democratic system designed to ease communal tensions via the principles of recognizing the existence of specific groups and granting some share of power in the central government to each, usually codified in specific legal or constitutional guarantees to each group (chapter 4)

constructivism   A theory of identity-group formation that argues identities are created through a complex process usually referred to as social construction; societies collectively "construct" identities as a wide array of actors continually discusses the question of who "we" are, identity groups are not frozen in time but change relatively slowly, and each individual can be part of more than one group (chapter 4)

convergence   Argument that globalization will force similar economic and social policies to be adopted across all countries (chapter 10)

coordinated market economies (CMEs)   In the varieties of capitalism approach, capitalist economies in which firms, financiers, unions, and government consciously coordinate their actions via interlocking ownership and participation; Germany and Japan are examples (chapter 10)

corporatism   Interest group system in which one organization represents each sector of society; originally from the Catholic belief in society as an organic whole; two subtypes are societal and state corporatism (chapter 3)

coup d'etat   Military takeover of a government (chapter 3)

cultural nationalism   National unity based on a common cultural characteristic; those people who don't share that particular cultural characteristic cannot be included in the nation (chapter 4)

deficit spending   Government spending exceeds what is collected in revenue (chapter 5)

delegative democracies   Democracies in which free and fair elections take place but neither vertical nor horizontal accountability is strong enough to prevent the emergence of elected executives with nearly unlimited power (chapter 9)

deliberative democracy   Democracy that asks citizens not only to assume their rights and minimally participate through voting but also to engage actively in democratic discussion in the effort to build a better society (chapter 12)

democracy   A regime in which citizens have basic rights of open association and expression and the ability to change the government through some sort of electoral process (chapter 1)

democratic centralism   The organization of a ruling party, primarily in communist regimes, in which lower organs of a party and state vote on issues and individuals to represent them at higher levels, ultimately reaching the top level, which makes final, binding decisions that all must then obey without question; key organizational innovation of Vladimir Lenin, leader of the Russian Communist Party (chapter 3)

democratic consolidation   The idea that democracy has become widely accepted as the permanent form of political activity in a particular country, and all significant political elites and their followers accept democratic rules and are confident everyone else does as well (chapter 9)

democratic deepening   Improvement in the quality of democracy, including the extent of participation, rule of law, and vertical and horizontal accountability (chapter 9)

developmental state   A state that seeks to create national strength by taking an active and conscious role in the development of specific sectors of the economy (chapter 5)

devolution   Partial decentralization of power from central government to subunits such as states or provinces, with subunits' power being dependent on central government and reversible (chapter 6)

dictator's dilemma An authoritarian ruler's repression creates fear, which then breeds uncertainty about how much support the ruler has; in response, the ruler spends more resources than is rational on coopting the opposition (chapter 8)

dictatorship of the proletariat The first stage of communism in Marxist thought, characterized by absolute rule by workers as a class over all other classes (chapter 3)

dominant-party system Party system in which multiple parties and free and fair elections exist but one party wins every election and governs continuously (chapter 7)

Duverger's Law French political scientist Maurice Duverger argued that "first-past-the-post" electoral systems will produce two major parties, eliminating smaller parties (chapter 7)

electoral democracy Political system in which opposition parties are legal and elections take place, but full civil and political rights of liberal democracy are not secure (chapter 3)

electoral systems Formal, legal mechanisms that translate votes into control over political offices and shares of political power (chapter 7)

elite theory Theory that all societies are ruled by a small group that has effective control over virtually all power; contrast to pluralist theory (chapter 1)

empirical theory An argument explaining what actually occurs; empirical theorists first notice and describe a pattern and then attempt to explain what causes it (chapter 1)

environmental justice movement A movement focused on exposing and fighting against racial and class inequalities in exposure to pollution, started in the United States in 1982 (chapter 11)

ethnic group A group of people who see themselves as united by one or more cultural attributes or a sense of common history but do not see themselves as a nation seeking their own state (chapter 4)

executive The branch of government that must exist in all modern states; it is the chief political power in a state and implements all laws (chapter 6)

export-oriented growth (EOG) Development policy based on encouraging economic growth via exports of goods and services, usually starting with light manufacturing such as textiles (chapter 10)

externality A cost or benefit of the production process that is not fully included in the price of the final market transaction when the product is sold (chapter 5)

external sovereignty Sovereignty relative to outside powers that is legally recognized in international law (chapter 2)

failed state A state that is so weak that it loses effective sovereignty over part or all of its territory (chapter 2)

fealty A relationship between lord and vassal in which the lord gave a vassal the right to rule a piece of land, its products, and people in exchange for political and military loyalty; the central relationship in feudal states (chapter 2)

federalism A system in which a state's power is legally and constitutionally divided among more than one level of government; in contrast to a unitary system (chapter 2)

federal systems Political systems in which a state's power is legally and constitutionally divided among more than one level of government; in contrast to a unitary system (chapter 6)

feudal states Premodern states in Europe in which power in a territory was divided among multiple and overlapping lords claiming sovereignty (chapter 2)

first dimension of power The ability of one person or group to get another person or group to do something it otherwise would not do (chapter 1)

"first-past-the-post" (FPTP) Electoral system in which individual candidates are elected in single-member districts; the candidate with the most votes, but not necessarily a majority, wins (chapter 7)

fiscal policy Government budgetary policy (chapter 5)

foreign direct investment (FDI) Investment from abroad in productive activity in another country (chapter 10)

founding election The first democratic election in many years (or ever), marking the completion of a transition to democracy (chapter 9)

free wage labor Labor that can move from place to place and is paid based on the time worked; required by capitalism (chapter 3)

globalization A rapid increase in the flow of cultural symbols, political ideas and movements, economic activity, technology, and communications around the globe (chapter 5)

guanxi In China, networks of personal supporters, including but not exclusively family, that are important for economic and political survival and advancement (chapter 8)

hardliners Leaders in an authoritarian regime who believe in repressing any opposition and preserving the status quo when faced with a demand for political liberalization or democratization (chapter 9)

head of government The key executive power in a state; usually a president or prime minister (chapter 6)

head of state The official, symbolic representative of a country, authorized to speak on its behalf and represent it, particularly in world affairs; usually a president or monarch (chapter 6)

Hindu nationalism In India, a movement to define the country as primarily Hindu; the founding ideology of the BJP party (chapter 7)

historical institutionalists Theorists who believe institutions explain political behavior, shape individuals' political preferences and their perceptions of their self-interests, evolve historically in particular countries, and change relatively slowly (chapter 1)

historical materialism The assumption that material forces are the prime movers of history and politics; a key philosophical tenet of Marxism (chapter 3)

horizontal accountability The ability of state institutions to hold one another accountable (chapter 6)

hyperglobalization Thesis that globalization is so powerful, it will overwhelm the power of nation-states, forcing convergence of economic policies (chapter 10)

ideal type Term used by Max Weber for a model of the purest version that a thing might be (chapter 2)

ideological hegemony The ruling class's ability to spread a set of ideas justifying and perpetuating its political dominance (chapter 1)

import-substitution industrialization (ISI) Development policy popular in the 1950s–1970s that uses trade policy, monetary policy, and currency rates to encourage the creation of new industries to produce goods domestically that the country imported in the past (chapter 5)

institutionalism An approach to explaining politics that argues that political institutions are crucial to understanding political behavior (chapter 1)

institutionalization The degree to which government processes and procedures are established, predictable, and routinized (chapter 8)

instrumentalism An elite theory of identity politics: rational and self-interested elites manipulate symbols and feelings of identity to mobilize a political following (chapter 4)

interest-group pluralism An interest group system in which many groups exist to represent particular interests and the government remains officially neutral among them; the United States is a key example (chapter 7)

internal sovereignty The sole authority within a territory capable of making and enforcing laws and policies; an essential element of a modern state (chapter 2)

international capital flows Movements of capital in the form of money across international borders (chapter 10)

international relations The study of politics among national governments and beyond national boundaries (chapter 1)

iron triangles Three-sided cooperative interaction among bureaucrats, legislators, and business leaders in a particular sector that serves the interest of all involved but keeps others out of the policy-making process (chapter 6)

Islamism The belief that Islamic law, as revealed by God to the Prophet Mohammed, can and should provide the basis for government in Muslim communities, with little equivocation or compromise (chapter 3)

jihad Derived from an Arabic word for "struggle"; an important concept in Islam; the Quran identifies three kinds of jihad: internal struggle to live faithfully, struggle to resist evil and right injustice, and struggle to protect the Muslim community (chapter 3)

judicial independence The belief and ability of judges to decide cases as they think appropriate, regardless of what other people, especially politically powerful officials or institutions, desire (chapter 6)

judicial review The right of the judiciary to decide whether a specific law contradicts a country's constitution (chapter 6)

judiciary Branch of government that interprets the law and applies it to individual cases (chapter 6)

jus sanguinis Citizenship based on "blood" ties; Germany is a key example (chapter 4)

jus soli Literally, citizenship dependent on "soil," or residence within the national territory; France is a key example (chapter 4)

Keynesian theory Named for British economist John Maynard Keynes, who argued that governments can reduce the "boom and bust" cycles of capitalism via active fiscal policy, including deficit spending when necessary (chapter 5)

legislative oversight Members of the legislature, usually in key committees, oversee the working of the bureaucracy by interviewing key leaders, examining budgets, and assessing how successfully a particular agency has carried out its mandate (chapter 6)

legislature Branch of government that makes the law in a democracy (chapter 6)

legitimacy The recognized right to rule (chapter 2)

liberal democracy A system of government that provides eight key guarantees: freedom of association, freedom of expression, the right to vote, broad citizen eligibility for public office, the right of political leaders to compete for support, alternative sources of information, free and fair elections, and institutions that make government policies depend on votes and other forms of citizen preferences (chapter 3)

liberal market economies (LMEs) In the varieties of capitalism approach, countries that rely heavily on market relationships to govern economic activity, meaning that firms interact with other firms and secure sources of finance through purely market-based transactions; the United States and United Kingdom are key examples (chapter 10)

liberal welfare states States whose social policies focus on ensuring that all who can do so gain their income in the market; more concerned with preserving individual autonomy via market participation than with reducing poverty or inequality; the United States is a key example (chapter 11)

liberationist approach Branch of the LGBT movement that seeks to transform sexual and gender norms, not simply to gain equal rights with heterosexuals but also to liberate all persons to express whatever sexual orientation and gender identity they wish in order to gain social acceptance and

respect for all regardless of their conformity to preexisting norms or institutions (chapter 12)

majoritarian democracy A type of democratic system that concentrates power relatively tightly in a single-party executive, with executive dominance over the legislature, a single legislative branch, and constitutions that can be easily amended (chapter 6)

market-based private insurance system Health care system that relies on private insurance for the bulk of the population; the United States is a key example (chapter 11)

market economy An economic system in which individuals and firms exchange goods and services in a largely unfettered manner (chapter 5)

market failure Phenomenon that occurs when markets fail to perform efficiently or they fail to perform according to other widely held social values; often caused by externalities, high risk, or imperfect information (chapter 5)

marketing boards Government entities with monopoly control over the domestic and international marketing of key crops; usually found in Africa (chapter 5)

Marxism Structuralist argument that says economic structures largely determine political behavior; the philosophical underpinning of communism (chapter 1)

mass parties Parties that recruit as many members as possible who expect to have some control and from whom the parties gain financial support, labor, and votes; in contrast to cadre parties (chapter 7)

means-tested public assistance Social programs that provide benefits to individuals who fall below a specific income level; TANF is an example in the United States (chapter 11)

member of parliament (MP) An elected member of the legislature in a parliamentary system (chapter 6)

military regime System of government in which military officers control power (chapter 3)

Millennium Development Goals (MDGs) Targets established by the United Nations to reduce poverty and hunger, improve education and health, improve the status of women, and achieve environmental sustainability (chapter 10)

mixed representation system Also called a semi-proportional representation system; an electoral system that combines single-member district representation with overall proportionality in allocation of legislative seats to parties; Germany is a key example (chapter 7)

mode of production   In Marxist theory, the economic system in any given historical era; feudalism and capitalism in the last millennium in Europe (chapter 3)

moderates   Leaders of democracy movements who are willing to compromise with the authoritarian regime to make some gains toward democracy, even if partial (chapter 9)

modernists   Theorists of political culture who believe that clear sets of attitudes, values, and beliefs can be identified in each country that change very rarely and explain much about politics there (chapter 1)

modernization   The transformation from poor agrarian to wealthy industrial societies, usually seen as the process of postcolonial societies becoming more like societies in the West (chapter 1)

modernization theory   Theory of development that argues that postcolonial societies need to go through the same process that the West underwent in order to develop (chapter 3)

monetarist theory   Economic theory that only monetary policy can affect economic well-being in capitalist economies; rejects Keynesian idea of using fiscal policy to regulate economy, arguing instead for reduced role for government (chapter 5)

monetary policy   The amount of money a government prints and puts into circulation and the basic interest rates the government sets (chapter 5)

monopoly   The control of the entire supply of a valued good or service by one economic actor (chapter 5)

moral hazard   Occurs when parties to a transaction behave in a particular way because they believe they will not have to pay the full costs of their actions (chapter 11)

most different systems design   A common approach of the comparative method that looks at countries that differ in many ways but are similar in terms of the particular political process or outcome in which the research is interested (chapter 1)

most similar systems design   A common approach of the comparative method that selects cases that are alike in a number of ways but differ on a key question under examination; often used

by comparativists who focus exclusively on one region of the world (chapter 1)

multicultural integration   Accepts that ethnocultural identities matter to citizens, will endure over time, and must be recognized and accommodated within political institutions; in contrast to assimilation (chapter 12)

multiculturalism   In general, the belief that different cultures in a society ought to be respected; in the United Kingdom, the policy governing how the state treats racial and religious minorities (chapter 12)

multiparty systems   Party systems in which more than two parties could potentially win a national election and govern (chapter 7)

nation   A group that proclaims itself a nation and has or seeks control of a state (chapter 4)

national health insurance (NHI)   A health care system in which the government mandates that virtually all citizens must have insurance; Germany is a key example (chapter 11)

national health system (NHS)   A government-financed and managed health care system, often called a single-payer system; the government creates a system into which all citizens pay, either through a separate insurance payment or via general taxation, and through which they gain medical care; the United Kingdom is a key example (chapter 11)

nationalism   The desire to be a nation and thus to control a national state (chapter 4)

natural monopolies   The control of the entire supply of valued goods or services by one economic actor in sectors of the economy in which competition would raise costs and reduce efficiency (chapter 5)

neocolonialism   Relationship between postcolonial societies and their former colonizers in which leaders benefit politically and economically by helping outside businesses and states maintain access to the former colonies' wealth and come to serve the interests of the former colonizers and corporations more than they serve their own people (chapter 1)

neocorporatism   Also called societal corporatism; corporatism that evolves historically and voluntarily rather than being mandated by the state; Germany is a key example (chapter 7)

neofascist   Description given to parties or political movements that espouse a virulent nationalism, often defined on a cultural or religious basis and opposed to immigrants as threats to national identity (chapter 3)

neofundamentalist Term coined by French scholar Olivier Roy; Islamic movements that focus only on implementing an extremely rigid vision of Sharia at the local level that dictates how people live their daily lives while ignoring the state; key example is the Taliban in Afghanistan (chapter 3)

neoliberalism Development theory supporting structural adjustment programs; argues that developing countries should reduce the role of government and open themselves to global trade to allow the market to allocate resources to maximize efficiency and thereby economic growth (chapter 5)

neopatrimonial authority Power based on a combination of the trappings of modern, bureaucratic states with underlying informal institutions of clientelism that work behind the scenes; most common in Africa (chapter 3)

New Public Management (NPM) Theory of reform of bureaucracies that argues for the privatizing of many government services so that they are provided by the market, creating competition among agencies and subagencies within the bureaucracy to simulate a market, focusing on customer satisfaction (via client surveys, among other things), and flattening administrative hierarchies to encourage more team-based activity and creativity (chapter 6)

New Public Service (NPS) Theory of reform of bureaucracies that argues for a more participatory and democratic process of determining regulations and service provision that fit local community needs; it relies on citizens' active participation in policymaking via networks of citizens interested in a particular policy area interacting with the bureaucracy (chapter 6)

normative theory An argument explaining what ought to occur rather than what does occur; contrast with empirical theory (chapter 1)

one-party regime A system of government in which a single party gains power, usually after independence in postcolonial states, and systematically eliminates all opposition in the name of development and national unity (chapter 3)

open-list proportional representation Electoral system with multiple candidates in each district; voters are presented with a list of all candidates and vote for the individual candidate of their choice; each party receives a number of legislative seats based on the total number of votes cast for all candidates from that party, and candidates with the most votes in the party get those seats; Brazil is a key example (chapter 7)

pact In a transition to democracy, a conscious agreement among the most important political actors in the authoritarian regime and in civil society to establish a new form of government (chapter 9)

pardo In Brazil, a mixed-race group (chapter 4)

parliamentarism A term for a parliamentary system of democracy (chapter 6)

parliamentary sovereignty Parliament is supreme in all matters; key example is the United Kingdom (chapter 3)

participatory democracy A form of democracy that encourages citizens to participate actively, in many ways beyond voting; usually focused at the local level (chapter 3)

party system The number of parties and each one's respective strength as an institution (chapter 7)

patriarchy Rule by men (chapter 1)

patron-client relationships Top leaders (patrons) mobilize political support by providing resources to their followers (clients) in exchange for political loyalty (chapter 1)

Peace of Westphalia Agreement among European powers in 1648 that codified the idea of states as legal equals that recognized each other's external and internal sovereignty within specified territories and that were prepared to defend that sovereignty and their interests via diplomacy if possible or war if necessary (chapter 2)

peak associations Organizations that bring together all interest groups in a particular sector to influence and negotiate agreements with the state; in the United States, an example is the AFL-CIO (chapter 7)

personalist regime System of government in which a central leader comes to dominate a state, typically not only eliminating all opposition but also weakening the state's institutions to centralize power in his hands (chapter 3)

personality cult Occurs in the most extreme cases of personalist rule; followers constantly glorify the ruler and attempt to turn his every utterance into not only government fiat but also divine wisdom; Mao Zedong in China was a key example (chapter 8)

pluralist theory Explanation of who has power that argues that society is divided into various political groups and power is dispersed among these groups so that no group has complete or permanent power; contrast to elite theory (chapter 1)

plurality The receipt of the most votes but not a majority (chapter 7)

politburo The chief decision-making organ in a communist party; China's politburo is a key example (chapter 3)

political accountability The ability of the citizenry, directly or indirectly, to control political leaders and institutions (chapter 6)

political actor Any person or group engaged in political behavior (chapter 1)

political appointees Officials who serve at the pleasure of the president or prime minister and, among other things, are assigned the task of overseeing their respective segments of the bureaucracy (chapter 6)

political culture A set of widely held attitudes, values, beliefs, and symbols about politics (chapter 1)

political development The processes through which modern nations and states arise and how political institutions and regimes evolve and the study of these processes (chapter 1)

political discourse The ways in which people speak and write about politics; postmodern theorists argue it influences political attitudes, identity, and actions (chapter 1)

political economy The study of the interaction between political and economic phenomena (chapter 1)

political ideology A systematic set of beliefs about how a political system ought to be structured (chapter 1)

political institution A set of rules, norms, or standard operating procedures that is widely recognized and accepted by the society and that structures and constrains political actions (chapter 1)

political liberalization The opening of the political system to greater participation; typically before a transition to democracy (chapter 9)

political rights The second of T. H. Marshall's rights of citizenship; those rights associated with active political participation: right to association, expression, voting, and running for office (chapter 3)

political saliency The degree to which something is of political importance (chapter 4)

political science The systematic study of politics and power (chapter 1)

political socialization The process through which people, especially young people, learn about politics and are taught a society's common political values and beliefs (chapter 1)

political violence The use of violence by nonstate actors for political ends (chapter 9)

politics The process by which human communities make collective decisions (chapter 1)

politics of recognition The demands for recognition and inclusion that have arisen since the 1960s in racial, religious, ethnic, gender, and other minority or socially marginalized groups (chapter 4)

populism A broad and charismatic appeal to poor people on the part of a leader to solve their problems directly via governmental largess; most common in Latin America in the early to mid-twentieth century (chapter 7)

postmaterialist Set of values in a society in which most citizens are economically secure enough to move beyond immediate economic (materialist) concerns to "quality of life" issues like human rights, civil rights, women's rights, environmentalism, and moral values (chapter 1)

postmodernist An approach that sees cultures not as sets of fixed and clearly defined values but rather as sets of symbols subject to interpretation (chapter 1)

precautionary principle A policy that emphasizes risk avoidance even when the science predicting a risk is uncertain (chapter 11)

presidentialism A term denoting a presidential system of democracy (chapter 6)

prime minister (PM) The head of government in parliamentary and semipresidential systems (chapter 6)

primordialism A theory of identity that sees identity groups as in some sense "natural" or God given, having existed since "time immemorial," and able to be defined unambiguously by such clear criteria as kinship, language, culture, or phenotype (chapter 4)

principal-agent problem A problem common in any hierarchical situation in which a superior (principal) hires someone (agent) to perform a task but the agent's self-interests do not necessarily align with the principal's, so the problem is how the principal makes sure the agent carries out the task as assigned; in politics, common when the elected or appointed political leadership in the executive or legislative branches assigns a bureaucrat a task to implement laws in a particular way (chapter 6)

privatize   Sell off public assets to the private sector (chapter 5)

proletariat   A term in Marxist theory for the class of free wage laborers who own no capital and must sell their labor to survive; communist parties claim to work on the proletariat's behalf (chapter 1)

proportional representation (PR)   Electoral system in which seats in a legislature are apportioned on a purely proportional basis, giving each party the share of seats that matches its share of the total vote (chapter 7)

psychological theories   Explanations of political behavior based on psychological analysis of political actors' motives (chapter 1)

public goods   Those goods or services that cannot or will not be provided via the market because their costs are too high or their benefits too diffuse (chapter 5)

quantitative statistical techniques   Research method used for large-scale studies that reduces evidence to sets of numbers that statistical methods can analyze to systematically compare a huge number of cases (chapter 1)

quasi-states   States that have legal sovereignty and international recognition but lack almost all the domestic attributes of a functioning modern state (chapter 2)

race   A people who sees itself as a group based primarily on one or more perceived common physical characteristics and common history (chapter 4)

radicals   In democratic transitions, members of civil society who wish to achieve immediate and complete democracy and are unwilling to compromise with the existing regime (chapter 9)

rational choice institutionalists   Institutionalist theorists who follow the assumptions of rational choice theory and argue that institutions are the products of the interaction and bargaining of rational actors (chapter 1)

rational choice theory   Explanation of political behavior that assumes that individuals are rational beings who bring a set of self-defined preferences and adequate knowledge and ability to pursue those preferences to the political arena;

these assumptions are then used to model political behavior in particular contexts (chapter 1)

rational-legal legitimacy   The right of leaders to rule based on their selection according to an accepted set of laws, standards, or procedures; one of Max Weber's three versions of legitimacy (chapter 2)

regime   A set of fundamental rules and institutions that govern political activity (chapter 3)

relative deprivation   A belief that a group or individual is not getting its share of something of value relative to others in the society or relative to members' own expectations (chapter 4)

rent seeking   Gaining an advantage in a market without engaging in equally productive activity; usually involves using government regulations to one's own benefit (chapter 6)

research methods   Systematic processes used to ensure that the study of a specific item or situation is as objective and unbiased as possible (chapter 1)

resource curse   Occurs when a state relies on a key resource for almost all of its revenue, allowing it to ignore its citizens and resulting in a weak state (chapter 2)

revolution   A relatively rapid transformation of the political system and social structure that results from the overthrow of the prior regime by mass participation in extra-legal political action, which is often (but not always) violent (chapter 9)

revolutions from above   Revolutions in which the outcomes are often negotiated among political elites, each with the backing of a segment of the populace (chapter 9)

revolutions from below   Revolutions that involve the mass uprising of the populace to overthrow the government as a central part of the process (chapter 9)

risk assessment   Analysis of what the risks of damaging outcomes are in a particular situation (chapter 11)

risk management   Policy used to keep risks to acceptable levels (chapter 11)

ruling class   An elite who possess adequate resources to control a regime; in Marxist theory, the class that controls key sources of wealth in a given epoch (chapter 1)

second dimension of power   The ability not only to make people do something but to keep them from doing something (chapter 1)

security dilemma A situation in which two or more groups do not trust one another, fear one another, and do not believe that institutional constraints will protect them (chapter 4)

semi-authoritarian regime A type of hybrid regime in which formal opposition and some open political debate exist and elections are held to select the executive and legislative branches but in which the ruling party controls electoral outcomes and the regime cannot be considered democratic in any real sense; also called competitive authoritarian and electoral authoritarian (chapter 3)

semipresidentialism A political system in which executive power is divided between a directly elected president and a prime minister elected by a parliament; Russia and France are key examples (chapter 6)

semiproportional representation system See *mixed representation system* (chapter 7)

separation of powers Constitutionally explicit division of power among the major branches of government (chapter 6)

Sharia Muslim law (chapter 3)

single, nontransferable vote (SNTV) An electoral system in which multiple seats exist in each legislative district but each voter only votes for one candidate; Japan prior to 1993 was a key example (chapter 7)

single case study Research method that examines a particular political phenomenon in just one country or community and can generate ideas for theories or test theories developed from different cases (chapter 1)

single-member district (SMD) Electoral system in which each geographic district elects a single representative to a legislature (chapter 7)

single-payer system See *national health system (NHS)* (chapter 11)

social capital Social networks and norms of reciprocity important for a strong civil society (chapter 7)

social classes In Marxist theory, groups of people with the same relationship to the means of production; more generally, groups of people with similar occupations, wealth, or income (chapter 1)

social construction Part of constructivist approach to identity; process through which societies collectively "construct" identities as a wide array of actors continually discusses the question of who "we" are (chapter 4)

social contract theory Philosophical approach underlying liberalism that begins from the premise that legitimate governments are formed when free and independent individuals join in a contract to permit representatives to govern over them in their common interests (chapter 3)

social democracy Combines liberal democracy with much greater provision of social rights of citizenship and typically greater public control of the economy (chapter 3)

social democratic welfare states States whose social policies strongly emphasize universal entitlements to achieve greater social equality and promote equal citizenship; Sweden is prime example (chapter 11)

social insurance Provides benefits to categories of people who have contributed to a (usually mandatory) public insurance fund; typically used to provide retirement pensions (chapter 11)

social market economy In Germany, postwar economic system that combines a highly productive market economy with an extensive and generous welfare state and unusually active involvement of both business and labor associations in setting and implementing economic policy (chapter 5)

social movements Part of civil society; have a loosely defined organizational structure and represent people who have been outside the bounds of formal institutions, seek major socioeconomic or political changes to the status quo, or employ noninstitutional forms of collective action (chapter 7)

social policy Policy focused on reducing poverty and income inequality and stabilizing individual or family income (chapter 11)

social revolution In Marxist theory, the transition from one mode of production to another; Marxist understanding of revolution (chapter 3)

social rights The third of T. H. Marshall's rights of citizenship; those rights related to basic well-being and socioeconomic equality (chapter 3)

societal corporatism See *neocorporatism* (chapter 7)

softliners In democratic transitions, members of the authoritarian regime willing to consider compromising with opponents as a means to survive demands for democratization (chapter 9)

sovereign Quality of a state in which it is legally recognized by the family of states as the sole legitimate governing authority within its territory and as the legal equal of other states (chapter 2)

soviets Legislative bodies in the communist regime of the Soviet Union (chapter 3)

stagflation Simultaneous high inflation and high unemployment; term coined in the 1970s (chapter 5)

stare decisis Literally, "let the the decision stand"; in common law, the practice of accepting the precedent of previous similar cases (chapter 6)

state A set of ongoing institutions that develops and administers laws and generates and implements public policies in a specific territory (chapter 2)

state corporatism Corporatism mandated by the state; common in fascist regimes (chapter 7)

structural adjustment programs (SAPs) Development programs created by the World Bank and International Monetary Fund beginning in the 1980s; based on neoliberalism (chapter 5)

structuralism Approach to explaining politics that argues that political behavior is at least influenced and limited, and perhaps even determined, by broader structures in a society such as class divisions or enduring institutions (chapter 1)

subcultures Groups that hold partially different beliefs and values from those of the main political culture of a country (chapter 1)

supreme leader Individual who wields executive power with few formal limits in an authoritarian regime; in the Islamic Republic of Iran, the formal title of the top ruling cleric (chapter 8)

sustainable development Economic development that can continue over the long term because it is not environmentally unsound or excessively dependent on uncertain foreign sources of support (chapter 10)

symmetrical federal system Division of constitutionally assigned power to national and subnational governments with all subnational governments (states or provinces) having the same relationship with and rights in relation to the national government (chapter 6)

tax expenditures Targeted tax breaks for specific groups of citizens or activities designed to achieve social policy goals (chapter 11)

technocratic legitimacy A claim to rule based on knowledge or expertise (chapter 3)

territory An area with clearly defined borders to which a state lays claim (chapter 2)

terrorism Political violence targeted at civilian noncombatants (chapter 9)

theocracy Rule by religious authorities (chapter 3)

theory An abstract argument that provides a systematic explanation of some phenomena (chapter 1)

third dimension of power The ability to shape or determine individual or group political demands by causing people to think about political issues in ways that are contrary to their own interests (chapter 1)

totalitarian regime A regime that controls virtually all aspects of society and eliminates all vestiges of civil society; Germany under Hitler and the Soviet Union under Stalin were key examples (chapter 3)

trade The flow of goods and services across national borders (chapter 10)

traditional legitimacy The right to rule based on a society's long-standing patterns and practices; one of Max Weber's three versions of legitimacy (chapter 2)

tragedy of the commons No individual has the incentive or ability to preserve a common, shared good that is free, so without collective effort, it is likely to be overused and perhaps ultimately destroyed (chapter 11)

transition to democracy A type of regime change typically involving a negotiated process that removes an authoritarian regime and concludes with a founding election for a new, democratic regime (chapter 9)

two-and-a-half-party system Party system in which two large parties win the most votes but typically neither gains a majority, thus requiring a third (the "half" party) to join one of the major parties to form a legislative majority; Germany is key example (chapter 7)

two-party system Party system in which only two parties are able to garner enough votes to win an election, though more may compete; the United Kingdom and United States are key examples (chapter 7)

typology A classification of some set of phenomena into distinct types for purposes of analysis (chapter 1)

umma The global Muslim community (chapter 3)

unitary systems Political systems in which the central government has sole constitutional sovereignty and power; contrast with federal systems (chapter 6)

universal entitlements Benefits that governments provide to all citizens more or less equally, usually funded through general taxation; in the United States, public education is an example (chapter 11)

vanguard party Vladimir Lenin's concept of a small party that claims legitimacy to rule based on its understanding of Marxist theory and its ability to represent the interests of the proletariat before they are a majority of the populace (chapter 3)

varieties of capitalism approach School of thought analyzing wealthy market economies that focuses primarily on business firms and how they are governed in terms of their interactions with government, each other, workers, and sources of finance; divides such economies into liberal market economies (LMEs) and coordinated market economies (CMEs) and argues that globalization will not produce convergence between them (chapter 10)

vertical accountability The ability of individuals and groups in a society to hold state institutions accountable (chapter 6)

veto player An individual or collective actor, such as a legislature or interest group, whose agreement is essential for any policy change (chapter 6)

vote of no confidence In parliamentary systems, parliament voting to remove a government (the prime minister and cabinet) from power (chapter 6)

weak state State that cannot provide adequate political goods to its population (chapter 2)

welfare states Distinct systems of social policies that arose after World War II in wealthy market economies, including social democratic welfare states, Christian democratic welfare states, and liberal welfare states (chapter 11)

Index

NOTE: Page numbers with *b, f, m,* or *t* indicate boxes, figures, maps, and tables, respectively. Italicized page numbers indicate photographs.

A

Abacha, Sani, *125, 390*
 control of Nigeria's judiciary by, 392–393
 corruption of, 234–235, *414*
 patronage by, 393
 political parties and, 415, 470
 repression and corruption under, 126–127, 469–470
Abiola, Moshood, 470
Abortion, 278, 631
Absolutism, 46–47, 97–98, 151–152
Abstract judicial review, 274, 276–278
Abuja, Nigeria, MEND violence in, 595
Abuse, women's movement and, 631
Accountability. *See also* Horizontal accountability; Vertical accountability
 in Brazil, 456
 executive system types and, 270
 popular control of government, effective governance and, 246
 of top leadership in China, 384–385
Acemoglu, Daron, 103*b*
Acephalous societies, 165
Acid rain, 589, 594
Act of Union (1542 & 1707, UK), 62–63

Adenauer, Konrad, 217, 348
Administration vs. government, 39
Administrative guidance (Japan), 224–225
AFDC (Aid to Families with Dependent Children, U.S.), 212, 559–560
Affirmative action, 174, 177, 181–182
Afghanistan
 as failed state, 56–58
 September 11 attacks and, 5
 Taliban in, 439*b*
 UK military presence in, 622
 voting system in, 353*b*
AFL-CIO, 331
Africa. *See also specific regions and countries*
 Asian miracle vs. malaise in, 514–515
 authoritarian regimes, 373, 397–398
 background conditions in, 514–515
 blessing of ancestors over the king in, 43
 citizens as children of "father-chief," 23–24
 corruption in, 291*b*
 coups d'etat by decade in, 432*b*
 from democracy to semi-authoritarianism, 476

 democratization in, 121–122, 444–445, 451
 development economists on free trade vs. terms of trade for, 199
 in economic crisis from Great Recession, 204
 European colonialism in, 49, 71
 failed states in, 51
 gap with developed countries and, 502–503
 gender gap in, 632
 globalization and development in, 513–518
 as homeland for U.S. blacks, 174
 interest groups' emergence in, 331, 397
 Latin Americans descended from people of, 179–180, 180*b*
 legislatures of one-party regimes in, 375
 military coups in, 426–427*b*, 427*m*, 428, 432*b*
 modern states in, 48
 moral matrix of legitimate governance, 23–24
 neocolonialism in, 31
 one-party regimes in, 121–122
 patron-client relationships in, 28, 338
 political behavior patterns, 14

Africa *(cont.)*
political development in, 7
political ideologies and regime types in, 138
political parties in, 323
postcolonial societies and secularism in, 616
quasi-states in, 56
quotas for women in elected positions, 635
Schatzberg's study of, 23–24
semipresidentialism in, 258*b*
state type and development in, 513–517
structural adjustment programs in, 201
tribes or ethnic groups in, 156*b*
women's rights in, 149*b*
African Americans
congressional representation, 173–174, 176*t*
discrimination laws, 173–174
environmental justice movement and, 588
racial disparity, 173–174, 176*t*
from slavery to assimilation, 171–175
terminology for, 173
as U.S. slaves, 65–66
African National Congress (ANC, South Africa), 323
African Renaissance, 517
Afrikaner identity construction, 148
Afrobarometer, on Ghana, 453
Afro-Brazilian cultural practices/ political movement, 178, 180–181
Agenda 2010 (Germany), 218, 555
Age of high mass consumption in modernizing authoritarianism, 119
Agrarian Party (Sweden), 546
Agrarian societies and individual political participation, 9
Agriculture
in Africa, 514
alternative strategies for, 502
in China, 519
China's household responsibility system and, 519
in India, 523–525
industrial society vs., 102–103*b*
in Mexico, 130, 230
in Nigeria, *232*, 233
in Turkey, 513
U.S. protectionist policies for, 215

Agriculture associations, 329, 331
Ahmadinejad, Mahmoud, *80, 410*
cabinet of, 388–389
election of, 136, 388, 409, 413, 532
government role and reforms under, 530–532
women's rights under, 640, 644
Ahmadiyah Muslims, 616
Ahmad Shah, King of Afghanistan (1747), 56
AIDS. *See* HIV/AIDS
AIDS Coalition to Unleash Power (ACT UP), 650
Aid to Dependent Children (ADC, U.S.), 559
Aid to Families with Dependent Children (AFDC, U.S.), 212, 559–560
Air pollution. *See also* Environment; Pollution
Beijing Summer Olympics and, 589–590, *590*
as economic externality, 193–194
by gas flaring in Nigeria, *593*, 594
globalization-induced, 581–582
U.S. improvements, 587–589
Air traffic controllers' strike (1981, U.S.), 212
Akali Dal (Sikh political party, India), 359
Alaska
environmental protections, 587
Exxon *Valdez* oil spill, 594
Alcohol use, as public health concern, 571
Alesina, Alberto, 548
Algerian Islamic Front (FIS), 133, 330
Ali, Iman, 134
Al Jazeera, 401
All-China Federation of Trade Unions (ACFTU), 405
Allen, Chris, 426
Allende, Salvador, 227
Allies, World War II, 71
All India Muslim Personal Law Board (AIMPLB), 624–625
All India Muslim Women's Personal Law Board, 624
All India Shia (Shiite) Personal Law Board, 624
Almond, Gabriel, 21–22, 102*b*, 444
al-Qaida, 133, 439*b*, 622
Alternative-vote (AV) system, 318–319
Altman, Roger, 206

Alvarez, Michael, 509–511
Amakudari, Japanese practice of, 287
American Revolution, 109, 436–437*b*
Americo-Liberian elite, 58–59
Ames, Barry, 458
Amin, Idi, 374*b*
Ancient hatreds, 160, 169
Anderson, Benedict, 151
Anderson, Perry, 47
Anglican Church. *See* Church of England
Anglo-American countries, 548–549. *See also* British colonies, former
Anglo-American law, 273
Anthias, Flora, 149*b*
Antiblack hate crimes during Obama's presidency, 177
Anti-child-poverty policy in UK, 495
Anticlericalism in Catholic Mexico, 626–629, *627*
Anticommunism in Brazil, 123–124
Antidiscrimination laws in UK, 618
Antinuclear movement, 348–349
Antiwar social movement, 325
Apartheid. *See also* Segregation
sexual, in Saudi Arabia, 633
in South Africa, 31–32, *32*, 148, 182, 323, 608
"Arab Spring," 136, 634
Arab states. *See* Middle East
Argentina
globalization and development in, 508
presidential term of office in, 260
same-sex marriage and, 647
social programs in, 510
Aristotle, 9
Armed Forces Ruling Council, Nigeria, 391
Aron, Leon, 468
Articles of Confederation (U.S.), 65
Aryan racial bloodlines, Nazis on, 153
Asia. *See also specific regions and countries*
authoritarian rule after independence, 397–398
comparative advantage policies in, 504
democratization in, 445
European colonialism in, 49

free trade vs. terms of trade for, 199
gap with developed countries and, 502–503
interest groups' emergence in, 331, 397
modern states in, 48
neocolonialism in, 31
political development in, 7
political ideologies in, 138
political parties in, 323
postcolonial societies and secularism in, 616
SAPs in, 504
women
    gender gap and, 632
    in power positions in, 317*b*
    quotas in elected positions, 635
Asian American Political Alliance, 175
Asian Americans, terminology for, 174–175
Assembly of Experts, Iran, 135, 386
Assimilation
    ethnic groups in U.S., 173
    French revolutionary nationalism as, 152
    LGBTs in U.S., 645, 649
    multicultural integration vs., 609–610
Assimilationist, defined, 152
Asymmetrical federal systems, 295
AT&T, 196
Ataturk, Kemal, 614
Atiku, Abubakar, 473–474
Austerlitz, Battle of (1805), 70
Australia
    deindustrialization in, 488
    as federalist country, 292
Austria-Hungary, Prussian wars with, 70
Authoritarianism/authoritarian regimes. *See also* Modernizing authoritarianism
    basic characteristics, 369–379
    of case countries, 416–419
    China's evolution as, 379–385
    civil society in, 397–398
    collective action problems for, 394
    controls on military institutions in, 425–426
    defined, 8
    democratic regimes vs., 102*b*, 309, 533
    development success under, 508–511*b*

economic growth
    in democracies vs., 533
    hypothesis, 508–509
    in Egypt, 373
    elections in, 394–397
    ethnic conflict under, 157
    executive power and institutionalization in, 372–379
    institutionalism/institutionalists in, 418
    institutions of, 396, 416
    in Iran, 385–390
    legislatures and judiciaries in, 372
    in Mexico, 78
    in Nigeria, 390–394, 413–416
    as outcome of revolution, 439
    patron-client relationships in, 398–399
    political parties in, 372–373, 374–375*b*, 394–398, 418–419
    in post-revolution China, 442
    power sharing in, *370*
    public displays of support for, 394–395, *403*
    religious conflict under, 163
    representation in, 9
    with revolution from below, 475
    security apparatus for, 372–373
    social movements in, 397–398
    succession in, 378–379
    traits of, 418
    transition to democracy in, 445
    types vs. political behavior, 417
    in Zaire, 377–378
    in Zimbabwe, *370*
Automobile industry. *See also specific manufacturers*
    bailouts under Obama, 214
    gas mileage standards
        in China, 592
        in U.S., 588
Autonomy. *See also* Nationalism
    black autonomy, 174
    of Brazilian military, Goulart's threats to, 430–431
    defined, 150
    equality vs., 543
    ethnic groups and, 155
    governing, for distinct cultural groups, 609
    identity groups and, 183, 608
    judicial, in authoritarian regimes, 376
    local, Russian federalism and, 299–301
    races and, 171
    regional, Nigerian ethnic groups and, 166

religious groups and, 163
of subnational governments, 293–295, 298
Awolowo, Obafemi, 166
Aylwin, Patricio, 228
Ayodhya, India, Hindu nationalists on temple site in, 360–361, 626
d'Azeglio, Massimo, 151
Azikiwe, Nnamdi, 166
Aztec people, 77

B
Babangida, Ibrahim, 126, 392–394, 415, 469
Baby boomers' political involvement, 325
Bachelet, Michele, 228
Bachrach, Peter, 10–11
Back to Africa movement, 174
Baer, Werner, 529
Bahrain, protests in, 402
Bailouts
    auto industry, 214
    in Greece, 221
    in Ireland, 221
Baird, Vanessa, 276
Banking regulations, 211–215
Bank nationalization in Germany, 498
Bank of Canada, 211*b*
Bank of England, 211*b*, 495
Bank of Japan, 211*b*
Bano, Shah, 624–625
Banque de France, 211*b*
Baratz, Morton, 10–11
Barre, Siad, 45
Basic Law, West Germany's, 71, 348
Basij (civilian militia in Iran), 388
Basques, 156*b*
Bates, Robert, 191
Bazaari groups (Iran), 442–443
BDA (German business organization), 348
BDI (German business organization), 348
Beijing, China
    elections in, 405
    hunger strike in, 407
    smog and pollution in, *590*
    Summer Olympics (2008) in, 384, *518*, *590*
    Tiananmen Square demonstrations, 86, 383, 407–408
    women's conference (1995) in, 630
Belfast Agreement (1998), 158
Belgium
    colonial rule in Rwanda, 169
    consociationalism in, 157

Belgium *(cont.)*
  federalism and consociational-
    ism in, 293
  same-sex marriage status in, 647
Ben Ali, Zine, 399–401
Beneficial roles in market econ-
    omy, 193–196, 204*b*
Benin as democratic success, 454
Berlin Wall, *70,* 71, 349, 444
Bermeo, Nancy, 447
Bharatiya Janata Party (BJP,
    India), 358–361, *623,* 625
Biafra, Nigeria and, 89, 166, 168
Bicameral legislatures
  in Brazil, 264
  in coalition governments, 247
  federalism and, 293
  in Germany, 500
  legislator terms of office in, 260
  in UK, 255
  in U.S., 262
Biden, Joe, *172*
Big Men (Nigeria), 471
Bill of Rights, British, 109
bin Laden, Osama, 56–57, 133–134
Birth rates in Russia, 637–638
Bisexuals. *See* Lesbian, gay, bisex-
    ual, and transgender (LGBT)
    people
Bismarck, Otto von
  German unification and, 70–71,
    153
  national health care system
    under, 571
  as ruler of Germany's first
    regime, 7
  social insurance under, 554
  social market economy and,
    216, 218
Black Hawk Down episode (Soma-
    lia, 1993), 55
Black Panthers, 174
Black Power movement (U.S.),
    174–175
Blacks. *See also* African Americans
  Black nationalism, 174, 177–178
  "Black" political movement in
    UK, 619–620
  in Brazil, 178
  terminology for, 172–173
Blair, Tony
  centralized decision making,
    254
  devolution and, 109–110
  EU Convention for Human
    Rights in UK, 110
  hereditary peers and, 255
  labor unions, relationship to,
    340–341

"New Labour" reform under,
    284, 341, 576
  welfare benefits and, 494–495
Blyth, Mark, 321, 324*b*
Boix, Carles, 327, 448*b*
Bolivia
  indigenous people, percentage
    of population, 180*b*
  leftist critics of neoliberal
    reforms in, 507–508
  women in power positions in,
    317*b*
Bolsa Familia and *Bolsa Escola* (Bra-
    zil), *562,* 562–563
Bolsheviks, 113
Bombay Club, India, 524–525
Bonyads (Islamic foundations),
    389, 530–532
Boom and bust economy, 198
Borders
  in identity politics, 148
  of postcolonial states, 49–50
  recognition of changes in, 42*b*
Bosnia
  genocide in, 143
  language and ethnic conflict in
    Yugoslavia for, 155
  Muslims in, 162
  Serbs and Croats, conflict
    with, 157
Botswana, as democratic success,
    454
Bourgeoisie, 25, 30–31, 92,
    110–111
Bowers v. Hardwick (1986, U.S.), 650
Bowling Alone (Putnam), 336–337
Brahmin caste, 82–83, 358,
    360–361
Branch Davidians, 43
Brass, Paul, 147
Bratton, Michael, 450
Braun, Carol Moseley, 176
Brazil
  bloodless coup as "Revolution"
    in, 431
  bureaucratic-authoritarian
    regime in, 374*b*
  condomblé in, 165
  coup d'etat in Nigeria vs.,
    429–431
  currency problems (1998), 507
  currency valuations in, 485
  democratization and demo-
    cratic deepening in,
    455–460
  development in, 119
  federalism in, 296–298
  as fragmented-multiclass state,
    510

Freedom House scores for, 456*b*
  globalization and development
    in, 507, 526–530
  heterodox reforms in, 507
  import-substitution industrial-
    ization and, 200
  industrialization in, 196
  institutionalization in, 374–375
  judiciary in, 278–280
  leftist critics of neoliberal
    reforms in, 507–508
  LGBT movement in, 647,
    652–655
  military-created legislature in,
    374
  modernizing authoritarianism
    in, 123–124
  as modern state, 72–74
  neoliberal model adapted by,
    518
  presidential system in, 263–265
  presidential term of office in,
    260
  race in, 178–182, *179*
  regime type and characteristics,
    138
  rotating presidency in military
    regime of, 371
  slavery in, 48
  social insurance and agriculture
    in, 562
  social movements under
    military regime of, 397
  social programs in, 510,
    562–563
  state formation, 73
  stock market problems in
    (1998), 507
  white elites in, 180
Brazilian Association of Lesbians,
    Gays, and Transvestites, 653
Brazilian Miracle (1967–1973),
    124, 527
Brezhnev, Leonid, 114
Bribery, 279, 285. *See also*
    Corruption
BRIC (Brazil, Russia, India,
    China) group, *72*
Brinton, Crane, 437*b*
Britain. *See* United Kingdom
British colonies, former. *See also*
    specific countries
  African coups in, 426–427*b*
  citizens' immigration to UK,
    618–619
  common law in, 273
  federalism in India and, 298
  first-past-the-post representation
    in, 343*b*

immigrants to UK from, 618–619
political institutions of, 258*b*, 259
religious diversity in India as, 623
British East India Company, 82
British Telephone, 196
British welfare state, 63
Brooks, Robin, 447
Brown, Gordon, 254, 340, 495
Brownlee, Jason, 374*b*, 396
Brubaker, Rogers, 152, 153
Buddhism, Indonesia's recognition of, 616
Budget deficits. *See also* Deficit spending
Mexico, 231
U.S., 213–214
Buhari, Muhammadu, 126, 392–393, 415, 433, 470–471, 474
Bulgaria, revolution in (1989–1990), 434
Bundesbank (Germany), 211*b*, 216, 218
Bundesrat (Germany), 294–295
Bureaucracy
accountability and, 301
in authoritarian regimes, 372, 376–377, 418
in Brazil, 72–74
characteristics of, 280–292
defined, 44
in India, 82–83, 288–292
in Iran, 387–388
in Japan, 67, 283, 286–288
in Mexico, 77
of modern states, 44–46, 246
in Nigeria, 125–127, 391–393
in Russia under Putin, 467
in U.S., 66, 263
welfare states and, 549
Bureaucracy hypotheses testing, 283
Bureaucratic-authoritarian regime (Brazil), 124, 374*b*, 429, 431
Burqa, wearing of, 614, 634
Burundi
border retention in, 50
Mobutu's downfall in Zaire and, 378
Bush, George W.
election of 2000 and, 262
on Kyoto Protocol, 584, 588
monetarist policies used by, 213
presidential power expansion under, 263

signing statements, 263
tax rebate, 213
unitary executive theories, 302
Business associations, 238, 329, 331, 334, 359. *See also* Civil society; Interest groups

C
Cabinet
in India, 255
in Iran, 386, 388–389
in parliamentary systems, 252
in presidential systems, 260–261, 262, 271
in Russia, 268–269
in UK, 255
Cadre parties. *See also* Political parties
defined, 319–320
in early U.S., 343
in Europe, 327
in Latin America, 322
mass parties vs., 320
in UK parliament, 339
Caesar, Julius, 156*b*
Cai, Yongshun, 407–408
Calderón, Felipe, 461, *461*, 628
California, air pollution from China in, 592
Caliphs, rulers of Iran, 133
Calles, Plutarco Elias, 129, 628
Calvinism, propensity against social welfare by, 548
Cameron, David
child allowance as social right, 110
economic reforms under, 493, *493*
health insurance reforms and, 574, *575*, 576, 598
multicultural policies in UK, 622
Cameroon, German colonialism in, 71
Campaign for Democracy (CD), Nigeria, 469
Campesinos (Mexican peasant class), 78
Canada
index of interest-group pluralism, 341
same-sex marriage status in, 647
Cancún, Mexico, environmental conference (2010), 584
Candeira, Gregory, 276
Cap and trade system for pollution control, 583–585, 587–588
Capitalism. *See also* Varieties of capitalism
as cause of nationalism, 151

defined, 191
developmental state in Japan, 67
Germany's social market economy and, 71, 217
as market economy with private property rights, 191
Marx on, 111
Capital mobility and globalization, 205
Capitation system for health care expenditures
in Germany, 573
moral hazards of, 567
in UK, 574–575
in U.S., 578
Carbon pollution, 542, 582, 584–586, 589, 592. *See also* Greenhouse gases
Cárdenas, Cuauhtémoc, 79, 131, 461–463
Cárdenas, Lázaro, 129, 229, 461
Cardoso, Fernando Henrique
Brazil's racial policy and, 181
economic policies of, 527–528
one-round election of, 264
popularity of, 458
presidential powers and, 302
reforms under, 297
Carnival (Brazil), 180
Cartel parties, 321
Carter, Jimmy, 212, 385, 443, 471
"Cash for clunkers" program (Germany), 219
Caste systems, 358, *360*, 360–361
Catholic Church
in Brazil, 124, 456, 652–654
Christian Democrats and, 322*b*, 326
feudalism and, 46–47
Henry VIII of England's break with, 109
Indonesia's recognition of, 616
liberation theology in Brazil, 74
in Mexico
anticlericalism, 626–629
elections, role in, 130
reforms under Santa Ana, 627
in Northern Ireland, 158–159
propensity for social welfare by, 548–549
secularism in France and Mexico and, 613, 657
theocracy in Europe, 132
Caudillos (Mexican strongmen), 78
CCP. *See* Chinese Communist Party
Cellular devices, social capital decline and, 326–327
CEN (National Executive Committee, Mexico), 129

Census Bureau, U.S., racial categories in, 175
Central America, rebellions in, 48–49. *See also* Latin America
Central Asian republics, democracy failure in, 440
Central Bank (Nigeria), 474
Central banks, 211*b*
Central Commission for Discipline Inspection (China), 384
Central Military Commission (CMC, China), 381–383
Central state planning as developmental policy, 288
Centre Party (France), 328
Centripetal approach, 157, 185
Chamber of Commerce (U.S.), 331
Chamber of Deputies, Brazil, 264, 297, 457
Chancellor, German, 117, 249
Charismatic legitimacy, 43
Charles I (King of England), 109
Charter 08 (China), 406
Chastity police (Iran), 640
Chavez, Hugo, 510
Chechnya, secession struggles with Russia, 268, *296*, 299, 466, 639
Checks and balances, 274. *See also* Separation of powers
Cheibub, Jose Antonio, 122, 272, 509–511
Chen Jo-hsi, 380
Chernenko, Konstantin, *30*
Chiang Kai-shek, 441
Chiapas, Mexico, guerrilla campaign in, 79
Chicago Boys (Chile), 227
Child allowances, 110, 544, 555
Children, caregivers for, 630–631, 637–638
Chile
  constitution under Pinochet, 446
  health care study in, 569
  Mexico's debt crisis and, 228
  neoliberal reform in, 227–228, 507, 516
  presidential term of office in, 260
  structural adjustment programs in, 201, 202*b*
  transition to democracy in, 26–27
China, People's Republic of. *See also* Chinese Communist Party
  authoritarian regime, evolution as, 379–385

Chinese Empire as modern state, 48
civilian control over military in, 383
civil war in, 441–442
communism in, 9, 434
Confucian ideas of merit in, 280
corruption in, 384–385
economy
  in crisis from Great Recession, 204, 206
  economic liberalization in, 138
  growth of, 5–6, 518–522
  legitimacy over political reform, 84–87
  market economy and participation and representation in, 404, 406, 408
election fraud in, 405
factional infighting in, 383
gap with developed countries and, 502–503
industrialization in, 196
inequality in, 505
interest groups in, 405–406
Internet use in, *85*
Japanese invasion of, 68, 85–86
judiciary institutionalization in, 383
Mao's personalist decision-making for, 380, 442
modernizing authoritarianism in, 408
as one-party Communist state, 379–385
participation, growth of, 402–408
party and state institutions in, 380–381, 381*f*, 383
patron-client networks in, 403–404
people's courts in, 383
pollution problem in, 582, 584–586
repression of civil society in, 397, 404
revolution (1911–1949), 434, 440–442
social revolution from below in, 442
state formation, 84–87
succession in, *379*, 379–380, 382–383, 385
voter turnout in, 405
women in power in, 405
China Family Planning Association, 406
Chinese Americans, 175

Chinese Communist Party (CCP)
  corruption in, 384–385
  economic development under, 382, 404
  factional infighting in, 383
  loosening in, 404
  under Mao, 85–86
  membership and patron-client networks in, 403–404
  modern state in China and, 86–88
  Party Congress secrecy, 379–380
  private business leaders and, 520
  reformers in, 138
  revolution (1911–1949), 434, 440–442
  role in state institutions of, 380, 381*f*
Chinn, Stuart, 275
Chirac, Jacques, 328, 614
Chopsticks tax (China), 591
Chou En Lai, *441*
Christian Democratic Union (CDU). *See also* Christian democratic welfare states
  in Chile, 228
  in Europe, 320–321, 322*b*
  in Germany, *554*
    France vs., 326
    health care equity concerns of, 572–574
    under Kohl, 500
    policy choices and reforms, 555
    social market economy development, 217–218
Christian Democratic Union/ Christian Social Union (CDU/CSU, Germany), 348–350
Christian democratic welfare states
  Catholics in population and, 548–549
  defined, 545, 547
  in Germany, reform of, *554*, 554–557
  maternity leave and child care in, 632
  as share of national economy, 551
  on welfare reform, 553
Christians/Christianity. *See also* Catholic Church
  in Africa, 616
  as missionaries, 49, 88
  in Nigeria, 87–89, 165–167, 183, 414, 473
  theocracies and, 138

in UK, 620–621

U.S. conservative, LGBT movement opposition by, *649,* 652

Churches. *See* Religious groups

Church of England, 63, 617, 620

Citizens/citizenship. *See also* Accountability; Inequality

for African Americans, 174

definition, evolution of, 97

demands for inclusion in, 656

early U.S. definitions of, 436–437*b*

on economic leadership in democracies, 189

enfranchisement rules for, 73, 180

fascism and, 116

in Germany, *153,* 153–154

inclusion policies and, 605, 654

in India, communal rights of religious law and practice and, 624–625

in Iran, powers of, 133, 136

in liberal democracies, 104–105, 107*b,* 109, 543

modernizing authoritarianism and, 118–120

political ideology and, 100–103, 137

presidential systems and, 258

regime variations and attitudes toward, 100

states and, 95

in Sweden, welfare state and, 546–547

in UK, 109

women's rights and, 630, 633–635, 645

Civic culture, 21

The Civic Culture (Almond & Verba), 21–22, 102*b,* 444

Civic nationalism, 151, 611

Civil action groups, 349

Civil codes for Muslims in India, 625

Civilians

control over military, 383, 460, 471–472, 475

military perceptions of, 425–426

Civilizing of native colonial population, 49

Civil law, 273, 383

Civil Liberties Organization (Nigeria), 469

Civil rights

American social movement for, 335, 343

Brazilian social movement for, 183

defined, 97

discrimination laws for African Americans, 173–174

legislation, 66, 174

for LGBT community in U.S., 649–650

in liberal democracy, 104

Marshall on citizenship and, 97–98

Civil Rights Act of 1964 (U.S.), 66, 174

Civil Service (U.S.), 346

Civil society. *See also* Interest groups

in authoritarian regimes, 372, 394, 397–398

in Brazil, 124, 460

under communism, 111, 113–114

defined, 9

ethnic and religious, 330

fascism and, 116

importance to democracy, 138

in India, 359, 362

interest group characteristics, 331, 333*f*

in Iran, 136, 411

Islamists and, 133

in Japan, 352, 356–357

in Mexico, 463

modern, emergence of, 98

modernizing authoritarianism and, 119–120

in Nazi Germany, 117

in Nigeria, 127, 415–416

participation and interest representation in, 310, 364–365

in postcolonial countries, 358

regime variations and attitudes toward, 99

in Russia, 467

social capital decline and, 336–337

social movements and, 329–330, 334–337, 341

transition to democracy and, 445

weak, democratic breakdown and, 447

women in Russia of early 1990s and, 637

Civil unions, 647, 651, 654–655. *See also* Same-sex marriage

Civil War (U.S.)

as challenge to internal sovereignty, 43

evolution of political parties and, 343

institutional instability and, 25–26

as revolution, 436*b*

state formation and, 64, 66–67

Civil wars. *See also* Civil War (U.S.)

as challenge to internal sovereignty, 42–43, 45–46

in China, 441–442

classification question, 13*b*

in Congo, 92, 377–378

in England, 109

ethnic fragmentation and, 164*m*

explanations for, 160

factors leading to, 13*b,* 14

in Liberia, 92

in Mexico, 78

in Nigeria, 89, 126, *165,* 166, 393, 433

religious differences and, 109, 612

in Somalia, 45–46, 92

in Zaire, 377

Cixi, Empress Dowager of China, 441

Clans in middle-income new democracies, 291*b*

Clark, John, 428

The Clash of Civilizations (Huntington), 147

Clean Air Act of 1970 (U.S.), 587–588

Clean Water Act of 1972 (U.S.), 587

Clegg, Nick, 255, 340

Clergy. *See* Iran

Clientelism

in Africa, 426, 450

in authoritarian regimes, 398

in Brazil, 73

defined, 73

in Mexico, 78, 129–131, 229

populism in Latin America and, 323

Climate change. *See also* Environment

in China, 589–593

globalization and, 207, 542, 584–586, 596–597

market failure and, 581–582

U.S. policies, 586–589

Clinton, Bill

on economy during 1992 presidential campaign, 189

environmental policy, 588

"family values" and, 23

on gays in military, 651

health care reform plan of, 578

Kyoto Protocol and, 584

Clinton, Bill *(cont.)*
  monetarist economic policies, 213–214
  NAFTA and, 215
  signing statements, 263
  welfare reform, 559–560
Clinton, Hillary Rodham, 385, 629
Closed-list proportional representation (PR) electoral system, 315, 466–467
Clouthier, Manuel, 461–462
Coalition governments
  defined, 247–250
  in Germany, 347, 349
  in India, *253*, 256–257, 298–299, 357–359, 361
  in Japan, 354, 357
  PM, powers of, 301
  in Turkey, 512
  in UK, 250, 257, 339, 340*t*, *493*, 495–496
Cocoa, *232*, 233
Code law
  in Brazil, 279
  countries with, 274*m*
  defined, 273
  in Germany, 276–278
Codetermination, in Germany's social market economy, 218, 348, 350, 498
Coffee industry, 73
Cohabitation, 266–267, 272
Cohesive-capitalist states, South Korea as, 510
Cold War
  Germany and, 7, 71
  Soviet states during, 448*b*
  U.S. aid to Liberia during, 58
  Zaire and, 377, 378
Collective action problem
  civil society and, 394
  defined, 310
  interest groups and, 319
  markets and, 598
  political behavior explanations, 363–364
  political parties and, 320
  voting and, 313
Collective responsibility, 254
Collier, Paul, 160, 162–163
Collor, Fernando, 264–265, 278, 458, 527
Colonialism. *See also* Postcolonial countries; *specific colonies*
  in Africa
    coups d'etat and, 426–427*b*
    political culture of corruption and, 233
    British, 63, 87–88

external sovereignty absent in, 41
  German, 71
  modern state development from, 48–49, 91
  political development and, 7
  Portuguese, 72–73
  Spanish, 73
  worldwide (circa 1900), 49, 50*m*
Colorado Party (Paraguay), 396
Colored. *See also* African Americans
  terminology for, 173
Color revolutions (Ukraine), 402
Colosio Murrieta, Luis Donaldo, 231, 462
Comité ¡Eureka!, 463
Command and control policies for pollution control, 583, 587, 591–592. *See also* Environment
Command economies
  communism and, 189, 191
  defined, 191
Commission on Racial Equality (CRE, UK), 619, 621
Commodity Futures Modernization Act of 2000 (U.S.), 213
Common currency, wisdom of using, 221–222
Common law, 273, 274*m*
Commonwealth, British. *See* British colonies, former
Communication forms of marginalized groups, 611. *See also* Internet; Mass communications; Media; Press
Communism/communist regimes. *See also* China, People's Republic of; Chinese Communist Party; Communist Party; Post-communist countries
  as authoritarian regime type, 8
  decline of, 382*b*, 435
  elections and electoral systems in, 395–396
  Hitler's opposition to, 117
  Marx's vs. Lenin's concept of, 137
  mass organizations in, 397
  in 1975 vs. 2008, 382*b*
  one-party states and, 382*b*
  party elites and leadership in, 371
  political identity and, 138
  as political ideology, 100*b*, 110–112
  political socialization
    for military in, 425–426
    of young people, 396

state power and citizens' rights under, 137
  succession in, 378
Communist Manifesto (Marx), 31, 111
Communist Party. *See also* Chinese Communist Party
  command economies and, 189, 191
  in Europe, 320–321, 322*b*
  in France, 328
  in Germany, 71, 348, 349
  importance in communist regimes, 396
  of India (CPI), factions in, 358–359
  institutionalized regimes and, 372
  in Russia, 113–114, 268, 465–466
Communitarianism, 610
Comparative (economic) advantage, 199
Comparative institutional advantage, of LMEs vs. CMEs, 489–492
Comparative method, controlled variables and, 13*b*, 14
Comparative politics, 10, 11–12, 15–16
Comparativists, 10, 16*b*, 160
Concrete judicial review in code law, 274
Conditional Cash Transfers (CCTs), 553, 561
Condomblé (Brazil), 165, 180
Confederación de Trabajadores de Mexico (Mexican Labor Confederation, CTM), 130
Confederation of British Industry (CBI), 341
Confederation of the Rhine, 70
Confucianism, 441, 515, 534
Congo, Democratic Republic of. *See also* Zaire
  ethnic cleansing in, 143
  as failed state, 51
  war in, 92
  as weak or failed state, 51, 53*b*, 92
Congress (U.S.). *See also* House of Representatives (U.S.); Senate (U.S.)
  British parliament vs., 255
  gridlock and, 262–264
  racial representation in, 176*t*
Congressional Budget Office and health care reform costs, 579
Congress of People's Deputies (Soviet Union), 465

Congress Party (India), 83, 251, 290, 523, 625. *See also* Indian National Congress
Consensus systems
  accountability and, 270
  consensus democracy, 247
  markets and, 598
  PR systems and, 314
"The Conservation of Races" (du Bois), 173
Conservative faction (Iran), 412
Conservative Party
  in Europe, 320–321, 322*b*
  in UK
    economic reform, *493*, 493–495
    NHS reforms by, 574–576
    parliamentary system, 253
    two-party system, 323
Conservative regime, Japan as, 225
Consociationalism/consociational system, 157–158, 185, 293, 450
Consolidation (Mexico), 463
Constituent Assembly (Brazil), 457
Constitution (U.S.). *See also specific Amendments*
  amendments to, 66
  on citizen qualifications, 174
  on electoral system details, 342
  on executive role, 261, 263
  on military role, 425
  right to privacy, 650
  slavery under, 436*b*
  Tea Party and, 326
  writing of, 65
Constitutional complaints (Germany), 276–277
Constitutional Courts
  in France, 614
  in Germany, 276–278, *277*, 280, 348, 556
  in Turkey, 615
Constitutional Reform Act (UK), 255
Constitutional signing statements, 263
Constitutions. *See also* Constitution (U.S.)
  Basic Law in Federal Republic of Germany as, 71
  in Brazil, 431, 562
    democratization and, 455–457
    federal system and, 296
    judicial independence and, 278–279
    nineteenth century, 73
    on sexual orientation, 654
  in Chile, 446

in China, 380, 520
in coalition governments, 247
European Union, rejection of, 220
of federal systems, 294
in France, 266, 328
in Ghana, 452
in India, 298, 623–624
in Iran, 80, 135, 389–390, 410, 443
  women and, 643–644
in Japan, 68–69
judicial review and, 275
in Mexico, 627–628
of modern states, 245
in Nigeria, 125, 167, 414, 469, 473
reform of, identity group redress of grievances through, 183
in Russia, 267–269, 299–300, 465, 638
on semipresidentialism, 266
in South Africa, 647
transition to democracy and, 445–446
in Turkey, 615
in UK, 109
in West Germany, 348
Constructivism/constructivists, 147–150, 184
Contact days for volunteerism (Sweden), 546
"Contagion" effect in Africa, 426
Continental law, 273
Continuity of institutions, 303
Contraception, women's movement and access to, 628, 630, 642
Contract rights, modern state, market economies and, 191, 192
Control, scientific concept of, 13*b*
Convention system, for U.S. political parties, 344
Convergence of economic policies, globalization and, 488
Convergence theory on CMEs vs. LMEs, 491
Converse, Nathan, 451
Conversion, religious identity and, 162–163
Co-optation
  in authoritarian regimes, 372–373, 375–376, 395–396, 399, 416–418
  in China, 404, 408
  in Iran, 386, 413
  in Kenya, 375–376

in Nigeria, 391, 416–417
in Russia, 468
Coordinated market economies (CMEs)
  characteristics, 489–492
  in Germany, 497–498, 500
  market openness in, 533–534
Copayments for health care expenditures, 567, 570, *572*, 573
Copenhagen, Denmark, environmental conference (2009), 584, 588, 592
Copper as Chilean product, 228
Cornell, Stephen, 170
Coroneis (colonels) and *coronelismo* (Brazil), 73, 455
Corporate finance, coordinated market economy of Germany and, 497
Corporate social responsibility program (Nigeria), 594
Corporate tax system (U.S.), 211
Corporatism. *See also* State corporatism
  defined, 115
  in Germany, 497, 498, 554, 571
  interest group, 332
Corpus Christi massacre (1971), 463
Corruption
  in Asia vs. Africa, capital investment risks with, 515
  in authoritarian regime bureaucracies, 376, 397
  in Brazil, 73, 264, 278–280, 458–460, 563
  in China, 87, 384–385, 591
  country scores globally, 285*m*
  in Egypt, 400
  elite integrity and, 449*b*
  environmental laws in Nigeria and, 594–596
  explanations for, 291*b*
  in Ghana, 453
  in India, 83, 256–257, 288–292, 358, 361–362
  in Iran, 390
  in Japan, 69, 226–227, 286–288, 292, 353–354, 356
  in Mexico, 78–79, 130, 231, 397, 464
  Mobutu and, 377
  in modernizing authoritarian regimes, 137
  in Nigeria
    from agricultural economy to oil wealth for elites, 232–236

Corruption (*cont.*)
  under Babangida, 415–416
  environmental damage and, 594
  under Gowon, 433–434
  neopatrimonialism and weak institutions, 469, 510b
  under Obasanjo, 89–90, 472–474
  by ruling military regimes, 125–127
  weak institutions and military rule, 391–394
  in Russia, 268–269, 300, 467–468
  in Tunisia, 401
  in U.S., 66, 346
  weak bureaucratic institutions and, 55, 281, 284, 391–394
Corruption Perception Index
  for Brazil, 459
  for Ghana, 453
  for Nigeria, 474
  for Russia, 468
Cortés, Hernán, 77
Costa Rica, women in power positions in, 317b
Cost control, in German NHI program, 571–573
Côte d'Ivoire
  one-party regime in, 120
  semipresidential system in, 258b
Cotton, 233
Council of Ministers (EU), 220–221
Council of Mosques (UK), 620
Country, terminology for, 39
Country and concept
  authoritarian rule, 369, 371t, 378
  ethnicity, race, and religion, 144–145t, 146
  globalization, deindustrialization, and development, 487t
  governing institutions of case countries, 248
  modern regimes, 95, 96t
  parties, elections, and civil society, 311t, 312–313
  policies and politics of inclusion, 606–607t, 632, 647
  regime change and outcome, 423–425, 424t
  snapshot of governing institutions, 248, 248t
  states and markets, 189–190, 190t

weak and failed states, 51, 61t
welfare, health, and the environment, 540–541t, 542, 545, 566, 570
Coups d'etat
  in Africa, 426–427b, 427m, 432b
  in Brazil, 124, 429–431, 434
  in Chile, 227
  defined, 120
  explanations for, 427–429
  in Latin America by decade, 431–432b
  in Mexico, 78
  in Nigeria, 125–126, 166, 432, 469
  personalist leaders and, 370, 373
  regime change through, 373, 377, 475–476
  in Rwanda, 169
  in Zaire, 377
Courts. *See* Judiciary/judicial systems
Cox, Robert Henry, 497
Credit default swaps, 194, 199, 213, 215
Crenshaw, Martha, 438b
Criminal law (China), 383
Cristero War (1926–1929), 628
Critical thinking, 17b
Croatia
  Catholicism and, 162
  language and ethnic conflict in Yugoslavia for, 155
  Serbia and Bosnia, conflict with, 157
Cromwell, Oliver, 63, 109
Cuba
  mass organizations in, 397
  revolution (1959), 434
Cultural groups, 609, 656. *See also* Identity politics; Inclusion
Cultural nationalism, 151–154, 157. *See also* Political culture
Cultural Revolution (China), 86, 380, 403, *403*
Cultural revolution, in U.S. after war of independence, 437b
Cultural theory
  on globalization, 534
  on inclusion and conflicting values, 658
Culture and political behavior, 18
Culture of dependency (Brazil), 563
Currency/currency valuations. *See also* Euro
  Argentine problems with, 507
  in Brazil, 485, 527–529
  China's revaluing of, 520

currency war prospect, 208
globalization and convertibility of, 205
in Indonesia, 485
in Malaysia, 485
in Mexico, 230–231
in Philippines, 485
in Russia, 485
in South Korea, 485
state provision of, market economies and, 191, 192
in Thailand, 485
Customs Union between Turkey and EU, 512
Czechoslovakia, revolution (1989–1990), 434
Czech Republic, revolution from above, 440

D

Dahl, Robert, 107b, 274
Daimyo, Japanese landlords, 68
Dalits (formerly, "untouchables") caste, *360*, 360–361
Dalton, Russell, 321, 337, 351
Davies, James, 436
Debt crisis (Mexico), 230
Decalo, Samuel, 428
Decentralization (Brazil), 296
Declaration of Independence (U.S.), 65, *65*, 104, 174
Defense of Marriage Act of 1996 (DOMA, U.S.), 651–652
Deficit spending. *See also* Budget deficits
  under Bush, 213
  defined, 198
  in Japan, 226
  Keynesian vs. monetary theories, 197–199
  in Mexico, 231
Deflation (Japan), 226
Deforestation, 582, 584, 591, 593
de Gaulle, Charles, 258b, 266
Deindustrialization, 488, 495. *See also* Welfare states
Delegative democracies, 446
Deliberative democracy, 610–611
Democracies/democratic countries. *See also* Democratization; Liberal democracy
  after revolutions, 436–437b, 439
  Algerian Islamic Front on, 133
  in Brazil, 72–74, 123–124, 263–265
  in case studies, 35
  in China, *85*
  consumption vs. investment, 508–509

corruption in, 291*b*

defined, 8

development success under, 508–511*b*

economic growth hypothesis, 508–509

economic growth in authoritarian regimes vs., 533

emancipative values, effect on, 449*b*

geographic clusters of, 138

in Germany after 1990, *70,* 71

globally by era, 106*m*

in India, 83–84

Islamist views on, 132–133

in Japan, 69

major types of, location of countries with, 258*b,* 259*m*

in Mexico, *77,* 79

modernizing authoritarianism and. *See* Modernizing authoritarianism

in Nigeria, 88–90, 125–127, 167, 234–235

normative theories on politics of inclusion in, 609

oil wealth as deterrent to, 448*b*

parliamentarism as model of, 249–257, 250*f*

participation, representation and, 309

political development and, 7

political parties, party systems and, 329

political socialization for military in, 425

power of majority in, 247

presidentialism as model of, 270

as regime type, 7–8

semi-authoritarian regimes and, 127–128

Third Wave, and governing institutions, 451*m*

in Turkey, 512

UK as cradle of, 108–109

Democratic breakdowns, 9, 446–447

Democratic centralism, 113

Democratic consolidation, 446, 460, 477

Democratic deepening

in Brazil, 455–460

defined, 446

in Ghana, 454

Democratic deficit in EU constitution, 220–221

Democratic Party (DPJ, Japan), 286, 352

Democratic Party (U.S.), 65, 343–345, 579

Democratic Republic of the Congo. *See* Congo, Democratic Republic of

Democratization. *See also* Democracies/democratic countries

in African neopatrimonial regimes, 450

authoritarian rule vs., 102*b*

demands for inclusion by identity groups and, 657

democratic consolidation with, 446

early theories on waves of, 444

economic reform and, 447

new type of, 445

regime change through, 396, *414,* 416, 475

revolution from above and, 475

in South Korea, economic miracle and, 508*b*

Third Wave democracies and governing institutions, 416, 451*m*

transition, 9

Deng Xiaoping, 86, 380–383, 519–520, 590

Denmark

Prussian wars with, 70

women in power in, 137*b*

Deobandi Sunni Islam, 624

Department, terminology for, 281

Dependent variable, scientific concept of, 13*b*

Deprivation, relative, of identity, 156, 184

Deregulation, Japan's bureaucracy and, 288

Derivatives markets, 194, 213, 215

Descriptive representation, 635–636

Developing countries. *See* Postcolonial countries

Development. *See also* Industrialization

in Africa, 513–518

Asian miracle vs. African malaise in, 514–515

assumptions about requirements for, 119

benefits in modernizing authoritarianism, 119

in China, 518–522

democracy transition and, 448*b*

in East and Southeast Asia, 503–504, 508–509

globalization, state role and, 501

in India, 522–526

in Latin America, 506–507

in Middle East and North Africa, 512, 517

in Nigeria, 126

quality of life as definition, 568

in South Korea, 503, 508*b*

Developmentalism (Turkey), 512

Developmental policy and central state planning, 288

Developmental states

defined, 224

East Asian miracle and, 504–506

globalization, policy convergence and, 488–489

Japan as, 67, 69, 222–227, 286

South Korea as, 503, 508*b*

Development economics, 199, 238

Deviant case studies, 12

Devolution

in Scotland and Wales, 109–110

in unitary vs. federal systems, 295

Diamond, Larry, 394

Diamond mining (Sierra Leone), 58–60

Diaz, Porfirio, 78, 229

Diaz-Cayeros, Alberto, 294

Dickson, Bruce, 404

Dictator's death as democracy opportunity (Nigeria), 379

Dictator's dilemma

in China, 384

defined, 373

in Nigeria, 414, 417

Dictatorship of the proletariat, 111–112

Dictatorships, 27–28. *See also* Authoritarianism/authoritarian regimes; Personalist regimes

Die Linke (The Left party, Germany), *347,* 350

Diet (Japanese parliament), 352–354

DIHT (German business organization), 348

Direct election hazards, 271

Direct primary elections (U.S.), 344

"Diretas já" campaign (Brazil), 456

Discrimination. *See* Civil rights; Race/racial groups

Divided societies in presidential systems, 271

Divine right of kings, 43, 132

Doe, Samuel, 59–56

Domestic partnerships, 647, 651, 654–655. *See also* Same-sex marriage

Dominant party system
  defined, 323
  in India, 357–358
  in Japan, 352–355
  in South Africa, 323
  in U.S., 343
"Don't ask, don't tell" policy
  (U.S.), 651
Douglass, Frederick, 174
Driving, women in Saudi Arabia,
  634
Drug cartels/drug wars (Mexico),
  79, 463–464
Dual legitimacy, 271–272
Dual-track market system (China),
  519
du Bois, W.E.B., 173
Duma (Russia's parliament),
  267–269, 466–467, 639
Dutch Republic of the United
  Provinces, as first modern
  federal system, 292
Duvalier, François "Papa Doc," 379
Duvalier, Jean-Claude "Baby Doc,"
  372, 379
Duverger, Maurice, 320, 326–327
Duverger's Law
  defined, 326
  in France, 326, 328
  in India, 361–362
  in Japan, 352, 354
  rational-choice theory and, 364
  in UK, 339
  in U.S., 339

E
Earned Income Tax Credit (EITC,
  U.S.), 545, 557, 560
Earning power for women in
  Russia, 638
Earth Day (U.S.), 586–587
EarthFirst!, 336
Earthquakes
  in Chile, 228
  in Japan, 226, 288, 356
East Asia. *See also* Asia
  East Asian miracle, *200*, 201,
    485, 503, 514–515
  economic growth in, 5–6,
    533–534
  financial crisis (1997–1998),
    485, 504–505, 517–518,
    520, 528
The East Asian Miracle (World
  Bank), 504
Easterly, William, 516–517
Eastern Europe
  border changes and state
    creations in, 41

democratization in, 445
ethnic violence and resentment
  in, 162
parliamentarism or semipresidentialism used in, 258*b*
presidentialism, 271–272
revolutions (1989–1990) in, 434
runaway bureaucracy in, 284–285
semipresidential systems, 258
East Germany. *See also* Germany
  communist regime in, 7–8, 71
  reunification with West Ger-
    many, 218, 278, 349
  revolution (1989–1990) in, 434
  unemployment in, 218, 555
Ebadi, Shirin, 640, 643
EC (European Community), 71
Echeverría, Luís, 229, 463
Ecology movement in Europe,
  320, 322*b*. *See also* Environment; Green Party
Economic crises. *See* East Asia;
  Great Depression; Great
  Recession
Economic development. *See also*
  Development; Economy;
  Gross domestic product
  (GDP); Political economy
  in Brazil, 430
  in China, 86–87
  in Germany, 70
  health care study, 569
  in India, 82–83
  in Iran, 410, 412–413
  in Japan, 67–69, 352
  political development and, 7
  political instability and, 510–511
  regime type vs., 508–511
Economic diversification and oil
  production/revenues, 517
Economic globalization index,
  503, 503*t*
Economic liberalization program
  (Iran), 642
Economic overview of case study
  countries, 208–209*t*
Economic policy convergence,
  globalization and, 488–489
Economic resources. *See also* Oil
  production/revenue
  in Germany, 71
  in Liberia, 59–60
  in Nigeria, 88–90
  in Sierra Leone, 59–60
  state strength and, 53*b*
Economic sovereignty, 63
Economy. *See also* Command
  economies; Economic development; Market economy

globalization of, 205–208
major theories about, 197–203
political leaders of democracies
  and citizen perceptions of,
  189
Ecuador
  indigenous people, percentage
    of population, 180*b*
  Left Turn and, 507–510
  women in power positions in,
    317*b*
Edo (Tokyo), 68
Education. *See also* Literacy
  in Brazil, 180
  in China, 522
  cultural homogeneity and, 153
  debate over scope of, 193
  in Germany, 154
  in Iran, 411, 642
  in Kuwait, 633–634
  market economies and provi-
    sion of, 193
  to promote nationalism, 152
  in Russia, 637–638
  in Saudi Arabia, 633–634
  state strength and, 55
  in UK, 496, 620–621
  as universal entitlement, 544
  university quotas, 181–182
  in U.S., 174, 175–176, 557–558,
    560–561
  of women, 631–634, 637–638,
    642
  World Bank on long-term
    development and, 201, 203
EEC (European Economic
  Community), 63, 220
Effective demand, 539–542
Effective democracy measures,
  449*b*
Effectiveness, executive-legislative
  institution comparisons,
  270–271
Egbe Omo Oduduwa (Nigeria),
  166
Egypt
  authoritarian regime in, 373
  election fraud in, 400
  emergency law under Mubarak,
    399
  international trade in, 400
  media use among young in,
    401
  primary elections under
    Mubarak, 399
  reforms promised, 399
  revolt and regime change
    (2011), 22, 401–402, 423,
    434, 477

semi-authoritarian regime in, 399–402
social network technology in, 337
Ekeh, Peter, 291*b*
Election fraud
in authoritarian regimes, 395–396
in China, 405
in Egypt, 400
in Ghana, 452
in Iran, 133
in Kenya, 395
in Mexico, 130, 395, 462
in Nigeria, 469–471
in Rwanda, 395
Elections
in authoritarian regimes, 394–398
in China, 404–405, 408
in democratic transitions, 445–446
in Ghana, 453–454
in Iran, 386, 389, 409–411, *410*, 412*b*, 413
majoritarian tendencies in, 271
in Mexico, 462
in Nigeria, 414, 469–471
in parliamentary systems, 249
in presidential systems, 262, 271
in UK, 340, 340*t*
in U.S., *172*, 214, 345
Electoral authoritarianism, 127
Electoral College (U.S.), 259, 262, 342–343
Electoral democracy. *See also* Democracies/democratic countries
defined, 107*b*, 446
demands for inclusion in, 657
democratization in Brazil and, 456
in Ghana, 454
in Nigeria, 125
semipresidentialism in, 265–269
Electoral districts. *See also* Single-member district electoral system
in Japan, 353
in U.S., 342
Electoral systems
accountability vs. representation, 363
in authoritarian regimes, 395–396
in Brazil, 457
consociationalism and, 157
counting votes, method of, 312
defined, 312

effective governance and, 362–363
inclusion guarantees for, 609
majoritarian, in British parliamentary system, 247, 249
in Nigeria, 469
participation, representation and, 312–319
in post–World War II Japan, 69
presidential, 259
proportional representation. *See* Proportional representation
race in U.S. and, 174
in Russia, Putin's changes to, 466–467
single, nontransferable vote, 352–353, 353*b*
single-member districts, 313, 342
women in office and type of, 315
world map of types, 318*m*
Electoral volatility
in Brazil, 458
political party realignments and, 325*b*
Electronic trading systems, 206–207
Elgie, Robert, 268*b*
Elias Calles, Plutarco, 78
Elites
in authoritarian regimes, 372, 374–375*b*, 376
business leaders' power in democracies, 108
cartels, corruption and, 291*b*
colonialism and, 48–49
democratization and, 445
identity politics and, 148–150, 183–185
interest group representation and, 334
in modernizing authoritarian regimes, 119
in postcolonial Nigeria, 233, 237–238
in postcolonial states, 49
Elite theory
contemporary political parties, 321, 324*b*
on corporate elite power in U.S., 34*b*
in democratic regimes, 310
on division of power, 32, 33*t*
effectiveness questions, 239–240
feminists on patriarchy, 31
identity politics and, 185
instrumentalism and, 147

Lindblom on, 31
Marx on, 30–31
Mills, C. Wright, 31
pluralist theory vs., 304
on public policy, 599
Elizabeth II (Queen of England), *62, 619*
Emancipation Proclamation (U.S.), 66
Emancipative values, democracy's effect on, 449*b*
Emergency room as health care for poor, 579
Emirs (Nigeria), 88
Empirical theory, 11–12
Employee training, CMEs vs. LMEs, 491
Employer-based health insurance, 578, 580
Employment Act of 1946 (U.S.), 212
Employment conditions. *See* Working conditions
Employment discrimination
sexual orientation and, 646, 649, 651
in UK, religion and, 621
women and
in Iran, 641–642
in Russia, *637*
Employment Non-discrimination Act (ENDA, U.S.), 651
Enabling Act (1933, Germany), 117
Endangered Species Act of 1973 (U.S.), 587, 589
Enfranchisement. *See also* Suffrage; Voting/voters
Jim Crow laws in U.S. and, *172*, 608
of women, 631, 634
England. *See* United Kingdom (UK)
Entitlements
AFDC in U.S. as, 559
universal, 543–584
Environment
environmental conferences, 584, 588
environmental justice movement
in Nigeria, 593–596
in U.S., 588
environmental policies
in China, 589–593
in Germany, 349
globalization and, 207
in India, 359
market failure and, 581–597

Environment *(cont.)*
in Nigeria, 593–596
social movement on, 335–341
as state intervention, 193–194
in U.S., 586–589
environmental protests
in China, 592
in Nigeria, 593, 595–596
market failures and, 539,
581–597
wealth and health, relationship
to, 540–541*t*, 542, 545
Environmental Protection Agency
(EPA, U.S.), 587
Environmental Protection
Bureaus (EPBs, China), 591
Equality, autonomy vs., 543
Equality and Human Rights Commission, UK, 621
Equal protection rights for gays in
military, 651
Erdogan, Tayyip, 615
Escola Superior de Guerra (ESG,
Brazil), 430
Eskridge, William, 649
Esping-Andersen, Gosta, 545
Estado Novo (New State, Brazil),
73–74, 123, 430, 527
Ethics and comparative politics, 15
Ethiopia, as Soviet Cold War ally, 53*b*
Ethnic cleansing
in Democratic Republic of the
Congo, 143
in Sudan, 143
Ethnicity/ethnic groups
defined, 155
demands for autonomy by, 608
distinguished from nation, 150,
156*b*
distinguished from race, 170
ethnic mobilization, 156–157,
160
ethnic pluralism, 447
ethnic violence, *146*, 160–163
federalism and, 295, 298–299
global picture, 164*m*
inclusion policies and, 605
in India, 298–299, 359, 361, 363
minority, federalism and protection of, 293
in Nigeria, 87–89, 125–126, 157,
165–168, 415, 432, 472
political identity and, 138, 143,
181
in Russia, 299
Rwandan genocide and,
168–169
societies divided by, 373, 432,
447, 473

special representation for,
311–312, 315
women's movement and, 149*b*,
645
Ethnocentrism, 22
Ethnocultural identities, 610
Eureka! Committee, 463
Euro
adoption of, 63, 192
in EU (2004), 192
Germany and creation of, 71,
216, *216*, 218
globalization, economic sovereignty and, 220–222
long-term stability of, 221–222
Eurocommunism, 322*b*
Europe. *See also* Eastern Europe;
European Union (EU); *specific countries*
breakdown of democracy in,
pre-WWII, 447
child allowances in, 544
colonialization of Africa by, 88
deindustrialization in, 488
divine right of kings in, 43
expansion of citizenship in,
105–93
Green Party in, 335
influence in China, 84–85
interest groups' emergence in,
331
Islamic veil as identity symbol
in, 149*b*
modern state development in,
47
national health insurance in,
565
parliamentarism in, 258*b*
political ideologies and regime
types in, 138
political parties in, 320–321, 322*b*
quotas for women in elected
positions, 635
revolutions of 1848 in, 48
secularism in, 617
social capital in, 326
social democratic parties in, 105
southern, democratization in,
445
subjects of monarchs in, 97
universal entitlements in, 584
welfare states in, 548
women in power positions in,
317*b*
European Central Bank (ECB),
71, 211*b*, 216, *216*, 218,
220–221
European Coal and Steel
Community, 220

European colonies. *See* Colonial-
ism; Postcolonial countries
European Commission, 221
European Community (EC), 71
European Convention on Human
Rights, 110
European Economic Community
(EEC), 63, 220
European Monetary Union
(EMU), 220, 501
European Parliament, 220, 341
European Union (EU)
British membership in, 63
economic sovereignty, globaliza-
tion and, 220–222
euro adopted (2004), 192
Germany
EU formation and, 71, 216,
216, 218, 220, 351
market economy and, 498,
500*b*
globalization and, 238
government and growth in
Germany and U.S. vs., 500*b*
Great Recession and, 238
labor unions and business regulation by, 206
postnational citizenship, 98–99
precautionary principle for
environmental risk avoid-
ance in, 583
Turkey and, 512–513
Exchange rate controls, globalization and, 206–207
Executive/executive branch.
See also Ruling entities
accountability of judges vs., 274
in authoritarian regimes,
372–379, 416, 418
in Brazil, 261–265, 460
bureaucracy's limitations of,
280
as chief political power of a
state, 246
in China, 380–382, 386
federalism and limitations on,
293
as head of government, 249
as head of state, 246, 248
in Iran, 386–387
in modern states, 246
in parliamentary systems,
249–250
presidential systems, 270
in Russia, 466
Expediency Council (Iran),
387–388, 389
Expenditure cap system for health
care (Germany), 573

Expert vs. red role in communist China, 404
Export-oriented growth (EOG)
in Asia vs. Africa, development and, 514–515
in China, 519
import-substitution industrialization vs., 502, 504–505
in South Korea, *504*
Externalities
environmental policies as, 193–194, 207, 581–582, 596
intergenerational externality of mineral and oil depletion, 584
market inefficiencies and, 539
External sovereignty
Peace of Westphalia and, 47
state recognition of, 41
UK, 19th century, 63
Extremism, 320, 322*b*
ExxonMobil oil spill (Nigeria), 594
Exxon *Valdez* oil spill, 594

F
Factionalism, 117, 412
Factions, internal, Soviet pluralism and, 27–28
Failed states. *See also* Weak states
Afghanistan as, 56–58
current international system and, 91–92
defined, 51
Liberia as, 58–60
Sierra Leone as, 58–60
Somalia as, 51, 55
in 2010, 54*b*
Failed States Index, 52*b*, 61*t*, 452
Fallacy of composition, 203*b*
Falun Gong, 407
Families. *See also* Welfare states; Welfare/welfare reform
African chiefs as heads of, 23
bank lending in Korea to, 505
in China
household responsibility system for, 519
one-child rule for, 406
citizenship and autonomy of, 543
civil society vs., 98
in early American churches, 437*b*
family values, under Reagan vs. Clinton, 23
in personalist regimes, 373, 375*b*, 392, 403–404
political culture transferred through, 148

of political parties in France, 328
religious groups and, 619
Family law, women's social status and, 608, 630, 632, 644
Family Protection Law (Iran), 642
Farming. *See* Agriculture
Fascism/fascist regimes
as authoritarian regime type, 8
Brazil and, 123–124
in Germany, 68, 71, 116–118, 138
on modernizing authoritarianism, 120
as political ideology and regime type, 24, 100*b*, 115–116
state power and citizens' rights under, 137
Fascism: Doctrine and Institutions (Mussolini), 115
Fatwa condemning Rushdie, 620
Fealty, 46
Feasibility variables, ethnic violence and, 161
Feder, Judith, 580
Federal Election Institute (IFE, Mexico), 462
Federal Election Tribunal (TRIFE, Mexico), 461–462
Federal Environmental Protection Agency (Nigeria), 594
Federal High Court, Germany, 276
Federalism/federal systems
in authoritarian regimes, 393–394
in Brazil, 265, 296–298, 457, 460
characteristics, 292–301
defined, 65, 292
ethnicity-based states or provinces under, 157–158
in Germany, 276, 500
in India, 253, 296, 298–299, 624
in Nigeria, 89, 167, 233, 393–394, 432–433, 473
parliamentary systems and, 253, 394
in Russia, 296, 299–301
statistical characteristics, 293*b*
symmetrical, 295–296
in U.S., 26, 65–66, 652
welfare state types and, 549
Federal Republic of Germany (FRG), 71. *See also* West Germany
Federal Reserve (U.S.), 199
Federal Reserve Board (U.S.), 66, 211–214
Federal Security Bureau (FSB, Russia), 467

Fedeyin (Iran), 442–443
Fee-for-service health care system, 573–574
Females in labor force, 550–551*t*, 551
Feminism/feminist theory, 611, 630. *See also* Women/women's rights
Feng, Yi, 509
Ferejohn, John, 275
Fetzer, Joel, 617
Feudal states
European, 46
Japanese, 67
Persian, 80
sovereignty and taxation in, 191–192
Fiefs, 46
Fifth Republic (France), 258*b*, 266, 327–328
Figueiredo, Argelina, 458
Financial crises
of 1997–1998 and East Asian model, *200*, 201, 485, 503, 505, 514–515
in Turkey, 512
of 2008–2009. *See* Great Recession
Finer, Samuel, 427
Finland
semipresidential powers in, 266
women in power in, 317*b*
Firestone Tire Company, 58
First Amendment rights for gays in military, 651
First dimension of power, 10
First-past-the-post representation (FPTP). *See also* Majoritarianism; Single-member district electoral system
characteristics, 313–314
country statistics, 343*b*
election of women and, 315, 317*b*
in India, 357–358, 361–362
in Nigeria, 469
in UK, 258*b*, 339–340, 342
in U.S., 339, 342
First Republic (Nigeria), 432
Fiscal decentralization (China), 520
Fiscal policy
deficit spending and, 197–199, 213, 226, 231
defined, 197–198
in EU, 220–221
globalization and, 205, 220–221
in Japan, 226
in Mexico, 231

Fiscal policy *(cont.)*
in UK, 494
in U.S., 213–214
Fiscal Responsibility, Brazil's Law
of, 297
Fish, Steven, 447, 451, 468
Fishing industry and oil damage
(Nigeria), 593–594
Five pillars of Islam, 133
Five-Year Development Plans
(Iran), 531
Five-Year Plans for Environmental
Protection (China), 590, 592
Flying geese model of economic
development, 515
Food aid, emergency, market
failure and, 542
Food Stamps (U.S.), 544, 560
Force, use of, in sovereign
states, 43
Foreclosures in Great Recession,
210, 213–214
Foreign Affairs (journal), 206
Foreign capital inflow (Latin
America), 507
Foreign currency inflows (Tur-
key), 513
Foreign direct investment (FDI),
487, 520
Foshan, China, Honda plant labor
issues in, 406
Fossil fuel exploration and devel-
opment in U.S., 588
Foucault, Michel, 23
Founders (U.S.), 263, 436–437*b*
Founding elections, 445–446
Fourth Republics
in France, 327
in Ghana, 453
Fox Quesada, Vicente, *77*, 79, 131,
462–463, 628
FPTP. *See* First-past-the-post repre-
sentation
Fragmented-multiclass states, 510
France. *See also* French colonies;
French Revolution
bureaucrat recruitment in,
281–284
civil unions in, 647
devolved institutions of, 295
European Monetary Union and,
220
Islamic headscarves in, 613–616
Japanese treaty with, 68
liberal revolution in, 434
Muslim immigration to, 118
National Front Party, 118
nationalism in, 151–152
neofascists in, 118

party system in, 327–328
post–World War II occupation
of Germany by, 71
Prussian wars with, 70
secularism in, 613
semipresidentialism in, 258*b*,
266–267, 268*b*
Vichy government in, 41
weak labor unions in, 334
Franchise Act (1884, UK), 109
Franco, Itamar, 527
Franz II (Emperor of Holy Roman
Empire), 70
Fraternité and the *burqa*, 614
Free Democrat Party (FDP),
Germany, 348, 350, 500, 573
Freedom House
on civil liberties and political
rights
in Iran vs. Middle East, 412*b*
in Nigeria vs. Africa, 469, 470*b*
on democracy in sub-Saharan
Africa, 450
on democratic norms in
Nigeria, 469, 470*b*
on democratization in Brazil,
456*b*
on Ghana, 452
on global democratization, 444
on Mexico, 463
on Russia's political rights and
civil liberties, 465
on semipresidential systems,
268*b*
seven point freedom scale, 449*b*
Free-market economies/free
market model
in Mexico, 79, 230
in U.S., 210–216, 236
Free trade. *See also* Market economy
in Chile, 228
comparative advantage as, 199
in U.S., 210–211
Free wage labor, 111
French colonies. *See also specific
countries*
code law in, 273
semipresidential systems and,
258*b*
in West Africa, 426–427*b*
French Revolution (1789), 48, 97,
97, 152, 434, 627
Frente Democrático Nacional
coalition (Mexico), 461
Freud, Sigmund, 170
Freyre, Gilberto, 180
FRG (Federal Republic of
Germany), 71
Friedman, Eli, 405

Friedman, Milton, 198, 227
Friends of the Earth, 336
Fukuyama, Francis, 5, 423
Fundamentalism, religious, 132
Fund for Peace, Failed States
Index of, 52*b*, 61*t*

G
G-8 organization, 516
G-20 organization, 207–208
Gaddafi, Muammar, 373
Gandhi, Indira
collective responsibility and, 257
corruption, factionalism and,
358
dominance of, 358
economic policies of, 523–524
emergency rule, and parliamentary elections, 358
as INC head and prime
minister, 256
politicization of bureaucracy
under, 290
as prime minister, 83
regional groups and institutions
and, 298–299
Sikh independence movement
and, 360
Gandhi, Jennifer, 128, 373, 375,
395, 405, 418
Gandhi, Mahatma, 82–83, 358,
360, 622–623
Gandhi, Rajiv, 256, 290, 298–299,
358
Garibi hatao (I. Gandhi's abolish
poverty slogan), 358, 523–524
Garrett, Geoffrey, 205
Garrido de Sierra, Sebastian, 462
Garvey, Marcus, 174
Gas flaring, *593*, 594
Gastarbeiters (guest workers), 153
Gatekeepers, in health care, 567,
572, 575, 578
Gaullists (France), 328
Gay, Lesbian, Bisexual, and Trans-
gender parade (São Paulo,
Brazil), *653*
Gay Activist Alliance, 649
Gay Liberation Front, 649
Gay marriage. *See* Same-sex
marriage
Gay rights. *See* Lesbian, gay, bisex-
ual, and transgender (LGBT)
people
GDR (German Democratic
Republic), 71
Geddes, Barbara, 396
Geisel, Ernesto, *430*
Gellner, Ernest, 151

Gender. *See also* Women/women's rights
  identity politics and, 149*b*
  inclusion policies and, 605, 606–607*t*
  segregation, 642, 644
General Agreement on Tariffs and Trade (GATT), 230
General secretaries (Russia), 113
Genetically modified organisms (GMOs), EU ban on, 583
Genocide
  in Bosnia, 143
  charges against Echeverría, 463
  identity group redress of grievances through, 184
  in Rwanda, 143
Geography
  in Africa vs. Asia, development and, 514–515
  majoritarian electoral systems and, 319
  political ideologies, regimes types and, 138
  state failures and, 52*b*
George III (King of England), 109
Georgia (former Soviet Republic of), South Ossetia and internal sovereignty in, 43
German colonies, 71
German Confederation, 70
German Democratic Republic (GDR), 71
German Evangelical Church, 118
German Labor Front, 117
German miracle, 216, 219, 499
German Trade Union Federation, 348
Germany. *See also* East Germany; West Germany
  abortion in, 278
  chancellor in, 249
  church-state relations and study of Islam in, 616
  codetermination, 218
  communism in, 217
  coordinated market economy of, 490
  election of women in, 317*b*
  European Monetary Union and, 220
  fascism in, 68, 71, 116–118, 138
  federalism in, 294
  globalization and, 496–501
  government and growth in EU and U.S. vs., 500*b*
  Great Recession and, 347, 351
  Green Party in, *310*, 322*b*, 327, 336

health care policy in, 565, 570, 571–574, *572*
  judiciary in, 276–278, *278*
  labor unions' strength in, 237–239
  mixed electoral system in, 316
  as modern welfare state, 69–71
  Muslim immigrants in, 154, 617
  nationalism in, 151–154
  neocorporatist interest group system in, 332, 348, 351
  "New Germany," discontent with, 348
  NPM and bureaucracy size in, 284
  regimes in, 7–8, 138
  religious group recognition and autonomy in, 616
  reunification, 218, 278, 349
  semiproportional electoral systems in, 316–318, 327, 348–349, 351
  social market economy of, 209, 216–219
  state formation, 69–70
  Swedish and U.S. welfare states compared to, 556*t*
  taxation in, 294
  two-and-a-half party system, 326, 347–351
Germany Does Away with Itself (Sarrazin), 154
Gerrymandering, 353, 395
Ghana
  as democratic success, 452–454
  economy, vs. South Korea, 504
  regimes in, 452
  structural adjustment programs in, 202*b*
Gibson, James, 276
Gil, Gilberto, 181
Gingerich, Daniel, 492
GINI Index of income inequality. *See also* Income inequality
  for Brazil, 529
  for case countries, 190*t*
  for China, 521
  for U.S., 213
Girls. *See* Women/women's rights
Glaeser, Edward, 548
Glasnost in Soviet Union, 114
Glass ceiling, 634
Global feminisms, 657
Global financial crisis. *See* Great Recession
Globalization
  in Africa, 513–518
  in Brazil, 526–530
  cartel parties and, 321

  in China, 405, 519
  cultural approaches to, 534
  defined, 204
  development and, 501–511
  East Asian financial crisis and, 485
  economic policies and, 485–486
  economic sovereignty and, 220–222
  environmental damage and, 581–582
  in European Union, 220–222
  factors contributing to, 206–207
  in Germany, 218–219, 347, 350–351, 496–501
  global currency markets and, 506
  inclusion policies and, 605, 657
  index, 503, 503*t*
  in India, 523–524
  in Iran, 530–532
  in Japan, 288, 356
  in Latin America, 506–507, 511
  in Middle East and North Africa, 512, 517
  nation-states and, 204–208
  in Nigeria, 530–532
  political party realignments and, 324*b*
  public health and, 571
  social market economies and, 216, 218–219, 496–501
  social movement opposing, 335
  in South Korea, 504
  state involvement in the market and, 238
  in Sweden, 546–547
  UK policy changes, 552
  U.S. as champion of, 207, 215
  welfare state reform and, 548, 551, 552–553
Global South, women's movement and, 630
Global warming. *See* Climate change; Environment
Glorious Revolution (England, 1688), 48, 63, 109
Gómez Farías, Valentin, 627
Gonzalez, Nathan, 388
Google, access in China, 384
Gorbachev, Mikhail, 57, 114, 464–465, 637–638
Gore, Al, 262, *587*, 588
Goulart, João, 123–124, 430–431
Governance, effective
  accountability, popular control of government and, 246
  participation, representation and, 362–363

Governing institutions. *See also* Political institutions
China's party institutions compared to, 381*f*
Iran's, 382*b*, 386–389, 387*f*
of Third Wave democracies, 451*m*
Government, administration vs., 39
Government Organized Nongovernmental Organizations (GONGOs, China), 406, 592
Government positions, buying and selling in China of, 405
Governments. *See also* Governing institutions
discrimination against LGBT community by, 646–647
electoral systems effects on, 313
states or nations vs., 39
Gowon, Yakubu "Jack" Dan-Yumma, 126, 391–393, 432–433
Graf, William, 433
Gramsci, Antonio, 24
Grand Ayatollah, Khomeini as, 389
Grassroots protests. *See* Social movements
Great Britain. *See* United Kingdom
Great Charter of Freedoms, 108
Great Depression
Germany and, 116
Keynes on, 197–198
New Deal and, 66
poverty reduction in U.S. and, 559, 561, 597
U.S. economic policy and, 210–211
Great Firewall of China, 406
Great Leap Forward, China, 86
Great Proletarian Cultural Revolution (China). *See* Cultural Revolution
Great Recession
in Africa, 517
beginnings (2007), 213
in Brazil, 486, 529
causes, 189
in China, 519–520
economic policy questions raised by, 203
EU and, 221–222, 238
euro, questions on use of, 222
in Germany, 216, 219, 347, 351, 497, 500
in Ghana, 453
housing bubble as cause, 195, 210

in India, 486, 523, 525–526
in Iran, 531–532
in Japan, 353, 355
Keynesian deficit spending and, 210, 214–215, 237
in Latin America, 507, 511
in Mexico, 229, 231
as one of series, 533
pollution in China and, 591
in Russia, 468
in Sweden, 546–547
in Turkey, 512
in UK, 340, 495–496, 574
U.S. image and, 215–216, 560
Great Society programs (U.S.), 66, 212, 215
The Great Transformation (Polanyi), 196
The Great War. *See* World War I
Greece
economic crisis in Great Recession, 204–205, 221
EU and IMF rescue package, 205
index of interest-group pluralism (Lijphart), 341
Greed variables and ethnic violence, 161
Green, Simon, 351
Green government. *See* Social Democratic Party (SDP)
Greenhouse gases. *See also* Environment
annual and global share of, for case countries, 540–541*t*
cap and trade system in U.S., 588
China's policies on, 592
management of, 584–585, 587–588
in Nigeria, 593, 594
Green Movement (Iran), 409, 410, 411, 413, 641
Green Party
in Europe, 335
in Germany, 310, 320–321, 322*b*, 327, 336, 348–349
green social movement and, 310
Green passage (China), 591
Green Revolution (India), 359, 523
Greenspan, Alan, 199
Gridlock
government stability and effectiveness and, 313
in Mexico, 463
in semipresidential systems, 267
in U.S.
electoral systems and, 313

participation and representation and, 342, 345
presidential system permits, 262–263, 270
Grievances in identity politics, 146, 182–183
Grievance variables and ethnic violence, 161
Griswold v. Connecticut (1965, U.S.), 650
Gross domestic product (GDP)
in Asia vs. sub-Saharan Africa, 514
case country statistics, 61*t*, 190*t*, 566
in Chile, 228
in China, 518–519
green GDP, 590, 593
New Deal programs and, 212
OECD study on health expenditures as percentage of, 566
social policy and growth in, 550–551, 550–551*t*
in Turkey, 512–513
Group behavior. *See also* Ethnicity/ethnic groups; Identity politics; Interest groups
political saliency and, 146
rational choice theories on, 18–19
Group rights. *See also* Identity politics; Inclusion; Representation
individual rights vs., 609–612
Grupo Somos (gay rights group, Brazil), 652–653
Guanajuato, Mexico
Catholic education funding in, 628
Fox as governor of, 463
Guanxi (China's patron-client networks), 403–404
Guardian Council (Iran), 135, 386–389, 409–410, 644
Guatemala
indigenous people, percentage of population, 180*b*
ladino in, 170
Native American marginalization in, 49
racial/ethnic indigenous groups, 170
Guerra sucia (dirty war, Mexico), 463
Guest workers (Germany), 154
Guinea
color revolution in, 423
first free election, 21
Gujarat, India, Hindus and Muslims clash in, 622, 623

Gul, Abdullah, 615
Guomindang (Taiwan), 397
Gurr, Ted Robert, 436
Gyimah-Boadi, E., 452, 453
Gysi, Gregor, *347*

H

Habyarimana, Juvenal, 378
Hadenius, Axel, 449*b*
Haggard, Stephan, 26
Hagopian, Francis, 458–459
Haider-Markel, Donald P., 650
Haiti
    Duvaliers in, 372, 379
    slave rebellion (1793), 48
    voodoo religion, 165
Hall, Anthony, 563
Hall, Peter, 490, 492
Hanafi school, of Sunni Muslims
    in UK, 620
Hardliners, 445
Hartman, Douglas, 170
Hartz reforms, of German social
    insurance system, *554,*
    555–556
Hausa (Nigeria), 165–166
Häusermann, Silja, 553
Hay, Colin, 488–489
Haymarket Riots (1886, U.S.), 211
Heads of government
    executive as, 249
    in parliamentary systems,
        249–252
    in presidential systems,
        258–259, 264
Heads of state
    executive as, 249
    in parliamentary systems,
        249–250
    in presidential systems, 258–259,
        261, 264
Head Start preschool program
    (U.S.), 545, 557, *558*
Health, wealth, and environment,
    relationship among, 540–541*t,*
    542, 545
Health care
    access to, 570
    cost control by increased pool
        size for, 566
    cost control strategies,
        566–570
    debate over scope of, 193
    expenditures of case countries
        for, 540–541*t*
    fee-for-service vs. HMO, 578
    in Germany, 571–574, *572*
    globalization and, 571
    market-based systems and, 599

market economies and provi-
    sion of, 193
market inefficiencies and, 542
market model in U.S., 577–580
moral hazard and, 564–565
NHI vs. NHS, 599
public health concerns, 570–571
public option system and, 579
as social right, 564
systems, 565–566
UK's National Health Service,
    574–576, 599
in U.S., 577–580
    in crisis, 577
    as employment benefit, 578
World Bank on long-term devel-
    opment and, 201, 203
Health maintenance organizations
    (HMOs)
    in Germany, 572
    in U.S., 567, 578
Heavily Indebted Poor Countries
    (HIPC) initiative, 516
Heclo, Hugh, 549
Hegemony, 24–25
Heilongjiang Province, *maiguan
    maiguan in,* 384
Henry VII (King of England), 63
Henry VIII (King of England), 63,
    109
Hen-Tov, Elliot, 388
Hereditary peers (UK), 255
Heroin, Afghan production of, 57
Heterodox policy, 507, 527
Hijab (Muslim head scarf),
    613–616, 642
Hindu Code Bill (India), 624
Hinduism
    culture expectations, 534
    India's political development
        and, 82, 83
    Indonesia's recognition of, 616
    Muslim clashes with, 622, *623*
Hindu nationalism, 358–361,
    625–626
Hindu Rastra (Hindu nation-state),
    626
Hindutva (BJP's ideology), 625
Hiroshima, Japan, U.S. atomic
    bombing of, 68
Hispanics/Latinos
    terminology for, 175
    in U.S., 174–175, 176*t,* 588
Historical institutionalists
    on authoritarian regimes,
        374–375*b,* 418–419
    on political behavior, 26, 304
Historical materialism, 110
Hitler, Adolf

conservative nationalists of
    Weimar Republic and, 348
defeat of, and Germany's
    division, 71
fascism and racism under, *116,*
    116–118
German economy and, 217
Weimar Republic instability
    and, 7
HIV/AIDS, 650, 653
Hobbes, Thomas, *47,* 104
Holocaust, 118
Holy Roman Empire, 70
Homeland concept, 184
Homophile movement (U.S.), 649
Homosexuals. *See* Lesbian, gay,
    bisexual, and transgender
    people
Honda automobile plant (China),
    521
Hong Kong
    East Asian miracle and economy
        in, 201, 503–504
    investments in China by, 522
Horizontal accountability. *See also*
    Accountability
    in authoritarian regimes, 379
    in Brazil, 279, 460
    of bureaucrats, 280
    consensual systems and, 270
    contexts for, 265
    democratic deepening and, 446
    executive-legislative institution
        comparisons, 270
    in Ghana, 454
    in India, 299
    judiciary and, 273–274, 301
    legislative oversight as, 281
    majoritarian systems and, 270
    in Russia, 269, 299
    of state institutions by other
        state institutions, 246–247
    in UK, 257
    Westminster model and, 301
Horowitz, David, 157
Hot button issues, global
    policymaking, 9
    political development, 6–7
    political economy, 10
    regime type and change, 7–9
    representation, 9
Hough, Dan, 351
House of Commons (UK), 255
House of Lords (UK), 255
House of Representatives (U.S.)
    autonomy from executive
        branch, 262
    cap and trade system for green-
        house gases and, 588

House of Representatives *(cont.)*
FPTP electoral system, 342, *342*
Pelosi and, 317*b*
Howard, Christopher, 560
How the Irish Became White
(Ignatiev), 173
Hu Jintao
as Chinese president and
supreme leader, *379*, 380
civilian control over military
under, 383
as core of the fourth genera-
tion, 382
executive authority of, 381
succession after, 380
Hu Yaobang, 407
Huang, Jing, 382
Huber, Evelyne, 24, 545, 548, 598
Huber, John, 282–283
Human capital
in Africa vs. Asia, 514–515
structural adjustment programs
and, 203*b*
Human Development Index
(UN), 60
Human Rights Campaign (HRC),
649
Human Rights Watch, 471
Hundred Flowers Campaign
(China, 1950s), 403
Hungary
revolution (1989–1990), 434
revolution from above, 440
Hunger strike in Beijing, China,
407
Huntington, Samuel, 147, 423,
427, 438, 446, 463
Hussein, Saddam, 373
Hutus (Rwanda), 168–169
Hybrid regimes, 127
Hyperglobalization, 488–489, 497,
501, 553, 598
Hyperinflation (Brazil), 264
Hypothesis, scientific concept of,
13*b*, 16*b*

I
Iceland, same-sex marriage and,
647
Ideal type, 51
Identity politics. *See also* Inclusion
in Brazil, 180*b*
challenges, 656
debate over, 147–150
democracy and, 9
ethnicity and ethnic conflicts,
153–155
inclusion policies and, 605,
606–607*t*, 609–612

nations and nationalism,
150–152
race in, 170–171, 183
religion as group identity, 157
shifting basis for, 143, 182–185
study theories, 184–185
Ideological hegemony, 24–25
Ideology. *See* Political ideology
Igboland, Nigeria, 88
Igbo peoples of Nigeria
as acephalous society, 165
coup by, 125–126, 432–433
as social construct, *165*, 165–166
as southern tribe, 87–89
Ignatiev, Noel, 173
Ihonvbere, Julius, 415–416
Ijaw ethnic group (Nigeria), 167
Ijtihad, Muslim concept of,
132–133, 643
Ikporukpo, Chris, 594
Illegitimacy
of communist regimes, 440
of East Germany, *70*
GMO foods and, 583
of inherited status in U.S., 437
of Nigerian governments, 235,
432, 473
Illiteracy. *See* Literacy
Imagined communities. *See also*
Social construction
ethnic groups as, 155
in identity politics, 148, 183
nations as, 150
Imam Charity Committee, 309
Immigrants and immigration
to Brazil, whitening policy and,
179–180
cultural protection from larger
society for, 610
France's FN party on, 152
between India and Pakistan, 83
rural-urban
in Brazil, 527
in China, 521
Turkish, as German citizens,
153, 154
to UK from its former colonies,
618–619
to U.S., 66, 73, 175–176, 178
Impeachment
of Collor in Brazil, 278, 459, 527
in presidential systems, 260
Imperialism, global (circa 1900),
49, 50*m*
Impersonal institutions, strong
states and, 52*b*
Import-substitution industrialization (ISI), *200*
in Africa vs. Asia, 514

in Brazil, 527
in Chile, 227
defined, 199–201
development of India's bureaucracy and, 288–289
East Asian miracle and, 504
globalization and, 501
in India, 290, 523
in Japan, 223
in Mexico, 229
in Nigeria, 232, 236
in South Korea, *504*, 505
in Turkey, 512
Inappropriate institutions, 450
Inclusion. *See also* Identity politics
challenges of, 655
inclusive democracy, 610–611
of LGBT community, 645–655
policies and politics of, 605,
606–607*t*, 655–656
of religious groups, 612–629
of women, 629–636
Income inequality. *See also*
Inequality
in Brazil, 74, 561
case country statistics, 190*t*
in Chile, 228
economic growth in China and,
86
in Mexico, 231
in Nigeria, ethnic divisions and,
167
in reunified Germany, 218
in Saudi Arabia, 634
in Southeast Asia, 504–505
states and markets and, 207
in UK, 495–496, 500
in U.S., 196–197, 213
Income redistribution. *See also*
Welfare states; Welfare/
welfare reform
in Europe and U.S., 196–197
by welfare state type, 549,
550–551
Income stabilization, Christian
democratic welfare states
and, 547
Income tax system in U.S., 211.
See also Taxation
An Inconvenient Truth (Gore), *587*
Independent candidates, single,
nontransferable vote systems
and, 352–353, 353*b*
Independent variable, defined,
13*b*
Index of interest-group pluralism
(Lijphart), 341
India
agriculture in, 523–525

asymmetrical federal system in, 296
bureaucratic control and corruption in, 288–292
centralized federal system in, 296
democracy in, 138, 446, 522–526
dominant-party to multiparty democracy, 357–362
in economic crisis from Great Recession, 204
federalism in, 292, 296, 298–299
as fragmented-multiclass state, 510
greenhouse gases produced by, 585
health care programs, 540–541*t*, 570–571
horizontal accountability with state government autonomy in, 299
Kashmir independence conflict and, 626
members of parliament (2005), *255–257*
parliamentary system in, 253–257
patron-client relationships in, 337–338
regime type and characteristics, 138
regional autonomy for linguistic groups in, 155
secularism and religion in, 622–626
state formation, 82–84
state-level parties in, 299
Indian Administrative Service (IAS), 289–290
Indian Civil Service (ICS), 288–289
Indian National Congress (INC). *See also* Congress Party (India)
corruption, factionalism and, 358
on democracy and secularism, 623
dominance of, 83, 256, 358
electoral defeats for, 358–359, 361–362
federalism in India and, 298
lower castes' status and, 358
Indigenization decree (Nigeria), 392
Indigenous people, 180*b*
Indirect rule, by British in Nigeria, 88

Individual motivation
among bureaucrats, corruption and, 281
theories for, 18–20, 28*t*
Individual rights. *See also* Citizens/ citizenship
constitutional complaints in Germany by, 276
group rights vs., 609–612
Islamist *jihad* and, 133
Indonesia
currency valuations in, 485
East Asian financial crisis and, 505–506
religions recognized in, 616
Industrial deepening (Turkey), 512
Industrialism, logic of, 548
Industrialization. *See also* Deindustrialization; Development
in Brazil, *72*, 74, 124
in China, 520–521
environmental damage and, 581–582, 585*m*
in Germany, 70, 216, 218
groups adversely affected, 548
in Japan, 222–223
in Latin America, 331
in Mexico, 78–79
in Nigeria, 233–234
rise of nations and, 151
in Russia, 113–114
in UK, 63–64
in U.S., 66, 210–211
Industrial societies
agricultural societies vs., 102–103*b*
civil societies and, 9
Inequality. *See also* Income inequality
in Asia, 505
in Brazil, 178, 279, 460, 527, *527*
in China, 505, 520–521
deindustrialization, welfare state and, 488
descriptive representation and, 635–636
expansion of citizenship and, 105
in Germany, 557, 572
in India, 523
in Latin America, 507
market failure and, 542
in Mexico, 231, 463
policy for reducing, 542–543
in South Korea, 505
in Taiwan, 505
in Turkey, 512
in U.S., 175–176, 176*t*, 560
in welfare states by type, 551, 552*f*

Infant mortality statistics, 540–541*t*, 568–570
Inflation
in Brazil, 458, 502, 527–528
case country statistics, 190*t*
in Chile, 227
in China, 519, 522
globalization and, 488
of health care costs in U.S., 578–579
in India, 524
in Iran, 530–532
in Mexico, 230–231
monetarist theory of, 198
in Russia, 465
in Turkey, 512–513
in UK, 493–494
Influence markets, corruption and, 287, 291*b*
Informal political institutions, 25. *See also* Political institutions; Social movements
British Parliament as, 109
corrupt rule and, 137
in postcolonial countries, 122–123
in semi-authoritarian regimes, 127
Information. *See also* Internet; Mass communications
imperfect, market inefficiencies and, 539
poor, health care system use and, 564–565
Information technology industry (India), 523, *523*, 525–526
Infosys (Bangalore, India), 522–523, *523*
Infrastructure
in Asia vs. Africa, 514–515
in Brazil, 527, 529
in China, 520, 522
debate over scope of, 193
German reunification and construction of, 218
in India, 524
market economies and provision of, 193
in Mexico, 229
Mobutu on deterioration of, 378
Nigerian investments in, 233–234
state strength and, 55
structural adjustment programs and, 203*b*
Inglehart, Ronald, 22–23, 324*b*, 447, 449*b*
Inherited presidentialism, newly democratic countries and, 258*b*

Insect-borne diseases, 571
Institutional Acts (Brazil), 431
Institutional breakdowns and democracy survival, 475–476
Institutionalism/institutionalists. *See also* Historical institutionalists
  in authoritarian regimes, 418
  on corporate elite power in U.S. democracy vs. other countries, 34*b*
  on coups d'etat, 427–429
  on development in Asia vs. Africa, 515
  on globalization and national economic sovereignty, 489, 534
  inappropriate institutions, 450
  on inclusion and conflicting values, 658
  on modern states, 92
  on party systems and political parties, 326–327
  on political behavior, 302, 304
  on public policy, 599–600
  rational choice institutionalists, 25–26
  on state involvement in the market, 238, 240
  on structural adjustment programs, 202–203*b*
  structuralism and, 25–27
  on welfare state reform, 553
Institutionalization. *See also* Political institutions
  after Brazil's coup of 1964, 429, 431, 434
  in authoritarian regimes, 370–373, 374–375*b*, 375–377
  in China, 380–383, 520, 522
  defined, 371
  limits on executive power in authoritarian regimes through, 371
  in Nigeria, 434, 471–472, 474
  succession in authoritarian regimes and, 378
Instituto Federal Electoral (IFE, Mexico), 462
Instrumentalism/instrumentalists
  ethnic mobilization by elites theory, 160
  identity politics and, 147, 184–185
  on leadership in ethnic groups, 160
Inter-American Development Bank, 563

Interest aggregation, political parties and, 312
Interest group pluralism
  characteristics, 331, 333*f*
  effective governance and, 362–363
  entry into political process, 346
  in Japan, 356
  in U.S., 339–340, 345–346
Interest groups. *See also* Civil society; Group behavior; Identity politics
  in authoritarian regimes, 373, 394, 397–398
  in Brazil, 653
  characteristics, 331, 333*f*
  in China, 405–406
  in India, 359, 361
  political participation through, 9
  types, 362–363
Intergenerational externality of mineral and oil depletion, 584
Intergovernmental Panel on Climate Change (IPCC), 582, *587*
Internal sovereignty
  challenges to, 41–43
  defined, 41
  Peace of Westphalia and, 47
International capital flows, 487
International Criminal Court, 98
International Energy Agency, 584
International financial institutions (IFIs), 563
International Monetary Fund (IMF)
  bailouts to Ireland and Greece, 221
  Brazil's debt and, 527–528
  East Asian financial crisis and, 505–506
  global economy and, 208, 505
  Heavily Indebted Poor Countries Initiative of World Bank and, 516
  India's appeal for emergency funding, 524
  Iranian theocracy and, 531
  Keynes and creation of, 199
  Latin American development and, 506–507
  Mexico, loans to, 231
  on Nigeria as oil exporter, 234
  structural adjustment programs under, 201, 202*b*, 238
  in Turkey, 512
International relations, defined, 11
International state system, 92

International Women's Day (Moscow), *637*
Internet. *See also* Mass communications
  in China, *85*, 384, 406
  globalization and, 205–206
  in Iran, 136
  Move On!, 337
  political mobilization in U.S., 345–346
  social capital and, 326–327, 336–337
  women's movement and, 634, 644
Interracial marriage. *See* Racial intermarriage
Interventionist economic development strategy, 79
Invasion, external sovereignty absent in, 41
IRA (Provisional Irish Republican Army), 158–159, 438–439*b*
Iran
  civil society in, 411–412
  factionalism in, 412
  globalization and oil wealth of, 530–532
  ideological factions in, 412
  Islamic revolution in, 434
  legitimacy in, 386
  military dictatorship or theocracy in, 385–390
  modernizing authoritarianism under Shah in, 410
  Muslim theocracy in, 132, 135
  nationalism, student interest in, 136
  as oil exporter, 235*b*
  as oil-industrializing nation, 530–532
  parliament of, 389, 409–410, 413
  political parties in, 408, 410
  reformist ascendency in, 411
  regime type and characteristics, 138
  repression in, 409–413
  Revolutionary Guard, 136, 385–390, 409, 412–413, 531–532
  revolution of 1979 in, 434
  secularization and Westernization in, 133
  social network technology in, 337
  state formation, 80–81
  succession in, *385*, 386
  territorial reduction of, 80
  theocracy with limited participation in, 80–81, 134–136, 385–390, 412–413
  women's rights in, 411, 640–644

Iran-Iraq War, 388, 524, 530, 532, 642

Iraq
  coalition leaders, *6*
  Hussein in, 373
  Iran-Iraq War economic impact, 524, 530
  nationalism and regional oil reserves, 157
  UK military presence in, 622
  U.S. invasion of, 5

Ireland. *See also* Northern Ireland
  economic crisis in Great Recession, 204–205, 221
  taxation in, 294
  unification into UK, 62

Irish, political identity of, 150

Irish Americans, 155, 173

Irish Republican Army (IRA), 158–159, 438–439*b*

Ironsi, Johnson Thomas Umunnakwe Aguiyi, 125, 392, 432

Iron triangles, 287, 356

IRP (Islamic Republican Party, Iran), 135

Isaaq clan, Somaliland, 45

ISI. *See* Import-substitution industrialization

Islam
  Arab invasion of Persia and, 80
  in Europe, policy differences toward, 617
  forced to Siberia by Stalin, 299
  foundations (*bonyads*), 530 532
  in France and Turkey, headscarves and, 613–616
  fundamentalism, terminology for, 132
  immigrants to France, 118
  immigrants to Germany, 154
  in India
    Hindu clashes with, 83–84, 622, *623*
    Moghul Empire, 82
    political participation by, 625
    Sikh Golden Temple invasion, 359–360
  Indonesia's recognition of, 616
  male guardianship in, 633
  military leaders and Kaduna mafia, 470
  in Nigeria, 87–89, 165–166, 183, 415, 470–471, 473
    Christian tensions with, 167
  in Pakistan, 83
  in Turkey, 513, 613
  in UK
    poverty among, 619
    in prison, 619

  radical Islam and, 622
  religious education in public schools, 620–621
  veil, as identity symbol, 149*b*
  women's rights, 656
    in Iran, 640–644
    in Saudi Arabia and Kuwait, 633–634

Islamic Republican Party (IRP, Iran), 135

Islamic Republic of Iran. *See* Iran

Islamic terrorists
  defined, 132
  internationalist movement of, 138, 143, 183
  radicalism of, 386, 412
  in Somalia, U.S. fears about, 55
  use of terrorism by, 438–439*b*

Islamist Renaissance Party (Tunisia), 400

Islamophobia, 614

Israel
  fragmented parliamentary systems, 272
  Israeli Arabs, policy on, 252
  Labour Party in, 251
  multiple parties in, 251
  Palestine, policy on, 252
  parliamentary system in, 251–252

Italian Americans, assimilation of, 173

Italy
  fascism in, 68, 115, 118
  fragmented parliamentary systems in, 272
  multiparty system in, 326
  nationalism in, 151
  parliamentary instability after World War II in, 313

J

Jackson, Andrew, 262, 343

Jackson, Jesse, 173–174

Jackson, Robert, 56

Jacksonian Revolution (U.S.), 65

Jalisco, Mexico, Christian rebellion in, 628

James I (King of England), 63

James II (King of England), 48, 109

James VI (King of Scotland), 63

Japan
  bank loan policies, 223, 226
  bureaucracy reform in, 286–288
  bureaucrat recruitment in, 281–284
  coordinated market economy of, 490

  deflation in, 226
  deindustrialization in, 488
  democratic consolidation in, 446
  as developmental state, 222–227, 239, 286, 504
  dominant-party to two-party system, 352–357
  earthquake and tsunami in, 226, 288
  economic success in, East Asian miracle and, 515
  economy of, 67, *67*, 209, 226*t*
  electoral reform in, 354
  health care programs, 540–541*t*, 570–571
  invasion and occupation of China, 68, 85–86, 441–442
  investments in China by, 522
  judicial review in, 275
  mixed electoral system in, 316
  national health insurance in, 565
  NPM and bureaucracy size in, 284
  patron-client relationships in, 337–338
  postal saving system, 224, 226
  SNTV system in, 318
  social capital in, 326
  as sovereignty, 67–69
  state formation, 68
  tsunamis in, 226
  weak civil society in, 352

Japanese miracle, 225

Japan Socialist Party (JSP), 356

Jasmine Revolution (Tunisia), 22, 384, 399, 401–402, 423, 434, 616

Jefferson, Thomas, 103, 261–263, 343

Jeffersonian Republicans, 343

Jews, 118, 173

Jiang Zemin, 382, 521

Jihad, Islamists on, 133

Jim Crow laws (U.S.), 32, 608.
  See also Enfranchisement

João VI (King of Portugal), 73

John (King of England), 108

Johnson, Chalmers, 224

Johnson, Lyndon, 212, 559

Johnson-Sirleaf, Ellen, *58,* 59

Johnston, Michael, 287, 291*b*

Jonathan, Goodluck, 89, 471–473

Jordan, voting system in, 353*b*

Jos, Nigeria, ethnic and religious mix in, 167

Journalism. *See* Press

Judges. *See also* Judiciary/judicial systems
in Brazil, scandals involving, 279
horizontal accountability to executives and legislatures of, 274
Judicial independence
in Brazil, 278–280
in parliamentary systems, 276
in presidential systems, 275–276
Judicialization of politics
in Brazil, 279
defined, 246–203
in Germany, 276–279
Judicial review
in Brazil, 278–280
under common law vs. code law, 273–274
defined, 273–274
in democracies, 273–280
federalism and, 293
in Germany, 276–278
Judiciary/judicial systems
in authoritarian regimes, 372, 376
in Brazil, 278–280, 460
in China, 383
in Germany, 276–278
horizontal accountability and, 301
as interpreter of executive power, 246
in Iran, 388
in Nigeria, 391–392
political role of, 273
Jus sanguinis laws, 152–154, *153*
Jus soli laws, 152, 153
Justice and Development Party (AKP, Turkey), 512, 615

K

Kabashima, Ikuo, 355
Kaduna mafia (Nigeria), 415, 433, 470–472
Kagame, Paul, 395
Kalenjin (Kenya), 156*b*
Kan, Naoto, *286, 352*
Kang, Alice, 635
Kapstein, Ethan B., 451
Karelia, as Russian republic, 300
Karlsruhe, Germany, *277*
Karzai, Hamid, 57
Kashmir, independence conflict in, 626
Katz, Richard, 321, 324*b*
Katzenstein, Peter, 548
Kaufman, Robert, 26
Keidanren (Japanese business interests group), 356

Keiretsu (Japanese business networks), 223–225, 224*b*, 356
Kenya
election fraud in, 395
Kalenjin people, 156*b*
Kenyatta's dictatorship, *8*, 376
one-party regime in, 120, 375–376
patron-client relationships in, 398
voter fraud in (2007), 396
Kenyatta, Jomo, *8*, 376
Kerala state, India, social services in, 526
Keynes, John Maynard, 197, 199, 542
Keynesian economic theory
boom and bust economy, 198
cartel parties and, 321
characteristics, 197–198
development economics and, 199
EU use of, 220
Japan's use of, 226
monetarism vs., 198–199, 237
social democratic parties and, 198
stagflation and, 198
U.S. use of, 210–212
Khakassia, as Russian republic, 300
Khamenei, Ali, 134, *385*, 389
Khan, Abdur Rahman, emir of Afghanistan, 56
Khatami, Mohammad, 136, 408–409, 412, 531–532, 644
Khomeini, Ruhollah
family law restrictions under, 642
fatwa condemning Rushdie by, 620
as Grand Ayatollah, 389
Khamenei and, *385*
opposition to shah by, 81, 442–443
political parties banned by, 410
as supreme leader in Iran, *134*, 135–136, *385*, 385–386
Khordad Front (Iranian party), 410
Khrushchev, Nikita, 114
"Kicking in Groups" (Lemann), 337
Kidnappings (Nigeria), 593, 595
Kim Il-Sung, 385
King, Martin Luther, Jr., 174, 335
Kirkpatrick, Jeane, 629
Kleptocracy, in Zaire under Mobutu, 377–378

Knesset (Israeli parliament), 251–252
Koenkai (Japanese local voter mobilization machine), 353, 355
Kohl, Helmut, 218, 349, 500, 555
Kohli, Atul, 299, 510–511, 524
Koizumi, Junichiro, 226–186, 287, 354
Koran (Quran), 132
Korea. *See also* North Korea; South Korea
as Japanese colony, 68
Kosovo, border changes in, 40–41
Krahn people (Liberia), 59
Kremlinology, 114
Krio (colonial elite of Sierra Leone), 58
Kristallnacht (Germany, 1937), 118
Krook, Mona Lena, 635
Kufuor, John, 453
Ku Klux Klan (KKK), 329–330
Kuomintang (Taiwan), 397
Kurds, 5, 157
Kurzarbeit program (Germany), 499
Kuwait, women in, 633–634
Kymlicka, Will, 609–610
Kyoto Protocol, 584–586, *587*, 588

L

Labastida, Francisco, 463
Laboratory control in political studies, 12–14
Labor Day, recognition of, 211
Labor/labor unions
in Brazil, 74, 124, 456
in China, 405–407
democracies vs. authoritarianism, 508–509
in Egypt, 401
in Germany, 117, 217–218, 348, 350–351
globalization and
collective bargaining and, 497–499
policy convergence and, 489–492
power of, 205–206
in India, 359, 524
in Japan, 225, 356
mass electoral democracy and emergence of, 331
in Mexico, 77–78, 129–131, 397, 463
modern welfare state and political demands of, 196
in Nigeria, 415

social democratic welfare states and, 548–549

social insurance in Christian democratic welfare states and, 547

strength of, state involvement in the market and, 237

in Sweden, 34b, 547

in UK, 493–494, 496

in U.S., 34b, 211–212, 215

Labour Party (Israel), 251–252

Labour Party (UK)
devolution under Blair, 109–110
economic reform and, 493–495
membership in unions and, 320
Muslim schools funding and, 621
NHS reforms and, 574–575
parliamentary system and, 253
social movement groups and, 341
strikes (1978–1979) and, 493
two-party system and, 323

Ladino (Guatemala), 170

Lafontaine, Oskar, *347*, 350

Laicismo (Mexico), *627*, 627–628

Laïcité (secularist ideology in France), 613–614, 617, 657

Laissez faire model of economic development, 210–211

Lambda Defense and Education Fund, 649

Lander (German states), 217, 276–278, 294

Land ownership conflict, 169

Languages
of ethnic groups in India, 359
federalism in India and conflict over, 298–299
French nationalism and, 152
German nationalism and, 153–154
Hispanics and Latinos in U.S. and, 175
identity group rights and, 83, 155, 165, 175, 183, 293, 359
Igbo and, 167
regional autonomy in India for groups based on, 155
Serbo-Croatian conflict and, 155

Latin America. *See also individual countries*
breakdown of democracy in (1960s), 447
clientelism and populism in, 323
democratization in, 445

development economists on free trade vs. terms of trade for, 199

ethnic and racial categorizations in, 170

foreign capital inflow, 507

Freedom House scores, 456b

gap with developed countries and, 502–503

gender gap in, 632

globalization and development in, 506–507

Great Recession in, 507

industrialization in, 331

interest groups' emergence in, 331

lost decade in, 507

MERCOSUR free trade zone, 228

military coups by decade in, 431b

neoliberal policies and poverty in, 534

North American colonial history compared to, 64

political behavior patterns, 14

political development in, 7

political ideologies and regime types in, 138

political parties in, 322–323

presidentialism used in, 258b, 272

race and ethnicity in, 180b

rebellions in, 48–49

social movements in authoritarian regimes of, 397

structural adjustment programs in, 201

subjugation of Native American states and empires in, 48

trade/investment with U.S., 507

on welfare reform, 553

Latinos. *See* Hispanics/Latinos

Lawrence v. Texas (2003, U.S.), 650

LDP (Liberal Democratic Party, Japan), 69

Leadership. *See also* Elites
in authoritarian regimes, 371–372
in identity politics, 150, 156, 183

League of Nations, 56

Lebanon, as consociational system, 157

Lee, Ching Kwan, 405

Lee, Frances, 345

Left-wing parties, 322b

Legal profession, Iranian women in, 642

Legal rights

of LGBT community in U.S., 649–650

of women. *See* Women/women's rights

Legal systems. *See* Judiciary/judicial systems

Legislative capacity testing, 283

Legislatures/legislative system. *See also* Bicameral legislatures; Congress (U.S.); *Duma*; Parliaments
accountability of judges vs., 274
in authoritarian regimes, 373–376
bicameral, 255
in China, 380, 383
fixed terms for, in presidential systems, 272
in France, 266–267
horizontal accountability and, 281
importance in democracies, 249
in Nigeria, 391
power of, 27
as power through which executive can be limited, 246
in presidential systems, 260–263, 272
quota laws for representation by women in, 635
strength of, in new democracies, 450–451
in Westminster system, 253–255
women representatives in, 636m

Legitimacy
in authoritarian regimes
institutionalization and, 372
judiciary and, 376
repression as disadvantage, 372
in Brazil, 72, 74, 279
in China, 408
corruption and, 291b
defined, 43
dual, in presidential systems, 271–272
FPTP system and, 319
in Germany, 69
in interest groups, 330–331
in Iran, 136, 386, 412–413, 532
in Japan, 67–69
of judiciary, 276
in Mexico, 77–79
national identity as source of, 43–44
in Nigeria, 234–235, 390–391, 416
popular sovereignty and, 99
in semi-authoritarian states, 428

Legitimacy *(cont.)*
state strength, correlation to, 91
as subject loyalty, 47
types of, 43–44
Lehman Brothers, 194, 213
Lemann, Nicholas, 337
Lenin, Vladimir, *112*, 112–114, 137–138
Le Pen, Jean-Marie, 118, 152
Le Pen, Marine, 118
Lesbian, gay, bisexual, and transgender (LGBT) people, 645–652
in Brazil, 652–655
gay rights, globally, 647, 648*m*
inclusion issues, 646–647
laws, rights, opinions about, in case countries, 655
legal discrimination against, 606–607*t*, 609–610
recognition of rights for, 645–646
terminology for, 645–646
in U.S., 649–652
Levendusky, Matthew, 345
Lewis-Beck, Michael, 177
Li Cheng, 383
Liberal democracy. *See also* Democracies/ democratic countries
civil rights and representative democracy in, 104
defined, 103–104, 107*b*
demands for inclusion in, 657
equal citizenship as core value of, 608–609, 611–612
Marx on, 111
nationalism and, 151–152
as political ideology and regime type, 100*b*, 103–104
social policies and market economies of, 543
state power and citizens' rights under, 137
voter eligibility, 104–105
Liberal Democratic Party (LDP, Japan), 226
bureaucratic control and corruption and, 286
corruption scandals, electoral reform and, 353–354
dominance of, 69, 352–356
on NPOs, 356–357
Liberal Democratic Party (UK), 254, 341–342
Liberalism
classical, 103
European, 48
Liberal Party and, 322*b*

political identity and, 138
as political ideology, 24
Liberalization (Turkey), 512–513
Liberal market economies (LMEs)
characteristics, 489–492
in Germany, 497
market openness in, 533–534
under Thatcher in UK, 493–495
Liberal Party
in Europe, 320, 322*b*
in UK, 323
Liberal welfare states
in Brazil, 562
characteristics, 549–550
defined, 549
maternity leave and child care in, 632
political behavior and, 598
as share of national economy, 549, 551
types of, 545
in U.S., reform of, 557–561
weakly organized working classes and, 549
Liberationist approach to LGBT inclusion, 646, 649
Liberation theology (Brazil), 74
Liberia
children as soldiers in, 59–60
civil war in, 92
as failed state, 51, 58–60
Libya
Gaddafi in, 373
Muslim organizations in UK and, 619
uprisings in, 402, 417
License raj, 289
Life expectancy
in Iran, 642
in Russia, 638
statistics, 540–541*t*, 570
Lifetime employment (Japan), 225
Lijphart, Arend, 247, 249, 257, 270, 302–303, 341, 450
Likud (conservative coalition in Israel), 251–252
Limited-participatory institutions, 416
Limongi, Fernando, 458, 509–511
Lincoln, Abraham, 66, 343
Lindberg, Staffan, 451
Lindblom, Charles, 31
Line-item veto (Brazil), 264
Linz, Juan, 271–272, 450
Lipset, Seymour Martin, 444
Lisbon Treaty (2007), 221
Literacy
in Asia vs. Africa, 515

black Brazilians in 1990s and, 180
East Asians and, 505
Indians and, 525–526
in Iran, 412*b*, 642
postcolonial elites on citizen rights and, 49, 119
in Tanzania, 121
voting rights in Brazil and, 73, 180
women in Iran and, 642
Little Tigers (East Asia), 505–506, 508*b*, 515*b*, 516
LMEs. *See* Liberal market economies
Lobbying, 183, 346
Local governments
elections in China, 404
in federal and unitary systems, 292, 293
in U.S., gay rights authorized by, 649
Locke, John, 103, 108–109
Logic of industrialism, 548
Logit regression, 161
Lok Sabha (India's parliament), *82*
London, England
as multicultural city, 618, *619*, 620
subway bombings (2005), 621–622
Long March (China), 85, *441*
Long-term health care, 568
López Obrador, Andrés Manuel, 461, 163
López Portillo, José, 230
"Lost decade" in Latin America, 507
Louisiana Purchase (U.S.), 262
Louis XIV (King of France), 47
Lowe, Chris, 156*b*
Loyalists in American Revolution, 437
Lu Yiyi, 406
Luan Xiuju, *518*
Lukes, Steven, 10–11, 170, 185
Lula da Silva, Luis Inácio, *261*, *527*
compromises on promises by, 455, 528–529
corruption scandals, 458–459
economic policies under, 526, *527*, 528–529
on hate crimes and civil unions, 654
judiciary and, 278–279
popularity of, 458–459
power-sharing with National Congress, 265
reelection of, 264
social policies of, *562*
Luther, Martin, 70

M

Maastricht Treaty (1992), 220
MacArthur, Douglas, 69
Macroeconomic stability, 494–495
Madagascar, color revolution in, 423
Madero, Francisco, 78
Madison, James, 343
Madrid Hurtado, Miguel de la, 230
Mafias
  market economies and, 191
  in Nigeria, 415, 433, 470–472
  in Russia, 76, 468
Magaloni, Beatriz, 395
Magna Carta, *108*, 108–109
Mahdavi, Pardis, 642
Maiguan maiguan (China), 384
Majlis (parliament), in Iran, 136, 389, 409–410, 413
Major, John, 254
Majoritarianism
  accountability and, 270
  electoral systems. *See also* First-past-the-post representation; Single-member district electoral system
    in British parliamentary system, 247–249
    compromise in divided societies with, 271
    in France, 328
    in Iran, 386, 409
    in Japan, 354
    participation and, 313
    representation vs. accountability in, 363
  majoritarian democracy, 247
  parliamentary system in UK, 496
  vertical accountability and, 270
  Westminster model, 302
Majority beliefs, judicial review as expression of, 275
Majority power
  in democracies, 247
  federalism and limitations on, 293–294
  in presidential systems, 271–272
Malaysia
  currency valuations in, 485
  East Asian financial crisis and, 505
  IMF recovery plan rejection in, 518
  neoliberal policies in, 201
Malcolm X, 335
Male guardianship (Saudi Arabia), 633
al-Maliki, Nouri, *6*

Malnutrition, as public health concern, 571
Managed advocacy groups, 346
Managerial competence, cartel parties and, 321
Manchukuo (Manchuria), Japanese control of, 41
Mandela, Nelson, 323, 444, 474
The Man on Horseback (Finer), 427–428
Mansbridge, Jane, 635
"Man without a country," 97
Mao Zedong
  charismatic legitimacy of, 43–44
  economic liberalization after death of, 138
  environmental policy under, 590
  military loyalty of, 383
  personalist decision-making by, 380, 520
  as personality cult, 380
  revolution under, 85–86, 441, *441*
  succession after, 382–383
Maquiladora (manufacturing) economy (Mexico), 79, 231
Marcos, Ferdinand, 120, 444
Market-based health care systems
  NHI and NHS systems vs., 580
  private health insurance systems, 566
  quality and economy of, 599
  in U.S., 577
Market-based policies
  New Public Service (NPS) and, 284
  political behavior and, 597
  pollution in China, 591
Market economy
  in Chile, 227–228
  in China, participation and representation and, 86, 404, 406, 408
  defined, 190
  in Germany, 216–219
  globalization, policy convergence and, 488–489
  government intervention effectiveness questions, 239–240
  in Japan, 222–227
  liberal vs. coordinated, 489–492
  modern states and, 191–197, 204*b*, 237
  in Nigeria, *232*, 232–234, 236
  in Russia, 465, 638
  social democracy and, 107*b*
  state controls on, 190–191
  theories applied to, 239–240
  in U.S., 210–211

Market failure. *See also* Welfare states; Welfare/welfare reform
  characteristics, 542
  defined, 193
  environmental damage and, 581–582
  in Keynesian theory, 199
  in monetarist theory, 199
  monopolies as, 195–196
  moral hazard with health insurance and, 546–565
  perfect information and, 194
  pollution as, 596–597
  zaibatsu in Japan as, 223
Marketing boards (Nigeria), *232*, 233
Market-oriented economic politics, 131
Markets as veto players, 598
Marshall, T. H., 97–99, 105, 107*b*, 543, 608
Marsiaj, Juan, 653
Marx, Karl, 25, 30–31, 110–112, 114, 137, 435
Marxism/Marxists
  on capitalism and modern state, 91–92, 151
  on corporate elite power in U.S., 34*b*
  defined, 25
  as elite theory example, 30–31
  in Iran, 443
  under Mao, 441
  on modernizing authoritarianism, 120
  as political structure, 25
  social democratic parties arising from, 105
  on state involvement in the market, 238
Mary Tudor (Mary Queen of Scots), 63
Mass communications. *See also* Information; Internet; Media; Press
  debate on impact on civil society of, 336–337
  demands for inclusion by identity groups and, 634, 643, 650
  newspapers in Iran, 411
  political parties in U.S. and, 344
  social capital decline and, 326–327
Mass media. *See* Media
Mass organizations, 397
Mass parties, 320

Maternity leave policy
  in Iran, 642
  in Papua New Guinea, lack of, 557
  in Russia, 637–638
  in Sweden, 546
Mattachine Society, 649–650
Mbembe, Achille, 394
McElwain, Kenneth, 324–325*b*
McGuire, James, 568
Means-tested public assistance, 544–545, 550, 555, 557–562. *See also* Welfare states; Welfare/welfare reform
Media. *See also* Mass communications
  Al Jazeera, 401
  in China, 406
  elite domination of, 312
  interest groups and, 341
  in Iran, 136, 411
  in Mexico, 462
  political party realignments and, 324*b*
  in Russia, 269, 467
  television, 326–327, 337
Medicaid (U.S.), 212, 559, 561, 578
Medicare (U.S.), 212, 215, 558, 561, 578
Medvedev, Dmitry Anatolyevich, *267*, 269, 468
Meer, Nasar, 622
Meiji Restoration (Japan, 1867–1868), 68, 222–223
Membership-based organizations, 336
Members of parliament (MPs), 249
  in Britain, 253–254
  defined, 249
  in Germany, neocorporatist ties of, 348, 350
  in India, *253*, 255–257
Men. *See* Gender
Menashri, David, 412
Mengistu Haile-Mariam, 53*b*
MERCOSUR free trade zone, 228
Merkel, Angela, 218–219, 347, 350, 572–573
Mestizo population (South America), 48
Mexican-American War (1846–1848), 78
Mexican Revolution (1910–1920), 78, 229, 627
Mexican War of Independence (1810), 627

Mexico
  anticlericalism in, 626–629
  debt crisis in, 230, 507
  democratic consolidation in, 446
  disparities, economic, 79
  election fraud in, 395
  electoral system in, 131
  GINI index, 231
  import-substitution industrialization and, *200*, 200–201, 229
  indigenous people, 180*b*
  internal sovereignty challenges, 77–79
  market-based private health insurance system in, 566, 570
  military coups in, 78
  obesity in, 571
  oil industry in, 461
  presidential election victories by PRI in, 395
  presidential term of office in, 260
  PRI weaknesses in, 397
  protectionism to neoliberalism, 229–231
  reforms under Santa Ana, 627
  regional inequality in, 229
  secularism in, 613
  from semi-authoritarianism to democracy, 461–464
  as semi-authoritarian regime, 128–131
  state corporatism under PRI in, 397
  state formation, 78–79
  stock market in, *229*
  taxation in, 294
  war with U.S., 67
Mexico City, Mexico
  abortion in, 628
  Catholic Church in, *627*
  Olympics (1968) in, 130
  same-sex marriage in, 628
Michigan, foreclosures in, *210*
Michoacan, Mexico, Christian rebellion in, 628
Microfinance, 502, 633
Middle East. *See also specific countries*
  inhibitions to industrialization in, 512
  political and social rights for women in, 149*b*
  women in power positions in, 317*b*
Migdal, Joel, 377
Military power/regimes. *See also* Coups d'etat; Security
  in authoritarian regimes, 372–373

  in Brazil, 73–74, *123*, 124, 181, *455*, 456
  bureaucracies in, 374*b*
  in Chile, 227
  in China, 85, 383, 407
  in civilian regimes, 383, 460, 471–472, 475
  in democracies, 425
  ethnic conflict and, 157
  formal institutionalization in, 122
  in Germany, 71
  institutionalization in, 376, 426–429
  in Iran, 136, 385–386
  in Japan, 68, 223
  multiple military institutions, 426
  in Nigeria, 89–90, 125–126, 166–168, 390–392, 391
  political institutions of, 396
  political parties' freedom under, 323
  Revolutionary Guard in Iran, 136, 385–390, 409, 412–413
  Russia, failed coup d'etat, 114
  in Rwanda, 169
  in sub-Saharan Africa (1970–2000), 392*b*
Military service of gays (U.S.), 651
Mill, John Stuart, 105
Millennium Development Goals (MDGs), UN's, 516
Millennium Promise (foundation), 516–517
Mills, C. Wright, 31
Mills, John Atta, 452–453
Milosevic, Slobodan, 157
Miners' strike (UK, 1984–1985), 493
Ministries, terminology for, 281
Ministry of Environment Protection (MEP, China), 590–591
Ministry of Finance (MOF, Japan), 224, 287
Ministry of International Trade and Industry (MITI, Japan), 224–225
Minority parties, single, nontransferable vote systems and, 353*b*
Minority rights. *See also* Identity politics; Inclusion
  in democracies, 247
  federalism and protection of, 293–295
  judicial review as protection for, 275
  political institutions and protection for, 301–302
  politics of inclusion and, 609

Miskimmon, Alister, 351

Mitchell, George, 158–159

Mixed electoral systems
in Germany, 347
in Japan, 352
women in power under, 317

Mixed-race population (South America), 48

Mixed representation systems, 316–318

Mobile phone licenses scandal (India), 290

Mobutu Sese Seko, 120, 377–378, 395

Mode of production, Marx on, 111

Moderate Party (Sweden), 546–547

Moderates, 445

Modern absolutist states. *See* Absolutism

Modernist theory of political culture, 21–22

Modernization
defined, 7
in India, 623
in Mexico, 463–464
in Nigeria, 233

Modernization, Cultural Change, and Democracy (Inglehart & Welzel), 449*b*

Modernization theory
on democracy, 448*b*
modern elite as ruler, 119
on regime change, 477
on revolution, 438–439

Modernizing authoritarianism.
See also Authoritarianism/authoritarian regimes;
Military power/regimes;
One-party regimes/states;
Personalist regimes
in Brazil, 74, 123–124, 527
in China, 86, 380, 408
core assumptions, 119–120
coups d'etat and, 428
defined, 101*b*
development benefits, 119
fascists on, 120
forms, 120
geographic clusters of, 138
in Iran under Shah, 8, 410
Marxists on, 120
in Mexico, 229
modern elite in, 119
national unity in, 119
neopatrimonialism, 122–123
in Nigeria, 125–127
political culture and, 24

state power and citizens' rights under, 137
in Tanzania, 121–122

Modern states. *See also* Failed states; State formation case studies; States
case country economic statistics, 190*t*
characteristics of, 33, 39–40
civil society development with development of, 97–98
historical origins of, 46–49
market economies and, 191–197, 204*b*, 237
terminology for, 39–40
timeline for development of, 91*t*
written constitutions of, 245

Modood, Tariq, 622

Moghul Empire, 82

Mohammed, Prophet of Islam, 132, 134, 643

Monarchs/monarchies
in Brazil, 179
as European absolutist rulers, 46–48
feudal, market economies and, 191–192
as heads of state, 249–250
in Japan, 67–68
in Nigeria, 169
in Persia, 80
subjects of, 97
in UK, 62, 62–63

Monetarist economic theory
cartel parties and, 321
in Chile, 227
development economics and, 201
EC/EU use of, 220
Japan's use of, 226
Keynesian theory vs., 198–199, 237
stagflation and, 198
U.S. use of, 210, 213

Monetary policy, 198, 494

Money. *See* Currency/currency valuations

Monopolies
market economies and prevention or regulation of, 193, 195
natural, 195
in Nigeria, 233
U.S. regulation of, 211
zaibatsu in Japan, 223

Monroe, James, 343

Monsiváis, Carlos, 628

Montesquieu, Baron de, 103

Montreal Protocol, 587

Moore, Barrington, 102, 102*b*, 436, 436*b*

Moral hazard, health insurance and, 564–565, 567

Morality/moral values
inclusion policies and, 605
postmaterialism and, 22

Morality police (Saudi Arabia), 634

Moral matrix of legitimate governance, 23–24

Moran, Donald, 580

Mortgage-backed securities (MBS), 194, 199

Mosaddeq, Mohammad, 81, 442–443

Moscow. *See also* Russia
as federal city, 299
mafias in, 76

MOSOP (Movement for the Survival of the Ogoni People), Nigeria, 393, 415, 595

Most different systems design, 14, 510

Most similar systems design, 14

Mother of Parliaments, 258

Motivation for political behavior, 18

Mousavi, Mir-Hossein, 409, 411

Movement for the Emancipation of the Niger Delta (MEND), 168, 473, 595

MoveOn!, 337

Movimento Negro Unificado (Unified Black Movement, Brazil), 181

Moyo, Dambisa, 516–517

Mubarak, Gamal, 400

Mubarak, Hosni, 373, 399–401

Mugabe, Robert, *370*

Mujahedeen, of Afghanistan, 56–57

Mujahedin, of Iran, 442–443

Mulatto group (Brazil), 180

Mulgan, Aurelia, 287, 288

Multiculturalism, 618–622
assimilation vs. integration, 609–610
Nigeria and, 165–168

Multiparty systems. *See also* Party systems
in Brazil, 263–264
characteristics, 326
in France, 327
in India, 255–257, 358–361

Mumbai, India, hotel bombing, 626

Muslim Brotherhood, 133, 400–401

Muslim League (India), 623, 625

Muslims. *See* Islam

Muslim Women's (Protection of Rights on Divorce) Bill, India, 625
Mussolini, Benito, 115
Myanmar, air pollution from China in, 592

N
al-Nabhani, Taqi al-Din, 132
Nagasaki, Japan, U.S. atomic bombing of, 68
Nairobi, Kenya, UN conference on women in, 630
Namibia, German colonialism in, 71
Nanjing, China, as capital after Taiping Rebellion, 85
Napoleon Bonaparte, 70, 153, 273, 627
Napoleonic Code, 273
National Action Party (PAN, Mexico), 461
National AIDS Program, Brazil, 653
National Assembly (France), 328
National Assembly (Northern Ireland), 159
National Association of Manufacturers, 331
National Congress (Brazil), 181
  corruption and resignations from, 459
  federalism and power of, 264–265
  Goulart opposition in, 430–431
  indirect presidential elections in, 456
  LGBT antidiscrimination law and, 654
  Lula's social insurance program and, 562–563
  provisional decrees of president and, 264–265
  race politics and, 181
  weak political parties and, 457–458
National Council of Nigeria and Cameroons, 166
National Democratic Coalition (NADECO, Nigeria), 470
National Democratic Congress party (NDC, Ghana), 452–453
National Democratic Front (Mexico), 461
National Executive Committee (CEN, Mexico), 129
National Executive Committee, Labour Party (NEC, UK), 340
National Front Party (FN, France), 118, 152, 328

National Gay and Lesbian Task Force (NGLTF), 649
National health insurance (NHI) system, 565–566, 570–574, *572*, 580
National Health System (NHS, UK)
  Cameron's reforms, 574–576, 598
  NHI and market-based systems, vs., 580, 599
  priorities of care, 570
  as single-payer system, 565–566
  Thatcher's proposed reforms, 494, 496
National identity
  European colonialism and, 49
  gender symbols for boundaries of, 149*b*
  globalization and, 205–208
  as source of legitimacy, 44–45
Nationalism. *See also* Autonomy
  causes for development of, 151
  defined, 150
  in France, 151–152
  in Germany, 151–154
  in Italy, 151
  nations and, 150–152
  political identity and, 143
  strong states and, 92
Nationalist Party. *See also* Right-wing extremists
  in China, 441–442
  in Germany, 117
Nationalization. *See* State-owned enterprises
Nationalization of banks (Mexico), 230
National Judicial Council (Brazil), 279
National Judicial Council (Nigeria), 472
National Mine Workers Union (UK), 493
National Organization of Women, 336
National Party Congress (China), 380, 382, 384
National People's Congress (China), 380, 383
National People's Party (NPP, Ghana), 453
National Priorities toxic waste sites (U.S.), 589
National Realtors Association, 331
National Revolutionary Party (Mexico), 129
National security as public good, 192

National Security Doctrine (Brazil), 430–431
National Socialists (Nazis), 71, 116–118, 153
National Socialist Youth (Germany), *116*, 117
National unity
  identity group challenges due to effort supporting, 184
  in Israel, 251
  in modernizing authoritarian regimes, 119
  in Nigeria, 126
Nations
  defined, 7, 150
  ethnicity or tribes vs., 156*b*
  nationalism and, 150–152
  states or governments vs., 39, 146
Native Americans
  cultural protection from larger U.S. society, 172, 609
  European colonialists and, 48, 65
  nation vs. tribe designation, 156*b*
  in Peru and Guatemala, national identity issues and, 49
  U.S. westward expansion and, 65, 67
NATO, Afghan government and, 57–58
Natural monopolies, 195
Nazi Party (Germany), 7, 71, 116–118, 153
Negro, terminology for, 173. *See also* African Americans
Nehru, Jawaharlal
  bureaucracy under, 289
  democracy and secularism under, 623
  dominance of, 358
  as INC head and prime minister, 83, 256
  regional groups and institutions and, 299
Neighborhood effects in Africa vs. Asia, 515
Neoclassical theory, Asian crisis and, 505–506
Neocolonialism in Africa and Asia, 31. *See also* Postcolonial countries
Neocorporatism
  in Germany, 347–348, 350–351, 498
  pluralism vs., 332–335, 333*f*
Neofascism, 118, 527
Neofundamentalism, 133

Neoliberalism/neoliberal policies.
   See also Structural adjustment
      programs
   in Africa vs. other regions,
      514–515, 516
   in Brazil, 527–529, 563
   in Chile, 227–228
   democratization and economic
      reform using, 447
   in Egypt, 400
   export-oriented growth, 502,
      504–505
   human capital and, 203*b*
   in India, 288–292, 361, 524–525
   infrastructure and, 203*b*
   in Iran, 532
   in Latin America, 506–511,
      517–518
   monetarist policy and, 201
   in Nigeria, 234
   opposition to social policies,
      543
   SAPs and, 501–502
   social policy and, 553
   success of, 239
Neopatrimonalism/neopatrimo-
      nial regimes
   characteristics, 122–123
   corruption in, 291*b*
   coups d'etat and, 428
   in Ghana, 453–454
   globalization and, 513, 515*b*
   modernizing authoritarian
      regimes as, 137
   in Nigeria, 122, 125–127,
      234–235, 471, 510
   structural adjustment program
      and, 202*b*
   transition to democracy in
      Africa and, 450
Netanyahu, Binyamin, 252
Netherlands
   child allowances in, 544
   as first modern federal system,
      292
   multicultural policies in, 622
   same-sex marriage status in, 647
New Deal (U.S.), 66, 210–213,
      344–345, 558
New developmentalism (Brazil),
      502
New Economic Policy (Russia),
      113, 138
New Frontier Party (NFP, Japan),
      354
"New Labour" Party (UK), 284,
      341
Newly-independent countries.
      See Postcolonial countries

New Partnership for Africa's
      Development (NEPAD), 517
New Public Management (NPM)
      theory, 284, 287, 290
New Public Service (NPS), 284
New Republic (Brazil), 74
Newspapers. *See* Mass communica-
      tions; Press
New York City
   mosque near World Trade
      Center site, 614–615
   Stock Exchange, *195*
New Zealand
   deindustrialization in, 488
   NPM and bureaucracy size in, 284
   women in power positions in,
      317*b*
Nguza Karl-i-Bond, 378
Nicaragua
   revolution of 1979 in, 434
   Samoza dynasty, 378–379
   Sandinista regime, 372
Niger, coup in (2010), 477
Niger Delta, 593–596
Niger Delta Development
      Commission (NDDC), 596
Nigeria
   authoritarian regimes in,
      390–394, 413–416
   Biafra and, 433
   co-optation in, 416–417
   coups d'etat in Brazil vs.,
      431–434
   debt forgiven, 235–236
   dictator's death as democracy
      opportunity, 379
   dictator's dilemma in, 414, 417
   economy of, 209
   ethnicity and religion, 165–168
   government employment in, 233
   health care programs in,
      540–541*t*, 570–571
   international investors and, 206
   military regimes in, 120, 390,
      392, 414–415
   neopatrimonial rule in, 122,
      125–127, 510
   neopatrimonial transition,
      469–474
   north-south schism, 88
   oil
      corruption, and dependence
         on, *232*, 232–234
      environmental justice, and
         sustainable development
         in, 593–596
      as exporter, 235*b*
   poverty and social insurance in,
      563

   president's death in office, 271
   removed from British Common-
      wealth, 393
   shifting identity politics in,
      165–168, 183
   Sierra Leone rebels and, 59
   state formation, 87–90
   timeline history of military
      intervention in, 391*b*
   tribes or ethnic groups in, 156*b*
   as weak state, 232–236, 237–238
Nigerian Bar Association, 415
Nigerianization policies, 233–234
Nigerian Labor Congress, 415
Nigerian Union of Journalists, 415
Night of the Long Knives
      (Germany, 1934), 117
9/11 attacks. *See* September 11,
      2001, attacks
Nineteenth Amendment, 317*b*
Nissan company, 223, 225
Nixon, Richard, 559
Niyazov, Saparmurat, 395
Nobel Peace Prize
   Gore as co-winner (2007), *587*
   for human rights, 640, 643
   Intergovernmental Panel on
      Climate Change Report
      (2007), 582, *587*
   for microfinance, 502
Nongovernmental organizations
      (NGOs)
   in China, 384, 406, 591–592
   social insurance system in
      Germany and, 554
   women
      in Iran, 643
      women's issues, 632–633
Non-indigenes (non-indigenous
      people, Nigeria), 168
Non-Profit Organizations (NPOs,
      Japan), 356–357
Nonproperty holders, enfranchise-
      ment rules on, 343. *See also*
      Property rights
Norman, Wayne, 610
Norman invasion (1066), 62–63
Normative theories, 12, 15, 609
Norris, Pippa, 337
North, Douglass, 55
North America. *See also* Canada;
      United States
   deindustrialization in, 488
   destruction of Native American
      states and empires in, 48
   political ideologies and regime
      types in, 138
   secularism in, 616
   social capital in, 326

North American Free Trade Agreement (NAFTA), 215, *229*, 230–231
Northern Ireland. *See also* Ireland
consociationalism in, 158–159
devolved institutions of, 295
nationalist party in, 341
religious conflicts in, 158
Northern People's Congress (Nigeria), 166
North Korea
air pollution from China in, 592
communism in, 115
personality cult in, 395
repression of civil society in, 397
Norway
same-sex marriage status in, 647
women in power in, *317b*
NPM. *See* New Public Management
Nuclear capabilities in Iran, 81, 413
Nyerere, Julius, 121–122

O

Obama, Barack
antiblack hate crimes during presidency of, 177
auto industry bailouts, 214
climate change agreements, 584
Defense of Marriage Act and, 652
domestic policy agenda, 189
Don't Ask, Don't Tell repeal, 425, 651
electoral divisions in campaign, 345
environmental policies, 588
free trade and globalization promotion, 215
health care reforms, 577, *577*, 579–580
in India, *253*
Keynesian vs. monetarist policies, 210, 214–215
on Lula in Brazil, 455
online campaign, 345
presidency's impact on African Americans, 177
signing statements, 263
stimulus spending program, 214
troop reduction in Afghanistan, 57
U.S. racial politics, 171–178
victory speech, *172*
Obama, Michelle, *172*
Obasanjo, Olusegun, *469*
anticorruption drive by, 89, 474
Kaduna mafia and, 470–472

opposed Jonathan for election, 473
political parties and, 414–415
regional support for, 167
Obesity, as public health concern, 571
October Revolution (1917) in Russia, 113
O'Donnell, Guillermo, 124, 245–246, 431, 446
OECD (Organisation for Economic Co-operation and Development), 504, 557, 560, 566, 571
"Official Mogul" in Russia, *291b*
Ogawa, Akihiro, 357
Ogoni Bill of Rights (Nigeria), 595
Ogoni movement (Nigeria), 89, 167, 393, 595
Ohmae, Kenichi, 205
Oil Mineral Producing Areas Development Commission (OMPADEC, Nigeria), 596
Oil production/revenue
in Africa and Middle East, economic policies and, 517
in Brazil, 530
in China, 442
corruption/patronage and, 517
import-substitution industrialization and, 200–201
in Iran, 388–389, 391–392, 530–532
in Latin America, 510–511
in Mexico, 229–230, 461
in Nigeria, *232*
in Biafra, 89
civil war and, *165*, 166
economy and, 209, 232–234, 236, 393
environmental impact of, 593–596
ethnic tensions and, 167–168
military rule and, 125–126
non-benefit to locals, 87, *87*
Supreme Court on control of, 472
in Russia
economy and, 465
Putin's power and, 467–468
taxation for nonrenewable resource extraction, 584
in UK, 493
wealth as deterrent to democracy, *448b*
Oil spills, 593–594
Oil Stabilization Fund (OSF), Iran, 531
Okinawa, Japan, U.S. military base, 356

Oligarchs, 76, 269, *291b*, 467–468
Olmec people (Mexico), 77
Olympics (Summer 2008), *518, 590*
"One drop" rule, U.S. racial identification and, 172–173
One-party regimes/states. *See also* China, People's Republic of
in Africa, 375–376
characteristics, 120, 121
in China, 380
development of, 373
ethnic conflict and, 157
institutionalization in, 372
military leaders' role in, 372–373
party weaknesses in, 396–397
in sub-Saharan Africa (1970–2010), *392b*
O'odua People's Congress (Nigeria), 168
Opacity of political world, *13b*
Open-list proportional representation, 315, 457
Opium Wars (China), 84, 440
Ordinary People in Extraordinary Times (Bermeo), 447
Organisation for Economic Co-operation and Development (OECD), 504, 557, 560, 566, 571
Organization of Petroleum Exporting Countries (OPEC), *235b*
Organization of the Islamic Conference (OIC), 415
Ortega, Daniel, 373
Ortega, Humberto, 372–373
Ottoway, Maria, 127
Our Home Is Russia party, 466
Outcomes, rational choice theories and explanations for, 19
Outsourcing, 215
Oversloot, Hans, 465–467
Ozawa, Ichiro, *352*, 356
Ozawa, Terutumo, 515

P

Pacific countries, women in power in, *317b*
Pacts, 445, 450
Pahlavi, Mohammed Reza Shah, 81, 135. *See also* Shahs of Iran
Paid maternity leave, lack of, 557
Paige, Jeffery, 435–436
Pakistan
Kashmir independence conflict and, 626
Muslim ICS officer migration to, 289

Muslim League and, 625
as separate Muslim state, 83, 623
Palestinians, political identity of, 150
Pan-German League, 153
Papua New Guinea, no paid maternity leave, 557
Paraguay, Colorado Party in, 396
"Parallel parliaments" in Russia, 467
Pardo (mixed-race) group, Brazil, 179–182
Parental leave, 638
Parliamentarism/parliamentary systems
  Brazilian referendum on presidentialism vs., 457
  Britain and India as examples of, 253–257
  bureaucracy hypotheses testing for, 283
  in former British colonies, 272
  in Israel, 251–252
  location of countries using, 258*b*, 259*m*
  as model of democratic power, 249–257
  for new democracies, 450–451
Parliamentary Front for Freedom of Sexual Expression, Brazil, 654
Parliamentary immunity, 376
Parliamentary sovereignty, 109
Parliaments. *See also* Members of parliament (MPs)
  European, 220, 341
  in Germany, 276
  in India, *82*
  in Iran
    cabinet ministers approved by, 388
    clergy as members, 386
    Majlis, 136, 389, 409–410, 413
    women in, 642, 644
  in Japan, 68, 352–354–355
  in Russia, 268, 465, 639
  in Tanzania, 121
  in UK, 108–109, 249–257, 314*t*
    devolution, 110
Participation. *See also* Political institutions; *specific participatory opportunities*
  in authoritarian regimes, 372, 374, 379, 394–399, 417–418
  in Brazil, 460
  in China, 380, 385, 402–408
  civil society and, 364–365
  democratic deepening and, 446
  effective governing and, 362–363

electoral systems and, 363–364
by identity groups, 608–609
interest group pluralism in U.S. and, 345–346
in Iran, 386
under Nigeria's military regimes, 413–416
political, 9
political institutions and shaping of, 309–312
proportional representation electoral systems and, 314–316
representation, power and, 362
in Russia, 637–638
in UK, 620
Participatory budgeting (PB, Brazil), 460
Participatory democracy, 107*b*
Partido Acción Nacional (PAN, Mexico), 79, 131, 627–628
Partido de la Revolución Democrática (PRD, Mexico), 131
Partido Revolucionario Institucional (PRI, Mexico), *79*
  anticlericalism stand, 627–628
  on Clouthier's death, 462
  formation and legitimacy of, 78–79
  reformation of, 463
  semi-authoritarianism under, 129–131, 394–397
Partisanship, declining, 321, 324*b*
Party-centric semi-authoritarianism, 129
Party loyalty vs. patronage, 458
Party of National Action (PAN). *See* Partido Acción Nacional
Party of Social Democracy (PDS, Germany), 349
Party of the Democratic Revolution (PRD, Mexico), 131, 461–462, 628
Party of the Mexican Revolution (PRM), 129
Party systems. *See also* Multiparty systems; Political parties
  in Brazil after 1964 coup, 431
  characteristics, 323–327
  defined, 319
  democratic rule and, 329
  electoral systems and, 312
  in France, 327–328
Pashtun, 56–57
Pasquino, Pasquale, 275
Pateman, Carole, 630
Paternity leave, 632
Patriarchy, 31

Patrimonial regimes, 121. *See also* Neopatrimonialism/ neopatrimonial regimes
Patronage, political
  in Africa, 513
  in Brazil
    corruption and, 458
    federalism and, 297, 457
    Law of Fiscal Responsibility and, 297
    party loyalty vs., 458
    politics of, 264
  development under, 509
  executive appointments to bureaucracy and, 280
  in India, 358, 523, 525–526
  in Iran, 532
  in Japan, 353–354
  in Mexico, 394–395
  in Nigeria, 390–391, 393–394, 471–472
  oil production/revenues and, 517
  in Russia, 467
  in Turkey, 512
  U.S. political parties and, 343–344
Patron-client relationships
  in Africa power-sharing, 28, 450
  in authoritarian regimes, 389–399, 417
  capitalist investment risks with, 515
  in China, 403
  co-optation in authoritarian regimes using, 372–373, 375–376, 395–396, 399, 416–418
  defined, 30
  informal participation and, 337–338
  in Iran, 389, 412
  in Japan, 353
  in Kenya, 398
  in neopatrimonial regimes, 122
  in Nigeria
    corrupt economy and, 234
    ethnic groups and, 166
    participation and survival by, 416
  in Russia, 468
  in sub-Saharan Africa, 398
  weak formal institutions and, 338
  in Zaire, 377–378
Peace of Westphalia (1648), 47
Peak associations, 332, 333*f*, 334–335, 350, 498

Pearl Harbor, Japanese attack on, 68
Peasants
    Chinese revolution (1911–1949) and, 440, 442
    social movements in India by, 358
Pedro I (Prince of Portugal), 73
Pedro II (Emperor of Brazil), 73
Pekkanen, Robert, 356
Pelé, 181
Pelosi, Nancy, 317b
Pempel, T. J., 225
Pensions. *See* Retirement benefits
People Power movement (Philippines), 444
People's courts (China), 383
People's Democratic Party (PDP, Nigeria), 470–471, 474
Per capita incomes, state failures and, 52–53b
Pereira, Luiz Carlos Bresser, 502
Perestroika (Soviet Union), 114
Perfect information, 194
"Perils of presidentialism," 450
Perot, Ross, 326
Perry, Matthew, 68
Persia, 80. *See also* Iran
Personalist coups (Nigeria), 476
Personalist regimes
    African, controls on military institutions in, 426
    bureaucracies in, 376–377, 418
    characteristics, 120
    corruption in, 291b
    elections in, 396
    institutionalization in, 372
    under Mao, 380
    in Nigeria, 126
    political parties of, 396
    in Russia under Putin, 468
    security apparatus for, 372
    succession in, 378–379
    weak political institutions of, 396, 398, 416–417
    in Zaire, 377–378
Personality cults, 380, 395, *403*
Peru
    indigenous people, percentage of population, 180b
    Native American marginalization in, 49
Perverse incentives, 559
Peso, valuation of, 230
Petersen, Roger, 147, 161–163
Petróleos Mexicanos (PEMEX), 229
Pharmaceuticals, 573
Phenotype, 147

Philip (Prince of England), *8*
Philippines
    currency valuations in, 485
    East Asian financial crisis and, 505
    People Power movement in, 444
Pierson, Christopher, 40
Pincus, Steven, 438
Pinochet, Augusto, 227–228, 446, 507
Pittsburgh, Pennsylvania, pollution problem in, 582
Plessy v. Ferguson (1896, U.S.), 172
Pluralism/pluralist theory. *See also* Interest group pluralism
    on division of power, 27–30, 32, 33t
    effectiveness questions, 239–240
    elite theory vs. on governing institutions, 304
    identity politics and, 185
    neocorporatism vs., 332–335
    on public policy, 599
    on state involvement in the market, 238, 240
Plurality electoral systems, 259, 313, 352
Poland
    revolution from above, 440
    revolution of 1989–1990 in, 434
Polanyi, Karl, 196
Police brutality, 456
Policymaking, 10
Polish Americans, assimilation of, 173
Politburo, 113, 380–381
Politburo Standing Committee (PSC), China's, 380–381
Political accountability of institutions, 245. *See also* Accountability
Political actors, 12, 18. *See also* Individual motivation
Political appointees, 281. *See also* Patronage, political
Political behavior
    in comparative politics, 16–17
    culture and ideology and, 21–25, 29t
    cultures and structures, 29b
    explanations for, 16–18, 29t
    individual motivation for, 18–20, 28t
    structuralism and, 26, 29t
Political culture
    Asian economic miracle vs. African malaise and, 514–515
    constructivism and, 147–148

corporate elite power in U.S. democracy theory, 34b
coups in West Africa and, 426–427b
defined, 21
democratization and, 425, 446–447
modernist theory of, 21–22, 29t, 476
political ideology theories, 24–25
postmodernist theory of, 23, 29t
primordialism and, 147
for transferring power, coups d'etat and, 427–428
U.S., women in power positions and, 317b
welfare states and, 549
Political development, as hot button issue, 6–7
Political discourse, postmodernist study of, 23
Political economy, 10, 197. *See also* Keynesian economic theory; Monetarist economic theory
Political goods, adequate, 51
Political identity. *See* Identity politics
Political ideology
    of authoritarian regimes, 372
    of Brazilian major parties, 457–458
    characteristics, 24–25, 29t
    communism, 100b
    fascism, 115–116
    Hindutva, of BJP (India), 625
    liberal democracy, 100b, 103–104
    major types of, 100–101b
    modernizing authoritarianism. *See* Modernizing authoritarianism
    as motivation for revolution, 434–435
    outcome of revolutions and, 439–440
    political behavior and, 18
    proportional representation electoral systems and, 319
    on public policy, 600
    regimes, citizens and, 95–96, 100–103, 100b
    theocracy, 132–134
Political instability, 511
Political institutions. *See also* Governing institutions; Institutionalization; Weak political institutions
    Asian economic miracle vs. African malaise and, 514–515

in Brazil, 460
bureaucracy, 280–281
civil society, 329–337
CMEs vs. LMEs, 491
continuity of, 303
defined, 26
electoral systems, 312–319,
    318*m*
executives and legislatures, 248*t*,
    249–252
federalism, 292–301
identity groups using to
    approach the state, 656
India from dominant party
    to multiparty democracy,
    357–362
informal, 109, 122–123
institutionalization in authori-
    tarian regimes, 371
Japan's dominant party system,
    weak civil society, and
    electoral reform, 352–355
judiciary, 273–280
of modern states, power and
    importance of, 245
Muslims in India and France
    and, 656
negative public opinion on, 335
neocorporatism in Germany
    under threat, 348
parliamentarism as democratic
    model of, 249–250
participation and, 310
party systems, 323–327
political behavior and, 25–27, 29*t*
political parties, 319–323, 329
presidentialism as democratic
    model of, 258–265
representation and, 310
semipresidentialism as demo-
    cratic model of, 265–269,
    266*f*
structures and contexts for, 303
timeline on development of,
    330–334, 330–334*f*
U.S. two-party, pluralist system
    evolution, 343
Political liberalization, 445–446
Politically generated roles in
    market economy, 196–197,
    204*b*
Political machines, 344
Political mobilization
    China's revolutions and,
        441–442
    in U.S. using Internet, 345–346
Political opportunity structures,
    and Muslim policy adoption
    in Europe, 617

Political parties. *See also* Party
    systems; *specific parties*
in authoritarian regimes,
    372–373, 374–375*b*,
    394–398, 418–419
in Brazil
    coalitions among, 458–460
    federalism and, 297, 457
characteristics and classification
    of, 319–323
democratic rule and, 329
electoral systems and, 312
European ideologies and,
    320–321, 322*b*
fragmentation and individual-
    ization of electorate and,
    336–337
in France, 327–328
functions in democracies, 319
in Germany
    abstract judicial review and,
        277–278
    after World War II, 348
    new social movements and,
        349
    reunification and, 349
in Ghana, 452–454
inclusion guarantees for, 609
in India, 301–302
in Iran, 136, 408, 410
in Japan, 69, 352–357
in Nigeria, 167, 414–415, 432,
    469–471
opposition, in transition to
    democracy, 116, 451
political participation through, 9
proportional representation
    and, 314–316, 315*t*
reasons to join, 320
in Russia, 76, 465–466
in UK, 253, 340–341
under- or over-representation in
    single-member districts of,
    314, 342–343
in U.S., 64, 262–263, 343
Political power questions, 17–18
Political rights
    citizenship and, 98
    of LGBT community in U.S.,
        649–652
    of women. *See* Women/women's
        rights
Political saliency
    of identity groups, 146
    of Nigerian regional, ethnic, and
        religious groups, 165–168
    of race, 171
Political science, defined, 10
Political socialization

defined, 21
democratic norms of military
    personnel and, 425
historical institutions and, 26
Political violence, 73–74,
    438–439*b*. *See also* Coups
    d'etat; War
Political will, structural adjust-
    ment program success and,
    201–202, 202–203*b*
Political Woman (Kirkpatrick), 629
Politicians' restraint on bureau-
    crats, 282–283
Politics, defined, 10
Politics of recognition, 155.
    See also Recognition
Politics of survival, 377
Pollution. *See also* Air pollution;
    Environment
    in China, 582, 584–586
    control policies, 583–584
    as market failure, 596–597
    U.S. environmental policy and,
        586–589
Polyarchy, 107*b*
Popular opinion, abstract judicial
    review in Germany and, 278
Popular sovereignty, 98. *See also*
    Sovereign states/sovereignty
Populism
    in Brazil, 73–74, 431, 455, 562
    clientelism in Latin America,
        323
    defined, 323
    in India, 524
    in Iran, 531
    in Turkey, 512
Porfiriato (Time of Porfirio),
    78, 229
Pork-barrel politics, 264
Portfolio investment equity, 487
Portfolios, in parliamentary
    systems, 252
Portugal
    colonial Brazil and, 72–73, 296
    colonies, code law in, 273
    economic crisis in Great
        Recession, 204, 221
    emigrants to Brazil, 179
    fascism in, 118
    same-sex marriage and, 647
    semipresidentialism in, 268*b*
Positive discrimination, 361
Postal saving system (Japan),
    224, 226
Postcolonial countries. *See also*
    specific countries
    civil society strength and effec-
        tiveness in, 358

Postcolonial countries *(cont.)*
dictatorships and pluralism in, 28
import-substitution industrialization of, 201
inherited political institutions of, 258*b*
interest groups' emergence in, 331
LGBT movements in, 647
modernizing authoritarianism in, 119, 138
obstacles and challenges for, 49–51
as quasi-states, 56
ruling class in, 31–32
secularism in, 616
state failures among, 52*b*
weaknesses in one-party systems of, 397
in West Africa, coups in, 426–427*b*
women in, 629–631
Post-communist countries. *See also specific countries*
in case studies, 35
judicial review in, 276
recognition of women's rights in, 656
semipresidentialism used in, 267–269
Postindustrial service economies and political party realignments, 324*b*
Postindustrial societies and globalization, 488
Postmaterialism, 22–23, 324*b*
Post-military dictatorship democratic countries, 35. *See also* China, People's Republic of; Russia
Postmodernist theory of political culture, 23
Postnational citizenship, 98–99
Poverty
in Africa, 513–514, 516–517
amelioration in Europe and U.S., 196–197
in Brazil, 460, 526–527, 529, 561
in Chile, 228
in China, 440–441, 518
crime and, 543
democracy vs. authoritarianism and, 511
in Germany, 557
in Ghana, 452–453
in India, 83–84, 523–525
in Iran, 442, 530–531
in Latin America, 180*b*, 507
market failure and, 539
minorities in U.S., 174
National Poverty Line statistics, 209*t*
in Nigeria, 89, 236, 415
political and social rights for women and, 149*b*
in Russia, 465, 638
social policy for reducing, 539
in Sweden, 546–547
in UK among Muslims, 619
in U.S., 212, 558–560
in welfare states by type, 551, 552*f*
women's movement and, 630
Powell, Bingham, 247, 270, 363
Powell, Enoch, 618
Power
defined, 10
elite theories on division of, 30–33
global, 66
informal, in U.S. presidential system, 262
limitations of, in modern state, 91–92
participation, representation and, 362
pluralist theories on division of, 27–30, 32
sovereignty enforcement and, 43
of subnational governments, federalism and, 293–295, 298
transfer mechanisms, coups d'etat and, 428
The Power Elite (Mills), 31
Power in Movement (Tarrow), 98
Pragmatist faction (Iran), 412
Precautionary principle, for EU environmental risk avoidance, 583
Predatory lending, 194
Preexisting medical conditions and health insurance, 579
Premier (China), 381
Preschool programs, 545, 638
Presidentialism
in Brazil, 263–265, 457
countries using, 258*b*, 259*m*, 302
defined, 258
failure, causes of, 272
as model of democratic power, 258–265, 270
for new democracies, 450–451
in Nigeria, 469–474
parliamentarism vs., 271–272, 457
"perils of presidentialism," 450
presidential systems, 260*f*, 283, 302
in Russia's semipresidential system, 268
in UK, 255
in U.S., 261–263
welfare states and, 549
Presidential representatives (Russia), 300
Presidents
in Brazil, 261–265
in China, *379*, 381–382
in France's semipresidential system, 266–267
in India's parliamentary system, 255–256
in Iran, 135–136, 386, 388
in parliamentary systems, 250
in U.S., 261–265
President's Rule (India), 298–299
Press
in Iran, 136
scandal in Japan, 288
self-censorship in Mexico, 130
PRI. *See* Pardido Revolucionario Institucional
Price, Melanye, 174
Primary elections (U.S.), 320, 344
Prime ministers (PMs)
defined, 249
in France's semipresidential system, 266–267
in India, 251–252, 255–257
in parliamentary systems, 249–257
in Russia's semipresidential system, 267–269
in UK, 109–110, 254
Prime Minister's Office (India), 256
Primordialism, 147, 156*b*, 184
Principal-agent problem, bureaucratic professionalism and, 281
Printing as precursor to nationalism, 151
Privacy/private aspects of life
U.S. sodomy laws and right to, 650
women's movement and defined, 631
Private insurance
in Germany, 572
in UK, 575
in U.S., 577–578
Privatization
in Brazil, 528
in China, 519–521

of government-owned industries, 201, 218
in India, 524
in Iran, 531
in Japan, 226
New Public Management and,
284
in Russia, 465
in UK, 493–494
Probit (statistics technique),
448*b*
Procurator, role in China's courts
of, 383
Production, Marx on mode of, 111
Professionalization, 280–281
Progressive movement (U.S.),
344, 346
Progressivism, 326
Proletariat, 25, 30–31, 111, 113
Property rights, 104–105
for LGBT people in Brazil, 654
modern state, market economies and, 191, 192, 202*b*
women's legal rights and, 608,
632, 637
Proportional representation (PR)
electoral system. *See also*
Mixed electoral systems
defined, 314
effective governance and,
362–363
election of women and, 315,
317*b*
in European parliaments, 258*b*
in France, 328
in Israel, 251
in Mexico, 131
multiparty systems and, 328
participation, representation
and, 314–316
party systems and, 327
Sweden's parliamentary election
(2006), 314, 315*t*
Proposition 8 (California), 652
Protectionism, 229
Protestantism
evangelical, in Brazil, 655
Indonesia's recognition of, 616
Luther and, 70
in Mexico, 628
in Northern Ireland, 158–159
social welfare attitudes in, 548
Protestant Reich Church, 118
Protestant work ethic, 534
Protests
in Brazil, military killing of
student, 123
in China
Falun Gong, 407

petrochemical plant construc-
tion, 592
Tiananmen Square, 86, 407
Xinjiang region, 407
in Germany, Hartz IV reforms,
554
in India
Gujarat train attack, 622
Shah Bono's divorce, 624–625
in Iran
mandatory veiling, 642
Mousavi's followers, 409, 410,
410
in Nigeria, Saro-Wiwa execution, 393
Provinces, as subnational governmental units, 292
Provisional decrees (PDs), of
Brazilian presidents, 264–265
Provisional Irish Republican Army
(IRA), 158–159, 438–439*b*
Pro-worker policies, 22
Prussia. *See also* Germany
German Confederation mem-
ber, 70
state-based nationalism in, 153
Przeworski, Adam, 447, 448–449*b*,
509–511
Psychological theories
authoritarian leaders and, 418
identity politics and, 184
for individual motivation, 19–20
Public displays of support, by
authoritarian regimes,
394–395, *403*
Public goods, state provision of, 192
Public housing in UK, 494
Public option system and health
care reform, 579
Public policy theories, 599–600
Punjab state, India
agriculture in, 524
Akali Dal in, 359–360
Puppet states, external sovereignty
absent in, 41
Purpose-built capitals, 39
Putin, Vladimir, *267, 296*
consolidation of rule, 465
corruption under, 467
federalism and, 300
as PM in Medvedev's presidency,
267, 269, 468
political parties and, 467
presidential powers used by,
268–269
semi-authoritarian regime
under, 76
women's rights in Russia and,
637, 639–670

Putnam, Robert, 336–337
Puyi (Chinese emperor), 41

Q
Qajar Empire, Iran, 80
Qom, Iran, demonstration in, 443
Quadros, Jânio, 123, 430
Quality of life, 22, 568
Quantitative easing (printing
money), 214
Quantitative statistical techniques,
13*b*, 14
Quasi-states, 56
Queer. *See* Lesbian, gay, bisexual,
and transgender (LGBT)
people
Question Time, for British Parlia-
ment, 255
Quotas
for Muslims in India, 625
women in elected positions,
315, 317*b*, 635, 639
Quran, 132
Qutb, Sayyid, 133

R
Race/racial groups. *See also* Civil
rights; Minority rights
American union movement
and, 238
antidiscrimination law in UK
on, 619–620
in Brazil, 178–182
defined, 170
discrimination/segregation
policies, 335–336
enfranchisement rules on, 343
fascism in Germany and, 116–
118, 153
gay rights movement in U.S.
and, 650
gender symbols for boundaries
of, 149*b*
identity politics and, 170–171
inclusion policies and, 605,
606–607*t*
interest groups on rights for,
331
political identity and, 143, 146,
148
racial democracy in Brazil, 180
racial elite, 31–32
U.S. politics and, 171–178, 176*t*
welfare states and divisions in,
548
women's movement and, 630
Race Relations Act (1976, UK),
619–620
Race to the bottom, 581–582

Racial intermarriage
  in Brazil, 179, *179*, 182
  in U.S., 177
Radical faction of Islam. *See*
  Islamic terrorists
*The Radicalism of the American
  Revolution* (Wood), 436–437*b*
Radicals (in democracy), 445
Rajya Sabha (India's upper house),
  298
Rama, Lord (Hindu deity), 360
Rao, Narasimha, 256
Rashtriya Swayamsevak Sangh
  (RSS, India), 360
Rational-actor analysis
  of authoritarianism, 418–419
  on coups d'etat, 429
  on democratization, 445
  on Germany's judiciary system,
    278
  identity politics and, 185
  on inclusion and conflicting
    values, 658
  on modern states and market
    economies, 191–192
  on participation in democra-
    cies, 309–310
  patronage vs. party loyalty,
    458
  for political behavior, 18–19
  on political ideology, 25
  on self-interest of bureaucrats,
    281, 284
Rational-choice theory
  on authoritarian regimes, 375*b*
  capitalist economic growth
    explained by, 191
  defined, 19–20
  effectiveness questions,
    239–240
  on formal rules of power, 301
  on globalization, 534
  identity politics and, 184–185
  instrumentalism, 147
  on political behavior, 304
  politicians' restraint on
    bureaucrats, 282–283
  on public policy, 600
  on regime change, 476
  regime type choices, 103*b*
  on Russia, 468
  security dilemma theory, 160
Rational-legal legitimacy, 44
Rawlings, Jerry, 452–453
Reagan, Ronald
  economic policy changes and,
    271
  economic reform under, 493,
    495

election of, 343
environmental policies under,
  587
"family values" and, 23
monetarist policies used by, 198,
  212–213
New Public Management and,
  284, 303
Republican ideology after, 345
signing statements, 263
Thatcher, compared to, 303
welfare reform proposals of, 559
Real Plan (Brazil), 527–528
Rebellions, 48, 399. *See also* Civil
  wars; Coups d'etat
Recognition. *See also* Identity
  politics; State recognition
  of ethnic groups, 155–158
  of gay rights, 645–646
  of identity groups, 608
  politics of, 155
  of racial groups, 171
Recruit Corporation scandal,
  Japan (1988), 286–287
Recycling, 589
Red brigades, China's, 403
Red vs. expert role in communist
  China, 404
"Red-Green Alliance," in Germany,
  349
Reform Act (1832, UK), 109
Reformist ascendency (Iran),
  388, 411
Reform Party (U.S.), 326
Regime change
  in Brazil, democratic deepening
    and, 455–460
  coups d'etat. *See* Coups d'etat
  democratization, 444, 451*m*,
    454–455, 475
  images of, 474
  in Nigeria, 471
  overview, 424*t*
  political development and, 7
  questions about, 8–9
  revolutions, 434–444, 436–437*b*,
    439*b*, 475–476
  in Russia, 464–468
  state existence and, 95
  theories on, 476
Regimes
  defined, 95
  democratic governments vs., 7
  economic growth by type,
    508–511
  governments vs., 95
  major types, 7–8, 100–101*b*
  modern, ideological justifica-
    tion for, 99

relationships to citizen rights and
  civil society among, 100*b*
  strength of, 375*b*
  welfare state types, 549
Regional inequality, 229
Regions, as subnational governmental units, 292
Regression analysis
  for bureaucracy hypotheses,
    282–283
  in health care study, 568–569
  political party realignment
    theories and, 324–325*b*
Reich (nation), 153
Reichsbank, Germany, 211*b*
Reichstag (legislature), Germany,
  117
Relative deprivation of identity,
  156, 184
Religion. *See also* Religious groups;
  Religious tensions; *specific
  religions*
  decline of as cause of national-
    ism, 151
  freedom of
    in case countries, 657
    in U.S., 64–65
  fundamentalism as political
    ideology, 22
  gender symbols for boundaries
    of, 149*b*
  as group identity, 157, 162–163
  political identity and, 143, 183
  political salience in Nigeria of,
    167
Religious groups. *See also* Religious
  tensions; Secular states/
  secularism
  challenge to multiculturalism in
    UK by, 618–622
  demands for autonomy by, 608
  inclusion policies and, 605,
    606–607*t*
  in India, 82–84, 622–626
  in Japan, 356
  as minorities, federalism and
    protection of, 295
  persecution of, in UK, 63
  rational-choice analysis of, 19
  recognition of, 157, 162–163
Religious political parties (Israel),
  251–252
Religious tensions
  in former Yugoslavia, 162
  in India, 83–84, 360
  in Iran, 443
  in Nigeria, 89, 166–168, 415
  in 19th century Europe, 326
  in Northern Ireland, 158

Remington, Thomas F., 468
Renan, Ernest, 150
Reno, Janet, 43
Rent-seeking, 285
Reporters without Borders, 384
Representation. *See also* Political
    institutions; Recognition
  civil society and, 364–365
  effective governing and,
      362–363
  electoral systems and, 312–313,
      362–363
  in European parliaments, 258*b*
  for identity groups, 608–609
  participation, power and, 362
  political institutions and
      shaping of, 309–312
  regime type and, 9
  in upper chambers of federal
      systems, 294–295
  of women in Russia, 637–638
  women's movements on,
      635–636
Representation of the People Act
    (1867, UK), 109
Representative democracy, 104.
    See also Liberal democracy
Repression
  in authoritarian regimes,
      372–373, 375
  under Bismarck in Germany, 70
  in Brazil, 73–74, 124
  in China, 85–86, 385, 404,
      407–408
  of civil society in authoritarian
      regimes, 397–398
  as expensive for dictators, 372
  by hardliners during transition
      to democracy, 445
  in Iran, 133, 136, 386, 409, 411,
      413, 443
  in Mexico, 463
  military role in authoritarian
      regimes for, 373
  in Nigeria, 125–126, 390, 415
  in Russia, 113, 467
Reproductive rights, 630–631
Republicanism and American
    Revolution, 437*b*
Republican Party (U.S.), 65,
    343–345, 579
Republicans in Northern Ireland,
    158
Republic of China (Taiwan)
  developmental state and indus-
      trialization in, 503–504
  East Asian miracle and, 201,
      503–504
  formation on mainland, 86

health care study in, 569
inequality in, 505
investments in mainland China
    by, 522
as Japanese colony, 68
recognized as government of
    China, 86
U.S. foreign aid for, 515
under Sun Yat-sen, 441
Research methods/projects
  defined, 12–14
  normative questions and, 15
  variable analysis, 15–16*b*
Residential segregation, 619
Resource curse, 53*b*, 58, 60, 92
Resource mobilization theory, and
    Muslim policy adoption in
    Europe, 617
Retirement benefits
  in Brazil, 562
  demographic changes and
      pressure on, 545, 552–553
  in Germany, 556
  as social insurance, 544–545
  in Sweden, 546–547
"Return to democracy" promises
    (Nigeria), 390
Reunification, West and East Ger-
    many, 218, 278, 349, 554–555
Reuter, Ora John, 468
Revolution, terminology for,
    436*b*
Revolutionary Guard (Iran),
    136, 385–390, 409, 412–413,
    531–532
Revolutionary parties, one-party
    states and, 373
Revolutions
  American, debate over, 436–437*b*
  in China vs. Iran, 440–443
  common elements of, 14
  communist, in Russia (1917), 76
  definitions and characteristics,
      434–444, 476
  European (1848), 48
  motivations for, 435
  outcomes of, 439–440
  regime changes through, 9
  Rwanda independence, 169
  terrorism vs., 438–439*b*
Revolutions from above, 435, 475
Revolutions from below, 435, 475
Right-wing extremists. *See also*
    Nationalist Party
  in Europe, 320, 322*b*
Riker, William, 292
Rio de Janeiro, Brazil
  environmental conference
      (1992), 584

investment and growth in, 527
Portuguese colonists in, 73
whitening policy in, 179–180
Risk assessment, of environmental
    damage, 583
Road maintenance in African
    authoritarian regimes, 373
Robinson, James, 103*b*
Roett, Riordon, 431
Romania
  democracy failure in, 440
  revolution (1989–1990), 434
Roman law, code law and, 273
Roosevelt, Franklin Delano
  New Deal and, 66, 211–212, 343
  presidential power expansion
      under, 262
  social insurance programs of,
      558
  two-term presidency and, 25
Rosenbluth, Frances, 275, 288
Rostow, Walt, 119
Rotberg, Robert, 51
Rousseau, Jean-Jacques, 103
Rousseff, Dilma, *261*, 265, 459,
    529
Roy, Olivier, 133
Ruffo Appel, Ernesto, 462
Rule by theft, in Zaire under
    Mobutu, 377–378
Rule of law
  in authoritarian regimes, 376,
      380, 415
  in Brazil, 456, 460
  democratic deepening and, 446
  precursors, in China, 380
  in Russia, 468
  state strength and, 55
Ruling class
  bourgeoisie as, 30–31
  ideology and dominance by, 24
  in postcolonial societies, 31–32
Ruling entities. *See also* Power
  elite theories on, 30–33
  environmental issues and, 596
  individual as state in absolutist
      states, 47
  individual or group power as,
      27–33
  pluralist theories on, 27–30
  venal, weak, or failed states and,
      55, 58–60
Runaway bureaucracy (Eastern
    Europe), 284–285
Rushdie, Salman, 620
Russia. *See also* Soviet Union
  asymmetrical federal system in,
      296, 299–300
  as autocratic regime, 9

Russia (cont.)
  centralized federal system in, 296
  Chechen rebels and, 161–162
  communism in, 112–115
  communist revolution in (1917), 434–435
  coup attempt (1991), 464, 464
  currency valuations in, 485
  federalism in, 292–293, 296, 296, 299–302
  media in, 269
  as oil exporter, 235b
  Persian dependence on, 80
  presidential control of ministries in, 268
  regime type and characteristics, 138
  republic as term, 299–300
  revolution to democracy, 435
  as semi-authoritarian regime, 128, 269, 464–468
  semipresidentialism in, 267, 267–269
  strong state with weak rule of law, 74–77
  Tatarstan demands resolved, 161
  territory covered by, 40
  transition to semi-authoritarian rule, 464–468
  women through social and political transformation in, 636–640
Russian Communist Party, 113–114
Russian Federation, 299
Russia's Choice party, 466
Rwanda
  ancient hatreds in, 169
  border retention, 50
  election fraud in, 395
  genocide in, 143, 163, 168–169
  land ownership conflict in, 169
  Mobutu and, 378

S
Sachs, Jeffrey, 515–517
Sadat, Anwar, 399
Safavids, first Iranian empire and, 80
Saich, Tony, 407
Saint Petersburg, Russia, as federal city, 299
Salinas de Gortari, Carlos, 79, 130–131, 230–231, 461–462
Samba (Brazil), 180
Same-sex marriage
  assimilationist vs. liberationist approach, 646–647

  in Brazil, 652, 653, 654, 655
  by country, 647, 648m
  in Mexico, 628
  San Francisco demonstrations, 649
  in U.S., 651–652, 658
Samuels, David, 271
Samurai, Japanese, 68
Sandinista army (Nicaragua), 372–373
Sandstorms, 590
San Francisco, California, same-sex marriage and, 649
Santa Ana, Antonio López de, 627
Santiso, Carlos, 279
São Paulo, Brazil
  gay pride parade in, 652, 653, 655
  as industrialization hub, 72
  investment and growth in, 527
SAPs. See Structural adjustment programs
Sarkozy, Nicolas, 614
Saro-Wiwa, Ken, 89, 167, 393, 415, 470, 595
Sarrazin, Thilo, 154
Satanic Verses (Rushdie), 620
Saudi Arabia
  curriculum from in UK schools, 621
  Muslim organizations in UK and, 619
  September 11 attacks and, 5
  Sharia law in, 616
  women's rights in, 633–634
Scandals, mobile phone licenses in India, 290
Schattschneider, E. E., 319
Schatzberg, Michael, 23
Schedler, Andreas, 127
Schneider, Aaron, 297
Schröder, Gerhard, 218
Scientific method, 12–13, 13b
Scotland
  devolution in, 109–110, 295
  nationalist party in, 341
  unification into UK, 63
Scots, as ethnic group, 156b
SDP. See Social Democratic Party
Secessionist movements, 183
Second dimension of power, 10–11
Second face of power, 656
Second Republic (Nigeria), 126, 393, 433, 469
Second shift, for women, 630, 639
Secret police, 28, 443
Secularization (Iran), 133

Secular states/secularism
  in Europe, policy differences toward Muslims and, 617
  in India, 622–626
  Islamic headscarves in France and Turkey, 613–615
  modern states and, 629
  neutral states and, 616
  primary models of, 612–613
  types of, 657
  in UK, religious challenge to multiculturalism and, 618–622
  in U.S., and recognition and autonomy of religious groups and churches, 612–613
Security. See also Military power/regimes
  apparatus for Mobutu in Zaire, 378
  apparatus for personalist regimes, 372–373
  ethnic violence and, 160
  modern state, market economies and, 191–192
Segregation
  in Brazil, 182
  in India, 82, 358–361, 360
  in Northern Ireland, 158–159
  in Saudi Arabia, 633
  in South Africa, 31–32, 32, 182, 608
  in U.S., 173, 178, 182
Seko, Mobutu Sese, 53b
Self-expression values, 447
Self-genocide by Hutus, 169
Semi-authoritarianism/semi-authoritarian regimes
  in China, 408
  defined, 8
  democratic transition in, 446
  development of, 127–128
  in Egypt, 399–402
  elections in, 396–397, 451
  informal political institutions in, 127
  in Iran, 386
  in Mexico, 77, 79, 461
  parties in surviving to democracy, 397
  party-centric type, 129
  as political ideology and regime type, 101b
  in Russia, 76, 464–468
Semipresidentialism
  dangers in, 272
  defined, 265
  in France, 266–267, 268b

in Iran, 386
location of countries using, 258b, 259m
as model of democratic power, 258, 265–269, 266f
in nonelectoral and free electoral democracies, 266–269
in Russia, 267–269
Semiproportional electoral systems
defined, 316–318
in Germany, 316–318, 327, 348–349, 351
Senate (Brazil), 264, 297
Senate (U.S.)
autonomy from executive branch, 262
cap and trade system blocked, 588
election system for, 342, 342–343
federalism and, 294–295
Separation of powers, 104, 249, 258–263, 270–271. See also Federalism/federal systems
Sepoy Rebellion (India), 82
September 11, 2001, attacks, 5–6, 57–58, 423, 612, 621
Serbia
Croatia and Bosnia, conflict with, 157
cultural nationalism war, 157
language and ethnic conflict in Yugoslavia for, 155
Orthodox religion and, 162
Settlement patterns and ethnic violence, 160
Sexenio (six-year presidential term, Mexico), 130
Sexual apartheid. See also Segregation
in Saudi Arabia, 633
Sexual citizenship, 646
Sexually transmitted diseases, 571
Sexual orientation, 605, 606–607t, 608, 645–647, 655. See also Lesbian, gay, bisexual, and transgender people
Sexual relationships, 642
Sezer, Ahmet Necdet, 615
Shagari, Shehu, 433
Shahs of Iran, 80–81, 385, 389, 442–443, 641. See also Pahlavi, Mohammed Reza Shah
Shambaugh, David, 408
Shanghai, China, environmental protection commitment, 591
Sharia (Muslim law)
adherence to by Muslims, 132–133

Hanafi school of Sunnis and, 620
in India, 624
in Iran, 135, 388, 410
in Nigeria, 167–168, 473–474
in Saudi Arabia, 616
Shell Petroleum, 594–595
Sherman Antitrust Act of 1890 (U.S.), 211
Shiite Muslims, 5, 80, 134–136, 157, 386
Shipan, Charles, 275, 282–283
"Shock therapy" in Russia, 465
Shoguns, of Japan, 68
Short-term health care, 568
Shura, Muslim concept of, 132, 135–136
Siam. See Thailand
Sichuan Province earthquake (2008), 384
Sick leave policy, 546
Sickness Insurance Act (Germany), 571
Sierra Leone
children as soldiers, 59–60
as failed state, 51, 58–60
Sikhs, 83, 359, 626
Sikkim, 298
Silva, Benedita da, 181
Singapore and East Asian miracle, 201, 503–504
Singh, Manmohan, 526
Single, nontransferable vote (SNTV) system, 318, 352–353, 353b
Single case studies, 12–14
Single European Act (1987), 220
Single-member district (SMD) electoral system. See also Electoral districts; Mixed electoral systems; United Kingdom
alternative-vote systems and, 318
defined, 313
election of women in, 317b
geographical representation, 319
in Germany, 354
in Ghana, 452, 454
in Iran, 409
in Japan, 354
in Russia, 466
semiproportional, representation system and, 316
in U.S., 342
Single-payer health care system, 565, 579
Single Transferable Vote (STV), 159
Sinn Fein, 158–159

Skocpol, Theda, 345–346, 437
Slavery. See also Civil War (U.S.)
after American war of independence, 436b
in Brazil, 72–73, 178–179
in colonial North America, 65
European colonists and, 48
independent nations in Americas and, 49
modern legacy in U.S., 67
Nigeria and, 88
19th century U.S., 66, 172, 178
Smith, Anthony, 151
SNM (Somali National Movement), 45
SNTV (single, nontransferable vote), 318, 352–353, 353b
Sobels (soldier/rebels), of Sierra Leone, 59
Social capital
defined, 336–337
in UK, 346–347
in U.S., 345–347
Social citizenship, 105
Social classes, 25, 548–549. See also Elites; Ruling class
Social construction. See also Imagined communities
of ethnic groups, 155
of ethnic identity under colonialism in Nigeria, 165
in identity politics, 148
of races, 170, 175, 177, 179–182
Social contract theory, 104
Social democracy
defined, 107b
in India, 358
social policies in, 545
Social democratic parties, Keynesianism and, 198
Social Democratic Party (SDP)
in Europe, 320, 322b
in Germany
Agenda 2010 under Schröder, 218
health care equity concerns of, 572–573
opposition to Bismarck, 70–71
social insurance under, 555–556
support of social market economy, 348–350
Weimar government involvement, 217
social democratic welfare states and, 548
in Sweden, welfare state and, 546–547

Social democratic welfare states
characteristics of, 545–547
maternity leave and child care
in, 632
poverty reduction in, 598–599
share of national economy, 551
Social development/programs,
528–529
Social expenditures and GDPs,
550–551, 550–551*t*
Social groups, 610
Social inequality, 460
Social insurance
characteristics, 544–545
in Christian democratic welfare
states, 547–548
in Germany, 554–555
in liberal welfare states, 549
Social Insurance Law (China), 521
Socialism
in Africa, 121–122
in Chile, 227
Lenin on, 113
Marx on, 111
Socialist parties. *See also* Social
Democratic Party
in Chile, 228
in Europe, 320–321, 322*b*
in France, 328
in Germany, 217
Social market economy, 71, 209,
216–219, 236, 348
Social movements. *See also* Lesbian,
gay, bisexual, and transgender
people; Religious groups;
Student movements; Women/
women's rights
in authoritarian regimes,
397–398
in China, 405–406
civil society and, 329–330,
334–337
established interest groups and
rise of, 335–337, 341
in Germany, 347, 349–351
inclusion policies and, 608
Muslim policy in Europe and,
617
in Nigeria, 469–470
Social network technology,
326–327, 337
*Social Origins of Dictatorship and
Democracy* (Moore), 102*b*
Social policy. *See also* Welfare/
welfare reform
in Brazil, 510
in China, 521
comparative perspective on,
542–545

economic growth and, 550–551*t*
neoliberal development strategies and, 553
Social revolution
identity groups and, 608
Marx on, 110–111, 114, 435
purpose for, 439*b*
in U.S. after war of independence, 436–437*b*
women and, 631
Social revolution from below
(China), 442
Social rights
defined, 98
health care as, 564
Marshall on citizenship and, 98,
107*b*, 543, 608
for women in Middle East, 149*b*
Social roles (Russia), 637, 639
Social Security Act of 1935 (U.S.),
558–559
Social Security system (U.S.), 212,
215, 557–559
Social spending
in CMEs vs. LMEs, 491
health care quality, relationship
to, 568
in UK, 493–495
in U.S., 557–561
Social values, market failure and,
539–541
Social welfare system. *See also*
Welfare states
European, EU constitution and,
222
in Germany, 70, 216–218, 497,
499–500
in Japan, 225
statistics for case countries,
540–541*t*
Societal corporatism, 332
Socioeconomic status. *See also*
Social classes
of identity groups, government
support for, 610
Sociological explanations. *See also*
Weber, Max
for declining partisanship,
336–337
for India's party system evolution, 361–362
for party systems emergence
and changes, 327
Sodomy laws, 650, 653
Softliners, 445
Soil erosion, 590
Sokoto caliphate, 166
Solidarity (social program,
Mexico), 231

Somalia
civil war in, 92
collapse (1991) and anarchy
in, 55
Somaliland and, 42*b*, 45–46
Somaliland
after Somalia's collapse, 55
case history, 45–46
Somalia and, 45–46
Somali National Movement
(SNM), 45
Somoza, Anastasio (father),
378–379
Somoza, Anastasio (son),
378–379
Somoza, Luis, 378–379
Somoza family dynasty (Nicaragua), 372–373, 378–379
Soper, Christopher, 617
Soros, George, 205, 485
Soskice, David, 490
South Africa
Afrikaner identity construction
in, 148
apartheid in, 31–32, *32*, 148,
182, 323, 608
democratic consolidation in,
446
as democratic success, 454
dominant party system in,
323
Mandela's election, 444
Nationalist Party, 148
same-sex marriage status in,
647
South Korea, cars imported
from, *504*
South America. *See* Latin America;
specific countries
Southeast Asia. *See also* Asia; East
Asia
economic crises of 1997, 205
structural adjustment programs
in, 201
Southern Democrats (U.S.), 343
South Korea
air pollution from China in,
592
as cohesive-capitalist state, 510
currency valuations in, 485
developmental state and
industrialization in,
503–504, *504*
East Asian miracle and, 201,
503–504
GDP growth in Ghana since
1957 vs., 503–504
health care study in, 569
inequality in, 505

political development in, 7
U.S. foreign aid for, 515
South Ossetia, internal sovereignty
in Georgia and, 43
Sovereign states/sovereignty.
See also State recognition
in Brazil, 72
bureaucracy of, 44–45
economic, European Union,
globalization and, 64, 97,
220–222
external sovereignty as standard
for, 41
internal sovereignty, and
challenges to, 41–43
legitimacy of, 41–43
in Mexico, 77
separation from sovereign of, 97
in theocracies, 132, 134
use of power/force in, 43
Soviet Union. *See also* Russia
Afghanistan invasion by, 56–57
under communism, pluralism
in, 27–28
coup attempt (1991), 435
creation of, 113
dissolution of, 114, 435, *464*,
464–465
ethnic political battles in, 143
expulsion of ethnic Germans,
154
federalism in, 299–301
former, semipresidentialism
in, 268
post–World War II German
occupation by, 71
repression of civil society in, 397
revolution in China and, 441
soviets (legislative bodies), 113
women's rights in, 637
Spain
economic crisis in Great
Recession, 221
fascism in, 118
Mexico, colonialization of,
77–78
Napoleon in, 627
same-sex marriage status in, 647
South American colonialization, 73
Spanish colonies, code law in,
273
Special Constitutional Court,
Germany. *See* Constitutional
Courts
Special economic zones (SEZs,
China), 519
Special interests, terminology
for, 18

Spodek, Howard, 626
Spy networks, 373. *See also* Secret
police
Sri Lanka, semipresidentialism
in, 266
Stability and executive-legislative
institution comparisons,
271–273
Stagflation, 198, 212
Stalin, Josef, 27, 113–114, 299, 637
Standard Oil monopoly, 211
Stare decisis, 273, 279
State Children's Health Insurance
Program (SCHIP, U.S.),
578
State corporatism, 332, 397, 404,
406, 408. *See also* Corporatism
State Council and its Standing
Committee, China, 380–381
State Environmental Protec-
tion Agency (SEPA, China),
590–591
State formation case studies
Brazil, 72–74
characteristics, 60–62
Germany, 69–71
India, 82–84
Iran, 80–81
Japan, 67–69
Mexico, 77–79
Nigeria, 87–90
UK, 62–64
U.S., 64–67
State governors
in Brazil, 296–297, 457
in Nigeria, 393, 472–473
Stateless nations, 39
State of nature and liberal
democracy, 104
State-owned enterprises (SOEs)
in Brazil, 528
in China, 519–520
in Iran, 530–532
State recognition, 41–42, 42*b*, 42*t*,
45–46
States. *See also* Modern states; State
formation case studies
citizens and. *See* Citizens/citi-
zenship
defined, 39
development diversification
neglect if oil-rich, 517
global economics and, 533
as "higher personality," 115
nations or governments vs.,
39–40, 143, 150
regime changes and, 95
role in development, 504–505,
508–511*b*

role in market economy,
192–197, 204*b*
U.S., central government power
vs. power of, 65–66
weak and failed, 51, 52*b*, 55,
58–60, 61*t*
States (subnational units). *See also*
State governors
Brazilian, on sexual orientation,
654
federalism and, 292, 298,
299–300
power and autonomy of,
293–295, 298
taxation and spending powers
of, 294, 296–298
U.S.
electoral systems of, 342
gay rights authorized by, 649,
651–652
State strength. *See also* Weak states
democratization and, 445
elements in, 53*b*, 55
state involvement in the market
and, 237
Statistical techniques, quantitative, 13
Steel, Gill, 355
Stephens, John D., 24, 545, 548,
598
Stevens, Siaka, 58
Stimulus spending programs
in Brazil, 529
in China, 521
EU and, 221
in Germany, 219
in India, 524
Mexico and, 231
in U.S., 214
Stock markets
in Germany, 497–498
Mexico, *229*
New York, *195*
Stokes, Susan, 448*b*
Stoner-Weiss, Kathryn, 299–300
Stonewall Inn (New York City),
gay rights riots at, 649
Stories, in identity politics,
148–150
Streeck, Wolfgang, 497
Stroessner, Alfredo, 396
Structural adjustment programs
(SAPs)
characteristics, 201, 202–203*b*
East Asian miracle and, 504
globalization and, 501
in Nigeria, 234, 236, 415
Structuralism, 25–27, 29*t*
Structural social groups, 610

Student movements. *See also* Social movements
in Germany (1960s & 1970s), 348–349
in Iran, 409, 411, 443
in Mexico, 463
in Nigeria, 415
Student participation, 407
STV (Single Transferable Vote), 159
Subcultures, 22
The Subjection of Women (Mill), 105
Subject loyalty, 47
Sub-Saharan Africa. *See also* Africa
authoritarian rule in (1970–2010), 392*b*
patron-client relationships in, 398
transition to democracy in, 447
women in power positions in, 317*b*
Succession
in authoritarian regimes, 378
in China, 379–380, 382, 385
in Iran, *385*, 386, 389
Sudan
border changes, 41
ethnic cleansing in, 143
as failed state, 51
religious to ethnic salience shift, 183
Suffrage. *See also* Enfranchisement
in Brazil, 73
classical liberal theorists on, 105
full suffrage recently granted, 197
in Japan, 68
in U.S., 65–66, 342, 344
Sugar industry, 72–73
Suharto, 505
Sulfur dioxide as pollutant, 587
Sunnah, Muslim holy book, 132
Sunni Arabs/Muslims
Hussein's patronage of, 373
in Iraq, 5–6
as nonhierarchical, 616
no oil reserves in area, 157
in UK, 618–622
Sunni Islamists, 134
Sun Yat-sen, 85, 441
Superfund Act of 1986 (U.S.), 587, 589
Superior War College (ESG), Brazil, 430
Supplemental Nutrition Assistance Program (SNAP, U.S.), 544, 560

Support, public displays of, by authoritarian regimes, 394–395, *403*
Supreme Court
in Brazil, 264
in India, 626
in Nigeria, 471–472
in UK, 255
in U.S., 274, 277
Supreme Federal Tribunal (STF, Brazil), 278–279
Supreme Justice Tribunal (Brazil), 278
Supreme leaders
in authoritarian regimes, 372, 374–375*b*, 376
in fascist regimes, 100*b*
institutionalization and limits on, 372, 374*b*, 394
in Iran, 135, *385*, 386–390
Supreme Military Council, Nigeria, 391–392
Supreme People's Court, China, 384
Supreme Soviet (Russian legislature), 465
Sustainable development
in China, 589–593
defined, 502
developing countries' dilemmas with, 582
in Nigeria, 593–596
Sustainable states (2010), 54*b*
Swaziland, no paid maternity leave in, 557
Sweden
labor unions in, 34*b*
parliamentary election (2010), 314, 315*t*
same-sex marriage and, 647
U.S. and German welfare states vs., 556*t*
as welfare state, 34*b*, 546–547, 598
women in power in, 317*b*
Switzerland
consociationalism in, 157
as federalist country, 292, 294
mosques with minarets ban, 614
Symbols, in identity politics, 148–150, 149*b*
Symmetrical federal systems, 295
Syndromes of Corruption: Wealth, Power, and Democracy (Johnston), 291*b*

Syria
protests in, 402
secularism in, 616

T
Tahmasebi-Birgani, Victoria, 644
Taiping Rebellion, China, 85
Taisho, Emperor of Japan, 68
Taiwan. *See* Republic of China
Taliban, 56–57, 133, 439*b*
"Talking about 'Tribe': Moving from Stereotypes to Analysis" (Lowe), 156*b*
Tamil Nadu (Indian state), Hindu temples in, 624
Tamils, federalism in India and, 299
Tanaka Giichi, 68
Tanzania
German colonialism in, 71
one-party regime in, 121–122
restricted political campaigns, 157
Tanzanian African National Union (TANU), 121–122
Taqlid, Muslim concept of, 132
Tariffs on imports
globalization and, 206, 488
in India, 525
TARP (Troubled Asset Relief Program), 213–214
Tarrow, Sidney, 98
Tate, C. Neal, 275
Taxation
in China, 591
in federal systems, 294
in Germany, 499–500
globalization and, 491
in India, 298
in Mexico, 294
for nonrenewable resource extraction, 584
for pollution, 583–584
in Russia, 300
as social policy, 544–545
subnational government power and, 294
in Sweden, 546–547
in UK, 494
in U.S., 66, 211–213, 545, 561
Taylor, Charles, 59, 155
Taylor, Matthew, 275
Tea Party movement (U.S.), 177, 325–326, 345
Technocratic legitimacy, 119
Technology
globalization and, 206
Indian castes, effect on, 361

Tehran, Iran
    demonstrations in, 409, 443
    political opposition rally in, *80*
Telephone service
    as natural monopoly, 195–196
    representation and participation and, 337
Television. *See also* Mass communications; Media
    representation and participation and, 337
    social capital decline and, 326–327
Temporary Assistance to Needy Families (TANF, U.S.), 544, 557, 559–560, 578
Teorell, Jan, 449*b*
Term of office
    for Brazilian president, 264
    for British prime ministers, 249, 254
    in presidential systems, 260, 272
Territory
    defining a state, 40
    Mexican loss of to U.S., 78
    of postcolonial states, 49–50
    recognition by external states of, 41
Terrorism. *See also* Islamic terrorists; September 11, 2001, attacks
    revolution vs., 438–439*b*
    Terrorism Acts (UK), 623
    Terrorist organizations in Germany, 349
Thailand
    border retention (as Siam), 49–50
    East Asian financial crisis and, 505
    floating currency, 485
    neoliberal policies in, 201
Thatcher, Margaret
    centralized decision making by, 254
    economic policy changes and, 271, 493–495
    miners' strike and, 493
    monetarist policies used by, 198
    New Public Management and, 284, 303
    NHS reforms by, 575
    Reagan, compared to, 303
    vote of no confidence, 249, 254
    welfare policy changes in UK, 552
    winter of discontent in UK, 341

Theocracy/theocratic regimes
    as authoritarian regime type, 8
    in case studies, 35
    defined, 132
    in Iran, 385–386, 412–413, 530, 532
    as political ideology and regime type, 101*b*, 132–134
    state power and citizens' rights under, 137
Theory. *See also individual theories*
    defined, 11, 13*b*
    ideologists vs. institutionalists, 138–139
    on inclusion and conflicting values, 658
Thies, Michael, 288
Third dimension of power, 11
Third party candidates (U.S.), 344
Third Republics
    France, 152, 327
    Nigeria, 126, 167, 472
Third wave of democratization, 444–446, 475
Three Gorges Dam (China), 383, 590
Tiananmen Square demonstrations (China), 86, 383, 407–408
Tibet, China's sovereignty dispute with, 86, 384, 407
Tigers
    East Asian, 503–504, 508–509
    Middle Eastern, 512–513
Tilly, Charles, 137
Time lines
    military intervention in Nigeria, 391*b*
    modern states' development, 91*t*
    political institutions' development, 330–334, 330–334*f*
Timmins, Graham, 351
Tito, Jozef, 191
Tobacco use, 571
Tocqueville, Alexis de, 345
Toft, Monica, 160–161, 163
Togo, German colonialism in, 71
Tokugawa Bakufu, 68
Tokugawa Ieyasu, 68
Tokyo (Edo), 68
Totalitarian regimes. *See also* Authoritarianism/authoritarian regimes; Personalist regimes
    civil society eliminated in, 397
    in Nazi Germany, 116–118
    in Russia, 113–114

Town and Village Enterprises (TVEs, China), 519
Toyota, 223, 225
Trade. *See also* Free trade; Tariffs on imports
    globalization and, 487
    Iranian reduction of barriers to, 530–531
Trades Union Congress (TUC, UK), 341, 493
Trade unions. *See* Labor/Labor unions
Traditional legitimacy, 43
Tragedy of the commons, 581, 584
Transgendered people. *See* Lesbian, gay, bisexual, and transgender people
"Transition" paradigm, 475
Transition-to-democracy theory, 9, 445, 476. *See also* Democratization
Translocal, locally rooted membership associations, 345–346
Transnational corporations (TNCs), *523*
Transparency International
    on Brazil, 459
    on Ghana, 453
    on India, 290
    on Nigeria, 234–235, 474
    on Russia, 468
Transvestites, 653. *See also* Lesbian, gay, bisexual, and transgender people
Treaty of Guadalupe Hidalgo (1848), 78
Treaty of Lisbon (2007), 221
Treaty powers, in presidential systems, 262
Tribes, ethnic groups or nations vs., 156*b*, 165
Tribunal Federal Electoral (TRIFE, Mexico), 462
Tribus (tribe), 156*b*
Tripp, Aili Mari, 635
Troubled Asset Relief Program (TARP), 213–214
"The Troubles" (Northern Ireland), 158
Trust in government, 336–337, 347
Tsebelis, George, 247
Tsunami and earthquake (Japan, 2011), 226, 288
Tunisia
    corruption in, 401
    international trade in, 400
    Islamist Renaissance Party in, 400

Tunisia *(cont.)*
protests in, 401–402
reforms promised, 399
revolt and regime change
(2011), 22, 384, 401–402,
423, 434, 477, 616
social network technology in,
337
suicide of street vendor, 400
Turkey
export-oriented industrialization in, 512–513
import-substitution industrialization and, 200
Islamic headscarves in, 613–615
market-based private health
insurance system in, 566
as Middle Eastern Tiger,
512–513
secularism in, 613
Turkish immigrants to Germany,
citizenship for, *153*, 154
Turkmenistan, personality cult in,
395
Tutsi, Rwandan, 168–169
Tuvalu, territory covered by, 40
Two-and-a-half party systems, 326,
347, 351
Two-party systems
characteristics, 323
in France, 328
in India, 362
majoritarian electoral system
and, 329
in U.S., 339
Two-round electoral systems, 259,
264, 267–268, 327–328
2008–2009 financial crisis. *See*
Great Recession
Two-turnover test, 446, 463
Typology, defined, 21

U
Udmurtia, as Russian republic,
300
Uganda
Idi Amin in, 374*b*
LGBT movement in, 647
Mobutu and, 378
SAPs in, 202*b*
Tutsi refugees in, 169
Ujamaa villages (Tanzania), 121
UK. *See* United Kingdom
Ukraine, color revolutions in, 402
Ulama (Islamic clergy), 443,
620–621
Umma (Islamic), 133–135, 439*b*
UNDP (United Nations Develop-
ment Programme), 181

Unemployment
in Chile, 228
deindustrialization and, 488
in Germany
employment growth (1997–
2007) and, 498–499, 499*f*
health care coverage for, 572
neocorporatism and, 349–350
social insurance system and,
554, 555–556
social market economy and,
216, 218
taxes, social benefits and,
497–500, 498*f*
Unemployment Benefit II,
555
in Great Recession, 214
in Iran, 530–531
in Nigeria, 415
in Russia, 465, 637
social insurance provisions for,
544
statistics, 190*t*
in Sweden, 546–547
in Turkey, 512
in UK, 494–495
in U.S., 211
Unified Black Movement (Brazil),
181
Union of Muslim Organizations
(UK), 620
Union of Soviet Socialist Republics (USSR). *See* Soviet Union
Union of Women in Russia, 639
Unitary executive theories, 302
Unitary systems, federal systems
vs., 292, 295
United Kingdom (UK). *See also*
British colonies, former
asymmetrical devolution in, 295
British Empire, 63
church-state relations and study
of Islam in, 617
common law in, 273
as cradle of democracy, 108–110
development as democracy, 369
election results in, 340, 340*t*
external sovereignty, 19th
century, 63
FPTP and pluralist systems,
339–342
Glorious Revolution and James
II's resignation, 48, 109
health care programs in,
540–541*t*, 570–571, 574–576
industrialization in, 63–64
Ireland, unification with, 62
Japanese treaty with, 68
judicial review absence in, 275

Labour Party, 109–110
languages in, 63
liberal market economy of, 489,
492–496
as modern state, 62–64
Muslim citizenship in, 617
National Health Service in,
565–566, 574–576, *575*,
597–598
nationalism in, 151
NPM and bureaucracy size in,
284
parliamentarism in, 249–257
parliamentary election results
(2005), 314*t*
Persian dependence on, 80
political appointees in, 281
post–World War II occupation
of Germany by, 71
power of majority in, 247
regime type and characteristics
in, 138
religious challenge to multiculturalism in, 618–622
rivalry with Germany and
France, 49
Scotland, unification with, 63
state formation, 62–64
Supreme Court established, 110
taxation in, 294
two-and-a-half-party system in,
326
two-party system in, 323, 327
unification with Scotland, 63
voting in U.S. vs., 340, 342
Wales, unification with, 63
welfare state, 63
United Nations (UN)
Afghan government and, 57
education as right, 193
global problems and civil society
pressure on, 208
on hostile takeovers of weak
states, 55
Human Development Index,
60, 513
Millennium Development
Goals, 516
new member states admitted by
decade, 41*b*
on oil's environmental impact
in Nigeria, 593–594
tribunals on Rwandan genocide,
169
on women's rights in Russia, 640
women's social status conferences, 630
World Conference on Racism
(2001), 181

United Nations Development Programme (UNDP), 181, 585, 593–594

United Nations Human Development Report (UNHDR) on climate change, 582

United Russia (political party), 269, 467–468

United States (U.S.). *See also* American Revolution

African slaves brought by colonists to, 48

Black Hawk Down episode in Somalia and, 55

Branch Davidians and internal sovereignty of, 43

Cold War foreign aid for Liberia, 58

as consciously crafted state, 64–67

Constitution. *See* Constitution (U.S.)

corruption in nineteenth century, 291*b*

democracy and welfare in Sweden vs., 34*b*

environmental policy and pollution in, 586–589

expansion of citizenship in, 105

federalism in, 292

FPTP and pluralist systems, 342–346

free market economic model of, 210–216

government and growth in EU and Germany vs., 500*b*

greenhouse gases produced by, 584–585

health care in, 540–541*t*, 557–561, 564, 566, 570–571, 577–580

interest group pluralism in, 331, 333*f*

Japanese treaty with, 68

Jim Crow laws in, 32, 608

judicial review in, 273

labor unions' weakness in, 237–239

LGBT movement in, 649–652

liberal market economy of, 489–492

market-based private health insurance system in, 566, 570

market economy of, 209

obesity in, 571

paid maternity leave, lack of, 557

patron-client relationships in, 338

political appointees in, 281

post–World War II occupation of Germany by, 71

power of majority in, 247

presidentialism in, 25, 95, 258–261

racial politics in, 170–178, 548

religious group recognition and autonomy in, 612–613, 616

social capital in, 326

social insurance in, 544, 597

Soviet invasion of Afghanistan and, 56–57

state formation, 64–67

states, power and autonomy of, 294

three government branches, importance of, 245

two-party, pluralist system evolution in, 343

two-term presidency in, 25

welfare state in, 34*b*, 544, 548, 557–561

women in power positions in, 317*b*

Unity party in Russia, 467

Universal Declaration of Human Rights of the United Nations, 99

Universal entitlements, 543–544

Universal family allowance (Sweden), 546

Universal health care program (U.S.), 579

Universities, 181–182

University of Tokyo, Faculty of Law, 286

"Untouchables" (*dalits*) caste, *360*, 360–361

User fees on public land, 584

Uyghurs, protest to China's rule, 384

Uzbeks, voting in Kyrgyzstan, *146*

V

Vallinder, Torbjörn, 275

Value-added tax (VAT) in UK, 494

Vanberg, Georg, 278

Van Buren, Martin, 343

van de Walle, Nicholas, 450

Vanguard party, Lenin on, 113

Vanuatu, voting system in, 353*b*

Vargas, Getulio, 73, 123, 180

Variable, scientific concept of, 13*b*

Varieties of capitalism, 489, 490*f*, 491, 493, 497

Varna (Indian castes), 360

Vector-borne diseases, 571

Venezuela

economy under Chavez, 510

leftist critics of neoliberal reforms in, 507–508

Verba, Sidney, 21–22, 102*b*, 444

Verheul, Ruben, 466–467

Vertical accountability. *See also* Accountability; Representation

in authoritarian regimes, 379

in Brazil, 279, 459–460

consensual systems and, 270

democratic deepening and, 446

executive-legislative institution comparisons, 270

executive power and, 301

majoritarian systems and, 270

in Russia, 269

of state institutions by individuals and groups, 245–247

in UK, 257

Veto players

in Brazil, 265, 280

consensual systems and, 270

defined, 247

in federal systems, 293, 300–301

in Germany, 280, 500

judicial review and, 273

markets as, 598

in parliamentary system, 249–250

in public policy, 600

in Russia, 269

separation of powers and, 259

in U.S., 265, 345

welfare states and, 549

in Westminster model, 257

Veto points and judicial review, 275

Veto power. *See also* Federalism/federal systems

in Brazil, 264

in U.S., 261

Vichy government of "free zone" France, 41

Vietnam, communism in, 115

Vietnam War, 212

Villa, Francisco "Pancho," 78

Volunteerism, 346, 357

von Beyme, Klaus, 320

Voodoo religion in Haiti, 165

Vote of no confidence, by British parliament, 249, 254

Voter fraud. *See* Election fraud

Voting Rights Act of 1965 (U.S.), 66, 174, 176

Voting/voters. *See also* Elections; Enfranchisement; Suffrage

aggregation and counting of votes, 312

Voting/voters *(cont.)*
British immigrants as, 620
identity group redress of
grievances through, 183
in Kyrgyzstan, *146*
power of, 27
in U.S. vs. UK, 340, 342
voter turnout
in China, 405
election fraud in Nigeria and,
471–472
electoral system effects on,
315, 316*f*
in Iran, 410
mobilization tactics, in
Mexico, 78
political party realignments
and, 325*b*
in U.S., 342–343, 345

W
Wales
devolution in, 109–110, 295
nationalist party in, 341
unification into UK, 63
Wallis, John, 55
War
social movement opposing,
329–330, 335, 341, 348
"War Against Indiscipline,"
Nigeria, 433
war declarations, in presidential
systems, 262
War of 1812, 67
War of Independence, Mexico
(1810–1821), 78
War on Poverty (U.S.), 559
war on terror, 263
Washington, George, 25
Water pollution, 582–583. *See also*
Environment; Pollution
Weak political institutions
of authoritarian regimes,
416–418
in Brazil, 278–280, 456
bureaucratic, corruption and,
281, 284
coups d'etat and, 427–428
democratic breakdown and,
447–450
in India, 288–290
in Iran, 412, 443
in Japan, 286–288
judicial independence and, 276
judiciary in new democracies
as, 273
in Nigeria, 391, 432, 434
patron-client relationships
and, 338

in Russia, 296, 300, 465–468
semipresidentialism and,
267–269
in Zaire, 377–378
in Zaire under Mobutu, 120
Weak states. *See also* Failed states
China's revolutions and,
440–442
colonialism and, 91
defined, 51
globalization and, 238
as international problems, 60
Nigeria as, 234–235, 474,
593–596
structural adjustment programs
and, 202–203*b*
venal leadership and, 55
Wealth. *See also* Income inequality;
Income redistribution
democratization and, 447, 448*b*
distribution of, after American
war of independence,
436–437*b*
health and environment, relationship to, 540–541*t*, 542,
545
in Sweden, 546
Wealthy countries. *See also specific
countries*
as case studies, 35, 61
corruption in, 291*b*
deindustrialization and welfare
state in, 488
democracies in, 22, 447, 448*b*
environmental damage/inter-
ventions, 581–583, 597
globalization's effects on economic policies of, 486,
488–492, 501, 533–534, 598
greenhouse gas production by,
584–585
health care in, 564–566, 567*b*,
571–580
"judicialization" of politics in,
246
macroeconomic stability in,
488
New Public Management in, 284
participation and representation in, 337
political parties in, 320
propensity for social welfare in,
548–549
public health issues for, 570–571
regime change in, 435, 444
rising health care costs in,
566–570, 567*b*
welfare state types in, 544, 564
women's movements in, 149*b*

Weber, Max, 43–44, 122, 280, 534
Weimar Republic, 7, 71, 117, 217,
348. *See also* Germany
Weingast, Barry, 25, 55
Welfare states. *See also* Christian
democratic welfare states;
Liberal welfare states; Social
democratic welfare states;
Social welfare system
deindustrialization and, 488
development of, 548–549
Germany, reform in, *554*,
554–557
globalization, policy convergence and, 488–489
institutional strength and,
238–239
modern, political demands for
protection under, 196
outcomes, 550–551, 550–551*t*
social insurance varieties of, 545
starting, in Brazil's developing
economy, 561–563
Sweden's, 546–547
in UK, 63, 110, 493–495
women's health care in, 630
Welfare/welfare reform
comparative perspective on,
542–545, 548–549,
550–551*t*, 550*t*
in Germany, 350, *554*, 554–557
market failure and, 539
in UK, 63, 552
in U.S., 557–561
welfare dependence, 559
Welzel, Christian, 447, 449*b*
Westernization
in Iran, 133, 641–642
in Turkey, 614–615
West Germany, *70. See also* Germany
democracy in, 7, 71
democratic consolidation in,
446
reunification with East
Germany, 218, 278, 349,
554–555
social market economy in, 348
Westminster model
accountability and, 301
of democratic power, 249–250,
253–255, 257
as majoritarian system, 270,
302
of parliamentarism, 249–257
Westphalia, Peace of (1648), 47
Whig Party (U.S.), 343
White ethnic identity
in Brazil, 179–182
in U.S., 173, 176*t*

Whitening policy (Brazil), 179–180
White Revolution (Iran), 442
WikiLeaks, 401
Wilhelm I, Kaiser, 7, 70
Winner-take-all electoral systems, 313, 319, 450. *See also* Single-member district electoral system
Winter of discontent (UK), 341, 493
Wintrobe, Ronald, 373
Wolferen, Karel van, 288
Women of Russia (political party), 639
Women/women's rights
  classical liberals on citizenship of, 105
  donor agency control in, 633
  enfranchisement rules on, 343
  gender as identity category, 149
  in Germany, 349, 555–557
  as global concern, 629–630
  in India, 624–626
  interest groups, 331
  in Iran, 411, 413, 640–644, 643*b*
  in Kuwait, 633–634
  labor force participation, by welfare state type, 549, 550–551*t*, 551
  legal discrimination against, 608
  Marx on, 111
  in Middle East, 643*b*
  military service and, 630
  political and social rights for, 149*b*, 629–645. *See also* Political rights
  in power, 317*b*, 363
  quotas, electoral, 315, 317*b*
  representation and participation of, 635–636
  in Russia, 636–640
  in Saudi Arabia, 633–634
  social movement on rights for, 329–330, 335–336, 341
  suffrage
    in UK, 109
    in U.S., 65
  women in power, PR systems and, 363
Wong, Cara, 177
Wood, Gordon, 436–437*b*
Workers' councils (Germany), 218
Workers' Party (PT, Brazil)
  discipline and success of, 458–459
  formation of, 456
  LGBT movement and, 653–654
  Lula's election and, 455

minimum income for citizens, 563
National Congress seats and compromises by, 265
participatory budgeting and, 460
on social development, 528
succession after Lula and, 265
Working conditions
  during German industrialization era, 216
  in Japan, 225
  market economies and regulation of, 196
  U.S.'s New Deal programs and, 212, 215
  during Weimar Republic, 217
World Bank
  Bolsa Família support by, 562, 562–563
  creation of, 199–200
  The East Asian Miracle, 504
  global economy and, 501–502
  global problems and civil society pressure on, 208
  good governance agenda, 501
  Heavily Indebted Poor Countries initiative, 516
  import-substitution industrialization and, 200
  on institutionalization by Chinese Communist Party, 520
  LGBT movement in Brazil and, 653
  neoliberal agenda of, 201, 203
  pollution in China and, 591
  on state role in development, 504
  structural adjustment programs under, 201, 202*b*, 238
World Conference on Racism, UN (2001), 181
World Trade Organization (WTO), 99, 206, 519, 583
World Values Survey, 449*b*
World War I, 71, 116, 223
World War II
  Germany during and after, 71, 118
  India's independence after, 83
  Japanese role in, 68
  revolution in China and, 86, 441–442
  U.S. modern bureaucracy after, 66
Wren, Anne, 324–325*b*
Wright, Teresa, 408

X
Xi Jinping, *379*, 380, 382
Xinjiang region, China, protests in, 407

Y
Yar'Adua, Umaru Musa, 89, *469*, 470, 472, 474, 595
Yellow River, China, 590
Yeltsin, Boris
  federalism in Russia and, 300
  military coup attempt and, 474
  military coup attempt confrontation, 464, *464*
  presidential powers used by, 268, 465–466
  Russian legislature and, 465
  on women's status, 640
Yemen, protests in, 402
Yoruba peoples, 87–89, 165–166, 168, 470
Young, Iris Marion, 609–611
Yugoslavia
  democracy failure in, 440
  fall of communism and, 162
  language and ethnic conflict in, 155
  modified market economy under Tito, 191
  religion and ethnic conflict in, 162
Yukos (Russian oil company), 467
Yunus, Mohamed, 502
Yuval-Davis, Nira, 149*b*

Z
Zaibatsu (Japanese industrial conglomerates), 223
Zaire. *See also* Congo, Democratic Republic of
  personalist regime under Mobutu, 120, 395
  survival politics, 377–378
Zanan (Women), Iranian publication, 643
Zapata, Emiliano, 78
Zapatista Army of National Liberation (EZLN), 78, 231, 463
Zedillo, Ernesto, 131, 231, 462
Zhao Ziyang, 383
Zheng Xiaoyu, 384
Zimbabwe
  LGBT movement in, 647
  Mugabe in, *370*
Zócalo Square, Mexico city, Obrador's speech in, 461
Zulus as ethnic group, 150, 156*b*